Computer users are not all alike.
Neither are SYBEX books.

We know our customers have a variety of needs. They've told us so. And because we've listened, we've developed several distinct types of books to meet the needs of each of our customers. What are you looking for in computer help?

If you're looking for the basics, try the **ABC's** series. You'll find short, unintimidating tutorials and helpful illustrations. For a more visual approach, select **Teach Yourself,** featuring screen-by-screen illustrations of how to use your latest software purchase.

Running Start books are really two books in one—a tutorial to get you off to a fast start and a reference to answer your questions when you're ready to tackle advanced tasks.

Mastering and **Understanding** titles offer you a step-by-step introduction, plus an in-depth examination of intermediate-level features, to use as you progress.

Our **Up & Running** series is designed for computer-literate consumers who want a no-nonsense overview of new programs. Just 20 basic lessons, and you're on your way.

We also publish two types of reference books. Our **Instant References** provide quick access to each of a program's commands and functions. SYBEX **Encyclopedias** and **Desktop References** provide a *comprehensive reference* and explanation of all of the commands, features, and functions of the subject software.

Our **Programming** books are specifically written for a technically sophisticated audience and provide a no-nonsense value-added approach to each topic covered, with plenty of tips, tricks, and time-saving hints.

Sometimes a subject requires a special treatment that our standard series doesn't provide. So you'll find we have titles like **Advanced Techniques, Handbooks, Tips & Tricks,** and others that are specifically tailored to satisfy a unique need.

We carefully select our authors for their in-depth understanding of the software they're writing about, as well as their ability to write clearly and communicate effectively. Each manuscript is thoroughly reviewed by our technical staff to ensure its complete accuracy. Our production department makes sure it's easy to use. All of this adds up to the highest quality books available, consistently appearing on best-seller charts worldwide.

You'll find SYBEX publishes a variety of books on every popular software package. Looking for computer help? Help yourself to SYBEX.

For a brochure of our best-selling publications:

SYBEX Inc. 2021 Challenger Drive, Alameda, CA 94501
Tel: (510) 523-8233/(800) 227-2346 Telex: 336311
Fax: (510) 523-2373

SYBEX®

SYBEX is committed to using natural resources wisely to preserve and improve our environment. As a leader in the computer book publishing industry, we are aware that over 40% of America's solid waste is paper. This is why we have been printing the text of books like this one on recycled paper since 1982.

This year our use of recycled paper will result in the saving of more than 15,300 trees. We will lower air pollution effluents by 54,000 pounds, save 6,300,000 gallons of water, and reduce landfill by 2,700 cubic yards.

In choosing a SYBEX book you are not only making a choice for the best in skills and information, you are also choosing to enhance the quality of life for all of us.

Mastering Windows NT Programming

Mastering
Windows™ NT
Programming

Brian Myers & Eric Hamer

SYBEX®

San Francisco • Paris • Düsseldorf • Soest

Acquisitions Editors: Dianne King, Dave Clark
Developmental Editor: Gary Masters
Editor: Dusty Bernard
Project Editor: Michelle Nance
Technical Editor: John Barrie
Book Designer: Suzanne Albertson
Production Artist: Charlotte Carter
Technical Artist: Cuong Le
Screen Graphics: Cuong Le
Typesetter: Ann Dunn
Proofreader/Production Assistant: David Silva
Indexer: Matthew Spence
Cover Designer: Archer Design
Cover Photographer: Richard Wahlstrom
Cover Photograph Art Director: Ingalls + Associates

Library of Congress Card Number: 93-60631
ISBN: 0-7821-1264-1

Manufactured in the United States of America

10 9 8 7 6 5 4 3 2 1

For Ellen

e quindi uscimmo a riveder le stelle.

B.G.M.

ACKNOWLEDGMENTS

Our colleagues at Access Softek contributed substantially to this book. For help with the OLE chapters we thank Stephen Crane, who generously gave us code from his Intellidraw program and drafts of the text. Michael Barnes crafted the Show-Wave program in Chapter 17. Chris Doner gave us the use of company resources and advised us out of quandaries. More than once we benefited from the advice of Ian Emmons and Eric van Vliet. Tania Wasser and Cynthia Townsend went out of their way to be helpful, and Jonathan Lemon drew the spiffy icons.

Without the help of Microsoft's technical support engineers in the MSWIN32 forum on CompuServe, this would have been a much less interesting book. We plied them with questions almost daily for seven months, and if the book doesn't brim with helpful information it certainly isn't their fault. We acknowledge particular debts to Rohan Phillips, for more answers than we can count; to Petrus Wong, GeDI knight; Doug Olson, for knowing the tools of the trade; David Brown, who tactfully exclaimed that we asked such *interesting* questions; and also Nancy Cluts, Jerry Drain, Steve Firebaugh, Pete Grey, Lee Hart, Dan Knudson, Bob Landau, Mike Markley, Bruce Ramsey, Paul Sanders, Eric Sassaman, Julie Solon, Colin Stuart, Dave Taniguchi, Paul Tissue, and Stu Wiley. Don't leave DOS without them. Our thanks also to the many forum participants who gladly shared their knowledge.

If it weren't for Arthur Knowles, hero of hardware hassles, we might still be crawling under the desk to flip switches, reconfigure ports, and mutter curses. The staff at U.C. Computer also deserve our special gratitude.

At SYBEX, we thank the many Rumpelstiltskins who spun our manuscript into a book. The editor, Dusty Bernard, was midwife to the book and to her grandchild at the same time. She gave accuracy and clarity to our text, but we don't mind if she likes her other project better. Michelle Nance, whose job title should be "eye of the storm," calmly coordinated all the various stages of production. John Barrie, technical editor, gave much-needed advice and encouragement. Dianne King and Gary Masters helped us conceive and plan the project. Others also contributed their expertise: Barbara Gordon, managing editor; David Silva, proofreader; Ann Dunn, typesetter; Cuong Le, technical and screen graphics artist; and Charlotte Carter, production artist.

CONTENTS AT A GLANCE

TABLE OF CONTENTS

8 Drawing Complex Shapes with the New GDI 393

INTRODUCTION

We began this book by asking ourselves which features of the new operating system would seem most powerful and least familiar to programmers moving from 16-bit to 32-bit Windows. The table of contents shows our answers: threads, synchronization, processes, pipes, structured exception handling, virtual memory management, memory-mapped files, enhanced metafiles, world coordinate transformations, system security, and Unicode. We have aimed to impart more, however, than a knowledge of features. This book's strength lies in the context it gives for new commands to make them understandable. If you haven't ever used pipes or performed asynchronous I/O in other systems, then their purpose may seem at first unclear and the details of their implementation confusing. Our explanations look for the logic that governs the details: the situations that would make a certain feature useful, the line of reasoning that accounts for an apparent inconsistency, and the larger context that joins a "why" to every "how."

The structure of the book's chapters reflects our emphasis on giving explanations to accompany the instructions. Most chapters have three sections: "Concepts," "Commands," and "Code." First comes the general idea, then specific routines, and finally practical examples. The divisions make it easy to find the passages that will help you most. For an overall view of the entire system, try reading just the "Concepts" section of every chapter. Then return to the chapters most relevant to your own work. Readers already familiar with structured exception handling might skip the concepts and go straight to the commands. Readers in a hurry to get their own code working might begin with the "Code" section and skim backward to find explanations for anything puzzling.

IS THIS BOOK FOR YOU?

This book was written for programmers who know C and have some Windows programming experience. We assume you do not need introductions to such basic concepts as message-driven programs, dialog boxes, and device contexts. Those features have not changed from earlier versions of Windows and other books are available to help you with them. This book opens directly with the major new features of Windows NT, such as threads and processes. If you are moving to a 32-bit system and want a comprehensive explanation of its new programming paradigms, this is the book for you. (For an introduction to the basic concepts and structures of Windows programming, we recommend the *Programmer's Introduction to Windows 3.1* by Brian Myers and Chris Doner, SYBEX, 1992.)

WHAT YOU NEED

To run Windows NT you need a machine with a 32-bit processor. NT runs on an Intel 80386/25 CPU as well as on some RISC-based CPUs such as the MIPS R4000 and the DEC Alpha. You also need a graphics adapter and display with at least VGA resolution, a hard disk with at least 70MB free, a high-density floppy drive (for Intel machines only), and 8MB of RAM. For programming you will need a mouse, a SCSI CD-ROM, twice as much memory, and at least another 30MB of disk space. A 32-bit C compiler with Windows NT programming libraries is also required.

Some features in the palette code from Chapter 10 won't be visible unless your video adapter supports 256 colors. The sound program in Chapter 16 runs anywhere but can't do much without a sound card such as SoundBlaster.

BORLAND USERS

Most of the source code on the accompanying disk comes with make files for the Borland C++ 4.0 compiler. As this book goes to press, Borland's first beta version has not yet incorporated all the features of Win32, so we are unable to test some of the programs. With a later version of the Borland tools, however, you should be able to follow the example make files we do provide and compile the few remaining programs as well.

WHAT IS WINDOWS NT?

Microsoft Windows NT is a 32-bit operating system and so takes full advantage of advanced CPU chips, as DOS never could. Unlike earlier versions of Windows, NT does not run on top of another system, so it is not always trying to overcome the limitations of an older base layer. Windows NT has the same graphical user interface as 16-bit Windows, but underneath the surface much has changed. New features include

- Preemptive multitasking
- 32-bit operations
- Virtual memory and protected address spaces
- Scalability to run on different platforms, including RISC workstations and computers with multiple processors
- A security system to identify users, protect system resources, and audit user's actions
- Built-in network capabilities for sharing files and printers
- Support for many networks (such as Banyan, Novell) and network transports (NetBEUI, TCP/IP)
- Subsystems to run programs written for DOS, 16-bit Windows, POSIX, and character-based OS/2
- A new file system (NTFS) that allows long names and better security
- New accessory applications for managing user accounts and network services

HOW THIS BOOK IS ORGANIZED

The first chapter describes the internal structure of the new system. Windows NT does not resemble DOS. It is designed from the ground up to be modular, extensible, device independent, multitasking, and secure. This chapter describes the system's basic components and their interactions.

Chapters 2 and 3 orient the programmer to new tools and new requirements. They survey the process of building a Windows NT program and explain the differences between code written for 16-bit Windows and for 32-bit Windows.

Chapters 4 through 7 describe the core elements of Windows NT programming, features that are entirely new to Windows programmers. When you master threads, processes, synchronization objects, pipes, structured exception handling, memory-mapped files, and virtual memory management, you'll be able to write 32-bit programs that take fullest advantage of the new features that make Windows NT exciting.

Chapters 8 through 12 turn to familiar features of the old API that Windows NT enhances and expands. The GDI now supports Bézier curves, paths, scalable regions, join styles, and cosmetic pens. Several new commands make bitmaps more flexible, and a new enhanced format makes metafiles more truly device independent. A new layer of coordinate transformations makes it easy to rotate, scale, and skew any image. Dynamic-link libraries have a better entry-point mechanism and improved memory management. The commands for file I/O have also grown into a full-featured API.

The subjects of Chapters 13 through 16 are not new to Windows. They are advanced features that acquire new prominence under Windows NT. The private address space that protects each program's memory prevents programs from sharing data directly, so the DDE Management Library (DDEML) becomes an important channel of interprocess communication. The OLE and multimedia chapters both integrate new data types into the system, and because Windows NT runs on more powerful workstations, it is better equipped to process some of the more CPU-intensive data such as waveform sounds and animation.

The final chapter turns to more specialized topics in Windows NT programming. Not every program will need to manipulate security structures, choose among different network APIs, use Unicode, or run in a character-based console window, but all of these features are among the attractions of the new system.

INSTALLING THE COMPANION DISK

At the back of this book is a floppy disk containing all the source code from the sample programs. There are over 35 of them, and they take up over a megabyte of space. They are stored as a self-extracting LHA archive called programs.exe. To unpack the contents onto your hard disk, enter a command like this:

```
programs c:\masternt
```

The archive will create chapter directories under whatever directory you name on the command line.

TYPOGRAPHIC CONVENTIONS

We have used two different fonts to distinguish between commands that are part of the C language and commands that come from the Windows libraries. The "Windows font," which is boldface, indicates names and symbols defined for the Win32 API: **CreateNamedPipe, LOWORD**. The "program font" is used for other elements in a program, including procedure and function names, C reserved words, and variables: WinMain, atoi, if, bResult.

Some symbols appear in all uppercase letters. These are identifiers defined in the Windows header files. They include data structures, such as **PAINTSTRUCT**, message names, such as **WM_COMMAND**, and new variable types, such as **HPEN** and **DWORD**.

Italics mark important words when they are introduced and defined. Angle brackets <like these> indicate a blank space in the syntax that the programmer fills in with any appropriate name or text.

In naming variables we have followed the common "Hungarian" convention of prefixing a few letters to indicate the data type. The prefixes include the following abbreviations:

Prefix	Type
a	Array
b	**BOOL** (int)
by	**BYTE** (unsigned char)
cb	Count of bytes
ch	char
d	double
dw	**DWORD** (unsigned long)
fl	float
fn	Function
h	**HANDLE** (void *)
i	int
l	**LONG** (long)
lp	Long (or far) pointer
n	short

Prefix	Type
p	Pointer
sz	String ending with 0 (null-terminated)
u	**UINT** (unsigned int)
w	**WORD** (unsigned short)
x	An x coordinate (usually int)
y	A y coordinate (usually int)

The pointer prefixes are usually added in front of some other prefix. For example, pdw is a pointer to a **DWORD**. The capitalized words are synonyms for normal C data types. Windows defines these synonyms in order to make variable declarations more informative. For example, **HANDLE** is more descriptive than unsigned int.

Windows NT does not distinguish between near and far pointers; all pointers are the same size. For compatibility, however, the header file definitions often retain the old "lp" prefixes (as in **LPSTR**).

The prefixes help you avoid type mismatches. Suppose bResult is a Boolean variable and dwWritten is a 4-byte double word. They would be declared like this:

```
BOOL  bResult;              // error detected?
DWORD dwWritten;            // bytes written
```

Deep down in some subprocedure you might forgetfully assign a value to the wrong variable:

```
dwWritten = bResult;
```

The prefixes make the mistake more obvious than it would be if you simply wrote

```
Written = Result;
```

The informative prefixes sometimes make code a little easier to understand, and a naming convention is doubly useful for programming teams developing a single application together.

Where a function is called, we always run the parentheses against the function name; where it is defined, a space separates the name from the opening parenthesis:

```
MyFunction( bMyFlag );                    // function call

void MyFunction ( BOOL bMyFlag )          // function definition
```

The space makes it easy to search through a program for the place where a function name is defined, skipping over all the places where it is only called.

Understanding the NT System

- Features of the new system

- Kernel mode and user mode

- Process, object, and virtual memory managers

- Multitasking mechanisms

- Subsystems

WINDOWS NT: NEW TECHNOLOGY

With the universalizing ambition of a true zealot, Windows NT aspires to calm the Babel of clamorous systems, environments, and standards confusedly striving for integration and cooperative harmony. In Microsoft's new promised land a single system will run programs written for MS-DOS, for OS/2, for POSIX, and for Windows; it will do this with a RISC chip or a CISC chip, on a PC or a minicomputer, with a single processor or with multiprocessors. And fulfilling the promise of its 16-bit predecessor, Windows NT will bring the Windows interface to many machines and many tribes: to laptops and LANs, to micros and minis, and to the Latin, Cyrillic, Greek, Hebrew, and Kanji nations. Your programs will speak in tongues, their **WORD**s shall double, and the New Technology will be heard throughout the lands.

The inauguration of a major operating system is bound to generate a certain millennial optimism, but Windows programmers catching sight of NT for the first time will no doubt feel a surge of excitement. Gone are the foolish memory segments, the precariously non-preemptive multitasking, the schizophrenic straddling of 16-bit and 32-bit modes, and even the repressive constraints of a strictly rectilinear drawing space. Programs written for Windows NT gain the advantage of full 32-bit processing, conveniently linear memory addresses, a protected virtual address space, true and robust multitasking, and substantially enhanced graphics capabilities. Even more, Windows NT boasts extensive built-in network facilities, a C2 security rating from the Department of Defense, the ability to run on many platforms, and support for internationalization, including the use of different alphabets. Programs written for NT can reach more platforms and more places more easily than programs written for many other systems.

This chapter explains how Windows NT works. It begins with an overview of the system's design goals and main components. Then it considers the more important components individually, explaining how each one works and how it interacts with the others. By the end of the chapter you'll understand how the system

- Schedules multitasking processes
- Provides protection and security
- Integrates competing protocols and execution environments
- Services your Windows programming calls

As a programmer your contact with the system will be filtered through NT's enhanced version of the Windows Application Programming Interface (API), and you will rarely be aware of the system at any lower level. Readers in a rush to get started can skip to the next chapter and wander back when they have leisure to be curious. Readers who like to know what's really going on should stick around. A single chapter can only aim to introduce the major concepts, so the explanations that follow often give a simplified view of complex operations. For a more comprehensive account of the system's internal design, consult Helen Custer's book *Inside Windows NT* (Microsoft Press, 1993).

What Windows NT Does

From the outset the Windows NT designers aimed to give the system a set of features that would bring Windows up to date with recent hardware and new design models. NT finally leaves behind the vestiges of the 8088 processor and its antiquated real-mode addressing. It performs full 32-bit processing, which substantially increases the speed of computations and memory access. It runs many programs at the same time, switching rapidly between them to perform multitasking. Furthermore, a single program can perform several tasks simultaneously by dividing itself into threads. Threads execute independently, like programs, but several threads can share the resources and global data of a single program. Windows NT incorporates sophisticated memory management using virtual addresses to prevent programs from interfering with each other and using page swapping to increase the apparent size of a computer's memory. Besides built-in support for sharing files and printers across a variety of networks, Windows NT permits distributed processing, allowing a program to divide its work among several different machines. Distributed processing effectively makes CPU power a network resource to be shared as easily as files and printers. Another major design goal was to write an operating system that could run on many different processors. To this end most of the system was, like UNIX, written in C. Those sections of code that rely on a particular machine architecture have been minimized and reside in independent modules, easily replaced.

Though written in C, much of the system code imitates the object architecture of C++, and a rigorous modularity pervades the system to accomplish three additional design goals: extensibility, robustness, and security. *Extensibility* means that the system easily incorporates changes to support new features or new hardware. Internal changes in one component have no effect on other components. The same modularity also makes the system both robust and secure. Errors in one component cannot corrupt another, and no one can reach a component's data without its permission. The use of structured exception handling also enhances the system's reliability. *Structured exception handling* is a method for uniformly trapping and handling errors wherever they occur. If any part of the software or hardware generates an error, some piece of code is always in place to respond. Nothing catches the system entirely by surprise.

Table 1.1 compares Windows NT to other operating systems feature by feature.

TABLE 1.1: A Comparison of Advanced Features in Several Operating Systems

	DOS	Windows 16	POSIX	OS/2	Windows NT
Multitasking		(non-preemptive)	x	x	x
Multiprocessing			x		x
Multiple platforms			x	x	x
32-bit			x	x	x
Protected address space			x	x	x
GUI		x	(X-Windows)	x	x
Built-in networking			x		x

OVERVIEW OF THE SYSTEM

The average user looking at the screen will have trouble distinguishing between 16-bit Windows (also called Windows for DOS and Windows 16) and Windows NT. Both use the same interface. NT even comes with 32-bit versions of the same familiar accessories such as the Program Manager, the File Manager, the Control Panel, and Notepad. But underneath this familiar chassis lies a much more powerful engine. We've already mentioned many features the new engine was built to provide. The form this engine took—the shape and design of the system—was influenced in part by the desire to support such diverse application programming interfaces as POSIX-compliant UNIX, MS-DOS, OS/2, and Windows. These APIs often have conflicting requirements. For example, POSIX distinguishes between lowercase and uppercase in naming files; MS-DOS does not. POSIX and the Win32 API both allow processes to inherit resources, but not all APIs do. POSIX maintains hierarchical parent/child relations between processes, but other APIs do not. Most operating systems perform input and output (I/O) synchronously, but some of these APIs also require asynchronous I/O. To resolve the conflicts, the core of the NT system provides a feature-rich collection of elemental services. The interpreters that manage each different API pick and choose among these native services to build support for the particular commands they offer their client programs.

Windows programmers will see NT primarily through the filter of the Win32 API, and from that superficial perspective NT looks very much like the message-driven system of 16-bit Windows (Win16). In fact, the Win32 protected subsystem does everything it can to mimic the older program interface as closely as possible. Only when you look under the hood does the magnitude of the change become apparent.

Kernel Mode and User Mode

Like many other operating systems, Windows NT protects itself by establishing two running modes for the processor. In the privileged *kernel mode*, the system allows access to hardware and system memory; only the system itself uses this mode. Applications always run in the ordinary *user mode* with fewer privileges. Applications manipulate system resources only by calling system routines. The system then switches to kernel mode, executes its own service routine, switches back to user mode, and returns control to the application. Collectively, the kernel-mode portions of Windows NT are called the *NT executive*. Figure 1.1 shows the kernel and user modes as layers in the system architecture.

Unlike other operating systems, Windows NT does not run *all* its own code in the privileged kernel mode. To support different programming APIs, Windows NT relies on a set of user-mode subsystems. Each subsystem translates API commands into Windows NT service calls. Currently NT comes with four subsystems to support Win32, POSIX, MS-DOS, and 16-bit Windows. (The 16-bit subsystem is often called Windows on Win32 or, more emphatically, WOW.) The API servers are *protected subsystems*. They are "protected" because each runs as a separate process with a private address space. Besides these protected environment subsystems, there is a security subsystem to log users on and keep track of their accounts. Some parts of the system's network support also run as user-mode subsystems.

FIGURE 1.1:

Kernel-mode services and user-mode subsystems

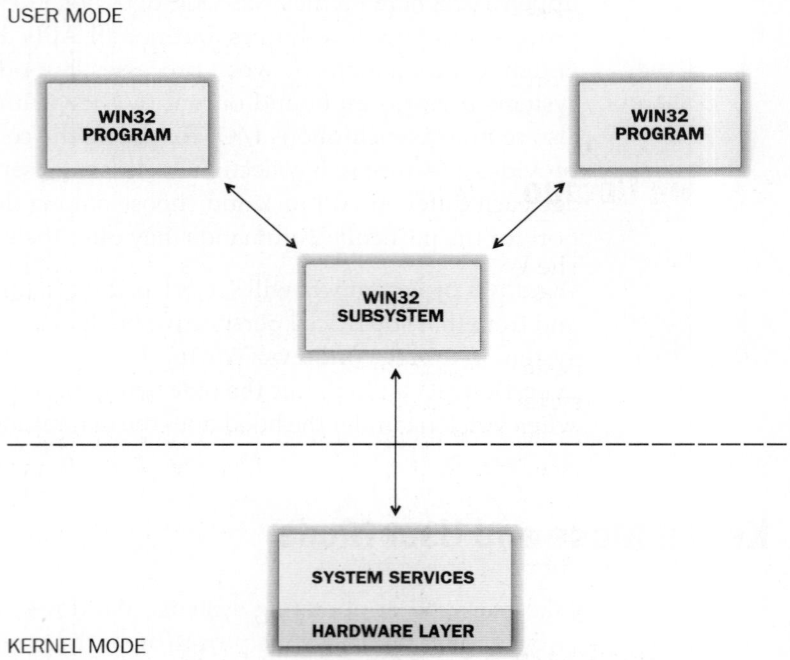

USER MODE

```
┌──────────────┐                              ┌──────────────┐
│   WIN32      │                              │   WIN32      │
│  PROGRAM     │                              │  PROGRAM     │
└──────────────┘                              └──────────────┘

              ┌──────────────┐
              │   WIN32      │
              │ SUBSYSTEM    │
              └──────────────┘

─ ─ ─ ─ ─ ─ ─ ─ ─ ─ ─ ─ ─ ─ ─ ─ ─ ─ ─ ─ ─ ─ ─ ─

              ┌──────────────────┐
              │ SYSTEM SERVICES  │
              ├──────────────────┤
              │ HARDWARE LAYER   │
              └──────────────────┘
```

KERNEL MODE

Clients and Servers

When applications want something done they call an environment subsystem to do it. A program that wants something done is a *client*, and the process it calls to do it is a *server*. A server is a separate program, an independent process that loops continuously while waiting for clients to request its services. The client/server paradigm contrasts with the more monolithic structure of DOS, where any process directly calls any hardware service it needs. Because clients and servers are separate processes, they do not share any memory. The separation protects each process's data from the actions of other processes and avoids embedding in the system assumptions about how a particular service is performed. The client/server model also extends to accommodate network operations where a server machine may do work on behalf of other client machines.

The environment subsystems that support different APIs are servers, and programs that use a particular API are clients. When a program makes a command it sends a message to the API server, which in turn calls on native NT services to perform the requested action. When the native service finishes, the API server sends back any return value in a concluding message.

System Components

The Windows NT system contains a set of highly modular components managing different tasks. The most elemental machine-dependent operations are localized in the kernel and the hardware abstraction layer. The object manager also provides basic services to many different modules. It creates, maintains, and protects all the system's data objects. Other parts of the system draw on these elemental modules to help them manage memory, I/O, interprocess communications, and the interface. The need to regulate the interaction of so many pieces has forced the system to develop in effect a bureaucracy of distinct units, each with its own departmental charter. The following sections briefly describe the major components shown in Figure 1.2.

Hardware Abstraction Layer (HAL)

The hardware abstraction layer (HAL) is the lowest layer in the kernel-mode executive services. It contains in the form of a dynamic-link library a set of platform-specific functions to handle low-level I/O, interrupts, hardware caches, and communication among multiprocessors.

Kernel

The NT kernel is another very low layer. It manages the processor by handling interrupts and exceptions, scheduling threads, and synchronizing multiprocessors. Kernel code must be rewritten for porting to different processors but works with different platforms built around the same processor. By hiding the details of hardware operations, the kernel and the hardware abstraction layer together allow other components to remain as portable as possible. Even device drivers can avoid processor-specific code by calling functions from HAL and the kernel.

FIGURE 1.2:

Components of the NT system

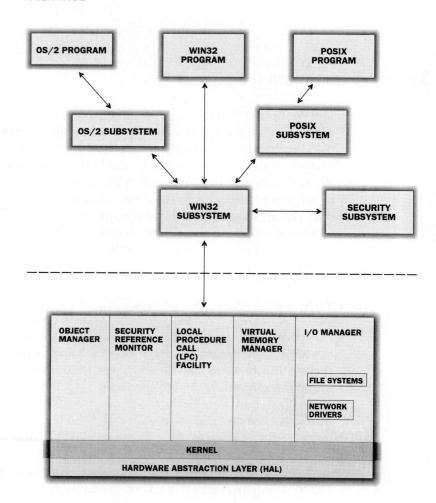

Object Manager

Although Windows NT is written largely in C, not C++, it still makes extensive use of objects and object classes. An *object* differs from other general data structures in that the data it contains cannot be manipulated directly. It can be manipulated only through procedures the object itself provides. An object, then, consists of both data, or *attributes,* and procedures, or *methods,* to manipulate the data. The primary benefit objects confer is to protect any code that uses the object from depending on the particular implementation of an abstract structure. For efficiency a singly linked list might be changed to a doubly linked list, but the parts of the program that use the list object could still call the same methods—delete, insert, and find. The methods attached to an object form a stable programming interface for dealing with the data in the object. Even if the implementation changes, the methods you call to use the object remain constant. Almost every part of the system relies on the object manager to create the structures it manipulates. For example, processes, files, events, and interprocess messages are all "objects" in NT.

Virtual Memory Manager

All the processes running on the system need to use memory, and the memory manager assigns it to them. As the clearing house for all memory allocations, the memory manager prevents two programs from trying to use the same space. Even more, it allows each program to ignore all the others and proceed as though it has complete control of a full address space. Each program is given its own set of memory addresses ranging from 0 to 4 gigabytes, and the memory manager takes care of translating these imaginary *virtual* addresses into actual physical addresses. The memory manager assigns an arbitrary physical location without the program's knowledge. Since a program never uses literal physical addresses, it cannot choose to modify any specific physical location. The memory manager prevents programs from seeing or changing any physical address in use by another program. This enforced isolation gives each program an effectively *private address space* and protects the entire system from erratic programs.

The memory manager also makes room for new memory objects by copying old ones to a disk file. Later, when it needs the objects again, it reads them back. Swapping parts of memory out to a disk is called *paging*.

Process Manager

The multitasking capabilities of Windows NT depend on the system's handling of processes and threads. Both terms designate ways of dividing labor in the operating system. The term *process* names an executable program and all the program's resources as it runs in the system: its virtual address space, the access token that assigns it a privilege level, the resource quotas determined by the user's privilege level, one or more threads of execution, and other objects as they are assigned dynamically, including perhaps an open file or a shared memory block. Every process has at least one *thread* of execution, one path the processor follows through its code. A process can also choose to divide its work into several tasks and create separate threads for each one. *Multitasking* happens when one machine runs several programs at once; *multithreading* happens when one program runs several threads at once. The process manager creates and destroys processes and their threads. It also suspends threads and resumes them.

I/O System

The I/O system handles the flow of information through a variety of peripheral devices including the mouse, the keyboard, printers, disk drives, CD-ROM drives, and networks. In the NT system the goal of providing a uniform, machine-independent interface results in a complex interlinking of many smaller I/O components that often pass I/O requests through several layers of abstraction. Among these components are the I/O manager, installable file systems, installable device drivers, and the cache manager. The I/O manager also routes network requests through a redirector and network transport drivers.

Security Reference Monitor

Whenever a thread asks to use an object, the object manager calls the security reference monitor to determine whether the thread is authorized to receive whatever access rights it has requested. The decision depends on the thread's authorization level, stored in an access token, and the object's access restrictions, stored in its access control list.

Local Procedure Call (LPC) Facility

The local procedure call facility passes messages between clients and servers when both reside on the same machine. NT also possesses a more generalized message facility for remote procedure calls (RPCs), capable of calling servers on remote machines, but the system gains significant speed by using an optimized local facility whenever possible.

Win32 Subsystem

The screen is a system resource all programs must share. The single component responsible for managing the screen, and with it all related input from the keyboard and the mouse, is the Win32 subsystem. Without it Windows NT would have no way of interacting with the user. When any program wants to draw on the screen, its server subsystem invokes window-management or graphics routines from the Win32 subsystem. Win32 includes a new set of console functions to imitate a terminal screen for character-based applications.

THE NT EXECUTIVE

The rest of this chapter explains in more detail how some of the system components perform their tasks. After considering how the NT executive manages objects, memory, multitasking, I/O, and networks, we'll turn finally to this book's *raison d'être*, the Win32 subsystem and its new API.

The Object Manager

A Windows NT object is a data structure with two main parts, a header and a body. Objects come in different types depending on what the data represents, but objects of all types have similar headers. Because all system objects share this one structure, a single set of code, the object manager, can maintain all of them. An object header contains the following information:

Object name	Optional tag that makes the object visible to other processes
Object directory	Node in the system's hierarchical tree of all objects
Security descriptor	Sets access requirements for processes that use the object
Quota charges	System resource charge a process pays to open the object
Open handle counter	Number of times the object has been opened
Open handle database	Processes that have opened the object
Status	Permanent/temporary flag permitting the system to delete the object when not in use
Mode	Kernel/user flag controlling whether the object is visible in user mode
Type object pointer	Pointer to an index of similar objects

The fields in the header are object attributes. The object manager also provides a small set of generic services, or methods, that work with the attributes from an object header. These services include, for example, retrieving information from the header, setting the security protection level, creating a duplicate handle to the object, and closing a handle to the object. More generally, the object manager is involved in creating objects, giving them names recognizable to humans, deciding which other processes can use them, and deducting from the resource quotas of processes that use the object. The object manager works with threads, files, memory blocks, ports, timers, I/O requests, and events, all of which—and more—are represented as objects.

Windows NT handles objects in much the way most programming languages customarily handle files. To use an object, first you open it by name. You can name either an existing or a new object. Like file names, object names can contain a full path indicating a position within the system's overall hierarchy of existing objects.

When you open an object you request particular access rights, just as you might request to read from or write to a file. The object manager returns a handle to the object, and subsequent operations refer to the object by its handle. Eventually you close the object handle. Two programs can share an object by opening handles to it at the same time.

The Type Object

One field in the standard object header points to something called a *type object*. The type object is an internal structure; the object manager creates it whenever an NT component registers a new kind of object. A type object defines the attributes that objects of a particular type share. One type object exists for each new kind of object. The type object holds three kinds of information: static attributes common to all objects of the type, standard procedures (methods) that the object manager calls at certain points in each object's life, and a list of all the objects that have been created of this type. The object manager uses the list to locate objects by type. For example, given the type object for processes, the object manager can enumerate all the different process objects currently running in the system.

The Object Body

Although all object headers are alike, the object body varies from type to type. All books have a cover, a title page, and a table of contents; these common elements are analogous to the object header. But a dictionary object would call for a body of 26 alphabetical sections, while a play object would call for a body of 5 acts. Figure 1.3 shows the parts of an object.

Most parts of the system create object types to suit their needs. The more primitive of these, called *kernel objects,* are not even visible to user-level processes. Others, called *executive objects,* are available to user-mode code, though they can be created and modified only by native NT services. The kernel objects are generally concerned with calling and scheduling processes and procedures. Here is a sampling of some more prominent executive objects:

- A *process* is a running program, including its address space. Processes are created by the process manager.

- A *thread* is an executing unit within a process. Threads are created by the process manager.

- A *section* is an area of memory shared between processes. Sections are created by the memory manager.

- A *file* is a disk file or an I/O device open for access. Files are created by the I/O manager.

- A *port* is a place to deliver messages for a process. Ports are created by the local procedure call (LPC) facility.

- An *access token* contains the security information that sets privileges for the logged-on user. Access tokens are created by the security system.

- A *semaphore* is a counter controlling the number of threads that use an object at one time. Semaphores are created by the executive support services.

The defining characteristics of any object type can be represented simply by diagrams like those in Figure 1.4.

FIGURE 1.3:

Header and body of an object

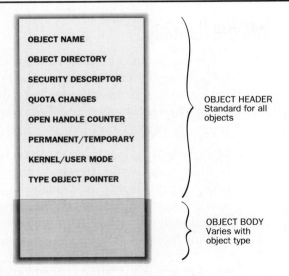

| OBJECT NAME |
| OBJECT DIRECTORY |
| SECURITY DESCRIPTOR |
| QUOTA CHANGES |
| OPEN HANDLE COUNTER |
| PERMANENT/TEMPORARY |
| KERNEL/USER MODE |
| TYPE OBJECT POINTER |

OBJECT HEADER
Standard for all
objects

OBJECT BODY
Varies with
object type

FIGURE 1.4:

Attributes and methods defining a process object

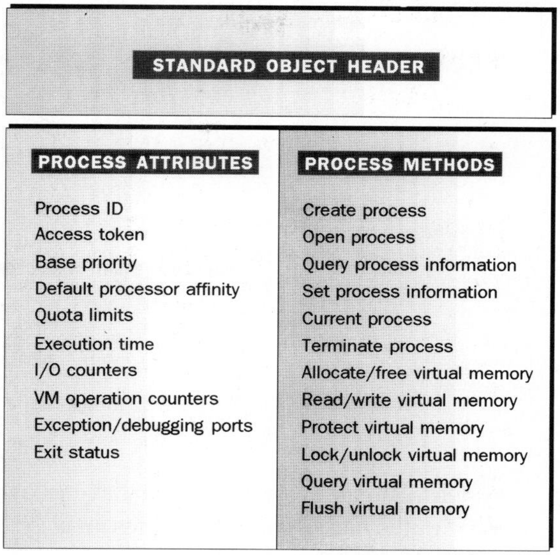

STANDARD OBJECT HEADER

PROCESS ATTRIBUTES

Process ID
Access token
Base priority
Default processor affinity
Quota limits
Execution time
I/O counters
VM operation counters
Exception/debugging ports
Exit status

PROCESS METHODS

Create process
Open process
Query process information
Set process information
Current process
Terminate process
Allocate/free virtual memory
Read/write virtual memory
Protect virtual memory
Lock/unlock virtual memory
Query virtual memory
Flush virtual memory

REPRESENTATION OF A PROCESS OBJECT

Naming Objects

In order to distinguish between objects, the system gives them names. In order to keep track of objects, the system stores all their names in a list. The list of named objects lives in global memory so one process can find and open objects made by another process. One constraint on the naming conventions and the object list structure was the need to support the file systems of MS-DOS and POSIX. Both operating systems store files in a hierarchical tree of directories.

The object name hierarchy begins with a root node designated by a backslash (\), as shown in Figure 1.5. The leaf nodes of the tree name individual objects. The inner nodes traversed in passing from the root to a leaf are object directories. An *object directory object* is the internal structure that represents a directory node. Its primary attribute is a list of object names, and of course some of those names may themselves be object directories from the next level down the tree.

The object manager's name hierarchy does not directly contain all the named objects in the system. It cannot because some objects use their own naming conventions. For example, each of the supported file systems—HPFS, NTFS, POSIX, and FAT—creates its own hierarchy with rules understood only by a driver in the I/O

FIGURE 1.5:

Object names stored in a tree

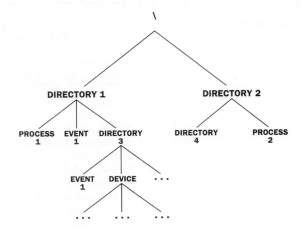

system. The file system is said to have its own *namespace*. The self-contained set of objects in this namespace constitutes an *object domain*. The I/O system manages the objects in its own domains. It creates a new domain for each disk device. The I/O system also creates an object to represent each device, and these *device objects* do appear in the global object hierarchy. Figure 1.6 shows how an object domain attaches to a device object in the global name hierarchy. When the object manager, searching for a file name, traverses the tree and encounters a disk device object, it notices that this object offers a *parse method*, a routine for reading object names from its own domain. The object manager passes the name to the parse method and waits for a result from the I/O system.

For example, consider a program that attempts to open a disk file called c:\word\diss\ch1.doc. The object manager receives a request to open the object at \device\harddisk0\word\diss\ch1.doc. It searches the global namespace until it reaches harddisk0. It discovers that the harddisk0 object has a parse method. It calls the parse method, passing to it the name \word\diss\ch1.doc. The I/O system receives the request and passes it to the appropriate file system driver. The driver locates the file and opens it.

Although the global name tree represents objects only from the local machine, it can link to object domains on other machines by the same method. A device object can represent remote machines. When parsing an object name leads the object manager to a network device object, the parse method invokes a part of the I/O system called the *redirector*. The redirector in turn calls the appropriate network driver to contact the remote file system.

FIGURE 1.6:

Device object node linking two
namespaces

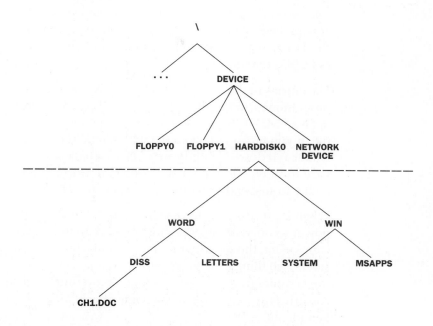

OBJECT MANAGER NAMESPACE

FILE SYSTEM NAMESPACE

Object Handles

To avoid searching through the entire tree every time a program refers to any object, Windows NT also supplies a handle mechanism. Each process remembers all the objects it uses in a private *object table.* Whenever the process creates or refers to a new object, a new entry is added to the object table. The process also receives a handle indexing an entry in its object table, and the table entry points to the object. The handle remains valid until the process closes the object. The object manager has to search its name tree only when processes create or open an object. Subsequent references to the object use the more direct handle.

The use of handles also benefits the system in other ways. Besides a pointer to an object, each entry in an object table holds information useful for object inheritance, access privileges, and resource accounting. When one process creates another process, the system examines the creator's object table. In each entry it finds an *inheritance designation* that may permit the handle to be copied into the object table of the new process. Windows NT does not enforce a hierarchical relation of parent and child for new processes, but the inheritance designation supports subsystems, such as POSIX, that do enforce a hierarchy.

The entries in the object table also record the process's access privileges. MS-DOS programmers know about access privileges from their experience with file I/O. To open an MS-DOS file you must say whether you intend to read or write with the file. If you try to write to a file with a read-only handle, the system prevents you. Under Windows NT all types of objects have access modes and privileges, which vary from type to type. For example, in opening a thread you might request the ability to suspend or terminate its execution.

When a process asks to open an object, the object manager, which has exclusive power to open all objects, must make a security decision. It calls another system component, the security monitor, to make the decision. The security monitor considers two things: the process's access token and the object's access list. The access token comes from the system's logon procedure. When the user logs on, the system constructs an access token object and attaches it to the user's process. The access token identifies the user to the system. Any new processes the user initiates inherit this access token.

An object protects itself with an *access control list* (ACL), a list of users and user groups along with the kinds of access each is allowed. When a process creates an object it attaches an ACL to the security descriptor in the object header (see Figure 1.3). The security monitor reads the access token, looks for the user in the object's ACL, determines whether the user is entitled to use the object in the way requested, and returns its decision to the object manager.

Besides allowing object inheritance and access security, object handles permit resource accounting. Multi-user systems typically need to track and limit the system resources each person uses. NT enforces its limits through the object manager by subtracting something from a process's system quota for each object it opens. The exact amount varies from object to object and generally reflects the object's use of memory. (The process manager also enforces a limit on how much CPU time a user's processes may consume.)

The Virtual Memory Manager

The fact that Windows NT is a 32-bit operating system marks it as part of a new generation of PC systems. The importance of those 32 bits, as we'll explain more thoroughly in Chapter 7, has to do with how the system handles memory. The new system differs fundamentally from MS-DOS in representing memory addresses by a simple linear sequence instead of using segments and offsets. The limits of working in 64K blocks have disappeared. But along with these linear addresses (also called a *flat address space*), the new system brings other sophisticated memory management techniques, of which the most important are virtual memory and page swapping.

When the first IBM PCs were limited to 640K of RAM—and most machines had less than that—ambitious programmers discovered they could still write very large programs by dividing the code into nearly independent sections to be loaded and discarded as needed. These sections were called overlays. Running with overlays, however, required a lot of housekeeping. You had to load and unload the overlays manually, and you had to be careful not to call a function from a part of the program no longer in memory. Virtual memory does the same thing much more conveniently. It allows the system to work with programs, or sets of programs, whose total size exceeds the machine's memory capacity. The system assumes the burden of noticing when a program refers to a section that needs to be loaded and it does the loading automatically. It also unloads unused memory objects to make room for new ones. Virtual memory allows the system to overcommit physical memory.

16-bit Windows programmers already know what it means to work with a virtual device. A device context, for example, represents to the programmer an idealized drawing space with axes extending 32K in every direction. You draw on this idealized space, and the system translates your commands for a specific printer or display adapter. 32-bit Windows virtualizes memory the same way. You write to an idealized memory space using linear addresses that range sequentially from 0 to 4 gigabytes, and the system translates your commands for whatever physical memory is actually installed. The system translates from a logical memory address (0–4GB) to a physical memory address just as when you draw and the Windows GDI translates from logical to device coordinates. The virtual memory system protects you from worrying about which other programs are running and which addresses they are using. Figure 1.7 shows how the virtual memory manager maps logical to physical memory.

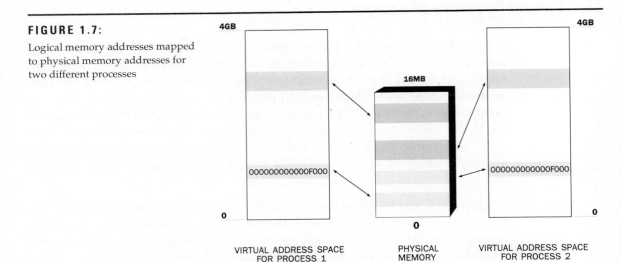

FIGURE 1.7:

Logical memory addresses mapped to physical memory addresses for two different processes

VIRTUAL ADDRESS SPACE FOR PROCESS 1   PHYSICAL MEMORY   VIRTUAL ADDRESS SPACE FOR PROCESS 2

Windows NT is designed for newer CPUs that support logical addresses in the hardware. That means you can't slip under the virtual memory manager and use a physical address to access another program's memory. No other program can interfere with the physical memory assigned to your program. The 4GB of logical memory that every application thinks it owns is a *private address space*. As you can see from Figure 1.7, even if two processes happen to use the same logical address—say 1000—neither will interfere with the other because each "1000" is mapped to a different part of physical memory. One consequence of this protection is that programs cannot exchange addresses with each other to share data. They must use other system-supported mechanisms for that.

When physical memory fills up, the virtual memory manager begins moving sections of memory into a large hard disk file dedicated to this purpose (pagefile.sys). For efficiency the memory manager avoids performing many small swaps by moving blocks of 4K at a time. These blocks are called *pages*. Advanced CPUs support pages as part of their built-in virtual memory capabilities. Whenever the CPU encounters an instruction with a logical address that refers to a page not currently present in memory, the CPU issues a *page fault*. The trap handler receives the fault signal and asks the virtual memory manager to restore the required page. Pages, much like files, can be set to allow only particular kinds of access such as read-only or read/write. Pages can also be locked into physical memory, protected, and even marked as guards so they emit a signal if any program reads them.

Sharing Memory

Processes can share memory by creating section objects. A *section object* is an area of physical memory that has been mapped into two virtual address spaces (see Figure 1.8). If a section is very large, a process may choose to open only a small window into the section, called a *view*. The view can be moved along the full length of the section so that through it the process can read all the shared data.

FIGURE 1.8:

How the virtual memory manager maps section objects and mapped files

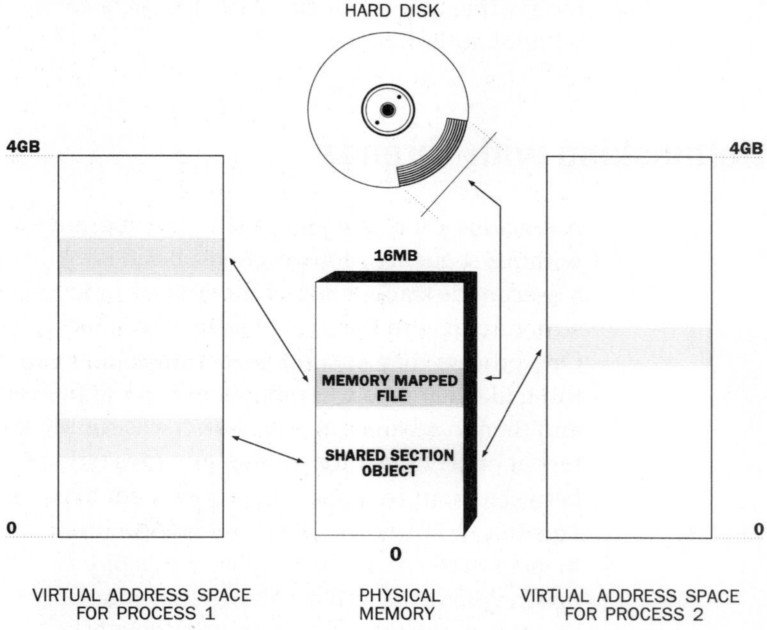

HARD DISK

4GB

4GB

16MB

MEMORY MAPPED FILE

SHARED SECTION OBJECT

0

0

0

VIRTUAL ADDRESS SPACE FOR PROCESS 1

PHYSICAL MEMORY

VIRTUAL ADDRESS SPACE FOR PROCESS 2

A remarkable possibility presents itself. The virtual memory manager possesses three capabilities. First, in converting logical to physical addresses it gains the power to make logical addresses point anywhere it likes. Second, it swaps data from memory to a disk file without the program knowing it. Third, it gives programs small views into shared memory objects. Why not let the system treat all disk files as sections of shared memory? It can page them in and out of memory, it can map logical addresses into file positions, and it can let several programs have views into the same file. The result is a *mapped file*. Programs can read from mapped files with the same ease, and the same syntax, as from an array. In fact, the Win32 subsystem implements all sections as *file-mapping objects*, whether or not they map to disk files. Figure 1.8 shows the virtual memory manager mapping a file section into a program's address space.

Windows NT protects memory in four ways. First, the distinction between kernel mode and user mode prevents nonsystem code from reading system memory. Second, the virtual address space firmly isolates programs from each other. Third, individual memory pages can be marked to limit access. Finally, section objects receive the same protection that all objects do: No process can open an object handle without authorization.

Multitasking with Threads

A thread is a sort of bookmark in the program's code, marking the current position within a sequence of instructions. Besides an instruction pointer, a thread includes a user-mode stack, a kernel-mode stack, and a set of register values. Together these structures record the current state of the machine as it follows one line of execution. One process may create many threads that run concurrently. The result is something like being able to put a bookmark at the beginning of each chapter in a book and then to advance all the bookmarks simultaneously, reading from all the chapters at once. In fact the system executes only one thread at a time, but it switches between them so quickly that they seem to execute simultaneously. Unlike earlier versions of Windows, Windows NT can interrupt threads arbitrarily and force one to yield to the next. This is called *preemptive multitasking*. The non-preemptive multitasking of Win16 systems allows switching only when one process pauses for a new message from the system. In Windows NT a recalcitrant program can no longer freeze the system by neglecting or refusing to take its next message.

Processes and threads are both objects. The object manager creates them, and they have attributes and services like any other object. Their attributes include an ID number so the system can tell them apart, a base priority governing how threads are scheduled, and a cumulative execution time to help the system monitor their use of system resources. A process is the building that houses a program. It contains all the resources a program needs to run, including a memory address space, a program image loaded from the disk, and ports for communicating with other processes. Threads inhabit the process building. They follow the instructions in the program, fill the rooms with data, issue commands, and send messages. Figure 1.9 shows the collection of resources united in a process. A process keeps track of its threads in an object table, along with all its other objects. Also, the virtual memory manager attaches to a process a list of the virtual addresses the process currently uses.

FIGURE 1.9:

The resources that compose a process

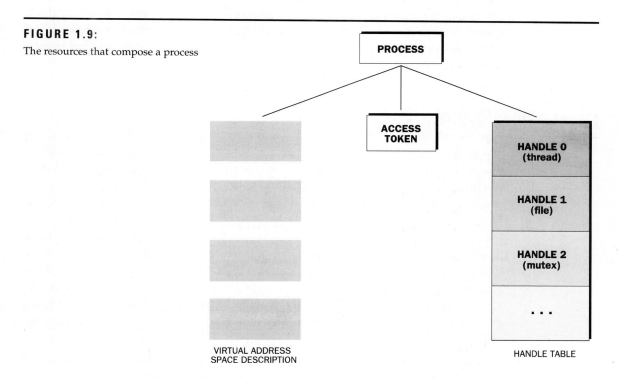

VIRTUAL ADDRESS
SPACE DESCRIPTION

HANDLE TABLE

Threads, being the fundamental unit of program execution, are in a sense the premier object that the rest of the system supports. Other system components such as the I/O manager and the memory manager exist to give threads whatever resources they need to perform their tasks, just as stage managers and set designers prepare for the appearance of actors. Threads are scheduled by the kernel, which, like a director, stages all their entrances and exits.

All the threads inhabiting one process have equal access to that process's resources, including memory addresses and object handles. Naturally, as in any crowded household, problems can arise if several threads want to modify one object at the same time or if one thread moves something without telling the others. *Synchronization* refers to letting a thread suspend itself until some condition is met or some signal received. Coordinating the work of multiple threads within a process usually requires a synchronizing mechanism. The other problem that arises in a system with multiple threads is *scheduling*, which refers to the complex task of switching from thread to thread so that each receives its share of time on the processor. The following sections explain some of the mechanisms in Windows NT that permit synchronization and scheduling.

Synchronizing

Threads can issue a "wait for object" command. When they do they enter a queue of any threads waiting for the same object. Periodically the system checks whether the object's status has changed. When it has, the system awakens the next thread sleeping in the queue. The system determines an object's synchronization status by examining its signal state. The signal state is either on or off, *signaled* or *nonsignaled*. Not all objects have a signal state—only those that a thread might have to wait for. Different synchronization objects use their signaled state to communicate different things. A thread, for example, has a signal state because other threads might need to wait for it to finish before proceeding with their own work. A thread that receives a command to terminate its program might need to wait for other threads in the same program to finish first. Threads remain in a nonsignaled state while they run and are set to a signaled state when they end. Here is a list of synchronization objects with descriptions of their signaled states:

Object	Signaled When...
Thread	A thread terminates
Process	All its threads terminate
File	An I/O operation ends
Event	A thread sets the event signal
Event pair	A thread sets the event signal
Semaphore	The counter reaches 0

Object	Signaled When...
Timer	A time arrives or an interval expires
Mutant	A thread releases the mutant

The last five objects exist only to aid in synchronization. An *event object* announces the occurrence of some system event. *Event pairs* are used only by the Win32 subsystem; they notify the subsystem when it receives certain kinds of messages. Semaphores, which we mentioned earlier in discussing objects, are counters that tally the number of threads using an object. Timers are also counters; they track the system time. The word "mutant" is colorfully derived from the original "mutex," short for *mut*ual *ex*clusion. A *mutant* guards a resource so that only one thread may use it at a time. Only the thread that currently owns the mutex may use the resource. The most famous mutant is probably the conch shell in *Lord of the Flies:* At assemblies only the boy who holds the shell may speak.

Scheduling

The kernel takes responsibility for scheduling threads. It must also assume the related burden of calling interrupt handlers when parts of the hardware need attention and, on multiprocessor systems, keeping each processor busy with a thread of its own. On any system, the kernel spends much of its time moving one thread's data out of a CPU and moving another thread's in. These swaps are called *context switches*. Context switches typically occur when a new thread is ready to execute, when the current thread uses up its turn on the CPU, when a thread terminates or suspends itself, or when something changes the priority of a thread. Deciding which thread to bring up next is one of the operating system's most important tasks.

Priority

Choosing a thread for execution is a matter of priority. The kernel recognizes 32 distinct levels of priority, numbered from 0 (lowest priority) to 31 (highest priority). Most program threads have priorities between 1 and 15 because 0 is only for system use and 16 through 31 are for processing more urgent real-time events. Every thread has a base priority and a dynamic priority. A thread receives its base priority from the process that creates it. The kernel schedules threads according to their dynamic priority, which begins at the base priority but changes as the thread runs according to the needs of its current task. The goal of dynamic priority adjustments is to enhance system response time. Threads engaged in interaction with the user receive priority boosts from the system.

The kernel tracks all threads in its *dispatcher database*. It remembers which threads are running, which processes own them, and which processor they are running on (in a multiprocessor system). Central to this database is the *dispatcher ready queue*, shown in Figure 1.10, which is really a set of 32 queues. Each queue contains all the threads waiting at one priority level. In rescheduling the processor the kernel begins with the high-priority real-time threads and works its way down the ready queue.

FIGURE 1.10:

Dispatcher ready queue

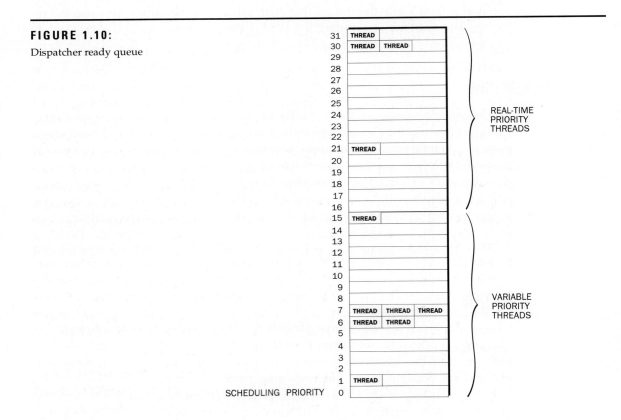

Traps and the Trap Handler

One other important consideration complicates the kernel's scheduling system. Besides switching from thread to thread, the kernel must respond to *interrupts* and *exceptions*. These are signals that arise within the system and interrupt the processor to handle some new condition. When the kernel detects an interrupt or an exception, it preempts the current thread and diverts control to a different part of the system. Which part depends on what condition the signal indicates. The *trap handler* is the part of the kernel invoked to answer interrupts and exceptions. It interprets the signal and transfers control to some procedure previously designated to handle the indicated condition.

Although the system's handling of interrupts will sound familiar to MS-DOS programmers, there are two important differences. First, MS-DOS uses only interrupts, not exceptions. Interrupts are asynchronous, meaning they may occur at any time, and their causes have nothing to do with any code the processor may be executing. Hardware devices, such as a mouse, a keyboard, and a network card, often generate interrupts to feed their input into the processor. Sometimes software generates interrupts, too. The kernel, for example, initiates a context switch by causing an interrupt. Exceptions, on the other hand, are synchronous, meaning they arise within a sequence of code as the result of executing a particular instruction. Often exceptions arise when some piece of code encounters an error it cannot handle. Divide-by-zero errors and memory access violations, for example, cause the system to raise an exception. But not all exceptions are errors. Windows NT also raises an exception when it encounters a call for a system service. In handling the exception, the kernel yields control to the part of the system that provides the requested service.

When it receives an interruption signal, the trap handler first records the machine's current state so it can be restored after the signal is processed. Then it determines whether the signal is an interrupt, a service call, or an exception and passes the signal accordingly to the interrupt dispatcher, the system service dispatcher, or the exception dispatcher. These subsidiary dispatchers locate the appropriate handler routine and transfer control there. Figure 1.11 diagrams the trap handler and its components.

In addition to the trapping of exceptions as well as interrupts, Windows NT differs from MS-DOS in assigning priority levels for each interrupt. The priority assigned to an interrupt is called its *interrupt request level* (IRQL). Do not confuse this with a thread's dynamic priority, which is assigned to a sequence of code; IRQLs are assigned to interrupt sources. The mouse has an IRQL, and its input is processed at

FIGURE 1.11:

Components of the trap handler

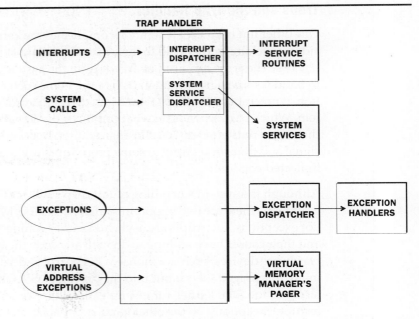

one level of priority. The system clock also generates interrupts, and its input is assigned another IRQL.

The CPU also has an IRQL, which changes as the system runs. Changing the CPU's IRQL allows the system to block out interrupts of lower priority. Only kernel-mode services, such as the trap handler, can alter the processor's IRQL. User-mode threads do not have that privilege. Blocked interrupts do not receive attention until some thread explicitly lowers the CPU's level. When the processor runs at the lowest IRQL, normal thread execution proceeds and all interrupts are permitted to occur. When the trap handler calls an interrupt service routine (ISR), it first sets the CPU to that interrupt's IRQL. Traps of a lower level are masked while the ISR runs in order to prevent relatively unimportant events, such as device input signals, from interfering with critical operations, such as the power-loss routines. When the processor's IRQL level drops, any interrupts that were masked are drawn from their queue and duly processed. Eventually the processor returns to the lowest IRQL and the interrupted thread resumes. Figure 1.12 shows the range of interrupt request levels and marks in gray those that are masked as the processor responds to a signal from the system clock.

FIGURE 1.12:

Lower IRQLs masked while the processor works at a high IRQL

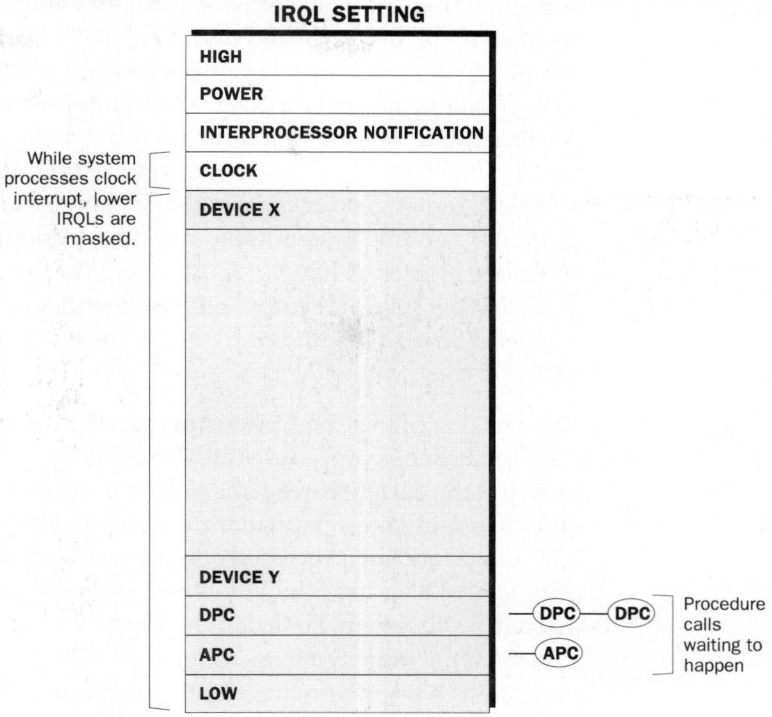

IRQL SETTING
HIGH
POWER
INTERPROCESSOR NOTIFICATION
CLOCK
DEVICE X
DEVICE Y
DPC
APC
LOW

While system processes clock interrupt, lower IRQLs are masked.

DPC — DPC
APC
Procedure calls waiting to happen

To process any interrupt the trap handler must first locate an appropriate handler routine somewhere in the system. It keeps track of interrupt handlers in the *interrupt dispatch table* (IDT). The IDT has 32 entries, one for each IRQ level. Each entry points to a handler, or possibly to a chain of handlers if several devices happen to use the same IRQL. When new device drivers are loaded into the system they immediately add their own handlers to the appropriate IDT entry. They do this by creating and connecting an *interrupt object,* a structure containing all the information the kernel needs to augment the IDT. By using an interrupt object, drivers are able to register their interrupt handlers without knowing anything about the interrupt hardware or the structure of the interrupt dispatch table.

Deferred and Asynchronous Procedure Calls

The kernel exploits the masking of low-level traps to defer low-priority actions until a convenient time. Whenever the kernel runs it raises the processor's IRQL just high enough to block all software-generated interrupts. If the kernel is several layers deep in its own code and discovers that a thread needs rescheduling, it generates a dispatch interrupt. Because all software interrupts are already masked, the dispatch interrupt will be deferred until the kernel finishes and reduces the processor's IRQL. Another variation on this delaying tactic occurs when an interrupt handler wants to initiate a system service that doesn't need high priority. In that case the handler gets an address to the system service, adds the address to a queue of similar pending system calls, and then requests a low-level software interrupt. When the high-level handler finishes and the processor level drops, the system accepts the low-level interrupt and removes the procedure call from the queue. This is called a *deferred procedure call* (DPC). The queued addresses are stored in *DPC objects*, and they wait in the *DPC queue*.

The masking of low-level interrupts permits one other useful deferral mechanism, the asynchronous procedure call (APC). Deferred procedure calls, when they occur, interrupt the current thread, displacing it to execute a system service. APCs, on the other hand, invoke a particular procedure *within* a thread. APC objects wait in the APC queue and are processed only when the processor sinks nearly to its base priority level. DPCs are largely internal, but user-mode processes can request APCs through a subsystem. For example, suppose a thread asks to read information from a file on a network. Such operations are often lengthy. The thread can designate a procedure to respond whenever the read operation happens to finish. Meanwhile the thread moves on to another task. When the I/O manager finishes collecting information from the network, it requests an APC interrupt to call the thread's response procedure. When the processor acknowledges the APC interrupt, it removes an APC object from the APC queue, finds the procedure address in the object, and calls the procedure.

Exceptions

Besides responding to hardware and software interrupts, the trap handler responds to exceptions. Conditions that raise exceptions include illegal instructions, privileged instructions, debugger breakpoints, and memory page read errors. The trap handler invokes the exception dispatcher to find a handler that will dispose of a particular exception. The system handles many exceptions by itself. Page read exceptions, for example, trigger the memory manager to locate a memory page that was swapped to disk. On those few occasions when the system cannot handle an exception, it passes the exception to a debugger, to the current process, or to the process's API subsystem, depending on how the subsystem chooses to implement exceptions. The Win32 subsystem allows programs to build their own high-level frame-based exception handlers. We'll say more about them in Chapter 6.

I/O System

Like other parts of the NT executive, the I/O system was partly shaped by the need to support a variety of APIs. To make the best use of CPU time, the executive implements all I/O asynchronously. In other words, at the system level functions that initiate I/O return immediately and resume program execution before the I/O task finishes. This means a program can still accomplish other work while it is waiting for the result of, say, a disk read. To order a pizza synchronously you would go to the restaurant, place your order, wait for it, and bring it home. To order asynchronously you would call the store, place your order, read a book or do other work, and receive the pizza when you hear the doorbell ring. Not all APIs support asynchronous operations. DOS programmers, for example, customarily wait for the operation to terminate before proceeding. An _lread command, for example, halts program execution until the system finishes reading the disk. Windows programmers too are more accustomed to synchronous I/O, although the multimedia APIs generally allow a choice of synchronous or asynchronous operation. The protected subsystems can choose to expose these asynchronous capabilities in their own APIs, or they can simulate their customary synchronous operation by waiting for a return value before allowing a thread to resume operation.

The central component of the I/O system is the I/O manager. Its purpose is to translate requests for information into a data structure called an *I/O request packet* (IRP) and pass the packet to the appropriate driver. When the driver responds, the I/O manager disposes of the return packet. The operations of the I/O manager create a uniform interface to handle many different kinds of I/O requests. All drivers are constructed to support the model this interface imposes. As a result, the term "driver" in NT designates a much more flexibly defined entity than "device driver" usually implies. Any component that translates a logical request for input into a more specifically physical request can be a driver. For example, a file system is supported by a driver. Windows NT includes drivers to support a number of common file systems, including the DOS file allocation table (FAT) system, the OS/2 high-performance file system (HPFS), and the new NT file system (NTFS). Typically a file system driver receives IRPs requesting to access a particular file and translates the file name into a logical disk address. The modified IRP is then passed to a disk driver, which translates the logical address to a physical sector. Some simple devices require only a single driver; for file-based devices NT typically uses *layered drivers*.

Unlike DOS device drivers, Windows NT drivers are written in a high-level language. This is possible because they rely on another part of the system—specifically the kernel and the hardware abstraction layer—to perform low-level operations. Also, NT drivers can be installed or removed dynamically, as the system runs.

Networks

Built in to Windows NT is the ability to share resources in a peer-to-peer network. Without installing any additional software, users of Windows NT can copy files between machines, send E-mail, and post jobs to a remote printer. The system allows for user accounts, resource security, and remote processing. It includes support for NetBEUI, TCP/IP, and other transports.

The core of the network services is again the I/O manager. Machines connected through a network function much like other file-based devices such as disk drives and are reached through a similar series of layered drivers. Two fundamental components in the layering are the redirector and the network transport drivers. The *redirector* behaves like a local file system but communicates with remote devices. In response to requests for remote I/O, the redirector opens a virtual circuit connecting with the remote device and sends *server message blocks* (SMBs) to the other machine. Below the redirector are transport drivers that determine how to implement the virtual circuit: how to establish a connection, how to begin and end transmission, and how to receive responses. Each network transport protocol uses a different transport driver. Figure 1.13 shows how an application's I/O request trickles down to the transport driver.

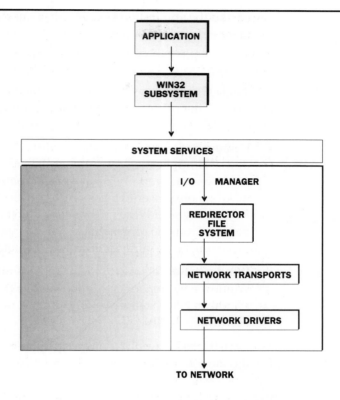

FIGURE 1.13:

How the I/O manager processes a
network I/O request

Multiple Network APIs

Applications can request network services through any of six different APIs. The
first four all provide different services; the last two provide compatibility for existing applications that rely on older network APIs.

- **Win32 I/O API:** The standard file I/O routines in the Win32 API automatically work across networks when their parameters name files on remote machines. Remote files are usually distinguishable because their name strings
  either refer to logical disk drives not present locally or else begin with the
  double backslash (\\) that indicates use of a network name format called the
  uniform naming convention (UNC).

- **Win32 network (WNet) API:** The WNet API is also part of the Win32 API. It
  supplies commands for browsing through remote file systems. These APIs

permit the application to establish connections with other machines and enumerate remote resources.

- **Win32 named pipe and mailslot APIs:** *Pipes* and *mailslots* are memory buffers where processes leave messages for each other. Information directed to a single recipient moves through a named pipe. Information broadcast to many other processes uses a mailslot. Pipes and mailslots can both work across network connections. The recipients may be local or remote.

- **Remote procedure call (RPC) facility:** By linking with the RPC library, a Windows NT application can arrange to divide its code between two or more computers on a network. Typically, smaller computers use remote procedure calls to make a more powerful machine execute the CPU-intensive parts of its code. The RPC facility shields the programmer from implementing the actual network connection. From the programmer's point of view a local procedure calls a remote procedure in the same intuitive way it would call any other procedure.

- **Windows Sockets API:** This set of APIs allows applications to interact with Windows NT networks through sockets that imitate UNIX-style networks. Windows NT systems can, for example, participate in the Internet wide-area network.

- **NetBIOS API:** Applications written for the IBM NetBIOS system can still use the same commands under Windows NT.

Open Architecture

Although network capabilities are built in to NT, they are not hard-wired. The underlying mechanisms that support the various network APIs may be combined with, or even replaced by, third-party components designed to support a variety of network equipment. We have already described the redirector, which intercepts I/O requests for remote files and sends them across the network. A system administrator may load additional redirectors for other networks. In that case, some part of the system must decide which redirector to call. The multiple provider router (MPR) and the multiple UNC provider (MUP) stand between the Win32 subsystem and the redirectors. The MPR supports the WNet API; the MUP steps in when the normal Win32 file I/O commands are used with network file names. The multiple provider router is implemented as a DLL, the MUP as a system driver. Both routers broadcast a request to any network support components installed below them searching for one that recognizes a particular network resource. The redirectors recognize and distinguish between different available networks. Nothing in the layers above—neither the Win32 subsystem nor the Win32 applications—ever needs to ask which networks and network protocols are installed. Network requests from the Win32 subsystem are filtered through several layers, each adding more specific information about the network connection.

Below the redirectors, which establish high-level links with a particular network, are the transport drivers, which perform the low-level chores of translating network connections and message streams into discrete packets according to some recognized protocol. Like the redirectors, the transport drivers are extensible. The system comes with some and allows others to be added. All transport drivers are written to support a single low-level API called the transport driver interface (TDI). This enforced standard ensures that any redirector can communicate with any transport driver. Windows NT comes with support for NetBEUI and TCP/IP transport. Support also exists or is in development for these transports: IPX/SPX (used by Novell's NetWare), DECnet, AppleTalk, and XNS (Xerox Network Systems).

Distributed Processing

Networks exist to share resources. They let a user on one machine make use of data, programs, printers, and other resources on other machines. Another resource that computers might usefully share is processor time. A program running on a small machine might benefit from passing some of its work to another machine, possibly a more powerful machine. Dividing a task so that parts of it run on different computers is called *distributed processing*. Typically the user loads the client half of an application on a small PC. The client half manages the user interface, receiving commands from the user and displaying results. Whenever the user requests a difficult or lengthy operation, such as a database query, the client passes the command to a remote server. The server probably contains the actual database and a search engine. The server is likely to be a workstation capable of much faster searches. The server runs in a loop waiting for commands from any of its clients. When it receives a data query, it performs the search and sends the result back to the client.

A consortium of companies known as the Open Software Foundation (OSF) has established standards for a complete distributed computing environment (DCE). One component of this standard is a remote procedure call (RPC) service. In a flurry of three-letter acronyms we can give this facility its full name: the OSF DCE RPC standard. The RPC standard defines specific protocols and transmission formats for compliant systems. Windows NT complies with this industry standard, so with it you can build clients for any DCE server and servers for any DCE client.

A program that wants to make remote procedure calls must be divided into two separate executable files, one for the client and one for the server. Clients call server procedures by name, just the way they normally would call other procedures in the same program. An RPC program also needs one new component: a file defining the server's network interface. The interface definition includes a function prototype and some additional information used to identify the server over the network. The definition is written in the Interface Design Language (IDL). A special compiler reads the interface definition and constructs from it a library of stub procedures. Each stub contains commands to initiate a network connection and send the server a request. The linker inserts these stubs into the client whenever the client calls a server procedure. The source code contains no reference to the network, but the executable file replaces some procedure calls with network calls. The result is distributed processing.

The special compiler that creates stubs from the interface definition is called the MIDL compiler because it implements Microsoft's version of the standard Interface Definition Language. The Windows NT remote procedure call tool kit also includes several runtime libraries. These DLLs must be in the path where the client and server run. The stub procedures call library functions to perform network operations. Figure 1.14 shows how a remote procedure call passes from client to server.

Chapter 14 explains more about networks and develops a sample RPC program.

THE SUBSYSTEMS

So far we have focused exclusively on the NT executive. Conspicuously absent from our account so far is a user interface. The Win32 subsystem provides that. NT cannot run without the Win32 subsystem to manage the screen. The Win32 subsystem also coordinates the interactive operations of all the other protected subsystems so that applications written for DOS, POSIX, OS/2, Win16, and Win32 can all share the screen harmoniously. The subsystems are integrated in other ways, as well. For example, using the clipboard, the user can cut data from a Win16 application and paste it into a Win32 program. A DDE conversation can include both Win16 and Win32 participants. At the command prompt in a shell window (see Figure 1.15) the user can start up any program, no matter what subsystem it uses, by typing its name and pressing Enter. This section explains how programs interact

FIGURE 1.14:

How a remote procedure call moves from a client application to a server on a different machine

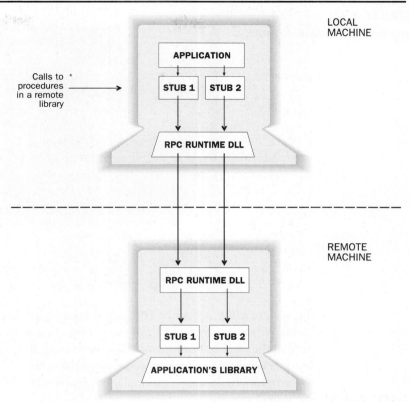

with their subsystem, how the other subsystems depend on and relate to the Win32 subsystem, and how the new Win32 API differs functionally and conceptually from its Win16 predecessor.

How Programs Use the Subsystem

The Win32 subsystem contrasts markedly with Windows on DOS in that it is not a DLL. API calls generally do not link dynamically to a Windows API service. Instead, they send messages to the Win32 server. The Win32 subsystem is an independent server process looping continuously and waiting for requests from client programs. It receives messages, processes them, and sends back responses. Turning

FIGURE 1.15:

Windows NT command shell window

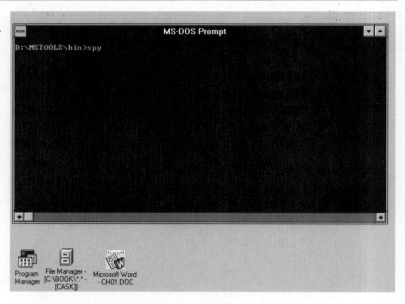

the system into a server has the advantage of protecting its global memory. Under 16-bit Windows every API call turns execution over to a DLL. DLLs are not programs; they are only libraries. They run using the caller's heap and stack. The library code and the program code share the same address space, and any mistakes the program makes can potentially corrupt the library's own internal data. Because the Win32 subsystem is an independent process like any other, it has a private address space. Its client programs can never accidentally modify memory assigned to the Win32 process. This makes the system very much more robust and secure. Figure 1.16 illustrates the interaction between a client program and its server subsystem.

Of course, sending a message to execute each API call could slow things down. Besides the overhead of queuing and reading messages, two context switches also intervene in every call as the kernel saves the status of the client thread and switches to the subsystem and then saves the subsystem status and switches back to the client. The system designers found several ways to optimize the API calls. First, the context switches themselves save and load only the minimum information and in the fastest possible order. Second, the mechanism for sending messages is flexible. Each message is sent as a local procedure call (LPC). An LPC works quickly because it

FIGURE 1.16:

How a Win32 program invokes
Win32 API routines from the Win32
subsystem

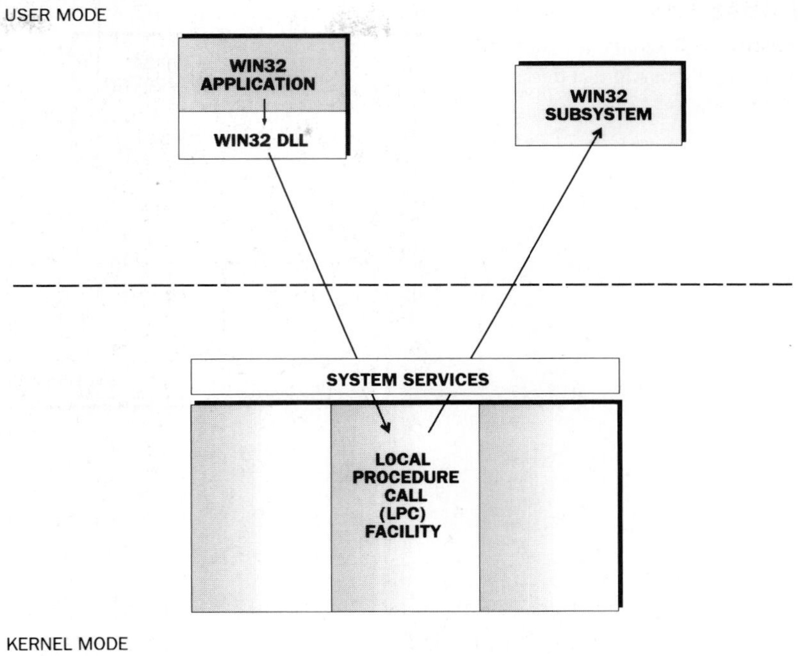

USER MODE

WIN32
APPLICATION

WIN32 DLL

WIN32
SUBSYSTEM

SYSTEM SERVICES

LOCAL
PROCEDURE
CALL
(LPC)
FACILITY

KERNEL MODE

carries only a short message. For those occasions when extra information must accompany a message, the LPC tells the server what information to look for and where to find it in a shared memory section constructed by the client. LPCs can also work with callbacks, where either client or server follows up one message with a request for more information in another. There is even a "quick LPC" used for the window manager and GDI in which the server dedicates a new thread and a stable section object for passing a series of high-priority messages.

The best way to speed up server calls, of course, is to avoid them altogether when possible. Since the purpose of making the subsystem a separate process is to protect global data, any API routines that do not use global data need not call the server. Some APIs still live in a DLL and run in the caller's address space. Figure 1.17 shows how a Win32 program reaches some NT executive services through a DLL instead of through the server.

FIGURE 1.17:

A program bypassing the subsystem when it calls an API that doesn't use global data

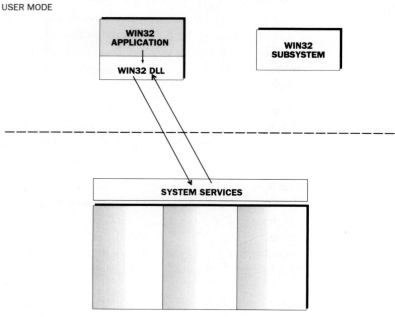

One other set of LPC optimizations involves the GDI and so comes up in Chapter 8. Aside from that one exception, as a programmer you will rarely be aware of the mechanisms that invoke a particular API. The linker handles them for you. For each API call in a program the linker automatically provides either a dynamic link reference or a stub that sends a message to the subsystem.

Coordinating the Subsystems

The command shell shown in Figure 1.15 resembles the DOS box from Windows 16 but has many new capabilities. Among them is the ability to start any program from the command line. Similarly, the icons in the new Program Manager may represent programs intended for any execution environment. To start any program, Win32 begins by creating a process object. If, however, Win32 does not recognize the executable file format, it passes the new process to one of the other subsystems. The new program becomes a client of the other subsystem.

The Win32 subsystem manages the screen for all subsystems. For character-based programs it creates a console window like the command shell. A new set of console APIs creates character-based output in a window, and the subsystems call these Win32 commands to put characters on the screen. Because Win32 draws all the consoles, it always knows which window has the focus and which subsystem should receive input from the mouse and the keyboard.

As an added benefit, the new console routines allow developers to produce 32-bit character-based native Windows NT applications. Many of the NT development tools, such as the compiler and linker, use the console services. It is also possible to cut and paste text to and from a console with the Windows clipboard.

The MS-DOS and WOW (Windows on Win32) subsystems work a little differently than the others. Neither is a server process. MS-DOS programs run in a virtual DOS machine (VDM), an application whose virtual address space contains the code and drivers for MS-DOS. Many VDMs can run simultaneously. A built-in instruction execution unit processes the assembly-language instructions, traps system calls, and forwards them to the appropriate VDM virtual drivers, Win32 routines, or native NT services. A VDM can even start up new 32-bit processes. When the user enters the name of any program to execute, the VDM simply asks Win32 to create a new process. The console window runs anything (no more "This program requires Microsoft Windows" warnings). Also, unlike the Win16 DOS windows, VDMs are not memory hogs. They can swap their memory to disk, and they load their code in pieces only as needed. Furthermore, multiple VDMs share much of their emulation code.

WOW applications also run in a virtual DOS machine. When the user starts a WOW program Win32 recognizes the DOS executable file format and initiates a VDM. The VDM in turn loads the WOW support into its own address space. All concurrent WOW applications effectively share a single VDM, just as they would normally share a single DOS machine. Although each WOW application is at some level an NT thread, the kernel still schedules them non-preemptively. Only the WOW subsystem can switch from one WOW thread to another; after running non-WOW applications, the kernel returns control only to whichever single WOW application it last interrupted. This allows the WOW subsystem to mimic exactly the old Windows environment.

The WOW subsystem does not really implement the Windows 16 API. Instead, the virtual system DLLs (GDI, Kernel, User) call 32-bit code high in the VDM's virtual address space. This 32-bit code translates any addresses to the flat 32-bit format and calls the corresponding Win32 API. WOW applications are really using the Win32 routines. Therefore, ill-behaved Windows 16 applications that depend on knowledge of internal system structures may not run in WOW.

The Win32 API

Finally we reach an overview of this book's real topic, the Win32 API. This API extends the old set of 16-bit Windows routines to accomplish the following design goals:

- A 32-bit flat memory model

- Preemptive multitasking

- Improved memory and security capabilities through the use of virtual memory and object management

- Multithreaded processes

- Enhanced graphics capabilities

- Support for internationalization

From 16-bit Windows the development team ported much of the old window management and user interface code, but the Graphics Device Interface (GDI) had to be rewritten. The new GDI is the only part of Windows NT written largely in C++.

Moving to 32 bits caused some of the more noticeable changes to the API. Since memory addresses and integer variables have doubled in size, many of the data structures that hold them have also changed. Handles, pointers, and logical drawing coordinates are now 32 bits wide. Some of the old routines can't accommodate the new sizes. **MoveTo**, for example, returns the x and y coordinates of the old pen position packed into a single 32-bit **DWORD**. Now that the x and y coordinates take up 32 bits *each*, a new "extended" function, **MoveToEx**, supercedes the old **MoveTo**. Similarly, a number of messages that carried handles and coordinates in their parameters have been restructured. In fact, message parameters no longer come in two sizes. Instead of a word parameter and a long parameter, Win32 messages have two 32-bit parameters. The name "wParam" anachronistically persists, but the

WPARAM type is defined as **UINT**, and unsigned integers are now 32-bit values. Far-sighted Windows 3.1 developers who coded with **STRICT** types and message crackers will hardly notice these changes. Others will benefit from the new PortTool utility described in Chapter 3.

More exciting than small changes to a familiar landscape are the vast new territories suddenly exposed in the Win32 API *Programmer's Reference* manual. Microsoft's documentation recognizes the groups of functions listed in Table 1.2. Asterisks mark groups that are new or significantly extended.

TABLE 1.2: Function Families in the Win32 API

Atoms	Dynamic data exchange	*Messages and message queues
*Bitmaps	Dynamic-link libraries	*Metafiles
Brushes	*Errors	Mouse input
Buttons	*Event logging	Multimedia file I/O
Carets	*File I/O	Multimedia timers
*Character-mode support	File installation library	Multiple Document Interface
Clipboard	File Manager extensions	*National language support
Clipping	*File mapping	*Networks
Colors and color palettes	Filled shapes	Object Linking and Embedding libraries (OLE)
Combo boxes	Fonts and text	Painting and drawing
Common dialog box library	High-level audio	*Paths
Communications	Hooks	Pens
Control Panel applications	Icons	*Performance monitoring
Controls	Keyboard accelerators	*Pipes
*Coordinates and transformations	Keyboard input	Printing
Cursors	*Lines and curves	Print spooler management
Data decompression library	List boxes	*Processes and threads
*Debugging	Low-level audio	Rectangles
*Device contexts	*Mailslots	Regions
Dialog boxes	Media control interface	*Registry and initialization files
Drag-and-drop interface	*Memory management	*Resources
Dynamic Data Exchange Library (DDEML)	Menus	Screen-saver library

TABLE 1.2: Function Families in the Win32 API (continued)

Scroll bars	*Synchronization	Window classes
Security	*System information	Window procedures
*Services	*Tape backup	Window property
Shell library	*Time	Windows
String manipulation	Timers	
*Structured exception handling	*Unicode	

Win32s

To assist developers in creating source code that runs in 16-bit Windows and in Windows NT, Microsoft offers Win32s, a set of dynamic-link libraries that implement a subset of the Win32 API and run under MS-DOS. Programs that link to Win32s can call any of the full Win32 APIs, but some of them, such as **CreateThread**, will always return an error code. By including all the API functions, even without all their functionality, Win32 makes it possible to write code that tries a 32-bit command, tests the return value, and if it fails calls some 16-bit alternative code instead. The extra work required to provide 16-bit alternatives for some sections may be justified if it helps a developer avoid creating and maintaining two entirely separate programs, one for each platform.

Windows NT brings a full-featured modern 32-bit operating system to desktop machines. In this niche it competes with UNIX and OS/2. Its hopes for success depend largely on the system's chameleon-like ability to run programs written for a variety of environments, including its desktop predecessors, MS-DOS and Windows 16, as well as its 32-bit competition, UNIX and OS/2. The system's scalability and security also enhance its appeal. Windows NT runs on RISC and CISC machines with single and multiprocessors, and it complies with government standards for a C2 security rating. (Future releases will probably improve that rating.) The distinction between kernel mode and user mode protects the system from the applications it runs. The pervasive design concepts of objects and client/server relations also help to make the system both modular and secure. Within the NT executive many independent components cooperate to isolate most of the system from device-dependent code. These components include the process manager, the object manager, the virtual memory manager, the I/O manager, the local procedure call facility, and the kernel.

Surprisingly, a few parts of the operating system run as separate processes in user mode. These are the protected subsystems that support programs written for different APIs. The Win32 subsystem creates the user interface for Windows NT and coordinates the actions of all the other subsystems.

Having looked under the hood, we next move behind the wheel and examine the dashboard. Chapter 2 describes the tools the Windows NT SDK provides for creating 32-bit programs that take full advantage of the new system. You'll see the compiler, the linker, the debugger, and other important utilities. The remaining chapters help you navigate through the new territories of the expanded Win32 API.

Compiling a
Windows NT Program

- Using the compilers and the linker

- Setting options for debugging and release versions

- Automating compilation with make files

- Recognizing differences between Win16 and Win32

Together, this chapter and the next explain what Windows programmers need to know in moving from the Windows 3.1 to the Windows NT development environment. Chapter 2 concentrates on the basic mechanisms of producing a Windows NT program: how to compile and link, what command options to use for debugging and release versions, and how to revise your NMake script files. In order to illustrate the pieces of a Windows program and to demonstrate how they fit together, the last part of the chapter presents our version of the conventional Hello program. Experienced programmers may choose to skim through the new compiler options (don't miss the make file) and jump to the end, where we describe a few important differences between Win16 programs and Win32 programs. Chapter 3 explores in more detail some subtle changes from the old Win16 API and offers strategies for porting old programs and for writing code that easily compiles for both environments.

TOOLS FOR BUILDING

To build a program you will have to invoke at least four separate tools: the compiler, the resource compiler, the resource converter, and the linker. This section explains how and when to use each one.

The Compiler

The Win32 SDK comes with several compilers. The CL compiler produces 16-bit code; to produce 32-bit NT code you will use the CL386 compiler. If you installed MIPS programming tools, then you have the CC compiler. The programs in this book use CL386. Like CL, CL386 automatically invokes the linker to connect a new object file to its libraries. You can pass linker options on the CL386 command line, or you can tell CL386 not to link and then invoke the linker later yourself.

Compiler command lines for 16-bit code typically begin with a memory model switch, such as −AS or −AM, indicating which version of the C runtime libraries the program uses. In the 32-bit flat address space of Windows NT, which lacks segments, different memory models serve no purpose. All pointers are the same size, so there is no distinction between near and far. In effect, CL386 programs always use the small memory model. The −AS switch would be redundant. Another familiar switch that no longer serves a purpose in NT is −GA, used with protected-mode-only programs to optimize the prolog and epilog code attached to every callback procedure. Windows NT does not have different running modes and does not need prologs for callback procedures.

For both the compiler and the linker we describe only those options of most interest for general Win32 programming on an Intel machine.

- **−c:** Forces the compiler not to link. The compiler stops after creating all the object files and does not create an executable file.

- **−D:** Defines constants for the source file. This switch has the same effect as a `#define` statement. Defining constants on the command line is often a convenient way to include or exclude sections of the source file bracketed by `#if` conditions. Defining DEBUG, for example, might make the program include lines that send output to the debugger. You should always define −D_X86_ because a few of the header files test that variable and compile some sections conditionally. To use the C runtime routines in a multithreading program, you must also set −D_MT. Microsoft's samples now conventionally define either −DWIN16 or −DWIN32, whether they use the variable or not, to establish a standard method for indicating the target environment. (As of this writing, only the dos.h header actually tests for `WIN32`.)

- **−G3:** Permits the compiler to generate code for an 80386 CPU. Since NT requires at least an 80386 to run, the 32-bit compiler defaults to −G3. Use −G4 for programs that want to support only an 80486 or higher processor.

- **−Gz:** Requests the new `_stdcall` calling convention for all procedures. `WinMain`, window, and callback procedures must use `_stdcall`; for other procedures it is optional. The default −Gd flag calls for the `_cdecl` calling convention. If you use that flag then you must explicitly declare all window and callback procedures as `_stdcall`. The old Windows 3.x constants **PAS-CAL**, **CALLBACK**, and **WINAPI** now uniformly resolve to `_stdcall`; you may continue to use them in all the usual places.

- **−Os:** Makes the compiler optimize for size. During debugging use the −Od flag to disable all optimizing. Optimized code confuses symbolic debuggers when they try to match lines of source code with machine instructions. Also, the compiler works faster with optimizing off. −Od is the default setting.

- **−W3:** Permits the compiler to give warnings even for situations that are not severe. −W4 is the most permissive setting, generating the most warnings. −W3 is sufficient for most purposes, though we recommend −W4 while debugging. (At −W4 the compiler issues many warnings about the contents of the standard Windows header files. They may disappear in future versions. Ignore them.)

- **−Zi:** Adds to the object file information for the debugger, including line numbers and function and variable names. CodeView (16-bit) and WinDebug (32-bit) need this information to associate source code symbols with machine instructions. −Zd does the same thing as −Zi but includes only global and external symbols. Use it to produce a smaller debugging executable file or to prepare for debugging with the NT Symbolic Debugger (NTSD).

- **−Zg:** Generates a list of function prototypes without compiling the program. If you don't normally add function prototypes to your code as you write, use −Zg on a command line by itself to extract prototypes for your header file.

- **−Zs:** Checks syntax without compiling. Run −Zs on a line by itself for early versions of a program before you start performing full compiles.

- **/link:** Introduces another set of switches for the compiler. If present, this switch must appear last on the command line. (We'll describe the linker options in a minute.)

Compiler Command Lines for NT Programs

To summarize, here are the command lines we recommend for compiling NT programs. First, the debugging version:

```
cl386 −c −Gz −W4 −Zi −D_X86_ −DWIN32 hello.c
```

Those switches inhibit linking, select the _stdcall calling convention, accept the default optimizing (none), ask to receive all warnings, and include full symbolic information for the debugger. For a release version you can optimize, reduce the warning level, and omit the debugging information:

```
cl386 −c −Gz −Os −W3 _D_X86_ −DWIN32 hello.c
```

Environment Variables

To avoid repeatedly typing out a long command line of all your favorite options, store some of them in an environment variable called CL386. The compiler then uses the environment switches as its default settings. You can still override the environment defaults on the command line. To set environment variables, go to the Control Panel and start up the System applet. Figure 2.1 shows the dialog box where you enter new variables. Variables you set here will be available in any virtual DOS machines you run.

FIGURE 2.1:

Using the System applet dialog box for setting environment variables

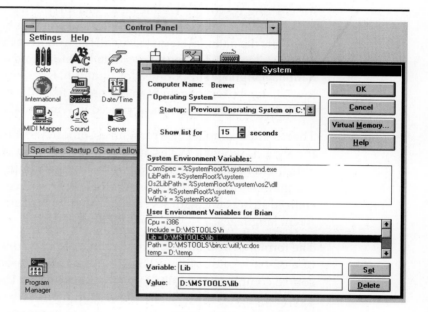

Normally, when you install NT on a single machine the system creates two accounts, one for the Administrator and one for a user. The installation program for the Win32 SDK sets programming environment variables for only one account. To compile from other accounts, you will need to set environment variables for CPU, LIB, INCLUDE, and PATH for each account from the system applet. (You will have to log out and log back in for the new settings to take effect.)

The Resource Compiler

Old Win16 resource scripts compile unmodified with NT. You will have to modify your make files, however, to avoid calling the resource compiler after the linker. Win16 requires running the resource compiler before linking to create a .RES file and after linking to put the resources in the .EXE file. Now the linker itself processes the resources along with the other object files.

Four new statements sometimes appear in Win32 resource scripts. Two of them, **CHARACTERISTICS** and **VERSION**, exist only for the convenience of utility programs for creating resources. Utilities may encode private information in a **DWORD** after either statement; the resource compiler itself ignores both. The new **LANGUAGE** statement sets the national language for all the resources that follow, up to the next **LANGUAGE** statement. The legal constants for indicating a language are defined in the national language support header, winnls.h. Finally, the new **EXSTYLE** statement allows dialog boxes to include in their style flags the extended window styles, such as **WS_EX_TOPMOST**, that first appeared in Windows 3.1.

The resource compiler also recognizes some new control types such as **AUTO3STATE**, for a check box that cycles automatically between checked, unchecked, and disabled, and **PUSHBOX**, which is identical to a push-button control but shows only text without a button face or frame. Another new resource type, **MESSAGETABLE**, is a specialized string table with several equivalent sets of error and message strings in different languages.

The format of a 32-bit resource file differs from a 16-bit resource file. The elements of a 32-bit resource file (.RES), for example, align on **DWORD** boundaries. The resource compiler internally converts all strings to Unicode with the **MultiByte-ToWideChar** function. The headers for each resource contain new information. The Win32 API contains new functions, such as **UpdateResource**, for enumerating and modifying individual resources within an executable file.

The 32-bit resource compiler requires no option flags. It ignores the old −r flag, which makes the 16-bit rc program stop after creating a .RES file. It accepts a −v flag for verbose operation, causing the compiler to generate messages as it proceeds. The flag is optional but educational.

To compile the resource list (.RC) for Hello, you would enter this command:

```
rc hello.rc
```

The Resource Conversion Utility (CvtRes)

Although the 32-bit resource compiler produces .RES files in a Win32 format, the linker cannot recognize them without a special COFF format header. Before the linker can read a .RES file, you must run a conversion utility called CvtRes. (Future releases may not require CvtRes.)

- **−[i386/mips]:** Tells the conversion utility which processor to set in the header. Don't omit this switch.
- **−o <filename>.RBJ:** Assigns a name for the converted resource file. By default, the conversion utility adds the .OBJ extension. To distinguish compiled source files from compiled resource files, it is conventional to use the .RBJ extension for resource objects.

The command line to convert hello.res would be

```
cvtres −i386 −o hello.rbj hello.res
```

The Microsoft Portable Executable Linker

Microsoft's 16-bit C development tools produce object files in a format called the Object Module Format (OMF). The 32-bit linker works with modules in a different format, called the Common Object File Format (COFF.) The COFF format originated in UNIX System V. The Microsoft version adds a few private records but is otherwise very much like UNIX COFF.

The format of executable files has also changed. The 32-bit linker does not create programs in the New Executable format of 16-bit Windows applications. Instead it uses the new Portable Executable (PE) format. The old MapSym program becomes MapSymPE; the new version converts map files to symbol files for PE executables.

The new command for linking is Link32. Options on the command line may come in any order.

- **−debug:*[MAPPED/NOMAPPED,][NONE/MINIMAL/PARTIAL/FULL]*:** Tells how much debugging information to include in the executable file and, optionally, whether to load the symbolic information into memory with the program when it starts up. The amount may be NONE, to omit debugging information; MINIMAL, to include only public symbols; PARTIAL, which adds line numbers and the program name; or FULL, which includes local variables and types.

- **−debugtype:*[COFF/CV/BOTH]*:** Tells which debugger format to use. CodeView and WinDebug use one format, indicated by the CV option. To prepare for the NT Symbolic Debugger (NTSD) or the Kernel Debugger (KD), use the default COFF option. Specifying BOTH includes both formats. Files that use the CV format debugging information must also be compacted with CVPack before debugging; the linker calls CVPack automatically.

- **−DLL:** Produces a dynamic-link library instead of an executable file.

- **−entry:<symbol>:** Sets the point in the program where execution will begin. The default value varies with different subsystems. For DLLs, it is the initialization routine. Normally a program can accept the default entry point. For Win32 programs that use the GDI interface, not the console functions, the default is WinMainCRTStartup, an initialization routine from the C runtime library.

- **−machine:*[i386/MIPS]*:** Lets the linker verify that all the object files, which already designate a target machine internally, have in fact been compiled for the correct machine. This switch is optional.

- **−out:*[filename]*:** Optionally specifies a name for the resulting executable file.

- **−subsystem:*[NATIVE/WINDOWS/CONSOLE/POSIX/OS2][version]*:** NATIVE programs (the default) are those that do not require a specific subsystem. WINDOWS programs are graphical applications that use the GDI API. CONSOLE programs use the console API for a character-based interface. POSIX and OS2 are obvious. Optionally, you can specify a minimum version number for the target system. The version number can be a single value ("3") or it can include a minor version number as well ("3.1"). The default value is "0.0".

- **−verbose:** Sends more information to the standard output as linking occurs. Optional but educational.

Linker Command Lines for an NT Program

Besides option switches, a linker command line specifies the names of the object files and the libraries with which to link them. For example, the linker command to produce a debugging version of a program called Hello looks like this:

```
link32 −debug:full −debugtype:cv −subsystem:windows hello.obj \
    hello.rbj libc.lib ntdll.lib kernel32.lib user32.lib gdi32.lib
```

The particular libraries you include depend on which subsystem the program uses and whether it performs multithreading. Multithreaded applications need reentrant versions of the C runtime functions, so they link to libcmt.lib instead of libc.lib. (They also define the constant _MT, typically on the compiler command line.) Compiled resource files are now linked along with the object files. Notice that hello.rbj appears on the linker command line. Most Windows programs that use the GDI for their output (instead of the console API) use the four libraries ntdll, kernel32, user32, and gdi32. Our Hello program happens not to call any functions in the GDI32 library, so the linker generates this warning:

```
warning 0505: No modules extracted from D:\MSTOOLS\lib\gdi32.lib
```

Most programs, however, do use all four libraries. It's generally easier to include them all than to check call by call which libraries your program actually uses. Compulsive programmers who really do want to know will be glad to find a master list of library symbols in the \mstools\lib directory. Look for win32api.csv.

Appendix A briefly describes all the libraries in the SDK \lib directory. There are of course no longer different C libraries for different memory models.

For a release version, omit the debugging options:

```
link32 −subsystem:windows hello.rbj hello.obj libc.lib ntdll.lib \
    kernel32.lib user32.lib gdi32.lib
```

"Make" Files

The NMake utility ("New Make") executes scripts to compile and link your programs automatically. The version of NMake that accompanies the Win32 SDK works exactly like previous versions, but because compiling an NT program requires different commands than compiling a Win16 program you will probably have to rewrite your old NMake files. The command-line options differ, you have to call CvtRes, and you can't call the resource compiler after linking. The rules for linking DLLs have also changed; they come up in Chapter 11.

Here's the make file that compiles Hello:

```
#
#   Compiles a debugging version of HELLO.EXE
#

all: hello.exe

# Update the object file if necessary
hello.obj: hello.c hello.h
    cl386 -c -Gz -Od -W4 -Zi -D_X86_ -DWIN32 hello.c

# Update the resources if necessary
hello.res: hello.rc hello.h
    rc hello.rc
    cvtres -i386 hello.res -o hello.rbj

# Update the executable file
hello.exe: hello.obj hello.res
    link32 -debug:full -debugtype:cv -subsystem:windows -out:hello.exe \
    hello.obj hello.rbj libc.lib ntdll.lib kernel32.lib user32.lib gdi32.lib
```

Microsoft provides a more complex make file on which to base your own. Look for ntwin32.mak in \mstools\h. It defines make-file macros to handle just about any program you might think of. Microsoft's sample programs rely on ntwin32.mak in constructing their own make files, so knowing about it will help you understand the samples. ntwin32.mak reads the CPU environment variable to determine whether the target is an i386 or MIPS machine. Then it defines macros to hold the compiler name, compiler options, debug flags, and a list of libraries for the linker. To use it, begin your own make file with !include <ntwin32.mak>. Here's the resulting NMake script to compile Hello. All the macro expressions—the ones beginning with a dollar sign and parentheses—are defined in ntwin32.mak:

```
#
#     Compiles a debugging version of HELLO.EXE
#     Relies on macros defined in NTWIN32.MAK
#

PROJ = hello
SRC = hello.c

!include <ntwin32.mak>

all: $(PROJ).exe

# Inference Rules:

.c.obj:
    $(cc) $(cdebug) $(cflags) $(cvars) $(cf) $<

.rc.res:
    $(rc) $(rcvars) r $<
    cvtres $(CPU) o $*.RBJ $*.RES

$(PROJ).hlp: $(PROJ).rtf $(PROJ).hpj
    $(hc) n $(PROJ).hpj

$(PROJ).exe: $(SRC:.C=.OBJ) $(PROJ).res $(PROJ).def
    $(link) $(linkdebug) $(conflags) out:$(PROJ).exe $(SRC:.C=.OBJ) \
    $(PROJ).rbj $(guilibs)
```

All the expressions in parentheses are defined in ntwin32.mak. By changing just the lines that define PROJ and SRC, you can use this same make file for many different programs.

Putting It All Together

Besides the header, source, resource script, module definition, and make files, Windows programs often have other parts. A glance through Microsoft's sample directories reveals a variety of different file types. Here's a list to help you identify the more common ones:

File Extension	Description	Created by
BMP	Bitmap image of icon (used for .hlp)	Programmer (using Paint or Image Editor)
C	Source	Programmer
DEF	Program characteristics	Programmer
DLG	Dialog template	Programmer (using Dialog Editor)
DLL	Dynamic-link library	Link32
EXE	Compiled program	Link32 linker
EXP	Export library	Lib32
H	Program-specific header	Programmer
HLP	Compiled help file	Help compiler
HPJ	Help project file (controls building of an .HLP file)	Programmer
ICO	Program icon	Programmer (using Image Editor)
LIB	Import library or static link library	Lib32
MAK	NMake script for automatic compiling	Programmer
OBJ	Compiled, unlinked code in COFF format	CL386 compiler
RBJ	Compiled resources in final COFF format	CvtRes

File Extension	Description	Created by
RC	Resource script	Programmer
RCV	Resource script containing only a VERSION template	Programmer
RES	Compiled resources in intermediate format	Resource compiler
RTF	Help topic file; a rich-text format (RTF) file containing text for an .HLP file	Programmer (using a word processor)

The compiler, the resource compiler, the help compiler, and the linker all cooperate to merge the many pieces into a single library or executable file. Figure 2.2 diagrams how all the pieces come together.

A SIMPLE WIN32 PROGRAM

Win32 programs follow the same basic structure as Win16 programs. They are message driven. They begin with a procedure called WinMain. WinMain initializes the program and enters a message loop. When the loop receives a **WM_QUIT** message, the program ends. When WinMain receives other messages, it forwards them to the program's window procedure. The window procedure sorts through them and responds to any it considers important, passing others back to the system to permit default responses.

Our first sample program, Hello, writes "Hello world!" in its window. It should be reassuring to find that Hello is nearly indistinguishable from a Win16 program. Hello requires four files:

- The program source code goes in the *source file*, labeled with the extension .C.

- The program's menu, dialog box, and string data go in the *resource list*, marked .RC.

- The header file (.H) holds function prototypes, global variable declarations, and manifest constants for the program and its resources.
- The make file contains a script for compiling and linking the program and its resources automatically.

FIGURE 2.2:

How the pieces of a Windows program fit together

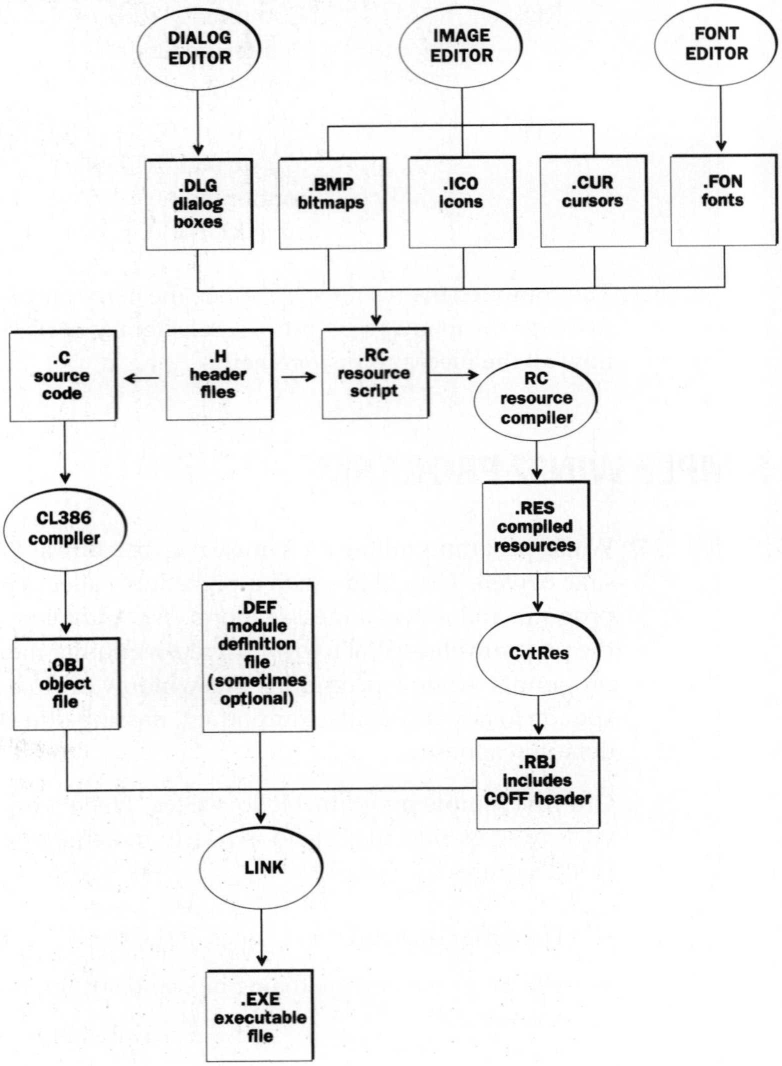

Figure 2.3 shows what the Hello program looks like when it runs.

FIGURE 2.3:

The Hello program

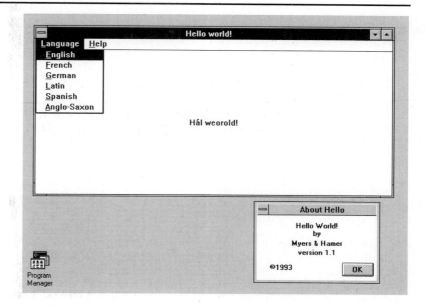

.DEF by Default

Module definition files (.DEF) written for Windows 3.x work fine under Windows NT without modification, but often they are not necessary. Exported functions no longer require special prologs; the stack can now grow dynamically just like the heap; and the linker assigns default loading attributes to the program's code and data. You need to provide only a .DEF file to override default values, to embed **DE-SCRIPTION** and **VERSION** text in the .EXE file, and to compile libraries. We'll say more about module definition files under NT when we come to building DLLs in Chapter 11.

The Header and Resource Files

This program's header and resource files have not changed at all from the version we wrote for Windows 3.1. It still needs function prototypes, constants to represent resources, string tables, and menu and dialog templates.

```
/*-------------------------------------------------------------------

        HELLO.H

        Header file for Hello. Defines program constants,
        resource identifiers, and function prototypes.

        ----------------------------------------------------------*/

/*-------------------------------------------------------------------
        FUNCTION PROTOTYPES for type checking
        ----------------------------------------------------------*/

int WinMain( HANDLE hinstThis, HANDLE hinstPrev, LPSTR lpszCmdLine,
    int iCmdShow );
BOOL Init( HANDLE hinstThis, int iCmdShow );
BOOL RegisterHelloClass( HANDLE hinstThis );
LONG Hello_WndProc( HWND hWnd, UINT uMessage, UINT uParam,
    LONG lParam );
void Hello_OnCommand( HWND hWnd, WORD wCmd );
void Hello_OnPaint( HWND hWnd );
void MakeAbout( HWND hWnd );
BOOL About_DlgProc( HWND hDlg, UINT uMessage, UINT uParam,
    LONG lParam );

/*-------------------------------------------------------------
        CONSTANTS
        ----------------------------------------------------------*/

#define NAME_BUFSIZE        10       /* max chars for IDS_APPNAME string */
#define TITLE_BUFSIZE       20       /* max chars for the window caption */
#define GREETING_BUFSIZE    30       /* max chars for the greeting strings */

/*-------------------------------------------------------------
        RESOURCE IDs
        ----------------------------------------------------------*/

#define IDM_MAIN            10               /* main menu template */
```

```
#define DLG_ABOUT           10                      /* DIALOG template */

/* MENUITEM command IDs */

#define IDM_ENGLISH         100                     /* Language menu commands */
#define IDM_FRENCH          110
#define IDM_GERMAN          120
#define IDM_LATIN           130
#define IDM_SPANISH         140
#define IDM_SAXON           150
#define IDM_ABOUT           200                     /* Help menu command */

/* STRING IDs */

#define IDS_APPNAME         10
#define IDS_TITLE           20
#define IDS_ENGLISH         IDM_ENGLISH             /* the idea is to be able to */
#define IDS_FRENCH          IDM_FRENCH              /* refer to each string by    */
#define IDS_GERMAN          IDM_GERMAN              /* the number of the menu     */
#define IDS_LATIN           IDM_LATIN               /* command that goes with it */
#define IDS_SPANISH         IDM_SPANISH
#define IDS_SAXON           IDM_SAXON
```

==

```
/*-----------------------------------------------------------------


        HELLO.RC
        Resource script file for the Hello program

---*/

#include <windows.h>
#include "hello.h"

/* a table of all the strings Hello uses */
STRINGTABLE
BEGIN
    IDS_APPNAME,     "hello"
    IDS_TITLE,       "Hello world!"
    IDS_ENGLISH,     "Hello world!"
    IDS_FRENCH,      "Bon jour, le monde!"
    IDS_GERMAN,      "Guten Tag, Welt?"
    IDS_LATIN,       "Salve munde!"
    IDS_SPANISH,     "¡Buenos díaz mundo!"
```

```
    IDS_SAXON,        "Hál weorold!"
END

/* a script for the menu Hello displays */
IDM_MAIN MENU PRELOAD
BEGIN
POPUP "&Language"
    BEGIN
        MENUITEM "&English",        IDM_ENGLISH
        MENUITEM "&French",         IDM_FRENCH
        MENUITEM "&German",         IDM_GERMAN
        MENUITEM "&Latin",          IDM_LATIN
        MENUITEM "&Spanish",        IDM_SPANISH
        MENUITEM "&Anglo-Saxon",    IDM_SAXON
    END
POPUP "&Help"
    BEGIN
        MENUITEM "&About Hello...", IDM_ABOUT
    END
END

/* a script for the "About" dialog box */
DLG_ABOUT DIALOG 17, 18, 114, 68
STYLE DS_MODALFRAME ¦ WS_POPUP ¦ WS_VISIBLE ¦ WS_CAPTION ¦ WS_SYSMENU
CAPTION "About Hello"
FONT 8, "Helv"
BEGIN
    CTEXT              "Hello World!",    -1, 0, 7, 114, 8
    CTEXT              "by",              -1, 0, 15, 114, 8
    CTEXT              "Myers && Hamer",  -1, 0, 25, 114, 8
    CTEXT              "version 1.0",     -1, 0, 35, 114, 8
    LTEXT              "©1993",           -1, 12, 51, 25, 8
    DEFPUSHBUTTON      "OK", IDOK, 81, 50, 30, 14, WS_GROUP
END
```

The Source File

The source code holds a few small surprises. One is the **UNREFERENCED_PARAMETER** macro that marks parameters a procedure declares but ignores. The macro prevents the compiler from issuing a –W4 warning about unused formal parameters. Instead the compiler warns that the "statement has no effect." Trading one warning for another doesn't make the compile any cleaner, but it does help you uncover formal parameters that really are unused and makes for clearer code. (For cleaner compiles you can suppress either warning, or both, with a warning #pragma.)

We'll point out a few more novelties after you look over the program.

```
/*-----------------------------------------------------------------

        HELLO.C

        Says "Hello world!" in different languages.

        Also provides a general template for other Windows NT
        programs.

        FUNCTIONS
                WinMain              receive and dispatch messages
                Init                 initialize program data
                RegisterHelloClass   register program's window class
                Hello_WndProc        sort out messages for main window
                Hello_OnCommand      process menu commands
                Hello_OnPaint        write "Hello" in program's window
                MakeAbout            invoke the About box
                About_DlgProc        sort out messages for About box

        from Programming for Windows NT
        copyright 1993 by Brian Myers & Eric Hamer

        -------------------------------------------------------------*/

#include <windows.h>
#include "hello.h"


/*-----------------------------------------------------------------
        GLOBAL VARIABLES
        -------------------------------------------------------------*/

char szAppName[NAME_BUFSIZE];          // application name
char szTitle[TITLE_BUFSIZE];           // caption for window
char szGreeting[GREETING_BUFSIZE];     // a "Hello world!" string
HANDLE hInst;                          // the current program instance


/*-----------------------------------------------------------------
        WIN MAIN
        Calls initializing procedures and runs the message loop
```

```
-----------------------------------------------------------*/

int WinMain (
    HANDLE hinstThis,                   // current instance
    HANDLE hinstPrev,                   // NULL if this is first instance
    LPSTR lpszCmdLine,                  // command-line string
    int iCmdShow )                      // window's initial state
{
    MSG msg;

    if (!Init( hinstThis, iCmdShow ))
    {
        return( FALSE );
    }

    // keep getting messages until one says "QUIT"
    while (GetMessage( &msg, NULL, 0, 0 ))
    {
        TranslateMessage( &msg );
        DispatchMessage( &msg );
    }

     return( msg.wParam );

    // ----- unused parameters -----
    UNREFERENCED_PARAMETER( hinstPrev );
    UNREFERENCED_PARAMETER( lpszCmdLine );
}

/*------------------------------------------------------------
        INIT
        Initializes window and data for the application, if
        necessary; then initializes data and creates the window
        for this instance.
    -----------------------------------------------------------*/

BOOL Init (
    HANDLE hinstThis,
    int iCmdShow )
{
    HWND hWnd;

    // initialize global variables
    hInst = hinstThis;                  // remember what instance this is
    LoadString( hInst, IDS_APPNAME, szAppName,  sizeof(szAppName)  );
```

```
        LoadString( hInst, IDS_TITLE,  szTitle,   sizeof(szTitle)   );

        // register the window class for program's main window
        if (!RegisterHelloClass( hinstThis ))
        {
            return( FALSE );
        }

        // Make a class "Hello" window exist for this instance
        hWnd = CreateWindow (
            szAppName,              // window class name
            szTitle,                // string for window caption
            WS_OVERLAPPEDWINDOW,    // window style
            CW_USEDEFAULT,          //  x  ( --WINDOW POSITION-- )
            CW_USEDEFAULT,          //  y  ( let Windows set a   )
            CW_USEDEFAULT,          // cx  ( default position    )
            CW_USEDEFAULT,          // cy  ( and size            )
            NULL,                   // no parent window
            NULL,                   // no menu for this window
            hInst,                  // who created this window
            NULL );                 // no parameters to pass on

        if (hWnd)
        {
            ShowWindow( hWnd, iCmdShow );
            UpdateWindow( hWnd );
        }

        return( hWnd != NULL );
}


/*------------------------------------------------------------------
        REGISTER HELLO CLASS
        Gives the system information about the type of window
        the program wants for its main window.
        -----------------------------------------------------------*/

BOOL RegisterHelloClass ( HANDLE hinstThis )
{
    WNDCLASS wc;

    // fill structure with information about this window class
    wc.lpszClassName  = szAppName;
    wc.hInstance      = hinstThis;
    wc.lpfnWndProc    = Hello_WndProc;
```

```
    wc.hCursor          = LoadCursor( NULL, IDC_ARROW );
    wc.hIcon            = LoadIcon( NULL, IDI_APPLICATION );
    wc.lpszMenuName     = MAKEINTRESOURCE( IDM_MAIN );
    wc.hbrBackground    = (HANDLE)(COLOR_WINDOW + 1);
    wc.style            = CS_HREDRAW | CS_VREDRAW;
    wc.cbClsExtra       = 0;
    wc.cbWndExtra       = 0;

    // tell Windows about the new window class
    return( RegisterClass(&wc) );
}


/*-----------------------------------------------------------------
        HELLO WINDOW PROCEDURE
        Every message for this program ends up here.
    -------------------------------------------------------------*/

LONG Hello_WndProc (
    HWND hWnd,              // message address
    UINT uMessage,         // message type
    UINT uParam,           // message contents
    LONG lParam )          // more contents
{
    WORD wCmd;             // number identifying a command from the menu

    switch (uMessage)
    {
        case WM_CREATE:
            // our window is about to be drawn; initialize settings
            LoadString( hInst, IDS_ENGLISH, szGreeting, sizeof(szGreeting) );
            break;

        case WM_COMMAND:
            // user made a choice from the menu
            wCmd = LOWORD(uParam);
            Hello_OnCommand( hWnd, wCmd );
            break;

        case WM_PAINT:
            // time to redraw the window
            Hello_OnPaint( hWnd );
            break;

        case WM_DESTROY:
            // Windows has removed this window from the screen
```

```
            PostQuitMessage( 0 );    // tell WinMain to quit
            break;

        default:
            return( DefWindowProc(hWnd, uMessage, uParam, lParam) );
    }

    return( 0 );                     // return 0 for success
}

/*-----------------------------------------------------------------
        COMMAND PROCEDURE
        Process WM_COMMAND messages here.
    ------------------------------------------------------------*/

void Hello_OnCommand (
    HWND hWnd,
    WORD wCmd )
{
    switch (wCmd)
    {
        case IDM_ABOUT:                    // user chose "About"
            MakeAbout( hWnd );             // create dialog box
            break;

        default:                           // user chose a language
            LoadString( hInst, wCmd, szGreeting, sizeof(szGreeting) );
            InvalidateRect( hWnd, NULL, TRUE );
            UpdateWindow( hWnd );
            break;
    }
    return;
}

/*-----------------------------------------------------------------
        PAINT PROCEDURE
        Process WM_PAINT messages here.
    ------------------------------------------------------------*/

void Hello_OnPaint ( HWND hWnd )
{
    PAINTSTRUCT ps;      // information about what to draw
    HDC hDC;             // display context = screen device settings
    RECT rect;           // coordinates of window's client area
```

```
    // establish a display context
    hDC = BeginPaint( hWnd, &ps );

    // make text foreground and background match default system colors
    SetBkColor( hDC, GetSysColor(COLOR_WINDOW) );
    SetTextColor( hDC, GetSysColor(COLOR_WINDOWTEXT) );

    GetClientRect( hWnd, &rect );    // get coordinates of drawing area

    DrawText( hDC, szGreeting, -1, &rect,
            DT_CENTER | DT_VCENTER | DT_SINGLELINE | DT_NOCLIP );

    // release memory allocated for the paint structure
    EndPaint( hWnd, &ps );
    return;
}

/*-------------------------------------------------------------------
        CREATE "ABOUT" DIALOG BOX
        Process requests to show the About box here.
    --------------------------------------------------------------*/

void MakeAbout ( HWND hWnd )
{
    DialogBox( hInst, MAKEINTRESOURCE(DLG_ABOUT), hWnd, About_DlgProc );
    return;
}

/*-------------------------------------------------------------------
        ABOUT BOX DIALOG PROCEDURE
        Process messages for the About box window here
    --------------------------------------------------------------*/

BOOL About_DlgProc (
    HWND hDlg,                          // handle to dialog window
    UINT uMessage,
    UINT uParam,
    LONG lParam )
{
    switch (uMessage)
    {
        case WM_INITDIALOG:             // about to show dialog box
            return( TRUE );             // yes, we processed the message

        case WM_COMMAND:                // message was a command
```

```
            EndDialog( hDlg, TRUE );      // only command is OK, so quit
            return( TRUE );               // yes, we processed the message
    }
    return( FALSE );                      // no, Windows must process it

    // ----- unused parameters -----
    UNREFERENCED_PARAMETER( uParam );
    UNREFERENCED_PARAMETER( lParam );
}
```

No, Pascal!

You may have noticed that no procedure in the program is marked with any special calling convention. In particular, nothing is marked _far or _pascal (or CALLBACK or WINAPI, which mean the same thing). That's because nothing can be _far when all pointers are the same size, and _pascal (along with _fortran and _syscall) is no longer supported either. In its place is _stdcall, which, like _pascal, assigns the task of removing parameters from the stack to the procedure that was called, not to the calling procedure. (Procedures that accept a variable number of arguments still require _cdecl because only the calling procedure can know in advance how many arguments there are to remove.) _stdcall also performs better type checking than _pascal. WinMain, Hello_WndProc, and About_DlgProc do require _stdcall, but we've set the compiler's –Gz switch to use _stdcall everywhere.

Getting the Message

Some other changes appear in the way Hello treats the two parameters that accompany every message. Instead of a **WORD** and a **LONG**, Hello declares a **UINT** and a **LONG**. A **WORD** is a 16-bit quantity, but under Win32 both message parameters are 32 bits. Both parameters are now the same size. Microsoft had to expand the small parameter because the information some messages carry has changed from 16-bit to 32-bit values. Windows outgrew the old parameter size.

Microsoft saw this change coming in 3.1 and urged programmers to begin declaring the first parameter a **UINT** instead of a **WORD**. A **WORD** is always 16 bits, but the size of a **UINT** changes to match the CPU environment. Wider CPUs like to work with wider integers, so 16-bit compilers create 16-bit **UINT**s and 32-bit compilers create 32-bit **UINT**s.

As a result, the declaration

```
UINT uParam;
```

works perfectly in the source code for either compiler but produces different results each time. On the other hand, a program that declares one of its window procedure's parameters to be a **WORD** will cause compiler errors under Win32. The "word" parameter must now be declared a **UINT**. (Alternatively, a STRICT-compliant program achieves the same compatibility by using the more specific variable types **WPARAM** and **LPARAM**. We'll say more about **STRICT** types in a few pages.)

Unfortunately, expanding the "word" parameter forces an atavistic inconsistency. The **MSG** structure still uses the old name:

```
/* Message structure, taken from winuser.h */
typedef struct tagMSG {
    HWND        hwnd;
    UINT        message;
    WPARAM      wParam;    // "wParam" is a misleading name--it's not a WORD!
    LPARAM      lParam;
    DWORD       time;
    POINT       pt;
} MSG, *PMSG, NEAR *NPMSG, FAR *LPMSG;
```

The **wParam** field is no longer a **WORD**, but for backward compatibility it must retain the old "w" prefix. Traditionalists may therefore choose to continue naming their message parameter variables wParam and lParam.

Win32 messages that carry newly widened information can't be read the same way as the old messages. The contents are different and must be parsed differently. For example, Hello doesn't read WM_COMMAND messages the same way a Win16 program would. A Win16 program would extract information this way:

```
wID           = wParam;                 // item, control, or accelerator ID
hwndCtl       = (HWND)LOWORD(lParam);   // handle of control
wNotifyCode   = HIWORD(lParam);         // notification code
```

But under Win32 window handles are 32 bits wide, so the hwndCtl value fills the entire LONG parameter by itself:

```
wID           = LOWORD(wParam);         // item, control, or accelerator ID
wNotifyCode   = HIWORD(wParam);         // notification code
hwndCtl       = (HWND)lParam;           // handle of control
```

To accommodate widened 32-bit variable types, many other messages have also restructured the information in their parameters. The next chapter identifies the affected messages and suggests several ways to deal with the changes.

An Instance of Perpetual Virginity

Another difference appears during the program's initialization. Hello never checks the hinstPrev parameter to determine whether other instances of the same program are already running. Every instance of Hello registers its window class anew. The reason is the private address space every program receives. Even new instances of old programs think they have the machine to themselves. The hinstPrev parameter remains only for compatibility with 16-bit programs that expect to find it. Under Win32, its value is always **NULL**. Every instance always thinks it is the first instance.

When a program registers a window class, that class is available only to processes that share the same address space—in other words, to the registering instance and any subsidiary processes it may spawn. Do not use **GetInstanceData**; it will always fail because programs in different address spaces cannot share memory directly. Always let each new instance load its own resources and generate its own initial data.

A Thunkless Task

To the eyes of a practiced Windows programmer, the MakeAbout procedure conspicuously lacks calls to **MakeProcInstance** and **FreeProcInstance**. Both APIs have become obsolete. The prolog ("thunk") that **MakeProcInstance** adds to a Win16 function call is necessary for switching between the system's data segment and the program's data segment. The 32-bit flat address space, of course, does not use segments to address different parts of memory, so there's no need to reset the DS register. An application shares its private address space with any DLLs it calls, and they all effectively use the same DS value. The compiler still recognizes the commands **MakeProcInstance** and **FreeProcInstance**, but it erases them. Here are the relevant definitions from the winbase.h header:

```
#define MakeProcInstance(lpProc, hInstance) (lpProc)
#define FreeProcInstance(lpProc) (lpProc)
```

The Balkanization of windows.h

One final difference is not actually visible in the source code. The windows.h header grew so unwieldy that its contents have split apart into a number of smaller header files. With a series of include directives, windows.h now musters a confederacy of other files. Here's the full list, with comments to explain each item. The list may differ slightly in your version.

```
#ifndef RC_INVOKED
#include <excpt.h>            // structured exception handling
#include <stdarg.h>           // variable argument functions
#endif /* RC_INVOKED */

#include <windef.h>           // typedefs for basic Windows types
#include <winbase.h>          // low-level system and memory
#include <wingdi.h>           // GDI
#include <winuser.h>          // USER
#include <winnls.h>           // national language support
#include <wincon.h>           // character mode (console)
#include <winver.h>           // version management
#include <winreg.h>           // registry and initialization files
#include <winnetwk.h>         // network API

#include <cderr.h>            // common dialog error returns
#include <dde.h>              // dynamic data exchange
#include <ddeml.h>            // DDE Management Library
#include <dlgs.h>             // common dialog control IDs
#include <lzexpand.h>         // file compression API
#include <mmsystem.h>         // multimedia
#include <nb30.h>             // NetBIOS 3.0
#if defined(INC_RPC)
#include <rpc.h>              // remote procedure calls
#endif // Include RPC
#include <shellapi.h>         // shell file association database
#include <winperf.h>          // peformance monitoring
#include <winsock.h>          // Windows Sockets
#ifndef NOGDI
#include <commdlg.h>          // common dialog library
#include <drivinit.h>         // printer driver initialization
#include <winspool.h>         // printing
#include <ole.h>              // Object Linking and Embedding
#endif // !NOGDI
```

```
#ifndef NOSERVICE
#include <winsvc.h>                  // service control manager
#endif
```

For dredging through these files to find particular definitions, a grep utility is invaluable. Microsoft includes with the Win32 SDK a utility called QGrep to search through files for any string of characters.

This chapter began with an explanation of the new compiler and linker commands. It summarized the most useful command-line switches, pointing out differences between the Win16 and Win32 tools. The linker switches in particular have changed greatly, and the resource compiler no longer copies resources into the .EXE file. You learned about the Common Object File Format (COFF) and the Portable Executable (PE) format. Finally, in considering a simple Windows NT program, you discovered some significant differences between Windows 3.x and Windows NT programs. There are no far addresses. The only calling convention any procedure requires is the new _stdcall. Some messages carry wider values than before, so the wParam has changed types and some messages require different parsing. Finally, **MakeProcInstance** has atrophied and, like an appendix, can be removed at will.

Chapter 3 sets out more systematically how some of the old familiar Windows routines have subtly changed and may surprise the unwary programmer. The chapter returns to the Hello program and suggests modifications that allow the program to compile equally well for both the 16-bit and the 32-bit compiler.

Porting from 16-Bit Windows to Win32

- **Adjusting to changes in the syntax and usage of old Win16 routines**

- **Porting from Win16 to Win32**

- **Writing programs that compile for Win16 *and* Win32**

Win32 modifies the Windows Application Programming Interface in two ways. First, and most alluringly, it expands the API with new functions that perform new tasks such as multithreading, drawing complex shapes, and interacting with networks. But the expanded API could not absorb all the old routines unchanged, and some of them had to be modified. The rest of this book explains how to take advantage of new functions and features, but this chapter focuses on unexpected stumbling blocks that may trip you up in old familiar functions. The many new functions don't cause porting problems, but changes to the old Win16 functions do. Though most routines work exactly the way they always did, some modifications could not be avoided.

DIFFERENCES BETWEEN 16-BIT AND 32-BIT WINDOWS PROGRAMMING

Chapter 2 presented a simple Windows NT program, and even there we discovered some significant differences between Win16 and Win32 code. This chapter lays out the differences more systematically and considers ways to allow for them. The first half presents a list of changes, both syntactic and semantic. It explains where and how to change 16-bit Windows programs to make them work as 32-bit programs. It includes reference lists of modified, enhanced, and obsolete window messages and API calls. The second half proposes several strategies for porting Win16 programs to Win32 and for writing portable code that compiles equally well either way without modification. The PortTool utility, Win32s, STRICT variable types, and the windowsx.h macro APIs all find a place in these discussions. Porting to 32-bit Windows won't be difficult as long as you follow the guidelines in this chapter.

This book was written before the public release of Windows NT. We have made every effort to describe accurately the final form NT will take, but your version may differ from ours in small ways. For the most current information check the NT "readme" files, the on-line help files, and the *Programming Techniques* manual.

Syntactic Changes

Syntactic changes are those that govern how you call a routine but not what the routine does. *Semantic changes,* described in the next section, affect the meaning of a function and the actions it performs. One series of syntactic changes in the API results from the fact that a 16-bit compiler treats integers (type int) as 16-bit quantities with a maximum unsigned value of 65,535, while a 32-bit compiler treats integers as 32-bit quantities with a maximum value of 4,294,967,295. Some variables are wider than they used to be, and the changes show up in messages, in structures, and in functions that assumed 16-bit quantities. After detailing the changes that result from widened variables, this section moves on to APIs that have become obsolete and been replaced either by enhanced routines or by entirely new programming services.

Widened Variable Types

A 32-bit processor can hold 32 bits of information in one register at a time. It works speedily with values that occupy exactly 32 bits and more slowly with quantities that occupy more or less space. Knowing that Windows would soon advance to a fully 32-bit system, in Windows 3.1 Microsoft changed many windows.h definitions from type **WORD** to type **UINT**. A **WORD** remains 16 bits in both systems, but **UINT**, defined as unsigned int, changes size. It is *polymorphic*. For the most part the expansion has no effect on what you write in your code. Whichever system you compile on, anything you declare as a **UINT** will automatically be made to fit the processor's registers.

For reference, here's a list of variable types showing which change size in the 32-bit operating system and which do not. These types have constant sizes:

Win16 Size	Signed	Unsigned
1 byte	char	BYTE
2 bytes	short	WORD
4 bytes	long	DWORD

These types change from 2 to 4 bytes:

Win16 Size	Signed	Unsigned
2 bytes	int	UINT
2 bytes	BOOL	

It's true—1-bit Boolean values now consume 4 full bytes. 32-bit processors, and especially RISC chips, often access 4 bytes much more quickly than smaller chunks.

Do not assume you know the size of a **UINT** or other polymorphic variable or of a structure that contains polymorphic variables. Do not, for example, allocate a **POINT** structure like this:

```
LPPOINT lppt = LocalAlloc( LPTR, 4 );              // not portable
```

The two fields in a **POINT** are defined as type int, so the size of the structure changes. Use sizeof to avoid hard-coding structure sizes:

```
LPPOINT lppt = LocalAlloc( LPTR, sizeof(POINT) );  // portable
```

Recommendations:

- Use **UINT**s in your own code wherever possible. Polymorphic variables make the best use of any target processor's capabilities.

- Never hard-code the size of a variable or structure. Use sizeof instead.

Message Parameter Changes

Because some common variable types have expanded, some of the structures and parameters expected to hold them have also been forced to expand. In particular, the 16-bit word parameter that every window message carries is too small for the new wider values. Win32 must instead pass two 32-bit parameters with each message. wParam and lParam are now the same size.

Most messages never filled all the space in their parameters anyway and remain unaffected by the change. The following list shows all the messages whose parameters had to be modified. Generally these are messages that formerly packed a handle into one half of the long parameter. Some edit control messages have also been repacked to permit working with a larger text buffer. Code that directly extracts the information from any of the messages in the list is not portable. Consult the on-line help file for descriptions of each message's new structure.

EM_GETSEL	WM_ACTIVATE
EM_LINESCROLL	WM_CHARTOITEM
EM_SETSEL	WM_COMMAND

WM_CTLCOLOR	WM_MENUSELECT
WM_HSCROLL	WM_PARENTNOTIFY
WM_MDIACTIVATE	WM_VKEYTOITEM
WM_MDISETMENU	WM_VSCROLL
WM_MENUCHAR	

Recommendations:

- Limit the number of unportable sections in your code by parsing all message parameters immediately in the window procedure where they are received.

- Avoid unportable sections entirely by using conditional #if statements for selective compiling or by using message cracker macros. Examples of both strategies appear in the second half of this chapter.

Window Procedure Prototype

When the message parameters changed, so did the prototype of the function that receives them. Under 16-bit Windows, a window procedure formerly declared the wParam to be a **WORD**. That prototype is not portable. Windows 3.1 changed the **WORD** to a polymorphic **UINT** and is therefore portable.

```
// Windows 3.0 prototype; not portable
LONG CALLBACK WndProc( HWND hWnd, UINT uMsg, WORD wParam, LONG lParam );

// Windows 3.1 and Windows NT prototype; portable
LONG CALLBACK WndProc( HWND hWnd, UINT uMsg, UINT wParam, LONG lParam );
```

Recommendation:

- Use the portable prototype for all window procedures.

Extended GDI Functions

Besides restructuring some messages, the widened variables also forced changes in some Windows commands. The GDI routines suffered the most because drawing coordinates, being integers, have also changed from 16 to 32 bits. For example, the old **MoveTo** function returns a double word (**DWORD**) containing both the coordinates of the pen's previous position—the point where the pen was before the **MoveTo** command. In the 32-bit API, however, a single *x* or *y* coordinate takes up an entire double word by itself, so the mechanism for returning a point had to change. In Windows 3.1 Microsoft added an alternative to **MoveTo** called **MoveToEx**. The "Ex" stands for "extended." The new version returns a Boolean value to indicate success or failure, and it also has a new **LPPOINT** parameter:

```
BOOL MoveToEx( HDC hDC, int x, int y, LPPOINT lppt );
```

If you provide a point structure for the fourth parameter, Windows fills it in with the old position. Alternatively, you can leave the last parameter **NULL**, and Windows ignores it.

Other functions that work with points have also been extended. These include

Obsolete Win16 Routine	Portable Windows 3.1/NT Routine
GetAspectRatioFilter	GetAspectRatioFilterEx
GetBitmapDimension	GetBitmapDimensionEx
GetBrushOrg	GetBrushOrgEx
GetCurrentPosition	GetCurrentPositionEx
GetTextExtent	GetTextExtentPoint
GetTextExtentEx	GetTextExtentExPoint
GetViewportExt	GetViewportExtEx
GetViewportOrg	GetViewportOrgEx
GetWindowExt	GetWindowExtEx
GetWindowOrg	GetWindowOrgExt
MoveTo	MoveToEx
OffsetViewportOrg	OffsetViewportOrgEx
OffsetWindowOrg	OffsetWindowOrgEx
ScaleViewportExt	ScaleViewportExtEx
ScaleWindowExt	ScaleWindowExtEx

Obsolete Win16 Routine	Portable Windows 3.1/NT Routine
SetBitmapDimension	SetBitmapDimensionEx
SetViewportExt	SetViewportExtEx
SetViewportOrg	SetViewportOrgEx
SetWindowExt	SetWindowExtEx
SetWindowOrg	SetWindowOrgEx

Recommendation:

- Replace obsolete GDI functions with their extended "Ex" replacements.

Window and Class Extra Words

Two more routines whose design does not port smoothly to a 32-bit world are **Get-WindowWord** and **GetClassWord**. While both still work, successfully retrieving **WORD** values from a **WNDCLASS** structure, the values they were usually asked to retrieve, such as **GCW_HICON** and **GWW_HINSTANCE**, are no longer **WORD**s. The **GCW_** and **GWW_** constants are obsolete. To retrieve the same data, call instead **GetWindowLong** or **GetClassLong** using a new set of **GCL_** and **GWL_** indices:

Obsolete Windows 3.x Index	Equivalent Win32 Index
GCW_HCURSOR	GCL_HCURSOR
GCW_HBRBACKGROUND	GCL_HBRBACKGROUND
GCW_HICON	GCL_HICON
GWW_HINSTANCE	GWL_HINSTANCE
GWW_HWNDPARENT	GWL_HWNDPARENT
GWW_ID	GWL_ID
GWW_USERDATA	GWL_USERDATA

To write portable code you have several choices.

Recommendations:

- Bracket calls to these functions with #if statements that compile differently depending on whether the WIN32 variable is defined on the command line.

- Where possible, use named API routines. For example:

```
GetWindowWord( hWnd, GWW_HWNDPARENT );          // not portable
GetParent( hWnd );                              // portable
```

- Define macros for retrieving any **WORD** values you need. When compiling for Win32, redefine the macro. For example:

```
#if defined(WIN32)
#define GetClassCursor( hWnd ) ((HCURSOR)GetClassLong((hWnd), GCL_HCURSOR))
#else
#define GetClassCursor( hWnd ) ((HCURSOR)GetClassWord((hWnd), GCW_HCURSOR))
#endif
```

- Include windowsx.h with your other program headers and rely on the macro APIs it provides, such as **GetWindowInstance**. These resemble our GetClassCursor macro and are completely portable.

The **GetWindowWord** and **SetWindowWord** routines survive in Win32, but only for use with window words that you define yourself. All predefined system information uses long values.

DDE Message Packing

Some DDE messages also required new packing arrangements. They are

    WM_DDE_ACK

    WM_DDE_ADVISE

    WM_DDE_DATA

    WM_DDE_POKE

All four messages now use the long parameter to pass a handle to an information structure.

Recommendation:

- Modify code that sends DDE messages to use the three new routines for packing and unpacking the contents of the long parameter. They are `PackDDElParam`, `UnPackDDElParam`, and `FreeDDElParam`.

DOS Calls

DOS interrupts have of course disappeared from Windows NT. The MS-DOS subsystem does interpret interrupt instructions for DOS programs, but you should not use them in Windows programs. The `DOS3Call` API is obsolete as well. Made available to speed up INT 21H functions under Windows, it was used most often for file access.

Recommendation:

- Replace `DOS3Call` with equivalent routines from the new API, such as `SetCurrentDirectory` or `GetDateAndTimeFile`.

Resources

Several of the less common resource functions have been changed or deleted. Because resources now are held in mapped image files, `SetResourceHandler` is unnecessary and has been dropped. `AccessResource` is gone as well; call `LoadResource`, `LockResource`, and `FindResource` instead. Finally, `AddFontResource` and `RemoveFontResource` still exist, but they require a string, not a handle, for the file name.

Obsolete API Routines

Besides the changes already described, a few small sets of Win16 functions have been dropped from the API either because they serve no purpose, like the segmented memory functions, or because they have been replaced by enhancements to other parts of the API, as the voice functions were replaced by multimedia. The lists in the following sections show routines that have been dropped.

System and Memory

Routines that refer to structures or mechanisms specific to MS-DOS or to Intel x86 processors have been dropped. These routines, which generally concern memory, instances, and segments, cannot be supported in NT's secure, hardware-independent environment.

AllocDSToCSAlias	GlobalDosAlloc
AllocResource	GlobalDosFree
AllocSelector	GlobalNotify
Catch	GlobalPageLock
ChangeSelector	GlobalPageUnlock
FreeSelector	LimitEMSPages
GetCodeHandle	SwitchStackBack
GetCodeInfo	SwitchStackTo
GetCurrentPDB	Throw
GetInstanceData	ValidateFreeSpaces
GetKBCodePage	ValidateCodeSegments

The Local and Global memory functions that persist in the API now both allocate from a single undifferentiated heap (see Chapter 7).

Sound

The original sound API was superseded in Windows 3.1 by multimedia sound support. The old functions have been dropped entirely from the Win32 API.

CloseSound	SetVoiceAccent
CountVoiceNotes	SetVoiceEnvelope
GetThresholdEvent	SetVoiceNote
GetThresholdStatus	SetVoiceQueueSize
OpenSound	SetVoiceSound
SetSoundNoise	SetVoiceThreshold

StartSound	SyncAllVoices
StopSound	WaitSoundState

The **sndPlaySound** function remains in Win32. Other sound operations must be converted to use wave audio or other multimedia capabilities (see Chapter 16).

Profiling

Application profiling now takes place through the system registration database. Retrieve performance information by querying the **HKEY_PERFORMANCE_DATA** key in the system registry. The following functions have been dropped:

ProfClear	ProfSampRate
ProfFinish	ProfSetup
ProfFlush	ProfStart
ProfInsChk	ProfStop

Disks and Devices

A few hardware and file system functions have become obsolete:

Obsolete Win16 Routine	Portable Win16/Win32 Routine
DeviceCapabilities	DeviceCapabilitiesEx
DeviceMode	DeviceModeEx
DlgDirSelect	DlgDirSelectEx
DlgDirSelectComboBox	DlgDirSelectComboBoxEx
ExtDeviceMode	ExtDeviceModeEx
GetTempDrive	GetTempPath (Win32 only)
NetBIOSCall	NetBios (Win32 only)

Communications

The serial communications API has been improved and standardized. Now a serial device is opened and closed with the same functions that open and close a file. Replace obsolete communications functions with equivalents from the Win32 API.

Obsolete Win16 Routine	New Win32 Routine
CloseComm	Closefile
FlushComm	PurgeComm
GetCommError	GetCommState
OpenComm	CreateFile
ReadComm	ReadFile
SetCommEventMask	SetCommMask
UngetCommChar	[no equivalent]
WriteComm	WriteFile

Just say NOP

Finally, here's a list of functions that remain in the API solely for compatibility with earlier source code. These instructions do nothing in a Win32 program. When porting old code you can simply omit them, or you can bracket them in #if statements so they compile only when WIN16 is defined. Or you can leave them alone; they reduce to harmless no-operation (NOP) instructions.

AnsiToOem	GlobalWire
DefineHandleTable	LocalCompact
FreeProcInstance	LocalShrink
GetFreeSpace	LockSegment
GlobalCompact	MakeProcInstance
GlobalFix	SetSwapAreaSize
GlobalUnfix	UnlockSegment
GlobalUnwire	

Obsolete C Runtime Routines

For some C runtime routines that manipulate files and memory, the 16-bit compiler defines alternate model-independent versions that always use far pointers. The alternates include functions like _fmemcpy and _fstrlen. In a flat memory model the alternates serve no purpose, and the 32-bit runtime libraries omit them. Rather than change each line where any of the alternates appears in your code, you can write macros like these, mapping them back to their original versions:

```
#define _fmemcpy memcpy
#define _fstrlen strlen
```

The optional header windowsx.h contains a complete set of these remapping macros.

Semantic Changes

Besides direct changes to the syntax of some messages and API routines, some semantic changes are necessary. This section covers new programming practices Windows NT requires and some other changes we recommend for the sake of creating portable code.

Instances

The Hello program in Chapter 2 never used the previous-instance parameter in WinMain, and we explained that because each program has a private address space each program thinks it is the only instance. As a consequence no program should attempt to retrieve data from other instances of itself. In particular, do not call Get-InstanceData. Win32 applications do not perform first-instance initialization. To share data, instances must now resort to the same means any application uses to share with any other, including DDEML, memory-mapped files, and pipes. (Not even the GMEM_SHARE flag permits common memory objects now.)

Recommendation:

- Let every instance initialize its own variables, load its own resources, and reregister the same window class.

Some applications, such as the Control Panel, need to allow only one instance to run at a time. Without the previous-instance parameter, they must use other means to locate other instances.

Recommendation:

- To determine if another instance of your application is running, use **FindWindow** or **GetWindow** instead of reading the hinstPrevious parameter.

Localized Input

Under 16-bit Windows, all input for any program is held in a single queue. Under 32-bit Windows, every individual thread has its own input state. The routines that set or query the input state now operate slightly differently. The routines are

SetFocus	GetCapture
GetFocus	SetCapture
SetActiveWindow	ReleaseCapture
GetActiveWindow	

These functions now affect the local state of a particular thread, not of a whole program. Formerly **GetFocus** could never return **NULL** because some window always had the input focus, but now that one program may have several threads, the thread with the focus may not own a window.

Recommendation:

- Be sure to check for a **NULL** return from **GetFocus**, **GetActiveWindow**, or **GetCapture**. Do not assume they return a valid handle.

The effect of **SetCapture** has changed slightly as well, depending on whether the mouse button is up or down. If the mouse is down when one thread captures input for a window, then the capturing window receives all input from the mouse until **ReleaseCapture** is called or the button goes up. If the mouse is up, however, then the capturing window sees mouse events only when the cursor passes over windows made by the capturing thread. Furthermore, since every thread gets its own asynchronous input queue, several threads may capture the input simultaneously. All of them receive the input they request.

GDI Objects

Win32 is phasing out the old device-dependent bitmaps (DDBs) and offers only a subset of the original DDB functionality. The header of a device-independent bitmap (DIB) includes much more information about the image's dimensions, color resolution, and palette. Monochrome DDBs work fine since all devices organize them internally the same way, but you can no longer create a color bitmap with `CreateBitmap` (see Chapter 10).

Recommendation:

• Use DIBs instead of DDBs wherever possible.

Win16 programs sometimes share GDI objects such as bitmaps and brushes by passing their handles from one program to another. Under Win32, handles are valid only in their original address space. A handle from one program is meaningless to another.

Recommendation:

• Do not pass object handles between applications. Use DDEML or mapped files to share objects. Also, read about `DuplicateHandle` in Chapter 4.

Pointers

All pointers, even pointers to the local heap, now occupy a full 32 bits. Pointers do not contain segments and offsets, and they do not "wrap" the same way. Some programmers, in performing pointer arithmetic, have been known to rely on the fact that when a pointer increments past 64K it cycles back to 0. Win32 pointers, however, cycle back only after reaching 4GB. Generally, any pointer arithmetic that uses segments is suspect.

Recommendations:

• Do not calculate an offset and add it to the high-order half of a pointer.

• Do not assume memory blocks are allocated on 64K boundaries.

• Do not rely on finding a base offset of 0 in the low-order word.

DLLs

The initialization and termination functions formerly required of all DLLs are optional in Windows NT. Furthermore, they are called at different times than the old `LibEntry` and `WEP` functions, and different information is available to them. DLLs now have more control over their data segments as well. Chapter 11 explains the changes in more detail.

Recommendation:

- Do not use libentry.asm, which is not portable. Revise `LibMain` to provide NT-compatible initialization code. (No assembly language is needed.)

File Names

Windows NT works with a variety of file systems. Each has different rules for naming files. Do not limit file name buffers to 13 characters, as you sometimes can for the DOS file system.

Recommendation:

- Use the constants from stdlib.h (shown below) to declare string buffers for file names. **GetVolumeInformation** returns information about the file system on a given device.

```
#define _MAX_PATH    260    /* max. length of full pathname */
#define _MAX_DRIVE   3      /* max. length of drive component */
#define _MAX_DIR     256    /* max. length of path component */
#define _MAX_FNAME   256    /* max. length of file name component */
#define _MAX_EXT     256    /* max. length of extension component */
```

Hardware Assumptions

The internal format of some simple variable types changes from machine to machine. Do not assume you know the alignment of fields within a structure, even one you define. The compiler may change the order to align fields on even boundaries.

We've already advised using `sizeof` to determine the size of any variable or structure type. Do not assume you know the maximum and minimum values for a given type, either.

Recommendation:

- Do not hard-code maximum or minimum values for a variable type. Refer instead to the manifest constants defined for each variable type in limits.h. Here are some examples:

limits.h constant	Value
CHAR_MIN	Least value for a char
CHAR_MAX	Greatest value for a char
UINT_MAX	Greatest value for an unsigned int
LONG_MIN	Least value for a long

More generally, don't assume anything about the device capabilities. Shaded dialog areas, for example, sometimes look terrible and are even unreadable on monochrome or gray-scale monitors. Windows NT will carry applications to an even larger variety of machines.

Recommendation:

- Don't limit your programs to specific hardware by hard-coding the pixel dimensions of dialog controls, scroll bars, or other interface features. Rely on **GetSystemMetrics** for measurements. To provide shading or three-dimensional effects, always use **GetSystemColors**.

Structure Alignment

An 80386 processor retrieves a **DWORD** from memory more quickly if the **DWORD** begins on an even 4-byte boundary. Otherwise it has to retrieve two 4-byte chunks and combine a part from each. The CPU works with any alignment, but misalignment degrades performance. The performance loss can be much greater on other processors, particularly on RISC chips (where Windows NT also runs). Consider this structure from wingdi.h:

```
typedef struct tagBITMAPFILEHEADER {
        WORD    bfType;         // 2 bytes (bytes 0-1)
        DWORD   bfSize;         // 4 bytes (bytes 2-5)
        WORD    bfReserved1;    // 2 bytes (bytes 6-7)
        WORD    bfReserved2;    // 2 bytes (bytes 8-9)
```

```
      DWORD    bfOffBits;         // 4 bytes (bytes 10-13)
} BITMAPFILEHEADER, FAR *LPBITMAPFILEHEADER, *PBITMAPFILEHEADER;
```

A 32-bit CPU will be hampered in retrieving either **DWORD** field because neither begins on a 4-byte boundary. (One begins at byte 2, another at byte 10.) It would have been more efficient to put the two **DWORD**s first in the declaration. Then they would begin at bytes 0 and 4.

Recommendation:

- When possible, arrange structure fields to align with 4-byte boundaries. Often, putting larger fields first helps. You can also influence structure alignment with the compiler's −Zp option.

STRATEGIES FOR PORTING AND PORTABILITY

You can aim for either of two levels of compatibility in moving your program to Windows NT. The first, and the easiest, is binary compatibility, which means that the binary code of a 3.1 application will run unmodified under Windows NT in the WOW subsystem. Win16 programs that follow good coding practices, that don't tamper with the hardware or write directly to the system configuration files, probably already run under WOW.

The second level is source code compatibility, meaning that a program can be recompiled to produce native 32-bit binary code. The preceding list of differences will help you recognize code that won't work in every environment. Here are a few more recommendations for easing the transition.

PortTool

Microsoft has achieved a high degree of success in making the Win32 API closely imitate the previous Windows API, but as you have seen, the task of porting is not always entirely trivial. More difficult than smoothing out any one wrinkle is the task of remembering all the possible snags to check for. The PortTool utility, included with the Win32 SDK, automates that chore.

PortTool works from a list of strings that might indicate trouble spots. The string might be, for example, "WM_COMMAND" or "MoveTo". Much like a spell checker, PortTool reads through each line of a file and shows in a dialog box, one by one, the lines that contain possible problems. (You can see the dialog box in Figure 3.1.) Along with each line, PortTool displays a short description of the potential problem. Pressing a button summons up the Win32 API help file and displays a relevant screen, such as **WM_COMMAND** or **MoveTo**. (You may have to modify the help path in port.ini.) The program's main window allows basic editing, so you can type in changes directly or mark lines and return to them later.

Not every line PortTool question needs attention. For example, PortTool doesn't recognize multiline comments marked by /* delimiters and may stop in the middle of one. Comments, of course, port just fine. PortTool also stops on any occurrence of "FAR" to advise you that NEAR and FAR make no difference in NT. But since a #define statement in the Win32 header files removes all occurrences of FAR anyway, you don't need to change anything. PortTool's list of search strings is, however, easily expanded or curtailed, and an Options box lets you include or exclude whole groups of strings for each run. You can even run PortTool in the background

FIGURE 3.1:

PortTool warning about a message that requires different handling in Win32

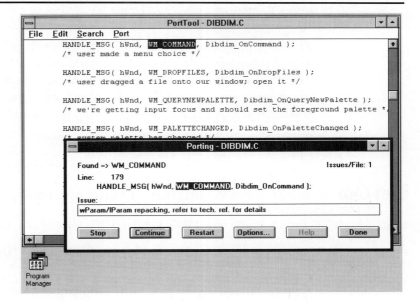

to search a series of files and insert comments marking string matches.

We worked with version 2.2 of PortTool. It may have other features in your release.

Recommendation:

- Run PortTool to identify potential problems when modifying a Win16 program to run under NT.

Source Code That Compiles Both Ways

The best way to avoid portage hassles is of course not to port at all. With a little thought you can write Win16 programs that compile under CL386 without any modifications. The Hello program in Chapter 2 won't compile under Win16. Its callback functions aren't declared _far, it assumes the Win32 packing for a **WM_COM-MAND** message, it omits **MakeProcInstance** when creating a dialog box, and its make file uses 32-bit compiler commands. This section details the changes that would allow Hello to compile equally well as a 16-bit or a 32-bit program.

Setting a Calling Convention

First the calling conventions. In Chapter 2 we set the compiler's -Gz switch to make all the procedures use the new _stdcall convention. Win32 programs must use _stdcall for WinMain, window procedures, and callback procedures. Win16 programs must use _pascal for WinMain and _far _pascal for window and callback procedures. Typically, a Win16 version of Hello would use these function prototypes:

```
/*-------------------------------------------------------------------
        FUNCTION PROTOTYPES for type checking
   --------------------------------------------------------------*/

int PASCAL WinMain( HANDLE hinstThis, HANDLE hinstPrev,
    LPSTR lpszCmdLine, int iCmdShow );
LONG CALLBACK Hello_WndProc( HWND hWnd, UINT uMessage, UINT uParam,
    LONG lParam );
BOOL CALLBACK About_DlgProc( HWND hDlg, UINT uMessage, UINT uParam,
    LONG lParam );
```

As it turns out, those three Win16 function prototypes are completely portable. Use them under Win32 with no modification. It works because Windows 3.1 and

Windows NT define **PASCAL** and **CALLBACK** differently. Windows 3.1 gives these definitions for three calling-convention constants:

```
#define CALLBACK          _far _pascal
#define WINAPI            _far _pascal
#define PASCAL            _pascal
```

But Windows NT defines all three constants as _stdcall (in windef.h), which is exactly what callbacks, window procedures, and WinMain should use for Win32:

```
#define CALLBACK      __stdcall
#define WINAPI        __stdcall
#define APIENTRY      WINAPI
#define PASCAL        __stdcall
```

In Win32 programs you may also see **APIENTRY** used to declare a function's calling convention. **APIENTRY** originates in OS/2, where it serves about the same purpose as **WINAPI** and **CALLBACK**. **CALLBACK** is meant for window procedures and callback procedures (like EnumFontProc). **WINAPI** is meant for exported DLL procedures. All three exist primarily for backward compatibility. Using these manifest constants makes code more portable to the environments where the terms originated, but otherwise they are interchangeable.

First Change:

• Modify the function prototypes in hello.h and the declarations in hello.c. Make WinMain and the window procedures use the **PASCAL** and **CALLBACK** manifest constants to designate calling conventions in a portable manner.

Checking for a Previous Instance

The first version of Hello reregisters its window class on every instance. A Win16 program must register the window class only once, for the first instance. Again, the normal Windows 3.1 syntax turns out to be perfectly portable:

```
if (!hinstPrev)     // is this the first instance of the program?
{
    if (!RegisterHelloClass( hinstThis ))      // yes, so register window class
    {
        return( FALSE );                       // registration failed
    }
}
```

Under Win32 `WinMain` still receives two instance handle parameters, but the handle for the previous instance is always **NULL**. The `if` statement that tests `hinstPrev` will always find its condition true, and every instance will register its window class. The first `if` condition is necessary only for Win16 but is perfectly portable to Win32.

Second Change:

- Pass the previous instance handle to `Init` and register the window class only if the handle is **NULL**.

Parsing Messages

The 32-bit version of the `WM_COMMAND` message packs its parameters differently, so a portable version must arrange for different parsing methods. Here's a version that works by checking the value of the `WIN32` constant, which NT programs conventionally define with the –D switch on the compiler's command line:

```
case WM_COMMAND:
    // the user chose something from the menu

    // uParam and lParam are packed differently in WIN32
    #if defined (WIN32)                    // parse the command
        wCmd   = LOWORD(uParam);
        wEvent = HIWORD(uParam);
        hCtrl  = (HWND)lParam;
    #else
        wCmd   = (WORD)uParam;
        wEvent = HIWORD(lParam);
        hCtrl  = (HWND)LOWORD(lParam);
    #endif

    Hello_OnCommand( hWnd, wCmd );         // interpret the command
    break;
```

Hello doesn't really need all three parts of the message. It uses only the command ID. We've extracted the notification code and originating control window as well for the sake of giving a complete example.

Third Change:

- Extract the information from the **WM_COMMAND** message immediately and use `#if` conditions to compile correctly for each environment.

Invoking the Dialog Box

Win32 programs have no use for **MakeProcInstance**, but portable programs must still call it. Neither **MakeProcInstance** nor **FreeProcInstance** exists as a Win32 API, but as we showed earlier, both are defined as empty macros for the sake of backward compatibility. Here's a portable version of the MakeAbout procedure that invokes the program's dialog box:

```
/*------------------------------------------------------------------
        MAKE "ABOUT" DIALOG BOX
        Process requests to show the About box here.
        --------------------------------------------------------------*/

void MakeAbout ( HWND hWnd )
{
    FARPROC lpfnAbout;

    // MakeProcInstance and FreeProcInstance do nothing in Win32
    lpfnAbout = MakeProcInstance((FARPROC)About_DlgProc, hInst );

    // show the dialog box
    DialogBox( hInst, MAKEINTRESOURCE(DLG_ABOUT), hWnd, (DLGPROC)lpfnAbout );

    // The box is modal. Execution stops here until OK button
    // is pressed, so now free the procedure's context.

    #if !defined (WIN32)              // avoids a -W4 warning
        FreeProcInstance( lpfnAbout );
    #endif
    return;
}
```

The #if condition surrounding **FreeProcInstance** isn't strictly necessary. It only prevents a −W4 warning from the CL386 compiler saying, "This line does nothing." The **MakeProcInstance** line does not generate a warning because even when the command disappears the line still assigns a value to lpfnAbout.

Fourth Change:

- Call **MakeProcInstance** and **FreeProcInstance** for dialog and callback procedures even though Win32 ignores them.

Adding a Module Definition File

The 32-bit linker does not require a module definition file (.DEF) for every program (only for libraries); the Win16 linker requires one for every program. For portability, Hello needs to provide one.

```
NAME     Hello
DESCRIPTION 'basic outline for Windows applications'

EXETYPE WINDOWS            ;needed for any Windows program
STUB 'WINSTUB.EXE'         ;provides error message if run w/o Windows

CODE PRELOAD MOVEABLE DISCARDABLE
DATA PRELOAD MOVEABLE MULTIPLE

HEAPSIZE    1024           ; room for local variables
STACKSIZE   5120           ; room needed for function calls

EXPORTS                    ; functions called by Windows must be exported
   Hello_WndProc   @1      ; main window procedure
   About_DlgProc   @2      ; window procedure for About dialog box
```

The 32-bit linker does recognizes some new .DEF file statements. They come up in Chapter 11 when we build dynamic-link libraries.

Fifth Change:

- Add a module definition file for linking the Win16 version of Hello.

Revising the Make File

Finally, we need a make file that decides whether to build a 16-bit or a 32-bit program, depending on whether NMake is running under Windows 3.1 or NT. The make file should determine which tools to call and give them the right command switches. Here it is:

```
#
#   Create a debugging version of Hello. According to the value
#   of the CPU environment variable, compile either a 16-bit
#   or a 32-bit version of Hello.
#
all: hello.exe

!if "$(CPU)" != ""
```

```
# Here we are generating code for Windows NT

#
# Update the resources if necessary
hello.res: hello.rc hello.h
    rc hello.rc
    cvtres -i386 hello.res -o hello.rbj

# Update the object file if necessary
hello.obj: hello.c hello.h
    cl386 -c -G2 -W4 -D_X86_=1 -DWIN32 -Zi -Od hello.c

# Create the executable file
hello.exe: hello.obj hello.res hello.def
    link32 -debug:full -debugtype:cv -subsystem:windows -out:hello.exe \
    hello.obj hello.rbj libc.lib ntdll.lib kernel32.lib user32.lib gdi32.lib

!ELSE

# Here we are generating code for Windows 3.1

# Update the object file if necessary
hello.obj: hello.c hello.h
    cl -c -AS -G2w -W4 -Zip -Od -DWIN16 hello.c

# Update the resource file if necessary
hello.res: hello.rc hello.h
rc -r hello.rc

# Create the executable file
hello.exe: hello.obj hello.def hello.res
    link  /NOD /CO /AL:16 hello.obj ,,, libw slibcew, hello.def
    rc hello.res

!ENDIF
```

This make file begins by testing the value of the environment variable CPU. Windows NT defines that variable on installation as either i386 or MIPS. If it is not defined, the make file realizes NT is not running and calls the 16-bit tools.

Sixth Change:

- Rewrite the make file to handle both sets of tools.

With those six changes, Hello acquires the discretion of a chameleon and compiles automatically to suit its environment. The changes should give you some helpful examples, but Hello hardly tests the full range of compatibility issues. We have some other suggestions as well.

A Function That Runs Under 3.0, 3.1, and NT

We've already explained that many graphics routines were replaced by extended versions to accommodate 32-bit drawing coordinates. The old functions, such as **MoveTo**, exist in Windows 3.0 and 3.1. The new versions, such as **MoveToEx**, exist in Windows 3.1 and Windows NT. It seems impossible to write a program with **MoveTo** that works in all three versions. Compatibility with 3.0 is of course becoming less important as more people upgrade, but for those to whom it still matters here's a **MoveTo** procedure that successfully compiles and runs for all three systems:

```
/*-------------------------------------------------------------
        MYMOVETOEX
        Performs a MoveTo command.

        Under 3.1 or later, calls MoveToEx. In earlier versions,
        calls MoveTo. Should run under 3.0, 3.1, and Win32.
        -----------------------------------------------------------*/

    BOOL MyMoveToEx (
    HDC hDC,
    int x,
    int y,
    LPPOINT lppt )
{
    DWORD dwPoint;                      // return from MoveTo
    UINT  uWinVer = LOWORD( GetVersion() );

    uWinVer = ((WORD)LOBYTE(uWinVer) << 8 ) | (WORD)HIBYTE(uWinVer);
    if (uWinVer >= 0x030A)
    {
        // running under version 3.1 or higher
        return( MoveToEx(hDC, x, y, lppt) );
    }
    else
```

```
{
    // running under version earlier than 3.1
    dwPoint = MoveTo( hDC, x, y );
    if (lppt)                     // does caller want return?
    {                             // yes; extract coordinates
        lppt->x = LOWORD( dwPoint );
        lppt->y = HIWORD( dwPoint );
    }
    return( TRUE );
}
}
```

Incidentally, Windows NT also considers itself to be version 3.1, and it returns that value to **GetVersion**. Windows NT, however, sets the high bit of **GetVersion**'s return value, while Windows 3.1 and Win32s do not. (Be careful, too, how you test the return value. Carelessly written tests might conclude that a hypothetical version 4.0 *precedes* 3.1 because the minor version number (0) is less than the minor version number of 3.1.)

Use Only the Published Windows API

Windows has always contained some functions, messages, and structures used internally by the system but not documented in the SDK literature. Undocumented features can sometimes make a particular task easier, and even some commercial programs use them.

Generally, Microsoft's unwillingness to document a feature, such as the internal structure of a device context or a region, indicates that the feature is likely to change in future versions. When the future version runs on an entirely different underlying system, the likelihood of internal changes becomes certainty. Reliance on "illegal" features may ease development in the short term but will cause "port bugs" that appear only under subsequent versions. The danger is greatest for functions related to hardware access because, as an independent and secure operating system, Windows NT has its own completely different methods for managing hardware and I/O.

Recommendation:

- Use only documented structures and commands.

Use the Profile Functions

Windows for DOS stores configuration information for the system and for individual applications in system.ini, win.ini, and various private initialization files. Even though the Windows API includes profile functions specifically to read and write initialization files, occasionally programmers have preferred to avoid the sometimes cumbersome profile functions and called standard I/O functions instead to manage the files.

Windows NT, however, replaces all the separate ASCII .INI files with a single configuration database. Procedures that try to manipulate the configuration files directly will fail. The database is not a text file and is not easily accessible to normal file I/O.

Recommendation:

- For portability, rely entirely on the profile functions, such as `WriteProfileString` and `WritePrivateProfileString`.

Files and Text

Data files rarely travel well between CPUs. The internal layout of a structure and the sizes of its fields are likely to vary. If a Windows 3.1 program saves an array of UINTs, each element in the file will occupy 16 bits. If a Windows NT program then reads the file back as a series of UINTs, it will be retrieving 32-bit values.

Recommendation:

- To avoid problems with polymorphic data types, consider reading and writing data files as one-dimensional arrays of characters.

In changing CPUs you may also encounter different character sets. Do not assume an ASCII character set.

Recommendation:

- To test character values, include the ctype.h header and rely on its portable functions such as `isalpha`, `isdigit`, `tolower`, and `toupper`.

Specific Type Definitions

Hello defined its Window procedure with **LONG**s and **UINT**s:

```
LONG Hello_WndProc (
    HWND hWnd,
    UINT uMsg,
    UINT uParam,
    LONG lParam )
```

But the Windows header files allow more specific data types to be used in the same places:

```
LRESULT Hello_WndProc (
    HWND hWnd,
    UINT uMsg,
    WPARAM wParam,        // (yes, this is still a 32-bit value)
    LPARAM lParam )
```

The type **LRESULT** is more specific than **LONG**, and **WPARAM** is more specific than **UINT**. **LRESULT** is the type for the value a window procedure returns, and **WPARAM** is the type for the third parameter of a window procedure. Source code gains an additional boost in portability by using unique type names for different kinds of objects. Rather than declaring everything a **HANDLE**, use more specific names like **HWND** and **HGLOBAL**. Rather than a simple **LONG**, use **LPARAM** or **LRESULT**. Rather than **FARPROC**, use **DLGPROC** and **HOOKPROC**. If any of the objects acquire new definitions when the code travels to a new environment, the unique names will apply the modifications selectively and automatically.

Recommendation:

- Use specific data types, such as **HINSTANCE**, instead of general types, such as **HANDLE**. In general you should also prefer defined types, such as **LONG**, to the basic C data types, such as long.

STRICT Type Definitions

Some of the specific variable types become more powerful when you also define the manifest constant **STRICT**. Starting with Windows 3.1, Microsoft included in windows.h sections that compile differently depending on whether **STRICT** has been defined. By pairing the two lines

```
#define STRICT
#include <windows.h>
```

you activate stronger type checking. Without **STRICT**, the compiler does not distinguish between, for example, **HBRUSH** and **HBITMAP**, which are both simply **HANDLE**s. **STRICT** influences a lot of definitions, including this one in winnt.h:

```
#ifdef STRICT                            // STRICT is defined
typedef const void *HANDLE;
#define DECLARE_HANDLE(name) \
    struct name##__ { int unused; }; \
    typedef const struct name##__ *name
#else                                    // STRICT is not defined
typedef PVOID HANDLE;
#define DECLARE_HANDLE(name) typedef HANDLE name
#endif
```

Those lines offer alternate versions of the **HANDLE** type and of a macro called **DECLARE_HANDLE**. Scattered through the rest of the header files are lines like these:

```
DECLARE_HANDLE(HWND);
DECLARE_HANDLE(HBITMAP);
DECLARE_HANDLE(HBRUSH);
DECLARE_HANDLE(HDC);
DECLARE_HANDLE(HFONT);
DECLARE_HANDLE(HMENU);
DECLARE_HANDLE(HINSTANCE);
DECLARE_HANDLE(HPALETTE);
DECLARE_HANDLE(HPEN);
```

Without **STRICT**, the compiler thinks of any handle as a pointer to type void. With **STRICT**, the compiler thinks of each handle as a pointer to a different kind of structure. Each structure has a name like **HPEN__** or **HBRUSH__**. Handles aren't really structures, of course, but by declaring them this way you enable the compiler to help you avoid passing a device context instead of a window handle. The fact that the compiler thinks handles are pointers may help you understand some of its error messages and the debugger's way of displaying them as structures.

Enforcing **STRICT** type distinctions will cause compiler warnings for functions such as **SelectObject**, which accept parameters of several different types. One solution is to cast the variables back to their generic types:

```
SelectObject( hDC, (HANDLE)hBitmap );
```

But of course that defeats the purpose of stronger type checking. A better solution is to include the optional supplementary header file windowsx.h, which defines macro versions of **SelectObject** for each type. The macros include **SelectPen**, **SelectBrush**, **SelectFont**, and **SelectBitmap**. All of them call the standard **SelectObject** API, but each provides the proper type casting to work with a specific **STRICT** type. Here, for example, is the one for selecting an **HPEN**:

```
#define SelectPen(hdc, hpen) \
    ((HPEN)SelectObject((hdc), (HGDIOBJ)(HPEN)(hpen)))
```

There is a matching set of deletion macros, such as **DeletePen** and **DeleteBrush**. The macro APIs produce clearer code, especially with **STRICT** defined, and we use them in this book. On the other hand, the type casting in the macros can conceal mismatches:

```
#define STRICT
#include <windows.h>
#include <windowsx.h>

HDC hDC;
int x;
SelectPen( hDC, x );            // compiler doesn't notice
SelectObject( hDC, x );         // compiler complains
```

Control Message APIs

STRICT types can also generate compiler errors when you pack information into message parameters for dialog controls. In order to prevent an accumulation of type casts around dialog control code, and to simplify your **SendMessage** commands, windowsx.h defines a long set of control macros, one for every control window message. The macros let you replace the code

```
int iNumChars;
iNumChars = (int)SendMessage( hwndEdit, EM_GETLINE, iLine, (LONG)(LPSTR)aCh );
```

with this code:

```
iNumChars = Edit_GetLine( hwndEdit, iLine, aCh, sizeof(aCh) );
```

The macro names are all generated by combining the name of the control (edit) with an underscore and the name of the message (EM_GETLINE). Similarly, there are macros for **Button_Enable**, **Static_SetIcon**, and **ListBox_AddString**.

The macros are defined for both Win16 and Win32. As an added benefit, using the macros makes code more portable by handling transparently any differences that result from the widened window message parameters of Win32. The macros correctly pack and unpack any control window messages in either environment.

Message Crackers

Not surprisingly, windowsx.h contains another set of macros to provide the same portability for unpacking regular window messages. Rather than cramming **#if** conditions into every case of a window procedure's lengthy switch statement, you can call a macro for each message. The macro unpacks the information from a message and calls whichever procedure you designate to process that particular message. The result looks like this:

```
LRESULT CALLBACK Hello_WndProc (
    HWND hWnd,
    UINT uMessage,
    WPARAM wParam,
    LPARAM lParam )
{
    switch (uMessage)
    {
        HANDLE_MSG( hWnd, WM_COMMAND, Hello_OnCommand );

        HANDLE_MSG( hWnd, WM_PAINT, Hello_OnPaint );

        HANDLE_MSG( hWnd, WM_DESTROY, Hello_OnDestroy );

        default:
```

```
        return( DefWindowProc(hWnd, uMessage, wParam, lParam) );
    }
}
```

If you're curious you can follow the intricate workings of the **HANDLE_MSG** macro in windowsx.h. It expands to insert a `case` statement for each message; it correctly parses, extracts, and type-casts information from the wParam and lParam of any message; and it passes the parsed information, along with the window handle, to the handler function named in the third parameter. (You must declare and define each handler function.) Finally, the macro accepts whatever value the handler passes back and places the value in a `return` statement. If the handler returns void, the macro returns OL. **HANDLE_MSG** is called a *message cracker* because it cracks apart the wParam and lParam values to extract information from them.

HANDLE_MSG has an important limitation. It assumes you have named your message parameters wParam and lParam. Those conventional names are hard-coded into the macro.

Since each window message contains different information, **HANDLE_MSG** passes different parameters to each handler function. To write a handler function, such as Hello_OnCommand, you normally begin by looking up its prototype in windowsx.h. Search for "oncommand" and you'll find this:

```
/* void Cls_OnCommand(HWND hwnd, int id, HWND hwndCtl, UINT codeNotify); */
```

That line shows how to declare a message handler function for **WM_COMMAND** messages.

```
void Hello_OnCommand (
    HWND hWnd,          // window that received WM_COMMAND message
    int iCmd,           // command ID number (such as IDM_FILEOPEN)
    HWND hCtl,          // where message originated (if not a menu)
    UINT uCode );       // notification message sent by control window
```

To write the comments for that prototype, we looked up **WM_COMMAND** in the on-line help file to see what information a **WM_COMMAND** message normally conveys.

The message cracker macro forces you to include all the parameters in your message handler even if you don't intend to use them. If you compile with the highest warning level, −W4, as we do, then unused parameters generate the warning "unreferenced formal parameter." You can safely ignore the warning. Long programs generate the warning over and over. If it bothers you then change to −W3, but we recommend the consistency that −W4 enforces. Alternatively, you can suppress the warning with this pragma:

```
#pragma warning (disable :4100)        // unused formal parameter warning
```

But of course the pragma suppresses the warning entirely, so the compiler won't tell you if you really do leave an extra parameter somewhere.

There's a new macro for such cases called **UNREFERENCED_PARAMETER**. Microsoft uses it in their sample programs. For example, programs that don't read arguments from the command line often end WinMain like this:

```
    return( msg.wParam );
    UNREFERENCED_PARAMETER( lpszCmdLine );
}
```

Instead of generating an unreferenced parameter warning here, the −W4 switch now warns that this instruction does nothing. Though it doesn't reduce warnings, the macro has the advantage of clarity. It reassures a reader that the programmer didn't simply forget to do something important with an unused parameter.

Occasionally you may discover gaps where windowsx.h fails to define a message cracker for some message you want to use. Or you may need a message cracker for a **WM_USER** message of your own. They are easy to write. The multimedia program in Chapter 16 defines a custom message cracker for **MCINOTIFY** messages.

In order to reveal the portability problems that restructured messages cause, we chose not to use message crackers (or **STRICT**, or unique variable types) in Hello. All the examples in later chapters make full use of these features.

Message Forwarders

Related to the message cracker macro is a series of message forwarder macros. After all, unpacking messages is only half the problem. You also create potentially unportable code when you pack information into messages and send them to other windows. Use the message cracker to receive messages and the message forwarders to send them. To find a message forwarder in windowsx.h, search for the message name. Searching for "wm_command" turns up this:

```
#define FORWARD_WM_COMMAND(hwnd, id, hwndCtl, codeNotify, fn) \
    (void)(fn)(    (hwnd), \
                WM_COMMAND, \
                MAKEWPARAM((UINT)(id), \
```

```
            (UINT)(codeNotify)), \
            (LPARAM)(HWND)(hwndCtl))
```

The message forwarder always has the same *signature*, or parameter list, as the corresponding message handler, with the addition of a message function (`fn`) at the end. To send a message, you might write this:

```
FORWARD_WM_COMMAND( hWnd, IDM_NEW, NULL, 0, SendMessage );
```

The final parameter could be **PostMessage** instead, depending on whether you want to wait for the message to be processed before continuing.

Dialog Procedures and Message Crackers

HANDLE_MSG works fine for window procedures but not for dialog procedures, which is unfortunate because dialog procedures receive and unpack messages too and are equally susceptible to the porting problems that message crackers solve.

Dialog procedures differ from window procedures in several ways. A true window procedure returns an **LRESULT** (a long integer), but a dialog procedure returns a Boolean value—**TRUE** if the message was processed and **FALSE** if it was not. **HANDLE_MSG** is designed to return **LRESULT** values. A window procedure must call **DefWindowProc** for any messages it ignores; a dialog box simply returns **FALSE** to make Windows execute the default response. Finally, dialog procedures do not need to answer **WM_PAINT** or **WM_DESTROY** messages, and they never receive **WM_CREATE** messages. (They get **WM_INITDIALOG** instead.) The differences result from the fact that a dialog procedure is not a true window procedure. The behavior of a dialog box is standard and largely determined by the system. The system itself contains a single window procedure for all the system's dialog boxes, and within the standard procedure the system calls your dialog procedure to permit some individual responses. A program's main overlapping window, in contrast, has fewer default standard behaviors. Window procedures define their own work and call the system occasionally for support, but dialog boxes run from a single standard window procedure and occasionally call you for support.

Microsoft's reasons for deciding to make dialog procedures differ from other window procedures remain obscure. There are no evident advantages. The differences prevent easy pasting of code between dialog and window procedures and heap one more arbitrary distinction in the path of the Windows apprentice.

There is a way to make dialog procedures that look like window procedures and that can use message crackers. Once again, the macros that allow this new structure come from windowsx.h. Since you can't return long results from a dialog procedure, the trick is to forward *all* messages from the real, old-style dialog procedure to an ersatz new-style dialog procedure. The old procedure with its Boolean returns becomes a mere transfer point, forwarding all messages to its replacement. The new procedure sorts them out, handles them, and returns an **LRESULT**. The old procedure caches the **LRESULT** in a place where it can be recovered, should anyone want it, and then returns **TRUE**.

The next problem is activating the default responses for the dialog box. Normally a dialog procedure returns **FALSE** to make Windows handle a dialog message, but the old dialog procedure can't tell from the **LRESULT** whether it ought to return **TRUE** or **FALSE**. Normal window procedures call **DefWindowProc** to trigger a default response. For a dialog window, though, a call to **DefDlgProc** initiates an endlessly recursive loop. **DefDlgProc** is the system's internal window procedure for all dialog boxes, and one of the things it does is call the program's dialog procedure. So if we call **DefDlgProc** it calls us right back, initiating an endless loop. If we can stop the recursion we can use **DefDlgProc** after all and make the new dialog procedure even more like a normal window procedure.

A static Boolean flag solves the problem. We set the flag to **TRUE** just before calling **DefDlgProc**, and whenever **DefDlgProc** calls our dialog procedure, the first thing we do is check the flag. If bRecursing is **TRUE**, then we know the system is trying to redeliver the message we just processed. We return **FALSE** and reset the flag, and **DefDlgProc** continues with its default processing.

Three macros in windowsx.h greatly simplify the creation of new-style dialog procedures. They are

- **CheckDefDlgRecursion:** Called at the beginning of the old stub dialog procedure, this macro checks the recursion flag and immediately returns **FALSE** if the flag is **TRUE**. It also resets the flag to **FALSE**.

- **SetDlgMsgResult:** This macro figures out what value the old stub procedure should return. Internally the macro calls the new window-like dialog procedure, receives and stores an **LRESULT**, and returns **TRUE**. A few special messages, such as **WM_CTLCOLOR**, must return something important other than **TRUE** (such as a brush handle.) **SetDlgMsgResult** checks for these special messages, casts their return value to a Boolean, and returns it intact.

- **DefDlgProcEx:** Called at the end of the new-style dialog procedure, this macro collapses the two steps of setting the recursion flag to **TRUE** and calling **DefDlgProc**.

The macros do most of the work. Here's how you'd build an About box with them:

```
/*------------------------------------------------------------------
        ABOUT BOX PROCEDURE (OLD-STYLE)
        Runs the dialog box that displays information about the
        program. This is the stub procedure. It checks and resets
        the recursion flag and forwards all messages to the new-style
        procedure. Win16 programs must still export this procedure in the
        .DEF file.
        ----------------------------------------------------------------*/

static BOOL bRecursing = FALSE;        // for aborting recursive calls

// Every dialog box incorporates DefDlgProcEx in its own DefProc macro
#define About_DefProc( hWnd, uMessage, wParam, lParam ) \
    DefDlgProcEx( hWnd, uMessage, wParam, lParam, &bRecursing )

BOOL CALLBACK About_OldDlgProc (
    HWND hDlg,
    UINT uMessage,
    WPARAM wParam,
    LPARAM lParam )
{
    // If bRecursing is TRUE, this macro ends the procedure
    // by returning FALSE. It also resets bRecursing.
    CheckDefDlgRecursion( &bRecursing );

    // The next line calls About_DlgProc and processes
    // the LRESULT return value.
    return( SetDlgMsgResult(hDlg, uMessage,
                    About_DlgProc(hDlg, uMessage, wParam, lParam)) );
}


/*------------------------------------------------------------------
        ABOUT BOX (NEW-STYLE PROCEDURE)
        ----------------------------------------------------------------*/
```

```
LRESULT About_DlgProc (                  // note the return value
                HWND hDlg,
                UINT uMessage,
                WPARAM wParam,
                LPARAM lParam )

            {
                switch (uMessage)
    {
        HANDLE_MSG( hDlg, WM_INITDIALOG, About_OnInitDialog );

        HANDLE_MSG( hDlg, WM_COMMAND, About_OnCommand );

        default:
            // set the bRecursing flag and call DefDlgProc
            return( AllDlg_DefProc(hDlg, uMessage, wParam, lParam) );
    }
}
```

We haven't defined **About_OnInitDialog** and **About_OnCommand** but they would look just like message handlers for any other window procedure. This version of the dialog procedure is entirely portable. It will, for example, parse **WM_COMMAND** correctly for Win16 and for Win32.

Win32s

Win32s is the name of a Microsoft product that lets a 16-bit Windows program call any of the Win32 API routines. The don't all work (most return errors) but you can at least call them. The Win32s subset DLLs allow the developer to write a single source file that compiles for both the 16-bit and 32-bit environments *and* when compiled for NT makes full use of the entire API. Also, the Win32s system does work internally in full 32-bit processing mode.

Win32s is a set of DLLs that contain at least a stub procedure for every Win32 API. Win32s doesn't actually perform all the new functions—no threads, no mapped files, no Bézier curves—but all the commands for those functions exist, and they return their proper error codes when they fail to perform their normal NT functions. Whenever a Win32s program calls a function that exists only in Win32, it must check the return value. It must be prepared for Win32 functions to fail. It might disable some options when a function fails, or it might branch to Win16 code that performs the same option a different way.

One new feature from NT does work in Win32s: structured exception handling. Microsoft included it to encourage developers to incorporate this new, more robust error-handling mechanism right from the start. Chapter 6 explains how to use structured exception handling.

Developers may distribute the Win32s system extensions to users along with their applications. The DLLs are also in the Win32 SDK. Win32s runs applications non-preemptively, so expect some minor differences from its behavior on NT. Win32s programs run more slowly, of course, than they do under NT, but more quickly than they would without the 32-bit processing of Win32s.

Now you've learned a number of differences between 16-bit and 32-bit Windows programs. Some variables have grown wider, and some messages and functions have changed to accommodate them. Many GDI functions have been replaced by extended versions. Class and window extra words grew into long values. Whole sets of functions have become obsolete, including the old system-specific memory functions, sound functions, and communications functions. Instances of the same program remain much more independent of each other now. They do not share data, and each reregisters its window class anew. Because Windows NT runs on different machines with different file systems, hard-coding specific information about file name sizes or pixel dimensions can prevent a program from running on some NT systems.

Fortunately you can run PortTool to help locate trouble spots when converting a 16-bit program to NT. You can also adopt some programming practices for writing portable code that needs little or no modification to compile for both environments. We particularly recommended restricting programs to documented features, using the most specific data types and enforcing them with **STRICT**, and calling message crackers to parse messages.

Having spent a chapter looking backward at all the old functions and making sure you would still be able to use them, we now turn forward to face new regions. Chapter 4 strides straight into the thick of it with multithreading.

Creating and Synchronizing Multiple Threads

- Creating multiple threads

- Changing a thread's priority

- Suspending and resuming threads

- Using object handles

- Synchronizing with mutexes, events, semaphores, and critical sections

Aprogram of any complexity at all is a maze of instructions that loop and branch, full of forks, jumps, and returns. The processor makes decisions as the program runs, and each decision leads down a different set of instructions. Each time the program executes, the processor follows a different path from start to termination. When Theseus fought the minotaur he marked his way through the labyrinth by unwinding a thread behind him. When an NT program wants to do several things at once, it creates objects called threads, and each thread winds its own way through the program's code.

Another way to look at it is to say that threads let a program be in two places at once. The system keeps a list of all the threads and cycles through them, giving each a slice of time on the processor. When a time slice ends the system records the current CPU register values in the thread object, including a pointer to whatever instruction the thread was about to execute. The system then selects another thread, restores *its* CPU registers, and resumes execution wherever the thread last left off. A thread marks a location in the program, and by marking several locations with different threads the program effectively clones itself and seems to execute in many places at the same time.

Like most of the book's remaining chapters, this one covers its topic in three steps: concepts, commands, and code. It begins with a conceptual introduction to threads, surveys the commands for using threads, and finishes with a sample program demonstrating threads. By the end of this chapter you will understand when and how to create threads in your programs, how to manage them while they run, and how to synchronize them so they don't interfere with each other. Mutexes, semaphores, events, and critical sections will hold no more mysteries for you.

CONCEPTS

Threads are closely related to processes. A process is a program loaded into memory, complete with all the resources assigned to the program, but a process is static and does nothing by itself. A thread executes program commands, following a path through the code. Every process possesses one initial thread. Optionally, the initial thread (also called the *primary thread*) may create other threads. All the threads belonging to one process share the assets of that process. They all follow instructions from the same code image, refer to the same global variables, write to the same private address space, and have access to the same objects. A process is a house inhabited by threads.

The WinPerf performance monitor, shown in Figure 4.1, counts, among other things, the total number of threads in the system. Even when you aren't running any programs the many threads of the system itself are busy at their work.

FIGURE 4.1:

WinPerf performance monitor

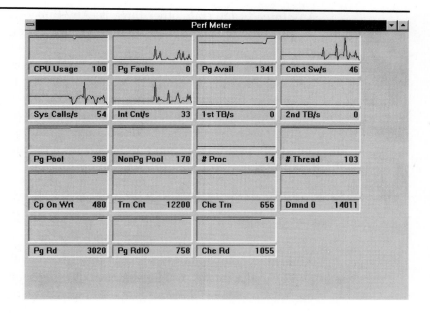

When to Create Threads and Processes

You should consider creating new threads anytime your program handles asynchronous activity. Programs with multiple windows, for example, generally benefit from creating a thread for each window. Most MDI (multi-document interface) applications will want to create threads for the child windows. A program that interacts with several asynchronous devices would create threads for responding to each device. A desktop publisher, for example, might assign responsibility for the main window to a single thread of high priority. When the user initiates a lengthy operation, such as pouring text into an empty layout, the program creates a new thread to do the formatting in the background. Meanwhile the first thread continues to manage the main window and responds quickly to new commands from the user. If the user then asks to cancel the formatting, the input thread can interrupt the formatting thread by terminating it. Threads can also be useful for performing slow disk operations in the background or for communicating with other processes. One thread sends messages and another waits to receive them.

Any thread can create other threads. Any thread can also create new processes. When a program needs to do several things at once, it must decide whether to create threads or processes to share the work. Choose threads whenever you can because the system creates them quickly and they interact with each other easily. Creating a process takes longer because the system must load a new executable file image from the disk, but a new process has the advantage of receiving its own private address space. You might choose processes over threads as a way of preventing them from interfering, even accidentally, with each other's resources. For more details about processes, refer to the section "Process Manager" in Chapter 1 and to Chapter 5.

Thread Objects

At the system level, a thread is an object created by the object manager. Like all system objects a thread contains data, or attributes, and functions, or methods. Figure 4.2 represents a thread object schematically, listing its attributes and methods.

Most of the thread methods have corresponding Win32 functions. When you call **SuspendThread**, for example, the Win32 subsystem responds by calling the thread's Suspend method. In other words, the Win32 API *exposes* the Suspend method to Win32 applications.

The Thread Context attribute is the data structure for saving the machine state whenever the thread stops executing. We'll explain other attributes as we proceed.

Objects and Handles

Programs that run at the system's user level (as opposed to the more privileged kernel level) may not directly examine or modify the inside of a system object. Only

FIGURE 4.2:

Attributes and methods contained in a thread object

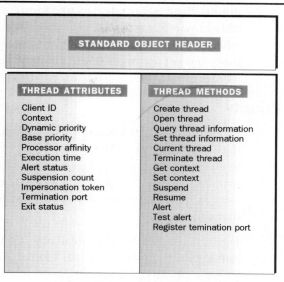

REPRESENTATION OF A THREAD OBJECT

by calling Win32 API routines can you do anything at all with an object. Windows has always protected some internal structures, such as windows and brushes, from direct manipulation. Windows gives you a handle to identify the object, and you pass the handle to functions that need it. Threads, too, have handles (as do processes, semaphores, files, and many other objects). Windows NT, designed from the ground up to be a secure system, protects its internal structures much more effectively than 16-bit Windows ever did. Only the object manager touches the inside of an object.

The function that creates a thread returns a handle to the new object. With the handle you can raise or lower the thread's scheduling priority, make the thread pause and resume, terminate the thread, and find out what value the thread returned when it ended.

Scheduling and Synchronizing Threads

Working with threads requires more than just starting and stopping them. You also have to make threads work together, and effective interaction requires control over timing. Timing control takes two forms: priority and synchronization. Priority controls how often a thread gets processor time. Synchronization regulates threads when they compete for shared resources and imposes a sequence when several threads must accomplish tasks in a certain order.

Priority

When the system scheduler preempts one thread and looks for another to run next, it gives preference to threads of high priority. Some activities, such as responding to an unexpected power loss, always execute at a very high priority. System interrupt handlers have a higher priority than user processes. Every process has a priority rating, and threads derive their base scheduling priority from the process that owns them.

Figure 4.2 showed that a thread object's attributes include a base priority and a dynamic priority. When you call commands to change a thread's priority, you change the base priority. You cannot push a thread's priority more than two steps above or below the priority of its process. Threads can't grow up to be very much more important than their parents.

Although a process cannot promote its threads very far, the system can. The system grants a sort of field promotion to threads that undertake important missions. When the user gives input to a window, for example, the system always elevates all the threads in the process that owns the window. When a thread waiting for data from a disk drive finally receives it, the system promotes that thread, too. These temporary boosts, added to the thread's current base priority, form the dynamic priority. The scheduler chooses threads to execute based on their dynamic priority. Process, base, and dynamic priorities are distinguished in Figure 4.3.

Dynamic priority boosts begin to degrade immediately. A thread's dynamic priority slips back one level each time the thread receives another time slice and finally stabilizes at the thread's base priority.

How Scheduling Happens

Figure 1.10 in Chapter 1 showed how the kernel's dispatcher ready queue holds all the system threads in 32 separate queues, one for all the threads at each priority level. To select the next thread, the scheduler begins at the highest priority queue, executes the threads there, and then works its way down the rest of the list. But the

FIGURE 4.3:

How the range of a thread's dynamic priority derives from the priority class of its process

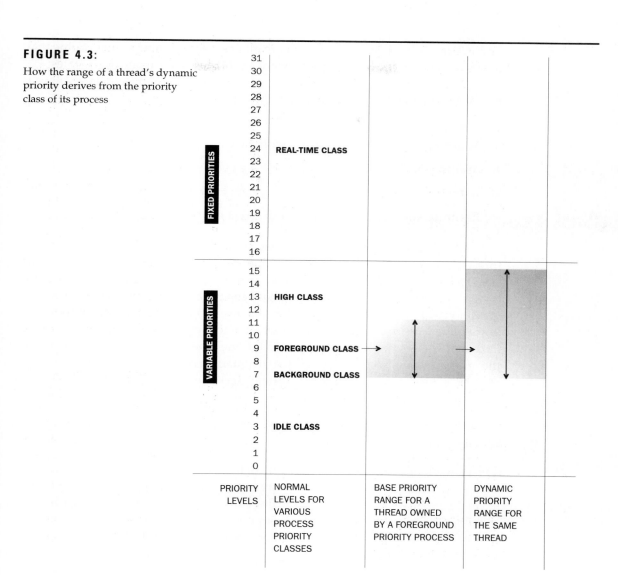

dispatcher ready queue may not contain all the threads in the system. Some may be suspended or blocked. At any moment a thread may be in one of six states:

- **Ready**: Queued, waiting to execute
- **Standby**: Ready to run next (in the batter's box)
- **Running**: Executing; interacting with the CPU
- **Waiting**: Not executing; waiting for a signal to resume
- **Transition**: About to execute when system loads its context
- **Terminated**: Through executing, but object not deleted

When the scheduler selects a ready thread from the queue, it loads a *context* for the thread. The context includes a set of values for the machine registers, the kernel stack, a thread environment block, and a user stack in the address space of the thread's process. (If part of the context has been paged to disk, the thread enters the transition state while the system gathers the pieces.) Changing threads means saving all the pieces of one context and loading in to the processor all the pieces of the next one. The newly loaded thread runs for one time slice, which is likely to be on the order of 20 milliseconds. The system maintains a counter measuring the current time slice. On each clock tick the system decrements the counter, and when it reaches 0 the scheduler performs a context switch and sets a new thread running.

Synchronization

To run at all, threads have to be scheduled; to run well, they often need to be synchronized. Suppose one thread creates a brush and then creates several threads that share the brush and draw with it. The first thread must not destroy the brush until the other threads finish drawing. Or suppose one thread accepts input from the user and writes it to a file, while another thread reads from the file and processes the text. The reading thread mustn't read while the writing thread is writing. Both situations require a means of coordinating the sequence of actions in several threads.

One solution would be to create a global Boolean variable that one thread uses to signal another. The writing thread might make bDone be **TRUE**, and the reading thread might loop until it sees the flag change. That would work, but the looping thread wastes a lot of processor time. Instead, Win32 supports a set of synchronization objects including mutexes, semaphores, events, and critical sections. All are system objects created by the object manager. Though each coordinates different interactions, they all work in a similar way. A thread that wants to perform some coordinated action waits for a response from one of these objects and proceeds only after receiving it. The scheduler removes waiting objects from the dispatch queue so they do not consume processor time. When the signal arrives, the scheduler allows the thread to resume.

How and when the signal arrives depends on the object. Take mutexes, for example. The one essential characteristic of a mutex is that only one thread can own it. A mutex doesn't do anything apart from letting itself be owned by one thread at a time. ("Mutex" stands for *mut*ual *ex*clusion.) If several threads need to work with a single file, you might create a mutex to protect the file. Whenever any thread begins a file operation, it first asks for the mutex. If no one else has the mutex the thread proceeds. If, on the other hand, another thread has just grabbed the mutex for itself, the request fails and the thread *blocks,* becoming suspended while it waits for ownership. When one thread finishes writing it releases the mutex, and the waiting thread revives, receives the mutex, and performs its own file operations.

The mutex does not actively protect anything. It only works because the threads that use it agree not to write to the file without owning the mutex first. Nothing actually prevents all the threads from trying to write at once. The mutex is just a signal, much like the Boolean bDone in our looping example. You might create a mutex to protect global variables, a hardware port, a handle to a pipe, or a window's client area. Whenever several threads share any system resource you should consider whether to synchronize their use of it.

- A mutex object works like a narrow gate for one thread to pass at a time.

- A semaphore object works like a multi-lane toll gate that a limited number of threads can pass through together.

- An event object broadcasts a public signal for any listening thread to hear.

- A critical section object works just like a mutex but only within a single process.

Mutexes, semaphores, and events can coordinate threads in different processes, but critical sections are only visible to threads in a single process. When one process creates a child process, the child often inherits handles to existing synchronization objects. Critical section objects cannot be inherited.

Fundamentally a synchronization object, like other system objects, is simply a data structure. Synchronization objects have two states, signaled and not signaled. Threads interact with synchronization objects by changing the signal or waiting for the signal. A waiting thread is blocked and does not execute. When the signal occurs the waiting thread receives the object, turns the signal off, performs some synchronized task, and turns the signal back on when it relinquishes the object.

Threads can wait for other objects besides mutexes, semaphores, events, and critical objects. Those four object types exist only for synchronization, but sometimes it makes sense to wait for a process, a thread, a timer, or a file. These objects serve other purposes as well, but like the synchronization objects they too possess a signal state. Processes and threads signal when they terminate. Timer objects signal when a certain interval passes. Files signal when a read or write operation finishes. Threads can wait for any of these signals.

Bad synchronization causes bugs. For example, a deadlock bug occurs when two threads wait for each other. Neither will end unless the other ends first. A race condition occurs when a program fails to synchronize its threads. Suppose one thread writes to a file and another thread reads the new contents. Whether the program works depends on which thread wins the race to its I/O operation. If the writing thread wins, the program works. If the reading thread tries to read first, the program fails.

About Win32 Object Handles

Under 16-bit Windows an object has only one handle. The handle may be copied into several variables, but it is still one handle, and when the object is destroyed all the copies of the handle become invalid. Some of the new objects in Win32, however, work differently. Several threads or processes may have different handles to the same object. Brushes and windows and device contexts still support only one handle, but a single thread or process or mutex, for example, may have many different handles. As each finishes with the object it calls **CloseHandle**. When the last handle closes the system destroys the object.

Incidentally, although the total number of handles in the system is limited only by available memory, no single process may possess more than 65,536 open handles.

COMMANDS

As an introduction to the features of multithreaded programming, this section surveys the parts of the Win32 API that relate to threads. The first half explains commands for creating and modifying threads, and the second half concentrates on synchronizing threads.

Making and Modifying Threads

The life cycle of a thread begins when you call **CreateThread**. Other functions let you examine the thread, suspend or resume it, change its priority, and terminate it.

Creating Threads

Any thread can create another thread by calling **CreateThread**. The arguments to **CreateThread** specify the properties a thread needs to begin life, primarily security privileges and a starting function. The starting function is to a thread what main or WinMain is to a full program. The thread's life coincides with the life of its main function. When the function returns, the thread ends. A thread can start at any function that receives a single 32-bit parameter and returns a 32-bit value.

The parameter and return value are for your convenience. You have to declare them, but you don't have to use them. **CreateThread** lets you pass a **DWORD** into the starting function. If several threads execute the same function you might pass each one a different argument. Each might receive a pointer to a different file name, for example, or a different object handle to wait on.

The Parameters

CreateThread takes six parameters:

```
// prototype for the CreateThread function
HANDLE CreateThread(
    LPSECURITY_ATTRIBUTES lpThreadAttributes,    // access privileges
    DWORD dwStackSize,                           // say 0 for default
    LPTHREAD_START_ROUTINE lpStartAddress,       // pointer to function
    LPVOID lpParameter,                          // value passed to function
```

```
        DWORD dwCreationFlags,                    // active or suspended
        LPDWORD lpThreadId );                     // system returns an ID here
```

The first parameter points to a **SECURITY_ATTRIBUTES** structure that determines who may share the object and whether other processes may be allowed to modify it. The structure contains a security descriptor that assigns access privileges for various system users and groups of users. Most programs simply accept the default descriptor that comes with the current process. The security structure also contains an inheritance flag. If you set the flag to **TRUE**, then any child processes you create will automatically inherit a handle to this object.

```
typedef struct _SECURITY_ATTRIBUTES { /* sa */
    DWORD nLength;                        //sizeof(SECURITY_ATTRIBUTES)
    LPVOID lpSecurityDescriptor;          // NULL to accept process's descriptor
    BOOL  bInheritHandle;                 // TRUE if children may inherit the object
} SECURITY_ATTRIBUTES;
```

You don't need to create a **SECURITY_ATTRIBUTES** structure unless you want the thread to be inherited. If you pass **NULL** as the first parameter to **CreateThread**, the new thread receives the default descriptor and will not be inherited. If you do want to create a handle with limited access rights to its object, investigate the four SetSecurity-Descriptor functions.

The next three parameters give the new thread material to work with. By default each thread receives a stack the same size as that of the primary thread. You can change the size with the second parameter. If the stack later needs more room, the system expands it automatically. The third parameter points to the function where the thread will start, and the value in the fourth parameter becomes the argument passed to the starting function.

Beware of using a local variable to pass a value to a new thread. The local variable will be destroyed when its procedure ends, and the thread may not have used it yet. Use global variables, allocate memory dynamically, or make the first thread wait for the new thread to terminate before it returns.

The dwCreationFlags parameter may be one of two values, either 0 or **CREATE_SUSPENDED**. A suspended thread does not actually begin to run until you give it a push with **ResumeThread**. A program that creates a number of threads might suspend them, accumulate their handles and, when ready, start them all off at once. That's what the sample program later in the chapter does.

The last parameter points to an empty **DWORD** where **CreateThread** places a number to identify the thread uniquely in the system. A few functions require you to identify threads by their ID number instead of by their handles.

The Return Value

CreateThread returns a handle to the new thread. If the thread could not be created, the handle will be **NULL**. Be aware that the system will create the thread even if the `lpStartAddress` or `lpParameter` values are invalid or point to inaccessible data. In that case **CreateThread** returns a valid handle but the new thread terminates immediately and returns an error code. You can test a thread's viability with **GetExit-CodeThread**, which returns **STILL_ACTIVE** if the thread has not ended.

Unless you give **CreateThread** an explicit security descriptor, the new handle comes with full access rights to the new object. In the case of threads, full access means that with this handle you can suspend, resume, terminate, or change the priority of the thread. The handle remains valid even after the thread terminates. To destroy the thread object, close its handle by calling **CloseHandle**. If more than one handle exists, the thread will not be destroyed until the last handle is closed. If you forget to close the handle, the system will do it automatically when your process ends.

Changing a Thread's Priority

High-priority threads get more time on the processor, finish their work more quickly, and are more responsive to the user. But making all your threads high priority entirely defeats the purpose of priorities. If a set of threads all have the same priority, whether their priority is high or low the scheduler must give them equal processor time. One thread can be more responsive only if others are less responsive. The same rule applies equally to processes. Restrict your threads and processes as much as possible to low or average priority levels, and stay at high levels only as long as you must.

```
// these functions retrieve or modify any thread's base priority
BOOL SetThreadPriority(
    HANDLE hThread                      // a thread to modify
    int iPriority );                    // its new priority level

int GetThreadPriority( HANDLE hThread );
```

SetThreadPriority returns TRUE or FALSE for success or failure. GetThreadPriority returns the thread's current priority. A set of constants names the possible priority values for both functions.

THREAD_PRIORITY_LOWEST	2 levels below process
THREAD_PRIORITY_BELOW_NORMAL	1 level below process
THREAD_PRIORITY_NORMAL	Same level as process
THREAD_PRIORITY_ABOVE_NORMAL	1 level above process
THREAD_PRIORITY_HIGHEST	2 levels above process
THREAD_PRIORITY_TIME_CRITICAL	15 (in normal user processes)
THREAD_PRIORITY_IDLE	1 (in normal user processes)

The first five values adjust the thread's base priority level with respect to the level of its parent process, as shown in Figure 4.3. The last two, for critical and idle priority, express absolute priority levels at the upper and lower extremes of the parent's priority class. (For real-time priority code, these extremes are 16 and 31.) The Idle priority level works well for screen savers since they should not execute unless nothing else is happening. Use the Time Critical level with extreme caution and only for short periods because it will starve lower-priority threads of processor time.

Suspending and Resuming a Thread's Execution

A suspended thread stops running and will not be scheduled for processor time. It continues in stasis until some other thread makes it resume. Suspending a thread might be useful if, for example, the user interrupts a task. You could suspend the thread while waiting for the user to confirm the cancellation. If the user chooses to continue, the interrupted thread can resume where it left off. The sample program later in this chapter suspends several drawing threads whenever the user resizes the window. When the window is repainted, the threads continue drawing.

```
// a thread calls these functions to make another thread pause and resume
DWORD SuspendThread( HANDLE hThread );
DWORD ResumeThread( HANDLE hThread );
```

A single thread may be suspended several times in succession without any intervening resume commands, but every **SuspendThread** must eventually be matched with a **ResumeThread**. The system counts the number of pending suspension commands for each thread. (See the Suspension Count attribute in Figure 4.2.) **SuspendThread** increments the counter and **ResumeThread** decrements it. Both functions return in a **DWORD** the previous value of the counter. Only when the counter returns to 0 does the thread resume execution.

A thread can suspend itself but obviously cannot resume itself. What a thread can do is put itself to sleep for a set amount of time. The **Sleep** command delays execution, removing the thread from the scheduler's queue until some interval passes. Interactive threads that write or draw information for the user often take short naps to give the user time to see the output. Sleep is better than an empty loop because it doesn't use processor time.

```
// a thread calls these functions to pause for a set time

VOID Sleep( DWORD dwMilliseconds );

DWORD SleepEx(
    DWORD dwMilliseconds,       // duration of pause
    BOOL bAlertable );          // TRUE to resume if I/O operation finishes
```

The extended **SleepEx** function typically works in conjunction with background I/O functions. As you'll see when we get to files in Chapter 12, Win32 allows you to initiate a read or write operation without waiting for it to finish. The operation continues in the background and when it finishes the system notifies you by invoking a callback procedure from your program. Background I/O (also called overlapping I/O) is particularly helpful in interactive programs that must remain responsive to the user while working with relatively slow devices such as tape drives and network disks. The Boolean parameter in **SleepEx** lets the system wake the thread prematurely if an overlapping I/O operation finishes before the sleep interval expires. **SleepEx** returns 0 if the interval passes uninterrupted and **WAIT_IO_COMPLETION** otherwise.

Getting Information about Existing Threads

A thread can easily retrieve the two pieces of its own identity: a handle and an identifier.

```
// these functions return information identifying the current thread
DWORD GetCurrentThreadID( VOID );
HANDLE GetCurrentThread( VOID );
```

The return value from **GetCurrentThreadID** matches the value in **lpIDThread** after a **CreateThread** command. It is the number that identifies the thread uniquely to the system. Although very few of the Win32 API commands require you to know a thread's ID, it can be useful for monitoring threads system-wide without having to keep handles open for each one. Open handles prevent threads from being destroyed.

The handle that **GetCurrentThread** returns serves the same purpose as the handle returned from **CreateThread**, and it works in the same functions that other handles work, but in fact it is a pseudohandle. A *pseudohandle* is a special constant that the system always interprets a certain way, much as a single dot (.) in DOS always refers to the current directory and this in C++ always points to the current object. The pseudohandle constant returned from **GetCurrentThread** always refers to the current thread. Unlike real handles, a pseudohandle does not work when passed to other threads. Here's what a thread must do to acquire a real, transferable handle to itself:

```
HANDLE hThread;

hThread = DuplicateHandle(
    GetCurrentProcess( ),        // source process
    GetCurrentThread( ),         // original handle
    GetCurrentProcess( ),        // destination process
    &hThread,                    // new duplicate handle
    0,                           // access rights (overridden by last parameter)
    FALSE,                       // children do not inherit the handle
    DUPLICATE_SAME_ACCESS );     // copy access rights from original handle
```

CloseHandle has no effect on a pseudohandle, but the handle **DuplicateHandle** creates is real and must eventually be closed. Using pseudohandles lets **GetCurrent-Thread** work more quickly because it simply assumes a thread should have full access to itself and returns its result without bothering about any security considerations.

Terminate the Execution of a Thread

Normally a thread meets its demise when it comes to the end of the function where it began, just as a Windows program ends when it comes to the end of WinMain. When a thread comes to the end of its starting function the system automatically calls **ExitThread**.

```
// a thread calls this function to stop itself after finishing its work
VOID ExitThread( DWORD dwExitCode );
```

Though the system calls **ExitThread** automatically, you may call it directly yourself if some condition forces a thread to an untimely end:

```
DWORD ThreadFunction( LPDWORD lpdwParam )
{
    HANDLE hThread = CreateThread( <parameters> );

    // initialization chores happen here
    // test to see if there was a problem

    if (<error condition>)
    {
        ExitThread( ERROR_CODE );        // cancel the thread
    }

    // no error, work continues

    return( SUCCESS_CODE );          // this line causes the system
                                     // to call ExitThread
}
```

ERROR_CODE and SUCCESS_CODE are whatever you define them to be. In this simple example, we could just as easily have canceled with a return command:

```
if (<error condition>)
{
    return( ERROR_CODE );               // cancel the thread
}
```

This return command has exactly the same effect as **ExitThread**; in fact, it even results in a call to **ExitThread**. The **ExitThread** command would be genuinely useful for canceling from within any subroutines ThreadFunction calls.

When a thread ends at a return statement, the 32-bit return value becomes the exit code passed automatically to **ExitThread**. After a thread terminates, its exit code is available through this function:

```
// one thread calls this to find out how another ended
BOOL GetExitCodeThread( HANDLE hThread, LPDWORD lpdwExitCode );
```

GetExitCodeThread returns **FALSE** if an error prevents it from determining the return value.

ExitThread, whether called explicitly or as an implicit consequence of `return`, permanently removes a thread from the dispatch queue and destroys the thread's stack. It does not, however, destroy the thread object. That's why you can still ask about the thread's exit status even after the thread stops running. When possible, you should close thread handles explicitly (call **CloseHandle**) to avoid wasting space in memory. The system destroys a thread when its last handle is closed. The system will not destroy a running thread even if all its handles are closed. (In that case, the thread is destroyed when it stops running.) If a process leaves handles open when it terminates, the system closes them automatically and removes orphaned objects no longer held by any process.

With **ExitThread** a thread stops itself gracefully at a place of its own choosing. Another function allows one thread to stop another abruptly and arbitrarily:

```
// one thread calls this to stop another
BOOL TerminateThread( HANDLE hThread, DWORD dwExitCode );
```

A thread cannot protect itself from termination. Anyone with a handle to the thread can force the thread to stop immediately, regardless of its current state—providing, of course, that the handle allows full access to the thread. Using the default security attributes in **CreateThread** produces a handle with full access privileges.

TerminateThread does not destroy the thread's stack, but it does provide an exit code. Both **ExitThread** and **TerminateThread** set the thread object to its signaled state so that any other threads waiting for this one to end may proceed. After either command the thread object lingers lifelessly until all its handles have been closed.

Equivalent C Runtime Functions

Several C runtime library commands duplicate some of the Win32 thread commands:

```
unsigned long _beginthread(
    void( *start_address )( void * ),     // starting function
```

```
    unsigned stack_size,                    // initial stack size
      void *arglist );                      // parameter for starting function
void _endthread( void );
void _sleep( unsigned long ulMilliseconds );
```

_beginthread performs some internal initialization for a new thread that other C runtime functions, such as signal, depend on. The rule is consistency: If your program manipulates threads with C runtime functions, then use only C runtime functions wherever you have a choice. If your program uses Win32 functions with its threads, then stick to **CreateThread** and **ExitThread**. Also, if the thread calls C runtime functions, then create it with the C functions rather than the Win32 API. A few C routines require the initialization _beginthread performs.

Threads and Message Queues

Each window a program creates belongs to the thread that creates it. When a thread creates a window the system gives it a message queue, and the thread must enter a message loop to read from its queue. If a single thread creates all a program's windows, then the program needs only a single message loop. Conversely, any thread that wants to receive messages must create a window for itself even if the window remains hidden. Only threads that create windows get message queues.

Synchronizing Threads

To work with threads you must be able to coordinate their actions. Sometimes coordination requires ensuring that certain actions happen in a specific order. Besides the functions to create threads and modify their scheduling priority, the Win32 API contains functions to make threads wait for signals from objects such as files and processes. It also supports special synchronization objects such as mutexes and semaphores.

Waiting

We'll start with the functions that wait for an object to reach its signaled state because they best illustrate how synchronization objects are used. With a single set of generic waiting commands you can wait for processes, threads, mutexes, semaphores, events, and a few other objects to reach their signaled states. This command waits for one object to turn on its signal:

```
DWORD WaitForSingleObject(
    HANDLE hObject,              // object to wait for
    DWORD dwMilliseconds );      // maximum time to wait
```

WaitForSingleObject allows a thread to suspend itself until a specific object gives its signal. In this command a thread also states how long it is willing to wait for the object. To wait indefinitely, set the interval to **INFINITE**. If the object is already available, or if it reaches its signal state within the designated time, then **Wait-ForSingleObject** returns 0 and execution resumes. If the interval passes and the object is still not signaled, the function returns **WAIT_TIMEOUT**.

Beware when setting the interval to **INFINITE**. If for any reason the object never reaches a signaled state, the thread will never resume. Also, if two threads establish a reciprocal infinite wait, they will deadlock.

To make a thread wait for several objects at once, call **WaitForMultipleObjects**. You can make this function return as soon as any one of the objects becomes available, or you can make it wait until all the requested objects reach their signaled states simultaneously. An event-driven program might set up an array of objects that interest it and respond when any of them signals.

```
DWORD WaitForMultipleObjects(
    DWORD dwNumObjects,          // number of objects to wait for
    LPHANDLE lpHandles,          // array of object handles
    BOOL bWaitAll,               // TRUE to wait for all; FALSE to wait for any
    DWORD dwMilliseconds );      // maximum waiting period
```

Again, a return value of **WAIT_TIMEOUT** indicates that the interval passed and no objects were signaled. If bWaitAll is **FALSE**, then a successful return value indicates which element of the lpHandles array has become signaled. (The first element is 0, the second is 1, and so on.)

Two extended versions of the wait functions add an alert status allowing a thread to resume if an asynchronous read or write command happens to end during the wait. In effect these functions say, "Wake me up if the object becomes available, if a certain time passes, or if a background I/O operation runs to completion." (Asynchronous I/O operations are covered in Chapter 12.)

```
DWORD WaitForSingleObjectEx(
    HANDLE hObject,              // object to wait for
    DWORD dwMilliseconds,        // maximum time to wait
    BOOL bAlertable );           // TRUE to end wait if I/O completes
```

```
DWORD WaitForMultipleObjectsEx(
    DWORD dwNumObjects,             // number of objects to wait for
    LPHANDLE lpHandles,             // array of object handles
    BOOL bWaitAll,                  // TRUE to wait for all; FALSE to wait for any
    DWORD dwMilliseconds,           // maximum waiting period
    BOOL bAlertable );              // TRUE to end wait if I/O completes
```

Successful wait commands usually modify the awaited object in some way. For example, when a thread waits for and acquires a mutex, the wait function restores the mutex to its unsignaled state so other threads will know it is in use. Wait commands also decrease the counter in a semaphore and reset some kinds of events.

Mutexes and Semaphores

Of course, you have to create an object before you can wait on it. We'll start with mutexes and semaphores because they have parallel API commands to create the objects, acquire or release them, get handles to them, and destroy them.

Creating

The creation functions for mutexes and semaphores need to be told what access privileges you want, some initial conditions for the object, and an optional name for the object.

```
HANDLE CreateMutex(
    LPSECURITY_ATTRIBUTES lpsa,    // optional security attributes
    BOOL bInitialOwner             // TRUE if creator wants ownership
    LPTSTR lpszMutexName )         // object's name

HANDLE CreateSemaphore(
    LPSECURITY_ATTRIBUTES lpsa,    // optional security attributes
    LONG lInitialCount,            // initial count (usually 0)
    LONG lMaxCount,                // maximum count (limits # of threads)
    LPTSTR lpszSemName );          // name of the semaphore (may be NULL)
```

If the security descriptor is **NULL**, the returned handle will possess all access privileges and will not be inherited by child processes. The names are optional and useful for identification only when several different processes want handles to the same object.

By setting the bInitialOwner flag to **TRUE**, a thread creates and acquires a mutex both at once. The new mutex remains unsignaled until the thread releases it.

Only one thread at a time may acquire a mutex, but a semaphore remains signaled until its acquisition count reaches `iMaxCount`. If any more threads try to wait for the semaphore, they will be suspended until some other thread decreases the acquisition count.

Acquiring and Releasing

Once a semaphore or a mutex exists, threads interact with it by acquiring and releasing it. To acquire either object, a thread calls **WaitForSingleObject** (or one of its variants). When a thread finishes whatever task the object synchronizes, it releases the object with one of these functions:

```
BOOL ReleaseMutex( HANDLE hMutex );

BOOL ReleaseSemaphore(
    HANDLE hSemaphore,
    LONG lRelease,              // amount to increment counter on release
                                // (usually 1)
    LPLONG lplPrevious );       // variable to receive the previous count
```

Releasing a mutex or a semaphore increments its counter. Whenever the counter rises above 0 the object assumes its signaled state and the system checks whether any other threads were waiting for it.

Only a thread that already owns a mutex—in other words, that already waited for it—can release it. **ReleaseSemaphore**, however, can be called by any thread and can adjust the acquisition counter by any amount up to its maximum value. Changing the counter by arbitrary amounts lets you vary the number of threads that may own a semaphore as your program runs. You may have noticed that **CreateSemaphore** allows you to set the counter for a new semaphore to something other than its maximum value. You might, for example, create it with an initial count of 0 to block all threads while your program initializes and then raise the counter with **ReleaseSemaphore**.

Remember to release synchronization objects. If you forget to release a mutex, for example, any threads that wait on it without specifying a maximum interval will deadlock. They will not be released.

A thread may wait for the same object more than once without blocking, but each wait must be matched with a release. This is true of mutexes, semaphores, and critical sections.

Events

An event is the object a program creates when it requires a mechanism for alerting threads if some action occurs. In its simplest form, a manual reset event, the event object turns its signal on and off in response to the two commands **SetEvent** (signal on) and **ResetEvent** (signal off.) When the signal is on, all threads that wait for the event will receive it. When the signal is off, all threads that wait for the event become blocked. Unlike mutexes and semaphores, manual reset events change their state only when some thread explicitly sets or resets them.

You might use a manual reset event to allow certain threads to execute only when the program is not painting its window or only after the user enters certain information. Here are the basic commands for working with events:

```
HANDLE CreateEvent(
    LPSECURITY_ATTRIBUTES lpsa,      // security privileges (NULL for default)
    BOOL bManualReset,               // TRUE if event must be reset manually
    BOOL bInitialState,              // TRUE to create event in signaled state
    LPTSTR lpszEventName );           // name of event (may be NULL)

BOOL SetEvent( HANDLE hEvent );

BOOL ResetEvent( HANDLE hEvent );
```

With the `bInitialState` parameter, **CreateEvent** allows the new event to arrive in the world already signaled. The Set and Reset functions return **TRUE** or **FALSE** to indicate success or failure.

With the `bManualReset` parameter, **CreateEvent** also lets you create an automatic reset event instead of a manual reset event. An automatic reset event returns immediately to its unsignaled state right after a **SetEvent** command. **ResetEvent** is redundant for an auto-reset event. Furthermore, an automatic reset button always releases only a single thread on each signal before resetting. An auto-reset event might be useful for a program where one master thread prepares data for other worker threads. Whenever a new set of data is ready, the master sets the event and a single worker thread is released. The other workers continue to wait in line for more assignments.

Besides setting and resetting events, you can pulse events.

```
BOOL PulseEvent( hEvent );
```

A pulse turns the signal on for a very short time and then turns it back off. Pulsing a manual event allows all waiting threads to pass and then resets the event. Pulsing an auto event lets one waiting thread pass and then resets the event. If no threads are waiting, none will pass. Setting an auto event, on the other hand, causes the event to leave its signal on until some thread waits for it. As soon as one thread passes, the event resets itself.

The sample named pipe program in Chapter 5 demonstrates the use of automatic and manual reset events.

Sharing Mutexes, Semaphores, and Events

Processes, even unrelated processes, can share mutexes, semaphores, and events. By sharing objects processes can coordinate their activities, just as threads do. There are three mechanisms for sharing. One is inheritance, where one process creates another and the new process receives copies of the parent's handles. Only those handles marked for inheritance when they were created will be passed on.

The other methods involve calling functions to create a second handle to an existing object. Which function you call depends on what information you already have. If you have handles to both the source and destination processes, then call **DuplicateHandle**. If you have only the name of the object, call one of the Open functions. Two programs might agree in advance on the name of the object they share, or one might pass the name to the other through shared memory, DDEML, or a pipe.

```
BOOL DuplicateHandle(
    HANDLE hSourceProcess,      // process that owns the original object
    HANDLE hSource,             // handle to the original object
    HANDLE hTargetProcess,      // process that wants a copy of the handle
    LPHANDLE lphTarget,         // place to store duplicated handle
    DWORD fdwAccess,            // requested access privileges
    BOOL bInherit,              // may the duplicate handle be inherited?
    DWORD fdwOptions );         // optional actions, e.g. close source handle

HANDLE OpenMutex(
    DWORD fdwAccess,            // requested access privileges
    BOOL bInherit,             // TRUE if children may inherit this handle
    LPTSTR lpszName );          // name of the mutex

HANDLE OpenSemaphore(
    DWORD fdwAccess,            // requested access privileges
```

```
    BOOL bInherit,              // TRUE if children may inherit this handle
    LPTSTR lpszName );          // name of the semaphore

HANDLE OpenEvent(
    DWORD fdwAccess,            // requested access privileges
    BOOL bInherit,              // TRUE if children may inherit this handle
    LPTSTR lpszName );          // name of the event
```

Those **LPTSTR** variable types are not a misprint, by the way. It's a generic text type that compiles differently depending on whether an application uses Unicode strings or ASCII strings. Unicode comes up in Chapter 17.

Destroying Mutexes, Semaphores, and Events

Mutexes, semaphores, and events persist in memory until all the processes that own them end or until all the object's handles have been closed with **CloseHandle**.

```
BOOL CloseHandle( hObject );
```

Critical Sections

A critical section object performs exactly the same function as a mutex except that critical sections may not be shared. They are visible only within a single process. Critical sections and mutexes both allow only one thread to own them at a time, but critical sections work more quickly and involve less overhead.

The functions for working with critical sections do not use the same terminology, but they do roughly the same things. Instead of creating a critical section, you initialize it. Instead of waiting for it, you enter it. Instead of releasing it, you leave it. Instead of closing its handle, you delete the object.

```
VOID InitializeCriticalSection( LPCRITICAL_SECTION lpcs );
VOID EnterCriticalSection( LPCRITICAL_SECTION lpcs );
VOID LeaveCriticalSection( LPCRITICAL_SECTION lpcs );
VOID DeleteCriticalSection( LPCRITICAL_SECTION lpcs );
```

The variable type **LPCRITICAL_SECTION** names a pointer (not a handle) to a critical section object. **InitializeCriticalSection** expects to receive a pointer to an empty object, which you can allocate like this:

```
CRITICAL_SECTION cs;
```

The Sprite library in Chapter 11 demonstrates the use of a critical section object.

CODE: THE THREADS PROGRAM

The Threads sample program, shown in Figure 4.4, puts into code some of the ideas we've been explaining. It creates four secondary threads, each of which draws rectangles in a child window until the program ends. The top fourth of the window is a list box showing information about all four threads. By selecting a thread and choosing a menu command, you can suspend, resume, and change the priority of any thread. From the Options menu you can also activate a mutex so that only one thread draws at a time.

FIGURE 4.4:

What the Threads program looks like as it runs

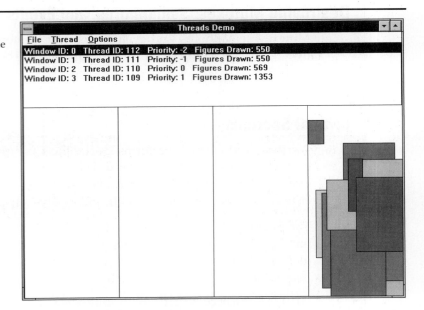

The Header and Resource Files

Threads.h and threads.rc define program constants and resources such as the string table, menu, and About box template.

```
/*--------------------------------------------------------------------

        THREADS.H
        Header file for the Threads program.

    --------------------------------------------------------------------*/

/*--------------------------------------------------------------------
        FUNCTION PROTOTYPES
    --------------------------------------------------------------------*/

/* window procedures */
LRESULT WINAPI Main_WndProc(HWND hWnd , UINT uMessage, WPARAM wParam,
    LPARAM lParam);
LRESULT WINAPI Thread_WndProc(HWND hWnd, UINT uMessage, WPARAM wParam,
    LPARAM lParam);
BOOL WINAPI About_DlgProc(HWND hDlg, UINT uMessage, WPARAM wParam,
    LPARAM lParam);

/* message handlers */
BOOL Main_OnCreate(HWND hWnd, LPCREATESTRUCT lpCreateStruct);
void Main_OnInitMenu(HWND hWnd, HMENU hMenu);
void Main_OnCommand(HWND hWnd, int iID, HWND hwndCtl, UINT uCode);
void Main_OnSize(HWND hWnd, UINT uState, int cxClient, int cyClient);
void Main_OnTimer(HWND hWnd, UINT uTimerID);
void Main_OnDestroy(HWND hWnd);

/* other procedures */
BOOL InitializeApp (void);
BOOL CreateWindows(void);
void ClearChildWindows(void);
void UpdateListBox(void);
void DoThread(int iCmd);
void DrawProc(DWORD dwThreadID);
long StartThread(LPVOID lpThreadData);
void MakeAbout(HWND hWnd);

/*--------------------------------------------------------------------
        CONSTANTS
    --------------------------------------------------------------------*/

/* maximum string size */
#define MAX_BUFFER      64
```

```
/*thread states*/
#define ACTIVE          100
#define SUSPENDED       200

/* timer ID */
#define TIMER           100

/*-------------------------------------------------------------------
        RESOURCE IDs
    -----------------------------------------------------------------*/


/* templates */
#define MENU_MAIN       10
#define DLG_ABOUT       10

/* menu IDs */
#define IDM_ABOUT       100
#define IDM_EXIT        200

#define IDM_SUSPEND     300
#define IDM_RESUME      400
#define IDM_INCREASE    500
#define IDM_DECREASE    600

#define IDM_USEMUTEX    700

/* string IDs */
#define IDS_APPNAME     100
#define IDS_TITLE       200
#define IDS_THREAD      300


=======================================================================


/*-------------------------------------------------------------------


        THREADS.RC
        Resource script file for the Threads program

    -----------------------------------------------------------------*/


#include <windows.h>
#include "threads.h"

/* a table of all the strings Threads uses */
STRINGTABLE
```

```
BEGIN
    IDS_APPNAME,      "Threads"
    IDS_TITLE,        "Threads Demo"
    IDS_THREAD,       "Thread"
END

MENU_MAIN MENU
BEGIN
    POPUP   "&File"
    BEGIN
        MENUITEM   "&About Threads...",          IDM_ABOUT
        MENUITEM   "E&xit",                      IDM_EXIT
        END

        POPUP "&Thread"
        BEGIN
        MENUITEM   "&Suspend",                   IDM_SUSPEND
        MENUITEM   "&Resume",                    IDM_RESUME
        MENUITEM   "&Increase Priority"          IDM_INCREASE
        MENUITEM   "&Decrease Priority",         IDM_DECREASE
    END

    POPUP "&Options"
    BEGIN
        MENUITEM "Use &Mutex",           IDM_USEMUTEX
    END
END

DLG_ABOUT DIALOG 17, 18, 114, 68
STYLE DS_MODALFRAME ¦ WS_POPUP ¦ WS_VISIBLE ¦ WS_CAPTION ¦ WS_SYSMENU
CAPTION "About Multithreaded"
FONT 8, "Helv"
BEGIN
    CTEXT             "Multi-threaded Demonstration!",-1, 0, 7, 114, 8
    CTEXT             "by",                  -1, 0, 15, 114, 8
    CTEXT             "Myers && Hamer",   -1, 0, 25, 114, 8
    CTEXT             "version 1.0",      -1, 0, 35, 114, 8
    LTEXT             "©1993",             -1, 12, 51, 25, 8
    DEFPUSHBUTTON     "OK", IDOK, 81, 50, 30, 14, WS_GROUP
END
```

Initialization Procedures

The initialization procedures register two window classes, one for the main overlapping window and one for the child windows where the threads draw. They also create a timer. At five-second intervals the list box updates the information about each thread. The CreateWindows function creates and positions all the windows, including the list box that shows information about each thread. The four threads are created during the **WM_CREATE** message handler.

Note the absence of a **PeekMessage** loop in WinMain. That's a clear sign that you have entered the world of preemptive multitasking. The threads can draw continuously without monopolizing the processor. Other programs can still run at the same time.

```
/*------------------------------------------------------------------

    THREADS.C

    Demonstrates Window NT's multithreading capabilities. Creates
    four threads to draw simultaneously in four windows.

    FUNCTIONS
        WinMain             main message loop
        InitializeApp       register windows, initialize variables
        CreateWindows       create all the windows (6 of them)
        Main_WndProc        process messages for main window
        Main_OnCreate       //
        Main_OnTimer        //          message handlers
        Main_OnSize         //
        Main_OnInitMenu     //
        Main_OnCommand      //
        DoThread            modify a thread according to user's command
        Main_OnDestroy      //

        ClearChildWindows   erase all shapes in all child windows
        StartThread         the function the secondary threads execute
        DrawProc            draw shapes in a child window
        Thread_WndProc      process messages for a child window

        MakeAbout           show the About box
        About_DlgProc       process messages for the About box
        About_OnInitDlg     //
        About_OnCommand     //
```

```
                from Mastering Windows NT Programming
                copyright 1993 by Brian Myers & Eric Hamer


    ------------------------------------------------------------*/

#define STRICT
#include <windows.h>
#include <windowsx.h>
#include <stdlib.h>                    // included for rand() and srand()
#include "threads.h"


/*------------------------------------------------------------------
        GLOBAL VARIABLES

    ------------------------------------------------------------*/


HWND            hwndChild[4];       // windows where threads draw
HANDLE          hThread[4];         // handles for the four threads
HWND            hwndParent;         // main window
HWND            hwndList;           // list box window
HINSTANCE       hInst;              // current instance

DWORD           dwThreadID[4];      // array of thread IDs
DWORD           dwThreadData[4];    // total shapes drawn by each thread
int             iRectCount[4];      // cumulative totals of shapes drawn
int             iRandSeed = 0;      // random number seed
int             iState[4];          // current state of each thread
BOOL            bTerminate = FALSE; // TRUE to quit
BOOL            bUseMutex = FALSE;  // TRUE to make one thread draw at a time
HANDLE          hDrawMutex;         // mutex synchronization object

/*------------------------------------------------------------------
        WIN MAIN
        Calls initializing procedures and runs the message loop
    ------------------------------------------------------------*/

int WINAPI WinMain (
    HINSTANCE hinstThis,            // handle to this instance
    HINSTANCE hinstPrev,            // NULL if no previous instance
    LPSTR lpszCmdLine,              // points to command line
    int iCmdShow )                  // initial window status
{
    MSG msg;

    hInst = hinstThis;              // store in global variable
```

```
    if (!InitializeApp( ))
    {
        // if the application was not initialized, exit here
        return( 0 );
    }

    ShowWindow( hwndParent, iCmdShow );
    UpdateWindow( hwndParent );

    /* receive and forward messages from our queue */
    while (GetMessage( &msg, NULL, 0, 0 ))
    {
        TranslateMessage( &msg );
        DispatchMessage( &msg );
    }

    return( msg.wParam );
}


/*-------------------------------------------------------------------
        INITIALIZE APP
        Register two window classes and then create the windows
    -----------------------------------------------------------------*/

BOOL InitializeApp ( void )
{
    WNDCLASS wc;
    char szAppName[MAX_BUFFER];
    char szTitle[MAX_BUFFER];
    char szThread[MAX_BUFFER];
    int iCount;

    /* load strings from the string table */
    LoadString( hInst, IDS_APPNAME, szAppName,  sizeof(szAppName));
    LoadString( hInst, IDS_TITLE,   szTitle,    sizeof(szTitle));
    LoadString( hInst, IDS_THREAD,  szThread,   sizeof(szThread));

    /* seed the random number generator */
    srand( iRandSeed++ );

    /* register the main window class*/
    wc.lpszClassName    = szAppName;
    wc.hInstance        = hInst;
    wc.lpfnWndProc      = Main_WndProc;
```

```
wc.hCursor          = LoadCursor( NULL, IDC_ARROW );
wc.hIcon            = LoadIcon( NULL, IDI_APPLICATION );
wc.lpszMenuName     = szAppName;
wc.hbrBackground    = (HBRUSH)(COLOR_WINDOW + 1);
wc.style            = CS_HREDRAW | CS_VREDRAW;
wc.cbClsExtra       = 0;
wc.cbWndExtra       = 0;

if (!RegisterClass( &wc ))
{
    return( FALSE );
}

/* register the class for child windows where threads draw */
wc.style            = CS_HREDRAW | CS_VREDRAW;
wc.lpfnWndProc      = (WNDPROC)Thread_WndProc;
wc.cbClsExtra       = 0;
wc.cbWndExtra       = 0;
wc.hInstance        = hInst;
wc.hIcon            = NULL;
wc.hCursor          = LoadCursor( NULL, IDC_ARROW );
wc.hbrBackground    = GetStockBrush( WHITE_BRUSH );
wc.lpszMenuName     = NULL;
wc.lpszClassName    = "ThreadClass";

if (!RegisterClass( &wc ))
{
    return( FALSE );
}

// Mark the initial state of each thread as SUSPENDED.
// That is how they will be created.
for(iCount = 0; iCount < 4; iCount++)
{
    iState[iCount] = SUSPENDED;
}

/* make the primary thread more important to facilitate user i/o */
SetThreadPriority( GetCurrentThread(), THREAD_PRIORITY_ABOVE_NORMAL );

/* create all the windows */
return( CreateWindows( ) );
}
```

The call to **SetThreadPriority** increases the priority of the primary thread. If all the secondary threads were busy working at the same priority as the main thread, the menus would respond sluggishly. You can test this yourself by raising the priority of the secondary threads as the program runs.

```
/*-----------------------------------------------------------------
        CREATE WINDOWS
        Create the parent window, the list box window, and the four
        child windows.
        ----------------------------------------------------------*/

BOOL CreateWindows ( void )
{
    char szAppName[MAX_BUFFER];
    char szTitle[MAX_BUFFER];
    char szThread[MAX_BUFFER];
    HMENU hMenu;
    int iCount;

    /* load the relevant strings */
    LoadString( hInst, IDS_APPNAME, szAppName,  sizeof(szAppName));
    LoadString( hInst, IDS_TITLE,   szTitle,    sizeof(szTitle));
    LoadString( hInst, IDS_THREAD,  szThread,   sizeof(szThread));

    /* create the parent window */
    hMenu = LoadMenu( hInst, MAKEINTRESOURCE(MENU_MAIN) );
    hwndParent = CreateWindow(
        szAppName, szTitle,
        WS_OVERLAPPEDWINDOW | WS_CLIPCHILDREN,
        CW_USEDEFAULT, CW_USEDEFAULT, CW_USEDEFAULT, CW_USEDEFAULT,
        NULL, hMenu, hInst, NULL );

    if (!hwndParent)
    {
        return( FALSE );
    }

    /* create the list box */
    hwndList = CreateWindow(
        "LISTBOX", NULL,
        WS_BORDER | WS_CHILD | WS_VISIBLE | LBS_STANDARD
        | LBS_NOINTEGRALHEIGHT,
        0, 0, 0, 0, hwndParent, (HMENU)1, hInst, NULL );
```

```
if (!hwndList)
{
    return( FALSE );
}

/* create the four child windows */
for (iCount = 0; iCount < 4; iCount++)
{
    hwndChild[iCount] = CreateWindow(
        "ThreadClass", NULL,
        WS_BORDER | WS_CHILD | WS_VISIBLE | WS_CLIPCHILDREN,
        0, 0, 0, 0, hwndParent, NULL, hInst, NULL );

    if (!hwndChild)
    {
        return( FALSE );
    }
}

return( TRUE );
}
```

Window Procedure and Message Handlers

The Threads program uses **HANDLE_MSG**, the message cracker macro we explained in Chapter 3. As a result, the compiler produces a series of warnings saying, "unreferenced formal parameter" for the message handlers. Ignore the warnings. They are unavoidable.

Most of the message handler functions are simple. Main_OnTimer calls a procedure to clear the list box, generate four new strings of information, and display them. The Main_OnSize function suspends all the secondary threads while the program repositions the child windows to accommodate the new size. Otherwise the busy threads would slow down the display operation. Main_OnCreate, besides creating threads, creates a mutex.

```
/*--------------------------------------------------------------
        MAIN_WNDPROC
        All messages for the main window are processed here.
    --------------------------------------------------------------*/
LRESULT WINAPI Main_WndProc (
    HWND hWnd,              // message address
    UINT uMessage,         // message type
    WPARAM wParam,         // message contents
    LPARAM lParam )        // more contents
  {
    switch (uMessage)
    {
        HANDLE_MSG( hWnd, WM_CREATE, Main_OnCreate );
        /* create the window and the threads */

        HANDLE_MSG( hWnd, WM_SIZE, Main_OnSize );
        /* reposition the child windows when the main window changes */

        HANDLE_MSG( hWnd, WM_TIMER, Main_OnTimer );
        /* update the list box every five seconds */

        HANDLE_MSG( hWnd, WM_INITMENU, Main_OnInitMenu );
        /* put a check by the Use Mutex menu item if bUseMutex is TRUE */

        HANDLE_MSG( hWnd, WM_COMMAND, Main_OnCommand );
        /* process menu commands */

        HANDLE_MSG( hWnd, WM_DESTROY, Main_OnDestroy );
        /* clean up and quit */

        default:
            return( DefWindowProc(hWnd, uMessage, wParam, lParam) );
    }

    return( OL );
}

/*--------------------------------------------------------------
        MAIN_ONCREATE
        Create the four threads and set the timer
    --------------------------------------------------------------*/
BOOL Main_OnCreate (
    HWND hWnd,
    LPCREATESTRUCT lpCreateStruct )
```

```
{
    UINT uRet;
    int iCount;

    /* create the four threads, initially suspended */
    for (iCount = 0; iCount < 4; iCount++)
    {
        iRectCount[iCount] = 0;
        dwThreadData[iCount] = iCount;
        hThread[iCount] = CreateThread(
            NULL,
            0,
            (LPTHREAD_START_ROUTINE)StartThread,
            (LPVOID)(&(dwThreadData[iCount])),
            CREATE_SUSPENDED,
            (LPDWORD)(&(dwThreadID[iCount])) );

        if (!hThread[iCount])           // was the thread created?
        {
            return( FALSE );
        }
    }

    // Create a timer with a five-second period.
    // The timer is used to update the list box.
    uRet = SetTimer( hWnd, TIMER, 5000, NULL );
    if (!uRet)
    {                                       // unable to create the timer
        return( FALSE );
    }

    /* create a mutex synchronization object */
    hDrawMutex = CreateMutex( NULL, FALSE, NULL );
    if (!hDrawMutex)
    {                                       // unable to create mutex
        KillTimer( hWnd, TIMER );   // stop the timer
        return( FALSE );
    }

    /* start the threads with a priority below normal */
    for (iCount = 0; iCount < 4; iCount++)
    {
        SetThreadPriority( hThread[iCount], THREAD_PRIORITY_BELOW_NORMAL );
        iState[iCount] = ACTIVE;
        ResumeThread( hThread[iCount] );
```

```
    }
    // Now all four threads are running!
    return( TRUE );
}


/*-------------------------------------------------------------
        MAIN_ONSIZE
        Position the list box and the four child windows.
    ----------------------------------------------------------*/
void Main_OnSize (
    HWND hWnd,
    UINT uState,
    int cxClient,
    int cyClient )
{
    char *szText = "No Thread Data";
    int iCount;

    // Suspend all active threads while the windows
    // resize and repaint themselves. This pause
    // enables the screen to update more quickly.

    for (iCount = 0; iCount < 4; iCount++)
    {
        if (iState[iCount] == ACTIVE)
        {
            SuspendThread( hThread[iCount] );
        }
    }

    /* place the list box across the top fourth of the window */
    MoveWindow( hwndList, 0, 0, cxClient, cyClient / 4, TRUE );

    // Spread the 4 child windows across the bottom 3/4 of the
    // window. (The left border of the first one should be 0.)

    MoveWindow( hwndChild[0], 0, cyClient / 4 - 1, cxClient / 4 + 1,
                cyClient, TRUE);

    for (iCount = 1; iCount < 4; iCount++)
    {
        MoveWindow( hwndChild[iCount], (iCount * cxClient) / 4,
                    cyClient / 4 - 1,  cxClient / 4 + 1, cyClient, TRUE);
    }
```

```
        // Add the default strings to the list box, and initialize
        // the number of figures drawn to zero

        for (iCount = 0; iCount < 4; iCount++)
        {
            iRectCount[iCount] = 0;
            ListBox_AddString(hwndList, szText);
        }

        ListBox_SetCurSel(hwndList, 0);

        /* reactivate the threads that were suspended while redrawing */
        for (iCount = 0; iCount < 4; iCount++)
        {
            if (iState[iCount] == ACTIVE)
            {
                ResumeThread( hThread[iCount] );
            }
        }
        return;
}


/*-------------------------------------------------------------------
        MAIN_ONTIMER
        Process the timer message by updating the list box.
   -------------------------------------------------------------------*/
void Main_OnTimer (
    HWND hWnd,
    UINT uTimerID )
{
    /* update the data shown in the list box */
    UpdateListBox( );
    return;
}


/*-------------------------------------------------------------------
        MAIN_ONINITMENU
        Check or uncheck the Use Mutex menu item based on the
        value of bUseMutex
   -------------------------------------------------------------------*/
void Main_OnInitMenu (
    HWND hWnd,
    HMENU hMenu )
```

155

```
{
    CheckMenuItem( hMenu, IDM_USEMUTEX,
                   MF_BYCOMMAND |
                   (UINT)(bUseMutex ? MF_CHECKED : MF_UNCHECKED) );
    return;
}

/*-------------------------------------------------------------------
        MAIN_ONCOMMAND
        Respond to commands from the user
   -----------------------------------------------------------------*/
void Main_OnCommand (
    HWND hWnd,
    int iCmd,
    HWND hwndCtl,
    UINT uCode )
{
    switch (iCmd)
    {
        /* display the about box */
        case IDM_ABOUT:
            MakeAbout( hWnd );
            break;

        /* exit this program */
        case IDM_EXIT:
            DestroyWindow( hWnd );
            break;

        /* modify the priority or state of one of the threads */
        case IDM_SUSPEND:
        case IDM_RESUME:
        case IDM_INCREASE:
        case IDM_DECREASE:
            DoThread( iCmd );               // adjust a thread
            break;

        /* toggle the use of the mutex */
        case IDM_USEMUTEX:
            ClearChildWindows( );           // make all thread windows white
            bUseMutex = !bUseMutex;         // toggle mutex setting
            break;
```

```
        default:
            break;
    }
    return;
}
```

Modifying the Threads

The DoThread procedure responds to menu commands by modifying whichever thread is currently selected in the list box. DoThread can raise or lower a thread's priority and suspend or resume threads. The iState array records the current state of each thread, either active or suspended. The hThreads array holds handles to each of the four secondary threads.

```
/*----------------------------------------------------------------
        DO THREAD
        Modify a thread's priority or change its state in response
        to commands from the menu.
    ------------------------------------------------------------*/
void DoThread ( int iCmd )
{
    int iThread;
    int iPriority;

    /* determine which thread to modify */
    iThread = ListBox_GetCurSel( hwndList );

    switch (iCmd)
    {
    case IDM_SUSPEND:
        /* if the thread is not suspended, then suspend it */
        if (iState[iThread] != SUSPENDED)
        {
            SuspendThread( hThread[iThread] );
            iState[iThread] = SUSPENDED;
        }
        break;

    case IDM_RESUME:
        /* if the thread is not active, then activate it */
        if (iState[iThread] != ACTIVE)
```

```
    {
        ResumeThread( hThread[iThread] );
        iState[iThread] = ACTIVE;
    }
    break;

case IDM_INCREASE:
    // Increase the thread's priority (unless it is
    // already at the highest level.)
    iPriority = GetThreadPriority(hThread[iThread]);

    switch (iPriority)
    {
        case THREAD_PRIORITY_LOWEST:
            SetThreadPriority( hThread[iThread],
                THREAD_PRIORITY_BELOW_NORMAL );
            break;

        case THREAD_PRIORITY_BELOW_NORMAL:
            SetThreadPriority( hThread[iThread],
                THREAD_PRIORITY_NORMAL );
            break;

        case THREAD_PRIORITY_NORMAL:
            SetThreadPriority( hThread[iThread],
                THREAD_PRIORITY_ABOVE_NORMAL );
            break;

        case THREAD_PRIORITY_ABOVE_NORMAL:
            SetThreadPriority( hThread[iThread],
                THREAD_PRIORITY_HIGHEST );
            break;

        default:
            break;
    }
    break;

case IDM_DECREASE:
    // Decrease the thread's priority (unless it is
    // already at the lowest level.)
    iPriority = GetThreadPriority( hThread[iThread] );

    switch (iPriority)
```

```
            {
                case THREAD_PRIORITY_BELOW_NORMAL:
                    SetThreadPriority( hThread[iThread],
                        THREAD_PRIORITY_LOWEST );
                    break;

                case THREAD_PRIORITY_NORMAL:
                    SetThreadPriority( hThread[iThread],
                        THREAD_PRIORITY_BELOW_NORMAL );
                    break;

                case THREAD_PRIORITY_ABOVE_NORMAL:
                    SetThreadPriority( hThread[iThread],
                        THREAD_PRIORITY_NORMAL );
                    break;

                case THREAD_PRIORITY_HIGHEST:
                    SetThreadPriority( hThread[iThread],
                        THREAD_PRIORITY_ABOVE_NORMAL );
                    break;

                default:
                    break;
            }
            break;

        default:
            break;
    }
    return;
}

/*-------------------------------------------------------------------
        MAIN_ONDESTROY
        Kill the timer, set the terminate flag to zero, and post
        the WM_QUIT message. When the process ends, the system automatically
        closes the thread and mutex handles.
    -------------------------------------------------------------------*/
void Main_OnDestroy ( HWND hWnd )
{
    bTerminate = TRUE;              // signal threads to stop
    KillTimer( hWnd, TIMER );      // destroy timer
    PostQuitMessage( 0 );          // post WM_QUIT to close app
    return;
}
```

```
/*-------------------------------------------------------------------
        CLEAR CHILD WINDOWS
        Paint all four child windows white
  ----------------------------------------------------------------*/
void ClearChildWindows ( void )
{
    int iCount;

    for (iCount=0; iCount<4; iCount++)
    {
        RECT rcClient;          // client area
        HDC hDC;                // dc for child window
        BOOL bError;            // for testing return value

        /* get the window's dimensions */
        bError = GetClientRect( hwndChild[iCount], &rcClient );
        if (!bError)
        {
            return;
        }

        hDC = GetDC( hwndChild[iCount] );
        if (!hDC)
        {
            return;
        }

        SelectBrush( hDC, GetStockBrush(WHITE_BRUSH) );
        PatBlt( hDC, (int)rcClient.left, (int)rcClient.top,
                     (int)rcClient.right, (int)rcClient.bottom, PATCOPY );

        ReleaseDC( hwndChild[iCount], hDC );
    }
    return;
}
```

The **ListBox_*** macros in UpdateListBox come from the windowsx.h file. In Chapter 3 we explained that these macros correctly port from Win16 to Win32. They are also easier to read than the alternative **SendMessage** commands.

```
/*-------------------------------------------------------------------
        UPDATE LIST BOX
        Show new values in the list box window
  ----------------------------------------------------------------*/
```

```
void UpdateListBox ( void )
{
    char szText[128];        // buffer for a list box string
    int iPriority;           // one thread's current priority level
    int iCount;              // control variable
    int iSel;                // position of currently selected list box item

    /* save the ID of the currently selected list box item */
    iSel = ListBox_GetCurSel( hwndList );

    /* empty the list box */
    ListBox_ResetContent( hwndList );

    /* add updated thread data to the list box */
    for (iCount = 0; iCount < 4; iCount++)
    {
        iPriority = GetThreadPriority( hThread[iCount] );

        /* format the thread information */
        wsprintf( szText,
            "Window ID: %d   Thread ID: %ld   Priority: %d   Figures Drawn: %d",
            iCount, dwThreadID[iCount], iPriority,
            iRectCount[iCount] );

        /* add the text to the list box */
        ListBox_AddString( hwndList, szText );
    }

    /* restore the list box selection */
    ListBox_SetCurSel( hwndList, iSel );
    return;
}
```

Thread Procedures

When Main_OnCreate constructs the secondary threads, in each call to **Create-Thread** it passes a pointer to the StartThread function. StartThread becomes the main procedure for all the threads. They begin and end executing here.

If bUseMutex is **TRUE**, then the threads will wait to acquire the mutex before they draw and only one thread will draw at a time.

```
/*-------------------------------------------------------------------
        START THREAD
        This is called when each thread begins execution
    ---------------------------------------------------------------*/
LONG StartThread ( LPVOID lpThreadData )
{
    DWORD *pdwThreadID;       // pointer to a DWORD for storing thread's ID
    DWORD dwWait;             // return value from WaitSingleObject

    /* retrieve the thread's ID */
    pdwThreadID = lpThreadData;

    /* draw continuously until bTerminate becomes TRUE */
    while (!bTerminate)
    {
        if (bUseMutex)        // are we using the mutex?
        {
            /* draw when this thread gets the mutex */
            dwWait = WaitForSingleObject( hDrawMutex, INFINITE );
            if (dwWait == 0)
            {
                DrawProc( *pdwThreadID );   // draw rectangles
                ReleaseMutex( hDrawMutex ); // let someone else draw
            }
        }
        else
        {
            /* not using mutex; let the thread draw */
            DrawProc( *pdwThreadID );
        }
    }

    // This return statement implicitly calls ExitThread.
    return( 0L );
}
```

DrawProc draws a batch of rectangles. As you'll learn in Chapter 8, GDI calls do not always occur immediately. To avoid the overhead of many small messages between a program and the Win32 subsystem, graphics commands are held in a queue and periodically flushed. These delays somewhat exaggerate the effect of changing priorities in Threads.

```
/*------------------------------------------------------------
        DRAW PROC
        Draw five random rectangles or ellipses
   -----------------------------------------------------------*/
void DrawProc ( DWORD dwID )
{
    HBRUSH hBrush;          // brush of a random color
    HBRUSH hbrOld;          // previously selected brush
    RECT rcClient;          // bounds of child window's client area
    HDC hDC;                // device context for child window
    LONG cxClient;          // client area dimensions (RECT members are LONG)
    LONG cyClient;
    int iCount;             // loop control variable
    int xStart;             // randomly generated coordinates
    int xStop;
    int yStart;
    int yStop;
    int iRed;               // randomly generated color values
    int iGreen;
    int iBlue;
    int iTotal;             // number of shapes to draw at a time
    BOOL bError;            // return value to test for error

    if (bUseMutex)
    {
        iTotal = 50;        // If only one thread draws at a time,
    }                       // let it draw more shapes at once.
    else
    {
        iTotal = 1;
    }

    /* reseed the random generator */
    srand( iRandSeed++ );

    /* get the window's dimensions */
    bError = GetClientRect( hwndChild[dwID], &rcClient );
    if (!bError)
    {
        return;
    }

    cxClient = rcClient.right - rcClient.left;
    cyClient = rcClient.bottom - rcClient.top;
```

```
/* do not draw if the window does not have any dimensions */
if ((!cxClient) || (!cyClient))
{
    return;
}

/* get a device context for drawing */
hDC = GetDC( hwndChild[dwID] );

if (hDC)
{
    /* draw the five random figures */
    for (iCount = 0; iCount < iTotal; iCount++)
    {
        iRectCount[dwID]++;

        /* set the coordinates */
        xStart = (int)(rand() % cxClient);
        xStop = (int)(rand() % cxClient);
        yStart = (int)(rand() % cyClient);
        yStop = (int)(rand() % cyClient);

        /* set the color */
        iRed = rand() & 255;
        iGreen = rand() & 255;
        iBlue = rand() & 255;

        /* create the solid brush */
        hBrush = CreateSolidBrush(              // avoid dithered colors
        GetNearestColor( hDC, RGB(iRed, iGreen, iBlue)) );
        hbrOld = SelectBrush( hDC, hBrush );

        /* draw a rectangle */
        Rectangle( hDC,
            min(xStart, xStop), max(xStart, xStop),
            min(yStart, yStop), max(yStart, yStop) );

        /* delete the brush */
        DeleteBrush( SelectBrush(hDC, hbrOld) );
    }

    // If only one thread is drawing at a time, clear
    // the child window before the next thread draws
```

```
        if (bUseMutex)
        {
            SelectBrush( hDC, GetStockBrush(WHITE_BRUSH) );
            PatBlt( hDC, (int)rcClient.left, (int)rcClient.top,
                         (int)rcClient.right, (int)rcClient.bottom, PATCOPY );
        }

        /* release the HDC */
        ReleaseDC( hwndChild[dwID], hDC );
    }
    return;
}


/*------------------------------------------------------------------
        THREAD_WNDPROC
        Process messages sent to the child windows. Because
        the threads constantly repaint the windows, very little
        needs to happen here.
   ------------------------------------------------------------------*/
LRESULT WINAPI Thread_WndProc (
    HWND hWnd,
    UINT uMessage,
    WPARAM wParam,
    LPARAM lParam )
{
    switch (uMessage)
    {
        default:
            return( DefWindowProc(hWnd, uMessage, wParam, lParam) );
    }
}
```

The About Box

We haven't used message crackers here because the dialog's simplicity hardly seems to merit constructing the new-style dialogs described in Chapter 3.

```
/*------------------------------------------------------------------
        MAKE ABOUT
        Process requests to show the About box here
   ------------------------------------------------------------------*/
```

```
void MakeAbout ( HWND hWnd )
{
    /* show the dialog box */
    DialogBox( hInst, MAKEINTRESOURCE(DLG_ABOUT), hWnd, About_DlgProc );
    return;
}

/*-------------------------------------------------------------------

        ABOUT_DLGPROC
        Process messages for the About box window here
    --------------------------------------------------------------*/

BOOL WINAPI About_DlgProc (
    HWND hDlg,
    UINT uMessage,
    WPARAM wParam,
    LPARAM lParam )
{
    switch (uMessage)
    {
        case WM_INITDIALOG:
            return( TRUE );

        case WM_COMMAND:
            EndDialog( hDlg, TRUE );
            return( TRUE );

        default:
            return( FALSE );
    }
}
```

Running Threads

After you run Threads and experiment with priorities, turn the mutex on and off, and suspend and resume a few threads, you might want to try running the PView process viewer that comes with the Win32 SDK. In Figure 4.5 you can see what PView says about Threads. Note that it shows five threads for the program because it includes the primary thread as well. Browsing with PView gives you a better sense of how Windows NT works.

PView process viewer showing
information about Threads

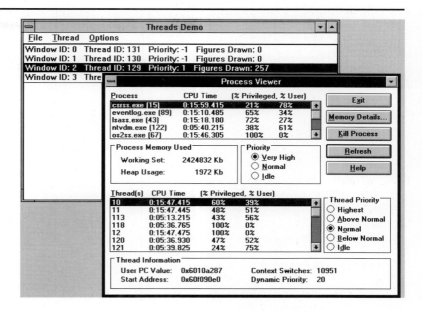

This chapter began with an introduction to threads, explaining what they are and how the system maintains and schedules them. Then we surveyed the Win32 functions for creating, modifying, and synchronizing threads. You learned about the base and dynamic priority of a thread, and you learned to distinguish mutexes, which pass one thread at a time; semaphores, which pass a several at once; events, which broadcast to all waiting threads; and critical sections, the local version of a mutex. Threads can wait for any of these objects. They remain blocked until they receive ownership. Blocked threads conserve processor time; they do not execute. The Threads program gave a practical example of threads in action.

We also spoke occasionally of processes and interprocess communication through pipes and shared memory. Chapter 5 explains how to create and manage processes.

Creating Processes and Pipes

- Creating child processes

- Coordinating processes

- Inheriting handles from a parent process

- Communicating through named and anonymous pipes

- Managing multiple instances of a pipe

In Chapter 4 you saw how one process can create many threads. A program that needs to do several things at once usually creates threads rather than whole new processes because threads are created more quickly with less overhead, they share resources such as handles and variables, and they are easy to synchronize. This chapter shows what happens when you decide instead to divide a task among several distinct processes, each with its own threads and its own private address space.

Processes and pipes are closely related topics. Processes often pass pipe handles to new processes they create in order to establish a channel for exchanging information. Along with the threads and synchronization objects you saw in Chapter 4, pipes and processes form the basic core of tools for multitasking in Windows NT. By the end of Chapter 5 you'll be able to launch a new child process, pass it handles, connect the parent to the child with a pipe, and send information through the pipe. In the process you'll encounter a whole new range of commands for governing all these interactions.

CONCEPTS: PROCESSES AND PIPES

The basic structure of a process object was explained in the section of Chapter 1 called "The Process Manager." Refer back to Figure 1.4 for a list of a process's attributes and methods and to Figure 1.9 for a diagram of the resources that make up a process. The resources include an access token, a virtual address space description, and a handle table. Every process has a primary thread—the one that begins execution at WinMain—and may create other threads as it runs. In many ways the commands for creating and managing processes resemble the commands for creating and managing threads, which you saw in Chapter 4. To create a process you specify security attributes and you receive a handle. With the handle you can, for example, change the priority of the process or terminate it. Even after a process stops running it continues to exist as long as any handles to it remain open. To destroy a process, close all its handles.

All the threads in one process share a single image of the executable file, but each new process requires the system to map the executable file into a new address space. The command for creating a process asks for the name of an .EXE file. An application that creates child processes to perform part of its work needs to be written and compiled as several distinct programs.

Inheritance

The documentation often refers to processes as parents, children, and siblings. A process that creates other processes is called the parent, and the new processes are its children. All the children of a single parent are siblings. Once a parent creates a child, the child no longer depends on the parent. If the parent terminates, the child may continue. The Win32 subsystem does not enforce any strong hierarchical dependence between parents and children.

The familial metaphor extends to one other action: inheritance. A new process *inherits* some attributes from its parent. Inherited attributes include an environment block with environment variables, a current working directory, standard input and output handles, and any other handles the parent may want its children to have. A child of a console process—that is, of a parent that uses the console API for drawing on the screen instead of the Windows GUI—also inherits its parent's console window. A child may inherit handles to processes, threads, mutexes, events, semaphores, pipes, and file-mapping objects. It may also inherit handles created with **CreateFile**, including files, console input buffers, console screen buffers, serial communication devices, and mailslots. When a child inherits a handle, both the parent and the child end up with handles to the same object. Whatever one does to the object affects the other. If a child's thread waits for and acquires a shared mutex, any parent threads that wait for the same object will be blocked. If a parent writes to a file, a child using the same handle will find its file position marker has moved forward, too.

When a child inherits a handle, it really only inherits access to the object. It does not inherit handle variables. When creating a child, the parent must both arrange for inheritance and pass the handles explicitly. These may be passed in several ways: on the command line, through a file, or through a pipe. An easier but less intuitive option involves the standard I/O channels. Recall that character-based C programs frequently direct their I/O through three standard channels called stdin, stdout, and stderr. Win32 processes automatically possess the same three channels, though they do not have the same predefined names. The standard I/O channels are generally useless to a GUI application because they are not actually connected to any device. (A GUI application may, however, open a console window and use its standard I/O devices there.) Normally a child inherits the same standard I/O devices its parent uses, but during creation the parent may specify a different set of handles for the child to receive. The child retrieves its inherited handles with

SetStdHandle. The parent may also change one or more of its own devices before creating the child. The child inherits the changes.

Children do not inherit all kinds of objects. Memory handles and pseudohandles are excluded from inheritance, for example. Each process has its own address space, so it cannot inherit memory objects from another process. Pseudohandles, such as the value returned by **GetCurrentThread**, are by definition valid only in the place where they originate. Nor do children inherit DLL module handles, GDI handles, or USER handles, including **HBRUSH** and **HWND** objects. Similarly, children do not inherit their parent's priority class. By default a child's priority will be **NORMAL_PRIORITY_CLASS**. There is one exception—the **IDLE_PRIORITY_CLASS** is inheritable. Parents of very low priority by default create children of very low priority; the poor stay poor. Parents of any other priority create children of normal priority.

Life Cycle of a Process

All Win32 processes begin life when some other process invokes them with **CreateProcess**. The Win32 subsystem starts up all its clients with that command. During **CreateProcess** the system sets up a virtual address space, loads an executable file image, and creates a primary thread. **CreateProcess** returns a handle to the new process and one to its primary thread. The parent may close the handles, relinquishing control over its child. Or the parent may keep them in order to change the child's priority class, terminate the child, or read the exit code when the child ends by itself. Like threads, processes remain in memory even after execution stops until all handles to the process have been closed.

A process remains active until its primary thread reaches the end of its starting procedure and stops execution or until any of its threads calls **ExitProcess**. **ExitProcess** causes the system to notify all supporting DLLs that this module has stopped. It also causes any other threads in the same process to terminate immediately.

Communication between Processes

Sometimes the processes the user runs have nothing to do with each other. A phone dialer and a paint program probably have little in common. But the ability to exchange information among processes sometimes produces a synergistic effect when their cooperation makes it possible to perform tasks neither program could manage alone. Windows allows many channels of communication including the clipboard, DDE, and OLE. Windows NT adds new channels. In Chapter 7, for example, you'll see how processes can share memory by opening views onto the same memory-mapped file. Pipes are another new and easy mechanism for different programs to exchange information. Unlike some other channels, pipes have no formal standards or protocols to govern how information is passed. That makes pipes easier to use and more flexible than, say, DDE conversations, but it also limits them to programs that recognize each other and know how to parse the information they agree to exchange.

A pipe is a section of shared memory where processes leave messages for each other. A pipe resembles a file where one program writes and another reads, but because a pipe is dedicated to interprocess communication the Win32 API can provide a range of commands to facilitate the exchange of information. Conceptually, a pipe is a cross between a computer file and a post office mailbox. One process writes something in the file and another process looks to see what was left behind.

The Life Cycle of a Pipe

A pipe appears when one program decides to create it. The program that creates a pipe is called the pipe's *server*. Other processes, called *clients,* may connect to the pipe's other end. The server assumes responsibility for the life of the pipe. Any process may be a server or a client, or both at once on different pipes. After the pipe is created and another process connects to it, either the client or the server—and sometimes both—writes into its end. Anything written at one end is read from the other. Reading and writing operations rely on the same commands you would use to work with any file: **ReadFile** and **WriteFile**. Typically a process that expects to receive a series of messages creates a new thread to wait for them. The thread repeatedly calls **ReadFile** and blocks, remaining suspended until each new message arrives.

Eventually the server decides the conversation has ended and breaks the connection. To destroy the pipe, the server calls **CloseHandle**. (The pipe will not actually be destroyed until all handles to it, both the server's and the client's, have been closed.) Alternatively, the server may decide to connect the old pipe with a new client.

Varieties of Pipes

Pipes come in several varieties: inbound, outbound, or duplex; byte or message; blocking or nonblocking; and named or anonymous. Most of these attributes are determined when the pipe is created. The first set of terms—inbound, outbound, and duplex—distinguishes the direction information flows through the pipe. "Inbound" and "outbound" describe one-directional pipes where one side only writes and the other side only reads. An inbound pipe lets the client send and the server receive. An outbound pipe lets the server send and the client receive. A duplex pipe allows both sides to send and receive. What the participants write determines whether the pipe should have a reading mode of type byte or type message. The reading mode helps the system decide when a read operation should stop. With a byte-mode pipe, a read operation stops when it either reaches the last byte of data in the pipe or else fills its reading buffer. With a message-mode pipe, however, a read operation stops when it reaches the end of a single message. Internally the system marks messages in a message-mode pipe by prefacing each newly written segment with a header stating its length. The programs on either end of the pipe never see the message headers, but **ReadFile** commands on a message-mode pipe automatically stop when they reach the end of a segment. Pipes may also be of a blocking or a nonblocking disposition. This attribute affects read, write, and connect commands. When any of these commands fails on a nonblocking pipe, the command returns immediately with an error result. On a pipe that allows blocking, the commands do not return until they succeed or an error occurs.

Operation	Blocking Mode	Nonblocking Mode
ConnectNamedPipe	Blocks until a client connects to the other end	Returns **FALSE** immediately
ReadFile	If pipe is empty, blocks until a message arrives	If pipe is empty, returns an error immediately

Operation	Blocking Mode	Nonblocking Mode
`WriteFile`	If pipe is nearly full, blocks until another process reads from the other end	If pipe is nearly full, returns immediately. For a byte-mode pipe, `WriteFile` will write as much as it can first. For a message-mode pipe, `WriteFile` returns **TRUE** and writes no bytes

Named and Anonymous Pipes

Finally, a pipe may be *named*, in which case the creator has endowed it with an identifying name string, or *anonymous*, meaning it has no name string. Like synchronization objects, such as mutexes and semaphores, a pipe may be given a name to help other processes identify it. Anonymous pipes require less overhead but perform only a limited subset of the services named pipes can perform. They pass messages in only one direction: either server to client or client to server, but not both. Also, anonymous pipes do not work over networks. Server and client must inhabit the same machine. Named pipes, on the other hand, may be bidirectional, may have multiple instances, and may pass messages between processes running on different machines.

The ability to exist in multiple instances permits a named pipe to connect one server with many clients. Each instance is an independent channel of communication. Messages in one instance do not interfere with messages in another instance. Multiple instances of a single pipe result when one or more servers pass the same identifying name to `CreateNamedPipe`.

COMMANDS

This section describes the Win32 API commands for creating processes and communicating through pipes. The process commands come first, followed by the pipe commands. Two sample programs in the final section of the chapter demonstrate most of the commands explained here.

Processes

Most of the effort in using the process API commands goes into the act of creating a process and determining what it inherits. Other commands change a process's priority, retrieve information about it, or terminate it.

Creating New Processes

Under NT, the **CreateProcess** command starts every new process. The old **WinExec** and **LoadModule** commands still exist for backward compatibility, but internally both now call **CreateProcess**.

```
BOOL CreateProcess(
    LPCTSTR lpszImageName,                  // image file (.EXE) name
    LPCTSTR lpszCmdLine,                     // command line for new process
    LPSECURITY_ATTRIBUTES lpsaProcess,       // how process will be shared
    LPSECURITY_ATTRIBUTES lpsaThread,        // how new thread will be shared
    BOOL bInheritHandles,                    // TRUE to inherit handles
    DWORD fdwCreate,                         // creation flags
    LPVOID lpvEnvironment,                   // new environment (NULL for default)
    LPTSTR lpszCurrentDir,                   // name of new current directory
    LPSTARTUPINFO lpStartupInfo,             // gives info about new process
    LPPROCESS_INFORMATION lpProcInfo )       // receives info about new process
```

The Parameters

The function's many parameters permit much control over the new process's starting conditions. First, every process requires code to execute. Together the first two parameters create a complete command line naming a program file and passing it arguments. Here, for example, is a command line you might type at the command prompt:

```
C> qgrep -L -y "ERROR_" *.h
```

The first parameter, lpszImageName, must point only to the name of the executable file (for example, "qgrep"). Do not include any arguments. In locating a file named in this parameter, the system does not search the PATH directories. The program must be in the current directory, or the string must contain a full path name.

The second parameter, lpszCmdLine, may be **NULL** if you have no arguments to pass. If you do pass arguments, the first item in the lpszCmdLine string must be what C programmers call the argv[0] value—again, "qgrep".

The first item is typically, but not necessarily, the name of the program, even if you have already given it in lpszImageName. You can omit the path and extension if they appear in the lpszImageName, but at any rate some item must precede the first argument, just as "qgrep" precedes "-L".

To make **CreateFile** search along the environment PATH for the file, leave the first parameter blank and pass the complete command line in the second parameter.

First Parameter	Second Parameter	Result
d:\dev\bin\qgrep	**NULL**	Runs qgrep, without arguments, only if qgrep is found in the \dev\bin directory
qgrep.exe	qgrep -L-y "ERROR_" *.h	Runs qgrep, with arguments, only if qgrep is in the current directory
NULL	qgrep -L-y "ERROR_" *.h	Runs qgrep, with arguments, if it can be found anywhere on the path

The next two parameters in **CreateProcess** provide security attributes for both the new process and its primary thread. (Every process receives an initial thread; otherwise nothing would ever execute.) You saw the same **SECURITY_ATTRIBUTES** structure when we created new threads in Chapter 4, and you will see it often in commands that create new objects. The information in this structure controls what another process may be permitted to do with the object if it opens a duplicate handle.

It also controls whether child processes may inherit a handle to the new object. By default other processes receive full access to the new object and children do not inherit it.

The bInheritHandles parameter of **CreateProcess** gives you a second chance to prevent a child from inheriting other handles you have already created. If bInheritHandles is **FALSE**, the new process inherits no handles, even if they were marked inheritable when created. Blocking inheritance is useful because many objects, including threads and processes, persist in memory until all the handles to them are closed. If every new child inherits a full set of handles from its parent, then many objects will stay in memory until all the child processes exit and their handles are destroyed. Children should be allowed to inherit only the handles they actually need.

The creation flags in the fdwCreate parameter govern the type and priority of the new process. The new process may be initially suspended; it may have a console or a GUI window; it may receive debugging information from its child; and it may receive a particular priority class. Here are some of the values that can be combined in the creation flag parameter:

DEBUG_PROCESS	Parent receives debugging information about the child and any of its children
DEBUG_ONLY_THIS_PROCESS	Parent receives debugging information about the child but not any of the child's children
CREATE_SUSPENDED	The primary thread of the new process is initially suspended
DETACHED_PROCESS	The new process does not use a console window
CREATE_NEW_CONSOLE	The new process receives its own new console window
IDLE_PRIORITY_CLASS	Runs only when the system is idle
NORMAL_PRIORITY_CLASS	No special scheduling needs

HIGH_PRIORITY_CLASS	Preempts all threads of lower priority in order to respond very quickly to some critical situation
REALTIME_PRIORITY_CLASS	Preempts even important system tasks

Each process has its own set of environment variables and its own current directory setting. If the `lpszEnvironment` and `lpszCurrentDir` parameters are **NULL**, the new process copies the block of environment variables and the directory setting from its parent. Environment variables are those defined with the SET command at the command prompt, typically in an autoexec file. Programmers usually define variables such as BIN, LIB, and INCLUDE to tell the compiler and linker where to find particular kinds of files. More generally, environment variables are a convenient way to customize programs by putting information where it is always available. A parent can send information to its children by defining environment variables. To give the child an entirely new environment, the parent should create a buffer and fill it with null-terminated strings of the form "<variable>=<setting>". The last string must be followed by two null characters. To give the child a slightly modified version of the parent's existing environment, the parent can temporarily modify its own settings with **GetEnvironmentVariable** and **SetEnvironment-Variable**, create the child, and then restore the old settings.

The last two parameters of **CreateProcess** point to structures. The parent fills out the **STARTUPINFO** structure before calling **CreateProcess** and receives information about the new process in the **PROCESS_INFORMATION** structure.

```
// You fill this out to describe a new process in advance
typedef struct _STARTUPINFO { /* si */
    DWORD   cb;                     // sizeof(STARTUPINFO)
    LPTSTR  lpReserved;             // should be NULL
    LPTSTR  lpDesktop;              // name of desktop object to run in
    LPSTR   lpTitle;                // caption for console title bar
    DWORD   dwX;                    // upper-left corner for new window
    DWORD   dwY;
    DWORD   dwXSize;                // width of new window
    DWORD   dwYSize;                // height of new window
    DWORD   dwXCountChars;          // width of new console window
    DWORD   dwYCountChars;          // height of new console window
    DWORD   dwFillAttribute;        // text/background colors for console
```

```
    DWORD    dwFlags;                  // activates fields in this structure
    WORD     wShowWindow;              // iCmdShow parameter value
    WORD     cbReserved2;              // zero
    LPBYTE   lpReserved2;              // NULL
    HANDLE   hStdInput;                // handles for the
    HANDLE   hStdOutput;               //   child's standard
    HANDLE   hStdError;                //   I/O devices
} STARTUPINFO, *LPSTARTUPINFO;
```

You must fill in the first field of the **STARTUPINFO** structure, but you can initialize all the rest to 0 or **NULL** to accept default values. The lpDesktop field names a feature not fully implemented in the first commercial release of NT. The desktop is the background window on which all a user's programs run. The current system allows only two desktops, one for logging on and one for the current user. Several features of the API, such as this lpDesktop field, suggest that in later releases NT may allow one user to work with multiple desktop windows. Until then, desktop-related fields and parameters serve little purpose. (Screen savers run on the logon desktop for security, to hide the user's data while the machine is idle. NT screen savers do not have access to the user's desktop.)

Many of the other fields in a **STARTUPINFO** structure matter only for nongraphics processes that will run in console windows instead of regular GUI windows. (The NT command shell, for example, runs in a console window. Consoles simulate character-based display.) Most of the fields are ignored in any case unless the values in dwFlags alert the system to use them. dwFlags may contain the following values, each activating a different field or set of fields from the **STARTUPINFO** structure:

Flag	Field(s) Activated
STARTF_USESHOWWINDOW	wShowWindow
STARTF_USESIZE	dwXSize, dwYSize
STARTF_USEPOSITION	dwX, dwY
STARTF_USECOUNTCHARS	dwXCountChars, dwYCountChars
STARTF_USEFILLATTRIBUTE	dwFillAttribute
STARTF_USESTDHANDLES	hStdInput, hStdOutput, hStdError

You don't need to initialize any of those 11 fields unless you activate them with a flag in dwFlags.

Three additional values for dwFlags do not activate specific fields. Two of them force the system to display or omit the waiting cursor that gives the user feedback as an application starts up. They are **STARTF_FORCEONFEEDBACK** and **STARTF_FORCE-OFFFEEDBACK**. The third, **STARTF_SCREENSAVER**, causes a screen saver program to initialize and terminate at a priority higher than its default idle priority level.

The last three fields allow you to specify standard I/O handles for the child that differ from those of the parent. Normally the child inherits whatever I/O devices the parent has. The I/O handles provide an easy way to pass the child any handles it needs to receive—one end of a pipe, for example. If you use any of the fields, you should set values in all of them. The child receives an invalid handle for any device you leave **NULL**. Call **GetStdHandle** to copy any of the parent's standard device handles into these fields.

Incidentally, a process created with the **DETACHED_PROCESS** flag cannot inherit its parent's standard I/O devices. The console program initialization procedures do not correctly receive the devices when the process has no console. Microsoft identified this limitation in an early release and added the handle fields as a workaround. They work for any child but are necessary for detached children.

Return Value

CreateProcess returns **TRUE** if it succeeds in creating the new object and **FALSE** if an error occurs. If **CreateProcess** returns **TRUE**, then it also returns information about the new process and its primary thread in the final parameter, the **PROCESS_INFORMATION** structure.

```
// CreateProcess fills this out to tell you what it created
typedef struct _PROCESS_INFORMATION { /* pi */
    HANDLE hProcess;              // handle to the new process
    HANDLE hThread;               // handle to its primary thread
    DWORD dwProcessId;            // number identifying new process
    DWORD dwThreadId;             // number identifying new thread
} PROCESS_INFORMATION;
```

If your program does not make use of the handles for the new process and its primary thread, you should close both right away. Otherwise, even if the **PROCESS_IN-FORMATION** structure is a local variable and goes out of scope, abandoning whatever it contained, the two object entries remain in your process's object table and the system counts them as open handles.

The size of physical system memory limits the total number of processes that can be created. Be sure to check for error returns. One of the early beta versions allowed a 16MB machine to create about 40 processes before failing for lack of memory. The limit will vary from version to version and machine to machine, but it is finite. Memory shortage can also cause **CreateThread** to fail, though threads consume significantly fewer resources than processes.

C Runtime Equivalents

The spawn and exec functions in the C runtime library also create new processes. Internally, however, they map to the same Win32 **CreateProcess** call. Through its parameters, **CreateProcess** offers more ways to customize the new process than do the C functions. The C runtime functions _getenv and _putenv, which work with a process's environment variables, also duplicate Win32 API functions.

Getting Information about a Process

Once a process starts up, it can call several commands to find out about itself. Like threads, processes are identified by a handle and an ID number. The parent receives both from the **CreateProcess** call; the child receives them by calling **GetCurrentProcess** and **GetCurrentProcessId**. Like **GetCurrentThread**, **GetCurrentProcess** returns a pseudohandle valid only in the current process. Pseudohandles may not be passed to other processes. To convert a pseudohandle to a real handle, use **DuplicateHandle**.

```
HANDLE GetCurrentProcess( void );
DWORD GetCurrentProcessId( void );
```

The C runtime function _getpid duplicates **GetCurrentProcessId**.

The next function retrieves the environment settings inherited from the parent.

```
DWORD GetEnvironmentVariable(
    LPTSTR lpszName,      // name of environment variable
    LPTSTR lpszValue,     // address of buffer for variable value
    DWORD dwValue )       // size of the lpszValue buffer in characters
```

You fill out the lpszName buffer with a variable name such as "PATH". The function looks up the corresponding value and copies it into lpszValue. The **DWORD** return value tells how many characters it copied into the `lpszValue` buffer. It is 0 if the variable was not found.

Another function retrieves a pointer to the command line, but the same information is usually available by other means as well. Console programs written in C can read the command line using `argc` and `argv`; GUI programs can retrieve it through the `lpszCmdLine` parameter of `WinMain`.

```
LPTSTR GetCommandLine( void )
```

Changing Priority

With the creation flags in **CreateProcess**, the parent can assign one of four base priority classes to a new process:

```
IDLE_PRIORITY_CLASS

NORMAL_PRIORITY_CLASS

HIGH_PRIORITY_CLASS

REALTIME_PRIORITY_CLASS
```

The default priority class is Normal. Do not use the high class, and especially not the real-time class, unless you must. Both levels impair the performance of lower-priority processes. Programs that do run at higher priorities should do so only for short periods of time. Here are the functions to find out and modify a process's priority class:

```
DWORD GetPriorityClass( HANDLE hProcess );

BOOL SetPriorityClass(
    HANDLE hProcess,            // process to modify
    DWORD fdwPriority );        // new priority class
```

The **DWORD** values in both functions should be one of the four **PRIORITY_CLASS** flags just listed. The priority class of a process becomes the base priority for all its threads. Refer to the discussion of thread priorities in Chapter 4 to see how the base priority influences a thread's dynamic priority. See especially Figure 4.3.

Synchronizing

Chapter 4 also explained how threads coordinate their separate tasks by waiting for signals from synchronization objects. Besides the four standard synchronization objects—mutexes, semaphores, events, and critical sections—threads can wait for other threads and for files, timers, and processes. Waiting for a thread or a process means waiting for it to stop execution. A thread waits for a process by passing the process handle to **WaitForSingleObject** or **WaitForMultipleObjects**. When the process terminates it enters its signaled state and all threads waiting for it resume execution.

One other synchronization command works only when waiting for processes. Instead of waiting for the process to terminate, you can wait for it to be idle. For this purpose, a process is considered idle when it is through initializing and no input from the user is waiting to reach it.

```
DWORD WaitForInputIdle(
    HANDLE hProcess,        // process to wait for
    DWORD dwTimeout );      // time-out time in milliseconds
```

Parents frequently call **WaitForInputIdle** immediately after creating a new process to allow the child time to establish itself. When the new process initializes and reaches its idle state the parent can try to communicate with it.

What **WaitForInputIdle** returns depends on how it ends. It returns 0 for a successful wait when the process becomes idle. If the time-out period elapses before the process idles, **WaitForInputIdle** returns **WAIT_TIMEOUT**. To indicate an error, it returns 0xFFFFFFFF.

WaitForInputIdle tests the child's message queue for pending messsages. It is intended only for GUI applications. Character-based console applications, lacking a message queue, are *always* idle by this definition.

Sharing Handles

Like handles to threads and synchronization objects, handles to processes can be shared. Several different processes might possess handles to any one process. As usual, you can't simply pass a handle directly from one process to another. You must instead rely on one of several transfer mechanisms to perform the conversion that makes a handle valid in a new address space. One mechanism is inheritance. If you tell **CreateProcess** to let the child inherit handles, the child receives copies of all your inheritable handles in its own object table. Children cannot use the handles there directly—they must still receive the handle on their command line or through a pipe—but inheritance makes the handle valid when it reaches the child process. If you pass to a child a handle it has not already inherited, the handle will not work.

Inheritance helps in passing handles only between related processes. To make a handle that can be passed to any other process, related or unrelated, call **DuplicateHandle**. You saw that function in Chapter 4. Given the original handle and a source and destination process, it creates a new handle valid in the destination process. **DuplicateHandle** also allows you to modify the attributes of a handle you want to keep. If, for example, you want only one of several children to inherit a particular handle, you create the first child, allowing inheritance, and then call **DuplicateHandle** to make a non-inheritable copy. Close the original inheritable handle and keep only the copy. Subsequent children will not inherit it. (One of the sample programs in this chapter uses **DuplicateHandle** to control inheritance. Look for the StartProcess procedure in the anonymous pipe program.)

Finally, another command allows any process to open a handle to any other process. The usual limits apply: You can open a process only if the security descriptor of your own process endows you with sufficient clearance.

```
HANDLE OpenProcess(
    DWORD fdwAccess,          // desired access privileges
    BOOL bInherit,            // TRUE for children to inherit the handle
    DWORD dwProcessId );      // number identifying the process
```

OpenProcess requires you to identify the process by its ID number. Normally you know the number only if you created the process or if the process itself, or one of its relatives, passes you the number—through a pipe, for example, or a DDE conversation. It is possible to generate a list of ID numbers for all the currently running processes, but the task is not trivial. It involves enumerating information stored in the system registry under the **HKEY_PERFORMANCE_DATA** key. The on-line help file contains example code showing how to search the registry with **RegEnumKey**, **RegEnumValue**, and **RegQueryInfoKey**. The structure of the **HKEY_PERFORMANCE_DATA** key is documented in winperf.h. The SDK comes with the source code for its Process Viewer utility (see Figure 4.5 in Chapter 4); it enumerates threads and processes.

Ending a Process

Normally you don't do anything special to end a process, just as you don't do anything to end a thread. When a thread reaches the `return` instruction at the end of its startup procedure, the system calls **ExitThread** and the thread terminates, leaving an exit code behind. When the primary thread in a process comes to the end of its starting procedure—usually `WinMain`—the system implicitly calls **ExitProcess** instead of **ExitThread**. **ExitProcess** forces all the threads in a process to end, no matter what they may be doing at the time. Any thread, however, may call **Exit-Process** explicitly to end its process at any time.

```
void ExitProcess( UINT fuExitCode );
```

You define the exit code to be whatever you like. Like threads, processes remain in memory even after they terminate until all the handles to them are closed. To determine a process's exit code, keep its handle and call **GetExitCodeProcess**.

```
BOOL GetExitCodeProcess(
    HANDLE hProcess,              // handle to the process
    LPDWORD lpdwExitCode )        // buffer to receive exit code
```

If the process has not ended, **GetExitCodeProcess** reports the exit code as **STILL_ACTIVE**.

Normally a process ends when its primary thread ends. The primary thread may, however, choose to quit without ending the process. If the primary thread ends with an explicit call to **ExitThread**, the system does not call **ExitProcess**. Other threads in the process continue to execute, and the process runs until any thread calls **ExitProcess** directly or until the last thread ends.

A number of things happen when a process ends. First, all the process's handles are closed—all its file handles, thread handles, event handles, and any other handles are destroyed. The objects they point to will also be destroyed, but only if no other processes also possess handles to them. Any dynamic-link libraries the process has called receive notification when the process terminates, giving them a chance to clean up and exit. Also, the terminating process acquires an exit code. More specifically, the "Exit Status" attribute of the process object (visible in Figure 1.4) changes from **STILL_ACTIVE** to whatever value **ExitProcess** assigns. Finally, the process object enters its signaled state and any threads waiting for it to end resume execution. Note that when a parent process dies, it does not take its children with it. The children, if any, continue to run independently.

Another command, **TerminateProcess**, also forces a process to exit. Actually this command brings the process to an abrupt and crashing halt, preventing some of the usual cleanup from happening. DLLs, for example, are not notified when **TerminateProcess** kills one of their clients. Like **TerminateThread**, **TerminateProcess** is abrupt, messy, and best avoided when possible.

```
BOOL TerminateProcess(
    HANDLE hProcess,            // handle to the process
    UINT fuExitCode );          // exit code for the process
```

Pipes

Pipes allow two processes to communicate with each other. A pipe is a memory buffer where the system preserves data between the time one process writes it and another process reads it. The API commands ask you to think of the buffer as a pipe, or conduit, through which information flows from one place to another. A pipe has two ends. A one-way pipe allows writing only at one end and reading only at the other; all the information flows from one process to the other. A two-way pipe allows both processes to read and write, so the information flows both ways at once. When you create a pipe you also decide whether it will be anonymous or named. Anonymous pipes are simpler, so we'll start with them.

Creating Anonymous Pipes

An anonymous pipe passes information in only one direction, and both ends of the pipe must be on the same machine. The process that creates an anonymous pipe receives two handles, one for reading and one for writing. In order to communicate with another process, the server must pass one of the handles to the other process.

```
BOOL CreatePipe(
    PHANDLE phRead,                    // variable for read handle (inbound)
    PHANDLE phWrite,                   // variable for write handle (outbound)
    LPSECURITY_ATTRIBUTES lpsa,        // access privileges
    DWORD dwPipeSize );                // size of pipe buffer (0=default)
```

The size of the pipe buffer determines how much information the pipe can hold before it overflows. No one can deposit messages in a full pipe until someone makes room by reading the old information from the other end.

If all goes well, **CreatePipe** returns **TRUE** and deposits two new valid handles in the variables indicated by the **PHANDLE** parameters. Next, the creating process usually needs to pass one of the handles to another process. Which handle you give away depends on whether you want the other process to send (write) or receive (read) information through the pipe. You can pass the handle to a child process on its command line or through its standard I/O handles. An unrelated process would have to receive the handle by other means, perhaps through a DDE conversation or a shared file. Connections through anonymous pipes are easier to arrange when the processes are related.

Creating Named Pipes

Many Windows NT system objects may be assigned name strings to identify them. Names allow other processes to locate objects more easily. Unnamed objects are known only by their handles, and handles are valid only in the process where they originate. Any process that knows the name of an object, however, can ask the system to search its object name hierarchy. (See the section "Naming Objects" in Chapter 1, and refer especially to Figure 1.5.) Given a name, the system can find any object on any connected machine.

If a pipe has a name, then the client program doesn't have to wait for the server to pass it a handle. Instead, the client can acquire a handle by calling **CreateFile** or **CallNamedPipe** (see below.) In either case, the client needs to know only the pipe's name string. A parent might pass the string to a child process on the command line, or any process might pass it to any other through a shared file or a DDE conversation. Most often, however, two processes sharing a named pipe have been written by the same developer and they simply agree on a name string in advance.

Named pipes can do several things that anonymous pipes cannot. They can pass information in both directions through one pipe, connect across a network to a process on a remote machine, exist in multiple instances, and use more pipe modes. In addition, the following commands work only with named pipes. Do not create an anonymous pipe if you need the functions these commands provide.

```
CallNamedPipe
ConnectNamedPipe
CreateFile
```

CreateNamedPipe

DisconnectNamedPipe

GetNamedPipeHandleState

GetNamedPipeInfo

ImpersonateNamedPipeClient

PeekNamedPipe

RevertToSelf

SetNamedPipeHandleState

TransactNamedPipe

WaitNamedPipe

Don't worry if you don't yet understand what all the commands do. We're about to explain them.

CreatePipe makes anonymous pipes and **CreateNamedPipe** makes pipes with names. Because named pipes have more features, **CreateNamedPipe** takes more parameters.

```
HANDLE CreateNamedPipe(
    LPTSTR lpszPipeName,          // string naming new pipe object
    DWORD fdwOpenMode,            // access, overlap, and write-through
    DWORD fdwPipeMode,            // type, read, and wait modes
    DWORD dwMaxInstances,         // maximum number of instances
    DWORD dwOutBuf,              // outbound buffer size in bytes
    DWORD dwInBuf,              // inbound buffer size in bytes
    DWORD dwTimeout,            // time-out interval in milliseconds
    LPSECURITY_ATTRIBUTES lpsa );  // access privileges
```

What's in a Name?

The first parameter points to the string you provide to name the new object. The system stores this name in its hierarchical tree of system object names. Pipe name strings should follow this form:

\\.\pipe\<pipename>

The first backslash designates the root node of the system's object name hierarchy. The other three backslashes separate the names of subsequent nodes. The period (.) stands for the local machine. Although pipes can connect with clients on other network servers, a new pipe object always appears on the local server where it was created. Under the server name is a node called "pipe", holding the names of all the pipe objects on the local machine. Within the name string, the substring <pipename> is the only section the programmer chooses. This substring may be as long as 256 characters.

Object names are not sensitive to case.

The period (.) stands in for the name of a server machine. Servers and clients both use . to represent the local server, but a client wishing to open a pipe on a remote server must know the server's name. One way to learn remote server names is to enumerate them with the **WNetOpenEnum**, **WNetEnumResource**, and **WNetCloseEnum** functions, but enumeration is bound to be slow. We'll suggest a better method in a few pages when we compare pipes to mailslots.

These functions require a pipe's name string as a parameter: **CreateNamedPipe**, **CreateFile**, **WaitNamedPipe**, and **CallNamedPipe**.

A Pipe's Access Mode

The next parameter after the name string, fdwOpenMode, combines flags to set several pipe attributes. The most important is the access mode, which determines the direction information flows through the pipe. fdwOpenMode must include one of the following three flags:

PIPE_ACCESS_OUTBOUND	Server only writes and client only reads
PIPE_ACCESS_INBOUND	Server only reads and client only writes
PIPE_ACCESS_DUPLEX	Server and client may both read and write

A Pipe's Write-Through and Overlapping Status

You must specify one of the three access flags for fdwOpenMode, and you can optionally add either or both of two additional flags in the same parameter:

FILE_FLAG_WRITE_THROUGH   Disables buffering over a
network

FILE_FLAG_OVERLAPPED   Enables asynchronous read and
write operations

For efficiency, when a pipe extends to a remote machine the system normally does not send every message immediately. Instead it tries to accumulate several short messages in a buffer and send them across the pipe in a single operation. If too much time passes and the buffer remains only partly full, the system eventually sends the buffer anyway. The write-through flag prevents the system from buffering; each new message is sent immediately, and write commands do not return until their output has been transmitted. Turn off the buffering if you expect to send messages only infrequently.

The second optional flag, **FILE_FLAG_OVERLAPPED**, allows read and write commands to return immediately while the action they initiate continues in the background. Read and write operations, because they involve physical devices, are usually slow. When we described the **SleepEx** function in Chapter 4, we explained that when a Windows NT program reads from a file, for example, it may choose simply to start the read process, name a procedure to be called when the read operation ends, and then continue executing while the system reads in the background. When the read operation finally ends the system schedules an asynchronous procedure call (see Chapter 1) and invokes the callback function you named in the read command. Your callback function then processes the newly retrieved information. Making the system do your reading and writing in the background is called *asynchronous I/O* or *overlapping I/O*. Pipes too support overlapping I/O. Overlapping I/O is harder to program because you have to write a callback function, but it's also more efficient. Chapter 12 includes an example of overlapping I/O.

A Pipe's Type and Its Read Mode

The fdwPipeMode parameter combines flags to designate another set of pipe features: the read mode, the type, and the wait flag. The type and the read mode are closely related; they might be better named the write mode and the read mode. Together they control how information in the pipe is organized and interpreted. Both modes offer a choice between "byte" and "message."

Pipe type (write mode) flags:

```
PIPE_TYPE_BYTE

PIPE_TYPE_MESSAGE
```

Read mode flags:

```
PIPE_READMODE_BYTE

PIPE_READMODE_MESSAGE
```

The information in a byte-mode pipe is read and written in the normal binary manner and understood as nothing more than a series of bytes. Sometimes it is more convenient to divide the information in a pipe into discrete messages, where the output from each separate write command constitutes a new message. A message-mode pipe automatically and transparently prefaces each new message with an invisible header specifying the length of the message. The header enables a read command to stop automatically when it reaches the end of one message. The recipient recovers messages one at a time, exactly as they were written. If one program sends to another a long series of integers, for example, it would probably use a byte-mode pipe because the receiver doesn't care how many integers were written at a time. Everything it retrieves is simply another integer. But if they were sending commands written in a script language, the receiver would have to retrieve the commands one at a time, exactly as written, in order to parse them. Since each command might be a different length, the two programs would use a message-mode pipe.

The write mode and read mode are designated independently, but not all combinations make sense. Specifically, you can't combine **PIPE_TYPE_BYTE** and **PIPE_READMODE_MESSAGE**. A byte-type pipe writes bytes without message headers, so the receiver can't recover message units. On the other hand, you can combine **PIPE_TYPE_MESSAGE** with **PIPE_READMODE_BYTE**. In that case the sender includes message headers but the receiver chooses to ignore them, retrieving the data as a series of undifferentiated bytes. (The receiver still does not see the invisible message headers.)

A Pipe's Wait Mode

Besides the flags to set the type and read mode for a pipe, the fdwPipeMode parameter accepts one other flag for the wait mode. The wait mode determines what happens when some condition temporarily prevents a pipe command from completing. For example, what should happen if you try to read from an empty pipe? Some programs might want to forget about reading and move on to the next instruction, but other programs might need to wait for a new message before proceeding. By default pipes cause reading threads to block and wait, but you can prevent blocking by adding the **PIPE_NOWAIT** flag to fdwPipeMode. (The default flag is **PIPE_WAIT**.) The wait mode affects write commands as well as read commands. A program that tries to write when the pipe buffer is full normally blocks until another program makes room by reading from the other end. The wait mode also affects a server trying to connect with a client. If the **ConnectNamedPipe** command finds no ready clients, the waiting mode determines whether the command waits for a client to connect or returns immediately.

The nonblocking mode is provided primarily for compatibility with LanMan 2.0.

Pipe Instances

A server program may wish to open pipes for more than one client. It may not know in advance how many clients it will have. It would be inconvenient to have to invent a new pipe name for each new client. How would all the clients know in advance what name to use when they open their end of the pipe? To circumvent this problem, Win32 permits the server to create the same pipe over and over. Each time you call **CreateNamedPipe** with the same name, you get a new instance of the same pipe. Each new instance provides an independent communication channel for another client. The server might begin by creating the same pipe four times. It would receive four different handles, and it could wait for a different client to connect to each one. All the clients would use the same pipe name to request their own handles, but each would receive a handle to a different instance. If a fifth client tried to connect, it would block until the server disconnected one of the first four instances.

The dwMaxInstances parameter of the **CreateNamedPipe** command sets an upper limit on the number of instances one pipe will support before **CreateNamedPipe** returns an error. The **PIPE_UNLIMITED_INSTANCES** flag indicates no upper limit. In that case the maximum number of instances is limited only by system resources. The value of dwMaxInstances may not exceed the value of **PIPE_UNLIMITED_IN-STANCES**, which our version of winbase.h defines as 255.

Buffer Sizes

dwOutBuf and dwInBuf set the initial size of the buffers that store anything written to the pipe from either end. For an outbound pipe (**PIPE_ACCESS_OUTBOUND**) only the output buffer matters; for an inbound pipe only the input buffer size is significant. The limits set by the buffer size parameters are flexible. Internally, every read or write operation on a pipe causes the system to allocate buffer space from the kernel's pool of system memory. The buffer size values are interpreted as a quota limiting these allocations. When the system allocates buffer space for a write operation, it charges the space consumed to the write buffer quota. If the new buffer size fits within the quota, all is well. If it does not, the system allocates the space anyway and charges it to the *process's* resource quota. In order to avoid excessive charges to the process quota, every **WriteFile** operation that causes the buffer to exceed its quota blocks. The writing thread suspends operation until the receiving thread reduces the buffer by reading from it.

In estimating buffer sizes, you'll need to take into account the fact that each buffer allocation is slightly larger than you expect because, besides the message contents, it includes an internal data structure of about 28 bytes. The exact size is undocumented and may vary from version to version.

To summarize, the system allocates buffer space dynamically as needed, but threads that frequently exceed their buffer size may block excessively. The sample programs at the end of this chapter leave the buffer size at 0 and suffer no apparent harm. Programs that send frequent messages or that expect the buffers to back up occasionally will benefit from increased buffer sizes.

Time-Out Period and Security Attributes

CreateNamedPipe takes two more parameters. The dwTimeout value matters only when a client calls **WaitNamedPipe** to make a connection, and it matters then only if the client accepts the default time-out period. The default period is the number the server sets in the dwTimeout parameter of **CreateNamedPipe**, but the client may set a different period in **WaitNamedPipe**.

The final parameter, a pointer to a **SECURITY_ATTRIBUTES** structure, should look very familiar by now. The values in it determine which operations the new handle allows you to perform on its object, and they also determine whether child processes may inherit the new handle. As usual, if you leave the field **NULL** the resulting handle has full access privileges and cannot be inherited.

Summary of Named Pipe Attributes

CreateNamedPipe allows you to set many potentially confusing characteristics of the new object. To add to the confusion, some of the characteristics must be exactly the same for every instance of a pipe, but some may vary with each instance. Table 5.1 summarizes these characteristics.

Anonymous pipes always have the characteristics that are the default state for named pipes: **PIPE_TYPE_BYTE**, **PIPE_READMODE_BYTE**, **PIPE_WAIT**, no overlapping I/O, and network buffering enabled.

Catching Errors

CreateNamedPipe returns a valid handle if it succeeds. If an error occurs, it returns the value (HANDLE)0xFFFFFFFF (also known as **INVALID_HANDLE_VALUE**).

You may have noticed that many of the functions we've described seem to have very rudimentary error returns. **CreateThread**, **CreateMutex**, **CreateProcess**, **CreatePipe**, and **CreateNamedPipe**, for example, all might fail for a variety of reasons. The system might be low on memory, or a particular mutex might already exist, or a network connection might fail, or a parameter might be invalid. Yet all of these creation functions indicate errors only by returning either **FALSE** or an invalid handle.

Better diagnostics are available. The system keeps a large set of error messages in a single collective message table and identifies each message with a different number. Whenever a command fails, it stores an error message number for the active thread. Immediately after a function fails you should call **GetLastError** to retrieve the message number. To translate the number into an explanatory string, suitable for showing in a message box, call **FormatMessage**. Even functions from the Windows 3.1 API sometimes set error codes under Win32. Microsoft's on-line help file regularly identifies error-setting commands in the descriptions of their return values: "To get extended error information, use the **GetLastError** function." The sample programs later in this chapter construct a procedure for displaying the appropriate message after any error. Look for ShowErrorMsg in the listings.

TABLE 5.1: Summary of Named Pipe Attributes

Characteristic	Parameter	Description	Possible Values	Constant for All Instances
Access mode	fdwOpenMode	Direction information flows	PIPE_ACCESS_OUTBOUND PIPE_ACCESS_INBOUND PIPE_ACCESS_DUPLEX	Yes
Type ("write mode")	fdwPipeMode	Whether to add a header to each new message	PIPE_TYPE_BYTE PIPE_TYPE_MESSAGE	Yes
Wait mode	fdwPipeMode	Whether to block when a command can't work immediately	PIPE_WAIT PIPE_NOWAIT	No
Overlapped I/O	fdwOpenMode	Whether to permit asynchronous I/O operations	FILE_FLAG_OVERLAPPED	No
Write-through	fdwOpenMode	Whether to buffer network transmissions	FILE_FLAG_WRITE_THROUGH	No

TABLE 5.1: Summary of Named Pipe Attributes (continued)

Characteristic	Parameter	Description	Possible Values	Constant for All Instances
Read mode	fdwPipeMode	Whether to end read operations on message boundaries	PIPE_READMODE_BYTE	No
			PIPE_READMODE_MESSAGE	
Maximum instances	dwMaxInstances	Most copies of one pipe allowed simultaneously	Number from 1 to PIPE_UNLIMITED_INSTANCES	Yes
Buffer sizes	dwOutBuf & dwInBuf	Size for buffers that hold messages in transit	Size in bytes	No
Time-out period	dwTimeout	Maximum waiting period for commands to succeed	0 for default Period in milliseconds	Yes
Security attributes	lpsa	Access privileges and inheritability	SECURITY_ATTRIBUTES structure NULL for defaults	No

Connecting to an Existing Pipe

After a server opens a named pipe it must wait for a client to open the other end. A client may open its end in any of several ways, but the most common is **Create-File**. This is the same function we'll use in Chapter 12 to open disk files. It also works with named pipes, communications devices, and the I/O buffers of a character-based console window. The **ReadFile** and **WriteFile** commands also work with the same set of objects. Using a single unified API for several different objects makes programming easier.

```
HANDLE CreateFile(
    LPCTSTR lpszName,                // name of the pipe (or file)
    DWORD fdwAccess,                 // read/write access (must match the pipe)
    DWORD fdwShareMode,              // usually 0 (no share) for pipes
    LPSECURITY_ATTRIBUTES lpsa,      // access privileges
    DWORD fdwCreate,                 // must be OPEN_EXISTING for pipes
    DWORD fdwAttrsAndFlags,          // write-through and overlapping modes
    HANDLE hTemplateFile );          // ignored with OPEN_EXISTING
```

The pipe name must match the string the server passed to **CreateNamedPipe**, but if the server and client programs are connecting over a network then the string must name the network server machine instead of using a dot (.). The fdwAccess parameter tells whether you want to read or write to the pipe. If the pipe was created with the **PIPE_ACCESS_OUTBOUND** flag, then you should specify **GENERIC_READ** in **CreateFile**. For an inbound pipe, the client needs **GENERIC_WRITE** privileges. For a duplex pipe, the client needs **GENERIC_READ | GENERIC_WRITE** privileges.

The fdwShareMode should generally be 0 to prohibit sharing the pipe with other processes. Occasionally, however, a client might use the share mode to duplicate the pipe handle for another client. In that case both clients would have handles to the same instance of the same pipe, and they might have to worry about synchronizing their read and write operations.

The security attributes in the lpsa parameter are by now familiar. The fdwCreate flag must be **OPEN_EXISTING** because **CreateFile** will not create a new pipe. It opens existing pipes. Other flags allow **CreateFile** to create new file objects where none existed before, but those flags produce errors when lpszName designates a pipe object. The last two parameters normally govern file attributes, such as hidden, read-only, and archive settings, but **CreateFile** uses the attributes only to create new files. When you open an existing object (with **OPEN_EXIST**), the object keeps whatever attributes it already has.

There are two exceptions. Two flags in the `fdwAttrsAndFlags` parameters do work when opening an existing named pipe. They are **FILE_FLAG_WRITE_THROUGH** and **FILE_FLAG_OVERLAPPED**. The client may set flags that differ from the server, enabling or disabling network buffering and asynchronous I/O to suit its own preferences.

Modifying an Existing Pipe

We've explained that two ends of the same pipe may have different read or wait modes, but **CreateFile** always copies the original attributes when it opens a handle for a client. Any process, however, can modify its pipe handle with **SetNamedPipeHandleState**.

```
BOOL SetNamedPipeHandleState(
    HANDLE hNamedPipe,                  // handle of a named pipe
    LPDWORD lpdwModes,                  // read and wait mode flags
    LPDWORD lpdwMaxCollect,             // transmission buffer size
    LPDWORD lpdwCollectDataTimeout );   // max time before transmission
```

The first parameter is a handle returned by **CreateNamedPipe** or **CreateFile**. The second parameter, like the `fdwPipeMode` parameter of **CreateNamedPipe**, combines flags to set several attributes at once. The `lpdwModes` parameter controls whether read operations use the byte or message mode and whether certain commands will block while they wait for the pipe to become available. The read mode may be **PIPE_READMODE_BYTE** or **PIPE_READMODE_MESSAGE**. (Specifying the message read mode for a pipe that was created with **PIPE_TYPE_BYTE** causes an error.) The read-mode pipe may be combined with either **PIPE_WAIT** or **PIPE_NOWAIT**.

The last two parameters matter only for pipes that connect with a remote machine. They control how the system buffers network transmissions. (They have no effect on pipes with the **PIPE_FLAG_WRITE_THROUGH** attribute, which disables network buffering.) Buffering allows the system to combine several messages into a single transmission. It holds outgoing messages in a buffer until either the buffer fills or a set time period elapses. `lpdwMaxCollect` sets the size of the collection buffer and `lpdwCollectDataTimeout` sets the time period in milliseconds.

Getting Information about an Existing Pipe

Three functions retrieve information about a pipe without changing any of its attributes. The first information command is the counterpart of **SetNamedPipe-HandleState**, but it retrieves more information than its partner sets:

```
BOOL GetNamedPipeHandleState(
    HANDLE hNamedPipe,              // handle of named pipe
    LPDWORD lpdwModes,             // read and wait modes
    LPDWORD lpdwCurInstances,      // number of current pipe instances
    LPDWORD lpcbMaxCollect,        // max bytes before remote transmission
    LPDWORD lpdwCollectTimeout,    // max time before remote transmission
    LPTSTR lpszUserName,           // user name of client process
    DWORD dwMaxUserNameBuff );     // size in characters of user name buffer
```

The lpdwModes parameter may contain the **PIPE_READMODE_MESSAGE** and **PIPE_NOWAIT** flags. To indicate the byte mode or wait mode, which are the default states, no flags are set. lpdwCurInstances counts the number of instances that currently exist for a pipe. In other words, it tells how many times the server has called **CreateNamedPipe** with the same name string. The collect and time-out parameters retrieve the same network buffering information that **SetNamedPipeHandleState** controls.

The last two parameters help a server learn about its client. They return the null-terminated string naming the user who is running the client application. User names are the names users give to log in. They are associated with particular configuration and security privileges. The server might want the name for a log or a report, but probably this parameter exists for compatibility with OS/2, which also makes the user name available. The lpszUserName parameter must be **NULL** if hNamedPipe belongs to a client—if, in other words, it was created with **CreateFile** rather than **CreateNamedPipe**.

Any of the pointer parameters may be set to **NULL** to ignore the value normally returned in that place.

A second function returns additional information about a pipe. **GetNamedPipeInfo** returns attributes that may not be changed, and **GetNamedPipeHandleState** returns attributes that may change during the life of a pipe.

```
BOOL GetNamedPipeInfo(
    HANDLE hNamedPipe,             // handle of named pipe
    LPDWORD lpdwType,             // type and server flags
    LPDWORD lpdwOutBuf,          // size in bytes of pipe's output buffer
```

```
    LPDWORD lpdwInBuf,          // size in bytes of pipe's input buffer
    LPDWORD lpdwMaxInstances ); // maximum number of pipe instances
```

The lpdwType parameter may contain either or both of two flags: **PIPE_TYPE_MES-SAGE** and **PIPE_SERVER_END**. If no flags are set, then the handle connects to the client end of a pipe that writes in bytes. The input and output buffer sizes are set in **CreateNamedPipe**. The lpdwMaxInstances parameter returns the value **CreateNamedPipe** set as an upper limit for the number of simultaneous instances allowed to exist for one pipe.

One final command also returns information about a pipe. Normally when you read from a pipe the read operation removes from the buffer the message it retrieves. With **PeekNamedPipe**, however, it is possible to retrieve a message without clearing it from the buffer.

```
BOOL PeekNamedPipe(
    HANDLE hPipe,               // handle of named or anonymous pipe
    LPVOID lpvBuffer,           // address of buffer to receive data
    DWORD dwBufferSize,         // size in bytes of data buffer
    LPDWORD lpdwBytesRead,      // returns number of bytes read
    LPDWORD lpdwAvailable,      // returns total number of bytes available
    LPDWORD lpdwMessage );      // returns unread bytes in this message
```

The inaptly named **PeekNamedPipe** command works with both named and anonymous pipes. The lpvBuffer parameter points to a place for the command to store whatever information it copies from the pipe. **PeekNamedPipe** cannot retrieve more than dwBufferSize bytes, even if more information remains in the pipe. lpdwBytesRead returns the number of bytes the function actually did read and lpdwMessage returns the number of bytes remaining in the current message, if any. lpdwMessage is ignored if the pipe's read mode is **PIPE_READMODE_BYTE**. In that case there are no message units to measure. (All anonymous pipes use the byte read mode.) The total number of available bytes returned in lpdwAvailable includes all bytes in all messages. If the buffer currently holds several messages, *lpdwAvailable may be greater than the sum of *lpdwBytesRead and *lpdwMessage.

It is legal to retrieve only a partial set of information by leaving some parameters **NULL**. You may, for example, set everything to 0 or **NULL** except the handle and lpdwAvailable if all you want to know is how many bytes are waiting in the buffer.

When reading from a pipe set to the message read mode, **PeekNamedPipe** always stops after reading the first message, even if the data buffer has room to hold several messages. Also, **PeekNamedPipe** never blocks on an empty pipe the way **Read-File** does if **PIPE_WAIT** is set. The wait mode has no effect on **PeekNamedPipe**, which always returns immediately.

Reading and Writing through a Pipe

All the choices you make to create a pipe—named or anonymous, byte or message, blocking or nonblocking—prepare for the moment when you actually send a message through the pipe. One program writes to its handle and the other program reads from its handle. This most basic transaction typically involves two functions, **WriteFile** and **ReadFile**.

```
BOOL WriteFile(
    HANDLE hFile,                  // place to write (pipe or file)
    CONST VOID *lpBuffer,          // points to data to put in file
    DWORD dwBytesToWrite,          // number of bytes to write
    LPDWORD lpdwBytesWritten,      // returns number of bytes written
    LPOVERLAPPED lpOverlapped );   // needed for asynchronous I/O

BOOL ReadFile(
    HANDLE hFile;                  // source for reading (pipe or file)
    LPVOID lpBuffer;               // buffer to hold data retrieved
    DWORD dwBytesToRead;           // number of bytes to read
    LPDWORD lpdwBytesRead;         // returns number of bytes read
    LPOVERLAPPED lpOverlapped;     // needed for asynchronous I/O
```

The number of bytes to read or write need not be as large as (but should not be larger than) the size of the buffer. If you call **ReadFile** on a message-mode pipe and give dwBytesToRead a value smaller than the size of the next message, **ReadFile** reads only part of the message and returns **FALSE**. A subsequent call to **GetLast-Error** discovers an error code of **ERROR_MORE_DATA**. Call **ReadFile** again, or **PeekNamedPipe**, to read the rest of the message. When **WriteFile** writes to a non-blocking byte-mode pipe and finds the buffer nearly full, it still returns **TRUE** but the value of *lpdwBytesWritten will be less than dwBytesToWrite.

Depending on the pipe's wait mode, both **WriteFile** and **ReadFile** may block. **WriteFile** might have to wait for a full pipe to empty out from the other end; an empty pipe causes **ReadFile** to block waiting for a new message.

Asynchronous I/O

The final parameter of both commands points to an **OVERLAPPED** structure that provides extra information for performing asynchronous (or overlapping) I/O. Asynchronous I/O allows the command to return immediately, even before the read or write operation runs to completion. Asynchronous commands do not automatically modify the position of the file pointer, so the **OVERLAPPED** structure includes an offset pointing to the place in the file where the operation should begin. The structure also contains a handle to an event object. A thread in the reading program can wait for the event's signal before examining what **ReadFile** placed in the retrieval buffer. You must supply an **OVERLAPPED** structure when using file handles that were created with the **FILE_FLAG_OVERLAPPED** attribute. Another method of performing asynchronous I/O involves the **ReadFileEx** and **WriteFileEx** commands. Instead of signaling completion with an event, these commands invoke a procedure you provide to be called at the end of each operation.

Chapter 12 shows how to set up overlapping file operations. With respect to pipes, overlapping I/O is a useful strategy for dealing with multiple clients connected to different instances of a single pipe. Synchronous I/O is easier to program, but slow read and write commands might hold up other waiting clients. A server can create a separate thread for each client, as our sample program does for simplicity, but that involves more overhead than the situation actually requires. A single thread can read and write simultaneously to different pipe instances with asynchronous I/O because each command always returns immediately, leaving the thread free while the system finishes in the background. With **WaitForMultipleObjects** a thread can arrange to block until any pending operation completes. The efficiency of asynchronous I/O can make a big difference over slow network connections. Also, it is easier to protect program resources when you have fewer threads to synchronize.

Synchronizing Connections

At any time a client may call **CreateFile** to open its end of a named pipe. Two problems, however, may arise. First, the server often needs to know when a client has connected to a pipe. Writing to an unconnected pipe serves little purpose, and **CreateFile** does not tell the server when a connection occurs. Second, if all the instances of a pipe are busy then **CreateFile** always immediately returns **INVAL-ID_HANDLE_VALUE** without establishing a connection. The client may prefer to wait for a pipe instance to become available when another client finishes. In short, both server and client must be able to block while waiting for conditions that permit a connection to occur. To do so, the server calls **ConnectNamedPipe** and the client calls **WaitNamedPipe**.

```
BOOL ConnectNamedPipe(
    HANDLE hNamedPipe,              // handle of an available named pipe
    LPOVERLAPPED lpOverlapped );    // info for asynchronous operation

BOOL WaitNamedPipe(
    LPTSTR lpszPipeName,            // points to string naming pipe object
    DWORD dwTimeout );              // maximum wait time in milliseconds
```

These coordinating functions work only with named pipes because a client cannot create its own handle to an anonymous pipe. It must receive a handle directly from the server, and in that case the connection is already made. **ConnectNamedPipe** can respond asynchronously, just as **ReadFile** and **WriteFile** can. The lpOverlapped parameter contains an event handle, and the event object signals when a client connects.

How **CreateNamedPipe** behaves depends on whether the pipe was created with, or subsequently modified to include, the **FILE_FLAG_OVERLAPPING** flag and the **PIPE_WAIT** mode. Its operation is most intuitive on pipes that allow waiting.

Wait Mode	Operation Mode	Results
PIPE_WAIT	Synchronous operation	Does not return until a client connects or an error occurs
		Returns **TRUE** if a client connects after the call begins
		Returns **FALSE** if a client is already connected or an error occurs
PIPE_WAIT	Asynchronous operation	Returns immediately
		Always returns **FALSE**

Wait Mode	Operation Mode	Results
		GetLastError signals ERROR_IO_PENDING if the wait is in progress
PIPE_NOWAIT	Synchronous operation	Always returns immediately
		Returns TRUE the first time it is called after a client disconnects. TRUE indicates the pipe is available. Otherwise the command always returns FALSE
		GetLastError indicates ERROR_PIPE_LISTENING if no connection was made or ERROR_PIPE_CONNECTED if a connection has already been made
PIPE_NOWAIT	Asynchronous mode	Should not be used with a no-wait mode pipe. The no-wait mode exists only for compatibility with LanMan 2.0

The unintuitive use of **TRUE** and **FALSE** returns results from the fact that **Connect-NamedPipe** returns **TRUE** only if the pipe begins in a listening state and a client connects after the connect command begins and before it returns. If the pipe is already connected, if the command responds asynchronously and so returns without waiting or is called for a pipe that does not allow waiting, the command generally returns **FALSE**.

The client's wait command, **WaitNamedPipe**, does not actually create a connection. It returns **TRUE** when a pipe is or becomes available, but it does not return a handle to the available pipe. It is common for a client to repeat the wait-then-create cycle in a loop until it acquires a valid handle. Normally **WaitNamedPipe** considers a pipe available only when the server calls **ConnectNamedPipe** to wait for a link. The two commands work together to synchronize server and client. If, however, the server creates a new pipe and has never connected to any client, **WaitNamedPipe** returns **TRUE** even without a matching **ConnectNamedPipe**. The purpose behind the apparent inconsistency is to guarantee that **WaitNamedPipe** connects only at times when the server knows its pipe is available. If a client breaks a connection the server may not realize it right away, and if another client connected immediately the server could not know it had a new partner. By recognizing only new pipes and pipes made available through **ConnectNamedPipe**, **WaitNamedPipe** prevents clients from sneaking in to the middle of a running conversation.

WaitForSingleObject does not work with pipes because pipes do not have signal states.

Closing a Connection

A client breaks its connection by calling **CloseHandle**. A server may do the same, but sometimes it may prefer to disconnect without destroying the pipe, saving it for later reuse. By calling **DisconnectNamedPipe** the server forces the conversation to end and invalidates the client's handle.

```
BOOL DisconnectNamedPipe( HANDLE hNamedPipe );
```

If the client tries to read or write with its handle after the server disconnects, the client receives an error result. The client must still call **CloseHandle**, however. Any data lingering unread in the pipe is lost when the connection ends. A friendly server can protect the last messages by calling **FlushFileBuffers** first.

```
BOOL FlushFileBuffers( HANDLE hFile );
```

When **FlushFileBuffers** receives a handle to a named pipe, it blocks until the pipe's buffers are empty.

Disconnecting a pipe from its client does not destroy the pipe object. After breaking a connection, the server should call **ConnectNamedPipe** to await a new connection on the freed pipe or else call **CloseHandle** to destroy that instance. Clients blocked on **WaitNamedPipe** do not unblock when a client closes its pipe handle. The server must disconnect its end and call **ConnectNamedPipe** to listen for a new client.

Making Transactions

Two more commands facilitate conversations through duplex pipes by combining a read and a write operation into a single *transaction*. Transactions are particularly efficient over networks because they minimize the number of transmissions. In order to support reciprocal transactions, a pipe must be named and must use the PIPE_ACCESS_DUPLEX flag, the message type, and the message-read mode. The server sets all those attributes with **CreateNamedPipe**. The client can adjust the attributes, if necessary, with **SetNamedPipeHandleState**. The blocking mode has no effect on transaction commands.

The first command, **TransactNamedPipe**, sends a request and waits for a response. Clients and servers both may use the command, though clients tend to find it more useful.

```
BOOL TransactNamedPipe(
    HANDLE hNamedPipe,              // handle of named pipe
    LPVOID lpvWriteBuf,            // buffer holding information to send
    DWORD dwWriteBufSize,         // size of the write buffer in bytes
    LPVOID lpvReadBuf,            // buffer for information received
    DWORD dwReadBufSize,         // size of the read buffer in bytes
    LPDWORD lpdwBytesRead,      // bytes actually read (value returned)
    LPOVERLAPPED lpOverlapped );  // info for asynchronous I/O
```

In spite of its many parameters, the function is straightforward. It writes the contents of lpvWriteBuf into the pipe, waits for the next response, and copies the message it receives into the lpvReadBuf buffer. The function fails if the pipe has the wrong attributes or if the read buffer is too small to accommodate the entire message. In that case **GetLastError** returns ERROR_MORE_DATA, and you should finish the reading with **ReadFile** or **PeekNamedPipe**.

TransactNamedPipe handles one exchange through a pipe. After establishing a connection, a program might call **TransactNamedPipe** many times before disconnecting. Another command, **CallNamedPipe**, works for clients that need a pipe for only a single transaction. **CallNamedPipe** connects, reads from, writes to, and closes the pipe handle all at once.

```
BOOL CallNamedPipe(
    LPTSTR lpszPipeName,     // points to string naming a pipe object
    LPVOID lpvWriteBuf,     // buffer holding information to send
    DWORD dwWriteBuf,      // size of the write buffer in bytes
```

```
LPVOID lpvReadBuf,        // buffer for information received
DWORD dwReadBuf,          // size of the read buffer in bytes
LPDWORD lpdwRead,         // bytes actually read (value returned)
DWORD dwTimeout );        // maximum wait time in milliseconds
```

CallNamedPipe expects in its first parameter the name of a pipe that already exists. Only clients call this function. Most of the other parameters supply the buffers needed to perform both halves of a transaction. **CallNamedPipe** condenses into a single call a whole series of commands: **WaitNamedPipe**, **CreateFile**, **WriteFile**, **ReadFile**, and **CloseHandle**. The final parameter, dwTimeout, sets the maximum waiting period for the **WaitNamedPipe** part of this transaction.

If the read buffer is too small to hold an entire message, the command reads what it can and returns **FALSE**. **GetLastError** reports **ERROR_MORE_DATA**, but because the pipe has already been closed the extra data is lost.

Disguising the Server

Often a client sends through a pipe commands or requests for the server to perform some action on its behalf. The client might, for example, ask the server to retrieve information from a file. Because the client and the server are different processes they may also have different security clearances. A server might want to refuse to perform commands for which the client lacks adequate clearance. The server may temporarily assume the client's security attributes before complying with a request and then restore its own attributes after responding. The commands that modify the server's security attributes are

```
BOOL ImpersonateNamedPipeClient( HANDLE hNamedPipe );

BOOL RevertToSelf( void );
```

The impersonation command fails on anonymous pipes, and it will not allow the server to impersonate the client on remote machines. The command temporarily modifies the security context of the thread that calls it. A similar function, **Dde-ImpersonateClient**, allows servers conversing with DDE clients to modify their own security context, too. (DDE conversations are the topic of Chapter 13.) **Revert-ToSelf** ends the masquerade and restores the original security context.

Destroying a Pipe

Like most of the objects we've discussed so far, a pipe object remains in memory until all the handles to it are closed. Whenever any process finishes with its end of a pipe, it should call **CloseHandle**. If you forget, the **ExitProcess** command closes all your remaining handles for you.

Distinguishing Pipes and Mailslots

Pipes are very similar to another object called a mailslot, so we offer here a short description to help you distinguish between them. Like a pipe, a mailslot is a buffer where processes leave messages for each other. Mailslots, however, always work in only one direction, and many applications may open the receiving end of the same mailslot. A program that opens a handle to receive messages in a mailslot is a mailslot server. A program that opens a handle to broadcast messages through a mailslot is the client. When a client writes to a mailslot, copies of the message are posted to every server with a handle to the same mailslot. A pipe takes information from one end and delivers it to the other end. A mailslot takes information from one end and delivers it to many other ends.

Mailslots have string names just as named pipes do. The commands for mailslot operations resemble the pipe API. To create a server's read-only mailslot handle, call **CreateMailslot**. To retrieve or modify its attributes, call **GetMailslotInfo** and **SetMailslotInfo**. To create the client's write-only mailslot handle, call **CreateFile**. To send and receive mailslot messages, call **WriteFile** and **ReadFile**. To destroy a mailslot, close its handles with **CloseHandle**.

Besides the advantage of broadcasting a message to multiple recipients, mailslots make it easier to connect with processes over a network. In order for a pipe client to connect with a remote server, the client must first ascertain the name of the server's machine, which may require a slow enumeration of network servers and repeated attempts to connect with each until the pipe is found. But in naming a mailslot for **CreateFile**, the mailslot client may use an asterisk (*) to represent the current network domain. (A *domain* is any group of linked workstations and network servers to which an administrator has assigned a common name. One network system may contain a single all-inclusive domain, or it may be divided into several associated domains.)

```
\\*\mailslot\<mailslotname>
```

The handle the client receives using a name of that form broadcasts messages to all processes in the current domain that have opened a mailslot using the <mailslotname> string. This ability to broadcast across a domain suggests one of the ways mailslots might be used. Processes that want to connect through a remote pipe link may prefer to find each other through a mailslot first. Both open a mailslot with the same name, and the client broadcasts the name of its pipe, including in the name string the name of its own network server. The recipient uses the broadcast string to connect with the pipe and avoids laboriously enumerating all the available servers. They find each other through a one-way mailslot and then establish a private two-way pipe to continue the conversation.

CODE: TWO VERSIONS OF THE PROCESS PROGRAM

We've written two versions of a sample program called Process. In both a parent process creates a child process and communicates with it through a pipe. The first version uses an anonymous pipe and the second a named pipe. A command on the parent's menu lets the user launch the child process. Once both are running, the user selects shapes, colors, and sizes from the parent program's menu. The parent sends the command information through a pipe and the client draws the requested shape. In the second version, the user may launch several children and the parent creates multiple instances of its pipe.

The Anonymous Pipe Version

Anonymous pipes are the easiest way to establish single-instance one-way communication between related processes on the same machine. (With two anonymous pipes you can communicate in both directions.) The Parent and Child program windows of the anonymous pipe program appear in Figure 5.1. The user has selected a small blue ellipse from the parent's menu and the resulting shape appears in the child's window.

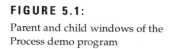

FIGURE 5.1:

Parent and child windows of the
Process demo program

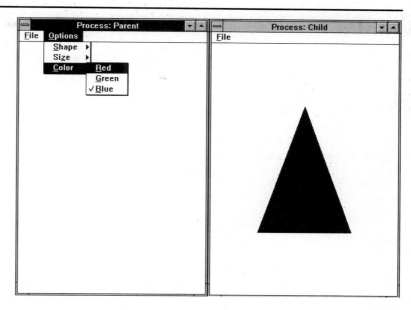

The Parent Process

The files that compose the parent process are parent.h, parent.rc, and parent.c. The child process files are child.h, child.rc, and child.c. The two programs together share an additional header, global.h, which defines structures and values both processes use to communicate with each other. When the parent puts command information into the pipe it uses a descriptive structure called FIGURE. A FIGURE variable holds values that represent commands from the parent's menu. The commands determine the shape, size, and color of the figure the child should draw. The global.h file, included at the top of both parent.c and child.c, makes the shared definitions available to both programs. The first listing includes a make file for the parent and child both, the parent and global headers, and the parent's resource script.

```
#
#   NMake file for the PARENT and CHILD halves of the PROCESS demo
#


#
#   Set targets and dependencies
#
```

```
all: parent.exe child.exe
parent.exe: parent.obj parent.rbj
child.exe: child.obj child.rbj

#
#   Define macros for command-line options and library modules
#

!IFDEF NODEBUG
CFLAGS = -c -G3 -Os -W3 -D_X86_=1 -DWIN32 =D_MT
LFLAGS = -subsystem:windows
!ELSE
CFLAGS = -c -G3 -Od -W4 -Zi -D_X86_=1 -DWIN32 =D_MT
LFLAGS = -debug:full -debugtype:cv -subsystem:windows
!ENDIF

LIBS = libcmt.lib ntdll.lib kernel32.lib user32.lib gdi32.lib


#
#   Define compiling rules
#

.c.obj:
   cl386 $(CFLAGS) $*.c

.rc.rbj:
   rc $*.rc
   cvtres -i386 $*.res -o $*.rbj

.obj.exe:
   link32 $(LFLAGS) -out:$*.exe $*.obj $*.rbj $(LIBS)

=======================================================================

/*---------------------------------------------------------------

       PARENT.H [anonymous pipe version]

       Header file for the parent process half of the PROCESS
       demo program.
       ---------------------------------------------------------*/


/*---------------------------------------------------------------

       CONSTANTS
       ---------------------------------------------------------*/
```

```
#define MAX_BUFFER          64          // maximum string size

/*-----------------------------------------------------------------
          RESOURCE IDs
-------------------------------------------------------------*/

#define DLG_ABOUT           100         // about box template
#define MENU_MAIN           200         // menu template

// A few menu command IDs are in this file. The others are in
// the global.h header, read by both child.c and parent.c

#define IDM_START           100         // menu command IDs
#define IDM_ABOUT           1100
#define IDM_EXIT            1200

#define IDS_APPNAME         100         // string IDs
#define IDS_TITLE           200
#define IDS_PROCESS         300

/*-----------------------------------------------------------------
          FUNCTION PROTOTYPES
-------------------------------------------------------------*/

BOOL Init( void );
LRESULT WINAPI Parent_WndProc( HWND hWnd , UINT uMessage, WPARAM wParam,
    LPARAM lParam );
void Parent_OnInitMenu( HWND hWnd, HMENU hMenu );
void Parent_OnCommand( HWND hWnd, int iCmd, HWND hWndCtl, UINT uCode );
void Parent_OnDestroy( HWND hWnd );
BOOL CreateMainWindow( void );
void StartProcess( void );
void ChangeShape( int iCmd );
void ChangeSize( int iCmd );
void ChangeColor( int iCmd );
BOOL SendCommand( void );
BOOL WINAPI About_DlgProc( HWND hDlg, UINT uMessage, WPARAM wParam,
    LPARAM lParam );
void ShowErrorMsg( void );

=================================================================
```

```
/*-------------------------------------------------------------------

        GLOBAL.H  [anonymous pipe version]

        Header file definitions common to both halves of the
        PROCESS demo program.
     --------------------------------------------------------------*/


// The parent process uses the following numbers as menu command IDs.
// It also records some of them in a FIGURE structure that gets passed
// through the pipe to the child. The child reads these values to
// find out what it should draw.

#define IDM_TERMINATE        200      // draw this "shape" to make child quit
#define IDM_ELLIPSE          300      // other shapes to draw
#define IDM_RECTANGLE        400
#define IDM_TRIANGLE         500

#define IDM_SMALL            600      // size of shape
#define IDM_LARGE            700

#define IDM_RED              800      // color for shape
#define IDM_GREEN            900
#define IDM_BLUE            1000

/* the structure used to pass information about a figure to the child */
typedef struct Figure
{
    int iShape;
    int iSize;
    int iColor;
} FIGURE, *PFIGURE;


=========================================================================


/*-------------------------------------------------------------------

        PARENT.RC  [anonymous pipe version]

        Resource script for the parent half of the PROCESS demo.
     --------------------------------------------------------------*/


#include <windows.h>
#include "parent.h"
#include "global.h"                  // values shared with the child program
```

```
/* a table of all the strings parent uses */
STRINGTABLE
BEGIN
    IDS_APPNAME,     "parent"
    IDS_TITLE,       "Process: Parent"
    IDS_PROCESS,     "child.exe"
END

MENU_MAIN MENU
BEGIN
    POPUP   "&File"
    BEGIN
        MENUITEM "&Start child",        IDM_START
        MENUITEM "&Terminate child",    IDM_TERMINATE
        MENUITEM SEPARATOR
        MENUITEM "&About...",           IDM_ABOUT
        MENUITEM "E&xit",               IDM_EXIT
    END

    POPUP     "&Options"
    BEGIN
        POPUP    "&Shape"
         BEGIN
            MENUITEM "&Ellipse",        IDM_ELLIPSE
            MENUITEM "&Rectangle",      IDM_RECTANGLE
            MENUITEM "&Triangle",       IDM_TRIANGLE
        END

        POPUP     "Si&ze"
        BEGIN
            MENUITEM "S&mall",          IDM_SMALL,
            MENUITEM "&Large",          IDM_LARGE
        END

        POPUP     "&Color"
        BEGIN
            MENUITEM "&Red",            IDM_RED,
            MENUITEM "&Green",          IDM_GREEN
            MENUITEM "&Blue",           IDM_BLUE
        END
    END
END

/* template for the about dialog box */
DLG_ABOUT DIALOG 17, 18, 114, 68
```

```
STYLE DS_MODALFRAME ¦ WS_POPUP ¦ WS_VISIBLE ¦ WS_CAPTION ¦ WS_SYSMENU
CAPTION "About Process"
FONT 8, "Helv"
BEGIN
    CTEXT               "Process Demonstration (Parent)",-1, 0, 7, 114, 8
    CTEXT               "by",               -1, 0, 15, 114, 8
    CTEXT               "Myers && Hamer",   -1, 0, 25, 114, 8
    CTEXT               "version 1.0",      -1, 0, 35, 114, 8
    LTEXT               "©1993",            -1, 12, 51, 25, 8
    DEFPUSHBUTTON       "OK", IDOK, 81, 50, 30, 14, WS_GROUP
END
```

Initializing

The global variables at the top of parent.c include a handle for the child process, a handle for the pipe, and a FIGURE variable. These are the three pieces of information the parent needs to communicate with its child. WinMain initializes figure to describe a small red rectangle.

```
/*-------------------------------------------------------------------

    PARENT.C   [anonymous pipe version]

    Contains the parent process for the PROCESS demo program.
    In this version, the two processes communicate through
    an anonymous pipe.

    FUNCTIONS
        WinMain             receive and dispatch messages
        Init                initialize program data
        CreateMainWindow    create main overlapping window
        Parent_WndProc      sort out messages for main window
        Parent_OnInitMenu   update status of all menu commands
        Parent_OnCommand    process menu commands
        Parent_OnDestroy    end program
        ChangeShape         store new shape choice
        ChangeSize          store new size choice
        ChangeColor         store new color choice
        StartProcess        start child process
        SendCommand         tell the child process what to draw
        About_DlgProc       sort out messages for About box
        ShowErrorMsg        call GetLastError and display the message
```

```
           from Programming for Windows NT
           copyright 1993 by Brian Myers & Eric Hamer

    ------------------------------------------------------------*/

#define STRICT
#include <windows.h>
#include <windowsx.h>
#include <memory.h>                    // memset()
#include "parent.h"
#include "global.h"

/*------------------------------------------------------------
          GLOBAL VARIABLES
    ------------------------------------------------------------*/
HWND          hwndMain;                // main overlapping window
HINSTANCE     hInst;                   // current instance
HANDLE        hProcess = NULL;         // the child process
HANDLE        hpipeWrite;              // handle for outbound pipe (uninheritable)
FIGURE        figure;                  // stores current menu choices

/*------------------------------------------------------------
          WIN MAIN
          Calls initializing procedures and runs the message loop
    ------------------------------------------------------------*/

int WINAPI WinMain (
    HINSTANCE hinstThis,               // handle to this instancee
    HINSTANCE hinstPrev,               // NULL if no previous instance
    LPSTR lpszCmdLine,                 // points to command line
    int iCmdShow )                     // initial window status
{
    MSG msg;

    hInst  = hinstThis;

    // This global FIGURE structure records whatever choices
    // the user makes to choose the shape, size, and color
    // of the figure drawn in the client's window. Here
    // we initialize it to the program's startup defaults.

    figure.iShape = IDM_RECTANGLE;        // draw a rectangle
    figure.iSize  = IDM_SMALL;            // don't fill the whole window
    figure.iColor = IDM_RED;              // make the rectangle red
```

217

```
    if (!Init( ))                          // register/create window
    {
        return( 0 );                       // initialization failed
    }

    /* show the main window */
    ShowWindow( hwndMain, iCmdShow );
    UpdateWindow( hwndMain );

    /* receive and translate messages */
    while (GetMessage( &msg, NULL, 0, 0 ))
    {
        TranslateMessage( &msg );
        DispatchMessage( &msg );
    }

    return( msg.wParam );
    UNREFERENCED_PARAMETER(hinstPrev);
    UNREFERENCED_PARAMETER(lpszCmdLine);
}

/*----------------------------------------------------------------
        INIT
        Register the window classes and then create the windows.
    ------------------------------------------------------------*/

BOOL Init ( void )
{
    WNDCLASS wc;
    char szAppName[MAX_BUFFER];
    char szTitle[MAX_BUFFER];

    LoadString( hInst, IDS_APPNAME, szAppName,  sizeof(szAppName) );
    LoadString( hInst, IDS_TITLE,   szTitle,    sizeof(szTitle) );

    /* register the main window class*/
    wc.lpszClassName   = szAppName;
    wc.hInstance       = hInst;
    wc.lpfnWndProc     = Parent_WndProc;
    wc.hCursor         = LoadCursor( NULL, IDC_ARROW );
    wc.hIcon           = LoadIcon( NULL, IDI_APPLICATION );
    wc.lpszMenuName    = MAKEINTRESOURCE( MENU_MAIN );
    wc.hbrBackground   = (HBRUSH)(COLOR_WINDOW + 1);
    wc.style           = CS_HREDRAW | CS_VREDRAW;
    wc.cbClsExtra      = 0;
```

```
    wc.cbWndExtra        = 0;

    if (!RegisterClass( &wc ))
    {
        return( FALSE );
    }

    return( CreateMainWindow( ) );
}

/*-------------------------------------------------------------------
        CREATE MAIN WINDOW
        Create the program's main overlapping window.
   ----------------------------------------------------------------*/

BOOL CreateMainWindow()
{
    char szAppName[MAX_BUFFER];
    char szTitle[MAX_BUFFER];

    /* load the relevant strings */
    LoadString( hInst, IDS_APPNAME, szAppName,  sizeof(szAppName));
    LoadString( hInst, IDS_TITLE,   szTitle,    sizeof(szTitle));

    /* create the parent window */
    hwndMain = CreateWindow( szAppName, szTitle,
        WS_OVERLAPPEDWINDOW | WS_CLIPCHILDREN,
        CW_USEDEFAULT, CW_USEDEFAULT, CW_USEDEFAULT, CW_USEDEFAULT,
        NULL, NULL, hInst, NULL );

    /* return FALSE for an error */
    return( hwndMain != NULL );
}
```

Responding to System Messages

The window procedure looks for only three messages. When the user begins to make a menu choice, the parent program intercepts **WM_INITMENU** to update the appearance of the menu. If the child process does not exist, then the parent disables the commands that work only with the child present: Terminate and all the shape options. The **WM_INITMENU** handler also puts check marks by all the options currently selected. The second message handler responds to **WM_COMMAND** messages from the menu. The user gives commands to start or terminate the child, to modify the shape the child draws, and to close the parent program. If the user makes any selection from the Options menu, SendCommand writes the updated figure variable into the pipe.

The third message handler ends the parent program in response to **WM_DESTROY**.

```
/*------------------------------------------------------------
        PARENT_WNDPROC
        This is where the messages for the main window are processed.
        ----------------------------------------------------------*/

LRESULT WINAPI Parent_WndProc (
    HWND hWnd,                       // message address
    UINT uMessage,                   // message type
    WPARAM wParam,                   // message contents
    LPARAM lParam )                  // more contents
{
    switch (uMessage)
    {
        HANDLE_MSG( hWnd, WM_INITMENU, Parent_OnInitMenu );

        HANDLE_MSG( hWnd, WM_COMMAND, Parent_OnCommand );

        HANDLE_MSG( hWnd, WM_DESTROY, Parent_OnDestroy );

        default:
            return( DefWindowProc(hWnd, uMessage, wParam, lParam );
    }

    return( OL );
}

/*------------------------------------------------------------
        PARENT_ONINITMENU
        Check whether the child process exists and enable or
        disable the Start, Terminate, and Options commands
        accordingly. Also put check marks on the option commands
        that reflect the user's most recent choices.
        ----------------------------------------------------------*/

void Parent_OnInitMenu (
    HWND hWnd,
    HMENU hMenu )
{
```

```
// While the child process does not exist, some of our
// menu commands make no sense and should be disabled.
// These include the Terminate command and the figure
// options commands.

/* get a handle to the options popup menu */
HMENU hmenuOptions = GetSubMenu( hMenu, 1 );

if (hProcess)
{
    /* child process exists; enable Terminate and shape options */
    EnableMenuItem( hMenu, IDM_START, MF_GRAYED );
    EnableMenuItem( hMenu, IDM_TERMINATE, MF_ENABLED );
    EnableMenuItem( hmenuOptions, 0, MF_ENABLED | MF_BYPOSITION );
    EnableMenuItem( hmenuOptions, 1, MF_ENABLED | MF_BYPOSITION );
    EnableMenuItem( hmenuOptions, 2, MF_ENABLED | MF_BYPOSITION );
}
else
{
    /* child process does not exist; disable Terminate and shape options */
    EnableMenuItem( hMenu, IDM_START, MF_ENABLED );
    EnableMenuItem( hMenu, IDM_TERMINATE, MF_GRAYED );
    EnableMenuItem( hmenuOptions, 0, MF_GRAYED | MF_BYPOSITION );
    EnableMenuItem( hmenuOptions, 1, MF_GRAYED | MF_BYPOSITION );
    EnableMenuItem( hmenuOptions, 2, MF_GRAYED | MF_BYPOSITION );
}

/* set a check mark on one of the three shape commands */
CheckMenuItem( hMenu, IDM_ELLIPSE, ((figure.iShape == IDM_ELLIPSE)
                ? (int)MF_CHECKED : (int)MF_UNCHECKED) );
CheckMenuItem( hMenu, IDM_RECTANGLE, ((figure.iShape == IDM_RECTANGLE)
                ? (int)MF_CHECKED : (int)MF_UNCHECKED) );
CheckMenuItem( hMenu, IDM_TRIANGLE, ((figure.iShape == IDM_TRIANGLE)
                ? (int)MF_CHECKED : (int)MF_UNCHECKED) );

/* set a check mark on one of the two size commands */
CheckMenuItem( hMenu, IDM_SMALL, ((figure.iSize == IDM_SMALL)
                ? (int)MF_CHECKED : (int)MF_UNCHECKED) );
CheckMenuItem( hMenu, IDM_LARGE, ((figure.iSize == IDM_LARGE)
                ? (int)MF_CHECKED : (int)MF_UNCHECKED) );

/* set a check mark on one of the three color commands */
CheckMenuItem( hMenu, IDM_RED, ((figure.iColor == IDM_RED)
                ? (int)MF_CHECKED : (int)MF_UNCHECKED) );
CheckMenuItem( hMenu, IDM_GREEN, ((figure.iColor == IDM_GREEN)
```

```
                     ? (int)MF_CHECKED : (int)MF_UNCHECKED) );
    CheckMenuItem( hMenu, IDM_BLUE, ((figure.iColor == IDM_BLUE)
                     ? (int)MF_CHECKED : (int)MF_UNCHECKED) );


    return;
    UNREFERENCED_PARAMETER( hWnd );
}
/*-------------------------------------------------------------------

        PARENT_ONCOMMAND
        Process commands from the menu.
    ---------------------------------------------------------------*/


void Parent_OnCommand (
    HWND hWnd,
    int iCmd,
    HWND hwndCtl,
    UINT uCode )
{
    switch (iCmd)
    {

        /* start the drawing process */
        case IDM_START:
            StartProcess( );
            break;

        /* send the figure data through the pipe */
        case IDM_ELLIPSE:
        case IDM_RECTANGLE:
        case IDM_TRIANGLE:
        case IDM_TERMINATE:           // when child sees TERMINATE it quits
            ChangeShape( iCmd );
            break;

        /* adjust the size of the figure */
        case IDM_SMALL:
        case IDM_LARGE:
            ChangeSize( iCmd );
            break;

        /* change the color of the figure */
        case IDM_RED:
        case IDM_BLUE:
        case IDM_GREEN:
```

```
            ChangeColor( iCmd );
            break;

        /* show the about dialog box */
        case IDM_ABOUT:
                    DialogBox( hInst, MAKEINTRESOURCE(DLG_ABOUT),
                               hWnd, About_DlgProc );
                    break;

        /* exit from the program */
        case IDM_EXIT:
            DestroyWindow( hWnd );                    // destroy program window
            break;

        default:
            break;
    }

    return;
    UNREFERENCED_PARAMETER( hwndCtl );
    UNREFERENCED_PARAMETER( uCode );
}

/*------------------------------------------------------------------
        PARENT_ONDESTROY
        Post the quit message.
    ------------------------------------------------------------*/

void Parent_OnDestroy ( HWND hWnd )
{
    PostQuitMessage(0);

    return;
    UNREFERENCED_PARAMETER( hWnd );
}

/*------------------------------------------------------------------
        CHANGE SHAPE
        Record a shape command from the user. If the user has
        chosen a new shape, send the updated FIGURE structure
        to the child.
    ------------------------------------------------------------*/

void ChangeShape ( int iCmd )
```

```
{
    if (iCmd != figure.iShape)        // new shape?
    {
        figure.iShape = iCmd;         // record it
        SendCommand( );               // tell child process
    }
    return;
}

/*-------------------------------------------------------------------
        CHANGE SIZE
        Record a size command from the user. If the user has
        chosen a new size, send the updated FIGURE structure to
        the child.
        ----------------------------------------------------------*/

void ChangeSize ( int iCmd )
{
    if (iCmd != figure.iSize)         // new size?
    {
        figure.iSize = iCmd;          // record it
        SendCommand( );               // tell child process
    }
    return;
}

/*-------------------------------------------------------------------
        CHANGE COLOR
        Record a color command from the user. If the user has
        chosen a new color, send the updated FIGURE structure
        to the child.
        ----------------------------------------------------------*/

void ChangeColor ( int iCmd )
{
    if (iCmd != figure.iColor)        // new color?
    {
        figure.iColor = iCmd;         // record it
        SendCommand( );               // tell child process
    }
    return;
}
```

Creating the Pipe and the Child

When the user chooses Start from the File menu, the program calls its **StartProcess** procedure to create the pipe, launch the child, and send the child its first command. Some complications arise in arranging for the child to inherit one end of the pipe.

The **CreatePipe** command must not simply accept the default security attributes, as we have done before, because by default the new handles cannot be inherited. **StartProcess** begins by filling out a **SECURITY_ATTRIBUTES** structure in order to set the **bInheritHandle** field to **TRUE**. If the next command were **CreateProcess**, the new child would automatically inherit copies of both handles, the reading end and the writing end of the pipe.

Unfortunately that's still not quite what we want to happen. The child needs only one handle. Anonymous pipes work only one way, and our child needs only to read from the pipe. It should not inherit **hpipeWrite**. The next command, **DuplicateHandle**, modifies the handle by changing its inheritance attribute. Because the parameter for the copied handle is **NULL**, the command does not actually make a copy; instead, it modifies the original. Now we have a reading handle that can be inherited and a writing handle that cannot.

Generally the child should not inherit handles it does not need. Most objects stay open as long as any process holds an open handle to them. If a child inherits an assortment of extraneous handles, many objects may be forced to linger in memory even after the parent ends. Furthermore, in this particular case, if the child owned handles for both ends of the pipe then it would not know when the parent destroyed its end of the pipe. From the child's point of view the pipe would remain open because someone (itself) still had a handle to the other end. Normally when one process closes its end of a pipe the other process notices because of error results from the read or write commands. That's why we went to the trouble of making sure the child inherits only one of the two pipe handles.

Inheriting a handle is not enough, however, for the handle to be useful. The child still needs to receive the handle explicitly from the parent. In effect, the child inherits only the *right* to use the handle, not the handle itself. More accurately, it receives an entry in its object table but no handle to the entry. The parent must still find a way to pass the handle to the new process. (The system considers the inherited object table entry to be an open handle even though the child has no direct access to it. The handle the parent later passes directly to the child connects with the inherited object table entry and does not count as a separate, new handle.)

Rather than passing a handle on the command line, we have chosen to set it in one of the child's standard I/O device channels. The **STARTUPINFO** procedure passed to **CreateProcess** contains three standard I/O handles. Two are the default handles returned by **GetStdHandle**, but the third is the pipe handle. The child will inherit all three devices. (It will use only the pipe handle, but it's best to pass all three handles through **STARTUPINFO**.)

All in all, the **StartProcess** procedure performs these steps:

1. Loads the string that names the child program's executable file ("child.exe").

2. Creates the pipe with inheritable handles.

3. Modifies the write-only handle with **DuplicateHandle** so it cannot be inherited.

4. Puts the read-only handle in a **STARTUPINFO** variable.

5. Creates the child process, which both inherits the read-only handle and receives a copy of the handle as its own stdin device. (The child inherits no other handles from this parent.)

6. Closes the parent's read-only handle to the pipe. The child has its own copy now, and the parent doesn't need it.

The **STARTUPINFO** structure allows the parent to decide how and where the child's window will appear. Many of the fields, however, apply only to character-based console windows. Our child program uses a graphics window, not a character window. Furthermore, because we have set only one activation flag in the dwFlags field, **CreateProcess** will ignore most of the values anyway. At a minimum, however, you should initialize the cb field, the lpDesktop field, the dwFlags field, and the three reserved fields.

StartProcess checks for errors after almost every command. If any command fails, **StartProcess** closes all the handles created to that point. The ShowErrorMsg procedure, which comes at the end of parent.c, displays a message box describing the last error that occurred.

```
/*-----------------------------------------------------------------
        START PROCESS
        In response to the IDM_START command, launch the child
        process and create the pipe for talking to it.
        -----------------------------------------------------------*/
void StartProcess ( void )
{
    char szProcess[MAX_BUFFER];      // name of child process image
    SECURITY_ATTRIBUTES sa;          // security privileges for handles
    STARTUPINFO sui;                 // info for starting a process
    PROCESS_INFORMATION pi;          // info returned about a process
    int iLen;                        // return value
    BOOL bTest;                      // return value
    HANDLE hpipeRead;                // inbound end of pipe (for client)

    /* load name of process image file from resources */
    iLen = LoadString( hInst, IDS_PROCESS, szProcess, sizeof(szProcess) );
    if (!iLen)
    {
        return;
    }

    /* fill out a SECURITY_ATTRIBUTES structure so handles can be inherited */
    sa.nLength = sizeof(SECURITY_ATTRIBUTES);   // structure size
    sa.lpSecurityDescriptor = NULL;             // default descriptor
    sa.bInheritHandle = TRUE;                   // inheritable

    /* create the pipe */
    bTest = CreatePipe( &hpipeRead,       // reading handle
                &hpipeWrite,              // writing handle
                &sa,                      // lets handles be inherited
                0 );                      // default buffer size
    if (!bTest)
    {
        ShowErrorMsg( );
        return;                           // error during pipe creation
    }

    /* make an uninheritable duplicate of the outbound (write) handle */
    bTest = DuplicateHandle( GetCurrentProcess( ),
        hpipeWrite,                           // original handle
        GetCurrentProcess( ),
        NULL,                                 // don't create new handle
        0,
```

```
    FALSE,                                  // not inheritable
    DUPLICATE_SAME_ACCESS );

if (!bTest)
{
    ShowErrorMsg( );
    CloseHandle( hpipeRead );
    CloseHandle( hpipeWrite );
    return;                                  // duplication failed
}

/* fill in the process's startup information */
memset( &sui, 0, sizeof(STARTUPINFO) );
sui.cb          = sizeof(STARTUPINFO);
sui.dwFlags     = STARTF_USESTDHANDLES;
sui.hStdInput   = hpipeRead;
sui.hStdOutput  = GetStdHandle( STD_OUTPUT_HANDLE );
sui.hStdError   = GetStdHandle( STD_ERROR_HANDLE );

/* create the drawing process */
bTest = CreateProcess( szProcess,           // .EXE image
            NULL,                           // command line
            NULL,                           // process security
            NULL,                           // thread security
            TRUE,                           // inherit handles--yes
            0,                              // creation flags
            NULL,                           // environment block
            NULL,                           // current directory
            &sui,                           // startup info
            &pi );                          // process info (returned)

/* did we succeed in launching the process? */
if (!bTest)
{
    ShowErrorMsg( );                        // creation failed
    CloseHandle( hpipeWrite );
}
else                                        // creation succeeded
{
    hProcess = pi.hProcess;                 // save new process handle
    CloseHandle( pi.hThread );              // discard new thread handle
    figure.iShape = IDM_RECTANGLE;          // reset to default shape
    SendCommand( );                         // tell child what to draw
}
```

```
        CloseHandle( hpipeRead );              // discard receiving end of pipe
        return;
}
```

If the **CreateProcess** command succeeds, StartProcess performs several final actions. First, it looks at the two handles returned in the **PROCESS_INFORMATION** structure. It moves the new process's handle to a global variable. The pi variable also holds a handle to the primary thread of the new child process. Having no use for that handle, the program closes it immediately. Then it closes the handle to the child's end of the pipe and calls SendCommand to tell the child what to draw first.

Resetting the figure variable before SendCommand is very important. The parent process can open and close a child many times in one session. To close the child, the parent puts IDM_TERMINATE in the figure variable and writes that to the pipe. The line that resets figure.iShape to IDM_RECTANGLE ensures that the child will not receive a leftover IDM_TERMINATE command as its first message.

Writing to the Pipe

The parent program sends the child a message immediately after launching the child whenever the user chooses a new shape attribute and when the user chooses Terminate from the Process menu. At each point the program calls SendCommand to put information in the pipe.

```
/*-------------------------------------------------------------------
        SEND COMMAND
        Tell the child program what to draw. Write the current
        contents of the global FIGURE variable into the pipe.

        Return
        TRUE indicates the write operation succeeded. FALSE means
        an error occurred and we have lost contact with the child.
        -------------------------------------------------------------*/

BOOL SendCommand ( void )
{
    BOOL bTest;                          // return value
    DWORD dwWritten;                     // number of bytes written to pipe

    /* pass the choices to the child through the pipe */
    bTest = WriteFile( hpipeWrite,  // anonymous pipe (outbound handle)
            &figure,                 // buffer to write
```

```
                sizeof(FIGURE),       // size of buffer
                &dwWritten,           // bytes written
                NULL );               // overlapping i/o structure

    if (!bTest)                       // did writing succeed?
    {
        // If the write operation failed because the user has
        // already closed the child program, then tell the user
        // the connection was broken. If some less predictable
        // error caused the failure, call ShowErrorMsg as usual
        // to display the system's error message.

        DWORD dwResult = GetLastError();

        if ((dwResult == ERROR_BROKEN_PIPE)    // pipe has been ended
            || (dwResult == ERROR_NO_DATA))    // pipe close in progress
        {
            /* presumably the user closed the child */
            MessageBox( hwndMain, "Connection with child was already broken.",
                "Parent Message", MB_ICONEXCLAMATION | MB_OK );
        }
        else    // an unpredictable error occurred
        {
            ShowErrorMsg( );
        }
    }

    // If a write error occurred, or if we just sent an IDM_TERMINATE
    // command to make the child quit, then in either case we break
    // off communication with the child process.

    if ((!bTest) || (figure.iShape == IDM_TERMINATE))
    {
        CloseHandle( hProcess );          // forget about the child
        hProcess = NULL;
        CloseHandle( hpipeWrite );        // destroy the pipe
    }

    return( bTest );
}
```

The **WriteFile** command may fail for any of several reasons. One likely problem arises if the user closes the child program from the child's menu. The parent does not know the child is gone until it tries to write to the pipe and receives an error. In that case the **GetLastError** function, which returns a number identifying whatever error last occurred in a given thread, indicates either **ERROR_BROKEN_PIPE** or **ERROR_NO_DATA**. Instead of handling these results like any other error, SendCommand raises a message box explaining that the connection has been broken. If the pipe fails for any reason at all, however, the parent makes no effort to reestablish contact. It closes the pipe handle and the child process handle. The program also resets the process handle to **NULL**, which **CloseHandle** does not do. The Parent_OnInitMenu message handler relies on the value of hProcess to determine whether the child still exists.

```
/*------------------------------------------------------------
        ABOUT BOX DIALOG PROCEDURE
        Process messages for the About box window here.
        ----------------------------------------------------------*/

BOOL WINAPI About_DlgProc (
    HWND hDlg,
    UINT uMessage,
    WPARAM wParam,
    LPARAM lParam )
{
    switch (uMessage)
    {
        case WM_INITDIALOG:
            return( TRUE );

        case WM_COMMAND:
            EndDialog( hDlg, TRUE );
            return( TRUE );
    }

    return( FALSE );
    UNREFERENCED_PARAMETER(wParam);
    UNREFERENCED_PARAMETER(lParam);
}


/*------------------------------------------------------------
        SHOW ERROR MESSAGE
        ----------------------------------------------------------*/

void ShowErrorMsg ( void )
{
    LPVOID lpvMessage;                          // temporary message buffer
```

```
/* retrieve a message from the system message table */
FormatMessage(
    FORMAT_MESSAGE_ALLOCATE_BUFFER ¦ FORMAT_MESSAGE_FROM_SYSTEM,
    NULL,                                   // ignored
    GetLastError(),                         // message ID
    MAKELANGID(LANG_ENGLISH, SUBLANG_ENGLISH_US),   // message language
    (LPTSTR)&lpvMessage,                    // address of buffer pointer
    0,                                      // minimum buffer size
    NULL );                                 // no other arguments

/* display the message in a message box */
MessageBox( hwndMain, lpvMessage, "Parent Message",
        MB_ICONEXCLAMATION ¦ MB_OK );

/* release the buffer FormatMessage allocated */
LocalFree( lpvMessage );

return;
}
```

ShowErrorMsg is built around the **FormatMessage** command, which chooses a message from the system's internal message table to describe the most recent error. (The most recent error value is maintained separately for each thread.) Given the flags we've set in its first parameter, **FormatMessage** dynamically allocates a message buffer and puts the address in the lpvMessage variable. Note that **FormatMessage** wants to receive the *address* of the buffer pointer, not the pointer itself.

The Child

The **CreateProcess** command in the parent's StartProcess procedure launches a program called Child. The parent stores the string "child.exe" in its table of string resources. Here are the auxiliary files for the child program:

```
/*-------------------------------------------------------------------

    CHILD.H   [anonymous pipe version]

    Header file for the child process half of the PROCESS
    demo program.
    -----------------------------------------------------------------*/
```

```
/*-------------------------------------------------------------------
          CONSTANTS
   ---------------------------------------------------------------*/

#define MAX_BUFFER          64        // maximum string size

/*-------------------------------------------------------------------
          RESOURCE IDs
   ---------------------------------------------------------------*/

#define DLG_ABOUT           100       // about box template
#define MENU_MAIN           200       // menu template

#define IDM_ABOUT           200       // menu command IDs
#define IDM_EXIT            300
#define IDM_READ            400

#define IDS_APPNAME         100       // string IDs
#define IDS_TITLE           200


/*-------------------------------------------------------------------
          FUNCTION PROTOTYPES
   ---------------------------------------------------------------*/

BOOL Init( void );
LRESULT WINAPI Child_WndProc( HWND hWnd , UINT uMessage, WPARAM wParam,
    LPARAM lParam );
BOOL Child_OnCreate( HWND hWnd, LPCREATESTRUCT lpCreateStruct );
void Child_OnPaint( HWND hWnd );
void Child_OnCommand( HWND hWnd, int iCmd, HWND hWndCtl, UINT uCode );
void Child_OnDestroy( HWND hWnd );
BOOL CreateMainWindow( void );
void DoRead( void );
LONG PipeThread( LPVOID lpThreadData );
BOOL WINAPI About_DlgProc( HWND hDlg, UINT uMessage, WPARAM wParam,
    LPARAM lParam );
void ShowErrorMsg( void );


===================================================================

/*-------------------------------------------------------------------
          CHILD.RC   [anonymous pipe version]
          Resource script for the child half of the PROCESS demo.
   ---------------------------------------------------------------*/
```

```
#include <windows.h>
#include "child.h"

/* a table of all the strings Child uses */
STRINGTABLE
BEGIN
    IDS_APPNAME,    "child"
    IDS_TITLE,      "Process: Child"
END

MENU_MAIN MENU
BEGIN
    POPUP   "&File"
    BEGIN
        MENUITEM "&About...",    IDM_ABOUT
        MENUITEM "E&xit",        IDM_EXIT
    END
END

/* template for the about dialog box */
DLG_ABOUT DIALOG 17, 18, 114, 68
STYLE DS_MODALFRAME | WS_POPUP | WS_VISIBLE | WS_CAPTION | WS_SYSMENU
CAPTION "About Process"
FONT 8, "Helv"
BEGIN
    CTEXT           "Process Demonstration (Child)",-1, 0, 7, 114, 8
    CTEXT           "by",               -1, 0, 15, 114, 8
    CTEXT           "Myers && Hamer",   -1, 0, 25, 114, 8
    CTEXT           "version 1.0",      -1, 0, 35, 114, 8
    LTEXT           "©1993",            -1, 12, 51, 25, 8
    DEFPUSHBUTTON   "OK", IDOK, 81, 50, 30, 14, WS_GROUP
END
```

Inheriting a Pipe Handle and Creating a Thread

The anonymous pipe version of Child dedicates a secondary thread to the task of waiting for data to arrive through the pipe. The primary thread processes system messages for the program's window. When the secondary thread receives a new command from the parent, it updates the global variables iShape, iSize, and iColor and then invalidates the window. The primary thread receives a **WM_PAINT** message and redraws the display using the new shape values. The secondary thread runs in a loop that ends when it reads an IDM_TERMINATE command from the pipe.

The first part of our child.c listing includes WinMain, the initialization procedures, and the message handlers. The child performs its most important initialization tasks in response to the **WM_CREATE** message. Child_OnCreate recovers the pipe handle inherited from the parent and creates a new thread to read from the pipe. If either action fails, the procedure returns **FALSE** and the process ends.

To retrieve the pipe handle, the child calls **GetStdHandle**. This command finds the handle that the parent told **CreateProcess** to deposit in the child's stdin device slot. The child creates its secondary pipe-reading thread in a suspended state in order to adjust the thread's priority. Because the primary thread responds to user input, we set the secondary thread to a lower priority. The difference ensures that the child will respond quickly to keyboard and menu input.

The paint procedure is long but straightforward. It simply reads the current values of iShape, iSize, and iColor, creates the pens and brushes it needs, and draws an ellipse, a rectangle, or a triangle.

```
/*------------------------------------------------------------------

    CHILD.C   [anonymous pipe version]

    Contains the child process for the PROCESS demo program.
    The program in parent.c creates this child process.
    In this version, the two processes communicate through
    an anonymous pipe.

    FUNCTIONS
        WinMain             receive and dispatch messages
        Init                initialize program data
        CreateMainWindow    create program's overlapping window
        Child_WndProc       sort out messages for main window
        Child_OnCreate      create named pipe
        Child_OnPaint       draw selected figure
        Child_OnCommand     process menu commands
        Child_OnDestroy     end program
        PipeThread          thread procedure for reading from pipe
        DoRead              procedure to read from pipe
        About_DlgProc       sort out messages for About box
        ShowErrorMsg        calls GetLastError and displays the message
```

```
        from Mastering Windows NT Programming
        copyright 1993 by Brian Myers & Eric Hamer

    ------------------------------------------------------------------*/

#define STRICT
#include <windows.h>
#include <windowsx.h>
#include "child.h"
#include "global.h"              // values common to both processes

/*-----------------------------------------------------------------
          GLOBAL VARIABLES
    ------------------------------------------------------------------*/

HWND        hwndMain;            // main window
HINSTANCE   hInst;              // current instance
HANDLE      hpipeRead;          // handle to the anonymous pipe
HANDLE      hThread;            // thread that reads from pipe
DWORD       dwThreadID;         // ID of pipe thread
int         iShape;            // figure to draw
int         iSize;             // size of figure to draw (SMALL/LARGE)
int         iColor;            // color of figure to draw
BOOL        bTerminate = FALSE; // TRUE when program should end

  /*-----------------------------------------------------------------
          WIN MAIN
          Calls initializing procedures and runs the message loop
    ------------------------------------------------------------------*/

int WINAPI WinMain (
    HINSTANCE hinstThis,        // handle to this instance
    HINSTANCE hinstPrev,        // NULL if no previous inst
    LPSTR lpszCmdLine,          // points to command line
    int iCmdShow )              // initial window status
{
    MSG msg;

    hInst = hinstThis;

    /* iShape = 0 do not draw anything during the first WM_PAINT message */
    iShape = 0;
```

```
    if (!Init( ))
    {
        /* if the application was not initialized, exit here */
        return( 0 );
    }

    /* display the main window */
    ShowWindow( hwndMain, iCmdShow );
    UpdateWindow( hwndMain );

    /* translate the message */
    while (GetMessage( &msg, NULL, 0, 0 ))
    {
        TranslateMessage( &msg );
        DispatchMessage( &msg );
    }

    return( msg.wParam );
    UNREFERENCED_PARAMETER(hinstPrev);
    UNREFERENCED_PARAMETER(lpszCmdLine);
}

/*-------------------------------------------------------------------
        INIT
        Register the window class and then create the window
    ---------------------------------------------------------------*/

BOOL Init ( void )
{
    WNDCLASS wc;
    char szAppName[MAX_BUFFER];
    char szTitle[MAX_BUFFER];

    LoadString( hInst, IDS_APPNAME, szAppName,  sizeof(szAppName) );
    LoadString( hInst, IDS_TITLE,   szTitle,    sizeof(szTitle) );

    /* register the main window class */
    wc.lpszClassName    = szAppName;
    wc.hInstance        = hInst;
    wc.lpfnWndProc      = Child_WndProc;
    wc.hCursor          = LoadCursor(NULL, IDC_ARROW);
    wc.hIcon            = LoadIcon( NULL, IDI_APPLICATION );
    wc.lpszMenuName     = MAKEINTRESOURCE( MENU_MAIN );
    wc.hbrBackground    = (HBRUSH)( COLOR_WINDOW + 1 );
```

237

```
    wc.style              = CS_HREDRAW | CS_VREDRAW;
    wc.cbClsExtra         = 0;
    wc.cbWndExtra         = 0;

    if (!RegisterClass( &wc ))
    {
        return( FALSE );
    }

    /* create the window */
    return( CreateMainWindow( ) );
}

/*------------------------------------------------------------------
        CREATE MAIN WINDOW
        Create the program's overlapping window.
    --------------------------------------------------------------*/

BOOL CreateMainWindow ( void )
{
    char szAppName[MAX_BUFFER];
    char szTitle[MAX_BUFFER];

    /* load the relevant strings */
    LoadString( hInst, IDS_APPNAME, szAppName,  sizeof(szAppName) );
    LoadString( hInst, IDS_TITLE,   szTitle,    sizeof(szTitle) );

    /* create the parent window */
    hwndMain = CreateWindow( szAppName, szTitle,
        WS_OVERLAPPEDWINDOW | WS_CLIPCHILDREN,
        CW_USEDEFAULT, CW_USEDEFAULT, CW_USEDEFAULT, CW_USEDEFAULT,
        NULL, NULL, hInst, NULL);

    /* return FALSE for an error */
    return( hwndMain != NULL );
}

/*------------------------------------------------------------------
        CHILD_WNDPROC
        This is where the messages for the main window are processed.
    --------------------------------------------------------------*/

LRESULT WINAPI Child_WndProc (
    HWND hWnd,                // message address
    UINT uMessage,            // message type
```

```
    WPARAM wParam,            // message contents
    LPARAM lParam )           // more contents
{
    switch (uMessage)
    {
        HANDLE_MSG( hWnd, WM_CREATE, Child_OnCreate );

        HANDLE_MSG( hWnd, WM_PAINT, Child_OnPaint );

        HANDLE_MSG( hWnd, WM_COMMAND, Child_OnCommand );

        HANDLE_MSG( hWnd, WM_DESTROY, Child_OnDestroy );

        default:
            return( DefWindowProc(hWnd, uMessage, wParam, lParam) );
    }

    return( OL );
}
/*-------------------------------------------------------------

        CHILD_ONCREATE
        On startup open the pipe and start the thread that will
        read from it.
    --------------------------------------------------------------*/
BOOL Child_OnCreate (
    HWND hWnd,
    LPCREATESTRUCT lpCreateStruct )
{
    /* open the pipe for reading */
    hpipeRead = GetStdHandle( STD_INPUT_HANDLE );
    if (hpipeRead == INVALID_HANDLE_VALUE)
    {
        ShowErrorMsg( );
        return( FALSE );
    }

    // Create the thread that will read from the pipe. It is created
    // suspended so its priority can be lowered before it starts.
    hThread = CreateThread( NULL,            // security attributes
                0,                           // initial stack size
                (LPTHREAD_START_ROUTINE)PipeThread,
                NULL,                        // argument
                CREATE_SUSPENDED,            // creation flag
                &dwThreadID );               // new thread's ID
    if (!hThread)
```

```
    {
        ShowErrorMsg( );
        return( FALSE );
    }

    /* lower the thread's priority and let it run */
    SetThreadPriority( hThread, THREAD_PRIORITY_BELOW_NORMAL );
    ResumeThread( hThread );

    return( TRUE );
    UNREFERENCED_PARAMETER(hWnd);
    UNREFERENCED_PARAMETER(lpCreateStruct);
}


/*------------------------------------------------------------------
        CHILD_ONPAINT
        Redraw the window, adding the figure indicated by iShape.
        The IDM_ constants used in this procedure are defined in
        global.h. In the parent process they represent menu
        commands. The parent uses the constants to tell the
        child what to draw.
        ----------------------------------------------------------*/

void Child_OnPaint ( HWND hWnd )
{
    HDC hDC;
    PAINTSTRUCT ps;
    RECT rcClient;          // client area
    COLORREF cr;            // a color
    HBRUSH hBrush;          // a new brush
    HBRUSH hBrushOld;       // the default brush
    HPEN hPen;              // a new pen
    HPEN hPenOld;           // the default pen
    POINT point[3];         // points defining a triangle
    int cxClient;           // width of client area
    int cyClient;           // height of client area

    /* do not draw anything if iShape is zero */
    if (iShape)
    {
        /* set the color according to the data read from the pipe */
        switch (iColor)
        {
            case IDM_RED:
                cr = RGB(255, 0, 0);
```

```
            break;

        case IDM_GREEN:
            cr = RGB(0, 255, 0);
            break;

        default:                         // IDM_BLUE
            cr = RGB(0, 0, 255);
            break;
    }
}

/* draw the figure */
hDC = BeginPaint( hWnd, &ps );
if (hDC)
{
    /* get the window's dimensions */
    GetClientRect( hWnd, &rcClient );
    cxClient = (int)(rcClient.right - rcClient.left);
    cyClient = (int)(rcClient.bottom - rcClient.top);

    /* set the pen and brush to the selected color */
    hBrush = CreateSolidBrush( cr );
    if (hBrush)
    {
        hBrushOld = SelectBrush( hDC, hBrush );
    }

    hPen = CreatePen( PS_SOLID, 0, cr );
    if (hPen)
    {
        hPenOld = SelectObject(hDC, hPen);
    }

    // If iShape is not zero draw either the large or
    // small version of the figure.

    switch (iShape)
    {
        case IDM_ELLIPSE:
            if (iSize == IDM_LARGE)
            {
                Ellipse( hDC,
                    (int)rcClient.left, (int)rcClient.top,
                    (int)rcClient.right, (int)rcClient.bottom );
```

```
    }
    else
    {
        Ellipse( hDC, cxClient / 4, cyClient / 4,
            (3 * cxClient) / 4,
            (3 * cyClient) / 4 );
    }
    break;

case IDM_RECTANGLE:
    if (iSize == IDM_LARGE)
    {
        Rectangle( hDC,
            (int)rcClient.left, (int)rcClient.top,
            (int)rcClient.right, (int)rcClient.bottom );
    }
    else
    {
        Rectangle( hDC, cxClient / 4, cyClient / 4,
            (3 * cxClient) / 4,
            (3 * cyClient) / 4 );
    }
    break;

case IDM_TRIANGLE:
    /* use the polygon function to draw the triangle */
    if (iSize == IDM_LARGE)
    {
        point[0].x = cxClient / 2;
        point[0].y = rcClient.top;

        point[1].x = rcClient.right;
        point[1].y = rcClient.bottom;

        point[2].x = rcClient.left;
        point[2].y = point[1].y;
    }
    else
    {
        point[0].x = cxClient / 2;
        point[0].y = cyClient / 4;

        point[1].x = (3 * cxClient) / 4;
        point[1].y = (3 * cyClient) / 4;
        point[2].x = cxClient / 4;
```

```
                    point[2].y = point[1].y;
                }

                Polygon( hDC, point, 3 );
                break;

            default:
                break;
        }

        /* free the resources */
        if (hBrush)
        {
            DeleteBrush( SelectBrush(hDC, hBrushOld) );
        }

        if (hPen)
        {
            DeletePen( SelectPen(hDC, hPenOld) );
        }
    }

    EndPaint( hWnd, ~ps );            // release the DC
    return;
}

/*------------------------------------------------------------------
        CHILD_ONCOMMAND
        Process commands from the menu.
    -----------------------------------------------------------------*/

void Child_OnCommand (
    HWND hWnd,
    int iCmd,
    HWND hwndCtl,
    UINT uCode)
{

    switch (iCmd)
    {
        /* show the about dialog box */
        case IDM_ABOUT:
            DialogBox( hInst, MAKEINTRESOURCE(DLG_ABOUT),
                    hWnd, About_DlgProc );
            break;
```

```
        /* exit this program */
        case IDM_EXIT:
            bTerminate = TRUE;
            DestroyWindow( hWnd );
            break;

        default:
            break;
    }

    return;
    UNREFERENCED_PARAMETER(hwndCtl);
    UNREFERENCED_PARAMETER(uCode);
}

/*-------------------------------------------------------------------

        CHILD_ONDESTROY
        Post the quit message.
    ----------------------------------------------------------------*/

void Child_OnDestroy ( HWND hWnd )
{
    PostQuitMessage(0);

    return;
    UNREFERENCED_PARAMETER(hWnd);
}
```

Reading from the Pipe

Child_OnCreate designates PipeThread as the main procedure for the secondary thread. The new thread immediately enters a while loop that ends when the global bTerminate flag becomes **TRUE**. The flag changes when the user chooses Exit from the child's menu, when the parent sends an IDM_TERMINATE command, or if the child encounters an error reading from the pipe. When the while loop finally does end, the thread posts a **WM_DESTROY** message to the program window. The secondary thread exits, the primary thread receives the destroy command, and the program ends.

```
/*-----------------------------------------------------------
        PIPE THREAD
        The WM_CREATE handler starts a thread with this procedure
        to manage the pipe connection. This thread waits for
        messages to arrive through the pipe and acts on them.
        ------------------------------------------------------*/

LONG PipeThread ( LPVOID lpThreadData )
{
    /* read from the named pipe until the terminate flag is set to true */
    while (!bTerminate)
    {
        DoRead( );
    }

    /* when bTerminate is TRUE, time to end program */
    FORWARD_WM_DESTROY( hwndMain, PostMessage );

    return( 0L );                          // implicit ExitThread()
    UNREFERENCED_PARAMETER(lpThreadData);
}


/*-----------------------------------------------------------
        DO READ
        Read from the pipe and set the figure to be drawn.
        ------------------------------------------------------*/

void DoRead ( void )
{
    FIGURE figure;
    DWORD dwRead;
    BOOL bTest;

    /* read from the pipe */
    bTest = ReadFile( hpipeRead,          // place to read from
                &figure,                  // buffer to store input
                sizeof(figure),           // bytes to read
                &dwRead,                  // bytes read
                NULL );
    if (bTest)
    {                                          // the read command succeeded
        if (figure.iShape == IDM_TERMINATE) // is the new command Terminate?
        {                                      // YES
            bTerminate = TRUE;                 // set flag to end this thread
        }                                  // NO
```

```
    else                              // thread continues; draw new shape
    {
        /* copy the new shape attributes to global variables */
        iShape = figure.iShape;
        iColor = figure.iColor;
        iSize  = figure.iSize;

        /* force the parent window to repaint itself */
        InvalidateRect( hwndMain, NULL, TRUE );
        UpdateWindow( hwndMain );
    }
}
else                                  // the read command failed
{
    ShowErrorMsg( );                  // tell user what happened
    bTerminate = TRUE;                // let the child end
}
return;
}
```

The while loop in the secondary thread does one thing: It calls DoRead over and over. The DoRead procedure performs one **ReadFile** command, interprets the message, and ends. Each call to DoRead retrieves one more message. Since all anonymous pipes use the waiting mode, the thread blocks on each call to **ReadFile** until data arrives. **ReadFile** may return immediately if the pipe is full or if an error occurs—if, for example, the parent program has already exited and the pipe handle has become invalid.

If the read command succeeds, the child must determine whether it has received a command to terminate or to draw a new shape. If the command fails, the child notifies the user by displaying the system's error message. The child also assumes the connection has been broken and exits.

Although this pipe, like all anonymous pipes, writes and reads in byte mode, our child program still manages always to retrieve exactly one message at a time, even if several messages are waiting. Because the parent always writes exactly sizeof(FIGURE) bytes into the pipe, the child always knows exactly where one message ends and the next begins.

The child program's About_DlgProc and ShowErrorMsg procedures duplicate the corresponding procedures in Parent almost exactly. The full listing of Child appears on the disk accompanying the book.

The Named Pipe Version

An anonymous pipe serves the needs of our Parent and Child programs perfectly well. They communicate in only one direction, use only one instance of the pipe at a time, and both run on the same machine. Our second version of the Process demo, however, allows the parent to create any number of children and communicate with several of them at once. Rather than creating a new anonymous pipe for each client, this version creates two instances of a single named pipe. If the user launches many child processes, only the first two will connect with the parent. The others will block waiting for one of the existing connections to break. Choosing Terminate from the Parent's menu causes all the currently connected children to quit. When the link with one child breaks, that instance of the pipe becomes available for one of the waiting children. In Figure 5.2 the Parent process has launched three children. Two are connected and have drawn the currently selected shape, while the third is waiting for an available pipe instance.

The listings that follow are partial and present only the most important changes for the new version, but the disk accompanying the book contains full listings for both versions.

FIGURE 5.2:

Parent process with three children, only two of which are connected to instances of the named pipe

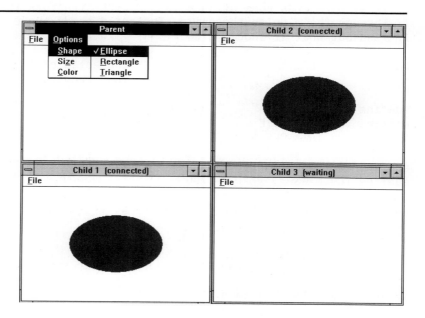

The Parent Process

In order to use a named pipe, both processes must agree on a string to name the pipe they will share. The name string belongs in the string table of both the parent and the child. We've set the string in a shared resource file, global.str, and modified both resource scripts to include it. The shared header file, global.h, adds a new constant to identify the common string resource. Notice that the name string in global.str contains double the expected number of backslashes:

```
IDS_PIPE,          "\\\\.\\pipe\\procdemo"       // name of pipe object
```

The resource compiler uses the backslash character to signal the beginning of an ASCII code sequence. Each pair of backslashes inserts a single literal backslash in the resource string.

```
/*------------------------------------------------------------------
        GLOBAL.H  [named pipe version]

        Header file definitions common to both halves of the
        PROCESS demo program.
        ----------------------------------------------------------*/

// The parent process uses the following numbers as menu command IDs.
// It also records some of them in a FIGURE structure that gets passed
// through the pipe to the child. The child reads these values to
// find out what it should draw.

#define IDM_TERMINATE         200      // connected children exit when
                                       // they receive this command

#define IDM_ELLIPSE           300      // other shapes to draw
#define IDM_RECTANGLE         400
#define IDM_TRIANGLE          500

#define IDM_SMALL             600      // size of shape
#define IDM_LARGE             700

#define IDM_RED               800      // color for shape
#define IDM_GREEN             900
#define IDM_BLUE             1000

// The parent and child share strings in their string table.
// The shared string names the pipe object. This number
// identifies the shared string.
```

```
#define IDS_PIPE              10000

/* the structure used to pass information about a figure to the child */
typedef struct Figure
{
    int iShape;
    int iSize;
    int iColor;
 } FIGURE, *PFIGURE;


=============================================================================

/*---------------------------------------------------------------------
        GLOBAL.STR

        Contains a string that should be included in the string
        tables of both the parent and child halves of the
        PROCESS demo program.
    ----------------------------------------------------------------*/

IDS_PIPE,          "\\\\.\\pipe\\procdemo"       // name of pipe object

=============================================================================

/*---------------------------------------------------------------------
        PARENT.RC [named pipe version]

        Resource script for the parent half of the PROCESS demo.
    ----------------------------------------------------------------*/

#include <windows.h>
#include "parent.h"
#include "global.h"                      // values shared with the child program

/* a table of all the strings list.c uses */
STRINGTABLE
BEGIN
    IDS_APPNAME,    "parent"
    IDS_TITLE,      "Parent"
    IDS_PROCESS,    "child.exe"
    #include "global.str"                // string to name the pipe object
END

MENU_MAIN MENU
BEGIN
```

```
    POPUP   "&File"
    BEGIN
        MENUITEM "&Start child",                IDM_START
        MENUITEM "&Terminate children",         IDM_TERMINATE
        MENUITEM SEPARATOR
        MENUITEM "&About...",                   IDM_ABOUT
        MENUITEM "E&xit",                       IDM_EXIT
    END

    POPUP    "&Options"
    BEGIN
        POPUP    "&Shape"
        BEGIN
            MENUITEM "&Ellipse",     IDM_ELLIPSE
            MENUITEM "&Rectangle",   IDM_RECTANGLE
            MENUITEM "&Triangle",    IDM_TRIANGLE
        END

        POPUP    "Si&ze"
        BEGIN
            MENUITEM "S&mall",       IDM_SMALL,
            MENUITEM "&Large",       IDM_LARGE
        END

        POPUP    "&Color"
        BEGIN
            MENUITEM "&Red",         IDM_RED,
            MENUITEM "&Green",       IDM_GREEN
            MENUITEM "&Blue",        IDM_BLUE
        END
    END
END

/* template for the about dialog box */
DLG_ABOUT DIALOG 17, 18, 114, 68
STYLE DS_MODALFRAME | WS_POPUP | WS_VISIBLE | WS_CAPTION | WS_SYSMENU
CAPTION "About Process"
FONT 8, "Helv"
BEGIN
    CTEXT           "Process Demonstration (Parent)",-1, 0, 7, 114, 8
    CTEXT           "by",                   -1, 0, 15, 114, 8
    CTEXT           "Myers && Hamer",    -1, 0, 25, 114, 8
    CTEXT           "version 1.0",          -1, 0, 35, 114, 8
    LTEXT           "©1993",                -1, 12, 51, 25, 8
    DEFPUSHBUTTON   "OK", IDOK, 81, 50, 30, 14, WS_GROUP
```

```
END

===========================================================================

/*-----------------------------------------------------------------------
          CHILD.RC   [named pipe version]

          Resource script for the child half of the PROCESS demo.
    ---------------------------------------------------------------------*/

#include <windows.h>
#include "child.h"
#include "global.h"

/* a table of all the strings list.c uses */
STRINGTABLE
BEGIN
    IDS_APPNAME,     "child"
    #include "global.str"                 // string to name the pipe object
END

MENU_MAIN MENU
BEGIN
    POPUP   "&File"
    BEGIN
        MENUITEM "&About...",     IDM_ABOUT
        MENUITEM "E&xit",         IDM_EXIT
    END
END

/* template for the about dialog box */
DLG_ABOUT DIALOG 17, 18, 114, 68
STYLE DS_MODALFRAME ¦ WS_POPUP ¦ WS_VISIBLE ¦ WS_CAPTION ¦ WS_SYSMENU
CAPTION "About Process"
FONT 8, "Helv"
BEGIN
    CTEXT              "Process Demonstration (Child)",-1, 0, 7, 114, 8
    CTEXT              "by",                -1, 0, 15, 114, 8
    CTEXT              "Myers && Hamer",   -1, 0, 25, 114, 8
    CTEXT              "version 1.0",      -1, 0, 35, 114, 8
    LTEXT              "©1993",            -1, 12, 51, 25, 8
    DEFPUSHBUTTON      "OK", IDOK, 81, 50, 30, 14, WS_GROUP
END
```

The new parent.h header defines the constant NUM_PIPE_INSTANCES, giving it the value of 2. To have the parent create more instances of its pipe and connect with more children simultaneously, modify the definition.

Creating the Named Pipe

The anonymous pipe parent destroys its pipe each time the child process terminates. If the user launches a new child, the parent creates a new pipe. A named pipe, however, more often lives through several connections with different clients. The named pipe parent creates its pipe instances only once, during initialization. The parent calls its MakePipeInstance procedure twice. Each successive call produces a handle to the program's pipe object and a new thread to support the new instance.

Parent_OnCreate also produces two other important objects, both events. As we explained in Chapter 4, an event object broadcasts a signal to as many threads as happen to be listening. The parent program uses one event to notify its pipe threads whenever the user makes a new choice from the menu. In response, the pipe threads send the new command to their clients. We choose to make it a manual reset event so that all listening pipes will unblock when the signal arrives. (Automatic reset events unblock only one thread on each signal.) The other event coordinates the threads while they are sending termination commands to multiple clients. It too is a manual reset event. This one, however, begins life already in its signaled state. You'll see why in the code for the pipe instance threads.

Because no other processes have any reason to use either event object, the events need no names.

```
/*-------------------------------------------------------------------

    PARENT.C  [named pipe version]

    Contains the parent process for the PROCESS demo program.
    This version communicates with its child process through
    a named pipe.

    FUNCTIONS
        WinMain              receive and dispatch messages
        Init                 initialize program data
        CreateMainWindow     create main overlapping window
        Parent_WndProc       sort out messages for main window
        Parent_OnCreate      create the named pipe
        Parent_OnInitMenu    update status of all menu commands
```

```
            Parent_OnCommand      process menu commands
            Parent_OnDestroy      end program
            ChangeShape           store new shape choice
            ChangeSize            store new size choice
            ChangeColor           store new color choice
            StartProcess          start child process
            MakePipeInstance      create a pipe and a thread to run it
            PipeInstanceThread    starting procedure for pipe-writing threads
            SendCommand           tell the child process what to draw
            About_DlgProc         sort out messages for About box
            ShowErrorMsg          call GetLastError and display the message

        from Mastering Windows NT Programming
        copyright 1993 by Brian Myers & Eric Hamer


    ------------------------------------------------------------------*/

#define STRICT
#include <windows.h>
#include <windowsx.h>
#include "parent.h"
#include "global.h"

/*-----------------------------------------------------------------
        GLOBAL VARIABLES
    ------------------------------------------------------------------*/

HWND        hwndMain;                   // main overlapping window
HINSTANCE   hInst;                      // current instance
FIGURE      figure;                     // stores current menu choices
int         iNumConnections = 0;        // number of connected children
int         iPrevShape;                 // records shape before terminating
HANDLE      hCmdEvent;                  // signals command from user
HANDLE      hNotTerminatingEvent;       // signals termination in progress

/*-----------------------------------------------------------------
        PARENT_WNDPROC
        This is where the messages for the main window are processed.
    ------------------------------------------------------------------*/

LRESULT WINAPI Parent_WndProc (
    HWND hWnd,                  // message address
    UINT uMessage,              // message type
```

```
    WPARAM wParam,              // message contents
    LPARAM lParam )            // more contents
{
    switch (uMessage)
    {
        HANDLE_MSG( hWnd, WM_CREATE, Parent_OnCreate );

        HANDLE_MSG( hWnd, WM_INITMENU, Parent_OnInitMenu );

        HANDLE_MSG( hWnd, WM_COMMAND, Parent_OnCommand );

        HANDLE_MSG( hWnd, WM_DESTROY, Parent_OnDestroy );

        default:
            return( DefWindowProc(hWnd, uMessage, wParam, lParam) );
    }
    return( OL );
}

/*------------------------------------------------------------------
        PARENT_ONCREATE
        Create all the pipe instances and the two event objects used
        to synchronize the program's threads
    ------------------------------------------------------------------*/

BOOL Parent_OnCreate (
    HWND hWnd,
    LPCREATESTRUCT lpcs )
{
    int i;
    int iNumInstances = 0;              // counts instances created

    // Create all the instances of the named pipe. The
    // MakePipeInstance command also starts up a new
    // thread to service each pipe instance.

    for (i = 1; i <= NUM_PIPE_INSTANCES; i++)
    {
        if (MakePipeInstance( ))           // make one instance
        {                                  // if successful,
            iNumInstances++;               // increment counter
        }
    }
```

```
if ( iNumInstances != NUM_PIPE_INSTANCES )   // did we make all of them?
{
    char szBuffer[128];
    wsprintf( szBuffer, "Created only %i instances\n\r", iNumInstances );
    MessageBox( hwndMain, szBuffer, "Parent Message",
                MB_ICONEXCLAMATION | MB_OK );
    return( FALSE );                    // creation failed
}

// Create the event object used for signaling the pipe
// instance threads when the user makes a command.

hCmdEvent = CreateEvent(
            NULL,                   // default security attributes
            TRUE,                   // manual reset event
            FALSE,                  // initially not signaled
            NULL );                 // no name

if (hCmdEvent == NULL)
{
    ShowErrorMsg( );                // event creation failed
    return( FALSE );
}

// Create the event that coordinates the pipe threads when
// the program terminates all linked children. The threads
// block on this event until all the clients have received
// the IDM_TERMINATE message.

hNotTerminatingEvent = CreateEvent(
            NULL,                   // default security attributes
            TRUE,                   // manual reset event
            TRUE,                   // initially signaled
            NULL );                 // no name

if (hNotTerminatingEvent == NULL)
{
    ShowErrorMsg( );                // event creation failed
    return( FALSE );
}

return( TRUE );
UNREFERENCED_PARAMETER(hWnd);
UNREFERENCED_PARAMETER(lpcs);
}
```

```
/*----------------------------------------------------------------
        MAKE PIPE INSTANCE
        Create a new instance of the named pipe.

        Return
        TRUE if the procedure creates a new instance; FALSE if an
        error prevents creation.
        --------------------------------------------------------------*/

BOOL MakePipeInstance ( void )
{
    char szPipe[MAX_BUFFER];        // name of pipe
    int iLen;                       // return value
    HANDLE hPipe;                   // handle to new pipe
    HANDLE hThread;                 // handle to new thread
    DWORD dwThreadID;               // ID of new thread

    /* get name to use for sharing pipe */
    iLen = LoadString( hInst, IDS_PIPE, szPipe, sizeof(szPipe) );
    if (!iLen)
    {
        return( FALSE );
    }

    // Create a new instance of the named pipe. This command will
    // fail if two instances already exist.

    hPipe = CreateNamedPipe( szPipe,            // name
                PIPE_ACCESS_OUTBOUND,           // open mode
                PIPE_TYPE_BYTE | PIPE_READMODE_BYTE | PIPE_WAIT,
                NUM_PIPE_INSTANCES,             // max instances
                0,                              // out buffer size
                0,                              // in buffer size
                0,                              // time out value
                NULL );                         // security attributes

    if (hPipe == INVALID_HANDLE_VALUE)
    {
        ShowErrorMsg( );                        // creation failed
        return( FALSE );
    }

    hThread = CreateThread( NULL,               // security attributes
                0,                              // initial stack size
```

```
                (LPTHREAD_START_ROUTINE)PipeInstanceThread,
                (LPVOID)hPipe,                // argument for thread proc
                CREATE_SUSPENDED,             // creation flag
                &dwThreadID );                // new thread's ID

    if (!hThread)
    {
        ShowErrorMsg( );
        CloseHandle( hPipe );
        return( FALSE );                      // thread creation failed
    }

    /* lower the thread's priority and let it run */
    SetThreadPriority( hThread, THREAD_PRIORITY_BELOW_NORMAL );
    ResumeThread( hThread );

    /* let go of the handle, for which we have no further use */
    CloseHandle( hThread );

    return( TRUE );
}
```

MakePipeInstance begins by loading the resource string that names the pipe object. The subsequent call to **CreateNamedPipe** sets the pipe's attributes. Because the parent and child send information in only one direction, we choose a one-way outbound pipe. For clarity we specify all three mode flags even though the particular characteristics we have chosen—byte mode and wait mode—happen to be the default values. We don't need the message mode because the parent's messages are always the same length. NUM_PIPE_INSTANCES prevents **CreateNamedPipe** from producing more than two handles to this pipe. The first call to **CreateNamedPipe** sets the pipe's maximum number of instances, and subsequent creation commands will fail if they specify a different number. The zero values for the buffer sizes instruct the system to allocate message space dynamically as needed.

For each pipe handle, MakePipeInstance also creates a new thread. The pipe instance thread waits for the user to choose commands from the parent menu and writes the new command into its pipe. We might equally well have stored the pipe handles in an array and created a single thread to write to all the instances on each new command. Again, as with the anonymous pipe child, the program sets secondary threads to a lower priority, reserving normal priority for the primary thread alone—the one thread that responds directly to the user.

This time we pass a parameter to the thread's starting function. A thread function always receives a 32-bit parameter when it starts up, but until now our programs have not used it. Each of our instance threads, however, requires a different pipe handle, so hPipe becomes the fourth parameter of CreateThread.

Launching the Child

When the user chooses the Start command from the parent's File menu, the program calls StartProcess. In this version the Start command is always enabled, permitting the user to launch any number of children. As an exercise in using the command line, the parent passes to each child an identifying number. The first child is 1, the second is 2, and so on. To pass arguments to a child on its command line, ignore the first parameter of CreateProcess and pass the entire command line, including the program name, in the second parameter. Our command-line parameter string looks like this:

```
child.exe 1
```

Use the first parameter, lpszImage, when you have no arguments to pass or do not want the system to search for the child's .EXE file along the system PATH.

Because the children can acquire their own pipe handles with CreateFile, there is no need to arrange for inheritance. Even if the parent program had created inheritable handles, the children would not inherit any of them because we pass **FALSE** as the fifth parameter to **CreateProcess**.

```
/*-------------------------------------------------------------
        START PROCESS
        In response to the IDM_START command, create a new
        child process. The user may create any number of children.
        -------------------------------------------------------------*/

void StartProcess ( void )
{
        static int iChildNum = 1;       // counts child processes

        char szProcess[MAX_BUFFER];     // name of child process image
        STARTUPINFO sui;                // info for starting a process
        PROCESS_INFORMATION pi;         // info returned about a process
        char szCmdLine[MAX_BUFFER];     // child's command line
        int iLen;                       // return value from LoadString
        BOOL bTest;                     // return value
```

```
/* load name of process image file from resources */
iLen = LoadString( hInst, IDS_PROCESS, szProcess, sizeof(szProcess) );
if (!iLen)
{
    return;                       // loading string failed
}

/* fill in the process's startup information */
sui.cb              = sizeof(STARTUPINFO);
sui.lpReserved      = NULL;          // must be NULL
sui.lpDesktop       = NULL;          // starting desktop
sui.lpTitle         = NULL;          // title for new console window
sui.dwX             = 0;             // window starting offsets
sui.dwY             = 0;
sui.dwXSize         = 0;             // window starting size
sui.dwYSize         = 0;
sui.dwXCountChars   = 0;             // console screen buffer size
sui.dwYCountChars   = 0;
sui.dwFillAttribute = 0;             // console text colors
sui.dwFlags         = 0;             // flags to activate startup fields
sui.wShowWindow     = 0;             // iCmdShow parameter
sui.cbReserved2     = 0;
sui.lpReserved2     = NULL;

/* prepare child's command-line argument, a window caption string */
wsprintf( szCmdLine, "%s %i", (LPSTR)szProcess, iChildNum++ );

/* create the drawing process */
bTest = CreateProcess( NULL,           // .EXE image
          szCmdLine,                   // command line
          NULL,                        // process security
          NULL,                        // thread security
          FALSE,                       // inherit handles
          0,                           // creation flags
          NULL,                        // environment block
          NULL,                        // current directory
          &sui,                        // startup info
          &pi );                       // process info (returned)

if (!bTest)
{
    ShowErrorMsg( );                   // creation failed
    return;
}
```

```
    WaitForInputIdle( pi.hProcess, 5000 );   // wait for child to start up
    CloseHandle( pi.hProcess );              // we don't need the handles
    CloseHandle( pi.hThread );
    return;
}
```

Synchronizing the Threads

Whenever the user changes the shape options by choosing a new figure, size, or color, the program must write new commands in all its pipes. The primary thread receives and processes the user's command. It needs a way to make all the pipe instance threads transmit the new information. One of the event objects created during initialization serves this purpose. When the user picks a new option, the procedures that store the command also pulse the event. The **PulseEvent** command combines the **SetEvent** and **ResetEvent** commands into one operation. The event remains signaled just long enough to unblock all waiting threads and then immediately returns to its unsignaled state.

The ChangeShape procedure incorporates one other modification. When it receives the IDM_TERMINATE command, it saves the old shape value in a global variable, iPrevShape. After all the connected children quit, the parent restores the iPrevShape value to the figure.iShape field. If children are waiting they will connect immediately to the newly released pipes, and if figure.iShape still held IDM_TERMINATE their first command would shut them down. The iPrevShape variable allows newly connected children to draw immediately whatever shape the user last selected.

```
/*-------------------------------------------------------------------
            CHANGE SHAPE
            Record a shape command from the user. If the user has chosen
            a new shape, send the updated FIGURE structure to the child.
            -----------------------------------------------------------------*/

void ChangeShape ( int iCmd )
{
    if (iCmd != figure.iShape)          // new shape?
    {
        // After sending a terminate command, we need to
        // restore the last shape drawn so that newly
        // connected clients can still draw whatever the
        // user last chose.
```

```
        if (iCmd == IDM_TERMINATE)
        {
            iPrevShape = figure.iShape; // save old shape command
        }

        figure.iShape = iCmd;          // record new shape command
        PulseEvent( hCmdEvent );       // tell threads shape has changed
    }
    return;
}

/*-------------------------------------------------------------------
        CHANGE SIZE
        Record a size command from the user. If the user has chosen
        a new size, send the updated FIGURE structure to the child.
        -----------------------------------------------------------*/

void ChangeSize ( int iCmd )
{
    if (iCmd != figure.iSize)          // new size?
    {
        figure.iSize = iCmd;           // record it
        PulseEvent( hCmdEvent );       // tell threads shape has changed
    }
    return;
}

/*-------------------------------------------------------------------
        CHANGE COLOR
        Record a color command from the user. If the user has chosen
        a new color, send the updated FIGURE structure to the child.
        -----------------------------------------------------------*/

void ChangeColor ( int iCmd )
{
    if (iCmd != figure.iColor)         // new color?
    {
        figure.iColor = iCmd;          // record it
        PulseEvent( hCmdEvent );       // tell threads shape has changed
    }
    return;
}
```

Connecting with Clients

The threads that run each pipe instance begin life at the PipeInstanceThread procedure. Each new thread enters an endless loop waiting for clients to connect with its instance of the pipe. When a client does connect, a smaller nested loop begins. While the connection lasts, the thread waits for command signals from the event object. Each time the event pulses, the thread unblocks, copies the current contents of the global figure variable into its pipe, and resumes its wait for a new command.

If for any reason the write operation fails, the thread assumes its client process has terminated. The thread calls **DisconnectNamedPipe**, returns to the top of its outer loop, and issues **ConnectNamedPipe** to wait for a new client. The loop also maintains a connection count in the global variable iNumConnections. Each time any thread succeeds in connecting, it increments the counter. When the connection breaks, it decrements the counter. The Parent_OnInitMenu procedure reads the counter to decide which menu options should be enabled. If the parent has no listening clients, then all the shape option commands are disabled.

The outer loop of PipeInstanceThread begins with a while (TRUE) command, so the loop can never break. The pipe threads stop running when the primary thread reaches the end of WinMain and the system calls **ExitProcess**. At our customary −W4 warning level, using a constant for a conditional expression causes the compiler to complain. The #pragma commands surrounding the procedure suppress the warning.

Adding to the complexity of this procedure is the task of coordinating the threads when they all disconnect their clients in response to a Terminate command from the user. Several potential problems arise along the way. First, the parent should not write its IDM_TERMINATE command to the pipe and then disconnect immediately because **DisconnectNamedPipe** destroys any data still lingering in the pipe's buffer. The command could be lost before the child had a chance to read it. **FlushFileBuffers**, when passed a pipe handle, blocks until the receiving program clears the pipe by reading all its contents. Only a program with write access to its pipe may call **FlushFileBuffers**. The command fails when passed a read-only handle.

As each thread disconnects from its terminated client, it returns to the top of the loop and waits for a new connection. As soon as it connects it sends the client an initial message to make it draw something right away. But if other threads are still terminating their clients, the global figure variable still contains the IDM_TERMINATE command. The thread will terminate its newly connected client by mistake.

We need a way to prevent any thread from sending that initial message to a new client until after all the old clients have been disconnected. The hNotTerminatingEvent object solves the problem. Near the top of the outer loop you'll find a **WaitForSingleObject** command that every thread passes before writing its first message to a new client. Most of the time the event remains signaled and all threads pass quickly by. As soon as one thread sends a termination command, however, it calls **ResetEvent** to turn off the signal, indicating that a termination sequence has started. Now when any thread finds a new client it will block before sending the first message. The last thread to terminate its client resets the figure.iShape command to iPrevShape, the value it last held before the termination began. The last thread also calls **SetEvent** to restore the event signal and unblock the other waiting threads. A thread knows when it is the last to terminate its client because the iNumConnections counter reaches 0.

```
/*-------------------------------------------------------------------
        PIPE INSTANCE THREAD
        MakePipeInstance starts a thread with this procedure
        to manage a connection for one instance of the pipe.
    -----------------------------------------------------------------*/

/* Tell the compiler not to complain about the "while (TRUE)" loop */
#pragma warning (disable :4127)

LONG PipeInstanceThread ( HANDLE hPipe )
{
    BOOL bConnected;    // true when a client connects to the pipe

    // This loop runs endlessly. When a client disappears, the
    // loop simply waits for a new client to connect. This thread is
    // terminated automatically when the program's primary thread exits.

    while (TRUE)
    {
        /* wait for a connection with some client */
        ConnectNamedPipe( hPipe, NULL );

        // If other threads are terminating their clients, then
        // figure.iShape still holds the IDM_TERMINATE command.
        // The thread blocks here until the last client is
        // terminated. The last terminating thread resets
        // figure.iShape to its previous value.

        WaitForSingleObject( hNotTerminatingEvent, INFINITE );
```

```
/* now the connection is made and a command message is ready */
iNumConnections++;                      // update global variable
SendCommand( hPipe );                   // give client its first command

/* send another message each time the Command event signals */
bConnected = TRUE;
while (bConnected)
{
    WaitForSingleObject( hCmdEvent, INFINITE ); // wait for signal
    if (!SendCommand( hPipe ))          // send new shape command
    {
        // The connection failed--probably
        // we just sent IDM_TERMINATE or
        // the user exited from the client.
        // Show no error message.

        bConnected = FALSE;
    }
}

FlushFileBuffers( hPipe );          // wait for child to read message
DisconnectNamedPipe( hPipe );       // break connection
iNumConnections--;                  // update global variable

// The following if condition coordinates threads when they
// are all terminating their clients. When a thread discovers
// it has just sent the IDM_TERMINATE command, it sets the
// hNotTerminatingEvent object to the nonsignaled state.
// Other threads will block until the last thread to disconnect
// restores the signal. The last thread also replaces the
// IDM_TERMINATE command with IDM_RECTANGLE so that all the
// threads will have a useful command to send in the first
// message to their new clients.

if (figure.iShape == IDM_TERMINATE) // did we just terminate?
{                                       // have all connections
    if (iNumConnections > 0)            // been terminated?
    {                                   // NO; block other threads
                                        // while terminating proceeds
        ResetEvent( hNotTerminatingEvent );
    }
    else                                // YES
    {
        figure.iShape = iPrevShape;         // restore previous command
```

```
                SetEvent( hNotTerminatingEvent );    // unblock threads
            }
        }
    }
    return( OL );
}

/* allow the "conditional expression constant" warning again */
#pragma warning (default :4127)
```

Writing to the Pipe

Within the PipeInstanceThread loops, the program repeatedly calls SendCommand to write the current values from figure into the pipe. If the connection with the client breaks, the procedure returns **FALSE**. The connection may break in either of two ways, and each has different consequences for the program's behavior. The program handles disconnection most gracefully when the user chooses Terminate and the parent breaks the links itself. In that case, SendCommand returns **FALSE** immediately after sending the message, and the program seeks new replacement clients immediately. But if a client closes its handle to the pipe's other end, the server does not know. If the user chooses Exit from the menu of a connected child process, the parent discovers the break only when it later tries to send a new message and **WriteFile** returns an error value. Furthermore, the broken pipe remains technically connected until the server calls **DisconnectNamedPipe**. As a consequence, if you end one of the connected child programs while a third child is blocked on **WaitNamedPipe**, the waiting child remains blocked until you issue another command. Using a two-way duplex pipe would smooth the transition because the client could send the server a termination message before it exits and the server could disconnect immediately. To accommodate that arrangement the server would probably dedicate two threads to each pipe instance, one to send and one to receive, or perhaps one thread to do all the writing for all instances and another to do the reading.

```
/*------------------------------------------------------------------
        SEND COMMAND
        Tell the child program what to draw. Write the current
        contents of the global FIGURE variable into the pipe.

        Return
        TRUE indicates the write operation succeeded. FALSE means
        an error occurred and we have lost contact with the child.
        ----------------------------------------------------------------*/
```

```
BOOL SendCommand ( HANDLE hPipe )
{
    BOOL bTest;                     // return value
    DWORD dwWritten;                // number of bytes written to pipe

    /* pass the choices to the child through the pipe */
    bTest = WriteFile( hPipe,       // named pipe (outbound handle)
                &figure,            // buffer to write
                sizeof(FIGURE),     // size of buffer
                &dwWritten,         // bytes written
                NULL );             // overlapping i/o structure

    if (!bTest)                     // did writing succeed?
    {
        // If the write operation failed because the user has
        // already closed the child program, then we don't need
        // to do anything special about the error. If, however,
        // some less predictable error caused the failure, call
        // ShowErrorMsg as usual to display the system's error
        // message.

        DWORD dwResult = GetLastError();

        if ((dwResult != ERROR_BROKEN_PIPE)      // pipe has been ended
            && (dwResult != ERROR_NO_DATA))      // pipe close in progress
        {
            ShowErrorMsg( );                      // unpredictable error
        }
    }

    // SendCommand returns FALSE on errors to indicate that the
    // connection has failed. SendCommand also returns FALSE after
    // it tells a child to quit because that too makes a connection
    // fail.

    return( (bTest) && (figure.iShape != IDM_TERMINATE) );
}
```

The Child Process

The child process requires fewer changes. One change is visible in Figure 5.2. Because the parent now creates multiple children, we distinguish each with a different number in its window caption. The parent passes each child its own number through the command-line parameter of **CreateProcess**. The child's window caption also states whether the child is connected to a pipe or waiting for a connection.

During initialization each child retrieves its assigned number with **GetCommand-Line**. This command returns a pointer to a string containing all the command-line arguments separated by spaces. The first item on the command line should be the name of the program (child.exe), so calling strtok twice extracts the child's sequence number, the second item on the command line. The program constructs a base string of the form "Child 1 %s" and calls **wsprintf** to replace the %s marker with a string describing the program's current status, which is initially "waiting" but may change to "connected."

```
/*----------------------------------------------------------------

        CHILD.C   [named pipe version]
        Contains the child process for the PROCESS demo program.
        The program in parent.c creates this child process. In this
        version, the two processes communicate through a named pipe.

        FUNCTIONS
            WinMain                 receive and dispatch messages
            Init                    initialize program data
            CreateMainWindow        create program's overlapping window
            Child_WndProc           sort out messages for main window
            Child_OnCreate          create named pipe
            Child_OnPaint           draw selected figure
            Child_OnCommand         process menu commands
            Child_OnDestroy         end program
            PipeThread              thread procedure for managing the pipe
            DoRead                  procedure to read from pipe
            About_DlgProc           sort out messages for About box
            ShowErrorMsg            calls GetLastError and displays the message

        from Mastering Windows NT Programming
        copyright 1993 by Brian Myers & Eric Hamer

    ----------------------------------------------------------------*/


#define STRICT
#include <windows.h>
#include <windowsx.h>
#include <string.h>                 // strcpy, strcat
#include "child.h"
#include "global.h"                 // values common to both processes
```

```
/*-------------------------------------------------------------------
        GLOBAL VARIABLES
      ----------------------------------------------------------*/

HWND            hwndMain;                   // main window
HINSTANCE       hInst;                      // current instance
int             iShape;                     // figure to draw
int             iSize;                      // size of figure to draw (SMALL/LARGE)
int             iColor;                     // color of figure to draw
BOOL            bTerminate = FALSE;         // TRUE when program should end
char            szTitle[MAX_BUFFER];        // window caption string

/*-------------------------------------------------------------------
        CREATE MAIN WINDOW
        Create the program's overlapping window.
      ----------------------------------------------------------*/

BOOL CreateMainWindow ( void )
{
    char szAppName[MAX_BUFFER];
    char szBuffer[MAX_BUFFER];
    char *pToken;

    /* load the relevant strings */
    LoadString( hInst, IDS_APPNAME, szAppName,  sizeof(szAppName) );

    // Create window's caption using command-line string from parent.
    // The basic caption has the form:
    //
    //      Child 1 %s
    //
    // The identifying number comes from the parent through the
    // command line. We'll use wsprintf to insert the phrase
    // "waiting" or "connected" into the title as appropriate.

    strcpy( szTitle, "Child " );            // begin with "Child "
    strtok( GetCommandLine(), " " );        // move past first word
    pToken = strtok( NULL, " " );           // get first argument
    if (pToken)                             // is there one?
    {
        strcat( szTitle, pToken );          // append it
    }
    strcat( szTitle, " %s" );               // append a wsprintf format mark
```

```
// The global szTitle now contains the base caption.
// Insert a current status marker in it.
wsprintf( szBuffer, szTitle, (LPSTR)" (waiting)" );

/* create the parent window */
hwndMain = CreateWindow( szAppName, szBuffer,
    WS_OVERLAPPEDWINDOW | WS_CLIPCHILDREN,
    CW_USEDEFAULT, CW_USEDEFAULT, CW_USEDEFAULT, CW_USEDEFAULT,
    NULL, NULL, hInst, NULL );

/* return FALSE for an error */
return( hwndMain != NULL );
}
```

Creating a Thread and Connecting to the Pipe

Because CreateMainWindow has already set the window caption, the new Child_OnCreate procedure no longer loads a caption from the resource string table. Because the child has not inherited a pipe handle, this version also omits the original call to **GetStdHandle**. Instead the new thread function, PipeThread, now coordinates all the pipe actions. It first loads the pipe name string both programs share in the global.str file, and then it passes the name to **CreateFile**. The system searches its object name tree and finds the pipe with this name. If an instance of the pipe is available, **CreateFile** returns a handle to it. Because the original pipe was created with the **PIPE_ACCESS_OUTBOUND** flag, the client must request **GENERIC_READ** access rights.

PipeThread embeds the **CreateFile** command in a while loop that runs until **CreateFile** returns a valid handle. The loop begins with a **WaitNamedPipe** command, causing the thread to block waiting for an available instance. **WaitNamedPipe** does not, however, initiate the connection. **CreateFile** does that. Between the execution of the **WaitNamedPipe** command and the execution of **CreateFile**, it is possible for the system to schedule another thread that grabs the pipe for itself. If that happens **CreateFile** will fail even though **WaitNamedPipe** returned **TRUE**. If **CreateFile** fails during PipeThread, the while loop notices the error and tries again. If **CreateFile** produces an error message indicating any problem other than busy pipes, the loop sets the bTerminate flag and the process ends a few lines later.

When the client child successfully links to the server parent, the procedure updates the window caption and enters another loop to wait for messages to arrive through the pipe. The receiving loop ends when the user chooses Exit from the child's menu or when the child receives an IDM_TERMINATE command from the parent.

The DoRead procedure calls **ReadFile** to read messages from the parent. It needs no revisions to work with a named pipe.

```
/*-------------------------------------------------------------------
        PIPE THREAD
        The WM_CREATE handler starts a thread with this procedure
        to manage the pipe connection.
        -------------------------------------------------------------*/

LONG PipeThread ( LPVOID lpThreadData )
{
    char szBuffer[MAX_BUFFER];      // used for pipe name and window caption
    int iLen;                       // length of a string
    BOOL bConnected;                // TRUE when we have a pipe handle
    HANDLE hpipeRead;               // receiving handle to 1-way pipe

    /* load the string that contains the name of the named pipe */
    iLen = LoadString( hInst, IDS_PIPE, szBuffer, sizeof(szBuffer) );
    if (!iLen)
    {
        return( FALSE );
    }

    // This while loop continues until an instance of the named
    // pipe becomes available. bConnected is a global variable,
    // and while it is FALSE the primary thread paints "Waiting..."
    // in the window's client area.

    // If an unpredictable error occurs, the loop sets the bTerminate
    // flag, this procedure ends quickly, and it kills the program
    // on its way out.

    bConnected = FALSE;
    while (!bConnected && !bTerminate)
    {
        /* wait for a pipe instance to become available */
        WaitNamedPipe( szBuffer, NMPWAIT_WAIT_FOREVER );

        /* open the named pipe for reading */
        hpipeRead = CreateFile( szBuffer,          // name of pipe
                GENERIC_READ,                      // access mode
                0,                                 // share mode
```

```
                    NULL,                          // security descriptor
                    OPEN_EXISTING,                 // do not create a new object
                    FILE_ATTRIBUTE_NORMAL,         // file attributes
                    NULL );                        // file from which to copy attributes

        /* check that the pipe's handle is valid */
        if (hpipeRead == INVALID_HANDLE_VALUE)
        {
            // If CreateFile failed simply because
            // other waiting threads grabbed the
            // pipe, don't bother the user with
            // an error message.

            if (GetLastError() != ERROR_PIPE_BUSY)
            {
                // an unpredictable error occurred; show message
                ShowErrorMsg( );
                bTerminate = TRUE;                 // break loop; end program
            }
        }
        else
        {
            bConnected = TRUE;                     // succeeded in connecting
        }
    }

    /* change window caption to show this window is connected */
    wsprintf( szBuffer, szTitle, (LPSTR)" (connected)" );
    SetWindowText( hwndMain, szBuffer );

    /* read messages from the pipe until we receive a terminate command */
    while (!bTerminate)
    {
        DoRead( hpipeRead );
    }

    /* when bTerminate is TRUE, end the program */
    FORWARD_WM_DESTROY( hwndMain, PostMessage );

    return( OL );                                  // implicit ExitThread()
    UNREFERENCED_PARAMETER(lpThreadData);
}
```

A process is a collection of system resources that support an executable file. It contains, among other things, its own virtual memory address space, a table of objects created, and one or more threads to execute its code. One process may create and launch other processes, called its children. Child processes inherit objects and attributes from their parents. Like threads, processes run at different scheduling priorities. A process ends when any of its threads calls **ExitProcess** or when its primary thread exits.

To communicate with each other, processes often create objects called pipes. A pipe is a conduit through which information flows. One process writes information at one end, and another process reads information out of the other end. Pipes come in many varieties. An anonymous pipe works in only one direction, with only one client at a time, and never over a network. Named pipes are more versatile. Any process on any machine can connect to the pipe if it knows the pipe's name. One named pipe may exist in many instances, serving many clients at once. Named pipes can organize their information as a byte stream or as a set of discrete messages; they may choose whether to block threads that try to read when the pipe is empty; they may or may not support asynchronous I/O operations. A set of pipe-related API commands regulates the connections and transactions among the server and clients of a named pipe.

The sample programs in this chapter also introduced the **GetLastError** and **FormatMessage** functions for signaling to the user when something goes wrong. The next chapter explores a more advanced mechanism for dealing with unexpected failures: structured exception handling.

Handling Exceptions

 Structured exception handling

Termination handling

Try blocks

Exception filters

Message tables

As a program runs, many conditions may disturb its normal flow of execution. The CPU may complain of an improper memory address; the user may interrupt by pressing Ctrl-C; a debugger may halt and resume a program arbitrarily; or an unexpected value may produce an overflow or underflow in a floating-point calculation. Exceptional conditions such as these may arise in user mode or kernel mode or on a RISC or an Intel chip, and either the hardware or the software may signal their occurrence. Furthermore, each programming language must find a way to cope with them. To unify the processing required for all these different situations, Windows NT builds structured exception-handling mechanisms into the system at a low level.

Different languages, and even different compilers, may choose to expose structured exception handling in different ways. Microsoft's C compilers supply the keywords `try`, `except`, and `finally`, each introducing a new block of code. A try block marks code that might raise exceptions. An `except` block contains code to run if an exception occurs. A `finally` block contains code to run when a `try` block ends, even if the try block fails or is interrupted. From the programmer's perspective, these syntax structures conveniently separate code that handles exceptional conditions from code that handles normal tasks.

CONCEPTS

Exceptions closely resemble interrupts. Both signals cause the CPU to transfer control to some other part of the system. We contrasted interrupts and exceptions in Chapter 1 under the heading "Traps and the Trap Handler." Briefly, an interrupt occurs asynchronously, often as a result of some hardware event such as a keypress or serial port input. A program has no control over such interruptions, and they may occur at any time. An exception, on the other hand, arises synchronously, as a direct result of executing a particular program instruction. Often exceptions indicate error conditions, and usually they can be reproduced by running the same code again with the same context. These generalizations are useful guidelines, though in practice the distinction is not quite as firm as it might at first appear. The decision to signal some API failures with error returns and others by raising exceptions must sometimes be arbitrary.

Structured Exception Handling

Any exception that arises must be handled, if not by the program then by the system itself. Some code somewhere must respond and clear it. Exception handling, then, means providing blocks of code to respond if an exception occurs. A program is likely to have many small handler blocks guarding different portions of code against different exceptions. In searching for a block of code prepared to deal with a particular condition, the system looks first in the current procedure, then backward through the stack to other active pending procedures in the same process, and finally to the system's own exception handlers. If the offending process happens to be under the scrutiny of a debugger, then the debugging program also gets a chance to handle the exception.

The provisions for handling errors differ with the subsystem and the programming language. The WOW subsystem, for example, must handle all exceptions directly because its Win16 clients have no way to do it themselves. Also, different languages may choose to expose exception handling through different syntaxes. But the name "structured exception handling" implies that the language itself must include some control structure for dealing with exceptions. The basic exception-handling statements in C are try and except. The try/except structure separates the code for exceptional situations from the code for normal situations.

```
try                                    // beginning of try block
{
     <guarded code statements>         // code that may produce exceptions
}
except (<filter>)                      // beginning of exception handling block
{
     <exception handling code>         // code to execute if an exception occurs
}
```

In any implementation, structured exception handling associates a block of code for handling exceptions with a block of code it is said to guard. If an exception occurs while the guarded block executes, control transfers to the filter expression. Usually the filter expression asks what the exception is and decides how to proceed. Exceptions that pass through the filter reach the exception-handling code. If the filter blocks an exception then the handler is not invoked. The system continues to search elsewhere for a handler that will take the exception.

The filter expression may be complex. It may even call a separate function. Sometimes the filter even does the real work of responding to an exception, leaving the except block empty.

Termination Handlers

An exception, by interrupting the execution of a guarded try block, may prevent the block from reaching its normal conclusion. If the block normally sets up something at the beginning and takes it down at the end, an exception in the middle may prevent the block from performing its final cleanup instructions. Since exceptions may potentially occur anywhere, no if statement can guarantee that cleanup code will execute. That is the job of a termination handler.

The syntax of a termination handler closely resembles that of an exception handler:

```
try                                     // beginning of try block
{
    <guarded code statements>           // code that may produce exceptions
}
finally                                 // beginning of termination-handling block
{
    <termination-handling code>         // code to execute when guarded block ends
}
```

A termination handler contains code that must execute after a guarded block ends, regardless of how the block ends. When the execution path leaves the guarded block, the termination block always runs. It doesn't matter if the guarded block calls return, is interrupted by an exception, or simply runs to the end and falls through into the finally block. Any of those events triggers the termination handler. A program typically uses termination handlers to guarantee that resources are released. A section of code that waits to own a mutex, for example, might guard itself with a termination handler to ensure the mutex's eventual release. Failure to release a mutex would freeze other waiting threads.

The only way to exit a try block without triggering its termination handler is to call **ExitThread** or **ExitProcess** (or abort, which calls **ExitProcess** internally).

What Is Exceptional?

Programmers new to structured exception handling sometimes have the false impression that they no longer need to check for error returns after executing each command. An error, however, is not the same thing as an exception. A function can fail without raising an exception. For example, consider these lines of code:

```
hBrush = CreateSolidBrush( RGB(255, 0, 0) );
hOldBrush = SelectObject( hDC, hBrush );
Rectangle( hDC, 0, 0, 100, 100 );
```

If the first command fails and returns **NULL** for the brush then **SelectObject** fails, too. The third command still draws a rectangle but does not color it correctly. No exceptions are raised. The only way to protect against those failures is to check the return values. Here's another example:

```
HANDLE hMemory;
char *pData;

hMemory = GlobalAlloc( GHND, 1000 );
pData = (char *)GlobalLock( hMemory );
```

If the allocation fails then hMemory becomes **NULL**, **GlobalLock** fails, and pData becomes **NULL**, too. Neither failure, however, produces an exception. But the next line does produce an exception when it tries to write to an invalid address:

```
pData[0] = 'a';                    // raises exception if pData = NULL
```

An exception is a kind of error that the command can't process. If **GlobalAlloc** can't find enough room, it simply returns **NULL**. But if the assignment operator has no valid destination to place a value, it can do nothing, not even return an error. It must raise an exception, and if the process cannot handle the exception then the system must close down the process.

The line between exceptions and errors is sometimes difficult to draw. The next chapter, for example, introduces another allocation command, **HeapAlloc**, that can be made to indicate normal failures by generating exceptions instead of returning **NULL**. The difference between an error and an exception is sometimes a matter of implementation. Recognizing commands that might raise exceptions takes a little practice. Learn which exceptions can arise and then imagine which operations might cause them. The faulty assignment statement causes an *access violation* exception. The list of possible exceptions varies on different machines, but here are some the Windows NT kernel defines universally:

Data type misalignment

Debugger breakpoint

Debugger single step

Floating-point divide by zero

Floating-point overflow and underflow

Floating-point reserved operand

Guard page violation

Illegal instruction

Integer divide by zero

Integer overflow

Memory access violation

Page read error

Paging file quota exceeded

Privileged instruction

Frame-Based Exception Handling

The exception-handling mechanisms in Microsoft C are *frame based*, meaning that each except block is associated with, or framed in, the procedure that contains it. The term *frame* describes a layer in the program stack. Each time a program calls a procedure, the program pushes a new set of information on the stack. The information includes, for example, parameters passed to the new procedure and an address showing where to return when the called procedure ends. If the second procedure calls a third and the third a fourth, each successive call pushes a new frame onto the stack, as you see in Figure 6.1.

Frames placed on the stack by
successive procedure calls

High Stack Addresses

```
void ProcA ( )
{
    ProcB ( );  ──────────>
}
```

| FRAME |
| for call to ProcB |
| PARAMETERS |
| RETURN ADDRESS |

```
void ProcB ( )
{
    ProcC ( );  ──────────>
}
```

| FRAME |
| for call to ProcC |
| PARAMETERS |
| RETURN ADDRESS |

Stack
grows
down
with
each
procedure
call

Low Stack Addresses

Each frame represents an activated procedure waiting for its subroutines to finish before resuming. At any point it is possible to trace back through the stack frames to discover which procedures have been called. When an exception occurs, the system traces back looking for exception handlers in each pending procedure.

The internal mechanisms that support exception handling vary from system to system. A MIPS machine, for example, implements handlers through tables, not stacks.

Order of Execution

When an exception arises, the system first saves the machine context of the interrupted thread, just as it does when it performs a context switch for normal multitasking. Depending on how the exception is eventually handled, the system may later use the saved context to resume execution at the beginning of the line where the exception occurred.

In response to an exception, the system generally tries to execute the following pieces of code, in this order:

1. Termination handler

2. Exception filter

3. Exception handler

If the exception arises in code guarded by a `try`/`finally` structure, the `finally` block executes first. The termination handler performs its duties *before* the system begins to look for an exception handler. Then the system traces backward through the stack looking for an exception filter that accepts the current exception. The system may have to execute several filters in its search. A filter usually identifies the current exception and always responds with one of three commands: **EXCEPTION_EXECUTE_HANDLER**, **EXCEPTION_CONTINUE_EXECUTION**, or **EXCEPTION_CONTINUE_SEARCH**. The Execute Handler command transfers control to the adjacent `except` block. When the `except` block ends, execution drops through the handler's closing bracket and continues on from the same place. The Resume Execution command does *not* execute any `except` block. A filter gives this command to resume execution at exactly the point where the exception first arose. (Resuming is useful when the filter function itself has cleared up whatever circumstances caused the exception to occur, permitting resumption.) The Continue Search command lets the filter refuse to handle an exception. The system continues its backward progress through the stack looking for another handler. When the system finds a filter that returns Execute Handler or Continue Execution, it considers the exception to have been handled. If the system cannot find an interested handler it displays a message box like the one in Figure 6.2 and terminates the process.

Debuggers

The task of finding a handler becomes more involved when a process is being debugged because the system transfers control to the debugger *before* seeking the program's own exception handlers. Typically the debugger uses this early alert to handle single-step and breakpoint exceptions, allowing the user to inspect the context before resuming. If the debugger decides *not* to handle an exception during the early alert the system returns to the process in search of a handler. If the process also

Message box from the system
warning of an unhandled exception

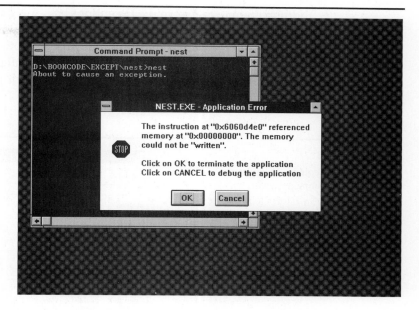

refuses the exception then the system gives the debugger a second chance to handle
what has now become a more serious situation. If the debugger refuses a second
time, then the system finally gives up and settles for providing its own default response, which is usually to terminate the process. To summarize:

1. The debugger gets an early alert. If it refuses the exception, then—

2. The program stack is searched for a suitable handler. If none is found, then—

3. The debugger gets a second chance to respond. If it still refuses the
   exception, then—

4. The system kills the procedure.

The WinDbg symbolic debugger gives the user control over how the program responds to its early and late exception notifications. The Debugger Exceptions dialog box, shown in Figure 6.3, allows you to select which exceptions to accept and
to specify debugger commands to execute when the exception occurs. You can also
make the debugger recognize private exceptions defined for a single program by

adding them to the list in the Exceptions box. Another option directs the debugger to ignore particular exceptions. The ignore option is useful when some part of a program relies on the arrival of a particular exception. The List program in Chapter 7, for example, depends on exceptions to commit pages of memory. If the debugger handles the exception first, then the program never gets its chance and the memory pages remain unavailable.

FIGURE 6.3:

Debugger Exceptions dialog box in the WinDbg debugger

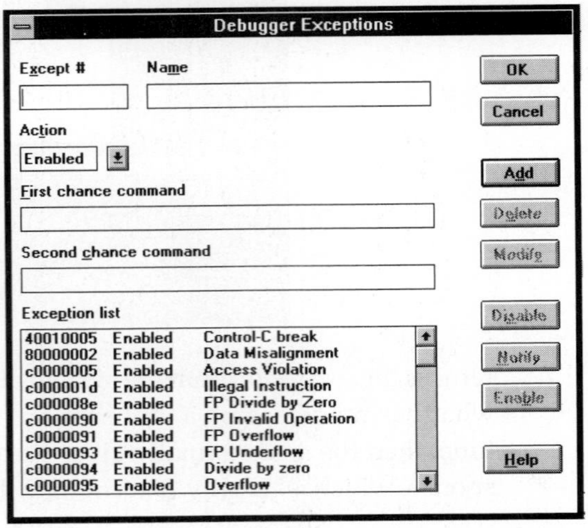

COMMANDS

This section introduces a few API commands commonly used with exception handlers. It begins with commands useful primarily for gathering information while handling an exception or executing a termination handler. Then it explains how to define custom exceptions to suit the error-handling needs of your own programs.

Filters

The filter expression determines whether or not the handler it accompanies will accept particular exceptions. The filter must ultimately resolve to one of three values:

- **EXCEPTION_EXECUTE_HANDLER**: Yes, do execute the `except` block. When the `except` block ends, execution continues on from its last statement in normal sequential fashion. In other words, if an exception arises in one procedure and is handled in another, the program does not return to where the exception occurred.

- **EXCEPTION_CONTINUE_SEARCH**: The handler refuses the exception. The `except` block does not execute. The system must continue to search for another handler.

- **EXCEPTION_CONTINUE_EXECUTION**: The handler accepts the exception but does not execute the `except` block. The system returns control to the point where the exception occurred.

In the simplest case, the filter expression may be one of these constants:

```
try
{
     <guarded code statements>
}
except (EXCEPTION_EXECUTE_HANDLER)         // always execute the handler code
{
     <exception handling code>
}
```

Of course, that filter expression doesn't really filter anything. It's a poor sentry that lets everyone pass. More flexible filters require a means of determining which exception has just been generated. For that you need a new command:

```
DWORD GetExceptionCode ( void );
```

The value returned by **GetExceptionCode** identifies the most recent exception by number. Exception constants are defined in winbase.h. Here are some of the more commonly encountered exceptions:

Return Value	Cause of Exception
`EXCEPTION_ACCESS_VIOLATION`	The thread used a memory address for which it is not privileged
`EXCEPTION_ARRAY_BOUNDS_EXCEEDED`	The thread tried to read outside the declared bounds of an array (Not all hardware supports bounds-checking.)
`EXCEPTION_BREAKPOINT`	A debugging breakpoint interrupted the thread
`EXCEPTION_DATATYPE_MISALIGNMENT`	The thread tried to read or write values not evenly aligned on logical address boundaries (Some systems provide automatic alignment.)
`EXCEPTION_PRIV_INSTRUCTION`	The thread tried to execute an instruction illegal in the current running mode
`EXCEPTION_SINGLE_STEP`	A debugging single-step breakpoint interrupted the thread
`STATUS_NONCONTINUABLE_EXCEPTION`	The thread tried to continue after receiving an exception that disallows continuation

In addition, another set of exceptions signals anomalies in math operations:

```
EXCEPTION_FLT_DENORMAL_OPERAND

EXCEPTION_FLT_DIVIDE_BY_ZERO

EXCEPTION_FLT_INEXACT_RESULT

EXCEPTION_FLT_INVALID_OPERATION
```

```
EXCEPTION_FLT_OVERFLOW

EXCEPTION_FLT_STACK_CHECK

EXCEPTION_FLT_UNDERFLOW

EXCEPTION_INT_DIVIDE_BY_ZERO

EXCEPTION_INT_OVERFLOW
```

By default, all the floating-point (FLT) exceptions are disabled, and errors announce themselves only by returning infinity or 0. To generate exceptions for any of the floating-point conditions, call _controlfp. These lines, for example, enable exception signals for all errors:

```
int iFPMask = _controlfp( 0 ,0 );            // save old control mask

iFPMask &= ~(EM_OVERFLOW | EM_UNDERFLOW | EM_INEXACT
        | EM_ZERODIVIDE | EM_DENORMAL );

_controlfp( iFPMask, MCW_EM );               // set new control mask
```

Beware, however, when turning on floating-point exceptions because any unhandled exceptions will, as always, cause the program to terminate abruptly.

GetExceptionCode enables a filter expression to execute its handler conditionally. The following example executes its handler only in response to a memory access violation. It refuses other exceptions, forcing the system to continue its search for a handler.

```
try
{
    <guarded code statements>
}
except ((GetExceptionCode() == EXCEPTION_ACCESS_VIOLATION)
        ? EXCEPTION_EXECUTE_HANDLER : EXCEPTION_CONTINUE_SEARCH)
{
    // this block executes only after an access violation
}
```

Filter Functions

For those occasions when a single line can't hold all the logic of your filter, define your own filter function. A filter function must return one of the three valid filter constants. Microsoft's examples assign the filter function a **DWORD** return value, but since **EXCEPTION_CONTINUE_EXECUTION** is defined in excpt.h as −1, it makes more sense—and avoids a −W4 warning—to return a signed **LONG** value. This example accepts two different exceptions and refuses all others:

```
try
{
    <guarded code statements>
}
except (MyFilter(GetExceptionCode()))
{
    // this block executes only after an access violation
}

LONG MyFilter ( DWORD dwException )
{
    switch (dwException)
    {
        case EXCEPTION_ACCESS_VIOLATION:
        case EXCEPTION_INT_DIVIDE_BY_ZERO:
            return( EXCEPTION_EXECUTE_HANDLER );

        default:
            return( EXCEPTION_CONTINUE_SEARCH );
    }
}
```

The code in a filter function may be as complex as you care to make it. Note, however, that we did not call **GetExceptionCode** from within the filter. It works only in the filter expression (on the same line as except) or within the exception-handling block, but not in other procedures, such as MyFilter.

Getting More Information

To discover more about an exception than its identifying number, call **GetExceptionInformation** instead of **GetExceptionCode**. **GetExceptionInformation** returns a pointer to an **EXCEPTION_POINTERS** structure, which itself holds pointers to two more structures: an **EXCEPTION_RECORD** and a **CONTEXT**. The **CONTEXT** structure contains all the machine-specific information about the state of the CPU at the moment the exception arose. **CONTEXT** is defined in winnt.h; its fields vary with the CPU. The structure of an **EXCEPTION_RECORD** does not vary:

```
LPEXCEPTION_POINTERS GetExceptionInformation( void );

typedef struct _EXCEPTION_POINTERS { /* exp */
    PEXCEPTION_RECORD ExceptionRecord;
    PCONTEXT ContextRecord;
} EXCEPTION_POINTERS;

typedef struct _EXCEPTION_RECORD { /* exr */
    DWORD ExceptionCode;                    // same as GetExceptionCode
    DWORD ExceptionFlags;                   // continuable?
    struct _EXCEPTION_RECORD *ExceptionRecord;  // link field
    PVOID ExceptionAddress;                 // where exception occurred
    DWORD NumberParameters;                 // number of params in final array
    DWORD ExceptionInformation[EXCEPTION_MAXIMUM_PARAMETERS];
} EXCEPTION_RECORD;
```

The **ExceptionFlags** field is most often 0 but, for exceptions so serious that the system will not permit the program to resume the field, contains **EXCEPTION_NONCONTINUABLE**. Any attempt to continue executing the program after handling a noncontinuable exception generates a second non-continuable exception, **STATUS_NONCONTINUABLE_EXCEPTION**. The **ExceptionRecord** field comes into play when several exceptions occur and accumulate before the system finishes handling any one of them. Traversing the links in this field leads back to records for previous exceptions. The **ExceptionAddress** field is the address of the code instruction where the exception arose. **NumberParameters** tells how many elements of the final **ExceptionInformation** array the current exception actually uses.

Usually **NumberParameters** is 0, but some exceptions do pass information through the array. If the exception code is **EXCEPTION_ACCESS_VIOLATION**, for example, then the first element of the **ExceptionInformation** array tells whether the offending element tried to read or write, and the second element contains the illegal memory address. An exception handler might use the information to fix the problem or to tell the user exactly what happened. Few of the standard system exceptions use the information array, but user-defined exceptions might need it, as you'll see in a few pages when we explain the **RaiseException** command.

GetExceptionCode works only when called within a filter or an except block, and GetExceptionInformation works only when called within a filter. Neither command works within a filter function; they work only within the filter expression. The restrictions have to do with losing information from the top of the stack when an exception is accepted by a handler. The only useful way to call GetExceptionInformation is to pass its result as a parameter to a filter function. If the filter function copies the received values to some other storage, then the exception handler can also read the values.

```
EXCEPTION_RECORD ExceptRecord;                    // a global variable

try
{
    <guarded code statements>
}
except (MyFilter( GetExceptionInformation() ))
{
    // This block can refer to values stored in
    // the ExceptRecord variable by the filter function.

    if (ExceptRecord.ExceptionCode == EXCEPTION_ACCESS_VIOLATION)
    {
        <code to handle access violations>
    }
}

DWORD MyFilter ( LPEXCEPTION_POINTERS lpEP )
{
    // Copy some of the exception information to a place
    // where the exception handler block can read it.
    CopyMemory( &ExceptRecord, lpEP->ExceptionRecord,
        sizeof(EXCEPTION_RECORD) );

    return( EXCEPTION_EXECUTE_HANDLER );
}
```

Abnormal Termination

One final information-gathering function works with termination handlers rather than exception handlers. If from inside a finally block you need to know whether the guarded block reached its natural end or was interrupted, call **AbnormalTermination**:

```
BOOL AbnormalTermination( void );
```

AbnormalTermination works only within a finally block. (Placing it elsewhere produces a compiler error.) It returns **FALSE** if the guarded try block executed its last line and reached the closing bracket (}). Exiting from any other point is considered abnormal and makes the function return **TRUE**. Abnormal exits occur when an exception arises within the block and also as a result of return, break, goto, or continue statements.

Abnormal termination from the first half of a try/finally structure is costly. When execution jumps out of a guarded block, the system must trace back through the stack to see how many termination handlers have been triggered. One jump can trigger several nested handlers. Tracing back through the stack costs hundreds of instructions. Wherever possible, design the try block of a termination handler to terminate normally.

To encourage normal termination of try blocks wherever possible, Microsoft's implementation of structured exception handling also includes a keyword called leave. Like the break instruction in loops and switches, leave jumps immediately to the closing bracket of a code structure. The leave command in this try block skips over intermediate code to exit the block immediately. If the subsequent finally block calls **AbnormalTermination**, it receives an answer of **FALSE**.

```
try
{
    if (<condition>)
    {
        leave;                          // jumps to end of try block
    }
    <more guarded code>
}
finally
{
    <termination-handling code>
}
```

leave is a valid instruction only within a try block.

Do-It-Yourself Exceptions

RaiseException generates an exception by hand. It causes the system to step in, save the context, and search for a handler, just as it would for any other exception. **RaiseException** can generate the predefined exceptions you already know, such as access violations, or it can generate exception codes that you define. By incorporating **RaiseException** in your own routines you can extend the mechanisms of exception handling to structure even more of your code.

```
void RaiseException(
    DWORD dwExceptionCode,          // exception code (you define it)
    DWORD dwExceptionFlags,         // 0 or non-continuable flag
    DWORD dwNumArgs,                // number of arguments in array
    LPDWORD lpArguments );          // array of optional arguments for handler
```

Introducing Console Applications

In order to avoid the extra code necessary for a graphics interface and to concentrate on the mechanisms of structured exception handling, the sample programs in the remainder of this chapter make use of the console application facilities in Windows NT. A console application does not use the standard graphics features of the Windows interface. It does not create its own windows or run message loops. It automatically receives a single main window that mimics the character-based output of a DOS screen. (Figure 1.16 in Chapter 1 shows the Windows NT command shell, which uses a console window.) Console programs follow the traditional structure of C programs, beginning with main rather than WinMain.

Chapter 17 summarizes the new API for creating and manipulating console windows, but for the simple case of a single window with normal text output knowledge of the APIs is unnecessary. The only special requirements come when linking. The linker must be told to use the console subsystem:

```
link -debug:full -debugtype:cv -subsystem:console example.obj \
    libc.lib ntdll.lib kernel32.lib
```

Changing the subsystem to console also changes the default entry point for the -entry switch from WinMainCRTStartup to mainCRTStartup. (It is not necessary to specify the default value on the command line.)

Most console applications do not use routines from gdi32.lib and user32.lib, but they can if they want to. A console program could call **CreateWindow** to create a second drawing area and paint it with GDI commands. It would probably also create a thread to run the window's message loop. Even without creating a GUI window, console applications may still call functions from the Win32 API. They may, for example, have resources, display message boxes, and play multimedia audio.

CODE

The best way to learn structured exception handling is to read programs that use it. The short programs that follow illustrate a variety of situations that arise when implementing the try, except, and finally structures. We'll consider basic syntax, nested blocks, blocks layered in successive frames, and customized exceptions.

Nesting Blocks

Let's begin with a simple termination handler. A termination handler cleans up when an exception interrupts a block of code, but it does not handle the exception. The finally block executes, but the system still must locate an except block to process the exception. This short program, for example, never reaches its final line:

```c
#include <windows.h>
#include <stdio.h>

int main ( )
{
    char *szText = NULL;

    try
    {
        puts("About to cause an exception." );
        lstrcpy( szText, "Error" );        // writes to NULL string
    }
    finally
    {
        puts( "Termination handler ran." );
    }
```

```
    // Because the exception is never handled, the
    // system terminates the program before it
    // reaches these lines.

    puts( "This line will never print." );
    return( 0 );
}
```

The faulty string copy command generates an exception that is never handled. When the program runs, the `finally` block prints its message, and then the system displays its error message (like the one in Figure 6.2) and the program ends. The final message is never printed, as you can see from the program's output.

```
About to cause an exception.

Termination handler ran.
```

Even without an exception handler a `finally` block can be quite useful, but the two are often paired. The next example nests a termination handler within an exception handler.

```
#include <windows.h>
#include <stdio.h>

int main ( )
{
    char *szText = NULL;

    try
    {
        try
        {
            puts("About to cause an exception." );
            lstrcpy( szText, "Error" );        // writes to NULL string
        }
        finally
        {
            puts( "Termination handler ran." );
        }
    }
    except (EXCEPTION_EXECUTE_HANDLER)
    {
        puts( "Handling exception." );
    }
```

```
    puts( "Program ending normally." );
    return( 0 );
}
```

The `finally` block executes whether or not an exception occurs. If an exception does occur, first the `finally` block executes and then the `except` block. Here's the output:

```
About to cause an exception.

Termination handler ran.

Handling exception.

Program ending normally.
```

As you see, one procedure may contain several `try` blocks. A procedure may contain any number of exception and termination handlers, and they may be nested as these are, or they may appear in succession.

A `finally` block always executes when its `try` block finishes, but it does not execute if an exception interrupts the thread before the `try` block begins. In this revision of the preceding program, for example, the termination handler does *not* execute:

```
#include <windows.h>
#include <stdio.h>

int main ( )
{
    char *szText = NULL;

    try
    {
        puts("About to cause an exception." );
        lstrcpy( szText, "Error" );          // writes to NULL string

        try
        {
            puts( "Entered try block." );
        }
        finally
        {
            puts( "Termination handler ran." );
        }
    }
```

```
except (EXCEPTION_EXECUTE_HANDLER)
{
    puts( "Handling exception." );
}

puts( "Program ending normally." );
return( 0 );
}
```

The except block handles the exception, but the finally block never runs. The trace message from the termination message does not appear in the output.

```
About to cause an exception.

Handling exception.

Program ending normally.
```

As a further illustration, here's how the Threads program from Chapter 4 ought to make use of nested exception and termination handlers. Because of the procedure's new exception handler, the thread will continue to run even after an exception occurs (provided the exception permits continuation). The termination handler guarantees that the mutex will be released in any case, so no matter what happens to one thread the others may still acquire the mutex that lets them continue drawing.

```
/*------------------------------------------------------------------
        START THREAD
        This is called when each thread begins execution
        ----------------------------------------------------------*/

LONG StartThread ( LPVOID lpThreadData )
{
    DWORD *pdwThreadID;      // pointer to a DWORD for storing thread's ID
    DWORD dwWait;            // return value from WaitSingleObject

    /* retrieve the thread's ID */
    pdwThreadID = lpThreadData;

    /* draw continuously until bTerminate becomes TRUE */
    while (!bTerminate)
    {
        if (bUseMutex)
        {
            /* draw when this thread gets the mutex */
            dwWait = WaitForSingleObject( hDrawMutex, INFINITE );
```

```
        if (dwWait == 0)                    // did wait succeed?
        {
            try
            {
                try
                {
                    DrawProc( *pdwThreadID );
                }
                finally
                {
                    ReleaseMutex( hDrawMutex );
                }
            }
            except (EXCEPTION_EXECUTE_HANDLER)
            {
                MessageBox( hwndParent, "A thread was unable to draw.",
                    "Threads Message", MB_OK | MB_ICONEXCLAMATION );
            }
        }
    }
    else
    {
        /* not using mutex; let the thread draw */
        DrawProc( *pdwThreadID );
    }
}

/* stop this thread and return */
ExitThread(0);                           // now thread is not running
CloseHandle(hThread[*pdwThreadID]);      // now thread is destroyed
return( 0L );
}
```

Leaps and Bounds

Jumping into and out of try blocks and handler blocks requires some care. First, no part of an exception or termination handler may be entered by jumping. Execution must flow in sequentially through the opening bracket of a try block, and the try block must be the only path into the handler. You may jump *out* of try, except, and finally blocks, but never in. Compiling the following example produces an error:

```
goto bumsteer;

try
{
    < guarded code here >
}
except (EXCEPTION_EXECUTE_HANDLER)
{
    bumsteer:
}
```

A goto statement that jumps out of a try block ends the block. In a try/finally sequence, the goto statement triggers the termination handler.

```
#include <windows.h>
#include <stdio.h>

int main ( )
{
    char *szText = NULL;

    try
    {
        puts( "In try block." );
        goto label1;                   // this jump ends the try block
    }
    finally
    {
        puts( "In finally block." );
    }

label1:
    puts( "Ending program." );
    return( 0 );
}
```

When that program runs it produces the following output:

```
In try block.

In finally block.

Ending program.
```

The code in the `finally` block executes before the `goto` statement even though `goto` comes first in the listing.

A `goto` statement leaving the `try` block of an exception handler also ends the `try` block. The exception this sample generates occurs too late to trigger the exception-handling code.

```c
#include <windows.h>
#include <stdio.h>

int main ( )
{
    char *szText = NULL;

    try
    {
        puts( "In try block." );
        goto label1;
    }
    except (EXCEPTION_EXECUTE_HANDLER)
    {
        puts( "In except block." );          // this line doesn't happen
    }

label1:
    puts( "Jumped to 'label1'; forcing an exception." );
    lstrcpy( szText, "Error" );              // writes to NULL pointer

    puts( "Ending program." );               // this line doesn't happen
    return( 0 );
}
```

The exception occurs outside the `try` block, so a run of this program should produce the following output:

```
In try block.

Jumped to 'label1'; forcing an exception.
```

We say "should" because in our version of the system a bug fails to end the `try` block after the `goto` and the exception *does* trigger its handler. The exception handler runs; execution flows forward and reaches the bad **lstrcpy** a second time. When the system correctly realizes that no `try` block is pending, it aborts the program and shows its own message box.

```
In try block.

Jumped to 'label1'; forcing an exception.

In except block.

Jumped to 'label1'; forcing an exception.
```

Then the program aborts. Microsoft has promised to fix this bug for the system's public release, so the program should work for you as we first described it.

Back-Stacking

We've said that when an exception occurs, the system backtracks through the stack seeking a hospitable handler. The next sample, Unwind, puts three frames on the stack, each with a different handler, and generates exceptions from the bottom level to see where they go.

```c
#include <windows.h>
#include <stdio.h>
#include <float.h>

//  Function prototypes.
//

void MiddleProc( void );            // intermediate function
void InnerProc( void );             // causes various exceptions

//  MAIN
//  Program entry point.

int main ( )
{
    puts( "Starting program." );

    try
    {
        MiddleProc();
    }

    // This exception handler responds if anything lower
    // down in the program generates an exception without
    // providing a handler.
```

```
    except (EXCEPTION_EXECUTE_HANDLER)
    {
        puts( "Unwind encountered an unknown error." );
    }

    puts( "Program ending normally." );
    return( 0 );
}

// MIDDLE PROC
// Calls the function that raises exceptions.

void MiddleProc ( void )
{
    puts( "Starting MiddleProc." );

    try
    {
        puts( "In try block of MiddleProc." );
        InnerProc();
    }
    except ((GetExceptionCode() == EXCEPTION_ACCESS_VIOLATION)
            ? EXCEPTION_EXECUTE_HANDLER : EXCEPTION_CONTINUE_SEARCH)
    {
        puts( "MiddleProc recognized an access violation." );
    }

    puts( "MiddleProc ending normally." );
    return;
}

// INNER PROC
// Causes exceptions.

void InnerProc ( void )
{
    char *szText = NULL;
    int i1;
    int i2 = 0;
    float f1 = FLT_MAX;
    UINT uFPMask;

    puts( "Starting InnerProc." );
```

```
uFPMask = _controlfp( 0, 0 );
uFPMask &= ~EM_OVERFLOW;
_controlfp( uFPMask, MCW_EM );

try
{
    // This block can produce any of three different
    // exceptions. Comment out some lines to test
    // how the program handles each exception.

    puts( "Forcing an integer divide-by-zero error." );
    i1 = i1 / i2;                        // handled in InnerProc

    // puts( "Forcing an access violation." );
    // lstrcpy( szText, "Hello" );       // handled in MiddleProc
    // puts( "Forcing a floating point overflow." );
    // f1 = f1 * f1;                     // handled in main

    puts( "This is never printed." );
}
except ((GetExceptionCode() == EXCEPTION_INT_DIVIDE_BY_ZERO)
        ? EXCEPTION_EXECUTE_HANDLER : EXCEPTION_CONTINUE_SEARCH)
{
    puts( "InnerProc encountered divide-by-zero error." );
}

puts( "InnerProc ending normally." );
return;
}
```

The innermost procedure, InnerProc, contains statements to generate any of three exceptions. Choose which exception by commenting out the lines you don't want. The handler in the InnerProc frame accepts only the integer divide-by-zero exception. The floating-point and access violation exceptions have to be handled in preceding frames.

Unwind issues trace messages as it proceeds, marking its progress through the code. Each of the exceptions produces a different set of trace messages.

Exception	Trace Messages
EXCEPTION_INT_ DIVIDE_BY_ZERO	Starting program.
	Starting MiddleProc.

Exception	Trace Messages
	In try block of MiddleProc.
	Starting InnerProc.
	Forcing an integer divide-by-zero error.
	InnerProc encountered divide-by-zero error.
	InnerProc ending normally.
	MiddleProc ending normally.
	Program ending normally.
EXCEPTION_ ACCESS_VIOLATION	Starting program.
	Starting MiddleProc.
	In try block of MiddleProc.
	Starting InnerProc.
	Forcing an access violation.
	MiddleProc recognized an access violation.
	MiddleProc ending normally.
	Program ending normally.
EXCEPTION_ FLT_OVERFLOW	Starting program.
	Starting MiddleProc.
	In try block of MiddleProc.
	Starting InnerProc.
	Forcing a floating point overflow.
	Unwind encountered an unknown error.
	Program ending normally.

The trace messages confirm that an exception handler gains complete control over execution of the program. No matter what procedure generates the exception, execution resumes in the procedure where the exception is handled. For example, when Unwind creates a memory access exception, `InnerProc` does not terminate normally. Only `main` and `MiddleProc` issue their closing trace messages

The outer `try` block, the one in `main`, serves as a catchall for any exceptions not handled elsewhere. Because the `except` block comes just before the closing `return` statement the program terminates whenever this handler runs, but the handler still manages to shield the user from the system's default message box with its cryptic exception addresses.

Incidentally, `InnerProc` would never generate a floating-point exception if it neglected to enable the exception with `_controlfp` first.

Our version of the compiler mistakenly generates a −W4 warning for this line of the Unwind program:

```
except (EXCEPTION_EXECUTE_HANDLER)
```

Apparently the compiler dislikes the use of a single constant as the filter expression and misinterprets the line as meaningless:

```
unwind.c(31) : warning C4705: statement has no effect
```

Microsoft is aware of the bug and has promised to fix it in time for the system's public release.

Having followed the intricacies of Unwind, you may find it easier now to understand how the system walks the stack for exceptions. First, an exception handler receives exceptions from only one thread. If a `try` block calls `CreateThread` or `CreateProcess`, the handler will not receive exceptions that arise when the new thread executes its own instructions. Second, while it is legal to put `return` in the middle of a `finally` block, the result may not be what you intend. When an exception occurs, the system may have to walk back through several frames to find a handler. When it does find one, it goes through the stack again to find and execute all the intervening termination handlers whose `try` blocks the jump interrupts. This is called *unwinding the stack*. Unwinding proceeds sequentially through all the pending handlers until the system reaches the target frame *or* until one of the `finally` blocks ends with `return`. Executing a `return` statement within a `finally` block halts any unwinding that may be in progress. This is called *colliding the stack*. Handlers and filters still waiting on the stack will be skipped over. Any actions they were expected to perform will not be performed, and that omission could conceivably impede the target handler at the end of the unwind operation.

A Filter Function

All the exception handlers in Unwind tenaciously transfer execution to their own frames when they execute. Sometimes it would be useful to determine the cause of the error, modify some data, and try to run the offending instruction again. This snippet revises Unwind's InnerProc procedure to modify variables and resume whenever a divide-by-zero exception occurs. Only a filter function can attempt to reexecute code that generated an exception.

```
//  INNER PROC
//  Causes exceptions.

void InnerProc ( void )
{
    char *szText = NULL;
    int i1;
    int i2 = 0;
    float f1 = FLT_MAX;
    UINT uFPMask;

    puts( "Starting InnerProc." );

    uFPMask = _controlfp( 0, 0 );
    uFPMask &= ~EM_OVERFLOW;
    _controlfp( uFPMask, MCW_EM );
    try
    {
        // This block can produce any of three different
        // exceptions. Comment out some lines to test
        // how the program handles each exception.

        puts( "Forcing an integer divide-by-zero error." );
        i1 = i1 / i2;                    // handled in InnerProc

        // puts( "Forcing an access violation." );
        // lstrcpy( szText, "Hello" );   // handled in MiddleProc
```

```
        // puts( "Forcing a floating-point overflow." );
        // f1 = f1 * f1;                    // handled in main
    }
    except (MyFilter( GetExceptionCode(), &i2 ))
    {};

    puts( "InnerProc ending normally." );
    return;
}


// MY FILTER
// Filter function for the exception handler in InnerProc

LONG MyFilter (
    DWORD dwCode,
    int *i )
{
    if (dwCode == EXCEPTION_INT_DIVIDE_BY_ZERO)
    {
        puts( "MyFilter fixed divide-by-zero exception." );
        *i = 1;                                 // modify offending variable
        return( EXCEPTION_CONTINUE_EXECUTION ); // try that instruction again
    }
    return( EXCEPTION_CONTINUE_SEARCH );
}
```

When this version of Unwind runs it produces these trace messages:

```
        Starting program.

        Starting MiddleProc.

        In try block of MiddleProc.

        Starting InnerProc.

        Forcing an integer divide-by-zero error.

        MyFilter fixed divide-by-zero exception.

        InnerProc ending normally.

        MiddleProc ending normally.

        Program ending normally.
```

An Error-Handling System

The final sample program, Errors, establishes a system for handling program errors. It stores descriptive error strings in a message table, defines two exceptions to signal private events within the program, and builds an exception handler that displays the message corresponding with each exception.

The Message Compiler

A message table resource is a specialized string table. It is intended for programs that log events and need several complete sets of all the possible messages, each set in a different language. A separate utility program called the Message Compiler facilitates numbering so that each message always has the same ID number in any language. The **FormatMessage** command, introduced in Chapter 5, displays messages from a custom table as easily as from the system table.

A message table begins as a text file, conventionally having the extension .MC, that contains several pieces of information describing each message. The Message Compiler reads the .MC file and generates three new files from it. The first is a binary resource file containing all the messages in compiled form. The message compiler creates one binary file, marked with the extension .BIN, for each language used in the .MC file. In addition, the Message Compiler produces a short resource file (.RC) that refers to the binary files and a header file with defined constants for the source modules that use the messages.

The make file that compiles Errors includes a Message Compiler command to create errors.rc from errors.mc. The same command also generates the files errors.h and msg00001.bin. Programs that use larger message tables with more languages often compile them all into a single DLL, but Errors simply leaves its table in the .EXE file. Although it is a console application, Errors does have resources and displays message boxes. In order to call **MessageBox**, the make file adds user32.lib to the Link32 command line.

```
#
#    NMake file for ERRORS program
#

#
#    Define macros for command-line options and library modules
#
```

```
!IFDEF NODEBUG
CFLAGS = -c -G3 -Os -W3 -D_X86_=1 -DWIN32
LFLAGS = -subsystem:console
!ELSE
CFLAGS = -c -G3 -Od -W4 -Zi -D_X86_=1 -DWIN32
LFLAGS = -debug:full -debugtype:cv -subsystem:console
!ENDIF

LIBS = libc.lib ntdll.lib kernel32.lib user32.lib


#
#    Create all the pieces
#

all: errors.exe

errors.rc: errors.mc
    mc $*.mc

errors.obj: errors.c errors.h errors.rbj
    cl386 $(CFLAGS) $*.c

errors.rbj: errors.rc errors.mc
    rc $*.rc
    cvtres -i386 $*.res -o $*.rbj

errors.exe: errors.obj errors.rbj
    link32 $(LFLAGS) -out:$*.exe $*.obj $*.rbj $(LIBS)
```

The message file, errors.mc, contains the text of two messages, each describing one privately defined program exception. Each message in the message table is accompanied by information describing its ID number, its degree of severity, the facility that invokes the message, a symbolic name, and a language indicator. We have chosen to leave the MessageID fields blank and permit the compiler to supply ID numbers. MessageID values are limited to 16 bits. (We'll say more about those bits in a moment.) The degree of severity and the facility name matter only if you want to define them in some way useful to your program. If your program wants to distinguish warnings from errors, perhaps with a different message box icon, then you need two degrees of severity. To distinguish messages from different program modules, define a facility to code to represent each module. These are the default severities and facilities:

```
SeverityNames=(
    Success=0x0
    Informational=0x1
    Warning=0x2
    Error=0x3 )

FacilityNames=(
    System=0x0FF
    Application=0xFFF )
```

Errors uses a single facility name to indicate that its exceptions arise from within the application. It redefines the two default facilities in order to associate a symbol, FACILITY_APP_ERRORS, with the one value it uses. It is also possible to define your own set of severity codes and attach symbols to them. Severity codes are 2-bit values; facility codes may use 12 bits. To put comments in the message header file you must use both semicolons and /* markers because the message compiler strips out the semicolons.

```
;/*
;        ERRORS.MC
;        Message strings for the Errors program message table.
;*/

FacilityNames=
(
    System=0x0FF
    Application=0xFFF:FACILITY_APP_ERRORS
)

;/* first message */
MessageID=
Severity=Error
Facility=Application
SymbolicName=ERRORS_ERROR_NO_NAME

Language=English
Rats. Another crook stays nameless.
file: %1
line: %2!1d!%0
    .
```

```
;/* second message */
MessageID=
Severity=Success
SymbolicName=ERRORS_SUCCESS_MASTERMIND

Language=English
Eureka!  We've found the mastermind.
file: %1
line: %2!ld!%0
.
```

Each message gets an ID, a severity, and a facility. An omitted field receives as a default value whatever value it had in the preceding message. Each of our messages has three text lines: an explanatory string, a file name, and a line number. The second and third text lines contain formatting codes to indicate where a file name and a line number will be inserted when the program runs. %1 and %2 mark the positions of each insertion. The string "!ld!" indicates a long integer in decimal format. Because the %1 marker does not specify a format, it uses the default "!s!" string format. %0 is not an argument like %1 and %2; it simply prevents the compiler from appending a newline character to the end of the message.

The Message Compiler automatically begins every message header file with a long standard comment explaining how it constructs error codes. Each error code combines several different values with a logical OR, so the ID value that identifies an error at run time encodes several pieces of information about the condition that produced it. The primary piece of information is, of course, the 16-bit MessageID value. Bits 16–27 carry the facility code, and the two high-order bits show the severity level. In addition, the system uses bit 29 to distinguish messages the system defines from custom messages a program defines. When bit 29 is set, you can safely use a single number to identify both an exception and an associated message; bit 29 prevents conflicts between your own message IDs and the system's predefined message IDs. Unfortunately, our sample program cannot demonstrate this feature because the beta version of the message compiler provides no way to set bit 29. Microsoft's engineers tell us to look for a command-line switch in the final version that turns the bit off or on. Check the online help file tools.hlp for more current information. Errors.h defines three manifest constants based on information in the .MC file. One identifies the only facility marker Errors uses, and the other two identify each of the two messages.

```
/*
        ERRORS.H
        Symbol definitions for the Errors program message table.
*/
/* first message */
//
//   Values are 32-bit values laid out as follows:
//
//    3 3 2 2 2 2 2 2 2 2 2 2 1 1 1 1 1 1 1 1 1 1
//    1 0 9 8 7 6 5 4 3 2 1 0 9 8 7 6 5 4 3 2 1 0 9 8 7 6 5 4 3 2 1 0
//   +---+-+-+---------------------+-----------------------------+
//   |Sev|C|R|       Facility      |              Code           |
//   +---+-+-+---------------------+-----------------------------+
//
//   where
//
//        Sev - is the severity code
//
//             00 - Success
//             01 - Informational
//             10 - Warning
//             11 - Error
//
//        C - is the Customer code flag
//
//        R - is a reserved bit
//
//        Facility - is the facility code
//
//        Code - is the facility's status code
//
//
// Define the facility codes
//
#define FACILITY_APP_ERRORS               0xFFF

//
// Define the severity codes
//
```

```
//
// MessageId: ERRORS_ERROR_NO_NAME
//
// MessageText:
//
//  Rats. Another crook stays nameless.
//  file: %1
//  line: %2!ld!%0
//
#define ERRORS_ERROR_NO_NAME                 0xCFFF0001L

/* second message */
//
// MessageId: ERRORS_SUCCESS_MASTERMIND
//
// MessageText:
//
//  Eureka!  We've found the mastermind.
//  file: %1
//  line: %2!ld!%0
//
#define ERRORS_SUCCESS_MASTERMIND            0x0FFF0002L
```

The Message Compiler produces a resource script as well as a header file. The resource script simply refers to the binary file where the compiled strings are. The resource compiler copies the binary message table into the program's executable file (or into a separate DLL if you wish). The resource file for Errors looks like this:

```
LANGUAGE 0x9,0x1
1 11 MSG00001.bin
```

The Source Code

The source code file begins by including the errors.h header that the Message Compiler just created. The program calls two subroutines. One asks the user to enter a name, and the other echoes the name back to the screen. Each subroutine sometimes raises an exception. GetName raises an exception if the user enters an empty string. For convenience we assign this exception the same ID number as the message that describes it, namely ERRORS_ERROR_NO_NAME. The second routine, Check-Name, raises an exception if the user happens to enter the name "Moriarty". The symbol identifying this exception is ERRORS_SUCCESS_MASTERMIND. A single exception handler in the main program responds to all exceptions. If the exception ID contains the `FACILITY_APP_ERRORS` code in its upper half then the exception handler calls a procedure to display the error message. Any unexpected system exceptions produce a single generic warning message.

In Figure 6.4 the user entered "Moriarty" and the Errors program raised one of its exceptions.

FIGURE 6.4:

Errors program displaying a message in response to a privately defined exception

```
/*------------------------------------------------------------------

        ERRORS.C

        Basic outline for using structured exception handling and
        message tables to process program errors.

        FUNCTIONS
                main                    main routine
                GetName                 ask user to enter a name
                CheckName               see whether user typed "Moriarty"
                MainFilter              interpret exception signals
                ShowExceptionMsg        show messages from message table
```

```
        from Programming for Windows NT
        copyright 1993 by Brian Myers & Eric Hamer


    ------------------------------------------------------------------*/

#include <windows.h>
#include <stdio.h>
#include "errors.h"

/*------------------------------------------------------------------
        FUNCTION PROTOTYPES
    ------------------------------------------------------------------*/

void GetName( void );
void CheckName( void );
LONG MainFilter( LPEXCEPTION_POINTERS lpEP );
void ShowExceptionMsg( DWORD dwMsgCode, LPVOID lpvArgs );

/*------------------------------------------------------------------
        GLOBAL VARIABLE
    ------------------------------------------------------------------*/

char szName[40];                         // string user enters

/*------------------------------------------------------------------
        MAIN
        Call two I/O procedures and check for exceptions.
    ------------------------------------------------------------------*/

int main ( )
{
    try
    {
        GetName( );                      // get name from user
        CheckName( );                    // see what the user typed
    }
    except (MainFilter( GetExceptionInformation() ))
    {
    }

    return( 0 );
}
```

```
/*-------------------------------------------------------------------
        GET NAME
        Ask user to enter a name string.
    -------------------------------------------------------------------*/

void GetName ( void )
{
    /* get name from user */
    printf( "Enter your name: " );
    gets( szName );

    /* check whether user entered any characters */
    if (lstrlen((LPSTR)szName) < 1)
    {
        /* user entered nothing; raise an exception */

        DWORD adwArgs[2];              // arguments for exception handler
        char szFile[FILENAME_MAX];   // buffer to store source file name

        /* store handler arguments in array */
        lstrcpy( szFile, __FILE__ );
        adwArgs[0] = (DWORD)szFile;
        adwArgs[1] = __LINE__;

        /* call for an exception handler */
        RaiseException(
            ERRORS_ERROR_NO_NAME,
            0,
            2,
            adwArgs );
    }
    return;
}


/*-------------------------------------------------------------------
        CHECK NAME
        Raise an exception if the user typed "Moriarty".
    -------------------------------------------------------------------*/

void CheckName ( void )
{
    /* did the user enter the name "Moriarty"? */
```

```
    if (lstrcmp( szName, "Moriarty" ) == 0)
    {
        DWORD adwArgs[2];               // arguments for exception handler
        char szFile[FILENAME_MAX];  // buffer to store source file name

        /* store handler arguments in array */
        lstrcpy( szFile, __FILE__ );
        adwArgs[0] = (DWORD)szFile;
        adwArgs[1] = __LINE__;

        /* call for an exception handler */
        RaiseException(
            ERRORS_SUCCESS_MASTERMIND,
            0,
            2,
            adwArgs );
    }
    else
    {
        printf( "Thank you, " );
        printf( szName );
    }
    return;
}


/*--------------------------------------------------------------------
        MAIN FILTER
        Interpret and respond to exceptions.
    ----------------------------------------------------------------*/

LONG MainFilter ( LPEXCEPTION_POINTERS lpEP )
{
    DWORD   dwCode  = lpEP->ExceptionRecord->ExceptionCode;
    LPDWORD lpdwArgs = lpEP->ExceptionRecord->ExceptionInformation;

    /* is this a private exception? */
    if (HIWORD(dwCode & 0x0FFF0000) == FACILITY_APP_ERRORS)
    {
        /* show a message from the message table */
        ShowExceptionMsg( dwCode, lpdwArgs );
    }
    else /* not a private exception */
    {
        char szMsg[40];
```

```
        /* tell the user something went wrong */
        wsprintf(
            szMsg,
            "Program received unknown exception #%lu",
            dwCode );

        MessageBox( NULL, szMsg, "Errors Message",
                    MB_ICONEXCLAMATION | MB_OK );

    }

    /* resume execution after the except block */
    return( EXCEPTION_EXECUTE_HANDLER );
}


/*-------------------------------------------------------------------
        SHOW EXCEPTION MESSAGE
        Display a message box with a string from the program's
        message table.
        -----------------------------------------------------------*/

void ShowExceptionMsg (
    DWORD dwMsgCode,
    LPVOID lpvArgs )
{
    LPTSTR lpMessage;

    /* pull string from message table and insert formatted arguments in it */
    FormatMessage(
        FORMAT_MESSAGE_FROM_HMODULE             // take message table string
      | FORMAT_MESSAGE_ALLOCATE_BUFFER          // allocate a buffer for it
      | FORMAT_MESSAGE_ARGUMENT_ARRAY,          // read lpvArgs as DWORD array
        NULL,                                   // message table is in this module
        dwMsgCode,                              // code identifying message
        MAKELANGID(LANG_ENGLISH, SUBLANG_ENGLISH_US),    // message's language
        (LPTSTR)&lpMessage,                     // pointer for new buffer
        0,                                      // ignored with _ALLOCATE_BUFFER
        lpvArgs );                              // values to insert in string

    // lpvArgs points to the DWORD array containing the location
    // of the source file name string and a line number. FormatMessage
    // inserts those values at the format markers (!s! and !ld!) in
    // the message string.
```

```
/* display the message in a message box */
MessageBox( NULL, lpMessage, "Errors Message",
            MB_ICONEXCLAMATION | MB_OK );

/* release the buffer allocated by FormatMessage */
LocalFree( lpMessage );

return;
}
```

Raising the exceptions takes a little work because we decided to pass information to the exception handler through the last parameter of **RaiseException**, an array of **DWORD**s. The first element of the array holds a pointer to a string naming the source file, in this case "errors.c". The second element holds the line number. (The macros __FILE__ and __LINE__ are predefined by Microsoft's compiler.) The exception filter receives a pointer to the array from **GetExceptionInformation** and passes the pointer on to ShowExceptionMsg.

ShowExceptionMsg is built around a **FormatMessage** command. **FormatMessage** is intended for situations exactly like this, but its parameters are sometimes frustrating to work with. In this procedure, **FormatMessage** retrieves a string from the program's message table, allocates a buffer the proper size, and inserts the file name and line number where they belong. The file name and line number serve no real purpose here, but they can be very useful when debugging larger programs.

In our version of the system, the message box raised during ShowExceptionMsg always appears *behind* the command shell window where the program runs. If the program seems to hang when you expect it to display an exception message, try looking behind the main window. This behavior is a system fault, and Microsoft may have fixed it for the final release.

The try, except, and finally blocks that perform structured exception handling unify the system's responses to a variety of exceptional conditions. They also clarify code by separating the exceptional from the usual. Whenever the system signals an exception, execution jumps to a new location. The system must find an exception handler willing to respond to the particular condition that has arisen. To find one it searches backward through the program stack, frame by frame, for any pending except blocks. Because exceptions cause execution to jump abruptly, a termination handler is sometimes needed to guarantee that cleanup operations occur even if a block of code terminates abnormally. A program can define private exception values and process its own error conditions in the same structured way it processes other exceptional conditions.

Occasionally exception-handling mechanisms are more than just convenient. The next chapter focuses on memory management, and one of its sample programs relies on a `try` block to perform a particular memory task in the most efficient way.

Managing Memory

- **Understanding the Virtual Memory Manager**

- **Reserving and committing virtual memory**

- **Working with multiple heaps**

- **Sharing memory through mapped file objects**

Besides the flashy interface and the multitasking, one of Windows' great attractions has always been memory management. From the 8086 target machine of version 1 all the way up through the 80486, 16-bit Windows has always helped programs make full use of whatever resources the system offers. But MS-DOS, the underlying trellis on which Windows grew, is inherently a 1-megabyte system, and much of the potential of a 32-bit processor remained untapped.

The first crack in the 1MB barrier came with the protected addressing mode of the 80286 processor, which offered access to more memory but was incompatible with the DOS "real" mode. The result was a flurry of proposed memory management standards and DOS extender programs blazing new routes into the frontiers. The methods were ingenious. Temporarily unneeded blocks of code or data were swung up like a Murphy bed into higher memory, and clever programmers insinuated their code into the lowest levels of the system software to hijack allocation requests and smuggle goods across the 1MB border. The original 80286 was never designed for one program to run in two modes. When switching from one to the other, the CPU ground to a halt and reset itself. Like Janus, the two-faced god of doorways, the DOS extender must stand with one leg on each side of the abyss. 16-bit Windows never entirely freed itself from this schizophrenic existence; it just became better adjusted to its inherent neuroses.

With the release of Windows NT, Windows finally transcends the restrictions of DOS and stands independently as a full 32-bit protected-mode operating system. This chapter begins by summarizing the hardware mechanisms and system policies that underlie the memory management of Windows NT. It explains the translation from virtual to physical memory and the paging scheme that supports the protected address spaces. A new set of virtual memory API routines gives you control over individual memory pages. Win32 also adds improved heap management and still preserves the old Global and Local memory functions from the Win16 API. After contrasting the advantages of all three command sets, we'll also explain how processes in protected address spaces can manage to share blocks of memory by creating file-mapping objects. The first of two sample programs constructs a dynamically allocated array using virtual memory functions, and the second shares a block of memory among instances of a program that lets the user view and edit the contents of the shared memory.

CONCEPTS

The Windows NT memory management API, working with an imagined logical address space of 4GB, is supported internally by the Virtual Memory Manager, which in turn bases its services on the features of advanced 32-bit processors. Windows NT requires its hardware to use 32-bit memory addresses, to map virtual to physical addresses, and to perform memory paging. From these basic capabilities, the Virtual Memory Manager constructs its own mechanisms and policies for managing virtual memory.

The Virtual Memory Manager

Like virtual reality, virtual memory isn't the real thing but does a good job of pretending to be. The 4GB of memory addresses every Windows NT program commands is a virtual space. The system does not contain 4GB of physical memory, yet somehow a program is able to use any address in the full range. Obviously a translator somewhere in the background must silently convert each memory reference into an existing physical address. From this silent conversion the memory manager draws much of its power.

The Virtual Memory Manager is the part of the Windows NT system responsible for mapping references to a program's virtual address space into physical memory. The VMM decides where to put each memory object and which memory pages should be written to disk. It also isolates each process in a separate address space by refusing to translate virtual addresses from one process into the physical memory used by another process. It supports the illusion of an idealized, logical space of 4GB, just as the GDI supports the illusion that every program draws to idealized logical display coordinates. The system translates logical addresses or coordinates into physical locations and prevents programs from colliding with each other by trying to use the same resource at the same time.

Pointers and Movable Memory

MS-DOS programmers customarily work with pointers to memory objects. If the object moves to another location, the pointer becomes invalid. On a machine that runs only one program at a time, pointers work fine, but multitasking systems need to manage system memory more actively, loading and discarding pieces on demand and moving pieces to make more room. The first versions of Windows got around the problem by substituting handles for pointers wherever possible. A handle points to an entry in an object table, and the table remembers where each object actually is at any given moment. When the system moves an object, it updates the table. The handles pointing to the table remain valid even when the object moves because they point to the place where the real pointer is kept, and the system keeps the real pointer current.

Processors running in a protected mode provide a similar layering mechanism for all memory addresses. Instead of working with pointers containing segments and offsets, Intel CPUs work with *selectors* and offsets. A selector is to memory what a handle is to Windows: a pointer to a pointer. To give a simplified account, the selector, with its offset, refers to a system table that keeps track of memory addresses. In a sense, protected mode has built-in memory handles. The difference is that selectors live at a much lower level in the system than handles do. The hardware knows what a selector is—the CPU can decode them—but only Windows knows what a handle is. Windows can have handles only where Windows itself creates them. You have to make an effort to use handles instead of pointers, but protected mode gives you selectors whether you want them or not. Even when you lock down memory, the system lets you see only the selector, not the physical address. Your program doesn't care. The code that worked with pointers works just as well with selectors, only now it doesn't matter if the system moves what your selector "points" to. The operating system can move objects through memory with impunity as long as it remembers to update the corresponding memory table entry. The entry may change but the selector does not. The selector always points to the same place in the table, and the table is guaranteed to point to your memory object. As a consequence, you can safely use and preserve a pointer without impeding any other program in the least.

The conversion from a selector and its offset to a physical address involves two stages: a trivial conversion from a logical to a virtual address, and a complex conversion from a linear address to a physical address. The first conversion, from a logical segmented address to a virtual linear address, simply adds an offset to a base address. NT makes this conversion trivial by keeping the base address set always to 0. If the segment is constant, only the offset matters. The 32-bit offset may range from 0 to 4GB, exactly the range of the system's flat linear addresses. Under NT, a 32-bit selector addresses all of virtual memory in much the same way that small-model programs address their entire segment with a single near pointer. But a linear address is still not a physical address. In the second and more complex conversion, the VMM parses the linear address into indices for the process's paging tables, which contain physical addresses.

Paging

The use of virtual addresses confers many benefits, among them the illusion of working in a very large space. Windows NT allows the virtual addresses to range from 0 to 4MB regardless of the physical memory actually installed on the current system. Obviously a problem arises if all the running programs try to allocate all the virtual memory they think they see all at once. Like a crooked bank, the system goes suddenly broke if all its customers cash in at the same time. Physical memory always imposes some kind of upper limit, but a paging system raises the limit considerably by setting off part of a hard disk to act as additional memory.

The CPUs on which Windows NT runs have built-in memory-paging capabilities. Small blocks of memory called pages can be saved to the disk when not in use to make more room. A page interrupt occurs whenever a program tries to read a part of memory that has been moved to the disk. The program doesn't ever know the memory is gone; the CPU generates an error, the operating system reloads the missing page, and the program resumes. If blocks of memory can be saved and restored as needed, nothing prevents the system from overcommitting memory. If you have a thousand pages of memory then you could have, for example, two thousand pages' worth of code. It can't all be in memory at once, but any block can always be loaded when needed. Of course, disks are slower than RAM. Virtual memory works best if your hard drive is large, fast, and partly empty.

Much of the Virtual Memory Manager's energy goes into moving and recovering pages of memory. Windows NT can work with pages of up to 64K, but the Intel CPU enforces a size of 4K. A 4K block of memory aligned on a 4K boundary is called a *page frame*. The term *page* refers to the data a program stores in a page frame. There are usually more pages than page frames; some of the pages have been saved in the paging file. Though the contents of a page remain the same, it may appear in different page frames at different times as the memory manager adjusts to the demands of all the current programs.

In order to satisfy requests for memory, the memory manager maintains several data structures. It must be able, for example, to traverse a list of page frames to see which are free and which are full and also to determine which process currently owns any given page. The structure that holds this set of information is the *page frame database*. Through the database the VMM, given any page, can find the process that owns it. Another data structure, called a *page table*, works in the other direction. Every process has at least one page table, so given any process the VMM can find all the pages it owns. When the memory manager assigns physical memory to a process, it updates the database and also adds an entry to a page table. Whenever a process refers to a virtual address, the memory manager looks up the address in a page table to find the associated memory. Besides a virtual address and its corresponding physical address, the page table entry records other information about each page, including whether the page is protected (read-only, for example) and whether it is in memory or swapped to the disk. A swapped page is marked invalid in the page table.

For the convenience of the hardware, a single page table takes up exactly 4K. One 4K page table has room for 1024 different entries. Each entry points to a single page. If one page table can point to 1024 pages and each page is 4K, then one page table can address 4MB of memory (1024 x 4096). A process that uses more memory receives more page tables. Each process has a single master table, called a *page directory*, pointing to all its page tables. A page directory also holds up to 1024 entries. With 1024 page tables, each addressing 4MB, a process can reach up to 4GB (4MB x 1024). Because each page directory and page table occupies exactly 4K, or one page frame, the system can easily swap the directory and tables in and out of memory along with all the other pages as needed. The diagram in Figure 7.1 should help clarify how page directories point to page tables that point to pages, and at the same time the page frame database keeps a separate list of each page's current status. Most memory operations occur more rapidly than this elaborate indexing scheme seems to allow because the CPU caches frequently used virtual address translations in a fast hardware buffer called the Translation Lookaside Buffer (TLB).

The page frame database records the current state of each page frame. A page frame is always in one of six states:

- **Valid:** Contains a page some process is using. A page table entry points to it.

- **Standby:** Contains a page that was in use, but the memory manager has decided to free it for some process. A standby page has been removed from the process's working set.

- **Modified:** A page the VMM wants to discard, but because the process has modified the page, it must first be saved to disk.

FIGURE 7.1:

How the system finds a process's physical memory through the page directory and page tables

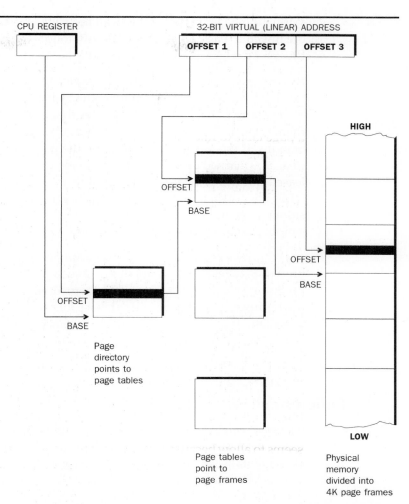

- **Free:** A frame that is no longer owned by any process. Anything it contained has been saved to disk.

- **Zeroed:** A frame belonging to no one and full of nothing but zeros. Only zeroed pages may be given to any process.

- **Bad:** A frame that generated a parity error or other hardware error and cannot be used.

Within the page frame database, all the page entries with the same status marker are linked to each other. The VMM can follow a different series of links to find all the zeroed pages, all the free pages, all the standby pages, and so on.

Releasing a page frame involves several steps, and the status marker reflects how far along the process the memory manager has come. When it needs to make room, the memory manager looks for frames that haven't been used recently and marks them for later disposal. If the page has not been changed by its process, it is marked Standby. If the process has written to the page so that it needs to be saved to the disk, it is marked Modified. Both markers indicate that the page is ready to be released but has not yet been released. If the owning process tries to use the page while it is still marked Standby or Modified, the system responds quickly to the resulting page fault because it does not have to read the page back from the disk. It simply changes the status back to Valid.

For security reasons, any page frame assigned to a process must be zeroed first. No process may receive memory that still contains information left behind by another program. When the list of available zeroed pages runs low, the memory manager reads through the page frame database following all the links to free pages and zeroes them. If memory is still low, the memory manager wakes one of its threads to find Modified pages and save them, slowly and one by one in the background, so as not to interfere with system performance.

Policies and Working Sets

It should be clear now that the memory manager keeps a constant watch over the status of all the system pages. If one process uses more physical memory than allowed in its security quota, the memory manager steps in and invalidates some of its pages by marking them Standby or Modified, and eventually their page frames may be released. The group of page frames currently in use by one process is the process's *working set*. Like an embezzler, the Virtual Memory Manager sneaks through the system and steals frames out from under processes as they run, hoping no one will notice. When a process begins to complain with a flurry of page faults, the memory manager placates it by enlarging its working set. Busy programs end up with bigger sets.

The memory manager follows defined policies in deciding when to retrieve swapped pages, where to place restored pages in memory, and what to swap out first when the system needs more room. NT's retrieval policy is called "demand paging with clustering." *Demand paging* means the memory manager loads pages only when a program asks for them rather than trying to minimize delays by anticipating what a program will need. The system does try to anticipate to some extent by *clustering*, which means that in response to each demand the system actually loads several adjacent pages, figuring that memory operations often center on a single region, so nearby pages may be needed soon.

The placement policy determines where reloaded pages are put. The memory manager tries to put them on the first zeroed page frames it finds in the page frame database, and when it runs out of zeroed frames it begins searching the lists of frames in other states. When deciding on pages to swap out, the memory manager follows a "local FIFO" replacement policy. *Local* in this context means that the system makes room for one page in a process by dropping another page from the same process. By keeping the working set for each process to a roughly constant size, the system prevents one program from monopolizing resources. *FIFO* means "first in first out." Within one process's working set, the pages that have been in memory longest are the first to go. Pages a program touches often may be marked invalid, but the process will probably recover them from their transitional standby or modified state before the VMM actually saves the contents and zeroes the frame.

Commitments and Reservations

Now that you know the Virtual Memory Manager is sneaky because it steals pages and lazy because it often invalidates them without bothering to discard them, perhaps you won't be surprised to learn that it sometimes only pretends to allocate the memory you request. To allocate memory, the VMM must construct page tables and search the page frame database for suitable zeroed areas. It may even have to find other invalidated pages and prepare them for use, possibly readjusting the working sets of other programs. If a program allocates a large virtual space but ends up using only parts of it, the memory manager's efforts will have been largely wasted. Instead of allocating physical memory, the memory manager often simply marks part of the process's virtual address space as being in use without securing physical memory to back it up. It *reserves* memory without *committing* it. Reserving memory is like paying with a promissory note. When a program later tries to use some of the reserved memory, cashing in its IOU, the hardware notices because it can't find a page table entry for the given virtual address. It issues a page fault. The memory manager steps in and finally pays its debt, committing physical pages to fulfill an allocation. Of course, even as it commits new page frames for one request it may be invalidating other pages to make room. The sequence of reserving addresses, receiving a page fault, and committing new memory may all be invisible to the oblivious process, which tours its virtual domain like an emperor who walks everywhere on rich carpets, barely noticing the servants who roll out the silk before him and gather it behind as he passes.

To support the illusion of a vast address space, the memory manager requires yet another data structure. A tree of Virtual Address Descriptors (VADs) records each allocation and suballocation the process makes in its range of virtual addresses. Whenever a program allocates memory, the memory manager creates a VAD and adds it to the tree, as shown in Figure 7.2. A VAD records the range of addresses an allocation claims, the protection status for all pages in the range, and whether child processes may inherit the object contained in the range. If a thread uses an address that falls outside the range of any of its VADs, the memory manager knows the address was never reserved and recognizes an access violation.

FIGURE 7.2:

Tree of Virtual Address
Descriptors (VADs)

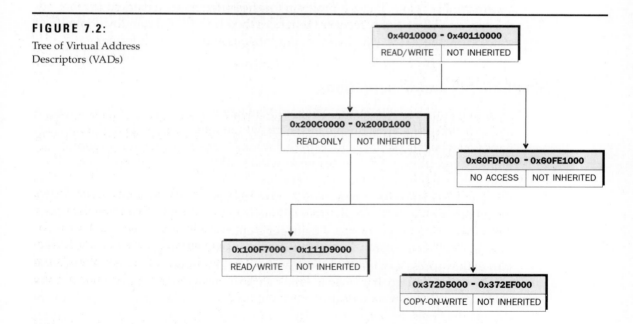

Constructing a Virtual Address Descriptor is much simpler than constructing a page table and filling it with valid page frame addresses. Furthermore, the size of the allocation has no effect on the speed of the response. Reserving 2K is no faster than reserving 2MB; each request produces a single VAD. When a thread actually uses the reserved memory, the memory manager commits page frames by copying information from the descriptor into new page table entries.

Often programs have no need to concern themselves with the differences between reserved and committed memory. Usually it's enough to know that memory will be available when you expect it to be. Among its new features, however, Win32 boasts a set of virtual memory APIs that give you precise control over reserving, committing, and protecting pages of memory. Using them you can allocate a very large memory object, fill it only partially, and waste no memory. The usual example is a spreadsheet because most of its cells are likely to be empty, with data clustering together in a few areas. If you reserve a large range of addresses to represent the entire spreadsheet as an array, the VMM commits physical memory only for the areas actually in use, and it still allows convenient access to any part of the array through a full range of continuous addresses.

The Address Space

Most of what we've explained so far goes on behind the scenes. From the perspective of a running program, what matters most are not the page tables and working sets but the 4GB of virtual address space. Figure 7.3 shows how the system organizes the space.

Although a process does indeed run in a 4GB address space, as the diagram shows the process gets to use only 2GB of those addresses. The system reserves the upper half of the addresses for itself. The high half of the address space is the same for every application, but only kernel-mode threads may use it. In other words, it is accessible only to the operating system. At the very highest addresses the system keeps critical system code that cannot be paged out of memory—for example, the part of the VMM that performs paging operations.

All the pieces of memory over which you have control are mapped into the lower 2GB of the address space. That's where the code and data for a process reside, along with a stack for each thread, at least one default heap, and the program's own DLLs. The system always loads a process's code near the bottom of the address space at

FIGURE 7.3:

Map showing which virtual addresses the system uses for different entities in the address space of a single process

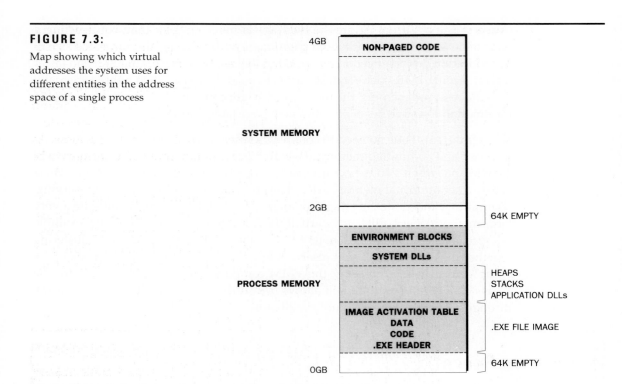

the 64K mark. The 64K at the top of a process's 2GB space also remain permanently empty. The no-man's-land at either end helps the system identify invalid pointers. For example, 0 is never a valid address.

At the lowest available address is an image of the process's .EXE file, including its header, code, data, and an *image activation table*. The activation table aids in dynamic linking. When the linker finds in your code, for example, a **CreateWindow** command, it cannot know in advance where in memory to find the **CreateWindow** code. For all such unresolved dynamic links, the linker creates an entry in the image activation table. When the system loads an executable file it searches for all the DLL entry points listed in the activation table, locates the appropriate DLL, and fixes the table to include the current entry addresses. The linker speeds loading by guessing where the DLLs will be and providing tentative addresses. The Win32 subsystem always tries to map its system DLLs to the same addresses near the top of the 2GB space. If on loading a program the system discovers that the DLLs are indeed in the expected place then the activation table does not need fixing. (You can specify a preferred loading address for your own DLLs too, as you'll see in Chapter 11.)

The loader may not actually copy an entire .EXE file into memory. It is more likely to reserve virtual addresses for the .EXE file and let the memory manager commit physical pages later if the code refers to those addresses. The Win32 subsystem DLLs have been structured to cluster related commands in adjacent addresses. As a result, common calling sequences usually require a minimum of new pages to be loaded.

An application's own DLLs, heaps, and stacks may be allocated anywhere in the address space between the .EXE file image and the system DLLs. The Process Walker, a sample program included with the Win32 SDK, scans through the address space of any process and shows the current status of all allocations. Figure 7.4 shows the Process Walker's view of one of our sample programs, List. As usual, the first allocation begins at 0x00010000, or 64K.

FIGURE 7.4:

What the Process Walker shows about a program's address space

Address	State	Prot	Size	BaseAddress	BaseProt
00000000	Free	NA	65536	00000000	NA
00010000	Commit	RW	4096	00010000	RW
00011000	Free	NA	61440	00000000	NA
00020000	Commit	RW	4096	00020000	RW
00021000	Free	NA	61440	00000000	NA
00030000	Reserve	NA	1036288	00030000	RW
0012d000	Commit	RW	4096	00030000	RW
0012e000	Commit	RW	8192	00030000	RW
00130000	Commit	RW	12288	00130000	RW
00133000	Reserve	NA	1036288	00130000	RW
00230000	Commit	RW	4096	00230000	RW
00231000	Reserve	NA	61440	00230000	RW
00240000	Commit	RO	16384	00240000	RO
00244000	Free	NA	49152	00000000	NA
00250000	Commit	RO	36864	00250000	RO
00259000	Free	NA	28672	00000000	NA
00260000	Commit	RO	266240	00260000	RO
002a1000	Free	NA	61440	00000000	NA
002b0000	Commit	RO	4096	002b0000	RO
002b1000	Free	NA	61440	00000000	NA
002c0000	Commit	RW	65536	002c0000	RW
002d0000	Reserve	NA	1048576	002d0000	NA
003d0000	Free	NA	196608	00000000	NA
00400000	Commit	RO	4096	00400000	NA
00401000	Commit	NA	61440	00400000	NA
00410000	Commit	NA	8192	00400000	NA
00412000	Commit	NA	57344	00400000	NA
00420000	Commit	RW	12288	00400000	NA
00423000	Commit	NA	53248	00400000	NA
00430000	Commit	RO	4096	00400000	NA
00431000	Commit	NA	61440	00400000	NA
00440000	Commit	RW	4096	00400000	NA

Mapped Files

Alert readers may already have wondered what happens when a user initiates several instances of a single program. Given that every process has its own secure address space, must the system load a new copy of the .EXE file for each new instance? If not, how do two processes share the block of memory that contains the file image? The situation calls for a new strategy and one widely useful in many other situations as well.

Normally the memory manager protects programs from each other by ensuring that a virtual address from one process never translates to a page frame in use by another process. Because the memory manager always translates every virtual address into a physical address, no program reaches memory directly and the memory manager easily routes every memory access to a safe location. The scheme also allows, however, for the memory manager to make a single page frame visible in the virtual addresses of different processes. Figure 1.7 in Chapter 1 shows a block of physical memory mapped into two different address spaces. At the operating-system level, a block of shared memory is called a *section object*.

The Win32 subsystem exposes the functionality of section objects to its clients in the form of *memory-mapped files.* Two programs cannot share memory directly, but they can share the same disk file. Of course most of what the process perceives as physical memory is already in a disk-swapping file. In effect, the memory manager lets you retrieve information from the swap file by reading from particular memory addresses. In fact, you can access any disk file the same way, using memory addresses, by creating a memory-mapped file. As an extension of this memory I/O capability, two processes may open the same block of memory as though it were a file, read from it, and write to it. To share memory without creating a new disk file, the programs link the shared object to the system's normal page-swapping file.

When the user launches multiple instances of a program, the system creates a mapped file object to enable all instances to share a single copy of the .EXE file image.

COMMANDS

The Win32 memory management commands fall into three main categories: virtual memory functions, heap functions, and the familiar Global and Local allocation functions. Each set includes commands to allocate and free blocks of memory, but each set manages memory a little differently. We'll survey each group and compare their advantages, look briefly at a few related commands, and finish this section with the API for memory-mapped files.

Virtual Memory

The virtual memory commands, which have names like **VirtualAlloc** and **VirtualFree**, expose some of the memory manager's operations that the other two command sets hide. With the virtual memory commands you can imitate the VMM by reserving addresses without committing memory to support them and by protecting ranges of memory with read-only, read/write, or no-access flags. You can also lock pages in memory to prevent them from being swapped to disk. The other command sets are built on top of the virtual memory commands; these are the basic operations from which the Win32 API builds its other memory services.

Allocating and Freeing

The **VirtualAlloc** command is the starting point for managing your own virtual address space. Its parameters tell how much memory to allocate, where in the address space to situate the new block, whether to commit physical memory, and what kind of protection to set.

```
LPVOID VirtualAlloc(
    LPVOID lpvAddress,              // desired address for new block
    DWORD dwSize,                   // size of new memory block
    DWORD fdwAllocationType,        // reserve addresses or commit memory
    DWORD fdwProtect );             // no access, read-only, or read/write
```

VirtualAlloc tries first to find a range of free addresses marking a block of dwSize bytes beginning at lpvAddress. To do this it searches the process's tree of Virtual Address Descriptors. If the requested range is free, the function returns lpvAddress. If some part of it is in use, the function searches the entire address space looking for any sufficiently large free block. If it finds one, it returns the starting address. Otherwise it returns **NULL**. Most often programs set the first parameter to **NULL** and allow **VirtualAlloc** to place the block anywhere. Controlling the placement of a block may occasionally be useful if, for example, you are debugging a

DLL that usually loads at a particular address. By using **VirtualAlloc** to reserve that address before the DLL loads, you can force it to another location.

The `fdwAllocationType` parameter may be **MEM_RESERVE**, **MEM_COMMIT**, or both combined. To reserve a range of addresses, **VirtualAlloc** simply makes a new Virtual Address Descriptor marking an area in use. It does not, however, allocate any physical memory, so the reserved addresses cannot yet be used for anything. Attempts to read or write reserved pages produce access violation exceptions. On the other hand, no other allocation command may use previously reserved addresses, either. **GlobalAlloc** and `malloc`, for example, cannot place new objects in a range that overlaps with reserved space. If you call **VirtualAlloc** to reserve your entire two gigabytes of address space, all subsequent allocations will fail, even though **VirtualAlloc** has not yet taken up any physical memory.

Reserving addresses has no effect on the system's physical memory. The memory manager makes no guarantee that physical pages will be available when you begin to commit a reserved area. Only when you commit memory does the memory manager find pages to support it. As a consequence, the system does not charge reserved memory against a process's system resource quotas. Only memory actually in use counts against the quota.

Memory cannot be committed without being reserved. By combining the **MEM_RE-SERVE** and **MEM_COMMIT** flags, you can reserve and commit at the same time. More often programs call **VirtualAlloc** once to reserve a large area and then many times subsequently to commit parts of the area piece by piece.

The `fdwProtect` flag determines how a page or range of pages may be used. For memory that is only reserved, the flag must be **PAGE_NOACCESS**. When committing memory, you can optionally change the protection to **PAGE_READONLY** or **PAGE_READWRITE**. No other programs can read memory in your address space anyway, so read-only protection guards against bugs in your own program that might accidentally corrupt some important part of your data. Protection levels apply to individual pages. The pages in a single range of memory may have different protection flags. You can, for example, apply **PAGE_READONLY** to an entire block and temporarily change single pages to allow write access as needed. You cannot write-protect just part of a page. The protection flags apply to entire pages.

VirtualAlloc cannot reserve more than 2GB because a process has control over only the bottom half of its 4GB address space. In fact the actual limit is slightly smaller because of the 64K free area at either end of a process's 2GB space (see Figure 7.4). Also, **VirtualAlloc** reserves memory in blocks of 64K and commits memory in blocks of one page. When reserving memory, **VirtualAlloc** rounds lpvAddress down to the nearest multiple of 64K. When committing memory, if lpvAddress is **NULL**, **VirtualAlloc** rounds dwSize up to the nearest page size boundary. If lpvAddress is not **NULL**, **VirtualAlloc** commits every page containing any bytes in the range lpvAddress to lpvAddress + dwSize. A 2-byte allocation, if it crosses a page boundary, would require the commitment of two entire pages. On most Windows NT systems a page is 4K, but if you need to know the size call **GetSystemInfo**.

Uses for Reserved Memory

The ability to reserve memory without committing it is useful primarily for dynamically allocated structures and sparse arrays. A thread that expands some structure, perhaps a list, as the program runs can reserve room to prevent other threads from using up addresses the structure may need as it expands. The reserved area does set an upper limit on the size of the structure because there is no such command as "VirtualReAlloc" to expand a reserved area. Resizing requires allocating a second block, copying the first block into it, and freeing the original. On the other hand, given a 2GB range of possible addresses, you can reasonably set the upper size limit of the original allocation quite high.

Reserved memory also makes it easy to create a sparse array—a large array with only a few elements full. We've already mentioned that a spreadsheet is a sparse array of empty cells with only a few positions occupied, and those positions are usually clustered in adjacent areas. With the virtual memory commands you can reserve a large address space for all the possible cells and commit memory only for the areas in use. Of course, spreadsheet programs in any system find ways to minimize their allocations, but the virtual memory solution to sparse arrays is particularly convenient because you can still address the array as a range of contiguous addresses.

A problem arises when you try to write to pages that have been reserved but never committed. The system generates an access violation exception. You might choose to call **VirtualQuery** before every read or write to be sure the page is committed, but that takes time. The usual practice, demonstrated in the List program below, is to let the exception arise and provide an exception handler to deal with it. The handler calls **VirtualAlloc** to commit the required page and lets the program continue.

When a process ends, the system automatically releases any memory that was still in use. To free memory sooner, call **VirtualFree**.

```
BOOL VirtualFree(
    LPVOID lpvAddress,          // address of memory to free
    DWORD dwSize,               // size of memory block
    DWORD fdwFreeType );        // decommit or release
```

VirtualFree can decommit a set of committed pages leaving their addresses still reserved, or it can release a range of reserved addresses, or both at once. Decommitting can release small blocks, and the blocks may include a mix of both reserved and committed pages. The rules differ for releasing reserved addresses. You must free the entire range of addresses as originally allocated, and all the pages in the range must be in the same state, either all reserved or all committed. **lpvAddress** must contain the base address previously returned by **VirtualAlloc**, and the value of **dwSize** is ignored because the whole range is freed at once. **dwSize** matters only when decommitting sections of a range.

Before decommitting a page, be sure no part of it is still in use. Our sample List program, for example, fits four list items on each 4K page. Deleting one item does not make it safe to delete a page because the other three items might still be in use. Programs that use the virtual memory commands usually need some kind of garbage-collection mechanism to decommit pages when they become empty. The mechanism could be a low-priority thread that occasionally cycles through an allocated area looking for entirely empty pages.

Protecting

After reserving address space, you call **VirtualAlloc** again to commit individual pages and **VirtualFree** to decommit or release them. When committing pages, **VirtualAlloc** also changes the protection state from no-access to read-only or read/write. To change the protection for a page already committed, call **Virtual-Protect**.

```
BOOL VirtualProtect(
    LPVOID lpvAddress,          // address of memory to protect
    DWORD dwSize,               // size of area to protect
    DWORD fdwNewProtect,        // new protection flags
    PDWORD pfdwOldProtect );     // variable to receive old flags
```

lpvAddress and dwSize indicate the range of addresses to protect. The two flag parameters each contain one of the familiar protection flags: **PAGE_NOACCESS**, **PAGE_READONLY**, or **PAGE_READWRITE**. Flags apply to whole pages. Any page even partially included in the given range will be changed. The **pfdwOldProtect** parameter returns the previous state of the first page in the range. **VirtualProtect** works only with pages already committed. If any page in the range is not committed, the function fails. The pages in the range do not, however, need to have identical protection flags.

The primary advantage of protection is in guarding against your own program bugs. For an example, refer to the revised AddItem and DeleteItem procedures that follow this chapter's sample List program.

Querying

Sometimes you need to get information about a block of memory. Before writing to a page, for example, you might want to find out whether the page has been committed. **VirtualQuery** fills a structured variable with information about a given block of memory:

```
DWORD VirtualQuery(
    LPVOID lpvAddress,                    // address of area to be described
    PMEMORY_BASIC_INFORMATION pmbiBuffer,  // address of description buffer
    DWORD dwLength );                     // size of description buffer

typedef struct _MEMORY_BASIC_INFORMATION { /* mbi */
    PVOID BaseAddress;                    // base address of page group
    PVOID AllocationBase;                 // address of larger allocation unit
    DWORD AllocationProtect;              // allocation's initial access protection
    DWORD RegionSize;                     // size, in bytes, of page group
    DWORD State;                          // committed, reserved, free
    DWORD Protect;                        // group's access protection
    DWORD Type;                           // type of pages (always private)
} MEMORY_BASIC_INFORMATION;
typedef MEMORY_BASIC_INFORMATION *PMEMORY_BASIC_INFORMATION;
```

The lpvAddress parameter of **VirtualQuery** points to an arbitrary address. Any given location in memory may be part of two different allocation units. It may be part of a large block of reserved pages, and it may also be part of a smaller region of pages subsequently committed, decommitted, or protected together. A region consists of all contiguous pages with the same attributes. In the **BaseAddress** field,

VirtualQuery returns the address of the first page in the smaller region that contains lpvAddress. The **AllocationBase** field returns the address of the larger allocation that first reserved lpvAddress. **AllocationBase** matches the value returned previously by **VirtualAlloc**. Whatever protection flags the original **VirtualAlloc** applied to the range are returned in **AllocationProtect** (**MEM_NOACCESS**, **MEM_READONLY**, or **MEM_READWRITE**). The other fields describe the smaller subgroup of like pages, giving its size, current status, and protection flag. The last field always returns **MEM_PRIVATE**, indicating that other processes cannot share this memory. The existence of this field suggests that Microsoft may later consider adding other mechanisms for processes to share memory.

Although they are not part of the virtual memory command set, two other commands also retrieve information about memory. **GlobalMemoryStatus** returns the total size and remaining space for physical memory, the page file, and the current address space. **GetSystemInfo** returns, among other things, the system's physical page size and the lowest and highest virtual addresses accessible to processes and DLLs. (Generally these values are 4K, 0x00010000, and 0x7FFEFFFF.)

Locking and Unlocking

The last two virtual memory commands lock and unlock pages. A locked page cannot be swapped to disk while your program executes. When your program is not currently executing, however, all of its pages, including locked pages, may be swapped to disk. In effect, locking a page guarantees that it will become a permanent part of the program's working page set. In a busy system, the working set manager may reduce the number of pages a process may lock. The maximum for any process is approximately 30 to 40 pages. The exact value varies slightly with the size of system memory and the application's working set.

Locking memory is discouraged because it constrains the memory manager and makes organizing physical memory more difficult. For the most part only device drivers and other system-level components lock any of their pages. A program that must respond very rapidly to system signals might lock some pages to ensure that unexpected disk reads don't delay the response.

```
BOOL VirtualLock(
    LPVOID lpvAddress,          // beginning of area to lock
    DWORD dwSize );             // size of area to lock
```

```
BOOL VirtualUnlock(
    LPVOID lpvAddress,          // beginning of area to unlock
    DWORD dwSize );             // size of area to unlock
```

There is no lock count on virtual memory. **VirtualLock** commands do not always require a matching **VirtualUnlock**. You can, for example, lock three contiguous pages with three different commands and then unlock them all with a single command. All the pages must already be locked, but the range does not need to correspond exactly with the range given in any previous lock command.

Before being locked, memory must be committed. When a process ends the system automatically unlocks any remaining locked pages. **VirtualFree** releases pages even if they are locked.

Be aware that **Globalloc** and **VirtualLock** do very different things. **Globalloc** simply translates handles into pointers. It locks an allocated object into a virtual address but has no effect at all on physical memory. **Virtual Lock**, on the other hand, is more severe. It locks pages, not objects, and the locked pages are forced into physical memory whenever the program runs.

Heap Functions

A *heap* is a block of memory from which a program allocates smaller pieces as needed. A 16-bit Windows program draws memory from both a global heap and a local heap. The local heap is faster but limited to 64K. A flat address space abolishes the difference between "global" and "local" and between "near" and "far." The entire address space is a single undifferentiated heap. Even so, working from a smaller heap sometimes still makes sense. Reserving and committing virtual memory has obvious advantages for large dynamic or sparse structures, but what about algorithms that call for many small allocations? The Heap memory commands allow you to create one or more private heaps in your address space and suballocate smaller blocks from them.

Creating a Heap

The memory you get from a heap is just like the memory you get any other way. In fact, you can write your own heap implementation using the virtual memory commands; that's exactly what the Windows subsystem does. Heap commands make internal calls to the virtual memory API. To create a heap, you give a starting size and an upper limit:

```
HANDLE HeapCreate(
    DWORD dwOptions,           // heap allocation flag
    DWORD dwInitialSize,       // initial heap size
    DWORD dwMaximumSize );      // maximum heap size
```

Behind the scenes, the Win32 subsystem responds by reserving a block of the maximum size and committing pages to support the initial size. Subsequent allocations make the heap grow from the bottom to the top. If any allocation calls for new pages, the Heap commands automatically commit them. Once committed, they remain committed until the program destroys the heap or ends. The system does not manage the inside of a private heap—it does not compact the heap or move objects within it—so a heap may become fragmented if you allocate and free many small objects. If allocations fill the heap to its maximum size, then subsequent allocations fail. If dwMaximumSize is 0, however, the heap size is limited only by available memory.

The dwOptions parameter allows a single flag to be set: **HEAP_NO_SERIALIZE**. By default, without this flag, the heap prevents threads that share memory handles from interfering with each other. A serialized heap disallows simultaneous operations on a single handle. One thread blocks until another finishes. Serialization slows performance slightly. A program's heap does not need to be serialized if the program has only one thread, if only one of its threads uses the heap, or if the program itself protects the heap, perhaps by creating a mutex or a critical section object.

Allocating from a Heap

HeapAlloc, **HeapReAlloc**, and **HeapFree**—like the Win16 commands their names recall—allocate, reallocate, and free blocks of memory from a heap. All of them take as one parameter a handle returned from **HeapCreate**.

```
LPSTR HeapAlloc(
    HANDLE hHeap,              // handle of a private heap
    DWORD dwFlags,            // control flags
    DWORD dwBytes );          // number of bytes to allocate
```

HeapAlloc returns a pointer to a block of the requested size. The control flags may include **HEAP_GENERATE_EXCEPTIONS** and **HEAP_ZERO_MEMORY**. The first flag influences how the command handles errors. Without the flag, **HeapAlloc** indicates failure by returning **NULL**. With the flag, it raises exceptions instead for all error conditions. The other flag causes **HeapAlloc** to initialize the newly allocated block with zeros. If the function succeeds, it allocates at least as much memory as requested and may allocate slightly more to reach a convenient boundary. To discover the exact size of any block, call **HeapSize**. Besides the bytes in the block itself, each allocation consumes a few extra bytes for an internal supporting structure. The exact size varies but is near 16 bytes. You need to know this only because it may prevent you from squeezing as many allocations out of one heap as you expect. If you create a 2MB heap and attempt two 1MB allocations, the second one is likely to fail.

To change the size of a memory block after it has been allocated, call **HeapReAlloc**.

```
LPSTR HeapReAlloc(
    HANDLE hHeap,            // handle of a private heap
    DWORD dwFlags,           // flags to influence reallocation
    LPSTR lpMem,             // address of memory block to reallocate
    DWORD dwBytes );         // new size for the memory block
```

Besides the two flags **HeapAlloc** uses to zero memory and to generate exceptions, the dwFlags parameter of **HeapReAlloc** accepts one other flag: **HEAP_REAL-LOC_IN_PLACE_ONLY**. (To the best of our knowledge, five words is a record for Microsoft's manifest constants.) This flag prevents **HeapReAlloc** from moving the memory block to a more spacious area. If other nearby allocations prevent the block from expanding in place, this flag makes **HeapReAlloc** fail rather than relocate.

Destroying a Heap

When you have no more use for an allocated block, release it with **HeapFree**. When you have no more use for the heap itself, release it with **HeapDestroy**.

```
BOOL HeapFree(
    HANDLE hHeap,            // handle of a private heap
    DWORD dwFlags,           // unused (must be zero)
    LPSTR lpMem );           // address of a memory block to free
```

```
BOOL HeapDestroy( HANDLE hHeap );
```

Freeing a memory block does not decommit the page it occupied, but it does make the space available for subsequent allocations in the same heap. **HeapDestroy** decommits and releases all the pages in the heap whether or not the heap still contains allocated blocks. After **HeapDestroy** the hHeap handle is invalid.

The Heap commands conveniently group allocations together in a small section of the address space. Clustering allocations serves several purposes. First, it can separate and protect related allocations. A program that makes many small allocations all the same size can pack memory most efficiently by making them contiguous. A heap allows that. Second, if all your linked-list nodes come from one heap and your binary-tree nodes come from another, then a mistake in one algorithm is less likely to interfere with the other. Third, memory objects used in conjunction with each other should be grouped together to minimize page swapping. If several addresses happen to reside on the same memory page, a single disk operation retrieves all of them.

Global and Local Memory Commands

In Chapter 3, under the heading "Obsolete API Routines," we listed system and memory commands dropped from the API in the transition from 16 to 32 bits. Most of the obsolete memory commands, such as **AllocSelector**, refer to low-level features specific to Win16 or to Intel CPUs. For backward compatibility, most of the more familiar memory commands are retained:

`GlobalAlloc`	`LocalAlloc`
`GlobalDiscard`	`LocalDiscard`
`GlobalFlags`	`LocalFlags`
`GlobalFree`	`LocalFree`
`GlobalHandle`	`LocalHandle`
`GlobalLock`	`LocalLock`
`GlobalMemoryStatus`	`LocalReAlloc`
`GlobalReAlloc`	`LocalSize`
`GlobalSize`	`LocalUnlock`
`GlobalUnlock`	

The Win32 environment forces a few semantic changes. Most important, both sets of commands, Global and Local, now work with the same heap. Every process on loading receives a default heap, and the old API commands work from that. It is legal, though confusing, to mix Global and Local commands in a single transaction. For example you could, just to be perverse, allocate an object with `GlobalAlloc` and release it with `LocalFree`. Also, the 32-bit pointer `LocalLock` now returns is indistinguishable from the 32-bit pointer `GlobalLock` returns.

The default heap expands as needed, limited only by physical memory. Even the humble `LocalAlloc` can allocate megabytes. The default heap automatically serializes operations to prevent different threads from corrupting the heap by using the same handle at the same time.

Pages allocated by `GlobalAlloc` or `LocalAlloc` are committed and marked for read/write access. Unlike `HeapFree`, `GlobalFree` checks for empty pages and releases them back to the system. The allocation commands still recognize the flags that make memory fixed or movable, but with NT's paging and virtual addressing, even "fixed" memory moves. The only practical use for `GMEM_FIXED` is to make `GlobalAlloc` return a pointer instead of a handle. A few of the other flags are now ignored, including LOWER, NOCOMPACT, NODISCARD, NOT_BANKED, and NOTIFY. More significant than the loss of these minor flags is the loss of `GMEM_DDESHARE`. Like other Win32 object handles, handles to allocated memory refer to the object table of a specific process. A handle passed from one program to another becomes invalid in the new address space. `DuplicateHandle` makes it possible for processes to share some handles, but it fails on memory handles. The `GMEM_DDESHARE` flag still exists because Microsoft apparently plans for it to signal some optimization appropriate for DDE conversations, but the old method of sharing memory handles is simply not supported. Sharing a block of memory now requires a memory-mapped file.

The Win32 Global and Local memory commands differ from the Heap commands in creating movable and discardable objects. Objects created by `HeapAlloc` do not change their virtual address (though their physical address may change). The Local and Global functions, at the expense of more memory management overhead, do move objects to minimize fragmentation. With a memory manager as flexible as the VMM, discardable memory is less important than it used to be, and a cryptic note in Microsoft's online help file warns that some versions of Win32 may not support it.

The primary advantage of the old API functions is the obvious one: They are portable. To write source code that ports easily from 16 bits to 32 bits, limit yourself to the Win16 memory commands. In Win32 the global and local sets are interchangeable, but you should pick the set that would make the most sense in a Win16 program.

For small, fast allocations, use the Local functions. For large allocations, use the Global functions. Under Windows NT both sets perform alike, but since their advantage is portability, you should use them in a portable fashion.

The heap and virtual memory command sets are faster and more efficient than the older commands. You can allocate from the default heap with less overhead by doing this:

```
HeapAlloc( GetProcessHeap(), 0, dwSize );
```

GetProcessHeap returns a handle to the default heap. (Do not pass that handle to **HeapDestroy**.)

What the System Can Handle

Because Windows NT does not use the descriptor tables that limited 16-bit Windows to a system-wide total of 8192 handles, the new system supports many more allocations. Nevertheless some limits remain. **VirtualAlloc** never reserves an area smaller than 64K, so allocating 32,767 blocks fills up the 2GB user address space. **VirtualAlloc** cannot create more than 32,767 (32K) handles in one process. **Heap-Alloc** has no such limit; Microsoft says it's created over a million handles on a single heap in tests. Also, under Windows NT **GlobalAlloc** and **LocalAlloc** combined cannot create more than 65,535 (64K) handles. The limit applies only to movable objects, however. Given the **GMEM_FIXED** or **LMEM_FIXED** flag, the allocation functions do not create handles. Instead they return direct pointers.

Validation

Another new set of commands tests the validity of pointers. Each receives a virtual address and returns **TRUE** if the process does not have a particular access privilege. Call these to make programs more robust by testing values before using them.

Function	Argument	Validation Test
IsBadCodePtr	Pointer to a function	Tests for read access to the beginning of the function

Function	Argument	Validation Test
IsBadReadPtr	Pointer to a memory block	Tests for read access to a range of addresses
IsBadStringPtr	Pointer to a string	Tests for read access to all bytes up to the end of the string
IsBadWritePtr	Pointer to a memory block	Tests for write access to a range of addresses

Be aware that other threads, and even other processes (such as debuggers), could conceivably change the contents or protection of a memory page between the time an IsBad function confirms validity and the time you try to touch the address yourself.

C Runtime Equivalents

Under Windows NT, the malloc family of C runtime functions call system Heap routines internally. The C routines work perfectly well in NT, though they do not perform the same suballocations they do in the 16-bit versions.

The runtime memory buffer commands such as memset now have competition from four new Win32 routines:

    CopyMemory

    FillMemory

    MoveMemory

    ZeroMemory

Only on a MIPS machine, however, do these commands link dynamically to the system DLLs. On an x86 machine, all four map back to the standard C runtime functions, memcopy, memmove, and memset.

Sharing Memory in Mapped Files

For two processes to share a block of memory, they must create a file-mapping object. Such objects have two purposes: They facilitate file I/O and they create a memory buffer processes can share. To explain sharing memory, we have to begin with files.

After opening a disk file, a program may optionally create an associated file-mapping object in order to treat the file as a block of memory. The system reserves a range of addresses from the process's space and maps them to the file instead of to physical memory. The process reads and writes to these addresses as it would to any other memory address, using functions like `lstrcpy` and **`FillMemory`**. You can even type-cast the base address to make an array pointer and retrieve file records by indexing the array. The memory manager responds to page faults in a file-mapping object by swapping pages from the disk file rather than the system's paging file.

This ingenious file I/O technique also allows processes to share memory. Two programs can open handles to the same file; what difference does it make if the file happens to be in memory? If the cooperating programs want to share memory but don't need to create a disk file, they can link their shared file-mapping object to the system's paging file. Then the memory in the mapped file is paged exactly the same way all other memory is paged.

Setting up a new mapped file requires three commands:

- **`CreateFile:`** Opens a disk file
- **`CreateFileMapping:`** Returns a handle to a file-mapping object
- **`MapViewOfFile:`** Links a region in the file to a range of virtual addresses and returns a pointer

`CreateFile` is familiar from Chapter 5, where we used it to open existing named pipes. **`CreateFileMapping`** creates a new system object, adds an entry to the process's object table, and returns a handle. The new object creates the potential for parts of the file to be held in memory, but you cannot actually read the file until you also create a view into it. A *view* is a small section of a larger object, a window into a section of the file. The third command, **`MapViewOfFile`**, creates a view by associating positions in the file with positions in the address space. Operations on that range of addresses become operations on the file. Certainly you can create a view big enough to contain the entire file, but in theory a file can be much larger than your entire address space, so an alternative is necessary. The alternative is to create a smaller view and move it when you need to reach new parts of the file. After creating a file-mapping object, you can map, unmap, and remap your view of it over and over. You can even map several simultaneous views of a single file. Figure 7.5 diagrams the relation between a file and its view.

FIGURE 7.5:

Two programs with different views of the same file-mapping object

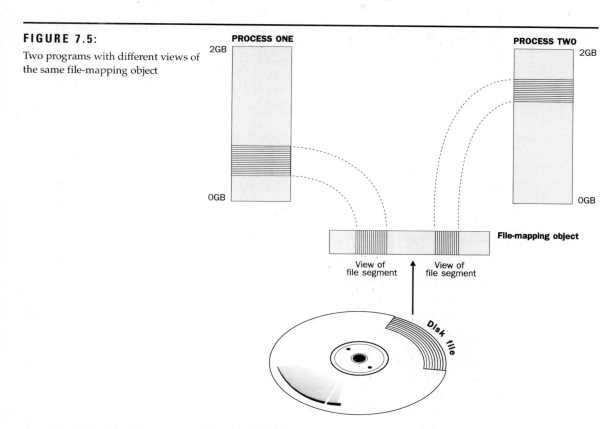

Creating a File-Mapping Object

CreateFileMapping requires a file handle to associate with the new object. Normally you receive the handle from **CreateFile**, but to share memory without creating a separate file you may instead pass 0xFFFFFFFF. The system then maps from the system paging file.

```
HANDLE CreateFileMapping(
    HANDLE hFile,                  // handle of file to map
```

```
LPSECURITY_ATTRIBUTES lpsa,    // optional security attributes
DWORD fdwProtect,              // protection for mapping object
DWORD dwMaxSizeHigh,           // high-order 32 bits of object size
DWORD dwMaxSizeLow,            // low-order 32 bits of object size
LPTSTR lpszMapName );          // name of file-mapping object
```

The `fdwProtect` parameter sets the protection flag for all the memory pages the mapped file uses. It may be **PAGE_READONLY**, **PAGE_READWRITE**, or **PAGE_WRITE-COPY**. The first two you know, but **PAGE_WRITECOPY** is new. We'll say more about it in a moment when we discuss coherent views.

The next two parameters of **CreateFileMapping**, both **DWORD**s, together tell the size of the file-mapping object. If the file-mapping object is smaller than the file it maps, then not all of the file is accessible through it. The last part of the file is excluded from sharing. The system interprets `dwMaxSizeHigh` and `dwMaxSizeLow` as the high and low halves of a single value. The size is an 8-byte quantity to allow for the possibility that disk files may exceed the value of ULONG_MAX (4GB). Programs that work only with files of sub-astronomical sizes always set `dwMaxSizeHigh` to 0. Setting both parameters to 0 instructs the system to set the maximum size from the file's current size. If `hFile` is 0xFFFFFFFF, however, the size may not be 0. You must set an explicit size in order to work from the system swap file.

The final parameter, `lpszMapName`, gives the new object a name. `lpszMapName` is not the name of a disk file; if there is a disk file, its name was passed to **CreateFile**. `lpszMapName` assigns a name to the new file-mapping object for the convenience of other processes. Processes use the name to share the object, just as they use pipe names to share pipes. Other processes open their handles to the same object by passing the name string to **OpenFileMapping**. The name of a file-mapping object may not exceed **MAX_PATH** characters (currently 260) and may not contain back-slashes. (**MAX_PATH** is defined in windef.h.)

The rule against backslashes in mapped file names contrasts with the rules for naming pipes. Pipe names, as you recall from Chapter 5, always begin with the sequence "\\.\pipe\" and may contain other backslashes indicating other subnodes. The names differ because pipes are implemented as a file system while mapped files belong to the heap management system.

CreateFileMapping returns a valid handle if it succeeds and **NULL** if it fails. If the name string in `lpszMapName` designates a mapping object that already exists and if the requested protection attributes match, then **CreateFileMapping** returns a valid handle to the existing object. That may not be what you want. A program trying to create a new mapping object may be surprised if another program happens to have used the same name for its own object. To detect whether your new handle belongs to an old object, call **GetLastError** even after **CreateFileMapping** *succeeds* and test for **ERROR_ALREADY_EXISTS**.

Mapping a View

MapViewOfFile connects a section of memory with a section of the file. It makes part of the file visible in memory. A mapped file is "mapped" because of what this function does: It associates every byte of the memory range with a corresponding byte in the file.

```
LPVOID MapViewOfFile(
    HANDLE hMapObject,        // mapped file to view
    DWORD fdwAccess,          // access mode
    DWORD dwOffsetHigh,       // high-order 32 bits of file offset
    DWORD dwOffsetLow,        // low-order 32 bits of file offset
    DWORD dwViewSize );       // size of view in bytes
```

The hMapObject handle has to be created with **CreateFileMapping** or **OpenFile-Mapping**. The second parameter requests access privileges for the pages within the view. The privileges requested here must not conflict with those already set in the original **CreateFileMapping** command. For example, a file-mapping object created with the **PAGE_READONLY** flag will not support a view with **FILE_MAP_WRITE** access. Many processes may open views to a single file-mapping object. The view access flags are

Flag	Purpose	Matching Creation Flag(s)
FILE_MAP_WRITE	Grants write access	Requires **PAGE_READWRITE**
FILE_MAP_READ	Grants read-only access	Requires **PAGE_READONLY** or **PAGE_READWRITE**
FILE_MAP_ALL_ACCESS	Synonym for **FILE_MAP_WRITE**	Requires **PAGE_READWRITE**
FILE_MAP_COPY	Grants copy-on-write access	Requires **PAGE_WRITECOPY**

When you finish with one view and want to inspect another region of the file, un-map the first view and call **MapViewOfFile** again.

```
BOOL UnmapViewOfFile( LPVOID lpvBaseAddress );
```

lpvBaseAddress is the same value earlier received from **MapViewOfFile**. **Un-mapViewOfFile** writes any modified pages in the view back to the disk and releases the virtual address space reserved for the mapping. (The **FlushViewOfFile** command also forces modifications to be saved.)

Sharing a Mapped-File Object

In order for two processes to share a file-mapping object, both must acquire a handle. Child processes may inherit file-mapping handles from their parents. If the second process is not a child and if the name string is not coded into both programs, then one must pass it to the other through a pipe, a mailslot, a DDE conversation, or by some other arrangement. **OpenFileMapping** converts a name string into a handle for an existing object.

```
HANDLE OpenFileMapping(
    DWORD dwAccess,              // access mode
    BOOL bInheritHandle,        // TRUE for children to inherit the handle
    LPTSTR lpszName );          // points to name of file-mapping object
```

After receiving its handle, the second process also calls **MapViewOfFile** to see what the file contains.

Preserving Coherence

If several processes open views on a shared file-mapping object, any changes one makes will be visible to the others. All their view pointers will point to different places in the same coherent object. The file-mapping object coordinates modifications from all its open views. The file may become incoherent, however, if the views derive from two different concurrent file-mapping objects linked to a single file. If the viewers write their changes to different file-mapping objects, then they create conflicting versions of the file. Figure 7.6 shows how two file-mapping objects may contain different versions of the disk file and fall out of synch. Any modifications the first two processes make will be deposited in the first file-mapping object, but the second file-mapping object holds separately any modi-fications made by process three. If all processes unmap their views and write their changes to the disk, only one set of changes is saved because one set writes over the other on the disk. When file views become incoherent, he who saves last saves best.

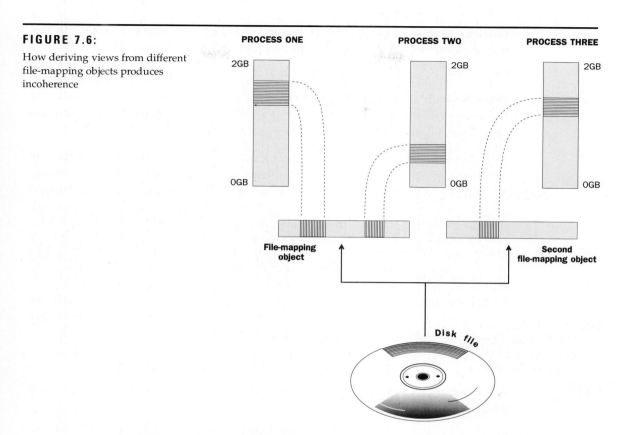

FIGURE 7.6:

How deriving views from different file-mapping objects produces incoherence

To enforce coherence, Microsoft recommends that the first program to open the file should specify exclusive access (set 0 in the share-mode parameter.) Then no other program can open the file to create a second mapping object.

Three other situations can also produce incoherence. First, normal I/O performed on a disk file that other processes are viewing as a mapped object causes incoherence. The changes will be lost when the file-mapping object saves its version of the file. Second, processes on different machines may share mapped files, but since they cannot share the same block of physical memory across a network, their views remain coherent only as long as neither process writes to its view.

Finally, a similar situation arises when views are created with copy-on-write protection. Copy-on-write protection means that when a process tries to write on a page the system copies the page and writes only to the copy. The original page cannot be modified. In other words, the process has read-only access to the original and gets automatic copies of any parts it decides to change. If two processes modify a copy-on-write mapped file, they are not writing to the same pages. The modified pages are no longer shared, and the views are not coherent.

Copy-on-write protection can be useful for preserving a buffer's original state until all the changes are final. A half-edited spreadsheet, for example, with all its formulas linking cells, might be useless in its unfinished state. Simply saving changed areas back to the original file could cause problems because the changes in one edited place might invalidate the data in another unedited place. Copy-on-write protection leaves the original buffer and its file intact while editing proceeds. Of course, the problem doesn't arise with unmapped files, but in that case you would have to keep an extra copy of the entire spreadsheet, not just the modified pieces.

Debuggers use copy-on-write protection when altering code to add a breakpoint, for example. If another instance of the process is running outside the debugger, both instances still share all of the source code image except the altered page.

CODE

Our two sample programs for this chapter, List and Browser, make use of the virtual memory API and file-mapping objects. Full listings of both programs, including two different versions of List, appear on the disk that accompanies the book. To save space, a few trivial procedures are not printed here.

The List Program

The List program, shown in Figure 7.7, creates a list by reserving virtual memory and committing it as the user enters new items. A list box filling the window's client area displays the entire list. From the menu the user adds items and deletes them.

FIGURE 7.7:

List program accepting
a new item entry

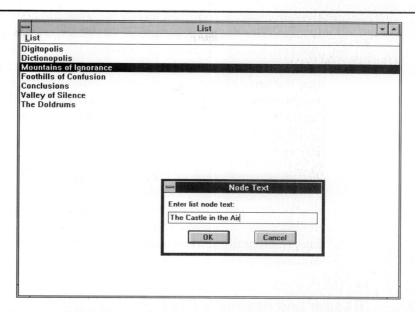

To create a dynamic list of identically sized nodes in 16-bit Windows you would probably create a structure of linked nodes.

```
typedef struct ListNode
{
    char szText[256];
    HANDLE hNext;
} LISTNODE, *PLISTNODE;
```

Each new entry would require an allocation something like this:

```
HANDLE hNode;
PLISTNODE pNode;
char szText[MAX_BUFFER];

/* allocate memory for the list node */
hNode = GlobalAlloc( GHND, sizeof(LISTNODE) );
pNode = GlobalLock( hNode );

 /* copy the text to the node and unlock the node */
lstrcpy( pNode->szText, szText );
GlobalUnlock( pNode );
```

A Win16 program compiled with MSC 7.0 would do better to substitute `malloc` for `GlobalAlloc` here because internally `malloc` creates something like a heap of its own and manages suballocations within it. By contrast, each new call to **Global-Alloc** uses up one more slot in the system's finite descriptor table. Either way, however, the basic algorithm remains the same. An array would be easier to program but much more wasteful since it would allocate more memory than it ever used. Under Windows NT, however, the virtual memory commands make a large dynamically allocated array quite practical, and that's how List implements its data structure.

Writing a virtual memory program calls for a decision about how to deal with uncommitted pages. List uses exception handling to commit pages on demand, as page faults occur. After the source files we show versions of the central procedures revised to use a different method. The revised procedures query the state of each page before writing. They also keep all pages write-protected except when writing to them.

Header and Resource Files

The header file defines two constants governing the size and structure of the list. Each array element has room for 1024 characters. Because the system's page size (4K) is a multiple of the element size (1K), no list item will cross a page boundary, and therefore retrieving an item never requires reading more than a single page from the disk. We've set the array's maximum size to a mere 500, figuring even that small number will challenge the patience of most readers to fill. Setting the limit to 20,000 would still tie up less than 1 percent of the 2GB user address space.

```
/*-------------------------------------------------------------------
        LIST.H
        Header file for the virtual memory List program.
        -----------------------------------------------------------*/


/*-------------------------------------------------------------------
        CONSTANTS
        -----------------------------------------------------------*/


#define MAX_ITEMS       500         // max number of entries in the list
#define ITEM_SIZE       1024        // max chars for one node's text
#define MAX_BUFFER      64
```

```
/*------------------------------------------------------------
          RESOURCE IDs
   --------------------------------------------------------------*/

#define MENU_MAIN          10        // menu template

#define DLG_ABOUT          10        // dialog templates
#define DLG_TEXTENTRY      20

#define IDD_EDIT           100       // edit control

#define IDM_ADD            100       // menu commands
#define IDM_DELETE         200
#define IDM_ABOUT          300
#define IDM_EXIT           400

#define IDS_APPNAME        100       // strings
#define IDS_TITLE          200

/*------------------------------------------------------------
          FUNCTION PROTOTYPES
   --------------------------------------------------------------*/

LRESULT WINAPI List_WndProc( HWND hWnd , UINT uMessage, WPARAM wParam,
    LPARAM lParam );
BOOL Init( void );
BOOL CreateWindows( void );
void List_OnInitMenu( HWND hWnd, HMENU hMenu );
void List_OnSize( HWND hWnd, UINT uState, int cxClient, int cyClient );
void List_OnSetFocus( HWND hWnd, HWND hwndOldFocus );
void List_OnCommand( HWND hWnd, int iCmd, HWND hwndCtl, UINT uCode );
void List_OnDestroy( HWND hWnd );
BOOL CreateList( void );
void AddItem( void );
LONG CommitMemFilter( DWORD dwExceptCode, int iIndex );
void DeleteItem( void );
void DeleteList( void );
int GetItemText( char *pszText );
int GetPageBaseEntry( int iPlace );
void AdjustLookupTable( int iStart );
BOOL WINAPI Text_DlgProc( HWND hDlg, UINT uMessage, WPARAM wParam,
    LPARAM lParam );
void Text_DoCommand( HWND hDlg, int iCmd );
BOOL WINAPI About_DlgProc( HWND hDlg, UINT uMessage, WPARAM wParam,
    LPARAM lParam );
```

```
void ShowErrorMsg( int iLine );
=========================================================================

/*-----------------------------------------------------------------------
        LIST.RC
        Resource script for the virtual memory List program.
        ------------------------------------------------------------------*/
#include <windows.h>
#include "list.h"

STRINGTABLE
BEGIN
    IDS_APPNAME,  "listdemo"
    IDS_TITLE,    "List"
END

MENU_MAIN MENU
BEGIN
    POPUP   "&List"
    BEGIN
        MENUITEM "Add &Item...",      IDM_ADD, GRAYED
        MENUITEM "&Delete Item",      IDM_DELETE, GRAYED
        MENUITEM SEPARATOR
        MENUITEM "&About List...",    IDM_ABOUT
        MENUITEM SEPARATOR
        MENUITEM "E&xit",             IDM_EXIT
    END
END

/* template for the About dialog box */
DLG_ABOUT DIALOG 17, 18, 114, 68
STYLE DS_MODALFRAME | WS_POPUP | WS_VISIBLE | WS_CAPTION | WS_SYSMENU
CAPTION "About List"
FONT 8, "Helv"
BEGIN
    CTEXT          "List",            -1, 0,  7, 114, 8
    CTEXT          "by",              -1, 0, 15, 114, 8
    CTEXT          "Myers && Hamer",  -1, 0, 25, 114, 8
    CTEXT          "version 1.0",     -1, 0, 35, 114, 8
    LTEXT          "©1993",           -1,12, 51,  25, 8
    DEFPUSHBUTTON  "OK", IDOK, 81, 50, 30, 14, WS_GROUP
END
```

```
/* template for the dialog box where the user enters text */
DLG_TEXTENTRY DIALOG 17, 18, 150, 64
STYLE DS_MODALFRAME | WS_POPUP | WS_VISIBLE | WS_CAPTION | WS_SYSMENU
CAPTION "List Item Text"
FONT 8, "Helv"
BEGIN
    LTEXT "Enter list item text:" -1, 4, 8, 64, 12
    EDITTEXT  IDD_EDIT, 4, 20, 142, 12, ES_AUTOHSCROLL
    DEFPUSHBUTTON "OK", IDOK, 23, 40, 40, 14, WS_GROUP
    PUSHBUTTON "Cancel", IDCANCEL, 86, 40, 40, 14, WS_GROUP
END
```

Initialization

Among the program's global variables are two arrays, iListLookup and bInUse. The lookup array links lines in the list box to elements in the dynamic array. If iListLookup[4] is 7, then string 4 in the list box is stored in element 7 of the array. (The list box and the array both begin numbering at 0.) The second array contains a Boolean value for each element in the dynamic array. Whenever the program adds or deletes a string, it changes the corresponding element of bInUse to **TRUE** for an occupied position and **FALSE** for an empty position. To add a new string, the program searches bInUse for an empty array element. To delete the currently selected string, the program locates the array element by referring to iListLookup.

```
/*-----------------------------------------------------------------

    LIST.C

    Creates a dynamic list using Windows NT's virtual memory
    management functions.

    FUNCTIONS
        WinMain              receive and dispatch messages
        Init                 initialize program data
        CreateWindows        make program window and list box
        List_WndProc         sort out messages for main window
        List_OnInitMenu      enable/disable menu choices
        List_OnSize          make list box fit new window size
        List_OnSetFocus      set focus on list box control
        List_OnCommand       process menu commands
        List_OnDestroy       end program
        CreateList           initialize list structures
        AddItem              create new list item
```

```
        DeleteItem              delete selected item
        DeleteList              destroy list structures
        GetItemText             get text from user for new item
        GetPageBaseEntry        find first entry on same page as given entry
        AdjustLookupTable       update global status variables after changes
        Text_DlgProc            text entry dialog box
        Text_DoCommand          copy text from edit control to buffer
        About_DlgProc           About box
        ShowErrorMsg            display message from system table


     from Programming for Windows NT
     copyright 1993 by Brian Myers & Eric Hamer


------------------------------------------------------------------*/

#define STRICT
#include <windows.h>
#include <windowsx.h>
#include <string.h>
#include "list.h"

/*-----------------------------------------------------------------
        GLOBAL VARIABLES
------------------------------------------------------------------*/

HWND hwndMain;                  // main program window
HWND hwndList;                  // list box window
HINSTANCE hInst;                // program instance
char szListText[ITEM_SIZE];     // holds text user enters
char *pBase;                    // bottom of list's virtual space
int iListLookup[MAX_ITEMS];     // matches list box index to array position
BOOL bInUse[MAX_ITEMS];         // marks array positions that are in use
BOOL bListEmpty = TRUE;         // Add/DeleteItem update these
BOOL bListFull = FALSE;         //    global status flags

/*-----------------------------------------------------------------
        WIN MAIN
        Calls initializing procedures and runs the message loop
------------------------------------------------------------------*/

int WINAPI WinMain (
    HINSTANCE hinstThis,
    HINSTANCE hinstPrev,
    LPSTR lpszCmdLine,
    int iCmdShow )
```

```
{
    MSG msg;

    hInst = hinstThis;

    /* initialize the application */
    if (!Init( ))
    {
        return( 0 );                            // initialization failed
    }

    ShowWindow( hwndMain, iCmdShow );       // show main window
    UpdateWindow( hwndMain );

    while (GetMessage( &msg, NULL, 0, 0 ))  // pull messages from queue
    {
        TranslateMessage( &msg );
        DispatchMessage( &msg );
    }

    return( msg.wParam );
    UNREFERENCED_PARAMETER( lpszCmdLine );
    UNREFERENCED_PARAMETER( hinstPrev );
}

/*------------------------------------------------------------------
        INIT
        Register the window class and call a procedure to create
        the program window and its list box.
        ----------------------------------------------------------------*/

BOOL Init ( void )
{
    WNDCLASS wc;
    char szAppName[MAX_BUFFER];

    LoadString( hInst, IDS_APPNAME, szAppName,  sizeof(szAppName));

    /* register the main window class*/
    wc.lpszClassName = szAppName;
    wc.hInstance     = hInst;
    wc.lpfnWndProc   = List_WndProc;
    wc.hCursor       = LoadCursor( NULL, IDC_ARROW );
    wc.hIcon         = LoadIcon( NULL, IDI_APPLICATION );
```

```
    wc.lpszMenuName  = szAppName;
    wc.hbrBackground = (HBRUSH)(COLOR_WINDOW + 1);
    wc.style         = CS_HREDRAW | CS_VREDRAW;
    wc.cbClsExtra    = 0;
    wc.cbWndExtra    = 0;

    if (!RegisterClass( &wc ))
    {
        return( FALSE );
    }

    /* create the windows */
    if (!CreateWindows( ))
    {
        return( FALSE );
    }

    /* reserve memory for the list */
    return( CreateList( ) );
}


/*-------------------------------------------------------------------
        CREATE WINDOWS
        Create the parent window and the list box window.
    ---------------------------------------------------------------*/

BOOL CreateWindows ( void )
{
    char szAppName[MAX_BUFFER];
    char szTitle[MAX_BUFFER];
    HMENU hMenu;

    /* load the relevant strings */
    LoadString( hInst, IDS_APPNAME, szAppName,  sizeof(szAppName));
    LoadString( hInst, IDS_TITLE,   szTitle,    sizeof(szTitle));

    /* create the parent window */
    hMenu = LoadMenu( hInst, MAKEINTRESOURCE(MENU_MAIN) );
    hwndMain = CreateWindow( szAppName, szTitle,
        WS_OVERLAPPEDWINDOW | WS_CLIPCHILDREN,
        CW_USEDEFAULT, CW_USEDEFAULT, CW_USEDEFAULT, CW_USEDEFAULT,
        NULL, hMenu, hInst, NULL);
```

```
    if (!hwndMain)
    {
        return( FALSE );        // an error occurred
    }

    /* create the list box */
    hwndList = CreateWindow( "LISTBOX", NULL,
        WS_CHILD | WS_VISIBLE | LBS_NOTIFY | LBS_NOINTEGRALHEIGHT,
        0, 0, 0, 0, hwndMain, (HMENU)1, hInst, NULL );

    return( hwndList != NULL );               // FALSE for errors
}

/*-----------------------------------------------------------------
        CREATE LIST
        Reserve the memory for the list and initialize the variables
        for the list box and memory status.
    -----------------------------------------------------------------*/

BOOL CreateList ( void )
{
    int i;
    /* reserve one meg of memory address space */
    pBase = VirtualAlloc( NULL,                 // starting address (anywhere)
                MAX_ITEMS * ITEM_SIZE,          // one megabyte
                MEM_RESERVE,                    // reserve; don't commit
                PAGE_NOACCESS );                // can't be touched

    if (pBase == NULL)
    {
        ShowErrorMsg( __LINE__ );
        return( FALSE );
    }

    /* initialize the status variables */
    for (i = 0; i < MAX_ITEMS; i++)
    {
        bInUse[i] = FALSE;                      // show no entries in use
        iListLookup[i] = 0;
    }

    bListEmpty = TRUE;                          // update global flags
    bListFull = FALSE;
    return( TRUE );
}
```

When the program starts it calls `CreateList` to reserve memory and initialize the supporting data structures. **VirtualAlloc** reserves a 1-megabyte range of addresses. Like all reserved pages, these must be marked **PAGE_NOACCESS** until they are committed.

Window Procedure and Message Handlers

The message handler functions perform basic housekeeping tasks. The **WM_INIT-MENU** handler disables or enables the Add and Delete commands if the list is empty or full. The **WM_SIZE** handler adjusts the list box control to fit exactly in the window's client area. The **WM_COMMAND** and **WM_DESTROY** handlers both call other procedures to manage the list.

```
/*------------------------------------------------------------------
        LIST_WNDPROC
        Process messages for the main window here.
     ----------------------------------------------------------------*/

LRESULT WINAPI List_WndProc (
    HWND hWnd,                              // message address
    UINT uMessage,                         // message type
    WPARAM wParam,                         // message contents
    LPARAM lParam )                        // more contents
{
    switch (uMessage)
    {
        HANDLE_MSG( hWnd, WM_INITMENU, List_OnInitMenu );

        HANDLE_MSG( hWnd, WM_SIZE, List_OnSize );

        HANDLE_MSG( hWnd, WM_SETFOCUS, List_OnSetFocus );

        HANDLE_MSG( hWnd, WM_COMMAND, List_OnCommand );

        HANDLE_MSG( hWnd, WM_DESTROY, List_OnDestroy );

        default:
            return( DefWindowProc(hWnd, uMessage, wParam, lParam) );
    }
    return( OL );
}
```

```
/*-------------------------------------------------------------
        LIST_ONINITMENU
        When the user begins to make a menu choice, update the
        status of menu items.
   -----------------------------------------------------------*/

void List_OnInitMenu (
    HWND hWnd,
    HMENU hMenu )
{
    if (bListFull)                          // is the list full?
    {                                       // disable Add Item
        EnableMenuItem( hMenu, IDM_ADD, MF_GRAYED );
    }
    else                                    // the list is not full
    {                                       // enable Add Item
        EnableMenuItem( hMenu, IDM_ADD, MF_ENABLED );
    }

    if (bListEmpty)                         // is the list empty?
    {                                       // disable Delete Item
        EnableMenuItem( hMenu, IDM_DELETE, MF_GRAYED );
    }
    else                                    // list is not empty
    {                                       // enable Delete Item
        EnableMenuItem( hMenu, IDM_DELETE, MF_ENABLED );
    }

    return;
    UNREFERENCED_PARAMETER( hWnd );
}


/*-------------------------------------------------------------
        LIST_ONSIZE
        Adjust the list box to fit in the main window's client area.
   -----------------------------------------------------------*/

void List_OnSize (
    HWND hWnd,
    UINT uState,
    int cxClient,
    int cyClient )
{
    if (hwndList)                   // does list box window exist?
```

```
    {
        /* reposition the list box and select the first item */
        MoveWindow( hwndList, 0, 0, cxClient, cyClient, TRUE );
        ListBox_SetCurSel( hwndList, 0 );
    }

    return;
    UNREFERENCED_PARAMETER( uState );
    UNREFERENCED_PARAMETER( hWnd );
}

/*-------------------------------------------------------------------
        LIST_ONSETFOCUS
        When main window receives the input focus, shift it to the
        list box so the user can reach it with the keyboard.
    -----------------------------------------------------------------*/

void List_OnSetFocus (
    HWND hWnd,
    HWND hwndOldFocus )
{
    SetFocus( hwndList );

    return;
    UNREFERENCED_PARAMETER( hWnd );
    UNREFERENCED_PARAMETER( hwndOldFocus );
}

/*-------------------------------------------------------------------
        LIST_ONCOMMAND
        Process menu commands.
    -----------------------------------------------------------------*/

void List_OnCommand (
    HWND hWnd,
    int iCmd,
    HWND hwndCtl,
    UINT uCode )
{
    switch (iCmd)
    {
        case IDM_ADD:                           // add item to list
            AddItem();
            break;
```

```
        case IDM_DELETE:                        // delete selected item
            DeleteItem();
            break;

        case IDM_ABOUT:                         // show the About box
            DialogBox( hInst, MAKEINTRESOURCE(DLG_ABOUT),
                    hWnd, About_DlgProc );
            break;

        case IDM_EXIT:
            DestroyWindow( hWnd );              // end program
            break;

        default:
            break;
    }

    return;
    UNREFERENCED_PARAMETER( hwndCtl );
    UNREFERENCED_PARAMETER( uCode );
}

/*------------------------------------------------------------------
        LIST_ONDESTROY
        Post the quit message
    ----------------------------------------------------------------*/
void List_OnDestroy ( HWND hWnd )
{
    DeleteList( );                              // release list structures
    PostQuitMessage(0);

    return;
    UNREFERENCED_PARAMETER( hWnd );
}
```

Adding an Item

When the user chooses Add Item from the menu, the AddItem procedure performs the following steps:

1. Locates the first empty slot in the array (iIndex)

2. Asks the user to enter the new string in a dialog box

3. Copies the new string into the memory allocated during `CreateList`

4. Updates the list box and several global variables

The first unused position in the array may happen to occupy an uncommitted memory page. In that case, the `lstrcpy` command that tries to put a string there generates an exception. The exception handler around `lstrcpy` looks for the **EXCEPTION_ACCESS_VIOLATION** signal and responds by calling **VirtualAlloc** to commit a single page from the previously reserved range.

```
/*------------------------------------------------------------------
        ADD ITEM
        Add a list entry.  MAX_ITEMS and ITEM_SIZE are both set
        to 1024.  With 1024 bytes per entry there are four entries
        per page.  With 500 entries, the list uses a maximum of
        125 pages.
        -----------------------------------------------------------*/

void AddItem ( void )
{
    char szText[ITEM_SIZE];            // text for one item
    int iLen;                          // string length
    int iIndex;                        // position in array
    int iPos;                          // position in list box
    int iCount;                        // count of entries in list box
    BOOL bDone;                        // TRUE when free array entry found

    /* determine the location of the first free entry */
    bDone = FALSE;
    iIndex = 0;
    while ((!bDone) && (iIndex < MAX_ITEMS))
    {
        if (!bInUse[iIndex])           // is entry in use?
        {
            bDone = TRUE;              // found an empty entry
        }
        else
        {
            iIndex++;                  // advance to next entry
        }
    }
```

```
/* ask user for new text string */
iLen = GetItemText(szText);
if (!iLen)
{
    return;
}

// The try block copies the new text to an empty place
// in the item array.  If that memory page is uncommitted,
// lstrcpy raises an exception.  The exception filter
// commits the page and the command continues.

try
{   /* put text in the item */
    lstrcpy( &(pBase[iIndex * ITEM_SIZE]), szText );
}
except (CommitMemFilter( GetExceptionCode(), iIndex ))
{
    /* the filter does all the work */
}

/* mark this entry as in use */
bInUse[iIndex] = TRUE;
bListEmpty = FALSE;

// Add the new text to the list box.  The string is inserted
// at iPos.  Update iListLookup[iPos] to indicate where in the
// item array the new entry was stored (iIndex).

iCount = ListBox_GetCount( hwndList );
iPos = ListBox_InsertString( hwndList, iCount, szText );
iCount++;
ListBox_SetCurSel( hwndList, iPos );
iListLookup[iPos] = iIndex;

if (iCount == MAX_ITEMS)                     // did we fill the last place?
{
    bListFull = TRUE;
}
return;
}
```

```
/*------------------------------------------------------------
        COMMIT MEM FILTER
        Exception-handling filter for AddItem.  If a page fault
        occurs, this function attempts to commit the page.  If
        it succeeds, the program returns to lstrcpy and proceeds
        from there.  If it fails, the search for an exception
        handler continues.
        ------------------------------------------------------------*/

LONG CommitMemFilter (
    DWORD dwExceptCode,                   // code identifying the exception
    int iIndex )                          // array element where fault occurred
{
    LPVOID lpvResult;

    // If the exception was not a page fault, then refuse
    // to handle it.  Make the system keep looking for
    // an exception handler.

    if (dwExceptCode != EXCEPTION_ACCESS_VIOLATION)
    {
        return( EXCEPTION_CONTINUE_SEARCH );
    }

    /* Try to commit the missing page. */
    lpvResult = VirtualAlloc(
        &(pBase[iIndex * ITEM_SIZE]),     // bottom of area to commit
        ITEM_SIZE,                        // size of area to commit
        MEM_COMMIT,                       // new status flag
        PAGE_READWRITE );                 // protection status

    if (!lpvResult)                       // did allocation fail?
    {
        /* if we can't commit the page then we can't handle the exception */
        return( EXCEPTION_CONTINUE_SEARCH );
    }

    // The missing page is now in place.  Tell the
    // system to go back and try again.

    return( EXCEPTION_CONTINUE_EXECUTION );
}
```

```
/*-------------------------------------------------------------------
        GET ITEM TEXT
        Display a dialog box where the user can enter the text
        for a new list item.  Returns the number of bytes in
        the new string.
        ----------------------------------------------------------*/

int GetItemText ( char *pszText )
{
    int iRet;                   // return value from dialog (1=OK)
    int iLen;                   // length of user's new text string

    /* show text entry dialog box */
    iRet = DialogBox( hInst, MAKEINTRESOURCE(DLG_TEXTENTRY),
                hwndMain, Text_DlgProc );

    if (iRet)                               // did user cancel?
    {
        lstrcpy( pszText, szListText );     // no; store text
        iLen = lstrlen( pszText );
    }
    else
    {
        pszText = NULL;                     // yes
        iLen = 0;                           // say string was empty
    }

    /* return the number of bytes in the text string */
    return( iLen );
}
```

Deleting an Item

When `DeleteItem` removes an element from the virtual array, it also checks to see whether any other entries remain on the same memory page. If all four entries are empty, it decommits the page, releasing 4K to the system. The virtual addresses that pointed to the page remain reserved. Whether or not it frees a page, `DeleteItem` then removes the string from the list box and updates the global status variables.

Two other procedures help with these tasks. `GetBasePageEntry` receives an array index and returns the index of the first element on the same page frame. In other words, it rounds down to the nearest multiple of four. `AdjustLookupTable` removes the entry it held for a newly deleted list box string and slides up all the following elements to fill in the gap.

```
/*-------------------------------------------------------------------
        DELETE ITEM
        Delete the item containing the text selected in the
        list box.
        -----------------------------------------------------------*/

void DeleteItem ( void )
{
    int iCurSel;            // position of current selection in list box
    int iPlace;             // position of current selection in item array
    int iStart;             // first position on same memory page as selection
    int i;                  // loop variable
    BOOL bFree;             // TRUE if all 4 entries on one page are unused
    BOOL bTest;             // for testing return results

    /* retrieve the memory offset of the currently selected entry */
    iCurSel = ListBox_GetCurSel( hwndList );
    iPlace = iListLookup[iCurSel];

    /* zero out the deleted entry */
    FillMemory( &(pBase[iPlace * ITEM_SIZE]), ITEM_SIZE, 0 );

    /* mark this entry as free */
    bInUse[iPlace] = FALSE;

    // Figure out which entry number is first on the current page.
    // If all four entries on the page are empty, we'll uncommit
    // the page to release memory.

    iStart = GetPageBaseEntry( iPlace );
    bFree = TRUE;

    for (i = 0; i < 4; i++)                         // check four entries
    {
        if (bInUse[i + iStart])                     // in use?
        {
            bFree = FALSE;                          // page is not free
        }
    }
```

```
    /* if a whole memory page is now unused, free it */
    if (bFree)                              // is page free?
    {                                       // YES; release it
        bTest = VirtualFree( &(pBase[iStart * ITEM_SIZE]),
                ITEM_SIZE, MEM_DECOMMIT );
        if (!bTest)
        {
            ShowErrorMsg( __LINE__ );
            ExitProcess( (UINT)GetLastError() );
        }
    }

    /* update the list box display and the lookup table array */
    ListBox_DeleteString( hwndList, iCurSel );
    AdjustLookupTable( iCurSel );

    /* check whether any entries remain in the list */
    bListEmpty = TRUE;
    i = 0;
    while ((i < MAX_ITEMS) && (bListEmpty))
    {
        /* if the item is in use then the list is not empty */
        bListEmpty = !bInUse[i++];
    }

    /* reposition the selection marker in the list box */
    if (!bListEmpty)
    {
        if (iCurSel)                    // did we delete the first item?
        {                               // no; select item above deletion
            ListBox_SetCurSel( hwndList, iCurSel-1 );
        }
        else                            // deleted item was at top
        {                               // select new top entry
            ListBox_SetCurSel( hwndList, iCurSel );
        }
    }
    return;
}

/*-------------------------------------------------------------------

        DELETE LIST
        Delete all the entries in the list and free the memory
        it occupied.  Called when the program ends.
        -----------------------------------------------------------*/
```

```
void DeleteList ( void )
{
    BOOL bTest;

    /* decommit the memory and then release the address space */
    bTest = VirtualFree( pBase, O, MEM_DECOMMIT );
    if (!bTest)
    {
        ShowErrorMsg( __LINE__ );
    }

    bTest = VirtualFree( pBase, O, MEM_RELEASE );
    if (!bTest)
    {
        ShowErrorMsg( __LINE__ );
    }

    return;
}

/*-------------------------------------------------------------------
        GET PAGE BASE ENTRY
        Given an index into the list, figure out which entry
        is first on the same page.  To do this, find the first
        integer that is divisible by four and is less than or
        equal to iPlace.
        ---------------------------------------------------------------*/

int GetPageBaseEntry ( int iPlace )
{
    while (iPlace % 4)
    {
        iPlace--;
    }

    return( iPlace );
}

/*-------------------------------------------------------------------
        ADJUST LOOKUP TABLE
        When a list box entry is deleted, the array that matches
        the list box entries and the memory offsets must be updated.
        The iStart parameter gives the position in the list box
        from which a string was just deleted.
        ---------------------------------------------------------------*/
```

```
void AdjustLookupTable ( int iStart )
{
    int i;

    // This loop starts at the position where an entry
    // was just deleted and works down the list, scooting
    // lower items up one space to fill in the gap.

    for (i = iStart; i < MAX_ITEMS - 1; i++)
    {
        iListLookup[i] = iListLookup[i + 1];
    }

    iListLookup[MAX_ITEMS - 1] = 0;
    return;
}
```

The remaining procedures run the dialog box where the user enters text, display the About box, and show error messages when something goes wrong. They appear on the disk.

Write-Protecting the List Pages

Instead of waiting for page faults and scurrying for last-minute commitments, the List program could invest a little overhead and manage its array in a more deliberate fashion. Here are versions of AddItem and DeleteItem that call **VirtualProtect** before and after each modification to ensure that every page is committed in advance and write-protected afterward.

```
/*-------------------------------------------------------------
        ADD ITEM
        Add a list entry.  MAX_ITEMS is 500 and ITEM_SIZE is set
        to 1024.  With 1024 bytes per entry there are four entries
        per page.  With 500 entries, the list uses 125 pages.
        ----------------------------------------------------------*/

void AddItem ( void )
{
    MEMORY_BASIC_INFORMATION MemInfo;     // info about a memory block
    char szText[ITEM_SIZE];               // text for one item
    DWORD dwOldState;                     // memory status flags
    int iLen;                             // string length
```

```
int iIndex;                      // position in array
int iPos;                        // position in list box
int iCount;                      // count of entries in list box
BOOL bDone;                      // TRUE when free array entry found
BOOL bTest;                      // for testing return values

/* determine the location of the first free entry */
bDone = FALSE;
iIndex = 0;
while ((!bDone) && (iIndex < MAX_ITEMS))
{
    if(bInUse[iIndex] == 0)      // is entry in use?
    {
        bDone = TRUE;            // found an empty entry
    }
    else
    {
        iIndex++;                // advance to next entry
    }
}

/* retrieve the text */
iLen = GetItemText(szText);
if (!iLen)
{
    return;
}

// Retrieve information about this entry's memory page.
// If it is committed, remove the access protection to
// allow reading and writing.  If it is not committed,
// allocate it.

/* fill out a MEMORY_BASIC_INFORMATION structure */
VirtualQuery( &(pBase[ITEM_SIZE * iIndex]),
              &MemInfo,
              sizeof(MemInfo) );

if (MemInfo.State == MEM_COMMIT)
{
    // The memory has already been committed.  Change the
    // access mode to permit reading and writing.
```

```
    bTest = VirtualProtect(
        &(pBase[ITEM_SIZE * iIndex]),    // bottom of area to protect
        ITEM_SIZE,                       // size of area to protect
        PAGE_READWRITE,                  // new protection status
        &dwOldState );                   // old protection status

    if (!bTest)
    {
        ShowErrorMsg( __LINE__ );        // protection failed
    }
}
else // this page is not yet committed
{
    LPVOID lpvResult;

    lpvResult = VirtualAlloc(
        &(pBase[iIndex * ITEM_SIZE]),    // bottom of area to commit
        ITEM_SIZE,                       // size of area to commit
        MEM_COMMIT,                      // new status flag
        PAGE_READWRITE );                // protection status

    if (!lpvResult)
    {
        ShowErrorMsg( __LINE__ );
        return;                          // allocation failed
    }
}

/* put text in the item */
lstrcpy( &(pBase[iIndex * ITEM_SIZE]), szText );

/* restore the protection state of this page to read-only */
bTest = VirtualProtect(
            &(pBase[iIndex * ITEM_SIZE]),    // bottom of area to protect
            ITEM_SIZE,                       // size of area to protect
            PAGE_READONLY,                   // new protection status
            &dwOldState );                   // previous protection status
if (!bTest)
{
    ShowErrorMsg( __LINE__ );
}

/* mark this entry as in use */
bInUse[iIndex] = 1;
bListEmpty = FALSE;
```

```
    // Add the new text to the list box.  The string is inserted
    // at iPos.  Update iListLookup[iPos] to indicate where in the
    // item array the new entry was stored (iIndex).

    iCount = ListBox_GetCount( hwndList );
    iPos = ListBox_InsertString( hwndList, iCount, szText );
    iCount++;
    ListBox_SetCurSel( hwndList, iPos );
    iListLookup[iPos] = iIndex;

    if (iCount == MAX_ITEMS)                 // did we fill the last place?
    {
        bListFull = TRUE;
    }
    return;
}


/*-------------------------------------------------------------
       DELETE ITEM
       Delete the item containing the text selected in the
       list box.
       ----------------------------------------------------------*/

void DeleteItem ( void )
{
    int iCurSel;        // position of current selection in list box
    int iPlace;         // position of current selection in item array
    DWORD dwOldState;   // previous memory-protection flags
    int iStart;         // first position on same memory page as selection
    int i;              // loop variable
    BOOL bFree;         // TRUE if all 4 entries on one page are unused
    BOOL bTest;         // for testing return results

    /* retrieve the memory offset of the currently selected entry */
    iCurSel = ListBox_GetCurSel( hwndList );
    iPlace = iListLookup[iCurSel];

    /* set the protection to read/write and zero out the entry */
    bTest = VirtualProtect(
                &(pBase[ITEM_SIZE * iPlace]),   // bottom of area to protect
                ITEM_SIZE,                      // size of area to protect
                PAGE_READWRITE,                 // new protection status
                &dwOldState );                  // previous protection status
```

```
if (!bTest)
{
    ShowErrorMsg( __LINE__ );
    return;
}
FillMemory( &(pBase[iPlace * ITEM_SIZE]), ITEM_SIZE, 0 );

/* mark this entry as free */
bInUse[iPlace] = 0;

// Figure out which entry number is first on the current page.
// If all four entries on the page are empty, we'll uncommit
// the page to release memory.

iStart = GetPageBaseEntry( iPlace );
bFree = TRUE;

for (i = 0; i < 4; i++)                    // check four entries
{
    if (bInUse[i + iStart])                // in use?
    {
        bFree = FALSE;                     // page is not free
    }
}

// If a whole memory page is now unused, free it.  If not,
// restore its read-only protection.

if (bFree)                                 // is page free?
{                                          // YES; release it
    bTest = VirtualFree( &(pBase[iStart * ITEM_SIZE]),
            ITEM_SIZE, MEM_DECOMMIT );
}
else
{                                          // NO; protect it
    bTest = VirtualProtect( &(pBase[ITEM_SIZE * iPlace]),
            ITEM_SIZE, PAGE_READONLY, &dwOldState );
}
if (!bTest)
{
    ShowErrorMsg( __LINE__ );
}
```

```
/* update the list box display and the lookup table array */
ListBox_DeleteString( hwndList, iCurSel );
AdjustLookupTable( iCurSel );

/* check whether any entries remain in the list */
bListEmpty = TRUE;
i = 0;
while ((i < MAX_ITEMS) && (bListEmpty))
{
    /* if the item is in use then the list is not empty */
    bListEmpty = !bInUse[i++];
}

/* reposition the selection marker in the list box */
if (!bListEmpty)
{
    if (iCurSel)                    // did we delete the first item?
    {                              // no; select item above deletion
        ListBox_SetCurSel( hwndList, iCurSel - 1 );
    }
    else                           // deleted item was at top
    {                              // select new top entry
        ListBox_SetCurSel( hwndList, iCurSel );
    }
}

    return;
}
```

Mapped Memory File Browser

Each instance of our next program, the Mapped File Browser, opens a handle to the same file-mapping object and maps a view of it. The object represents a small buffer of only 6K and is backed by the system's paging file. A multiline edit box in the program window shows the contents of the shared buffer. A set of six radio buttons permits the user to inspect different sections of the shared buffer. When the user selects a new section, the program copies part of the shared buffer into the edit control where it can be examined and modified. In Figure 7.8, several instances of Browser have written information to different parts of the same buffer.

FIGURE 7.8:

Two instances of the Mapped File Browser sharing views of the same mapped file

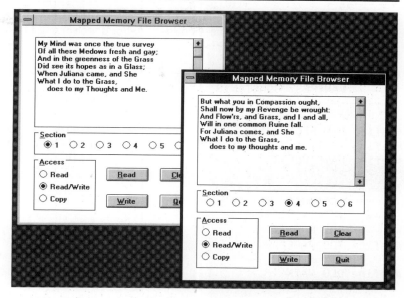

Push buttons issue commands to write from the screen back to the buffer, read from the buffer to refresh the screen, clear text from the edit window, and quit the program. Three more radio buttons set the page protection for the current page to read, read/write, or copy-on-write. If the user pushes the Write button while viewing a read-only page, the program traps the resulting exception.

Header and Resource Files

Two constants in the header file direct the program in creating and using the mapped file. The program's window has room for six radio buttons across its width, so we want to divide the buffer into six sections. Each section should roughly fill the buffer so that as the user switches from section to section new contents come into view. SECTION_SIZE tells how big one section is (1K) and NUM_SEC-TIONS tells how many sections there are (6).

The resource script includes a string to name the file-mapping object. Because all instances use the same name string, all receive handles to the same object. Also in the resources is a dialog template describing the program's main window, which is a dialog box. The **AUTORADIOBUTTON** statement is new in Windows NT, but it duplicates the effect of the old **BS_AUTORADIOBUTTON** style.

```
/*-------------------------------------------------------------------

          BROWSER.H
          Header file for the Browser mapped memory file demo program.
          ------------------------------------------------------------*/


/*-------------------------------------------------------------------

          MANIFEST CONSTANTS
          ------------------------------------------------------------*/


#define NUM_SECTIONS            6          // dialog supports 6 section buttons
#define SECTION_SIZE            1024       // each section shows 1K of buffer
#define NAME_BUFFER             80         // size of mapping object name string


/*-------------------------------------------------------------------

          RESOURCE IDs
          ------------------------------------------------------------*/


#define IDS_MAPFILE             10         // string

#define DLG_MAIN                10         // main window dialog template

#define IDD_EDIT                100        // edit control

#define IDD_READ                110        // push buttons
#define IDD_WRITE               120
#define IDD_CLEAR               130
#define IDD_QUIT                140

#define IDD_READ_ACCESS         150        // page protection radio buttons
#define IDD_READWRITE_ACCESS    160
#define IDD_WRITECOPY_ACCESS    170

#define IDD_SECTION1            200        // file section radio buttons
#define IDD_SECTION2            201        // (must be consecutive numbers)
#define IDD_SECTION3            202
#define IDD_SECTION4            203
#define IDD_SECTION5            204
#define IDD_SECTION6            205


/*-------------------------------------------------------------------

          FUNCTION PROTOTYPES
          ------------------------------------------------------------*/
```

```
BOOL InitApp( HINSTANCE hInst );
BOOL WINAPI Browser_DlgProc( HWND hDlg, UINT uMsg, WPARAM wParam,
        LPARAM lParam );
void Browser_DoInitDialog( HWND hDlg );
void Browser_DoCommand( HWND hDlg, UINT uCmd );
void DoWrite( HWND hWnd, int iSection );
void DoRead( HWND hWnd, int iSection );
void DoClear( HWND hWnd );
void ChangeAccess( int iNewAccess );
void ShowErrorMsg( int iLine );


=======================================================================

/*---------------------------------------------------------------------

        BROWSER.RC
        Resource script for the Browser mapped file demo program.
        ---------------------------------------------------------------*/

#include <windows.h>
#include "browser.h"


STRINGTABLE
BEGIN
    IDS_MAPFILE,      "browser_mapped_file"
END


DLG_MAIN DIALOG DISCARDABLE  6, 24, 192, 209
LANGUAGE LANG_NEUTRAL, SUBLANG_NEUTRAL
STYLE DS_MODALFRAME | WS_POPUP | WS_VISIBLE | WS_CAPTION | WS_SYSMENU
CAPTION "Mapped Memory File Browser"
FONT 8, "MS Sans Serif"
BEGIN
    EDITTEXT            IDD_EDIT,13,12,160,96,ES_MULTILINE | WS_VSCROLL
    GROUPBOX            "&Section",-1,13,110,160,27,WS_GROUP | WS_TABSTOP
    AUTORADIOBUTTON     "1",IDD_SECTION1,22,122,21,10
    AUTORADIOBUTTON     "2",IDD_SECTION2,47,122,21,10
    AUTORADIOBUTTON     "3",IDD_SECTION3,72,122,21,10
    AUTORADIOBUTTON     "4",IDD_SECTION4,97,122,21,10
    AUTORADIOBUTTON     "5",IDD_SECTION5,122,122,21,10
    AUTORADIOBUTTON     "6",IDD_SECTION6,147,122,21,10
    GROUPBOX            "&Access",-1,13,139,59,57,WS_GROUP | WS_TABSTOP
    AUTORADIOBUTTON     "Read",IDD_READ_ACCESS,18,153,39,10
    AUTORADIOBUTTON     "Read/Write",IDD_READWRITE_ACCESS,18,166,52,10
    AUTORADIOBUTTON     "Copy",IDD_WRITECOPY_ACCESS,18,179,52,10
```

```
PUSHBUTTON              "&Read",IDD_READ,82,151,40,14
PUSHBUTTON              "&Write",IDD_WRITE,82,179,40,14
PUSHBUTTON              "&Clear",IDD_CLEAR,133,151,40,14
PUSHBUTTON              "&Quit",IDD_QUIT,133,179,40,14
END
```

Initializing the Mapped File

Browser keeps information about its file-mapping object in two global variables. hMapFile is a handle to the object, and lpView points to a mapped view of the object.

Because the program's main window is a dialog box, WinMain omits the usual message loop. Instead it simply calls an initialization procedure and invokes a modal dialog box. When the dialog box quits, WinMain releases its objects and ends.

InitApp creates the file-mapping object and maps a view of it. Because the instances of Browser want only to share memory, not to create a disk file, the **CreateFileMapping** command passes 0xFFFFFFFF as the file handle. The buffer will be mapped from the system's paging file. Had we chosen to create a new disk file for the Browser instances to share, we would have had to call **CreateFile** first:

```
/* create the file to be mapped */
hFile = CreateFile( szFileName,            // file name string
    GENERIC_READ | GENERIC_WRITE,          // access rights
    0,                                     // don't share files being mapped
    (LPSECURITY_ATTRIBUTES)NULL,           // default attributes
    CREATE_ALWAYS,                         // if file doesn't exist create it
    FILE_ATTRIBUTE_NORMAL,                 // no special attributes
    NULL );                                // no special attributes
```

The file-mapping object allows read/write access, but individual views may request different protection flags. **PAGE_READWRITE** is compatible with all the possible view access flags.

After creating the file-mapping object, InitApp next maps a view of it. Initially, the view allows the user both read and write privileges by specifying **FILE_MAP_ALL_ACCESS**. The next two zeros make the beginning of the mapped view begin with the first byte of the file, and the final zero parameter causes the view to extend to the end of the file. **CreateFileMapping** sets the file's size to NUM_SECTIONS * SECTION_SIZE, which happens to be 6K. The size and starting point of the view never change in this program. The starting point can't change because it must be a multiple of 64K. For a 6K file, the view must begin at byte 0. To show different sections of the 6K shared buffer, Browser uses `lpView` to treat the buffer as an array of characters.

```
/*-------------------------------------------------------------------

        BROWSER.C

        Demonstrates sharing memory through mapped files.  Different
        instances of this program share a single mapped file.  The
        user reads and writes from any instance and other instances
        see the changes.

        FUNCTIONS
              WinMain                    receive and dispatch messages
              InitApp                    create file mapping object
              Browser_DlgProc            main window (dialog) procedure
              Browser_DoInitDialog       initialize dialog window
              Browser_DoCommand          respond to dialog controls
              DoWrite                    write to the shared file
              DoRead                     read from the shared file
              DoClear                    clear the edit control buffer
              ChangeAccess               change read/write flags
              ShowErrorMsg               display message box after errors

        from Mastering Windows NT Programming
        copyright 1993 by Brian Myers & Eric Hamer

        -------------------------------------------------------------*/

#define STRICT
#include <windows.h>
#include <windowsx.h>
#include "browser.h"

/*-------------------------------------------------------------------
         GLOBAL VARIABLES
        -------------------------------------------------------------*/

HANDLE hMapFile;                   // file-mapping object
char *lpView;                      // base address of a mapped file view
```

```
/*-------------------------------------------------------------------
        WIN MAIN
        Calls initializing procedures and creates the Browser
        dialog window.
    ------------------------------------------------------------------*/

int WINAPI WinMain (
    HINSTANCE hInstance,
    HINSTANCE hPrevInstance,
    LPSTR lpszCmdLine,
    int iCmdShow )
{
    int iDlgRet;

    /* create the file-mapping object and its view */
    if (!InitApp( hInstance ))
    {
        return( 0 );
    }

    /* display the browser dialog box */
    iDlgRet = DialogBox( hInstance, MAKEINTRESOURCE(DLG_MAIN), NULL,
                        (DLGPROC)Browser_DlgProc );

    /* clean up */
    UnmapViewOfFile( lpView );      // (optional:  the system
    CloseHandle( hMapFile );        // cleans up on exit anyway)

    return( iDlgRet );
    UNREFERENCED_PARAMETER( hPrevInstance );
    UNREFERENCED_PARAMETER( lpszCmdLine );
    UNREFERENCED_PARAMETER( iCmdShow );
}

/*-------------------------------------------------------------------
        INIT APP
        Create the program's file mapping object and map a view
        of it.
    ------------------------------------------------------------------*/

BOOL InitApp ( HINSTANCE hInst )
{
    char szMapFile[NAME_BUFFER];

    /* load the string to name the file-mapping object */
```

```
int iLen = LoadString( hInst, IDS_MAPFILE,
                    szMapFile, sizeof(szMapFile) );
if (!iLen)
{
    return( FALSE );
}

// Create the file-mapping object.  Secondary instances
// will receive a handle to the object the first instance
// has already created.

hMapFile = CreateFileMapping(
            (HANDLE)0xFFFFFFFF,              // use system swap file
            (LPSECURITY_ATTRIBUTES)NULL,     // default attributes
            PAGE_READWRITE,                  // read and write to buffer
            0,                               // high half of size
            NUM_SECTIONS*SECTION_SIZE,       // low half of size
            szMapFile );                     // name of new object
if (hMapFile == NULL)                        // any error?
{
    ShowErrorMsg( __LINE__ );
    return( FALSE );                         // yes; give up
}

/* map a view of the file */
lpView = MapViewOfFile( hMapFile,            // handle to file-mapping object
            FILE_MAP_ALL_ACCESS,             // access privileges
            0, 0,                            // start at beginning of file
            0 );                             // size of view area (all of file)

if (!lpView)                                 // any error?
{
    CloseHandle( hMapFile );                 // yes; free handle
    ShowErrorMsg( __LINE__ );
    return( FALSE );
}

return( TRUE );
}
```

All instances of Browser initialize alike. If the program mapped its buffer to an independent disk file, the first instance would have to initialize differently. Only the first instance would call **CreateFile**, and subsequent instances could be made to call **OpenFileMapping** rather than repeating the original **CreateFileMapping** command.

```
/* get a handle for an existing file-mapping object */
hMapFile = OpenFileMapping(
                FILE_MAP_ALL_ACCESS,     // access privileges
                FALSE,                   // inheritable?
                szMapFile );             // name of object
if (!hMapFile)
{
    ShowErrorMsg( __LINE__ );            // initialization failed
    return( FALSE );
}
```

Because Windows NT always passes **NULL** to WinMain for the hPrevInstance parameter, Browser would need another mechanism to check for other instances. **FindWindow** works for overlapping windows, but standard dialog windows don't have a documented class name. (The class for standard dialog windows seems to be #32770, as you can verify with Microsoft's Spy utility, but undocumented features may change in future releases.) Successive instances of Browser could also identify their precedence if the first instance created a named pipe or added a string to the global atom table. Each instance could determine whether it has a predecessor by checking for the existence of the signal object.

Running the Dialog Box

The next procedures receive and respond to messages for the dialog box. The Browser dialog initializes its controls when it receives **WM_INITDIALOG**. Among other things, Browser_DoInitDialog sets a limit on the number of characters the user may enter in the edit control. The limit prevents the user from entering more text than the current section of the mapped file can hold. Browser_DoCommand calls other procedures to manipulate the mapped file view in response to input from the user.

```
void Browser_DoCommand (
    HWND hDlg,
    UINT uCmd )                         // control ID of the button pressed
{
    // The static variable iCurSection records the user's
    // most current selection from the Section radio buttons.

    static int iCurSection = 0;

    switch (uCmd)
    {
```

```
        case IDD_WRITE:
            DoWrite( hDlg, iCurSection );
            break;

        case IDD_READ:
            DoRead( hDlg, iCurSection );
            break;

        case IDD_CLEAR:
            DoClear( hDlg );
            break;

        case IDD_SECTION1:
        case IDD_SECTION2:
        case IDD_SECTION3:
        case IDD_SECTION4:
        case IDD_SECTION5:
        case IDD_SECTION6:
            iCurSection = uCmd - IDD_SECTION1;  // save current choice
            DoClear( hDlg );                    // clear edit box
            DoRead( hDlg, iCurSection );         // show new file section
            break;

        case IDD_READ_ACCESS:
        case IDD_READWRITE_ACCESS:
        case IDD_WRITECOPY_ACCESS:
            ChangeAccess( uCmd );
            break;

        case IDCANCEL:
        case IDD_QUIT:
            EndDialog( hDlg, TRUE );
            break;
    }
    return;
}
```

Modifying the Shared Object

When the user presses the Write, Read, or Clear button the program calls DoWrite, DoRead, or DoClear. In response to commands from the Access radio buttons, the program calls ChangeAccess.

DoWrite and DoRead send **WM_GETTEXT** and **WM_SETTEXT** messages to the edit control. DoWrite copies the contents of the edit buffer to a section of the mapped file, and DoRead copies a section of the mapped file to the edit control. In both procedures, this expression points to the beginning of the current section of the mapped view:

```
&(lpView[iSection*SECTION_SIZE])
```

lpView is type **LPSTR**, so it points to an array of characters. iSection tells which radio button is currently checked. The first button is 0, so the result of iSection*SECTION_SIZE is the number of the first byte in the given file section. lpView[] evaluates to a character, and &(lpView[]) gives the address of the character.

The exception handler in DoWrite is designed to catch the error when the user write-protects the mapped view and then tries to use the Write button. We could of course disable the button, but allowing the error to occur seemed more instructive and a better demonstration of what write protection does.

ChangeAccess unmaps the current view of the file-mapping object in order to re-map it with a different access privilege. Every instance of the program may choose different access flags because each has its own independent view of the object. An instance that uses **FILE_MAP_COPY** remains synchronized with the other instances' views until it writes to the buffer. At that moment the system intervenes and creates a copy of the protected page for the program to modify. From then on, the program never sees the original unmodified page again, even though the other instances do. Since Browser shows the buffer in 1K sections, four sections fill one page frame. If one instance writes to the first section with copy-on-write protection, then it loses synchronization in the first four sections (one page frame). Its view of sections 5 and 6, however, will continue to reflect changes made by other instances. Also, changes the first program makes to its copy-on-write buffer will never be visible to other instances. The copied pages are private.

```
/*-----------------------------------------------------------------
        DO WRITE
        Copy text from the edit control to the mapped file.  Beware
        of possible write-protection errors.
    -------------------------------------------------------------*/

void DoWrite (
    HWND hDlg,
    int iSection )
{
```

```
    /* get the edit control handle */
    HWND hwndEdit = GetDlgItem( hDlg, IDD_EDIT );

    if (hwndEdit)
    {
        try
        {
            /* copy the text from the edit buffer to the mapped file */
            Edit_GetText( hwndEdit,                    // edit control
                &(lpView[iSection*SECTION_SIZE]),      // pointer into the view
                SECTION_SIZE );                        // bytes in section
        }
        except (EXCEPTION_ACCESS_VIOLATION)
        {
            /* assume the exception was due to read-only access */
            MessageBox( hDlg, "Memory is read only.\n\rNo data was written.",
                "Browser Message", MB_OK | MB_ICONEXCLAMATION );
        }
    }
    return;
}

/*-------------------------------------------------------------
        DO READ
        Read text from the mapped file and copy it to the edit
        control buffer.
    -------------------------------------------------------------*/

void DoRead (
    HWND hDlg,
    int iSection )
{
    HWND hwndEdit;

    /* get the edit control handle */
    hwndEdit = GetDlgItem( hDlg, IDD_EDIT );

    if (hwndEdit)
    {
        /* retrieve the text from memory and display it */
        Edit_SetText( hwndEdit,
                &(lpView[iSection*SECTION_SIZE]) ); // pointer into view
    }
     return;
}
```

```
/*------------------------------------------------------------------
        DO CLEAR
        Clear the text in the edit control.  This procedure does not
        read or modify the mapped file, only the edit buffer.
        ----------------------------------------------------------*/

void DoClear ( HWND hWnd )
{
    HWND hwndEdit;
    char *szText = "\0";

    /* empty the edit buffer by filling it with a null string */
    hwndEdit = GetDlgItem( hWnd, IDD_EDIT );
    if (hwndEdit)
    {
        Edit_SetText( hwndEdit, szText );
    }
    return;
}

/*------------------------------------------------------------------
        CHANGE ACCESS
        Destroy the current view of the map file and create a new
        one using the values passed to indicate which access
        rights to grant and which part of the file to show.
        ----------------------------------------------------------*/

void ChangeAccess ( int iNewAccess )            // requested access rights
{
    DWORD fdwAccess;                            // new access flag

    /* close the previous mapping */
    UnmapViewOfFile( lpView );

    /* choose new access flag */
    switch (iNewAccess)
    {
        case IDD_READWRITE_ACCESS:
            fdwAccess = FILE_MAP_ALL_ACCESS;
            break;

        case IDD_READ_ACCESS:
            fdwAccess = FILE_MAP_READ;
            break;
```

```
    default: // IDD_WRITECOPY_ACCESS
        fdwAccess = FILE_MAP_COPY;
        break;
}

/* remap the view using the requested access and view number */
 lpView = MapViewOfFile( hMapFile,         // handle to mapping object
            fdwAccess,                     // access privileges
            0, 0,                          // starting offset in file
            0 );                           // size of view area (all of file)

if (lpView == NULL)                        // error?
{
    ShowErrorMsg( __LINE__ );             // yes; tell user
}
return;
}
```

To manage memory so concurrent programs may run smoothly together, the Windows NT Virtual Memory Manager relies on hardware to provide the protected addressing and paging capabilities from which it constructs for each process the illusion of a 4GB address space. The virtual memory API passes on to you some of the VMM's new powers, especially the ability to reserve a range of addresses without immediately committing physical memory to support them. The ability to guarantee that a range of contiguous addresses will be available as an object grows, or as an array slowly fills in, makes working with sparse memory structures easy.

The Win32 API also supplies two sets of commands for working with heaps. The Global and Local allocation commands carried forward from 16-bit Windows operate on a default process heap, but for managing a series of small, related allocations you may prefer to create other private heaps with the Heap API commands. The Heap commands work more efficiently with less overhead, but the Global and Local commands are the only choice for writing portable code.

Given the memory manager's effectiveness in isolating each process from memory used by any other process, sharing blocks of memory becomes problematic. Programs have moved apart into private address spaces. Gone are the neighborly days of passing memory handles from program to program. In their place are the high-tech miracles of memory-mapped files, and with them come all the modern concerns for protection, coherence, and point of view.

Drawing Complex Shapes with the New GDI

New features of the GDI

Bézier curves

Paths

Join styles and end caps

Parallelogram block transfers

Readers who have followed the book this far now know the fundamental mechanisms that distinguish Windows NT from Windows for DOS. From the programmer's point of view, threads and processes form the core of the system's multitasking ability. Synchronization objects and pipes coordinate concurrent tasks and pass information from program to program. Structured exception handling and virtual memory management also give you new powers. These basic tools have their place in most Win32 programs. The remaining chapters turn to some of the system's other more specialized features, such as file I/O, multimedia, and security. We begin with the Graphics Device Interface. Chapters 8, 9, and 10 concern themselves with new and advanced drawing features in the GDI.

This chapter first briefly surveys changes to the GDI and then explains in more detail four particular features: Bézier curves, wideline pens, paths, and bitmap distortions. A sample paint program at the end of the chapter demonstrates all four features. Subsequent chapters explain coordinate transformations, enhanced metafiles, and common bitmap operations.

CHANGES TO THE GDI

The GDI was largely rewritten for Windows NT, and many changes, both small and large, have found their way into the new version. We'll summarize them briefly first and then consider the more important changes individually.

- The GDI now draws true Bézier curves. Until now the only way to draw non-conic curves was to calculate the points and approximate the shape with `Polyline`.

- The GDI now supports wide lines. It was always possible to draw wide lines with a fat pen, but now the GDI supports a variety of settings to control how wide lines are drawn. Join styles change the way the GDI draws corners where end points overlap. Pen styles and brushes now apply to wide lines, as well.

- The Digital Differential Analyzer (DDA) has been improved. The GDI uses this algorithm to decide which pixels should be colored in when you ask for a line connecting two points. The code that makes the decisions no longer rounds its internal results to integers, so its decisions are more accurate.

- The new path commands make it easy to define irregular areas enclosed by any combination of curves and lines. Path shapes can be outlined, filled, or converted to regions.

- Region objects have been improved. 16-bit Windows defines a region by breaking it down into a set of rectangles. To define a circle requires a large collection of very narrow rectangles. Windows NT defines regions with trapezoids instead of rectangles, resulting in smaller definitions and faster processing. Also, regions now scale correctly if you create them with paths.

- The addition of world coordinate transformations makes mapping much more versatile. You can draw any figure using coordinates for the easiest head-on perspective and have the system scale, rotate, shear, translate, and reflect the image to any degree and in any direction.

- Font users benefit from an improved font mapper based on PANOSE numbers. The new algorithm makes better choices when asked to find a font most closely matching a particular set of attributes.

- Font character widths can now be fractional values, allowing more precise placement for advanced design and publishing requirements. Character outlines can be made into paths, brushed, outlined with pens, and even used as clipping regions.

- Logical coordinates are now 32-bit values, making the logical coordinate space stretch 2GB in each direction. The change benefits high-resolution design programs that work internally with a large coordinate system to guarantee precise alignment on any display device. The widened values also benefit the processor, which handles 32-bit quantities very efficiently. The change forced some modifications to GDI routines that work with co-ordinate values; for a summary, refer back to the section "Extended GDI Functions" in Chapter 2.

- New bitmap commands make it easy to rotate and distort a bitmap and to perform block transfers with an intermediate masking bitmap.

- With halftone support, the GDI does a better job of simulating colors it doesn't actually have.

- Metafiles have been enhanced to handle all the new GDI features, including paths and transformations. Also, the new metafile format automatically includes in its header some of the placement information that Win16 programmers often have to attach as a separate structure.

- All GDI objects, such as bitmaps and brushes, are deleted automatically when the program ends. The system now marks objects internally with a process ID, so the system easily identifies orphaned objects. A sloppy program no longer leaves behind an unwanted legacy of allocations.

- Device contexts are no longer in short supply. Now only available memory limits the number of simultaneous common device contexts.

As an orientation to the new API, we list in Table 8.1 all the GDI functions new in Win32.

The following functions no longer exist in Win32. Most of them have been replaced by extended versions that perform the same actions using 32-bit coordinates.

GetAspectRatioFilter	OffsetWindowOrg
GetBitmapDimension	ScaleViewportExt
GetBrushOrg	ScaleWindowExt
GetCurrentPosition	SetBitmapDimension
GetMetaFileBits	SetBrushOrg
GetTextExtent	SetMetaFileBits
GetViewportExt	SetViewportExt
GetViewportOrg	SetViewportOrg
GetWindowExt	SetWindowExt
GetWindowOrg	SetWindowOrg
MoveTo	UnrealizeObject
OffsetViewportOrg	

In addition, a few functions remain in the Win32 API for compatibility only. Windows NT programs should avoid these and call the more current replacement functions instead.

TABLE 8.1: GDI Functions New in Win32

Lines, Curves, and Shapes

AngleArc	PolyBezier	PolylineTo	SetArcDirection
ArcTo	PolyBezierTo	PolyPolyline	SetPixelV
GetArcDirection	PolyDraw	PolyTextOut	

GDI Command Batching (see Chapter 8)

GdiFlush	GdiGetBatchLimit	GdiSetBatchLimit

Device Access

DeviceCapabilitiesEx	DrawEscape	ExtEscape

Coordinate Transformations (see Chapter 9)

CombineTransform	SetGraphicsMode	ModifyWorldTransform
GetWorldTransform	GetGraphicsMode	SetWorldTransform

TABLE 8.1: GDI Functions New in Win32 (continued)

Paths

AbortPath	EndPath	GetPath	StrokeAndFillPath
BeginPath	FillPath	PathToRegion	StrokePath
CloseFigure	FlattenPath	SelectClipPath	WidenPath

Fonts

AddFontModule	GetCharABCWidthsFloat	GetTextExtentExPoint
ExtCreateFontIndirect	GetCharWidthFloat	RemoveFontModule

Metafiles (see Chapter 9)

CloseEnhMetaFile	GdiComment	GetEnhMetaFilePaletteEntries	SetEnhMetaFileBits
CopyEnhMetaFile	GetEnhMetaFile	GetMetaFileBitsEx	SetMetaFileBitsEx
CreateEnhMetaFile	GetEnhMetaFileBits	GetWinMetaFileBits	SetWinMetaFileBits
DeleteEnhMetaFile	GetEnhMetaFileDescription	PlayEnhMetaFile	
EnumEnhMetaFile	GetEnhMetaFileHeader	PlayEnhMetaFileRecord	

TABLE 8.1: GDI Functions New in Win32 (continued)

Bitmaps (*see Chapter 10*)			
CreateDIBPattern-BrushPt	CreateDIBSection	MaskBlt	PlgBlt
Clipping			
ExtSelectClipRgn	GetClipRgn	GetMetaRgn	SetMetaRgn
Other GDI Objects			
CreateHalftone-Palette	ExtCreateRegion	GetObjectType	SetBrushOrgEx
ExtCreatePen	GetCurrentObject	GetRegionData	
Device Contexts			
CancelDC	GetColorAdjustment	GetMiterLimit	
SetColorAdjustment	SetMiterLimit		

Don't Call This	Call This Instead
CreateBitmap	CreateDIBitmap
CreateBitmapIndirect	CreateDIBitmap
CreateDIBPatternBrush	CreateDIBPatternBrushPt
CreateDiscardableBitmap	CreateCompatibleBitmap
FloodFill	ExtFloodFill
GetBitmapBits	GetDIBits
SetBitmapBits	SetDIBits

CreateDiscardableBitmap now maps internally to **CreateCompatibleBitmap**. The bits retrieved by **GetBitmapBits** depend on the device and may not be the same under NT as they are for 16-bit Windows. Do not call **GetBitmapBits** and save the result under an old version of Windows and then expect to load the same file back under the new version. In general, use device-dependent bitmaps only for temporary images and buffers that are re-created for each session. Never save them or pass them to other programs. Use device-independent bitmaps (DIBs) instead. Similarly, although the old metafile commands remain in the API, you should use enhanced metafiles instead.

CONCEPTS

This section explains some of the new concepts important for understanding extensions to the Win32 GDI. It introduces the GDI command buffer, wideline support, Bézier curves, and paths. The API routines for working with these objects appear later under the "Commands" heading. For explanations of world coordinate transformations and enhanced metafiles, turn to Chapter 9.

GDI Command Buffer

Whenever possible, the Win32 subsystem implements its services through DLLs that communicate directly with the system. The client program calls the DLL and the DLL calls the system. But this direct method works only for commands that do not use any of the Win32 subsystem's internal variables or settings. Drawing commands do require information from the subsystem. Clipping regions, for example, are stored within the subsystem, and all output must be clipped to some program's window. Output commands must therefore be routed through the subsystem in a local procedure call. Figures 1.16 and 1.17 in Chapter 1 diagram both forms of interaction. LPCs are naturally slower than system calls through a DLL. To respond as quickly as possible to the high volume of output requests its clients generate through the USER and GDI libraries, the Win32 subsystem services each client with a section object (the system-level version of a file-mapping object) and dedicates a thread to reading commands the client leaves there. Rather than routing service requests through the system, the client-side DLLs write directly to the shared block, and the dedicated thread retrieves them.

The interactions of client and server also gain speed when the DLLs save commands in a buffer and pass them to the subsystem in batches. A series of individual commands requires more read and write operations than does a single batch of combined commands. The Win32 subsystem buffers all GDI commands. As a result, GDI commands usually return before the subsystem has received them. Your program may draw an ellipse, receive a **TRUE** return value, and move to the next instruction without the ellipse being drawn. **TRUE** signals only that the command was placed in the queue, not that the operation succeeded. Most of the time this semantic difference is trivial.

The buffer speeds operations by processing commands together in a batch. You can improve speed even more by avoiding the overhead of many successive calls within your own program. The "Poly" functions, some old and some new, operate on an array of points to produce a series of lines or curves all at once. They are listed here. Paths are explained below; they too efficiently group sequential commands into a single operation.

PolyBezier	PolyBezierTo
PolyDraw	PolyLine
PolyLineTo	PolyPolygon
PolyPolyLine	PolyTextOut

Bézier Curves

Originally the word "spline" referred to a flexible instrument used by draftsmen for drawing irregular curves. Mathematicians adopted the word to describe a family of related curves. An engineer named Pierre Bézier developed the mathematical definition of a particular spline curve known since as a Bézier curve. The Bézier spline curve is particularly useful for visual design and fonts. (TrueType fonts use spline curves to define characters.)

It takes four points to determine a Bézier curve: two end points and two control points. A line connects the two end points; the control points influence the line's curvature. Figure 8.1 shows several examples. Usually the curve does not pass through its control points, but it always fits inside the four-sided polygon the four points together describe. Where it starts, the curve runs tangent to a line from the starting point to the first control point. Where it ends, the curve runs tangent to a line from the second control point to the end point. The curve may reverse its orientation twice, at the two points where it most closely approaches the control points.

FIGURE 8.1:

Examples of Bézier curves

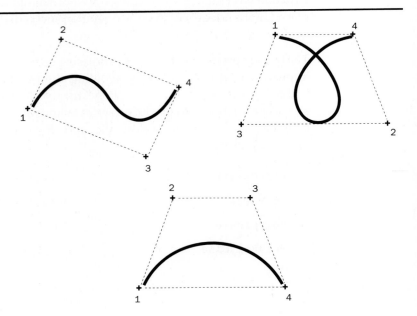

Paths

Now that the GDI can draw non-conic curves, it needs a new way to create regions. `CreateRectRgn`, `CreateEllipticRgn`, and `CreatePolygonRgn` understand only ellipses and polygons. An area partially bounded by a Bézier curve cannot be made into a region using the old routines. Win32 makes it possible to describe areas by combining sequences of line and curve commands into something called a *path*. Every display context has room to hold one path. Once a path has been created for a DC, it can be outlined with the current pen, filled in with the current brush, modified or flattened to change curves to line segments, or made into a region object and even used to clip output. In some ways a path resembles a metafile. Both are created by recording a series of GDI commands; both later reproduce the recorded commands. But in other respects paths and metafiles are very different objects. Here are the important differences.

- A path records output from fewer commands than does a metafile. It does not record region commands, object creation commands, or commands that modify the DC. It does record shape and line commands, including `TextOut` and `ExtTextOut`.

- A path may not be detached from its device context. It may not be swapped in and out, saved to disk, or passed to other programs.

- The records in a path may not be enumerated or modified individually.

- A path can be converted into a region object. A metafile cannot become a region.

COMMANDS

This section explains how to use the GDI command buffer, draw Bézier curves, put joins and end caps on wide lines, make paths, and distort bitmaps.

Controlling the GDI Command Buffer

The command buffer accumulates GDI function calls and passes them to the subsystem in bunches. Batching the commands reduces the number of separate send and receive operations necessary for transmitting successive calls, but it also prevents functions from passing values back to the program after they execute. By the time the command executes, the program has moved on to another instruction. Therefore batching works only with commands that return Boolean values. A command like **SetPixel**, which returns a **COLORREF**, cannot be batched because some programs may depend on using the return value. The Boolean returns from drawing functions, however, usually *are* ignored. (A new version of **SetPixel**, called **SetPixelV**, does return a Boolean value. It exists to permit batching.)

GDI commands accumulate in their batch buffer until one of four events triggers their transmission:

- The buffer fills.
- The program calls any GDI function that does not return a Boolean value.
- The program calls **GdiFlush**.
- A USER library command causes the buffer to empty.

Some of the USER32 library routines also make use of the GDI batch buffer. The USER32 library takes care of windows and messages. When a thread calls a routine to draw a window, for example, USER ends up placing GDI commands in the thread's buffer. These are held for batching just like the thread's own direct commands. Some other USER commands, such as **PeekMessage**, do not issue GDI commands but do go through the buffer. These commands are *not* batched, and they immediately flush all other pending commands as they pass through. As a result of the USER activity, the buffer generally empties frequently, and you cannot exercise precise control over it. Fortunately, precise control is not necessary; few programs need even an occasional **GdiFlush**.

GdiSetBatchLimit also influences the buffer's behavior by setting the maximum number of commands the buffer may hold. The matching function **GdiGetBatchLimit** retrieves the current limit. Setting the limit to 0 selects the default limit value, which on our system is 10. Setting the limit to 1 in effect disables batching. Each thread has its own buffer and its own buffer limit.

```
BOOL GdiFlush( void );
DWORD GdiGetBatchLimit( void );
DWORD GdiSetBatchLimit( DWORD dwLimit );
```

Speaking practically, the existence of the GDI buffer means that you can't rely on return values from Boolean GDI functions to report errors accurately and that very occasionally you may have to call **GdiFlush** to ensure a timely screen update. For example, an idling screen saver that updates a clock face every minute should either disable buffering or call **GdiFlush** after each update. Otherwise the update command might sit in the buffer long enough for the delay to be noticeable.

Drawing Bézier Curves

Two commands draw Bézier curves. Both accept a potentially large array of points and will draw many curves all at once. The last point of one curve becomes the first point of the next, so the result is always continuous. **PolyBezierTo** updates the pen position; **PolyBezier** does not.

```
BOOL PolyBezier(
    HDC hDC,                    // device context
    LPPOINT lppt,               // address of an array of points
    DWORD dwNumPoints );        // number of points in lppt array

BOOL PolyBezierTo(
    HDC hDC,                    // device context
    LPPOINT lppt,               // address of an array of points
    DWORD dwNumPoints );        // number of points in lppt array
```

If the lppt array is large, both commands draw more than one curve. The last point in one curve becomes the first point in the next. It takes four points to define the first curve but only three more for each successive curve. The number of points you pass must be exact, without leftovers. If dwNumPoints is not 1 more than a multiple of 3, neither command draws anything, even though both still return **TRUE**.

Although successive curves share an end point and therefore are continuous, their intersection may form a sharp corner. If you want a smooth transition from one curve into the next, then the control points around the intersection must all fall on a straight line. Specifically, the second control point of the first curve, the shared end point, and the first control point of the second curve must be colinear. The closer they are to a line, the smoother the join will be. Figure 8.2 diagrams a smooth curve.

FIGURE 8.2:

How to place control points to ensure
a smooth join between continuous
Bézier curves

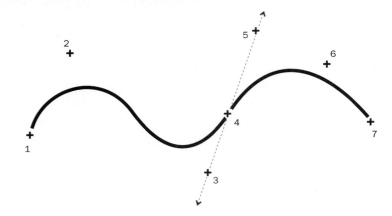

Drawing Wide Lines

The Windows NT GDI offers *wideline support,* a set of vastly improved capabilities
for controlling how lines are colored, styled, and scaled. Because the GDI draws
lines with pens, the new wideline features require new kinds of pens. The
ExtCreatePen command creates cosmetic pens and geometric pens. A *cosmetic pen*
has the features that Windows programmers already expect: a width, a color, and a
style. *Geometric* pens possess four additional attributes: a pattern, a hatch style, an
end style, and a join style. Cosmetic pens maintain a constant physical width of 1
pixel no matter how the image they paint is transformed or scaled. The width of a
geometric pen, on the other hand, is measured in logical units, may be very large,
and always obeys scaling and transformation rules. Use cosmetic pens for fast output at a constant width. Use geometric pens for brushed lines, end cap and line join
styles, and scaling. A cosmetic pen might be valuable for internal lines in a CAD
cross section; a wide geometric pen would work well for drawing bars in a chart
that must be scaled.

```
HPEN ExtCreatePen(
    DWORD dwPenStyle,          // pen type and style flags
    DWORD dwWidth,             // pen width (must be 1 for PS_COSMETIC)
    LPLOGBRUSH lpLogBrush,     // structure for brush attributes
    DWORD dwStyleCount,        // length (in DWORDs) of style array
    LPDWORD lpdwStyle );       // array of DWORDs for custom styles (optional)
```

The first parameter, dwPenStyle, combines flags that determine whether the pen is cosmetic or geometric, whether it draws solid or dashed lines, how corners are drawn when two lines meet, and how the end of a line segment is capped off. dwPenStyle may include one flag from each category. Asterisks mark the default values.

Type

PS_COSMETIC*	Creates a cosmetic pen
PS_GEOMETRIC	Creates a geometric pen

Style

PS_ALTERNATE	Pen draws on every other pixel (cosmetic only)
PS_DASH	Pen draws a dashed line
PS_DOT	Pen draws a dotted line
PS_DASHDOT	Pen draws alternating dashes and dots
PS_DASHDOTDOT	Pen repeatedly draws a dash and two dots
PS_INSIDEFRAME	Pen draws a solid line that is always made to fit entirely inside the bounding rectangle of any geometric figure it is used to outline (geometric only)
PS_NULL	Pen draws an invisible line
PS_SOLID*	Pen draws a solid line
PS_USERSTYLE	Pen draws with a styling array supplied by the user

End cap

PS_ENDCAP_FLAT	Line ends are flat
PS_ENDCAP_ROUND*	Line ends are rounded
PS_ENDCAP_SQUARE	Line ends are square

Line join

`PS_JOIN_BEVEL`	Joins are beveled
`PS_JOIN_MITER`	Joins are mitered (or beveled if they are outside the current miter limit)
`PS_JOIN_ROUND`*	Joins are rounded

Most of the pen styles are familiar from older versions of Windows. Figure 8.3 illustrates the different styles for end caps and line joins. Because cosmetic pens are only 1 pixel wide, end caps and join styles have no effect on them.

FIGURE 8.3:

End cap and line join styles

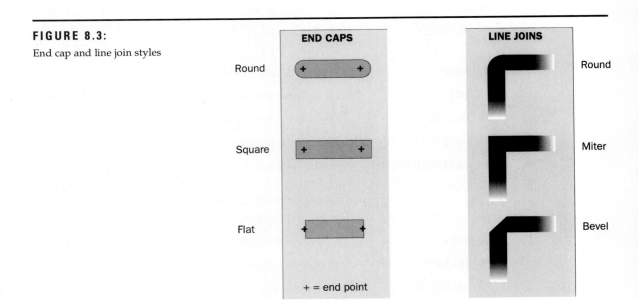

The second parameter of `ExtCreatePen`, `dwWidth`, determines how wide a line drawn by this pen will be. For geometric pens, the value is interpreted in logical units. For cosmetic pens, the only valid width is 1. `lpLogBrush` points to a **LOGBRUSH** structure, listed below. From this structure a cosmetic pen derives its color, which must be solid. (The **lbStyle** field of the **LOGBRUSH** structure must be **BS_SOLID**.) A cosmetic pen ignores the other fields.

```
typedef struct tagLOGBRUSH { /* lb */
    UINT     lbStyle;            // hatched, DIB, pattern, solid, or hollow
    COLORREF lbColor;            // foreground color for the brush
    LONG     lbHatch;            // hatch style, bitmap handle, or DIB pointer
} LOGBRUSH;
```

Geometric pens, however, may be colored with any brush, solid or not. They may be brushed with a pattern drawn from a custom bitmap or hatched with parallel lines.

With the last two parameters of **ExtCreatePen** you can define a custom style, spacing the dots and dashes to suit your preference. lpdwStyle points to an array of **DWORD** values. The array has dwStyleCount elements. The first element tells how many successive units to color in for the first dash. The second element defines the length of the first space. The third element defines the second dash, the fourth element the second space, and so on. These parameters matter only if dwPenStyle includes the **PS_USERSTYLE** flag. Without that flag, the last two parameters should be 0 and **NULL**. How the units in lpdwStyle are understood depends on the type of pen. For cosmetic pens, the units are physical pixels. Geometric pens define their styles in logical units. As a result, the dots and dashes in a cosmetic pen remain the same size no matter how the image is scaled or transformed. The dots and dashes in a geometric pen shrink and expand when scaled or transformed.

ExtCreatePen returns a pen handle (**HPEN**) that may be selected into a device context (**SelectObject**). Subsequent lines and curves drawn to that device will use the new pen. (Note that text output does not use the pen, but text characters in a stroked path do use the pen. See the next section.) When you finish with the pen, remove it from the DC and destroy it (**SelectObject**, **DeleteObject**.)

The old **CreatePen** and **CreatePenIndirect** commands survive in the API for compatibility, but they are anomalies. Though these commands are documented as cosmetic pens, the objects they create are really hybrids. They are not really cosmetic because they can be wider than a pixel, but neither are they geometric because they don't scale and can't have end caps or join styles. Internally the system flags old-style pens and imitates old-style functionality for them.

Two functions influence the drawing of mitered joins. The distance from the internal vertex of the join to the external vertex is called the *join length*. As you can see in Figure 8.4, when two wide lines join at a very acute angle the miter join can potentially grow very long. The device context holds a miter join limit, and if the join length exceeds the limit, the system uses a beveled join instead.

FIGURE 8.4:

Vertex with long join length that could be prevented by reducing the miter limit

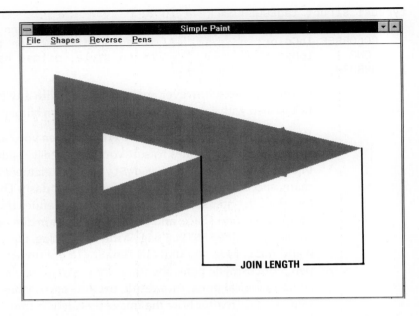

```
BOOL SetMiterLimit(
    HDC hDC,                    // device context
    FLOAT pflNewLimit,          // new miter limit
    PFLOAT pflOldLimit );       // previous miter limit

BOOL GetMiterLimit(
    HDC hDC,                    // device context
    PFLOAT pflLimit );          // current miter limit (returned)
```

The floating-point number that limits the miter join represents a ratio of the join length to the line width. The default limit is 10.0.

Making Paths

A path contains a series of commands for drawing lines and curves. To create a path, call **BeginPath**. Then call output routines for the lines and curves. Conclude by calling **EndPath**. **BeginPath** and **EndPath** mark off a *path bracket*. Line and curve commands within the path bracket do not produce output on the screen. Instead the device context accumulates them in a path object. **EndPath** automatically selects the new path into the device context. If the DC already held a path, the old path is destroyed.

```
BOOL BeginPath( HDC hDC );
BOOL EndPath( HDC hDC );
```

If either function fails it returns **FALSE** and sets an error code for **GetLastError**.

Within a path bracket, the following functions add points to the path:

AngleArc	Arc	ArcTo
Chord	CloseFigure	Ellipse
ExtTextOut	LineTo	MoveToEx
Pie	PolyBezier	PolyBezierTo
PolyDraw	Polygon	PolyLine
PolylineTo	PolyPolygon	PolyPolyline
Rectangle	RoundRect	TextOut

The commands whose names end in "To" all take the current pen position as the first point of a shape. The difference between **Arc** and **ArcTo**, for example, is that **ArcTo** begins by drawing a line from the current pen position to the arc's starting point. **ArcTo** also changes the pen position to be the arc's ending point. **Arc** makes no use of, and has no effect on, the pen position. The "To" functions can be useful for connecting pieces of a path.

MoveToEx does not, of course, draw any new lines, but it does move the pen. It produces a discontinuity in the path. Each discontinuity is said to begin a new subpath. A *subpath* is a set of connected lines and curves. A *closed* subpath begins and ends at the same point. An *open* subpath does not connect the first point to the last point and so does not completely surround any area. **CloseFigure** seals off a subpath, connecting its last point to its first point. Any subsequent drawing command begins a new subpath.

```
BOOL CloseFigure( HDC hDC );
```

To close off a subpath you must call **CloseFigure**. Even if you finish a subpath with a **LineTo** ending precisely at the starting point, the subpath is considered open without **CloseFigure**. For wide lines, the line endings at the final intersection will be drawn with end caps unless you call **CloseFigure** to indicate they should be joined.

AbortPath interrupts the path in progress and clears the DC's path object. After aborting a path, **EndPath** is superfluous. If the path bracket has already been closed, **AbortPath** still discards the currently selected path.

```
BOOL AbortPath( HDC hDC );
```

The internal format of a path object is undocumented, but **GetPath** returns the set of points that compose the path along with type flags explaining how to interpret the points.

```
int GetPath(
    HDC hDC,                  // device context where path is selected
    LPPOINT lpPoints,         // address of array to receive path points
    LPBYTE lpTypes,           // address of array to receive point types
    int iSize );              // number of points in the path
```

If the last parameter, iSize, is 0, then **GetPath** does not fill the arrays. Instead it returns the total number of points contained in the path. Use that value to allocate space for the arrays. When iSize is not 0, **GetPath** copies points from the path to lpPoints and fills lpTypes with flags indicating which shapes to draw with each point. The flags may be **PT_MOVETO**, **PT_LINETO**, or **PT_BEZIERTO**. The last two flags may be combined with **PT_CLOSEFIGURE** to indicate the end of a closed subpath. The **PolyDraw** function, also new in Win32, can draw from the information **GetPath** returns. It expects the same two array parameters and draws all the lines according to the flags in lpTypes.

There are two ways to modify an existing path: flattening and widening.

```
BOOL FlattenPath( HDC hDC );
BOOL WidenPath( HDC hDC );
```

FlattenPath straightens out all the curves, replacing them with line segments. This might be useful, for example, in positioning text along the lines of a path. You could flatten the curves, retrieve the resulting coordinates with **GetPath**, measure the line segments, and position the text.

WidenPath redefines the path to be the area that a wide pen would color in if it followed the path. The two sides of the wide pen stroke become the boundary lines of the figure, and the area in between them where the pen would draw becomes the interior of the figure. The width is taken from the pen currently selected in the DC. The pen must have a width greater than 1. The DC must already contain a closed path; in other words, don't call **WidenPath** before **EndPath**. In order to perform its modifications, **WidenPath** converts any Bézier curves it encounters into an approximating series of line segments. Also, the changes are permanent. Selecting a new pen does not cause an already widened path to change again.

The process of creating and adjusting a path usually culminates in one of these five functions:

```
BOOL StrokePath( HDC hDC );          // draw all the lines in the path
BOOL FillPath( HDC hDC );            // fill in all the figures in the path
BOOL StrokeAndFillPath( HDC hDC );   // outline path and fill in figures
HRGN PathToRegion( HDC hDC );        // construct a region from the path
BOOL SelectClipPath(                 // merge path into DC's clipping region
    HDC hdc,                         // device context where path is selected
    int iMode );                     // how to combine path with existing clip rgn
```

Stroking a path draws all the lines and curves in the path. The lines are drawn with the currently selected pen. Filling a path colors its interior with the current brush. The current polygon filling mode (alternate or winding) affects the result of a **Fill-Path** command. **FillPath** begins by closing off any figures or subpaths in the path that remain open. **StrokeAndFillPath** outlines the path with the pen and colors it in with the brush. You cannot achieve the same result by calling **StrokePath** and **FillPath** sequentially because *all five functions finish by destroying the path* they operate on. To preserve a path for use in a series of operations, convert it to a region and work with the region instead. **PathToRegion** requires that all figures in the path already be closed. **SelectClipPath** is a shortcut for **PathToRegion** and **ExtSelectClipRgn** together. It combines the path region with any existing clipping region according to a rule given in the iMode parameter.

- **RGN_AND:** Includes only the areas where both regions overlap

- **RGN_XOR:** Includes only the areas where the regions do not overlap

- **RGN_OR:** Includes all areas of both regions

- **RGN_DIFF:** Includes only those areas of the clipping region that do not overlap the path region

- **RGN_COPY:** Replaces the clipping region with the path region

Paths confer many benefits. They allow more flexibility in defining closed areas than do the old polygon, ellipse, and region commands. Also, **StrokePath** effectually groups a series of line and curve commands into a single operation for more efficient GDI batching. The ability to close off a subpath ensures correct line joins in irregular figures. An unexpected benefit of paths is that they make outlined text possible. When **TextOut** and **ExtTextOut** add their output to a path, the GDI converts the outline of each character into a series of line and curve strokes. A subsequent call to **StrokePath** produces outline text, like that in Figure 8.5. If the text is drawn from a bitmap font, the GDI first converts the bitmap to a vector font because it cannot produce strokes from a bitmap. To draw outlined text from a stroked path, the GDI uses the current pen.

FIGURE 8.5:

Outline characters produced by drawing the text into a path and stroking the path

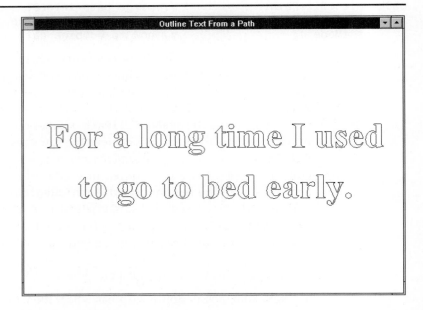

Finally, the new enhanced metafiles (discussed in the next chapter) also benefit from paths. Unlike other region creation functions, **PathToRegion** and **Select-ClipPath** work from logical coordinates, not physical coordinates, so the resulting region scales correctly when it is mapped to the screen in different modes or with different transformations. **CreateRectRgn**, for example, does not even ask for a DC as one parameter. Without the DC it cannot know the mapping mode, and without the mapping mode it is limited to physical pixel coordinates. Physical coordinates do not scale well. Such a region can be selected into a metafile and played back successfully, but if you play it back to a different area or a different adapter, the region does not scale with the other elements of the metafile image. The ability to define regions with logical coordinates removes a significant limitation of the old Windows API. When working with NT's enhanced metafiles, always use **PathToRegion** or **SelectClipPath** to create any region you use. To make rectangular or elliptical regions that scale correctly, draw the shape into a path instead of passing it to **CreateRectRgn** or **CreateEllipticRgn**.

Fitting Bitmaps in Parallelograms

PlgBlt copies a source image into a given parallelogram. It stretches or compresses the image to fit the destination and can also mirror or reverse it. The current stretch mode (**SetStretchBltMode**) influences any stretching **PlgBlt** performs.

```
BOOL PlgBlt(
    HDC hdcDest,              // handle of destination device context
    LPPOINT lpPoints,         // vertices of destination parallelogram
    HDC hdcSrc,               // handle of source device context
    int xSrc,                 // (xSrc, ySrc) gives the upper-left
    int ySrc,                 //     point of the source rectangle
    int iWidth,               // width of source rectangle
    int iHeight,              // height of source rectangle
    HBITMAP hbmMask,          // a monochrome bitmap mask (optional)
    int xMask,                // (xMask, yMask) gives the point in the mask
    int yMask );              //     to align with (xSrc, ySrc)
```

The lpPoints parameter points to an array of three **POINT** structures defining the parallelogram where the distorted image should appear. (Given any three corners of a parallelogram, the fourth is always implicit because opposite sides are parallel and have equal lengths.) **PlgBlt** copies an image from device hdcSrc to device hdcDest. The DC, origin, and extent parameters have the same meaning here they do in the familiar **BitBlt** command. The final three parameters allow for a third monochrome bitmap to act as a filter in transferring the image. The filter is optional. We'll say more about how to use bitmap masks in Chapter 10 when we introduce the new **MaskBlt** command.

Chapter 9 presents the world coordinate transformation mechanisms. **PlgBlt** cannot cope with all of them. If the source device rotates or shears as it draws, **PlgBlt** fails. Scaling, translating, and reflecting are allowed. Any transformations are allowed in the destination device. Also, the source device cannot be a metafile. Finally, be aware that **PlgBlt** is one of the slowest GDI functions.

The images in Figure 8.6 were all produced with **PlgBlt**. The first one sets the destination parallelogram to a rectangle, producing the same result as **BitBlt**. The fourth image specifies the destination points out of order and so reverses the image. Here's the code that produced the illustration.

FIGURE 8.6:

Bitmap sheared, stretched, and reversed with PlgBlt

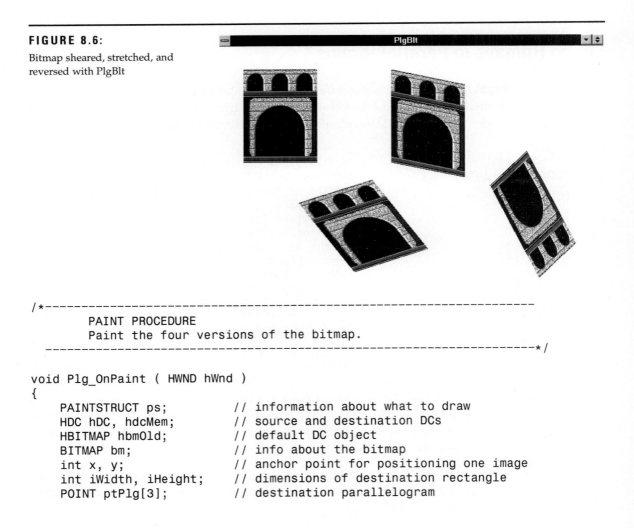

```
/*-----------------------------------------------------------
        PAINT PROCEDURE
        Paint the four versions of the bitmap.
    -------------------------------------------------------*/

void Plg_OnPaint ( HWND hWnd )
{
    PAINTSTRUCT ps;             // information about what to draw
    HDC hDC, hdcMem;            // source and destination DCs
    HBITMAP hbmOld;             // default DC object
    BITMAP bm;                  // info about the bitmap
    int x, y;                   // anchor point for positioning one image
    int iWidth, iHeight;        // dimensions of destination rectangle
    POINT ptPlg[3];             // destination parallelogram
```

```
/* create screen and memory DCs for destination and source */
hDC = BeginPaint( hWnd, &ps );
hdcMem = CreateCompatibleDC( hDC );
hbmOld = SelectBitmap( hdcMem, hBitmap );

/* get bitmap dimensions */
GetObject( hBitmap, sizeof(BITMAP), &bm );
iWidth  = (int)bm.bmWidth;
iHeight = (int)bm.bmHeight;

// DRAW THE FIRST IMAGE
// copy the image directly, with no distortion

x = 40;                          // set anchor point
y = 40;

/* these values describe a rectangle */
ptPlg[0].x = x;                  // 1. top left
ptPlg[0].y = y;
ptPlg[1].x = x + iWidth;         // 2. top right
ptPlg[1].y = y;
ptPlg[2].x = x;                  // 3. bottom left
ptPlg[2].y = y + iHeight;

/* display the image; copy it to the rectangle */
PlgBlt( hDC,                     // destination device
    ptPlg,                       // points defining destination area
    hdcMem,                      // source device
    0, 0,                        // source image origin
    iWidth, iHeight,             // source image extents
    NULL, 0, 0 );                // monochrome mask bitmap

// DRAW THE SECOND IMAGE
// shear the image horizontally and vertically

x = x + iWidth/2;                // set anchor point
y = y + iHeight + 70;

ptPlg[0].x = x + iWidth/4;
ptPlg[0].y = y;
ptPlg[1].x = ptPlg[0].x + iWidth;
ptPlg[1].y = ptPlg[0].y - iHeight/4;
ptPlg[2].x = x + iWidth;
ptPlg[2].y = ptPlg[1].y + iHeight;
```

```
/* display the image */
PlgBlt( hDC,                         // destination device
    ptPlg,                           // points defining destination area
    hdcMem,                          // source device
    0, 0,                            // source image origin
    iWidth, iHeight,                 // source image extents
    NULL, 0, 0 );                    // monochrome mask bitmap

// DRAW THE THIRD IMAGE
// shear the image vertically by dropping its right side

x = 40 + 2*iWidth;                   // set anchor point
y = 40;

ptPlg[0].x = x;                      // define a parallelogram
ptPlg[0].y = y;
ptPlg[1].x = x + iWidth;
ptPlg[1].y = y + iHeight/6;
ptPlg[2].x = x;
ptPlg[2].y = y + iHeight;

/* display the image */
PlgBlt( hDC,                         // destination device
    ptPlg,                           // points defining destination area
    hdcMem,                          // source device
    0, 0,                            // source image origin
    iWidth, iHeight,                 // source image extents
    NULL, 0, 0 );                    // monochrome mask bitmap

// DRAW THE FOURTH IMAGE
// stretch, shear, and invert image

x = x + iWidth;                      // set anchor point
y = y + 3*iHeight/4;

iHeight = 3*iHeight/2;               // stretch this image
iWidth = 2*iWidth;
ptPlg[0].x = x + iWidth/2;           // describe the parallelogram
ptPlg[0].y = y + iHeight;
ptPlg[1].x = x + iWidth;
ptPlg[1].y = y + iHeight/2;
ptPlg[2].x = x;
ptPlg[2].y = y;
```

```
/* display the image */
PlgBlt( hDC,                    // destination device
    ptPlg,                      // points defining destination area
    hdcMem,                     // source device
    0, 0,                       // source image origin
    iWidth, iHeight,            // source image extents
    NULL, 0, 0 );               // monochrome mask bitmap

/* clean up */
SelectBitmap( hdcMem, hbmOld );
DeleteDC( hdcMem );
EndPaint( hWnd, &ps );
return;
}
```

CODE: SIMPLE PAINT

The Simple Paint program, shown in Figure 8.7, is an interactive drawing program. The user draws with the mouse using shape tools selected from a menu. An off-screen bitmap stores everything the user draws. The program's main purpose is to experiment with wide lines. The Pens menu allows the user to create geometric pens with a wide range of attributes, including end caps and line joins, and view the pen's effect in drawings. The program also flips and reverses the picture with **PlgBlt**.

The Shapes menu also offers a Bézier tool and a Path tool. To draw a Bézier curve, choose four points on the screen by clicking with the left mouse button. The program marks each point with a small cross. Click the right button to draw the curve. You can select up to 100 different points to draw a series of Béziers all together. The fourth point of the first curve becomes the first point of the second, so all the curves together are continuous. When you press the right button, the program draws as many curves as it can and ignores any leftover points at the end. (If, for example, you click five points, only the first four can be used.)

Simple Paint drawing shapes with a wide pen

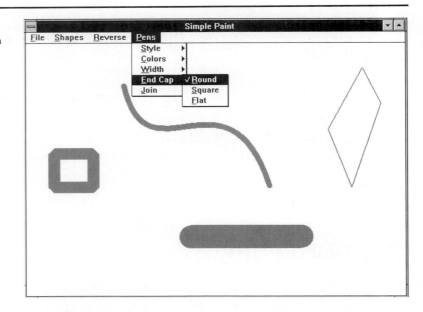

The Path tool waits for you to mark points, just as the Bézier tool does. After marking points with the left button, press the right button. Simple Paint passes all the points to the Polygon command, draws the Polygon into a path, widens the path using the current pen, and strokes the path to outline it on the screen.

Header and Resource Files

The header and resource script show the program's menus. The File menu offers commands to clear the drawing space and to restore default options. The Shapes menu contains tools for freehand sketching, lines, rectangles, ellipses, Béziers, and paths. The Reverse menu commands reverse the image by mirroring it or turning it upside down. The submenus under Pens offer choices for style, colors, width, end caps, and line joins.

```
/*------------------------------------------------------------------

        SIMPAINT.H
        Header file for SIMPAINT--defines identifiers for the
        application's resources and constants

        -----------------------------------------------------------*/

/*------------------------------------------------------------------
        PROGRAM SYMBOLS AND CONSTANTS
        -----------------------------------------------------------*/

/* RGB color constants */
#define RGB_BLACK           RGB(0x00, 0x00, 0x00)
#define RGB_WHITE           RGB(0xFF, 0xFF, 0xFF)
#define RGB_GRAY            RGB(0x80, 0x80, 0x80)
#define RGB_RED             RGB(0xFF, 0x00, 0x00)
#define RGB_YELLOW          RGB(0xFF, 0xFF, 0x00)
#define RGB_GREEN           RGB(0x00, 0xFF, 0x00)
#define RGB_CYAN            RGB(0x00, 0xFF, 0xFF)
#define RGB_BLUE            RGB(0x00, 0x00, 0xFF)
#define RGB_MAGENTA         RGB(0xFF, 0x00, 0xFF)

/*------------------------------------------------------------------
        RESOURCE IDENTIFIERS
        -----------------------------------------------------------*/

#define DLG_ABOUT               10
#define MENU_MAIN               10

/* identifiers for string resources */
#define IDS_APPNAME             10
#define IDS_TITLE               20

/* identifiers for popup COMMANDS menu */
#define IDM_ERASE               100
#define IDM_DEFAULTS            120
#define IDM_ABOUT               140
#define IDM_EXIT                160

/* shapes menu */
#define IDM_PENCIL              300
#define IDM_LINE                320
#define IDM_RECT                340
#define IDM_ELLIPSE             360
```

```
#define IDM_BEZIER              380
#define IDM_PATH                400

/* rotation menu */
#define IDM_MIRROR              500
#define IDM_FLIP                520
#define IDM_MIRROR_AND_FLIP     540

/* pen styles */
#define IDM_PEN_DOTTED          1200
#define IDM_PEN_SOLID           1220
#define IDM_PEN_DASHED          1240
#define IDM_PEN_DASHDOT         1260
#define IDM_PEN_DASHDOTDOT      1280
#define IDM_PEN_INSIDEFRAME     1300
#define IDM_PEN_NULL            1320
#define IDM_PEN_HATCH           1340

/* pen end cap styles */
#define IDM_PEN_ROUND           1400
#define IDM_PEN_SQUARE          1420
#define IDM_PEN_FLAT            1440

/* pen join styles */
#define IDM_PEN_BEVEL           1600
#define IDM_PEN_JROUND          1620
#define IDM_PEN_MITRE           1640

/* pen colors */
#define IDM_PEN_WHITE           1800
#define IDM_PEN_GRAY            1820
#define IDM_PEN_BLACK           1840
#define IDM_PEN_RED             1860
#define IDM_PEN_YELLOW          1880
#define IDM_PEN_GREEN           1900
#define IDM_PEN_CYAN            1920
#define IDM_PEN_BLUE            1940
#define IDM_PEN_MAGENTA         1960

/* pen widths */
#define IDM_PEN_ONE             2100
#define IDM_PEN_FIVE            2120
#define IDM_PEN_TEN             2140
#define IDM_PEN_TWENTY          2160
#define IDM_PEN_FORTY           2180
```

```
/*----------------------------------------------------------------
          FUNCTIONS
          prototypes for type checking
     -------------------------------------------------------------*/

int WINAPI WinMain( HINSTANCE hinstThis, HINSTANCE hinstPrev,
LPSTR lpszCmdLine, int iCmdShow );
LONG WINAPI WndProc( HWND hWnd , UINT uMessage, WPARAM wParam,
     LPARAM lParam );
BOOL WINAPI About_DlgProc( HWND hDlg, UINT uMessage, WPARAM wParam,
     LPARAM lParam );

/* initialization functions */
BOOL Init( HINSTANCE hInstance, int iCmdShow );
BOOL CreateBits( HWND hWnd );
BOOL Simpaint_OnCreate( HWND hWnd, LPCREATESTRUCT lpCreateStruct );
void Simpaint_OnPaint( HWND hWnd );
void Simpaint_OnCommand( HWND hWnd, int iCmd, HWND hwndCntl, UINT uCode );
void Simpaint_OnLeftButtonDown( HWND hWnd, BOOL bDoubleClick, int x, int y,
     UINT uKeyFlags );
void Simpaint_OnRightButtonDown( HWND hWnd, BOOL bDoubleClick, int x, int y,
     UINT uKeyFlags );
void Simpaint_OnMouseMove( HWND hWnd, int x, int y, UINT uKeyFlags );
void Simpaint_OnLeftButtonUp( HWND hWnd, int x, int y, UINT uKeyFlags );
 void Simpaint_OnDestroy( HWND hWnd );

/* command functions */
HPEN GetPenHandle( void );
COLORREF GetColorRef( int iColorCmd );
DWORD GetEndCap( void );
DWORD GetJoinStyle( void );
DWORD GetPenStyle( void );
DWORD GetPenWidth( void );
void DoReverse( int iCmd );

/* paint functions */
void FinalDraw( POINT ptBegin, POINT ptPrev, POINT ptMouse );
void PhantomDraw( HDC hDC, POINT ptBegin, POINT ptMouse );

/* functions to draw shapes */
void PencilDraw( POINT ptPrev, POINT ptEnd );
void DrawLine( HDC hDC, POINT ptBegin, POINT ptEnd );
void DrawRect( HDC hDC, POINT ptBegin, POINT ptEnd );
void DrawEllipse( HDC hDC, POINT ptBegin, POINT ptEnd );
```

```
void DrawHashMark( HWND hWnd, LPPOINT lppt );
void DrawBezier( void );
void DrawPath( void );

/* subfunctions */
void Repaint( void );
void SetDefaults( HWND hWnd );
void ClearBits( HDC hDC, HBITMAP hBitmap );

=============================================================================

/*-------------------------------------------------------------------

        SIMPAINT.RC
        Resource script file for SIMPAINT program.

    ----------------------------------------------------------------*/


#include <windows.h>
#include "simpaint.h"

STRINGTABLE
BEGIN
    IDS_APPNAME,       "simpaint"
    IDS_TITLE,         "Simple Paint"
END

MENU_MAIN MENU
BEGIN
    POPUP "&File"
    BEGIN
        MENUITEM "&Erase All"          IDM_ERASE
        MENUITEM "&Defaults"           IDM_DEFAULTS
        MENUITEM SEPARATOR
        MENUITEM "&About...",          IDM_ABOUT
        MENUITEM SEPARATOR
        MENUITEM "E&xit",              IDM_EXIT
    END

    POPUP "&Shapes"
    BEGIN
        MENUITEM "Pen&cil",            IDM_PENCIL
        MENUITEM "&Line",              IDM_LINE
        MENUITEM "&Rectangle",         IDM_RECT
```

```
        MENUITEM "&Ellipse",            IDM_ELLIPSE
        MENUITEM "&Bezier",             IDM_BEZIER
        MENUITEM "&Path",               IDM_PATH
END

POPUP "&Reverse"
BEGIN
        MENUITEM "&Mirror"              IDM_MIRROR
        MENUITEM "&Flip"                IDM_FLIP
        MENUITEM "&Both"                IDM_MIRROR_AND_FLIP
END

POPUP "&Pens"
BEGIN
    POPUP "&Style"
    BEGIN
        MENUITEM "&Solid"               IDM_PEN_SOLID
        MENUITEM "&Dotted"              IDM_PEN_DOTTED
        MENUITEM "D&ashed"              IDM_PEN_DASHED
        MENUITEM "Dash-D&ot"            IDM_PEN_DASHDOT
        MENUITEM "Dash-Do&t-Dot"        IDM_PEN_DASHDOTDOT
        MENUITEM "&InsideFrame"         IDM_PEN_INSIDEFRAME
        MENUITEM "&Empty"               IDM_PEN_NULL
        MENUITEM "&Hatch"               IDM_PEN_HATCH
    END

    POPUP "&Colors"
    BEGIN
        MENUITEM "&White",              IDM_PEN_WHITE
        MENUITEM "&Gray",               IDM_PEN_GRAY
        MENUITEM "&Black",              IDM_PEN_BLACK
        MENUITEM "&Red",                IDM_PEN_RED
        MENUITEM "&Yellow",             IDM_PEN_YELLOW
        MENUITEM "Gree&n",              IDM_PEN_GREEN
        MENUITEM "&Cyan",               IDM_PEN_CYAN
        MENUITEM "Bl&ue",               IDM_PEN_BLUE
        MENUITEM "&Magenta",            IDM_PEN_MAGENTA
    END

    POPUP "&Width"
    BEGIN
        MENUITEM "&One",                IDM_PEN_ONE
        MENUITEM "&Five",               IDM_PEN_FIVE
        MENUITEM "&Ten",                IDM_PEN_TEN
        MENUITEM "T&wenty",             IDM_PEN_TWENTY
```

```
        MENUITEM "Fo&rty",                IDM_PEN_FORTY
    END

    POPUP "&End Cap"
    BEGIN
        MENUITEM "&Round"                 IDM_PEN_ROUND
        MENUITEM "&Square"                IDM_PEN_SQUARE
        MENUITEM "&Flat"                  IDM_PEN_FLAT
    END

    POPUP "&Join"
    BEGIN
        MENUITEM "&Bevel"                 IDM_PEN_BEVEL
        MENUITEM "&Round"                 IDM_PEN_JROUND
        MENUITEM "&Mitre"                 IDM_PEN_MITRE
    END
  END
END

/* template for the About dialog box */
DLG_ABOUT DIALOG 17, 18, 114, 68
STYLE DS_MODALFRAME ¦ WS_POPUP ¦ WS_VISIBLE ¦ WS_CAPTION ¦ WS_SYSMENU
CAPTION "About Simple Paint"
FONT 8, "Helv"
BEGIN
    CTEXT           "Simple Paint",    -1, 0, 7, 114, 8
    CTEXT           "by",              -1, 0, 15, 114, 8
    CTEXT           "Myers && Hamer",  -1, 0, 25, 114, 8
    CTEXT           "version 1.0",     -1, 0, 35, 114, 8
    LTEXT           "©1993",           -1, 12, 51, 25, 8
    DEFPUSHBUTTON   "OK", IDOK, 81, 50, 30, 14, WS_GROUP
END
```

Initialization Procedures

WinMain and Init create the program window and start the message-polling loop. Along the way they also end up calling CreateBits to make the bitmap where the program records the user's actions. When the program window receives its initialization message, **WM_CREATE**, it calls SetDefaults to initialize all the program settings before the window gets painted.

Of these procedures, `CreateBits` probably deserves the most attention. First it must find out how big a bitmap it needs; this will vary from one display to another. The bitmap must be just big enough to store an image of the entire screen, the size of a window zoomed to maximum area. `GetDeviceCaps` returns the screen's horizontal and vertical resolution measured in pixels. The bitmap doesn't really have to store the whole screen. A maximized window still has caption and menu bars. By omitting their heights from the screen's vertical resolution and making a shorter bitmap, we can save memory. On a VGA using 16 colors, `GetSystemMetrics` reports that the client area of a maximized window is 460 pixels high.

Before returning, `CreateBits` calls `ClearBits`. It's perfectly legal to display a bitmap that hasn't been initialized, but the result usually looks like garbage. Whatever old data was in the bitmap's newly allocated memory space will be misinterpreted as pixel values. `PatBlt` fills the bitmap with the default white brush.

```
/*------------------------------------------------------------------

   SIMPAINT.C

   A paint program that lets the user draw on the screen.  It
   draws Bezier curves and offers a range of geometric pen
   styles, including end caps and join styles.  User can also
   draw a path and reverse or flip the image with PlgBlt.

   WinMain                      poll for messages
   Init                         create window
   CreateBits                   create bitmap to store drawings
   WndProc                      receive messages
   Simpaint_OnCreate            set program defaults
   Simpaint_OnPaint             refresh screen
   Simpaint_OnCommand           respond to menu commands
   Simpaint_OnLeftButtonDown    initiate a drawing operation
   Simpaint_OnMouseMove         track mouse while drawing
   Simpaint_OnLeftButtonUp      end a drawing operation
   Simpaint_OnRightButtonDown   draw a Bezier or a path
   Simpaint_OnDestroy           clean up and quit program
   FinalDraw                    draw new shapes to the bitmap
   PhantomDraw                  draw temporary shapes to the screen
   PencilDraw                   sketch wherever user moves mouse
   DrawLine                     let user draw line segments
   DrawRect                     let user draw rectangles
```

```
        DrawEllipse                  let user draw ellipses
        DrawBezier                   let user draw Bezier curves
        DrawPath                     let user draw a path
        DrawHashMark                 mark points user selects for a path
        DoReverse                    mirror or flip entire client area
        GetPenHandle                 return HPEN based on menu choices
        GetEndCap                    read setting, return PS_ value
        GetJoinStyle                 read setting, return PS_ value
        GetPenStyle                  read setting, return PS_ value
        GetPenWidth                  read setting, return PS_ value
        GetColorRef                  read setting, return PS_ value
        Repaint                      determine area of screen to invalidate
        SetDefaults                  select default options
        ClearBits                    erase contents of bitmap
        About_DlgProc                process About box messages

    from Mastering Windows NT Programming
    copyright 1993 by Brian Myers & Eric Hamer


    --------------------------------------------------------------------*/

#define STRICT

#include <windows.h>
#include <windowsx.h>
#include "simpaint.h"

/*--------------------------------------------------------------------
          GLOBAL VARIABLES
    --------------------------------------------------------------------*/

typedef struct tagSETTINGS {        // structure to hold current settings
    UINT shape;                     // shape to draw
    UINT penStyle;                  // pen style
    UINT penEnd;                    // pen end cap style
    UINT penJoin;                   // pen join style
    UINT penColor;                  // color to draw lines with
    UINT penWidth;                  // width of the pen
} SETTINGS;

SETTINGS   current;                 // current program settings
HWND       hwndMain;                // handle to the main program window
POINT      ptPoly[100];             // points for PolyBezier or Polygon
```

```
POINT       ptBegin;                // where mouse went down
POINT       ptMouse;                // where mouse is now
POINT       ptPrev;                 // where mouse was last
HBITMAP     hBitmap;                // bitmap same size as screen
HDC         hdcBit;                 // DC for the bitmap
int         iPolyCount = 0;         // number of points marked
BOOL        bMouseDown = FALSE;     // is the mouse button down?
BOOL        bJustUp = FALSE;        // was the button just released?
BOOL        bPolyDone = FALSE;      // TRUE when user finishes picking points

/*------------------------------------------------------------------
    WINMAIN
    Initialize the application and process the messages
    ------------------------------------------------------------------*/

int WINAPI WinMain (
    HINSTANCE hinstThis,
    HINSTANCE hinstPrev,
    LPSTR lpszCmdLine,
    int iCmdShow )
{
    MSG msg;

    /* initialization routine */
    if (!Init( hinstThis, iCmdShow ))
    {
        return( FALSE );
    }

    /* main loop, terminated by a quit message */
    while (GetMessage( &msg, NULL, 0, 0 ))
    {
        TranslateMessage( &msg );
        DispatchMessage( &msg );
    }

    return( msg.wParam );
    UNREFERENCED_PARAMETER( hinstPrev );
    UNREFERENCED_PARAMETER( lpszCmdLine );
}
```

```
/*-------------------------------------------------------------
        INIT
        Initialize the application.
     ---------------------------------------------------------*/

BOOL Init (
    HINSTANCE hInstance,
    int iCmdShow )
{

    WNDCLASS wc;
    char szAppName[10];             // application name
    char szTitle[25];               // caption for window

    /* load strings from resource */
    LoadString( hInstance, IDS_APPNAME, szAppName, sizeof(szAppName) );
    LoadString( hInstance, IDS_TITLE,   szTitle,   sizeof(szTitle)   );

    /* fill structure with information about this window class */
    wc.lpszClassName  = szAppName;
    wc.hInstance      = hInstance;
    wc.lpfnWndProc    = WndProc;
    wc.hCursor        = LoadCursor( NULL, IDC_ARROW );
    wc.hIcon          = LoadIcon( NULL, IDI_APPLICATION );
    wc.lpszMenuName   = MAKEINTRESOURCE( MENU_MAIN );
    wc.hbrBackground  = GetStockBrush( WHITE_BRUSH );
    wc.style          = CS_HREDRAW | CS_VREDRAW;
    wc.cbClsExtra     = 0;
    wc.cbWndExtra     = 0;

    /* register the class */
    if (!RegisterClass( &wc ))
    {
        return( FALSE );            // initialization failed
    }

    /* create the main window */
    hwndMain = CreateWindow( szAppName, szTitle, WS_OVERLAPPEDWINDOW,
        CW_USEDEFAULT, CW_USEDEFAULT, CW_USEDEFAULT, CW_USEDEFAULT,
        NULL, NULL, hInstance, NULL );

    if (hwndMain)
    {
        ShowWindow( hwndMain, iCmdShow );
        UpdateWindow( hwndMain );
    }
```

```
        return( hwndMain != NULL );
}

/*------------------------------------------------------------------
        CREATE BITS
        Create the bitmap where SimPaint keeps a permanent image of
        what the user has drawn.
        ------------------------------------------------------------*/
BOOL CreateBits ( HWND hWnd )
{
    HDC hDC;
    POINT ptBitDim;                         // physical dimensions of bitmap

    hDC = GetDC( hWnd );
    if (!hDC)
    {
        return( FALSE );
    }

    /* get screen size and make a bitmap to match it */
    ptBitDim.x = GetDeviceCaps( hDC, HORZRES );     // width in pixels
    ptBitDim.y = GetDeviceCaps( hDC, VERTRES );     // height in pixels

    /* subtract space for caption and menu bars */
    ptBitDim.y = GetSystemMetrics( SM_CYFULLSCREEN );

    /* create a bitmap compatible with the display device */
    hBitmap = CreateCompatibleBitmap( hDC,          // device
                (int)ptBitDim.x,                    // width
                (int)ptBitDim.y );                  // height
    if (!hBitmap)
    {
        ReleaseDC( hWnd, hDC );
        return( FALSE );            /* couldn't create bitmap */
    }

    /* make a display context for the bitmap */
    hdcBit = CreateCompatibleDC( hDC );
    if (!hdcBit)
    {
        ReleaseDC( hWnd, hDC );
        DeleteBitmap( hBitmap );
        return( FALSE );
```

```
    }
    SelectBitmap( hdcBit, hBitmap );

    ReleaseDC( hWnd, hDC );                  // we don't need this anymore

    /* initialize the bitmap to white */
    ClearBits( hdcBit, hBitmap );

    return( TRUE );
}

/*-------------------------------------------------------------------
        CLEAR BITS
        Erase everything in the bitmap.  Uses no global variables and
        makes no assumptions about the state of the DC.  The bitmap
        must not be selected into any other DC, though it may already
        be selected into this one.
    ----------------------------------------------------------------*/

void ClearBits (
    HDC hDC,
    HBITMAP hBitmap )
{
    BITMAP bm;                  // info about the bitmap
    HBRUSH hbrOld;              // default DC objects
    HBITMAP hbmOld;
    int iOldMapMode;           // default DC setting

    /* prepare the DC; remember its original settings */
    hbrOld      = SelectBrush( hDC, GetStockBrush(WHITE_BRUSH) );
    hbmOld      = SelectBitmap( hDC, hBitmap );
    iOldMapMode = SetMapMode( hDC, MM_TEXT );

    /* get the bitmap's dimensions */
    GetObject( hBitmap, sizeof(BITMAP), &bm );

    /* clear the bitmap with the white brush */
    PatBlt( hdcBit, 0, 0, (int)bm.bmWidth, (int)bm.bmHeight, PATCOPY );

    /* restore the original DC settings */
    SelectBrush( hdcBit, hbrOld );
    SelectBitmap( hDC, hbmOld );
    SetMapMode( hDC, iOldMapMode );
    return;
}
```

```
/*-----------------------------------------------------------------
        SIMPAINT_ONCREATE
        Create the global bitmap and set the default menu items.
        --------------------------------------------------------------*/

BOOL Simpaint_OnCreate (
    HWND hWnd,
    LPCREATESTRUCT lpCreateStruct )
{
    if (!CreateBits( hWnd ))
    {
        /* quit if we couldn't make the bitmap */
        MessageBox( hWnd, "Couldn't create bitmap.",
            "Simpaint Message", MB_OK | MB_ICONEXCLAMATION );
        return( FALSE );
    }

    /* set all menu choices to default values */
    SetDefaults( hWnd );

    return( TRUE );
    UNREFERENCED_PARAMETER( lpCreateStruct );
}

/*-----------------------------------------------------------------
        SET DEFAULTS
        Send menu command messages to select the default options.
        --------------------------------------------------------------*/

void SetDefaults ( HWND hWnd )
{
    /* shape */
    FORWARD_WM_COMMAND( hWnd, IDM_RECT, NULL, NULL, SendMessage );

    /* pen style */
    FORWARD_WM_COMMAND( hWnd, IDM_PEN_SOLID, NULL, NULL, SendMessage );

    /* pen end cap style */
    FORWARD_WM_COMMAND( hWnd, IDM_PEN_FLAT, NULL, NULL, SendMessage );

    /* pen join style */
    FORWARD_WM_COMMAND( hWnd, IDM_PEN_MITRE, NULL, NULL, SendMessage );
```

```
/* pen color */
FORWARD_WM_COMMAND( hWnd, IDM_PEN_BLACK, NULL, NULL, SendMessage );

/* pen width */
FORWARD_WM_COMMAND( hWnd, IDM_PEN_ONE, NULL, NULL, SendMessage );

    return;
}
```

Message Handlers

The WM_COMMAND message handler devotes most of its energy to remembering which choices the user has made from the menu. Each new menu choice updates a value in current, a global structure for program settings. The command handler also adjusts check marks in the menus that indicate the current settings. Most of the other handlers worry about what the mouse is doing. Three global variables, ptBegin, ptMouse, and ptPrev, store coordinates for the mouse at various key moments. The user initiates shapes by pressing the left button, so ptBegin remembers where that initial event occurred. ptMouse, continually updated in response to WM_MOUSEMOVE, remembers where the mouse is at each moment while the button is down. ptPrev remembers where the mouse was last seen before its current position; we'll explain why in the section "Knowing What to Repaint" later in this chapter.

Generally the user defines a shape by dragging the mouse. When the user releases the button, the program draws the shape. The mouse message handlers maintain two Boolean flags, bMouseDown and bJustUp. From reading them, the paint procedure determines whether the mouse is dragging or releasing. While the user drags, the paint procedure draws temporary ghost images on the screen to mark the changing figure. When the user releases the button, the paint procedure draws the final shape to the bitmap where it becomes a permanent part of the drawing.

If the user has chosen to draw a Bézier curve or a polygon path, the mouse message handlers accumulate the coordinates of successive mouse clicks in the ptPoly array. DrawHashMark puts a cross on the screen at each new point. Pressing the right button causes the WM_RBUTTONDOWN handler to set a flag and invalidate the window. When the paint procedure notices the flag, it reads the coordinates in ptPoly and draws the appropriate figure.

```
/*---------------------------------------------------------------
        WNDPROC
        Process the window's messages
    --------------------------------------------------------------*/

LRESULT WINAPI WndProc (
    HWND hWnd,
    UINT uMessage,
    WPARAM wParam,
    LPARAM lParam )
{
    switch (uMessage)
    {
        /* window is about to appear on screen */
        HANDLE_MSG( hWnd, WM_CREATE, Simpaint_OnCreate );

        /* window needs to be repainted */
        HANDLE_MSG( hWnd, WM_PAINT, Simpaint_OnPaint );

        /* user has chosen something from the program menu */
        HANDLE_MSG( hWnd, WM_COMMAND, Simpaint_OnCommand );

        /* user has pressed the left mouse button */
        HANDLE_MSG( hWnd, WM_LBUTTONDOWN, Simpaint_OnLeftButtonDown );

        /* user has pressed the right mouse button */
        HANDLE_MSG( hWnd, WM_RBUTTONDOWN, Simpaint_OnRightButtonDown );

        /* the mouse has moved on our window */
        HANDLE_MSG( hWnd, WM_MOUSEMOVE, Simpaint_OnMouseMove );

        /* user has released the left mouse button */
        HANDLE_MSG( hWnd, WM_LBUTTONUP, Simpaint_OnLeftButtonUp );

        /* our window has been destroyed */
        HANDLE_MSG( hWnd, WM_DESTROY, Simpaint_OnDestroy );

        default:
            return( DefWindowProc(hWnd, uMessage, wParam, lParam) );
    }
    return( OL );
}
```

```
/*----------------------------------------------------------------
        SIMPAINT_ONCOMMAND
        Process the WM_COMMAND messages here.  Call procedures to
        respond when the user selects menu commands.
   ----------------------------------------------------------------*/

void Simpaint_OnCommand (
    HWND hWnd,
    int iCmd,
    HWND hwndCtl,
    UINT uCode )
{
    HMENU hMenu;
    HINSTANCE hInst;

    /* retrieve a handle to the menu */
    hMenu = GetMenu( hWnd );
    if (!hMenu)
    {
        return;
    }

    switch (iCmd)
    {
        case IDM_ERASE:                         // remove all signs of drawing
            ClearBits( hdcBit, hBitmap );       // erase the bitmap
            ptBegin.x = ptMouse.x = 0;          // reset the mouse coordinates
            ptBegin.y = ptMouse.y = 0;
            iPolyCount = 0;                     // forget any figures in progress
            InvalidateRect( hWnd, NULL, FALSE );
            UpdateWindow( hWnd );               // redraw the window
            break;

        case IDM_DEFAULTS:                      // set all options to defaults
            SetDefaults( hWnd );
            break;

        case IDM_ABOUT:                         // display the About box
            hInst = GetWindowInstance( hWnd );
            DialogBox( hInst, MAKEINTRESOURCE(DLG_ABOUT),
                hWnd, About_DlgProc );
            break;

        case IDM_PENCIL:                        // choose a figure
        case IDM_LINE:                          // for drawing
```

```
case IDM_RECT:
case IDM_ELLIPSE:
case IDM_BEZIER:
case IDM_PATH:
    CheckMenuItem( hMenu, current.shape, MF_UNCHECKED );
    current.shape = iCmd;
    CheckMenuItem( hMenu, current.shape, MF_CHECKED );
    break;

case IDM_MIRROR:                        // rotate the image
case IDM_FLIP:
case IDM_MIRROR_AND_FLIP:
    DoReverse( iCmd );
    break;

case IDM_PEN_DOTTED:                    // change the pen style
case IDM_PEN_SOLID:
case IDM_PEN_DASHED:
case IDM_PEN_DASHDOT:
case IDM_PEN_DASHDOTDOT:
case IDM_PEN_INSIDEFRAME:
case IDM_PEN_HATCH:
    CheckMenuItem( hMenu, current.penStyle, MF_UNCHECKED );
    current.penStyle = iCmd;
    CheckMenuItem( hMenu, current.penStyle, MF_CHECKED );
    break;

case IDM_PEN_ROUND:                     // change the end cap style
case IDM_PEN_SQUARE:
case IDM_PEN_FLAT:
    CheckMenuItem( hMenu, current.penEnd, MF_UNCHECKED );
    current.penEnd = iCmd;
    CheckMenuItem( hMenu, current.penEnd, MF_CHECKED );
    break;

case IDM_PEN_JROUND:                    // change the join style
case IDM_PEN_BEVEL:
case IDM_PEN_MITRE:
    CheckMenuItem( hMenu, current.penJoin, MF_UNCHECKED );
    current.penJoin = iCmd;
```

```
        CheckMenuItem( hMenu, current.penJoin, MF_CHECKED );
        break;

    case IDM_PEN_WHITE:                    // change the pen color
    case IDM_PEN_GRAY:
    case IDM_PEN_BLACK:
    case IDM_PEN_RED:
    case IDM_PEN_YELLOW:
    case IDM_PEN_GREEN:
    case IDM_PEN_CYAN:
    case IDM_PEN_BLUE:
    case IDM_PEN_MAGENTA:
    case IDM_PEN_NULL:
        CheckMenuItem( hMenu, current.penColor, MF_UNCHECKED );
        current.penColor = iCmd;
        CheckMenuItem( hMenu, current.penColor, MF_CHECKED );
        break;

    case IDM_PEN_ONE:                      // change the pen width
    case IDM_PEN_FIVE:
    case IDM_PEN_TEN:
    case IDM_PEN_TWENTY:
    case IDM_PEN_FORTY:
        CheckMenuItem( hMenu, current.penWidth, MF_UNCHECKED );
        current.penWidth = iCmd;
        CheckMenuItem( hMenu, current.penWidth, MF_CHECKED );
        break;

    case IDM_EXIT:                         // exit the program
        DestroyWindow( hWnd );
        break;

    default:
        break;
    }

    return;
    UNREFERENCED_PARAMETER( uCode );
    UNREFERENCED_PARAMETER( hwndCtl );
}
```

```
/*-----------------------------------------------------------------
        SIMPAINT_ONLEFTBUTTONDOWN
        Process WM_LBUTTONDOWN messages here.  Save mouse coordinates.
        Capture input if the user begins dragging.
    -------------------------------------------------------------*/

void Simpaint_OnLeftButtonDown (
    HWND hWnd,
    BOOL bDoubleClick,
    int x,
    int y,
    UINT uKeyFlags )
{
    if ((current.shape == IDM_BEZIER) || (current.shape == IDM_PATH))
    {
        // If the user wants to draw Beziers or a polygon
        // path, then store the point where the button was
        // clicked and draw a hash mark there.

        /* limit the poly-point collection to 100 points */
        if (iPolyCount == 99)
        {
            return;
        }

        ptPoly[iPolyCount].x = x;                    // save coordinates
        ptPoly[iPolyCount].y = y;

        DrawHashMark( hWnd, &ptPoly[iPolyCount] ); // mark point with cross

        iPolyCount++;                               // advance counter

        /* mark where the user clicked */
        return;
    }

    /* store mouse position in global variable */
    ptBegin.x = ptPrev.x = ptMouse.x = x;
    ptBegin.y = ptPrev.y = ptMouse.y = y;

    /* for non-Bezier shapes, capture the mouse */
    SetCapture( hWnd );
```

```
    bMouseDown = TRUE;

    return;
    UNREFERENCED_PARAMETER( bDoubleClick );
    UNREFERENCED_PARAMETER( uKeyFlags );
}

/*------------------------------------------------------------------
        SIMPAINT_ONMOUSEMOVE
        Process WM_MOUSEMOVE messages here.  Update mouse position
        variables and draw any temporary images that mark an
        operation in progress.
    ----------------------------------------------------------------*/

void Simpaint_OnMouseMove (
    HWND hWnd,
    int x,
    int y,
    UINT uKeyFlags )
{
    // No need to track mouse movements while accumulating
    // points for a Bezier or polygon path.

    if ((current.shape == IDM_BEZIER) || (current.shape == IDM_PATH))
    {
        return;
    }

    /* if any button is down, update mouse position */
    if (bMouseDown)
    {
        ptPrev = ptMouse;
        ptMouse.x = x;
        ptMouse.y = y;

        /* force a repaint so the phantom image can be drawn */
        Repaint( );
    }

    return;
    UNREFERENCED_PARAMETER( uKeyFlags );
    UNREFERENCED_PARAMETER( hWnd );
}
```

```
/*-------------------------------------------------------------------
        SIMPAINT_ONLEFTBUTTONUP
        Process the WM_LBUTTONUP messages here.  When the button goes
        up, the user has finished drawing a shape.
        -------------------------------------------------------------*/

void Simpaint_OnLeftButtonUp (
    HWND hWnd,
    int x,
    int y,
    UINT uKeyFlags )
{
    /* stop tracking mouse and draw shape in final form */
    bMouseDown = FALSE;
    bJustUp = TRUE;

    if ((current.shape != IDM_BEZIER) && (current.shape != IDM_PATH))
    {
        /* the mouse was not captured for Beziers or paths */
        ReleaseCapture( );
        Repaint( );
    }

    return;
    UNREFERENCED_PARAMETER( x );
    UNREFERENCED_PARAMETER( y );
    UNREFERENCED_PARAMETER( uKeyFlags );
    UNREFERENCED_PARAMETER( hWnd );
}


/*-------------------------------------------------------------------
        SIMPAINT_ONRIGHTBUTTONDOWN
        Process WM_RBUTTONDOWN messages here.
        -------------------------------------------------------------*/

void Simpaint_OnRightButtonDown (
    HWND hWnd,
    BOOL bDoubleClick,
    int x,
    int y,
    UINT uKeyFlags )
{
    switch (current.shape)
```

```
{
    case IDM_BEZIER:                    // drawing a Bezier?
        if (iPolyCount < 4)
        {
            return;                     // not enough points; do nothing
        }
        else
        {
            // Round iPolyCount down to the nearest
            // (multiple of three) + 1.  This ignores
            // any extra points that can't be used in
            // drawing a Bezier curve.

            iPolyCount = iPolyCount - ((iPolyCount-1) % 3);
        }
        break;

    case IDM_PATH:                      // drawing a path?
        if (iPolyCount < 2)
        {
            return;                     // not enough points; do nothing
        }
        break;

    default:
        return;
}

// We get here only if the user has entered enough points
// and is ready to draw a Bezier or a path.  Set a flag
// to tell the paint procedure to draw something.

bPolyDone = TRUE;

/* erase the hash marks and draw the shape */
InvalidateRect( hWnd, NULL, FALSE );
UpdateWindow( hWnd );

return;
UNREFERENCED_PARAMETER( bDoubleClick );
UNREFERENCED_PARAMETER( x );
UNREFERENCED_PARAMETER( y );
UNREFERENCED_PARAMETER( uKeyFlags );
```

```
}
/*-------------------------------------------------------------------
        SIMPAINT_ONDESTROY
        Free the bitmap and the DC and post a WM_QUIT message.
   ----------------------------------------------------------------*/

void Simpaint_OnDestroy ( HWND hWnd )
{
    DeleteDC( hdcBit );
    DeleteBitmap( hBitmap );

    PostQuitMessage( 0 );

    return;
    UNREFERENCED_PARAMETER( hWnd );
}


/*-------------------------------------------------------------------
        DRAW HASH MARK
        Draw marks where the user adds points for a polygon
        path or a Bezier curve.
   ----------------------------------------------------------------*/

void DrawHashMark (
    HWND hWnd,
    LPPOINT lppt )
  {
    HDC hDC;
    POINT pt1, pt2;      // end points for the bars of the cross mark

    /* retrieve the window's device context */
    hDC = GetDC( hWnd );

    if (hDC)
    {
        // Calculate end points for the horizontal
        // bar of the hash mark.

        pt1.x = lppt->x - 8;
        pt1.y = lppt->y;
        pt2.x = lppt->x + 8;
        pt2.y = lppt->y;
```

```
    DrawLine( hDC, pt1, pt2 );                    // draw horizontal bar

    // Repeat for the vertical segment.

    pt1.x = lppt->x;
    pt1.y = lppt->y - 8;
    pt2.x = lppt->x;
    pt2.y = lppt->y + 8;
    DrawLine( hDC, pt1, pt2 );                     // draw vertical bar

    ReleaseDC( hWnd, hDC );
  }
  return;
}
```

Reversing the Image

In response to commands from the Reverse menu, Simple Paint calls DoReverse. This procedure flips the image in the client area, reversing it horizontally, vertically, or both. It reverses only the visible area, not the entire bitmap. **StretchBlt** could flip the image, but we've chosen the new **PlgBlt** command instead. Since we're reversing the image in place, the source and destination rectangles are identical. The trick is to state the boundary points in the proper order. Imagine that the drawing space is a piece of transparent paper with corners numbered as in Figure 8.8. You have to give **PlgBlt** three destination points. The first point you name becomes the upper-left corner of the new image. Imagine lifting the transparent paper, flipping it over so the corner labeled "4" assumes the upper-left position, and putting the paper back down. Reading clockwise, the corners now come in the order 4, 3, 2, 1. Passing the points to **PlgBlt** in that order causes the image to flip upside down and backwards.

PlgBlt is slow. We could create a secondary thread and let it churn through the block transfer in the background, but there's very little the user can do in Simple Paint until the operation finishes anyway.

FIGURE 8.8:

How to order the coordinates for
PlgBlt to reverse an image

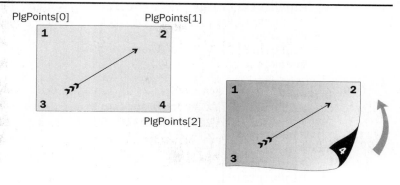

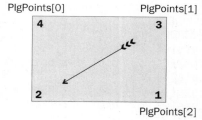

```
/*-----------------------------------------------------------------
        DO REVERSE
        Use PlgBlt to flip the image.  This procedure draws its
        coordinates from the current size of the client area.  Only
        the part of the bitmap corresponding to the current client
        area will be modified.
        -----------------------------------------------------------*/

void DoReverse ( int iCmd )
{
    RECT rcClient;
    POINT PlgPoints[3];

    /* get the client rect */
    GetClientRect( hwndMain, &rcClient );

    /* calculate the rectangle that the image will be rotated into */
    switch (iCmd)
    {
        case IDM_MIRROR:
            PlgPoints[0].x = rcClient.right;
            PlgPoints[0].y = rcClient.top;
```

```
            PlgPoints[1].x = rcClient.left;
            PlgPoints[1].y = rcClient.top;
            PlgPoints[2].x = rcClient.right;
            PlgPoints[2].y = rcClient.bottom;
            break;

        case IDM_FLIP:
            PlgPoints[0].x = rcClient.left;
            PlgPoints[0].y = rcClient.bottom;
            PlgPoints[1].x = rcClient.right;
            PlgPoints[1].y = rcClient.bottom;
            PlgPoints[2].x = rcClient.left;
            PlgPoints[2].y = rcClient.top;
            break;

        case IDM_MIRROR_AND_FLIP:
            PlgPoints[0].x = rcClient.right;
            PlgPoints[0].y = rcClient.bottom;
            PlgPoints[1].x = rcClient.left;
            PlgPoints[1].y = rcClient.bottom;
            PlgPoints[2].x = rcClient.right;
            PlgPoints[2].y = rcClient.top;
            break;
    }

    /* transfer the bits */
    PlgBlt( hdcBit,                             // destination device
            PlgPoints,                          // destination parallelogram
            hdcBit,                             // source device
            (int)rcClient.left,                 // source origin and extents
            (int)rcClient.top,
            (int)(rcClient.right - rcClient.left),
            (int)(rcClient.bottom - rcClient.top),
            NULL, 0, 0 );                       // monochrome mask bitmap

    InvalidateRect( hwndMain, NULL, FALSE );
    UpdateWindow( hwndMain );
    return;
}
```

Paint Procedures

Although the user draws on the screen with the mouse, the program's bitmap is the real sketch pad. Whenever the display or the bitmap changes and the paint procedure needs to update the display, it simply copies from the bitmap. The paint procedure has two basic steps: It draws any new shapes to the bitmap, and then it copies the revised bitmap to the program's client area. Both steps are easy, but complications arise from showing temporary shapes on the screen as the user stretches a line, a rectangle, or an ellipse to its final size. If we draw all the intermediate images to the bitmap, they won't go away when the mouse button is released. They'll remain in the bitmap until it's entirely cleared. But if we draw the temporary shapes on the screen before we copy the bitmap to the screen, the subsequent **BitBlt** will immediately erase them. Therefore, the paint procedure really has three steps instead of two, and they must happen in this order:

1. Check to see if the user has just completed a shape. If so, draw it permanently on the bitmap. A procedure called FinalDraw paints shapes on the bitmap.

2. Copy the bitmap to the window's client area. Any new shapes will then appear on the screen. **BitBlt** performs the block transfer.

3. Check to see if the user is in the process of drawing a shape. If so, draw a temporary "phantom" image on the screen. A procedure called PhantomDraw does this job.

Of course, before any of this takes place, the paint procedure must read the current settings and adjust the device contexts for the screen and the bitmap.

```
/*-------------------------------------------------------------------
        SIMPAINT_ONPAINT
        Process WM_PAINT messages here.  Initialize the DC according
        to the user's current menu choices.  Call BitBlt to
        refresh the screen from the bitmap.  Call PhantomDraw to
        show any temporary images to mark a drawing in progress.
        -------------------------------------------------------------*/

void Simpaint_OnPaint ( HWND hWnd )
{
    PAINTSTRUCT ps;
    HDC hdcScr;                          // display context for the screen
```

```
HPEN hpenScr;                    // default screen and bitmap pens
HPEN hpenBit;
HPEN hPen;                       // new pen from user's selections
BOOL bResult;                    // for testing return values
int i;                           // loop control variable

/* initialize screen DC */
hdcScr = BeginPaint( hWnd, &ps );

if (hdcScr)
{
    /* retrieve the pen handle based on the menu choices */
    hPen = GetPenHandle();

    /* select the current pen to draw the outline of the image */
    hpenScr = SelectPen( hdcScr, hPen );

    /* initialize bitmap display context */
    hpenBit = SelectPen( hdcBit, hPen );

    /* draw permanent images to bitmap */
    FinalDraw( ptBegin, ptPrev, ptMouse );

    /* transfer invalidated block from bitmap to screen */
    bResult = BitBlt( hdcScr,                            // dest. device
        (int)ps.rcPaint.left, (int)ps.rcPaint.top,      // dest. origin
        (int)(ps.rcPaint.right - ps.rcPaint.left),      // block's x extent
        (int)(ps.rcPaint.bottom - ps.rcPaint.top),      // block's y extent
        hdcBit,                                          // source device
        (int)ps.rcPaint.left, (int)ps.rcPaint.top,      // source origin
        SRCCOPY );
    if (!bResult)
    {
        /* an error occurred performing the bitmap operation */
        MessageBox( hWnd, "Couldn't transfer image to screen.",
            "Simpaint Message", MB_OK | MB_ICONEXCLAMATION );
    }

    /* draw intermediate phantom images to screen */
    if (bMouseDown)
    {
        PhantomDraw( hdcScr, ptBegin, ptMouse );
    }
```

```
    /* repaint the user's accumulated hash marks, if any */
    for (i=0; i<iPolyCount; i++)
    {
        DrawHashMark( hWnd, &ptPoly[i] );
    }

    bJustUp = FALSE;

    SelectPen( hdcScr, hpenScr );          // remove pen from DCs
    SelectPen( hdcBit, hpenBit );
    DeletePen( hPen );                      // delete the pen
 }

EndPaint( hWnd, &ps );
return;
}
```

BitBlt is a fairly fast operation, but the larger the area the longer the transfer takes. Simple Paint picks up a little speed by refreshing only the part of the screen that was invalid instead of always repainting the entire client area. When a menu or dialog box covers part of the display, only that part needs to be fixed. **BitBlt** finds the coordinates of the invalid area in the **PAINTSTRUCT** that comes with the **WM_PAINT** message.

FinalDraw and PhantomDraw

FinalDraw determines which tool is being used and calls a procedure to draw the requested shape. All the drawing procedures read the three mouse point variables to decide where the shape should appear. PhantomDraw paints the ghost outlines of rectangles, ellipses, and lines while the user drags the mouse with the button down. It calls the same subroutines that FinalDraw calls, but instead of passing them a DC for the bitmap, it passes a DC to the program's window. Permanent images get drawn only when the user releases the button (bJustUp == TRUE), and phantom images get drawn only while the button is down (bMouseDown == TRUE).

```
/*-------------------------------------------------------------
    FINAL DRAW
    Called when the user has finished creating a shape, this
    procedure draws the shape into the program's bitmap.
    ---------------------------------------------------------*/
```

```
void FinalDraw (
    POINT ptBegin,
    POINT ptPrev,
    POINT ptMouse )
{
    switch (current.shape)
    {
        case IDM_PENCIL:                            // PENCIL
            if (bMouseDown)
            {
                PencilDraw( ptPrev, ptMouse );
            }
            break;

        case IDM_LINE:                              // LINE
            if (bJustUp)
            {
                DrawLine( hdcBit, ptBegin, ptMouse );
            }
            break;

        case IDM_RECT:                              // RECTANGLE
            if (bJustUp)
            {
                DrawRect( hdcBit, ptBegin, ptMouse );
            }
            break;

        case IDM_ELLIPSE:                           // ELLIPSE
            if (bJustUp)
            {
                DrawEllipse( hdcBit, ptBegin, ptMouse );
            }
            break;

        case IDM_BEZIER:                            // BEZIER
            if (bPolyDone)
            {
                DrawBezier( );
            }
            break;
```

```
        case IDM_PATH:                                  // PATH
            if (bPolyDone)
            {
                DrawPath( );
            }
            break;

        default:
            break;
    }
    return;
}

/*-----------------------------------------------------------------
        PHANTOM DRAW
        If drawing is in progress, draw temporary shape to screen
    ------------------------------------------------------------*/

void PhantomDraw (
    HDC hDC,
    POINT ptBegin,
    POINT ptMouse )

{
    switch (current.shape)
    {
        case IDM_LINE:                                  // LINE
            if (bMouseDown)
            {
                DrawLine( hDC, ptBegin, ptMouse );
            }
            break;

        case IDM_RECT:                                  // RECTANGLE
            if (bMouseDown)
            {
                DrawRect( hDC, ptBegin, ptMouse );
             }
            break;

        case IDM_ELLIPSE:                               // ELLIPSE
            if (bMouseDown)
            {
                DrawEllipse( hDC, ptBegin, ptMouse );
```

```
        }
        break;

    default:
        break;
    }
    return;
}
```

Drawing Shapes

The draw procedures each interpret the mouse coordinates and draw a particular shape. DrawBezier and DrawPath use coordinates accumulated in the ptPoly array, feeding them to either **PolyBezier** or **Polygon**. The iPolyCount variable tells how many points the user has marked. After drawing either shape, the procedures reset the counter to 0 in preparation for a new shape to begin.

DrawPath opens a path bracket and draws one shape into it. The **Polygon** command automatically connects the last point to the first point to produce a closed shape. Simple Paint doesn't really need a path to connect the user's points. Selecting a wide pen and drawing with **Polygon** produces the same result. The path would be necessary if we included curves as well as lines and wanted to color or clip the resulting complex area. It is included here for demonstration.

```
/*-------------------------------------------------------------------
        FUNCTIONS TO DRAW SHAPES
    ---------------------------------------------------------------*/

void PencilDraw (
    POINT ptPrev,
    POINT ptEnd )
{
    /* draw a line on the bitmap */
    MoveToEx( hdcBit, (int)ptPrev.x, (int)ptPrev.y, NULL );
    LineTo( hdcBit, (int)ptEnd.x, (int)ptEnd.y );

    // Keep Repaint from invalidating way back to the
    // point where the pencil line originally began.

    ptBegin = ptMouse;
    return;
}
```

```c
void DrawLine (
    HDC hDC,                        // bitmap or device DC //
    POINT ptBegin,
    POINT ptEnd )
{
    MoveToEx( hDC, (int)ptBegin.x, (int)ptBegin.y, NULL );
    LineTo( hDC, (int)ptEnd.x,  (int) ptEnd.y);
    return;
}

void DrawRect (
    HDC hDC,                        // bitmap or device DC
    POINT ptBegin,
    POINT ptEnd )
{
    Rectangle( hDC, (int)ptBegin.x, (int)ptBegin.y, (int)ptEnd.x,
        (int)ptEnd.y );
    return;
}

void DrawEllipse (
    HDC hDC,                        // bitmap or device DC
    POINT ptBegin,
    POINT ptEnd )
{
    Ellipse( hDC, (int)ptBegin.x, (int)ptBegin.y, (int)ptEnd.x,
        (int)ptEnd.y );
    return;
}

void DrawBezier ( void )
{
    /* add the Bezier curve to the bitmap */
    PolyBezier( hdcBit, ptPoly, iPolyCount );

    /* reset the poly-point variables so another figure can be drawn */
    iPolyCount = 0;
    bPolyDone = FALSE;
    return;
}

void DrawPath ( void )
{
```

```
/* create a path and draw it in the bitmap */
BeginPath( hdcBit );                    // open path bracket
Polygon( hdcBit, ptPoly, iPolyCount );  // draw to the path
CloseFigure( hdcBit );                  // join lines at final vertex
EndPath( hdcBit );                      // close bracket
StrokePath( hdcBit );                   // draw the path

/* reset the poly-point variables so another figure can be drawn */
iPolyCount = 0;
bPolyDone = FALSE;
return;
}
```

Pen Style Procedures

The paint procedure draws with a pen created according to choices made from the menu. Each menu option represents a different style, such as **PS_DASH** or **PS_JOIN_MITER**. To convert from menu commands to pen style flags, the paint procedure relies on a set of functions with switch statements to interpret the settings for each style. All of them receive a menu command ID and return a pen style value.

GetPenStyle pulls together all the settings and calls **ExtCreatePen** to create a geometric pen with all the user's desired features. One possible feature is a hatched brush style. Using the **LOGFONT** parameter you can assign any brush for the pen to draw with. When the user asks for a hatch brush, we set the **BS_HATCH** style and choose the standard **HS_CROSS** pattern. When you run Simple Paint, don't forget to try out this feature.

```
/*-------------------------------------------------------------------
        GET PEN HANDLE
        Return a handle to a pen with the currently selected color,
        style, and attributes.
        -----------------------------------------------------------*/

HPEN GetPenHandle ( void )
{
    LOGBRUSH lb;                        // set of brush attributes
    DWORD dwPenStyle;                   // dash/dot flag
    DWORD dwEndCap;                     // round/square/flat flag
    DWORD dwJoinStyle;                  // miter/bevel/round flag
```

```
        DWORD dwPenWidth;                       // logical width for new pen
        HPEN hPen;                              // new drawing object

        /* get the PS_ values for the user's current attribute choices */
        dwEndCap    = GetEndCap( );
        dwJoinStyle = GetJoinStyle( );
        dwPenStyle  = GetPenStyle( );
        dwPenWidth  = GetPenWidth( );

        /* geometric pens derive some attributes from a LOGBRUSH structure */
        lb.lbStyle = (current.penStyle == IDM_PEN_HATCH) ? BS_HATCHED : BS_SOLID;
        lb.lbColor = GetColorRef( current.penColor );
        lb.lbHatch = HS_CROSS;                  // ignored without BS_HATCH

        /* create a geometric pen that matches the user's choices */
        hPen = ExtCreatePen( PS_GEOMETRIC      // scalable pen with joins
                    ¦ dwPenStyle               // dash/dot style
                    ¦ dwJoinStyle              // miter/bevel/round
                    ¦ dwEndCap,                // flat/square/round
                  dwPenWidth,                  // logical width of pen
                  &lb,                         // brush for color
                  0, NULL );                   // no custom style

        return( hPen );
    }

/*-------------------------------------------------------------------
        GET END CAP
        Return the pen's end cap style flag according to the current
        menu selection.
    -----------------------------------------------------------------*/

DWORD GetEndCap ( void )
{
    switch (current.penEnd)
    {
        case IDM_PEN_SQUARE:
            return( PS_ENDCAP_SQUARE );

        case IDM_PEN_FLAT:
            return( PS_ENDCAP_FLAT );

        case IDM_PEN_ROUND:
            return( PS_ENDCAP_ROUND );
```

```
        default:
            return( PS_ENDCAP_FLAT );        // should never happen
            break;                           // (but just in case)
    }
}

/*-------------------------------------------------------------------
        GET JOIN STYLE
        Return the pen's join style flag according to the current
        menu selection.
        ---------------------------------------------------------------*/
DWORD GetJoinStyle ( void )
{
    switch (current.penJoin)
    {
        case IDM_PEN_MITRE:
            return( PS_JOIN_MITER );

        case IDM_PEN_BEVEL:
            return( PS_JOIN_BEVEL );

        case IDM_PEN_JROUND:
            return( PS_JOIN_ROUND );

        default:                             // should never happen
            return( PS_JOIN_MITER );         // (but just in case)
    }
}

/*-------------------------------------------------------------------
        GET PEN STYLE
        Return the pen's style flag according to the current menu
        selection.
        ---------------------------------------------------------------*/

DWORD GetPenStyle ( void )
{
    switch (current.penStyle)
    {
        case IDM_PEN_SOLID:
            return( PS_SOLID );

        case IDM_PEN_DOTTED:
            return( PS_DOT );
```

```
        case IDM_PEN_DASHED:
            return( PS_DASH );

        case IDM_PEN_DASHDOT:
            return( PS_DASHDOT );

        case IDM_PEN_DASHDOTDOT:
            return( PS_DASHDOTDOT );

        case IDM_PEN_INSIDEFRAME:
            return( PS_INSIDEFRAME );

        case IDM_PEN_NULL:
            return( PS_NULL );

        default:                              // should never happen
            return( PS_SOLID );               // (but just in case)
    }
}

/*------------------------------------------------------------------

        GET PEN WIDTH
        Return the pen's width according to the current menu
        selection.
    ----------------------------------------------------------------*/

DWORD GetPenWidth ( void )
{
    switch (current.penWidth)
    {
        case IDM_PEN_ONE:
            return( 1 );

        case IDM_PEN_FIVE:
            return( 5 );

        case IDM_PEN_TEN:
            return( 10 );

        case IDM_PEN_TWENTY:
            return( 20 );

        case IDM_PEN_FORTY:
            return( 40 );
```

```
        default:                             // should never happen
            return( 1 );                     // (but just in case)
    }
}


/*------------------------------------------------------------------
        GET COLORREF
        Return the RGB value for the pen's color according to the
        current menu selection.
    ----------------------------------------------------------------*/

COLORREF GetColorRef ( int iColorCmd )
{

    switch (iColorCmd)
    {
        case IDM_PEN_WHITE:
            return( RGB_WHITE );

        case IDM_PEN_GRAY:
            return( RGB_GRAY );

        case IDM_PEN_BLACK:
            return( RGB_BLACK );

        case IDM_PEN_RED:
            return( RGB_RED );

        case IDM_PEN_YELLOW:
            return( RGB_YELLOW );

        case IDM_PEN_GREEN:
            return( RGB_GREEN );

        case IDM_PEN_CYAN:
            return( RGB_CYAN );

        case IDM_PEN_BLUE:
            return( RGB_BLUE );

        case IDM_PEN_MAGENTA:
            return( RGB_MAGENTA );
```

```
    default:                             // Should never happen
        return( RGB_BLACK );             // (but just in case)
    }
}
```

Invalidating Part of the Client Area

As the user drags the mouse to draw a line or a rectangle, Simple Paint repeatedly calls **InvalidateRect** and updates the screen to stretch the growing figure. We can make the updates speedier by invalidating only the part of the screen that needs to be redrawn. Our **BitBlt** command is already prepared to benefit from partial invalidations. The problem is describing the smaller area to **InvalidateRect**. Obviously the solution must involve ptBegin and ptMouse since those two variables always control where the output appears. We might try something like this:

```
SetRect( &rect, ptBegin.x, ptBegin.y, ptMouse.x, ptMouse.y );
InvalidateRect( hwndMain, &rect, FALSE );
```

That is indeed part of the answer, and sometimes those two lines of code would be enough in themselves. But as they stand they will sometimes fail for a reason that is not obvious.

Knowing What to Repaint

Suppose the user starts to make a very large rectangle but then decides not to and begins to drag back toward the starting point. The invalidation area first gets very big, and then it starts to shrink. As it grows, the successively larger **BitBlt**s blot out the earlier, smaller phantom images. But as it shrinks, the smaller **BitBlt**s do not erase the larger rectangles left behind. Figure 8.9 shows the result. We had assumed that transferring a new area to the screen would erase the old one, but it doesn't always. We can't even just pick the larger of the two, as the figure demonstrates; the phantom shapes might shrink in one direction as they grow in another. Instead, we have to combine the two areas—the previous rectangle and the current rectangle—and invalidate their union.

FIGURE 8.9:

Result of a flawed algorithm for erasing phantom images

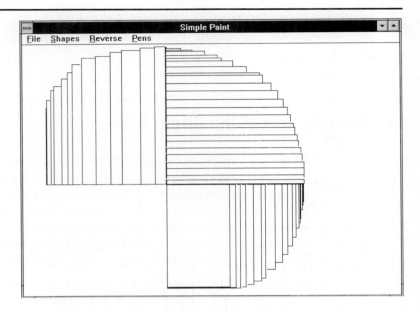

This is the reason for the third global mouse point variable, ptPrev. ptBeginDP and ptMouseDP describe only the current area. ptPrev stores the previous position of the mouse, the place where it was last seen before its current position. Maintaining the new variable poses no problem: At every **WM_MOUSEMOVE** message, before updating ptMouse, we copy the obsolete value into ptPrev. Now we can construct the two rectangles. One stretches from ptBegin to ptPrev, and one from ptBegin to ptMouse. **UnionRect** calculates the smallest rectangle that contains both of them. The Repaint procedure assumes responsibility for calculating what area to invalidate while the user is dragging the mouse to create a shape. It sorts the coordinates of two rectangles, combines them, and passes the result to **InvalidateRect.**

```
/*------------------------------------------------------------------

    REPAINT
    Calculate rectangle to invalidate, and send a message to
    repaint it.  Call this procedure for continual repainting
    while the user drags the mouse to create a shape.  It speeds
    repainting by invalidating the smallest area possible.
    ------------------------------------------------------------*/
```

```
 void Repaint ( void )
{
    RECT rNew;        // from buttondown point to current mouse position
    RECT rOld;        // from buttondown point to previous mouse position
    RECT rClient;     // client area

    /* calculate the area where the mouse has been */
    SetRect( &rNew, (int)ptBegin.x, (int)ptBegin.y,
                    (int)ptMouse.x, (int)ptMouse.y );
    SetRect( &rOld, (int)ptBegin.x, (int)ptBegin.y,
                    (int)ptPrev.x,  (int)ptPrev.y );

    /* be sure the rectangles are not null */
    InflateRect( &rNew, current.penWidth, current.penWidth );
    InflateRect( &rOld, current.penWidth, current.penWidth );

    /* exclude anything outside the client rectangle */
    GetClientRect( hwndMain, &rClient );
    IntersectRect( &rNew, &rNew, &rClient );
    IntersectRect( &rOld, &rOld, &rClient );

    /* expand rNew to include both areas and then invalidate them */
    UnionRect( &rNew, &rNew, &rOld );
    InvalidateRect( hwndMain, &rNew, FALSE );
    UpdateWindow( hwndMain );
    return;
}

/*-------------------------------------------------------------------
        ABOUT BOX DIALOG PROCEDURE
        Process messages for the About box window here.
    ----------------------------------------------------------------*/

BOOL WINAPI About_DlgProc (
    HWND hDlg,
    UINT uMessage,
    WPARAM wParam,
    LPARAM lParam )
{
    switch (uMessage)
    {
        case WM_INITDIALOG:
            return( TRUE );
```

```
    case WM_COMMAND:
        EndDialog( hDlg, TRUE );
        break;
    }

    return( FALSE );
    UNREFERENCED_PARAMETER( wParam );
    UNREFERENCED_PARAMETER( lParam );
}
```

The Win32 GDI benefits from a number of important improvements. A few smaller changes merit attention. The GDI command buffer sometimes makes the return value of a Boolean output function inaccessible. The system no longer imposes a limit on the number of concurrent device contexts. Regions work more quickly now because they are stored as sets of trapezoids. But most of this chapter presented more important additions to the API. You can now draw Bézier curves, wide lines with join styles and end caps, irregular regions constructed from paths, and bitmaps distorted to fit non-rectilinear destinations. Paths turn out to be versatile objects. Besides making it possible to create regions bounded by irregular Bézier curves, they create regions that scale correctly in metafiles and they create outlines of text characters for special effects. You might, for example, turn the character outlines into a clipping region and shade them in with colors from a custom palette.

The next two chapters continue to pursue GDI topics. Chapter 9 covers enhanced metafiles and the new coordinate transformations, while Chapter 10 turns to the topic of bitmaps.

### NINE

Transforming Enhanced Metafiles

- **World coordinates**

- **Translating, scaling, rotating, reflecting, and shearing images**

- **Enhanced metafiles**

Any Win16 programmer who ever struggled with mapping modes may not at first rejoice to learn that Windows NT flings yet another coordinate space into the mapping maelstrom. The news is genuinely good, however, because the new "world" coordinate space makes all the GDI drawing commands more versatile and rationalizes a complete set of transformations, including rotation and scaling, in a single coherent mechanism. Metafiles have been improved as well, and the two topics go hand in hand. Working with metafiles always required some knowledge of mapping modes, and one big advantage of metafiles over bitmaps is that they scale better. The enhanced metafiles of Windows NT are more genuinely device independent even than DIBs, and they work with all the new commands you read about in Chapter 8, such as paths and Bézier curves. The sample program at the end of the chapter, Metafile Transform, interactively applies transformations to metafiles and in the process develops generalized utility procedures to use in your own programs.

CONCEPTS

We'll begin by explaining what world coordinates are, what it means to transform them, and how the transformation alters images. Then we'll turn to metafiles, explaining what they are and how the new enhanced ones differ from the old ones.

World Coordinate Transformations

As a Windows programmer you already know about the difference between the logical coordinate space and the physical coordinate space. By selecting the mapping mode you choose different logical units, such as inches or millimeters. The system conveniently accepts the chosen units for subsequent drawing commands, silently converting to pixel units to produce the output. The logical points exist in one imagined coordinate system, and the GDI converts them to points in the physical coordinate system of the display device. Though the distinction seldom matters to programmers, there are really three coordinate systems at work, not two: the logical space, the device space, and the physical device space. The device space uses physical units—pixels—and extends 2^{27} pixels in each direction. The *physical* device space is an area on the screen. The distinction between device space and physical device space accommodates the need of each program to situate the device origin within its own client area.

Conceptually, the program draws on a logical space. In converting from logical units to physical pixels, the GDI moves the image from the logical space to the device space. Then, in a separate step, it moves the image from the device space to the physical device space by sliding the image over to situate it with respect to a new origin. Each step performs a straightforward mathematical conversion on the image's coordinates. The image advances from space to space like a product on an assembly line, and at each step the GDI transforms the image until the final product reaches the user's screen.

From these layered conversions, the system gains device independence and a piece of its windowing mechanism. Windows NT greatly enhances the system's power to transform images by inserting a new coordinate space before the logical space. The new space, called the *world space,* is also logical, so to distinguish between them the coordinate system that Win16 programmers customarily call the logical space is now called the *page space.* The new world coordinate system precedes the page space in the order of conversions. GDI commands now draw with world coordinates, no longer with page coordinates. To display the image, the GDI converts world coordinates to page coordinates, page coordinates to device coordinates, and device coordinates to physical device coordinates.

Transformation Equations

The advantage of the additional layer lies in the mathematical operations the GDI performs to translate world coordinates into page coordinates. A program can modify the equations that convert from world to page to produce a variety of useful transformations. A *transformation* is an algorithm for altering coordinate points, for moving them from one place to another. Suppose, for example, you want to scale an image, to stretch it or squash it. (The `StretchBlt` command, for example, scales its source image.) Figure 9.1 shows a square before and after scaling. Scaling makes some of the points on the square move. In this example, two corners have shifted sideways. It is possible to write equations that describe the change. If (x, y) names a point on the original square and (x', y') names the new location of the transformed point, the equations look like this:

```
x' = x * Dx
y' = y * Dy
```

Dx and Dy are scaling factors. If the factor is 1, no scaling occurs. As the scaling factor increases, the image stretches more and more. If the factor is a fractional amount and shrinks toward 0, the image shrinks too. If you apply only the first equation, the image scales horizontally and retains its original height. If you apply only the second equation, the image stretches in the vertical direction. If you apply both, it stretches in both directions at once.

FIGURE 9.1:

A square before and after a scaling transformation

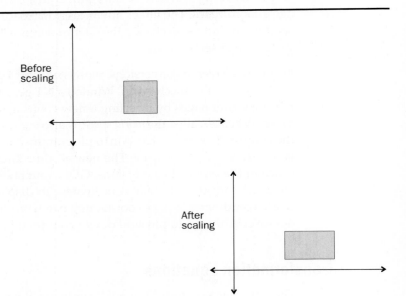

The same transformation equations can be expressed as an equivalent operation on a 2 x 2 matrix:

$$|x'\ y'| = |x\ y| * \begin{vmatrix} Dx & 0 \\ 0 & Dy \end{vmatrix}$$

In case your matrix math is rusty, that operation requires multiplying x times each item in the first row and adding the products to get x'. To get y', add the products of y times each item in the second row.

```
x' = (x * Dx) + (x * 0)
y' = (y * Dy) + (y * 0)
```

We began with equations for scaling images, but other operations are possible. With other equations you can translate, rotate, shear, and reflect images. Translating an image means shifting it from one place to another. Rotating an image means making it revolve a certain number of degrees around the coordinate origin. Shearing an image twists or distorts it, and reflecting it makes the image turn upside down or backwards. Examples of all five transformations appear in Figure 9.2.

FIGURE 9.2:

Scaling, translating, rotating, shearing, and reflecting an image

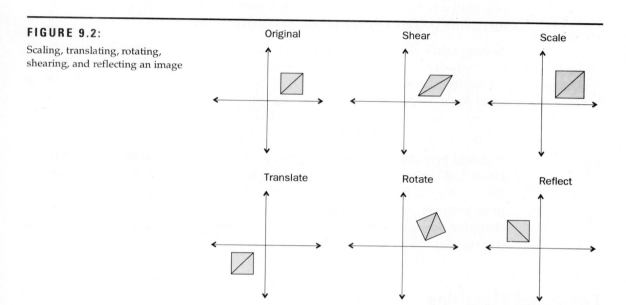

A different set of equations defines each operation. If you go to the trouble of generating and comparing each set, eventually you discover that all five sets of transformation equations can be combined into a single operation on a 3 x 3 matrix. By adjusting the factors in the matrix, you can scale, translate, rotate, shear, and reflect an image all at the same time.

$$|x'\ y'\ 1| = |x\ y\ 1| * \begin{vmatrix} eM11 & eM12 & 0 \\ eM21 & eM22 & 0 \\ eDx & eDy & 1 \end{vmatrix}$$

The quantities in the first two columns of the matrix change to produce different results. The quantities in the third column remain constant. (We'll explain the names—eM11 and eDx—in the section "World Coordinate Transformations" later in this chapter.) Under NT, each device context now contains a matrix. The default

467

matrix is an identity matrix, one that results in no change to x or y:

$$|x'\ y'\ 1| = |x\ y\ 1| * \begin{vmatrix} 1 & 0 & 0 \\ 0 & 1 & 0 \\ 0 & 0 & 1 \end{vmatrix}$$

By filling out a structure called an **XFORM**, you can change the values in the first two columns to produce any of the five possible transformations, alone or in combination with others. You can shear rectangles into parallelograms, tilt text, rotate bitmaps, turn polygons upside down, and stretch Bézier curves.

To summarize, the GDI now normally performs three transformations on every set of coordinates it receives. In converting from world to page coordinates, the GDI rotates, translates, scales, shears, and reflects the original image. In moving from page space to device space, the GDI converts logical units to pixels. In moving from device space to physical device space, the GDI shifts the image over to match the origin of a particular client area.

It should be noted that the old mapping mode commands can also perform translation and scaling transformations. By redefining the viewport and window origins, a program translates the image across the client area. In choosing the isotropic or anisotropic mapping mode, a program defines its own logical units, and by changing the units it scales the image. Only the rotation, shearing, and reflection transformations are entirely new.

Enhanced Metafiles

The paint program in Chapter 8 stores its picture in a bitmap. Useful as bitmaps are, they do have limitations. They consume large amounts of memory, for example. And although they can be stretched, the process is relatively slow and the image quality suffers. The apparent size of a bitmap depends on the size of the pixels that compose it, so even a device-independent bitmap changes size on displays of different resolutions.

There is another option. Pictures can also be stored in a metafile. The name can be misleading; "metafile" does not refer to a disk file (although metafiles are often stored on disks). A *metafile* is a data structure resembling an array of records. Each record describes a GDI command. One metafile contains all the commands for drawing a picture—all the **LineTo**s, **Rectangle**s, and **TextOut**s—and plays them back as often as you like. It's like a script, a list of actions for the drawing device to carry out. A metafile that draws a circle, for example, contains only one record to describe an **Ellipse** command. It does not specify all the bits that make up the circle, only the four coordinates needed to draw it. The command

```
Ellipse( hDC, 0, 0, 200, 200 );
```

naturally takes up much less room in memory than a bitmap image of the 40,000 pixels in a 200 x 200 area.

A metafile works like a tape recorder. You speak into the microphone, the machine records what you say, and then you play back the tape. The manuals say you "record" commands in a metafile and then "play" them back. In fact, a metafile is something like a simple procedure: You "program" the metafile and it executes your commands. But a metafile is *not* code. It is data, stored in a format that the GDI can translate into commands. Because a metafile is data, it can be swapped through the clipboard, saved in files, and read by other programs, just like bitmaps and other data structures.

Furthermore, metafiles can be scaled to any size when you play them back. Choose either of the unconstrained mapping modes, isotropic or anisotropic, and you can squeeze the metafile image into any area by adjusting the viewport extents. With the new world coordinate transformations, you can also rotate, reflect, and shear a metafile. The GDI transformation equations map the image to its new coordinates without losing detail.

Metafiles, then, often take up much less memory than bitmaps, and they scale more easily. Of course, metafiles have their own drawbacks. Displaying a large metafile usually takes much longer than displaying a single bitmap, particularly when the metafile contains many relatively slow commands, such as **Ellipse** and **StretchBlt**. Metafiles also lack the versatility that ROP codes give to bitmaps, and modifying the records in a metafile is much more difficult than modifying the image in a bitmap. Which format you choose depends on what you want to do. In general, metafiles are most commonly used for exchanging pictures with other programs through the clipboard, through disk files, or through DDE and OLE.

Windows Metafiles and Enhanced Metafiles

Win32 recognizes two different types of metafiles: enhanced metafiles and Windows metafiles. Metafiles created by the old Windows 3.x API are *Windows metafiles*.

The old format suffered from some limitations that Win32 overcomes in a new *enhanced metafile* format. A set of new commands works with metafiles in the new format. **CreateMetaFile** returns a device context to a Windows metafile; **CreateEnhMetaFile** returns a device context to an enhanced metafile. The old routines remain in the Win32 API only for the sake of compatibility. Windows NT programs should always use enhanced metafiles. The new format provides these improvements:

- Enhanced metafiles recognize the new GDI commands for paths, Bézier curves, and world coordinate transformations.

- The expanded header of an enhanced metafile provides true device independence by including more information about the image's physical dimensions and the device where it was created.

- Enhanced metafiles offer a palette to the program that plays them back. The receiving program can guarantee the best possible presentation of the image by realizing the metafile's palette before playing it.

A disk file for a Windows metafile conventionally receives the extension .WMF. The extension for an enhanced metafile is .EMF.

What Can't Go into a Metafile

Metafiles only draw; they can't test conditions or control execution flow the way program code can. A metafile can't hold expressions like ptMF.x or (iRow * WIDTH); it can store only the value each expression represents at the time the metafile is created. The coordinates in a metafile are hard-wired.

Nor can a metafile test return values. It cannot interrogate the DC. It can *set* the mapping mode, the ROP2 code, the pen, the brush, and the background color, but it can't *get* them—metafiles don't record any functions that begin with "Get." You can call Get functions while you create the metafile. You can, for example, select a font into a metafile DC and then call **GetTextMetrics** to find out which font was actually selected. But the call to **GetTextMetrics** does not generate a new record in the metafile, and any coordinates you calculate based on the **TEXTMETRIC** values become hard-coded in the metafile records. When the metafile is played back on a different display, **CreateFont** and **SelectObject** may end up putting a different font in the display's device context, but the hard-wired coordinates would still be based on the original font.

Most of the drawing functions do work in metafiles, but a few do not. **DrawText** fails, for example, as do **DrawFocusRect**, **FillRect**, **FrameRect**, and **GrayString**. All of these exceptional functions belong to the User segment of the system and not to the GDI.

Metafile Records

Examining the internal records for each command is a good way to understand just what a metafile can and cannot do. Every metafile begins with a header. Like the **BITMAP** structure that begins a bitmap, this header contains information the system needs to read the object: the physical dimensions of its image, the number of instruction records in the metafile, the resolution of the device where the image was created, and other descriptive facts.

```
typedef struct tagENHMETAHEADER { /* enmh */
    DWORD iType;                // must be MR_METAFILE
    DWORD nSize;                // sizeof( ENHMETAHEADER )
    RECTL rclBounds;            // bounding rect in device units (from GDI)
    RECTL rclFrame;             // bounding rect in .01 mm (from creator)
    DWORD dSignature;           // must be ENHMETA_SIGNATURE
    DWORD nVersion;             // creator's version number for the picture
    DWORD nBytes;               // size of the enhanced metafile
    DWORD nRecords;             // number of records in enhanced metafile
    WORD  nHandles;             // number of handles in the metafile's table
    WORD  sReserved;            // reserved; must be 0
    DWORD nDescription;         // number of bytes in following array
    DWORD offDescription;       // offset to an optional description string
    DWORD nPalEntries;          // number of entries in emf's palette
    SIZEL szlDevice;            // resolution of reference device in pixels
    SIZEL szlMillimeters;       // resolution of reference device in mm
} ENHMETAHEADER;
```

The metafile API commands fill out the header for you as you create a metafile. The **rclBounds** field, for example, is filled by the GDI when you close the metafile. The **rclFrame** field, on the other hand, is based on information you provide when creating the metafile. The two rectangles do not necessarily coincide. **rclFrame** describes the area the creator requests for the metafile, but the creator may include room for an empty margin, or a careless creator may negligently draw outside the requested area. **rclFrame** is not necessarily the smallest possible rectangle that completely contains all of the metafile output. That information is calculated by the GDI and placed in **rclBounds**.

iType identifies the data as the header of an enhanced metafile. **dSignature** indicates an internal version of metafile support (much like the **palVersion** field of a **LOGPALETTE** structure). The types **SIZEL** and **RECTL** are synonymous with **SIZE** and **RECT**; at some point Microsoft apparently intended to distinguish between versions that did or did not use long values, but since there's no need for 16-bit versions, both structures always use long values. **nHandles** tells how many GDI objects (such as pens and brushes) the metafile creates as it runs. During playback, the metafile holds the necessary handles in a table, and the metafile's records refer to the handles by their position in the table. The **nPalEntries** and **nDescription** fields give the size of several optional blocks of information that may follow the header. The description string, if present, typically tells who created the metafile, when it was created, and what it contains. A program might show the descriptions in the File Open dialog box to help the user identify the files. The palette entries describe the colors the metafile needs in order to display correctly. If a metafile contains any palette entries, you should create a palette from them and realize it before playing back the metafile. The metafile itself may select and realize palettes as it runs, but the system always forces a metafile's palettes into the background so they cannot interfere with any color arrangements the program may already have made. By realizing the palette in advance you give the metafile's desired colors foreground priority and increase the chances of producing an accurate image.

The individual records begin immediately after the description string and palette entries. Each record is an **ENHMETARECORD** structure.

```
typedef struct tagENHMETARECORD { /* enmr */
    DWORD iType;                    // number identifying a GDI routine
    DWORD nSize;                    // size of the record in bytes
    DWORD dParm[1];                 // parameters passed to the GDI routine
} ENHMETARECORD;
```

iType contains a constant, defined in wingdi.h, that identifies a GDI command. The complete list of constants shown in Table 9.1 is useful in determining which commands do generate records in a metafile.

TABLE 9.1: Record Type Constants for Enhanced Metafiles

EMR_ABORTPATH	EMR_FILLRGN	EMR_POLYLINETO	EMR_SETCOLORADJUSTMENT
EMR_ANGLEARC	EMR_FLATTENPATH	EMR_POLYLINETO16	EMR_SETDIBITSTODEVICE
EMR_ARC	EMR_FRAMERGN	EMR_POLYPOLYGON	EMR_SETMAPMODE
EMR_ARCTO	EMR_GDICOMMENT	EMR_POLYPOLYGON16	EMR_SETMAPPERFLAGS
EMR_BEGINPATH	EMR_INTERSECTCLIPRECT	EMR_POLYPOLYLINE	EMR_SETMETARGN
EMR_BITBLT	EMR_INVERTRGN	EMR_POLYPOLYLINE16	EMR_SETMITERLIMIT
EMR_CHORD	EMR_LINETO	EMR_POLYTEXTOUTA	EMR_SETPALETTEENTRIES
EMR_CLOSEFIGURE	EMR_MASKBLT	EMR_POLYTEXTOUTW	EMR_SETPIXELV
EMR_CREATEBRUSHINDIRECT	EMR_MODIFYWORLDTRANSFORM	EMR_REALIZEPALETTE	EMR_SETPOLYFILLMODE
EMR_CREATEDIBPATTERNBRUSHPT	EMR_MOVETOEX	EMR_REALIZEPALETTE	EMR_SETROP2
EMR_CREATEMONOBRUSH	EMR_OFFSETCLIPRGN	EMR_RECTANGLE	EMR_SETSTRETCHBLTMODE
EMR_CREATEPALETTE	EMR_PAINTRGN	EMR_RESIZEPALETTE	EMR_SETTEXTALIGN
EMR_CREATEPEN	EMR_PIE	EMR_RESTOREDC	EMR_SETTEXTCOLOR
EMR_DELETEOBJECT	EMR_PLGBLT	EMR_ROUNDRECT	EMR_SETVIEWPORTEXTEX
EMR_ELLIPSE	EMR_POLYBEZIER	EMR_SAVEDC	EMR_SETVIEWPORTORGEX
EMR_ENDPATH	EMR_POLYBEZIER16	EMR_SCALEVIEWPORTEXTEX	EMR_SETWINDOWEXTEX
EMR_EXCLUDECLIPRECT	EMR_POLYBEZIERTO	EMR_SCALEWINDOWEXTEX	EMR_SETWINDOWORGEX
EMR_EXTCREATEFONTINDIRECTW	EMR_POLYBEZIERTO16	EMR_SELECTCLIPPATH	EMR_SETWORLDTRANSFORM
EMR_EXTCREATEPEN	EMR_POLYDRAW	EMR_SELECTOBJECT	EMR_STRETCHBLT
EMR_EXTFLOODFILL	EMR_POLYDRAW16	EMR_SELECTPALETTE	EMR_STRETCHDIBITS
EMR_EXTSELECTCLIPRGN	EMR_POLYGON	EMR_SETARCDIRECTION	EMR_STROKEANDFILLPATH
EMR_EXTTEXTOUTA	EMR_POLYGON16	EMR_SETBKCOLOR	EMR_STROKEPATH
EMR_EXTTEXTOUTW	EMR_POLYLINE	EMR_SETBKMODE	EMR_WIDENPATH
EMR_FILLPATH	EMR_POLYLINE16	EMR_SETBRUSHORGEX	

Microsoft's support engineers confirm that the existence of records such as **EMR_POLYLINE16** and **EMR_POLYBEZIER16** indicate that an enhanced metafile internally converts records to a 16-bit form where possible. This revealing detail suggests that Microsoft envisions a future version of 16-bit Windows that supports enhanced metafiles and new GDI commands. Using 16-bit records where possible would let metafiles travel between 16-bit and 32-bit systems.

Some GDI commands don't produce the record you might expect. A call to **TextOut**, for example, produces an **ExtTextOut** record, and where you call **CreatePen** to make an object, the metafile may call **ExtCreatePen**. Don't be alarmed. The metafile is optimizing the commands, and the results will be exactly what you want.

The values in the **dParm[]** field of a metafile record vary from one command to the next. For **SetMapMode**, the field contains the mapping mode number. For commands that require more parameters, **dParm[]** extends to several words—**Arc**, for example, takes eight integer parameters. Still other commands fit whole structures into the parameters field of a metafile record: **CreatePenIndirect** uses a **LOGPEN** structure, and **ExtTextOut** stores the entire output string along with its other parameters. **BitBlt** and **StretchDIBits** pack whole bitmaps into the parameters field. Figure 9.3 shows a metafile header and the metafile records for several GDI commands. The numbers are hexadecimal.

Incidentally, whenever you play **BitBlt** or **StretchBlt** into a metafile, the GDI automatically converts the device-dependent bitmap (DDB) into a device-independent bitmap. Since metafiles contain only DIBs, they transfer very well from one system to another.

How Metafiles Handle Drawing Objects

Often to create a picture you need to create objects for the device context. Commands like **CreatePen**, **CreateSolidBrush**, and **GetStockObject** do not affect any device context. The new objects have to be selected first. Commands that create objects have no effect on a metafile DC, either. If you create objects while recording a metafile, the creation commands do not generate metafile records. Metafiles don't create an object until it's selected. Each **SelectObject** command generates two separate metafile records, one to create the new object and one to select it. When the metafile plays back it builds a table of all the objects it uses and refers to them by number. When Windows records **SelectObject** in a metafile, it always converts the second parameter from a handle to an index for an item in the object table.

FIGURE 9.3:

Examples of a metafile header and records

```
ENHMETAHEADER

   Contents           Type      Field Name      Description
   --------           ----      ----------      -----------

   01 00 00 00        DWORD     iType           MR_METAFILE
   58 00 00 00        DWORD     nSize           sizeof(ENHMETAHEADER) = 88
   04 00 00 00        RECTL     rclBounds       GDI's bounding rectangle
   13 00 00 00                                  device units
   47 00 00 00
   5D 00 00 00
   00 00 00 00        RECTL     rclFrame        creator's bounding rectangle
   00 00 00 00                                  in hundredths of a millimeter
   80 0E 00 00
   18 15 00 00
   20 45 4D 46        DWORD     dSignature      ENHMETA_SIGNATURE
   00 00 01 00        DWORD     nVersion
   00 11 00 00        DWORD     nBytes          4,352 bytes for entire metafile
   12 00 00 00        DWORD     nRecords        18 records in the metafile
   03 00              WORD      nHandles        metafile creates 3 objects
   00 00              WORD      sReserved
   00 00 00 00        DWORD     nDescription    no description string
   00 00 00 00        DWORD     offDescription
   00 00 00 00        DWORD     nPalEntries     no palette colors
   80 02 00 00        SIZEL     szlDevice       reference device pixel dimensions
   E0 01 00 00                                  640 x 480
   4A 01 00 00        SIZEL     szlMillimeters  resolution of reference device
   F0 00 00 00                                  in millimeters

RECORD FOR: SetBkMode( hdcMF, TRANSPARENT );

   12 00 00 00        DWORD     iType           EMR_SETBKMODE
   0C 00 00 00        DWORD     nSize           12 bytes
   01 00 00 00        DWORD     dParm[1]        TRANSPARENT

RECORD FOR: BeginPath( hdcMF );

   3B 00 00 00        DWORD     iType           EMR_BEGINPATH
   08 00 00 00        DWORD     nSize           8 bytes (no parameters)

RECORD FOR: MoveToEx( hdcMF, 1, 1, NULL );

   1B 00 00 00        DWORD     iType           EMR_MOVETOEX
   10 00 00 00        DWORD     nSize           16 bytes
                      DWORD     dParm[2]
   01 00 00 00        int       x coordinate
   01 00 00 00        int       y coordinate

RECORD FOR: LineTo( hdcMF, 127, 1 );

   36 00 00 00        DWORD     iType           EMR_LINETO
   10 00 00 00        DWORD     nSize
   7F 00 00 00        int       x coordinate
   01 00 00 00        int       y coordinate

RECORD FOR: EndPath( hdcMF );

   3C 00 00 00        DWORD     iType           EMR_ENDPATH
   08 00 00 00        DWORD     nSize           8 bytes (no parameters)

----------------------------------------------------------------
All values under Contents are hexadecimal.  Bytes are ordered from
least significant to most significant.
```

475

`SelectObject` has one other peculiarity in metafiles: it no longer returns a handle to the previously selected object. Instead it returns **TRUE** if the object is selected and **FALSE** otherwise. Don't expect to do this in a metafile:

```
DeleteObject( SelectObject(hdcMeta, hBrush) );
```

When a metafile finishes playing back, Windows automatically deletes all the objects in the metafile's table and restores the DC's previous objects. The system also restores other DC attributes, such as clipping regions, window extents, and pen position. Playing a metafile never permanently disturbs the program's initial DC settings.

COMMANDS

This section describes first the commands for performing world coordinate transformations and then the commands for creating enhanced metafiles. After that, we'll demonstrate both sets of commands in a sample program that performs any transformation on a set of metafiles designed to reveal how different GDI features behave when transformed.

World Coordinate Transformations

The new commands for working with world-to-page transformations are few. They enable world transformations, set the transformation matrix, get the transformation matrix, and combine different matrices. By default, a device context uses the identity matrix to translate from world to page coordinates. In effect, the identity matrix disables transformations. Transformation equations based on the identity matrix return the same values passed in. To change the matrix and produce more interesting transformations, a program must first alter the device context's new graphics mode attribute. By default the graphics mode is set to **GM_COMPATIBLE**, which maintains compatibility with Windows 3.1 by disallowing world coordinate transformations. Changing to **GM_ADVANCED** allows you subsequently to alter the transformation matrix.

```
int SetGraphicsMode(
    HDC hDC,                    // device context
    int iMode );                // graphics mode (GM_COMPATIBLE, GM_ADVANCED)
```

Enabling the advanced graphics mode also has several smaller consequences. Subsequent rectangle commands, for example, will contain their right and bottom sides. Normally those sides are considered outside the rectangle. Also, in advanced mode the GDI always draws arcs in the counter-clockwise direction.

The other transformation routines all work with a new data structure for holding matrix values:

```
typedef struct  tagXFORM {  /* xfrm */
    FLOAT eM11;
    FLOAT eM12;
    FLOAT eM21;
    FLOAT eM22;
    FLOAT eDx;
    FLOAT eDy;
} XFORM;
```

The numbers in the field names indicate positions in the matrix. **eM21**, for example, is in column 2, row 1. The "e" prefix indicates a data type Microsoft uses internally for performing arithmetic with large numbers. "M" stands for "matrix," and "D" stands for "delta." **eDx** and **eDy** are the delta values for sliding the image in a translation.

$$\begin{vmatrix} eM11 & eM12 & 0 \\ eM21 & eM22 & 0 \\ eDx & eDy & 1 \end{vmatrix}$$

To change the transformation matrix in a device context, first set all the values in an **XFORM**. Note that the fields hold floating-point values and so may be fractions. Then pass the new values to **SetWorldTransform**.

```
BOOL SetWorldTransform(
    HDC hDC,                 // device context
    LPXFORM lpXform );       // transformation data
```

SetWorldTransform fails if the device context is set to the default **GM_COMPATIBLE** graphics mode.

To determine the current transformation values, call **GetWorldTransform**.

```
BOOL GetWorldTransform(
     HDC hDC,                    // device context
     LPXFORM lpXform );          // structure to receive transformation data
```

This snippet of code calls both functions in order to modify two values in the matrix without altering the others.

```
XFORM xform;

GetWorldTransform( hDC, &xform );
xform.eM11 *= -1;
xform.em22 *= -1;
SetWorldTransform( hDC, &xform );
```

Reversing the sign of those two fields flips the image both upside down and backwards. The next section explains which fields to change to produce particular effects.

Performing Specific Transformations

The 3 x 3 matrix allows five different transformations. The trick is knowing which fields to change and what values to put in them. This list should help:

Transformation	Field(s)	Effect
Translate	eDx, eDy	Slides the image along the x axis (eDx) or the y axis (eDy). Measured in logical units. The sign of each value controls the direction of the slide
Scale	eM11, eM22	Stretches the image along the x axis (eM11) or the y axis (eM22). Values from 0 to 1 shrink the image. Larger values expand the image more and more. Negative values invert the image (see Reflect)

Transformation	Field(s)	Effect
Shear	eM12, eM21	Distorts the image by sliding one side in a direction parallel to itself. The values in these fields control the degree of displacement. A shear constant of 1 skews straight lines 45 degrees from their original position. Values between 0 and 1 produce smaller angles; values greater than 1 produce larger angles that eventually converge on 90 degrees. The sign of the value controls the direction of the shear
Rotate	eM11, eM12, eM21, eM22	Rotates the image around the origin. The values determine the angle of rotation. They derive from the sine and cosine of the angle, as described below
Reflect	eM11, eM22	Turns the image backwards (eM11) or upside down (eM22). A negative value in either field inverts the image along one axis. −1 inverts without stretching (see Scale)

When you run the Metafile Transform sample program you can experiment with different values for each transformation and see how the image responds.

Rotation requires some extra comment. As Figure 9.4 shows, rotating an image spins the entire coordinate space around the origin. The amount of rotation can be measured in degrees. In the example, the angle θ describes how far the space rotated to

FIGURE 9.4:

Image rotated around the coordinate system's origin

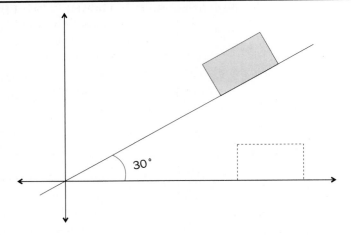

move the image to its second position. To rotate an image, you need to specify an angle.

$$eM11 = \cos \theta$$

$$eM12 = \sin \theta$$

$$eM21 = -\sin \theta$$

$$eM22 = \cos \theta$$

Those values rotate an image in a counter-clockwise direction, assuming that the positive y axis points up. In the **MM_TEXT** mapping mode, however, the positive y axis points down, and a slightly different matrix is required to produce counter-clockwise motion.

$$eM11 = \cos \theta$$

$$eM12 = -\sin \theta$$

$$eM21 = \sin \theta$$

$$eM22 = \cos \theta$$

Rotation does not spin images in place. If you have several images scattered across your client area and rotate them, the ones farther from the origin move greater distances. A rotation of more than 90 degrees normally moves everything completely out of view. More often you want rotation to reorient an image and show it at the same place on the screen. The easiest way is to draw the image around the origin with (0,0) at its center. Then with `SetViewportOrgEx` you can position the rotated image anywhere in the client area. To rotate several images, you can shift the origin from place to place with `SetWindowOrgEx` as you begin each new image. In effect, this method translates each image to the origin before rotating. It is also possible to build a single transformation matrix that translates an image to the origin, rotates it, and translates it back to its original position. That requires merging several transformations into a single matrix.

Combining Successive Transformations

Mathematically, combining transformations is simple. Given two different matrices, you simply multiply them. The product is a single matrix that combines the instructions for both operations. If you know how to multiply matrices you can do it by hand and set the results in an **XFORM** structure, or you can accomplish the same thing by calling `CombineTransform`.

```
BOOL CombineTransform(
    LPXFORM lpxformResult,   // combined transformation matrix
    LPXFORM lpxform1,        // first transformation matrix
    LPXFORM lpxform2 );      // second transformation matrix
```

Note that while multiplication is commutative, matrix multiplication is not. In other words, MatrixA x MatrixB is not necessarily the same as MatrixB x MatrixA. Suppose, for example, that you want to shear and rotate a rectangle. Figure 9.5 shows the difference between shearing first and rotating first.

The order is not always significant. Reflecting and translating an image, for example, produces the same result in either order. But sometimes it matters whether MatrixA is passed as `lpxform1` or `lpxform2`.

`CombineTransform` does not modify the device context. It has no effect on subsequent drawing commands. After calling `CombineTransform`, you probably want to pass `lpxFormResult` to `SetWorldTransform`. To superimpose a new transformation on the existing matrix, you would have to call `GetWorldTransform` to get the current values, `CombineTransform` to merge the two matrices, and `SetWorldTransform` to replace the old values with the new merged values. Another command, `ModifyWorldTransform`, combines all three operations into a single step.

```
BOOL ModifyWorldTransform(
     HDC hDC,                      // device context
     LPXFORM lpXform,              // transformation data to merge into DC
     DWORD dwMode );               // modification mode (left, right, or identity)
```

The value of dwMode may be **MWT_LEFTMULTIPLY**, **MWT_RIGHTMULTIPLY**, or **MWT_IDENTITY**. The left and right flags direct the function to combine the matrices in a particular order. Left multiplication applies the new transformation before the existing transformation. Right multiplication applies the existing transformation first. In other words, **MWT_LEFTMULTIPLY** makes the lpXform matrix the left multiplicand and **MWT_RIGHTMULTIPLY** makes lpXform the right multiplicand.

MWT_IDENTITY is a quick way to restore the default identity matrix, clearing all transformations. When dwMode is **MWT_IDENTITY**, lpXform is ignored.

Returning to the problem we proposed in the last section, you can rotate an object in place by combining, in order, the three matrices to translate the image to the center, rotate it, and translate it back to its starting place.

FIGURE 9.5:

Different results from combining
transformations in a different order

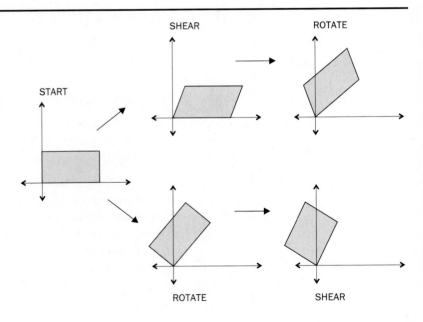

```
/*----------------------------------------------------------
        SYMBOL
----------------------------------------------------------*/

#define PI 3.141592653589793

/*----------------------------------------------------------
        ROTATE IN PLACE
        Sets the world coordinate transformation matrix to cause
        rotation around a point other than the origin.  All output
        commands called after RotateInPlace will be rotated around
        the point (x,y).  To rotate several figures in different
        places, call RotateInPlace once for each new figure.
----------------------------------------------------------*/

void RotateInPlace (
    HDC hDC,                        // device context
    int x,                          // x coordinate of new center
    int y,                          // y coordinate of new center
    int iAngle )                    // amount to spin (measured
{                                   //    in degrees counterclockwise)
    XFORM xForm;
    FLOAT flCos, flSin;

    // RotateInPlace works by combining three transformations.
    //    1. Shift image to origin
    //    2. Spin image around origin
    //    3. Shift rotated image back to starting point (x,y)

    /* TRANSLATE TO ORIGIN */

    ModifyWorldTransform( hDC, NULL, MWT_IDENTITY );
    GetWorldTransform( hDC, &xForm );
    xForm.eDx = (FLOAT)-x;
    xForm.eDy = (FLOAT)-y;
    SetWorldTransform( hDC, &xForm );

    /* ROTATE */

    /* convert degrees to radians and figure sine/cosine */
    flCos = (FLOAT)cos( ((double)iAngle)*(PI/180) );
    flSin = (FLOAT)sin( ((double)iAngle)*(PI/180) );
```

```
// The values for rotating counter-clockwise differ
// slightly depending on the direction of the y axis,
// which in MM_TEXT points down and in all other
// modes points up.

if (GetMapMode(hDC) == MM_TEXT)          // positive y points down
{
    xForm.eM12 = -flSin;
    xForm.eM21 = flSin;
}
else                                     // positive y points up
{
    xForm.eM12 = flSin;
    xForm.eM21 = -flSin;
}

xForm.eM11 = flCos;
xForm.eM22 = flCos;
xForm.eDx = (FLOAT)0;
xForm.eDy = (FLOAT)0;
ModifyWorldTransform( hDC, &xForm, MWT_RIGHTMULTIPLY );

/* TRANSLATE BACK TO STARTING POINT (x,y) */

xForm.eM11 = (FLOAT)1;
xForm.eM12 = (FLOAT)0;
xForm.eM21 = (FLOAT)0;
xForm.eM22 = (FLOAT)1;
xForm.eDx = (FLOAT)x;
xForm.eDy = (FLOAT)y;
ModifyWorldTransform( hDC, &xForm, MWT_RIGHTMULTIPLY );

return;
}
```

Figure 9.6 shows the effect of RotateInPlace. The dotted lines show the square's original position before rotation. As you can see from the code below, the two **Rectangle** commands that draw the image use exactly the same coordinates, but a new transformation matrix changes the effect of the second command.

FIGURE 9.6:

A square rotated by a single
compound transformation matrix

```
/*------------------------------------------------------------------
        PAINT PROCEDURE
        Process WM_PAINT messages here.
  ----------------------------------------------------------------*/


void InPlace_OnPaint ( HWND hWnd )
{
    PAINTSTRUCT ps;      // information about what to draw
    HDC hDC;             // display context = screen device settings
    HPEN hPen;

    // establish a display context
    hDC = BeginPaint( hWnd, &ps );

    SetGraphicsMode( hDC, GM_ADVANCED );

    /* outline the original unrotated rectangle */
    hPen = CreatePen( PS_DOT, 1, RGB(0,0,0) );
    if (hPen)
    {
        HPEN hpenOld = SelectPen( hDC, hPen );
        Rectangle( hDC, 260, 170, 380, 290 );
        SelectPen( hDC, hpenOld );
        DeletePen( hPen );
    }

    /* using the same coordinates, rotate the rectangle in place */
    RotateInPlace( hDC, 320, 230, 30 );
```

```
SelectBrush( hDC, GetStockBrush(GRAY_BRUSH) );
Rectangle( hDC, 260, 170, 380, 290 );

EndPaint( hWnd, &ps );
return;
}
```

Enhanced Metafiles

Creating and playing a metafile are straightforward tasks. When you create a metafile, the GDI gives you a device context. While you have the DC, the metafile is "open" and you can draw on it with most of the normal GDI functions. When given the DC of a metafile, however, the GDI functions produce no real output—not even invisible output to a memory bitmap. Instead, Windows registers each command, with its parameters, as a record in the metafile. You can create drawing objects and change the DC settings, just as you would with any device context. When the drawing is complete, you "close" the metafile. At this point the metafile DC is no longer valid. The function that closes a metafile returns a handle, and from then on the handle is all you need. The "play" function takes the metafile handle and feeds all the metafile commands to the display device. Unneeded metafiles should be deleted, just like brushes, bitmaps, and other objects. These four functions perform the basic operations for working with any metafile.

```
HDC CreateEnhMetaFile(
    HDC hdcRef,                     // reference device context
    LPTSTR lpszFileName,            // string naming a new disk file (optional)
    LPRECT lpRect,                  // bounding rectangle in .01 mm
    LPTSTR lpDescription );         // optional description string

HENHMETAFILE CloseEnhMetaFile( HDC hdcMF );

BOOL PlayEnhMetaFile(
    HDC hDC,                        // device context where metafile will display
    HENHMETAFILE hEMF,              // the metafile
    LPRECT lpRect );                // bounding rectangle in logical units

BOOL DeleteEnhMetaFile( HENHMETAFILE hEMF );
```

To fill in the new metafile's header structure, **CreateEnhMetaFile** needs to know what device the image will be displayed on. If the metafile is transferred to other machines, the header information ensures that the image will retain its original size and proportions.

This section of code illustrates the basic steps for creating and playing an enhanced metafile:

```
HDC hDC, hdcMF;                             // screen and metafile DCs
RECT rBounds;                               // area where image is drawn
HENHMETAFILE hEMF;                          // handle to the metafile

// CREATE the metafile
hDC = GetDC( hWnd );                        // create the reference DC
rBounds.left   = 0;                         // declare the image's boundaries
rBounds.top    = 0;
rBounds.right  = 200;
rBounds.bottom = 200;
PixToMm( hDC, (LPPOINT)&rBounds, 2 );       // convert boundaries to .01 mm
hdcMF = CreateEnhMetaFile(
                hDC,                        // reference DC
                NULL,                       // disk file for storage
                &rBounds,                   // bounding area in .01 mm
                NULL );                     // name string

// DRAW in the metafile by calling GDI output
// commands here; each one takes hdcMF as its
// first parameter
Ellipse( hdcMF, 0, 0, 200,200 );

// CLOSE the metafile to get a handle
hEMF = CloseEnhMetaFile( hdcMF );           // this invalidates hdcMF

// PLAY the metafile to draw it on the screen
PlayEnhMetaFile( hDC, hMF );                // now you see the image
ReleaseDC( hWnd, hDC );

// DELETE the metafile to release memory when you're done
DeleteEnhMetaFile( hMF );
```

The PixToMm conversion procedure appears in the Metafile Transform program at the end of the chapter.

Memory- and Disk-Based Metafiles

Windows metafiles and enhanced metafiles both come in two varieties: memory based and disk based. Because the preceding example passes **NULL** as the file parameter to **CreateEnhMetaFile**, the function creates the metafile in memory. If we passed a file name instead, the function would store the metafile's records on the disk. Disk-based and memory-based metafiles function exactly alike: You open them the same way, build them the same way, and close them and play them back exactly the same way. The only difference is where the contents are actually stored. Under Windows 3.1, disk-based metafiles play back more slowly than memory-based metafiles, but file mapping largely eliminates the performance penalty of disk access. When working with disk-based metafiles, the system maps the file into memory, a process we described in Chapter 7. The metafile's disk file is paged in and out of memory just like any other memory page. Under Windows NT, even the old-style unenhanced metafiles gain speed from file mapping. Because disk-based and memory-based metafiles now perform alike, any metafile destined for the disk might as well begin straight off as a disk-based metafile. Choose memory-based metafiles for temporary objects or for objects that later will be embedded in a larger file.

Win16 programmers have another reason for preferring memory-based metafiles. Because the old format does not include any information about the device where the image originated or the image's original size, old .WMF files do not transfer well from one system to another. The receiving program has no way of knowing how to scale the image. To make metafiles less dependent on a particular device, Win16 programmers often preface .WMF files with a header structure to provide the missing information. But the new **ENHMETAHEADER** structure already includes enough information for device independence, so the disk-based form of an enhanced metafile (.EMF) is more useful than the disk-based form of a Windows metafile (.WMF). One is portable, the other is not.

The **DeleteEnhMetaFile** command does not erase the file where a disk-based metafile resides; it only unmaps the file from memory and invalidates the metafile's handle. Unless you call **DeleteFile** (or _unlink or remove), the .EMF file survives even after the handle is invalid. To use the metafile again you would need to recover its handle. **GetEnhMetaFile** creates a handle for an existing disk-based metafile.

```
HENHMETAFILE GetEnhMetaFile( LPTSTR lpszFileName );
```

lpszFileName points to the name of the disk file where the metafile is stored.

488

Querying a Metafile

Three functions return information about a metafile. **GetEnhMetaFileDescription** retrieves the optional description string that may have been incorporated in the metafile by its creator. **GetEnhMetaFileHeader** retrieves the **ENHMETAHEADER** structure that begins every enhanced metafile. **GetEnhMetaFilePaletteEntries** retrieves the array of color descriptions that may optionally accompany a metafile.

```
UINT GetEnhMetaFileDescription(
    HENHMETAFILE hEMF,              // the metafile
    UINT uBuffSize,                // size of text buffer in characters
    LPTSTR lpszDescription );      // buffer to receive test

UINT GetEnhMetaFileHeader(
    HENHMETAFILE hEMF,              // the metafile
    UINT uBuffSize,                // size of buffer in bytes
    LPENHMETAHEADER lpEMH );       // buffer to receive header data

UINT GetEnhMetaFilePaletteEntries(
    HENHMETAFILE hEMF,              // the metafile
    UINT uNumEntries,              // number of palette entries
    LPPALETTEENTRY lpPE );         // array to receive palette entry data
```

All three functions copy data into a buffer. The buffer size for the header is always the same, but the buffer size for the description string and the palette entries varies from one metafile to another. To find out how large the buffer should be, call either command with a **NULL** buffer pointer; it returns a size in bytes. Allocate a buffer that size and pass the new buffer pointer in a second call to the same function. For example, this code sequence calls **GetEnhMetaFilePaletteEntries** twice, once to find out whether the metafile has a palette and again while creating and realizing the metafile's palette:

```
// Assume hEMF (a metafile) and hDC (a display device context)
// have already been created.

UINT uNumColors;
LPPALETTEENTRY lpPE;

/* find out how large the metafile's palette is */
uNumColors = GetEnhMetaFilePaletteEntries( hEMF, 0, NULL );
if (uNumColors > 0)                          // does it have a palette at all?
{
    /* allocate room for a logical palette structure with all the colors */
    lpPE = GlobalAlloc( GMEM_FIXED, sizeof(LOGPALETTE)
```

```
                                        + sizeof(PALETTEENTRY)
                                        * uNumColors );
    if (lpPE)                                   // did the allocation succeed?
    {
        UINT uResult;                           // return value for error testing

        /* initialize the new LOGPALETTE structure */
        lpPE->palVersion    = 0x300;
        lpPE->palNumEntries = uNumColors;

        /* fill in the palette entries */
        uResult = GetEnhMetaFilePaletteEntries( hEMF, uNumColors, lpPE );
        if (uResult == uNumColors)              // be sure the command worked
        {
            HPALETTE hPal, hpalOld;
            hPal = CreatePalette( lpPE );
            if (hPal)
            {
                hpalOld = SelectPalette( hDC, hPal, FALSE );
                RealizePalette( hDC );
                SelectPalette( hDC, hPalOld, FALSE );
                DeletePalette( hPal );
            }
        }
        GlobalFree( lpPE );
    }
}

/* now you can play the metafile and be sure of seeing all its colors */
```

Editing a Metafile

To inspect the contents of a metafile and modify its output, you need functions that work with individual records: **EnumEnhMetaFile** and **PlayEnhMetaFileRecord**.

```
BOOL EnumEnhMetaFile(
    HDC hDC,                            // device context
    HENHMETAFILE hEMF,                  // enhanced metafile
    ENHMFENUMPROC lpEnhMetaProc,        // address of callback function
    LPVOID lpData,                      // optional data for callback function
    LPRECT lpRect );                    // image's bounding rectangle
```

```
BOOL PlayEnhMetaFileRecord(
    HDC hDC,                          // device context
    LPHANDLETABLE lpHandleTable,      // address of metafile handle table
    LPENHMETARECORD lpEnhMetaRecord,   // address of metafile record
    UINT uNumHandles );              // number of handles in table
```

These two functions work along with a callback procedure you write to process individual metafile records. You give **EnumEnhMetaFile** a pointer to your callback function, and it calls the function once for each record in the metafile. The callback function must use this prototype:

```
int CALLBACK EnhMetaFileProc(
    HDC hDC,                          // device context
    LPHANDLETABLE lpHTable,           // address of metafile handle table
    LPMETARECORD lpEMR,               // address of metafile record
    int iNumHandles,                  // number of handles in table
    LPARAM lpData );                 // address of optional data
```

Your function can do whatever it likes with each record. It will probably test the **iType** field to identify the command.

```
switch (lpEMR->iType)
{
    case EMR_LINETO:
        // process LineTo commands
        break;

    case EMR_POLYBEZIER:
        // process PolyBezier commands
        break;
}
```

The callback function can even change the parameters stored in a metafile, provided the new values occupy the same number of storage bytes as the old parameters.

```
    case EMR_LINETO:
        lpMFR->dParm[0] = 0;     // x coordinate
        lpMFR->dParm[1] = 0;     // y coordinate
        break;
```

The modification is trivial but illustrative: If you make all the **LineTo** coordinates $(0, 0)$, then whenever the metafile plays, all the lines it draws will end at the origin.

Metafiles rarely need to be modified this way. Rather than permanently changing certain records, you are more likely to intercept a few commands and adjust the output for one playback only.

```
int CALLBACK EnhMetaFileProc(
    HDC hDC,                          // device context
    LPHANDLETABLE lpHTable,           // address of metafile handle table
    LPMETARECORD lpEMR,               // address of metafile record
    int iNumHandles,                  // number of handles in table
    LPARAM lpData )                   // address of optional data
{

    HPEN hpenOld;
    HPEN hpenDot = CreatePen( 2, 1, OL );            // dotted lines

    switch (lpEMR->iType)
    {
        case EMR_LINETO:
            hpenOld = SelectPen( hDC, hpenDot );
            PlayEnhMetaFileRecord( hDC, lpHT, lpEMR, iNumHandles );
            SelectPen( hDC, hpenOld );
            break;

        case EMR_TEXTOUT:
            // eliminate text output by doing nothing
            break;

        default:
            PlayEnhMetaFileRecord( hDC, lpHTable, lpEMR, iNumHandles );
            break;
    }
    DeletePen( hpenDot );
    return( 1 );                      // a non-zero value means continue
}
```

Every time this callback function discovers a **LineTo** command, it selects a dotted-line pen before executing that record, so all the lines drawn with **LineTo** will be dotted. Since the procedure restores the old pen before continuing, other output commands are not affected; they draw with whatever pen the metafile itself selects.

PlayEnhMetaFileRecord executes the GDI command in a single record. By refusing to call **PlayEnhMetaFileRecord** for **TextOut** records, our enumeration procedure removes text from the output. The enumeration procedure could also play individual records selectively into a new metafile to produce a modified or edited version of the original. It is also permissible to play one metafile into another.

Copying Metafile Data

You can duplicate a metafile with **CopyEnhMetaFile**. Duplicates are useful for passing to the clipboard and for saving a backup when modifying the original. Also, by copying a metafile you can convert between the disk-based and memory-based forms.

```
HENHMETAFILE CopyEnhMetaFile(
    HENHMETAFILE hEMF,              // handle of source metafile
    LPTSTR lpszFileName );          // string naming a disk file (may be NULL)
```

If `lpszFileName` points to a string, the command uses it to create a disk file and copies the original metafile there. If `lpszFileName` is **NULL**, the duplicate metafile is memory based.

CopyEnhMetaFile combines two steps into a single command. First it extracts the raw bits from the original metafile, and then it feeds them back into a new metafile. Two other commands make these steps available individually. **GetEnhMetaFile-Bits** copies the contents of a metafile object into a buffer, and **SetEnhMetaFileBits** copies the contents of a buffer into a new metafile object.

```
UINT GetEnhMetaFileBits(
    HENHMETAFILE hEMF,             // handle of source metafile
    UINT uBuffSize,                // size of data buffer in bytes
    LPBYTE lpbBuffer );            // buffer to receive the metafile data

HENHMETAFILE SetEnhMetaFileBits(
    UINT uBuffSize,                // size of data buffer in bytes
    LPBYTE lpbBuffer );            // raw bits from the enhanced metafile
```

GetEnhMetaFileBits cannot copy more bits than the buffer will hold. To find out how big the buffer should be, call **GetEnhMetaFileBits** with `lpbBuffer` set to **NULL**. The return value gives the size of the metafile data. When you allocate a buffer and pass a valid pointer in `lpbBuffer`, the function returns the number of bytes actually copied from the metafile to the buffer.

The ability to extract the data from metafiles makes it possible to embed a metafile inside another document and save the compound result in a single file. A desktop publisher, for example, might embed metafile images within the data that represents a page.

Although the enumeration and playback process permits limited modifications to a metafile, the metafile format and the metafile APIs do not lend themselves to substantial editing. You cannot easily shift sections of the data and reconstitute the metafile. Such operations are possible but only through brute-force manual methods. It is possible to extract the bits, build new metafile records by hand, shift parts of the buffer to make room, recalculate the **ENHMETAHEADER**, and reconstitute the metafile, but if you're doing that much work you might as well invent a new and more flexible internal data structure, one that might allow other editing capabilities. You might want to group subsets of related commands, for example, and permit point-and-click editing where the user clicks and drags to stretch or move shapes. Metafiles are not well suited to extensive editing.

Converting between Metafile Formats

Enhanced metafiles have many advantages over the old Windows metafiles, but until the enhanced metafile API trickles back down into Windows for DOS, expect to deal with the old format as well. Remember that the user may be running 16-bit Windows programs under the WOW subsystem. The user may wish to save a metafile from an NT program and reopen it with a Windows 3.1 program. An NT program should be able to offer its data in both formats.

Fortunately, converting is easy. To create a Windows metafile from an enhanced metafile, call **GetWinMetaFileBits**. It reaches into the enhanced metafile to extract its header and records, converting them along the way to the old format. Records for new NT functions are converted to approximately equivalent functions from the old API. **PolyBezier** and **AngleArc**, for example, are converted to **Polyline** (with the possible loss of some points from the original curve).

```
UINT GetWinMetaFileBits(
    HENHMETAFILE hEMF,          // enhanced metafile (source)
    UINT uBuffSize,             // buffer size in bytes
    LPBYTE lpbBuffer,           // buffer for converted bits (target)
    INT iMapMode,               // mapping mode
    HDC hdcRef ),               // device context for reference device
```

Windows metafiles conventionally begin with calls to **SetWindowOrgEx** and **SetWindowExtEx**. The program that plays them back first calls **SetViewportOrgEx** and **SetViewportExtEx**. As part of the conversion process, **GetWinMetaFileBits** prefixes the metafile with the appropriate commands to set the mapping mode and adjust the logical window, drawing the necessary information from the enhanced metafile's header and from the `iMapMode` and `hdcRef` parameters. To create a scalable metafile, set `iMapMode` to **MM_ANISOTROPIC**.

The return value tells how many bytes were copied into `lpbBuffer`. Zero indicates an error. If you pass **NULL** for `lpbBuffer`, the return value tells how many bytes the converted metafile would require. After a successful conversion, `lpbBuffer` points to the raw bits for a Windows metafile. If you write the bits directly to the disk, then you can call **GetMetaFile** to create a disk-based Windows metafile. Or you can create a memory-based metafile by passing `lpbBuffer` directly to **SetMetaFileBitsEx**.

To convert an old Windows metafile to the new enhanced format, call **SetWinMetaFileBits**.

```
HENHMETAFILE SetWinMetaFileBits(
    UINT uBuffSize,              // buffer size in bytes
    LPBYTE lpbBuffer,            // Windows metafile data (source)
    HDC hdcRef,                  // device context for reference device
    LPMETAFILEPICT lpMFP ),      // suggested size of metafile picture
```

`lpbBuffer` points to the raw bits from a Windows metafile. Initialize the buffer by reading the data from a file with **ReadFile** or by calling **GetMetaFileBitsEx**. The system constructs an **ENHMETAHEADER** structure from information in the original header, the `lpMFP` parameter, and the reference DC. It returns a handle to a new memory-based enhanced metafile. If `hdcRef` is **NULL**, the system draws information from the current display device. If the reference device is not the device where the Windows metafile actually originated, some commands in the metafile may not execute as intended. If `lpMFP` is **NULL**, the system sets the mapping mode to **MM_ANISOTROPIC** and scales the picture to fill the reference device's display.

The commands for working with enhanced metafiles do not accept Windows metafiles, and vice versa. The two command sets run largely parallel: **GetMetaFile** and **GetEnhMetaFile**; **PlayMetaFile** and **PlayEnhMetaFile**. This chapter focuses on the enhanced metafile API, but for review here is a list of the old command set. These commands survive in the Win32 API only for compatibility.

- **CloseMetaFile:** Closes a metafile DC and returns an HMETAFILE handle

- **CopyMetaFile:** Duplicates a metafile

- **CreateMetaFile:** Creates a metafile DC, ready for recording

- **DeleteMetaFile:** Removes a metafile from memory and invalidates its handle

- **EnumMetaFile:** Passes records from a metafile one by one to a callback function

- **GetMetaFile:** Opens a disk file as a disk-based metafile

- **GetMetaFileBitsEx:** Copies the raw bits from a metafile into a buffer

- **PlayMetaFile:** Executes all the commands described in the metafile records

- **PlayMetaFileRecord:** Executes the command stored in one metafile record

- **SetMetaFileBitsEx:** Takes raw bits from a buffer and copies them into a new metafile object

Reading and Writing Windows Metafiles

Often the point of converting between old and new formats is to import or export disk files. File I/O with a Windows metafile takes a little extra effort. As we've already observed, its skimpy header renders inadequate the simple disk-based form of an old metafile. If you open a normal .WMF file with **GetMetaFile**, you have no way of knowing the image's mapping mode or its intended dimensions.

The solution is to read and write metafiles manually, with standard file functions, and add a header at the beginning. **METAFILEPICT** would be a logical choice for the header structure, but Aldus Corporation devised a more detailed alternative, which has become standard:

```
// file header for placeable metafiles
typedef struct
{
    DWORD   key;                // identifies file type
    HANDLE  hmf;                // unused
    RECT    bbox;               // bounding rectangle
    WORD    inch;               // units per inch
    DWORD   reserved;           // unused
    WORD    checksum;           // XOR of previous fields
} METAFILEHEADER;
typedef METAFILEHEADER FAR* LPMETAFILEHEADER;
```

Some programs call this structure an APMFILEHEADER, for "Aldus Placeable Metafile." A metafile with this header is "placeable" because the header tells how to place it on the screen. Microsoft subsequently documented the same structure for Windows 3.1 under the name METAFILEHEADER, and some of Microsoft's programs, including Word for Windows 2.0, require metafiles to have this header. METAFILE-HEADER does not, however, appear in any Microsoft header files; you must define it yourself.

Placeable metafiles also use the .WMF extension. To tell whether a metafile is placeable or simply disk based, you must open the file and read the data. Read the key field and, optionally, the checksum field to identify a placeable metafile. .WMF files with the placeable header do not work with **GetMetaFile**; you cannot open them and play them through the normal API functions. You must read in the file by hand and convert it to an enhanced metafile with **SetWinMetaFileBits**.

The first field, key, marks the file type. It must be 0x9AC6CDD7L. The second field, hmf, is unused and must be 0. The third and fourth fields tell the receiving application how big the picture should be. The value in inch defines an arbitrary number of metafile units per inch, and the values in bbox use those units to define the smallest rectangle that completely encloses the metafile picture. To avoid overflow, don't make inch more than 1440, the value for measuring in **MM_TWIPS** mapping mode (1440 twips per inch). The following lines define a box for a metafile 1 inch wide and 2 inches tall:

```
METAFILEHEADER mfh;

mfh.inch = 1000;                      // MM_HIENGLISH units
SetRect( mfh.bbox, 0, 0, 1000, 2000 );
```

The reserved field is also unused and must be 0. The checksum field helps to verify the integrity of the information in the header. Calculate it by XORing 0 with the ten preceding words:

```
WORD GetChecksum ( LPMETAFILEHEADER lpMFH )
{
    LPWORD lpw;                       // pointer to words in header
    WORD wChecksum = 0;

    for (lpw = (LPWORD)lpMFH;
         lpw < (LPWORD)&lpMFH->checksum;
         ++lpw )
    {
        /* XOR current checksum with next field */
        wChecksum ^= *lpw;
    }
    return( wChecksum );
}
```

If you need to save a metafile in the old format, perform this calculation to create the checksum value. When you load a metafile, call this procedure again and compare the result to the checksum value read from the file. If the values do not match, the file is invalid because either it does not contain a metafile or its data has become corrupt.

After the last field of the header, the actual metafile data begins. To determine the size of the data, call **GetFileSize** and subtract sizeof(METAFILEHEADER), which is 22.

Since a placeable metafile begins with a header and ends with a large block of binary data, reading or writing one takes two separate operations. To read a metafile into memory, follow these steps:

1. Open the file (**CreateFile**).

2. Read the METAFILEHEADER information (**ReadFile**).

3. Verify that the file contains a metafile by examining the key and checksum fields.

4. Calculate the size of the metafile data and allocate memory for it (**GetFileSize** and **GlobalAlloc**).

5. Read the actual metafile bits (**ReadFile**).

6. Close the file (**CloseHandle**).

7. Convert the bits into a metafile (**SetWinMetaFileBits**).

SetWinMetaFileBits constructs a metafile from the data in a memory buffer and returns a handle to the new object. You then have two handles to the same data—the old memory handle and the new metafile handle. Do not use the old handle; set it to **NULL** and forget about it entirely.

To save a .WMF file with a placeable header, first fill a buffer with the metafile data by calling either **GetMetaFileBitsEx** or **GetWinMetaFileBits**, depending on whether the original metafile object is in the old or new format. Then follow these steps:

1. Open the file (**CreateFile**).

2. Initialize the METAFILEHEADER structure, including the checksum field.

3. Write the METAFILEHEADER information (**WriteFile**).

4. Copy the bits from the metafile into a memory buffer (**GetWinMetaFileBits**).

5. Write the metafile data (**WriteFile**).

6. Close the file (**CloseHandle**).

Passing Metafiles through the Clipboard

Besides passing metafiles as disk files, programs may pass them through the clipboard. The need for conversion arises again if the user cuts and pastes metafiles between 16-bit and 32-bit programs running simultaneously. Exchanging through the clipboard is easier, though, because the system converts automatically between the old and new formats. The NT clipboard recognizes two distinct metafile data formats: **CF_METAFILEPICT** and **CF_ENHMETAFILE**. If the user copies to the clipboard an enhanced metafile from one program and tries to paste it into another program that accepts only the Windows format, the system itself converts the object and the paste operation succeeds. The system is said to *synthesize* the missing format. If the default arrangements would produce an unsatisfactory image, the donor program may choose to perform the conversion and offer both formats itself. When the donor explicitly places both formats on the clipboard with successive calls to **SetClipboardData**, the system does not perform conversions.

Incidentally, the system also synthesizes text formats. If a program offers **CF_TEXT** data and closes the clipboard, the system also makes available **CF_OEMTEXT** and **CF_UNICODETEXT** formats. Given text in one form the system can always synthesize the other two.

CODE: THE METAFILE TRANSFORMATION PROGRAM

The Metafile Transform program (MFX) creates several metafiles, each displaying different features of the GDI. One shows pens, one shows fonts, one a 256-color bitmap, and one a brushed region made from a path. The user selects a metafile from the menu and then opens a dialog box to toggle on and off each of the five possible world coordinate transformations. In Figure 9.7 the user has opened the dialog box to transform the metafile that draws a region.

FIGURE 9.7:

What the Metafile Transform
program does

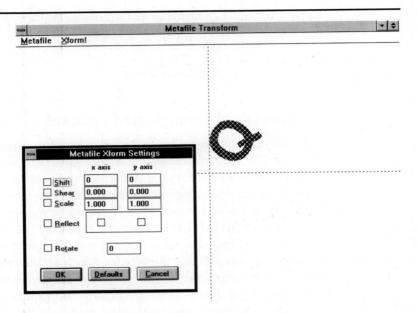

Reading the source code will familiarize you with many operations on metafiles
and matrices, and running the program should help you get a feel for how different
matrix values affect the image.

Auxiliary Files

The code for Metafile Transform is divided into four modules. If this were a 16-bit
program we would compile it as a medium-model program, but since the operating
system no longer distinguishes between near and far addresses, any routine in any
module can always call any other public routine without the need for special compiler support. The make file simply bunches all the object files onto the linker's
command line to produce a single .EXE file.

```
#
#   NMake file for the METAFILE XFORM program
#
```

```
#
#     Set targets and dependencies
#

all: mfx.exe
mfx.exe: mfx.obj init.obj xform.obj dlg.obj mfx.rbj mfx.h
mfx.obj: mfx.c mfx.h
init.obj: init.c mfx.h
xform.obj: xform.c mfx.h
dlg.obj: dlg.c mfx.h dlg.h
mfx.rbj: mfx.rc mfx.h dlg.h

#
#     Define macros for command-line options and library modules
#

!IFDEF NODEBUG
CFLAGS = -c -G3 -Os -W4 -D_X86_=1 -DWIN32
LFLAGS = -subsystem:windows
!ELSE
CFLAGS = -c -G3 -Od -W4 -Zi -D_X86_=1 -DWIN32
LFLAGS = -debug:full -debugtype:cv -subsystem:windows
!ENDIF

INCS = mfx.h
OBJS = mfx.obj init.obj xform.obj dlg.obj mfx.rbj
LIBS = libc.lib ntdll.lib kernel32.lib user32.lib gdi32.lib

#
#     Define compiling rules
#

.c.obj:
    cl386 $(CFLAGS) $*.c

.rc.rbj:
    rc $*.rc
    cvtres -i386 $*.res -o $*.rbj

.obj.exe:
    link32 $(LFLAGS) -out:$*.exe $(OBJS) $(LIBS)
```

```
=========================================================================

/*-----------------------------------------------------------------


        MFX.H

        Header file for MFX. Defines program constants, resource
        identifiers, and function prototypes.

     ----------------------------------------------------------------*/


/*-----------------------------------------------------------------
        TYPE DECLARATION
     ----------------------------------------------------------------*/

typedef struct tagSETTINGS {
    BOOL bShift;
    int iShiftX;
    int iShiftY;
    BOOL bShear;
    FLOAT flShearX;
    FLOAT flShearY;
    BOOL bScale;
    FLOAT flScaleX;
    FLOAT flScaleY;
    BOOL bReflect;
    BOOL bFlipX;
    BOOL bFlipY;
    BOOL bRotate;
    int iAngle;
} SETTINGS, *PSETTINGS;

/*-----------------------------------------------------------------
        PROTOTYPES of routines called from other modules
     ----------------------------------------------------------------*/


/* MFX module */

LRESULT WINAPI Mfx_WndProc( HWND hWnd, UINT uMessage, WPARAM wParam,
    LPARAM lParam );

/* XFORM module */
void Scale( HDC hDC, FLOAT flFactorX, FLOAT flFactorY, BOOL bCombine );
void Shift( HDC hDC, int cx, int cy, BOOL bCombine );
void Reflect( HDC hDC, BOOL bFlipX, BOOL bFlipY, BOOL bCombine );
```

```
void Rotate( HDC hDC, int iAngle, BOOL bCombine );
void Shear( HDC hDC, FLOAT flShearX, FLOAT flShearY, BOOL bCombine );
void DefaultXform( HDC hDC );
void RotateInPlace( HDC hDC, int x, int y, int iAngle );

/* INIT module */

BOOL Init( HINSTANCE hinstThis, int iCmdShow );
void SetDefaults( PSETTINGS pData );
HENHMETAFILE MakeBitmapMF( HWND hWnd );
HENHMETAFILE MakeFontsMF( HWND hWnd );
HENHMETAFILE MakePathMF( HWND hWnd );
HENHMETAFILE MakePensMF( HWND hWnd );

/* DLG module */

void DoTransformDlg( HWND hWnd );
BOOL WINAPI About_DlgProc( HWND hDlg, UINT uMessage, WPARAM wParam,
    LPARAM lParam );

/*-------------------------------------------------------------
          CONSTANTS
   ----------------------------------------------------------*/

#define NAME_BUFSIZE        10       /* max chars for IDS_APPNAME string */
#define TITLE_BUFSIZE       20       /* max chars for the window caption */
#define PALVERSION          0x300    /* needed for a LOGPALETTE structure */

/*-------------------------------------------------------------
          MACROS
   ----------------------------------------------------------*/

#define RGB_BLACK           RGB(0,0,0)
#define RGB_GRAY            RGB(127,127,127);
#define RGB_WHITE           RGB(255,255,255);

/*-------------------------------------------------------------
          RESOURCE IDs
   ----------------------------------------------------------*/

#define BMP_256COLOR        10
#define MENU_MAIN           10
#define DLG_XFORM           10
#define DLG_ABOUT           20
```

```
/* MENUITEM command IDs */

#define IDM_BITMAP          100
#define IDM_FONTS           110
#define IDM_PATH            120
#define IDM_PENS            130

#define IDM_ABOUT           200

#define IDM_XFORM           300

/* STRINGS */

#define IDS_APPNAME         10
#define IDS_TITLE           20
```

===

```
/*----------------------------------------------------------------


        DLG.H

        Header file for the Xform dialog in the Metafile Transform
        program.

    --------------------------------------------------------------*/


#define IDD_DEFAULT             10

#define IDD_TOGGLE_SHIFT        20
#define IDD_EDIT_SHIFTX         30
#define IDD_EDIT_SHIFTY         40

#define IDD_TOGGLE_SHEAR        50
#define IDD_EDIT_SHEARX         60
#define IDD_EDIT_SHEARY         70

#define IDD_TOGGLE_SCALE        80
#define IDD_EDIT_SCALEX         90
#define IDD_EDIT_SCALEY         100

#define IDD_TOGGLE_REFLECT      110
#define IDD_FLIPX               120
#define IDD_FLIPY               130
```

```
#define IDD_TOGGLE_ROTATE              140
#define IDD_EDIT_ROTATE                150


========================================================================

/*-----------------------------------------------------------------

        MFX.RC
        Resource script file for the Metafile Transform program

    -------------------------------------------------------------*/

#include <windows.h>
#include "mfx.h"
#include "dlg.h"

BMP_256COLOR     BITMAP        256color.bmp

/* a table of all the strings Test uses */
STRINGTABLE
BEGIN
    IDS_APPNAME,       "MFXF"
    IDS_TITLE,         "Metafile Transform"
END


/* a script for the menu Test displays */
MENU_MAIN MENU
BEGIN
    POPUP "&Metafile"
    BEGIN
        MENUITEM "&Bitmap"         IDM_BITMAP
        MENUITEM "&Fonts"          IDM_FONTS
        MENUITEM "&Path"           IDM_PATH
        MENUITEM "Pe&ns"           IDM_PENS
        MENUITEM SEPARATOR
        MENUITEM "&About"          IDM_ABOUT
    END
    MENUITEM "&Xform!"             IDM_XFORM
END

DLG_XFORM DIALOG 6, 18, 160, 139
STYLE DS_MODALFRAME | WS_POPUP | WS_VISIBLE | WS_CAPTION | WS_SYSMENU
CAPTION "Metafile Xform Settings"
FONT 8, "Helv"
```

```
BEGIN
    LTEXT           "x axis", -1, 63, 4, 20, 8
    LTEXT           "y axis", -1, 103, 4, 20, 8
    AUTOCHECKBOX    "&Shift", IDD_TOGGLE_SHIFT, 17, 19, 33, 10, \
                    WS_GROUP | WS_TABSTOP
    EDITTEXT        IDD_EDIT_SHIFTX, 56, 16, 32, 12, ES_AUTOHSCROLL
    EDITTEXT        IDD_EDIT_SHIFTY, 97, 16, 32, 12, ES_AUTOHSCROLL
    AUTOCHECKBOX    "Shea&r", IDD_TOGGLE_SHEAR, 17, 30, 30, 10
    EDITTEXT        IDD_EDIT_SHEARX, 56, 29, 32, 12, ES_AUTOHSCROLL
    EDITTEXT        IDD_EDIT_SHEARY, 97, 29, 32, 12, ES_AUTOHSCROLL
    AUTOCHECKBOX    "&Scale", IDD_TOGGLE_SCALE, 17, 41, 30, 10
    EDITTEXT        IDD_EDIT_SCALEX, 56, 42, 32, 12, ES_AUTOHSCROLL
    EDITTEXT        IDD_EDIT_SCALEY, 97, 42, 32, 12, ES_AUTOHSCROLL
    AUTOCHECKBOX    "&Reflect", IDD_TOGGLE_REFLECT, 17, 63, 34, 10
    GROUPBOX        "", -1, 57, 52, 72, 26
    AUTOCHECKBOX    "", IDD_FLIPX, 68, 63, 14, 10
    AUTOCHECKBOX    "", IDD_FLIPY, 106, 63, 19, 10
    AUTOCHECKBOX    "Ro&tate", IDD_TOGGLE_ROTATE, 17, 89, 32, 10
    EDITTEXT        IDD_EDIT_ROTATE, 77, 89, 32, 12, ES_AUTOHSCROLL
    DEFPUSHBUTTON   "OK", IDOK, 13, 115, 40, 14, WS_GROUP
    PUSHBUTTON      "&Defaults", IDD_DEFAULT, 59, 115, 40, 14
    PUSHBUTTON      "&Cancel", IDCANCEL, 105, 115, 40, 14, WS_TABSTOP
END

/* template for the about dialog box */
DLG_ABOUT DIALOG 17, 18, 114, 68
STYLE DS_MODALFRAME | WS_POPUP | WS_VISIBLE | WS_CAPTION | WS_SYSMENU
CAPTION "About MFX"
FONT 8, "Helv"
BEGIN
    CTEXT           "Metafile Transform", -1, 0, 7, 114, 8
    CTEXT           "by",               -1, 0, 15, 114, 8
    CTEXT           "Myers && Hamer",   -1, 0, 25, 114, 8
    CTEXT           "version 1.0",      -1, 0, 35, 114, 8
    LTEXT           "©1993",            -1, 12, 51, 25, 8
    DEFPUSHBUTTON   "OK", IDOK, 81, 50, 30, 14, WS_GROUP
END
```

The Main Module

The main module concerns itself primarily with Windows messages. Other modules set matrix transformations, initialize the program and the metafiles, and run the dialog box. mfx.c contains WinMain, the window procedure, all the message handlers, and utility procedures for setting transformations, realizing palettes, and responding to errors.

```
/*------------------------------------------------------------------

          MFX.C

          A program to display metafiles and observe their response
          to various global coordinate transformations.

          FUNCTIONS
               WinMain                    receive and dispatch messages
               Init                       initialize program data
               RegisterMfxClass           register program's window class
               Mfx_WndProc                sort out messages for main window
               Mfx_OnCommand              process menu commands
               Mfx_OnPaint                display currently selected metafile
               Mfx_OnDestroy              end program
               DoTransform                set world transformation matrix
               RealizeEnhMetaFilePalette   realize metafile's palette
               ShowErrorMsg               tell user when something goes wrong

          from Mastering Windows NT Programming
          copyright 1993 by Brian Myers & Eric Hamer


          --------------------------------------------------------------*/

#define STRICT
#include <windows.h>
#include <windowsx.h>
#include "mfx.h"


/*------------------------------------------------------------------
          PROTOTYPES of local procedures
          --------------------------------------------------------------*/

int WINAPI WinMain( HINSTANCE hinstThis, HINSTANCE hinstPrev,
     LPSTR lpszCmdLine, int iCmdShow );
```

```
static void Mfx_OnCommand( HWND hWnd, int iCmd, HWND hwndCtl, UINT uCode );
static void Mfx_OnPaint( HWND hWnd );
static void Mfx_OnDestroy( HWND hWnd );
static void DoTransform( HDC hDC );
static BOOL RealizeEnhMetaFilePalette( HDC hDC, HENHMETAFILE hEMF );
static void ShowErrorMsg( LPSTR lpszFile, int iLine );

/*----------------------------------------------------------------
          GLOBAL VARIABLE
     ------------------------------------------------------------*/

SETTINGS current;                      // XFORM settings from Xform dialog

/*----------------------------------------------------------------
          STATIC VARIABLES
     ------------------------------------------------------------*/

char szTitle[TITLE_BUFSIZE];          // caption for window

HENHMETAFILE hEMF;
/*----------------------------------------------------------------
          WIN MAIN
          Calls initializing procedures and runs the message loop
     ------------------------------------------------------------*/

int WINAPI WinMain (
    HINSTANCE hinstThis,
    HINSTANCE hinstPrev,
    LPSTR lpszCmdLine,
    int iCmdShow )
{
    MSG msg;

    SetDefaults( &current );

    if (!Init( hinstThis, iCmdShow ))
    {
        return( FALSE );
    }

    // keep getting messages until one says "QUIT"
    while (GetMessage( &msg, NULL, 0, 0 ))
    {
        TranslateMessage( &msg );
        DispatchMessage( &msg );
```

```
    }

    return( msg.wParam );
    UNREFERENCED_PARAMETER( hinstPrev );
    UNREFERENCED_PARAMETER( lpszCmdLine );
}

/*------------------------------------------------------------
        MFX WINDOW PROCEDURE
        Every message for this program ends up here.
   --------------------------------------------------------------*/

LRESULT WINAPI Mfx_WndProc (
    HWND hWnd,
    UINT uMessage,
    WPARAM wParam,
    LPARAM lParam )
{

    switch (uMessage)
    {
        HANDLE_MSG( hWnd, WM_PAINT, Mfx_OnPaint );

        HANDLE_MSG(hWnd, WM_COMMAND, Mfx_OnCommand );

        HANDLE_MSG( hWnd, WM_DESTROY, Mfx_OnDestroy );

        default:
            return( DefWindowProc(hWnd, uMessage, wParam, lParam) );
    }

    return( 0 );                    // return 0 for success
}

/*------------------------------------------------------------
        COMMAND PROCEDURE
        Process WM_COMMAND messages here.
   --------------------------------------------------------------*/

static void Mfx_OnCommand (
    HWND hWnd,
    int iCmd,
    HWND hwndCtl,
    UINT uCode )
```

```
{
    HENHMETAFILE hemfTemp;

    switch (iCmd)
    {
        case IDM_BITMAP:        // show bitmap metafile
            hemfTemp = MakeBitmapMF( hWnd );
            if (hemfTemp)
            {
                DeleteEnhMetaFile( hEMF );
                hEMF = hemfTemp;
                InvalidateRect( hWnd, NULL, TRUE );
                UpdateWindow( hWnd );
            }
            else
            {
                ShowErrorMsg( __FILE__, __LINE__ );
            }
            break;

        case IDM_FONTS:        // show fonts metafile
            hemfTemp = MakeFontsMF( hWnd );
            if (hemfTemp)
            {
                DeleteEnhMetaFile( hEMF );
                hEMF = hemfTemp;
                InvalidateRect( hWnd, NULL, TRUE );
                UpdateWindow( hWnd );
            }
            else
            {
                ShowErrorMsg( __FILE__, __LINE__ );
            }
            break;

        case IDM_PATH:        // show path metafile
            hemfTemp = MakePathMF( hWnd );
            if (hemfTemp)
            {
                DeleteEnhMetaFile( hEMF );
                hEMF = hemfTemp;
                InvalidateRect( hWnd, NULL, TRUE );
                UpdateWindow( hWnd );
            }
            else
```

```
            {
                ShowErrorMsg( __FILE__, __LINE__ );
            }
            break;

        case IDM_PENS:              // show pens metafile
            hemfTemp = MakePensMF( hWnd );
            if (hemfTemp)
            {
                DeleteEnhMetaFile( hEMF );
                hEMF = hemfTemp;
                InvalidateRect( hWnd, NULL, TRUE );
                UpdateWindow( hWnd );
            }
            else
            {
                ShowErrorMsg( __FILE__, __LINE__ );
            }
            break;

        case IDM_XFORM:                         // change transformation matrix
            DoTransformDlg( hWnd );
            break;

        case IDM_ABOUT:                     // show about box
            DialogBox( GetWindowInstance(hWnd),
                MAKEINTRESOURCE(DLG_ABOUT), hWnd, About_DlgProc );
            break;
    }

    return;
    UNREFERENCED_PARAMETER( hwndCtl );
    UNREFERENCED_PARAMETER( uCode );
}


/*-----------------------------------------------------------------
        PAINT PROCEDURE
        Process WM_PAINT messages here.
    -----------------------------------------------------------------*/

static void Mfx_OnPaint ( HWND hWnd )
{
    HINSTANCE hInst;            // current instance
    PAINTSTRUCT ps;             // information about what to draw
    HDC hDC;                    // display context
```

```
RECT rClient;                 // coordinates of window's client area
ENHMETAHEADER emh;            // info from the metafile
RECT rBounds;                 // area to display metafile
HPEN hPen, hpenOld;           // pen for drawing quadrant lines
int iHorzSize, iVertSize;     // screen dimensions

hInst = GetWindowInstance( hWnd );
hDC = BeginPaint( hWnd, &ps );

/* allow transformations */
SetGraphicsMode( hDC, GM_ADVANCED );

/* use hundredths of a millimeter for logical units */
SetMapMode( hDC, MM_HIMETRIC );

/* set origin to center of client area */
GetClientRect( hWnd, &rClient );
SetViewportOrgEx( hDC, rClient.right/2, rClient.bottom/2, NULL );

/* make a dotted pen for drawing x and y axes */
hPen = CreatePen( PS_DOT, 1, RGB(0,0,0) );
if (hPen)
{
    hpenOld = SelectPen( hDC, hPen );
}

/* get screen dimensions in hundredths of a millimeter */
iHorzSize = GetDeviceCaps( hDC, HORZSIZE ) * 100;
iVertSize = GetDeviceCaps( hDC, VERTSIZE ) * 100;

/* draw the x and y axes, marking quadrants in the client area */
MoveToEx( hDC, -iHorzSize/2, 0, NULL );
LineTo( hDC, iHorzSize/2, 0 );
MoveToEx( hDC, 0, -iVertSize/2, NULL );
LineTo( hDC, 0, iVertSize/2 );

if (hPen)
{
    SelectPen( hDC, hpenOld );
    DeletePen( hPen );
}

/* set the world transformation matrix */
DoTransform( hDC );
```

```c
    /* get info from the metafile */
    GetEnhMetaFileHeader( hEMF, sizeof(ENHMETAHEADER), &emh );

    /* set the area where the metafile will appear */
    rBounds.left   = 0;
    rBounds.top    = emh.rclFrame.bottom - emh.rclFrame.top;
    rBounds.right  = emh.rclFrame.right - emh.rclFrame.left;
    rBounds.bottom = 0;

    /* ask the system to provide any colors the metafile needs */
    RealizeEnhMetaFilePalette( hDC, hEMF );

    /* display the metafile */
    SetCursor( LoadCursor(hInst, IDC_WAIT) );
    PlayEnhMetaFile( hDC, hEMF, (LPRECT)&rBounds );
    SetCursor( LoadCursor(hInst, IDC_ARROW) );

    EndPaint( hWnd, &ps );
    return;
}

/*-------------------------------------------------------------------
        MFX_ONDESTROY
   --------------------------------------------------------------------*/

static void Mfx_OnDestroy ( HWND hWnd )
{
    if (hEMF)
    {
        DeleteEnhMetaFile( hEMF );
    }
    PostQuitMessage( 0 );   // tell WinMain to quit

    return;
    UNREFERENCED_PARAMETER( hWnd );
}

/*-------------------------------------------------------------------
        DO TRANSFORM
        Read the global settings variable ("current") and modify
        the world transformation matrix accordingly.
   --------------------------------------------------------------------*/
```

```
static void DoTransform ( HDC hDC )
{
    BOOL bDoneFirst = FALSE;

    // After the first matrix entry is set, bDone will be TRUE, so all
    // remaining matrix modifications will use a right multiply.

    /* if the user selected shift, modify the transformation matrix */
    if (current.bShift)
    {
        Shift( hDC, current.iShiftX, current.iShiftY, FALSE );
        bDoneFirst = TRUE;
    }

    /* if the user selected shear, modify the transformation matrix */
    if (current.bShear)
    {
        Shear( hDC, current.flShearX, current.flShearY, bDoneFirst );
        bDoneFirst = TRUE;
    }

    /* if the user selected scale, modify the transformation matrix */
    if (current.bScale)
    {
        Scale( hDC, current.flScaleX, current.flScaleY, bDoneFirst );
        bDoneFirst = TRUE;
    }

    /* if the user selected reflect, modify the transformation matrix */
    if (current.bReflect)
    {
        Reflect( hDC, current.bFlipX, current.bFlipY, bDoneFirst );
        bDoneFirst = TRUE;
    }

    /* if the user selected rotate, modify the transformation matrix */
    if (current.bRotate)
    {
        Rotate( hDC, current.iAngle, bDoneFirst );
        bDoneFirst = TRUE;
    }

    return;
}
```

```
/*-------------------------------------------------------------------
        REALIZE ENHANCED METAFILE PALETTE
        If the metafile carries palette information, create
        and realize a palette.
    ----------------------------------------------------------------*/

static BOOL RealizeEnhMetaFilePalette (
    HDC hDC,
    HENHMETAFILE hEMF )
{
    ENHMETAHEADER emh;                  // info from the metafile
    PLOGPALETTE pPal;                   // data from metafile's color table
    HPALETTE hPal, hpalOld;             // new palette and default palette
    UINT uResult;                       // return value for error mfxing

    /* extract information from the metafile */
    uResult = GetEnhMetaFileHeader( hEMF, sizeof(ENHMETAHEADER), &emh );
    if (uResult == 0)
    {
        return( FALSE );                // FAIL: couldn't get info
    }

    /* does the metafile have a palette to realize? */
    if (emh.nPalEntries == 0)
    {
        return( TRUE );                 // SUCCEED: no need for palette at all
    }

    /* allocate space to hold the metafile's logical palette info */
    pPal = GlobalAllocPtr( GHND, sizeof(LOGPALETTE)
                                + sizeof(PALETTEENTRY)
                                * emh.nPalEntries );
    if (!pPal)
    {
        return( FALSE );                // FAIL: allocation error
    }

    /* initialize the LOGPALETTE structure */
    pPal->palVersion    = PALVERSION;
    pPal->palNumEntries = (WORD)emh.nPalEntries;
    uResult = GetEnhMetaFilePaletteEntries(
                    hEMF,
                    (UINT)emh.nPalEntries,
                    pPal->palPalEntry );
```

515

```
    if (uResult == GDI_ERROR)
    {
        GlobalFreePtr( pPal );
        return( FALSE );                 // FAIL: couldn't get palette info
    }

    /* create a palette object from the LOGPALETTE */
    hPal = CreatePalette( pPal );
    if (!hPal)
    {
        GlobalFreePtr( pPal );
        return( FALSE );                 // FAIL: couldn't create palette
    }

    /* select and realize the palette */
    hpalOld = SelectPalette( hDC, hPal, FALSE );
    uResult = RealizePalette( hDC );

    /* clean up */
    SelectPalette( hDC, hpalOld, FALSE );
    DeletePalette( hPal );
    GlobalFreePtr( pPal );
    return( uResult != GDI_ERROR );      // did RealizePalette succeed?
}

/*-------------------------------------------------------------------
        SHOW ERROR MESSAGE
        Receives line number where error occurred and displays it
        as part of a system error message describing the most
        recent error. Relies on a global variable, hwndMain.
    -------------------------------------------------------------------*/

static void ShowErrorMsg (
    LPSTR lpszFile,
    int iLine )
{
    LPVOID lpvMessage;                       // temporary message buffer
    char *pMsg;

    /* retrieve a message from the system message table */
    FormatMessage(
        FORMAT_MESSAGE_ALLOCATE_BUFFER | FORMAT_MESSAGE_FROM_SYSTEM,
        NULL,                                    // ignored
        GetLastError(),                          // message ID
        MAKELANGID(LANG_ENGLISH, SUBLANG_ENGLISH_US),    // message language
```

```
     (LPTSTR)&lpvMessage,              // address of buffer pointer
     0,                                // minimum buffer size
     NULL );                          // no other arguments

/* allocate a larger buffer and append the line number to the end */
pMsg = LocalAlloc( LHND, lstrlen(lpvMessage) + lstrlen(lpszFile) + 10 );
wsprintf( pMsg, "%s (%s : %u)",
            (LPSTR)lpvMessage, (LPSTR)lpszFile, iLine );

/* display the message in a message box */
MessageBox( NULL, pMsg, "Metafile Xform Message",
            MB_ICONEXCLAMATION ¦ MB_OK );

/* release the buffers allocated by FormatMessage and by us */
LocalFree( lpvMessage );
LocalFree( pMsg );

return;
}
```

The Transformations Module

The paint procedure in the main module relies on routines from xform.c to set the values for the transformation matrix. Together the routines featured here make it easy to select and merge transformations without needing to remember, for example, whether the y-scaling field is **eM21** or **eM22**. Most of the routines accept a device context, one or two transformation values, and a Boolean variable named bCombine. When the Boolean variable is **FALSE**, the routines replace the existing matrix with a new transformation. When it is **TRUE**, they merge the new transformation into the existing matrix. Because they always use right-hand multiplication, successive transformations are applied in the order you set them. Metafile Transform feeds values from the Xform dialog controls directly into these procedures to let you call them interactively.

The Rotate procedure accepts a signed integer indicating the number of degrees to spin the coordinate space. Rotate takes into account the current mapping mode to ensure that the spin is always counter-clockwise.

Reflect flips the coordinate space horizontally (backwards) and vertically (upside down) in response to two Boolean variables. Setting either to **TRUE** inverts one axis.

RotateInPlace is another version of the procedure listed earlier in the chapter. This version is shorter because it can call the Shift and Rotate routines to do most of the work. The path metafile in init.c rotates its image by calling RotateInPlace.

```
/*------------------------------------------------------------------

        XFORM.C
        A set of procedures for setting the XFORM transformation
        values in a DC. (The DC must already be set to the
        GM_ADVANCED graphics mode.)

        FUNCTIONS
                Scale           stretch image
                Shift           translate image
                Rotate          spin coordinate space
                Reflect         invert coordinate space
                Shear           skew or distort image
                DefaultXform    clear all transformations
                RotateInPlace   rotate around a given point

        from Mastering Windows NT Programming
        copyright 1993 by Brian Myers & Eric Hamer

        ------------------------------------------------------------------*/

#define STRICT
#include <windows.h>
#include <windowsx.h>
#include <math.h>                       // sin() cos()
#include "mfx.h"

/*------------------------------------------------------------------
        MANIFEST CONSTANT
        ------------------------------------------------------------------*/

#define PI 3.141592653589793

/*------------------------------------------------------------------
        SCALE
        Set a matrix to stretch or shrink an image along either axis
        ------------------------------------------------------------------*/

void Scale (
    HDC hDC,                            // device context
```

```
        FLOAT flFactorX,                    // horizontal scaling factor
        FLOAT flFactorY,                    // vertical scaling factor
        BOOL bCombine )                     // TRUE to merge with current matrix
{
        XFORM xForm;

        xForm.eM11 = flFactorX;
        xForm.eM12 = (FLOAT)0.0;
        xForm.eM21 = (FLOAT)0.0;
        xForm.eM22 = flFactorY;
        xForm.eDx  = (FLOAT)0.0;
        xForm.eDy  = (FLOAT)0.0;

        if (bCombine)
        {
            ModifyWorldTransform( hDC, &xForm, MWT_RIGHTMULTIPLY );
        }
        else
        {
            SetWorldTransform( hDC, &xForm );
        }
         return;
}


/*-------------------------------------------------------------------
        SHIFT
        Translate an image, sliding it intact from one part of the
        coordinate space to another.
        -------------------------------------------------------------*/

void Shift (
    HDC hDC,                                // device context
    int cx,                                 // horizontal displacement
    int cy,                                 // vertical displacement
    BOOL bCombine )                         // TRUE to merge with current matrix
{
    XFORM xForm;

    xForm.eM11 = (FLOAT)1.0;
    xForm.eM12 = (FLOAT)0.0;
    xForm.eM21 = (FLOAT)0.0;
    xForm.eM22 = (FLOAT)1.0;
    xForm.eDx  = (FLOAT)cx;
    xForm.eDy  = (FLOAT)cy;
```

```
    if (bCombine)
    {
        ModifyWorldTransform( hDC, &xForm, MWT_RIGHTMULTIPLY );
    }
    else
    {
        SetWorldTransform( hDC, &xForm );
    }
    return;
}


/*-----------------------------------------------------------------
        REFLECT
        Invert the x or y axis to produce mirror images
    ---------------------------------------------------------------*/

void Reflect (
    HDC hDC,
    BOOL bFlipX,
    BOOL bFlipY,
    BOOL bCombine )
{
    XFORM xForm;

    xForm.eM11 = (FLOAT)(bFlipX ? -1 : 1);
    xForm.eM12 = (FLOAT)0;
    xForm.eM21 = (FLOAT)0;
    xForm.eM22 = (FLOAT)(bFlipY ? -1 : 1);
    xForm.eDx  = (FLOAT)0;
    xForm.eDy  = (FLOAT)0;

    if (bCombine)
    {
        ModifyWorldTransform( hDC, &xForm, MWT_RIGHTMULTIPLY );
    }
    else
    {
        SetWorldTransform( hDC, &xForm );
    }
    return;
}
```

```
/*---------------------------------------------------------------
        ROTATE
        Spin the coordinate space a given number of degrees counter-
        clockwise around the origin.
    -----------------------------------------------------------------*/

void Rotate (
    HDC hDC,                            // device context
    int iAngle,                         // distance to rotate
    BOOL bCombine )                     // TRUE to merge with current matrix
{
    XFORM xForm;
    FLOAT flCos, flSin;

    flCos = (FLOAT)cos( ((double)iAngle)*(PI/180) );
    flSin = (FLOAT)sin( ((double)iAngle)*(PI/180) );

    // The values for rotating counter-clockwise differ
    // slightly depending on the direction of the y axis,
    // which in MM_TEXT points down and in all other
    // modes points up.

    if (GetMapMode(hDC) == MM_TEXT)              // positive y points down
    {
        xForm.eM12 = -flSin;
        xForm.eM21 = flSin;
    }
    else                                         // positive y points up
    {
        xForm.eM12 = flSin;
        xForm.eM21 = -flSin;
    }

    xForm.eM11 = flCos;
    xForm.eM22 = flCos;
    xForm.eDx  = (FLOAT)0;
    xForm.eDy  = (FLOAT)0;

    if (bCombine)
    {
        ModifyWorldTransform( hDC, &xForm, MWT_RIGHTMULTIPLY );
    }
    else
    {
        SetWorldTransform( hDC, &xForm );
```

```
    }
    return;
}

/*----------------------------------------------------------------
        SHEAR
        Twist or distort the image, skewing it so the sides no
        longer align.
    ------------------------------------------------------------*/

void Shear (
    HDC hDC,                        // device context
    FLOAT flShearX,                 // degree of horizontal skew
    FLOAT flShearY,                 // degree of vertical skew
    BOOL bCombine )                 // TRUE to merge with current matrix
{
    XFORM xForm;
    xForm.eM11 = (FLOAT)1;
    xForm.eM12 = (FLOAT)flShearY;
    xForm.eM21 = (FLOAT)flShearX;
    xForm.eM22 = (FLOAT)1;
    xForm.eDx  = (FLOAT)0;
    xForm.eDy  = (FLOAT)0;

    if (bCombine)
    {
        ModifyWorldTransform( hDC, &xForm, MWT_RIGHTMULTIPLY );
    }
    else
    {
        SetWorldTransform( hDC, &xForm );
    }
    return;
}

/*----------------------------------------------------------------
        DEFAULT XFORM
        Restore the default identity matrix to the DC. (Note that
        SetGraphicsMode( hDC, GM_COMPATIBLE ) fails unless the
        current matrix is the identity matrix.)
    ------------------------------------------------------------*/

void DefaultXform ( HDC hDC )
{
    ModifyWorldTransform( hDC, NULL, MWT_IDENTITY );
```

```
        return;
}

/*------------------------------------------------------------------
        ROTATE IN PLACE
        Sets the world coordinate transformation matrix to cause
        rotation around a point other than the origin. All output
        commands called after RotateInPlace will be rotated around
        the point (x,y). To rotate several figures in different
        places, call RotateInPlace once for each new figure.
        ----------------------------------------------------------*/

void RotateInPlace (
    HDC hDC,                        // device context
    int x,                          // x coordinate of new center
    int y,                          // y coordinate of new center
    int iAngle )                    // distance to spin
{
    // RotateInPlace works by combining three transformations.
    //    1. Shift image to origin
    //    2. Spin image around origin
    //    3. Shift rotated image back to starting point (x,y)

    Shift( hDC, -x, -y, FALSE );    // translate to origin
    Rotate( hDC, iAngle, TRUE );    // spin
    Shift( hDC, x, y, TRUE );       // return to starting place
    return;
}
```

The Initialization Module

The procedures in this module register and create the program window, initialize the global settings variable, current, and create the program's four metafiles on demand. Each metafile uses different GDI features.

The bitmap metafile displays a 256-color bitmap. Although the bitmap is attached to the program's resources, MFX does not call **LoadBitmap** to get it. That's because **LoadBitmap** always converts the resource to a device-dependent bitmap (DDB), and it pays no attention to the palette in the process. That means a 256-color DIB loses color information if you retrieve it with **LoadBitmap**. To load a DIB resource without converting it to a DDB, call **LoadResource** instead. We've written a short procedure called `LoadDIBResource` to handle the task. It returns a handle to a packed DIB. Chapter 10 explains more about DIBs and DDBs. As you can see from the code, though, working with DIBs requires a set of utilities to parse the DIB header structure and retrieve useful bits of information such as the number of colors and the address where the image bits begin.

The most complex of these utilities, `PaletteFromDIB`, reads the RGB values from the DIB's color table and creates a palette object from them. `MakeBitmapMF` realizes the palette as it creates the metafile. When the GDI adds a **`RealizePalette`** instruction to the metafile, it also modifies the **`nPalEntries`** field of the metafile's header and inserts a color table based on the palette between the metafile's header and its records. The paint procedure in mfx.c checks for the presence of a color table and, if it finds one, calls `RealizeEnhMetaFilePalette` to make the system select the necessary colors. As mentioned earlier, the **`EMR_REALIZEPALETTE`** record always gets low background priority. If one program plays several colorful metafiles, it can't give them all foreground priority. Realizing the metafile's palette in advance ensures that the metafile receives all the colors it needs, not just whatever approximations the current color set allows.

The font metafile creates three fonts—one TrueType, one vector, and one raster—to show that raster fonts do not transform as well as the other two. The GDI can scale raster fonts only to even multiples of the original size, and it cannot rotate them. Figure 9.8 shows the fonts metafile before and after a transformation that enlarged the image, inverted the x axis, and rotated the image 20 degrees. The GDI correctly calculated the point where the raster font string should begin, but it can't rotate or invert raster fonts. Also, the raster font does not scale as well as the TrueType and vector fonts.

The path metafile, visible in Figure 9.7, creates a region in the shape of the letter "Q" and colors the region with a hatched brush. Figure 9.9 shows the same metafile translated, scaled, and sheared. Regions in Windows metafiles do not scale well, but regions created from paths, like this one, work from logical coordinates and scale perfectly. Notice too that the hatch marks in the brush do *not* scale. They look the same in both figures.

FIGURE 9.8:

The fonts metafile before and after a series of transformations

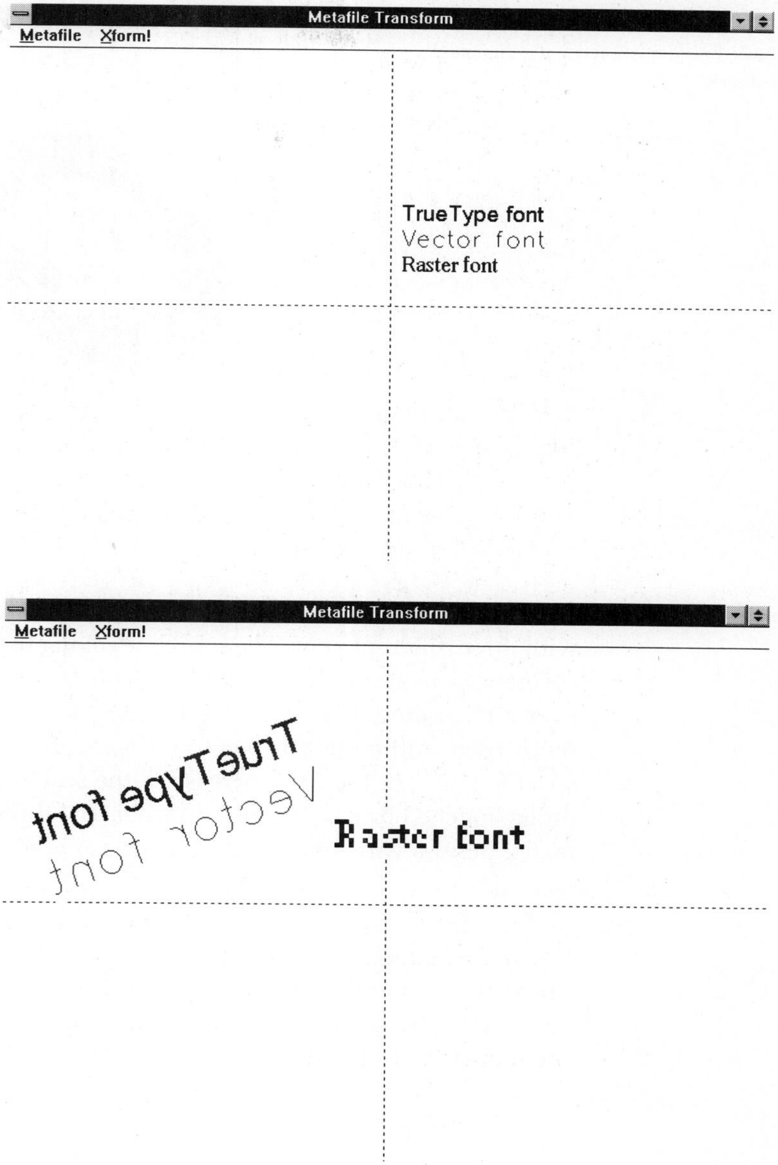

FIGURE 9.9:

Scaled region colored with a hatched brush

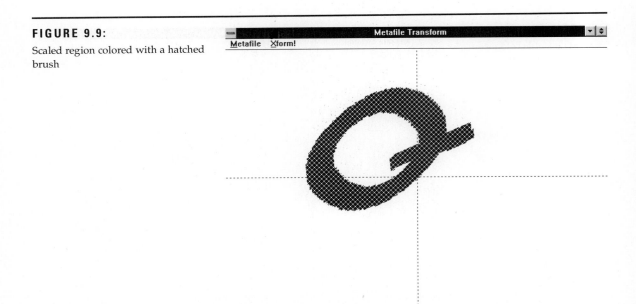

Figure 9.10 shows the pen metafile before and after scaling. This metafile draws with three different pens. The solid lines along the left and bottom sides come from cosmetic pens. Because cosmetic pens do not scale, the lines remain 1 pixel wide even after scaling. The top and right sides, however, were drawn with a dotted geometric pen. Although this pen too has a width of 1, the width of the line and the spacing between the dots increase in the scaled version. Geometric pen patterns, unlike hatched brush patterns, do scale. The three bars are also drawn with a geometric pen—a wide one—and they scale as well.

FIGURE 9.10:

Pen metafile before and after scaling

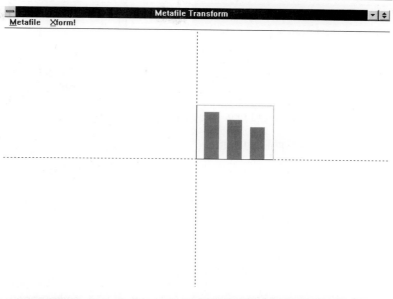

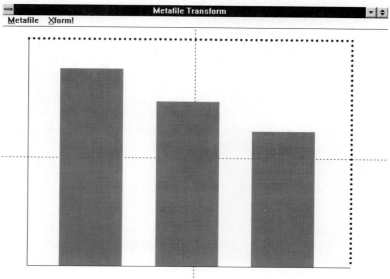

```
/*-----------------------------------------------------------------

        INIT.C

        Initialization module for the Metafile Transform program.
        On startup, registers the window class and creates the window.
        Also creates various metafiles on demand. The bitmap metafile
        works with a DIB and requires a number of supporting DIB-
        related utility procedures.

        PUBLIC FUNCTIONS
                Init                    initialize program data
                SetDefaults             initialize transformation settings
                MakeBitmapMF            create a metafile with a bitmap
                MakeFontsMF             create a metafile with fonts
                MakePathMF              create a metafile with a path
                MakePensMF              create a metafile with pens

        STATIC FUNCTIONS
                RegisterMfxClass        register program's window class
                PixToMm                 convert pixels to .01 mm
                LoadDIBResource         load a DIB from resources
                GetDIBImagePtr          find first byte of image data in a DIB
                GetClrTableSize         determine size of DIB's color table
                GetNumColors            count number of colors in DIB's color table
                PaletteFromDIB          create a palette from DIB's color table

        from Mastering Windows NT Programming
        copyright 1993 by Brian Myers & Eric Hamer

        -----------------------------------------------------------------*/

#define STRICT
#include <windows.h>
#include <windowsx.h>
#include "mfx.h"

/*-----------------------------------------------------------------
        EXTERNAL and STATIC VARIABLES
        -----------------------------------------------------------------*/

extern HENHMETAFILE hEMF;

char szAppName[NAME_BUFSIZE];           // application name
```

```
/*------------------------------------------------------------------
        PROTOTYPES for static functions
    ----------------------------------------------------------------*/

static BOOL RegisterMfxClass( HINSTANCE hinstThis );
static void PixToMm( HDC hDC, LPPOINT lppt, int iNumPoints );
static LPVOID LoadDIBResource( HWND hWnd, LPTSTR lpszResName );
static LPVOID GetDIBImagePtr( LPBITMAPINFOHEADER lpbih );
static WORD GetClrTableSize( LPBITMAPINFOHEADER lpbih );
static WORD GetNumColors( LPBITMAPINFOHEADER lpbih );
static HPALETTE PaletteFromDIB( LPBITMAPINFO lpbi );


/*------------------------------------------------------------------
        INIT
        Initializes window and data for the application, if
        necessary; then initializes data and creates the window
        for this instance.
    ----------------------------------------------------------------*/
BOOL Init (
    HINSTANCE hinstThis,
    int iCmdShow )
{

    HWND hWnd;
     char szTitle[TITLE_BUFSIZE];        // caption for window

    // initialize global variables
    LoadString( hinstThis, IDS_APPNAME, szAppName, sizeof(szAppName) );
    LoadString( hinstThis, IDS_TITLE,   szTitle,   sizeof(szTitle)   );

    // register the window class for program's main window
    if (!RegisterMfxClass( hinstThis ))
    {
        return( FALSE );
    }

    // Make a class "Mfx" window exist for this instance
    hWnd = CreateWindow (
        szAppName,                      // window class name
        szTitle,                        // string for window caption
        WS_OVERLAPPEDWINDOW,            // window style
        CW_USEDEFAULT,                  //   x  ( --WINDOW POSITION-- )
        CW_USEDEFAULT,                  //   y  ( let Windows set a   )
        CW_USEDEFAULT,                  //   cx ( default position    )
        CW_USEDEFAULT,                  //   cy ( and size            )
```

529

```
            NULL,                           // no parent window
            NULL,                           // no menu for this window
            hinstThis,                      // who created this window
            NULL );                         // no parameters to pass on
    if (!hWnd)
    {
        return( FALSE );
    }

    hEMF = MakeFontsMF( hWnd );
    if (!hEMF)
    {
        MessageBox( hWnd, "Metafile Xform", "Couldn't make metafile", MB_OK );
        return( FALSE );
    }

    ShowWindow( hWnd, iCmdShow );
    UpdateWindow( hWnd );
    return( TRUE );
}


/*-------------------------------------------------------------------
        REGISTER MFX CLASS
        Gives the system information about the type of window
        the program wants for its main window.
        -----------------------------------------------------------*/

static BOOL RegisterMfxClass ( HINSTANCE hinstThis )
{
    WNDCLASS wc;

    // fill structure with information about this window class
    wc.lpszClassName  = szAppName;
    wc.hInstance      = hinstThis;
    wc.lpfnWndProc    = Mfx_WndProc;
    wc.hCursor        = LoadCursor( NULL, IDC_ARROW );
    wc.hIcon          = LoadIcon( NULL, IDI_APPLICATION );
    wc.lpszMenuName   = MAKEINTRESOURCE( MENU_MAIN );
    wc.hbrBackground  = (HBRUSH)(COLOR_WINDOW + 1);
    wc.style          = CS_HREDRAW | CS_VREDRAW;
    wc.cbClsExtra     = 0;
    wc.cbWndExtra     = 0;

    return( RegisterClass(&wc) );
}
```

```
/*------------------------------------------------------------------
        SET DEFAULTS
        Initialize the global settings variable to clear all
        values and disable all transformations.
        ---------------------------------------------------------------*/

void SetDefaults ( PSETTINGS pData )

return;
{
    pData->bShift   = FALSE;
    pData->iShiftX  = 0;
    pData->iShiftY  = 0;
    pData->bShear   = FALSE;
    pData->flShearX = (FLOAT)0;
    pData->flShearY = (FLOAT)0;
    pData->bScale   = FALSE;
    pData->flScaleX = (FLOAT)1;
    pData->flScaleY = (FLOAT)1;
    pData->bReflect = FALSE;
    pData->bFlipX   = FALSE;
    pData->bFlipY   = FALSE;
    pData->bRotate  = FALSE;
    pData->iAngle   = 0;
}


/*------------------------------------------------------------------
        MAKE BITMAP METAFILE
        Create a metafile that displays a 256-color DIB to show how
        metafiles deal with palettes.
        ---------------------------------------------------------------*/

HENHMETAFILE MakeBitmapMF ( HWND hWnd )
{
    HDC hDC, hdcMF;                     // metafile and reference DCs
    HPALETTE hPal = NULL;               // palette for the bitmap
    HENHMETAFILE hEMF = NULL;           // new metafile
    RECT rBounds;                       // rectangle surrounding the image
    LPBITMAPINFOHEADER lpbih;           // info from the bitmaps

    /* load a resource bitmap as a DIB, not as DDB */
    lpbih = LoadDIBResource( hWnd, MAKEINTRESOURCE(BMP_256COLOR) );
    if (!lpbih)
    {
```

```
    return( NULL );
}

/* create a palette based on information in the DIB's color table */
hPal = PaletteFromDIB( (LPBITMAPINFO)lpbih );

hDC = GetDC( hWnd );                    // create the reference DC
if (!hDC)
{
    return( NULL );
}
/* rBounds describes the image's boundaries in .01ths of a mm */
rBounds.left   = 0;
rBounds.top    = 0;
rBounds.right  = lpbih->biWidth;
rBounds.bottom = lpbih->biHeight;
PixToMm( hDC, (LPPOINT)&rBounds, 2 );

hdcMF = CreateEnhMetaFile(
            hDC,                        // reference DC
            NULL,                       // disk file for storage
            &rBounds,                   // bounding area in .01 mm
            NULL );                     // description string

if (hdcMF)
{
    HPALETTE hpalOld;

    if (hPal)
    {
        /* if the bitmap has a palette, begin by realizing it */
        hpalOld = SelectPalette( hdcMF, hPal, FALSE );
        RealizePalette( hdcMF );
    }

    SetDIBitsToDevice( hdcMF,           // display the bitmap
        0, 0,
        (DWORD)lpbih->biWidth,
        lpbih->biHeight,
        0, 0,
        0, (UINT)lpbih->biHeight,
        GetDIBImagePtr( lpbih ),
        (LPBITMAPINFO)lpbih,
        DIB_RGB_COLORS );
```

```
        if (hPal)                                    // clean up
        {
            SelectPalette( hDC, hpalOld, FALSE );
            DeletePalette( hPal );
        }
        hEMF = CloseEnhMetaFile( hdcMF );          // finish drawing
    }

    ReleaseDC( hWnd, hDC );
    return( hEMF );
}

/*---------------------------------------------------------------
        MAKE FONTS METAFILE
        Create a metafile with several lines of text, each written
        with a different kind of font, to show how different fonts
        respond to transformations.
        ---------------------------------------------------------*/
HENHMETAFILE MakeFontsMF ( HWND hWnd )
{
    HDC hDC, hdcMF;                     // metafile and reference DCs
    HENHMETAFILE hEMF = NULL;           // new metafile
    RECT rBounds;                       // rectangle surrounding the image

    hDC = GetDC( hWnd );                // create the reference DC
    if (!hDC)
    {
        return( NULL );
    }

    /* rBounds describes the image's boundaries in .01ths of a mm */
    rBounds.left   = 0;
    rBounds.top    = 0;
    rBounds.right  = GetSystemMetrics( SM_CXFULLSCREEN ) / 5;
    rBounds.bottom = GetSystemMetrics( SM_CYFULLSCREEN ) / 5;
    PixToMm( hDC, (LPPOINT)&rBounds, 2 );

    hdcMF = CreateEnhMetaFile(
                hDC,                     // reference DC
                NULL,                    // disk file for storage
                &rBounds,                // bounding area in .01 mm
                NULL );                  // description string
```

```
if (hdcMF)
{
    LOGFONT lf;                          // info about a requested font
    HFONT hFont, hfontOld;               // font objects
    TEXTMETRIC tm;                       // info about a physical font
    int x, y;                            // drawing coordinates

    /* create a TrueType font and write one line with it */

    FillMemory( &lf, sizeof(LOGFONT), 0 );
    lf.lfHeight = 22;                    // describe font
    lf.lfWeight = FW_NORMAL;
    lf.lfCharSet = ANSI_CHARSET;
    lf.lfOutPrecision = OUT_TT_ONLY_PRECIS;
    lf.lfPitchAndFamily = VARIABLE_PITCH | FF_SWISS;
    lstrcpy( lf.lfFaceName, "Arial" );
    hFont = CreateFontIndirect( &lf );              // create the font
    if (hFont)
    {
        hfontOld = SelectFont( hdcMF, hFont );      // select the font
        GetTextMetrics( hdcMF, &tm );

        x = (int)tm.tmAveCharWidth;                 // write the text
        y = (int)rBounds.top;
        TextOut( hdcMF, x, y, "TrueType font", 13 );

        /* adjust the y coordinate for the next line of text */
        y += (int)(tm.tmHeight + tm.tmExternalLeading);

        SelectFont( hdcMF, hfontOld );              // clean up
        DeleteFont( hFont );
    }

    /* create a vector font and write one line with it */
    lf.lfCharSet = OEM_CHARSET;                     // describe font
    lf.lfOutPrecision = OUT_DEFAULT_PRECIS;
    lf.lfPitchAndFamily = VARIABLE_PITCH | FF_MODERN;
    lstrcpy( lf.lfFaceName, "Modern" );
    hFont = CreateFontIndirect( &lf );              // create the font
    if (hFont)
    {
        hfontOld = SelectFont( hdcMF, hFont );      // select font
        GetTextMetrics( hdcMF, &tm );
```

```
        TextOut( hdcMF, x, y, "Vector font", 11 );      // write text
        y += (int)(tm.tmHeight + tm.tmExternalLeading);

        SelectFont( hdcMF, hfontOld );              // clean up
        DeleteFont( hFont );
    }

    /* create a raster font and write one line with it */

    lf.lfCharSet = ANSI_CHARSET;                     // describe font
    lf.lfOutPrecision = OUT_RASTER_PRECIS;
    lf.lfPitchAndFamily = VARIABLE_PITCH | FF_ROMAN;
    lstrcpy( lf.lfFaceName, "MS Serif" );
    hFont = CreateFontIndirect( &lf );              // create the font
    if (hFont)
    {
        hfontOld = SelectFont( hdcMF, hFont );      // select font

        TextOut( hdcMF, x, y, "Raster font", 11 );  // write text

        SelectFont( hdcMF, hfontOld );              // clean up
        DeleteFont( hFont );
    }

    hEMF = CloseEnhMetaFile( hdcMF );               // stop drawing
    }

    ReleaseDC( hWnd, hDC );
    return( hEMF );
}

/*-----------------------------------------------------------------
        MAKE PATH METAFILE
        Create a metafile containing a brushed region derived from
        a path. Let the metafile rotate the image. This metafile
        shows that regions scale well, that brush patterns never
        scale, and that a metafile may contain internal transformation
        instructions.
        --------------------------------------------------------------*/

HENHMETAFILE MakePathMF ( HWND hWnd )
{
    HDC hDC, hdcMF;                          // reference and metafile dcs
    HENHMETAFILE hEMF = NULL;                // a new metafile
    RECT rBounds, rBoundsMm;                 // rectangle surrounding the image
```

```
LOGFONT lf;                                      // font for writing "Q"
HFONT hFont, hfontOld;
SIZE sExtent;                                    // size of the character

hDC = GetDC( hWnd );                             // create the reference DC
if (!hDC)
{
    return( NULL );
}

/* create a large font for drawing the letter "Q" */
FillMemory( &lf, sizeof(LOGFONT), 0 );
lf.lfHeight = 108;
lf.lfWeight = 700;
lf.lfCharSet = ANSI_CHARSET;
lf.lfOutPrecision = OUT_TT_ONLY_PRECIS;
lf.lfPitchAndFamily = VARIABLE_PITCH | FF_SWISS;
lstrcpy( lf.lfFaceName, "Arial" );
hFont = CreateFontIndirect( &lf );
if (hFont)
{
    hfontOld = SelectFont( hDC, hFont );
}

// The bounding rectangle of the metafile will
// be the character cell surrounding the letter.
// Get the dimensions and convert them to
// hundredths of a millimeter.

GetTextExtentPoint( hDC, "Q", 1, &SExtent );
if (hFont)
{
    SelectFont( hDC, hfontOld );
}
rBounds.left   = 0;
rBounds.top    = 0;
rBounds.right  = sExtent.cx;
rBounds.bottom = sExtent.cy;
CopyRect( &rBoundsMm, &rBounds );
PixToMm( hDC, (LPPOINT)&rBoundsMm, 2 );

/* open a metafile for recording */
hdcMF = CreateEnhMetaFile(
          hDC,                                   // reference DC
          NULL,                                  // disk file for storage
```

```
            &rBoundsMm,                    // bounding area in .01 mm
            NULL );                        // description string

if (hdcMF)
{
    LOGBRUSH lb;                           // brush for coloring the letter
    HBRUSH hBrush, hbrOld;
    HRGN hRgn;                             // region outlining the letter

    if (hFont)                             // select the large font
    {
        hfontOld = SelectFont( hdcMF, hFont );
    }

    /* cause the image to appear rotated around its own center */
    SetGraphicsMode( hdcMF, GM_ADVANCED );
    RotateInPlace( hdcMF,                  // DC to modify
        rBounds.right/2,                   // x coordinate of center point
        rBounds.bottom/2,                  // y coordinate of center point
        30 );                              // degrees counter-clockwise

    /* create a path by drawing one large "Q" */
    BeginPath( hdcMF );
    SetBkMode( hdcMF, TRANSPARENT );       // don't include char cell
    TextOut( hdcMF, 0, 0, "Q", 1 );
    EndPath( hdcMF );
    // Construct a brush for coloring in the large Q.
    // The letter will be brushed with a hatch pattern.
    // The hatch lines will be white, and the space
    // between them will be black. The background mode
    // must be OPAQUE or the black part will not be drawn.

    lb.lbStyle = BS_HATCHED;
    lb.lbColor = RGB_WHITE;
    lb.lbHatch = HS_DIAGCROSS;
    hBrush = CreateBrushIndirect( &lb );
    if (hBrush)
    {
        hbrOld = SelectBrush( hdcMF, hBrush );
    }
    SetBkMode( hdcMF, OPAQUE );
    SetBkColor( hdcMF, RGB_BLACK );
```

```
        // Color in the large Q. Do this by converting it
        // to a region, outlining the region, and then
        // brushing the region's interior.

        hRgn = PathToRegion( hdcMF );
        FrameRgn( hdcMF, hRgn, GetStockBrush(BLACK_BRUSH), 1, 1 );
        PaintRgn( hdcMF, hRgn );

        /* we're through drawing; clean up */
        if (hBrush)
        {
            SelectBrush( hdcMF, hbrOld );
            DeleteBrush( hBrush );
        }
        if (hFont)
        {
            SelectFont( hdcMF, hfontOld );
        }

        /* close the metafile DC and create a metafile object */
        hEMF = CloseEnhMetaFile( hdcMF );
    }

    if (hFont)
    {
        DeleteFont( hFont );
    }

    return( hEMF );
}

/*---------------------------------------------------------------------
        MAKE PENS METAFILE
        Create a metafile that draws with several different kinds
        of pens to show how different pens respond to scaling.
    ------------------------------------------------------------------*/

HENHMETAFILE MakePensMF ( HWND hWnd )
{
    HDC hDC, hdcMF;                    // reference and metafile dcs
    HENHMETAFILE hEMF = NULL;          // new metafile
    RECT rBounds, rBoundsMm;           // rectangle around the image
```

```
hDC = GetDC( hWnd );                    // create the reference DC
if (!hDC)
{
    return( NULL );
}

// rBounds describes the image's boundaries in device units.
// rBoundsMm describes the same rectangle in .01ths of a mm.
rBounds.left   = 0;
rBounds.top    = 0;
rBounds.right  = GetSystemMetrics( SM_CXFULLSCREEN ) / 5;
rBounds.bottom = GetSystemMetrics( SM_CYFULLSCREEN ) / 5;
CopyRect( &rBoundsMm, &rBounds );
PixToMm( hDC, (LPPOINT)&rBoundsMm, 2 );

hdcMF = CreateEnhMetaFile(
            hDC,                        // reference DC
            NULL,                       // disk file for storage
            &rBoundsMm,                 // bounding area in .01 mm
            NULL );                     // description string

if (hdcMF)
{
    LOGBRUSH lb;                    // structure for setting pen attibutes
    HPEN hpenWide;                  // a wide gray geometric pen
    HPEN hpenNarrow;                // a narrow dotted geometric pen
    HPEN hpenCosmetic;              // a black cosmetic pen
    HPEN hpenOld;                   // the default pen
    UINT uPenWidth;                 // width of hpenWide
    int x;                          // an x coordinate

    /* geometric pens derive some attributes from a LOGBRUSH structure */
    lb.lbStyle = BS_SOLID;
    lb.lbColor = RGB_BLACK;
    lb.lbHatch = 0;                         // ignored without BS_HATCH

    /* create a geometric pen that matches the user's choices */
    hpenNarrow = ExtCreatePen(
            PS_GEOMETRIC | PS_DOT,
            1,                              // logical width of pen
            &lb,                            // brush for color
            0, NULL );                      // no custom style

    hpenCosmetic = ExtCreatePen(
            PS_COSMETIC | PS_SOLID,
```

```
                1,
                &lb,
                0, NULL );

lb.lbColor = RGB_GRAY;
uPenWidth = (rBounds.right - rBounds.left) / 5;
hpenWide = ExtCreatePen(
                PS_GEOMETRIC | PS_SOLID
                | PS_ENDCAP_FLAT,
                uPenWidth,
                &lb,
                0, NULL );

hpenOld = SelectPen( hdcMF, hpenNarrow );
MoveToEx( hdcMF, (int)rBounds.left, (int)rBounds.top, NULL );
LineTo( hdcMF, (int)rBounds.right, (int)rBounds.top );
LineTo( hdcMF, (int)rBounds.right, (int)rBounds.bottom );

SelectPen( hdcMF, hpenCosmetic );
LineTo( hdcMF, (int)rBounds.left, (int)rBounds.bottom );
LineTo( hdcMF, (int)rBounds.left, (int)rBounds.top );

SelectPen( hdcMF, hpenWide );
x = (int)rBounds.left + uPenWidth;
MoveToEx( hdcMF, x, (int)rBounds.bottom, NULL );
LineTo( hdcMF, x, (int)rBounds.top + (uPenWidth/2) );
x += MulDiv( 3, uPenWidth, 2 );
MoveToEx( hdcMF, x, (int)rBounds.bottom, NULL );
LineTo( hdcMF, x, (int)rBounds.top + uPenWidth );

x += MulDiv( 3, uPenWidth, 2 );
MoveToEx( hdcMF, x, (int)rBounds.bottom, NULL );
LineTo( hdcMF, x, (int)rBounds.top + (int)(uPenWidth * 1.5F) );

SelectPen( hdcMF, hpenOld );
DeletePen( hpenWide );
DeletePen( hpenNarrow );
DeletePen( hpenCosmetic );
hpenOld = NULL;

hEMF = CloseEnhMetaFile( hdcMF );
}
```

```
        ReleaseDC( hWnd, hDC );
        return( hEMF );
}

/*-------------------------------------------------------------------
        PIXELS TO MILLIMETERS
        Convert an array of point coordinates from
        pixel units to millimeters.
    -----------------------------------------------------------------*/

static void PixToMm (
    HDC hDC,
    LPPOINT lppt,
    int iNumPoints )
 {
    int iWidthMM, iHeightMM;
    int iWidthPels, iHeightPels;
    double dMMPerPelX, dMMPerPelY;
    int i;

    iWidthMM  = GetDeviceCaps( hDC, HORZSIZE );
    iHeightMM = GetDeviceCaps( hDC, VERTSIZE );
    iWidthPels  = GetDeviceCaps( hDC, HORZRES );
    iHeightPels = GetDeviceCaps( hDC, VERTRES );
    dMMPerPelX = ((double)(iWidthMM * 100)) / iWidthPels;
    dMMPerPelY = ((double)(iHeightMM * 100)) / iHeightPels;

    for  (i=0; i<iNumPoints; i++)
    {
        lppt[i].x = (LONG)(lppt[i].x * dMMPerPelX );
        lppt[i].y = (LONG)(lppt[i].y * dMMPerPelY );
    }
    return;
}

/*-------------------------------------------------------------------
        LOAD DIB RESOURCE
        Load a DIB from the program's resources without
        converting it to a DDB.
    -----------------------------------------------------------------*/

static LPVOID LoadDIBResource (
    HWND hWnd,
    LPTSTR lpszResName )
```

```
{
    HINSTANCE hInst;
    HRSRC hRes;

    hInst = GetWindowInstance( hWnd );

    hRes = FindResource( hInst, lpszResName, RT_BITMAP );
    if (!hRes)
    {
        return( NULL );
    }

    hRes = LoadResource( hInst, hRes );
    if (!hRes)
    {
        return( NULL );
    }
    return( LockResource(hRes) );
}

/*----------------------------------------------------------------
        GET POINTER TO DIB BITS
        Calculates where in a DIB the info structures end and the
        image bits begin. Assumes the DIB is packed.
    ----------------------------------------------------------------*/

static LPVOID GetDIBImagePtr ( LPBITMAPINFOHEADER lpbih )
{
    return( (LPSTR)lpbih + lpbih->biSize + GetClrTableSize(lpbih) );
}


/*----------------------------------------------------------------
        GET COLOR TABLE SIZE
        Given a pointer to the bitmap info header, determines the
        number of bytes that intercede between the header and the
        DIB's actual image bits. These bytes contain information
        about the colors used in the bitmap.

        Does not need a packed bitmap.
    ----------------------------------------------------------------*/

static WORD GetClrTableSize ( LPBITMAPINFOHEADER lpbih )
{
    WORD wNumEntries;    // number of RGBQUADS or DWORDs in color table
```

```
    if (!lpbih)
    {
        return( 0 );
    }

    if (lpbih>biCompression == BI_BITFIELDS)       // color table holds
    {                                              // 3 bit masks
        wNumEntries = 3;
    }
    else                                           // color table holds
    {                                              // RGB values
        wNumEntries = GetNumColors( lpbih );
    }
    return( (WORD)(wNumEntries * sizeof(RGBQUAD)) );
}

/*------------------------------------------------------------------
        GET NUMBER OF COLORS
        Determines how many color specifications are given in
        a DIB's color table. Does not need a packed bitmap.
        ------------------------------------------------------------*/

static WORD GetNumColors ( LPBITMAPINFOHEADER lpbih )
{
    if ( lpbih>biClrUsed != 0 )           // if the ClrUsed field is not 0,
    {                                     // then it tells how many colors
        return( (WORD)lpbih>biClrUsed );  // the bitmap actually uses
    }

    switch (lpbih>biBitCount)             // given bits per pixel, figure
    {                                     // number of colors
        case 1:
            return( 2 );

        case 4:
            return( 16 );

        case 8:
            return( 256 );

        default:                          // 16, 24, or 32 bpp: no
            return( 0 );                  // colors in color table
    }
}
```

```
/*--------------------------------------------------------------------
        PALETTE FROM DIB
        Constructs a logical palette from the color table in a
        given DIB. Needs only to see the BITMAPINFO structure.

        RETURN
        A handle to the new palette, or NULL in case of error.
   --------------------------------------------------------------------*/

static HPALETTE PaletteFromDIB ( LPBITMAPINFO lpbi )
{
    PLOGPALETTE pPal;
    HPALETTE    hPal = NULL;
    WORD        wNumColors, i;

    if (!lpbi)
    {
        return( NULL );
    }

    wNumColors = GetNumColors( (LPBITMAPINFOHEADER)lpbi );

    /* make room in memory for a LOGPALETTE structure */
    pPal = GlobalAllocPtr( GHND, sizeof(LOGPALETTE)
                          + sizeof(PALETTEENTRY)
                          * wNumColors );
    if (!pPal)
    {
        return( NULL );
    }

    /* initialize the new LOGPALETTE structure */
    pPal->palVersion    = PALVERSION;
    pPal->palNumEntries = wNumColors;

    /* copy colors from the DIB table to the LOGPALETTE */
    for (i = 0;  i < wNumColors;  i++)
    {
        pPal->palPalEntry[i].peRed   = lpbi->bmiColors[i].rgbRed;
        pPal->palPalEntry[i].peGreen = lpbi->bmiColors[i].rgbGreen;
        pPal->palPalEntry[i].peBlue  = lpbi->bmiColors[i].rgbBlue;
        pPal->palPalEntry[i].peFlags = 0;
    }
```

```
    hPal = CreatePalette( pPal );        /* create the palette */
    GlobalFreePtr( pPal );               /* free LOGPALETTE */
    return( hPal );
}
```

The Dialog Module

Besides displaying the dialog box on the screen, this module copies settings from the current variable into dialog controls and then copies the user's changes from the controls back into current. SetCurrentData and RetrieveData perform those chores.

```
/*-------------------------------------------------------------

        DLG.C

        Runs the XFORM dialog for the Metafile Transform Program.

        FUNCTIONS
                DoTransformDlg      initiate the options dialog box
                Xform_DlgProc       process dialog window messages
                RetrieveData        read data from dialog controls
                SetCurrentData      put data in dialog controls
                About_DlgProc       process dialog window messages

        from Mastering Windows NT Programming
        copyright 1993 by Brian Myers & Eric Hamer

        -----------------------------------------------------------*/

#define STRICT
#include <windows.h>
#include <windowsx.h>
#include <stdlib.h>                  // atof()
#include <stdio.h>                   // sprintf()
#include "mfx.h"
#include "dlg.h"
```

```
/*------------------------------------------------------------
        PROTOTYPES of local routines
  ------------------------------------------------------------*/

BOOL WINAPI Xform_DlgProc( HWND hDlg, UINT uMessage, WPARAM wParam,
    LPARAM lParam );
static void SetCurrentData( HWND hWnd );
static void RetrieveData( HWND hWnd );

/*------------------------------------------------------------
        GLOBAL VARIABLES
  ------------------------------------------------------------*/

extern SETTINGS current;              // XFORM settings from Xform dialog

 /*------------------------------------------------------------
        DO TRANSFORM DLG
        Display the transform dialog and redraw the window if necessary
   -----------------------------------------------------------*/

void DoTransformDlg ( HWND hWnd )
{
    HINSTANCE hInst;
    int iTest;

    hInst = GetWindowInstance( hWnd );
    if (hInst)
    {
        /* show dialog box */
        iTest = DialogBox( hInst, MAKEINTRESOURCE(DLG_XFORM),
                           hWnd, Xform_DlgProc );
        if (iTest)
        {
            /* redraw the client window if the user selected OK */
            InvalidateRect( hWnd, NULL, TRUE );
            UpdateWindow( hWnd );
        }
    }
    return;
}
```

```
/*------------------------------------------------------------------
        XFORM_DLGPROC
        Process the dialog box messages
   ---------------------------------------------------------------*/

BOOL WINAPI Xform_DlgProc (
    HWND hDlg,
    UINT uMessage,
    WPARAM wParam,
    LPARAM lParam )
{
    switch (uMessage)
    {
        case WM_INITDIALOG:
            /* display the current data */
            SetCurrentData( hDlg );
            return( TRUE );

        case WM_COMMAND:
            switch (LOWORD(wParam))
            {
                case IDOK:
                    /* retrieve the new data */
                    RetrieveData( hDlg );
                    EndDialog( hDlg, TRUE );
                    return( TRUE );

                case IDCANCEL:
                    /* remove the dialog box */
                    EndDialog( hDlg, FALSE );
                    return( TRUE );

                case IDD_DEFAULT:
                    /* set and display the default data */
                    SetDefaults( &current );
                    SetCurrentData( hDlg );
                    return( TRUE );

                default:
                    return( TRUE );
            }
    }
```

```
        return( FALSE );
        UNREFERENCED_PARAMETER( lParam );
}


/*------------------------------------------------------------------
        RETRIEVE DATA
        Read the new data from the dialog box controls
    --------------------------------------------------------------*/

static void RetrieveData ( HWND hWnd )
{
        char szBuffer[16];
        UINT uTest;
        BOOL bTest;

        current.bShift = IsDlgButtonChecked( hWnd, IDD_TOGGLE_SHIFT );
        if (current.bShift)
        {
            /* if the shift check box is checked, read the data */
            current.iShiftX = GetDlgItemInt( hWnd, IDD_EDIT_SHIFTX, &bTest, TRUE );
            current.iShiftY = GetDlgItemInt( hWnd, IDD_EDIT_SHIFTY, &bTest, TRUE );
        }

        current.bShear = IsDlgButtonChecked( hWnd, IDD_TOGGLE_SHEAR );
        if (current.bShear)
        {
            /* if the shear check box is checked, read the data */
            uTest = GetDlgItemText( hWnd, IDD_EDIT_SHEARX, szBuffer,
                sizeof(szBuffer) );
            if (uTest)
            {
                current.flShearX = (FLOAT)atof( szBuffer );
            }

            uTest = GetDlgItemText( hWnd, IDD_EDIT_SHEARY, szBuffer,
                sizeof(szBuffer) );
            if (uTest)
            {
                current.flShearY = (FLOAT)atof( szBuffer );
            }
        }

        current.bScale = IsDlgButtonChecked( hWnd, IDD_TOGGLE_SCALE );
        if (current.bScale)
```

```
    {
        /* if the scale check box is checked, read the data */
        uTest = GetDlgItemText( hWnd, IDD_EDIT_SCALEX, szBuffer,
            sizeof(szBuffer) );
        if (uTest)
        {
            current.flScaleX = (FLOAT)atof( szBuffer );
        }

        uTest = GetDlgItemText( hWnd, IDD_EDIT_SCALEY, szBuffer,
            sizeof(szBuffer) );
        if (uTest)
        {
            current.flScaleY = (FLOAT)atof( szBuffer );
        }
    }

    current.bRotate = IsDlgButtonChecked( hWnd, IDD_TOGGLE_ROTATE );
    if( current.bRotate )
    {
        /* if the rotate check box is checked, read the data */
        current.iAngle = GetDlgItemInt( hWnd, IDD_EDIT_ROTATE, &bTest, TRUE );
    }

    /* set the flip Booleans according to the check box states */
    current.bReflect = IsDlgButtonChecked( hWnd, IDD_TOGGLE_REFLECT );
    current.bFlipX   = IsDlgButtonChecked( hWnd, IDD_FLIPX );
    current.bFlipY   = IsDlgButtonChecked( hWnd, IDD_FLIPY );
    return;
}

/*-------------------------------------------------------------------
        SET CURRENT DATA
        Set the dialog controls to reflect the values in the
        global variable current.
    -------------------------------------------------------------------*/

static void SetCurrentData ( HWND hWnd )
{
    char szBuffer[16];

    /* set the shift data */
    CheckDlgButton( hWnd, IDD_TOGGLE_SHIFT, current.bShift );
    SetDlgItemInt( hWnd, IDD_EDIT_SHIFTX, current.iShiftX, TRUE );
    SetDlgItemInt( hWnd, IDD_EDIT_SHIFTY, current.iShiftY, TRUE );
```

```
    /* set the shear data */
    CheckDlgButton( hWnd, IDD_TOGGLE_SHEAR, current.bShear );
    sprintf( szBuffer, "%1.3f", current.flShearX );
    SetDlgItemText( hWnd, IDD_EDIT_SHEARX, szBuffer );
    sprintf( szBuffer, "%1.3f", current.flShearY );
    SetDlgItemText( hWnd, IDD_EDIT_SHEARY, szBuffer );

    /* set the scale data */
    CheckDlgButton( hWnd, IDD_TOGGLE_SCALE, current.bScale );
    sprintf( szBuffer, "%1.3f", current.flScaleX );
    SetDlgItemText( hWnd, IDD_EDIT_SCALEX, szBuffer );
    sprintf( szBuffer, "%1.3f", current.flScaleY );
    SetDlgItemText( hWnd, IDD_EDIT_SCALEY, szBuffer );

    /* set the flip check boxes */
    CheckDlgButton( hWnd, IDD_TOGGLE_REFLECT, current.bReflect );
    CheckDlgButton( hWnd, IDD_FLIPX, current.bFlipX );
    CheckDlgButton( hWnd, IDD_FLIPY, current.bFlipY );

    /* Set the rotation data */
    CheckDlgButton( hWnd, IDD_TOGGLE_ROTATE, current.bRotate );
    SetDlgItemInt( hWnd, IDD_EDIT_ROTATE, current.iAngle, TRUE ):

    return;
}


/*-----------------------------------------------------------------
        ABOUT BOX DIALOG PROCEDURE
        Process messages for the About box window here.
    ---------------------------------------------------------------*/

BOOL WINAPI About_DlgProc (
    HWND hDlg,
    UINT uMessage,
    WPARAM wParam,
    LPARAM lParam )
{
    switch (uMessage)
    {
      case WM_INITDIALOG;
          return( TRUE );
```

```
    case WM_COMMAND:
        EndDialog( hDlg, TRUE );
        return( TRUE );
    }

    return( FALSE );
    UNREFERENCED_PARAMETER( wParam );
    UNREFERENCED_PARAMETER( lParam );
}
```

Chapter 8 surveyed the new features of the Graphics Device Interface, and this chapter focused on two particular features: world coordinate space and enhanced metafiles. The addition of a logical world space preceding the logical page space enables the GDI to shift and distort images in ways that the 16-bit GDI never allowed. The transformation matrix liberates you from the rectilinear tyranny that forced every rectangle to keep all four sides parallel to the coordinate axes. You can repeat a single rectangle command, never varying its coordinates, and transform the output each time to draw a square, a bigger rectangle, a parallelogram, or a diamond, and situate each figure anywhere on the screen.

The greater flexibility in scaling complements the greater device independence of enhanced metafiles. The new metafile format includes a more comprehensive header so any program on any device can show any metafile at its original size, and usually with its original colors. The new metafiles also recognize the expanded capabilities of the Win32 GDI, including coordinate transformations, Bézier curves, **PlgBlt**, and wide line styles.

Chapter 10 continues our focus on GDI issues by building a library of utilities for working with bitmaps and palettes.

Creating Special Effects with Bitmaps and Palettes

■ **Device-independent bitmaps (DIBs)**

■ **Palettes**

■ **Loading and saving bitmaps**

■ **Using bitmap masks**

■ **Transparent backgrounds**

■ **Palette animation**

In our third and final chapter on the Graphics Device Interface, we turn from metafiles, which store an image as a series of repeatable graphics commands, to bitmaps, which store images as a set of colored dots to be copied from place to place. Win32 continues to support the same two kinds of bitmaps familiar from Win16, namely device-dependent bitmaps (DDBs) and device-independent bitmaps (DIBs). The 32-bit system places even more emphasis on using DIBs wherever possible. The commands for working with DIBs, however, require more work from the programmer—including, on occasion, creating palette objects to make the image's colors display correctly. The explanations in this chapter lead to a collection of modular utility routines we've written to facilitate your work with bitmap images. Besides general routines for parsing and displaying DIBs, the collection includes procedures to read and write DIB disk files, several more to help you work with the new **MaskBlt** command, and routines to make a bitmap image slowly fade to black. The next chapter gathers all the routines into a library you can call from your own programs.

Windows NT introduces new 16- and 32-bit DIB formats, two new block transfer commands, ROP4 codes, and halftone palettes. All of these are described here.

CONCEPTS

This section sets out the concepts required for working with bitmaps and palettes. It explains the advantages and disadvantages of DDBs and DIBs and the internal format of a DIB and introduces palettes as a way to control the system's color set.

Bitmaps

A bitmap stores a graphics image pixel by pixel in a block of memory. In the simple case of a monochrome graphics display, every pixel on the screen corresponds to a bit in memory that is either on or off, black or white. Programs that draw pictures on the screen do so by changing the bits that control each pixel. The machine's display circuitry reads that part of memory something like 60 times a second, depending on the hardware, and so reflects changes to the display memory almost immediately. Color systems complicate the situation because they require more than 1 bit to describe the color of each pixel. In either case, though, there is always an image in memory that the screen copies. Unfortunately, the information necessary to describe color information is not stored the same way in every adapter. The internal format of the screen image varies, so a video image stored on one machine is often incompatible with other displays.

Device-Dependent Bitmaps

Any screen that shows graphics can display a monochrome bitmap, but a monochrome screen cannot show a color bitmap. Obviously it lacks the ability to produce red, green, and blue, but that's only part of the problem. Monochrome bitmaps match 1 bit to 1 pixel, but color bitmaps match several bits to each pixel. If you patch bits from a color bitmap into a monochrome screen image, the screen will misinterpret the new image. Color bitmaps generally organize their information one of two ways: chunky or planar. Chunky bitmaps put all the bits for each pixel next to each other in clumps something like this:

Pixel 1	Red bit; green bit; blue bit
Pixel 2	Red bit; green bit; blue bit
Pixel 3	Red bit; green bit; blue bit
...	

With three bits describing each pixel you get a total of eight colors: black, red (R), green (G), blue (B), yellow (RG), cyan (GB), magenta (RB), and white (RGB).

Planar bitmaps store the same information in a different format, devoting one plane to each primary color. (The primary colors may not be red, green, and blue, but the principle is the same.) Think of the different ink plates required to print a colored illustration. Each adds a new color to the page, and the final image appears only when the three layers are superimposed. Planar bitmaps are organized like this:

Red plane	Pixel 1 bit; pixel 2 bit; pixel 3 bit...
Green plane	Pixel 1 bit; pixel 2 bit; pixel 3 bit...
Blue plane	Pixel 1 bit; pixel 2 bit; pixel 3 bit...

The installed video adapter determines whether a system uses chunky or planar bitmaps, and the adapter's color capabilities determine the number of planes or the size of the chunks. As a consequence, bit images cannot be copied directly from one display to another; they must be translated into the Native format of each system.

Device-Independent Bitmaps

With the release of Windows 3.0, Microsoft chose a standard for the internal representation of bitmaps. Bitmaps stored in the standard way are not compatible with any particular device, but they can be translated for any device. Standardized images are called device-independent bitmaps, or more often DIBs. DIBs carry information about the device resolution and color palette for which they were created.

The programming commands that work with DDBs do not work with DIBs; the two are very different objects. DDBs tend to be smaller and faster. For images that do not travel, DDBs are often still the better choice. Don't be afraid to use DDBs when speed matters. Our samples in this chapter include procedures to convert between the two, so you can load a DIB from a file and convert it to a DDB for faster processing.

Device-independent bitmaps are meant for transferring graphics between programs and between machines. The Simple Paint program we wrote in Chapter 8 never saves bitmaps in files or gives bitmaps to other programs, so it has no need for DIBs. Images you create on the fly and don't need to save should be handled as device-dependent bitmaps. Images you want to save and reuse or make available for others to use should always be saved in device-independent format. All the .BMP files that come with Windows and all the .BMP files you create with Paintbrush or the Image Editor are DIBs. Any bitmap you save to a file should first be converted to device-independent format. Any bitmap you want to include in your program's resources should also be a DIB so that the program can run well on different displays. Microsoft strongly encourages Windows NT programmers to use device-independent bitmaps wherever possible.

What's in a DIB?

The essential fact about a device-independent bitmap—the one quality that produces its independence—is that it always stores the data representing pixel colors in one of several related standard formats. DIBs always have only one color plane, but depending on the number of colors they use the bits may be organized in clumps of 1, 4, 8, 16, 24, or 32. Large clumps take longer to process but allow more colors. Naturally, DIBs require their own display functions to translate their data into the display adapter's native format.

The bits that contain the pixel-by-pixel bitmap image are only part of the DIB. Every DIB has three basic parts: an information structure, a color table, and a set of image bits. The information structure tells about the bitmap's width and height; the color table lists the colors needed for the bitmap; and the actual picture comes last. The first two parts are defined as fields in a **BITMAPINFO** structure:

```
typedef struct tagBITMAPINFO {
    BITMAPINFOHEADER    bmiHeader;          // bitmap specifications
    RGBQUAD             bmiColors[1];       // color table
} BITMAPINFO;
```

The first field holds the bitmap's dimensions and the second is an array of colors. Here are their definitions:

```
typedef struct tagBITMAPINFOHEADER /* bmih */
{
    DWORD biSize;                   // size of the structure
    LONG  biWidth;                  // bitmap width
    LONG  biHeight;                 // bitmap height
    WORD  biPlanes;                 // color planes (1)
    WORD  biBitCount;               // bits per pixel
    DWORD biCompression;            // compression flag
    DWORD biSizeImage;              // count of image bits
    LONG  biXPelsPerMeter;          // horizontal resolution
    LONG  biYPelsPerMeter;          // vertical resolution
    DWORD biClrUsed;                // count of colors
    DWORD biClrImportant;           // how many colors matter?
} BITMAPINFOHEADER;

typedef struct tagRGBQUAD /* rgbq */
{
    BYTE rgbBlue;                   // blue intensity
    BYTE rgbGreen;                  // green intensity
    BYTE rgbRed;                    // red intensity
    BYTE rgbReserved;               // must be zero
} RGBQUAD;
```

The first seven fields of the information header matter the most, and the others are more or less optional. The first field should always contain the value sizeof(BIT-MAPINFOHEADER). The value in this field lets you distinguish Windows DIBs from OS/2 DIBs, which begin with a similar structure called a **BITMAPCOREHEADER**. Core headers also start with a **DWORD** field containing their own size, so by examining this field you can tell which format you have. All the Windows DIB functions support either format. Core headers are smaller, and their color tables use **RGBTRIPLE** structures instead of **RGBQUAD**s. Both are documented in the online help file.

The **biWidth** and **biHeight** fields give the dimensions of the bitmap image in pixels. **biPlanes** is always 1 and **biBitCount** tells how many bits the bitmap devotes to describing each pixel, which determines how many colors the bitmap distinguishes. The **biCompression** field tells whether the image bits have been compressed. We'll say more about both bit counts and compression methods after we finish describing the **BITMAPINFOHEADER** structure, but for now let us reassure you that all the DIB functions work with any of these internal formats, so normally you don't need to know which format a particular bitmap uses.

The other fields are technically optional. You should always fill them in yourself when you make new DIBs, but in our experience many programs are not conscientious about providing the optional values. **biSizeImage** should tell the size of the image in bytes. (If it is missing, you can calculate this value from the other fields.) The XPels and YPels fields tell what screen resolution the bitmap is intended for. The size and shape of a pixel varies greatly from machine to machine, so device-independent bitmaps are not really entirely device independent. The resolution values are measured in pixels per meter, and they are useful when a program is provided with several versions of one image intended for different screens. The resolution of the current device is always available through **GetDeviceCaps**, although you have to play with the **HORZSIZE**, **VERTSIZE**, **HORZRES**, and **VERTRES** indices to determine resolution in pixels per meter:

```
// how to calculate the screen's XPel and YPel values
LONG lXppm, lYppm                      // screen resolution in pixels per meter

// horizontal resolution
lXppm = GetDeviceCaps( hDC, HORZRES )      // pixels
        / GetDeviceCaps( hDC, HORZSIZE )   // millimeters
        * 1000;                            // mm per meter

// vertical resolution
lYppm = GetDeviceCaps( hDC, VERTRES )      // pixels
        / GetDeviceCaps( hDC, VERTSIZE )   // millimeters
        * 1000;                            // mm per meter
```

The last two fields, **biClrUsed** and **biClrImportant**, describe the **RGBQUAD** values that follow. Each **RGBQUAD** value designates one color needed for the bitmap.

biClrUsed tells how many **RGBQUAD** values the bitmap contains, and **biClrImportant** tells how many of the colors are considered important for displaying the bitmap. If **biClrUsed** is 0 and **biBitCount** is less than 24, the bitmap is assumed to contain the maximum number of colors possible given the value in **biBitCount**. If **biClrImportant** is 0, all colors are important.

After the **BITMAPINFOHEADER** comes the color table, an array of **RGBQUAD** values. Each **RGBQUAD** names one color. The image bits that follow do not themselves contain color values. Instead, each clump of bits representing a pixel points to an **RGBQUAD** entry in the color table. To understand why the table is necessary, take the case of a DIB with 8 bits per pixel. It can handle only 256 different color values, but the display screen may be capable of showing many more. The color table lets the bitmap select any 256 colors it likes from a larger assortment without having to be large enough to address all the colors at once. If the bitmap uses fewer than 256 colors, the color table may contain fewer than 256 **RGBQUAD**s.

24-bit DIBs are a different case. With 24 bits dedicated to each pixel, the DIB has enough room to express a complete RGB value for each pixel (including 8 bits for the red, for the green, and for the blue intensity components). The pixel entries in a 24-bit DIB are absolute color values, not indices into a color table, so the color table is not necessary.

New DIB Formats

Before NT, Windows permitted only four possible values for the bit count of a DIB, but the new GDI actively supports two more formats—16 bits and 32 bits per pixel.

System	Field	Values
Windows 3.1	biBitCount	1, 4, 8, 24
	biCompression	BI_RGB, BI_RLE4, BI_RLE8
Windows NT	biBitCount	1, 4, 8, 16, 24, 32
	biCompression	BI_RGB, BI_RLE4, BI_RLE8, BI_BITFIELDS

The 16-bpp format will become more common now that adapters come with more memory and are beginning to use a 16-bpp format internally. The most common adapter format allots only 8 bits per pixel in order to have twice as many pixels and a higher resolution. Users historically have preferred higher pixel resolution over higher color resolution, more room over more colors. The addition of a 16-bpp DIB format allows for an anticipated shift toward more colors as adapters with a lot of memory become more common.

The 32-bit format does not use the extra byte of information; after all, 16 million different colors you get from 24 bpp are really quite enough even for very demanding artwork. 32-bit DIBs merely pad out each 3-byte color value with an extra empty byte to align evenly on 32-bit boundaries. 32-bit processors work substantially more quickly with 32-bit quantities.

Table 10.1 lists the memory requirements for a 640x480 display.

TABLE 10.1: Memory Requirements for a 640x480 Display

Depth (bits per pixel)	Colors	Memory (in bytes)
1	2	38,400
4	16	153,600
8	256	307,200
16	32,768*	614,400
24	16,777,216	921,600
32	16,777,216**	1,228,800

* assuming a 5-5-5 format
** the fourth byte is unused

Color Value Masks

In color bitmaps of any depth, each numeric color value contains three separate components representing a particular combination of three primary colors, usually red, green, and blue. Since 16 does not divide evenly by 3, a DIB with 16 bits per pixel leaves 1 bit undefined. In the discussions over how to dispose of the odd pixel, programmers generally wanted to make it an extra green pixel (a 5-6-5 format) in order to squeeze as much information as possible into the available space. Hardware companies, on the other hand, favored leaving the pixel empty because a symmetrical 5-5-5 format poses fewer complications for the adapter. Microsoft compromised by creating color value masks that allow a 16- or 32-bit DIB to specify its own color format.

A color value mask is a 4-byte quantity used to extract the red, green, or blue component from a **COLORREF** value. By setting 1's in the bits that represent just red, just green, or just blue, you can extract a single color component with a logical AND operation. The following lines show how a mask extracts the green component from a 16-bit color value stored in a 5-6-5 format. The middle 6 bits representing green are 111100. The mask is stored as a 32-bit quantity.

16-bit 5-6-5 RGB value	00011111 10001111
Green color mask	00000000 00000000 00000111 11100000
Filtered result	00000000 00000000 00000111 10000000

You would still need to shift the bits right to interpret the resulting value.

Because 16- and 32-bit DIBs don't use their color tables anyway, Microsoft decided to insert three **DWORD**s after their header and fill each of the three with a mask for extracting one component from the color values in the image data. With the masks, every bitmap can set its own internal format for the color components. Display drivers look for the masks and extract the colors accordingly. As a programmer you can ignore the masks unless you decide for some reason to manipulate the image bits directly. You do need to remember the three mask values when calculating the size of a 16- or 32-bit DIB, however. Look for the `GetClrTableSize` procedure in this chapter's sample code. 16- and 32-bit DIBs always set the **biCompression** field of their header to **BI_BITFIELDS** to indicate the presence of the masks.

Compressing DIBs

The **biCompression** field in a **BITMAPINFOHEADER** tells whether the bitmap is compressed. Uncompressed bitmaps contain **BI_RGB** in this field. If **biBitCount** is 4 or 8, then the bitmap may be compressed with run-length encoding (RLE). 4-bit DIBs signal their compression by setting **BI_RLE4** in **biCompression**; 8-bit DIBs set the **BI_RLE8** flag. *Run-length encoding* is a way of compressing bitmaps by replacing strings of like-colored pixels with one number and one color, indicating repetitions of the color. This method works well with bitmaps that have areas of solid color but poorly with more realistic "noisy" images. In the worst possible case, an image where no 2 pixels adjacent in a row ever have the same color, compression actually expands the bitmap to twice its original size. It is certainly possible, and not uncommon, to *increase* the size of a bitmap by "compressing" it.

Choosing the format involves a trade-off between space and speed of display. RLE bitmaps display a little more slowly than uncompressed bitmaps. The speed difference shows more clearly on some screen drivers than others. Of course, compressed bitmaps can save space on the disk and in memory. Small files load more quickly, too. For bitmaps that compress well, the difference can be dramatic. An image with a large mono-colored background may compress to a tenth, or even less, of its original size.

Besides the three compression flags just described—**BI_RGB**, **BI_RLE4**, and **BI_RLE8**—Windows NT introduces the new **BI_BITFIELDS** flag. It represents a flexible new convention for indicating alternative compression methods such as JPEG. Alternative compression methods, however, are useful under Windows only for specialized applications because the system does not support them and drivers are not required to. Only programs that can assume the presence of a known, enhanced display driver should consider using other compression methods. The two RLE compression formats are always available because if the driver doesn't support them the system will. All the bitmap APIs work even when passed run-length encoded DIBs. They work most quickly when the driver itself supports compression and more slowly when the system must cover for the driver's deficiency. But the system can't cover for the driver when it encounters more exotic compression algorithms.

Palettes

Along with the other objects that can be selected into a device context, such as pens, brushes, and fonts, the GDI includes palettes for choosing colors. A palette contains the working set of color values with which an image or an application paints its display. The need for palettes arises with mid-range display devices, typically 8-bit adapters that show only 256 colors at once. With only a few colors, no one expects to see true color images. With 32,768 colors, all the windows on the screen can show all the colors they need simultaneously without competing for precedence. But 256 colors are often just enough to show only one picture with reasonable accuracy. No 8-bit digital museum could ever hang Gainsborough's *Blue Boy* on the same wall with Matisse's *Harmony in Red*, but with 24 bits you can probably display the entire Louvre.

The word "palette" refers of course to the board on which an artist mixes paints. An artist probably has many tubes of paint but not enough room on the palette for all of them at once; in the same way, 8-bit video adapters are often capable of showing many different colors but have only enough memory to use a few of them at one time. The colors in the group may change from time to time as we squeeze out new ones or wipe off old ones, but the number of colors in the group does not change.

Not every adapter supports multiple palettes. The standard Windows 16-color VGA driver does not permit the palette to be changed at all. The VGA is a palette device, but a palette of only 16 would be quite small. Windows requires some constant colors so that, for example, the window frames and caption bars don't all change whenever anyone adjusts the palette. This would leave only a few slots on a 16-color palette for programs to manipulate. On the other hand, high-color displays don't have palettes either because with many colors available every program always gets whatever it requests. But for the moment 256-color displays are still more common than high-color displays, and Windows needs a way to regulate the competing claims of concurrent applications.

Foreground and Background Palettes

Each program constructs a logical palette to describe its needs, and by a complicated set of rules the GDI adjusts the current system colors dynamically to reach the best compromise. The most basic rule of color assignments is that first choice goes to the currently active application. Windows that don't have the input focus must use the active application's colors or compete with each other for the few remaining slots. When the user moves to another window, the newly activated application requests its palette again and this time receives priority. The other applications may lose or gain colors as the focus changes.

The active application is said to realize its palette in the *foreground;* the others have *background* priority. The system reserves 20 permanent system colors to itself, leaving 236 available. The foreground application's colors are copied into the system palette, sequentially filling up available spaces. If the foreground application requests, for example, 240 colors, then the last four will not find an empty slot— unless some of them happen to match any of the 20 permanent system colors. Otherwise, pixels using any of the last four colors will instead receive whichever colors among the first 236 most closely match them. Background applications also must settle for the best matches from the first 236 colors. But if the first bitmap uses only 100 colors, then 136 more empty slots remain for the background palettes to fill up.

COMMANDS

There are only a few new functions in the Win32 API for bitmaps and palettes. We'll consider the bitmaps first and then the palettes, briefly reviewing some of the more important older functions along the way.

Bitmap Commands

The basic operation for a device-dependent bitmap is a block transfer, or "blit," where pixel values from one location are copied to another. A blit moves an image from place to place. The Win32 API contains five functions for performing different kinds of block transfers. Besides the familiar trio of **PatBlt**, **BitBlt**, and **StretchBlt**, you now have **PlgBlt** and **MaskBlt** as well. **PlgBlt**, which appeared in Chapter 8, skews the source image into a parallelogram (see Figure 8.6). Like **StretchBlt**, it can also mirror or invert the image. And like the new **MaskBlt**, **PlgBlt** can work with two source bitmaps at once, filtering one image through a monochrome mask to its destination. Although **MaskBlt** cannot scale an image, it does accept a ROP code, which **PlgBlt** does not, allowing the mask to modify the original image in a variety of ways.

Command	ROP Codes	Bitmap Mask	Image Scaling
PatBlt	x		
BitBlt	x		
StretchBlt	x		x
PlgBlt		x	x
MaskBlt	x	x	

Bitmap Masks

Although icon resources display pixel images, just as bitmaps do, an icon is a more complex object than a bitmap. Parts of an icon can be made transparent to let the window background show through behind. Internally, an icon contains several bitmaps. Besides the basic opaque image bitmap, it contains a monochrome *mask* bitmap derived from the original image. The mask becomes a filter for the image, allowing some pixels from the original to pass through to the destination and blocking others. The icon makes part of the mask act opaque and part of it act transparent, like a wall with windows in it. A mask can also act translucent, like a stained-glass window, modifying the original image selectively as it passes through different parts of the surface.

Any monochrome bitmap from any source can be used as a mask, but usually a mask is a kind of shadow echoing the original image, all in black and white. If you make a mask that has white pixels (bit = 1) that match your image's foreground and black pixels (bit = 0) for the background, then an AND operation filters out the background. The destination receives color from the original only in places where the mask is white. Remember that the ROP codes passed to most of the block transfer functions are logical Boolean rules for combining the source, pattern, and destination layers in a block transfer.

You can create a mask by copying a color image into a monochrome bitmap. You have to choose a color for the system to consider as the background. Suppose you have an image of a ghost, like the one in Figure 10.1. The image has a black background. To make a mask you would

1. Select the ghost bitmap into a DC (**SelectObject**).

2. Create a monochrome bitmap the same size (**CreateBitmap**).

3. Select the empty monochrome bitmap into its own destination DC.

4. Set black as the background color in the ghost's source DC (**SetBkColor**).

5. Copy the ghost image to the mask (**BitBlt**).

In the final step all the pixels of the color chosen with **SetBkColor** become white. All other pixels become black. By copying the source, the mask, and the destination area into a mixing buffer bitmap, and from there back to the screen—being careful to choose the right sequence of ROP codes—you can merge the source into the destination with a transparent background.

FIGURE 10.1:

Ghost drawn in the Image Editor

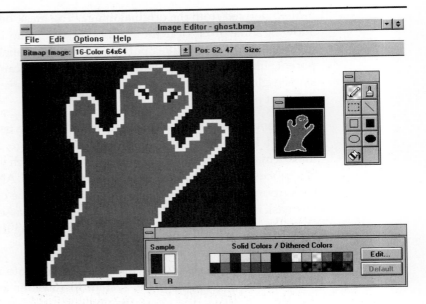

MaskBlt

MaskBlt combines into a single command the effect of the several **BitBlt**s required to filter a source image through a mask onto a destination surface. Besides the usual parameters for a block transfer, which include source and destination devices, the image's dimensions, and a position on each drawing surface, **MaskBlt** requires a handle to the mask bitmap.

```
BOOL MaskBlt(
    HDC hdcDest,            // destination device context
    int xDest,             // upper-left corner of destination rectangle
    int yDest,
    int iWidth,            // dimensions of source and
    int iHeight,           //     destination rectangles
    HDC hdcSrc,            // source device context
    int xSrc,              // upper-left corner of source rectangle
    int ySrc,
    HBITMAP hbmMask,       // monochrome mask bitmap
    int xMask,             // upper-left corner of mask rectangle
    int yMask,
    DWORD dwROP );         // raster operation code
```

The three points are made to align. The pixel at (xSrc, ySrc) is filtered through the pixel at (xMask, yMask) onto the pixel at (xDest, yDest). Notice that **MaskBlt** asks not for a mask bitmap DC but for an actual **HBITMAP** handle. The mask does not need to be selected into a device context. The GDI considers monochrome bitmaps compatible with any device and can use the mask directly with both the source and the destination. The mask may be larger than the transfer area, but if it is too small then **MaskBlt** fails with any ROP code that uses the mask. (Some, such as **SRCCOPY** and **DESTINATION**, ignore the mask.)

The Boolean return value indicates the function's success. Like **PlgBlt**, **MaskBlt** fails if either the source or the destination has set a shearing or rotating transformation matrix. To overcome this limit, set a memory DC as the destination for **MaskBlt** and then call **BitBlt** to copy the final result onto the transformed display surface. Passing a color bitmap for the mask also causes **MaskBlt** to fail.

ROP4 Codes

Windows 3.1 programmers are familiar with the ROP3 codes that alter the effect of **BitBlit**. Although they are always written as 4-byte quantities, there are only 256 possible ways to combine the source, the pattern, and the destination. Not all the bytes are used. Furthermore, the "3" in ROP3 indicates that the logical operations describe how to combine three different elements, but **MaskBlt** really combines four: source, mask, brush, and destination. The value in the dwROP parameter of **MaskBlt** is interpreted as a ROP4 code. A ROP4 code combines two ROP3 codes in the manner described by the following macro:

```
#define ROP4(black, white) ((((white) << 8) & 0xFF000000) | (black))
```

The macro shifts the "white" ROP3 code left 1 byte and ORs the high-order byte with the "black" ROP3 code. The two ROP3 codes merged in a single ROP4 code are applied according to information in the mask. Where the mask pixel is white (1), the white code applies. Where the mask pixel is black (0), the black code applies. This command would make the black areas of the mask transparent and color the white areas with the current brush.

```
MaskBlt( hdcDest,
    xDest, yDest,
    iWidth, iHeight,
    hdcSource,
    xSource, ySource,
    hbmMask,
```

```
    xMask, yMask,
    ROP4(PATCOPY, SRCCOPY) );
```

The source image passes through white pixels unfiltered, but black pixels block the source and draw the pattern instead. Here's another useful definition:

```
#define DESTINATION (DWORD)0x00AA0029
```

That gives a name to the ROP3 code that ignores both source and pattern, leaving the destination area intact. Can you see what this ROP4 code will do?

```
ROP4( DESTINATION, SRCCOPY )
```

The part of the destination under the black pixels is protected, and the source image is copied only where the mask is white. The result is a transparent background, just like an icon has. Try it yourself with our sample Mask program at the end of the chapter.

PlgBlt accepts a mask but has no parameter for the ROP code. The only ROP code it ever uses is exactly this transparency rule.

The ROP4 macro, as you may have noticed, really takes only one word from the first ROP3 code and merges it into another 4-word value. In fact, only the second-most-significant word of a ROP3 code indicates a combination rule. In these two sample definitions from wingdi.h, for example, 0xF0 and 0xCC encode truth tables for different logical operations. 0x20 and 0x21 simply give each rule a number.

```
#define SRCCOPY  (DWORD)0x00CC0020
#define PATCOPY  (DWORD)0x00F00021
```

The effect of combining **SRCCOPY** and **PATCOPY** appears in Figure 10.2, which shows Microsoft's sample program MaskBlt. The source image is in the middle, the mask on the right, and the merged image on the left. The controls at the top of the window reveal that a gray brush has been selected and that the ROP4 code is 0xF0CC0000. The black pixels do **PATCOPY**, producing gray. The white pixels do **SRCCOPY**, transferring parts of the original image.

DIB Commands

Although they are not new to Win32, the DIB commands merit a brief review here to help readers who haven't used them much understand the DIB code in our sample

FIGURE 10.2:

MaskBlt sample program merging
two bitmaps with a ROP4 code

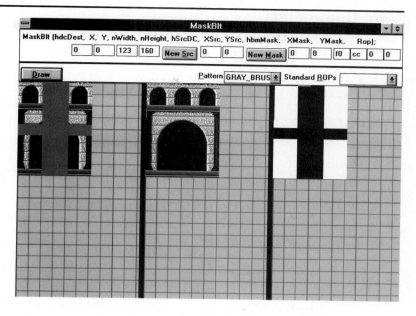

library routines. Here are the five most important commands:

- The **GetDIBits** function copies a device-dependent bitmap into a device-independent bitmap (DDB→DIB).

- **SetDIBits** copies a device-independent bitmap into a device-dependent bitmap (DIB→DDB).

- **CreateDIBitmap** would have been better named "CreateBitmapFromDIB." Given a **BITMAPINFOHEADER** specifying the format of a DIB, this function creates an entirely new corresponding device-dependent bitmap. (**SetDIBits** also converts from DIB to DDB, but it requires that the DDB already exist.)

- **SetDIBitsToDevice** displays a DIB on any device. Unlike **BitBlt**, **SetDIBitsToDevice** requires only one device context parameter (for the destination). DIBs, since they are independent of devices, cannot be selected into a device context.

- **StretchDIBits** is the **StretchBlt** function for DIBs, again with only one DC.

Palette Commands

Like other GDI objects, the logical palette object is really a structure in memory:

```
typedef struct tagLOGPALETTE { /* lgpl */
    WORD palVersion;                // structure version number (0x0300)
    WORD palNumEntries;             // elements in palPalEntry array
    PALETTEENTRY palPalEntry[1];    // array of color values
} LOGPALETTE;

typedef struct tagPALETTEENTRY { /* pe */
    BYTE peRed;                     // intensity values for color components
    BYTE peGreen;
    BYTE peBlue;
    BYTE peFlags;                   // directions for realizing a color
} PALETTEENTRY;
```

The **palVersion** field should hold the version number 0x0300. If Microsoft ever modifies the palette technology, newer palettes will use a higher version number. The **palPalEntry** field holds an array of color specifications, much like the **RGBQUAD** array in the **bmiColors** field of a **BITMAPINFOHEADER** (although the colors come in a different order and the fourth field is used for flags, not reserved). The size of a **LOGPALETTE** variable depends on the number of colors it contains.

A palette object is not the same thing as the structure that you fill out to describe it, just as a **LOGBRUSH** is not an **HBRUSH**. To create a palette from a **LOGPALETTE** variable you need the **CreatePalette** function. Working with palettes requires four basic functions:

- **CreatePalette** returns a handle to a palette object (**HPALETTE**) constructed from the information provided in a **LOGPALETTE** variable.

- **SelectPalette** inserts its object into a device context and returns a handle to the previously selected object. (**SelectPalette** is not a macro, like **SelectBrush** and **SelectBitmap**; it is an actual API function. **SelectObject** does not work with palettes.)

- **RealizePalette** maps colors from a particular device context into the system palette. Selecting a palette into a DC does not make new colors available for drawing because the system cannot promise to satisfy simultaneously all the palette requests from every program. Only when you realize the palette does the GDI try to place your colors in the system palette.

- **DeleteObject** destroys a palette you no longer need. (**SelectObject** does not work with palettes, but **DeleteObject** does.) Every **CreatePalette** must eventually be matched with **DeleteObject**. As usual, **DeleteObject** fails if the object is still selected into a device context.

An Example: The Gray Wash Palette

As an example of basic palette operations, this piece of code produces the screen shown in Figure 10.3. Using paths, as explained in Chapter 8, we converted the letters into a clipping region and drew gradually lighter vertical bars across the screen to fill it in. The effect requires a range of gray colors called a gray *wash*. The following two procedures create the gray wash palette and paint the screen. They show how to create a logical palette, select it, realize it, paint with it, and destroy it. The actual colors in our gray wash palette are visible in the smaller window at the bottom of the figure. Microsoft's sample program MyPal always shows the system palette. When the program realized its gray palette it was assigned the first 64 slots after the 10 static system colors at the left end of the palette. (The other 10 static colors are always at the other end.) In the figure, you can see the 64 shades of steadily lighter grays in a single block near the left.

The commands that create a new logical brush for each new shade in the gray wash palette use a macro called **PALETTEINDEX**. A palette index substitutes for an RGB value in any function that expects a color. An index number designates colors by their position in the currently selected logical palette instead of by absolute color value. If we put RGB values in the **LOGBRUSH** structure then the system must search the palette for reasonable matches, but if we put a palette index in the **LOGBRUSH**, then the system automatically uses a particular palette entry no matter what color it points to. That is the best way to request colors from the range of shades in our 64-entry gray wash palette.

FIGURE 10.3:

Colors drawn with a gray wash palette

```
/*-----------------------------------------------------------------
        PAINT PROCEDURE
        Write "King Lear" with a gray wash palette.
        -----------------------------------------------------------*/

#define INCREMENT        4
#define NUM_COLORS       256/INCREMENT

void Test_OnPaint ( HWND hWnd )
{
    PAINTSTRUCT ps;
    HDC hDC;
    LOGFONT lf;                  // logical font structure
    HFONT hFont, hfontOld;       // hFont is the program's text font
    SIZE size;                   // holds text string extents
    RECT rClient;                // client area dimensions
    int x, y;                    // starting point for text string
    HPALETTE hPal, hpalOld;      // gray-scale palette
    int i;                       // loop control variable
    int iIndex;                  // points to a position in the logical palette
    int iWidth;                  // width of one gray vertical stripe
```

```
hDC = BeginPaint( hWnd, &ps );

FillMemory( &lf, sizeof(LOGFONT), 0 );         // create a large font
lstrcpy( lf.lfFaceName, "Times Roman" );
lf.lfHeight = -132;
lf.lfWeight = 800;
lf.lfCharSet = ANSI_CHARSET;
lf.lfItalic = TRUE;
lf.lfPitchAndFamily = FF_ROMAN;
hFont = CreateFontIndirect( &lf );
if (hFont)
{
    hfontOld = SelectFont( hDC, hFont );       // adjust the DC
}
SetBkMode( hDC, TRANSPARENT );                 // no char cells in path

GetClientRect( hWnd, &rClient );               // in client area
GetTextExtentPoint( hDC, "King Lear", 9, &size );
x = (rClient.right / 2) - (size.cx / 2);
y = (rClient.bottom / 2) - (size.cy / 2);

BeginPath( hDC );                              // create path
TextOut( hDC, x, y, "King Lear", 9 );
EndPath( hDC );
SelectClipPath( hDC, RGN_COPY );

hPal = MakeGrayPalette( );  // put many grays in the system palette
if (hPal)
{
    hpalOld = SelectPalette( hDC, hPal, FALSE );
    RealizePalette( hDC );
}
iIndex = 0;

// Loop from one end of the string to the other, drawing a
// vertical line at each new point to color in the text.
// The lines grow successively lighter, black to white, from
// left to right.  (Our width calculations ignore the 10 darkest
// and the 10 lightest shades of gray because they are too
// close to black and white and don't look as good in our gray scale.

iWidth = max( 1, (int)( (double)size.cx / (double)(64-20) + 0.99 ));
iIndex = 9;
for (i = x; i <= (x+size.cx); i+=iWidth)
```

```
    {
        LOGBRUSH lb;
        HBRUSH hBrush, hbrOld;

        lb.lbStyle = BS_SOLID;
        lb.lbColor = PALETTEINDEX( iIndex );
        hBrush = CreateBrushIndirect( &lb );
        hbrOld = SelectBrush( hDC, hBrush );

        PatBlt( hDC, i, y, iWidth, (int)size.cy, PATCOPY );

        SelectBrush( hDC, hbrOld );
        DeleteBrush( hBrush );

        iIndex++;
        if (iIndex > 63)
        {
            iIndex = 0;
        }
    }

    if (hPal)                                   // clean up
    {
        SelectPalette( hDC, hpalOld, FALSE );
        DeletePalette( hPal );
    }
    if (hFont)
    {
        SelectFont( hDC, hfontOld );
        DeleteFont( hFont );
    }
    EndPaint( hWnd, &ps );
    return;
}


/*----------------------------------------------------------------
        MAKE GRAY PALETTE
        Create a logical palette containing shades of gray.
    -------------------------------------------------------------*/

HPALETTE MakeGrayPalette ( void )
{
    LPLOGPALETTE lpLogPal;      // logical palette structure
    HPALETTE hPal;              // new palette object
    int iIntensity = 0;         // color intensity value
```

```
int i;                          // loop control variable

/* allocate room for a logical palette */
lpLogPal = (LPLOGPALETTE)GlobalAllocPtr( GHND,
            sizeof(LOGPALETTE) + NUM_COLORS * sizeof(PALETTEENTRY) );
if (!lpLogPal)
{
    return( FALSE );
}

/* fill the LOGPALETTE structure with information */
lpLogPal->palVersion    = PALVERSION;
lpLogPal->palNumEntries = NUM_COLORS;

for (i = 0;   i < NUM_COLORS;   i++)
{
    /* each iteration slightly raises the color intensity */
    lpLogPal->palPalEntry[i].peRed   = (BYTE)iIntensity;
    lpLogPal->palPalEntry[i].peGreen = (BYTE)iIntensity;
    lpLogPal->palPalEntry[i].peBlue  = (BYTE)iIntensity;
    lpLogPal->palPalEntry[i].peFlags = PC_NOCOLLAPSE;

    iIntensity += INCREMENT;
}

hPal = CreatePalette( lpLogPal );                // create palette object
GlobalFreePtr( lpLogPal );
return( hPal );
}
```

Halftone Palettes

When a program asks for colors the device does not have, the GDI does the best it can with the available palette. It can approximate many colors by evenly mixing dots of several hues. These improvised shades are called *dithered* colors. For example, on a monochrome screen Windows can dither shades of gray by combining black and white pixels in different proportions. Windows printer drivers have long used a special kind of dithering called halftoning. Originally halftoning was used by newspapers to imitate the effect of several dyes when working only with black dye. Windows NT promotes the system's halftoning engine to work with displays as well as printers.

Halftoning on the display happens only during calls to **StretchDIBits**, and only if you select the proper settings in advance. It requires two sets of color information in order to work. The first is the original color table from the source image, and the second is a palette with particular groups of related shades. All halftoning operations on one device use an identical halftone palette. Its colors, unlike those of other palettes, do not derive from the source image. It contains a spread of colors necessary for halftoning on the given device. Halftoning does not work with DDBs because without internal image color tables the system has no ideal logical image to approximate and no need to dither. Halftoning has no effect on **SetDIBits-ToDevice** because that command performs a straight translation from source dot to destination dot. Only when you stretch a DIB can the GDI improve its color representation by producing blocks of pixels whose *average* color approximates that of the original color in the source.

To activate halftoning requires four steps:

1. Create a halftone palette for the DC (**CreateHalftonePalette**).

2. Select and realize the palette.

3. Set the stretching mode to the new **HALFTONE** setting (**SetStretchBltMode**).

4. Call **SetDIBits** to display an image on the device where the palette was realized.

CreateHalftonePalette is new in Win32.

```
HPALETTE CreateHalftonePalette( HDC hDC );
```

Incidentally, our copy of the documentation incorrectly states that **StretchBlt** also causes halftoning. As we said, halftoning requires the color table from a DIB.

Figure 10.4 shows a small bitmap stretched twice, once with normal dithering and once with halftoning. Here's the code that produced the halftone version:

```
void Halftone_OnPaint ( HWND hWnd )
{
    PAINTSTRUCT ps;       // information about what to draw
    HDC hDC;              // display context = screen device settings
    RECT rect;            // coordinates of window's client area
    HPALETTE hPal, hpalOld;    // halftone and default palettes
```

```
    // establish a display context
    hDC = BeginPaint( hWnd, &ps );
    GetClientRect( hWnd, &rect );    // get coordinates of drawing area

    hPal = CreateHalftonePalette( hDC );
    hpalOld = SelectPalette( hDC, hPal, FALSE );
    RealizePalette( hDC );
    SetStretchBltMode( hDC, HALFTONE );

    StretchDIBits( hDC, 0, 0,
            (int)rect.right, (int)rect.bottom,
            0, 0,
            (int)((LPBITMAPINFOHEADER)pvDIB)>biWidth,
            (int)((LPBITMAPINFOHEADER)pvDIB)>biHeight,
            GetDIBImagePtr(pvDIB),
            (LPBITMAPINFO)pvDIB,
            DIB_RGB_COLORS,
            SRCCOPY );

    SelectPalette( hDC, hpalOld, FALSE );
    DeletePalette( hPal );
    EndPaint( hWnd, &ps );
    return;
}
```

FIGURE 10.4:

Two bitmaps showing the difference between the standard stretching mode and the halftone stretching mode

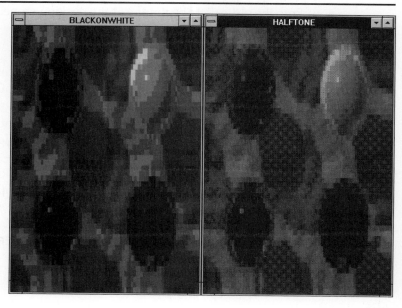

Palette Animation

The FadeOut procedure in our library of bitmap routines uses palette animation to make a bitmap fade to black. It replaces the bitmap's palette entries with successively dimmer color values until gradually they all reach 0. FadeIn performs the same operation in reverse.

Palette animation does not erase and redraw anything. It takes a single screen image and repeatedly changes the way the system interprets the image's color values. For example, you might draw a Christmas tree and give it light bulbs colored blue, yellow, and red. Then you can modify your palette to make everything that was blue change to yellow, all the yellow to red, and all the red to blue. The lights will seem to twinkle. Palette animation works very much like painting by numbers, only after the painting is done you tell the system that you've changed your mind and perhaps you want the number that meant "blue" to mean "yellow" instead. The system makes the change for you, and all the blue pixels turn yellow. **AnimatePalette** performs the substitution.

```
BOOL AnimatePalette(
    HPALETTE hPal,              // palette to change
    UINT uStartIndex,          // first entry to change
    UINT uNumEntries,          // number of entries to change
    CONST PALETTEENTRY *ppe ); // new entries
```

The last parameter points to an array of palette entries. The new entries are spliced into the old palette beginning at the position named in uStartIndex.

The PC_RESERVED Flag

AnimatePalette works only with a palette that contains the **PC_RESERVED** flag in the **peFlags** field of its **LOGPALETTE** structure. (You'll see how to set the flag later in the FadeOut procedure.) Flags tell the system how to interpret the value in each palette entry. Usually each entry contains a straightforward RGB value, and in that case no flag is necessary. But any entry you intend to change while the program runs—in other words, any entry you will animate—should be marked with **PC_RE-SERVED**. The **PC_RESERVED** flag protects other applications. All programs, no matter what logical palettes they construct of their own, must share a single system palette. Often several programs requesting similar colors must share a single entry in the system palette. If a shared palette entry changes (if, for example, it is animated), the display in both windows will change. The **PC_RESERVED** flag prevents the GDI from letting anyone else share a particular color entry.

Coping with Displays That Don't Support Palettes

Although the palette commands generally produce the desired effect even on non-palette devices, **AnimatePalette** is an exception. Selecting and realizing a palette may not serve much purpose on a high-color device, but the commands don't fail and the program gets all the colors it requires. 16-color devices, which also do not support palettes, have too few colors for lifelike representations and again produce the same results with or without a palette. But **AnimatePalette** exploits the hardware lookup table that supports the system palette, and without the hardware support it does not work well. On a non-palette device, **AnimatePalette** does change the values in the palette, but the hardware does not automatically update the screen. On a high-color device, repainting the window immediately after **AnimatePalette** does show the result of the change, but repainting is much slower than genuine palette animation. Still, the strategy of following each **AnimatePalette** command with **InvalidateRect** does give you an alternative to canceling the operation entirely on non-palette displays.

CODE: THE DIBLIB LIBRARY

Programming with bitmaps sometimes becomes complicated, so for this chapter we've written a library of bitmap routines to simplify the task and help you write your own programs. The library code comes in several modules of related procedures: one of general utility routines, one of file operations, one of special effects, and one of routines internal to the library. The first three are listed and explained here; the internal routines appear separately in Chapter 11, where they illustrate techniques for building a dynamic-link library. Along with the three library modules in this chapter we also list substantial excerpts from three client programs that show off what the library can do. (The full listings for all three programs appear on the accompanying disk.)

An Overview of the Library

The library's make file, module definition file, and its header file make a good introduction to its contents and structure. These files show only the exported routines, the ones other programs may call. All the routines should work with DIBs of any color depth or standard compression format; they do not, however, support OS/2-style bitmaps. We have written the routines with an eye to modularity, hoping to make them useful tools for general bitmap programming.

```
#
#    NMake file for the DIBLIB library
#


#
#    Set targets and dependencies
#

all: diblib.dll

diblib.dll: dibfile.obj dibfx.obj dibutil.obj diblib.obj diblib.exp
diblib.exp: dibfile.obj dibfx.obj dibutil.obj diblib.obj diblib.def
dibutil.obj: dibutil.c diblib.h
diblib.obj: diblib.c diblib.h
dibfile.obj: dibfile.c diblib.h
dibfx.obj: dibfx.c diblib.h

#
#    Define macros for command-line options and library modules
#

!IFDEF NODEBUG
CFLAGS = -c -G3 -Os -W3 -D_X86_=1 -DWIN32 -D_MT
LFLAGS = -subsystem:windows
!ELSE
CFLAGS = -c -G3 -Od -W4 -Zi -D_X86_=1 -DWIN32 -D_MT
LFLAGS = -debug:full -debugtype:cv -subsystem:windows
!ENDIF

OBJS = dibutil.obj diblib.obj dibfile.obj dibfx.obj
LIBS = libcmt.lib ntdll.lib kernel32.lib user32.lib gdi32.lib comdlg32.lib

#
#    Define compiling rules
#
```

```
.c.obj:
    cl386 $(CFLAGS) $*.c

.obj.exp:
    lib32 -machine:$(CPU) $(OBJS) -out:$*.lib -def:$*.def

.obj.dll:
    link32 $(LFLAGS) -DLL -entry:DllEntryPoint@12 \
        -out:$*.dll $(OBJS) $*.exp $(LIBS)
```

===

```
;
;    DIBLIB.DEF
;    Module definition file for diblib.dll
;

LIBRARY diblib BASE=0x2C000000

EXPORTS
    ReadDIB                 @1          ; DIBFILE module
    WriteDIB                @2

    PaletteFromDIB          @3          ; DIBUTIL module
    DIBBlt                  @4
    DIBtoDDB                @5
    DIBtoMonoDDB            @6
    DDBtoDIB                @7
    LoadDIBResource         @8
    GetNumColors            @9
    GetDIBImagePtr          @10
    GetClrTableSize         @11
    GetDIBSize              @12
    GetDIBImageSize         @13
    SetDIBColorUsage        @14

    FadeOut                 @15         ; DIBFX module
    FadeIn                  @16
    CreateMask              @17
    ClearBlt                @18
```

===

```
/*------------------------------------------------------------------

        DIBLIB.H

        Prototypes for compiling the DIBLIB dynamic-link library.

        ----------------------------------------------------------*/

/*------------------------------------------------------------------
        DIBLIB module
        ----------------------------------------------------------*/
BOOL InitMapping( void );
void TerminateMapping( void );
void GetDefaultNames( LPSTR lpszName, LPSTR lpszPath );
void SetDefaultNames( LPSTR lpszName, LPSTR lpszPath );

/*------------------------------------------------------------------
        DIBUTIL module
        ----------------------------------------------------------*/

HPALETTE PaletteFromDIB( PBITMAPINFO pBitmapInfo, BYTE byFlag );
void DIBBlt( HDC hDC, HPALETTE hPalDIB, int xDest, int yDest, int xExtent,
    int yExtent, PBITMAPINFOHEADER pBitmapInfoHeader, int xSource,
    int ySource, DWORD dwROP );
HBITMAP DIBtoDDB( HDC hDC, HPALETTE hPalette,
    PBITMAPINFOHEADER pbiHeader );
HBITMAP DIBtoMonoDDB( HDC hDC, HPALETTE hPalette,
    PBITMAPINFOHEADER pbiHeader );
PVOID DDBtoDIB( HPALETTE hPal, HBITMAP hBitmap,
    PBITMAPINFOHEADER pbmiSpecHeader );
PVOID LoadDIBResource( HINSTANCE hInst, LPSTR lpszResName );
LPVOID GetDIBImagePtr( PBITMAPINFOHEADER pBitmapInfoHeader );
WORD GetClrTableSize( PBITMAPINFOHEADER pbiHeader );
DWORD GetDIBSize( PBITMAPINFOHEADER pbiHeader );
DWORD GetDIBImageSize( PBITMAPINFOHEADER pbiHeader );
int GetNumColors( PBITMAPINFOHEADER pbiHeader );
BOOL SetDIBColorUsage( PVOID pDIB, HPALETTE hPal, UINT uUsage );

/*------------------------------------------------------------------
        DIBFX module
        ----------------------------------------------------------*/
```

```
BOOL FadeOut( HDC hDC, PVOID pDIBCurrent, HPALETTE hpalReserved );
BOOL FadeIn( HDC hDC, PVOID pDIBCurrent, HPALETTE hpalReserved, int x, int y );
HBITMAP CreateMask( HDC hDC, HBITMAP hbmImage, COLORREF cBkgnd );

/*------------------------------------------------------------------
          DIBFILE module
   ---------------------------------------------------------------*/

PVOID ReadDIB( HWND hWnd, LPSTR lpszPath, LPSTR lpszName, BOOL bAsk );
BOOL WriteDIB( HWND hWnd, LPSTR lpszPath, LPSTR lpszName, BOOL bAsk,
    PVOID pDIB );
BOOL ClearBlt( HDC hdcDest, int xDest, int yDest, HBITMAP hbmSource,
    COLORREF cTransparent );
BOOL GetFileName( HWND hWnd, BOOL bOpenName, LPSTR lpszFile,
    LPSTR lpszFileTitle );
```

The DIBUTIL Module

DIBUTIL is the longest and most complex of the program's modules. The larger
functions at the beginning rely on an array of smaller utility functions for examining the three individual parts of a DIB: the header, the color table, and the image
bits. The parsing functions appear together at the end of the module. We used some
of them in Chapter 9, but now they appear in a context where their code should be
more comprehensible.

```
/*------------------------------------------------------------------

        DIBUTIL.C

        Utility functions for performing common operations with
        device-independent bitmaps.  Part of the DIBLIB dynamic-
        link library.

        These functions assume they are working with Windows-style
        BITMAPINFOHEADER bitmaps and not OS/2-style BITMAPCOREINFO
        bitmaps.

        FUNCTIONS

            PaletteFromDIB        build a palette from a DIB's color table
            DIBBlt               convert DIB to DDB for fast display
```

```
        DIBtoDDB              convert DIB to HBITMAP
        DIBtoMonoDDB          convert to a monochrome HBITMAP
        DDBtoDIB              convert HBITMAP to DIB
        LoadDIBResource       load bitmap as a DIB from resources
        GetDIBImagePtr        get pointer to beginning of image bits
        GetClrTableSize       figure size of DIB's color table
        GetDIBSize            figure size of entire DIB
        GetDIBImageSize       figure size of image bits
        GetNumColors          get number of colors in bitmap
        SetDIBColorUsage      set palette indices in color table


    from Mastering Windows NT Programming
    copyright 1993 by Brian Myers & Eric Hamer

    ------------------------------------------------------------------*/


#define STRICT
#include <windows.h>
#include <windowsx.h>
#include "diblib.h"


/*-----------------------------------------------------------------
        SYMBOLS
    ------------------------------------------------------------------*/


#define PALVERSION          0x0300  // needed for a LOGPALETTE structure
```

PaletteFromDIB

PaletteFromDIB reads a DIB's color table and copies all the color values into a
LOGPALETTE structure. From that structure **CreatePalette** derives an actual palette object, which the procedure returns. Surprisingly, the Windows API does not
include a function to perform this very common action. Most programs that work
with DIBs will need this procedure in order to display bitmap images with the
proper colors.

The first field of a **LOGPALETTE** must contain a version number. Windows NT uses
the same version of palette support that first appeared in Windows 3.0, so this field
should always be set to 0x0300.

A simple **CopyMemory** command would fill the array of **PALETTEENTRY**s if only the RGB components of an **RGBQUAD** were stored in the same order as those of a **PALETTE-ENTRY**. Instead, a for loop must transfer the fields of each record individually.

After creating the palette we free the memory allocated for the **LOGPALETTE** structure since all its information has been copied into the palette. The palette remains unaffected.

```
/*-------------------------------------------------------------------
        PALETTE FROM DIB
        Constructs a logical palette from the color table in a given
        DIB.  Reads the data from a DIB's color table, copying it into
        a LOGPALETTE structure.

        Also, a palette flag (0, PC_NOCOLLAPSE, or PC_RESERVED) may be
        passed to this function for insertion in the new palette
        object.

        RETURN
        A handle to the new palette, or NULL in case of error.
        The caller should eventually delete the palette.
        ----------------------------------------------------------------*/

HPALETTE PaletteFromDIB (
    PBITMAPINFO pBitmapInfo,            // pointer to a DIB header
    BYTE byFlag )                       // flag to insert in palette entries
{
    LPLOGPALETTE pLogPalette;           // structure to hold info from DIB
    HPALETTE hPalette;                  // new palette object
    int iNumColors;                     // count of color entries in DIB
    int i;                              // loop variable

    /* confirm that the DIB pointer is not NULL */
    if (!pBitmapInfo)
    {
        return( NULL );
    }

    iNumColors = GetNumColors( (PBITMAPINFOHEADER)pBitmapInfo );

    /* make room in memory for a LOGPALETTE structure */
    pLogPalette = GlobalAllocPtr( GHND,
        sizeof(LOGPALETTE) + sizeof(PALETTEENTRY) * iNumColors );
```

```
    if (!pLogPalette)
    {
        return( NULL );
    }

    /* initialize the new LOGPALETTE structure */
    pLogPalette->palVersion    = PALVERSION;
    pLogPalette->palNumEntries = (WORD)iNumColors;

    /* copy colors from the DIB table to the LOGPALETTE */
    for (i = 0;  i < iNumColors;  i++)
    {
        pLogPalette->palPalEntry[i].peRed   =
            pBitmapInfo->bmiColors[i].rgbRed;
        pLogPalette->palPalEntry[i].peGreen =
            pBitmapInfo->bmiColors[i].rgbGreen;
        pLogPalette->palPalEntry[i].peBlue  =
            pBitmapInfo->bmiColors[i].rgbBlue;
        pLogPalette->palPalEntry[i].peFlags = byFlag;
    }

    hPalette = CreatePalette( pLogPalette );    // create the palette //

    GlobalFreePtr( pLogPalette );               // free LOGPALETTE //
    return( hPalette );
}
```

DIBBlt

DIBs cannot be selected in or blitted onto any device. Since you can't blit DIBs, Windows provides another function for displaying them directly. A typical call would look like this:

```
SetDIBitsToDevice(
    hDC,                        // destination device context
    xOrg,                       // x origin of dest. rect
    yOrg,                       // y origin of dest. rect
    (int)lpbih->biWidth,        // rectangle width
    (int)lpbih->biHeight,       // rectangle height
    0,                          // x origin of source rect
    0,                          // y origin of source rect
    0                           // num. of first scan line
```

```
(int)lpbih->biHeight,          // num. of scan lines
GetDIBImagePtr(lpbih),         // address of image bits
(LPBITMAPINFO)lpbih,           // BITMAPINFO structure needed
DIB_RGB_COLORS );              // explicit RGB colors
```

Just to emphasize one last time the difference between DIB commands and DDB commands, notice that **SetDIBitsToDevice** requires only one DC, for the destination. DIBs don't have devices. Another unusual thing about **SetDIBitsToDevice** is that it does not ask for a handle to the DIB; it asks instead for a pointer to the **BITMAPINFO** structure and a pointer to the image bits (here calculated by our own GetDIBImagePtr routine). **SetDIBitsToDevice** doesn't even care if the header and the image bits are contiguous in memory; you can have different headers with different color tables and use them for the same image, if you like. A DIB with contiguous pieces, which can therefore be referenced with a single pointer, is called a *packed bitmap*. DIBs are nearly always referred to by pointers rather than handles; no DIB function requires a handle. The Windows headers even lack an HDIB variable type. By contrast, device-dependent bitmap functions nearly always ask for a handle.

SetDIBitsToDevice is ideal when memory runs low or bitmaps run large because it can work with a bitmap in small pieces. The scan line parameters in the **SetDIBitsToDevice** call identify rows in the bitmap and determine which horizontal band will be displayed. By writing a loop that reads sections of a bitmap from a file and sets them piece by piece on the screen, you can display an image that would otherwise consume more memory than is actually available.

SetDIBitsToDevice is, however, comparatively slow. DIBBlt works more quickly by converting the DIB to a device-dependent bitmap and blitting that to the screen. This method takes more code and more memory but paints the image more quickly. It requires us briefly to hold in memory two copies of the same bitmap, one a DIB and the other a DDB.

```
/*-------------------------------------------------------------------
    DIB BLT
    Converts a DIB to a temporary DDB for faster display, then
    blits it to the screen.  Assumes the DIB is packed.  The
    parameters are meant to resemble BitBlt, but instead of a
    source DC you pass a pointer to the DIB.

    RETURN
    The result of the BitBlt--TRUE for image displayed,
    FALSE for error.
-------------------------------------------------------------------*/
```

```
void DIBBlt (
    HDC hDC,                             // destination device
    HPALETTE hPalDIB,                    // palette for DIB
    int xDest,                           // destination origin
    int yDest,
    int xExtent,                         // destination dimensions
    int yExtent,
    PBITMAPINFOHEADER pbiHeader,         // the DIB
    int xSource,                         // source origin
    int ySource,
    DWORD dwROP )                        // ROP3 code
{
    HDC hdcMem;
    HBITMAP hBitmap;
    HBITMAP hbmOld;

    if (!pbiHeader)
    {
        return;
    }

    hBitmap = DIBtoDDB( hDC, hPalDIB, pbiHeader );
    if (!hBitmap)
    {
        return;
    }

    hdcMem  = CreateCompatibleDC( hDC );        // put bitmap in a DC
    if (!hdcMem)
    {
        DeleteBitmap( hBitmap );
        return;
    }
    hbmOld = SelectBitmap( hdcMem, hBitmap );

    if (xExtent == 0)                           // default extents are
    {                                           // width and height
        xExtent = (int)pbiHeader->biWidth;
    }
    if (yExtent == 0)
    {
        yExtent = (int)pbiHeader->biHeight;
    }
```

```
BitBlt( hDC, xDest, yDest,              // display the image
    xExtent, yExtent,
    hdcMem, xSource, ySource,
    dwROP );

SelectBitmap( hdcMem, hbmOld );         // clean up
DeleteDC( hdcMem );
DeleteBitmap( hBitmap );
return;
}
```

DIBtoDDB

The DIBtoDDB procedure receives a pointer to a DIB and returns a handle to a new device-dependent bitmap containing the same image. DIBBlt calls this routine to construct the DDB it blits to the screen. Because DDBs generally work more quickly than DIBs, you might consider storing images as DIBs and converting them to DDBs at run time.

CreateDIBitmap easily accomplishes the task of transferring a DIB image into a device-dependent bitmap. It needs to be told the device for which the bitmap is intended; the hDC variable provides that information. The DIB is passed as a set of three pointers in different parameters: one to a **BITMAPINFOHEADER**, one to the image bits, and one to a **BITMAPINFO** structure (with its color table). The third parameter, **CBM_INIT**, tells the function to initialize the new bitmap by copying the image from the DIB. If the initialization parameter and the image pointer were both **NULL**, **CreateDIBitmap** would make a bitmap big enough to hold the image but would leave the bitmap blank. The last parameter tells what kind of values are in the **BITMAPINFO** color table. Usually they are absolute RGB values, but it is also possible to substitute indices that point to entries in the currently selected palette or the system palette. The possibilities are signaled by **DIB_RGB_COLORS, DIB_PAL_COLORS**, and **DIB_PAL_INDICES**. Palette indices are occasionally convenient for your own DIBs, but for saving and exchanging information with other programs absolute color entries are essential.

The color table with its RGB values contains the raw material for creating a GDI palette object, but remember that the system won't automatically use those colors. It can use only the colors in the system palette, and to get different colors you have to put them there yourself. The PaletteFromDIB procedure creates a palette from the bitmap's color table, and DIBtoDDB carefully realizes this palette before translating the bits into a device-dependent format. When **CreateDIBits** draws the new image on the surface of the device-dependent bitmap it has to choose colors available on the device. By first realizing the DIB's palette we ensure that the system offers **CreateDIBits** colors that match the DIB's palette as closely as possible.

The new DIB palette must be removed from the device context (by **SelectObject**) before it can be destroyed.

```
/*-------------------------------------------------------------------
      DIB TO DDB
      Convert a device-independent bitmap (DIB) to a device-dependent
      bitmap (DDB).  The DIB must be packed.

      RETURN
      A handle to the DDB (HBITMAP).  If an error occurs, the return
      value will be NULL.
      -----------------------------------------------------------------*/

HBITMAP DIBtoDDB (
    HDC hDC,
    HPALETTE hPalette,
    PBITMAPINFOHEADER pbiHeader )
{
    HBITMAP   hBitmap;
    HPALETTE hpalOld = NULL;

    if (hPalette)
    {
        hpalOld = SelectPalette( hDC, hPalette, FALSE );
        RealizePalette( hDC );
    }

    hBitmap = CreateDIBitmap( hDC,
                              pbiHeader,
                              CBM_INIT,
                              GetDIBImagePtr(pbiHeader),
                              (PBITMAPINFO)pbiHeader,
                              DIB_RGB_COLORS );

    if (hpalOld)
    {
        SelectPalette( hDC, hpalOld, FALSE );
    }
    return( hBitmap );
}
```

DIBtoMonoDDB

This function performs the same conversion as DIBtoDDB, but it always produces a 1-plane, 1-bit-per-pixel monochrome bitmap. DIBtoDDB generally produces a bitmap that matches the color depth of the current display, even if the source image contains only black and white pixels. Now that two GDI routines, **PlgBlt** and **MaskBlt**, accept only 1-bpp monochrome bitmaps in one parameter, DIBtoMonoDDB may be useful. A bitmap that uses only black and white is not a true monochrome bitmap if its internal format would still permit other colors as well.

```
/*------------------------------------------------------------
        DIB TO MONO DDB
        Convert a device-independent bitmap (DIB) to a monochrome
        device-dependent bitmap (DDB), suitable for use as a mask.
        The DIB must be packed.

        RETURN
        A handle to the DDB (HBITMAP).  If an error occurs, the return
        value will be NULL.
    -------------------------------------------------------------*/

HBITMAP DIBtoMonoDDB (
    HDC hDC,
    HPALETTE hPalette,
    PBITMAPINFOHEADER pbiHeader )
{
    HBITMAP hbmMono, hbmOld;                    // monochrome bitmap
    HDC hdcMono;                                // memory DC
    HPALETTE hpalOld;

    hbmMono = CreateBitmap(                     // create an empty bitmap
                (int)pbiHeader->biWidth,
                (int)pbiHeader->biHeight,
                1, 1, NULL );
    if (!hbmMono)
    {
        return( NULL );
    }

    hdcMono = CreateCompatibleDC( hDC );        // put bitmap in a memory DC
    if (!hdcMono)
```

```
{
    DeleteBitmap( hbmMono );
    return( NULL );
}
hbmOld = SelectBitmap( hdcMono, hbmMono );

if (hPalette)                                    // realize DIB's palette
{
    hpalOld = SelectPalette( hdcMono, hPalette, FALSE );
    RealizePalette( hdcMono );
}

SetDIBits( hdcMono, hbmMono,                     // copy image to mono bitmap
        0, (int)pbiHeader->biHeight,
        GetDIBImagePtr(pbiHeader),
        (PBITMAPINFO)pbiHeader,
        DIB_RGB_COLORS );

if (hPalette)                                    // clean up
{
    SelectPalette( hDC, hpalOld, FALSE );
}
SelectBitmap( hdcMono, hbmOld );
DeleteDC( hdcMono );
return( hbmMono );
}
```

DDBtoDIB

Converting a device-dependent bitmap to a DIB poses a bigger challenge. **Get-DIBits** will perform the conversion, but first we have to allocate space in memory for the new bitmap—a step that **CreateDIBitmap** performed automatically going the other way. Allocating memory would be easier if we knew how big the new DIB will be, but we can't tell the size of a compressed bitmap from its header. This means another function call to find out the size before we can allocate memory. We must

1. Allocate a block of memory for the normal DIB structures and fill them in with information about the DIB we want to create.

2. Determine the size of the future DIB by calling **GetDIBits** with a **NULL** pointer for the image bits parameter. **GetDIBits** returns the projected size.

3. Reallocate the DIB block to make it the right size.

4. Copy the device-dependent bitmap into the DIB by calling **GetDIBits** again, this time with all its parameters.

Specifications for the DIB that DDBtoDIB should create are passed in through the **pbiSpecHeader** parameter. To fill out the header you need to know some details about the original bitmap. A device-dependent bitmap, remember, consists of two parts. The first part, a **BITMAP** data structure, contains information about how the actual image bits are organized. The last field points to the bits themselves. Normally you can't read the information in the **BITMAP** structure because you have only a handle to it. Windows does the dirty work. But there are times when you need that information, and **GetObject** is the answer. **GetObject** copies the object's data structure into a buffer you provide.

```
BITMAP bm;

GetObject( hBitmap, sizeof(BITMAP), &bm );
```

GetObject copies values from the logical structure in the given handle to the structured variable. It works with pens, brushes, and fonts as well as bitmaps.

From the information in a **BITMAP** structure you can derive the necessary values for the pbiSpecHeader that DDBtoDIB requires.

```
typedef struct tagBITMAP {   /* bm */
    LONG   bmType;                      // type of bitmap; always 0
    LONG   bmWidth;                     // image width in device units
    LONG   bmHeight;                    // image height in device units
    LONG   bmWidthBytes;               // bmWidth rounded up to nearest DWORD
    WORD   bmPlanes;                    // color planes in the bitmaps
    WORD   bmBitsPixel;                 // bits per pixel
    LPVOID bmBits;                      // pointer to image bits
} BITMAP;
```

The **bmWidth** and **bmHeight** fields give the dimensions needed to convert the bitmap to a DIB. Put the product of **bmPlanes** and **bmBitsPixel** in the DIB's **biBitCount** field. You should also initialize **biSize** and **biCompression**.

Besides the measurements in pbiSpecHeader, DDBtoDIB receives an optional palette. **GetDIBits** puts colors from the system palette into the color table of the new DIB, so realizing a palette before converting influences the color values stored in the new DIB.

GetDIBits calls the display driver to get information about the bitmap. In theory the display driver should fill out the **biSizeImage** field of the new DIB for us. In practice it may not always. Check to be sure you get a value. If the image size field remains 0 assume the bitmap is not compressed and calculate the size by hand. The calculation we supply will fail, however, in the unlikely event that **biSizeImage** remains 0 for a compressed DIB that *expands* under run-length encoding. If you encounter problems, modify the calculation to something like

```
pbiHeader->biSizeImage = GetDIBImageSize(pbiHeader) * 3 / 2;
```

GlobalReallocPtr is a windowsx.h macro calling the API function **GlobalRealloc**. **GlobalRealloc** can cause problems if you forget that when Windows changes the size of a memory block it may also be necessary to change its location. Even if the reallocation succeeds, the old pointer may become invalid. Store the return value in a temporary variable. If the return was not **NULL** then the function worked, and you can safely copy the result back into your permanent pointer:

```
pTemp = GlobalReAllocPtr( <parameters> );
if (pTemp)                                    // did reallocation work?
{
    /* the temporary variable protects us if the address changed */
    pbmiNewHeader = pTemp;                     // yes; mark new address
}
```

The block can be moved only if reallocated with the **GMEM_MOVEABLE** attribute.

```
/*-------------------------------------------------------------------
        DDB TO DIB
        Convert a device-dependent bitmap (DDB) to a device-independent
        bitmap (DIB)

        RETURN
        A pointer to the packed DIB.  If an error occurs, the return
        value will be NULL.
        ----------------------------------------------------------------*/


PVOID DDBtoDIB (
        HPALETTE hPal,                         // palette to use for DIB
        HBITMAP hBitmap,                       // bitmap to convert
        PBITMAPINFOHEADER pbmiSpecHeader )  // header info for DIB
```

```
{
    PVOID pTemp;                             // temporary pointer memory buffer
    PBITMAPINFOHEADER pbmiNewHeader;         // pointer to the new DIB
    HPALETTE hpalOld;                        // current palette from hDC
    HDC hDC;

    if (!pbmiSpecHeader)
    {
        return( NULL );
    }

    hDC = GetDC( NULL );
    if (!hDC)
    {
        return( NULL );                      // return if we couldn't get a DC
    }

    if (hPal)                                // was a palette provided?
    {
        hpalOld = SelectPalette( hDC, hPal, FALSE );    // use it
        RealizePalette( hDC );
    }

    /* allocate estimated space for the new DIB */
    pbmiNewHeader = GlobalAllocPtr( GHND, GetDIBSize(pbmiSpecHeader) );
    if (!pbmiNewHeader)
    {
        ReleaseDC( NULL, hDC );
        return( NULL );
    }

    /* copy the given DIB specifications into the new space */
    CopyMemory( pbmiNewHeader, pbmiSpecHeader,
                (size_t)pbmiSpecHeader->biSize );

    /* ask GetDIBits how much room we'll really need */
    GetDIBits( hDC, hBitmap, 0, (UINT)pbmiNewHeader->biHeight,
               NULL, (LPBITMAPINFO)pbmiNewHeader, DIB_RGB_COLORS );

    // No test for an error here since we expect GetDIBits to
    // return 0 on that last call.

    /* did the screen driver put an answer in biSizeImage? */
    if (pbmiNewHeader->biSizeImage == 0)
```

```
{
    /* if biSizeImage is still blank, figure it by hand */
    pbmiNewHeader->biSizeImage = GetDIBImageSize( pbmiNewHeader );
}

/* reallocate our global block to fit the size we were just given */
pTemp = GlobalReAllocPtr( pbmiNewHeader,
                          GetDIBSize(pbmiNewHeader),
                          GMEM_MOVEABLE );
if (pTemp)                                      // did reallocation work?
{
    /* the temporary variable protects us if the address changed */
    pbmiNewHeader = pTemp;                      // yes; mark new address
}
else
{
    GlobalFreePtr( pbmiNewHeader );             // no; bail out
    ReleaseDC( NULL, hDC );
    return( NULL );
}

/* ask GetDIBits to fill pbmiNewHeader with the new image bits */
if (!GetDIBits( hDC, hBitmap, O, (WORD)pbmiNewHeader->biHeight,
                GetDIBImagePtr(pbmiNewHeader),
                (LPBITMAPINFO)pbmiNewHeader,
                DIB_RGB_COLORS ))
{
    /* GetDIBits failed */
    GlobalFreePtr( pbmiNewHeader );
    pbmiNewHeader = NULL;
}

if (hPal)                                       // did we use a palette?
{                                               // yes
    SelectPalette( hDC, hpalOld, FALSE );       // restore default
}

ReleaseDC( NULL, hDC );
return( pbmiNewHeader );
}
```

LoadDIBResource

Now that you know more about device-independent bitmaps we can return to a potentially confusing point that first came up in Chapter 9. Any bitmap resources compiled into the executable file of a Windows program are likely to be DIBs, but when you load them with **LoadBitmap** what you get is a handle to a device-*dependent* bitmap. **LoadBitmap** automatically converts the bitmap to be compatible with the display and returns an **HBITMAP** handle. Often that's exactly what you want; DDBs take up less room and can be displayed more quickly. Unfortunately, in the conversion process **LoadBitmap** completely ignores the information in the DIB's color table.

This little-known fact about **LoadBitmap** often causes trouble. Programmers learning Windows often ask why their bitmaps do not display with the correct colors after a call to **LoadBitmap**. To preserve the appearance of a bitmap resource on a palette device you need to load it as a DIB. (A DIB may also be necessary if you intend to put the bitmap on the clipboard for another program.) To load a DIB, call **FindResource** (specifying the **RT_BITMAP** type); **LoadResource**, to get a handle; and **LockResource**, which loads the bitmap into memory (no, **LoadResource** didn't do that) and converts the resource handle into a pointer suitable for use with DIB functions. Later you can undo **LoadResource** and free up memory with **FreeResource**.

```
/*---------------------------------------------------------------
        LOAD DIB RESOURCE
        Load a DIB from the caller's resources.  Preserves the
        DIB intact--it is not converted to a DDB, as LoadBitmap
        would do.

        RETURN
        A pointer to a packed DIB (or NULL to signal errors).
        The caller should eventually release the DIB by calling
        FreeResource().
        ---------------------------------------------------------*/

PVOID LoadDIBResource (
    HINSTANCE hInst,                    // caller's instance
    LPSTR lpszResName )                 // string identifying the resource
{
    HRSRC hRes;                         // handle to the resource
```

```
/* locate the resource in the file */
hRes = FindResource( hInst, lpszResName, RT_BITMAP );
if (!hRes)
{
    return( NULL );
}

hRes = LoadResource( hInst, hRes );
if (!hRes)
{
    return( NULL );
}

return( LockResource(hRes) );
}
```

SetDIBColorUsage

Normally the values in a DIB's color table are RGB values, each number giving explicit instructions about the varying red, green, and blue intensities desired for a particular hue. The image bits do not themselves contain RGB values. Rather, they point to items in the color table. If the first byte of an 8 bits-per-pixel image is 00000010, then the first pixel should be drawn with the second color in the color table. Normally the GDI, to draw a bitmap, reads a color index from the image bits, finds the appropriate RGB value in the color table, and consults the selected palette to find the physical system color that best matches the RGB value.

These layers of indirection allow an internal representation of the image that is independent of the hardware, but of course they also take time. Once a bitmap's color table has been copied into a logical palette and realized in its display context, the indirections no longer serve any purpose. In particular, if the color table could be made to point directly to the corresponding logical palette entry then the system could avoid unnecessary searches for the best match in the palette. SetDIBColor-Usage performs that optimization. It loops through the color table putting 0 in the first **RGBQUAD**, 1 in the second, and so on, pointing the GDI to palette entries by their position in the logical palette. (The two structures coincide because we constructed one from a copy of the other.) The bitmap now contains palette indexes instead of color values. **SetDIBitsToDevice** and **StretchDIBits** operate more quickly with bitmaps in this format, and the last parameter of both functions indicates the bitmap's internal status as either **DIB_RGB_COLORS** or **DIB_PAL_COLORS**.

Of course, a bitmap with the **DIB_PAL_COLORS** format is no longer device independent. It should not be saved, passed to other programs, or used with any other palette realized in the DC. You should restore the original RGB values before saving the bitmap. SetDIBColorUsage shows how to read them back from the palette.

The palette animation procedures in the DIBFX module call SetDIBColorUsage to circumvent the system's normal color-mapping process and force a stable link with particular palette entries even when the colors change.

```
/*--------------------------------------------------------------------
        SET DIB COLOR USAGE
        Alters the color table data inside a DIB, converting between
        the DIB_RGB_COLORS and DIB_PAL_COLORS format.  The latter
        format optimizes color translations.

        The hPal palette object must have been built from
        the DIB's original color table.  The palette is ignored
        in the conversion to DIB_PAL_COLORS.  It is read when
        restoring RGB values.

        The algorithm assumes a DIB of 8 bits per pixel.
        (DIBs with more colors lack color tables.) The
        function fails when passed other color depths.
        --------------------------------------------------------------*/

BOOL SetDIBColorUsage (
    PVOID pDIB,                         // DIB to alter
    HPALETTE hPal,                      // palette built from DIB
    UINT uUsage )                       // desired color usage
{
    PBITMAPINFOHEADER pbiHeader;        // alias for pDIB
    PPALETTEENTRY ppe;                  // pointer to colors from hPal
    RGBQUAD * pRGBQ;                    // pointer to DIB's color table
    PWORD pWord;                        // pointer to data for one pixel
    int iNumColors;                     // number of colors in color table
    int i;                              // loop variable

    pbiHeader = (LPBITMAPINFOHEADER)pDIB;
    iNumColors = GetNumColors( pbiHeader );
```

```
if (pbiHeader->biBitCount != 8)        // is this a 256-color depth DIB?
{
    return( FALSE );                   // no, so don't use palette indices
}

if (iNumColors > 0)
{
    /* make pRGBQ point to the beginning of the color table */
    pRGBQ = (RGBQUAD*)((LPSTR)pbiHeader + (WORD)pbiHeader->biSize);

    switch (uUsage)
    {
        // Fill the color table with indices into the palette.
        // This is easy because the first RGBQUAD corresponds
        // with the first palette entry, the next with the
        // second, and so on.

        case DIB_PAL_COLORS:
            pWord = (PWORD)pRGBQ;
            for (i = 0; i < iNumColors; i++)
            {
                *pWord++ = (WORD)i;
            }
            break;

        // Fill the color table with the color values taken
        // from the palette.  (We presume the palette was
        // originally constructed from the DIB's color table.)

        case DIB_RGB_COLORS:
        default:
            /* allocate room to hold color values from the palette */
            ppe = GlobalAllocPtr( GHND,
                        sizeof(PALETTEENTRY) * iNumColors );
            if (!ppe)
            {
                return( FALSE );
            }

            /* copy PALETTEENTRYs from the palette object */
            GetPaletteEntries( hPal, 0, iNumColors, ppe );
```

```
        /* copy the color intensities into the RGBQUADs */
        for (i = 0; i < iNumColors; i++)
        {
            pRGBQ[i].rgbRed      = ppe[i].peRed;
            pRGBQ[i].rgbGreen    = ppe[i].peGreen;
            pRGBQ[i].rgbBlue     = ppe[i].peBlue;
            pRGBQ[i].rgbReserved = 0;
        }

        GlobalFreePtr( ppe );
        break;
    }
}
return( TRUE );
}
```

DIB Parsing Functions

As you have certainly noticed, the code in this module relies on a small battery of utility functions for parsing the structure of a DIB. Some of them appeared in the INIT module in Chapter 9. We will explain them briefly here.

GetDIBImagePtr	get pointer to beginning of image bits
GetClrTableSize	figure size of DIB's color table
GetDIBSize	figure size of entire DIB
GetDIBImageSize	figure size of image bits
GetNumColors	get number of colors in bitmap
SetDIBColorUsage	set palette indices in color table

GetDIBImagePtr returns a pointer to the place where the DIB's image bits begin. Most of the Windows DIB functions require an image pointer. Starting with a pointer to the bitmap header, GetDIBImagePtr adds to that the size of the header and the color table. Obviously it's assuming the bitmap is packed and its pieces are contiguous in memory.

GetClrTableSize simply multiplies the number of colors times the size of an RGBQUAD and returns the result. A program that needed to take into account OS/2 bitmaps would have to use sizeof(RGBTRIPLE) in computing the size.

GetDIBSize, which calculates the total size of all the parts of a DIB, first tests the compression state. If the bitmap is not compressed, GetDIBSize fills in biSize-Image with the value from GetDIBImageSize. Whether or not biSizeImage was blank, this move ensures that its value is accurate. If the DIB is compressed, Get-DIBSize must rely on the bitmap's creator to have set the correct value in the size field when the image was compressed. GetDIBSize adds the sizes of the header, the color table, and the image bits and returns their sum.

GetDIBImageSize determines how many bytes the actual image, excluding header and color table, occupy in memory. Its calculations assume the bitmap is not compressed. The function multiplies width times height to get number of pixels and then multiplies by bits per pixel and divides by 8 to get bytes. The only tricky thing is that the value in biWidth describes the width of the image but not necessarily the width of the bitmap, which must be aligned on 32-bit **DWORD** boundaries. In other words, the width of the bitmap's scan lines must be evenly divisible by 32.

GetNumColors finds out how many **RGBQUAD** values there are in a DIB's color table. The task would seem to be a simple matter of looking in the **biClrUsed** field, but as it turns out that field is normally set to 0 and holds a positive value only if the DIB uses fewer colors than it could. How many it *can* use depends on the value in the **biBitCount** field. A monochrome bitmap (**biBitCount** = 1) has two colors; a 4-bits-per-pixel bitmap needs 16 **RGBQUAD**s for its colors; and a bitmap with 8 bits per pixel can use 256 **RGBQUAD**s. As we said earlier, a bitmap with 16, 24, or 32 bits per pixel contains absolute RGB values for each pixel and has no need of a color table.

```
/*---------------------------------------------------------------
        GET DIB IMAGE POINTER
        Calculates where in a DIB the info structures end and the
        image bits begin.  Assumes the DIB is packed.
        -----------------------------------------------------------*/
PVOID GetDIBImagePtr ( PBITMAPINFOHEADER pbiHeader )
{
    return( (LPSTR)pbiHeader + pbiHeader->biSize
        + GetClrTableSize(pbiHeader) );
}


/*---------------------------------------------------------------
        GET COLOR TABLE SIZE
        Given a pointer to the bitmap info header, determines the
        number of bytes that intercede between the header and the
        DIB's actual image bits.  These bytes contain information
        about the colors used in the bitmap.

        Does not need a packed bitmap.
        -----------------------------------------------------------*/
```

```
WORD GetClrTableSize ( PBITMAPINFOHEADER pbiHeader )
{
    int iNumQuads;                     // number of RGBQUADs present

    if (!pbiHeader)
    {
        return( 0 );
    }

    /* count number of RGBQUADs in the color table */
    switch (pbiHeader>biBitCount)
    {
        case 16:                       // These DIBs do not have a normal
        case 32:                       // color table.  Their three RGBQUADs
            iNumQuads = 3;             // each contain a bit mask for extracting
            break;                     // R, G, and B values from the image data.

        case 24:
            iNumQuads = 0;             // no color table at all
            break;

        default:                       // bit count = 1, 4, or 8
            iNumQuads = GetNumColors( pbiHeader );
            break;
    }

    /* calculate size of color table in bytes */
    return( (WORD)(iNumQuads * sizeof(RGBQUAD)) );
}

/*-------------------------------------------------------------------
        GET DIB SIZE
        Calculates the total size of a DIB, including all structures
        and the image bits.  Does not need a packed bitmap.

        RETURN
        The total number of bytes, or 0 if there is an error
        ---------------------------------------------------------------*/

DWORD GetDIBSize ( PBITMAPINFOHEADER pbiHeader )
{
```

```
    if (!pbiHeader)                 // terminate if the pointer's no good
    {
        return( 0 );
    }

    //  If the DIB is not compressed, we can calculate the size
    //  of its image bits from other info in the INFO structure,
    //  but if it is compressed, we can only rely on the value
    //  already stored in pbiHeader->biSizeImage.

    if (pbiHeader->biCompression == BI_RGB)      // if not compressed
    {                                            // then calculate size
        pbiHeader->biSizeImage = GetDIBImageSize( pbiHeader );
    }

    /* add INFO structure and color table to image bits */
    return( pbiHeader->biSize
            + (DWORD)GetClrTableSize( pbiHeader )
            + pbiHeader->biSizeImage );
}

/*-------------------------------------------------------------------
        GET NUM COLORS
        Determines how many PALETTEENTRY structures you would need
        to build a palette for a given DIB.  Returns 0 for DIBs of
        high color depth that don't have colors in their tables.
        -----------------------------------------------------------*/

int GetNumColors ( PBITMAPINFOHEADER pbiHeader )
{
    if ( pbiHeader>biClrUsed != 0 )
    {
        return((WORD)pbiHeader>biClrUsed );
    }

    switch (pbiHeader>biBitCount)
    {
        case 1:
            return( 2 );

        case 4:
            return( 16 );
```

```
    case 8:
        return( 256 );

    default:                                    // bits per pixel > 8:
        return( 0 );                            // no colors in table
    }
}


/*--------------------------------------------------------------------
        GET DIB IMAGE SIZE
        Calculates the total size of all the image bits in a DIB.
        Assumes the DIB is not in a compressed RLE format.
        Does not need a packed bitmap.

        RETURN
        The total number of bytes, or 0 if there is an error.
    ------------------------------------------------------------------*/

DWORD GetDIBImageSize ( PBITMAPINFOHEADER pbiHeader )
{
    DWORD dwWidth;                      // width of image row in bytes

    /* figure width in bits */
    /* (bit width) = (pixel width) * (bits/pixel) */
    dwWidth = pbiHeader->biWidth * pbiHeader->biBitCount;

    /* convert to bytes, rounding up to align with DWORD boundary */
    /* (byte width) = (bit width) + (31) / (32 bits/DWORD) * (4 bytes/DWORD) */
    dwWidth = ( dwWidth + 31 ) / 32 * 4;

    return( dwWidth * pbiHeader->biHeight );
}
```

The DIBFILE Module

The DIBFILE module contains two primary procedures: ReadDIB and WriteDIB. One loads DIBs from files, the other saves DIBs into files. Two smaller functions are called to invoke the common dialog boxes for choosing a file to open or save.

```
/*-----------------------------------------------------------------


            DIBFILE.C

            File I/O routines for loading and saving bitmaps.  Part of
            the DIBLIB dynamic-link library.

            FUNCTIONS

                ReadDIB                 load DIB from file
                WriteDIB                save DIB to file
                DoOpenFileDlg           let user select a file name
                GetFileName             show common dialog box

            from Mastering Windows NT Programming
            copyright 1993 by Brian Myers & Eric Hamer

        ---------------------------------------------------------------*/

#define STRICT
#include <windows.h>
#include <windowsx.h>
#include <commdlg.h>
#include <stdlib.h>                        // MAX_ constants
#include "diblib.h"

/*-----------------------------------------------------------
        PROTOTYPE of private function
    -----------------------------------------------------------*/

static BOOL DoOpenFileDlg( HWND hWnd, LPSTR lpszName, LPSTR lpszPath );

/*-----------------------------------------------------------
        SYMBOL
    -----------------------------------------------------------*/

#define DIB_FILE_ID     0x4D42            // "BM" value marks DIB files
```

ReadDIB

Forgetting for a moment the error-checking steps that verify the success of each function before proceeding, ReadDIB works like this:

1. Open the file.

2. Read the **BITMAPFILEHEADER** structure.

3. Verify the header contents. The value in the **bmfType** field should be "BM" or, seen as an unsigned integer, 0x4D42.

4. Determine the size in bytes of the data we have to load.

5. Allocate that much room in global memory and lock it.

6. Read the bits from the file into the new global memory object.

7. Verify that we have loaded a Windows bitmap and not an OS/2 bitmap (which is very similar).

8. Destroy the previous bitmap, if any, and set the new one in its place.

Voilà! now you have a DIB.

Reading the Header and Data Structure

After an aerial view of the forest, we now approach the individual trees. **Create-File** opens the resource file. You've seen **CreateFile** open pipes and file-mapping objects; finally here it opens a disk file. DIBFILE does not call for any of **Create-File**'s special abilities because the file remains open only long enough to read its contents. All the operations in ReadDIB and WriteDIB could be done with the **OpenFile**, **_lread**, **_lwrite**, and **_lclose** commands instead of the new NT file commands, but we have written them with new NT functions instead. Chapter 12 tells more about file I/O.

The first **ReadFile** command reads the **BITMAPFILEHEADER** structure. We don't have much use for the file header, but the file pointer needs to advance past it. The **bfSize** field could be used to determine the size of the file we are about to read, but in case someone calculated the size incorrectly when the image was saved we prefer to determine the size by hand:

```
/* (size of bitmap) = (file size) - (file header size) */
dwDIBSize = (DWORD)FileInfo.nFileSizeLow - sizeof( BITMAPFILEHEADER );
```

Next ReadDIB allocates room for the DIB data and calls **ReadFile** again to fill the newly allocated buffer. The procedure then checks for another possible error: It may be that we have loaded a .BMP file created in OS/2, where bitmap headers have a slightly different format. OS/2 bitmaps have the same **BITMAPFILEHEADER** and the same image bits, but their **BITMAPINFO** structures begin with a **BITMAPCOREHEADER** instead of a **BITMAPINFOHEADER**. Also, the color table of an OS/2 bitmap uses **RGBTRIPLE**s instead of **RGBQUAD**s. All the Windows DIB functions work with either format, but we have decided not to complicate our demonstration program unnecessarily by checking in every procedure to see which format the current bitmap follows. If **ReadFile** succeeds in loading a Windows DIB then ReadDIB has accomplished its task. If the caller passed valid pointers as parameters, ReadDIB ends by copying the name and path of the newly opened file into the caller's buffers.

```
/*-------------------------------------------------------------------
        READ DIB
        Ask the user what file to open.  Load the DIB data from the
        file into memory.  Return a pointer to a valid DIB (or NULL
        for errors).

        RETURN
        A valid DIB pointer for success; NULL for failure.  Also,
        if lpszName and lpszPath are not NULL ReadDIB passes back the
        name and path of the file opened.
        -------------------------------------------------------------*/

PVOID ReadDIB (
    HWND hWnd,
    LPSTR lpszName,                     // path name of disk file
    LPSTR lpszPath,
    BOOL bAsk )                         // TRUE to ask user for name
{
    char szName[_MAX_FNAME];            // name of the disk file
    char szPath[MAX_PATH];              // full path of the disk file
    BITMAPFILEHEADER bfHeader;          // info about the image
    PBITMAPINFOHEADER pbiHeader;        // pointer to recast the same header
```

```
BY_HANDLE_FILE_INFORMATION FileInfo;     // info about an open file
HANDLE hFile;                            // handle to the file
DWORD dwDIBSize;                         // number of bytes in the DIB
DWORD dwBytesRead;                       // number of bytes read from DIB
UINT dwHeaderSize;                       // size of DIB header
LPVOID pDIB;                             // pointer to the loaded DIB
BOOL bTest;                              // for testing function returns

/* ask user for name of file to open */
if (bAsk)
{
    bTest = DoOpenFileDlg( hWnd, szName, szPath );
    if (!bTest)
    {
        return( NULL );                         // the user pressed Cancel
    }
}

/* open the file */
hFile = CreateFile( szPath,              // name of file
            GENERIC_READ,                // read-only access
            FILE_SHARE_READ,             // others may still read
            NULL,                        // default security
            OPEN_EXISTING,               // do not create new file
            FILE_ATTRIBUTE_NORMAL,       // file attributes
            NULL );                      // template for attributes
if (hFile == INVALID_HANDLE_VALUE)
{
    MessageBox( hWnd, "Cannot open file", "Error", MB_OK );
    return( NULL );
}

/* read BITMAPFILEHEADER structure from file */
dwHeaderSize = sizeof( BITMAPFILEHEADER );
bTest = ReadFile( hFile,                 // file to read from
            (LPVOID)&bfHeader,           // buffer to fill
            dwHeaderSize,                // num bytes to read
            &dwBytesRead,                // value returned
            NULL );                      // no overlapping I/O
if ((!bTest) || (dwBytesRead != dwHeaderSize))
```

```
{
    MessageBox( hWnd, "Could not read file", "Error", MB_OK );
    CloseHandle( hFile );
    return( NULL );
}

/* determine the number of data bytes in the file */
bTest = GetFileInformationByHandle( hFile, &FileInfo );
if (!bTest)
{
    CloseHandle( hFile );
    MessageBox( hWnd, "Could not get file info", "Error", MB_OK );
    return( NULL );
}

/* (size of bitmap) = (file size) - (file header size) */
dwDIBSize = (DWORD)FileInfo.nFileSizeLow - sizeof( BITMAPFILEHEADER );

/* allocate space in memory for an object that size */
pDIB = GlobalAllocPtr( GHND, dwDIBSize );
if (!pDIB)
{
    CloseHandle( hFile );
    MessageBox( hWnd, "Could allocate memory", "Error", MB_OK );
    return( NULL );
}

/* read all the data into the new buffer */
bTest = ReadFile( hFile,                        // file to read from
            pDIB,                               // buffer to fill
            dwDIBSize,                          // num bytes to read
            &dwBytesRead,                       // value returned
            NULL );                             // no overlapping I/O
if ((!bTest) || (dwBytesRead != dwDIBSize))
{
    CloseHandle( hFile );
    GlobalFreePtr( pDIB );

    MessageBox( hWnd, "Could not read bits", "Error", MB_OK );
    return( NULL );
}
```

```
/* verify that we have retrieved a Windows DIB, not an OS/2 DIB */
pbiHeader = (PBITMAPINFOHEADER)pDIB;
if (pbiHeader->biSize == sizeof(BITMAPCOREHEADER))
{
    CloseHandle( hFile );
    MessageBox( hWnd, "OS/2 bitmap", "Error", MB_OK );
    return( NULL );
}

/* if the caller gave name pointers, use them to return strings */
if (lpszName)
{
    lstrcpy( lpszName, szName );
}
if (lpszPath)
{
    lstrcpy( lpszPath, szPath );
}

return( pDIB );
}
```

WriteDIB

WriteDIB copies a DIB to a file. Not having to allocate any new memory blocks makes WriteDIB simpler than ReadDIB. Like ReadDIB, this procedure too accepts two string pointers and a Boolean parameter from the caller. bAsk instructs each procedure whether to ask the user for the name of a file to open or create. If requested, both procedures rely on another one—GetFileName—to raise one of the common dialog boxes and ask the user for a file name. In any case, if the file operation succeeds both procedures return the name of the file just used through the string parameters. The calling program may use the string pointers to pass Write-DIB a suggested name for the file or to retrieve and save the name either ReadDIB or WriteDIB ends up using for the file.

1. Initialize a **BITMAPFILEHEADER** structure for the new file.

2. Open the file.

3. Write the header, the bitmap, and the bits to the file.

4. Close the file.

```
/*-----------------------------------------------------------------
        WRITE DIB
        Write all the DIB data into a disk file.  If the caller
        sets bAsk to TRUE, show the save file dialog first to let the
        user pick a file name.  If the pointer parameters are
        non-null, their contents are used to initialize the dialog
        box settings.

        RETURN
        TRUE for success; FALSE for errors.  Also, if the function
        returns TRUE and lpszName and lpszFile are non-null, then
        afterward they point to the name and path the user chose.
        -----------------------------------------------------------*/

BOOL WriteDIB (
    HWND hWnd,
    LPSTR lpszName,                  // name of file
    LPSTR lpszPath,                  // full path of file
    BOOL bAsk,                       // ask user for file name?
    PVOID pDIB )                     // the DIB
{
    BITMAPFILEHEADER bmfHeader;      // header for bitmap file
    PBITMAPINFOHEADER pbiHeader;     // pointer to recast info in header
    HANDLE hFile;                    // handle to the file
    DWORD dwDIBSize;                 // number of bytes in bitmap
    UINT dwHeaderSize;               // number of bytes in file header
    BOOL bError = FALSE;             // TRUE if an error occurs
    char szName[_MAX_FNAME];         // name of disk file
    char szPath[MAX_PATH];           // full path of disk file
    DWORD dwBytesWritten;            // number of bytes written to disk
    BOOL bTest;                      // for testing function returns

    /* copy user's strings to full-sized buffers */
    if (lpszName)
    {
        lstrcpy( szName, lpszName );
    }
    if (lpszPath)
    {
        lstrcpy( szPath, lpszPath );
    }
```

```
/* if caller said to confirm name, show dialog */
if (bAsk)
{
    bTest = GetFileName( hWnd,        // ask the user for a file name
        FALSE,                        // FALSE to save (not to open)
        szPath,                       // buffer for path name
        szName );                     // buffer for file name

    if (!bTest)
    {
        return( FALSE );              // the user pressed Cancel
    }
}

/* make a pointer for referring to BITMAPINFOHEADER fields */
pbiHeader = (PBITMAPINFOHEADER)pDIB;

/* fill out a file header for the disk file */
bmfHeader.bfType = DIB_FILE_ID;               // the bytes "BM"
bmfHeader.bfSize = GetDIBSize( pDIB )
    + sizeof( BITMAPFILEHEADER );
bmfHeader.bfReserved1 = 0;
bmfHeader.bfReserved2 = 0;
bmfHeader.bfOffBits = (DWORD)sizeof( BITMAPFILEHEADER )
    + pbiHeader->biSize + (DWORD)GetClrTableSize(pbiHeader);

/* open the file */
hFile = CreateFile( szPath,                // path of file
            GENERIC_WRITE,                 // write-only access
            0,                             // prohibit file sharing
            NULL,                          // default security
            CREATE_ALWAYS,                 // overwrite old file
            FILE_ATTRIBUTE_NORMAL,         // file attributes
            NULL );                        // template for attributes
if (hFile == INVALID_HANDLE_VALUE)
{
    MessageBox(hWnd, "Could not open file", "Error", MB_OK);
    return( FALSE );
}

/* write header to disk */
dwHeaderSize = sizeof( BITMAPFILEHEADER );
bTest = WriteFile( hFile,                  // file to write in
            (const void *)&bmfHeader,      // data to write
            dwHeaderSize,                  // num bytes to write
```

```
                &dwBytesWritten,              // value returned
                NULL );                       // no overlapping I/O
if ((!bTest) || (dwBytesWritten != dwHeaderSize))
{
    CloseHandle( hFile );
    MessageBox( hWnd, "Could not write header", "Error", MB_OK );
    return( FALSE );
}

/* write the rest of the DIB to the file */
dwDIBSize = GetDIBSize( pDIB );
bTest = WriteFile( hFile,                     // file to write in
                (const void *)pDIB,           // data to write
                dwDIBSize,                    // num bytes to write
                &dwBytesWritten,              // value returned
                NULL );                       // no overlapping I/O
CloseHandle( hFile );
if ((!bTest) || (dwBytesWritten != dwDIBSize))
{
    MessageBox( hWnd, "Could not write header", "Error", MB_OK );
    return( FALSE );
}

/* if the caller gave name pointers, use them to return strings */
if (lpszName)
{
    lstrcpy( lpszName, szName );
}
if (lpszPath)
{
    lstrcpy( lpszPath, szPath );
}

return( TRUE );
}
```

Getting File Names

A single procedure, GetFileName, calls either the Open dialog or the Save As dialog, depending on the state of its Boolean parameter, bOpen. Both dialogs require a variable of type **OPENFILENAME** to store information about the current path, the suggested file name, the possible default file extensions, and the kind of response we want from the user. The library's needs are quite simple so we don't use all of the features in an **OPENFILENAME**. Unused fields should, however, be initialized explicitly to 0 or **NULL**.

The first field of the **OPENFILENAME** structure must hold its own size (just as the first field of a **BITMAPHEADERINFO** structure does.) hWnd identifies the parent of the new dialog box. The hInstance field matters only if you want to modify the standard template for the common dialog box, which we do not. **lpstrFilter** points to an array of descriptions and file extensions that will be offered to the user in a list box to use in filtering the list of files displayed. Bitmaps usually have the .BMP extension but sometimes also end in .DIB or .RLE. **lpstrFile** is a string buffer for storing the full path name of the user's choice. **lpstrFileTitle**, if not **NULL**, will receive just the name of the file, without its path. If you put a name in **lpstrFileTitle** before the dialog box runs, it appears in the dialog box's edit box as a default choice. In the **Flags** field we set markers to remove the Read Only check box from the dialog box, since it is irrelevant for our purposes, and to make the dialog box check that the user does not return the name of a path that doesn't exist.

The dialog box functions return a Boolean value to indicate success or failure. Whenever one fails, you can call **CommDlgExtendedError** to get a more precise error indicator. If the return value is 0, the user merely canceled the dialog box. When the function succeeds, GetFileName returns to its caller the file and path name used for the file operation.

One last procedure, DoOpenFileDlg, is called from ReadDIB as an intermediary to invoke GetFileName and raise a dialog box. DoOpenFileDlg brackets the call to GetFileName with GetDefaultNames and SetDefaultNames. Both procedures appear in the DibLib module listing in Chapter 11. SetDefaultNames writes the name and path of a file into a shared memory buffer from which GetDefaultNames later retrieves it. The DIB library creates a single shared memory buffer for all its clients, so they all set and get the same default value. If one program opens a file called pinkie.bmp, then the next program to display the Open File dialog box also offers "pinkie.bmp" as the default response.

```
/*-------------------------------------------------------------
    GET FILE NAME
    Invoke the Open File or Save As common dialog box.
    If the bOpenName parameter is TRUE, the procedure runs
    the OpenFileName dialog box.

    The lpszFile and lpszFileTitle parameters should point to
    buffers of size MAX_PATH and _MAX_FNAME, respectively.
```

```
        RETURN
        TRUE if the dialog box closes without error.  If the dialog
        box returns TRUE, then lpszFile and lpszFileTitle point to
        the new file path and name, respectively.
    ------------------------------------------------------------*/

BOOL GetFileName (
    HWND   hWnd,
    BOOL   bOpenName,                   // open file dlg or save as dlg
    LPSTR  lpszFile,                    // buffer for file path
    LPSTR  lpszFileTitle )              // buffer for file name
{
    OPENFILENAME ofn;
    CONST char *szFilter[] =    // filters for the file name combo box
    {
        "bitmaps (*.bmp)\0 *.bmp\0 All Files (*.*)\0 *.* \0\0",
    };

    /* initialize structure for the common dialog box */
    ofn.lStructSize       = sizeof( OPENFILENAME );
    ofn.hwndOwner         = hWnd;
    ofn.hInstance         = GetWindowInstance( hWnd );
    ofn.lpstrFilter       = szFilter[0];
    ofn.lpstrCustomFilter = NULL;
    ofn.nMaxCustFilter    = 0;
    ofn.nFilterIndex      = 1;
    ofn.lpstrFile         = lpszFile;
    ofn.nMaxFile          = _MAX_PATH;
    ofn.lpstrFileTitle    = lpszFileTitle;
    ofn.nMaxFileTitle     = _MAX_FNAME;
    ofn.lpstrInitialDir   = NULL;
    ofn.lpstrTitle        = NULL;
    ofn.nFileOffset       = 0;
    ofn.nFileExtension    = 0;
    ofn.lpstrDefExt       = "bmp";
    ofn.lCustData         = 0;
    ofn.lpfnHook          = NULL;
    ofn.lpTemplateName    = NULL;
```

```
    /* invoke the common dialog box */
    if (bOpenName)                              // Open a file
    {
        ofn.Flags = OFN_HIDEREADONLY | OFN_PATHMUSTEXIST |
                    OFN_FILEMUSTEXIST;
        return( GetOpenFileName(&ofn) );
    }
    else                                        // Save As...
    {
        ofn.Flags = OFN_HIDEREADONLY | OFN_OVERWRITEPROMPT;
        return( GetSaveFileName(&ofn) );
    }
}

/*-------------------------------------------------------------------
        DO OPEN FILE DLG
        Let the user select a file from the open file name
        common dialog.
    -------------------------------------------------------------*/

static BOOL DoOpenFileDlg (
    HWND hWnd,
    LPSTR lpszName,                     // file name from caller
    LPSTR lpszPath )                    // file path from caller
{
    BOOL bTest;                         // for testing return values

    // Retrieve a file name from the mapped memory object
    // the library shares among all its clients.  Offer
    // the retrieved name as the default response in the
    // dialog box.  The file holds two separate names:
    // the most recently loaded image bitmap and the most
    // recently loaded monochrome mask bitmap.

    GetDefaultNames( lpszName, lpszPath );

    bTest = GetFileName( hWnd,          // ask the user for a file name
                TRUE,                   // TRUE to open (not to save)
                lpszPath,               // buffer for path name
                lpszName );             // buffer for file name
    if (!bTest)
    {
        return( FALSE );                // assume user pressed Cancel
    }
```

```
    // Write the new file name to the mapped file object
    // where the next client can find it if needed.

    SetDefaultNames( lpszName, lpszPath );

    return( TRUE );
}
```

The DIBFX Module

The procedures in this module produce special effects with palette animation and bitmap masks.

```
/*-----------------------------------------------------------------

        DIBFX.C

        Utility functions for creating special effects with
        bitmaps and palettes.  Part of the DIBLIB dynamic-
        link library.

        FUNCTIONS

            FadeOut         makes an image fade to black
            FadeOnce        performs one step in the gradual fade
            FadeIn          makes an image fade in from blackness
            BrightenOnce    performs one step in the gradual brightening
            CopyColorTable  copies colors from DIB to PALETTEENTRY array
            CreateMask      create a mono mask bitmap from a color DDB
            ClearBlt        block transfer with transparent background

        from Mastering Windows NT Programming
        copyright 1993 by Brian Myers & Eric Hamer

    -----------------------------------------------------------------*/

#define STRICT
#include <windows.h>
#include <windowsx.h>
#include "diblib.h"
```

```
/*-----------------------------------------------------------------
          SYMBOLS
     ---------------------------------------------------------------*/

#define MAX_INTENSITY         255            // max R, G, or B value
#define FADE_INCREMENT          4            // used in palette fade routines
#define DESTINATION (DWORD)0x00AA0029        // a ROP3 code for ClearBlt

/*-----------------------------------------------------------------
          MACRO
     ---------------------------------------------------------------*/

// Combine two ROP3 codes into one ROP4 code.  The "black" code
// is applied to pixels in the source image that correspond to
// a black pixel in the mask.  The "white" code is applied to
// pixels that match up with a white pixel in the mask.

#define ROP4(black, white) ((((white) << 8) & 0xFF000000) | (black))

/*-----------------------------------------------------------------
          PROTOTYPES for private functions
     ---------------------------------------------------------------*/

static BOOL FadeOnce( HPALETTE hPal, PPALETTEENTRY ppeAnimate, int iNumColors,
    int iIncrement );
static BOOL BrightenOnce( HPALETTE hPal, PPALETTEENTRY ppeAnimate,
    PPALETTEENTRY ppeFinal, int iNumColors, int iIncrement );
static PPALETTEENTRY CopyColorTable( PVOID pDIB, BYTE byFlags );
```

Animating the Palette

The first four procedures modify the system palette so that whatever bitmap is being displayed appears to grow gradually dimmer or brighter, fading out from bright to black or fading back in from black to bright. Because **AnimatePalette** works only on devices that support palettes, not all systems can perform fades. Don't expect to see much if you run the code with a 16-color VGA adapter.

CopyColorTable

Both the fade routines make use of a utility called CopyColorTable. Its simple services are basic to the process of palette animation. First it allocates space for an array of **PALETTEENTRY** structures matching the **RGBQUAD** structures in the DIB's own color table. Then it copies the individual red, green, and blue color intensity values from the DIB into the new array. The result is the body of a logical palette containing all the colors without the preliminary **LOGPALETTE** header fields. The whole trick of palette animation is that you can graft new palette entries directly into a selected palette and have the screen reflect the changes immediately. FadeOut and FadeIn each create a copy of the DIB's color entries, increase or decrease them incrementally, and after each step load the changed values into the selected palette. All the pixels map to palette entries. When a pixel's palette entry changes, so does the pixel.

```
/*--------------------------------------------------------------------
        COPY COLOR TABLE
        Copy all the color information from the header of a DIB.
        This procecure allocates room for the new array of
        PALETTEENTRYs.  The caller is responsible for releasing
        the memory.
        ---------------------------------------------------------------*/

static PPALETTEENTRY CopyColorTable (
    PVOID pDIB,                         // DIB with color info to copy
    BYTE byFlag )                       // flag to insert in peFlags
{
    int iNumColors;                     // count of colors in DIB table
    int i;                              // loop variable
    PPALETTEENTRY ppeCopy;              // array of copied colors

    /* allocate space for a copy of the DIB's color table */
    iNumColors = GetNumColors( pDIB );
    ppeCopy = GlobalAllocPtr( GHND, sizeof(PALETTEENTRY) * iNumColors );
    if (ppeCopy)
    {
        /* copy the DIB's color table */
        for (i = 0;  i < iNumColors;  i++)
        {
            ppeCopy[i].peRed   =
                    ((PBITMAPINFO)pDIB)->bmiColors[i].rgbRed;
            ppeCopy[i].peGreen =
                    ((PBITMAPINFO)pDIB)->bmiColors[i].rgbGreen;
            ppeCopy[i].peBlue  =
                    ((PBITMAPINFO)pDIB)->bmiColors[i].rgbBlue;
            ppeCopy[i].peFlags = byFlag;
        }
    }
    return( ppeCopy );
}
```

FadeOnce

FadeOnce takes the array of palette entries copied from the bitmap and subtracts a small amount from each color value in it. After slightly reducing all the color intensities for all the **PALETTEENTRY**s, FadeOnce calls **AnimatePalette** to install the new values in the hpalDIB palette. (It assumes the palette has already been selected and realized.) The min macro prevents any color value from falling below 0, the lowest possible value. An RGB value of 0x000000L is black.

```
/*-----------------------------------------------------------------
        FADE ONCE
        Decrease the values of the bitmap's colors on step.
   ----------------------------------------------------------------*/
BOOL FadeOnce (
    HPALETTE hPal,
    PPALETTEENTRY ppeAnimate,
    int iNumColors,
    int iIncrement )
{
    int i;
    int iRed;
    int iGreen;
    int iBlue;
    BOOL bReturn;

    /* reduce the color intensities by one step */
    for (i = 0; i < iNumColors; i++)
    {
        iRed   = ppeAnimate[i].peRed   - iIncrement;
        iGreen = ppeAnimate[i].peGreen - iIncrement;
        iBlue  = ppeAnimate[i].peBlue  - iIncrement;

        ppeAnimate[i].peRed   = (BYTE)max( iRed,   0 );
        ppeAnimate[i].peGreen = (BYTE)max( iGreen, 0 );
        ppeAnimate[i].peBlue  = (BYTE)max( iBlue,  0 );
    }

    /* copy modified colors into the system palette */
    bReturn = AnimatePalette( hPal, 0, iNumColors, ppeAnimate );

    return( bReturn );
}
```

FadeOut

With `CopyColorTable` and `FadeOnce` understood, the procedure that runs the fade effect from start to finish is almost trivial. It copies the color table and then repeatedly passes the copy to `FadeOnce` in a loop.

`FadeOut`'s parameters include a DC, a palette handle, and a DIB pointer. `FadeOut` assumes the palette contains **PC_RESERVED** entries, that it has already been selected and realized in the DC, and that the DIB image has already been drawn. An animated palette must set the **PC_RESERVED** flag in order to protect other programs from accidentally mapping into an unstable color and having parts of their own images fade or brighten too. Even the changing palette entries repeatedly loaded into the logical palette must continue to set the **PC_RESERVED** flag, and you may have noticed that calls to `CopyColorTable` pass it the reserve flag to set in each entry.

```
/*-----------------------------------------------------------------
        FADE OUT
        Call FadeOnce repeatedly until the current image fades
        to black.  hpalReserved should be constructed from pDIB
        by calling PaletteFromDIB with the PC_RESERVED flag.
        FadeOut assumes that hpalReserved has already been selected
        and realized and that the DIB is currently displayed.
        -------------------------------------------------------------*/

BOOL FadeOut (
    HDC hDC,                         // device where pDIB is displayed
    PVOID pDIB,                      // currently displayed DIB
    HPALETTE hpalReserved )          // palette with PC_RESERVED entries
{
    int iNumColors;                  // number of colors in pDIB
    int i;                           // loop variable
    PPALETTEENTRY ppeAnimate;        // array of color intensities to reduce
    int iNumFades;                   // number of times to call FadeOnce

    if (!GetDeviceCaps(hDC, RASTERCAPS) & RC_PALETTE)
    {
        // AnimatePalette does not work well on devices
        // that do not support palettes.
        return( FALSE );
    }

    /* create array of color values copied from the DIB */
    ppeAnimate = CopyColorTable( pDIB, PC_RESERVED );
```

```
/* gradually reduce the intensities of the reserved colors */
iNumColors = GetNumColors( pDIB );
iNumFades = (MAX_INTENSITY+1) / FADE_INCREMENT;
for (i = 0; i < iNumFades; i++)
{
    FadeOnce( hpalReserved, ppeAnimate, iNumColors, FADE_INCREMENT );
}

/* clean up */
GlobalFreePtr( ppeAnimate );
return( TRUE );
}
```

Fading In

Two more procedures, FadeIn and BrightenOnce, manage the reverse process of starting an image from black and slowly raising all the color intensities until they reach full brightness. Though as their names suggest they closely resemble the fade-out routines, there is one significant difference. When an image fades out, all the pixels dim until they reach 0, but when an image fades in, each pixel stops brightening at a different point. All the colors increase from 0 until they reach their original values, which are not all the same. So FadeIn makes *two* sets of palette entries. The ppeAnimate set is the one that changes, as it did before, only this time starting at 0 and moving up. The new ppeFinal copy remains static and holds the final target value for each palette entry. When an entry in ppeAnimate matches the corresponding value in ppeFinal, it stops increasing. At each step of the fade-in BrightenOnce compares each animated color entry to its target value.

FadeIn does not assume, as FadeOut does, that the DIB has already been drawn, because the black version of the DIB can't be drawn without some of the tools FadeIn creates internally. You can't start a fade-in from a black screen; you must draw the image with an all-black palette first. To return to our paint-by-numbers analogy, a blank black window has only one color, one numbered area to paint. All the pixels map to the same black palette entry. What you need instead is a section of the screen where the pixels map to many different palette entries, but the entries all happen to be black. In effect, you have perhaps 236 different kinds of black, and you can reassign them all to different colors. FadeIn splices black into the logical palette, realizes the modified palette, and paints the DIB before it begins the fade-in. The **SetDIBitsToDevice** command produces no visible output on the screen because the window is already black, but it does remap parts of the video memory to a variety of different palette entries.

Even so, the system's normal impulse would be to avoid drawing so much black by mapping all the DIB's RGB values to the best possible color matches among the small set of static colors the system permanently shields from animation. FadeIn averts this disastrous mapping by changing the DIB to use palette indices instead of RGB colors. When the color table points directly to entries in the logical palette, the system sees no RGB values and is forced to use the palette colors.

```
/*---------------------------------------------------------------
        FADE IN
        Sets the current palette to black and gradually increases
        intensities in all palette entries until they reach the
        the normal values for pDIB.

        ppeAnimate contains the slowly increasing color values.
        ppeFinal contains the target color values for the normal
        DIB image.  No color intensity is allowed to increase
        beyond the maximum set for it in ppeFinal.

        Assumes that the hpalReserved palette contains PC_RESERVED
        entries, that this palette has already been selected and
        realized in the hDC device, and that the screen is already
        black.
        ------------------------------------------------------------*/

BOOL FadeIn (
    HDC hDC,                            // device where pDIB is displayed
    PVOID pDIB,                         // currently displayed DIB
    HPALETTE hpalReserved,              // palette with PC_RESERVED entries
    int x,                              // upper-left coordinates of place
    int y )                            //    where image should appear
{
    PBITMAPINFOHEADER pbiHeader;        // alias for pDIB
    PPALETTEENTRY ppeAnimate;           // array of color intensities to raise
    PPALETTEENTRY ppeFinal;             // copy of the DIB's own color table
    int iNumFades;                      // number of times to call BrightenOnce
    int iNumColors;                     // number of colors in pDIB
    int i;                              // loop variable

    pbiHeader = (PBITMAPINFOHEADER)pDIB;

    if (!GetDeviceCaps(hDC, RASTERCAPS) & RC_PALETTE)
    {
        // AnimatePalette does not work well on devices
        // that do not support palettes.
```

```
        return( FALSE );
}

/* create and initialize the array of target colors */
ppeFinal = CopyColorTable( pDIB, PC_RESERVED );

/* allocate space for another copy of the DIB's color table */
iNumColors = GetNumColors( pDIB );
ppeAnimate = GlobalAllocPtr( GHND, sizeof(PALETTEENTRY) * iNumColors );
if (!ppeAnimate)
{
        return( FALSE );
}

/* initialize the fade-in array by filling it with zeros (all black) */
FillMemory( ppeAnimate, sizeof(PALETTEENTRY)*iNumColors, 0 );
for (i = 0; i < iNumColors; i++)
{
        ppeAnimate[i].peFlags = PC_RESERVED;
}

/* fill the currently selected palette with black entries */
SetPaletteEntries( hpalReserved, 0, iNumColors, ppeAnimate );
RealizePalette( hDC );

// Draw the DIB so that screen pixels get matched to the new
// black palette.  If the screen is already black, this command
// should have no visible result.

SetDIBColorUsage( pDIB, hpalReserved, DIB_PAL_COLORS );
SetDIBitsToDevice( hDC,                   // destination
        x, y,                             // dest. origin
        pbiHeader->biWidth,               // dest. extents
        pbiHeader->biHeight,
        0, 0,                             // source origin
        0,                                // first scan line
        (UINT)pbiHeader->biHeight,        // last scan line
        GetDIBImagePtr( pDIB ),           // image bits
        (PBITMAPINFO)pDIB,                // DIB header
        DIB_PAL_COLORS );                 // color table usage

/* gradually increase the intensities of the reserved colors */
iNumFades = (MAX_INTENSITY+1) / FADE_INCREMENT;
for (i = 0; i < iNumFades; i++)
```

```
    {
        BrightenOnce( hpalReserved,          // palette to animate
                ppeAnimate,                  // array of colors that brighten
                ppeFinal,                    // stop when colors match this
                iNumColors,                  // number of colors in arrays
                FADE_INCREMENT );            // degree of brightness to add
    }

    /* clean up */
    SetPaletteEntries( hpalReserved, O, iNumColors, ppeFinal );
    SetDIBColorUsage( pDIB, hpalReserved, DIB_RGB_COLORS );
    GlobalFreePtr( ppeAnimate );
    return( TRUE );
}

/*------------------------------------------------------------------
        BRIGHTEN ONCE
        Increase the values of the bitmap's colors by one step.
    ------------------------------------------------------------------*/

static BOOL BrightenOnce (
    HPALETTE hPal,                           // palette to animate
    PPALETTEENTRY ppeAnimate,                // array of changing colors
    PPALETTEENTRY ppeFinal,                  // array of target colors
    int iNumColors,                          // number of colors in both arrays
    int iIncrement )                         // amount to increase color intensity
{
    int i;
    int iRed;
    int iGreen;
    int iBlue;
    BOOL bReturn;

    /* reduce the color intensities by one step */
    for (i = 0; i < iNumColors; i++)
    {
        iRed   = ppeAnimate[i].peRed   + iIncrement;
        iGreen = ppeAnimate[i].peGreen + iIncrement;
        iBlue  = ppeAnimate[i].peBlue  + iIncrement;

        ppeAnimate[i].peRed   = (BYTE)min( iRed,   ppeFinal[i].peRed );
        ppeAnimate[i].peGreen = (BYTE)min( iGreen, ppeFinal[i].peGreen );
        ppeAnimate[i].peBlue  = (BYTE)min( iBlue,  ppeFinal[i].peBlue );
    }
```

```
/* copy modified colors into the system palette */
bReturn = AnimatePalette( hPal, 0, iNumColors, ppeAnimate );

return( bReturn );
}
```

Making Masks

The last two routines in DIBFX, `CreateMask` and `ClearBlt`, help you make use of bitmap masks. `CreateMask`, given any device-dependent bitmap, constructs a monochrome bitmap of the same dimensions and performs a **BitBlt** to copy the color image onto the black-and-white surface. `CreateMask` controls which pixels turn black and which turn white by setting the background color in the source device. If, for example, **SetBkColor** chooses blue for the background, then all the blue pixels become white during the conversion and all the other pixels turn black. If the original bitmap held, for example, a blue circle on a white background, then the converted mask would show a white circle on a black background. A mask derived from an image in this way can be used to filter out sections of the original image or to modify the image selectively. The sample Mask program, which we'll reach in a moment, calls this procedure to let you make masks for any bitmap image.

The other procedure, `ClearBlt`, performs a block transfer but endows the source image with a transparent background. We have patterned its parameters after **BitBlt** with the addition of a color value designating the pixels that should become transparent. If, for example, the source image shows a chess board and the color value is black, then none of the black squares will be copied to the destination. The black squares will show in the new image only as gaps through which the original background is visible. `ClearBlt` first calls `CreateMask` to produce a filter with all the transparent pixel places set to white. It passes the mask to **MaskBlt** along with a ROP4 code that copies the original image only through the black pixels in the mask. The white pixels don't transmit; they remain opaque and block parts of the image during the transfer.

```
/*--------------------------------------------------------------------
    CREATE MASK
    Creates a monochrome mask bitmap derived from the image in
    a source image bitmap.  The mask will be white everywhere
    the image has the color given in cBkgnd.  The mask will be
    black everywhere else.
```

```
            RETURN
            A new bitmap handle, or NULL for errors. _____*/
------------------------------------------------------------------*/

HBITMAP CreateMask (
    HDC hDC,
    HBITMAP hbmImage,              // source image (color)
    COLORREF cBkgnd )              // color of hbmImage background
{
    BITMAP bm;                     // info about image bitmap
    HBITMAP hbmMask, hbmOld;       // monochrome bitmap
    HDC hdcMask, hdcImage;         // DCs for image and its mask

    /* create a memory DC for the image bitmap and one for the mask */
    hdcImage = CreateCompatibleDC( hDC );
    if (!hdcImage)
    {
        return( NULL );
    }

    hdcMask = CreateCompatibleDC( hDC );
    if (!hdcMask)
    {
        DeleteDC( hdcImage );
        return( NULL );
    }

    /* create a monochrome bitmap with same dimensions as hbmImage */
    GetObject( hbmImage, sizeof(BITMAP), &bm );
    hbmMask = CreateBitmap(
                (int)bm.bmWidth,           // bitmap dimensions
                (int)bm.bmHeight,
                1, 1, NULL );              // bitmap depth and initial bits
    if (!hbmMask)
    {
        DeleteDC( hdcImage );
        DeleteDC( hdcMask );
        return( NULL );
    }

    /* prepare both device contexts for the BitBlt */
    hbmOld = SelectBitmap( hdcImage, hbmImage );
    hbmOld = SelectBitmap( hdcMask, hbmMask );
    SetBkColor( hdcImage, cBkgnd );        // this color will be white
```

```
        BitBlt( hdcMask, 0, 0,                    // copy image to mask
            (int)bm.bmWidth,
            (int)bm.bmHeight,
            hdcImage, 0, 0,
            SRCCOPY );

        SelectBitmap( hdcImage, hbmOld );         // clean up
        SelectBitmap( hdcMask, hbmOld );
        DeleteDC( hdcImage );
        DeleteDC( hdcMask );
        return( hbmMask );
}

/*-----------------------------------------------------------------
        CLEAR BLT
        Performs a block transfer treating the background color of
        the source image as a transparent area.  Whatever is already
        on the destination surface will show through the image's
        background.

        The last parameter is a COLORREF value which should be an RGB
        number naming the source image's background color.  Pixels
        that color will not be copied to the destination.
        ------------------------------------------------------------*/

BOOL ClearBlt (
        HDC hdcDest,                      // device where image will appear
        int xDest,                        // position for image to appear
        int yDest,
        HBITMAP hbmSource,                // the image
        COLORREF cTransparent )           // the color not to copy
{
        BITMAP bm;                        // info about source bitmap
        HBITMAP hbmMask, hbmOld;          // new mono mask bitmap
        HDC hdcSource;                    // DC for source image
        BOOL bResult;                     // return from MaskBlt

        /* create the monochrome mask bitmap */
        hbmMask = CreateMask( hdcDest, hbmSource, cTransparent );
        if (!hbmMask)
        {
            return( FALSE );
        }

        hdcSource = CreateCompatibleDC( hdcDest );        // put image in a DC
```

```
if (!hdcSource)
{
    DeleteBitmap( hbmMask );
    return( FALSE );
}
hbmOld = SelectBitmap( hdcSource, hbmSource );

GetObject( hbmSource, sizeof(BITMAP), &bm );
bResult = MaskBlt( hdcDest, xDest, yDest,          // display image
    (int)bm.bmWidth, (int)bm.bmHeight,
    hdcSource, 0, 0,
    hbmMask,
    0, 0,
    ROP4(DESTINATION, SRCCOPY) );                  // white acts transparent

SelectBitmap( hdcSource, hbmOld );                 // clean up
DeleteDC( hdcSource );
DeleteBitmap( hbmMask );
return( bResult );
}
```

Figure 10.5 demonstrates the effect of transparency by drawing some ghosts randomly on a patterned background. Here's the procedure that draws the ghosts in response to mouse clicks.

FIGURE 10.5:

Ghosts drawn with ClearBlt

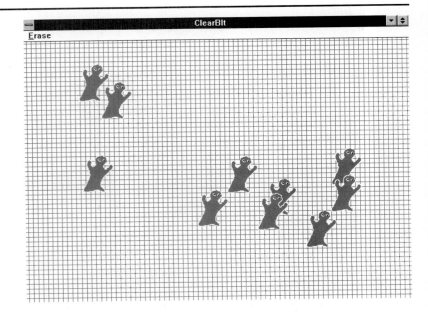

```
/*-----------------------------------------------------------------
        BUTTONDOWN PROCEDURE
        Draws the bitmap where the user clicks the mouse button.
        The background color of the source image is not copied,
        making it effectively transparent.
   -----------------------------------------------------------------*/

void ClearBlt_OnButtonDown ( HWND hWnd,
                             BOOL bDoubleClick,
                              int x,
                              int y,
                             UINT uKeyFlags )
{
    HDC hDC = GetDC( hWnd );
    if (!hDC)
    {
        return;
    }

    ClearBlt( hDC, x, y,
              hbmSource,
              RGB_BLACK );

    ReleaseDC( hWnd, hDC );
    return;
}
```

The Client Programs

The Ghost program from which we excerpted that last piece of source code is one of three client programs we wrote to use the DibLib library. All three appear on the accompanying disk. The other two are Fade, which uses the library's palette animation routines, and Mask, which allows the user to create masks from any bitmap and explore the effect of different ROP codes when source and mask are combined in a **MaskBlt** command.

The Fade Program

The Fade program demonstrates palette operations. The user loads any DIB and then makes it fade in or fade out. Figure 10.6 shows the Fade program window. The image is displayed at the center of a black client area. It fades in and out of the black background. The Fade program calls the following routines from the DIB Library: `FadeOut`, `FadeIn`, `PaletteFromDIB`, `DIBBlt`, `ReadDIB`, and `GetDIBImagePtr`. To call library routines, all a client has to do is link to the import library, diblib.lib. Chapter 11 explains more about building and using libraries. The make file, header, and resource template for Fade are all on the disk that accompanies the book; we have omitted from the listings here these and other files and procedures of no immediate relevance to bitmaps or palettes.

Message Procedures

Of the message-handling routines, perhaps the two palette message procedures require some comment. The **WM_QUERYNEWPALETTE** message arrives when the Fade window becomes active. It offers an opportunity to choose the colors we want by realizing a palette. Other applications may have put different colors into the system for their images and we may need to reset them. Whenever Fade loads a new bitmap, it creates a palette for the bitmap and stores it in the global variable `hpalDIB`.

FIGURE 10.6:

Fade program window

When a **WM_QUERYNEWPALETTE** message arrives, the program selects the palette into the device context and tells Windows to realize those colors, putting them into the system palette. Any subsequent GDI function calls will use the new colors.

The situation differs when our program does not have the input focus. The program with the focus gets top priority for its palette requests. Windows generally reserves a few palette entries for the system to use in drawing windows, but the foreground application gets first pick on everything else. Background applications get their chance when they receive **WM_PALETTECHANGED**. A program must first verify that it hasn't caused the message itself with its own previous palette changes. Compare your own window handle to the one that comes with the message to avoid recursion. Then you have two choices: a slow repaint or a faster but less accurate update. Usually neither action will give you every color you want. If the system has its usual 20 static colors and the foreground program fills up 200 more entries, the background applications may have only 36 more to share among them.

When a program's paint procedure does something slow, like displaying a large bitmap, repainting the client area for each palette change is cumbersome. Rather than redrawing a complex picture, you can choose instead to call **UpdateColors** and ask Windows to loop through all the pixels in your client area and find the best matches. **UpdateColors** usually works more quickly than repainting, but it is not entirely accurate. It works by considering what color each pixel mapped to before the palette changed and finding the best approximation in the new palette. Because each new update is based on the previous approximation, the picture deteriorates with successive updates. Fade_OnPaletteChanged avoids excessive deterioration by counting the updates and forcing a periodic repaint.

You must use the same palette each time you call **UpdateColors** for one image. Do not call PaletteFromDIB to extract a new palette for each **WM_PALETTECHANGED** message. Internally, each palette object remembers three distinct ways to map its colors into the system palette: how it is currently mapped, how it was last mapped, and how it will always be mapped whenever the palette has foreground priority. When you generate a new palette, you lose some of those mappings. Since every DDB, including the screen, remembers colors by their position in the system palette, switching palettes before **UpdateColors** produces unwanted psychedelic effects. **UpdateColors** must see the correct previous palette mapping in order to work.

Any application that uses palettes should consider responding to these two messages. Applications that don't use palettes can safely ignore both of them. Systems that don't use palettes ignore the messages too. A high-color adapter has no need for palettes and the system dispenses with delivering palette messages when it can.

You can test the efficacy of these two message-handling procedures by running two instances of Fade simultaneously on a 256-color adapter. Load a different 256-color DIB into each instance and then switch between them, clicking first one and then the other to shift the input focus. When an image moves to the background it turns to psychedelic mush as the other instance realizes its palette. But the background application then partially regains its composure by calling **UpdateColors** and the image becomes at least recognizable again. The Mask program, which we'll come to next, lacks procedures to handle palette changes and does not perform well when it shares the screen with other palette-hungry programs.

```
/*-----------------------------------------------------------------


        FADE.C

    Demonstrates palette animation.  The user loads any DIB
    and the program makes it fade to black or brighten from
    black back to visibility.

    Calls routines from the DIBLIB dynamic-link library.

    FUNCTIONS

            WinMain                 receive window messages
            Init                    register/create program window
            Fade_WndProc            respond to window messages
            Fade_OnInitMenu         update menu item check marks
            Fade_OnQueryNewPalette  realize palette on receiving focus
            Fade_OnPaletteChanged   update colors in the background
            Fade_OnPaint            repaint the display
            Fade_OnCommand          respond to menu commands
            Fade_OnDestroy          clean up and quit
            DoOpen                  load a DIB file
            DoFade                  make the image fade to black
            About_DlgProc           run the About box window

    from Mastering Windows NT Programming
    copyright 1993 by Brian Myers & Eric Hamer


------------------------------------------------------------------*/
```

```
#define STRICT
#include <windows.h>
#include <windowsx.h>
#include "fade.h"
#include "diblib.h"                    // DLL interface header

/*-----------------------------------------------------------------
        SYMBOL
  ---------------------------------------------------------------*/

#define MAX_PAL_UPDATES      5         // used in OnPaletteChanged

/*-----------------------------------------------------------------
        GLOBAL VARIABLES
  ---------------------------------------------------------------*/

PVOID     pDIBCurrent = NULL;          // bitmap read from the file
HPALETTE  hpalDIB;                     // palette made from the DIB

// ==========================================
//  Look for these procedures on the disk:
//  WinMain, Init, and About_DlgProc
// ==========================================

/*-----------------------------------------------------------------
        FADE_WNDPROC
        Respond to window messages.
  ---------------------------------------------------------------*/

LRESULT WINAPI Fade_WndProc (
    HWND hWnd,
    UINT uMessage,
    WPARAM wParam,
    LPARAM lParam )
{
    switch (uMessage)
    {
        /* window needs to be repainted */
        HANDLE_MSG( hWnd, WM_PAINT, Fade_OnPaint );

        /* update the menu */
        HANDLE_MSG( hWnd, WM_INITMENU, Fade_OnInitMenu );

        /* we're getting input focus and should set the foreground palette */
        HANDLE_MSG( hWnd, WM_QUERYNEWPALETTE, Fade_OnQueryNewPalette );
```

```
        /* system palette has changed */
        HANDLE_MSG( hWnd, WM_PALETTECHANGED, Fade_OnPaletteChanged );

        /* user has chosen something from the program menu */
        HANDLE_MSG( hWnd, WM_COMMAND, Fade_OnCommand );

        /* our window has been destroyed */
        HANDLE_MSG( hWnd, WM_DESTROY, Fade_OnDestroy );

        default:
            return( DefWindowProc(hWnd, uMessage, wParam, lParam) );
    }

    return( OL );
}

/*--------------------------------------------------------------------
        FADE_ONINITMENU
        Enable and disable commands according to whether the user has
        loaded a bitmap.
    --------------------------------------------------------------------*/

void Fade_OnInitMenu (
    HWND hWnd,
    HMENU hMenu )
{
    if (pDIBCurrent)
    {
        EnableMenuItem( hMenu, IDM_FADEIN,  MF_ENABLED );
        EnableMenuItem( hMenu, IDM_FADEOUT, MF_ENABLED );
        EnableMenuItem( hMenu, IDM_RESTORE, MF_ENABLED );
    }
    else
    {
        EnableMenuItem( hMenu, IDM_FADEIN,  MF_GRAYED );
        EnableMenuItem( hMenu, IDM_FADEOUT, MF_GRAYED );
        EnableMenuItem( hMenu, IDM_RESTORE, MF_GRAYED );
    }

    return;
    UNREFERENCED_PARAMETER( hWnd );
}
```

```
/*--------------------------------------------------------------------
        FADE_ONQUERYNEWPALETTE
        Process WM_QUERYNEWPALETTE messages here by realizing our
        palette as our program receives the input focus.  This
        restores any damage other programs' palettes may have done.

        RETURN
        TRUE if we change the system palette and FALSE if we don't
    ----------------------------------------------------------------*/
BOOL NEAR Fade_OnQueryNewPalette ( HWND hWnd )
{
    HPALETTE hpalOld;
    HDC hDC;
    BOOL bChanges;

    if (!pDIBCurrent)
    {
        /* no current DIB to draw; nothing to do */
        return( FALSE );
    }

    /* make the system use the DIB's palette */
    hDC = GetDC( hWnd );
    hpalOld = SelectPalette( hDC, hpalDIB, FALSE );
    bChanges = RealizePalette( hDC );
    SelectPalette( hDC, hpalOld, FALSE );
    ReleaseDC( hWnd, hDC );

    if (bChanges)
    {
        /* realization did modify the system palette, so redraw */
        InvalidateRect( hWnd, NULL, TRUE );
        UpdateWindow( hWnd );
    }
    return( bChanges );
}


/*--------------------------------------------------------------------
        FADE_ONPALETTECHANGED
        Process WM_PALETTECHANGED messages here by realizing our
        palette and calling UpdateColors to make quick, reasonable
        matches with the new system palette.
    ----------------------------------------------------------------*/
```

```
void Fade_OnPaletteChanged (
    HWND hWnd,
    HWND hwndPaletteChange )
{
    static short nUpdates = 0;        // number of times UpdateColors called
    HPALETTE hpalOld;
    HDC hDC;

    if ((!pDIBCurrent) ||                     // no current DIB?
        (hWnd == hwndPaletteChange))          // message from ourself?
    {
        return;                               // do nothing
    }

    /* merge the DIB's palette colors into the system palette */
    hDC     = GetDC( hWnd );
    hpalOld = SelectPalette( hDC, hpalDIB, FALSE );

    if (RealizePalette( hDC ))      // does this modify the system palette?
    {                                         // yes
        if (nUpdates < MAX_PAL_UPDATES)       // too many updates?
        {                                     // no, not too many
            UpdateColors( hDC );              // do another update
            nUpdates++;                       // increase counter
        }
        else                                  // yes, too many
        {
            InvalidateRect( hWnd, NULL, TRUE ); // force repainting
            nUpdates = 0;                       // reset counter
        }
    }
    SelectPalette( hDC, hpalOld, FALSE );
    ReleaseDC( hWnd, hDC );
    return;
}

/*------------------------------------------------------------------

        FADE_ONPAINT
        Redisplay the current DIB, if any.
    ------------------------------------------------------------*/
```

```
void Fade_OnPaint ( HWND hWnd )
{
    PAINTSTRUCT ps;
    HDC hDC;
    LPBITMAPINFOHEADER pbiHeader;          // alias for pDIBCurrent
    RECT rClient;
    int x, y;                              // coor's for centering DIB

    hDC = BeginPaint( hWnd, &ps );
    GetClientRect( hWnd, &rClient );

    if (pDIBCurrent && hDC)                // is a DIB loaded?
    {
        pbiHeader = (LPBITMAPINFOHEADER)pDIBCurrent;

        /* figure upper-left coordinate for centering DIB in client area */
        x = (rClient.right/2) - (pbiHeader->biWidth/2);
        y = (rClient.bottom/2) - (pbiHeader->biHeight/2);

        DIBBlt( hDC,
            hpalDIB,
            x, y,
            (int)pbiHeader->biWidth,
            (int)pbiHeader->biHeight,
            pbiHeader,
            0, 0,
            SRCCOPY );
    }

    EndPaint( hWnd, &ps );
    return;
}

/*-----------------------------------------------------------------
        FADE_ONCOMMAND
        Interpret command messages from the menu and call other
        procedures to respond.
    -------------------------------------------------------------*/

void Fade_OnCommand (
    HWND hWnd,
    int iCmd,
    HWND hwndCtl,
    UINT uCode )
```

```
{
    HINSTANCE hInst;
    HDC hDC;

    switch (iCmd)
    {
        case IDM_OPEN:                              // load a bitmap from a file
            DoOpen( hWnd );
            break;

        case IDM_FADEOUT:                           // make image fade to black
        case IDM_FADEIN:
            DoFade( hWnd, iCmd );
            break;

        case IDM_RESTORE:                           // repaint with normal colors
            hDC = GetDC( hWnd );
            if (hDC)
            {
                HPALETTE hpalOld;
                                                    // realize palette
                hpalOld = SelectPalette( hDC, hpalDIB, FALSE );
                RealizePalette( hDC );
                SelectPalette( hDC, hpalOld, FALSE );
                ReleaseDC( hWnd, hDC );
            }
            InvalidateRect( hWnd, NULL, TRUE );     // repaint
            UpdateWindow( hWnd );
            break;

        case IDM_ABOUT:                             // display the About box
            hInst = GetWindowInstance( hWnd );
            DialogBox( hInst, MAKEINTRESOURCE(DLG_ABOUT),
                hWnd, About_DlgProc );
            break;
    }

    return;
    UNREFERENCED_PARAMETER( uCode );
    UNREFERENCED_PARAMETER( hwndCtl );
}
```

```
/*-------------------------------------------------------------------
        FADE_ONDESTROY
        Free the bitmap and post the quit message.
    ----------------------------------------------------------------*/
void Fade_OnDestroy ( HWND hWnd )
{
    if (pDIBCurrent)                        // delete the DIB
    {
        GlobalFreePtr(pDIBCurrent);
    }

    if (hpalDIB)                            // delete its palette
    {
        DeletePalette( hpalDIB );
    }

    PostQuitMessage( 0 );

    return;
    UNREFERENCED_PARAMETER( hWnd );
}
```

Command Procedures

DoFade is the most important of the procedures that execute menu commands. It makes all the preliminary arrangements for fading the image into or out of its black background. First it creates a new palette for the DIB in order to add the **PC_RESERVED** flag to all the palette entries—**AnimatePalette** does not work without the flag. We could of course create a **PC_RESERVED** palette immediately on loading each new image, but that puts an unnecessary strain on the system if several colorful programs run at once.

Incidentally, the strain would not be insupportable. A "reserved" palette entry is not permanently locked in the system. As soon as any other application realizes its own palette in the foreground, all our reserved entries may be wiped out, to be restored only when Fade regains the foreground and re-realizes its own palette. Using a permanently reserved palette would not make Fade interfere with any application in the foreground; it would only intensify the competition among the background applications for the remaining system palette entries.

At any rate, Fade creates and realizes the reserved palette anew each time it calls DoFade. When it realizes the new palette, the system remaps all the logical palette colors. Even though the new palette contains exactly the same color values as the old one, it almost certainly has to be mapped differently now that all its entries must be reserved. The system will not, for example, let a **PC_RESERVED** palette entry map to any of the static system colors. They are protected from animation. Because the palette mapping has changed, the DIB must be redisplayed before animation begins. Even the color values for screen pixels, remember, refer to the system palette, and when the palette changes the entries they referenced no longer point to the same colors. That's why DIBBlt precedes our call to FadeOut.

FadeIn, as we explained earlier, has to take responsibility for drawing the initial black-palette image itself, so calling it takes less preparation.

```
/*------------------------------------------------------------
        DO OPEN
        Ask the user for the name of a BMP file.  Open the file,
        load the contents, and display the DIB.
        ----------------------------------------------------------*/

void DoOpen ( HWND hWnd )
{
    PVOID pDIBNew;                          // new DIB
    HDC hDC;                                // screen DC
    HPALETTE hpalOld;                       // default palette

    pDIBNew = ReadDIB( hWnd, NULL, NULL, TRUE );  // read DIB from file
    if (!pDIBNew)
    {
        return;                             // user pressed Cancel
    }

    if (pDIBCurrent)                        // delete previous objects
    {
        GlobalFreePtr( pDIBCurrent );
    }
    if (hpalDIB)
    {
        DeletePalette( hpalDIB );
    }

    pDIBCurrent = pDIBNew;                          // remember new objects
    hpalDIB = PaletteFromDIB( pDIBCurrent, O );
```

```
    hDC = GetDC( hWnd );                        // realize new palette
    if (hDC)
    {
        hpalOld = SelectPalette( hDC, hpalDIB, FALSE );
        RealizePalette( hDC );
        SelectPalette( hDC, hpalOld, FALSE );
        ReleaseDC( hWnd, hDC );
    }

    InvalidateRect( hWnd, NULL, TRUE );     // redraw the screen
    UpdateWindow( hWnd );
    return;
}

/*-------------------------------------------------------------------
        DO FADE
        Make the bitmap image fade gradually until all its colors
        are black.
   ------------------------------------------------------------------*/

BOOL DoFade (
    HWND hWnd,
    int iCmd )                          // IDM_FADEIN  or IDM_FADEOUT
{
    HDC hDC;
    BOOL bSuccess;                      // true if DoFade finds no errors
    PBITMAPINFOHEADER pbiHeader;       // alias for pDIBCurrent
    HPALETTE hpalReserved, hpalOld;    // palette with PC_RESERVED entries
    int iRealized;                      // return value from RealizePalette
    RECT rClient;                       // client area
    int x, y;                           // coor's for centering bitmap

    pbiHeader = (PBITMAPINFOHEADER)pDIBCurrent;
    hDC = GetDC( hWnd );

    /* create a palette for the DIB using all PC_RESERVED entries */
    hpalReserved = PaletteFromDIB( pDIBCurrent, PC_RESERVED );
    if (!hpalReserved)
    {
        ReleaseDC( hWnd, hDC );
        return( FALSE );
    }

    /* select and realize the new PC_RESERVED palette */
    hpalOld = SelectPalette( hDC, hpalReserved, FALSE );
```

```
iRealized = RealizePalette( hDC );
if (iRealized < GetNumColors(pDIBCurrent))
{
    MessageBox( hWnd, "Image uses many colors; not all may animate.",
        "Warning", MB_OK );
}

/* figure upper-left coordinate for centering DIB in client area */
GetClientRect( hWnd, &rClient );
x = (rClient.right/2) - (pbiHeader->biWidth/2);
y = (rClient.bottom/2) - (pbiHeader->biHeight/2);

/* make the palette slowly fade */
switch (iCmd)
{
    case IDM_FADEOUT:

        /* display the bitmap using its new palette */
        DIBBlt( hDC,                              // destination
            hpalReserved,                         // animation palette
            x, y,                                 // dest. origin
            (int)pbiHeader>biWidth,               // x extent
            (int)pbiHeader>biHeight,              // y extent
            pbiHeader,                            // DIB header
            0, 0,                                 // source origin
            SRCCOPY );                            // ROP3 code

        /* make the image fade to black */
        bSuccess = FadeOut( hDC, pDIBCurrent, hpalReserved );
        break;

    case IDM_FADEIN:
        /* make the image fade in from black to full color */
        bSuccess = FadeIn( hDC,                   // destination
            pDIBCurrent,                          // the image
            hpalReserved,                         // palette for animation
            x, y );                               // place to appear
        break;
}

if (!bSuccess)
{
    MessageBox( hWnd, "Cannot perform palette animation",
        "Error", MB_OK );
}
```

```
    SelectPalette( hDC, hpalOld, FALSE );    // clean up and quit
    DeletePalette( hpalReserved );
    ReleaseDC( hWnd, hDC );
    return( bSuccess );
}
```

The Mask Program

The Mask program also links with the DibLib library. It allows the user to load two bitmaps, one monochrome, and calls **MaskBlt** to filter the image through the mask and display the result. In Figure 10.7, Mask has loaded a picture, visible in the window's upper-left quadrant; created a mask bitmap, appearing at the lower left; and chosen a gray brush and a ROP4 code that combines **PATCOPY** with **SRCINVERT** to produce the image at the upper right. Once loaded the image and mask remain visible; the merged image appears whenever the user clicks MaskBlt! on the menu bar. The Brush menu offers a small selection of stock brushes to be used as the pattern for ROP combinations. The BlackROP menu lists common ROP3 codes and applies the current selection to source colors that filter through black mask pixels. The ROP3 code selected from the WhiteROP menu applies to colors that filter through white mask pixels.

FIGURE 10.7:

A bitmap, its mask, and an image MaskBlt produces by combining them

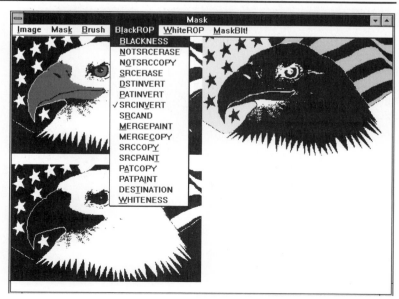

The Image popup menu offers Open and Clear commands to load new source images. The Mask menu, besides Open and Clear, includes commands to derive a new mask by converting the source image to monochrome and to load a standard checkerboard pattern from the program's resources.

To do all this, Mask calls a number of routines from the DIB Library: `ReadDIB`, `WriteDIB`, `CreateMask`, `PaletteFromDIB`, `DIBtoDDB`, and `DIBtoMonoDDB`.

```
// ============================================
//  The make file and header appear on the disk.
//  Look for mask.mak and mask.h.
// ============================================

/*-------------------------------------------------------------

        MASK.RC

        Resource script file for MASK program.

    ------------------------------------------------------------*/

#include <windows.h>
#include "mask.h"

BMP_MASK BITMAP "mask.bmp"

STRINGTABLE
BEGIN
    IDS_APPNAME,       "mask_class"
    IDS_TITLE,         "Mask"
END

MENU_MAIN MENU
BEGIN
    POPUP "&Image"
    BEGIN
        MENUITEM "&Open..."            IDM_LOADSOURCE
        MENUITEM "&Clear"              IDM_CLEARSOURCE
        MENUITEM SEPARATOR
        MENUITEM "&About...",          IDM_ABOUT
    END
```

```
POPUP "Mas&k"
BEGIN
    MENUITEM "&Open..."             IDM_LOADMASK
    MENUITEM "&Save..."             IDM_SAVEMASK
    MENUITEM "&Clear"               IDM_CLEARMASK
    MENUITEM "&Make"                IDM_MAKEMASK
    MENUITEM "&Squares"             IDM_LOADRESMASK
END

POPUP "&Brush"
BEGIN
    MENUITEM "&Black"               IDM_BR_BLACK
    MENUITEM "&Gray"                IDM_BR_GRAY
    MENUITEM "&White"               IDM_BR_WHITE
END

POPUP "B&lackROP"
BEGIN
    MENUITEM "&BLACKNESS",          IDM_BROP_BLACKNESS
    MENUITEM "&NOTSRCERASE",        IDM_BROP_NOTSRCERASE
    MENUITEM "N&OTSRCCOPY",         IDM_BROP_NOTSRCCOPY
    MENUITEM "&SRCERASE",           IDM_BROP_SRCERASE
    MENUITEM "&DSTINVERT",          IDM_BROP_DSTINVERT
    MENUITEM "&PATINVERT",          IDM_BROP_PATINVERT
    MENUITEM "SRCIN&VERT",          IDM_BROP_SRCINVERT
    MENUITEM "S&RCAND",             IDM_BROP_SRCAND
    MENUITEM "&MERGEPAINT",         IDM_BROP_MERGEPAINT
    MENUITEM "MERGE&COPY",          IDM_BROP_MERGECOPY
    MENUITEM "SRCCOP&Y",            IDM_BROP_SRCCOPY
    MENUITEM "SRCPAIN&T",           IDM_BROP_SRCPAINT
    MENUITEM "P&ATCOPY",            IDM_BROP_PATCOPY
    MENUITEM "PATPA&INT",           IDM_BROP_PATPAINT
    MENUITEM "DES&TINATION",        IDM_BROP_DESTINATION
    MENUITEM "&WHITENESS",          IDM_BROP_WHITENESS
END

POPUP "&WhiteROP"
BEGIN
    MENUITEM "&BLACKNESS",          IDM_WROP_BLACKNESS
    MENUITEM "&NOTSRCERASE",        IDM_WROP_NOTSRCERASE
    MENUITEM "N&OTSRCCOPY",         IDM_WROP_NOTSRCCOPY
    MENUITEM "&SRCERASE",           IDM_WROP_SRCERASE
    MENUITEM "&DSTINVERT",          IDM_WROP_DSTINVERT
    MENUITEM "&PATINVERT",          IDM_WROP_PATINVERT
    MENUITEM "SRCIN&VERT",          IDM_WROP_SRCINVERT
```

```
        MENUITEM "S&RCAND",              IDM_WROP_SRCAND
        MENUITEM "&MERGEPAINT",          IDM_WROP_MERGEPAINT
        MENUITEM "MERGE&COPY",           IDM_WROP_MERGECOPY
        MENUITEM "SRCCOP&Y",             IDM_WROP_SRCCOPY
        MENUITEM "SRCPAIN&T",            IDM_WROP_SRCPAINT
        MENUITEM "P&ATCOPY",             IDM_WROP_PATCOPY
        MENUITEM "PATPA&INT",            IDM_WROP_PATPAINT
        MENUITEM "DES&TINATION",         IDM_WROP_DESTINATION
        MENUITEM "&WHITENESS",           IDM_WROP_WHITENESS
    END
    MENUITEM "&MaskBlt!"                 IDM_MASKBLT
END


/* template for the about dialog box */
DLG_ABOUT DIALOG 17, 18, 114, 68
STYLE DS_MODALFRAME | WS_POPUP | WS_VISIBLE | WS_CAPTION | WS_SYSMENU
CAPTION "About Mask"
FONT 8, "Helv"
BEGIN
    CTEXT           "Mask",-1, 0, 7, 114, 8
    CTEXT           "by",            -1, 0, 15, 114, 8
    CTEXT           "Myers && Hamer",  -1, 0, 25, 114, 8
    CTEXT           "version 1.0",   -1, 0, 35, 114, 8
    LTEXT           "©1993",         -1,12, 51,  25, 8
    DEFPUSHBUTTON   "OK", IDOK, 81, 50, 30, 14, WS_GROUP
END
```

Message Procedures

Of the message handlers, the **WM_PAINT** procedure is the most complex. When only one bitmap is loaded, the bitmap appears at the window's upper left. When both a source and mask are present, however, the paint procedure clips each to one fourth of the client area, placing the mask below the original source image. The **BitBlt** commands always draw to the point (0, 0), but the **SetViewportOrgEx** commands move the origin to the position where the bitmap should appear.

After processing any menu command, the **WM_COMMAND** handler ends by calling EnableMaskBlt. Because the MaskBlt! command appears directly on the menu bar, it cannot be enabled and disabled like popup menu commands in response to **WM_INITMENU**. EnableMaskBlt checks for the presence of source and mask and disables MaskBlt! if necessary.

```
/*------------------------------------------------------------

      MASK.C

      Loads a bitmap and a mask and performs MaskBlt operations
      to merge them on the screen.  User may select different
      brushes and ROP codes to alter the result.

      Demonstrates bitmap operations using functions exported
      from the DIBLIB dynamic-link library.

      FUNCTIONS

            WinMain              receive window messages
            Init                 register/create program window
            Mask_WndProc         respond to window messages
            Mask_OnCreate        establish default settings
            Mask_OnInitMenu      update menu item check marks
            Mask_OnPaint         repaint the display
            Mask_OnCommand       respond to menu commands
            Mask_OnDestroy       clean up and quit
            LoadSource           load a DIB file
            LoadMask             load a mono mask bitmap for MaskBlt
            SaveMask             save the mask bitmap in a file
            MakeMask             create a mono mask bitmap from the image
            LoadResMask          load a resource bitmap for the mask
            DoMaskBlt            merge source with mask in block transfer
            EnableMaskBlt        check whether we have source and mask bmps
            GetROPCode           translate menu command into ROP3 code
            GetBrush             translate menu command into brush handle
            About_DlgProc        run the About box window

      from Mastering Windows NT Programming
      copyright 1993 by Brian Myers & Eric Hamer

      ------------------------------------------------------------*/

#define STRICT
#include <windows.h>
#include <windowsx.h>
#include <stdlib.h>               // MAX_ constants
#include "mask.h"
#include "diblib.h"               // DLL interface header
```

```
/*-------------------------------------------------------------------
        SYMBOL
    -----------------------------------------------------------------*/

/* a ROP3 code that blocks copying, leaving the destination intact */
#define DESTINATION (DWORD)0x00AA0029

/*-------------------------------------------------------------------
        MACRO
    -----------------------------------------------------------------*/

// Combine two ROP3 codes into one ROP4 code.  The "black" code
// is applied to pixels in the source image that correspond to
// a black pixel in the mask.  The "white" code is applied to
// pixels that match up with a white pixel in the mask.

#define ROP4(black, white) ((((white) << 8) & 0xFF000000) | (black))

/*-------------------------------------------------------------------
        GLOBAL VARIABLES
    -----------------------------------------------------------------*/

struct {                          // holds current program settings
    int iBlackROP;                // user's choice from BlackROP menu
    int iWhiteROP;                // user's choice from WhiteROP menu
    int iBrush;                   // user's choice from Brush menu
} current;

HBITMAP hbmSource = NULL;         // bitmap read from file
HBITMAP hbmMask   = NULL;         // monochrome bitmap
HPALETTE hPal;                    // palette for the source bitmap
char szMaskName[_MAX_FNAME];      // file name for mask bitmap
char szMaskPath[MAX_PATH];        // full path for mask bitmap

// ============================================
// Look for these procedures on the disk:
// WinMain, Init, GetROPCode, GetBrush,
// and About_DlgProc
// ============================================

/*-------------------------------------------------------------------
        MASK_WNDPROC
        Respond to window messages.
    -----------------------------------------------------------------*/
```

```
LRESULT WINAPI Mask_WndProc (
    HWND hWnd,
    UINT uMessage,
    WPARAM wParam,
    LPARAM lParam )
{
    switch (uMessage)
    {
        /* window has been created but is not visible */
        HANDLE_MSG( hWnd, WM_CREATE, Mask_OnCreate );

        /* window needs to be repainted */
        HANDLE_MSG( hWnd, WM_PAINT, Mask_OnPaint );

        /* update the menu */
        HANDLE_MSG( hWnd, WM_INITMENU, Mask_OnInitMenu );

        /* user has chosen something from the program menu */
         HANDLE_MSG( hWnd, WM_COMMAND, Mask_OnCommand );

        /* our window has been destroyed */
        HANDLE_MSG( hWnd, WM_DESTROY, Mask_OnDestroy );

        default:
            return( DefWindowProc(hWnd, uMessage, wParam, lParam) );
    }

    return( OL );
}


/*-------------------------------------------------------------------
        MASK_ONCREATE
        Send messages to give the menus initial settings.
    -----------------------------------------------------------------*/

BOOL Mask_OnCreate (
    HWND hWnd,
    LPCREATESTRUCT lpcs )
{
    /* choose default ROP codes and brush */
    FORWARD_WM_COMMAND( hWnd, IDM_BROP_SRCCOPY, NULL, 0, SendMessage );
    FORWARD_WM_COMMAND( hWnd, IDM_WROP_SRCCOPY, NULL, 0, SendMessage );
    FORWARD_WM_COMMAND( hWnd, IDM_BR_GRAY, NULL, 0, SendMessage );
```

```
    /* disable the MaskBlt! command */
    EnableMaskBlt( hWnd );
    return( TRUE );
    UNREFERENCED_PARAMETER( lpcs );
}


/*-------------------------------------------------------------------
        MASK_ONINITMENU
        Enable and disable the Save and Mask commands according
        to whether the program has a bitmap to save and a mask
        for MaskBlt.
    -------------------------------------------------------------------*/

void Mask_OnInitMenu (
    HWND hWnd,
    HMENU hMenu )
{
    if (hbmSource)
    {
        EnableMenuItem( hMenu, IDM_CLEARSOURCE, MF_ENABLED );
    }
    else
    {
        EnableMenuItem( hMenu, IDM_CLEARSOURCE, MF_GRAYED );
    }

     if (hbmMask)
    {
        EnableMenuItem( hMenu, IDM_SAVEMASK,  MF_ENABLED );
        EnableMenuItem( hMenu, IDM_CLEARMASK, MF_ENABLED );
    }
    else
    {
        EnableMenuItem( hMenu, IDM_SAVEMASK,  MF_GRAYED );
        EnableMenuItem( hMenu, IDM_CLEARMASK, MF_GRAYED );
    }

    return;
    UNREFERENCED_PARAMETER( hWnd );
}

/*-------------------------------------------------------------------
        MASK_ONPAINT
        Redisplay the current DIB, if any.
    -------------------------------------------------------------------*/
```

652

```
void Mask_OnPaint ( HWND hWnd )
{
    PAINTSTRUCT ps;                        // painting information
    HDC hDC;                               // display device
    RECT rClient;                          // window's client area
    RECT rClip;                            // clipping area for a blit
    HRGN hrgnClip;                         // clipping region for a blit
    BITMAP bmSource;                       // info about source bitmap
    BITMAP bmMask;                         // info about mask bitmap
    HDC hdcSource;                         // source device
    HDC hdcMask;                           // mask device
    HBITMAP hbmOld;                        // default device

    hDC = BeginPaint( hWnd, &ps );
    GetClientRect( hWnd, &rClient );

    // Select a brush to be the pattern element for MaskBlt.
    // Note that GetBrush returns only stock objects, so
    // there's no need to delete the brush later.
    SelectBrush( hDC, GetBrush(current.iBrush) );

    if (hbmSource)
    {
        GetObject( hbmSource, sizeof(BITMAP), &bmSource );
        hdcSource = CreateCompatibleDC( hDC );
        hbmOld = SelectBitmap( hdcSource, hbmSource );
    }

    if (hbmMask)
    {
        GetObject( hbmMask, sizeof(BITMAP), &bmMask );
        hdcMask = CreateCompatibleDC( hDC );
        hbmOld = SelectBitmap( hdcMask, hbmMask );
    }

    if (hbmSource)
    {
        if (hbmMask)
        {
            /* set origin and clipping to upper-left quadrant of window */
            SetViewportOrgEx( hDC, 0, 0, NULL );
            rClip.left   = 0;
            rClip.right  = rClient.right / 2;
            rClip.top    = rClient.top;
```

```
            rClip.bottom = rClient.bottom / 2;
            hrgnClip = CreateRectRgnIndirect( &rClip );
            SelectClipRgn( hDC, hrgnClip );
            DeleteObject( hrgnClip );
        }

        BitBlt( hDC, 0, 0,                      // display the source image
                (int)bmSource.bmWidth,
                (int)bmSource.bmHeight,
                hdcSource, 0, 0,
                SRCCOPY );
    }

    if (hbmMask)                                // if there's a mask, show it
    {
        if (hbmSource)                          // if there's a source, move mask
        {
            /* set origin and clipping to lower-right quadrant of window */
            SetViewportOrgEx( hDC, 0, rClient.bottom / 2, NULL );
            rClip.left   = rClient.left;
            rClip.right  = rClient.right / 2;
            rClip.top    = rClient.bottom / 2;
            rClip.bottom = rClient.bottom;
            hrgnClip = CreateRectRgnIndirect( &rClip );
            SelectClipRgn( hDC, hrgnClip );
            DeleteObject( hrgnClip );
        }

        BitBlt( hDC, 0, 0,                      // display the mask
                (int)bmMask.bmWidth,
                (int)bmMask.bmHeight,
                hdcMask, 0, 0,
                SRCCOPY );
    }

    if (hbmSource)                              // clean up
    {
        SelectBitmap( hdcSource, hbmOld );
        DeleteDC( hdcSource );
    }
    if (hbmMask)
    {
        SelectBitmap( hdcMask, hbmOld );
        DeleteDC( hdcMask );
    }
```

```
        EndPaint( hWnd, &ps );
        return;
}

/*-------------------------------------------------------------------

        MASK_ONCOMMAND
        Interpret command messages from the menu and call other
        procedures to respond.
        -----------------------------------------------------------*/

void Mask_OnCommand (
    HWND hWnd,
    int iCmd,
    HWND hwndCtl,
    UINT uCode )
{
    HINSTANCE hInst;
    HMENU hMenu;

    hMenu = GetMenu( hWnd );

    switch (iCmd)
    {
        case IDM_LOADSOURCE:                // load a bitmap from a file
            LoadSource( hWnd );
            break;

        case IDM_CLEARSOURCE:               // delete source bitmap
            DeleteBitmap( hbmSource );
            hbmSource = NULL;
            InvalidateRect( hWnd, NULL, TRUE );
            UpdateWindow( hWnd );
            break;

        case IDM_MASKBLT:                   // filter display through mask
            DoMaskBlt( hWnd );
            break;

        case IDM_LOADMASK:                  // load monochrome bitmap
            LoadMask( hWnd );
            break;

        case IDM_SAVEMASK:
            SaveMask( hWnd );
            break;
```

```
case IDM_CLEARMASK:
    DeleteBitmap( hbmMask );
    hbmMask = NULL;
    InvalidateRect( hWnd, NULL, TRUE );
    UpdateWindow( hWnd );
    break;

case IDM_MAKEMASK:
    MakeMask( hWnd );
    break;

case IDM_LOADRESMASK:
    LoadResMask( hWnd );
    break;

case IDM_BR_BLACK:                      // Brush menu
case IDM_BR_GRAY:
case IDM_BR_WHITE:
    CheckMenuItem( hMenu, current.iBrush, MF_UNCHECKED );
    current.iBrush = iCmd;
    CheckMenuItem( hMenu, current.iBrush, MF_CHECKED );
    break;

case IDM_BROP_BLACKNESS:                // Black ROP code
case IDM_BROP_NOTSRCERASE:
case IDM_BROP_NOTSRCCOPY:
case IDM_BROP_SRCERASE:
case IDM_BROP_DSTINVERT:
case IDM_BROP_PATINVERT:
case IDM_BROP_SRCINVERT:
case IDM_BROP_SRCAND:
case IDM_BROP_MERGEPAINT:
case IDM_BROP_MERGECOPY:
case IDM_BROP_SRCCOPY:
case IDM_BROP_SRCPAINT:
case IDM_BROP_PATCOPY:
case IDM_BROP_PATPAINT:
case IDM_BROP_DESTINATION:
case IDM_BROP_WHITENESS:
    CheckMenuItem( hMenu, current.iBlackROP, MF_UNCHECKED );
    current.iBlackROP = iCmd;
    CheckMenuItem( hMenu, current.iBlackROP, MF_CHECKED );
    break;
```

```
        case IDM_WROP_BLACKNESS:                        // White ROP code
        case IDM_WROP_NOTSRCERASE:
        case IDM_WROP_NOTSRCCOPY:
        case IDM_WROP_SRCERASE:
        case IDM_WROP_DSTINVERT:
        case IDM_WROP_PATINVERT:
        case IDM_WROP_SRCINVERT:
        case IDM_WROP_SRCAND:
        case IDM_WROP_MERGEPAINT:
        case IDM_WROP_MERGECOPY:
        case IDM_WROP_SRCCOPY:
        case IDM_WROP_SRCPAINT:
        case IDM_WROP_PATCOPY:
        case IDM_WROP_PATPAINT:
        case IDM_WROP_DESTINATION:
        case IDM_WROP_WHITENESS:
            CheckMenuItem( hMenu, current.iWhiteROP, MF_UNCHECKED );
            current.iWhiteROP = iCmd;
            CheckMenuItem( hMenu, current.iWhiteROP, MF_CHECKED );
            break;

        case IDM_ABOUT:                         // display the About box
            hInst = GetWindowInstance( hWnd );
            DialogBox( hInst, MAKEINTRESOURCE(DLG_ABOUT),
                hWnd, About_DlgProc );
            break;
    }

    EnableMaskBlt( hWnd );                       // update menu bar

    return;
    UNREFERENCED_PARAMETER( uCode );
    UNREFERENCED_PARAMETER( hwndCtl );
}

/*--------------------------------------------------------------------
        MASK_ONDESTROY
        Free the bitmap resources and post the quit message.
  --------------------------------------------------------------------*/

void Mask_OnDestroy ( HWND hWnd )
{
    if (hbmSource)                              // delete image bitmap
```

```
{
    DeleteBitmap( hbmSource );
}

if (hbmMask)                              // delete mask bitmap
{
    DeleteBitmap( hbmMask );
}

if (hPal)                                 // delete image's palette
{
    DeletePalette( hPal );
}

PostQuitMessage( 0 );

return;
UNREFERENCED_PARAMETER( hWnd );
}
```

Command Procedures

The rest of the routines in Mask are called in response to commands from the user. The first few have to do with acquiring source and mask images. They are Load-Source, LoadMask, SaveMask, MakeMask, and LoadResMask. There is no SaveSource procedure because Mask never modifies the source bitmap. It does, however, create new masks from them, like the one in Figure 10.7, and it makes sense to save them.

Although the images Mask loads from files are always and only device-independent bitmaps—as indeed they should be—the **MaskBlt** command expects to work with DDB bitmaps. After loading any bitmap Mask converts it to a DDB, and before saving any bitmap it restores the image to the DIB format. The program's global variables, then, include two **HBITMAP**s and one **HPALETTE**. (The monochrome bitmap doesn't need a palette.)

The procedure that calls CreateMask to make a black-and-white version of the source image must choose a color from the original bitmap to become white in the mask. A more sophisticated program might let the user click anywhere on the original to choose a color, or perhaps display the ChooseColor common dialog, but for simplicity MakeMask arbitrarily chooses the color of the source's upper-left pixel. Naturally this choice works better when the upper-left pixel contains a color also present elsewhere in the bitmap!

The real action occurs in DoMaskBlt, where the program sets up all the parameters for a **MaskBlt** command, drawing them from the global variables that reflect the user's choices, and merges the images. We chose this two-menu format for the ROP commands to match the two-code ROP4 macro that combines two familiar ROP3 codes. The double ROP menus let you mix your own combinations in a way that may seem more intuitive than simply entering the eight hexadecimal digits of a ROP4 code.

```
/*--------------------------------------------------------------------

        LOAD SOURCE
        Ask the user for the name of a BMP file.  Open the file,
        load the contents, and display the image.
    ----------------------------------------------------------------*/

void LoadSource ( HWND hWnd )
{
    PVOID pDIB;                              // DIB loaded from file
    HPALETTE hpalNew;                        // palette made from DIB
    HBITMAP hbmNew;                          // DIB converted to DDB
    HDC hDC;

    pDIB = ReadDIB( hWnd, NULL, NULL, TRUE );   // load DIB from file
    if (!pDIB)
    {
        return;                              // assume user canceled
    }

    try
    {
        hpalNew = PaletteFromDIB( (LPBITMAPINFO)pDIB, FALSE );

        hDC = GetDC( hWnd );
        if (!hDC)
        {
            DeletePalette( hpalNew );
            return;
        }

        hbmNew = DIBtoDDB( hDC, hpalNew, pDIB );    // convert to DDB
        ReleaseDC( hWnd, hDC );
        if (!hbmNew)
        {
```

```
            DeletePalette( hpalNew );
            return;
        }

        if (hbmSource)                        // delete previous objects
        {
            DeleteBitmap( hbmSource );
        }
        if (hPal)
        {
            DeletePalette( hPal );
        }

        hbmSource = hbmNew;                    // update globals
        hPal = hpalNew;
    }
    finally
    {
        GlobalFreePtr( pDIB );
    }

    InvalidateRect( hWnd, NULL, TRUE );
    UpdateWindow( hWnd );
    return;
}

/*-------------------------------------------------------------------
        LOAD MASK
        Load a monochrome bitmap.  The file is assumed to be in
        DIB format, and LoadMask converts it to a DDB. It will be
        passed to MaskBlt when the user chooses MaskBlt from the menu.
        --------------------------------------------------------------*/

void LoadMask ( HWND hWnd )
{
    PVOID pDIB = NULL;
    HDC hDC;
    HBITMAP hbmNew;

    pDIB = ReadDIB( hWnd,                      // load DIB from file
            szMaskName,                        // store file name here
            szMaskPath,                        // store file path here
            TRUE );                            // do ask user to choose file
```

```
    if (!pDIB)
    {
        return;                                 // assume user canceled
    }

    try
    {
        if (((PBITMAPINFOHEADER)pDIB)->biBitCount > 1)
        {
            GlobalFreePtr( pDIB );
            MessageBox( hWnd, "Mask bitmap must be monochrome.",
                "Error", MB_OK );
            return;                             // mask must be monochrome
        }

        hDC = GetDC( hWnd );                    // get DC for conversion
        if (!hDC)
        {
            return;
        }

        /* create a monochrome DDB version of the DIB */
        hbmNew = DIBtoMonoDDB( hDC, NULL, pDIB );
        ReleaseDC( hWnd, hDC );
        if (!hbmNew)
        {
            return;
        }

        if (hbmMask)                            // destroy old mask
        {
            DeleteBitmap( hbmMask );
        }

        hbmMask = hbmNew;                       // save new handle
    }
    finally
    {
        GlobalFreePtr( pDIB );                  // release DIB
    }

    InvalidateRect( hWnd, NULL, TRUE );         // update display
    UpdateWindow( hWnd );
    return;
}
```

```
/*----------------------------------------------------------------
        SAVE MASK
        Convert the hbmMask bitmap to a DIB and write it to a file.
    -------------------------------------------------------------*/

void SaveMask( HWND hWnd )
{
    PVOID pDIB;                             // converted mask
    BITMAP bm;                              // info about hbmMask
    BITMAPINFOHEADER biHeader;              // prescription for a DIB

    /* fill out biHeader with info about the DIB we want to create */
    GetObject( hbmMask, sizeof(BITMAP), &bm );
    FillMemory( &biHeader, sizeof(BITMAPINFOHEADER), O );
    biHeader.biSize = sizeof(BITMAPINFOHEADER);
    biHeader.biWidth = bm.bmWidth;
    biHeader.biHeight = bm.bmHeight;
    biHeader.biPlanes = 1;
    biHeader.biBitCount = 1;
    biHeader.biCompression = BI_RGB;

    /* convert hbmMask to a DIB */
    pDIB = DDBtoDIB( NULL, hbmMask, &biHeader );
    if (pDIB)
    {
        /* save the DIB in a file */
        WriteDIB( hWnd, szMaskName, szMaskPath, TRUE, pDIB );
    }
    return;
}


/*----------------------------------------------------------------
        MAKE MASK
        Create a monochrome bitmap derived from the current
        hbmSource. Replaces the current hbmMask.
    -------------------------------------------------------------*/

void MakeMask ( HWND hWnd )
{
    HDC hDC, hdcMem;
    HBITMAP hbmNew, hbmOld;
    COLORREF cBkgnd;
```

```
// The first half of this procedure determines the color value
// of the pixel in the source image's upper-left corner.  This
// color will become white in the mask; all others will be black.
// A more fully developed program might let the user select the
// background color by clicking somewhere on the bitmap.

hDC = GetDC( hWnd );                        // get display device context
if (!hDC)
{
    return;
}

hdcMem = CreateCompatibleDC( hDC );     // create memory device context
if (!hdcMem)
{
    ReleaseDC( hWnd, hDC );
    return;
}

/* determine color of pixel at (0, 0) */
hbmOld = SelectBitmap( hdcMem, hbmSource );
cBkgnd = GetPixel( hdcMem, 0, 0 );
SelectBitmap( hdcMem, hbmOld );
DeleteDC( hdcMem );

/* create the mask bitmap */
hbmNew = CreateMask( hDC, hbmSource, cBkgnd );
ReleaseDC( hWnd, hDC );
if (!hbmNew)
{
    return;
}

if (hbmMask)                                // delete previous mask
{
    DeleteBitmap( hbmMask );
}
hbmMask = hbmNew;                           // update global variable

InvalidateRect( hWnd, NULL, TRUE );        // display new mask
UpdateWindow( hWnd );
return;
}
```

```
/*--------------------------------------------------------------
        LOAD RESOURCE MASK
        Load a monochrome DDB from the program's resources to be
        the mask bitmap.
        ----------------------------------------------------------*/

void LoadResMask ( HWND hWnd )
{
    HBITMAP hbmNew;

    /* fetch the resource */
    hbmNew = LoadBitmap( GetWindowInstance(hWnd),
                         MAKEINTRESOURCE(BMP_MASK) );
    if (!hbmNew)
    {
        MessageBox( hWnd, "Cannot load mask.", "Error", MB_OK );
        return;
    }

    if (hbmMask)                               // delete previous objects
    {
        DeleteBitmap( hbmMask );
    }

    hbmMask = hbmNew;                          // save the new handle

    InvalidateRect( hWnd, NULL, TRUE );        // update the display
    UpdateWindow( hWnd );
    return;
}

/*--------------------------------------------------------------
        DO MASK BLT
        Perform a MaskBlt operation combining the source and the
        mask, taking into account the user's current ROP and brush
        selections.
        ----------------------------------------------------------*/

void DoMaskBlt ( HWND hWnd )
{
    HDC hdcSource, hDC;                 // source and dest. devices
    HBITMAP hbmOld;                     // default object
    BITMAP bmSource, bmMask;            // info about source and mask
    RECT rClient;                       // window's client area
    RECT rClip;                         // clipping area for blit
```

```
HRGN hrgnClip;                          // clipping region for blit
DWORD dwROP4;                           // ROP4 code for MaskBlt
int xExtent, yExtent;                   // blit area dimensions
hDC = GetDC( hWnd );                    // create the destination DC
if (!hDC)
{
    return;
}

/* prepare the source DC */
hdcSource = CreateCompatibleDC( hDC );
if (!hdcSource)
{
    ReleaseDC( hWnd, hDC );
    return;
}
hbmOld = SelectBitmap( hdcSource, hbmSource );

/* gather measurements */
GetClientRect( hWnd, &rClient );
GetObject( hbmSource, sizeof(BITMAP), &bmSource );
GetObject( hbmMask, sizeof(BITMAP), &bmMask );

/* set origin and clipping to upper-right quadrant of window */
SetViewportOrgEx( hDC, rClient.right / 2, 0, NULL );
rClip.left   = rClient.right / 2;
rClip.right  = rClient.right;
rClip.top    = rClient.top;
rClip.bottom = rClient.bottom / 2;
FillRect( hDC, &rClient, GetStockBrush(WHITE_BRUSH) );
hrgnClip = CreateRectRgnIndirect( &rClip );
SelectClipRgn( hDC, hrgnClip );
DeleteObject( hrgnClip );

/* limit output to smallest of mask or source */
xExtent = (int)min( bmSource.bmWidth, bmMask.bmWidth );
yExtent = (int)min( bmSource.bmHeight, bmMask.bmHeight );

/* determine the user's chosen ROP4 code */
dwROP4 = ROP4( GetROPCode(current.iBlackROP),
               GetROPCode(current.iWhiteROP) );

MaskBlt( hDC, 0, 0,                     // destination origin
         xExtent, yExtent,             // image extents
         hdcSource, 0, 0,              // source origin
```

```
                hbmMask,                        // mask
                0, 0,                           // mask origin
                dwROP4 );                       // ROP code

        SelectBitmap( hdcSource, hbmOld );      // clean up
        DeleteDC( hdcSource );
        ReleaseDC( hWnd, hDC );
        return;
}


/*-------------------------------------------------------------------
        ENABLE MASKBLT
        Check for the presence of source and mask bitmaps and
        enable or disable the MaskBlt command on the menu bar
        accordingly.
    -----------------------------------------------------------------*/

void EnableMaskBlt ( HWND hWnd )
{
    HMENU hMenu;
    hMenu = GetMenu( hWnd );

    if (hbmSource && hbmMask)                   // set the MaskBlt command
    {
        EnableMenuItem( hMenu, IDM_MASKBLT, MF_ENABLED );
    }
    else
    {
        EnableMenuItem( hMenu, IDM_MASKBLT, MF_GRAYED );
    }

    DrawMenuBar( hWnd );                        // update the display
    return;
}
```

In this chapter first we surveyed the basic features of device-independent bitmaps (DIBs) and color palettes, observing once again how Windows shields you from the physical limitations of the hardware by creating generalized data structures to hold color and image information. Windows then accepts the responsibility of translating the generalized information into a format acceptable to the local hardware. We contrasted programming for device-dependent bitmaps and for DIBs. DDBs use handles; DIBs don't. DDBs can be selected into a device; DIBs can't. DDBs can be moved with speedy block transfers; DIBs can't. DDBs do not travel well from one video adapter to another, but DIBs can move from machine to machine without loss of color or detail. DIBs contain colors that must be made into a palette and realized in the system before the DIB can be displayed properly.

From our discussions of internal bitmap structures we developed a set of short utility routines for parsing and interpreting the parts of a DIB, and from them we built larger procedures to convert between device-dependent and device-independent formats, to read and write DIB files, and to extract palettes from DIBs. For flash we added procedures for masking and palette animation. Along the way you picked up details about how palettes work, about some DIB formats new in NT, about half-tone dithering, and about the new **PlgBlt** and **MaskBlt** commands.

Most of the procedures we explained in this chapter are intended to form a library of routines useful for other programs. We showed you code from three programs that call some of these library routines, but we haven't explained how to build the library. Chapter 11 explains all about dynamic-link libraries, and at the end it presents the final module for the DibLib library and a make file to combine all the pieces.

Designing Dynamic-Link Libraries for Windows NT

Building DLLs

Calling DLLs

Shared and private DLL memory

Thread-local storage (TLS)

This chapter explains how dynamic-link libraries exist in memory, how they use memory when they run, how to build them, and how to load and execute them. Windows NT significantly improves the usefulness of DLLs in several ways. First, under a flat memory model the problems that arose from the library routines using the caller's stack simply disappear. There are no segments—or everything is in one segment, depending on how you look at it—so it's not possible for a pointer to confuse the stack with the data. The data segment and the stack segment are always the same (DS=SS). *All* the C runtime library functions now work in DLLs. Second, the entry-point mechanism is simplified. `LibMain` and `WEP` are gone; in their place is a single optional routine to respond whenever any thread or process calls or frees the library. Finally, using new memory management techniques, a DLL has complete control over which parts of memory are private to each client or shared among all clients. There are now ways to share or protect any memory, whether allocated statically or dynamically. It is even possible to give private variable values to each thread in a single process.

CONCEPTS

Before looking at the instructions for building a DLL and the code for calling one, it may be useful to review what DLLs are, why you might choose to make them, and how the system manages them in memory.

Three Kinds of Libraries

Windows programmers use the term "library files" for three very different objects. All libraries are groups of functions lumped together into one file. The three different kinds of libraries store and reference the code in different ways.

Windows, of course, did not invent the idea of function libraries. The C language, for example, depends heavily on libraries to implement standard functions for different systems. The linker copies runtime library functions, such as `malloc` and `printf`, into a program's executable file. The program can then call library functions just the way it would any of its own functions. The library saves each programmer from having to write a new procedure for common operations such as allocating memory and formatting output. Programmers can even build their own libraries to include functions for justifying text or sorting a database. Making the function available as a general tool eliminates redundant effort.

Since these function libraries contain binary object code they are sometimes called *object libraries*. Windows programmers also call them *static-link libraries* since the functions become a permanent, static part of the program's .EXE file when the linker copies them there.

For Windows, however, static linking presents a problem. As a multitasking system, Windows aims to let many applications run at the same time. If two of those programs run the same static-linked function at the same time then two copies of the function have to be in memory at once, and memory is wasted. The problem is particularly acute for the large functions necessary to a graphics interface.

Windows improves on the idea of a library in two ways. First of all, Windows libraries are *dynamically linked*. In other words, the linker does not copy library functions into the program's executable file. Instead, a program calls functions from the *dynamic-link library* as it runs. DLLs save memory because no matter how many programs are using a library, only one copy of the library is in memory at a time. By using DLLs a program can load and execute external code at run time.

Windows also changes the format of a library. Windows libraries have exactly the same format as any other DOS executable file (although they cannot themselves be executed). As a result, libraries can hold anything programs hold. Besides functions, libraries can encode data and even resources such as bitmaps and cursor shapes. Windows libraries are more versatile, expanding the range of shared resources to save you even more time.

Dynamically linked libraries can be loaded into memory as the program calls them and removed from memory immediately after use. Of course, this means the library must be available to the system while the program runs. A single copy of one library can service several applications simultaneously. Dynamic linking reduces both the memory and disk space requirements of Windows programs.

Some dynamic-link libraries are built into the system. Files such as kernel32.dll, user32.dll, and gdi32.dll are dynamic-link libraries. The subsystem exposes all the Win32 API routines to its clients through DLLs. Device drivers, such as keyboard.drv and comm.drv, are also dynamic-link libraries. They contain low-level procedures that the API functions call to control hardware. Most dynamic-link libraries, however, use the extension .DLL.

The third kind of library, an import library, helps the linker use DLLs. Even though the linker doesn't copy dynamically linked functions into an .EXE file, it still needs to know where the functions live and how they should be called. An import library is a small file containing skeletal reference points for the functions in a corresponding DLL. The declarations in an import library tell the linker what functions exist and which DLL to find them in.

For example, the file user32.lib contains references to all the Windows API functions referenced through user32.dll, a system library. If you tried to call a User function such as **CreateWindowEx** without naming user32.lib on the Link32 command line, you would get an "Unresolved external" error. (You may recall from Chapter 1 that the subsystem DLLs no longer contain the code to perform many of the API commands. Instead, they contain interface stubs that send service requests to the subsystem process through the Local Procedure Call facility. It is still true, however, that programs must link to DLLs to call Win32 APIs.)

Reasons to Use DLLs

The DLLs that come with Windows are not, of course, the only possible DLLs. You can write DLLs for your own applications. DLLs are an important part of the growing modularity of the Windows environment.

One reason for writing DLLs is to make customized versions of a program. Say, for example, you want to sell your application in the U.S. and overseas. Normally you would compile several versions of the application, each using a different language for all its strings. For a Windows program, you might instead store all the English-specific routines and resources in a file called english.dll. Another file, say french.dll, might hold code for the same functions but with French-language strings. Microsoft, for example, put the code and resources for all the common dialog boxes into a DLL called comdlg32.dll. The SDK comes with other versions of the same library written for other languages. A user can make all the standard dialog boxes that any program produces use French, Dutch, or Italian simply by copying a different version of comdlg32.dll into the system directory.

A more common use for DLLs is to share code among several applications. A well-designed DLL that performs some useful set of functions needed for several programs can save a lot of development overhead. Separating common code into a DLL improves consistency by ensuring that all applications have the latest version of the code and that all perform a task the same way. For these reasons, custom dialog controls such as spinners and progress bars usually end up in DLLs. That way even the Dialog Editor can use them.

Developers with expertise in a certain area can create DLLs for other developers. There might be a market for a library of animation-related functions or for three-dimensional graphics functions. Several programs written by Access Softek, for example, display graphics data files from many different programs. A single set of filter DLLs parses a large number of common graphics-file formats, such as PCX, CGM, and HPGL, and converts the data into a Windows metafile suitable for importing into other programs and documents.

Large software projects must be divided into modules for individual programmers to write. A single module of the application needs to have a well-defined interface for other modules to call. At the same time, within each module the programmer needs some freedom to be creative and to optimize the code. By splitting an application into different DLLs, the developer can provide programmers the freedom to implement their own parts of the task. Each DLL controls its own data blocks in memory, so the actions of one cannot easily interfere with another. Furthermore, using a prototype application, each DLL can be tested without linking to anyone else's object files. The high degree of modularity helps to isolate problems early in the process and speed the overall development time. And a DLL can be changed and recompiled without recompiling or relinking the entire application.

Encapsulating code in a DLL is a particularly good idea for system-level programming, such as device drivers and system-wide hooks. If portability or hardware concerns later necessitate changes, then only the DLL needs updating. Abstract data types are also good candidates for encapsulation.

Of course, DLLs don't solve every problem. They do have disadvantages. A DLL doesn't save much space if only one program uses it, for example. It may even consume *more* space if the DLL and its client program both use many of the same C runtime routines because both will contain statically linked copies of the same code. Also, using DLLs increases the number of files that must be present for a program to run and contributes to the clutter of files the user must manage. But two of the biggest inconveniences of Win16 DLLs have been eliminated in Win32—namely the difficulty of determining whether the client or the library is responsible for dynamically allocated objects and the need to avoid code that assumes DS=SS.

How DLLs Work

Because a DLL contains code that several processes may share, you won't be surprised to learn that the Windows subsystem loads them into memory-mapped files (which were covered in Chapter 7). The code from a DLL is mapped into the address space of each process that uses it, as you can see in Figure 11.1.

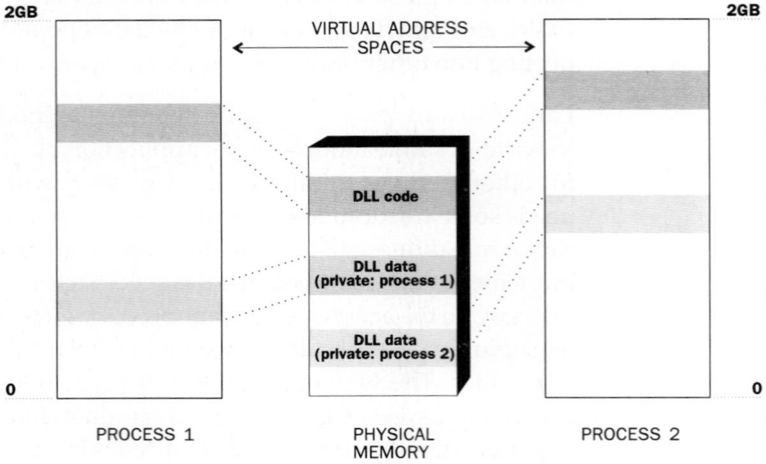

FIGURE 11.1:

One DLL mapped into the address space of several calling processes

When a program summons a DLL, the system searches the caller's address space to find room for the DLL. After mapping the file into place, the system examines reference tables in both the caller and the DLL, inserting the newly assigned virtual addresses for each DLL procedure into the caller's imports directory (part of the new PE image format). The memory in the DLL's memory-mapped file is given copy-on-write protection (also explained in Chapter 7). If the system needs to adjust any references within the DLL, the modified memory pages are copied. If several callers share a DLL, the system may have to map the library to different virtual addresses in each address space. That means each caller needs to modify the DLL's module differently. Copy-on-write protection duplicates just the minimum number of pages necessary to give each caller a private copy of the individually tailored area.

By default, all the memory a DLL allocates for variables is taken from the heap of the calling process. If two processes call a DLL then all the variables are allocated twice, once in each address space. Suppose, for example, you've written a DLL that accepts a text buffer and prints its contents. While it prints, the DLL displays a Cancel dialog box allowing the user to interrupt the print job. Your code declares a Boolean flag to signal if the user wants to stop:

```
BOOL bCancel;              // TRUE if user clicks Cancel button
```

The question is, what happens if two programs call your DLL to print at the same time? What happens if two Cancel dialog boxes are visible and the user clicks only one of them? When bCancel becomes **TRUE**, do both print operations stop?

The answer is no, only one print operation stops. When the second program loaded the DLL, the system created a new set of variables in the second address space. Although both programs share a single copy of the DLL code, each program has its own copy of the DLL data. There are two variables named bCancel, one in each process, and only one of them becomes **FALSE**. Each process has a private copy of the DLL's data.

It is also possible to create a single public copy of the data for all processes to share. If you wrote a DLL to replace the print spooler, for example, the DLL might declare a bBusy variable to indicate when a print job is in progress. bBusy would have to be public, shared by all applications, so that all applications could tell if any one of them was using the printer. Figure 11.2 shows how the system handles a DLL that uses both public and private data. Each calling process receives its own copy of private data, but a single copy of the public data is mapped into all the processes.

FIGURE 11.2:

How the public and private data segments of a single DLL are mapped into different processes

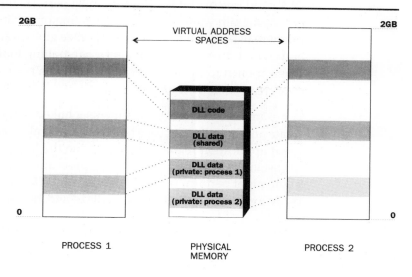

COMMANDS

The code inside a DLL differs only slightly from the code in an executable file. A DLL lacks a WinMain or main procedure, of course, and it may have a special entry point for handling initialization and termination, but otherwise the differences are trivial. First we'll present the basic steps for designing and compiling any DLL, and then we'll consider more advanced options for managing the memory in a DLL. The last part of the chapter looks at two examples that use memory in different ways.

Building DLLs

This section tells when and how to create an entry-point procedure, how to export public procedures by writing a module definition file, and how to link and compile a DLL.

The Entry Point

To turn a collection of procedures into a DLL, you may need to add an entry point. An *entry point* is a procedure the system calls whenever it loads a module into memory. WinMain is the entry point of a Windows program. An executable program must have an entry point, but under Windows NT the entry point is optional for a DLL. Add one only if your library must perform initialization tasks whenever another program wants to use it. Depending on what the DLL does, the entry point might register a window class or initialize global variables. Unlike WinMain, a DLL entry point does not contain a message-polling loop. Library routines speak only when spoken to by an application; they don't get messages of their own (unless they create their own windows).

For example, a DLL that implements a linked list would use the entry point to allocate and initialize the base node. Windows also calls the entry procedure when a client application releases the library, so the linked-list library could also destroy the list in the same routine. An entry procedure performs the same tasks that a program might perform in response to WM_CREATE and WM_DESTROY messages. The entry procedure replaces the old LibMain and WEP procedures used in 16-bit DLLs.

```
BOOL WINAPI DllEntryPoint (          // name this function anything you like
    HINSTANCE hinstDLL,              // a handle to the DLL module
    DWORD dwReason,                  // why DllEntryPoint has been called
    LPVOID lpReserved )              // not used
{
    hDLL = hinstDLL;                 // save in static variable

    switch (dwReason)
    {
        case DLL_PROCESS_ATTACH:     // a process is loading the DLL
            break;

        case DLL_THREAD_ATTACH:      // a process created a new thread
            break;

        case DLL_THREAD_DETACH:      // a thread exited
            break;

        case DLL_PROCESS_DETACH:     // a process is freeing the DLL
            break;
    }
    return( TRUE );
}
```

The entry-point procedure may have any name, but it must conform to this proto-type. The first parameter is a handle to the DLL module. If other procedures in your library have any use for the handle, you should save it here in a global variable because calling **GetModuleHandle** from a DLL returns the handle for the client program, not for the DLL.

A handle to a module and a handle to an instance are, by the way, largely interchangeable. Functions that ask for one as a parameter will usually accept the other, as well. Technically there is a difference, and we'll digress for a moment to explain it. A module is composed of all the items that define a program—everything you find in an .EXE file, including code, static variables, data, and resources. The form these objects take in memory is a *module*. An *instance* of something includes the module and a copy of the data values currently associated with it. Every instance of a program shares the same copy of the code; what makes different instances is individualized versions of all the associated data. A single module may support many instances; all instances of one program share the same module.

Returning to the entry-point prototype, the next parameter, dwReason, signals the particular occasion for calling the entry point. It may be one of the four values you see in the switch statement. The entry point is called when new threads want the library as well as when new procedures call it. This enables the entry point to perform any initialization appropriate to individual threads. In a multi-document program, for example, which creates a new thread for each new document window, a DLL might need to allocate space for data about each document. A DLL is not obligated to respond to all the possible values of dwReason. It can choose to handle some and ignore others.

The entry point returns a Boolean value, but the system pays attention to it only after a **DLL_ATTACH_PROCESS** call. If for any reason the DLL finds it cannot complete necessary initialization tasks, it should return **FALSE**.

```
switch (dwReason)
{
    case DLL_PROCESS_ATTACH:    // a process is loading the DLL
        if (!Initialize( ))
        {
            return( FALSE );
        }
        break;
```

If the DLL returns **FALSE**, the client's attempt to link with the DLL fails. In all other cases the return value is irrelevant.

As in earlier versions of Windows, the system keeps a reference count for each DLL. The count increases each time an application loads the library and decreases when an application frees it. When the count returns to 0, the system unmaps the DLL from memory. As long as any process still wants the DLL, it remains in physical memory, but as each client detaches itself the DLL frees the resources it allocated for that process.

If a calling process exits abruptly, the DLL does not receive all the normal notifications. If a client application causes a system error and dies, or if it ends from a call to **TerminateProcess** rather than **ExitProcess**, then its DLLs do not receive **DLL_PROCESS_DETACH** messages. (Back in Chapter 5 we warned against using **TerminateProcess** for exactly this reason.) Similarly, if a thread dies from a call to **TerminateThread**, DLLs do not receive **DLL_THREAD_DETACH** messages. The DLL does not have a chance to release resources it may have allocated. Those that were owned by the client will be destroyed anyway; resources owned by the DLL will not. When all the other clients release the DLL, however, the system does remove the DLL from memory.

The chance to initialize data for each new thread in a process is new with NT. After a program links to a DLL, any threads it subsequently creates automatically signal their presence to the DLL by sending **DLL_THREAD_ATTACH**. The DLL does not receive any notification from threads that already existed when the DLL was first called. Furthermore, the thread that calls **LoadLibrary** to attach the DLL produces only a **DLL_PROCESS_ATTACH** signal, not a **DLL_THREAD_ATTACH**. To include the calling thread in your thread initializations, omit the break from the first case statement:

```
switch (dwReason)
{
case DLL_PROCESS_ATTACH:    // a process is loading the DLL
        if (!InitProc( ))
        {
            return( FALSE );
        }
        /* omit break and fall through for starting thread */

    case DLL_THREAD_ATTACH:
        InitThread( );
        break;
```

DLLs that initialize for each thread often use thread-local storage, explained later in this chapter in the section "Managing Memory in a DLL."

Initializing for the C Runtime Library

A DLL that links with the C runtime library and calls functions from it must allow the C library a chance to perform its own initialization. The C libraries have a built-in entry point called _CRT_INIT. It has the same prototype as any other DLL entry point. A DLL with no entry point of its own can simply name _CRT_INIT as the entry point on the linker command line. (We'll get there in a minute.) A DLL that writes its own entry point, however, should call _CRT_INIT directly if it wants to use C runtime routines.

```
/* function prototype */
BOOL WINAPI _CRT_INIT( HINSTANCE hinstDLL, DWORD dwReason,
    LPVOID lpvReserved );

/* library's entry procedure */
BOOL WINAPI DllEntryPoint (              // name this function anything you like
    HINSTANCE hinstDLL,                  // a handle to the DLL module
    DWORD dwReason,                      // why DllEntryPoint has been called
    LPVOID lpReserved )                  // not used
{
    BOOL bSuccess;

    switch (dwReason)
    {
        case DLL_PROCESS_ATTACH:        // a process is loading the DLL

            /* allow the C runtime routines to initialize first */
            bSuccess = _CRT_INIT( hinstDLL, dwReason, lpReserved );
            if (!bSuccess)
            {
                return( FALSE );        // C runtime initialization failed
            }

            /* attempt the library's own initialization */
            bSuccess = MyInitProc( );
            if (!bSuccess)
            {
                return( FALSE );        // library's own initialization failed
            }
            break;

        case DLL_THREAD_ATTACH:         // a process created a new thread
            _CRT_INIT( hinstDLL, dwReason, lpReserved );
            MyInitThread( );
            break;

        // When detaching, call them in reverse order. Clean up
        // your own allocations first, then call _CRT_INIT.

        case DLL_THREAD_DETACH:         // a thread exited
            MyDetachThread( );
            _CRT_INIT( hinstDLL, dwReason, lpReserved );
            break;
```

```
    case DLL_PROCESS_DETACH:     // a process is freeing the DLL
        MyDetachProc( );
        _CRT_INIT( hinstDLL, dwReason, lpReserved );
        break;
    }
    return( TRUE );
}
```

As with any entry point, the return value from _CRT_INIT matters only in response to **DLL_ATTACH_PROCESS**. Also, the prototype for _CRT_INIT must appear in your code before you call it; otherwise the linker will fail to resolve the call. (Remember to include **WINAPI** in the prototype.)

Exporting Routines from a DLL

After writing the source code, the next step is to designate which procedures in the DLL should be available for other programs to call. Some of the DLL's procedures may be internal, for private use only. Public procedures must be exported. To *export* procedures means to tell the linker which routines are public. Usually a DLL exports procedures by listing them in a module definition file.

Module Definition Files

The primary use for module definition files in Windows NT is to export DLL procedures. Most of the other definition file features can now be handled through linker options, pragmas, and type declarations. First we'll explain definition files and then the alternatives.

In this sample module definition file, a dynamic-link library is exporting two functions for other programs to use. It is not necessary to provide a name with the **LIBRARY** statement. By default, the library module receives the base name of its source file.

```
LIBRARY
EXPORTS
    MyFunction1     @1
    MyFunction2     @2
```

The EXPORTS statement lists the procedures other code modules can call. These exports are the DLL's door to the outside world. A DLL that uses a .DEF file must have at least one export. Under 32-bit Windows, exporting a procedure does not alter the code; there's no need for the assembly prolog that introduces a Win16 export function—another bump smoothed out by the flat memory model. The linker constructs a table of exported functions as part of the DLL's file image. When a client loads the DLL, the system reads the table to resolve references in the client. Exporting a function adds it to this internal table.

Module definition files written for earlier versions of Windows work fine under Windows NT without modification. Most NT programs, however, have no need for a definition file because, as we explained in Chapter 2, callback procedures no longer need to be exported. The linker doesn't even read definition files; only the library utility does. Some of the old Win16 .DEF statements have become obsolete, but Lib32 simply ignores them. It also recognizes some new .DEF statements. We'll digress for a moment to summarize the changes before continuing with DLLs.

STUB and EXETYPE have no effect on an NT module. The stub procedure—the one that prints a warning when the user mistakenly tries to start a Windows program from the DOS command line—is now hard coded in the linker. It prints, "This program cannot be run in DOS mode." Microsoft has not provided a way to change the stub of an NT program. Later releases may add that feature. The EXETYPE statement serves no purpose because the linker now produces files only in the PE format. The VERSION statement is new. Like DESCRIPTION, it embeds informative text in the executable file.

Finally, the syntax of the HEAPSIZE and STACKSIZE statements has changed to permit a distinction between reserved and committed memory. (See the discussion of virtual memory in Chapter 7.) Reserved memory is set aside in the program's virtual address space, but no physical memory is assigned to the reserved addresses. Only when the program tries to use the reserved address does the system commit memory and supply pages from physical memory. This statement—

```
HEAPSIZE 0x10000, 0x2000
```

—reserves 64K for the heap and allocates it 8K at a time. Generally you should indicate only the reserve amount and accept the default commitment value of 4K. A program that uses a lot of memory immediately on loading might gain from boosting the commit level. Sometimes you can optimize performance by experimenting with quick but large allocations or slower but small allocations. This fine-tuning, however, produces only slight benefits.

The STACKSIZE value is now treated with the same flexibility Windows 3.1 allowed for HEAPSIZE. Now the system can adjust both values dynamically according to the needs of the program as it runs.

DLLs borrow stacks and heaps from their callers, so they don't use STACKSIZE and HEAPSIZE. The only two statements a DLL requires are LIBRARY and EXPORTS, both shown in the short sample above. Some other statements, though optional, can be useful. The old SEGMENTS statement doesn't make sense in an unsegmented architecture, so it has become a synonym for the new SECTIONS statement. A PE program (or DLL) may divide itself into sections and mark them individually with different kinds of memory protection indicating READ, WRITE, EXECUTE, or SHARED status. Also, using the BASE statement sometimes makes the calling program load more quickly.

```
LIBRARY MyDll BASE = 0x50000000
```

BASE introduces a requested location for the DLL. Whenever the system loads the DLL, it tries to place it at the requested base address. Normally the linker cannot know where a DLL will reside at run time, so when the system loads a program it must look up the current location of all the DLL procedures and copy the addresses into the program code. When you request a base address, the linker pencils in tentative addresses in advance. If the system manages to load the DLL at the requested location, then it can skip the lookup process and leave the tentative addresses intact.

Here are a few more small details for the curious. Even if the DLL does load at the requested address, the client's executable image may still have to be touched up. If, for example, the library has been rebuilt more recently than the client, the tentative addresses in the client's file may no longer be accurate. Also, sometimes the DLL image requires updating when it is first mapped into the address space. One DLL can call routines from another DLL (such as user32.dll or crtdll.dll), and its own import table may need revising.

Exporting Data

A dynamic-link library may export variables as well as procedures. To do so, it adds the CONSTANT keyword to exports in the definition file. The calling procedure reaches the public variables by pointers, not by name.

First, the DLL declares its variables in the source code:

```
// two variables to export
BOOL bTruthIsBeauty = FALSE;
char szProudhon[] = "Property is theft";
```

The module definition then lists the variables along with the library's other exports.

```
EXPORTS
    MyFunction1     @1                      ; functions
    MyFunction2     @2
    bTruthIsBeauty  CONSTANT                ; pointers to variables
    szProudhon      CONSTANT
```

The CONSTANT keyword marks exports as variables rather than procedures. What the library exports is a constant pointer. Calling programs declare pointers to the same variables, using the exported names:

```
extern BOOL *bTruthIsBeauty
extern char *szProudhon[];
```

To use the exported values, dereference the pointers:

```
if (!(*bTruthIsBeauty))
{
    printf( "%s\n\r", *szProudhon );
}
```

The need to use indirection invalidates the Hungarian notation prefix. bTruthIs-Beauty should really be pbTruthIsBeauty, but you have to use the exported name. As a convenience you might add #define statements to hide the discrepancy:

```
#define bTruthIsBeauty *bTruthIsBeauty
#define szProudhon *szProudhon
```

The newly defined constants allow you to write the variable names exactly the way they are used in the DLL:

```
if (!bTruthIsBeauty)
{
    printf( "%s\n\r", szProudhon );
}
```

Exporting variables gives clients a pointer directly into the library's own internal static data. If one client sets the Boolean variable to **FALSE**, then all the other clients can see the change. The value of each client's pointer is different because the DLL may occupy a different virtual address in each process. But all the pointers are mapped to the same memory-mapped file object where the DLL's module resides. They all lead to the same location and read the same value. There are other ways to share data among many clients, as you'll see shortly.

Compiling and Linking the DLL

Compiling a DLL is just like compiling any other program. The compiler needs no special instructions for a DLL. Linking does require some new steps, however. Much of the information in this section is particular to Microsoft's development tools.

First, Link32 never reads module definition files. Instead it needs to read an export library for every DLL it links. The library manager, Lib32, builds export libraries by combining information from the module definition file with the object files. A single run of Lib32 produces both an export library (.EXP) and an import library (.LIB). The export library is used only once, when the linker builds the DLL. Like .OBJ, .RES, and .RBJ files, the .EXP file is an intermediate byproduct, of no use after the DLL is finished. The import library, on the other hand, is used in building every program that calls the DLL. The export library contributes to linking the DLL, and the import library contributes to linking DLL clients. This command makes import and export libraries for MyDll:

```
lib32 -machine:i386 -def:mydll.def -out:mydll.lib mydll.obj
```

The results are mydll.lib and mydll.exp. The steps for building a DLL appear in Figure 11.3.

To link a DLL requires a new command line switch, –dll, telling the linker not to produce an executable file. In addition, a few of the old switches require new settings. The –entry switch must name the DLL's entry-point procedure; the –out switch receives a name with the .DLL extension instead of .EXE, and the export library must appear with the object files.

```
link32 -debug:full -debugtype:cv -machine:i386 -entry:DllEntryPoint@12  \
    -DLL -out:mydll.dll  mydll.exp mydll.obj mydll.rbj libc.lib ntdll.lib
```

In the –entry switch, the linker needs to see the "decorated" form of the procedure name. The compiler, when making object files, modifies procedure names by adding prefixes and suffixes that encode information about the procedure. When using the __stdcall calling convention, which is what **WINAPI** designates, the compiler appends a number telling how many bytes the procedure's parameters occupy. Because the three parameters of a DLL entry procedure take 4 bytes each, the linker switch must look like this:

```
-/entry:DllEntryPoint@12
```

FIGURE 11.3:

Steps for building a DLL

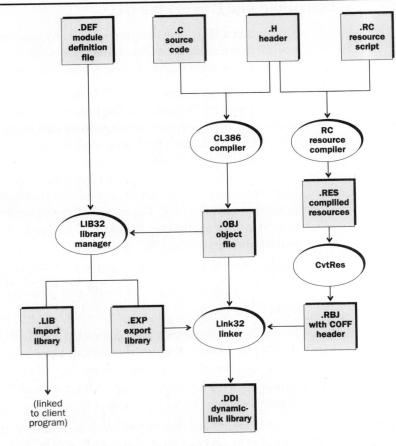

A program that has no entry-point procedure of its own but does call routines from the C runtime libraries should name _CRT_INIT as its entry point. A program with no entry point and no C routines may omit the −entry switch.

The Win32 SDK comes with three different versions of the C runtime library. Because the DS!=SS problem has disappeared, no version is particular to dynamic-link libraries. Programs and DLLs link to the same libraries.

Library	Description	Symbols to Define
libc.lib	Static-link library; does not support multithreading	[none]
libcmt.lib	Static-link library; designed to allow reentrancy for multiple threads in a single process	_MT
crtdll.lib	Dynamic-link library; supports multiple threads	_MT and _DLL

The libc.lib library provides the traditional support familiar to C programmers. The linker copies code for C runtime routines from the library into the program's .EXE file. libcmt.lib also links statically, but all its routines are reentrant to support multithreading. Any DLL that might be called by a multithreading program should use libcmt.lib or crtdll.lib. If you use either of those, you should also add this switch to the compiler command line: –D_MT. Some of the C runtime header files alter their declarations for multithreading modules.

Static linking with the C runtime libraries poses a potential inconvenience. If a DLL and its client both call, for example, `printf`, and both link to either libc or libcmt, then the `printf` code is duplicated in them. Duplicated code is merely inefficient; a more serious problem is that the C routines in the client do not share internal data with the library. If, for example, something goes wrong in the library, the client cannot report the problem by calling `perror` because it has a different copy of the `errno` variable. Similar problems arise if the client and the library try to share handles to buffered I/O streams.

One solution is to link with crtdll.lib instead. crtdll.lib is an import library for a new dynamic-link version of the standard C runtime routines. Windows NT keeps a copy of the DLL, crtdll.dll, in one of its system directories. If the client and server both link to the DLL version of the C runtime routines, then they share a single instance of the internal runtime data. Even programs that don't call DLLs benefit from linking to crtdll.lib. They achieve smaller .EXE files by leaving out the runtime routines, which are now permanently available through the system. Linking with crtdll.lib requires setting two compiler symbol definition switches: –D_MT, because crtdll.dll supports multithreading, and –D_DLL, because some of the header files alter their declarations to accommodate dynamic linking. The _DLL symbol is required for any modules, whether programs or libraries, that link with crtdll.lib. It indicates that you are linking to a DLL, not that you are trying to create one.

The only catch in linking a library to crtdll.lib. is that all its clients must also use crtdll.lib. A program that links to a static C runtime library and calls a DLL that uses the dynamic-link version may encounter unpredictable results. Do not use crtdll.lib for a DLL unless you are certain that all its clients also use crtdll.lib. DLLs that don't know their clients should use libcmt.lib. Also, in our version, crtdll.lib does not yet implement the thread-local storage features described below. Microsoft hopes to implement them for the final release.

Exporting without a .DEF File

Microsoft has already documented its plans for a new storage class declaration to make the EXPORTS statement unnecessary. When fully implemented, it will enable a program to designate all its exports in the source file and largely eliminate the need for a .DEF file. In our version of the SDK the linker has not yet incorporated this anticipated feature, so we are unable to test it. It may be available in your version, so we will describe it here.

The export feature is part of a new, more generalized method for designating storage class attributes. For the moment there are only three possible storage class attributes: dllimport, dllexport, and thread. We'll explain thread later when we get to thread-local storage, but all three designations alter the scope of a function or variable. Apparently Microsoft envisions future additions to the list of storage class attributes and has generalized the syntax to accommodate extensions. The new keyword __declspec introduces an extended storage attribute.

```
__declspec( dllexport ) int MyFunction( void );
__declspec( dllexport ) char szProudhon[] = "Property is theft";
```

The corresponding declarations in the client program use the dllimport keyword.

```
__declspec( dllimport ) int MyFunction( void );
__declspec( dllimport ) char *szProudhon[];
```

The __declspec keywords are analogous to static and extern, which also modify an item's storage class. static and extern, however, belong to the ANSI specification for C and C++. With __declspec, Microsoft introduces its own extensions to the language.

A DLL with many exported functions may benefit from using the .DEF file rather than __declspec to mark exports. The extended attribute syntax does not allow for the programmer to designate ordinal number synonyms, such as @1 and @2, for each export. Performing string searches to locate an exported function takes longer than jumping straight to a particular entry in the library's exports directory.

Most of the information that normally goes in a .DEF file can already be fed to the linker directly through the command line, making the .DEF file unnecessary. The −dll and −out switches duplicate the effect of a LIBRARY statement. The −base switch makes the BASE statement unnecessary for setting a default loading address. −section sets the same protection attributes that SECTIONS does. −version and VERSION also do the same thing. To embed descriptive text in the final file image, as DESCRIPTION does, the #pragma comment directive works equally well, and __declspec provides the alternative to an EXPORTS list. Microsoft seems to be moving away from the use of .DEF files.

A Note on Making .DEF Files for Programs

The compiler and the linker, as we said, pay no attention to the .DEF file. Only the Lib32 utility reads it. That poses a small problem if you decide to create a .DEF file for a regular .EXE module. Though normally a program doesn't need a .DEF file, you might want it to adjust the stack size or embed DESCRIPTION information. Also, programs ported from Win16 may want to use their old .DEF files. But how can you call Lib32 for a non-library program?

The solution is to pretend to export something. Add an empty dummy procedure or declare a dummy variable to list under the EXPORTS statement in the .DEF file. If Lib32 finds something to export, it will create an export library file (.EXP) incorporating all the definition file settings. Add the .EXP file to the linker command line, just as you would to link a library.

Calling a DLL

A program has two choices for calling procedures from a DLL. The easiest way is simply to add the DLL to the program's other libraries on the link line. Here, for example, is the command to let a program named Client call routines exported from MyDll:

```
link32 -debug:none -subsystem:console -out:client.exe client.obj    \
    libc.lib ntdll.lib kernel32.lib mydll.lib
```

The command line includes a reference to the import library associated with MyDll. The rest is automatic. The linker includes the name of the DLL in the Client program's executable file. When the system loads Client, it also searches for MyDll in the current directory, the system directory, and the path directories. If MyDll cannot be found, the system considers the Client program incomplete and cancels the loading operation. Client cannot run without MyDll. If MyDll is present, the system loads both modules. The DLL remains in memory as long as Client runs. When Client terminates, the library receives its detach process signal and both are removed from memory (unless other programs are using MyDll at the same time; then only the program is removed).

This method of connecting client to library is called *implicit linking* or *load-time linking* because the system loads the DLL and resolves calls into it when the program loads. The alternative is *runtime linking*, where the program does not link to the DLL at all. Instead, as the program runs it issues explicit commands to load and release the library when needed. **LoadLibrary** attaches a DLL to the current process, **GetProcAddress** finds the address of an exported function, and **FreeLibrary** detaches the DLL when the program is through with it. These lines load MyDll, call a Boolean function it exports, and release MyDll. (The prototype of the exported function serves here only for reference.)

```
BOOL IsTruthBeauty( void ); // prototype of exported function

HINSTANCE hLibrary;          // handle to the library
FARPROC lpfnTruth;           // pointer to exported function
BOOL bResult;                // value returned from function

hLibrary = LoadLibrary( "mydll" );
lpfnTruth = GetProcAddress( hLibrary, "IsTruthBeauty" );
bResult = (*lpfnTruth)();   // call the exported function using its address
FreeLibrary( hLibrary );
```

Of course, you should check for errors after each function. In fact, that's one of the main reasons to prefer runtime linking. If the careless user has misplaced the DLL, the program still loads and runs. If the missing DLL contains, for example, printing routines, then the client won't be able to print, but it can still show a warning message, disable a few menu options, and keep running. Implicit linking, on the other hand, makes the client entirely dependent on the presence of the DLL. Also, a client that calls DLL routines only very occasionally saves system resources by freeing the DLL whenever it is not in use.

Runtime linking is the only choice in situations where the name of the DLL can't be known in advance. To call a routine from the printer driver, for example, you can determine the name of the routine in advance because all printer drivers support a standard interface, but you can't know which printer driver to call until the program runs and checks the system settings.

The winbase.h header gives the handles in all three functions type **HINSTANCE** even though **HMODULE** would be more accurate for libraries. **HINSTANCE** is retained for compatibility with Win16. As we mentioned before, module and instance handles are usually interchangeable.

```
HINSTANCE LoadLibrary( LPCSTR lpszLibFile );      // library's file name

FARPROC GetProcAddress(
    HINSTANCE hLibrary,              // loaded library module
    LPCSTR lpszProc );               // name or ordinal value of export item

BOOL FreeLibrary( HINSTANCE hLibrary );          // loaded library module
```

GetProcAddress identifies exports more quickly by ordinal number than by name. Ordinal numbers are assigned in the .DEF file.

```
EXPORTS
    IsTruthBeauty    @1
```

Given that declaration, the most efficient call to **GetProcAddress** would identify the requested procedure by the number 1.

```
lpfnTruth = GetProcAddress( hLibrary, MAKEINTRESOURCE(1) );
```

After you call **LoadLibrary** and before the function returns, the DLL is loaded and receives a **DLL_PROCESS_ATTACH** signal. If the library's entry point returns **FALSE**, then **LoadLibrary** fails and returns **NULL**. **FreeLibrary** sends the **DLL_PROCESS_DE-TACH** notification.

Incidentally, **LoadLibrary** works with executable files, as well. Use it in combination with **FindResource** and **LoadResource** to read resources from other programs. In such cases you may prefer to call **LoadLibraryEx**, which retrieves a module handle without actually mapping the module into virtual memory. Use

LoadLibraryEx when you don't intend to call any functions from the library—if, for example, you only want to read its resources. It would also be useful when you don't know in advance which version of a DLL will be present. You can load the library without mapping it and call GetProcAddress to determine whether particular exports are present before deciding to use it.

Managing Memory in a DLL

By default, the variables declared in a DLL are reinstantiated each time another client calls the library. References to the variables always automatically refer to the values stored in the caller's instance because the library code runs in the context of the caller's process. In other words, the caller's CPU registers and stack remain in effect while the caller's threads follow their own paths through the DLL code. But as we mentioned earlier, sometimes a library needs to establish a single variable to service all its clients. Data that is copied anew for each client is said to be *private* because only one client sees it. Data that is never duplicated, that always exists in only a single instance, is said to be *shared* because all clients see the same copy.

Sometimes it is convenient to give every thread its own copy of certain variables, as well. Normally all the threads in one process share the same copy of any private data from the DLL, but *thread-local storage* (TLS) gives each thread its own private copy.

This section explains how a DLL arranges to declare variables that are shared among all processes, private to a process, or private to each thread, and also how a DLL allocates memory dynamically at any scope. Figure 11.4 summarizes the methods for allocating static or dynamic memory and making it shared in private. A single DLL may use one, several, or all of these methods.

Data Private to a Process

As a starting point to consider different storage attributes, here is a simple DLL that accepts the defaults. All its data is private to the caller. The one exported procedure returns the number of threads that have attached to the DLL. If called by several processes at once, the library totals the number of threads for each process separately because each process has a different copy of uNumThreads.

FIGURE 11.4:

Methods available to a DLL for
allocating memory with particular
attributes

SCOPE	ALLOCATION METHOD	
	STATIC	**DYNAMIC**
SHARED	#pragma data_seg( ) SECTION READ WRITE SHARED	Create File Mapping( )
PRIVATE TO ONE PROCESS	default for all declared variables	VirtualAlloc( ) HeapAlloc( ) GlobalAlloc( )
PRIVATE TO ONE THREAD	declspec(thread)	TlsAlloc( )

```
UINT uNumThreads = 0;                   // count of threads attached to DLL

BOOL WINAPI DllEntryPoint (
    HINSTANCE hinstDLL,                 // a handle to the DLL module
    DWORD dwReason,                     // why DllEntryPoint has been called
    LPVOID lpReserved )                 // not used
{
    switch (dwReason)
    {
        case DLL_PROCESS_ATTACH:        // this indicates a thread, too
        case DLL_THREAD_ATTACH:         // the client created a new thread
            uNumThreads++;
            break;

        case DLL_THREAD_DETACH:         // a thread exited
            uNumThreads--;
            break;
    }
    return( TRUE );
}
```

```
// Tell the calling process how many threads it
// has created since loading the DLL.

UINT GetNumThreads ( void )
{
    return( uNumThreads );
}
```

Most of the situations we've considered so far call for a library to use declared variables. Dynamically allocated memory is also private. The values returned by **VirtualAlloc**, **HeapAlloc**, and **GlobalAlloc** always refer to private objects. If a library allocates a block of memory, perhaps to receive data from a file, only one process has access to the buffer. Only one address space sees that part of memory.

Shared Data

Private data presents no challenge since the system provides it by default. To get shared data, you have to ask for it explicitly. The request goes either in the module definition file or on the linker command line. To change the storage attributes of a DLL's data, you must mark a data section, name it, and set the section's attributes in the module definition file.

Here's a version of our sample DLL revised to count the number of processes that attach to it:

```
#include <windows.h>
#include "countdll.h"

#pragma data_seg( ".Total" )        // beginning of section named .Total
UINT uNumClients = 0;
#pragma data_seg( )                 // end of section

BOOL WINAPI DllEntryPoint (
    HINSTANCE hinstDLL,             // a handle to the DLL module
    DWORD dwReason,                 // why DllEntryPoint has been called
    LPVOID lpReserved )             // not used
{
    switch (dwReason)
    {
        case DLL_PROCESS_ATTACH:    // a process is loading the DLL
            uNumClients++;
            break;
```

```
        case DLL_PROCESS_DETACH:      // a process is freeing the DLL
            uNumClients--;
            break;
    }
    return( TRUE );
}


// Tell the calling process how many
// clients are using the DLL.

UINT GetNumClients ( void )
{
    return( uNumClients );
}
```

Under Windows NT, data section names conventionally begin with a period to distinguish them easily from code sections, which begin with an underscore (".data" and "_code"). Though the documentation does not remark on it, our experience shows—and Microsoft confirms—that a section name may not contain more than eight characters. Longer names do not generate any helpful warnings; they just don't work.

The exported GetNumClients routine works as advertised only if the DLL declares its .Total data section to be SHARED. If data were private and each caller had its own copy of uNumClients, then GetNumClients would always return 1. This module definition file sets the necessary attribute:

```
LIBRARY
SECTIONS
    .Total READ WRITE SHARED
EXPORTS
    GetNumClients    @1
```

The possible attributes for a section are READ, WRITE, EXECUTE, and SHARED. The default values are READ and WRITE. To be compatible with Win16, if porting is a concern, a DLL must declare all its data SHARED.

You can choose to set the data attributes on the linker command line instead. The –sections switch applies attributes to a section of data identified by name. The linker command line would look like this:

```
link32 -debug:none -dll -out:countdll.dll countdll.obj \
    crtdll.lib ntdll.lib kernel32.lib \
    -entry:DllEntryPoint@12 -section:.Total,RWS
```

"RWS" stands for read, write, and shared.

If a DLL exports data items from a shared section, then its clients can import pointers to read and write shared data directly. In this limited way, a DLL can punch small holes in the boundaries between address spaces, effectively mapping one physical address into several processes. Many variables, however, are useless when shared—namely, pointers and handles. You can't, for example, declare an lpGlobal variable and share a pointer to some buffer. The value placed in lpGlobal will be a virtual address from the process that was active when the DLL allocated the buffer. Other processes might be able to retrieve the pointer value stored in lpGlobal, but the allocated object doesn't exist in their address spaces, and for them lpGlobal dangerously points to a random address. Handles too are invalid except in the process where they originate.

Microsoft's documentation and samples sometimes refer to the DATA statement as a simple way to alter the default attributes for all sections in a library.

```
DATA READ WRITE SHARED
```

In fact, the DATA statement has been dropped from Win32 and is no longer supported.

Combining Public and Private Data

The ability to mark off a data section and assign it attributes is the key to giving one DLL both public and private memory. The same pragma can designate several sections in a single DLL, and each segment may have different attributes. This version of CountDll creates both public and private sections in order to keep local totals for individual callers and a global total for all callers.

```
#include <windows.h>
#include "testdll.h"

#pragma data_seg( ".Global" )        // SHARED section
UINT uNumClients = 0;                 // count processes attached to DLL
UINT uNumThreadsGlobal = 0;           // count all attached threads
#pragma data_seg( )
```

```
#pragma data_seg( ".Local" )          // PRIVATE section
UINT uNumThreadsLocal = 0;            // count threads in current process
#pragma data_seg( )

BOOL WINAPI DllEntryPoint (
    HINSTANCE hinstDLL,               // a handle to the DLL module
    DWORD dwReason,                   // why DllEntryPoint has been called
    LPVOID lpReserved )               // not used
{
    switch (dwReason)
    {
        case DLL_PROCESS_ATTACH:      // a process is loading the DLL
            uNumClients++;
            /* fall through to process first thread */

        case DLL_THREAD_ATTACH:       // a new thread was created
            uNumThreadsLocal++;       // increment counter for this process
            uNumThreadsGlobal++;      // increment counter for all processes
            break;

        case DLL_THREAD_DETACH:       // a thread exited
            uNumThreadsLocal--;       // decrement counter for this process
            uNumThreadsGlobal--;      // decrement counter for all processes
            break;

        case DLL_PROCESS_DETACH:      // a process is freeing the DLL
            uNumClients--;
            break;
    }
    return( TRUE );
}

UINT GetNumClients ( void )
{
    return( uNumClients );
}

UINT GetNumThreadsLocal ( void )
{
    return( uNumThreadsLocal );
}
```

```
UINT GetNumThreadsGlobal ( void )
{
    return( uNumThreadsGlobal );
}
```

For this DLL to work, it must declare different attributes for both of its data sections. The module definition file would do it this way:

```
LIBRARY
SECTIONS
    .Global            READ WRITE SHARED
    .Local             READ WRITE
EXPORTS
    GetNumClients         @1
    GetNumThreadsLocal    @2
    GetNumThreadsGlobal   @3
```

The .Local line isn't strictly necessary since it merely accepts the default attributes. There is no PRIVATE keyword. In fact, CountDll really has no need to mark off and name the .Local section. We did it for symmetry and to demonstrate that one program may contain several named sections.

The link line can accomplish the same attribute assignments.

```
link32 -debug:none -dll -out:countdll.dll countdll.obj \
    crtdll.lib ntdll.lib kernel32.lib \
    -entry:DllEntryPoint@12 -section:.Global,RWS -section:.Local,RW
```

Again, in this particular case the second −section switch is optional because it requests default attributes.

Allocating Shared Memory Dynamically

Normally when a DLL allocates memory dynamically, the memory object it creates belongs to the calling process. Even if the DLL and the caller both forget to free the object, the system destroys it automatically when the calling process exits. 16-bit DLLs behave the same way. In 16-bit Windows, the alternative is to allocate with the **GMEM_DDESHARE** flag, assigning ownership to the DLL module instead of the caller's module. The resulting object then persists while clients come and go until the DLL frees it or exits.

The private address spaces of Windows NT do not permit the same behavior for dynamic allocations. Dynamically allocated buffers must be mapped into some process's address space, and they cannot be reached from other address spaces. As we mentioned in Chapter 7, **GMEM_DDESHARE** no longer functions the same way and is useful only for some DDE operations.

When a Win32 DLL needs to create at run time a buffer of shared data for several clients, it must resort to the same mechanism that supports shared memory for any processes: memory-mapped files (described in Chapter 7). When the first caller invokes a DLL, during its initialization the DLL might create a memory-mapped file. For each subsequent caller, the initialization routine opens a new handle to the existing object. Each process gets its own handle. When a particular thread asks to read or modify the data in the file, the DLL maps a view of the file and uses the resulting pointer to reach the shared buffer. When the thread finishes, the DLL unmaps the view. When a process finishes, the DLL closes the file handle for that process. When the last process finishes, the last handle is closed and the file-mapping object is released. One of the sample libraries later in this chapter demonstrates the use of memory-mapped files for sharing memory through a DLL.

Thread-Local Storage (TLS)

When several processes share a single memory object, care must be taken to ensure that the processes don't interfere with each other. If two write to the buffer at the same time, for example, the result may be garbage. The same problem can arise when multiple threads in a process share a single copy of the global variables in a DLL. With another __declspec extension, a DLL can declare static variables that are duplicated for each thread that uses the library. The thread storage class creates *thread-local storage*. (Unlike dllexport, thread is implemented in our version, but only in libcmt.dll, not yet in crtdll.dll.)

```
__declspec( thread ) char szMatch[BUFF_SIZE];
```

Now each thread sees a different copy of szMatch. One procedure in the DLL might scan a database file looking for a customer number.

```
BOOL FindName( int iID )                         // given number, find name
{
    BOOL bFound = FALSE;
    int iRecID;                                  // number read from file

    MoveToFirstRecord( ) ;                       // start of file
    while (!eof(hFile) && !bFound)
    {
        iRecID = ReadRecordID( );                // get id# from file
```

```
    if (iID = iRecID)
    {
        bFound = TRUE;
        lstrcpy( szMatch, ReadRecordName( ) );   // store associated name
    }
}

if (!bFound)
{
    szMatch[0] = 0;                              // null string
}
return( bFound );
}
```

Every thread stores a different value in the static variable szMatch. Any thread may read szMatch to get the result of its most recent search. Every thread always sees its own search result in szMatch, never anyone else's. Without the extended declaration, szMatch would record the result of the single most recent search made by any thread, not the most recent search for every thread. The sample library called Sprite later in this chapter also uses the thread storage class.

The TLS Functions

Our search procedure could accomplish the same thread-local storage with four Win32 API commands: **TlsAlloc**, **TlsSetValue**, **TlsGetValue**, and **TlsFree**. The storage class modifier is much easier to use, but the APIs come in handy when each thread needs to allocate a buffer dynamically and the buffers are large or different sizes. In cases where the thread-local data cannot be handled in a static variable, you must use the TLS commands.

TlsAlloc creates something called a *thread index*, which is basically an array of **DWORD** values. The array holds one **DWORD** slot for each thread in the current process. If the process creates more threads, the index automatically expands to accommodate them.

```
DWORD TlsAlloc( void );
```

TlsAlloc returns a number to identify the new index array. One process may open several thread indices. One index might hold an object handle for each thread; another might hold a Boolean value for each thread. If **TlsAlloc** fails, it returns 0xFFFFFFFF.

To store and retrieve values in the index, call **TlsSetValue** and **TlsGetValue**. Pass either one the number of an index created with **TlsAlloc**. Neither function requires a thread handle or ID. Both functions always work with the index entry for the current thread.

```
BOOL TlsSetValue(
    DWORD dwTlsIndex,                // set value for this index
    LPVOID lpvTlsValue );            // value to be stored (32 bits)

LPVOID TlsGetValue( DWORD dwTlsIndex ); // retrieve value from this index
```

Finally, to free the memory occupied by the index array, call **TlsFree**.

```
BOOL TlsFree( DWORD dwTlsIndex );        // TLS index to free
```

An index may store any value up to 32 bits, such as handles, integers, Booleans, BYTEs, or characters. Often it stores pointers. These lines show how to put a value in an index and retrieve it:

```
PSTR pBuffer;

/* allocate a buffer and store the pointer in the index */
TlsSetValue( dwIndex, LocalAlloc(LMEM_FIXED, sizeof(dwBuffSize) );

pBuffer = TlsGetValue( dwIndex );
```

DLLs and Reentrancy

Thread-local storage helps make DLLs reentrant to support multithreading. It protects the actions of one thread from interfering with the data of another. Private data in a multithreaded library and shared data in a library that supports multiple processes are vulnerable in the same way. DLLs commonly need synchronization objects to protect certain variables and resources. An animation library, for example, would use the caller's display DC frequently. If several threads use the DC simultaneously, they might interfere with each other. One might select a red brush, be interrupted by a thread that selects a blue brush, regain control, and draw a blue shape by accident. The library should create a critical section or a mutex, and every section of code that modifies the DC should wait for the object first. Code that draws might need to be synchronized too. The Sprite sample at the end of the chapter creates a critical section to protect its DC. (Don't forget that when a multithreading program calls C runtime functions it must link to a multithreading version of the runtime library and define _MT on the compiler command line.)

CODE

The first sample, Sprite, is a DLL for animating font characters and moving them randomly around the client area. The second sample, DibLib, shows how to share dynamically allocated memory among library clients by creating a memory-mapped file.

The Sprite DLL

Sprite demonstrates all the steps for building and linking a DLL, uses thread-local storage, and performs initialization tasks in its entry-point procedure. A client program called Wingdings calls procedures exported from Sprite to animate characters from the Wingdings font. Figure 11.5 shows Wingdings in action.

FIGURE 11.5:

Wingdings calling the Sprite library to animate characters

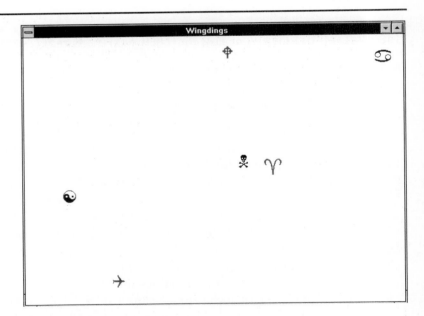

The Make File

This make file follows the guidelines we've described for building a DLL and its client program. The compiler command line defines the _MT symbol because Sprite allows (in fact, expects) multithreading clients. Both the DLL and its client must link to the same C runtime library. In this case, libcmt.lib is the only choice because Sprite supports multithreading and uses thread-local storage. (crtdll.lib does not allow thread-local storage in our version of the system.) Lib32 builds the import and export libraries that Link32 reads as it creates the final .EXE and .DLL files. In linking the DLL, Link32 also requires the –DLL and –entry switches. Wingdings links with the DLL at load time, not run time, so we specify sprite.dll on its linker command line.

```
#
#    NMake file for the SPRITE library and its client, WINGDINGS
#


#
#    Set targets and dependencies
#
all: wingding.exe sprite.dll
wingding.exe: wingding.obj wingding.rbj sprite.lib wingding.h sprite.h
sprite.lib: sprite.obj sprite.def
sprite.dll: sprite.obj sprite.exp


#
#    Define macros for command-line options and library modules
#


!IFDEF NODEBUG
CFLAGS = -c -G3 -Os -W3 -D_X86_=1 -DWIN32 -D_MT
LFLAGS =
!ELSE
CFLAGS = -c -G3 -Od -W4 -Zi -D_X86_=1 -DWIN32 -D_MT
LFLAGS = -debug:full -debugtype:cv
!ENDIF
SUBSYS = -subsystem:windows


# can't use crtdll.lib because it doesn't yet support thread-local storage
LIBS = libcmt.lib ntdll.lib kernel32.lib user32.lib gdi32.lib
```

```
#
#    Define compiling rules
#
.c.obj:
      cl386 $(CFLAGS) $*.c

.rc.rbj:
      rc $*.rc
      cvtres -i386 $*.res -o $*.rbj

.obj.lib:
      lib32 -machine:$(CPU) $*.obj -out:$*.lib -def:$*.def

.obj.exe:
      link32 $(LFLAGS) $(SUBSYS) -out:$*.exe $*.obj $*.rbj $(LIBS) sprite.lib

.obj.dll:
      link32 $(LFLAGS) -DLL -entry:DllEntryPoint@12 \
          -out:$*.dll $*.obj $*.exp $(LIBS)
```

The Module Definition File

Sprite's data section is private to each client, so the module definition file names this as a DLL (LIBRARY) and lists the exports. Lib32 reads the export list to build the import and export libraries, which eventually feed into the import and export reference tables in the final file images.

```
/*-------------------------------------------------------------------
        SPRITE.DEF
        Module definition file for the SPRITE.DLL library.
    ------------------------------------------------------------------*/

LIBRARY sprite BASE=0x1C000000

EXPORTS
        InitSprite        @1
        DrawSprite        @2
        MoveSprite        @3
        EraseSprite       @4
        GetSpritePos      @5
        SetSpritePos      @6
        GetSpriteSpeed    @7
        SetSpriteSpeed    @8
```

The Source Code

For the purpose of understanding DLLs, the most important parts of the source code are the global variable declarations and the entry-point procedure.

```
/*-------------------------------------------------------------------
        GLOBAL VARIABLES
    ---------------------------------------------------------------*/

CRITICAL_SECTION csDrawing;          // threads acquire this to use the hDC
__declspec( thread ) SPRITE sprite;  // one sprite per thread
```

The critical section, as you will see, is used in the drawing procedures to serialize access to the program's device context. Only one thread may use it at a time. (We explained critical sections, along with other synchronization objects, in Chapter 4.)

The other global variable, sprite, is a structure holding all the information about a single sprite image, including for example its present position and direction. Although we declare only a single variable, the thread designation means that in fact there will be many copies of sprite, one for each thread the client creates. Wingdings creates a new thread to run each sprite in its window, and when any thread calls procedures from the Sprite library, the code always automatically refers to the copy of sprite allocated for that thread. Without the thread-local storage class, all the threads would try to push the same single sprite around the screen. The critical section object, on the other hand, must *not* be local to each thread. If each thread had its own thread-local critical section, invisible to all the others, then waiting for it would serve no purpose.

The entry point initializes for each new client process by creating the critical section object. It also calls _CRT_INIT to initialize the C runtime libraries. Although Sprite does not call any routines from libcmt.lib, the thread keyword and try/finally termination handler do rely on C library definitions. Notice the prototype for _CRT_INIT, which must be present for linking to succeed.

```
/*---------------------------------------------------------------


        SPRITE.C

    A collection of routines for creating and animating
    sprite images (font characters) that move around
    the client area.

    FUNCTIONS
        DllEntryPoint          initializes the DLL's data
        InitSprite             puts starting values in a SPRITE structure
        DrawSprite             draws one thread's sprite
        EraseSprite            erases one thread's sprite
        MoveSprite             moves a sprite to its next position
        GetSpritePos           returns the sprite's current position
        SetSpritePos           sets the sprite's current position
        GetSpriteSpeed         returns the sprite's current speed
        SetSpriteSpeed         sets the sprite's current speed

    from Mastering Windows NT Programming
    copyright 1993 by Brian Myers & Eric Hamer

    ---------------------------------------------------------------*/

#define STRICT
#include <windows.h>
#include <windowsx.h>
#include "sprite.h"

/*---------------------------------------------------------------
        PROTOTYPE for the C runtime initialization function
    ---------------------------------------------------------------*/


BOOL WINAPI _CRT_INIT( HINSTANCE hinstDLL, DWORD dwReason,
    LPVOID lpvReserved );


/*---------------------------------------------------------------
        TYPE DEFINITION
    ---------------------------------------------------------------*/


typedef struct tagSPRITE
{
    int x;                  // sprite's current position
    int y;
    int dx;                 // sprite's horizontal speed
```

```
        int dy;                      // sprite's vertical speed
        int width;
        int height;
        char ch[1];                  // each "sprite" is a character from a font
        COLORREF crColor;            // color for drawing the sprite
    } SPRITE;

/*------------------------------------------------------------------
          GLOBAL VARIABLES
    --------------------------------------------------------------*/

CRITICAL_SECTION csDrawing;          // threads acquire this to use the hDC
__declspec( thread ) SPRITE sprite;  // one sprite per thread

/*------------------------------------------------------------------
          DLL ENTRY POINT
          Initializes any resources the DLL needs. Creates and
          destroys the critical section object; calls the
          C runtime initialization function.
    --------------------------------------------------------------*/

BOOL WINAPI DllEntryPoint (
    HINSTANCE hinstDLL,
    DWORD dwReason,
    LPVOID lpvReserved )
{
    switch (dwReason)
    {
        case DLL_PROCESS_ATTACH:     // create crit. section to protect DC
            if (!_CRT_INIT( hinstDLL, dwReason, lpvReserved ))
            {
                return( FALSE );
            }

            InitializeCriticalSection( &csDrawing );
            // The first thread does not create a sprite; no need
            // to fall through to the thread attach
            break;

        case DLL_THREAD_ATTACH:
            _CRT_INIT( hinstDLL, dwReason, lpvReserved );
            sprite.ch[0] = 0;
            break;
```

```
        case DLL_THREAD_DETACH:
            _CRT_INIT( hinstDLL, dwReason, lpvReserved );
            break;

        case DLL_PROCESS_DETACH:
            DeleteCriticalSection( &csDrawing );
            _CRT_INIT( hinstDLL, dwReason, lpvReserved );
            break;
    }

    return( TRUE );
    UNREFERENCED_PARAMETER( hinstDLL );
    UNREFERENCED_PARAMETER( lpvReserved );
}

/*--------------------------------------------------------------------
        INIT SPRITE
        Store initial values in a SPRITE structure.
    ------------------------------------------------------------------*/

BOOL InitSprite (
    HDC hDC,
    int x,
    int y,
    int dx,
    int dy,
    char* pch,
    COLORREF cr )
{
    TEXTMETRIC tm;                    // measurements for current font
    SIZE sExtent;                     // dimensions of one sprite character
    BOOL bSuccess;                    // TRUE for successful initialization
    /* give the sprite a position and a shape */
    sprite.x       = x;
    sprite.y       = y;
    sprite.dx      = dx;
    sprite.dy      = dy;
    sprite.ch[O]   = *pch;
    sprite.crColor = cr;

    /* calculate the character's dimensions */
    GetTextMetrics( hDC, &tm );
    GetTextExtentPoint( hDC, pch, 1, &sExtent );
    sprite.width   = (int)sExtent.cx;
    sprite.height  = (int)(tm.tmHeight + tm.tmInternalLeading);
```

```
    /* draw the shape at the position */
    bSuccess = DrawSprite( hDC );

    return( bSuccess );
}


/*-----------------------------------------------------------------
        DRAW SPRITE
        Draw one thread's sprite at its current position.
    ----------------------------------------------------------------*/
BOOL DrawSprite ( HDC hDC )
{
    BOOL bSuccess;

    /* confirm that the sprite has been initialized */
    if (sprite.ch[0] == 0)
    {
        return( FALSE );
    }

    EnterCriticalSection( &csDrawing );
    try
    {
        SaveDC( hDC );
        SetTextAlign( hDC, TA_TOP | TA_LEFT );
        SetTextColor( hDC, sprite.crColor );
        SetBkMode( hDC, TRANSPARENT );

        /* draw the sprite */
        bSuccess = ExtTextOut( hDC, sprite.x, sprite.y, 0, NULL,
                        sprite.ch, 1, NULL );

        RestoreDC( hDC, -1 );
    }
    finally
    {
        LeaveCriticalSection( &csDrawing );
    }

    return( bSuccess );
}
```

```
/*-------------------------------------------------------------------
        ERASE SPRITE
        Erase one thread's sprite from its current position.
  ------------------------------------------------------------------*/

BOOL EraseSprite ( HDC hDC )
{
    BOOL bSuccess;

    /* confirm that the sprite has been initialized */
    if (sprite.ch[0] == 0)
    {
        return( FALSE );
    }

    EnterCriticalSection( &csDrawing );
    try
    {
        SaveDC( hDC );
        SetTextAlign( hDC, TA_TOP | TA_LEFT );
        SetTextColor( hDC, GetSysColor(COLOR_WINDOW) );
        SetBkMode( hDC, TRANSPARENT );

        /* clear a box the size of the largest possible character */
        bSuccess = ExtTextOut( hDC, sprite.x, sprite.y, 0, NULL,
            sprite.ch, 1, NULL );

        RestoreDC( hDC, -1 );
    }
    finally
    {
        LeaveCriticalSection( &csDrawing );
    }

    return( bSuccess );
}


/*-------------------------------------------------------------------
        MOVE SPRITE
        Advance one thread's sprite from its current position
        by moving it the distance and direction indicated in its
        speed fields (.dx and .dy). Do not allow the sprite to
        leave a bounding rectangle passed by the caller.
  ------------------------------------------------------------------*/
```

```
BOOL MoveSprite (
    HDC hDC,
    LPRECT lprBounds )
{
    BOOL bSuccess = FALSE;
    RECT rBounds;                // boundaries adjusted for character size

    // Adjust boundary rectangle so the sprite cannot
    // slip partly out of view on the right or bottom
    // edges. (Remember sprite.x and sprite.y name the
    // image's top-left corner.)

    CopyRect( &rBounds, lprBounds );
    rBounds.right  -= sprite.width;
    rBounds.bottom -= sprite.height;

    /* erase the sprite from its old position */
    if (EraseSprite( hDC ))
    {
        /* advance the sprite position and draw it in a new place */
        sprite.x += sprite.dx;
        sprite.y += sprite.dy;

        // If the caller provided a bounding rectangle,
        // keep the sprite from leaving the defined area.

        if (lprBounds)
        {
            if (sprite.x <= rBounds.left)             // left boundary
            {
                sprite.x = (int)rBounds.left;
                sprite.dx = -sprite.dx;
            }
            if (sprite.y <= rBounds.top)              // top boundary
            {
                sprite.y = (int)rBounds.top;
                sprite.dy = -sprite.dy;
            }
            if (sprite.x >= rBounds.right)            // right boundary
            {
                sprite.x = (int)rBounds.right;
                sprite.dx = -sprite.dx;
            }
```

```
            if (sprite.y >= rBounds.bottom)              // bottom boundary
            {
                sprite.y = (int)rBounds.bottom;
                sprite.dy = -sprite.dy;
            }
        }
        bSuccess = DrawSprite( hDC );
    }
    return( bSuccess );
}

/*-------------------------------------------------------------------
        SPRITE POSITION FUNCTIONS
        Get and set the sprite's current position.
    --------------------------------------------------------------*/

void GetSpritePos ( LPPOINT lppt )
{
    lppt->x = sprite.x;
    lppt->y = sprite.y;
    return;
}

void SetSpritePos ( LPPOINT lppt )
{
    sprite.x = (int)lppt->x;
    sprite.y = (int)lppt->y;
    return;
}


/*-------------------------------------------------------------------
        SPRITE SPEED FUNCTIONS
        Get and set the sprite's current speed.
    --------------------------------------------------------------*/

void GetSpriteSpeed ( LPPOINT lppt )
{
    lppt->x = sprite.dx;
    lppt->y = sprite.dy;
    return;
}

void SetSpriteSpeed ( LPPOINT lppt )
{
    sprite.dx = (int)lppt->x;
```

```
    sprite.dy = (int)lppt->y;
    return;
}
```

The Interface Header

The header file for a DLL, containing prototypes for all its exported functions, commonly becomes the interface document for the client programs. Wingdings includes sprite.h along with its own header so the compiler can perform type-checking when Wingdings calls library functions.

```
/*------------------------------------------------------------

        SPRITE.H
        Interface declarations for the SPRITE.DLL library.
    ----------------------------------------------------------*/

BOOL InitSprite( HDC hDC, int x, int y, int dx, int dy, char *pch,
    COLORREF cr );
BOOL DrawSprite( HDC hDC );
BOOL MoveSprite( HDC hDC, LPRECT lprBounds );
BOOL EraseSprite( HDC hDC );
void GetSpritePos( LPPOINT lppt );
void SetSpritePos( LPPOINT lppt );
void GetSpriteSpeed( LPPOINT lppt );
void SetSpriteSpeed( LPPOINT lppt );
```

The Client Program

As part of its initialization sequence, Wingdings creates several threads. NUM_THREADS, defined in the header file, sets the number of threads created. The threads all execute the same procedure, SpriteThread, which initializes a new sprite, giving it a speed, position, color, and character value, and then calls MoveSprite in a loop to keep its sprite in motion. The DLL calls occur in the two procedures SpriteThread and NewSprite.

```
/*------------------------------------------------------------

        WINGDING.H
        Header file for WINGDINGS.

    ----------------------------------------------------------*/
```

713

```
/*-----------------------------------------------------------------
        PROTOTYPES
   --------------------------------------------------------------*/

int WINAPI WinMain( HINSTANCE hinstThis, HINSTANCE hinstPrev,
        LPSTR lpszCmdLine, int iCmdShow );
BOOL Init( HINSTANCE hinstThis, int iCmdShow );
BOOL MakeThreads( void );
LONG WINAPI Wingds_WndProc( HWND hWnd, UINT uMessage, WPARAM wParam,
     LPARAM lParam );
void Wingds_OnSize( HWND hWnd, UINT uState, int cx, int cy );
void Wingds_OnDestroy( HWND hWnd );
LONG SpriteThread( LPVOID lpv );
void NewSprite( HDC hDC, LPRECT lprClient );

/*-----------------------------------------------------------------
        CONSTANTS
   --------------------------------------------------------------*/

#define NAME_BUFSIZE       10      /* max chars for IDS_APPNAME string */
#define TITLE_BUFSIZE      20      /* max chars for the window caption */
#define NUM_SPRITES        5

  /*-----------------------------------------------------------------
          RESOURCE IDs
     --------------------------------------------------------------*/

/* STRINGS */

#define IDS_APPNAME        10
#define IDS_TITLE          20


=====================================================================

/*-----------------------------------------------------------------

        WINGDING.RC
        Resource script file for the Wingdings program

   --------------------------------------------------------------*/

#include <windows.h>
#include "wingding.h"
```

```
/* a table of all the strings Wingdings uses */
STRINGTABLE
BEGIN
    IDS_APPNAME,    "wingds"
    IDS_TITLE,      "Wingdings"
END


================================================================================

/*-------------------------------------------------------------------


        WINGDING.C

        A client program for the SPRITE.DLL, this program makes
        random Wingdings font characters move around the screen.

        FUNCTIONS
            WinMain             receive and dispatch messages
            Init                initialize program data
            MakeThreads         create a thread for each sprite
            Wingds_WndProc      sort out messages for main window
            Wingds_OnSize       update rClient global variable
            Wingds_OnDestroy    end the program
            SpriteThread        thread procedure for each sprite
            NewSprite           initialize a new sprite


        from Mastering Windows NT Programming
        copyright 1993 by Brian Myers & Eric Hamer

        ---------------------------------------------------------------*/

#define STRICT
#include <mywin.h>
#include <windowsx.h>
#include <stdlib.h>              // srand() rand()
#include <time.h>               // time()
#include "sprite.h"             // prototypes of DLL's exported functions
#include "wingding.h"

/*-------------------------------------------------------------
        GLOBAL VARIABLES
        ---------------------------------------------------------*/

BOOL bContinue = TRUE;          // FALSE to signal threads should stop
RECT rClient;                   // updated on WM_SIZE messages
```

```
HWND hwndMain;
HDC hDC;
HFONT hFont, hfontOld;          // Wingdings and default fonts

/*-----------------------------------------------------------------
        WIN MAIN
        Calls initializing procedures and runs the message loop
   -----------------------------------------------------------*/

int WINAPI WinMain (
    HINSTANCE hinstThis,
    HINSTANCE hinstPrev,
    LPSTR lpszCmdLine,
    int iCmdShow )
{
    MSG msg;

    if (!Init( hinstThis, iCmdShow ))
    {
        return( FALSE );
    }

    // keep getting messages until one says "QUIT"
    while (GetMessage( &msg, NULL, 0, 0 ))
    {
        TranslateMessage( &msg );
        DispatchMessage( &msg );
    }

    return( msg.wParam );
    UNREFERENCED_PARAMETER( hinstPrev );
    UNREFERENCED_PARAMETER( lpszCmdLine );
}

/*-----------------------------------------------------------------
        INIT
        Initializes window and data for the application, if
        necessary; then initializes data and creates the window
        for this instance.
   -----------------------------------------------------------*/

BOOL Init (
    HINSTANCE hInst,
    int iCmdShow )
```

```
{
    char szAppName[NAME_BUFSIZE];          // application name
    char szTitle[TITLE_BUFSIZE];           // caption for window
    WNDCLASS wc;
    HWND hWnd;
    LOGFONT lf;

    // load application name and caption
    LoadString( hInst, IDS_APPNAME, szAppName, sizeof(szAppName) );
    LoadString( hInst, IDS_TITLE,   szTitle,   sizeof(szTitle)   );

    // fill structure with information about this window class
    wc.lpszClassName = szAppName;
    wc.hInstance     = hInst;
    wc.lpfnWndProc   = Wingds_WndProc;
    wc.hCursor       = LoadCursor( NULL, IDC_ARROW );
    wc.hIcon         = LoadIcon( NULL, IDI_APPLICATION );
    wc.lpszMenuName  = NULL;
    wc.hbrBackground = (HANDLE)(COLOR_WINDOW + 1);
    wc.style         = CS_HREDRAW | CS_VREDRAW;
    wc.cbClsExtra    = 0;
    wc.cbWndExtra    = 0;

    // register the window class for program's main window
    RegisterClass( &wc );

    // Make a class "Wingds" window exist for this instance
    hWnd = CreateWindow ( szAppName, szTitle, WS_OVERLAPPEDWINDOW,
                CW_USEDEFAULT, CW_USEDEFAULT, CW_USEDEFAULT, CW_USEDEFAULT,
                NULL, NULL, hInst, NULL );
    if (!hWnd)
    {
        return( FALSE );
    }

    ShowWindow( hWnd, iCmdShow );            // make window visible
    UpdateWindow( hWnd );
    hwndMain = hWnd;

    hDC = GetDC( hWnd );                      // make a device context
    if (!hDC)                                 // (store in global variable)
    {
        return( FALSE );
    }
```

```
    FillMemory( &lf, sizeof(LOGFONT), 0 );   //create and select the font
    lf.lfHeight = 18;
    lf.lfCharSet = SYMBOL_CHARSET;
    lf.lfOutPrecision = OUT_TT_ONLY_PRECIS;
    lf.lfPitchAndFamily = VARIABLE_PITCH ¦ FF_DONTCARE;
    lstrcpy( lf.lfFaceName, "Wingdings" );
    hFont = CreateFontIndirect( &lf );
    if (hFont)
    {
        SelectFont( hDC, hFont );
    }

    if (!MakeThreads( ))                          // initiate sprite threads
    {
        return( FALSE );
    }

    return( TRUE );
}


/*-------------------------------------------------------------------
        MAKE THREADS
        Create all the threads, one for each sprite.
    ----------------------------------------------------------------*/

BOOL MakeThreads ( void )
{
    int i;
    int iCount = 0;
    DWORD dwThreadID;
    HANDLE hThread = NULL;

    for (i = 0; i < NUM_SPRITES; i++)
    {
        hThread = CreateThread(
                NULL,                                 // security
                0,                                    // stack
                (LPTHREAD_START_ROUTINE)SpriteThread, // start
                NULL,                                 // parameter
                0,                                    // flags
                &dwThreadID );                        // ID number
        if (hThread)
        {
            iCount++;
            CloseHandle( hThread );
```

```
        }
    }
    return( iCount > 0 );
}

/*------------------------------------------------------------------
        HELLO WINDOW PROCEDURE
        Every message for this program ends up here.
    ------------------------------------------------------------------*/

LRESULT WINAPI Wingds_WndProc (
    HWND hWnd,
    UINT uMessage,
    WPARAM wParam,
    LPARAM lParam )
{
    switch (uMessage)
    {
        HANDLE_MSG( hWnd, WM_SIZE, Wingds_OnSize );

        HANDLE_MSG( hWnd, WM_DESTROY, Wingds_OnDestroy );

        default:
            return( DefWindowProc(hWnd, uMessage, wParam, lParam) );
    }

    return( 0 );
}

/*------------------------------------------------------------------
        WINGDS_ONSIZE
        Update the global variable rClient whenever the window
        changes size.
    ------------------------------------------------------------------*/

void Wingds_OnSize (
    HWND hWnd,
    UINT uState,
    int cx,
    int cy )
{
    GetClientRect( hWnd, &rClient );

    return;
    UNREFERENCED_PARAMETER( uState );
```

```
    UNREFERENCED_PARAMETER( cx );
    UNREFERENCED_PARAMETER( cy );
}


/*----------------------------------------------------------------
        WINGDS_ONDESTROY
        Window is gone from the screen. Release global DC, end
        threads, quit.
    ----------------------------------------------------------------*/

void Wingds_OnDestroy ( HWND hWnd )
{
    if (hFont)                          // if we created a Wingdings
    {                                   //   font, delete it here.
        SelectFont( hDC, hfontOld );
        DeleteFont( hFont );
    }
    ReleaseDC( hWnd, hDC );             // hDC is global
    bContinue = FALSE;                  // halt the threads
    Sleep( 0 );                         // force a context switch
    PostQuitMessage( 0 );               // tell WinMain to quit
    return;
 }


/*----------------------------------------------------------------
        SPRITE THREAD
        Keep one sprite moving around the screen.
    ----------------------------------------------------------------*/

LONG SpriteThread ( LPVOID lpv )
{
    TEXTMETRIC tm;

    GetTextMetrics( hDC, &tm );

    NewSprite( hDC, &rClient );

    while (bContinue)
    {
        MoveSprite( hDC, &rClient );
        Sleep( 0 );
    }

    return( 0L );
    UNREFERENCED_PARAMETER( lpv );
```

```
}

/*-------------------------------------------------------------------
        NEW SPRITE
        Create a sprite and assign it random attributes.
    ----------------------------------------------------------------*/

void NewSprite (
    HDC hDC,
    LPRECT lprClient )
{
    char ch[1];                         // randomly generated character
    static iSeed = 0;                   // for seeding rand() numbers

    srand( iSeed++ );
    ch[0] = (char)((rand() % 95) + 33); // char from 33 - 127

    InitSprite( hDC,
        rand() % (int)lprClient->right,   // position
        rand() % (int)lprClient->bottom,
        (rand() % 5) - 2,
        (rand() % 5) - 2,                 // speed
        ch,                               // sprite character
        GetNearestColor(hDC, RGB(rand()%256, rand()%256, rand()%256)) );

    return;
}
```

The DibLib DLL

In Chapter 10 we presented a number of bitmap utility procedures and promised to give you one more module for building them into a library. DibLib is that module. The library's interface header file appeared in Chapter 10. Here we present the source code for the entry point, along with five new procedures for the library. The new procedures show how a DLL can allocate memory dynamically to share among all its clients. DibLib works with a file-mapping object to save the user's settings whenever any of them opens a common dialog to load a bitmap. The library stores the path and file name for the most recently loaded file in a section of memory that is visible to all the client processes. Whenever the user opens or saves a file in any client program, the file name most recently used *in any client process* appears automatically as the default.

The `DllEntryPoint` procedure initializes the file-mapping object when the first process attaches. Subsequent processes receive duplicate handles to the same object. When a process detaches, the entry point closes its handle. Of the five new procedures, two are called to create or release the file-mapping object, and the other three store and retrieve data from it.

```
/*-------------------------------------------------------------------

          DIBLIB.C

       Main module of the DIBLIB library.  Contains the entry
       point and functions that maintain the library's shared
       file-mapping object.

       FUNCTIONS

            DllEntryPoint
            InitMapping
            WriteInitialData
            SetDefaultNames
            GetDefaultNames
            TerminateMapping

       from Mastering Windows NT Programming
       copyright 1993 by Brian Myers & Eric Hamer


       ---------------------------------------------------------------*/


#define STRICT
#include <windows.h>
#include <windowsx.h>
#include <stdlib.h>                       // MAX_ constants
#include "diblib.h"


/*-------------------------------------------------------------------
          SYMBOLS
       ---------------------------------------------------------------*/


#define PATH_OFFSET      0           // place in buffer where path begins
#define FNAME_OFFSET     MAX_PATH    // place in buffer where name begins
```

```c
/*-----------------------------------------------------------------
          LOCAL FUNCTION PROTOTYPE
    -------------------------------------------------------------*/

void WriteInitialData( void );

/*-----------------------------------------------------------------
          STATIC VARIABLES
    -------------------------------------------------------------*/

HANDLE hMapFile;                                // file mapping object
char szMapObjName[] = "diblib_mapfile";         // shared object name
char *lpMapView;                                // pointer to a view

/*-----------------------------------------------------------------
          DLL ENTRY POINT
          This is where each process attaches and detaches from the DLL.
    -------------------------------------------------------------*/
BOOL WINAPI DllEntryPoint (
    HINSTANCE hDLL,
    DWORD dwReason,
    LPVOID lpvReserved )
{
    BOOL bTest;
    switch (dwReason)
    {
        case DLL_PROCESS_ATTACH:
            bTest = InitMapping( );         // create the file-mapping object
            if (!bTest)
            {
                MessageBox( NULL, "Unable to initialize the DLL",
                    "Error", MB_OK );
            }
            return( bTest );

        case DLL_PROCESS_DETACH:
            TerminateMapping( );            // release file-mapping object
            break;
    }

    return( TRUE );
    UNREFERENCED_PARAMETER( hDLL );
    UNREFERENCED_PARAMETER( lpvReserved );
}
```

```
/*------------------------------------------------------------------
        INIT MAPPING
        Create the file-mapping object.  Called whenever a client
        links to the library.  When the first client links, this
        procedure creates the object from scratch.  For subsequent
        clients, CreateFileMapping returns a handle to the already
        existing object.
    ------------------------------------------------------------------*/

BOOL InitMapping ( void )
{
    DWORD dwError;                              // return from GetLastError()

    /* create the file to be mapped */
    hMapFile = CreateFileMapping(
                    (HANDLE)OXFFFFFFFF,           // backed by page file
                    NULL,                         // security (default)
                    PAGE_READWRITE,               // access modes
                    0, (MAX_PATH + _MAX_FNAME),   // total size
                    szMapObjName );               // name of object
    if (!hMapFile)
    {
        return( FALSE );
    }

    /* map the view of the file */
    lpMapView = MapViewOfFile( hMapFile,          // object
                    FILE_MAP_ALL_ACCESS,          // access
                    0, 0, 0 );                    // size and offsets
    if (!lpMapView)
    {
        CloseHandle( hMapFile );                  // error: abort
        return( FALSE );
    }

    dwError = GetLastError( );
    if (dwError != ERROR_ALREADY_EXISTS)          // is this the first instance?
    {
        WriteInitialData();                       // initialize the buffer
    }

    return( TRUE );
}
```

```
/*--------------------------------------------------------------
        WRITE INITIAL DATA
        Initially the buffer contains two empty null-terminated strings.
   --------------------------------------------------------------*/

void WriteInitialData ( void )
{
    lpMapView[PATH_OFFSET] = '\0';
    lpMapView[FNAME_OFFSET] = '\0';
    return;
}

/*--------------------------------------------------------------
        DO WRITE
        Store in the mapped file the path and file name for
        the most recently opened file.
   --------------------------------------------------------------*/

void SetDefaultNames (
    LPSTR lpszName,
    LPSTR lpszPath )
{
    lstrcpy( &lpMapView[PATH_OFFSET], lpszPath );
    lstrcpy( &lpMapView[FNAME_OFFSET], lpszName );
    return;
}

/*--------------------------------------------------------------
        DO READ
        Read from the mapped file the path and file name of
        the most recently opened file.
   --------------------------------------------------------------*/

void GetDefaultNames (
    LPSTR lpszName,
    LPSTR lpszPath )
{
    lstrcpy( lpszPath, &lpMapView[PATH_OFFSET] );
    lstrcpy( lpszName, &lpMapView[FNAME_OFFSET] );
    return;
}
```

```
/*-----------------------------------------------------------------

        TERMINATE MAPPING
        Unmap the file and close the file handle.
    ------------------------------------------------------------*/


void TerminateMapping ( void )
{
    UnmapViewOfFile( lpMapView );
    CloseHandle( hMapFile );
    return;
}
```

The constants MAX_PATH and _MAX_FNAME are defined in stdlib.h. Using them to allocate space for file name buffers ensures that the buffer will accommodate the longest names from any file system Windows NT supports.

Dynamic-link libraries hold collections of useful routines for programs to load and execute as they run. DLLs written for Windows NT automatically receive a private data space for each client, eliminating the need to track each client and dynamically allocate space for the private data each one needs. With thread-local storage, a DLL painlessly achieves the same effect for all threads in one process, giving each one a private copy of particular variables. By bracketing some declarations with #pragma data_seg, you control precisely which variables are private and which are shared. Memory allocated dynamically is always private. To share blocks of memory among several clients, a DLL must create memory-mapped files. Windows NT DLLs also benefit from a single consistent entry-point mechanism that permits initialization and cleanup for each process and each thread.

DLLs compile with the same options as programs, but they link differently. Lib32 creates import and export libraries for the linker, and Link32 requires a –dll switch and an –entry switch to identify the entry-point procedure, if there is one. The steps for calling routines from a DLL have changed very little. The caller chooses load-time or runtime linking by building with the export library or calling **LoadLibrary** and **GetProcAddress.**

In Chapters 10 and 11 we've skirted around the topic of file I/O, which Chapter 12 addresses more fully.

### TWELVE

Working with Files

 FAT, NTFS, and HPFS file systems

Asynchronous I/O

Directory operations

Locking and unlocking files

Though successive versions of 16-bit Windows have become better and better at shielding the programmer from the mechanisms of the underlying operating system, DOS always pokes through when it comes to files. The Win16 API lacks commands of its own for common file operations, such as renaming or deleting a file. It would lack read and write commands if the C runtime routines accepted far buffer addresses, and even the `OpenFile` command is only a wrapper around the DOS 21H interrupt.

The Win32 API contains a full set of file I/O routines that reveal the power of NT's I/O manager. There are file commands to create and delete, read and write, rename and resize, lock and unlock, and also to read directories, search for file names, and even track changes in a directory tree as they occur. Windows NT also builds in the multitasking file management capabilities that DOS lacks. Even more, Windows NT can load drivers to interact with different file systems.

Besides multiple file systems, Windows NT features memory-mapped files and asynchronous I/O. Chapter 7 demonstrated memory-mapped files in connection with memory management; the sample code in this chapter demonstrates asynchronous I/O.

CONCEPTS

A *volume* is a formatted storage device, such as a disk or a tape. A *logical volume*, also called a *partition*, is a section of a larger physical volume treated as a separate device. Every logical volume has a single root directory named by a string such as "A:\" or "F:\". A *directory* is a container for holding files and other directories. Any directory may contain other directories forming a hierarchical tree. Directories also contain *files*, which are sets of information grouped together and given a name. Each volume may organize its files in accordance with a different system. A *file system* is the operating system software that manages the low-level organization of files on a volume. Windows NT delegates the file system tasks to a device driver, a smaller unit within the I/O manager. Several file system drivers may be installed concurrently, permitting the system to work with different file systems on different volumes at the same time. The terms "volume," "directory," and "file" all retain their meanings in each of the three file systems Windows NT supports.

File Systems

A file system governs how files are named, how they are protected, whether they can be recovered after system errors, and where on a particular medium they are stored. File systems don't always support the same features. The DOS file system, called *FAT* for its File Allocation Table structure, does not support the security features that other systems provide to protect files from unauthorized access. The file commands in the Win32 API support a large set of possible features, but some options are not available in some file systems.

Windows NT presently supports three file systems. The installation program always installs the FAT file system, but options allow it to install drivers for HPFS and NTFS as well. HPFS, for "high-performance file system," comes from OS/2. NTFS, for "New Technology file system," is the preferred system for Windows NT, and with it the operating system delivers its best performance and fullest set of features.

You are already familiar with the FAT system from DOS. It names files in an 8-3 format, with an eight-letter name preceding a three-letter extension, and it does not preserve any distinction between upper- and lowercase. A colon follows the drive letter and backslashes separate directory names. Besides alphanumeric characters, the following additional characters are legal in a FAT name:

$ % ' - _ @ { } ~ ` ! # ( )

FAT has several advantages over both NTFS and HPFS. It is the only file system whose directories can be read in all three operating systems—DOS, Windows NT, and OS/2—and only FAT supports floppy disks and other removable media. HPFS and NTFS can be installed only on fixed media such as hard drives.

The earliest versions of DOS were designed primarily for floppies, and the linear list format in which it stores file names is not efficient on hard disks with large directories. HPFS and NTFS organize file names in Btrees for faster access. They also permit longer file names (255 characters for NTFS; 254 for HPFS), and the names may contain spaces and periods. Both systems preserve case when storing file names but ignore case when performing searches. "CHAPTER 12" and "Chapter 12" refer to the same file.

HPFS in its native habitat, running under OS/2, always caches disk I/O. Because of this, by the time a write operation actually reaches the disk, the application may no longer be able to cope with a write error. The system itself responds with a technique called *hotfixing*. It pulls a good sector from a reserved hotfix pool, writes the data there, and replaces the bad sector with the good sector in disk and file maps. Under Windows NT, the operating system itself takes over disk caching and handles errors. Hotfixing does not occur.

Only NTFS permits Unicode characters in file names. It also supports more security features and recovers better from disk errors than do the other systems. After a CPU failure, a system crash, or an I/O error it restores consistency to a disk quickly by referring to its log of file changes. A disk-caching system runs the danger of corrupting files when a serious error leaves incomplete transactions in the buffer. NTFS guards against the problem by recording every file transaction in a log file. For each transaction, the system records *redo* information, which tells how to repeat the transaction, and *undo* information, which tells how to reverse the transaction. A background process records and caches information about the completion of each transaction. If an operation fails and is not completed, the system reverses it with the undo information. Every few seconds, the system checks the status of the cache and marks a checkpoint in the log. If the system crashes, it restores consistency by running through the transactions logged after the last checkpoint.

NTFS can mimic a POSIX file system. It can be made sensitive to case in file names, it allows the hard links that give one file several names, and it records multiple time stamps. For the convenience of OS/2 and MS-DOS stations that may share the same network, NTFS also automatically assigns to each file a short name in the 8-3 format derived from the file's full name. The files remain accessible to any station.

A special file holds the system's organizational data. Called the Master File Table (MFT), it contains records for each file and directory on the disk. The first 16 records hold system information including a file record for the MFT itself, a mirror of the MFT entry, and the log file for recording file transactions. The information for other files and directories begins with record 17. All of a file's attributes are stored in its record, including its name, its security descriptor, and its attribute flags; in fact, the MFT considers even a file's data to be an attribute. If the file is short and its data fits in the record, then the record itself is the file. For larger files, the data attribute points to other disk sectors where the actual data resides. The data attribute of a directory record contains file indexes. Large directories contain pointers to sectors with more directory entries organized in a Btree. Figure 12.1 diagrams records in a Master File Table.

The Master File Table and one large file whose data attribute points to data clusters elsewhere on the same volume

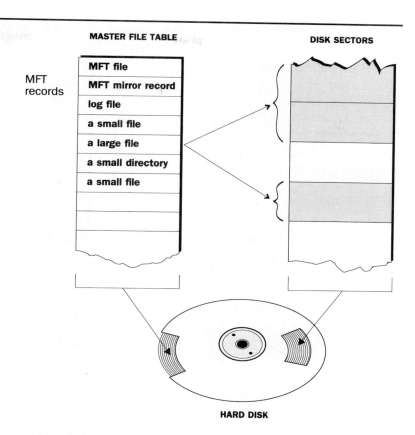

MASTER FILE TABLE

MFT records

| MFT file |
| MFT mirror record |
| log file |
| a small file |
| a large file |
| a small directory |
| a small file |

DISK SECTORS

HARD DISK

All three systems have directory trees and path names. All recognize "." as short-hand for the current directory and ".." as the parent directory. None permit these characters to appear in file names:

< > : " / \ |

You should also avoid using reserved words such as aux, con, and prn in a file name.

The three systems differ in their maximum partition and file capacities.

File System	Maximum Partition Size	Maximum File Size
FAT	2^{32}	2^{32}
HPFS	2^{41}	2^{32}
NTFS	2^{64}	2^{64}

COMMANDS

As an orientation to the Windows NT file API, the following list aligns familiar C runtime routines with their Win32 equivalents. The equivalence is often approximate rather than exact. **SetFileSecurity**, for example, controls many more access privileges than does _chmod. Win32 programs may call the C routines if they prefer but should avoid mixing calls from one API with calls from another.

C Routine	Win32 Equivalent	Description
File I/O routines:		
_chsize	SetEndOfFile	Change size of file
_close	CloseHandle	Close a file
_commit	FlushFileBuffers	Empty I/O buffers
_creat	CreateFile	Create a new file
_dup	DuplicateHandle	Create a second handle for a file
_eof	[no equivalent]	Test for end-of-file
_filelength	GetFileSize	Get length of file in bytes
_isatty	GetFileType	Check for character-stream device or file
_locking	LockFile, UnlockFile	Protect areas within a file

C Routine	Win32 Equivalent	Description
_lseek	SetFilePosition	Move the file pointer
_open, _sopen	CreateFile	Open an existing file
_read	ReadFile, ReadFileEx	Read data from a file
setmode	[no equivalent]	Choose text or binary file mode
_tell	SetFilePointer	Get position of file pointer
_write	WriteFile, WriteFileEx	Write data to a file

File management routines:

_access	GetFileSecurity	Check file access permission
_chmod	SetFileSecurity	Change file access permission
_dos_findfirst	FindFirstFile	Find first file matching a pattern
_dos_findnext	FindNextFile	Find subsequent files matching a pattern
_mktemp	GetTempFileName, GetTempPath	Create a unique file name
remove, _unlink	DeleteFile	Delete a file
rename	MoveFile, MoveFileEx	Rename a file

_stat, _fstat	GetFileInformation-ByHandle	Fill structure with info about file
[no equivalent]	CopyFile	Duplicate a file
[no equivalent]	MoveFile, MoveFileEx	Change the location of a file

Directory commands:

_chdir, _chdrive	SetCurrent-Directory	Change the working directory for a drive or a program
_getcwd, _getdcwd, _getdrive	GetCurrent-Directory	Get the current directory for a drive or a program
_mkdir	CreateDirectory	Make a new directory
_rmdir	RemoveDirectory	Remove a directory
_searchenv	SearchPath	Search for a file on a specified path
[no equivalent]	MoveFile	Rename a directory

Creating and Opening Files

We introduced **CreateFile**, the command for opening files, in Chapter 5. The client of a named pipe calls **CreateFile** to get the pipe's handle. To review:

```
HANDLE CreateFile(
    LPCTSTR lpszName,                  // name of the file
    DWORD fdwAccess,                   // read/write access
    DWORD fdwShareMode,                // may others use the file too?
    LPSECURITY_ATTRIBUTES lpsa,        // access privileges
    DWORD fdwCreate,                   // create new or use existing file?
    DWORD fdwAttrsAndFlags,            // file attributes; function modes
    HANDLE hTemplateFile );            // imitate attributes of this HPFS file
```

CreateFile opens a handle to a disk file, a named pipe, a communications port, or a console. **ReadFile** and **WriteFile** work with the same set of objects. Some parameter settings don't apply to some objects. You can't open a named pipe with any creation flag other than **OPEN_EXISTING**, for example, and you can't open a console's input stream with **GENERIC_WRITE** privileges. The ability to reach a variety of resources through a single API is meant to simplify the programmer's job.

We've already explained many of the **CreateFile** parameters, but those that have no bearing on pipes require a few more words in the context of file I/O. Pipes, for example, generally leave the share mode set to 0, but often a file can be shared with other processes. **FILE_SHARE_READ** and **FILE_SHARE_WRITE** grant read and write privileges to any other processes that may attempt to use the same file while you are working with it. Also, with pipes the fdwCreate flag must always be **OPEN_EXISTING**, but with disk files other flags also make sense.

- **CREATE_NEW:** Succeeds only if **CreateFile** can create a new file. Fails if the given file name is already in use.

- **CREATE_ALWAYS:** Forces **CreateFile** to create a new file no matter what. If the file already exists, **CreateFile** writes over it.

- **OPEN_ALWAYS:** Makes **CreateFile** open a file no matter what. If the file already exists, **CreateFile** uses it.

- **OPEN_EXISTING:** Succeeds only if a file with the given name already exists. Fails if it can't find the file.

- **TRUNCATE_EXISTING:** Succeeds only if the file already exists and resets the file so it starts out empty again.

The fdwAttrsAndFlags parameter governs the file's system attributes and the function's operating mode. Only the NTFS system supports all the flags and attributes. **CreateFile** ignores flags it cannot support on a particular volume. **FILE_ATTRIBUTE_TEMPORARY**, for example, has no effect on a FAT volume, and **FILE_FLAG_POSIX_SEMANTICS** has no effect on FAT or HPFS volumes.

- **FILE_ATTRIBUTE_ARCHIVE:** Marks a file that has not been backed up.

- **FILE_ATTRIBUTE_NORMAL:** Marks a file that has no special attributes. Setting any other flag overrides this one.

- **FILE_ATTRIBUTE_HIDDEN:** Marks a file that should be excluded from ordinary directory listings.

- **FILE_ATTRIBUTE_READONLY:** Marks a file that cannot be modified or deleted. Attempts to open a read-only file with **GENERIC_WRITE** privileges will fail.

- **FILE_ATTRIBUTE_SYSTEM:** Marks a file that belongs to the operating system.

- **FILE_ATTRIBUTE_TEMPORARY:** Marks a file that will soon be deleted. Programs should avoid writing to temporary files they did not create.

Two more attributes appear in our documentation but have no effect in our version of the system. They are **FILE_ATTRIBUTE_ATOMIC_WRITE** and **FILE_ATTRIBUTE_XACTION_WRITE**. Microsoft has not explained their intended purpose.

Besides file attributes, the dwAttrsAndFlags parameter controls several operating modes. Many of these flags affect the system's use of a disk buffer to cache file operations. Normally the system buffers both read and write operations to improve performance. Read commands retrieve whole chunks from the file in case nearby information is requested next; write commands are queued until several can be performed at once. Some of the flags tell the system how you intend to use the file so it can arrange the most efficient buffering mechanism.

- **FILE_FLAG_BACKUP_SEMANTICS:** Allows the calling process to override certain security checks for the sake of creating or restoring a backup archive.

- **FILE_FLAG_DELETE_ON_CLOSE:** Causes the system to delete the file when all its handles are closed. Useful for temporary files.

- **FILE_FLAG_NO_BUFFERING:** Turns off all buffering and caching for the file. Read and write operations can work only with chunks the size of a media sector and must begin on even sector boundaries. Call **GetDiskFreeSpace** to determine the size of a media sector.

- **FILE_FLAG_OVERLAPPED:** Initializes a file to operate asynchronously. File I/O commands execute in the background while the I/O thread continues to do other work.

- **FILE_FLAG_POSIX_SEMANTICS:** Reads file names according to POSIX rules.

- **FILE_FLAG_RANDOM_ACCESS:** Optimizes caching for random file access.

- **FILE_FLAG_SEQUENTIAL_SCAN:** Optimizes caching for a sequential file access that moves directly from beginning to end.

- **FILE_FLAG_WRITE_THROUGH:** Flushes the buffers after every write operation. Output is not held in a queue.

The sequential scan and random-access flags optimize the system's caching for particular kinds of access, but they do not restrict access to a single kind. **SetFile-Pointer** works even on files created with **FILE_FLAG_SEQUENTIAL_SCAN**.

Under Windows NT, the POSIX subsystem does not require its own file system. It uses instead the NTFS file system with special rules to support case-sensitive names and links allowing one file to have several names. NTFS preserves case in file names but ignores case in searches unless you set the POSIX flag. Also, to use POSIX names, separate the components with forward slashes.

POSIX form:	`//c/subdir/executable.exe`
Non-POSIX form:	`c:\subdir\executable.exe`

The final parameter of **CreateFile**, hTemplateFile, survives as an artifact from OS/2. It works only with HPFS files and is ignored in other file systems. It copies application- or user-defined key-value pairs from a previous file.

Creating Temporary Files

When creating temporary files, you can rely on the system to generate unique names that won't collide with other files in the directory. **GetTempFileName** builds file names and, if you wish, incorporates in the name a prefix and identifying number you supply.

```
UINT GetTempFileName(
    LPCTSTR lpszPath,           // directory for temporary file
    LPCTSTR lpszPrefix,         // app-supplied prefix for temporary name
    UINT uUnique,               // app-supplied number for use in name
    LPTSTR lpszTempFile );      // buffer to receive the temporary file name
```

To place the temporary file in the current directory, use "." for lpszPath. If you don't care where the temporary file is located, call **GetTempPath** to find out where the system prefers to locate temporary files. **GetTempFileName** concatenates the lpszPath string, the first three characters of the prefix string, the hexadecimal digits of uUnique (up to four of them), and a .TMP extension. The result has the form "path\pppuuuu.tmp", where "ppp" is the prefix and "uuuu" is the identifying number. The prefix and the number are optional parameters. If uUnique is 0, the command derives a number from the system time and ensures that the resulting name does not already exist in the given directory. If uUnique is not 0, the command does not check for uniqueness.

```
DWORD GetTempPath(
    DWORD dwBuffer,              // size, in characters, of the buffer
    LPTSTR lpszTempPath );       // buffer to receive temporary path name
```

When placing any file in the current path, you may find **GetFullPathName** useful. It accepts a file name and combines it with the current volume and directory names to produce a full path. **GetFullPathName** does not, however, verify that the resulting string is a valid name or that it refers to an existing file.

Reading from and Writing to a File

We introduced **ReadFile** and **WriteFile** with pipes in Chapter 5 (in the section "Reading and Writing through a Pipe"). They reappeared in Chapter 10 in the code for loading and saving bitmaps. Little remains to be said of them. So far, however, we've used them only for sequential operations, reading or writing straight through from the beginning to the end of a file. In order to read and write arbitrary locations in a file, we need a mechanism for moving the file pointer. The file pointer marks the current position in the file. Normally, **ReadFile** and **WriteFile** commands begin at the pointer's current position and advance the pointer automatically to the first byte after the area read or written. Each subsequent command begins where the last one left off. But a database, for example, must skip from place to place within a file as the user searches for records and modifies them in random, nonsequential order. Random file access requires a means of moving the pointer to an arbitrary position, just as you position a phonograph needle to play different parts of a record.

```
DWORD SetFilePointer(
    HANDLE hFile,                  // handle of an open file
    LONG lDistanceToMove,          // number of bytes to move file pointer
    PLONG plDistanceToMoveHigh,    // points to high-order word of distance
    DWORD dwStartFlag );           // starting position for pointer motion
```

The **DWORD** return value is the low-order word of the pointer's new position. The high-order word comes from plDistanceToMoveHigh, an unusual two-way parameter that holds both input and output. You pass in the high-order word of the distance to move, and the command passes out the high-order word of the new position. If `plDistanceToMoveHigh` is **NULL**, then **SetFilePointer** works only on files of no more than $2^{32}-2$ bytes.

The distance to move is interpreted as an offset from the beginning of the file, from the end of the file, or from the pointer's current position, according to the value of `dwStartFlag`. The flag's possible values are **FILE_BEGIN**, **FILE_END**, and **FILE_CURRENT**. Negative values are legal for `lDistanceToMove`. They move the pointer closer to the beginning of the file.

If a read operation reaches the end of the file and attempts to continue, no error occurs but no bytes are read. One way to check for the end of the file is to wait for **ReadFile** to return **TRUE** along with a `dwBytesRead` value of 0. Another method requires determining the file pointer's current position. The Win32 API does not include a separate function for that, but you can get the information from **SetFilePosition** by having it move a distance of 0 and checking the return value.

```
#define GetFilePointer( hFile ) \
    SetFilePointer( (hFile), 0, NULL, FILE_CURRENT )
```

From this, we can build another macro to test for the end of the file.

```
#define eof( hFile ) \
    (GetFilePointer(hFile) == GetFileSize(hFile, NULL))
```

Both macros are limited to files no larger than 2GB. For files up to 4GB, you could write functions similar to the macros using the high-order words passed back through the parameters of **SetFilePointer** and **GetFileSize**.

While it is possible to expand a file by pushing the pointer beyond the last byte written, it is never possible to read the preexisting data from the newly exposed area of the disk. For reasons of security, the system always fills any newly opened area of the disk with zeros. No process can ever read the garbage left behind when other processes delete their files. Windows NT enforces this rule in all the file systems it supports. In FAT files NT must physically fill empty spaces with zeros, but in NTFS and HPFS files NT simply remembers how far into a file you have written and delivers zeros if you try to read past the high-water mark. (Anyone with physical access to the machine and the ability to boot it with a different operating system could still recover deleted data, however.)

Unless you set flags to prevent it, Windows NT buffers all file operations. The system's caching algorithm determines when the buffer contents are written to the disk; even closing a file does not necessarily clear the buffers. You can force all of one file's pending output to the disk with **FlushFileBuffers**.

```
BOOL FlushFileBuffers( HANDLE hFile );
```

Resizing a File

Moving the file pointer past the end-of-file mark does not change the end-of-file mark. Write commands can push the mark forward, of course. You can also move it with **SetEndOfFile**, which either expands or truncates the file to make it end at the file pointer's current position.

```
BOOL SetEndOfFile( HANDLE hFile );
```

Asynchronous I/O

Disk access is much slower than most operations a program performs. A read or write command cannot finish its work until the disk head moves to the proper position, the disk sector rotates into place, data transfers, and the return result filters through the layers of the I/O manager back to the Win32 subsystem and eventually to the program itself. Physical devices always respond more slowly than most other system resources, and network file I/O in particular is notoriously slow.

If your toaster broke down, you could take it to the appliance store, wait for it to be fixed, and bring it home. This algorithm is synchronous. Only one thing happens at a time, and each step follows sequentially from the one before. A more efficient use of your time, however, would be to leave the toaster at the store and pick it up later when the store calls to say it's ready. In the meantime you could be gardening, paying bills, and learning to program for Windows NT. This algorithm is asynchronous. The steps do not follow one after the other, and one of the steps—the phone call—may come at any time, without any logical relation to the activities it interrupts.

So far, all our examples using **ReadFile** and **WriteFile** have followed a synchronous model. They issue a command, wait for the operation to finish, and move on to the next step. But all the I/O operations in Windows NT are, at the system level, asynchronous. Normally the Win32 subsystem simulates synchronous operations by holding a client program in suspension until its command finishes, but the subsystem also permits a program to request asynchronous operation. You can initiate an I/O operation without waiting for the result. Asynchronous I/O is useful to programs that do not immediately need the return value from a data transfer. Programs whose subsequent actions depend on the return value should use synchronous commands.

The system pursues an asynchronous I/O command in the background and notifies the thread when the operation finishes. The thread provides either an event object or a callback procedure, and the system signals completion by setting the event or calling the procedure. **ReadFile** and **WriteFile** support the event-notification version of asynchronous I/O. **ReadFileEx** and **WriteFileEx** work with a callback procedure.

Event Notification

The last parameter of both **ReadFile** and **WriteFile**, which we have ignored until now, points to an **OVERLAPPED** structure containing information for an asynchronous command. Whether a given command operates asynchronously depends on the value of the lpOverlapped parameter and on the file's original creation flags. Asynchronous operation occurs only if the file was created with **FILE_FLAG_OVER-LAPPED** and lpOverlapped is not **NULL**.

```
BOOL ReadFile(
    HANDLE hFile,                    // source for reading (pipe or file)
    LPVOID lpBuffer,                 // buffer to hold data retrieved
    DWORD dwBytesToRead,             // number of bytes to read
    LPDWORD lpdwBytesRead,           // returns number of bytes read
    LPOVERLAPPED lpOverlapped );     // needed for asynchronous I/O

BOOL WriteFile(
    HANDLE hFile,                    // place to write (pipe or file)
    CONST VOID *lpBuffer,            // points to data to put in file
    DWORD dwBytesToWrite,            // number of bytes to write
    LPDWORD lpdwBytesWritten,        // returns number of bytes written
    LPOVERLAPPED lpOverlapped );     // needed for asynchronous I/O

typedef struct _OVERLAPPED {   /* o */
    DWORD Internal;                  // system status
    DWORD InternalHigh;              // length of data transferred
```

```
    DWORD Offset;              // low-order word of start location
    DWORD OffsetHigh;          // high-order word of start location
    HANDLE hEvent;             // event object to set when finished
} OVERLAPPED;
```

The transfer buffer (lpBuffer) and the **OVERLAPPED** structure must both remain allocated while the I/O operation works in the background. Do not allocate either one as a local variable unless the variable remains in scope until the event signals completion. Also, do not attempt to modify the data buffer before the transfer operation finishes.

The first two fields of an **OVERLAPPED** structure are used by the system. The next two Offset fields indicate the point in the file where the read or write operation should begin. Synchronous operations do not need this information because they get it from the file pointer. Asynchronous operations, however, ignore the file pointer and so need to receive an explicit position. Asynchronous commands require explicit offsets because when several operations occur at once, their order is unpredictable.

For the final hEvent parameter, the program creates its own manual reset event object. The system sets the event to the signaled state when the read or write operation finishes its work. The application receives the notification by passing hEvent to **WaitForSingleObject** or **WaitForMultipleObjects** (see Chapter 4) or to **GetOverlappedResult** (see below).

When you initiate an asynchronous operation, the **ReadFile** or **WriteFile** command returns **FALSE** because the operation has not yet succeeded. A subsequent call to **GetLastError** confirms that the operation has not failed, either, by returning the value **ERROR_IO_PENDING**. Do not assume that every command on an asynchronous file always runs asynchronously. If the command can execute quickly, it may return immediately. Always check for **ERROR_IO_PENDING** to confirm asynchronous operation. When the operation finishes and the system sets the event signal, you should determine the outcome by calling **GetOverlappedResult**.

```
BOOL GetOverlappedResult(
    HANDLE hFile,              // handle of file, pipe, or comm. device
    LPOVERLAPPED lpOverlapped, // overlapped structure from earlier command
    LPDWORD lpdwBytesDone,     // place to store count of bytes transferred
    BOOL bWait );              // TRUE to wait for completion
```

If **GetOverlappedResult** discovers the operation has not yet completed, and if bWait is **TRUE**, then it calls **WaitForSingleObject** and blocks until the event in lpOverlapped is signaled. You might initiate an asynchronous operation, continue with other work, and then when you need the I/O result call **GetOverlapped-Result** with bWait set to **TRUE** to finish the background operation. If bWait is **FALSE** and the I/O operation has not finished, **GetOverlappedResult** returns **FALSE** immediately and **GetLastError** continues to indicate **ERROR_IO_PENDING**. When **GetOverlappedResult** returns **TRUE**, *lpdwBytesDone tells how many bytes were actually read or written. Because asynchronous I/O commands ignore the file pointer, the program itself must use the lpdwBytesDone value to update the offset in the **OVERLAPPED** structure for the next operation.

During our description of synchronization objects in Chapter 4, we mentioned that a thread may wait on a file handle in the same way it waits on events and semaphores. When an I/O operation ends, the system sets the signal on a file's handle. It is therefore possible to finish an asynchronous data transfer by passing hFile instead of hEvent to **WaitForSingleObject**. Waiting for the file handle is not recommended, however, because of what happens if several asynchronous commands queue up together. A signal from the hFile object cannot indicate *which* command finished. If one or more threads issue several asynchronous commands and then the program sits back to wait for an hFile signal, it cannot determine from the signal which operation is done or which transfer buffer to read from. Creating a new event object for each asynchronous command solves the problem.

Callback Notification

Instead of waiting for the system to set an event signal, some programs prefer to supply a completion routine to run when an asynchronous operation finishes its work. **ReadFileEx** and **WriteFileEx** initiate asynchronous I/O with a callback notification procedure.

```
BOOL ReadFileEx(
    HANDLE hFile,                              // handle of file to read
    LPVOID lpBuffer,                           // buffer to fill from file
    DWORD dwBytesToRead,                       // number of bytes to read
    LPOVERLAPPED lpOverlapped,                 // location to begin reading
    LPOVERLAPPED_COMPLETION_ROUTINE lpcr );    // address of completion routine
```

```
BOOL WriteFileEx(
    HANDLE hFile,                              // handle of file to write
    LPVOID lpBuffer,                           // buffer to copy to disk
    DWORD dwBytesToWrite,                      // number of bytes to write
    LPOVERLAPPED lpOverlapped,                 // location to begin writing
    LPOVERLAPPED_COMPLETION_ROUTINE lpcr );    // address of completion routine
```

Both functions require the hFile handle to have been opened with the **FILE_ FLAG_OVERLAPPED** flag. As before, the transfer buffer (lpBuffer) should not be modified until the operation runs to completion. And again, the **OVERLAPPED** structure substitutes for the file pointer in designating a place in the file for the data transfer to begin.

lpcr points to a completion routine that conforms to this prototype:

```
VOID WINAPI FileIOCompletionRoutine(
    DWORD fdwError,                  // completion code
    DWORD dwBytesDone,               // number of bytes transferred
    LPOVERLAPPED lpOverlapped );     // structure with I/O information
```

The system passes 0 for fdwError if the operation succeeded and **ERROR_HANDLE_EOF** if a **ReadFileEx** command tries to read beyond the end-of-file mark. A 0 for dwBytesDone indicates an error. lpOverlapped is the same pointer passed to **ReadFileEx** or **WriteFileEx**. Both commands ignore the hEvent field of the **OVER- LAPPED** structure, so it is available for passing operation-specific data into the completion routine.

The system will not call the completion routine while the I/O thread is running, only when it is waiting. To receive callback notification, a thread must enter an *alertable wait state* by calling one of the three functions that make a thread block but allow I/O results to interrupt the wait. The three are **SleepEx**, **WaitForSingle- ObjectEx**, and **WaitForMultipleObjectsEx**; they were introduced in Chapter 4. To determine whether one of them ended normally or was interrupted by a callback notification, look for a return value of **WAIT_IO_COMPLETION**.

The need to enter an alertable wait state in order for the system to call your completion routine feels to us like a limitation. Both the event and the callback versions of asynchronous I/O are really semi-synchronous since both require that the program eventually enter a wait state synchronously in order to receive the I/O result. In developing the logic to handle this wait, it may help to remember that with commands like these you can check for an I/O result without blocking:

```
WaitForSingleObject( hEvent, 0 );

SleepEx( 0, TRUE );
```

Both commands return immediately. The first simply checks the object's state, which you can determine afterward from the return value. The second gives the system a chance to call the completion routine and then moves straight on to the next command.

The semi-synchronous need to wait for results has the advantage of avoiding problems that can arise, especially on RISC machines, if the completion routine is allowed to interrupt anywhere between any machine instructions in your program.

It should be apparent that you can achieve the effect of asynchronous I/O by creating a new thread to execute each I/O command. One advantage of creating threads is that you can interrupt them, either by a prearranged signal or with **TerminateThread**. There is no way to cancel an asynchronous **ReadFile** or **WriteFile** command. But asynchronous commands transfer the burden of creating threads from you to the system.

Locking and Unlocking Files

Conflicts sometimes arise on a multitasking system when several threads attempt to manipulate a file at the same time. This issue arose in Chapter 7 when we discussed coherent views of a memory-mapped file. There we recommended that when a process creates a file-mapping object it should open the disk file with the sharing mode set to 0, thus preventing any other process from opening the same file. Establishing exclusive access to an entire file is one way to avoid the corruption that results when two processes write different changes to a single file simultaneously, but protecting the whole file is sometimes a drastic solution. Consider the case of a bank's database for customer accounts. If only one user at a time could write to the file, then the response time for entering transactions would slow enormously. On the other hand, if two people sharing an account made simultaneous withdrawals from different bank machines, the balance entry could become corrupted.

A mechanism for protecting one record at a time would solve the problem. The Win32 API permits you to protect a limited region within a file by locking it. No other process can write to or read from a locked region.

```
BOOL LockFile(
    HANDLE hFile,                // handle of file to lock
    DWORD dwFileOffsetLow,       // low-order word of offset to lock region
    DWORD dwFileOffsetHigh,      // high-order word of offset to lock region
    DWORD dwLengthLow,           // low-order word of region length
    DWORD dwLengthHigh );        // high-order word of region length

BOOL UnlockFile(
    HANDLE hFile,                // handle of file to unlock
    DWORD dwFileOffsetLow,       // low-order word of offset to locked region
    DWORD dwFileOffsetHigh,      // high-order word of offset to locked region
    DWORD dwLengthLow,           // low-order word of region length
    DWORD dwLengthHigh,          // high-order word of region length
```

Both functions call for the same parameters. In both cases, hFile must have been returned by **CreateFile** and must allow **GENERIC_READ** or **GENERIC_WRITE** access (or both). The offset parameters point to the beginning of the section to lock, and the length parameters tell how many bytes to lock, starting at the offset.

The length and offset in every **UnlockFile** command must match exactly the values passed in a previous **LockFile** command. You cannot, for example, separately lock three adjacent areas and then unlock them with a single command. Nor is it permitted to lock one region twice or to lock overlapping regions. A region may, however, extend beyond the end of the file. You must remove all locks before closing the file. Children that inherit a handle to a file with locked regions do not inherit the locks. They cannot read, modify, or unlock regions locked by the parent.

Locking works in all three file systems. The Share command that supports file sharing for MS-DOS is built in to the Windows NT kernel, so even FAT volumes always support locking and unlocking.

The lock you create with **LockFile** grants *exclusive access* to the locked region, preventing other processes from reading or writing. It is also possible to create a lock that guards only against write operations. Other processes may still read from a region locked for *shared access*. By default, the **LockFileEx** command creates a shared-access lock. It has one other advantage, too: It waits. If another process has already locked part of the area you want to protect, then **LockFileEx** waits for the region to become available.

```
BOOL LockFileEx(
    HANDLE hFile,                   // handle of file to lock
    DWORD dwFlags,                  // wait and access flags
    DWORD dwReserved,               // reserved, must be set to 0
    DWORD dwLengthLow,              // low-order word of region length
    DWORD dwLengthHigh,             // high-order word of region length
    LPOVERLAPPED lpOverlapped );    // structure with offset of region to lock
```

The two possible values for dwFlags are **LOCKFILE_FAIL_IMMEDIATELY** and **LOCK-FILE_EXCLUSIVE_LOCK**. Together they make **LockFileEx** work exactly the way **LockFile** does: The first prevents **LockFileEx** from waiting for the region to become available, and the second prevents other processes from reading as well as writing. The matching function **UnlockFileEx** seems to exist more for symmetry than necessity. The only difference between it and **UnlockFile** is that **UnlockFileEx** receives the file offset through an **OVERLAPPED** structure.

```
BOOL UnlockFileEx
    HANDLE hFile,                   // handle of file to lock
    DWORD dwReserved,               // reserved, must be set to 0
    DWORD dwLengthLow,              // low-order word of region length
    DWORD dwLengthHigh,             // high-order word of region length
    LPOVERLAPPED lpOverlapped );    // structure holding locked region offset
```

Closing and Deleting Files

When you're through with a file, close its handle with **CloseHandle**. Closing the handle does not delete the file (unless it was created with the delete-on-close flag). To erase a file from the disk, call **DeleteFile**.

```
BOOL DeleteFile( LPTSTR lpszFileName );      // name of the file to delete
```

DeleteFile returns **TRUE** if it succeeds and **FALSE** if it fails—if, for example, the file is still open or does not exist.

Moving and Copying Files

Another set of functions copies, renames, and moves files. Each one receives an old name and a new name for the file. **CopyFile** duplicates the original file. Its Boolean parameter instructs the routine whether to write over any existing file that already uses the new name. **MoveFile** changes the name of a file or a directory. For a file, the new name may indicate any device, but if the new name is already in use the command fails. If the new name points to a different volume, **MoveFile** copies the file and erases the original. For a directory, the new name must be on the same volume, and the command also renames all the dependent subdirectories. **MoveFileEx** works just like **MoveFile** but with a few extra options. It can be made to delete a file, to overwrite an existing file, and to fail if the source and destination are on different devices. Leaving the new name **NULL** erases the file. **MOVEFILE_REPLACE_ EXISTING** overwrites any file already using the new name, and omitting **MOVE- FILE_COPY_ALLOWED** prevents moving to a different device.

```
BOOL CopyFile(
    LPTSTR lpszExisting,          // name of an existing file
    LPTSTR lpszNew,               // file name to copy to
    BOOL bFailIfExists );         // TRUE to avoid writing over another file

BOOL MoveFile(
    LPTSTR lpszExisting,          // name of the existing file
    LPTSTR lpszNew );             // new name for the file

BOOL MoveFileEx(
    LPTSTR lpszExisting,          // name of the existing file
    LPTSTR lpszNew,               // new name for the file
    DWORD fdwFlags );             // flag to determine how to move file
```

Searching for Files

Most programs don't have to search for files. The bitmap DLL from Chapter 10, for example, asks the user to do the searching. The program shows a common dialog box and the user browses through the directories in search of a bitmap. But some programs need to search the directories themselves. A font manager, for example, would have to locate the system directory and search for .TTF and .FON files. A grep program or a file management shell would need to find all the files in a given directory. C programmers use the findfirst, findnext, and findclose routines. Under DOS, they map to an interrupt 21H service. In the 32-bit libraries, however, they map to new system calls—the same ones exposed in these three Win32 routines:

```
HANDLE FindFirstFile(
    LPTSTR lpszSearchFile,              // file to locate
```

```
    LPWIN32_FIND_DATA lpWFData );    // information returned

BOOL FindNextFile(
    HANDLE hFindFile,                // handle returned by FindFirstFile
    LPWIN32_FIND_DATA lpWFData );    // information returned

BOOL FindClose( HANDLE hFindFile ); // file search handle
```

The lpszSearchFile parameter points to a string naming the file to be found. The string may include a path, and it may include wildcard characters (* and ?). If the string ends with *.* then the search retrieves all the names from one directory. FindFirstFile by itself, however, retrieves information about only one file, the first one in the directory list to match the search string. FindFirstFile returns a valid handle if it discovers a match, and if not it returns INVALID_HANDLE_VALUE. If the returned handle is valid, then lpWFData contains further information about the newly located file.

If your search name contains wildcards, then you probably want to locate all the files that fit the pattern. The handle returned from FindFirstFile names a file search object, an internal structure that keeps track of a search's progress. Passing the handle to FindNextFile locates the next matching name from the given directory. Successive calls to FindNextFile turn up more matches. To locate all the matching files in a directory, continue calling FindNextFile until it returns FALSE. To determine whether FALSE indicates the end of the search or an error, call Get-LastError and check for ERROR_NO_MORE_FILES.

End the search by calling FindClose to release the search structure. Every call to FindFirstFile must have a matching FindClose. After FindClose, the search handle is no longer valid and may not be used in subsequent calls.

For each matching file, FindFirstFile and FindNextFile fill a structure of type WIN32_FIND_DATA with information describing the newly located file.

```
typedef struct _WIN32_FIND_DATA {   /* wfd */
    DWORD dwFileAttributes;          // FILE_ATTRIBUTE flags
    FILETIME ftCreationTime;         // when file was created
    FILETIME ftLastAccessTime;       // when file was last used
    FILETIME ftLastWriteTime;        // when file was last modified
    DWORD nFileSizeHigh;             // high-order half of size
    DWORD nFileSizeLow;              // low-order half of size
    DWORD dwReserved0;               // not used
    DWORD dwReserved1;               // not used
```

```
    CHAR cFileName[ MAX_PATH ];      // full path name
    CHAR cAlternateFileName[ 14 ];   // DOS alias
} WIN32_FIND_DATA;
```

FindFirstFile and **FindNextFile** return all matches, regardless of attributes. To produce a normal directory listing, you should skip over files marked with hidden or system attributes. The following program gives the functional equivalent of a simple dir command.

```c
#include <windows.h>
#include <stdio.h>

int main (
    int argc,
    char** argv )                    // user-supplied search pattern
{
    char szMatch[ _MAX_FNAME ];      // file name pattern to search for
    BOOL bContinue = TRUE;           // TRUE while matches are found
    HANDLE hSearch;                  // search object handle
    WIN32_FIND_DATA wfData;          // info about a matching file

    if (!argv[1])                    // check command line for a pattern
    {
        lstrcpy( szMatch, "*.*" );   // no pattern; show all files
    }
    else
    {
        lstrcpy( szMatch, argv[1] );    // use pattern from command line
    }

    /* look for first matching file */
    hSearch = FindFirstFile(
        szMatch,                     // file or file pattern to match
        &wfData );                   // information returned

    /* if no match was found, quit */
    if (hSearch == INVALID_HANDLE_VALUE)
    {
        return( 1 );
    }

    /* loop prints file names until all matches are found */
    while (bContinue)                // while we have a match, continue
    {
```

```
    /* skip over hidden and system files */
    if (!(wfData.dwFileAttributes & FILE_ATTRIBUTE_HIDDEN)
        && !(wfData.dwFileAttributes & FILE_ATTRIBUTE_SYSTEM))
    {
        /* display the file name */
        puts( wfData.cFileName );
    }

    /* look for the next matching file */
    bContinue = FindNextFile( hSearch, &wfData );
}

FindClose( hSearch );

return( 0 );
}
```

A Note on Time Formats

Three of the fields in a **WIN32_FIND_DATA** structure store times in a **FILETIME** structure. Windows NT represents times as 64-bit quantities measuring the number of 100-nanosecond intervals since January 1, 1601. (The upper range for this value is somewhere around 60,000 AD.) The **FILETIME** structure conveniently divides the 64-bit value into its high- and low-order halves.

```
typedef struct _FILETIME {    /* ft */
    DWORD dwLowDateTime;
    DWORD dwHighDateTime;
} FILETIME;
```

Internally, Windows NT always works with Coordinated Universal Time, also called UTC from its French acronym. UTC is basically Greenwich Mean Time (GMT). Working from a single standard time benefits wide-area networks that may span time zones. To consider an extreme example, imagine a file created in Melbourne, Australia. The file is sent by E-mail to someone in London who modifies it and sends it back. Because of the time difference, the modification date would be 10 hours earlier than the creation date.

To avoid such problems, Windows NT asks for a local time zone during installation. From then on in its own internal work NT always converts the system clock time into UTC. NTFS file dates are recorded in UTC but converted back to local time every time the directory is displayed. If you mail a file from your machine to another time zone, the system at the other end will show different values for the creation time. It will show what time it was in *that* zone when the file was created.

Most programs that concern themselves with times will convert the **FILETIME** value to a more readable format. The Win32 API recognizes a variety of time formats and provides functions to convert from one to another.

Time Format	Format Description	Variable Type
File time	100-nanosecond intervals since January 1, 1601	**FILETIME**
Local file time	Same as file time but converted to the system's local time zone	**FILETIME**
System time	Year, month, day, hour, second, and millisecond taken from internal hardware clock	**SYSTEMTIME**
Local time	Same as system time but converted to the system's local time zone	**SYSTEMTIME**
MS-DOS date and time	Two packed 16-bit values, one for the date and one for the time	**WORD**
Windows time	Number of milliseconds since the system booted; a 32-bit quantity that cycles every 49.7 days	**DWORD**

The Windows time format exists primarily for backward compatibility, and NT programs should have little other use for the old **GetCurrentTime** and **GetTickCount** functions. The new time API includes the following commands:

```
CompareFileTime

DosDateTimeToFileTime

FileTimeToDosDateTime
```

```
FileTimeToLocalFileTime

FileTimeToSystemTime

GetCurrentTime

GetFileTime

GetLocalTime

GetSystemTime

GetTickCount

GetTimeZoneInformation

LocalFileTimeToFileTime

SetFileTime

SetLocalTime

SetSystemTime

SetTimeZoneInformation

SystemTimeToFileTime
```

GetFileTime and **SetFileTime** do not perform any time conversions. When retrieving and setting times, be sure to call **FileTimeToLocalFileTime** and **LocalFileTimeToFileTime**.

Searching along a Path

The **FindFirstFile** loop works well for reading directories but is cumbersome when the task involves searching all the directories in a path to locate a single file. The alternative is **SearchPath**.

```
DWORD SearchPath(
    LPCTSTR lpszPath,            // name of path to search
    LPCTSTR lpszFile,            // name of file to find
    LPCTSTR lpszExtension,       // default file name extension
    DWORD dwReturnBuffer,        // size, in characters, of the return buffer
    LPTSTR lpszReturnBuffer,     // buffer for full path name of found file
    LPTSTR *plpszFileName );     // pointer to the file name within the path
```

The first parameter names a directory. **SearchPath** scans the directory and returns in `lpszReturnBuffer` the name of the first file that matches `lpszFile`. If the target string supplied in `lpszFile` lacks a three-letter extension, **SearchPath** automatically appends to the name the default extension optionally supplied in `lpszExtension`. If `lpszPath` is **NULL**, **SearchPath** seeks the file in all the normal default directories: the directory where the application resides, the current directory, the Windows system directory (\winnt\system32), the Windows directory (\winnt), and finally the directories listed in the environment path variable.

When `lpszPath` is not **NULL**, **SearchPath** scans only one directory and works very much like **FindFirstFile**. It differs in a few respects:

- It does not accept wildcards.

- It finds only the first match.

- It does not return any file times or attributes.

- It doesn't leave behind a handle to close.

- It allows for a default extension.

- It returns the full path name as well as the file name.

Directory Operations

Part of the data that comprises a process is its current directory setting. By default, the current directory is the one from which the user invoked the program. If you are in c:\word\data and type c:\word\winword.exe, c:\word\data becomes the current directory. A program may retrieve or reset its current directory with **GetCurrentDirectory** and **SetCurrentDirectory**. Also, a program may create or delete directories with **CreateDirectory** and **DeleteDirectory**. To rename a directory, call **MoveFile**.

To determine where the system is installed, call **GetSystemDirectory**. This retrieves the name of the directory that the installation program usually calls \winnt\system32. **GetWindowsDirectory** retrieves the name of the directory that is usually called \winnt.

Monitoring Directories

Another Win32 feature new to Windows programmers is the ability to watch for changes in a directory or directory tree. You can create a change notification object that signals whenever files or directories are created, deleted, renamed, resized, rewritten, or given new attributes. You can limit the watch to include only particular changes in a particular directory or subtree. The syntax resembles that used when searching for a file. **FindFirstChangeNotification** returns a handle to an object that signals when a change occurs. **FindNextChangeNotification** resets the same object to await the next change. **FindCloseChangeNotification** closes the notification object and ends the watch.

```
HANDLE FindFirstChangeNotification(
    LPTSTR lpszPath,              // directory to watch
    BOOL bWatchSubTree,           // TRUE to monitor subdirectories
    DWORD fdwFilter );            // changes to watch for

BOOL FindNextChangeNotification( HANDLE hChange );

BOOL FindCloseChangeNotification( HANDLE hChange);
```

FindFirstChangeNotification returns a handle to a change notification object. Pass the handle to **WaitForSingleObject** or **WaitForMultipleObjects**, just as you would an event handle. When changes occur in the directory or directories you specify, the system sets the change notification object to its signaled state. **FindNextChangeNotification** resets the object to its unsignaled state in preparation for another wait. If any change occurs in the brief period before you reset the object, the system remembers the change and the next Wait command returns immediately.

The fdwFilter parameter of **FindFirstChangeNotification** combines flags to request notification when particular kinds of changes occur.

- **FILE_NOTIFY_CHANGE_ATTRIBUTES:** File attributes are changed; for example, an archive marker is set.

- **FILE_NOTIFY_CHANGE_DIR_NAME:** Directories are renamed, created, or deleted.

- **FILE_NOTIFY_CHANGE_FILE_NAME:** Files are renamed, created, or deleted.

- **FILE_NOTIFY_CHANGE_LAST_WRITE:** A write operation changes the time recorded for a file's most recent modification.

- **FILE_NOTIFY_CHANGE_SECURITY:** The security descriptor for a file or directory changes.

- **FILE_NOTIFY_CHANGE_SIZE:** The end-of-file mark moves.

The flags for size and last-write changes differ because a write operation can modify a file without changing its size, and **SetEndOfFile** can alter a file's size without writing to it. Disk caching can delay the arrival of both notifications. Only when the buffers are flushed and the changes written to the disk does the system mark changes for these flags.

A program that watches for more than one kind of change can distinguish among them by creating a different notification object for each FILE_NOTIFY flag, storing the handles in an array, and passing the array to **WaitForMultipleObjects**. The signal from any change event, however, conveys only the fact that something has changed; it does not tell *what* has changed. The monitor signal is helpful for knowing when to refresh a directory display but awkward for logging information about the changes.

Getting Information about Files and Devices

A generous selection of routines retrieves or modifies information about files and file-related resources.

GetFileInformationByHandle fills out all the fields in a **BY_HANDLE_INFORMATION_STRUCTURE**. The fields include file attributes; creation, access, and last-write times; volume serial number; file size; number of NTFS links to the file; and a unique identifying number for the file. The identifying number, assigned by the system, remains constant while a file is open and enables you to determine whether two handles belong to the same file. Some of the functions that follow duplicate information that is also available from **GetFileInformationByHandle**.

GetFileAttributes returns a **DWORD** value containing a set of attribute flags. **SetFileAttributes** assigns a new set of flags to the file. For a list of file attribute flags, refer back to the description of the **CreateFile** command in the section "Creating and Opening Files" earlier in this chapter.

GetFileTime fills out three **FILETIME** structures giving the time the file was created, the time it was last used, and the time it was last modified. **SetFileTime** can modify any of the stored times, but to change them a process must either own the file or have the proper access privileges. Note that all file systems support the last-modified time, but the FAT file system does not record the other two times for its files. Some parameters are ignored when working with FAT files.

GetFileSize returns a file's size in bytes.

GetFileType tests a file handle to determine whether it refers to a pipe, a character stream such as a console or I/O port, a disk file, or some other unknown file type. Many file functions work only with disk files. A pipe, for example, doesn't have a creation time or a file size. **GetFileType** makes it possible to verify that a given handle refers to a seeking device—one with a file pointer—before attempting actions that involve seeking.

GetVolumeInformation, given the root directory of a volume, tells the volume's name, its serial number, the name of the volume's file system ("NTFS", "HPFS", or "FAT"), the largest permissible size for file names on the volume, and flags indicating whether the file system is sensitive to case in file names and whether file names may contain Unicode characters. To change the volume's name, if you have security privileges that allow it, call **SetVolumeLabel**.

GetDiskFreeSpace returns the number of bytes per sector for a given disk, the number of sectors per cluster, the total number of clusters on the disk, and the number of free clusters. Converting this information into the total number of bytes free requires some calculation:

```
DWORD GetFreeBytes( LPSTR lpszRootDir )
{
    DWORD dwBytesPerSector;
    DWORD dwSectorsPerCluster;
    DWORD dwTotalClusters;
    DWORD dwFreeClusters;

    GetDiskFreeSpace( lpszRootDir,
        &dwSectorsPerCluster,
        &dwBytesPerSector,
        &dwFreeClusters,
        &dwTotalClusters );

    return( dwFreeClusters * dwSectorsPerCluster * dwBytesPerSector );
}
```

GetDriveType returns one of the following flags:

DRIVE_REMOVABLE	Fixed disk drive
DRIVE_FIXED	Floppy or other removable media drive
DRIVE_REMOTE	Network drive
DRIVE_CDROM	CD-ROM drive
DRIVE_RAMDISK	RAM simulating a disk

GetLogicalDrives sets bits in a bitmask to indicate which logical drives are present in the system. Bit 0 represents drive A, bit 1 drive B, and so on.

GetLogicalDriveStrings fills a buffer with null-terminated strings naming the root directories of all the system's logical drives. Several other commands, such as GetDriveType and GetVolumeInformation, ask you to identify a device by the name of its root directory.

The Win32 API does not include a function to determine whether any medium is currently present in a given device, such as a floppy drive or tape drive. Here's a procedure to do the job:

```
/*--------------------------------------------------------------

       IS MEDIUM PRESENT
       Tests whether a removable-media device currently contains
       a disk or tape. Works by testing for the existence of
       an entry present in every FAT directory ("."). Suppresses
       the system's normal message box that appears when a program
       attempts to read from an empty drive.

       RETURN
       TRUE if the device contains any medium; FALSE if it is empty.
       --------------------------------------------------------------*/

BOOL IsMediumPresent( LPSTR lpszRootDir )    // string such as "A:\"
{
    HFILE hFile;                            // returned from OpenFile
    OFSTRUCT ofs;                           // info passed back from OpenFile
    char szFileName[10];                    // name for test file
    UINT uOldErrMode;                       // default error mode setting
    BOOL bSuccess = FALSE;                  // TRUE if we create a file
```

```
/* add a dot (".") to the end of the root directory */
lstrcpy( szFileName, lpszRootDir );
lstrcat( szFileName, "." );

/* suppress the system's error message box */
uOldErrMode = SetErrorMode( SEM_FAILCRITICALERRORS );

/* check for the dot entry (".") on the given device */
hFile = OpenFile( szFileName, &ofs, OF_EXIST );

/* clean up and return result */
SetErrorMode( uOldErrMode );
_lclose( hFile );
return( hFile != HFILE_ERROR );        // TRUE if medium is present
}
```

IsMediumPresent must call **OpenFile** instead of **CreateFile** to avoid a message box. If **CreateFile** discovers an open drive door or an empty drive, it asks the user to provide a disk. **OpenFile** does not. It generates a system error, which **SetError-Mode** can suppress.

File Security

Files and other securable objects in Windows NT have security descriptors attached to them. The fundamental element of a security descriptor is an access-control entry (ACE), a structure associating a list of privileges with a particular user or group of users. To examine the ACEs attached to a file, call **GetFileSecurity**. To attach new ACEs to a file, call **SetFileSecurity**. Chapter 17 explains ACEs in more detail.

C Runtime Equivalents

A Win32 program may choose to call routines from the C runtime libraries instead of the Win32 API. The Win32 routines are usually faster, however, because the C routines call them internally. Another difference between the two command sets is the limit they impose on the number of open files. The C libraries implement files as streams, and the **_NSTREAM_** constant in stdio.h sets the maximum number of simultaneous streams. Here is the definition from Microsoft's header file:

```
/*
* Number of supported streams.
*/
#ifdef _MT
#define _NSTREAM_    40
#else
#define _NSTREAM_    20
#endif
```

When _MT is defined (for a multithreading application), the libraries support 40 streams. Single-threaded applications have only 20 streams. Remembering that stdin, stdout, and stderr always take up three stream resources, the true limits on new files are 37 and 17.

The old **OpenFile** command from 16-bit Windows survives in the Win32 API for backward compatibility. New NT programs should have little use for it. Note that **OpenFile** returns an **HFILE** handle, defined in windef.h as an integer, while **CreateFile** returns a **HANDLE**. All the old file I/O functions, such as **_lwrite** and **remove**, expect an **HFILE** handle. **HFILE** is a carry-over naming the type for a DOS file handle. Of course true DOS file handles do not exist under Windows NT. Even C programs run from the command prompt only emulate them. But the two kinds of handles are conceptually heterogenous. **OpenFile** returns a handle to a file, and **CreateFile** returns a handle to a system object. In practice the two handles are sometimes interchangeable. A **HANDLE** from **CreateFile** may in fact work with **_lwrite**, for example, but then it may fail with close. Mixing the two APIs works unpredictably and should be avoided.

It is possible to convert a handle from one API into a handle for the other. _open_osfhandle receives an object handle returned by **CreateFile** and returns a file handle for the same open file. _get_osfhandle receives a C runtime handle and returns an operating system object handle. The conversion helps when only one API has a feature you need. The Win32 API, for example, does not support a distinction between binary and text mode. Its operations are in effect always binary. To put a Win32 file in text mode, pass its **HANDLE** to _open_osfhandle along with the _O_TEXT flag.

CODE

The two program modules listed here come from a larger program, called Database Server, that Chapter 13 completes. The program, a DDEML server, maintains a file of records holding names and phone numbers. Clients send messages asking the server to retrieve old records and add new ones. The record structure is very simple.

```
typedef struct _DBData
{
    char szName[MAX_NAME];          // name field
    char szPhone[MAX_PHONE];        // telephone number field
    int iStatus;                    // record status field
} DBDATA, *PDBDATA;
```

The two modules in this chapter, search.c and write.c, contain some of the program's file I/O operations. In search.c, a search thread scans the database sequentially from beginning to end looking for a record that matches the search criteria. In write.c, the program launches a single thread to handle all the Add Record commands from any client as long as the program runs. The search module reads synchronously, and the write module writes asynchronously.

The Search Module

The main program passes to FindRecord a pointer to a record structure containing the search criteria. The record's iStatus field contains flags to show whether the client wants to find a record that matches the given name, the given phone number, or both. **FindRecord** creates a new thread to perform each new search so that one long search won't cause delays in several concurrent client programs. Because several search threads may be running at once, the program must allocate a new buffer for each new search criteria record. If all the threads stored their criteria in the same variable, then the program would remember only one search goal at a time and concurrent searches would interfere with each other.

SearchThread is the thread procedure that carries out individual searches. First it opens the file, being careful to specify that the file may be shared for both reading and writing. If the thread prevented sharing, then it would block read and write operations in other DBServer threads. SearchThread checks the iStatus field of each record it reads for the STATUS_DELETED flag, which marks records the user has deleted but the program has not physically removed from the file. CompareRecords checks each new record against the search criteria. The search loop stops when CompareRecords returns **TRUE** or when it reaches the end of the file.

When the loop ends, the procedure must copy the results into a global variable and tell the main program thread it should send the new data to the waiting client. A mutex protects the global variable so that only one instance of the search thread may write to it at a time. The thread blocks until it has the mutex and then copies its result into the global variable. For reasons we'll explain in Chapter 13, the search thread cannot itself send the result to the client; the thread that manages DDEML operations must do that. The **IDM_UPDATE** command tells the main thread that a search has finished.

If the search did not turn up a match, the search thread places an empty string in the name field of the result buffer. The thread determines the success of the search by examining the number of bytes written in the most recent **ReadFile** operation. If dwRead is 0, then the loop tried to read past the end of the file.

The search thread cannot release the mutex until the main program has copied the data from DBFoundData and sent it to the client. The part of the program that sends the data pulses the heventDataSent event when it is safe to release the mutex. The search thread then cleans up and exits.

```
/*--------------------------------------------------------------------


        SEARCH.C

        Part of the DBSERVER program, this module contains the
        thread that locates particular records requested by
        a client by scanning the file record by record.

        FUNCTIONS
                FindRecord          initiate the thread that searches
                SearchThread        pull records one by one from file
                CompareRecords      compare one record to criteria

        from Mastering Windows NT Programming
        copyright 1993 by Brian Myers & Eric Hamer


        --------------------------------------------------------------*/
```

```
#define STRICT
#include <windows.h>
#include <windowsx.h>
#include "db.h"
#include "dbserver.h"

/*------------------------------------------------------------------
            FUNCTION PROTOTYPES
     ------------------------------------------------------------------*/

LONG SearchThread( CONST PDBDATA pdbCriteria );
BOOL CompareRecords( CONST PDBDATA pdbCriteria,
    CONST PDBDATA pdbRecord );

/*------------------------------------------------------------------
            FIND RECORD
            Create the thread that searches for a record. Returns
            TRUE if it successfully launches the thread.
     ------------------------------------------------------------------*/

BOOL FindRecord ( PDBDATA pData )
{
    HANDLE hThread;                        // thread handle
    DWORD dwThread;                        // thread ID number
    PDBDATA pdbCriteria;                   // buffer for thread's data

    if (!pData)                            // is pointer valid?
    {
        return( FALSE );
    }

    // Protect the search criteria from other searches by
    // copying them into a new buffer, one per thread

    pdbCriteria = LocalAlloc( LPTR, sizeof(DBDATA) );
    if (!pdbCriteria)
    {
        return( FALSE );
    }
    lstrcpy(pdbCriteria->szName, pData->szName);
    lstrcpy(pdbCriteria->szPhone, pData->szPhone);
    pdbCriteria->iStatus = pData->iStatus;
```

```
    /* create the thread that performs a search */
    hThread = CreateThread( NULL, 0, (LPTHREAD_START_ROUTINE)SearchThread,
        pdbCriteria, CREATE_SUSPENDED, (LPDWORD)&dwThread );
    if (!hThread)
    {
        return( FALSE );                        // CreateThread failed
    }

    /* set thread to low priority and start it running */
    SetThreadPriority( hThread, THREAD_PRIORITY_BELOW_NORMAL );
    ResumeThread( hThread );

    CloseHandle( hThread );                     // no further need for this
    return( TRUE );
}


/*-------------------------------------------------------------------

        SEARCH THREAD
        Scan the records in the file, beginning with the first,
        looking for one that matches the criteria stored in
        pdbCriteria. The search ends as soon as the first match
        is found.
        -------------------------------------------------------------*/

LONG SearchThread( CONST PDBDATA pdbCriteria )
{
    HANDLE hFile;                               // file handle
    DBDATA DBData;                              // data read from one record
    DWORD dwRead;                               // number of bytes read
    BOOL bContinue;                             // loop control variable
    BOOL bTest;                                 // function return values
    DWORD dwResult;

    /* create the file handle */
    hFile = CreateFile( szFile,                 // name of file
        GENERIC_READ,                           // read only
        FILE_SHARE_READ | FILE_SHARE_WRITE,     // others may read and write
        (LPSECURITY_ATTRIBUTES)NULL,            // default security
        OPEN_EXISTING,                          // always open, never overwrite
        FILE_ATTRIBUTE_NORMAL,                  // no special attributes
        NULL);                                  // no file template
    if (hFile == INVALID_HANDLE_VALUE)
    {
        return( 0L );                           // error: end thread
    }
```

```
// Loop through the file, reading them one by one, until
// we locate one matching the values in DBSearchData or
// we reach the end of the file.

bContinue = TRUE;                    // FALSE to abort search
while (bContinue)
{
    /* read a record */
    bTest = ReadFile( hFile,         // file handle
        &DBData,                     // destination buffer
        sizeof(DBDATA),              // size of buffer
        &dwRead,                     // bytes read (returned)
        NULL );                      // do synchronous I/O

    if (dwRead == 0)
    {
        bContinue = FALSE;           // failure or end of file
    }
    else
    {
        if (DBData.iStatus != STATUS_DELETED)
        {
            // ReadFile succeeded and the record has not
            // been marked for deletion. Check for a match.

            bContinue = !CompareRecords( pdbCriteria, &DBData );
        }
    }
}

// Wait for the mutex that protects the global buffer where
// the search thread transfers its results to the DDEML thread.
dwResult = WaitForSingleObject( hmxSearchResult, 60000 );
if (dwResult == 0xFFFFFFFF)
{
    // Abandon the search if we can't get the mutex. Abandoning
    // is not good, however, because it will leave a hot link open
    // until either the client or the server closes.

    return( 0L );
}
```

```
    /* prepare the global DBFoundData buffer to signal the search result */
    if (dwRead == 0)                         // did we reach end of file?
    {
        /* no match; return an empty record */
        DBFoundData.szName[0] = 0;
    }
    else                                     // a match was found
    {
        /* copy the found data into the buffer */
        lstrcpy( DBFoundData.szName, DBData.szName );
        lstrcpy( DBFoundData.szPhone, DBData.szPhone );
    }

    /* tell the main thread that a search has ended */
    SendMessage( hwndMain, WM_COMMAND, IDM_UPDATE, OL );

    /* wait for the DDE callback procedure to send the found record */
    WaitForSingleObject( heventDataSent, 60000 );
    ResetEvent( heventDataSent );

    // Now the search has ended, its result has been transmitted, and
    // another instance of the search thread may use the DBFoundData
    // buffer if one happens to be waiting.
    ReleaseMutex( hmxSearchResult );         // clean up
    LocalFree( pdbCriteria );
    CloseHandle( hFile );
    return( OL );                            // end thread
}

/*-------------------------------------------------------------------
        COMPARE RECORDS
        Compare a newly read record to the data in pdbCriteria.
        Note whether either data field matches. Look for records
        that match the client's name and/or phone number.
        Returns TRUE if a match is found.
    -------------------------------------------------------------------*/

BOOL CompareRecords (
    CONST PDBDATA pdbCriteria,
    CONST PDBDATA pdbRecord )
{
    BOOL bMatch = TRUE;                      // FALSE when a comparison fails

    // Check phone number field if we are looking for
    // a phone number.
```

```
if (pdbCriteria->iStatus == STATUS_SEARCHNUMBER)
{
    /* compare phone fields */
    if (lstrcmp( pdbRecord->szPhone, pdbCriteria->szPhone ))
    {
        bMatch = FALSE;                // they don't match
    }
}

// Check name field if we are looking for a name and if
// no previous comparisons have already proved this a mismatch

if ((pdbCriteria->iStatus == STATUS_SEARCHNAME) && bMatch)
{
    /* compare name fields */
    if (lstrcmp( pdbRecord->szName, pdbCriteria->szName ))
    {
        bMatch = FALSE;                // they don't match
    }
}

    return( bMatch );
}
```

The Write Module

A server might potentially handle many requests from different clients in rapid succession. If the server performs lengthy operations it could become a bottleneck, slowing response time in all its clients. The problem would be more acute for a server that accepted remote clients across a network because it might have many more clients, and network operations tend to be slow anyway.

The situation calls for asynchronous I/O. One way to achieve it would be to create a new thread to process every client request, leaving the main thread free to respond if new requests arrive. The search module follows that strategy. For the write module, which appends new records to the end of the file, we have chosen instead to use asynchronous I/O. This has the advantage of using only a single program thread (though the system creates background threads invisibly to complete the asynchronous commands.) One disadvantage is that you can't cancel asynchronous

ReadFile and WriteFile commands in progress. We could cancel a long search operation by calling TerminateThread to terminate the SearchThread procedure, but no command exists to interrupt overlapping read and write commands.

The first procedure, StartWritingThread, merely launches the thread. The writing thread runs below normal priority because it does not respond directly to clients or the user. It is meant to be a background thread, spending most of its time blocked as it waits for signals. WritingThread begins by opening the file. The CreateFile parameters allow the file to be shared for reading and writing. Since this thread leaves the file open as long as the program runs, it must share in order to allow other threads to do their work. This CreateFile command also sets FILE_FLAG_OVERLAPPED in preparation for the asynchronous write operations. WriteFileEx fails when passed a file handle that was acquired without the overlapped flag.

The system does not maintain a file pointer for asynchronous I/O file handles. The program must keep track of file offsets itself. When WritingThread adds records to the file, it always adds them to the end. A call to GetFileSize determines the starting byte for the first new record. To calculate subsequent offsets, the module counts all the records it writes and adds their combined lengths to the original size. The offset for each operation goes into an OVERLAPPED structure where Write-FileEx expects to find it. Because several write operations might run concurrently, we must allocate a new structure for each new command. When a command finishes, the system calls our IOCompletionRoutine, which releases each structure after the data is written.

Before each write command, WritingThread locks one record in the file to prevent other threads from reading or writing to the same location while the record changes. The lock is removed in the completion routine. Within this program the lock serves little purpose because the write command always writes to the end of the file, extending the end-of-file mark. This LockFileEx command is protecting a record that doesn't even exist until the write operation finishes. Locking beyond the end does not produce an error, however, and if the program's algorithm for finding empty record spaces were more sophisticated, the locking would be necessary.

At the top of the I/O loop, the thread waits for either of two event objects to be set. One of them, heventWrite, pulses whenever the main program receives a new record from a client. The thread wakes up, initiates the write command, and goes back to sleep. The other event, heventTerminate, is set just before the program closes down. It ends the loop so the thread can flush the file buffers before the program dies. Flushing the buffers is not strictly necessary; the system would do it eventually anyway. Besides responding to signals, the wait command serves one other important purpose. The system won't call the completion routine unless the thread is in an alertable wait state. A wait state means blocking, and an alertable wait state means blocking with one of the commands that specifically watch for I/O events: **WaitForSingleObjectEx**, **WaitForMultipleObjectsEx**, and **SleepEx**. A thread that performs asynchronous I/O must arrange to spend time waiting by calling one of these three commands.

The completion routine checks for errors, frees the **OVERLAPPED** structure, unlocks the locked record, and increments the counter used in calculating offsets.

```
/*-------------------------------------------------------------------

        WRITE.C

        Part of the DBSERVER program, this module contains the
        thread that performs asynchronous write operations to add
        records to the database file. A single thread can handle
        requests from many clients without creating a bottleneck
        because the write operations are carried out in the
        background.

        FUNCTIONS
                StartWritingThread      create thread that writes records
                WritingThread           write records when event pulses
                IOCompletionRoutine     check for errors after I/O

        from Mastering Windows NT Programming
        copyright 1993 by Brian Myers & Eric Hamer

        -----------------------------------------------------------------*/

#define STRICT
#include <windows.h>
#include <windowsx.h>
#include "db.h"                          // shared by client and server
#include "dbserver.h"

/*-------------------------------------------------------------
        FUNCTION PROTOTYPES
        -----------------------------------------------------------*/
```

```
void CALLBACK IOCompletionRoutine( DWORD dwError, DWORD dwBytes,
    LPOVERLAPPED lpOverlapped );
LONG WritingThread( LPVOID lpThreadData );

/*-------------------------------------------------------------------
        STATIC VARIABLE
    ----------------------------------------------------------------*/

DWORD dwRecsDone;          // counts records written by completion routine

/*-------------------------------------------------------------------
        START WRITING THREAD
        Create the thread that is responsible for entering new data.
    ----------------------------------------------------------------*/

BOOL StartWritingThread ( void )
{
    HANDLE hThread;                      // handle to writing thread
    DWORD dwThread;                      // ID of writing thread

    dwRecsDone = 0;                      // increases whenever I/O completes

    /* create the thread */
    hThread = CreateThread(
        NULL, 0,                         // default security and stack
        (LPTHREAD_START_ROUTINE)WritingThread,  // starting point
        NULL,                            // data for the thread
        CREATE_SUSPENDED,                // creation flag
        (LPDWORD)&dwThread );            // thread ID (returned)
    if (!hThread)
    {
        return( FALSE );
    }

    /* lower the thread's priority and let it run */
    SetThreadPriority( hThread, THREAD_PRIORITY_BELOW_NORMAL );
    ResumeThread( hThread );
    CloseHandle( hThread );              // no need for the handle now
    return( TRUE );
}
```

```
/*-------------------------------------------------------------------
        WRITING THREAD
        Block indefinitely until the event is signaled and then
        write a record at the end of the file.
        ----------------------------------------------------------*/

LONG WritingThread ( LPVOID lpThreadData )
{
    HANDLE hFile;                       // handle to database file
    HANDLE hEvents[2];                  // Write and Terminate events
    LPOVERLAPPED pOverlapped;           // info for overlapping I/O
    DBDATA DBLocal;                     // buffer for one record
    DWORD dwWaitResult;                 // return value from Wait command
    DWORD dwSize;                       // size of file
    DWORD dwRecsBegun;                  // count of records written
    BOOL bDone;                         // TRUE to end the thread

    /* put the events in an array for WaitMultipleObjectsEx */
    hEvents[0] = heventWrite;           // signals need for a Write command
    hEvents[1] = heventTerminate;       // signals program termination

    /* create the file handle */
    hFile = CreateFile( szFile,         // file name
        GENERIC_WRITE,                  // write-only permission
        FILE_SHARE_READ                 // others may read and write
        | FILE_SHARE_WRITE,
        (LPSECURITY_ATTRIBUTES)NULL,    // default security
        OPEN_ALWAYS,                    // create but don't overwrite
        FILE_ATTRIBUTE_NORMAL           // no special attributes
        | FILE_FLAG_OVERLAPPED,         // use asynchronous I/O
        NULL );                         // no template file
    if (hFile == INVALID_HANDLE_VALUE)
    {
        return( 0L );
    }

    /* how big is the file as we start? */
    dwSize = GetFileSize( hFile, NULL );

    dwRecsBegun = 0;                    // we have written 0 records
    bDone = FALSE;                      // TRUE to end thread
    while (!bDone)
    {
        /* wait on the Write and Terminate events */
        dwWaitResult = WaitForMultipleObjectsEx(
```

```
     2, hEvents,                    // array of 2 event handles
     FALSE,                         // don't wait for all at once
     INFINITE,                      // timeout period
     TRUE );                        // do interrupt when I/O finishes

/* did an error end the wait? */
switch (dwWaitResult)
{
    case WAIT_IO_COMPLETION:    // IOCompletionRoutine was called
        break;                  // do nothing

    case 0:                     // heventWrite was pulsed
        /* clear record buffer */
        FillMemory( &DBLocal, sizeof(DBLocal), 0 );

        /* copy data to a local buffer for overlapped operation */
        lstrcpy( DBLocal.szPhone, DBData.szPhone );
        lstrcpy( DBLocal.szName, DBData.szName );
        DBLocal.iStatus = STATUS_VALID;       // not deleted

        /* allocate memory for the overlapped structure */
        pOverlapped = GlobalAllocPtr( GHND, sizeof(OVERLAPPED) );
        pOverlapped->OffsetHigh = 0;          // high word is 0

        // Since WriteFileEx uses a completion routine, it has
        // no use for the hEvent field. The completion routine,
        // however, needs the file handle in order to unlock
        // the record once it's written.

        pOverlapped->hEvent = hFile;

        // The offset tells where in the file to write the new
        // record. DBSERVER always writes to the end of the file.
        // Its calculation is based on the file's starting size
        // and adds one record length for each increment of
        // dwRecsBegun.

        pOverlapped->Offset = dwSize + (dwRecsBegun * sizeof(DBDATA));

        // Lock the record first so that no other thread will read
        // or write it while it is being modified. If the same
        // record is already locked, LockFileEx will wait for it
        // to be released before continuing.
```

```
            LockFileEx( hFile,
                LOCKFILE_EXCLUSIVE_LOCK,     // prevent any other access
                0,                           // reserved
                sizeof(DBDATA),              // size of block to lock
                0,                           // high-order word of block size
                pOverlapped );               // file offset stored here

            // Commence an asynchronous write operation

            WriteFileEx( hFile,              // file handle
                &DBLocal,                    // source buffer
                sizeof(DBDATA),              // size of source buffer
                pOverlapped,                 // info for asynchronous I/O
                IOCompletionRoutine );       // call this when done

            dwRecsBegun++;
            break;

        case 1:                          // heventTerminate was pulsed
            bDone = TRUE;                // terminate thread
            break;

        default:                         // dwWaitResult == error
            bDone = TRUE;                // end thread
    }

} /* end of while loop */

// Check whether there are any pending I/O events by comparing
// this procedure's record count with that of the completion
// routine. Flush the file buffers if necessary.

if (dwRecsBegun != dwRecsDone)
{
    FlushFileBuffers( hFile );
}

CloseHandle( hFile );                    // clean up
return( OL );                            // end thread
UNREFERENCED_PARAMETER( lpThreadData );
}
```

```
/*-------------------------------------------------------------------
        I/O COMPLETION ROUTINE
        After an asynchronous write operation finishes, the system
        calls this routine to check for errors, update counters,
        and release the OVERLAPPED structure.
        ----------------------------------------------------------*/

void CALLBACK IOCompletionRoutine(
    DWORD dwError,                      // return result from I/O
    DWORD dwBytes,                      // count of bytes written
    LPOVERLAPPED lpOverlapped )         // info about the I/O command
{
    /* did an error occur while writing? */
    if (dwError)
    {
        MessageBox( NULL, "Error while writing to disk",
            szCaption, MB_OK | MB_ICONEXCLAMATION );
    }

    /* was a complete record written? */
    if (dwBytes != sizeof(DBDATA))
    {
        MessageBox( NULL, "Write operation was incomplete",
            szCaption, MB_OK | MB_ICONEXCLAMATION );
    }

    /* unlock the record that was just added */
    UnlockFileEx( lpOverlapped->hEvent, // file handle (not an event!)
        0,                              // reserved
        sizeof(DBDATA),                 // size of block to unlock
        0,                              // high-order word of block size
        lpOverlapped );                 // file offset stored here

    GlobalFreePtr( lpOverlapped );      // free this OVERLAPPED structure
    dwRecsDone++;                       // one more record written
    return;
}
```

This chapter covered file systems and the file I/O API. Windows NT currently supports FAT, HPFS, and NTFS file systems and may support others later. The FAT system works with floppy drives and can be read by both OS/2 and NT systems. NTFS, however, provides much fuller security features, longer file names, better recovery safeguards, and faster file access.

Unlike the Win16 API, the Win32 API includes a full set of routines for all aspects of file I/O. Besides opening, reading, writing, and closing, you can lock parts of files, read and write asynchronously, and expand files or truncate them. There are commands to locate files and to copy, move, and delete them. Each file is stored with several relevant times, and another set of routines converts between the absolute times stored on the disk and the machine's local time. Directories can be created, deleted, and monitored for changes.

As examples of file I/O, we presented two sections from a longer program that Chapter 13 explains fully. One section performed synchronous read operations, creating a new thread for each search, and the other performed asynchronous write operations, all from a single thread that handles many clients at once. The system handles all I/O operations asynchronously, but whether a particular program may depends on the API available through its subsystem. The asynchronous commands you learned in this chapter work with pipes as well as files, as we mentioned in Chapter 5. Chapter 16 shows asynchronous I/O using the multimedia API for RIFF files, and you'll encounter another form of asynchronous command when you read about the DDEML in the next chapter.

Communicating through the DDEML

- Dynamic Data Exchange

- DDEML servers and clients

- Cold, warm, and hot data links

- Poke and Execute transactions

- String and data objects

Isolated in private address spaces, Windows NT applications cannot share data directly. All sharing must work through established protocols such as Dynamic Data Exchange (DDE), the clipboard, and OLE. Chapters 14 and 15 show how to use OLE and the clipboard; this chapter investigates DDE through the DDE Management Library (DDEML). Dynamic data exchange is a message-based protocol for sharing information among applications. Because DDE is a standard protocol, any DDE program can communicate with any other. Users can link DDE applications to process data more efficiently. Also, DDE programs can send commands to each other. The Program Manager, for example, defines a set of DDE messages any application can send to create, modify, and delete groups of program icons. Through DDE, applications can achieve a high level of integration.

The DDE protocol can be difficult to manage. It is too "loose"—that is, it allows too much free play between the applications that participate in a DDE conversation. It does not provide enough structure for interaction or a robust error-checking mechanism. Many programmers also feel that DDE is hampered by the message system, that the information and commands exchanged in a DDE conversation must be compressed awkwardly to fit into the window message parameters.

The DDE Management Library, which first appeared in Windows 3.1, addresses these problems and makes DDE a more accessible protocol. The DDEML is a library of functions that give your program a new API for the old DDE transactions. Instead of sending messages, a DDEML application calls functions. The functions manage all the low-level details of atoms, messages, and memory management. Function-based DDEML calls are completely compatible with message-based DDE transactions. In other words, any DDEML program can communicate perfectly with any DDE program. The DDEML is a more convenient front end for the same message-based DDE operations.

Convenience is only one reason to prefer the DDEML over plain DDE. Another is that future enhancements may be available only through the library and not through the message-based protocol. OLE 1.0, for example, runs on top of DDE, but the next version of OLE will use a new, more efficient interprocess communication method, one that builds on the system's procedure call facilities. Future versions of the DDEML will probably also leave the old DDE behind. If that happens, even preexisting DDEML programs will benefit from the new mechanism, but plain DDE programs will not. Message-based DDE will still be supported in any case, but it may become obsolete. The DDEML will not.

CONCEPTS

Although the DDEML shields the programmer from the low-level details of a DDE interaction, the structure of the interaction and the required sequence of exchanges persist in the DDEML API. We'll first review the basic concepts of DDE and then explain the improvements the DDEML offers.

DDE Interactions

Any explanation of how to program DDEML exchanges eventually devolves into a painstaking step-by-step description of who does what when. Before we reach that level of detail, it may help to have a simple overview of what can happen in a DDE conversation. A DDEML exchange begins when the client initiates a conversation and the server application responds. Until one of them decides to disconnect, they continue to exchange data in one or more of the following ways:

- The client requests data and the server sends it.

- The client asks to be told whenever a certain data item changes.

- The client asks to receive the new value whenever a certain data item changes.

- The client sends a command and the server carries it out.

- The client sends unsolicited data to the server.

DDE and the DDEML, with all their transaction names, functions, messages, data handles, and flags, exist to support those five basic actions.

Dynamic Data Exchange (DDE)

An exchange of information or commands between two applications using DDE is called a DDE *conversation*. Each conversation is made up of two sides. The application that requests and receives the information is called the *client*. The application that responds to requests and provides information is called the *server*. A *link*, in DDE terms, is a series of messages that conveys a particular piece of information.

A single conversation may establish several links of different kinds. A link may be cold, hot, or warm; the client application determines which link to use for each data request.

All links begin when the client initiates a conversation by asking for data—say, a monthly regional sales figure. In a *cold link* the server immediately returns the data and the exchange ends. In a *hot link* the server continues to send the same piece of information automatically whenever the information changes—when, for example, another sale is recorded. In a *warm link* the server does not send the new data after each change; it merely notifies the client that a change occurred. The client may optionally ask to see the new value.

Clients and Servers

What sorts of applications should take each side in a DDE conversation? Perhaps the best way to differentiate clients and servers is to say that servers usually maintain data in its rawest form, while clients concern themselves with presentation. An application that performs both functions might support both the client and server sides of DDE.

A good example of a server would be a database of addresses. Such an application would maintain a list of names, addresses, phone and fax numbers, and other related items. All the entries would need to be up to date. Other office programs for mailing lists, faxing, writing letters, and tracking contacts could be clients and rely on the single central database for current information. If the address list is current then all the other applications will have current data.

An example of a client might be a word processor. Word processors are good for formatting and displaying information. By pasting hot links into a sales report, you can let DDE perform the tedious task of updating all the figures.

A spreadsheet might act as both client and server. Spreadsheets manipulate data, which is a common function of servers, and they present data, which clients often do. For example, a spreadsheet might pull sales figures from a database to calculate a regional sales total; it could in turn pass the results to a word processor for use in a monthly report.

How DDE Works

Windows defines nine messages for DDE, all beginning with the prefix WM_DDE_. A DDE program sends messages to signal each stage in a DDE conversation. The message parameters carry information.

Each piece of application data passed in a DDE conversation is uniquely identified by three strings: the application name, the topic name, and the item name. For example, to identify the value stored in one cell of a spreadsheet the application name might be "SPRDSHT.EXE", the topic might be the "SALES.DAT" file, and the item name might be a cell, such as "A12". A phone number may be defined by "ADDRBOOK.EXE", "Fred Jones", "Phone Number". Within a DDE conversation, the three strings are represented by three atoms. An *atom* is a **WORD** value that identifies a string stored in a hash table. Windows manages the hash table for you with a set of atom functions, of which the most useful are these:

- **GlobalAddAtom** puts a string in the table and returns an atom identifying it.

- **GlobalGetAtomName** retrieves a string from the table, given its atom.

- **GlobalDeleteAtom** removes the string from the global atom table.

An application can also have private strings in a local atom table, but they cannot be shared. The global atom functions work from a globally shared table. During a DDE conversation, the server and client send each other atoms. The server puts all three strings in the global atom table and sends the client three atoms. The client looks up the corresponding strings with **GlobalGetAtomName**. How the three fields identify an item is defined by the server. When designing your server, make sure that any given combination of application, topic, and item represents one unique value or range of values.

DDE conversations occur when programs send each other DDE messages. A client begins by calling **SendMessage** to broadcast **WM_DDE_INITIATE** to all the top-level windows. Interested servers respond by sending back **WM_DDE_INITIATE**. The client packs an item name atom and a clipboard format into a **WM_DDE_REQUEST** message, and if the server can satisfy the request, it copies the data into a memory object and returns the object handle in a **WM_DDE_DATA** message. If the client wants to know whenever the value of an item changes, it sends **WM_DDE_ADVISE** and the server continues to send updates in **WM_DDE_DATA** messages until the client breaks off the link with **WM_DDE_UNADVISE**. DDE exchanges may carry out other transactions as well, but they all involve sending a sequence of messages that carry atoms and handles. Some of the messages appear in Figure 13.1, where Microsoft's Spy utility has captured an exchange between Word for Windows and Excel.

FIGURE 13.1:

Exchange of DDE messages as Word for Windows establishes a link with an Excel spreadsheet

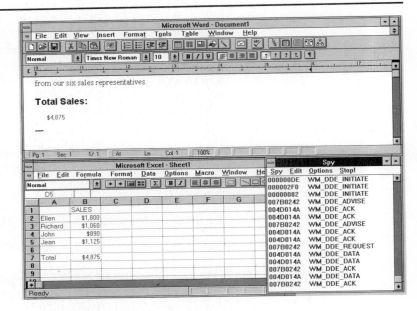

What the DDEML Adds to DDE

Three main points distinguish the DDEML from message-based DDE. First and most apparent, DDEML programs call functions instead of sending messages. The DDEML provides 27 functions for engaging in DDE transactions. The new functions are more specific than the DDE messages and provide a more comprehensive service. They form a high-level interface for the old mechanisms, but internally the DDEML still sends DDE messages with atoms and handles.

Second, DDEML applications must provide a callback procedure dedicated to DDEML transactions. Clients and servers alike interact directly with the DDE Management Library, which acts as a clearinghouse for DDE activity. When the library has information for any DDEML program, it delivers a message to the program's callback procedure. For example, a client initiates a conversation by choosing a topic and calling **DdeConnect**. The DDEML locates a server that supports the topic.

It passes **XTYP_CONNECT** as a parameter to the server's callback function, and the server recognizes a connection. This sequence illustrates the common pattern where a DDEML function call in one program causes a DDEML message to go to another program.

Third, instead of storing atoms in an atom table, DDEML programs create string objects and pass their handles. To create a string handle, pass a string to **DdeCreateStringHandle**. To retrieve the string associated with a handle, call **DdeQueryString**. To release a string you no longer need, call **DdeFreeStringHandle**. Each creation command should be matched by a freeing command. String handles have data type **HSZ**, defined as a **DWORD**.

The need for a client application to delete atoms it receives from the server causes some confusion in DDE programming. A string handle, however, belongs to the system, and the system assumes responsibility for releasing the string when all the programs have freed their handles to it.

Service, Topic, and Item Names

The purpose of most DDE conversations is to exchange data. The client requests a piece of information from the server, and the server provides it. In basic DDE, as we said, the three strings that identify any one piece of information are called the application name, the topic name, and the item name. The term *application name* is confusing because it refers to a broad category of information provided by a server, and although many servers do provide only one kind of information, some provide more and so require several "application" names. To avoid confusion, the DDE Management Library uses the term *service name* instead. The server defines its own strings and decides what they mean, but their usage generally conforms to these descriptions.

- **Service name:** A broad category of information
- **Topic name:** An information context, typically a file name
- **Item name:** A piece of information to pass in a DDE transaction

An item might identify a page, a string, a bitmap, a spreadsheet cell, or any other data that transfers from one program to another.

To consider an example, a spreadsheet might support two services called "spreadsheet" and "chart". As topics, both services might use file names. Items in the spreadsheet service might be cell ranges and take the form B3:E5. Items in the chart service might name presentation formats such as "pie" or "bar".

Limiting a server to a single service has some advantages. If the service and the server have the same name, then a client who knows one also knows the other. Given just the .EXE file name, a client can begin a conversation. If your server and its service have different names, or if there are several services, then you have to provide more documentation for clients. Clients sometimes ask users to enter the name of a desired service, topic, and item, so the more intuitive the names are, the better. Also, the System topic, described later in this chapter, lets the client retrieve a list of topics and items for any service and display it to the user. If the client knows your service name, further documentation may not be necessary.

If the client knows the program name as well as the service name, then when the client launches it can attempt to resume links from the last session by starting the server process (with **CreateProcess**). Links with Excel documents, for example, can be easily resumed. The client launches Excel with a file name on the command line. Excel appears and loads the requested file. Excel also treats the path names of open files as DDE topics, so the client begins a conversation with the "excel" service on the topic of "c:\data\myfile.xls". Word for Windows uses the same conventions. Its .EXE file and service name are "winword", and its topics are full path names for each open document or document template. In a WinWord topic, the items are bookmark names.

Interprocess Communication (IPC) Mechanisms

Dynamic Data Exchange is one of many methods for Windows programs to communicate with each other. The clipboard is another more rudimentary IPC mechanism, as are the pipes and mailslots discussed in Chapter 5 and the memory-mapped files of Chapter 7. Table 13.1 lists some others and tells which Windows NT code environments support them. Not all mechanisms can communicate between environments. For example, the POSIX equivalent of a named pipe, a FIFO queue, cannot communicate with pipes in other subsystems. Also, Win32s does not yet fully support memory-mapped files, but it does support shared section objects that map to the page-swapping file, just like the ones we created in Chapters 7 and 11.

TABLE 13.1: Interprocess Communication (IPC) Mechanisms and the Environments Where They Are Supported

Facility	Win32	Win32s	Win16	MS-DOS	POSIX	OS/2
DDE	X	X	X			
OLE	X	X	X			
OLE 2.0	X		X			
Named pipes	X	X	X	X	X	X
Mailslots	X	X				X
Semaphores	X				X	X
Memory-mapped files	X	X				
Remote procedure calls	X	X	X	X		
NetBIOS	X	X	X			X
Window sockets	X	X	X			

The standard DDEML API does not connect remote programs. Microsoft's technicians tell us that the first public release of Windows NT will include an alternate network DDEML API resembling the NetDDE facility in Windows for Workgroups.

COMMANDS

This section explains the commands, messages, and structures a DDEML program requires to communicate through the DDEML. We begin with some basic methods: how to write a DDEML callback function and how to create string handles and data objects. Then we'll work through the typical actions in the life cycle of a DDEML program, including initialization, conversations, and termination. Each interaction calls for a different sequence of functions, and the sequence differs for the client and server. We'll describe each transaction and explain who does what. The chapter closes with two sample programs, a DDEML database server and a DDEML client that uses it to store and retrieve names and phone numbers. Some parts of the server were explained in Chapter 12.

To use the DDEML functions you must include the ddeml.h header file in your source code, link with the user32.lib import library, and be sure the ddeml.dll library lies in the system path when your program runs.

The DDEML Callback Function

Every DDEML program contains a callback procedure where it processes signals sent from the DDE Management Library. The first parameter of the callback function, uType, indicates a type of transaction and tells the procedure what to do. The transaction symbol types begin with the prefix XTYP_, for "transaction type." All DDEML callback functions have the same prototype, and generally they contain a switch statement.

```
HDDEDATA WINAPI DdeCallback (
    UINT uType,              // transaction type
    UINT uFmt,               // clipboard format
    HCONV hConv,             // conversation handle
    HSZ hsz1,                // a string handle
    HSZ hsz2,                // another string handle
    HDDEDATA hData,          // global memory object handle
    DWORD dwData1,           // transaction data
    DWORD dwData2 );         // more transaction data
{
    switch (uType)
    {
        case XTYP_REGISTER:
        case XTYP_UNREGISTER:
            // registration code goes here
            return( (HDDEDATA)NULL );

        case XTYP_ADVDATA:
            // code for updating an item goes here
            return( (HDDEDATA)DDE_FACK );

        // add more cases for more messages

        default:
            return( (HDDEDATA)NULL );
    }
}
```

Some of the parameters will become clearer as we proceed. uFmt is a clipboard format for the current transaction. hConv is a handle to the current conversation. The contents of the other parameters depend on what kind of transaction the message represents. Not all transactions use all the parameters; some parameters may be **NULL** or 0. But in the parameter list you have room to pass two string handles, a global data handle, and two **DWORD**s full of data.

Which XTYP messages the procedure receives depends on whether the program is a client, a server, or both and also on what messages were filtered in the **Dde-Initialize** command.

The callback procedure's return value depends on the message. Some messages call for the procedure to return a data handle of type **HDDEDATA**, but some call for a response flag, some for a Boolean value, and some messages require no response at all. For reference, here are all the messages grouped according to the response they expect.

Boolean:	XTYP_ADVSTART
TRUE or FALSE	XTYP_CONNECT
Data handle (or NULL):	XTYP_ADVREQ
	XTYP_REQUEST
	XTYP_WILDCONNECT
Transaction flag:	XTYP_ADVDATA
DDE_FACK, DDE_FBUSY, or	XTYP_EXECUTE
DDE_FNOTPROCESSED	XTYP_POKE
None (notifications):	XTYP_ADVSTOP
	XTYP_CONNECT_CONFIRM
	XTYP_DISCONNECT
	XTYP_ERROR
	XTYP_REGISTER
	XTYP_UNREGISTER
	XTYP_XACT_COMPLETE

Managing Strings

Two of the parameters passed to a DDEML callback function are string handles. Many of the DDEML functions, such as **DdeConnect**, also use string handle parameters. The strings are usually service, topic, and item names. To avoid confusion about who owns a string and who releases it, the DDEML manages all the strings itself. To pass a string through a DDEML function, you must first register the string with the library and receive a handle to it. The handle is a value assigned by the system to identify a particular string. The system keeps all the strings together in an internal table and releases them when they are no longer needed. DDEML applications tell the library when they want to use a string and when they are through with it, and the library manages the rest.

DDEML programs require several functions for working with strings and string handles. The first two create a handle and destroy a handle.

```
HSZ DdeCreateStringHandle(
    DWORD dwInstID,            // instance identifier
    LPTSTR lpszString,         // address of null-terminated string
    int iCodePage );           // CP_WINANSI or CP_WINUNICODE

BOOL DdeFreeStringHandle(
    DWORD dwInstID,            // DDEML instance identifier
    HSZ hsz );                 // handle of string to free
```

In response to **DdeCreateStringHandle**, the library installs the string in a table and gives it a usage count of 1. **DdeFreeStringHandle** decrements the usage count. If the count reaches 0, the string is deleted. If several applications coincidentally register the same string, the library enters only one string and returns the same handle to both applications, raising the counter to 2. Every call to **DdeCreateStringHandle** must be matched by one and only one call to **DdeFreeStringHandle**.

Given a handle, a DDEML program must be able to read the associated string.

```
DWORD DdeQueryString(
    DWORD dwInstID,            // DDEML instance identifier
    HSZ hsz,                   // handle to a string
    LPTSTR lpsz,               // place to copy the string
    DWORD dwMax,               // length of buffer for string
    int iCodePage );           // CP_WINANSI or CP_WINUNICODE
```

DdeQueryString copies the string to the buffer addressed with lpsz. If the buffer is too small, it copies only as much of the string as will fit. If lpsz is **NULL**, the function returns the size of the string in bytes, which is useful for allocating a buffer sufficiently large. Here's a procedure that accepts a string handle, allocates a buffer, and returns a pointer to a copy of the string:

```
/*-----------------------------------------------------------------

    GET STRING FROM HSZ
    Extract a string from its HSZ handle.  Allocate a best-fit
    buffer, copy the string to it, and return the pointer.  The
    caller must release the buffer.
    -------------------------------------------------------------*/

PSTR GetStringFromHSZ (
    DWORD dwID,
    HSZ hsz )
{
    DWORD dwLength;                      // length of string in hsz
    DWORD dwResult;                      // function return value
    PSTR pStr = NULL;                    // pointer to copy of string

    dwLength = DdeQueryString( dwID, hsz, NULL, 0, CP_WINANSI );

    if (dwLength)
    {
        /* allocate space for the string (add 1 for \0) */
        pStr = GlobalAlloc( LPTR, dwLength + 1 );
        if (pStr)
        {
            /* copy the string into the new buffer */
            dwResult = DdeQueryString( dwID,    // instance ID
                hsz,                            // source object
                pStr,                           // destination buffer
                dwLength + 1,                   // buffer size
                CP_WINANSI );                   // code page

            /* compare string length to characters copied */
            if (dwResult != dwLength)
            {
                GlobalFree( pStr );
                pStr = NULL;
            }
        }
    }
```

```
    }

    return( pStr );
}
```

The string handles a server sometimes receives as parameters in its callback function remain valid only until the server returns from the callback function. The library may release the string handle any time after that. In order to preserve a string, the server needs to make the library increment the handle's usage count.

```
BOOL DdeKeepStringHandle(
    DWORD dwInstID,             // DDEML instance identifier
    HSZ hsz );                  // handle of string to preserve
```

The function returns **TRUE** if it succeeds in incrementing the counter. To release the string later, the program should call **DdeFreeStringHandle**.

Internally, the DDEML creates its string table using the Atom API. Atom operations preserve the case of strings they store but ignore the case when performing comparisons. As a result, DDE service, topic, and item names are not sensitive to case. If several applications register the same string using different cases, only the first version of the string is stored in the table, and all queries return the string in that initial form.

Managing Data Objects

Clients pass strings to request an item from the server, and servers pass items to their clients. Because the value associated with an item often is not a string—it may be anything—the DDEML requires another mechanism for packaging data as it passes from one program to another. The functions for managing DDE data objects resemble those for managing strings. You put the data in a buffer, let the DDEML make a data handle, and pass the handle as a function parameter. Anything that can be stored in a memory buffer can be passed through the DDEML.

The **DdeCreateDataHandle** function receives a pointer to a buffer and allocates memory of its own for a copy of the data. It returns a handle of type **HDDEDATA**, the type for any data object exchanged through the DDEML. The DDEML automatically frees its copy of the data when no one needs it anymore.

```
HDDEDATA DdeCreateDataHandle(
    DWORD dwInstID,                    // DDEML instance identifier
    LPBYTE lpbSrcBuffer,               // address of data source buffer
    DWORD dwObjSize,                   // length of data in bytes
    DWORD dwOffset,                    // offset into source buffer
    HSZ hszItem,                       // handle of item-name string
    UINT uFmt,                         // data format (clipboard constant)
    UINT uFlags );                     // creation flags
```

The dwObjSize and dwOffset parameters index a block of data within the source buffer. To create its data object, the DDEML copies dwObjSize bytes from the buffer beginning with the byte at offset dwOffset. hszItem gives the item name, if any, to which the new data object belongs, and uFmt indicates the format of the data with a clipboard format constant. If lpbSrcBuffer is **NULL**, **DdeCreateDataHandle** allocates an empty object of dwObjSize bytes.

By default, the new **HDDEDATA** handle remains valid only until it is passed to a DDEML function. Once passed to the DDEML, the handle becomes invalid. The DDEML assumes the burden of freeing the object later. Sometimes losing the object handle is inconvenient, however, as when the server intends to send the same object more than once, perhaps to several clients. To avoid reconstructing the same data object several times over, set the **HDATA_APPOWNED** flag in the uFlags parameter of **DdeCreateDataHandle**. Then the handle remains valid until the program frees it.

A program does not destroy data objects it has passed to the DDEML, but it should destroy objects that it owns. A program owns anything it has not yet passed to a DDEML function and anything created with the **HDATA_APPOWNED** flag. Call **DdeFreeDataHandle** to release a data object.

```
BOOL DdeFreeDataHandle( HDDEDATA hData );          // handle of a DDE object
```

A program may modify the data in a DDE object it owns with **DdeAddData**, which is useful for filling uninitialized structures. **DdeAddData** even reallocates the object if necessary to accommodate more data. Once the object has been passed to the DDEML, however, its contents cannot be modified, not even by the application that created it. It becomes a read-only object.

When the DDEML receives a data object, it passes the handle to another program, usually from a server to a client. In order to read the data, the client calls **DdeAccessData** or **DdeGetData**. **DdeAccessData** works like **GlobalLock**: It locks the object and returns a pointer. When through with the object, the client calls **DdeUnaccessData** to release the lock and invalidate the pointer. The handle remains valid.

```
LPBYTE DdeAccessData(
    HDDEDATA hData,                    // handle of data object
    LPDWORD lpdwDataLength ),          // place to return data length

BOOL DdeUnaccessData( HDDEDATA hData ); // handle of data object
```

Because the DDEML makes all its objects read-only, the recipient cannot modify any data object it receives. The pointer returned from **DdeAccessData** points to read-only memory. The client may prefer to make its own read/write copy of the object; **DdeGetData** does that.

```
DWORD DdeGetData(
    HDDEDATA hData,                    // handle of data object
    LPBYTE lpbDestBuffer,              // address of destination buffer
    DWORD dwMax,                       // max number of bytes to copy
    DWORD dwOffset ),                  // offset to beginning of data
```

Passing **NULL** for the buffer makes **DdeGetData** return the size of the object in bytes. When lpbDestBuffer is not **NULL**, **DdeGetData** copies up to dwMax bytes to the destination beginning with byte number dwOffset in the source. It returns the number of bytes copied, which may not exceed dwMax, or 0 to indicate failure.

Initializing an Application

Before a DDEML program attempts to contact another program, it must first register itself with the DDE Management Library. The library keeps a table of all active DDE participants. After terminating contact, an application must notify the library that it will no longer participate in DDE conversations. Registering with the DDEML table is called *initializing,* and withdrawing from it is called *uninitializing.* Initializing an application for the DDEML simply means calling **DdeInitialize**. In this call you tell the library where to send your transaction messages and which messages you do not want to receive. The function passes back an instance identifier, a value needed to identify your program instance when calling other DDEML functions.

```
UINT DdeInitialize(
    LPDWORD lpdwInstID,               // address of instance identifier
    PFNCALLBACK pfnCallback,          // address of DDEML callback function
    DWORD dwFlags,                    // command and filter flags
    DWORD dwRes );                    // reserved
```

The flags in dwFlags filter the information the program receives from the DDEML. The parameter may combine values from three sets of flags: application flags, callback flags, and monitor flags. The two application flags describe the program to the DDEML. With **APPCLASS_MONITOR** or **APPCLASS_STANDARD**, a program announces itself as a DDEML debugging monitor or a standard DDEML program. A set of callback flags tells the DDEML not to send certain messages. For example, an application that does not support the Execute or Poke transaction (both of which are described shortly) should include the **CBF_FAIL_EXECUTES** and **CBF_FAIL_POKES** flags. Then the program never receives **XTYP_EXECUTE** or **XTYP_POKE** messages. Filtering unsupported messages improves system performance. A monitor program receives notification when any DDEML event occurs. The monitor flags allow a DDEML monitor to request notification selectively for particular events. **MF_CONV**, for example, asks for information about each DDEML conversation; **MF_ERRORS** asks to be told about any DDE errors. Microsoft's DDESpy utility is a DDEML monitor. You can see it in Figure 13.7 further on in this chapter.

The value passed back through lpdwInstID identifies each DDEML participant to the library. It exists to resolve the conflict that arises when a DDEML program happens to call a dynamic-link library that also uses the DDEML. From the system's point of view, a process and its libraries belong to the same task and share instance data, but the DDEML sees the program and its library as distinct DDEML participants, each with its own list of services and topics. The DDEML relies on the instance identifier to distinguish them. "Instance identifier" is a misleading name because one program instance may support several DDEML participants, each with its own identifier. "Callback identifier" is more accurate since a program must call **DdeInitialize** once for each DDEML callback procedure it contains. A server may register several callback procedures to support different services.

Normally if a DDEML function fails and returns **NULL** or **FALSE**, you can get extended error information by calling **DdeGetLastError**.

```
UINT DdeGetLastError( DWORD dwInstID );
```

Because **DdeGetLastError** takes an instance identifier, you can't call it if **DdeInitialize** fails. Therefore **DdeInitialize** itself returns extended error codes.

- **DMLERR_NO_ERROR:** Initialization succeeded.

- **DMLERR_DLL_USAGE:** The program is registered as a monitor and cannot use the DDEML for transactions.

- **DMLERR_INVALIDPARAMETER:** A parameter contained invalid information.

- **DMLERR_SYS_ERROR:** An internal error occurred in the DDEML.

When any program calls **DdeInitialize**, the DDE library notifies other programs by sending **XTYP_REGISTER** to their callback functions. Sometimes clients use **XTYP_REGISTER** to maintain a list of available services.

The instance identifier puts a new constraint on Windows NT programmers because it is local to a thread. Only the thread that calls **DdeInitialize** may use the identifier, and no child process may inherit it. As a result, most of a program's DDEML operations for a particular service must happen in the same thread because most of the DDEML functions require the instance identifier as a parameter. For example, the thread that initializes a DDEML session must not terminate until the session ends; otherwise there is no way to call **DdeUninitialize** and no graceful way to end the session. Also, if you create threads to respond to DDEML transactions, the threads may not use the instance identifier to signal the result of their operations. The searching code in Chapter 12 cannot pass its discoveries directly to the DDEML because the search happens in a separate thread. Instead, the search procedure sends a message to the primary thread, and in response to the message the main thread passes the data.

Registering Services

After initializing, server applications should also register the names of the services they provide. The DDEML sends an **XTYP_REGISTER** message to other DDEML callback procedures to broadcast the registration of each new service. Clients might use the information to maintain a list of available DDEML services for the user. To register services, a server program calls **DdeNameService** with a handle to the string that names the service and an instance identifier for the service. From the instance identifier, the DDEML knows which callback procedure supports the service. A service may include several topics; it should always include at least the standard System topic. Through the System topic, DDEML services enumerate the other topics and data they provide.

```
HDDEDATA DdeNameService(
    DWORD dwInstID,               // instance identifier
    HSZ hsz1,                     // handle of string-naming service
    HSZ hszRes,                   // reserved
    UINT uFlags );                // service-name flags
```

The value in dwInstID must be obtained from **DdeInitialize**. The flags in the final parameter choose between registering or unregistering a name and between blocking or receiving connection signals for services the server has not registered.

- **DNS_REGISTER:** Register the service name.

- **DNS_UNREGISTER:** Unregister the service name. If hsz1 is **NULL**, unregister all services for this server.

- **DNS_FILTERON:** Prevent the server from receiving **XTYP_CONNECT** messages for services it has not registered.

- **DNS_FILTEROFF:** Allow the server to receive **XTYP_CONNECT** messages whenever any DDE program calls **DdeConnect**.

The value returned from **DdeNameService** is really Boolean—0 (or **NULL**) for failure, nonzero for success. It is typed as **HDDEDATA** to allow for possible improvements in the return indicator.

Initiating a Conversation

Once initialized, a DDEML program participates in conversations that typically follow three steps: connecting, transferring data, and disconnecting. Only client programs initiate conversations. A *conversation* is a sequence of transactions between one client and one server on a single DDEML topic. A client that needs information items from several topics must initiate several conversations. A client that needs several information items from a single topic may acquire them through a single conversation.

In the simplest case, a client converses with a single server. To begin, the client calls **DdeConnect**, including as parameters two string handles naming a service and topic. The DDEML consults its table of registered servers and sends an **XTYP_CONNECT** transaction message to all that support the requested service. (It also sends the same message to active servers that have not registered any services.) Servers receive the topic string handle in the hsz1 parameter of their callback procedure and the service string handle in hsz2. For topics they support, servers return **TRUE**, and for unsupported topics, **FALSE**. If a server returns **TRUE**, DdeConnect passes back to the client a conversation handle. (If several servers respond, the system picks one of them arbitrarily.) The DDEML also sends the server a follow-up message, **XTYP_CONNECT_CONFIRM**, so that the server too receives a handle to the same conversation. The diagram in Figure 13.2 follows the sequence of function calls and messages as a client and server initialize themselves and begin a conversation. The first two steps, **DdeInitialize** and **DdeNameService**, happen only once per session. The third step, connecting the client to a server, may happen many times in one session if a client participates in many conversations.

Sometimes the client does not know in advance the name of the service and the topic it wants. It may know only one of them or neither of them. A client requests a *wildcard connection* by setting either or both of the string handles to **NULL**. The DDEML sends an **XTYP_WILDCONNECT** message to each server. The servers return

FIGURE 13.2:

How a client and a server initialize themselves and begin a DDEML conversation

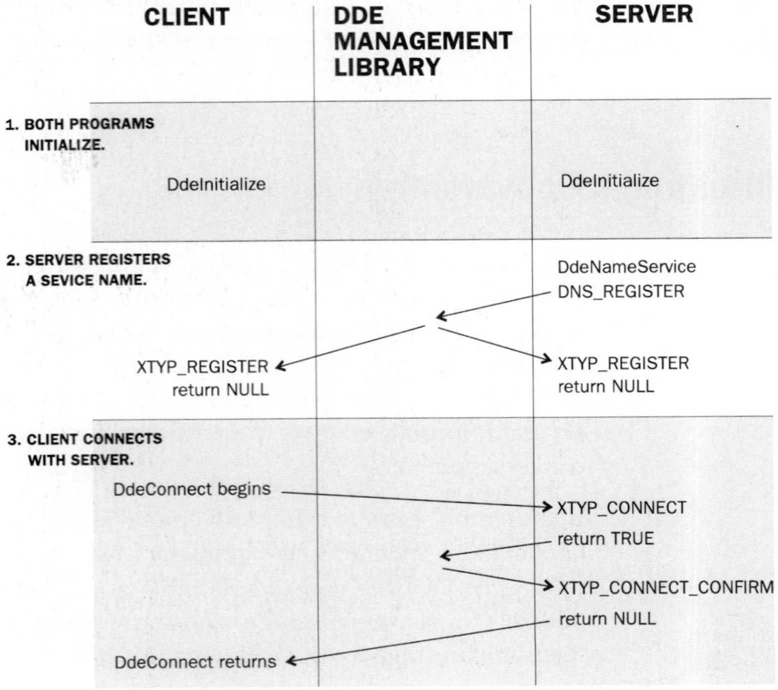

CLIENT	DDE MANAGEMENT LIBRARY	SERVER
1. BOTH PROGRAMS INITIALIZE.		
DdeInitialize		DdeInitialize
2. SERVER REGISTERS A SEVICE NAME.		DdeNameService DNS_REGISTER
XTYP_REGISTER return NULL		XTYP_REGISTER return NULL
3. CLIENT CONNECTS WITH SERVER.		
DdeConnect begins		XTYP_CONNECT return TRUE
		XTYP_CONNECT_CONFIRM return NULL
DdeConnect returns		

arrays of **HSZPAIR** structures naming all the service and topic pairs they support that might match the client's request. The system selects one of the servers, returns a conversation handle to the client, and sends an **XTYP_CONNECT_CONFIRM** transaction to the server.

```
HCONV DdeConnect(
    DWORD dwInstID,                 // DDEML instance identifier
    HSZ hszService,                 // handle of service-name string
    HSZ hszTopic,                   // handle of topic-name string
    PCONVCONTEXT pCC ),             // structure with context data
```

The value in dwInstID must be acquired through **DdeInitialize**. The **CONVCONTEXT** structure carries information about the client's locale and security requirements.

```
typedef struct tagCONVCONTEXT {   /* cc */
    UINT cb;                        // sizeof(CONVCONTEXT)
    UINT wFlags;                    // unused
    UINT wCountryID;                // country for topic and name strings
    int iCodePage;                  // CP_WINANSI or CP_WINUNICODE
    DWORD dwLangID;                 // language for topic and name strings
    DWORD dwSecurity;               // code defined by application
    SECURITY_QUALITY_OF_SERVICE qos; // client impersonation information
} CONVCONTEXT;
```

The structure in the last field determines what the server may be told about the client in order to impersonate its security attributes and act on its behalf. We'll say more about security in Chapter 17. The client application may leave the pCC parameter of **DdeConnect** **NULL** to request a default conversation context. The system then provides the server a **CONVCONTEXT** structure with all fields set to 0 except **cb** and **iCodePage**, which is **CP_WINANSI**. If **DdeConnect** succeeds, it returns a handle to the newly established conversation. A client may carry out several conversations simultaneously with a single server, so the conversation handle is necessary to identify resources the DDEML uses internally to manage each series of related transactions.

To extract successive conversation handles from the list, the client calls **DdeQuery-NextServer**.

Multiple Conversations

DdeConnect begins a conversation with a single server. Even if more than one server supports the requested service and topic, the DDEML begins a conversation with only one of them. If several servers respond, the system chooses one and the client has no control over the choice. To retrieve a full list of all the servers that support a certain service or topic, the client calls **DdeConnectList**. The DDEML then initiates conversations with *all* the servers that respond and returns to the client a handle to the list of conversations (**HCONVLIST**). To extract individual conversations from the list, call **DdeQueryNextServer**. Successive calls extract successive handles. The client may keep the list intact and converse with all the servers, or it may interrogate their System topics for more information and discard some from the list. Call **DdeDisconnect** to terminate individual conversations or **DdeDisconnectList** to terminate all of them.

How the Client Starts Transactions

A DDEML conversation consists of transactions in which the client calls a function and the server responds. The three possible transactions are link, poke, and execute.

Links

A transaction in which the client requests a data item from the server is called a *link*. If the transaction ends as soon as the client receives the item, it is a *cold link*. Not all transactions end immediately, however. The client may request an ongoing, continuous link to be apprised whenever the value of the item changes. An ongoing transaction is called a *hot link* if the server sends the new data for each change and a *warm link* if the server sends only a notification of each change. A single conversation may create several links of different sorts. Each link transfers a single item of data. (Hot and warm links transmit the same item over and over as its value changes.) All the items transferred in a single conversation must belong to the same service and topic.

A single command initiates any type of transaction. In the case of a link, the client chooses the kind of link it requires.

```
HDDEDATA DdeClientTransaction(
    LPBYTE lpbData,            // address of data to pass to server
    DWORD dwDataSize,          // length of data, in bytes
    HCONV hConv,               // handle of conversation
    HSZ hszItem,               // handle of item-name string
    UINT uFmt,                 // clipboard data format
```

```
UINT uType,            // transaction type
DWORD dwTimeout,       // time-out duration
LPDWORD lpdwResult );  // points to transaction result
```

The first two parameters, lpbData and dwDataSize, are not used for links. They should be **NULL** and 0. hConv is the value returned from a preceding **DdeConnect**. hszItem identifies an item name already passed to the DDE library in a call to **DdeCreateStringHandle**. The client must know something about the server in order to form item-name strings. Usually the programmer works from knowledge of a particular server. Microsoft Word for Windows and Excel, for example, both have published DDE specifications. Sometimes item names can be acquired at run time though the System topic, described below.

For links, uFmt names a data format the client would like the server to use. Its value is a clipboard format constant such as **CF_TEXT** or **CF_BITMAP**. The programmer usually knows in advance which formats a given server uses, but if the service has a System topic then the client can request a list of supported formats at run time. dwTimeOut tells how long the client is willing to wait for a response, measured in milliseconds. When it returns, the function sets result flags in *lpdwResult, but Microsoft recommends against reading them because they may not be supported in future versions.

We have saved uType for last because it is the most complex of the function's parameters. Here the client sets flags to specify a particular kind of transaction. We'll explain the link flags here and flags for other transactions in the next section.

XTYP_REQUEST	Cold link:	Transaction ends on receipt of item
XTYP_ADVSTART	Hot link:	Server sends new data in an **XTYP_ADVDATA** message whenever the item changes
XTYP_ADVSTART | XTYPF_ADVNODATA	Warm link:	Server sends an empty **XTYP_ADVDATA** message whenever the item changes

XTYP_ADVSTART signals the beginning of an *advise loop,* named for the underlying DDE message, which is **WM_DDE_ADVISE**. Hot and warm links are advise loops, and in them the server repeatedly advises the client when an item changes. When **DdeClientTransaction** initiates an advise loop, it does not return a data handle. To learn the item's current value, the client should send **XTYP_REQUEST** first. An advise loop continues until the client ends it with another **DdeClientTransaction** command, this time with the **XTYP_ADVSTOP** flag. Advise loops also end if either participant uninitializes itself from the DDEML.

For items that change frequently, the client may add the **XTYP_ACKREQ** flag to the uType parameter. The server then paces its signals by waiting for the client to acknowledge each one before it sends the next.

Poke and Execute Transactions

The DDEML defines two other transaction messages. With **XTYP_POKE** the client sends an item to the server. With **XTYP_EXECUTE** the client sends the server a command or series of commands. The **DdeClientTransaction** function can initiate either action.

How the Server Responds to Transactions

Every call to **DdeClientTransaction** causes the DDE library to send the server a message. The message differs according to the type of transaction the client requested. The server's callback function deals with each message in a separate switch case.

Message	Transaction
XTYP_REQUEST	Cold link (send an item)
XTYP_ADVISE	Warm or hot link (send an item and updates)
XTYP_POKE	Poke (receive data)
XTYP_EXECUTE	Execute (perform an action)

Request Transactions

When the server receives an **XTYP_REQUEST** message, it reads the topic and item names from the two string handle parameters and checks the requested data format. If it recognizes the item and supports the format, it creates a data object for the item's current value and returns the handle (**HDDEDATA**). If it does not support the item or the format, it returns **NULL**. Whatever value the server returns is passed to the client as the return value from **DdeClientTransaction**. Figure 13.3 diagrams the interaction. In the first step the client calls **DdeClientTransaction**, and the second step occurs in the server before the function returns.

FIGURE 13.3:

Sequence of events that follow when a client requests an item from the server

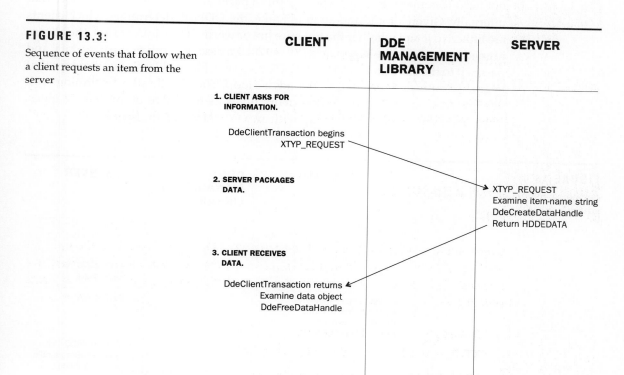

A server that does not support request transactions should set the **CBF_FAIL_REQUESTS** flag in **DdeInitialize** to avoid receiving unwanted **XTYP_REQUEST** messages.

Advise Transactions

When the client requests a link with updates, the server's callback procedure receives the **XTYP_ADVSTART** message. If the server recognizes the topic and item names and supports the requested format, it returns **TRUE** to allow the link or **FALSE** to prevent it. Note that the server cannot determine from the **XTYP_ADVSTART** message whether the link will be hot or warm. The server does not return data yet, but only when the item next changes. In response to **XTYP_ADVSTART**, the server often sets a flag to remind itself that updates have been requested. Whenever an item changes, the server checks the state of the flag and, if it is on, calls **DdePostAdvise** to notify the DDEML that it has new data for an interested client. The server does not need to remember which client wants a particular item; the DDEML does that internally. Given a topic and an item name, the DDEML determines which clients are linked to it and whether the links are hot or warm. If the links are hot, the library immediately sends the server an **XTYP_ADVREQ** message, receives the new data, and passes it to the client in an **XTYP_ADVDATA** message. Figure 13.4 shows the steps that begin, execute, and terminate a hot advise loop. The middle step, beginning with **DdePostAdvise**, may be repeated many times as the value of an item changes. Eventually the client ends the loop with an **XTYP_ADVSTOP** message.

FIGURE 13.4:

Beginning, middle, and end of a hot advise loop

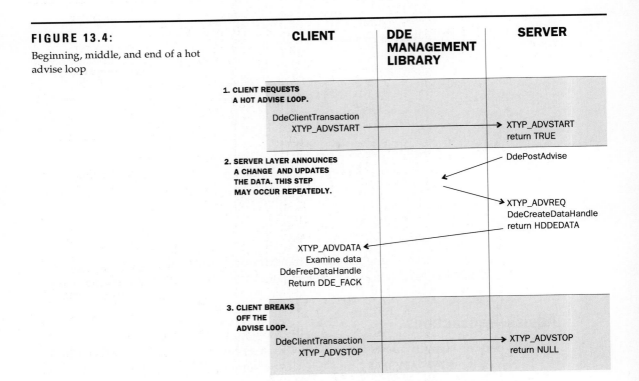

When the server calls **DdePostAdvise** for a warm advise loop, the DDEML does not send the server a data request message. Instead it sends the client an empty **XTYP_ADVDATA** message with a **NULL** data handle. To see the item's new value, the client must perform a request transaction, just like the one in Figure 13.3. Alternatively, the client may ignore the change by returning without requesting the new data. Empty **XTYP_ADVDATA** messages continue to signal updates until the link ends. Because warm and hot links begin and end with the same sequence of commands, Figure 13.5 tracks only the middle step of a warm link. The two versions show what happens if the client does or does not request the new value.

A server that does not support advise loops of any kind should set the **CBF_FAIL_ADVISES** flag in **DdeInitialize** to avoid receiving unwanted **XTYP_ADV-START** and **XTYP_ADVSTOP** messages.

FIGURE 13.5:

Advisory stage of a warm loop where the client decides whether or not to request an updated data item

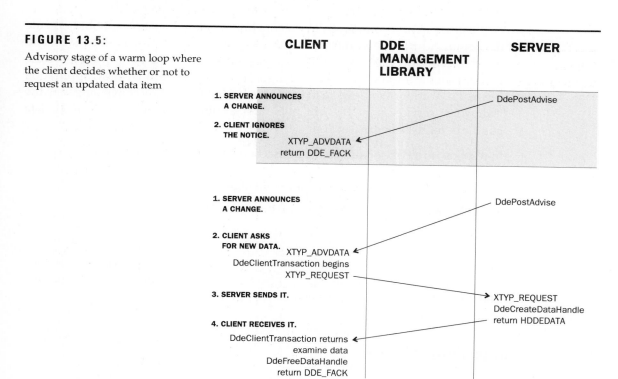

CLIENT	DDE MANAGEMENT LIBRARY	SERVER
1. SERVER ANNOUNCES A CHANGE.		DdePostAdvise
2. CLIENT IGNORES THE NOTICE. XTYP_ADVDATA return DDE_FACK		
1. SERVER ANNOUNCES A CHANGE.		DdePostAdvise
2. CLIENT ASKS FOR NEW DATA. XTYP_ADVDATA DdeClientTransaction begins XTYP_REQUEST		
3. SERVER SENDS IT.		XTYP_REQUEST DdeCreateDataHandle return HDDEDATA
4. CLIENT RECEIVES IT. DdeClientTransaction returns examine data DdeFreeDataHandle return DDE_FACK		

Poke and Execute Transactions

Some servers accept data from the client, reversing the usual transfer direction. A client wishing to send data to the server needs an **XTYP_POKE** transaction. In response to this message, the server checks the topic and item and, if it wants the information, reads the data object. A DDEML program can, for example, insert words into an open Word for Windows document by sending **XTYP_POKE**. The server is "winword", the item is a file name such as "c:\book\ch13.doc", and the item name is the name of a bookmark. The new text replaces whatever the bookmark previously contained.

Some servers accept commands from their clients. The commands arrive in the form of data handles. The server locks the object, parses the command string it contains, and performs some action. It must also free the data handle that carries the string, being sure to duplicate the string first if it will be needed later. Because clients usually expect commands to execute immediately, the server should execute the command from the callback function before returning, if possible. Excel and Word for Windows both accept Execute messages where the item string is a command from the application's macro language. For example, a DDEML application can make Word for Windows load its most recently used file by conversing with the "winword" service on the "system" topic and sending the string "[file1]" in the data handle of an Execute transaction.

In response to a Poke or an Execute transaction, the server returns one of three values:

- **DDE_FACK:** Data received and acknowledged
- **DDE_FBUSY:** Too busy to process; try again later
- **DDE_FNOTPROCESSED:** Data refused

Flags set in **DdeInitialize** can filter out Poke and Execute messages for servers that do not support them. **CBF_FAIL_POKES** blocks poke transaction messages and **CBF_FAIL_EXECUTES** blocks execute messages.

Asynchronous Transactions

Chapter 12 showed how a program can choose between synchronous I/O operations, which execute immediately and return results to the line that initiates them, and asynchronous operations, which run in the background and reach completion long after the read or write command returns. A DDEML client may choose between synchronous and asynchronous transactions. When `DdeClientTransaction` performs a synchronous action, it makes the client wait until the server answers, and then it passes the response back to the client as a return value. If the server makes the client wait longer than the client's time-out period, `DdeClientTransaction` cancels the transaction and returns.

To make `DdeClientTransaction` work asynchronously, set the time-out period to `TIMEOUT_ASYNCH`. In an asynchronous transaction, `DdeClientTransaction` returns `TRUE` immediately, placing a transaction ID at `lpdwResult`. The client continues executing other code while the DDEML pursues the transaction in the background. When the transaction ends, the DDEML sends an `XTYP_XACT_COMPLETE` message to the client's callback procedure. The completion message carries the ID number in its `dwData1` parameter, and with it the client determines which request has finished. The DDEML also provides an alternative mechanism for identifying transactions from their completion messages. The client may register a `DWORD` of its own to associate with each asynchronous transaction. `DdeSetUserHandle` accepts a conversation handle, an asynchronous transaction ID, and a custom `DWORD` value, and it stores them together internally. When an `XTYP_XACT_COMPLETE` message arrives, the client retrieves its private identifier by calling `DdeQueryConvInfo`.

While waiting for a synchronous transaction to finish, `DdeClientTransaction` enters a modal loop and polls for window messages, so the client may still respond to input from the user. The client may not, however, execute another DDEML function. `DdeClientTransaction` fails if another synchronous operation is already in progress for the same client.

To cancel an asynchronous operation before it finishes, call `DdeAbandonTransaction`. The DDEML then discards all its resources associated with the transaction and discards the result when the server eventually returns it. (The same thing happens when a synchronous operation exceeds the time-out period.)

The difference between synchronous and asynchronous operations matters only to client programs. From the server's end they look alike. Most clients use synchronous transactions because they are faster and easier to program. Asynchronous transactions are useful for very busy programs that need to perform substantial amounts of processing while interacting with a DDEML server or to programs that regularly interact with a particularly slow server and wish to avoid remaining idle.

Releasing a Client's Data Objects

The rules for freeing data objects differ depending on whether the client acquires them from a synchronous or an asynchronous transaction. In an asynchronous transaction, the DDEML delivers the data object handle to the client's callback function. When the callback function returns, the DDEML reasonably assumes the data is no longer needed and frees the object automatically. If the client needs to preserve the data, it can make a copy (**DdeGetData**) before returning. The client must not free data handles received asynchronously.

In a synchronous transaction, on the other hand, the DDEML passes the data handle as a return value from **DdeClientTransaction** and has no way of knowing when the data can be freed. The client owns data objects it receives synchronously from **DdeClientTransaction** and must eventually call **DdeFreeDataHandle** to release them.

Terminating a Conversation

To terminate a conversation, either the client or the server calls **DdeDisconnect**, specifying the handle of the conversation to terminate. This causes the DDE Management Library to send an **XTYP_DISCONNECT** transaction to the other application.

```
BOOL DdeDisconnect( HCONV hConv );        // handle of conversation
```

The conversation handle comes from **DdeConnect**. When the DDEML receives this command, it abandons any transactions still in progress for the given conversation. By convention, only clients break off conversations, though sometimes the server must—if, for example, the user closes the server application. **DdeDisconnect** sends **XTYP_DISCONNECT** to the other program's callback procedure. Clients and servers alike should be prepared to receive a disconnect message at any time during the conversation and close up data structures accordingly.

Uninitializing a DDEML Service

When the application closes or when it no longer wants to converse with other applications, it should uninitialize all its DDEML callback procedures. (Remember that a server typically has one procedure for each service.) Calling **DdeUninitialize** removes a service from the DDEML tables. It also terminates any conversations still in progress and sends **XTYP_UNREGISTER** to all DDEML callback procedures. Figure 13.6 shows the steps for breaking off a conversation and withdrawing from the DDEML.

```
BOOL DdeUninitialize( DWORD dwInstID );
```

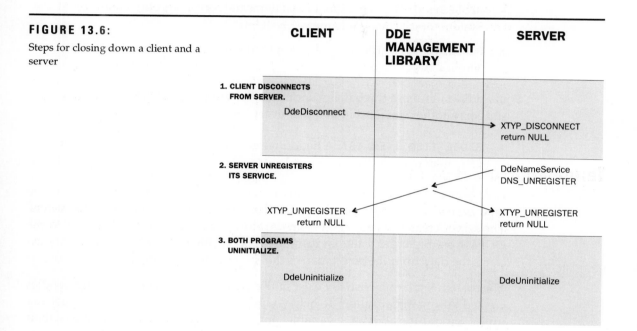

FIGURE 13.6:

Steps for closing down a client and a server

The System Topic

The usual sequence for initiating a conversation requires the client to know in advance which service or topic it needs. To make it possible for a client to survey available topics, DDEML servers conventionally include in each service a topic called System, under which name they support a set of standard informational items. Through the System topic a client obtains information about a particular service.

The strings identifying standard system items are defined in ddeml.h and identified by constants. Here are three that every program should support:

- **SZDDESYS_ITEM_FORMATS:** List of strings, separated by tabs, indicating the clipboard formats the server supports (The actual item name string is "Formats".)

- **SZDDESYS_ITEM_SYSITEMS:** List of items the server supports under the System topic (The item name is "SysItems".)

- **SZDDESYS_ITEM_TOPICS:** List of topics the server supports (The item name is "Topics".)

In addition to these three items under the System topic, a DDEML server should support another standard item under every topic.

- **SZDDE_ITEM_ITEMLIST:** A list of items from a topic other than System (The item name is TopicItemList.)

In response to requests for these items, the server is expected to concatenate all the topic, item, or format names into a single long string delimited by tab characters. The server creates a data object from the string and passes the handle back to the DDEML as the return value in response to **XTYP_REQUEST**. The client usually extracts the data from the object, parses the list, and displays the items for the user.

The system list strings usually exist in the server as a collection of string handles created during initialization. To help you form the tab-delimited lists, the TabList utility procedure accepts a variable number of **HSZ** parameters, extracts their strings, concatenates them, and passes back an **HDDEDATA** handle with data properly formatted for a System item. TabList calls the GetStringFromHSZ procedure we showed you earlier.

```
/*----------------------------------------------------------------
    TAB LIST
    Receives a variable number of HSZ string handles and
    concatenates all the strings into a single tab-delimited
    list.  Then constructs a data object (HDDEDATA) to contain
    the new list.

    Useful in responding to requests for items under the
    System topic.
```

```
        Returns a handle to the new data object, or NULL if an
        error occurs.
   ------------------------------------------------------------*/

HDDEDATA _cdecl TabList (
    DWORD dwID,                          // instance ID
    HSZ hszSysItem,                      // handle for a System item
    int iNumHandles,                     // number of arguments that follow
    ... )                                // HSZ handles for list items
{
    PSTR pList;                          // pointer to tab-delimited list
    char *pch;                           // index into the list string
    va_list vaArg;                       // pointer to an argument
    int iLength = 0;                     // length of list
    HDDEDATA hdde = 0;                   // new data object
    int i;                               // loop control variable

    va_start( vaArg, iNumHandles );
    pList = LocalAlloc( LPTR, 512 );     // LPTR includes ZEROINT
    pch = pList;
    for (i = 0; i < iNumHandles; i++)
    {
        HSZ hsz;                         // a string handle
        PSTR pStr;                       // pointer to data in an HSZ
        UINT uStrLen;                    // length of one string + tab

        hsz = va_arg( vaArg, HSZ );      // get next HSZ argument

        /* copy the handle's string into a buffer */
        pStr = GetStringFromHSZ( dwID, hsz );

        /* be sure adding this string+tab won't exceed buffer size */
        uStrLen = lstrlen( pStr );
        if ((iLength + uStrLen + 1) > 512)
        {
            LocalFree( pList );          // parameters exceed allocation
            pList = NULL;
            break;
        }

        /* append the string and a tab to end of list */
        lstrcat( pList, pStr );          // copy string to list
        pch += uStrLen;                  // point to terminating NULL
        *pch++ = '\t';                   // replace NULL with tab
        iLength += uStrLen + 1;          // update length counter
```

```
    GlobalFree( pStr );                 // release the string buffer
}
va_end( vaArg );                        // reset argument pointer

if (pList)
{
    *--pch = '\0';                      // undo the last tab

    hdde = DdeCreateDataHandle( dwID,    // instance ID
        (LPBYTE)pList,                  // source buffer
        iLength,                        // data length
        0,                              // offset into source
        hszSysItem,                     // associated item
        CF_TEXT,                        // format of buffer data
        0 );                            // creation flags

    LocalFree( pList );
}

return( hdde );
}
```

The DDEML Shell

As an example of what the DDEML can do, consider the Shell DDE Interface. Often when a Windows program installs itself, it asks the user whether to create a new group for the program in the Program Manager. If you say yes, the installation program converses with the Program Manager through the DDEML and passes information to create the new group. The Program Manager supports a small set of eight commands that other programs can send through Execute transactions. Together these functions form an API for manipulating the shell program. (A shell program is one that boots automatically when you log on and helps you launch other programs.) To initiate a conversation with the shell, give PROGMAN as both the service and topic name.

AddItem	ExitProgman
CreateGroup	Reload
DeleteGroup	ReplaceItem
DeleteItem	ShowGroup

These commands cause the shell to create and destroy MDI child windows for groups and to add, delete, or replace program icons within the group. They take parameters. You build a string containing the command and its parameters and pass the string in an Execute transaction. The Program Manager parses the string and performs the requested command. These lines, for example, if sent as part of an Execute message, would add the program DBServer to the group called Main:

```
[ShowGroup(Main,1)]
[AddItem(d:\bookcode\ddeml\dbserver.exe, DB Server)]
```

The alternative shell program in the Norton Desktop Utilities supports the same DDEML interface.

CODE

Chapter 12 presented two file I/O modules of the Database Server program. DBServer maintains a database of names and phone numbers. Its DDEML clients can add, delete, and search for records with Advise and Poke transactions. The client and server appear together in Figure 13.7, along with several windows from Microsoft's DDESpy program. The server needs no user interface, so its window is always minimized. The client has just completed a Search command and located a record in the database. One of the DDESpy windows records the ADVREQ and ADVDATA messages from the server's answering transmission. Another lists the DDEML conversation in which the search took place, and the third DDESpy window lists information about the link created when the client asked for information.

The client and server share two auxiliary files, db.h and db.rc. The shared resource file contains the strings the programs use to name a service, a topic, and items for DDEML transactions. The server's one service is called "dbserver". The one topic in that service is "database", and within that topic are three items: "add", "delete", and "search". DBServer transmits data in record structures, so the record structure for the database file also appears in the shared header. The iStatus field of a record can hold any of the four STATUS flags also defined in db.h. STATUS_VALID and STATUS_DELETED indicate whether the data in the other fields is in use or has been discarded. Only the server uses these flags. The client sets the STATUS_SEARCHNAME and STATUS_SEARCHNUMBER flags in order to request a search for a matching name, number, or both.

FIGURE 13.7:

DBClient and DBServer programs
being monitored by DDESpy

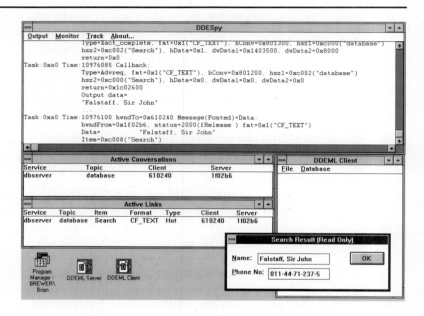

```
/*------------------------------------------------------------------


        DB.H

        Header file for both the client and server halves of
        the Database program.

        -------------------------------------------------------------*/

#ifndef DB_INC
#define DB_INC

/*------------------------------------------------------------------
        SYMBOLS
        -------------------------------------------------------------*/

#define DDE_TIMEOUT 1000                 // maximum wait for DDEML commands

#define DB_ADD        100                // dialog box function parameters
#define DB_DELETE     200
```

```
#define DB_SEARCH      300
#define DB_RESULT      400

#define MAX_NAME       25                  // max name string length
#define MAX_PHONE      16                  // max phone string length
```

```
// These flags are set in the iStatus field of a database record.
// The first two are used only in the disk file to mark records
// when they are deleted.  The other three are used only in variables
// to direct the action of procedures that receive a record.
```

```
#define STATUS_DELETED        0x0000      // user deleted the record
#define STATUS_VALID          0x0001      // record contains data
#define STATUS_SEARCHNAME     0x0002      // search file for matching name
#define STATUS_SEARCHNUMBER   0x0004      // search file for matching number

#define IDS_SERVICE       1               // DDEML service name string
#define IDS_DBTOPIC       2               // database topic name string
#define IDS_ADD           3               // item name strings
#define IDS_DELETE        4
#define IDS_SEARCH        5
```

```
/*-------------------------------------------------------------------
          DATABASE RECORD STRUCTURE
   ----------------------------------------------------------------*/

typedef struct _DBData
{
    char szName[MAX_NAME];               // name field
    char szPhone[MAX_PHONE];             // telephone number field
    int iStatus;                         // record status field
} DBDATA, *PDBDATA;

#endif  // DB_INC
```

```
===============================================================================
```

```
/*-------------------------------------------------------------------
          DB.RC
          Strings that belong in the string table of both the client
          and server database programs.
   ----------------------------------------------------------------*/

#include "db.h"
```

```
IDS_SERVICE,        "dbserver"      // DDEML service name
IDS_DBTOPIC,        "database"      // DDEML topic
IDS_ADD,            "Add"           // item names
IDS_DELETE,         "Delete"
IDS_SEARCH,         "Search"
```

The Database Server

DBServer interacts only with DDEML clients, so its user interface is minimal. It has no menu and remains permanently iconized. A user can do no more than launch it and close it. The program removes the Maximize, Restore, and Size commands from the system menu and always returns **FALSE** in response to the **WM_QUERYOPEN** message. The program's resource script accordingly contains only an icon and a few strings.

```
#
#    NMake file for the DATABASE SERVER program
#

#
#    Set targets and dependencies
#

all: dbserver.exe
dbserver.exe: dbserver.obj write.obj search.obj delete.obj dbserver.rbj
dbserver.obj: dbserver.c dbserver.h db.h
write.obj: write.c dbserver.h db.h
search.obj: search.c dbserver.h db.h
delete.obj: delete.c dbserver.h db.h
dbserver.rbj: dbserver.rc db.rc dbserver.h db.h

#
#    Define macros for command-line options and library modules
#

!IFDEF NODEBUG
CFLAGS = -c -G3 -Os -W4 -D_X86_=1 -DWIN32
LFLAGS = -subsystem:windows
!ELSE
CFLAGS = -c -G3 -Od -W4 -Zi -D_X86_=1 -DWIN32
```

```
LFLAGS = -debug:full -debugtype:cv -subsystem:windows
!ENDIF

OBJS = dbserver.obj write.obj search.obj delete.obj dbserver.rbj
LIBS = libc.lib ntdll.lib kernel32.lib user32.lib

#
#    Define compiling rules
#

.c.obj:
    cl386 $(CFLAGS) $*.c

.rc.rbj:
    rc $*.rc
    cvtres -i386 $*.res -o $*.rbj

.obj.exe:
    link32 $(LFLAGS) -out:$*.exe $(OBJS) $(LIBS)
```

===

```
/*-------------------------------------------------------------------


        DBSERVER.H

        Header file for the DBSERVER program.


        --------------------------------------------------------------*/
/*-------------------------------------------------------------------
        SYMBOLS
        --------------------------------------------------------------*/

#define MAX_RSRC_STRING      256

/*-------------------------------------------------------------------
        RESOURCE IDENTIFIERS
        Note that IDM_UPDATE is an internal WM_COMMAND, not a
        menu item.
        --------------------------------------------------------------*/

#define ICON_APP             100          // application icon
```

```
#define   MENU_SERVER          100          // menu template
#define   IDM_EXIT             100          // menu command
#define   IDM_UPDATE           200          // request for DdePostAdvise

#define   IDS_APPCLASS         100          // strings
#define   IDS_CAPTION          200


/*-------------------------------------------------------------------
          GLOBAL VARIABLES
   -----------------------------------------------------------------*/


extern char szFile[MAX_PATH];             // name of the database file
extern char szCaption[MAX_RSRC_STRING];   // string for window caption
extern DBDATA DBData;                     // pass records to modules here
extern HANDLE heventWrite;                // pulse this to write a record
extern HANDLE heventTerminate;            // set this to end the thread
extern HANDLE hmxSearchResult;            // protects DBFoundData
extern HANDLE heventDataSent;             // pulse this when ADVREQ is done
extern HANDLE hwndMain;                   // main program window
extern DBDATA DBFoundData;                // data found in a search


/*-------------------------------------------------------------------
          PROTOTYPES for functions used outside their own module
   -----------------------------------------------------------------*/


/* WRITE.C */
BOOL StartWritingThread( void );

/* SEARCH.C */
BOOL FindRecord( PDBDATA pDBData );

/* DELETE.C */
BOOL DeleteRecord( PDBDATA pData );

====================================================================


/*-------------------------------------------------------------------


          DBSERVER.RC

          Resource script for the DBSERVER program.

   -----------------------------------------------------------------*/
```

```
#include <windows.h>
#include "dbserver.h"

ICON_APP     ICON            dbserver.ico

STRINGTABLE
BEGIN
    IDS_APPCLASS,           "DDEML_Server"
    IDS_CAPTION,            "DDEML Server"
    #include "db.rc"        // strings for client and server
END
```

The DBServer Module

The server's global variables include three events and a mutex to coordinate operations with threads that search for records and the thread that writes records. The synchronization objects and the two modules that use them—write.c and search.c—were explained in Chapter 12. The server always works with the same file, database.dat. The intrepid reader might add a DDE item allowing the client to select a different file. The point of the server, though, is for many clients to share a single file.

The StartDDE and StopDDE procedures called from WinMain initialize and uninitialize the program as a DDEML participant. The server creates its set of string handles and registers its service from the WM_CREATE message handler. Most DDEML programs end up with a collection of global string handles. Putting them in an array is often a good strategy. The DdeNameService call includes the DNS_FILTERON flag to block Connect messages for services the program does not support.

The DbSrv_OnCommand message handler looks for only one command. IDM_UPDATE does not come from a menu; it is a purely internal signal. It originates in the SearchThread procedure, listed in Chapter 12, and indicates the end of a search operation. The command procedure calls DdePostAdvise to tell the DDE library that new data is available. The search procedure cannot call DdePostAdvise directly because the instance ID, dwID, works only in the thread that calls DdeInitialize. In response to DdePostAdvise, the DDEML sends a message to the callback procedure requesting the data. That comes next.

```
/*-------------------------------------------------------------

          DBSERVER.C

     Main module for a DDEML server program that lets clients
     add, delete, and search for names and phone numbers.

     FUNCTIONS
          WinMain               receive and dispatch messages
          Init                  initialize program data
          DbSrv_WndProc         sort out messages for main window
          DbSrv_OnCreate        load service, topic, and item strings
          DbSrv_OnQueryOpen     make the window stay iconized
          DbSrv_OnCommand       process menu commands
          DbSrv_OnDestroy       end program
          StartDDE              initialize with the DDEML
          StopDDE               withdraw from the DDEML
          DdeCallback           receive messages from the DDEML
          AddRecord             add a new record
          DoPoke                interpret XTYP_POKE transactions

     from Mastering Windows NT Programming
     copyright 1993 by Brian Myers & Eric Hamer

     -------------------------------------------------------------*/

#define STRICT
#include <windows.h>
#include <windowsx.h>
#include <ddeml.h>
#include "db.h"
#include "dbserver.h"

/*-------------------------------------------------------------
          FUNCTION PROTOTYPES
     -------------------------------------------------------------*/

int WINAPI WinMain( HINSTANCE hinstThis, HINSTANCE hinstPrev,
     LPSTR lpszCmdLine, int iCmdShow );
BOOL Init( HINSTANCE hInst );
LRESULT WINAPI DbSrv_WndProc( HWND hWnd, UINT uMessage, WPARAM wParam,
     LPARAM lParam );
BOOL DbSrv_OnCreate( HWND hWnd, LPCREATESTRUCT lpcs );
BOOL DbSrv_OnQueryOpen( HWND hWnd );
void DbSrv_OnCommand( HWND hWnd, int iCmd, HWND hWndCtl, UINT uNotify );
```

```
void DbSrv_OnDestroy( HWND hWnd );
void AddRecord( PDBEDATA pData );
BOOL DoPoke( HSZ hszCommand, HDDEDATA hData );
BOOL StartDDE( void );
void StopDDE( void );
HDDEDATA CALLBACK DdeCallback( UINT uType, UINT uFmt, HCONV hConv, HSZ hsz1,
    HSZ hsz2, HDDEDATA hData, DWORD lData1, DWORD lData2 );
```

```
/*-------------------------------------------------------------------
        GLOBAL VARIABLES
    -----------------------------------------------------------------*/
```

```
char szFile[] = "database.dat";       // name of the database file
char szCaption[MAX_RSRC_STRING];      // string for window caption
DBDATA DBData;                        // pass records to modules here
HANDLE heventWrite;                   // pulse this to write a record
HANDLE heventTerminate;               // set this to end the thread
HANDLE hmxSearchResult;               // protects DBFoundData
HANDLE heventDataSent;                // set this when ADVREQ is done
HANDLE hwndMain;                      // main program window
DBDATA DBFoundData;                   // data found in a search
```

```
/*-------------------------------------------------------------------
        STATIC VARIABLES
    -----------------------------------------------------------------*/
```

```
HSZ hszTopic;                         // DDE string handles
HSZ hszAdd;
HSZ hszDelete;
HSZ hszSearch;
HSZ hszService;
DWORD dwID;                           // DDEML instance identifier

DBDATA DBFoundData;                   // holds a record when found
```

```
/*-------------------------------------------------------------------
        WINMAIN
        Initialize program and poll for messages until user quits.
    -----------------------------------------------------------------*/
```

```
int WINAPI WinMain (
    HINSTANCE hinstThis,
    HINSTANCE hinstPrev,
```

```
       LPSTR lpszCmdLine,
       int iCmdShow )
{
       MSG msg;
       BOOL bTest;

       bTest = StartDDE( );                    // initialize for DDEML
       if (!bTest)
       {
           StopDDE( );
           return( FALSE );                    // initialization failed
       }

       bTest = Init( hinstThis );              // initialize program window
       if (!bTest)
       {
           StopDDE( );
           return( FALSE );                    // initialization failed
       }

       while (GetMessage( &msg, NULL, 0, 0 ))
       {
           TranslateMessage( &msg );
           DispatchMessage( &msg );
       }

       StopDDE( );                             // withdraw from DDEML

       return( msg.wParam );
       UNREFERENCED_PARAMETER( hinstPrev );
       UNREFERENCED_PARAMETER( lpszCmdLine );
       UNREFERENCED_PARAMETER( iCmdShow );
}

/*-------------------------------------------------------------------
         INIT
         Register class and create main program window
   ---------------------------------------------------------------*/

BOOL Init ( HINSTANCE hInst )
{
     WNDCLASS wc;
     char szAppClass[MAX_RSRC_STRING];     // progam's window class
     char szCaption[MAX_RSRC_STRING];      // program's window caption
     HMENU hMenu;                          // handle to system menu
```

```
int iLen;                                    // for testing return values
BOOL bTest;

iLen = LoadString( hInst, IDS_APPCLASS, szAppClass, sizeof(szAppClass) );
if (!iLen)
{
    return( FALSE );
}

iLen = LoadString( hInst, IDS_CAPTION, szCaption, sizeof(szCaption) );
if (!iLen)
{
    return( FALSE );
}

/* register window class */
wc.lpszClassName  = szAppClass;
wc.hInstance      = hInst;
wc.lpfnWndProc    = DbSrv_WndProc;
wc.hCursor        = LoadCursor( NULL, IDC_ARROW );
wc.hIcon          = LoadIcon( hInst, MAKEINTRESOURCE(ICON_APP) );
wc.lpszMenuName   = NULL;
wc.hbrBackground  = (HBRUSH)(COLOR_WINDOW + 1);
wc.style          = CS_HREDRAW | CS_VREDRAW;
wc.cbClsExtra     = 0;
wc.cbWndExtra     = 0;

if (!RegisterClass( &wc ))
{
    return( FALSE );
}

// This manual reset event signals the Writing thread
// when data for a new record needs to be written.

heventWrite = CreateEvent( NULL, TRUE, FALSE, NULL );
if (!heventWrite)
{
    return( FALSE );
}

// This manual reset event signals the Writing thread
// when the program is about to terminate.
```

```
heventTerminate = CreateEvent( NULL, TRUE, FALSE, NULL );
if (!heventTerminate)
{
    CloseHandle( heventWrite );
    return( FALSE );
}

// This mutex guards DBFoundData, the global buffer where
// the Search thread transfers the data it retrieves to
// the DDEML thread (the thread that calls DdeInitialize).

hmxSearchResult = CreateMutex( NULL, FALSE, NULL );
if (!hmxSearchResult)
{
    CloseHandle( heventWrite );
    CloseHandle( heventTerminate );
    return( FALSE );
}

// This manual reset event tells the Search thread when
// the data it retrieved has been sent to the client.
// After it is set, the Search thread releases the
// DBFoundData mutex.

heventDataSent = CreateEvent( NULL, TRUE, FALSE, NULL );
if (!heventDataSent)
{
    CloseHandle( heventWrite );
    CloseHandle( heventTerminate );
    CloseHandle( hmxSearchResult )
    return( FALSE );
}

// While the program runs, the writing thread blocks waiting
// for any write commands to arrive from a client.  Start the
// thread running now.

bTest = StartWritingThread( );
if (!bTest)
{
    CloseHandle( heventWrite );
    CloseHandle( heventTerminate );
    CloseHandle( hmxSearchResult )
```

```
            CloseHandle( heventDataSent )
            return( FALSE );
        }

        /* create the program window */
        hwndMain = CreateWindow( szAppClass, szCaption, WS_OVERLAPPEDWINDOW,
            CW_USEDEFAULT, CW_USEDEFAULT, CW_USEDEFAULT, CW_USEDEFAULT,
            NULL, NULL, hInst, NULL );
        if (!hwndMain)
        {
            CloseHandle( heventWrite );
            CloseHandle( heventTerminate );
            CloseHandle( hmxSearchResult )
            CloseHandle( heventDataSent )
            return( FALSE );
        }

        // The DBServer window always displays as an
        // icon.  It has almost no user interface.

        /* remove the system menu commands for resizing the window */
        hMenu = GetSystemMenu( hwndMain, FALSE );
        DeleteMenu( hMenu, SC_RESTORE, MF_BYCOMMAND );
        DeleteMenu( hMenu, SC_MAXIMIZE, MF_BYCOMMAND );
        DeleteMenu( hMenu, SC_MINIMIZE, MF_BYCOMMAND );
        DeleteMenu( hMenu, SC_SIZE, MF_BYCOMMAND );

        /* display the minimized server icon */
        ShowWindow( hwndMain, SW_MINIMIZE );
        UpdateWindow( hwndMain );

        return( TRUE );
}


/*--------------------------------------------------------------------
        DBSRV_WNDPROC
        Process all messages for the program's main window.
  ------------------------------------------------------------------*/

LRESULT WINAPI DbSrv_WndProc (
    HWND hWnd,
    UINT uMessage,
    WPARAM wParam,
    LPARAM lParam )
{
```

```
    switch (uMessage)
    {
        HANDLE_MSG( hWnd, WM_CREATE, DbSrv_OnCreate );

        HANDLE_MSG( hWnd, WM_QUERYOPEN, DbSrv_OnQueryOpen );

        HANDLE_MSG( hWnd, WM_COMMAND, DbSrv_OnCommand );

        HANDLE_MSG( hWnd, WM_DESTROY, DbSrv_OnDestroy );

        default:
            return( DefWindowProc(hWnd, uMessage, wParam, lParam) );
    }

    return( 0 );
}


/*-------------------------------------------------------------------
        DBSRV_ONCREATE
        Load all the DDEML server, topic, and item strings and
        create handles for them.
    ----------------------------------------------------------------*/

BOOL DbSrv_OnCreate (
    HWND hWnd,
    LPCREATESTRUCT lpcs )
{
    char szBuffer[MAX_RSRC_STRING];     // place to put one string
    HDDEDATA hdde;                       // return from DdeNameService
    HINSTANCE hInst;
    int iLen;

    hInst = GetWindowInstance( hWnd );

    if (!hInst)
    {
        return( FALSE );
    }

    iLen = LoadString( hInst, IDS_SERVICE, szBuffer, sizeof(szBuffer) );
    if (!iLen)
    {
        return( FALSE );
    }
```

```
hszService = DdeCreateStringHandle( dwID, szBuffer, CP_WINANSI );
if (!hszService)
{
    return( FALSE );
}

iLen = LoadString( hInst, IDS_DBTOPIC, szBuffer, sizeof(szBuffer) );
if (!iLen)
{
    return( FALSE );
}

hszTopic = DdeCreateStringHandle( dwID, szBuffer, CP_WINANSI );
if (!hszTopic)
{
    return( FALSE );
}

iLen = LoadString( hInst, IDS_ADD, szBuffer, sizeof(szBuffer) );

if (!iLen)
{
    return( FALSE );
}

hszAdd = DdeCreateStringHandle( dwID, szBuffer, CP_WINANSI );
if (!hszAdd)
{
    return( FALSE );
}

iLen = LoadString( hInst, IDS_DELETE, szBuffer, sizeof(szBuffer) );
if (!iLen)
{
    return( FALSE );
}

hszDelete = DdeCreateStringHandle( dwID, szBuffer, CP_WINANSI );
if (!hszDelete)
{
    return( FALSE );
}

iLen = LoadString( hInst, IDS_SEARCH, szBuffer, sizeof(szBuffer) );
```

```
    if (!iLen)
    {
        return( FALSE );
    }

    hszSearch = DdeCreateStringHandle( dwID, szBuffer, CP_WINANSI );
    if (!hszSearch)
    {
        return( FALSE );
    }

    // Register our service name with the DDEML.  The return value
    // is not a true handle; read it as a Boolean value.

    hdde = DdeNameService( dwID,           // instance ID
        hszService,                        // service name string
        (HSZ)NULL,                         // reserved
        DNS_REGISTER                       // register new name
        | DNS_FILTERON );                  // filter unwanted XTYP_CONNECTs
    if (!hdde)
    {
        return( FALSE );                   // registration failed
    }

    return( TRUE );
    UNREFERENCED_PARAMETER( lpcs );
}

/*--------------------------------------------------------------------
        DBSRV_ONQUERYOPEN
        Prevent the system from restoring this window to an open
        state.  The DBServer window remains minimized at all times.
    ----------------------------------------------------------------*/

BOOL DbSrv_OnQueryOpen ( HWND hWnd )
{
    return( FALSE );
    UNREFERENCED_PARAMETER( hWnd );
}

/*--------------------------------------------------------------------
        DBSRV_ONCOMMAND
        DBServer does not have a menu, but it does define one
        WM_COMMAND value for internal use.  Process it here.
    ----------------------------------------------------------------*/
```

```c
void DbSrv_OnCommand (
    HWND hWnd,
    int iCmd,
    HWND hwndCtl,
    UINT uNotify )
{
    switch (iCmd)
    {
        // The Update command comes as a message from the
        // input module.  When the search thread locates a
        // match, it sends a WM_COMMAND back to the main
        // thread requesting a DdePostAdvise be called.  Because
        // dwInst is local to this thread, the search thread
        // cannot call DdePostAdvise itself.

        case IDM_UPDATE:
            DdePostAdvise( dwID, hszTopic, hszSearch );
            break;

        default:
            break;
    }
    return;
    UNREFERENCED_PARAMETER( hWnd );
    UNREFERENCED_PARAMETER( hwndCtl );
    UNREFERENCED_PARAMETER( uNotify );
}

/*-------------------------------------------------------------------
        DBSRV_ONDESTROY
        Respond to WM_DESTROY by releasing objects and posting
        a WM_QUIT message.
    -----------------------------------------------------------------*/

void DbSrv_OnDestroy ( HWND hWnd )
{
    SetEvent( heventTerminate );         // tell Writing thread to end
    Sleep( 0 );                          // allow context switch

    CloseHandle( heventWrite );
    CloseHandle( heventTerminate );
    CloseHandle( heventDataSent );
    CloseHandle( hmxSearchResult );
```

```
    PostQuitMessage( 0 );
    return;
    UNREFERENCED_PARAMETER( hWnd );
}


/*---------------------------------------------------------------------
        START DDE
        Register the server with the DDEML.
    ---------------------------------------------------------------*/

BOOL StartDDE ( void )
{
    UINT uErr;                          // return value

    /* tell the DDEML who we are */
    uErr = DdeInitialize( &dwID,        // instance ID (returned)
        (PFNCALLBACK)DdeCallback,       // program's DDEML callback
        APPCLASS_STANDARD               // standard DDEML application
          ¦ CBF_FAIL_EXECUTES           // filter out XTYP_EXECUTE
          ¦ CBF_FAIL_REQUESTS           // filter out XTYP_REQUEST
          ¦ CBF_SKIP_ALLNOTIFICATIONS,  // filter notification messages
        0L );                           // reserved

    if (uErr != DMLERR_NO_ERROR)
    {
        return( FALSE );                // initialization failed
    }

    return( TRUE );
}


/*---------------------------------------------------------------------
        STOP DDE
        End the current conversation, release all DDE-related
        resources, and withdraw from the DDEML.
    ---------------------------------------------------------------*/

void StopDDE ( void )
{
    /* withdraw the service from the DDEML */
    DdeNameService( dwID, hszService, (HSZ)NULL, DNS_UNREGISTER );

    if (hszService)
    {
        DdeFreeStringHandle( dwID, hszService );
    }
```

```
if (hszSearch)
{
    DdeFreeStringHandle( dwID, hszSearch );
}

if (hszAdd)
{
    DdeFreeStringHandle( dwID, hszAdd );
}

if (hszDelete)
{
    DdeFreeStringHandle( dwID, hszDelete );
}

if (hszTopic)
{
    DdeFreeStringHandle( dwID, hszTopic );
}

DdeUninitialize( dwID );                // withdraw program from DDEML
return;
}
```

DdeCallback handles five messages. When a client wants to connect, the procedure checks the service and topic names. If the service is "dbserver" and the topic is "database" then the server returns **TRUE** and a conversation begins. When the server registered its service it asked to filter notification messages, so it never receives the follow-up **XTYP_CONNECT_CONFIRM** message.

The Poke message arrives when the client wants to add, delete, or search for a record. The item string selects one of the three possible actions. DdeCallback invokes DoPoke to interpret the string and call the appropriate procedure.

We have chosen to provide the search function to clients as a hot link. The search may be lengthy, so an asynchronous transaction seems useful. An asynchronous **XTYP_REQUEST**, however, is asynchronous only for the client. The server has to satisfy the request before the callback procedure ends. To make the server begin a search, the client pokes the server's Search item, sending a partially filled record containing search criteria. DBServer sets off a search thread to look for the data. Meanwhile the client establishes a hot link asking to be advised when the Search item has a value. When the server is ready, it calls **DdePostAdvise**. As soon as the client receives the search result, it cancels the link. Only one value passes through this hot link.

During the course of a search, then, DdeCallback receives four messages.

- **XTYP_POKE:** Poking the search item with search criteria causes the server to generate a searching thread.

- **XTYP_ADVSTART:** The client creates a link for passing the data back. The server merely acknowledges the link.

- **XTYP_ADVREQ:** The server generates this message indirectly by calling **DdePostAdvise** when a search operation signals completion. The server passes a data object to the DDEML.

- **XTYP_ADVSTOP:** As soon as the client receives the data it breaks off the connection and the server receives this message.

AddRecord copies the information for a new record and pulses an event. The signal awakens the writing thread, which copies the data to the file and promptly falls back asleep, waiting for more data. The code for the write.c module appears in Chapter 12.

```
/*-------------------------------------------------------------
        DDE CALLBACK
        Respond to messages from the DDEML.
        ----------------------------------------------------------*/

HDDEDATA CALLBACK DdeCallback (
        UINT uType,                             // message type
        UINT uFmt,                              // data format
        HCONV hConv,                            // conversation handle
        HSZ hsz1,                               // first string handle (topic)
        HSZ hsz2,                               // second string handle (item)
        HDDEDATA hData,                         // a data object
        DWORD dwData1,                          // transaction-specific data
        DWORD dwData2 )                         // transaction-specific data
{
        HDDEDATA hDDEData;                      // data packaged for the client
        BOOL bTest;                             // function return value

        switch (uType)
        {
```

```
        case XTYP_CONNECT:                       // client wants to converse
            if (!DdeCmpStringHandles( hsz2, hszService )
                && !DdeCmpStringHandles( hsz1, hszTopic ))
            {
                return( (HDDEDATA)TRUE );
            }
            break;

        case XTYP_POKE:                          // client sending information
            bTest = DoPoke( hsz2, hData );
            return( (HDDEDATA)bTest );

        case XTYP_ADVSTART:                      // client wants to search
            return( (HDDEDATA)TRUE );

        case XTYP_ADVREQ:
            hDDEData = DdeCreateDataHandle(
                dwID,                            // instance ID
                (LPBYTE)&DBFoundData,            // data to be sent
                sizeof(DBDATA),                  // size of data
                0,                               // offset into source buffer
                hszSearch,                       // associated item name
                CF_TEXT,                         // format of data
                0 );                             // creation flags

            /* tell the Search thread to release the DBFoundData mutex */
            SetEvent( heventDataSent );
            return( hDDEData );

        case XTYP_ADVSTOP:                       // client ends search link
            return( (HDDEDATA)NULL );

        default:
            break;
    }

    return( FALSE );
    UNREFERENCED_PARAMETER( uFmt );
    UNREFERENCED_PARAMETER( hConv );
    UNREFERENCED_PARAMETER( dwData1 );
    UNREFERENCED_PARAMETER( dwData2 );
}
```

```
/*-------------------------------------------------------------------
        ADD RECORD
        Copy a record from a data object to the DBData buffer and
        signal the Writing thread that we have data to store.
   ------------------------------------------------------------------*/

void AddRecord ( PDBDATA pData )
{
    /* copy data to global buffer for Write thread */
    CopyMemory( &DBData, pData, sizeof(DBDATA) );

    /* signal the Writing thread */
    PulseEvent( heventWrite );
    Sleep( 0 );                         // allow context switch
                                        // for thread to begin

    return;
}

/*-------------------------------------------------------------------
        DO POKE
        Invoked in response to XTYP_POKE, this procedure determines
        what item was poked and calls other procedures to perform
        the appropriate processing.  Returns TRUE if it recognizes
        the item and FALSE if it doesn't.
   ------------------------------------------------------------------*/

BOOL DoPoke (
    HSZ hszCommand,             // string handle for item that was poked
    HDDEDATA hData )            // new data from the client
{
    DBDATA DBRecord;                        // holds info for one record

    /* extract the data from the data handle */
    DdeGetData( hData,                  // handle to new data
        (LPBYTE)&DBRecord,              // place to put the data
        sizeof(DBDATA),                 // size of buffer
        0 );                            // offset into the data

    if (hszCommand == hszAdd)           // was Add item poked?
    {
        AddRecord( &DBRecord );
        return( TRUE );
    }
    else if (hszCommand == hszDelete)   // was Delete item poked?
    {
```

```
      DeleteRecord( &DBRecord );
      return( TRUE );
   }
   else if (hszCommand == hszSearch)      // was Search item poked?
   {
      FindRecord( &DBRecord );
      return( TRUE );
   }

   return( FALSE );                       // did not recognize the item
}
```

The Delete Module

The procedures for deleting a record work very much like those for finding a record. DeleteRecord creates a new thread to scan the file looking for a record that matches the criteria received from the client. If a matching record is found, DeletionThread sets the STATUS_DELETED flag in its iStatus field. Searches in DBServer ignore records marked for deletion.

A more fully realized database server could create another background thread for garbage collection. It would wake up every few minutes and, working at very low priority, scan through the database for deleted records and remove them physically by sliding all the subsequent records forward.

```
/*-----------------------------------------------------------------

      DELETE.C

      Part of the DBSERVER program, this module marks records
      when they are deleted.  A more fully implemented program
      would create a garbage-collecting thread that would cycle
      through the file periodically, working at low priority,
      to remove deleted records physically from the file.

      FUNCTIONS
            DeleteRecord        start a thread to delete a record
            DeletionThread      search for a record and delete it

      from Mastering Windows NT Programming
      copyright 1993 by Brian Myers & Eric Hamer

      ----------------------------------------------------------*/
```

```
#define STRICT
#include <windows.h>
#include <windowsx.h>
#include "db.h"
#include "dbserver.h"

/*-------------------------------------------------------------------
        FUNCTION PROTOTYPE
    ---------------------------------------------------------------*/

LONG DeletionThread( PDBDATA pdbCriteria );

/*-------------------------------------------------------------------
        DELETE RECORD
        Starts a thread that searches through the file for a
        particular record to delete.  The search criteria are passed
        through the parameter.  A record must match both fields
        of the search criteria in order to be deleted.

        Returns TRUE if it succeeds in starting the thread.
    ---------------------------------------------------------------*/

BOOL DeleteRecord ( PDBDATA pData )             // data from client
{
    HANDLE hThread;                             // handle to the new thread
    DWORD dwThread;                             // thread's ID number
    PDBDATA pdbCriteria;                        // search criteria

    if (!pData)                                 // is pointer valid?
    {
        return( FALSE );
    }

    // Protect the search criteria from other searches by
    // copying them into a new buffer, one per thread

    pdbCriteria = LocalAlloc( LPTR, sizeof(DBDATA) );
    if (!pdbCriteria)
    {
        return( FALSE );
    }
    lstrcpy( pdbCriteria>szName, pData>szName );
    lstrcpy( pdbCriteria>szPhone, pData>szPhone );
    pdbCriteria>iStatus = pData>iStatus;
```

```
    /* create the deletion thread */
    hThread = CreateThread( NULL, O, (LPTHREAD_START_ROUTINE)DeletionThread,
        pdbCriteria, CREATE_SUSPENDED, (LPDWORD)&dwThread );
    if (!hThread)
    {
        return( FALSE );
    }

    /* lower the thread's priority and start it running */
    SetThreadPriority( hThread, THREAD_PRIORITY_BELOW_NORMAL );
    ResumeThread( hThread );
    CloseHandle( hThread );                       // no use for the handle

    return( TRUE );
}

/*-------------------------------------------------------------------
        DELETION THREAD
        The thread procedure for reading through the file in search
        of a particular record to delete.  The search ends after
        it deletes one record or reaches the end of the file.
    -----------------------------------------------------------------*/
LONG DeletionThread ( PDBDATA pdbCriteria )
{
    HANDLE hFile;                             // handle to the file
    DBDATA DBData;                            // holds one record
    DWORD dwRead;                             // number of bytes read
    DWORD dwWrite;                            // number of bytes written
    DWORD dwPos;                              // offset into file
    BOOL bContinue;                           // TRUE while searching

    /* create the file handle */
    hFile = CreateFile( szFile,               // file name
        GENERIC_READ | GENERIC_WRITE,         // access privileges
        FILE_SHARE_READ | FILE_SHARE_WRITE,   // share privileges
        (LPSECURITY_ATTRIBUTES)NULL,          // security privileges
        OPEN_EXISTING,                        // file already exists
        FILE_ATTRIBUTE_NORMAL,                // no special attributes
        (HANDLE)NULL );                       // no template file
    if (hFile == INVALID_HANDLE_VALUE)
    {
        return( OL );                         // error: end thread
    }
```

```
/* loop through the file to find the record */
bContinue = TRUE;                           // FALSE when search ends
while (bContinue)
{
    /* read a record */
    ReadFile( hFile,                        // file handle
        &DBData,                            // destination buffer
        sizeof(DBDATA),                     // buffer size
        &dwRead,                            // bytes read
        NULL );                             // do synchronous I/O

    if (!dwRead)
    {
        bContinue = FALSE;                  // ReadFile failed
    }
    else
    {
        /* is this the record we're looking for? */
        if ((!lstrcmp(DBData.szName, pdbCriteria>szName)) &&
            (!lstrcmp(DBData.szPhone, pdbCriteria>szPhone)) &&
            (DBData.iStatus != STATUS_DELETED))
        {
            /* mark it deleted */
            DBData.iStatus = STATUS_DELETED;

            /* set pointer to beginning of record */
            dwPos = SetFilePointer( hFile, (int)sizeof(DBDATA), NULL,
                FILE_CURRENT );

            /* if no error, write modified record back to disk */
            if (dwPos != 0xFFFFFFFF)
            {
                WriteFile( hFile,           // file handle
                    &DBData,                // source buffer
                    sizeof(DBDATA),         // size of data
                    &dwWrite,               // bytes written
                    NULL );                 // synchronous I/O

                bContinue = FALSE;          // end search
            }
        }
    }
}
```

```
        CloseHandle( hFile );                // clean up
        return( OL );                        // end thread
}
```

The Database Client

The DBClient program interacts with the user through one menu and four dialog boxes. When the program starts, the user first chooses Connect from the Database menu to begin a DDEML conversation with the server. The other menu commands include Add, Delete, and Search. Each command brings up a dialog box where the user enters a name or a phone number or both, depending on the command. A fourth dialog box appears to display the matching record located by a Search command. All four dialog boxes are defined in the program's resource script.

```
#
#    NMake file for the DATABASE CLIENT program
#

#
#    Set targets and dependencies
#

all: dbclient.exe
dbclient.exe: dbclient.obj dialog.obj dbclient.rbj
dbclient.obj: dbclient.c dbclient.h db.h
dialog.obj: dialog.c dbclient.h db.h
dbclient.rbj: dbclient.rc db.rc dbclient.h db.h

#
#    Define macros for command-line options and library modules
#

!IFDEF NODEBUG
CFLAGS = -c -G3 -Os -W4 -D_X86_=1 -DWIN32
LFLAGS = -subsystem:windows
!ELSE
CFLAGS = -c -G3 -Od -W4 -Zi -D_X86_=1 -DWIN32
LFLAGS = -debug:full -debugtype:cv -subsystem:windows
!ENDIF
```

```
INCS = dbclient.h
OBJS = dbclient.obj dialog.obj dbclient.rbj
LIBS = libc.lib ntdll.lib kernel32.lib user32.lib


#
#    Define compiling rules
#

.c.obj:
    cl386 $(CFLAGS) $*.c

.rc.rbj:
    rc $*.rc
    cvtres -i386 $*.res -o $*.rbj

.obj.exe:
    link32 $(LFLAGS) -out:$*.exe $(OBJS) $(LIBS)


============================================================================

/*----------------------------------------------------------------


        DBCLIENT.H

        Header file for the Database Client program.

    ----------------------------------------------------------------*/

/*----------------------------------------------------------------
        SYMBOLS
    ----------------------------------------------------------------*/

#define MAX_RSRC_STRING      256

/*----------------------------------------------------------------
        RESOURCE IDENTIFIERS
    ----------------------------------------------------------------*/

#define ICON_APP            100         // application icon

#define MENU_CLIENT         100         // templates
#define DLG_ADDDATA         200
#define DLG_DELETEDATA      300
#define DLG_SEARCHDATA      400
#define DLG_RESULTDATA      500
```

```
#define IDS_APPCLASS        100         // strings in string table
#define IDS_CAPTION         200

#define IDM_EXIT            300         // menu commands
#define IDM_CONNECT         400
#define IDM_DISCONNECT      500
#define IDM_ADD             600
#define IDM_DELETE          700
#define IDM_SEARCH          800

#define IDD_NAMEEDIT        1006        // dialog controls
#define IDD_PHONEEDIT       1007

/*-------------------------------------------------------------------
          GLOBAL VARIABLE
          ---------------------------------------------------------*/

extern char szCaption[MAX_RSRC_STRING];          // window caption

/*-------------------------------------------------------------------
          PROTOTYPES for functions used outside their own module
          ---------------------------------------------------------*/

/* DBCLIENT.C */
BOOL StoreData( HWND hDlg );

/* DIALOG.H */
int DoDialog( HWND hWnd, PDBDATA pData, int iType );

============================================================================

/*-------------------------------------------------------------------


          DBCLIENT.RC

          Resource script for the DBCLIENT program.

          ---------------------------------------------------------*/

#include <windows.h>
#include "dbclient.h"

ICON_APP    ICON        dbclient.ico
```

```
STRINGTABLE
BEGIN
    #include "db.rc"                // db.rc has strings shared with server
    IDS_APPCLASS,                   "DDEML_Client"      // window class
    IDS_CAPTION,                    "DDEML Client"      // window caption
END

MENU_CLIENT MENU
BEGIN
    POPUP "&File"
    BEGIN
        MENUITEM "E&xit"            IDM_EXIT
    END
    POPUP "&Database"
    BEGIN
        MENUITEM "Co&nnect",        IDM_CONNECT
        MENUITEM "&Disconnect",     IDM_DISCONNECT, GRAYED
        MENUITEM SEPARATOR
        MENUITEM "&Add...",         IDM_ADD, GRAYED
        MENUITEM "&Delete...",      IDM_DELETE, GRAYED
        MENUITEM "&Search...",      IDM_SEARCH, GRAYED
    END
END

DLG_ADDDATA DIALOG 36, 55, 168, 48
STYLE DS_MODALFRAME | WS_POPUP | WS_CAPTION | WS_SYSMENU
CAPTION "Add Data"
BEGIN
    LTEXT "&Name:", -1, 5, 11, 25, 8, WS_CHILD | WS_VISIBLE | WS_GROUP
    EDITTEXT IDD_NAMEEDIT, 32, 10, 75, 12
    LTEXT "&Phone No:", -1, 5, 26, 38, 8, WS_CHILD | WS_VISIBLE | WS_GROUP
    EDITTEXT IDD_PHONEEDIT, 43, 26, 64, 12
    DEFPUSHBUTTON "OK", IDOK, 128, 8, 36, 14, WS_CHILD | WS_VISIBLE
        | WS_TABSTOP
    PUSHBUTTON "Cancel", IDCANCEL, 128, 26, 36, 14, WS_CHILD | WS_VISIBLE |
WS_TABSTOP
END

DLG_DELETEDATA DIALOG 36, 55, 168, 48
STYLE DS_MODALFRAME | WS_POPUP | WS_CAPTION | WS_SYSMENU
CAPTION "Delete Data"
BEGIN
    LTEXT "&Name:", -1, 5, 11, 25, 8, WS_CHILD | WS_VISIBLE | WS_GROUP
    EDITTEXT IDD_NAMEEDIT, 32, 10, 75, 12
    LTEXT "&Phone No:", -1, 5, 26, 38, 8, WS_CHILD | WS_VISIBLE | WS_GROUP
```

```
    EDITTEXT IDD_PHONEEDIT, 43, 26, 64, 12
    DEFPUSHBUTTON "OK", IDOK, 128, 8, 36, 14, WS_CHILD | WS_VISIBLE
        | WS_TABSTOP
    PUSHBUTTON "Cancel", IDCANCEL, 128, 26, 36, 14, WS_CHILD | WS_VISIBLE |
WS_TABSTOP
END

DLG_SEARCHDATA DIALOG 36, 55, 168, 48
STYLE DS_MODALFRAME | WS_POPUP | WS_CAPTION | WS_SYSMENU
CAPTION "Search Data"
BEGIN
    LTEXT "&Name:", -1, 5, 11, 25, 8, WS_CHILD | WS_VISIBLE | WS_GROUP
    EDITTEXT IDD_NAMEEDIT, 32, 10, 75, 12
    LTEXT "&Phone No:", -1, 5, 26, 38, 8, WS_CHILD | WS_VISIBLE | WS_GROUP
    EDITTEXT IDD_PHONEEDIT, 43, 26, 64, 12
    DEFPUSHBUTTON "OK", IDOK, 128, 8, 36, 14, WS_CHILD | WS_VISIBLE
        | WS_TABSTOP
    PUSHBUTTON "Cancel", IDCANCEL, 128, 26, 36, 14, WS_CHILD | WS_VISIBLE |
WS_TABSTOP
END

DLG_RESULTDATA DIALOG 36, 55, 168, 48
STYLE DS_MODALFRAME | WS_POPUP | WS_CAPTION | WS_SYSMENU
CAPTION "Search Result (Read Only)"
BEGIN
    DEFPUSHBUTTON "OK", IDOK, 128, 8, 36, 14, WS_CHILD | WS_VISIBLE
        | WS_TABSTOP
    LTEXT "&Name:", -1, 5, 11, 25, 8, WS_CHILD | WS_VISIBLE | WS_GROUP
    EDITTEXT IDD_NAMEEDIT, 32, 10, 75, 12, ES_READONLY
    LTEXT "&Phone No:", -1, 5, 26, 38, 8, WS_CHILD | WS_VISIBLE | WS_GROUP
    EDITTEXT IDD_PHONEEDIT, 43, 26, 64, 12, ES_READONLY
END
```

The DBClient Module

The client declares the same set of static **HSZ** variables as the server does, naming the service, topic, and items about which the two programs converse. The client also keeps a handle to any conversation it starts; the server does not need one. The StartDDE, StopDDE, and DbCli_OnCreate procedures initialize this program and wind it down in much the same way the corresponding procedures do for the server.

```
/*------------------------------------------------------------------

        DBCLIENT.C

        Main module for a DDEML client program that connects
        with a database server to let the user add, delete,
        and search for names and phone numbers.

        FUNCTIONS
                WinMain                 receive and dispatch messages
                Init                    initialize program data
                DbCli_WndProc           sort out messages for main window
                DbCli_OnCreate          load service, topic, and item strings
                DbCli_OnCommand         process menu commands
                DbCli_OnDestroy         end program
                DoSearch                search for a record
                DoDelete                delete a record
                AddData                 add a new record
                DisplayData             display data received from the server
                DoConnect               begin a new conversation
                DoDisconnect            end a conversation
                StartDDE                initialize with the DDEML
                StopDDE                 withdraw from the DDEML
                DdeCallback             receive messages from the DDEML

        from Mastering Windows NT Programming
        copyright 1993 by Brian Myers & Eric Hamer

        ------------------------------------------------------------*/


#define STRICT
#include <windows.h>
#include <windowsx.h>
#include <ddeml.h>                      // needed for any DDEML program
#include "db.h"                         // global to client and server
#include "dbclient.h"                   // header for this file


/*------------------------------------------------------------
        FUNCTION PROTOTYPES
        ------------------------------------------------------------*/


int WINAPI WinMain( HINSTANCE hinstThis, HINSTANCE hinstPrev,
    LPSTR lpszCmdLine, int iCmdShow );
LRESULT WINAPI DbCli_WndProc( HWND hWnd, UINT uMessage, WPARAM wParam,
    LPARAM lParam );
```

```
BOOL Init( HINSTANCE hInst, int iCmdShow );
BOOL DbCli_OnCreate( HWND hWnd, LPCREATESTRUCT lpcs );
void DbCli_OnCommand( HWND hWnd, int iCmd, HWND hwndCtl, UINT uNotify );
void DbCli_OnDestroy( HWND hWnd );
BOOL StartDDE( void );
void StopDDE( void );
void DoConnect( HWND hWnd );
void DoDisconnect( HWND hWnd );
void AddData( HWND hWnd );
void DoDelete( HWND hWnd );
void DoSearch( HWND hWnd );
HDDEDATA CALLBACK DdeCallback( UINT uType, UINT uFmt, HCONV hConv, HSZ hsz1,
    HSZ hsz2, HDDEDATA hData, DWORD lData1, DWORD lData2 );

/*----------------------------------------------------------------
        GLOBAL VARIABLE
        ------------------------------------------------------*/

char szCaption[MAX_RSRC_STRING];          // string for window caption

/*----------------------------------------------------------------
        STATIC VARIABLES
        ------------------------------------------------------*/

/* DDE string handles */
HSZ hszService;                           // service name
HSZ hszTopic;                             // topic name
HSZ hszAdd;                               // item names (for poking)
HSZ hszDelete;
HSZ hszSearch;

HCONV hconvDB;                            // conversation handle
HWND hwndMain;                            // main window
DWORD dwID;                               // DDEML instance identifier

/*----------------------------------------------------------------
        WINMAIN
        Initialize program and poll for messages until user quits.
        ------------------------------------------------------*/

int WINAPI WinMain (
    HINSTANCE hinstThis,
    HINSTANCE hinstPrev,
    LPSTR lpszCmdLine,
    int iCmdShow )
```

```
{
    MSG msg;
    BOOL bTest;
    bTest = StartDDE( );               // initialize for DDEML
    if (!bTest)
    {
        StopDDE( );
        return( FALSE );               // initialization failed
    }

    bTest = Init( hinstThis, iCmdShow );    // initialize program window
    if (!bTest)
    {
        StopDDE( );
        return( FALSE );               // initialization failed
    }

    /* receive and route messages */
    while (GetMessage( &msg, NULL, 0, 0 ))
    {
        TranslateMessage( &msg );
        DispatchMessage( &msg );
    }

    StopDDE( );                        // withdraw from DDEML

    return( msg.wParam );
    UNREFERENCED_PARAMETER( hinstPrev );
    UNREFERENCED_PARAMETER( lpszCmdLine );
}

/*-------------------------------------------------------------------
        INIT
        Register class and create main program window
    ---------------------------------------------------------------*/

BOOL Init (
    HINSTANCE hInst,
    int iCmdShow )
{
    WNDCLASS wc;
    char szAppClass[MAX_RSRC_STRING];
    int iLen;                          // return value from LoadString
```

```
iLen = LoadString(hInst, IDS_APPCLASS, szAppClass, sizeof(szAppClass) );
if (!iLen)
{
    return( FALSE );
}
iLen = LoadString( hInst, IDS_CAPTION, szCaption, sizeof(szCaption) );
if (!iLen)
{
    return( FALSE );
}

/* register the main window class */
wc.lpszClassName  = szAppClass;
wc.hInstance      = hInst;
wc.lpfnWndProc    = DbCli_WndProc;
wc.hCursor        = LoadCursor( NULL, IDC_ARROW );
wc.hIcon          = LoadIcon( hInst, MAKEINTRESOURCE(ICON_APP) );
wc.lpszMenuName   = MAKEINTRESOURCE( MENU_CLIENT );
wc.hbrBackground  = (HBRUSH)(COLOR_WINDOW + 1);
wc.style          = CS_HREDRAW | CS_VREDRAW;
wc.cbClsExtra     = 0;
wc.cbWndExtra     = 0;

if (!RegisterClass( &wc ))
{
    return( FALSE );
}

/* create the program window */
hwndMain = CreateWindow( szAppClass, szCaption, WS_OVERLAPPEDWINDOW,
    CW_USEDEFAULT, CW_USEDEFAULT, CW_USEDEFAULT, CW_USEDEFAULT,
    NULL, NULL, hInst, NULL );
if (!hwndMain)
{
    return( FALSE );
}

/* show the program window  */
ShowWindow( hwndMain, iCmdShow );
UpdateWindow( hwndMain );

return( TRUE );
}
```

```
/*-------------------------------------------------------------------
        DBCLI_WNDPROC
        Process all messages for the program's main window.
    ------------------------------------------------------------------*/

LRESULT WINAPI DbCli_WndProc (
    HWND hWnd,
    UINT uMessage,
    WPARAM wParam,
    LPARAM lParam )
{
    switch (uMessage)
    {
        HANDLE_MSG( hWnd, WM_CREATE, DbCli_OnCreate );

        HANDLE_MSG( hWnd, WM_COMMAND, DbCli_OnCommand );

        HANDLE_MSG( hWnd, WM_DESTROY, DbCli_OnDestroy );

        default:
            return( DefWindowProc(hWnd, uMessage, wParam, lParam) );
    }

    return( 0 );
}

/*-------------------------------------------------------------------
        DBCLI_ONCREATE
        Load all the DDEML server, topic, and item strings and
        create handles for them.
    ------------------------------------------------------------------*/

BOOL DbCli_OnCreate (
    HWND hWnd,
    LPCREATESTRUCT lpcs )
{
    char szBuffer[MAX_RSRC_STRING];
    HINSTANCE hInst;
    int iLen;

    hInst = GetWindowInstance( hWnd );
```

```
if (!hInst)
{
    return( FALSE );
}

iLen = LoadString( hInst, IDS_SERVICE, szBuffer, sizeof(szBuffer) );
if (!iLen)
{
    return( FALSE );
}

hszService = DdeCreateStringHandle( dwID, szBuffer, CP_WINANSI );
if (!hszService)
{
    return( FALSE );
}

iLen = LoadString( hInst, IDS_DBTOPIC, szBuffer, sizeof(szBuffer) );
if (!iLen)
{
    return( FALSE );
}

hszTopic = DdeCreateStringHandle( dwID, szBuffer, CP_WINANSI );
if (!hszTopic)
{
    return( FALSE );
}

iLen = LoadString( hInst, IDS_ADD, szBuffer, sizeof(szBuffer) );
if (!iLen)
{
    return( FALSE );
}

hszAdd = DdeCreateStringHandle( dwID, szBuffer, CP_WINANSI );
if (!hszAdd)
{
    return( FALSE );
}

iLen = LoadString( hInst, IDS_DELETE, szBuffer, sizeof(szBuffer) );
```

```
    if (!iLen)
    {
        return( FALSE );
    }

    hszDelete = DdeCreateStringHandle( dwID, szBuffer, CP_WINANSI );
    if (!hszDelete)
    {
        return( FALSE );
    }

    iLen = LoadString( hInst, IDS_SEARCH, szBuffer, sizeof(szBuffer) );
    if (!iLen)
    {
        return( FALSE );
    }
    hszSearch = DdeCreateStringHandle( dwID, szBuffer, CP_WINANSI );
    if (!hszSearch)
    {
        return( FALSE );
    }

    return( TRUE );
    UNREFERENCED_PARAMETER( lpcs );
}

/*---------------------------------------------------------------
        DBCLI_ONCOMMAND
        Respond to WM_COMMAND messages from the program's menu.
    ---------------------------------------------------------------*/

void DbCli_OnCommand (
    HWND hWnd,
    int iCmd,
    HWND hwndCtl,
    UINT uNotify )
{
    switch (iCmd)
    {
        case IDM_EXIT:                      // end program
            DestroyWindow( hWnd );
            break;
```

```
        case IDM_CONNECT:                    // connect to server
            DoConnect( hWnd );
            break;

        case IDM_DISCONNECT:                 // end a conversation
            DoDisconnect( hWnd );
            break;

        case IDM_ADD:                        // add a new record
            AddData( hWnd );
            break;

        case IDM_DELETE:                     // delete an old record
            DoDelete( hWnd );
            break;

        case IDM_SEARCH:                     // find a record in the database
            DoSearch( hWnd );
            break;

        default:
            break;
    }

    return;
    UNREFERENCED_PARAMETER( hwndCtl );
    UNREFERENCED_PARAMETER( uNotify );
}

/*---------------------------------------------------------------------
        DBCLI_ONDESTROY
        Respond to WM_DESTROY by posting a WM_QUIT message.
    ---------------------------------------------------------------*/

void DbCli_OnDestroy ( HWND hWnd )
{
    PostQuitMessage( 0 );

    return;
    UNREFERENCED_PARAMETER( hWnd );
}
```

Each of the menu commands leads to a procedure that invokes its dialog box, examines the user's entries, and executes a DDEML transaction with the server. DoDelete and AddData each perform a single Poke, passing the server a record to remove or append. Because the search operation requires a response from the server, it is more complex. DoSearch pokes the search criteria to the server and then initiates a hot advise loop. The loop tells the DDEML to anticipate that more data will arrive from the server for this same item. The **XTYP_ADVDATA** case in DdeCallback waits for the server's response.

DoConnect and DoDisconnect also respond to menu commands. Most of the program's menu items remain disabled until a connection is established. The callback procedure is short because, like most client programs, this one sends more DDEML signals than it receives.

```
/*------------------------------------------------------------------
        DO SEARCH
        Poke search data into the server and wait for the server to
        return the matching record.
    ----------------------------------------------------------------*/

void DoSearch ( HWND hWnd )
{
    DBDATA dbData;                      // one record
    DWORD dwResult;                     // function return values
    int iLen;
    int iRet;

    FillMemory( &dbData, sizeof(DBDATA), 0 );

    /* get record information from the user */
    iRet = DoDialog( hWnd, &dbData, DB_SEARCH );
    if (!iRet)
    {
        return;                         // user entered nothing
    }

    /* set record status */
    dbData.iStatus = 0;                 // no fields contain valid data

    /* if user entered a phone string, change field status */
    iLen = lstrlen( dbData.szPhone );
    if (iLen)
```

```
{
    dbData.iStatus = STATUS_SEARCHNUMBER;
}

/* if user entered a name string, change field status */
iLen = lstrlen( dbData.szName );
if (iLen)
{
    dbData.iStatus = dbData.iStatus | STATUS_SEARCHNAME;
}

// Give the target information to the server in a Poke
// transaction. Poking into the Search item causes the server
// to seek a matching record.

DdeClientTransaction(
    (LPBYTE)&dbData,              // data to pass
    sizeof(dbData),              // size of data in bytes
    hconvDB,                     // handle to existing conversation
    hszSearch,                   // string handle for item name
    CF_TEXT,                     // format of data in dbData
    XTYP_POKE,                   // transaction type
    DDE_TIMEOUT,                 // maximum wait period
    &dwResult );                 // status flags (returned)

// Begin a hot advise loop waiting for the search to end.
// The server treats a successful search as a change in the
// "Search" item value and calls DdePostAdvise in order to
// return the found information.

DdeClientTransaction(
    NULL,                        // data to pass
    0,                           // size of data
    hconvDB,                     // handle to existing conversation
    hszSearch,                   // string handle for item name
    CF_TEXT,                     // format for requested data
    XTYP_ADVSTART,               // transaction type
    TIMEOUT_ASYNC,               // send response to DdeCallback
    &dwResult );                 // status flags (returned)

    return;
}
```

```
/*-----------------------------------------------------------------
        DO DELETE
        Ask the user for record information, search for the
        record, and delete it when found.
    ------------------------------------------------------------*/

void DoDelete ( HWND hWnd )
{
    DBDATA dbData;                          // describes the record to delete
    DWORD dwResult;                         // function return values
    int iRet;

    FillMemory( &dbData, sizeof(DBDATA), 0 );

    /* get info from user */
    iRet = DoDialog( hWnd, &dbData, DB_DELETE );
    if (!iRet)
    {
        return;
    }

    // Pass the information to the server in a Poke transaction.
    // Poking the Delete item causes the server to search and delete.

    DdeClientTransaction(
        (LPBYTE)&dbData,                    // data to pass
        sizeof(dbData),                     // size of data
        hconvDB,                            // current conversation
        hszDelete,                          // string handle for item name
        CF_TEXT,                            // format of info in dbData
        XTYP_POKE,                          // transaction type
        DDE_TIMEOUT,                        // maximum wait period
        &dwResult );                        // status flags (returned)

    return;
}


/*-----------------------------------------------------------------
        ADD DATA
        Get information from the user and have the server add a
        new record to the data file.
    ------------------------------------------------------------*/
```

```
void AddData ( HWND hWnd )
{
    DBDATA dbData;                          // info from the user
    HDDEDATA hDDEData;                      // data object containing dbData
    DWORD dwResult;                         // return values
    int iRet;

    FillMemory( &dbData, sizeof(DBDATA), 0 );

    /* get information from the user */
    iRet = DoDialog( hWnd, &dbData, DB_ADD );
    if (!iRet)
    {
        return;             // user pressed Cancel on the Add Data dialog box
    }

    // Poking data on the Add item causes the server to append the
    // new record to the end of the file.

    hDDEData = DdeClientTransaction(
        (LPBYTE)&dbData,                    // new data
        sizeof(dbData),                     // size of data
        hconvDB,                            // conversation
        hszAdd,                             // string handle for item name
        CF_TEXT,                            // format of data in dbData
        XTYP_POKE,                          // type of transaction
        DDE_TIMEOUT,                        // max time to wait
        &dwResult );                        // status flags (returned)
    return;
}

/*------------------------------------------------------------------
        DISPLAY DATA
        Given a handle to a data object from the server, call a
        dialog box to display the contents.
    --------------------------------------------------------------*/

void DisplayData ( HDDEDATA hData )
{
    DBDATA DBData;                          // buffer for hData information

    /* copy the data into DBData */
    DdeGetData( hData,                      // data object
        (LPBYTE)&DBData,                    // buffer for copied data
        sizeof(DBDATA),                     // size of buffer
```

```
        0 );                                    // offset to beginning of data

    /* is the record empty? */
    if (lstrlen(DBData.szName) == 0)
    {
        MessageBox( NULL, "No match was found", szCaption,
            MB_OK | MB_ICONINFORMATION );
    }
    else
    {
        /* show data in a dialog box */
        DoDialog( hwndMain, &DBData, DB_RESULT );
    }
    return;
}


/*--------------------------------------------------------------------
        DO CONNECT
        Begin a conversation with a server on the topic "DB Topic".
    --------------------------------------------------------------------*/

void DoConnect ( HWND hWnd )
{
    HMENU hMenu;

    hconvDB = DdeConnect(                   // find a server
        dwID,                               // instance identifer
        hszService,                         // service name
        hszTopic,                           // topic name ("DB Topic")
        (PCONVCONTEXT)NULL );               // default context
    if (!hconvDB)
    {
        MessageBox( hWnd, "Unable to connect to the server", szCaption,
            MB_OK | MB_ICONEXCLAMATION );
        return;
    }

    /* enable menu items that work only with an existing conversation */
    hMenu = GetMenu( hWnd );
    if (hMenu)
    {
        EnableMenuItem( hMenu, IDM_CONNECT, MF_GRAYED );
        EnableMenuItem( hMenu, IDM_DISCONNECT, MF_ENABLED );
        EnableMenuItem( hMenu, IDM_ADD, MF_ENABLED );
        EnableMenuItem( hMenu, IDM_DELETE, MF_ENABLED );
```

```
            EnableMenuItem( hMenu, IDM_SEARCH, MF_ENABLED );
        }
        return;
    }

/*------------------------------------------------------------------
        DO DISCONNECT
        Disconnects from a server, ending any pending transactions.
    ------------------------------------------------------------------*/

void DoDisconnect ( HWND hWnd )
{
    HMENU hMenu;
    BOOL bTest;

    if (hconvDB)                                    // are we having a conversation?
    {
        bTest = DdeDisconnect( hconvDB );   // end a conversation
        if (!bTest)
        {
            MessageBox( hWnd, "Unable to disconnect from the server",
                szCaption, MB_OK | MB_ICONEXCLAMATION );
            return;
        }
    }

    hconvDB = (HCONV)NULL;                           // remove all traces

    /* disable menu choices that require a conversation */
    hMenu = GetMenu( hWnd );
    if (hMenu)
    {
        EnableMenuItem( hMenu, IDM_DISCONNECT, MF_GRAYED );
        EnableMenuItem( hMenu, IDM_CONNECT, MF_ENABLED );
        EnableMenuItem( hMenu, IDM_ADD, MF_GRAYED );
        EnableMenuItem( hMenu, IDM_DELETE, MF_GRAYED );
        EnableMenuItem( hMenu, IDM_SEARCH, MF_GRAYED );
    }
    return;
}


/*------------------------------------------------------------------
        START DDE
        Register DBCLIENT with the DDEML.
    ------------------------------------------------------------------*/
```

```
BOOL StartDDE ( void )
{
    UINT uErr;                          // return value

    /* tell the DDEML who we are */
    uErr = DdeInitialize( &dwID,        // instance ID (returned)
        (PFNCALLBACK)DdeCallback,       // program's DDEML callback
        APPCLASS_STANDARD               // not a DDEML monitor
        | APPCMD_CLIENTONLY,            // no server functions
        0L );                           // reserved

    if (uErr != DMLERR_NO_ERROR)
    {
        return( FALSE );
    }

    return( TRUE );
}

/*-----------------------------------------------------------------
        STOP DDE
        End the current conversation, release all DDE-related
        resources, and withdraw from the DDEML.
    -----------------------------------------------------------*/

void StopDDE( void )
{
    if (hconvDB)                                // end conversation
    {
        DdeDisconnect( hconvDB );
    }

    if (hszService)
    {
        DdeFreeStringHandle( dwID, hszService );
    }

    if (hszTopic)
    {
        DdeFreeStringHandle( dwID, hszTopic );
    }
```

```
    if (hszAdd)
    {
        DdeFreeStringHandle( dwID, hszAdd );
    }

    if (hszDelete)
    {
        DdeFreeStringHandle( dwID, hszDelete );
    }

    if (hszSearch)
    {
        DdeFreeStringHandle( dwID, hszSearch );
    }

    DdeUninitialize( dwID );                // end DDEML session
    return;
}

/*-------------------------------------------------------------------
        DDE CALLBACK
        Respond to messages from the DDEML.
   -------------------------------------------------------------------*/
HDDEDATA CALLBACK DdeCallback (
    UINT uType,                         // message type
    UINT uFmt,                          // data format
    HCONV hConv,                        // conversation handle
    HSZ hsz1,                           // first string handle (topic)
    HSZ hsz2,                           // second string handle (item)
    HDDEDATA hData,                     // a data object
    DWORD dwData1,                      // transaction-specific data
    DWORD dwData2 )                     // transaction-specific data
{

    switch (uType)
    {
        // When the client asks the server to search for a
        // record, it starts a hot advise loop.  When the
        // search ends, the server sends an ADVDATA message.
        // After the client receives the data, it ends
        // the loop.
```

```
    case XTYP_ADVDATA:                    // hot link update
        DisplayData( hData );             // display new data

        /* end the advise loop */
        DdeClientTransaction(
            NULL, 0,                      // no data
            hConv,                        // conversation
            hsz2,                         // item name
            CF_TEXT,                      // format of data
            XTYP_ADVSTOP,                 // type of transaction
            DDE_TIMEOUT,                  // max time to wait
            (LPDWORD)NULL );              // ignore status flags

        return( (HDDEDATA)TRUE );

    case XTYP_DISCONNECT:                 // server is leaving
        hconvDB = (HCONV)NULL;
        DoDisconnect( hwndMain );
        return( (HDDEDATA)NULL );

    default:
        break;
    }

    return( FALSE );
    UNREFERENCED_PARAMETER( uFmt );
    UNREFERENCED_PARAMETER( hConv );
    UNREFERENCED_PARAMETER( hsz1 );
    UNREFERENCED_PARAMETER( hsz2 );
    UNREFERENCED_PARAMETER( dwData1 );
    UNREFERENCED_PARAMETER( dwData2 );
}
```

The Dialog Module

Many of the client's command procedures invoke one of the program's four dialog boxes. The four boxes are very much alike, so a single dialog procedure can manage any of them. Before DoDialog creates a dialog box, it sets the static variable iDialogType to one of the four values DB_ADD, DB_DELETE, DB_SEARCH, or DB_RESULT. The dialog procedure refers to iDialogType to decide, for example, whether the user must enter both a name and a phone number string. Add and Delete require both fields, but either field by itself works for the Search command. The global variable DBData passes a record between the dialog module and the main program. DisplayResult passes information into its dialog box, but the other three use the buffer to pass information back to the main program. SetData takes information from the buffer to initialize the dialog controls. StoreData copies information from the controls to the buffer.

```
/*------------------------------------------------------------------

        DIALOG.C

        Part of DBCLIENT, a DDEML client of a database program.
        Raises dialog boxes for the user to enter and view
        records from the database.

        FUNCTIONS
                DoDialog                invoke one of 4 dialog boxes
                Data_DlgProc            run any of the dialog boxes
                Data_OnCommand          respond to push buttons
                SetData                 put data in dialog box controls
                StoreData               copy data from dialog box controls

        from Mastering Windows NT Programming
        copyright 1993 by Brian Myers & Eric Hamer

        ----------------------------------------------------------------*/

#define STRICT
#include <windows.h>
#include <windowsx.h>
#include "db.h"                         // global to client and server
#include "dbclient.h"

/*------------------------------------------------------------------
        PROTOTYPES
        ----------------------------------------------------------------*/

BOOL WINAPI Data_DlgProc( HWND hDlg, UINT uMessage, WPARAM wParam,
    LPARAM lParam );
void Data_OnCommand( HWND hDlg, int iCmd, HWND hwndCtl, UINT uNotify );
void SetData( HWND hDlg );
BOOL StoreData( HWND hDlg );
```

```
/*---------------------------------------------------------------
        STATIC VARIABLES
        -------------------------------------------------------*/

DBDATA DBData;                              // holds one record
int iDialogType;                            // identifies current dialog

/*---------------------------------------------------------------
        DO DIALOG
        Create a dialog box.  The iType parameter controls which
        dialog box will be created.
        -------------------------------------------------------*/

int DoDialog (
    HWND hWnd,                              // program window
    PDBDATA pDBData,                        // data for one record
    int iType )                            // Add, Search, Delete?
{
    HINSTANCE hInst;
    int iRet;

    hInst = GetWindowInstance( hWnd );

    switch (iType)
    {
        case DB_ADD:
            iDialogType = DB_ADD;
            iRet = DialogBox( hInst, MAKEINTRESOURCE(DLG_ADDDATA), hWnd,
                    (DLGPROC)Data_DlgProc);
            break;

        case DB_DELETE:
            iDialogType = DB_DELETE;
            iRet = DialogBox( hInst, MAKEINTRESOURCE(DLG_DELETEDATA), hWnd,
                    (DLGPROC)Data_DlgProc);
            break;

        case DB_SEARCH:
            iDialogType = DB_SEARCH;
            iRet = DialogBox( hInst, MAKEINTRESOURCE(DLG_SEARCHDATA), hWnd,
                    (DLGPROC)Data_DlgProc);
            break;
```

```
        case DB_RESULT:
            iDialogType = DB_RESULT;
            lstrcpy( DBData.szName, pDBData->szName );
            lstrcpy( DBData.szPhone, pDBData->szPhone);
            iRet = DialogBox(hInst, MAKEINTRESOURCE(DLG_RESULTDATA), hWnd,
                        (DLGPROC)Data_DlgProc);
            break;

        default:
            break;
    }

    if ((iRet) && (iDialogType != DB_RESULT))
    {
        lstrcpy( pDBData->szName, DBData.szName );
        lstrcpy( pDBData->szPhone, DBData.szPhone );
        pDBData->iStatus = STATUS_VALID;    // mark record in use
    }

    return( iRet );
}


/*-------------------------------------------------------------------
        ADD DIALOG PROCEDURE
        Process messages for any of the data dialog boxes
    -----------------------------------------------------------------*/
BOOL WINAPI Data_DlgProc (
    HWND hDlg,
    UINT uMessage,
    WPARAM wParam,
    LPARAM lParam )
{
    switch (uMessage)
    {
        case WM_INITDIALOG:
            if (iDialogType == DB_RESULT)
            {
                SetData( hDlg );
            }
            return( TRUE );

        case WM_COMMAND:
            Data_OnCommand( hDlg,
                (int)(LOWORD(wParam)),          // command ID
```

```
                    (HWND)(lParam),              // control window
                    (UINT)HIWORD(wParam) );      // notification code
                break;
        }

    return( FALSE );
}

/*--------------------------------------------------------------------
        Data_OnCommand
        Respond to WM_COMMAND messages from the dialog push buttons.
    ----------------------------------------------------------------*/

void Data_OnCommand (
    HWND hDlg,
    int iCmd,
    HWND hwndCtl,
    UINT uNotify )
{
    BOOL bTest;

    if (iCmd == IDOK)
    {
        bTest = StoreData( hDlg );
        if (bTest)
        {
            EndDialog( hDlg, TRUE );
        }
        return;
    }
    else if (iCmd == IDCANCEL)
    {
        EndDialog( hDlg, FALSE );
        return;
    }

    UNREFERENCED_PARAMETER( hwndCtl );
    UNREFERENCED_PARAMETER( uNotify );
}

/*--------------------------------------------------------------------
        SET DATA
        Copy name and phone number from DBData to the dialog's
        edit controls.
    ----------------------------------------------------------------*/
```

```
void SetData ( HWND hDlg )
{
    SetDlgItemText( hDlg, IDD_NAMEEDIT, DBData.szName );
    SetDlgItemText( hDlg, IDD_PHONEEDIT, DBData.szPhone );

    return;
}

/*-------------------------------------------------------------------
        STORE DATA
        Copy data from the dialog's edit controls to the DBData
        static variable.  Confirm that the user has entered
        the strings the program expects.  Return FALSE if the
        dialog needs more information to complete a particular
        command.
    -----------------------------------------------------------------*/

BOOL StoreData ( HWND hDlg )
{
    int iNameLen;                           // length of name entry
    int iNumLen;                            // length of phone number entry
    BOOL bValid = TRUE;                     // FALSE if more info is needed

    iNameLen = GetDlgItemText( hDlg, IDD_NAMEEDIT, DBData.szName,
        sizeof(DBData.szName) );

    iNumLen = GetDlgItemText( hDlg, IDD_PHONEEDIT, DBData.szPhone,
        sizeof(DBData.szPhone) );

    // To add or delete a record, force the user to
    // provide both a name and a phone number.

    if ((iDialogType == DB_ADD)             // adding a record
        || (iDialogType == DB_DELETE))      // deleting a record
    {
        if ((!iNameLen) || (!iNumLen))      // prevent empty fields
        {
            MessageBox( hDlg, "Please fill both fields.", szCaption,
                MB_OK | MB_ICONEXCLAMATION );
            bValid = FALSE;
        }
    }
```

```
// In the Search dialog box, force the user to enter
// at least one search criterion.

else if (iDialogType != DB_RESULT)        // not showing search result
{
    if ((!iNameLen) && (!iNumLen))        // insist on getting some data
    {
        MessageBox( hDlg, "Please fill one field", szCaption,
            MB_OK | MB_ICONEXCLAMATION );
        bValid = FALSE;
    }
}


// If more information is needed, set the input focus
// on an empty field so the user can start typing
// right away.

if (!bValid)
{
    if (!iNameLen)                             // name field empty?
    {
        SetFocus( GetDlgItem(hDlg, IDD_NAMEEDIT) );
    }
    else if (!iNumLen)                         // phone field empty?
    {
        SetFocus( GetDlgItem(hDlg, IDD_PHONEEDIT) );
    }
}

return( bValid );
}
```

To review, the DDEML is an interprocess communication (IPC) facility. It supports conversations between different programs. Programs converse with each other in order to share data or to give each other commands. Link transactions pass information from the server to the client, Pokes carry data from the client to the server, and Executes give the server commands to carry out.

To use the DDEML, a program must create many string handles and data objects. These standard objects accommodate data in a variety of formats and allow the DDE library to manage the details of allocating and releasing shared objects. Knowing when to release what has always been one of the difficulties in DDE programs. The DDEML simplifies the rules.

- Always call **DdeFreeStringHandle** eventually for any string handle you create.

- A server calls **DdeFreeDataHandle** only for data objects it owns. The server owns any objects that have never been passed to a DDEML function, and it owns anything created with the **HDATA_APPOWNED** flag.

- A client does not free the data handle it receives as a parameter in its **DdeCallback** procedure. A client must free any data handle it receives as the immediate return value from a synchronous DDEML command.

When programming the DDEML under Windows NT, don't forget that the instance identifier required by most DDEML commands is local to the thread where it was created. As a result, a single thread must manage most of the DDEML commands for any one service. If you create other threads to work in the background, they must pass their results back to the main thread, not to the DDE Library.

The next two chapters present another IPC facility. Like DDE, the OLE protocol exists to integrate programs by letting them share data. The DDEML works well for programs that require many small data links, the transmission of command strings, or other interactions actively initiated and maintained by programs rather than the user. Object linking and embedding, as you will see, integrate programs in ways that are more complex and more powerful.

Writing an OLE Client

- Object Linking and Embedding

- Storing compound documents

- Virtual tables

- Link mechanisms

- Reading the registry

Object Linking and Embedding (OLE) is a set of protocols and procedures proposed by Aldus Corporation in 1988 to simplify the creation and maintenance of compound documents. A *compound document* is a file belonging to one application (for example, a word processor) that also includes data created by another application (such as a graphics editor). Blocks of foreign data in a compound document are called *objects*. An application that receives data objects and builds compound documents is called an OLE *client*, and one that exports objects for other applications to use is called an OLE *server*.

When Microsoft built OLE into Windows, it took a big step toward making the user's work center on documents rather than applications. Traditionally, the user invokes a single application for each new document. Changing from one data format to another—from text to numbers or from pictures to sounds—usually means quitting one application and starting another. Typically, in an application-based environment, a document makes sense only when read by the application that created it.

A document-based environment, on the other hand, lets several applications cooperate in creating a single document. No one application understands all the objects in the document, but as you move from piece to piece the system automatically invokes the appropriate applications. You edit the pieces separately in their native applications, and the master document automatically receives updates from every contributor. You have more freedom to exercise creativity in combining sounds, video, pictures, numbers, and text in a single, integrated document. You can show pictures in your word processor or attach video clips to records in a database.

Compound documents existed in Windows before OLE, but their capabilities were very limited. A user would create a compound document by copying data to the clipboard and pasting it into another application. In this common transaction a data object moves from a server to a client program. But whenever the server subsequently edits its copy of the object, the cut-and-paste operation must be repeated *for all documents into which the object has been pasted*.

OLE provides two more powerful ways of storing server data in a client's document. The first is *embedding*. Embedding, just like pasting, gives the client a complete and independent copy of the data. An embedded object, however, remembers its origin, and the user can edit an embedded document by double-clicking it. The double-click invokes the server application and the editing happens there. When the user closes the server, the client receives the updated object. The second way of storing objects is to *link* them. Linking does not give the client its own independent copy of the data; instead the client receives a live connection to a piece of the server's document, a kind of window opening into a view of the server's data. If the object is modified in the server, the modifications appear automatically in the client. If several clients link to the same object, an update in one place is visible in all the others.

Whether an application is a client or a server depends on its role in a particular interaction. One application may act simultaneously as a client and a server in different interactions.

To create a document-based environment, the system must offer substantial facilities for coordinating applications. For example, the system must know which applications can operate on which kinds of data. As the user moves from object to object through a document, the system must recognize and support links to various other programs. In Windows, the OLE extension libraries assume these complex chores. The three libraries that implement OLE currently contain about 70 functions to help you create programs that handle virtually any kind of data object through a seamless cooperation with the program that created it.

In our experience, programming for OLE is one of the most complex tasks facing a Windows developer. The OLE APIs enforce a particular structure on the program, and one not readily familiar to most programmers when they first encounter it. Although the large command set includes many commands to accomplish high-level tasks, learning the vocabulary of the new commands can be a slow process. At first the semantics of the new command names seem fuzzy and discovering which are necessary for a given action difficult. Also, many of the structures and commands must be in place before you can begin testing any of the code. The overview that follows should help you find your way. This chapter leads up to a sample client program. Chapter 15 covers more briefly the design of an OLE server and ends with a description of the new features expected from OLE 2.0.

CONCEPTS

Like the DDEML, OLE gives you high-level functions to implement low-level data-sharing processes. The OLE functions reside in three dynamic link libraries. ole-cli32.dll contains all the functions for an OLE client, and olesvr32.dll contains the functions for an OLE server. In OLE 1.0, these two libraries exchange data and commands through DDE messages. The third library, shell32.dll, maintains a database of servers and data types to ensure that requests for assistance are routed correctly. When a client asks for help changing a bitmap, the OLE system searches the system registry for an appropriate editor. When a client wants to play a sound package, the system knows which server plays sounds.

Interacting through the OLE Libraries

OLE applications interact with each other through the libraries. When a client, for example, decides to edit a picture object, it passes the request to the OleCli DLL. OleCli sends a message to OleSvr. OleSvr locates a server and asks it to begin an editing session. The interaction of client and server through the OLE libraries is shown schematically in Figure 14.1.

FIGURE 14.1:

How the three OLE libraries interact with client and server applications

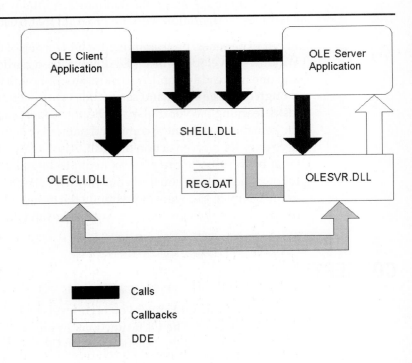

When a user initiates an OLE operation in the client application—for example, by double-clicking an embedded graphic—the client issues a sequence of calls to Ole-Cli, the client library. OleCli forwards the request to OleSvr, which in turn invokes the server application to perform the operation. When the operation has completed, OleSvr passes the results back to OleCli, and OleCli passes them on to the client. When the user activates an object, the OleSvr library must determine which server application corresponds to the given data format. To identify servers, OleSvr consults the Shell library. The Shell functions manage the system registry, which maps each data type to a server application name. Servers add their own names to the registry during their installation.

Incidentally, the registry also holds other information about integrating files in the Windows system. The File Manager reads registration information when you ask to open or run files. The Shell library also contains the drag-and-drop commands. Although the drag-and-drop commands do not use the registry, they, like OLE and the File Manager, all provide different services for integrating applications. You can examine and modify your system's registry with regedt32.exe, the Registry Editor.

Comparing the DDEML and OLE

Like the DDEML, the OLE libraries work through the DDE protocol. OLE commands send DDE messages. The complicated links OLE creates form a superstructure over the basic cold, hot, and warm links of DDE. The underlying DDE processes are invisible to an OLE application. Because Microsoft developed the DDEML and OLE systems in parallel, neither relies on the other. Also, neither OLE 1.0 nor the DDEML is fully multithreading; all of a server's DDEML or OLE calls should be made from a single thread.

To choose between the DDEML and OLE, consider what your application needs to do. For maintaining many links and updating them all frequently, choose the DDEML. One DDEML conversation can establish many links, but each OLE conversation transfers only a single object. OLE clients can of course initiate several conversations with one server, but this incurs an overhead that the DDEML avoids. DDEML links, however, die when either participant terminates. Choose OLE when you want to support persistent embedding and linking, rendering of common data formats, rendering of specialized data formats through the server, transferring data through the clipboard and through files, or activating objects.

Defining Terms

An object is any set of data from one application treated as a unit. OLE applications create compound documents when they combine several objects in one file. The user sees all the objects from one document displayed together in a single window. To the client program, each object looks like a black box full of incomprehensible data. The program calls OLE functions to manipulate objects; it does not need to understand them. When importing an object, a client chooses between linking and embedding. When a document file contains all the data for an object, the object is embedded. When a document contains only a reference pointing to data in another document, the object is linked.

Both methods produce the same result on the screen, but only linked objects receive updates. Embedded objects are transferred through the equivalent of a cold DDE link; when you copy them into your document they become independent of their source. By contrast, if you link an object into several documents, changing the object in one place causes it to change in all the others. Linked objects take less space in the document file, but documents that contain only embedded objects can move from system to system and carry all their data with them. The user can change linked objects into embedded objects at will.

If you embed a Paintbrush picture in a Write document, Paintbrush is the server and Write is the client. Write does not need to understand the data that makes up the image file. Write calls OLE functions to display the data. If the OLE system doesn't know how, it calls on the server, Paintbrush, to display data in the Write window. It's true that many word processors can import graphics images into a text document, but they don't have any commands to let you edit the image once it's there—and if they did, they could supply only rudimentary editing tools. But OLE draws on the full power and flexibility of the object's originator to manipulate the disparate objects in a compound document. If you link video clips into a database, you can still play the clips even though the database program knows nothing about video formats. The client database calls on the server video program to handle its own data.

The type of data a server exports is called an *object class*. Paintbrush, for example, exports objects of the PBrush class. Different classes contain different kinds of data. Excel supports the classes ExcelWorksheet and ExcelChart. Servers register their classes in the system registry. Only one server may handle each class.

For each of its object classes, a server also registers a set of verbs. A *verb* is something a server can do to an object. Two common verbs are Edit and Play. When the user selects an object in a compound document, the client application retrieves the list of verbs for that object class and makes the verbs available on one of its menus. The user manipulates objects by executing their verbs.

OLE is virtually unlimited in its scope. An OLE application you write now will work perfectly well even if it encounters a server that supplies data in a format Microsoft hasn't anticipated. Microsoft doesn't need to anticipate formats; if a server can handle the data, any client can receive it. A user may well apply OLE programs to tasks the developer never imagined.

Sample Interactions

The process of adding an object to a container document is simple. From within the client application, the user chooses the type of object to insert. A list box might offer, for example, picture data, spreadsheet data, and video clips; the list varies with the available servers. If you're running Write and decide to embed a drawing in your document, you might begin by starting Paintbrush, the registered server for bitmap objects. Open a .BMP file, select part of the image, and copy it to the clipboard. Then you enter Write and open the destination file. Pull down the Edit menu and you'll have a choice of three commands: Paste, Paste Link, and Paste Special. All of them bring the drawing into the text file. The easiest one, Paste, embeds the object. (If Paintbrush did not support OLE then the Paste command would merely copy the object, not embed it.) Later, if the object needs changes the user double-clicks it to recall the server. The illustrations in Figure 14.2 show the process of linking a picture into a text document, editing the picture, and having the changes appear in the linked document.

1. Create the picture using a graphics program and copy it to the clipboard.

2. Create the container document using an editor and paste-link the picture.

3. Activate the linked object and update the picture from inside the graphics program.

4. The changes appear in the editor.

FIGURE 14.2:

Linking a picture into a text document and activating the picture to edit it

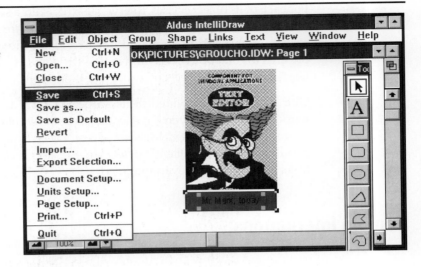

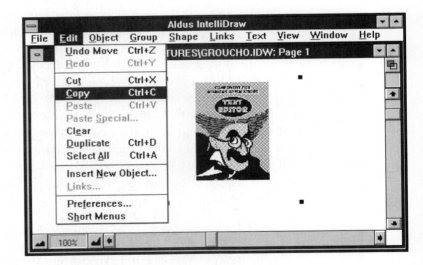

FIGURE 14.2:

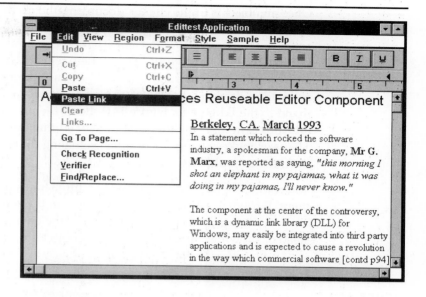

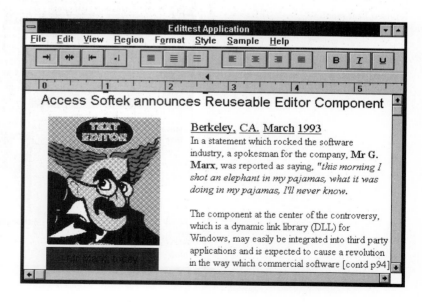

Once an object is in the client's document, the client provides ways to activate it. Usually double-clicking activates an object. An activated object performs whatever action is appropriate to its format. The server defines actions appropriate to its objects by listing a set of verbs in the system registry. Different objects respond to different verbs. A Paintbrush drawing has only the verb Edit. When you select an embedded drawing, the client application adds an Edit Paintbrush Picture command to the Edit menu. Figure 14.3 shows the revised menu. The Edit verb for an OLE object invokes another program for editing the data and copies the object to it. The user makes changes and quits, signaling on termination that the compound document should be updated.

You could also embed a .WAV file (a multimedia sound file) in a compound document. But what would a sound look like on the screen when you paste it? You'd have to use a graphical representation of the data, and this is called a *package*. Instead of showing a linked or embedded object directly, you can choose to represent

FIGURE 14.3:

Revised Edit menu

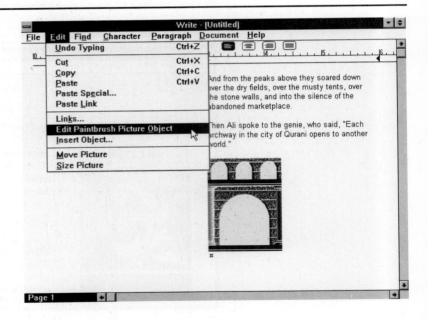

it with an icon. A package is an icon that represents an OLE object. When you double-click the icon, the OLE libraries determine what data the object contains and perform the appropriate verb action. For some data types, such as .WAV files, only packages make sense. By default, the package icon comes from the program that created the data, as shown in Figure 14.4. There, a sound package has been pasted into a Cardfile entry, and the Edit menu now offers two verbs associated with sound data: Play and Edit. Using the Object Packager program that comes with Windows, you can customize both the icon and the label of any package.

Eventually, with the help of some OLE functions, the client application saves the compound document. The document can then be transferred from user to user and read by the same client application on other computers. If the new system lacks some servers, all the objects will still display correctly because the OLE system itself handles standard clipboard formats like bitmaps and metafiles in any client without calling a server. You can't activate objects without a server, though. You can't do much with .WAV packages, for example, unless you have the Sound Recorder.

FIGURE 14.4:

Edit menu with sound verbs

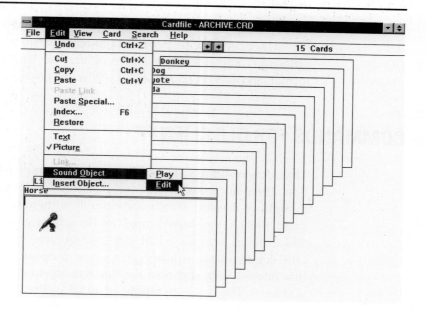

Presentation and Native Data Formats

Two of OLE's goals seem to place contradictory demands on data objects. In order to display the object in any application, whether or not the original server is present in the system, the object must contain data in some common, recognizable display format, such as metafiles or bitmaps. On the other hand, OLE also lets the user continue to edit objects even *after* they are pasted into a new application, and in order for the server to edit objects they must contain whatever data the server uses to represent them internally. Excel, for example, can't continue to edit spreadsheet cells that have been converted for display as a metafile, but neither can client programs—or even the OLE libraries—be expected to understand Excel's internal data well enough to display the cells by themselves on systems where Excel is not installed.

The solution, of course, is to supply two copies of the data for every OLE object. You'll read more in the next chapter about how the server does this, but essentially every OLE object contains data in a *Native* format, as the server created it, and in one of several standard *presentation* formats—usually a metafile—so anyone can display it.

There are not many differences between 16-bit and 32-bit versions of OLE 1.0, but one of them is that OLE benefits automatically from the enhanced metafiles we described in Chapter 9. 32-bit OLE recognizes `CF_ENHMETAFILE` as a new presentation format, and servers should use it whenever possible.

COMMANDS FOR OLE CLIENTS

This section summarizes the procedures for implementing an OLE client application. There are too many new OLE commands for us to treat all of them in detail, though we do stop to examine enough of them to show you how they work. Instead, this section steps through all the actions an OLE client commonly performs and explains how the client implements each one. Our narration encounters the OLE commands in clusters grouped by purpose. Scan the headers for operations that interest you, and read the descriptions to determine which OLE commands you need. The basic operations of an OLE client include registering with the system, opening container documents, receiving objects through the clipboard, putting objects on the clipboard, activating objects, removing objects from documents, and storing files that include objects. To perform any of these actions the client calls functions from the OleCli library. To write an OLE client you must include the ole.h header file in your source code and link with the olecli32.lib import library.

Installing an OLE Application

When any OLE application, client or server, is first installed, it should check the version numbers of the current olecli32.dll, olesvr32.dll, and shell32.dll files. OLE programs are usually distributed with their own copies of these three libraries, enabling them to upgrade any system if necessary. Two functions return the version numbers of the client and server libraries: **OleQueryClientVersion** and **OleQueryServerVersion**.

Initializing the Client

An OLE client performs two standard tasks as it starts up. It registers the three clipboard data formats all OLE applications must request. OLE transactions rely on several new clipboard formats. Since the formats are peculiar to OLE and not standard for the Windows system, OLE programs must register the new formats when they initialize. **RegisterClipboardFormat** tells Windows you intend to transfer data in a new format. The function receives a string naming the format and returns a number identifying it. If several applications register the same format, they all receive the same identifying number.

The three formats every OLE application supports are Native, OwnerLink, and ObjectLink. Native data refers to the internal format a server uses when creating an object. Excel, for example, can't directly read Lotus data files because the two spreadsheet programs use different Native formats. Only the server understands its native data, and generally the server edits data only in Native format. OwnerLink is the format for creating an embedded object from the clipboard, and ObjectLink is the format for creating a linked object.

The data for ObjectLink and OwnerLink is simply a set of three null-terminated strings naming an object. The strings give the object's class, the document name, and the item name. An extra null marks the end of the third string. For example, "SERVER\0SVRDOC01.SVR\0PARAGRAPH1\0\0" is valid as ObjectLink or

OwnerLink data. In this case, the item name identifies a paragraph. The contents of an ObjectLink or OwnerLink string are created and understood only by a particular OLE server.

Virtual Tables and Wrapper Structures

Often the OLE libraries need to call some of your procedures directly. The server library, for example, must be able to call functions from the server to perform common operations such as displaying or copying an object. The client library calls procedures in the client, too. OleCli commonly sends event codes to a client callback function, much as the system delivers messages to window procedures.

The OLE libraries need to be given addresses for each of the standard OLE callback functions your program supplies. As part of its initialization, each OLE program passes to either the client or server library several arrays of function pointers. Each array, called a *virtual table* or VTBL, groups together a set of semantically related functions. Borrowing a term from object-oriented programming, the functions in each virtual table are sometimes called *methods*. They are methods for working with a kind of object—a server, a document, or an OLE data object. If you know C++, think of the functions in a VTBL as members of a base class.

A client application needs only three callback procedures and two virtual tables to hold them.

OLESTREAMVTBL	OLECLIENTVTBL
Get	CallBack
Put	

The **OLESTREAMVTBL** table contains two members, Get and Put. These functions are called when OleCli requires the client to load or save an object. They form the core of an I/O stream.

The **OLECLIENTVTBL** holds only one callback procedure. It responds when OleCli signals any of several events concerning a particular object. The events include a change in the status of the object, a request for permission to continue a lengthy operation, or the completion of an asynchronous operation.

A VTBL becomes the core of a larger structure containing all the information the client needs to manipulate a stream or a data object. Usually a client adds other data fields to fill out the description of an object. Think of the virtual table as the basis for defining a C++ class—for example, **_OLESTREAM** and **_OLECLIENT**:

```
typedef struct _OLESTREAM              // one per client document
{
  LPOLESTREAMVTBL pOleStreamTable;
};


typedef struct _OLECLIENT              // one per client object
{
  LPOLECLIENTVTBL pOleClientVTable;
};
```

These structures are defined in ole.h. They are called *wrappers* because they enfold a virtual table. You can think of them as base classes containing methods for handling an I/O stream and a data object. Every client defines its own wrapper structure by adding its own private fields, but the wrappers always begin with an **LPOLESTREAMVTBL** or an **LPOLECLIENTVTBL**. By adding other fields the client program in effect defines its own types derived from base classes. Typically the added fields describe the state of an object. You would then allocate a separate structured variable to represent each new data object.

The Object Wrapper (_OLECLIENT)

Here, for example, is a complete wrapper describing the methods and attributes for an OLE object in the sample program at the end of the chapter:

```
typedef struct tagAPPOLECLIENT        // one per OLE object in client
{
    OLECLIENT OleClient;              // virtual table structure
    LPOLEOBJECT pObjectData;          // an OLE object
    HWND hwndObject;                  // the object's container window
    DWORD dwType;                     // object's type (link/embed/static)
    BOOL bBusy;                       // TRUE if asynch. op. in progress
} APPOLECLIENT, *PAPPOLECLIENT;
```

A compound document contains many objects. To manipulate one of them, the client passes OleCli a pointer to a wrapper structure. OleCli, when it receives the pointer, performs a type-safe conversion casting your object back to its superclass (_OLECLIENT *). In processing the command, OleCli may call functions from the VTBL contained in the wrapper. If the library sends a message back to the client, the message carries the same pointer. The client casts it back into its own type (here, PAPP-OLECLIENT) and regains access to all the application-specific fields. By examining the structure, you can determine the state of the object in question and respond accordingly.

The virtual table in an **_OLECLIENT** wrapper points to the client's callback function where the OleCli library sends signals when something happens that the client should know about. If an object changes, for example, the client receives an **OLE_CHANGED** message. The client might need to respond if an object is closed (**OLE_CLOSED**), renamed (**OLE_RENAMED**), saved (**OLE_SAVED**), or released (**OLE_RE-LEASE**). Also, OleCli paints objects for the client. If the paint operation takes a substantial amount of time, the client receives periodic **OLE_QUERY_PAINT** messages asking whether to continue. And if the server is too busy to respond to a request, the client gets an **OLE_QUERY_RETRY** message.

The I/O Stream Wrapper (_OLESTREAM)

The client's other virtual table, **OLESTREAMVTBL**, implements an OLE stream, a method of reading and writing OLE objects. To the client application, an object is only a set of binary data. A client must have some way to store OLE objects in its own document files, and each client must be able to define its own markers and header structures; the system can't impose a standard for every program's internal files.

The solution is for you to provide your own input and output routines, Get and Put, for OLE objects. The system calls your functions when it needs to write objects to, or read them from, the container document file. Get and Put must be able to read or write any private header you design for marking off foreign objects in your data files, followed by the stream of binary data that comprises an object. Your header information should include the size of the object, passed to your function by OleCli or determined by calling **OleQuerySize**. If you decide to collect all the objects in a file separate from the main document, the header should also indicate the object's location.

The declaration of a stream's virtual table structure shows the prototypes for Get and Put commands:

```
typedef struct _OLESTREAMVTBL
{
    DWORD(CALLBACK* Get)(LPOLESTREAM, void FAR*, DWORD);
    DWORD(CALLBACK* Put)(LPOLESTREAM, OLE_CONST void FAR*, DWORD);
} OLESTREAMVTBL;
typedef OLESTREAMVTBL FAR* LPOLESTREAMVTBL;
```

Again, the virtual table becomes the mandatory first field of a larger wrapper structure. The extra fields in your stream wrapper might, for example, include a file handle. To read or write an object, you pass a stream structure pointer to **OleLoadFromStream** or **OleSaveToStream**, and the client library passes the pointer to either Get or Put. The second parameter of each function points to the object data, and the third tells the object's size in bytes.

Here's an example, again drawn from the sample program, of fields you might add to an OLE stream wrapper:

```
typedef struct tagAPPOLESTREAM          // the document wrapper structure
{
    OLESTREAM OleStream;                 // virtual table structure
    LHCLIENTDOC OleDocHandle;            // OLE document handle
    POBJWINDOWINFO pCurObject;           // currently active object window
    POBJWINDOWINFO pObWindowList;        // base node for document's obj list
    char szDocName[_MAX_PATH];           // document's name
    char szAppClass[MAX_RSRCLEN];        // application name
    HANDLE hFile;                        // handle to a disk file
    int iObjects;                        // total number of objects
    int iBusyObject;                     // number of active objects
}   APPOLESTREAM, *PAPPOLESTREAM;
```

Opening a Document

A client application tells OleCli about each document it opens by calling **OleRegisterClientDoc**. This function has nothing to do with the system registry; OleCli itself maintains registration data for each active client document. **OleRegisterClientDoc** returns a document handle needed to identify the document for other OLE functions.

When opening a compound document that already contains OLE objects, the client calls **OleLoadFromStream** for any objects that should be immediately visible. The client also looks for all the linked objects in the document and updates them. A linked object may be out of date if, for example, the user has recently edited its source document. Some objects are marked to be updated manually; the client lists them for the user and asks whether to freshen them. Objects marked for automatic updates the client freshens immediately, without asking. The **OleUpdate** function changes an object's data and its display.

We lack space to consider in detail all of the roughly 70 functions in the OLE 1.0 API, but we will examine a few along the way to give you a feel for how they work.

```
OLESTATUS OleLoadFromStream(
    LPOLESTREAM lpStream;            // the client's stream wrapper
    LPSTR lpszProtocol;              // StdFileEditing or Static
    LPOLECLIENT lpClient;            // a newly made object wrapper
    LHCLIENTDOC lhClientDoc;         // document handle
    LPSTR lpszObjName;               // client's ID string for the object
    LPOLEOBJECT FAR * lplpObject )   // place to put an object pointer
```

The client calls **OleLoadFromStream** each time it needs to read an OLE object from a file. While the function is running, the OleCli library calls the Get function pointed to from the virtual table in the `lpStream` wrapper structure. It tries to load the object using the protocol in the second parameter. Normal OLE objects use StdFileEditing, but sometimes the user creates static objects, which take up less disk space but cannot be edited as linked and embedded objects can. `lpClient` points to the client's other kind of virtual table, an **OLECLIENTVTBL**, with its callback function. If later the server changes the original object, for example, OleCli notifies the linked client by sending an update code to the callback function. The document handle must already have been created by calling **OleRegisterClientDoc**; it tells the library which document the new object will belong to. When the OLE library finishes loading the OLE object, it places a pointer to the object's data in the last parameter. A client should not try to read or modify the data in an OLE object. Keep the pointer and pass it to OLE functions whenever you want something done to the object.

OLE functions return an **OLESTATUS** value, which is one of a set of defined constants such as **OLE_OK**, **OLE_ERRORSTREAM**, and **OLE_WAIT_FOR_RELEASE**. **OLE_OK** indicates success. Error constants such as **OLE_ERRORSTREAM** indicate a particular problem—in this case, an invalid `lpStream` parameter. **OLE_WAIT_FOR_RELEASE** means the operation will be lengthy and proceed in the background while the program continues. Until the library sends a release notice to the callback function in the lpClient virtual table, the program should consider the new object busy and avoid working with it. We'll show you how in our sample program. Look for the heading "Asynchronous Operations."

Adding New Objects

New OLE objects most commonly arrive through the clipboard. The server copies an object there and the client pastes it into the container document. To embed an object from the clipboard, call **OleCreateFromClip**. To link the object into the document, call **OleCreateLinkFromClip**. The first function copies the entire object into your document, including OwnerLink information and native as well as presentation data; the second writes only the ObjectLink information and a set of presentation data. One difference between DDE and OLE is that DDE makes no provision for using data from a file. **OleCreateFromFile** creates an OLE object by embedding the contents of a disk file. **OleCreateLinkFromFile** imports a linked object, copying in just enough information to indicate the file where the object lives.

New objects, besides coming from the clipboard and disk files, can come from old objects. **OleClone** makes an exact copy of an embedded object. **OleCopyFromLink** makes an embedded copy of an object already linked into a document. **OleCreate-FromTemplate** creates a new object based on an existing one and opens the server to edit the new object.

Finally, an OLE client can create new objects from scratch by calling **OleCreate**. This command starts up a server for any object class. When the user finishes creating the new object, **OleCreate** embeds it in the container document.

Displaying an Object

To display an object, the client must first decide on a bounding rectangle. **OleQueryBounds** returns measurements provided by the server in **MM_HIMETRIC** units (hundredths of a millimeter). The client cannot of course draw data it does not understand; it calls **OleDraw** to display any object in a given rectangle. OleCli understands the presentation formats, such as bitmaps and metafiles, and can render them by itself.

```
OLESTATUS OleDraw(
    LPOLEOBJECT lpObject,            // pointer to the object data
    HDC hDC,                         // destination DC
    const RECT FAR* lprBounds,       // destination rectangle
    const RECT FAR* lprWBounds,      // logical window origin and extents
    HDC hdcFormat );                 // DC for formatting
```

The first parameter must be a value returned by another OLE function such as `OleLoadFromStream` or `OleCreateFromClip`. The first DC parameter tells where the image will appear, and the other DC (rarely different from the first) allows the image to be formatted as though for a different device. The image will be scaled, stretched, or clipped to fit the rectangle in `lprBounds`. The other rectangle, `lprWBounds`, matters only when hDC is a metafile. For metafiles, OleCli needs to be told what window origin and extents it should set first (with `SetWindowOrgEx` and `SetWindowExtEx`). These four values are passed in `lprWBounds`.

To print an object, call `OleDraw` with a printer DC.

Executing an Object's Verbs

The server registers a set of actions called *verbs* for each object class it supports. When the user double-clicks an object to activate it, the client should execute the object's primary verb, or the first in the object's list of verbs. To execute a verb, call `OleActivate`. You specify the verb by number, and the primary verb is always 0. When the user activates an object, call `OleActivate` with a verb value of 0.

```
OLESTATUS OleActivate(
    LPOLEOBJECT lpObject,          // an OLE object
    UINT uVerb,                    // index into verb list
    BOOL bShow,                    // TRUE to show server window
    BOOL bTakeFocus,               // TRUE to give server the focus
    HWND hWnd,                     // document window where object appears
    const RECT FAR* lpBounds );    // bounding rectangle in document window
```

Again, `lpObject` points to the black-box data buffer returned previously when another OLE function inserted a new object in a document. uVerb is a number telling which of the object's verbs `OleActivate` should have the server execute. The client may if it wishes retrieve a full list of an object's verbs from the registry with `RegQueryValue`. (See the section "Insert Object" a little later in this chapter.) Often, however, this value is simply 0 to request the primary verb, the object's default action. The Boolean variables control whether the server window should become visible to perform the action (it should to edit, for example) and whether the server should be given the input focus as soon as it appears. The last two parameters describe the object's current location. The rectangle coordinates in `lpBounds` are expressed in whatever logical units the client uses in its device context.

Running the Edit Menu

As part of its duties, an OLE client application supports an expanded Edit menu like the ones in Figures 14.3 and 14.4. Note how the menus in those figures change depending on the object selected. The OLE libraries include some commands to make operating the Edit menu easy. To copy an object to the clipboard, call `OleCopyToClipboard`. To cut an object from a document to the clipboard, call `OleCopyToClipboard` followed by `OleDelete`. Here's what OLE applications do for the other commands.

Undo

Even though the client can't edit its linked and embedded objects, you can still have an Undo command if you call `OleClone` before you activate an object and save a copy in its original state. If the user then chooses Undo, `OleDelete` removes the modified version and you replace it with the saved original.

Paste

The Paste menu option should be enabled whenever an object is on the clipboard. Use the `OleQueryCreateFromClip` function to determine whether the clipboard data is an OLE object. If the user selects Paste when the clipboard contains an OLE object, call `OleCreateFromClip` to embed the object.

Paste Link

The Paste Link option should be enabled whenever `OleQueryLinkFromClip` returns `OLE_OK`. If the user selects Paste Link, call `OleCreateLinkFromClip` to add the object to your compound document.

Normally `OleCreateFromClip` creates an embedded object and `OleCreateLink-FromClip` creates a linked object, but the actual result depends on the order of the data on the clipboard. Follow up either creation function with `OleQueryType` to find out exactly what happened.

Paste Special

Often a server provides data in a variety of formats and the client indicates a default preference. A single server may, for example, offer a piece of text on the clipboard as formatted text, ASCII text, a bitmap, and a metafile. The client chooses a presentation format. The optional Paste Special command lets the user choose the format, overriding the client's default choice. A typical Paste Special dialog box offers a choice of formats and buttons for embedding (Paste) or linking (Paste Link), as shown in Figure 14.5. In response to this command the client calls **EnumClipboard-Formats** to generate a list of all the formats currently available. It displays the list in a dialog box. The user picks a format and presses a button either to link or to embed the object.

FIGURE 14.5:

Typical Paste Special dialog box

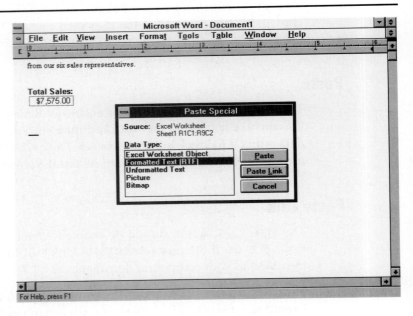

Class Name Object

When the user selects an object in a compound document, the client adds a menu command to activate the object by executing its verbs. If the object has more than one verb, they appear in a cascading submenu, as shown in Figure 14.4. When the user selects a verb, call **OleActivate** to perform it.

The string naming the object's class is part of the **_OLEOBJECT** structure the client receives from the OleCli library. The verb names come from the registry, and you read them the same way you read object class names for the Insert Object command.

Insert Object

Like Paste Special, the Insert Object command is optional. The command lets the user create a new object from scratch by choosing an object class. The client begins by producing a dialog box listing all the object classes available on the current system.

The names are stored hierarchically as keys and subkeys in the registry. A loop based on the **RegEnumKeys** and **RegQueryValue** commands generates a list of descriptive class names suitable for a list box. When the user selects one of the names, you call **RegQueryValue** again to retrieve the associated class name, which you pass to **OleCreate** or **OleCreateInvisible**. **OleCreate** causes the OLE system to open and display the server application so the user can begin editing the new object immediately. **OleCreateInvisible** does not show the server; it inserts a blank object that the user may activate to edit.

The registry organizes its information conceptually as a hierarchical tree, much like a disk directory. The branch nodes are called *keys* and most are identified by a name string. Besides a name string, each node may contain data, called a *value*. You open keys by name to read their values. Four standard keys near the root are always open, and starting from one of them an application works its way down to any value node by opening successively lower keys and enumerating the next set of subkeys. The standard root keys are named with symbols defined in winreg.h:

Entry-Point Keys	Uses for Subkeys
HKEY_CLASSES_ROOT	Types of document files and the properties associated with them, including file name extension associations and OLE server information
HKEY_CURRENT_USER	Preferences for the current user, including environment variables, program groups, and hardware connections

Entry-Point Keys	Uses for Subkeys
HKEY_LOCAL_MACHINE	The system's physical configuration
HKEY_USERS	Default configuration information assigned to new users

These are the most basic keys. Though other keys are also predefined, only these four are always open.

OLE clients read the registry to get lists of verbs for objects they import and sometimes to generate a list of available servers. Reading from the registry requires these four functions:

- **RegEnumKey:** Given the handle of an open key and a numeric index to a subkey, this function returns the string naming the subkey. Called with increasing index values, it retrieves all the subkey strings.

- **RegOpenKey:** Given the handle of an open key and a string naming a subkey, this function returns a handle to the subkey.

- **RegQueryValue:** Given the handle of an open key and the name of a subkey, this function fills a buffer with data stored in the subkey.

- **RegCloseKey:** This function closes an open key, releasing resources and invalidating the key's handle.

The clip.c module in our sample program Client uses these commands to read from the registry. Programs that use the registry commands must link to the advapi32.lib import library.

Links

A compound document may contain many objects with different kinds of links to a variety of servers. The user needs a way to modify and maintain the links. The Links dialog box in Figure 14.6 lists all the links in a document and lets the user update objects, change between automatic and manual links, cancel links, and enter new source file names to repair broken links.

The radio buttons allow the user to change how the link is updated. *Automatic* means that changes to the object automatically propagate to other documents linked to the same object. *Manual* links reflect recent changes only when the user

Links dialog box

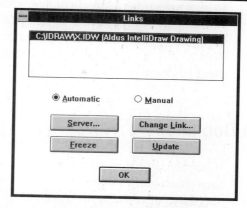

gives the Update command. The Server button invokes the server; it is synonymous with double-clicking the object. Change Link allows the user to change the name of the file in which the object is stored. This restores the connection after the source document is moved or renamed. Freeze converts the link into a static object that can no longer be edited using OLE. A frozen object takes up less disk space than an embedded one, however, and compound files quickly become very large.

To list the links for the dialog box, scan the document file for objects. How you recognize objects depends on how you stored them. To determine whether a link is automatic or manual, call **OleGetLinkUpdateOptions**. To change the update frequency, call **OleSetLinkUpdateOptions**. **OleUpdate** copies new information from the link's source. If the user clicks Cancel Link, call **OleObjectConvert** to embed the object, ending its association with a source file. To retrieve or modify information about the source of a specific link, call **OleGetData** or **OleSetData**, naming the ObjectLink format.

In practice, implementing the Links dialog is very time consuming. (It would be a good candidate for inclusion in the common dialog library.)

Saving a Document

When you register a newly opened document with OleCli by calling **OleRegister-ClientDoc**, you receive a document handle. Subsequent commands for saving objects or closing a document expect the handle as a parameter.

To save a document, the client first writes to disk all the non-object data. It then calls **OleSaveToStream** for each object. (You may want to call **OleQuerySize** first.) Ole-Cli in turn calls your own Put function to save each object. After all the data has been written, the application calls **OleSavedClientDoc** to tell OleCli that the document has been recently saved.

Closing a Document

When the user closes a document, the client application first calls **OleRelease** for each object in the document. This releases any memory the OLE libraries or servers may have devoted to an object. Next the client calls **OleSavedClientDoc** so that OleCli knows the file has been saved. Finally, the application tells OleCli that the document is no longer open by calling **OleRevokeClientDoc**. This invalidates the document's handle, ends the document's OLE session, and releases memory in the OleCli library.

Closing the Application

Before a client application ends, it should query the user about saving any modified open documents and then follow the standard procedures for closing all documents. As it calls **OleRelease** for all the objects in open documents, the client should check the return value. **OLE_OK** indicates the object was successfully released, but if the server is still editing the object then **OleRelease** returns **OLE_WAIT_FOR_RELEASE**. The client may continue to perform other cleanup chores but should not actually terminate until OleCli sends a follow-up notification code, **OLE_RELEASE**, to say the object has been released. When the **OLE_RELEASE** notification code arrives at the client's callback procedure, it does not indicate which object was released. To check on the status of a particular object, call **OleQueryRelease-Status**. To determine the success of a delayed release, call **OleQueryReleaseError**.

CODE: THE CLIENT PROGRAM

The Client program we present here creates compound documents by accepting objects from other servers. In Figure 14.7, Client has received objects from Paintbrush, the Sound Recorder, Excel, and Microsoft's Server Test program.

The most important items in the header file are three structure types, and understanding them will take you a long way toward being able to read the program code. Almost every procedure uses them. APPOLESTREAM describes our wrapper for the stream virtual table. The **OLESTREAM** field at the beginning holds pointers to our Get and Put functions, OLEGet and OLEPut. Whenever we ask OleCli to load or save an object, the library requests a pointer to the stream wrapper so it can reach the two low-level I/O routines. An OLE client needs one stream wrapper for each document it opens. A multi-document interface (MDI) program would initialize a new stream wrapper for each window it opened. The other fields in the wrapper contain information specific to a particular document, such as a file handle, a document name string, and the number of OLE objects in the document.

FIGURE 14.7:

Client program displaying objects from a variety of servers

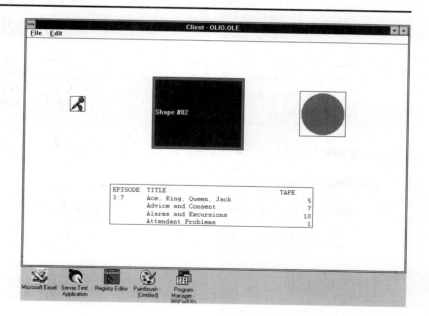

The APPOLECLIENT structure defines our wrapper for the **OLECLIENT** virtual table with its pointer to the client's callback function for notification messages. The program allocates and initializes one of these structures for each new OLE object it receives. The extra fields include a pointer to the actual object data, a flag saying whether the library is busy doing something with the object, and a type indicator to show which objects are linked and which embedded.

The object wrapper also holds a window handle. Our Client program creates a new child window for each object it imports. Much of the code for handling objects goes into the code for handling these windows. The third structure, OBJWINDOWINFO, defines a linked-list node for keeping all the object windows chained together. The windows attach OLE objects to themselves as window properties. Each window receives a PAPPOLECLIENT pointer for one object, and in response to **WM_PAINT** messages the child calls **OleDraw** to draw its object. When the user clicks an object, Client shows it is active by moving its window to the front. To save a document, Client traverses the list and calls **OleSaveToStream** for each successive object.

The make file shows that the Client program is divided into four files:

- client.c holds WinMain, the message handlers, and a collection of utility routines.

- document.c maintains the stream wrapper (PAPPOLESTREAM) for the current document and reads and writes document files.

- obwin.c manages the object windows and includes a window procedure for the object window class.

- clip.c handles all interactions with the clipboard, including cutting and pasting OLE objects.

```
#
#    Make file for the CLIENT program
#


#
#    Set targets and dependencies
#

all: client.exe
client.exe: client.obj document.obj obwin.obj clip.obj client.rbj
client.obj: client.c client.h
```

```
document.obj: document.c client.h
obwin.obj: obwin.c client.h
clip.obj: clip.c client.h
client.rbj: client.rc rsrc.h


#
#    Define macros for command-line options and library modules
#


!IFDEF NODEBUG
CFLAGS = -c -G3 -Os -W3 -D_X86_=1 -DWIN32 -D_MT -D_DLL
LFLAGS = -subsystem:windows
!ELSE
CFLAGS = -c -G3 -Od -W4 -Zi -D_X86_=1 -DWIN32 -D_MT -D_DLL
LFLAGS = -debug:full -debugtype:cv -subsystem:windows
!ENDIF


OBJS = client.obj document.obj obwin.obj clip.obj
LIBS = crtdll.lib kernel32.lib user32.lib gdi32.lib olecli32.lib \
       comdlg32.lib advapi32.lib


#
#    Define compiling rules
#

.c.obj:
    cl386 $(CFLAGS) $*.c

.rc.rbj:
    rc $*.rc
    cvtres -i386 $*.res -o $*.rbj

.obj.exe:
    link32 $(LFLAGS) -out:$*.exe $(OBJS) $*.rbj $(LIBS)

================================================================================

/*------------------------------------------------------------------


        CLIENT.H

        Header file for all modules of the CLIENT program.


        ----------------------------------------------------------*/
```

```
#ifndef _INC_STDLIB
#include <stdlib.h>                        // _MAX_FNAME
#endif

/*-------------------------------------------------------------
            PRIVATE APPLICATION MESSAGES (WM_USER)
      ------------------------------------------------------------*/


/* messages sent from the application to the object windows */

/* attach an object to an object window */
#define OBWIN_MSG_SETDATA (WM_USER + 800)
    // WPARAM: carries a pointer to an OLE object
    // LPARAM: unused
    // RETURN: none

/* get a pointer to the object in a window */
#define OBWIN_MSG_GETDATA (WM_USER + 801)
    // WPARAM and LPARAM: unused
    // RETURN: the window returns a pointer to its OLE object


/*-------------------------------------------------------------
            SYMBOLS
      ------------------------------------------------------------*/


#define MAX_RSRCLEN        64            // buffer size for resource strings
#define MAX_OBJNAME        64            // buffer size for object names
#define MAX_WINCAPTION    _MAX_FNAME+15  // buffer size for window caption
#define PROTOCOL_STRLEN    15            // buffer size for protocol strings


/*-------------------------------------------------------------
            TYPE DEFINITIONS
      ------------------------------------------------------------*/


typedef struct tagOBJWINDOWINFO          // nodes in list of obj windows
{
    struct tagOBJWINDOWINFO *pNext;      // next node
    HWND hwndObject;                     // object's child window
}   OBJWINDOWINFO, *POBJWINDOWINFO;

typedef struct tagAPPOLESTREAM           // the document wrapper structure
{
    OLESTREAM OleStream;                 // virtual table structure
    LHCLIENTDOC OleDocHandle;            // OLE document handle
    POBJWINDOWINFO pCurObject;           // currently active object window
```

```
        POBJWINDOWINFO pObWindowList;          // base node for document's obj list
        char szDocName[_MAX_PATH];             // document's name
        char szAppClass[MAX_RSRCLEN];          // application name
        HANDLE hFile;                          // handle to a disk file
        int iObjects;                          // total number of objects
        int iBusyObject;                       // number of active objects
} APPOLESTREAM, *PAPPOLESTREAM;


typedef struct tagAPPOLECLIENT                 // the object wrapper structure
{
    OLECLIENT OleClient;                       // virtual table structure
    LPOLEOBJECT pObjectData;                   // an OLE object
    HWND hwndObject;                           // the object's container window
    DWORD dwType;                              // object's type (link/embed/static)
    BOOL bBusy;                                // TRUE if asynch. op. in progress
} APPOLEOBJECT, *PAPPOLECLIENT;


typedef struct tagOBJECT_HEADER                // header for each object in a file
{
    char szProtocol[PROTOCOL_STRLEN+1];        // storage protocol string
    char szName[MAX_OBJNAME];                  // object name, unique in document
    RECT rObject;                              // position in HIMETRIC units
} OBJECT_HEADER, *POBJECT_HEADER;

/*---------------------------------------------------------------------
            GLOBAL VARIABLE
    ---------------------------------------------------------------------*/

extern char szObwinClass[MAX_RSRCLEN];   // object window class name

/*---------------------------------------------------------------------
        PROTOTYPES for functions called from other modules
    ---------------------------------------------------------------------*/

/* CLIENT module */

PAPPOLESTREAM GetOleStream( void );
PAPPOLECLIENT NewAppObject( void );
BOOL InitAppObject( HWND hWnd, PAPPOLECLIENT pAppObject, PRECT prPosition );
void DeleteAppObject( PAPPOLECLIENT pAppObject );
PSTR UniqueName( PSTR pszBuffer );
BOOL ValidateName( PSTR pszName );
void MmToPix( PPOINT pPts, int iNumPoints );
```

```
void PixToMm( PPOINT pPts, int iNumPoints );
void MoveRect( PRECT pRect, int x, int y );
void MarkIfBusy( OLESTATUS* pStatus, PAPPOLECLIENT pAppObject );
void OLEWait( PAPPOLECLIENT pAppObject );
void OLEWaitAll( void );

/* OBWIN module */

LRESULT WINAPI Obwin_WndProc( HWND hWnd, UINT uMessage, WPARAM wParam,
    LPARAM lParam );
POBJWINDOWINFO GetObjWindowInfo( HWND hWnd );
void InsertObjWindow( PAPPOLESTREAM pStream, OBJWINDOWINFO *pObWindow );
POBJWINDOWINFO SetCurrentObject( PAPPOLESTREAM pStream,
    OBJWINDOWINFO *pNewObWindow );
POBJWINDOWINFO CreateObjWindow( HWND hWndParent, LPRECT lpObWindowRect );
POBJWINDOWINFO DeleteObjWindow( PAPPOLESTREAM pStream,
    POBJWINDOWINFO pObWindow );

/* DOCUMENT module */

PAPPOLESTREAM InitOLEDoc( LPSTR lpszObjectClass, LPSTR lpszDocName );
void TermOLEDoc( PAPPOLESTREAM pStream );
BOOL ReadDocFile( HWND hWnd, PAPPOLESTREAM pStream );
BOOL WriteDocFile( PAPPOLESTREAM pStream );
DWORD WINAPI OLEGet( LPOLESTREAM pStream, PVOID pData, DWORD dwBytes );
DWORD WINAPI OLEPut( LPOLESTREAM pStream, OLE_CONST VOID *pData,
    DWORD dwBytes );
int WINAPI OLEEvent( LPOLECLIENT pOleObject, OLE_NOTIFICATION OleNotify,
    LPOLEOBJECT pObjectData );

/* CLIP module */

BOOL CanPasteObject( void );
BOOL CanPasteLink( void );
BOOL PasteObject( HWND hWnd, BOOL bLink );
BOOL CopyObject( HWND hWnd, POBJWINDOWINFO pObjWindow );
BOOL CutObject( HWND hWnd, POBJWINDOWINFO pObjWindow );
BOOL ClearObject( POBJWINDOWINFO pObjWindow );
BOOL InsertObject( HWND hWnd, PSTR pszCaption );
```

```
================================================================================
/*-----------------------------------------------------------------------

        RSRC.H

        Resource IDs for the CLIENT program.

        -------------------  ----------------------------------------------*/

#define MENU_MAIN            10          // templates
#define DLG_ABOUT            10
#define DLG_INSERT           20

#define IDD_SERVERLIST       10          // dialog control ID

#define IDM_NEW              100         // file menu commands
#define IDM_OPEN             200
#define IDM_SAVE             300
#define IDM_SAVEAS           400
#define IDM_EXIT             500
#define IDM_ABOUT            600
#define IDM_CUT              700         // edit menu commands
#define IDM_COPY             800
#define IDM_PASTE            900
#define IDM_PASTELINK        1000
#define IDM_DELETE           1100
#define IDM_INSERT           1200
#define IDS_APPCLASS         10          // strings
#define IDS_CAPTION          20
#define IDS_OBJECTCLASS      30
#define IDS_UNTITLED         40
#define IDS_UPDATELINKS      50


================================================================================

/*-----------------------------------------------------------------------

        CLIENT.RC

        Resource script file for the CLIENT program.

        ------------------------------------------------------------------*/

#include <windows.h>
```

```
#include "rsrc.h"

/* a script for the menu */
MENU_MAIN MENU PRELOAD
BEGIN
    POPUP "&File"
     BEGIN
        MENUITEM "&New",                    IDM_NEW
        MENUITEM "&Open...",                IDM_OPEN
        MENUITEM "&Save",                   IDM_SAVE
        MENUITEM "Save &As...",             IDM_SAVEAS
        MENUITEM SEPARATOR
        MENUITEM "E&xit",                   IDM_EXIT
        MENUITEM "&About...",               IDM_ABOUT
     END

    POPUP "&Edit"
    BEGIN
        MENUITEM "Cu&t",                    IDM_CUT
        MENUITEM "&Copy",                   IDM_COPY
        MENUITEM "&Paste",                  IDM_PASTE
        MENUITEM "&Paste &Link",            IDM_PASTELINK
        MENUITEM SEPARATOR
        MENUITEM "&Delete",                 IDM_DELETE
        MENUITEM "&Insert Object...",       IDM_INSERT
    END
END

/* a table of all the program's strings */
STRINGTABLE
BEGIN
    IDS_APPCLASS,         "clientapp_class"
    IDS_CAPTION,          "Client"
    IDS_OBJECTCLASS,      "objwindow_class"
    IDS_UNTITLED,         "Untitled"
    IDS_UPDATELINKS,
        "This file contains links to other\ndocuments.\n\nUpdate links now?"
END

DLG_INSERT DIALOG 19, 30, 160, 90
STYLE DS_MODALFRAME | WS_POPUP | WS_VISIBLE | WS_CAPTION | WS_SYSMENU
CAPTION "Insert Object"
FONT 8, "Helv"
BEGIN
    LTEXT           "&Object Type:", -1, 4, 4, 52, 8
```

```
        LISTBOX            IDD_SERVERLIST, 4, 16, 114, 76,
                           LBS_SORT | WS_VSCROLL | WS_TABSTOP
        DEFPUSHBUTTON      "OK", IDOK, 121, 9, 36, 14
        PUSHBUTTON         "&Cancel", IDCANCEL, 121, 26, 36, 14
END

DLG_ABOUT DIALOG 17, 18, 114, 68
STYLE DS_MODALFRAME | WS_POPUP | WS_VISIBLE | WS_CAPTION | WS_SYSMENU
CAPTION "About Client"
FONT 8, "Helv"
BEGIN
        CTEXT              "OLE Demo: Client", -1, 0, 7, 114, 8
        CTEXT              "by",             -1, 0, 15, 114, 8
        CTEXT              "Myers && Hamer", -1, 0, 25, 114, 8
        CTEXT              "version 1.0",    -1, 0, 35, 114, 8
        LTEXT              "©1993",          -1, 12, 51, 25, 8
        DEFPUSHBUTTON      "OK", IDOK, 81, 50, 30, 14, WS_GROUP
END
```

The Client Module

The program's initialization and message-handling procedures show how the program is structured, but they do little that is specific to OLE. The Init procedure registers the three OLE clipboard formats so the system knows Client is prepared to accept data in those formats. RegisterWndClasses registers a class for the object child windows as well as the parent window. WinMain calls InitOLEDoc to initialize an I/O stream wrapper structure for the initial empty document. When Client receives **WM_DESTROY**, it calls TermOLEDoc to release all the resources held for the current document, including all its objects.

```
/*-------------------------------------------------------------------

    CLIENT.C

    The main module of the Client program.  Client shows the
    basic operations of an OLE client, including clipboard
    and file I/O.

    FUNCTIONS

        WinMain                    receive all messages for this app
```

```
        Init                      initialize globals
        RegisterWndClasses        register window classes

        Client_WndProc            process messages for main window
        Client_OnInitMenu         enable/disable clipboard commands
        Client_OnCommand          process menu commands
        Client_OnDestroy          end the program

        NewDoc                    start new empty document
        OpenDoc                   initialize and load a new document
        SaveDoc                   save all objects to disk file
        GetFileName               get name of file to read or write
        UpdateLinks               freshen linked objects when loaded

        NewAppObject              allocate new object wrapper structure
        InitAppObject             fill wrapper with info about new object
        DeleteAppObject           release memory used for wrapper
        MarkIfBusy                process OLESTATUS return values
        OLEWait                   poll for messages
        OLEWaitAll                wait for all pending OLE ops to finish
        UniqueName                build strings to identify objects
        ValidateName              confirm string conforms to name format
        MmToPix                   convert from HIMETRIC to device coor's
        PixToMm                   convert from device coor's to HIMETRIC
        MoveRect                  slide rectangle to new position
        GetOleStream              return pointer to stream structure
        SetWindowTitle            add file name to window title bar
        About_DlgProc             process messages for the About box

    from Mastering Windows NT Programming
    copyright 1993 by Brian Myers & Eric Hamer

-----------------------------------------------------------------------*/


#define STRICT
#include <windows.h>
#include <windowsx.h>
#include <string.h>                         // strupr() stricmp()
#include "client.h"
#include "rsrc.h"


/*---------------------------------------------------------------------
          PROTOTYPES for functions internal to this module
-----------------------------------------------------------------------*/
```

```
static BOOL Init( HINSTANCE hinstThis, int iCmdShow );
static BOOL RegisterWndClasses( HINSTANCE hInst );

LRESULT WINAPI Client_WndProc( HWND hWnd, UINT uMessage, WPARAM wParam,
    LPARAM lParam );
static void Client_OnInitMenu( HWND hWnd, HMENU hMenu );
static void Client_OnCommand( HWND hWnd, int iID, HWND hwndCtl,
    UINT uCodeNotify );
static void Client_OnDestroy( HWND hWnd );

static PAPPOLESTREAM NewDoc( HWND hWnd, PSTR pszDocName );
static BOOL OpenDoc( HWND hWnd );
static BOOL SaveDoc( HWND hWnd );
static BOOL GetFileName( HWND hWnd, BOOL bOpenName, PSTR pszFilePath,
    PSTR pszFileName );
static void UpdateLinks( HWND hWnd );

static void SetTitle( HWND hWnd );
BOOL WINAPI About_DlgProc( HWND hDlg, UINT uMessage, WPARAM wParam,
    LPARAM lParam );

/*------------------------------------------------------------------
        SYMBOLS
   --------------------------------------------------------------*/

#define MAX_MESSAGELEN          256     // length for MessageBox text
#define HMM_PER_INCH            2540    // hundredths of a mm per inch

/*------------------------------------------------------------------
        GLOBAL VARIABLE for all modules
   --------------------------------------------------------------*/

char szObwinClass[MAX_RSRCLEN];         // object window class name

/*------------------------------------------------------------------
        STATIC VARIABLES for this module
   --------------------------------------------------------------*/

PAPPOLESTREAM pAppStream;               // stream info for current document
char szAppClass[MAX_RSRCLEN];           // application window class name
char szAppCaption[MAX_RSRCLEN];         // window caption
char szUntitled[MAX_RSRCLEN];           // name for untitled documents
char szDocName[_MAX_FNAME];             // current file name; no path
char szDocPath[_MAX_PATH];              // full file name
WORD wID = 1;                           // counter for making unique names
```

```
OLECLIPFORMAT cfLink;                    // OLE clipboard formats
OLECLIPFORMAT cfNative;
OLECLIPFORMAT cfOwnerLink;

/*-----------------------------------------------------------------
        WIN MAIN
        Calls initializing procedures and runs the message loop
    ---------------------------------------------------------------*/

int WINAPI WinMain (
    HINSTANCE hinstThis,
    HINSTANCE hinstPrev,
    LPSTR lpszCmdLine,
    int iCmdShow )
{
    MSG msg;

    /* initialize data and create the program's window */
    if (!Init( hinstThis, iCmdShow ))
    {
        return( FALSE );
    }

    // Initialize the OLE stream for a new empty document
    // and register the document with the OLE library.

    pAppStream = InitOLEDoc( szObwinClass, szDocName );
    if (!pAppStream)
    {
        return( FALSE );
    }

    /* process this window's messages */
    while (GetMessage( &msg, NULL, 0, 0 ))
    {
        TranslateMessage( &msg );
        DispatchMessage( &msg );
    }

    return( msg.wParam );
    UNREFERENCED_PARAMETER( hinstPrev );
    UNREFERENCED_PARAMETER( lpszCmdLine );
}
```

```
/*------------------------------------------------------------------
            INIT
            Initializes window and data for the application.
   ----------------------------------------------------------------*/
static BOOL Init (
     HINSTANCE hInst,
     int iCmdShow )
{
     HWND hWnd;                          // program window
     int iLen;                           // for testing
     BOOL bTest;                         // return values

     /* load the class, caption, and "Untitled" strings */
     iLen = LoadString( hInst, IDS_APPCLASS, szAppClass, sizeof(szAppClass) );
     if (!iLen)
     {
          return( FALSE );
     }

     iLen = LoadString( hInst, IDS_CAPTION, szAppCaption, sizeof(szAppCaption) );
     if (!iLen)
     {
          return( FALSE );
     }

     iLen = LoadString( hInst, IDS_UNTITLED, szUntitled, sizeof(szUntitled) );
     if (!iLen)
     {
          return( FALSE );
     }
     lstrcpy( szDocName, szUntitled );

     iLen =  LoadString( hInst, IDS_OBJECTCLASS, szObwinClass,
          sizeof(szObwinClass) );
     if (!iLen)
     {
          return( FALSE );
     }

     /* initialize this instance of the application */
     bTest = RegisterWndClasses( hInst );
     if (!bTest)
     {
```

```
        return( FALSE );
    }

    /* create the frame window that will contain the OLE objects */
    hWnd = CreateWindow( szAppClass, szAppCaption, WS_OVERLAPPEDWINDOW,
        CW_USEDEFAULT, CW_USEDEFAULT, CW_USEDEFAULT, CW_USEDEFAULT,
        NULL, NULL, hInst, NULL );
    if (!hWnd)
    {
        return( FALSE );
    }

    /* show the main window */
    SetTitle( hWnd );                        // starting caption is "UNTITLED"
    ShowWindow( hWnd, iCmdShow );
    UpdateWindow( hWnd );

    /* register the three clipboard formats used by OLE */
    cfLink      = (OLECLIPFORMAT)RegisterClipboardFormat( "ObjectLink" );
    cfNative    = (OLECLIPFORMAT)RegisterClipboardFormat( "Native" );
    cfOwnerLink = (OLECLIPFORMAT)RegisterClipboardFormat( "OwnerLink" );

    return( TRUE );
}

/*-------------------------------------------------------------------
        REGISTER WINDOW CLASSES
        Register classes for the program's main window and its
        object container windows.
    ---------------------------------------------------------------*/

static BOOL RegisterWndClasses ( HINSTANCE hInst )
{
    WNDCLASS wc;

    /* register the frame window class */
    wc.lpszClassName  = szAppClass;
    wc.hInstance      = hInst;
    wc.lpfnWndProc    = Client_WndProc;
    wc.hCursor        = LoadCursor( NULL, IDC_ARROW );
    wc.hIcon          = LoadIcon( NULL, IDI_APPLICATION );
    wc.lpszMenuName   = MAKEINTRESOURCE( MENU_MAIN );
    wc.hbrBackground  = (HBRUSH)(COLOR_WINDOW + 1);
    wc.style          = CS_HREDRAW | CS_VREDRAW;
```

```
    wc.cbClsExtra      = 0;
    wc.cbWndExtra      = 0;

    if (!RegisterClass( &wc ))
    {
        return( FALSE );
    }

    /* register the OLE object container class */
    wc.style           = CS_DBLCLKS | CS_VREDRAW | CS_HREDRAW;
    wc.lpfnWndProc     = Obwin_WndProc;
    wc.hIcon           = NULL;
    wc.cbWndExtra      = 4;
    wc.lpszMenuName    = NULL;
    wc.lpszClassName   = szObwinClass;

    if (!RegisterClass( &wc ))
    {
        return( FALSE );
    }

    return( TRUE );                          // initialization succeeded
}

/*-----------------------------------------------------------------
        CLIENT_WNDPROC
        Every message for the program's main window ends up here.
    -------------------------------------------------------------*/
LRESULT WINAPI Client_WndProc (
    HWND hWnd,
    UINT uMessage,
    WPARAM wParam,
    LPARAM lParam )
{
    switch (uMessage)
    {
        HANDLE_MSG( hWnd, WM_INITMENU, Client_OnInitMenu );

        HANDLE_MSG( hWnd, WM_COMMAND, Client_OnCommand );

        HANDLE_MSG( hWnd, WM_DESTROY, Client_OnDestroy );

        default:
            return( DefWindowProc(hWnd, uMessage, wParam, lParam) );
```

```
            break;
    }
    return( 0 );
}

/*-------------------------------------------------------------------
        CLIENT_ONINITMENU
        Enable or disable menu items according to the status of
        the clipboard and the current document.
    ------------------------------------------------------------------*/

static void Client_OnInitMenu (
    HWND hWnd,
    HMENU hMenu )
{
    BOOL bTest;

    /* check what is on the clipboard */
    bTest = CanPasteObject();
    if (bTest)
    {
        EnableMenuItem( hMenu, IDM_PASTE, MF_ENABLED );
    }
    else
    {
        EnableMenuItem( hMenu, IDM_PASTE, MF_GRAYED );
    }

    bTest = CanPasteLink();
    if (bTest)
    {
        EnableMenuItem( hMenu, IDM_PASTELINK, MF_ENABLED );
    }
    else
    {
        EnableMenuItem( hMenu, IDM_PASTELINK, MF_GRAYED );
    }

    /* if the document contains any objects, it can be saved */
    if (pAppStream->iObjects > 0)
    {
        EnableMenuItem( hMenu, IDM_SAVE,   MF_ENABLED );
        EnableMenuItem( hMenu, IDM_SAVEAS, MF_ENABLED );
    }
```

```
        else
        {
            EnableMenuItem( hMenu, IDM_SAVE,   MF_GRAYED );
            EnableMenuItem( hMenu, IDM_SAVEAS, MF_GRAYED );
        }

        /* if an object is active, it can be deleted, copied, or cut */
        if (pAppStream->pCurObject != NULL)
        {
            EnableMenuItem( hMenu, IDM_DELETE, MF_ENABLED );
            EnableMenuItem( hMenu, IDM_COPY,   MF_ENABLED );
            EnableMenuItem( hMenu, IDM_CUT,    MF_ENABLED );
        }
        else
        {
            EnableMenuItem( hMenu, IDM_DELETE, MF_GRAYED );
            EnableMenuItem( hMenu, IDM_COPY,   MF_GRAYED );
            EnableMenuItem( hMenu, IDM_CUT,    MF_GRAYED );
        }

    return;
    UNREFERENCED_PARAMETER( hWnd );
}

/*-------------------------------------------------------------------
        CLIENT_ONCOMMAND
        Process commands from the menu.
    -----------------------------------------------------------------*/
static void Client_OnCommand (
    HWND hWnd,
    int iID,
    HWND hwndCtl,
    UINT uCodeNotify )
{
    switch (iID)
    {
        case IDM_NEW:                           // make fresh empty document
            NewDoc( hWnd, szUntitled );
            break;

        case IDM_OPEN:                          // load a file from disk
            OpenDoc( hWnd );
            break;
```

```
    case IDM_SAVE:                          // save all objects to disk
        SaveDoc( hWnd );
        break;

    case IDM_SAVEAS:                        // save and rename
        if (GetFileName( hWnd, FALSE, szDocPath, szDocName ))
        {
            SaveDoc( hWnd );
        }
        break;

    case IDM_COPY:                          // copy object to clipboard
        CopyObject( hWnd, pAppStream->pCurObject );
        break;

    case IDM_CUT:                           // move object to clipboard
        CutObject( hWnd, pAppStream->pCurObject );
        break;

    case IDM_PASTE:                         // embed object from clipboard
        PasteObject( hWnd, FALSE );
        break;

    case IDM_PASTELINK:                     // link object from clipboard
        PasteObject( hWnd, TRUE );
        break;

    case IDM_DELETE:                        // remove active object
        ClearObject( pAppStream->pCurObject );
        break;

    case IDM_INSERT:                        // insert new object from server
        InsertObject( hWnd, szAppCaption );
        break;

    case IDM_EXIT:                          // terminate the program
        DestroyWindow( hWnd );
        break;

    case IDM_ABOUT:                         // show About box
        DialogBox(
            GetWindowInstance(hWnd),
            MAKEINTRESOURCE(DLG_ABOUT),
            hWnd, About_DlgProc );
        break;
```

```
    }
    return;
    UNREFERENCED_PARAMETER( hwndCtl );
    UNREFERENCED_PARAMETER( uCodeNotify );
}

/*-------------------------------------------------------------------

        CLIENT_ONDESTROY
        Frees up all program resources before program ends.
    -----------------------------------------------------------*/

static void Client_OnDestroy ( HWND hWnd )
{
    TermOLEDoc( pAppStream );              // terminate all OLE connections
    PostQuitMessage( 0 );                  // send WM_QUIT

    return;
    UNREFERENCED_PARAMETER( hWnd );
}
```

Document Commands

The next procedures respond to commands on the File menu. NewDoc, OpenDoc, and SaveDoc call procedures to perform the New, Open, and Save commands. One of the procedures they call is GetFileName, which runs the common dialog box to let the user select a file to load or save.

To create a new document, NewDoc performs three actions. It calls TermOLEDoc to release all the resources held for the current document, it sets the static file name variables back to "Untitled," and it initializes a new stream by calling InitOLEDoc.

OpenDoc begins by asking the user for a new file name. If the user provides one, Open-Doc calls NewDoc to reset all the program data structures. It then opens the file and adds the new file handle to the stream wrapper. ReadDocFile finds the handle there and reads all the data from the file. (Client reads only its own data files.)

SaveDoc follows the same steps but ends with a call to WriteDocFile instead. Both the Open and Save procedures rely on GetFileName when the user needs to choose a file. You saw a version of this procedure in Chapter 10. This time we've added temporary string buffers in order to avoid resetting the static file name variables when the user cancels.

Whenever a program opens documents containing OLE objects, the program should determine whether any of the objects are linked and, if so, whether the user wants to update them. *Updating* means determining whether the file containing the original native data has been modified since the link was made. The **OleUpdate** command copies fresh data into a linked object. If OpenFile succeeds in loading a document, it finishes by calling UpdateLinks to freshen any linked objects in the file.

```
/*-------------------------------------------------------------------
        NEW DOCUMENT
        Throw out any current objects and start again with a fresh,
        untitled document.

        Returns a pointer to a new stream, or NULL for errors.
        -----------------------------------------------------------*/

static PAPPOLESTREAM NewDoc (
    HWND hWnd,                              // main window
    PSTR pszNewName )                       // name for new document
{

    /* release objects and destroy object windows */
    TermOLEDoc( pAppStream );

    lstrcpy( szDocName, pszNewName );        // set new document name

    /* initialize new settings, register new document */
    pAppStream = InitOLEDoc( szObwinClass, szDocName );
    if (!pAppStream)
    {
        MessageBox( hWnd, "Cannot initialize document", szAppCaption, MB_OK );
        DestroyWindow( hWnd );
    }

    SetTitle( hWnd );
    return( pAppStream );
}

/*-------------------------------------------------------------------
        OPEN DOCUMENT
        Load a document file from disk.

        Modifies the global variable pAppStream.
        -----------------------------------------------------------*/
```

```
static BOOL OpenDoc ( HWND hWnd )
{
    HANDLE hFile;                                // file handle
    BOOL bSuccess;                               // return from Boolean function

    /* ask user what file to open */
    bSuccess = GetFileName( hWnd, TRUE, szDocPath, szDocName );
    if (!bSuccess)
    {
        return( FALSE );                         // user canceled
    }

    /* destroy the old stream and create a new one for this document */
    NewDoc( hWnd, szDocName );

    /* open the requested file */
    hFile = CreateFile( szDocPath,               // name of file
                GENERIC_READ,                    // read-only access
                FILE_SHARE_READ,                 // others may still read
                NULL,                            // default security
                OPEN_EXISTING,                   // do not create new file
                FILE_ATTRIBUTE_NORMAL,           // file attributes
                NULL );                          // template for attributes
    if (hFile == INVALID_HANDLE_VALUE)
    {
        MessageBox( hWnd, "Cannot open file", szAppCaption, MB_OK );
        return( FALSE );
    }

    pAppStream->hFile = hFile;                    // save file handle

    /* read all the data from the file */
    bSuccess = ReadDocFile( hWnd, pAppStream );
    CloseHandle( hFile );                         // close file
    if (!bSuccess)
    {
        MessageBox( hWnd, "Cannot read from file", szAppCaption, MB_OK );
        lstrcpy( szDocName, szUntitled );
    }

    SetTitle( hWnd );                             // update title bar
    UpdateLinks( hWnd );                          // freshen any linked objects
    return( bSuccess );
}
```

```
/*-----------------------------------------------------------------
        SAVE DOCUMENT
        Write all the data for all the current objects into a
        disk file.
        ----------------------------------------------------------*/

BOOL SaveDoc ( HWND hWnd )
{
    HANDLE hFile;                               // document file
    BOOL bSuccess;                              // for testing returns

    /* if szDocName still says "Untitled", ask for a file name */
    if (stricmp(szDocName, szUntitled) == 0)
    {
        bSuccess = GetFileName( hWnd, FALSE, szDocPath, szDocName );
        if (!bSuccess)
        {
            return( FALSE );                    // user canceled
        }
    }

    /* open the requested file */
    hFile = CreateFile( szDocPath,              // name of file
                GENERIC_WRITE,                  // read-only access
                FILE_SHARE_READ,                // others may still read
                NULL,                           // default security
                CREATE_ALWAYS,                  // create new or overwrite old
                FILE_ATTRIBUTE_NORMAL,          // file attributes
                NULL );                         // template for attributes
    if (hFile == INVALID_HANDLE_VALUE)
    {
        MessageBox( hWnd, "Cannot open file", szAppCaption, MB_OK );
        return( FALSE );
    }

    pAppStream->hFile = hFile;                  // save the new handle

    /* write to the open file */
    bSuccess = WriteDocFile( pAppStream );
    CloseHandle( hFile );                       // close the file
    if (!bSuccess)
```

```
    {
        MessageBox( hWnd, "Cannot write to file", szAppCaption, MB_OK );
        lstrcpy( szDocName, szUntitled );
    }

    SetTitle( hWnd );                               // update title bar
    return( bSuccess );
}


/*-------------------------------------------------------------------
        GET FILE NAME
        Invoke the File Open or File Save As common dialog box.
        If the bOpenName parameter is TRUE, the procedure runs
        the OpenFileName dialog box.

        The value passed in through pszFilePath will appear
        as a default response in the dialog box.  The two
        string pointers are assumed to point to buffers of
        size _MAX_PATH and _MAX_FNAME.

        Returns TRUE if the dialog box closes without error.  If
        it returns TRUE, then pszFilePath and pszFileName point to
        the user's choices.
        --------------------------------------------------------------*/
static BOOL GetFileName (
    HWND hWnd,                              // main program window
    BOOL bOpenName,                         // open file or save as
    PSTR pszFilePath,                       // buffer for file path
    PSTR pszFileName )                      // buffer for file name
{
    /* STATIC variables */
    static CONST char szDefExt[] = "OLE";   // default data file extension
    static CONST char *szFilter[] =         // file filters for dialog box
    {
        "Client files (*.OLE)\0 *.OLE\0 All Files (*.*)\0 *.* \0\0"
    };

    /* DYNAMIC variables */
    OPENFILENAME ofn;                       // common dialog structure
    char szTempPath[_MAX_PATH];             // temporary name buffers
    char szTempName[_MAX_FNAME];
    BOOL bSuccess;                          // TRUE if user picks a name
```

```
// Give the dialog copies of the names so that if the user
// cancels it hasn't disturbed the current settings.
lstrcpy( szTempPath, pszFilePath );
lstrcpy( szTempName, pszFileName );

/* initialize structure for the common dialog box */
FillMemory( &ofn, sizeof(OPENFILENAME), 0 );
ofn.lStructSize        = sizeof( OPENFILENAME );
ofn.hwndOwner          = hWnd;
ofn.lpstrFilter        = szFilter[0];
ofn.nFilterIndex       = 1;
ofn.lpstrFile          = szTempPath;
ofn.nMaxFile           = sizeof(szTempPath);
ofn.lpstrFileTitle     = szTempName;
ofn.nMaxFileTitle      = sizeof(szTempName);
ofn.lpstrDefExt        = szDefExt;

/* invoke the common dialog box */
if (bOpenName)                              // Open a file
{
    ofn.Flags = OFN_HIDEREADONLY | OFN_PATHMUSTEXIST |
                OFN_FILEMUSTEXIST;
    bSuccess = GetOpenFileName( &ofn );
}
else                                        // Save As...
{
    ofn.Flags = OFN_HIDEREADONLY | OFN_OVERWRITEPROMPT;
    bSuccess = GetSaveFileName( &ofn );
}
if (bSuccess)
{
    /* copy new names to permanent space */
    lstrcpy( pszFileName, szTempName );
    lstrcpy( pszFilePath, szTempPath );

    /* store new file name with the stream */
    lstrcpy( pAppStream->szDocName, szTempName );
}

return( bSuccess );
}
```

```
/*------------------------------------------------------------

        UPDATE LINKS
        Check all objects in current document.  If any are linked,
        ask the user whether to update them.  If the user says
        yes, call OleUpdate to be sure each linked object contains
        the most current data.
        ------------------------------------------------------------*/
static void UpdateLinks ( HWND hWnd )
{
    BOOL bFirst = TRUE;                      // FALSE after finding first link
    HINSTANCE hInst;                         // program instance
    PAPPOLECLIENT pAppObject;                // temporary item pointer
    POBJWINDOWINFO pObWindow;                // node in linked list
    char szUpdate[MAX_MESSAGELEN];           // update query message
    int iResponse;                           // MessageBox return
    OLESTATUS OleStatus;                     // Ole function return

    hInst = GetWindowInstance( hWnd );

    pObWindow = pAppStream->pObWindowList;
    while (pObWindow)
    {
        pAppObject = (PAPPOLECLIENT)SendMessage( pObWindow->hwndObject,
            OBWIN_MSG_GETDATA, 0, 0 );
        if (pAppObject->dwType == OT_LINK)
        {
            if (bFirst)
            {
                // On encountering the first linked object,
                // ask the user whether to update all links.
                // For subsequent links, skip the message.

                LoadString( hInst, IDS_UPDATELINKS, szUpdate,
                    sizeof(szUpdate) );
                iResponse = MessageBox( hWnd, szUpdate, szAppCaption,
                    MB_YESNO | MB_ICONEXCLAMATION);
                if (iResponse != IDYES)
                break;
```

917

```
        bFirst = FALSE;
    }
    OleStatus = OleUpdate( pAppObject->pObjectData );
    MarkIfBusy( &OleStatus, pAppObject );
    }
    pObWindow = pObWindow->pNext;        // advance to next list node
    }
}

OLEWaitAll( );
return;
}
```

Application Objects

Most of the remaining procedures in client.c work with the application's object wrappers. In naming object variables, we distinguish between those that point to an **OLECLIENT** structure, which we think of as OLE objects, and those that point to the derived APPOLECLIENT wrapper, which we think of as application objects. The two kinds of pointers give two ways to refer to the same object; the pointer type is the only difference between them. OleCli thinks of the object as an **OLECLIENT**, and Client thinks of it as an APPOLECLIENT.

The next three procedures allocate, initialize, and destroy object wrappers. Before the program loads or inserts a new object, it calls NewAppObject to allocate a new APPOLECLIENT structure and initialize its virtual table field with a pointer to the OLEEvent callback function. Creating a wrapper structure requires two allocations: one for the structure itself and one for the virtual table pointed to in the **OLECLIENT** field. The program passes the new object wrapper to the OLE functions, such as **OleCreate** and **OleLoadFromStream**, that create new objects. After the OLE libraries create the object, Client calls InitAppObject to fill in the other wrapper fields. InitAppObject determines the new object's type (**OT_LINK**, **OT_EMBEDDED**, or **OT_STATIC**) and its position. It also creates a new child window and tells the window which object it is responsible for displaying. It inserts the new window in the linked list and makes the window active.

DeleteAppObject first calls **OleRelease**, telling the library to deallocate any memory and resources held for the object. After this call finishes the object no longer exists (unless you have already saved it to the disk). Then DeleteAppObject destroys the child window and releases the memory allocated for the object's wrapper. Unmaking the wrapper takes two steps, just as allocating it did.

```
/*--------------------------------------------------------------
        NEW APPLICATION OBJECT
        Allocates a new object wrapper and initializes (only) its
        virtual table.  Returns TRUE for success.
        ----------------------------------------------------------*/

PAPPOLECLIENT NewAppObject ( void )
{
    PAPPOLECLIENT pAppObject;

    try
    {
        /* allocate the wrapper */
        pAppObject = GlobalAllocPtr( GPTR, sizeof(APPOLEOBJECT) );

        /* allocate the place for the VTBL */
        pAppObject->OleClient.lpvtbl =
            GlobalAllocPtr( GPTR, sizeof(OLECLIENTVTBL) );

        /* initialize the VTBL */
        pAppObject->OleClient.lpvtbl->CallBack = OLEEvent;
    }
    except ((GetExceptionCode() == EXCEPTION_ACCESS_VIOLATION)
            ? EXCEPTION_EXECUTE_HANDLER : EXCEPTION_CONTINUE_SEARCH)
    {
        DeleteAppObject( pAppObject );
        return( NULL );
    }
    return( pAppObject );
}

/*--------------------------------------------------------------
        INIT APPLICATION OBJECT
        Fills in the fields of a PAPPOLECLIENT wrapper structure.
        The structure should already have been created with
        NewAppObject, which you call before creating or inserting
        an OLE object.  Call InitAppObject after creating the
        OLE object to fill in the fields that depend on the
        object for their data.

        If prPosition == NULL, the object is placed at the
        client area origin.  If prPosition != NULL, then it
        should use HIMETRIC coordinates.
        ----------------------------------------------------------*/
```

```
BOOL InitAppObject (
    HWND hWnd,                              // main program window
    PAPPOLECLIENT pAppObject,               // the object
    PRECT prPosition )                      // where to position the object
{
    RECT rObject;                           // bounding rectangle for object
    POBJWINDOWINFO pObWindow;               // info about object's window

    if (!pAppObject->pObjectData)           // is there an object?
    {
        return( FALSE );
    }

    OLEWait( pAppObject );                  // can't work with busy object

    /* is the object linked, embedded, or static? */
    OleQueryType( pAppObject->pObjectData, (PLONG)&(pAppObject->dwType) );

    /* how big is it and where should it appear? */
    if (prPosition)                         // did caller give a position?
    {
        CopyRect( &rObject, prPosition );   // yes; use it
    }
    else                                    // no; retrieve one from OleCli
    {
        OleQueryBounds( pAppObject->pObjectData, &rObject );
        MmToPix( (PPOINT)&rObject, 2 );
        MoveRect( &rObject, 0, 0 );         // move rect to origin
    }

    /* create object window to display new object */
    pObWindow = CreateObjWindow( hWnd, &rObject );
    pAppObject->hwndObject = pObWindow->hwndObject;
    if (!pObWindow->hwndObject)
    {
        return( FALSE );                    // couldn't create object window
    }

    /* send the window its data to display */
    SendMessage( pObWindow->hwndObject, OBWIN_MSG_SETDATA,
        (WPARAM)pAppObject, 0 );
    InsertObjWindow( pAppStream, pObWindow );
    SetCurrentObject( pAppStream, pObWindow );
```

```
    pAppStream->iObjects++;                          // increment object counter
    return( TRUE );
}

/*-------------------------------------------------------------------
        DELETE APPLICATION OBJECT
        Releases the memory allocated for an object wrapper.
    ------------------------------------------------------------------*/
void DeleteAppObject ( PAPPOLECLIENT pAppObject )
{
    OLESTATUS OleStatus;

    /* be sure the pointer is valid and the object free */
    if (!pAppObject)
    {
        return;
    }
    OLEWait( pAppObject );

    /* if the wrapper contains a valid OLE object, release it */
    if (pAppObject->pObjectData)
    {
        OleStatus = OleRelease( pAppObject->pObjectData );
        MarkIfBusy( &OleStatus, pAppObject );

        // Wait for the release command to finish before deleting
        // the object's wrapper with its virtual table

        OLEWait( pAppObject );
    }

    // The if statements allow this to be called for errors in
    // NewAppObject; the wrapper may have been only partially
    // constructed.

    if (pAppObject->OleClient.lpvtbl)
    {
        GlobalFreePtr( pAppObject->OleClient.lpvtbl );
    }
    if (pAppObject)
    {
        GlobalFreePtr( pAppObject );
    }
    pAppObject = NULL;
```

```
pAppStream->iObjects--;                    // decrement object counter
return;
}
```

Asynchronous Operations

The next three procedures cope with the fact that some OLE commands return and allow execution to resume before they have finished performing the required action. Because OleCli must often communicate with OleSvr, which in turn must sometimes launch an inactive server in order to respond, some OLE commands can be comparatively slow. Just as **PostMessage** sends a message to a window and returns before the window has a chance to respond, so the OLE commands too sometimes only initiate an action and allow it to proceed in the background. When that happens, the OLE functions return a value of **OLE_WAIT_FOR_RELEASE**, indicating that an asynchronous operation has begun.

Asynchronous operations provide some definite speed advantages. For example, when the user closes a document the client must find all the open objects and release them one by one. There may be many objects actively linked to a variety of servers. Waiting for each release to conclude before beginning the next release could cause a tedious delay. Instead, each **OleRelease** command in effect posts a message to the server. Once the message is in the mail, the client can move straight on to its next task.

A potential problem arises, however, when foreground actions might conflict with pending asynchronous operations. To continue the same example, the client might reasonably expect to deallocate all its object wrappers once it has called **OleRelease** to destroy the actual objects the wrappers represent. But if the barrage of release messages is still trickling through the system after the last **OleRelease** command returns, then destroying the wrappers immediately will prevent the servers from responding. If the object's virtual table has been destroyed, then the OLE libraries no longer have a callback address to send the eventual return results. So after the client loops through a series of **OleRelease** commands, it must have a way to wait for all of them to conclude before it continues to shut down.

Similar problems may arise after any asynchronous operation begins. The documentation indicates that **OleSetHostNames**, for example, can return **OLE_WAIT_FOR_RELEASE**. While any background operation is in progress, the object is considered busy and cannot participate in other operations. If you follow up **Ole-SetHostNames** with, say, **OleActivate**, the second operation will simply fail if the first one still pends.

To deal with asynchronous operations, the client must maintain its own counters noting when objects are busy and when they are free. The logic expressed in the following code recurs throughout most OLE clients:

```
/* write the object data to the file */
OleStatus = OleSaveToStream( pAppObject->pObjectData, (LPOLESTREAM)pStream );

// In checking the result of the operation, recognize that not getting
// OLE_OK does not mean an error occurred. It may be that the command
// initiated an asynchronous operation. If so, update the program's
// busy object flags.

if (OleStatus == OLE_WAIT_FOR_RELEASE)
{
    pAppStream.iBusyObject++;           // count of all busy objects
    pAppObject.bBusy = TRUE;            // mark this object busy
}
else if (OleStatus != OLE_OK)          // abort if load failed
{
    return( FALSE );
}
```

The bBusy flag and the iBusyObject counter are reset in the callback function, which you'll see when we reach Client's document.c source file. Not all OLE commands can return **OLE_WAIT_FOR_RELEASE**, so not all need this special handling. Microsoft's on-line help file lists the possible error return values for each OLE function.

Setting the counters for busy objects solves only half the problem, of course. While it gives the program a way to determine whether any objects are busy, it does not give the program a way to wait for the object to become free before executing a particular command. The obvious solution in Windows NT would be a mutex protecting each object, but of course OLE 1.0 was developed for earlier versions of Windows and must remain compatible with the original API.

The next three procedures in Client cope with the problems of asynchronous operations. MarkIfBusy replaces the cumbersome if/else logic that must follow every potentially asynchronous OLE command. OLEWait polls for messages until a particular object is free. OLEWaitAll polls for messages until all objects are free.

```
/*-------------------------------------------------------------------
        MARK IF BUSY
        Called immediately after any OLE API to check for the
        wait-for-release result and update program counters.
        Also changes the OLESTATUS return from wait-for-release
        to OLE_OK to indicate that the situation has been handled
        and no error occurred.  This makes error checking after
        an OLE call a little easier.
        ----------------------------------------------------------*/

void MarkIfBusy (
    OLESTATUS* pStatus,            // value just returned from an OLE function
    PAPPOLECLIENT pAppObject )     // the object the function operated on
{
    if ((*pStatus) == OLE_WAIT_FOR_RELEASE)
    {
        pAppObject->bBusy = TRUE;
        pAppStream->iBusyObject++;
        *pStatus = OLE_OK;
    }

    // The "busy" flags are undone in the OLEEvent callback
    // in response to OLE_RELEASE.
    return;
}

/*-------------------------------------------------------------------
        OLE WAIT
        Process messages while some asynchronous operation
        is pending for a particular OLE object.
        ----------------------------------------------------------*/

void OLEWait ( PAPPOLECLIENT pAppObject )        // object to wait for
{
    MSG msg;

    while ((pAppObject->bBusy > 0) && GetMessage( &msg, NULL, 0, 0 ))
    {
        TranslateMessage( &msg );
        DispatchMessage( &msg );
    }

    return;
}
```

```
/*-----------------------------------------------------------------
        OLE WAIT ALL
        Process messages while any asynchronous operations are
        still pending for any OLE objects.
    -----------------------------------------------------------*/
void OLEWaitAll ( void )
{
    MSG msg;

    while ((pAppStream->iBusyObject > 0) && GetMessage( &msg, NULL, 0, 0 ))
    {
        TranslateMessage( &msg );
        DispatchMessage( &msg );
    }
    return;
}
```

Returning to the original example, with these procedures you can now mark the busy status and even wait for the object to be free, and do both with fewer lines of code.

```
/* write the object data to the file */
OleStatus = OleSaveToStream( pAppObject->pObjectData, (LPOLESTREAM)pStream );
MarkIfBusy( &OleStatus, pAppObject );      // set flags
if (OleStatus != OLE_OK)                    // check for errors
{
    return( FALSE );
}
OLEWait( pAppObject );                       // proceed when object is free
```

Controlling asynchronous operations in OLE is undoubtedly tedious. The code is repetitious and cumbersome. If OLE had been designed originally for NT, perhaps they would have added timeout parameters so the client could recognize when a server simply fails to respond. OLE 2.0 redresses part of the problem by moving the message loop inside the OLE libraries. We'll say more about OLE 2.0 in the next chapter.

Utilities

The other procedures in client.c perform a variety of small but useful tasks. Of these, only two operations need much comment. First, UniqueName generates a different string each time it is called. The string combines the name of the current document with a five-digit number. The OLE libraries ask you to name each new object you import, and the names must be unique within a single document. The user never sees these names so they do not need to be intelligible, merely unique. The name becomes a part of the object's internal data. You can find an object's name with `OleQueryName` and change it with `OleRename`.

The two conversion procedures, `PixToMm` and `MmToPix`, convert point coordinates between device units and hundredths of a millimeter. To help you display objects, the OLE libraries provide on request a bounding rectangle describing the object's area. To achieve device independence, the rectangle always arrives measured in metric units. When Client saves a document it saves along with each object a rectangle describing its current position in the client area, and for the same reason this rectangle too should be in absolute units. The conversion procedures convert the coordinates between **MM_HIMETRIC** units and **MM_TEXT** units. They even invert the sign of the y coordinates, just as the conversion between those two mapping modes does.

A Note on Scaling

Many programs scale their data differently for display on the screen than they do for a printer. Text programs, in particular, render their text more legibly on the screen by basing their sizes on the exaggerated measurements that **GetDeviceCaps** returns for **LOGPIXELSX** and **LOGPIXELSY**. The practice of scaling to logical sizes causes some minor problems for OLE clients because they know nothing about the contents of any OLE object and cannot tell whether or not it would best be scaled. We tried both methods, writing two versions of the conversion routines. Neither method was a uniform success. OLE package icons definitely require logical scaling to achieve the size of normal icons, but logical scaling made linked Excel cells look too large. Microsoft's technicians inform us that logical scaling is the preferred method, and we have followed their advice.

```
/*-------------------------------------------------------------------
    UNIQUE NAME
    Construct a name string, unique within the current document,
    for identifying objects to OleCli.  No one ever has to
    read the names, so they need only be unique, not intelligible.
    Client's object names are 5-character ASCII strings
    representing unsigned short values.
    -------------------------------------------------------------*/
```

```
PSTR UniqueName ( PSTR pszBuffer )
{
    wsprintf( pszBuffer, "%05d", wID++ );
    return( pszBuffer );
}


/*-------------------------------------------------------------------

        VALIDATE NAME
        Inspect an object name string to be sure it matches
        the program's usual 5-character ASCII string format.  Updates
        wID so it always contains a number higher than any
        it has seen in any validated name.  This ensures that wID
        always produces unique values in UniqueName.
        -----------------------------------------------------------*/

BOOL ValidateName ( PSTR pszName )
{
    if (lstrlen(pszName) == 5)              // is it standard length?
    {
        int i = atoi( pszName );            // is number in valid range?

        if (i > 0)
        {
            wID = (WORD)max( wID, i+1 );    // update wID
            return( TRUE );                 // yes, name is valid
        }
    }

    return( FALSE );                        // no, name is not valid
}


/*-------------------------------------------------------------------

        MILLIMETERS TO PIXELS
        Converts an array of point coordinates from hundredths of
        a millimeter (MM_HIMETRIC units) to pixel coordinates
        (MM_TEXT units).

        Both this procedure and its companion, PixToMm, base their
        conversion on the device driver's recommended scaling ratio as
```

reported by GetDeviceCaps. Measuring in pixels per "logical"
inch slightly enlarges the image for easier viewing.
Both procedures also assume the image is destined for the
display device, not a printer.

```
------------------------------------------------------------------*/

void MmToPix (
    PPOINT pPts,                            // array of points in HIMETRIC units
    int iNumPoints )                        // number of points in array
{
    HDC hDC;                                // screen DC
    int iXRes, iYRes;                       // screen's horz and vert resolution
    int i;                                  // loop variable

    hDC = GetDC( NULL );                    // get display device
    if (!hDC)
    {
        return;
    }

    /* determine screen's logical resolution */
    iXRes = GetDeviceCaps( hDC, LOGPIXELSX );
    iYRes = GetDeviceCaps( hDC, LOGPIXELSY );
    ReleaseDC( NULL, hDC );

    /* perform the conversion */
    for (i = 0; i < iNumPoints; i++)
    {
        pPts[i].x = MulDiv( iXRes, (int)pPts[i].x, HMM_PER_INCH );
        pPts[i].y = MulDiv( iYRes, (int)-pPts[i].y, HMM_PER_INCH );
    }

    return;
}

/*------------------------------------------------------------------
        PIXELS TO MILLIMETERS
        Convert display device coordinates into HIMETRIC coordinates
        (hundredths of a millimeter).  See preceding function header.
------------------------------------------------------------------*/

void PixToMm (
    PPOINT pPts,                            // array of points in device coor's
    int iNumPoints )                        // number of points in array
{
```

```
    HDC hDC;                            // screen display
    int iXRes, iYRes;                   // screen's horz and vert resolution
    int i;                              // loop variable

    hDC = GetDC( NULL );
    if (!hDC)
    {
        return;
    }

    /* determine screen's logical resolution */
    iXRes = GetDeviceCaps( hDC, LOGPIXELSX );
    iYRes = GetDeviceCaps( hDC, LOGPIXELSY );
    ReleaseDC( NULL, hDC );

    /* perform the conversion */
    for (i = 0;  i < iNumPoints; i++)
    {
        pPts[i].x = MulDiv( (int)pPts[i].x, HMM_PER_INCH, iXRes );
        pPts[i].y = MulDiv( (int)-pPts[i].y, HMM_PER_INCH, iYRes );
    }

    return;
}


/*-------------------------------------------------------------------
        MOVE RECT
        Offset a rectangle to position its upper-left corner
        at the given point.
    ----------------------------------------------------------------*/
void MoveRect (
    PRECT pRect,                        // the rectangle
    int x,                              // new left coordinate
    int y )                             // new top coordinate
{
    pRect->right  = x + (pRect->right - pRect->left);
    pRect->bottom = y + (pRect->bottom - pRect->top);
    pRect->top = y;
    pRect->left = x;

    return;
}
```

```
/*-----------------------------------------------------------------
        GET OLE STREAM
        Pass the static pointer to other modules.
  ------------------------------------------------------------*/

PAPPOLESTREAM GetOleStream ( void )
{
    return( pAppStream );
}

/*-----------------------------------------------------------------
        SET WINDOW TITLE
        Add the current file name to the window's caption bar.
  ------------------------------------------------------------*/

static void SetTitle ( HWND hWnd )
{
    char szBuffer[MAX_WINCAPTION];

    /* create a string that says "Client - FILENAME.OLE" */
    strupr( szDocName );
    wsprintf( szBuffer, "%s - %s", (LPSTR)szAppCaption, (LPSTR)szDocName );
    SetWindowText( hWnd, szBuffer );
    return;
}

/*-----------------------------------------------------------------
        ABOUT BOX DIALOG PROCEDURE
        Process messages for the About box window here.
  ------------------------------------------------------------*/

BOOL WINAPI About_DlgProc (
    HWND hDlg,
    UINT uMessage,
    WPARAM wParam,
    LPARAM lParam )
{
    switch (uMessage)
    {
        case WM_INITDIALOG:
            return( TRUE );

        case WM_COMMAND:
            EndDialog( hDlg, TRUE );
```

```
        break;
    }

    return( FALSE );
    UNREFERENCED_PARAMETER( wParam );
    UNREFERENCED_PARAMETER( lParam );
}
```

The Document Module

Most of the procedures in the document module deal with loading, saving, and maintaining documents. A Client program document contains the set of objects the user has pasted or loaded into the client area. A more sophisticated program, such as a word processor, would have to find ways to integrate the data from OLE objects with its own native data. Programs can either write all the data to disk in a single long stream with headers to mark different sections in the document or divide the data among several files, perhaps one for OLE objects and one for its own data. In either case, our sample code makes a good introduction to the basic process of loading and saving OLE objects.

Making and Unmaking the Stream Wrapper

A "stream" in OLE represents the channel through which objects flow to and from the disk. Because our stream wrapper holds information specific to the current document, we destroy and re-create it for each new document. One of the odd things about OLE is that although the API is meant to provide high-level commands to simplify managing foreign objects in your documents, it also requires you to be involved at the very lowest level of stream operations. The two commands **OleLoadFromStream** and **OleSaveToStream** seem to promise easy file I/O for any object, but to use them you have to create a virtual table first and define low-level I/O routines for the libraries to call. The OLE Load and Save commands do not read or write anything themselves; they call your Get and Put functions to do that work. Get and Put together function like a very simple device driver for the OLE libraries, enabling you to channel the read and write operations to any device and in any format you choose. For simple disk files Get and Put can be very brief, as you'll see. The two OLE stream functions convert an object's internal data to and from a series of bytes, which Get and Put process for storage. They transfer undifferentiated bytes between the disk and a buffer the OLE libraries pass to them.

Although the libraries seem to fail here in protecting you from low-level operations, they do succeed admirably at protecting you from the insides of an object. Get and Put are given bytes to store; they have no idea what the bytes mean, and they can represent the bytes in any way they choose. They might, for example, convert the bytes to the ASCII-Hex representation of the Rich Text Format convention, allowing the files to transfer more easily from system to system. On the other end of the file commands, your stream and object wrappers also have no idea what the OLE object contains; they know only where it is in memory.

The four procedures listed next implement the client's parts of a stream. InitOLEDoc allocates and initializes a stream wrapper structure, including the virtual table pointing to OLEGet and OLEPut. TermOLEDoc releases all the objects from a document and destroys all the program's supporting data structures.

TermOLEDoc includes one of the situations where remembering about asynchronous operations becomes very important. Before a client document may be closed, the client must wait until all pending operations have been completed on all of the objects it contains. TermOLEDoc calls OLEWaitAll to be sure the libraries have finished all their work before it walks the list and destroys everything.

```
/*--------------------------------------------------------------------


    DOCUMENT.C

    This module of the CLIENT program includes procedures
    for managing a document with OLE objects and performing
    file I/O.  InitOLEDoc and TermOLEDoc initialize and
    destroy the virtual table and wrapper structure for
    the OLE I/O stream.  The three callback functions
    that OleCli calls directly also live here.  OLEGet
    and OLEPut belong to the stream's virtual table, while
    OLEEvent belongs to the virtual table of each object.


    FUNCTIONS

        InitOLEDoc      set up a fresh empty document
        TermOLEDoc      clear all document data structures

        ReadDocFile     read in a document from the disk
        WriteDocFile    write current document to the disk
```

```
        ReadObject          read one object from the file
        WriteObject         write one object to the file

        OLEGet              read data byte by byte
        OLEPut              write data byte by byte

        OLEEvent            process OLE events

    from Mastering Windows NT Programming
    copyright 1993 by Brian Myers & Eric Hamer


    ------------------------------------------------------------------*/

#define STRICT
#include <windows.h>
#include <windowsx.h>
#include "client.h"

/*-------------------------------------------------------------------
        PROTOTYPES for functions local to this module
    ------------------------------------------------------------------*/

static BOOL ReadObject( HWND hWnd, PAPPOLESTREAM pStream );
static BOOL WriteObject( PAPPOLESTREAM pStream, PAPPOLECLIENT pAppObject );

/*-------------------------------------------------------------------
        MACRO
    ------------------------------------------------------------------*/

#define GetFilePosition( hFile ) \
    SetFilePointer( (hFile), 0, NULL, FILE_CURRENT )

/*-------------------------------------------------------------------
        INIT OLE DOC
        Initialize the OLE I/O stream wrapper for a new document.
        Allocate and initialize the OLESTREAMVTBL and register
        the new document with the OleCli DLL.
    ------------------------------------------------------------------*/

PAPPOLESTREAM InitOLEDoc (
    LPSTR lpszObwinClass,                   // object class name
    LPSTR lpszDocName )                     // document name
{
```

```
OLESTATUS OleStatus;                    // Ole function return value
PAPPOLESTREAM pStream;                  // InitOLEDoc return value

try
{
    /* allocate memory for the application-wide OLE stream structure */
    pStream = GlobalAllocPtr( GPTR, sizeof(APPOLESTREAM) );

    /* allocate room for the stream VTBL */
    pStream->OleStream.lpstbl =
        GlobalAllocPtr( GPTR, sizeof(OLESTREAMVTBL) );

    /* store the function used to load files */
    pStream->OleStream.lpstbl->Get =
        (DWORD(CALLBACK *)(LPOLESTREAM, PVOID, DWORD))OLEGet;

    /* store the function used to save files */
    pStream->OleStream.lpstbl->Put =
        (DWORD(CALLBACK *)(LPOLESTREAM, OLE_CONST VOID *, DWORD))OLEPut;
}
except ((GetExceptionCode() == EXCEPTION_ACCESS_VIOLATION)
        ? EXCEPTION_EXECUTE_HANDLER : EXCEPTION_CONTINUE_SEARCH)
{
    /* if an error occurs, release anything that was allocated */
    if (pStream->OleStream.lpstbl)
    {
        GlobalFreePtr( pStream->OleStream.lpstbl );
    }
    if (pStream)
    {
        GlobalFreePtr( pStream );
    }
    return( NULL );
}

lstrcpy( pStream->szDocName, lpszDocName );
pStream->iObjects = 0;
lstrcpy( pStream->szAppClass, lpszObwinClass );

/* register the new document with the OleCli DLL */
OleStatus = OleRegisterClientDoc(
                pStream->szAppClass,        // document class
                pStream->szDocName,         // document path name
                0,                          // reserved
                &pStream->OleDocHandle );   // new document handle
```

```
    if (OleStatus != OLE_OK)
    {
        GlobalFreePtr( pStream->OleStream.lpstbl );
        GlobalFreePtr( pStream );
        pStream = NULL;
    }

    return( pStream );
}

/*--------------------------------------------------------------
        TERMINATE OLE DOCUMENT
        Terminate all the OLE objects.  Unregister the current
        document.  After TermOLEDoc runs, the entire pStream wrapper
        structure is invalid.  (Call InitOLEDoc to create a new one.)
    --------------------------------------------------------------*/
void TermOLEDoc ( PAPPOLESTREAM pStream )
{
    if (!pStream)
    {
        return;                                 // nothing's open; return
    }

    OLEWaitAll( );              // wait for any asynchronous operations to end

    /* walk the linked list of object windows destroying each one */
    while (pStream->pObWindowList)
    {
        // Delete a node from the list, closing up the gap.
        // When a child window is destroyed, it also releases
        // its associated object, waits for the release to
        // reach completion, and deletes the object wrapper.

        DeleteObjWindow( pStream, pStream->pObWindowList );
    }

    /* tell OleCli we are through with the document */
    OleSavedClientDoc( pStream->OleDocHandle );     // doesn't need to be saved
    OleRevokeClientDoc( pStream->OleDocHandle );    // no longer in use

    /* release the stream wrapper */
    GlobalFreePtr( pStream->OleStream.lpstbl );
```

```
    GlobalFreePtr( pStream );
    pStream = NULL;

    return;
}

/*------------------------------------------------------------------
        OLE GET
        OLE callback function ("Get") for reading from a file.
        This function is pointed to in the OLESTREAMVTBL.  It
        returns a DWORD telling how many bytes were read from
        the file.
        ----------------------------------------------------------*/

DWORD WINAPI OLEGet (
    LPOLESTREAM lpOleStream,                    // stream wrapper
    PVOID pBuffer,                              // buffer to fill
    DWORD dwBytes )                            // count of bytes to read
{
    DWORD dwBytesRead;
    PAPPOLESTREAM pStream = (PAPPOLESTREAM)lpOleStream;

    ReadFile( pStream->hFile,                   // file handle
        pBuffer,                               // data buffer
        dwBytes,                               // size of buffer
        &dwBytesRead,                          // count of bytes read
        NULL );                                // no overlapping I/O

    return( dwBytesRead );
    // OleLoadFromStream will return an error if dwBytesRead
    // is any value other than dwBytes.
}

/*------------------------------------------------------------------
        OLE PUT
        OLE callback function ("Put") for writing to a file.
        This function is pointed to in the OLESTREAMVTBL.  It
        returns a DWORD telling how many bytes were written
        to the file.
        ----------------------------------------------------------*/

DWORD WINAPI OLEPut (
    LPOLESTREAM lpOleStream,                    // stream wrapper
```

```
OLE_CONST PVOID pData,                        // data buffer
DWORD dwBytes )                               // count of bytes in buffer
{
    DWORD dwBytesWritten;
    PAPPOLESTREAM pStream = (PAPPOLESTREAM)lpOleStream;

    WriteFile( pStream->hFile,                // file handle
        pData,                                // data buffer
        dwBytes,                              // size of buffer
        &dwBytesWritten,                      // count of bytes written
        NULL );                               // no overlapping I/O

    return( dwBytesWritten );
    // OleSaveToStream will return an error if dwBytesWritten
    // is any value other than dwBytes.
}
```

Reading and Writing Objects

ReadDocFile and WriteDocFile are high-level commands that loop through all the objects in a document and load them or save them one by one. They call Read-Object and WriteObject to perform most of the disk operations. They do perform one operation directly. Each Client data file begins with a single 4-byte unsigned integer indicating the number of objects in the document. WriteDocFile writes that quantity before storing the objects, and ReadDocFile begins by reading it.

ReadObject and WriteObject are built around **OleLoadFromStream** and **Ole-SaveToStream**. Before calling either of those, however, the object I/O procedures must account for a header. ReadObject reads the header and loads the object. WriteObject writes the header and saves the object. The header contains three items. The first, a string, names the object's storage protocol, which may be either "StdFileEditing" or "Static". Static objects contain only presentation data with no reference back to the original server. They may not be edited. "StdFileEditing" is the normal protocol for linked and embedded objects. **OleLoadFromStream** requires a protocol as one of its parameters, so store the protocol with each object. You could omit this field from the header and try first to load with StdFileEditing and then, if that failed, try again with Static. That's the approach normally used when pasting a new object from the clipboard, as you'll see in the clip.c module.

The second field in the Client object header records the unique name assigned to the object when it was received. The OLE libraries use the name internally to identify its data stream, and an object should be given the same name each time it is loaded. The third field contains a rectangle describing the object's position in hundredths of a millimeter. Client uses this information to position each object exactly where the user left it. We could instead call **OleQueryBounds** to get a display rectangle for each new object, but that returns only the object's size, not its position in the window.

```
/*-------------------------------------------------------------------
      READ DOCUMENT FILE
      Reads OLE objects from a file.  Reads the file header to see
      how many objects the file contains and then runs a loop
      to read each one.  Returns TRUE if all the objects load
      successfully.
      ---------------------------------------------------------------*/

BOOL ReadDocFile (
    HWND hWnd,
    PAPPOLESTREAM pStream )
{
    int iNumObjects;                        // objects in file
    DWORD dwBytesRead;                      // return from ReadFile
    BOOL bSuccess;                          // function return value

    /* move to beginning of file */
    SetFilePointer( pStream->hFile, 0, NULL, FILE_BEGIN );

    /* first four bytes tell number of objects in file */
    bSuccess = ReadFile( pStream->hFile,
                &iNumObjects,               // buffer to fill
                sizeof(int),                // num bytes to read
                &dwBytesRead,               // value returned
                NULL );                     // no overlapping I/O
    if ((!bSuccess) || (dwBytesRead != sizeof(int)))
    {
        return( FALSE );
    }

    /* loop through all the objects, loading each one */
    while ((iNumObjects > 0) && bSuccess)
```

```
        {
            bSuccess = ReadObject( hWnd, pStream );
            iNumObjects--;
        }
        return( bSuccess );
    }

/*-------------------------------------------------------------------
        WRITE DOCUMENT FILE
        Saves all the objects in the current document into a disk
        file.  Returns TRUE for success.
    -----------------------------------------------------------------*/
BOOL WriteDocFile ( PAPPOLESTREAM pStream )      // application stream pointer
{
    int iObjectsWritten = 0;                // counter of objects written to file
    DWORD dwBytesWritten;                   // returned from WriteFile
    POBJWINDOWINFO pWindow;                 // info about an object window
    PAPPOLECLIENT pAppObject;               // an object wrapper
    BOOL bSuccess;                          // returned from Boolean functions
    if (pStream->iObjects == 0)
    {
        return( FALSE );                    // nothing to write
    }

    /* move to beginning of file */
    SetFilePointer( pStream->hFile, 0, NULL, FILE_BEGIN );

    /* begin file with an integer saying how many objects it contains */
    bSuccess = WriteFile( pStream->hFile,
            &pStream->iObjects,             // buffer to save
            sizeof(int),                    // count of bytes to write
            &dwBytesWritten,                // count of bytes written
            NULL );                         // no overlapping I/O
    if (!bSuccess || (dwBytesWritten != sizeof(int)))
    {
        return( FALSE );
    }

    /* loop through all the windows retrieving and writing object data */
    pWindow = pStream->pObWindowList;        // select first window
    while ((iObjectsWritten < pStream->iObjects) && bSuccess)
    {
```

```
    /* retrieve object data associated with the window */
    pAppObject = (PAPPOLECLIENT)SendMessage( pWindow->hwndObject,
                            OBWIN_MSG_GETDATA, 0, 0 );

    if (pAppObject)
    {
        /* write the object data to the file */
        bSuccess = WriteObject( pStream, pAppObject );
        if (bSuccess)
        {
            iObjectsWritten++;           // increment counter
            pWindow = pWindow->pNext;   // select next window
        }
    }
    else
    {
        bSuccess = FALSE;                // failed to retrieve data
    }
    }

    return( bSuccess );
}


/*------------------------------------------------------------------
        READ OBJECT
        Read one object from the stream.
    --------------------------------------------------------------*/

static BOOL ReadObject (
    HWND hWnd,                          // main program window
    PAPPOLESTREAM pStream )             // current I/O stream
{
    PAPPOLECLIENT pAppObject;           // info about an object
    OBJECT_HEADER obHeader;             // precedes each object in file
    DWORD dwBytesRead;                  // count of bytes read from file
    OLESTATUS OleStatus;                // return value from Ole function
    BOOL bTest;                         // return from ReadFile

    /* initialize an object wrapper */
    pAppObject = NewAppObject( );
    if (!pAppObject)
    {
        return( FALSE );
    }
```

```
// Next read application-specific header info the program
// uses to mark the beginning of an object in the file.  This
// program heads each with an OBJECT_HEADER structure.

bTest = ReadFile( pStream->hFile,
        &obHeader,                      // buffer to fill
        sizeof(OBJECT_HEADER),          // num bytes to read
        &dwBytesRead,                   // value returned
        NULL );                         // no overlapping I/O
if ((!bTest) || (dwBytesRead != sizeof(OBJECT_HEADER)))
{
    return( FALSE );
}

/* verify that header contains a valid name string */
if (!ValidateName( obHeader.szName ))
{
    return( FALSE );                    // not a valid name
}

/* convert the position rectangle to device units */
MmToPix( (LPPOINT)&obHeader.rObject, 2 );

OleStatus = OleLoadFromStream(          // read data from file
    &pStream>OleStream,                 // I/O stream
    obHeader.szProtocol,                // I/O protocol
    &pAppObject>OleClient,              // new object's VTBL
    &pStream>OleDocHandle,              // container document
    obHeader.szName,                    // our name for new object
    &pAppObject>pObjectData );          // place for pointer to new buffer

/* note if the operation continues asynchronously */
MarkIfBusy( &OleStatus, pAppObject );
if (OleStatus != OLE_OK)                // abort if load failed
{
    DeleteAppObject( pAppObject );
    return( FALSE );
}

/* initialize the rest of the object wrapper fields */
InitAppObject( hWnd, pAppObject, &obHeader.rObject );

return( TRUE );
}
```

```
/*-------------------------------------------------------------------
        WRITE OBJECT
        Saves one object to the stream, writing its header and data.
        The header for this simple client program is a 15-character
        string naming the document's storage protocol, which should
        be either "StdFileEditing" or "Static".
        -----------------------------------------------------------*/

BOOL WriteObject (
        PAPPOLESTREAM pStream,                  // the I/O stream
        PAPPOLECLIENT pAppObject )              // the object to save
{
        BOOL bSuccess;                          // return from WriteFile
        DWORD dwBytesWritten;                   // count of bytes written
        OLESTATUS OleStatus;                    // return from Ole function
        POBJWINDOWINFO pObWinInfo;              // info about an object window
        OBJECT_HEADER obHeader;                 // precedes each object in file
        HWND hWnd;                              // main program window
        UINT uSize;                             // size of name string buffer

        if (!pAppObject)                        // check for invalid pointer
        {
            return( FALSE );
        }

        /* choose a string naming the object's protocol */
        if (pAppObject->dwType == OT_STATIC)
        {
            lstrcpy( obHeader.szProtocol, "Static" );
        }
        else
        {
            lstrcpy( obHeader.szProtocol, "StdFileEditing" );
        }

        /* copy object's name to szName field of object header */
        uSize = sizeof(obHeader.szName);
        OleQueryName( pAppObject>pObjectData, obHeader.szName, &uSize );

        /* initialize header with object window rectangle coordinates */
        pObWinInfo = GetObjWindowInfo( pAppObject->hwndObject );
        GetWindowRect( pAppObject->hwndObject, &obHeader.rObject );

        /* convert to HIMETRIC units for the parent window's client area */
        hWnd = GetParent( pAppObject->hwndObject );
```

```
ScreenToClient( hWnd, (LPPOINT)&obHeader.rObject );
ScreenToClient( hWnd, (LPPOINT)&obHeader.rObject.right );
PixToMm( (PPOINT)&obHeader.rObject, 2 );

/* write the header to the file */
bSuccess = WriteFile( pStream->hFile,
    &obHeader,
    sizeof(OBJECT_HEADER),
    &dwBytesWritten,
    NULL );
if (!bSuccess || (dwBytesWritten != sizeof(OBJECT_HEADER)))
{
    return( FALSE );
}

/* write the object data to the file */
OleStatus = OleSaveToStream( pAppObject->pObjectData,
    (LPOLESTREAM)pStream );

// The write operation is likely to be lengthy.  While the
// OLE libraries summon up the server, if necessary, poll
// for messages here so our windows continue to get messages

MarkIfBusy( &OleStatus, pAppObject );
OLEWait( pAppObject );

return( OleStatus == OLE_OK );
}
```

Event Notification

The virtual table wrapped in every APPOLECLIENT structure contains a pointer to a single callback function. The OleCli library needs to see this pointer when it works with your objects. If something happens to the object, the library sends a notification code to the callback procedure. In Client, this procedure is called OLEEvent, and you saw it mentioned in the code where NewAppObject initializes each new object wrapper. We've already discussed asynchronous OLE operations. When an asynchronous background command eventually does terminate, the library announces the event to the callback function. Responding to the **OLE_RELEASE** signal is the only way to maintain the program's flags for busy objects.

The OLE client callback function must follow this prototype:

```
int (CALLBACK* CallBack)(
    LPOLECLIENT lpOleClient,            // the client's object wrapper
    OLE_NOTIFICATION onNotification,    // the event code
    LPOLEOBJECT lpOleObject );          // the OLE object itself
```

Client has no use for some of the possible messages—all of which do appear in the switch statement—but if the object has been changed in the server it should be redrawn, and if the library wants to continue a lengthy paint operation it should be allowed.

```
/*-----------------------------------------------------------------
        OLE EVENT
        Process OLE events.  This is the callback function pointed to
        in the OLECLIENTVTBL.  When something beyond our control
        happens to an object, OleCli sends a message here.
        -------------------------------------------------------------*/

int WINAPI OLEEvent (
    LPOLECLIENT pOleObject,          // object wrapper
    OLE_NOTIFICATION OleNotify,      // event code
    LPOLEOBJECT pObjectData )        // OLE object data
{
    PAPPOLECLIENT pAppObject;        // alias for pOleObject wrapper
    PAPPOLESTREAM pStream;           // document I/O stream
    RECT rObject;                    // bounding rectangle
    HWND hWnd;                       // an object window
    DWORD dwSize;                    // size of the OLE object

    /* retrieve the pointers to the OLE object and the OLE stream */
    pAppObject = (PAPPOLECLIENT)pOleObject;
    pStream = GetOleStream( );

    switch (OleNotify)
    {
        case OLE_SAVED:              // object was saved in server
        case OLE_CHANGED:            // object was edited in server
            hWnd = pAppObject->hwndObject;
            OleQueryBounds( pAppObject->pObjectData, &rObject );
            MmToPix( (PPOINT)&rObject, 2 );
            SetWindowPos( hWnd, NULL,
                (int)rObject.left, (int)rObject.top,
```

```
                    (int)rObject.right, (int)rObject.bottom,
                    SWP_NOMOVE );
                break;

            case OLE_RELEASE:                        // asynchronous op. completed
                pAppObject->bBusy = FALSE;           // this object isn't busy
                pStream->iBusyObject--;              // one fewer busy objects
                break;

        case OLE_QUERY_PAINT:
            /* let OLE continue with a lengthy paint operation */
            return( TRUE );

        // If the user chooses Insert Object and then exits from
        // the server without finishing the new object, the only
        // notice we get is the usual indication that an actively
        // linked server has closed.  We can check the size, however,
        // to see whether we really received an object.

        case OLE_CLOSED:                             // server closed object
            OleQuerySize( pAppObject->pObjectData, &dwSize );
            if (dwSize == 0)                         // is object empty?
            {
                DeleteObjWindow( pStream, pStream->pObjWindowList );
            }
            break;

        /* this program makes no use of these other notifications */
        case OLE_QUERY_RETRY:                        // server no longer busy
        case OLE_RENAMED:                            // server renamed object
            break;
    }

    return( FALSE );
    UNREFERENCED_PARAMETER( pObjectData );
}
```

The Clipboard Module

The primary method of linking or embedding objects in a document is pasting from the clipboard. The ordinary Paste operation generally causes an object to be embedded, if the correct format is on the clipboard. To allow a user to link an object, an application provides a new menu item, Paste Link. (Alternatively it may provide Paste Special, which invokes a dialog box allowing a user to specify explicitly the type of pasting desired.) Two other OLE clipboard commands are optional, and Client includes one of them. The Links command allows the user to inspect, update, and modify all the link mechanisms in a document. The Insert Object command presents the user with a list of servers and invokes the selected one to create a new object. Client includes Insert Object on its menu. Some servers, such as the Draw program that comes with Microsoft Word for Windows, do not run as stand-alone applications and can be reached only through the Insert Object command on client menus.

Pasting from the Clipboard

You may have noticed that the `Client_OnInitMenu` message handler calls two Boolean functions, `CanPaste` and `CanPasteLink`, to decide whether Paste and Paste Link should be enabled. Both call OLE functions to test for the presence of OLE objects on the clipboard. Note that a **FALSE** return from `CanPaste` does not mean the clipboard is necessarily empty; it means only that the clipboard does not contain OLE objects. A full-featured program would check for progressively more primitive formats on the clipboard—first **CF_ENHMETAFILE**, then **CF_METAFILEPICT**, then **CF_BITMAP**, and finally **CF_TEXT**. Client, however, works only with OLE objects.

```
/*------------------------------------------------------------------

    CLIP.C

    Clipboard-related procedures for the CLIENT program.
    These functions move objects to and from the clipboard.
    Also included are those that read from the system
    registry in order to fill the server list box on the
    Insert dialog box.

    FUNCTIONS

        CanPasteObject          TRUE if Paste should be enabled
        CanPasteLink            TRUE if Paste Link should be enabled
        PasteObject             paste object from clipboard
        CopyObject              copy object to clipboard
        CutObject               remove object to clipboard
        ClearObject             remove object from document
```

```
            InsertObject              let user choose an object class
            DoInsertDlg               summon Insert dialog box
            Insert_DlgProc            process dialog box messages
            AddEntries                place list of servers in list box
            RetrieveData              convert description to class name
            GetOleClass               find class name in registry

        from Mastering Windows NT Programming
        copyright 1993 by Brian Myers & Eric Hamer


    ---------------------------------------------------------------------*/

#include <windows.h>
#include <windowsx.h>
#include <ole.h>
#include "client.h"
#include "rsrc.h"

/*-------------------------------------------------------------------
            PROTOTYPES
    ---------------------------------------------------------------------*/

static BOOL DoInsertDlg( HWND hWnd, LPSTR lpszText );
BOOL WINAPI Insert_DlgProc( HWND hDlg, UINT uMsg, WPARAM wParam,
    LPARAM lParam );
static BOOL AddEntries( HWND hwndList );
static void RetrieveData( HWND hDlg );
static BOOL GetOleClass( LPSTR lpszText );

/*-------------------------------------------------------------------
            STATIC VARIABLE
    ---------------------------------------------------------------------*/

char szServerClass[256];                         // string from registry

/*-------------------------------------------------------------------
            CAN PASTE OBJECT
            Determine whether there are any objects to be pasted.
    ---------------------------------------------------------------------*/

BOOL CanPasteObject ( void )
{
    OLESTATUS OleStatus;

    OleStatus = OleQueryCreateFromClip( "StdFileEditing", olerender_draw, 0 );
```

```
    if (OleStatus == OLE_OK)
    {
        return( TRUE );
    }

    OleStatus = OleQueryCreateFromClip( "Static", olerender_draw, 0 );
    if (OleStatus == OLE_OK)
    {
        return( TRUE );
    }

    return( FALSE );
}

/*------------------------------------------------------------------
        CAN PASTE LINK
        Determine whether there are any objects to be paste-linked.
    ------------------------------------------------------------------*/

BOOL CanPasteLink ( void )
{
    OLESTATUS OleStatus;

    OleStatus = OleQueryLinkFromClip( "StdFileEditing", olerender_draw, 0 );
    if (OleStatus == OLE_OK)
    {
        return( TRUE );
    }

    return( FALSE );
}
```

When the user issues a Paste command, the program calls `PasteObject`, which follows these steps:

1. Open the clipboard (with `OpenClipboard`).

2. Allocate a new object wrapper (with `NewAppObject`).

3. Try to take the object (with one of several OLE commands).

4. Close the clipboard (with `CloseClipboard`).

5. Test the return value from the OLE command.

6. Initialize the object wrapper (with `InitAppObject`).

The choice of OLE commands in step 3 depends on whether you want to link the object or embed it. **OleCreateLinkFromClip** pastes just the link information and the presentation data; **OleCreateFromClip** takes the original native data as well. If **OleCreateFromClip** fails, Client tries a second time with a less demanding protocol, Static. (Statically embedded objects cannot be edited as OLE objects; they retain absolutely no connection back to the original server or their native data.)

The call to `InitAppObject` takes care of determining the new object's display size, creating a window for it, and inserting the window in the program's list.

```
/*-----------------------------------------------------------------
        PASTE OBJECT
        Paste an object from the clipboard.
        -----------------------------------------------------------*/
BOOL PasteObject (
    HWND hWnd,                              // main program window
    BOOL bLink )                            // TRUE to link (not embed)
{
    char szName[MAX_OBJNAME];               // name to identify new object
    PAPPOLECLIENT pAppObject;               // object wrapper structure
    OLESTATUS OleStatus;                    // OLE function return value
    PAPPOLESTREAM pStream;                  // the I/O stream wrapper

    if (!OpenClipboard( hWnd ))             // ask for clipboard
    {
        return( FALSE );
    }

    pAppObject = NewAppObject( );           // allocate new wrapper
    if (!pAppObject)
    {
        CloseClipboard( );
        return( FALSE );
    }

    pStream = GetOleStream( );              // get the stream wrapper

    UniqueName( szName );                   // build identifier string
```

```
/* make an OLE call to link or embed the object */
if (bLink)                                   // user wants to link
{
    OleStatus = OleCreateLinkFromClip(
            "StdFileEditing",                // protocol
            (LPOLECLIENT)pAppObject,         // object VTBL
            pStream->OleDocHandle,           // receiving document
            szName,                          // client's name for object
            &pAppObject->pObjectData,        // place to put object
            olerender_draw,                  // preferred presentation format
            0 );                             // clipboard format (unused)
}
else                                         // user wants to embed
{
    /* try to embed the live object */
    OleStatus = OleCreateFromClip(
            "StdFileEditing",                // protocol
            (LPOLECLIENT)pAppObject,         // object VTBL
            pStream->OleDocHandle,           // receiving document
            szName,                          // client's name for object
            &pAppObject->pObjectData,        // place to put object
            olerender_draw,                  // preferred presentation format
            0 );                             // clipboard format (unused)

    /* if that failed, try for a static object instead */
    if (OleStatus != OLE_OK)
    {
        OleStatus = OleCreateFromClip(
            "Static",                        // protocol
            (LPOLECLIENT)pAppObject,         // object VTBL
            pStream->OleDocHandle,           // receiving document
            szName,                          // client's name for object
            &pAppObject->pObjectData,        // place to put object
            olerender_draw,                  // preferred presentation format
            0 );                             // clipboard format (unused)
    }
}
CloseClipboard( );                           // we're done with the clipboard

MarkIfBusy( &OleStatus, pAppObject );        // WAIT_FOR_RELEASE?
if (OleStatus != OLE_OK)
{
    DeleteAppObject( pAppObject );           // paste operation failed
    return( FALSE );
}
```

```
    /* fill in all the other fields of the object wrapper */
    if (!InitAppObject( hWnd, pAppObject, NULL ))
    {
        DeleteAppObject( pAppObject );
    }

    return( TRUE );
}
```

Copying, Clearing, and Cutting

CopyObject, CutObject, and ClearObject are short procedures. The first two put an object on the clipboard, and the last one deletes an object from the current document. CutObject works by calling CopyObject and then ClearObject. The only OLE command in all this is the very straightforward **OleCopyToClipboard**.

```
/*-------------------------------------------------------------------
        COPY OBJECT
        Copy an object to the clipboard.
   -------------------------------------------------------------------*/

BOOL CopyObject (
    HWND hWnd,
    POBJWINDOWINFO pObWindow )
{
    PAPPOLECLIENT pAppObject;
    OLESTATUS OleStatus;

    /* get object associated with current child window */
    pAppObject = (PAPPOLECLIENT)SendMessage( pObWindow->hwndObject,
                 OBWIN_MSG_GETDATA, 0, 0 );

    if (!OpenClipboard( hWnd ))              // get the clipboard
    {
        return( FALSE );
    }

    EmptyClipboard();                        // clear the clipboard

    OleStatus = OleCopyToClipboard( pAppObject->pObjectData );

    CloseClipboard();                        // close the clipboard
```

```
        return( OleStatus == OLE_OK );
}

/*-----------------------------------------------------------------
        CUT OBJECT
        Cut an object to the clipboard by first copying it there
        and then clearing it from the document.
    ------------------------------------------------------------*/

BOOL CutObject (
    HWND hWnd,
    POBJWINDOWINFO pObWindow )
{
    BOOL bTest;

    bTest = CopyObject( hWnd, pObWindow );
    if (bTest)
    {
        bTest = ClearObject( pObWindow );
    }

    return( bTest );
}

/*-----------------------------------------------------------------
        CLEAR OBJECT
        Delete the current object from the document.
    ------------------------------------------------------------*/

BOOL ClearObject ( POBJWINDOWINFO pObWindow )
{
    PAPPOLESTREAM pStream;                    // the I/O stream wrapper

    if (!pObWindow)                           // did we get a valid window?
    {
        return( TRUE );                       // no window is active
    }

    /* delete one window and make the next active */
    pStream = GetOleStream( );
    SetCurrentObject( pStream, DeleteObjWindow(pStream, pObWindow) );
```

```
        // DeleteObjWindow does all the work of deallocating
        // structures, releasing the object, and resetting variables.

        return( TRUE );
    }
```

The Insert Object Command

The final command on the Edit menu, Insert Object, asks the user to choose a server from a list of those registered in the system. Client invokes the selected server for the user to create and edit a new object. The code for inserting the object is easy; it appears in `InsertObject` and leads up to an **OleCreate** command. After creating the new object, Client calls **OleSetHostNames** to establish strings for the server's title bar. While the user works in the server, the name of Client's document appears in the server window. The name helps the user see which windows on the screen are working on the same project.

(Incidentally, Microsoft's documentation sometimes misleadingly refers to the third parameter of **OleSetHostNames** as `lpszClientObj` and seems to ask you for a name that uniquely identifies the object itself. But the user has no use for these individual names; what belongs here is the name of the compound document where the user has inserted the object.)

```
/*-----------------------------------------------------------------
        INSERT OBJECT
        Display Insert Object dialog box to let the user choose
        an object class from any registered server.  Invoke
        the server and receive a new object from it.
    ------------------------------------------------------------*/

BOOL InsertObject (
    HWND hWnd,                            // main window
    PSTR pszCaption )                     // main window title
{
    PAPPOLECLIENT pAppObject;             // object wrapper
    PAPPOLESTREAM pStream;                // stream wrapper
    char szObjClass[256];                 // object class name
    char szObjName[MAX_OBJNAME];          // our name for the object
    OLESTATUS OleStatus;                  // returned from Ole functions
    BOOL bTest;                           // Boolean return value
```

```
pStream = GetOleStream( );                      // get the stream wrapper

bTest = DoInsertDlg( hWnd, szObjClass );        // get class name from user
if (!bTest)
{
    return( FALSE );
}

pAppObject = NewAppObject( );                   // allocate new object wrapper
if (!pAppObject)
{
    return( FALSE );
}

UniqueName( szObjName );                         // make an identifying name

// Create a new object of the chosen class.  This command invokes
// the server and lets the user create the object there.  When
// the object is ready, this command embeds it in our document.

OleStatus = OleCreate(
    "StdFileEditing",                           // protocol
    (LPOLECLIENT)pAppObject,                    // client VTBL
    szObjClass,                                 // object class name
    pStream->OleDocHandle,                      // destination document
    szObjName,                                  // our name for the new object
    &pAppObject->pObjectData,                   // place to put object pointer
    olerender_draw,                             // preferred display format
    0 );                                        // clipboard format (not used)

MarkIfBusy( &OleStatus, pAppObject );           // WAIT_FOR_RELEASE?
if (OleStatus != OLE_OK)                         // success?
{
    DeleteAppObject( pAppObject );              // undo object creation
    return( FALSE );
}

// Tell the OleCli library how the server should identify
// this object to the user on its window title bar.
OLEWait( pAppObject );
OleStatus = OleSetHostNames(
    pAppObject->pObjectData,                    // the object
    pszCaption,                                 // application name
    pStream->szDocName );                       // document name
MarkIfBusy( &OleStatus, pAppObject );
```

```
/* initialize the rest of the fields in the object wrapper */
InitAppObject( hWnd, pAppObject, NULL );

    return( TRUE );
}
```

The Insert Object Dialog Box

Figure 14.8 shows the dialog box where the user selects an available server. This information is kept in the system registry, and the user may edit it with the Registry Editor accessory program, also visible in the same figure.

Five functions support the dialog box:

- `DoInsertDlg` invokes the Insert dialog box.

- `Insert_DlgProc` processes messages for the dialog box.

- `AddEntries` reads the registry and fills the list box with descriptive strings naming the kinds of objects supported by the currently installed servers.

FIGURE 14.8:

Dialog box showing information from the system registry, along with the Registry Editor's view of the same information

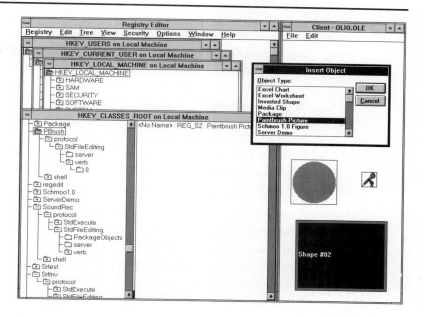

- `RetrieveData` finds the user's selection in the list box and returns the corresponding object class name.

- `GetOleClass` searches the registry for the object class name that matches a particular descriptive string.

The registry stores two strings for each object type. One is long and descriptive, meant to be readable for humans. It might be "Paintbrush Picture." The second one is the real class name, the one recognized by the OLE libraries. It might be "PBrush". (You can see all the classes and descriptions in your system with the RegEdit accessory program.)

Client reads only two subkeys from the registry. One subkey is the name of an object class and contains as its value the descriptive string for that class. The other subkey, several levels lower in the hierarchy, is named "server" and contains the full path of the server's executable file.

- `HKEY_CLASSES_ROOT\<classname>`: Stored in the class name subkey is a string naming the same class more descriptively. If the subkey is Pbrush, the value might be Paintbrush Picture.

- `KEY_CLASSES_ROOT\<classname>\protocol\StdFileEditing\server`: The value in the server subkey is the full path name of the server's executable file.

The `AddEntries` procedure enumerates the keys immediately under **HKEY_CLASSES_ ROOT**. Not all of the keys at this level are class names. Some are file name extensions, for example, and the values they contain are associated object classes. To determine whether a given key is an object class name, `AddEntries` checks for the existence of the server subkey further down the same branch. Client has no interest in the executable file name stored in the server node; the server node's mere existence confirms that the first node is indeed a class name. `AddEntries` returns to the class name node and queries its value, retrieves the descriptive string, and places that in the list box.

If the user does select a string from the list box, Client must return to the registry to recover the actual class name, which is the name of the subkey where the description was discovered. `GetObjectClass` enumerates the subkeys under the root a second time, comparing the value stored in each to the description string. When it finds a match, it deposits the subkey name in the static variable `szServerClass`, where it can be found after the dialog box ends.

```
/*------------------------------------------------------------------
        DO INSERT DIALOG
        Invoke the Insert dialog box.  Returns TRUE if the user
        makes a selection.  If DoInsertDlg returns TRUE, then
        lpszReturn will point to a string naming an object class
        chosen by the user from the system registry.
    ------------------------------------------------------------------*/
static BOOL DoInsertDlg (
    HWND hWnd,                          // main program window
    LPSTR lpszReturn )                  // place to return server's class name
{
    HINSTANCE hInst;
    int iResult;

    if (!lpszReturn)                    // did we get a return buffer?
    {
        return( FALSE );
    }

    /* show the dialog box */
    hInst = GetWindowInstance( hWnd );
    iResult = DialogBox( hInst, MAKEINTRESOURCE(DLG_INSERT), hWnd,
        (DLGPROC)Insert_DlgProc );

    if (!iResult)
    {
        return( FALSE );                          // user canceled
    }

    /* copy the user's choice where the calling procedure can find it */
    lstrcpy( lpszReturn, szServerClass );

    return( TRUE );
}


/*------------------------------------------------------------------
        INSERT_DLGPROC
        Process messages for the Insert Object dialog box.
    ------------------------------------------------------------------*/
BOOL WINAPI Insert_DlgProc (
    HWND hDlg,
    UINT uMsg,
```

```
    WPARAM wParam,
    LPARAM lParam )
{
    HWND hwndList;                              // control window
    BOOL bTest;                                 // return value for testing
    WORD wCmdID;                                // menu command ID
    WORD wCode;                                 // command info code

    switch (uMsg)
    {
        case WM_INITDIALOG:
            hwndList = GetDlgItem( hDlg, IDD_SERVERLIST );
            bTest = AddEntries( hwndList );
            return( bTest );

        case WM_COMMAND:
            wCmdID = LOWORD( wParam );           // parse message params
            wCode = HIWORD( wParam );

            switch (wCmdID)
            {
                case IDCANCEL:
                    EndDialog( hDlg, FALSE );
                    break;

                case IDD_SERVERLIST:
                    if (wCode == LBN_DBLCLK)
                    {
                        /* double-clicking is the same as clicking OK */
                        RetrieveData( hDlg );
                        EndDialog( hDlg, TRUE );
                    }
                    break;

                case IDOK:
                    RetrieveData( hDlg );
                    EndDialog( hDlg, TRUE );
                    break;
            }
            break;
    }

    return( FALSE );
    UNREFERENCED_PARAMETER( lParam );
}
```

```
/*------------------------------------------------------------------
        ADD ENTRIES
        Reads the system registry and fills the list box with
        descriptive strings naming the kinds of objects supported
        by currently installed servers.
        ---------------------------------------------------------------*/
static BOOL AddEntries ( HWND hwndList )
{
    char szServerKey[_MAX_PATH];        // string naming the server subkey
    char szKeyName[_MAX_PATH];          // subkey under HKEY_CLASSES_ROOT
    char szValue[_MAX_PATH];            // data stored in a key
    HKEY hKey;                          // handle to a registry key
    LONG lResult;                       // for testing returns
    LONG lLength;                       // size of a string buffer
    UINT uIndex;                        // counts enumerated subkeys

    ListBox_ResetContent( hwndList );

    /* acquire a handle for HKEY_CLASSES_ROOT */
    lResult = RegOpenKey( HKEY_CLASSES_ROOT, NULL, &hKey );
    if (lResult != (LONG)ERROR_SUCCESS)
    {
        return( FALSE );
    }

    /* retrieve the name of the first subkey under HKEY_CLASSES_ROOT */
    uIndex = 0;
    lResult = RegEnumKey( hKey, uIndex++, szKeyName, _MAX_PATH ) ;
    if (lResult != (LONG)ERROR_SUCCESS)
    {
        return( FALSE );
    }

    // Enumerate all the subkeys, testing whether
    // each one is an object class name.

    while (lResult == (LONG)ERROR_SUCCESS)
    {
        /* construct a string naming the hypothetical server subkey */
        lstrcpy( szServerKey, szKeyName );
        lstrcat( szServerKey, "\\protocol\\StdFileEditing\\server" );

        /* find out whether server subkey exists under szKeyName node */
```

```
        lLength = _MAX_PATH;
        lResult = RegQueryValue( hKey, szServerKey, szValue, &lLength );

        /* if the query retrieved a value, then the server subkey exists */
        if (lResult == (LONG)ERROR_SUCCESS)
        {
            // Now we know szKeyName is an object class name.  Get the
            // description string and give it to the list box.

            lLength = _MAX_PATH;
            lResult = RegQueryValue( hKey, szKeyName, szValue, &lLength );

            /* if the query succeeded, put the object class in the list box */
            if (lResult == (LONG)ERROR_SUCCESS)
            {
                ListBox_AddString( hwndList, szValue );
            }
        }

        /* continue with the next key */
        lResult = RegEnumKey( hKey, uIndex++, szKeyName, _MAX_PATH );
    }

    RegCloseKey( hKey );                        // release the handle
    return( TRUE );
}

/*-------------------------------------------------------------------
        RETRIEVE DATA
        Called when the user clicks OK, RetrieveData determines
        which item the user chose and returns the actual object
        class name corresponding to the user's choice.
    ---------------------------------------------------------------*/

static void RetrieveData ( HWND hDlg )
{
    HWND hwndList;                              // control window
    char szText[256];                           // class name
    int iIndex;                                 // position in list box

    /* retrieve the string the user selected */
    hwndList = GetDlgItem( hDlg, IDD_SERVERLIST );
    iIndex = ListBox_GetCurSel( hwndList );
    ListBox_GetText( hwndList, iIndex, szText );
```

```
        /* convert the descriptive name to a real class name */
        GetOleClass( szText );
        return;
}

/*-----------------------------------------------------------------
        GET OLE CLASS
        Round up the usual subkeys looking for one that matches
        our description string.
        ---------------------------------------------------------------*/
static BOOL GetOleClass ( LPSTR lpszText )  // string to find
{
    HKEY hKey;                              // an open key
    char szKeyName[_MAX_PATH];              // name of a subkey
    LONG lLength;                           // length of retrieved value
    UINT uIndex;                            // points to successive subkeys
    LONG lResult;                           // return value for testing
    BOOL bSuccess;                          // TRUE if the key is found

    /* acquire a handle for HKEY_CLASSES_ROOT */
    lResult = RegOpenKey( HKEY_CLASSES_ROOT, NULL, &hKey );
    if (lResult != (LONG)ERROR_SUCCESS)
    {
        return( FALSE );
    }

    /* retrieve the name of the first subkey under HKEY_CLASSES_ROOT */
    uIndex = 0;
    lResult = RegEnumKey( hKey, uIndex++, szKeyName, sizeof(szKeyName) );

    // Enumerate all the subkeys, testing whether
    // each one contains the string in lpszText.

    while (lResult == (LONG)ERROR_SUCCESS)
    {
        /* get the value of the current key */
        lLength = _MAX_PATH;
        lResult = RegQueryValue( hKey, szKeyName, szServerClass, &lLength );

        if ((LONG)ERROR_SUCCESS == lResult)
        {
            /* if there was a value, test it */
```

```
        if (!lstrcmp( szServerClass, lpszText ))
        {
            break;                              // a match! stop looking
        }
    }

    /* continue with the next key */
    lResult = RegEnumKey( hKey, uIndex++, szKeyName, sizeof(szKeyName) );
}

RegCloseKey( hKey );

if (lResult == (LONG)ERROR_SUCCESS)        // was a match found?
{
    lstrcpy( szServerClass, szKeyName );       // put the class name
    bSuccess = TRUE;                           // in a safe place
}
else
{
    bSuccess = FALSE;
}

return( bSuccess );
}
```

The Object Window Module

Enclosing an object in its own window has many advantages. It simplifies drawing the objects together on the screen, dragging them from place to place, moving the active object in front of the others, and repainting the objects as needed. The first set of procedures in this module creates and destroys windows, makes them active, and inserts them into the linked list of object windows whose root is kept in the document's stream wrapper. The rest of the module contains a window procedure and message handlers to maintain the child windows as they run.

Managing the Object Windows

CreateObjWindow and DeleteObjWindow create, initialize, and delete a single OBJ-WINDOWINFO structure to help the program keep track of a newly created child window. Each object window structure stores a handle to one child window and a pointer to the next node in a linked list. The application's stream wrapper holds the base node in its pObWindowList field. CreateObjWindow allocates memory for a single node, creates a new window, and stores the window handle in one field of the new node. InsertObjWindow walks to the end of the list and hangs the new node at the end. GetObjWindowInfo takes a window handle and returns a pointer to the associated list node. SetCurrentObject moves a given window to the front and marks it active by storing its node pointer in another part of the stream structure. When the user gives a command such as Copy or Delete, the program performs the requested action on the window whose handle is in pAppStream->pCurObject. DeleteObjWindow has to worry about the window itself, the linked list, and the memory allocated for the node. It sends the window a **WM_DESTROY** message, removes the node from the list, and releases the node structure.

None of these procedures assigns an OLE object to a particular window. A user-defined window message handles that task, as you'll see in the next section.

```
/*-------------------------------------------------------------------


    OBWIN.C


    The client program creates a new child window to display
    each new object it imports.  The user can drag the
    windows around the screen and double-click them to
    activate the object.


    The functions in this module create and delete windows,
    activate them, maintain a linked list of all the windows,
    and process system messages for them.


    Each window receives a pointer to a new object's wrapper
    structure (PAPPOLECLIENT) and stores the pointer as
    a window property.  Two application-defined window messages
    give the window its object pointer and ask to retrieve
    the pointer.
```

FUNCTIONS

CreateObjWindow	create a window for the new object
InsertObjWindow	append a window to the linked list
GetObjWindowInfo	return info from given window
SetCurrentObject	bring window front and give it focus
DeleteObjWindow	remove a window from the list
Obwin_WndProc	process messages for an object window
Obwin_OnPaint	display object
Obwin_OnLeftButtonDown	begin dragging
DoDoubleClick	activate object
Obwin_OnMouseMove	drag object window
Obwin_OnLeftButtonUp	stop dragging
Obwin_OnDestoy	kill window and release object

    from Mastering Windows NT Programming
    copyright 1993 by Brian Myers & Eric Hamer

```
-------------------------------------------------------------------*/

#define STRICT
#include <windows.h>
#include <windowsx.h>
#include "client.h"
#include "rsrc.h"


/*------------------------------------------------------------------
          PROTOTYPES for functions local to this module
    --------------------------------------------------------------*/


static void Obwin_OnPaint( HWND hWnd );
static void Obwin_OnLeftButtonDown( HWND hWnd, BOOL bDoubleClick, int x,
    int y, UINT uKeyFlags );
static void DoDoubleClick( HWND hWnd );
static void Obwin_OnMouseMove( HWND hWnd, int x, int y, UINT uKeyFlags );
static void Obwin_OnLeftButtonUp( HWND hWnd, int x, int y, UINT uKeyFlags );
static void Obwin_OnDestroy( HWND hWnd );


/*------------------------------------------------------------------
          STATIC VARIABLES for this module
    --------------------------------------------------------------*/


BOOL bMouseDown;                          // TRUE while user drags
POINT ptPrev;                             // where mouse was last
```

```
POINT ptMouse;                               // where mouse is now
RECT rObject;                                // set when dragging begins

/*-------------------------------------------------------------------
        CREATE OBJECT WINDOW
        Create a child window to display a new object.
   ------------------------------------------------------------------*/

POBJWINDOWINFO CreateObjWindow (
    HWND hwndParent,                         // main program window
    LPRECT lpObWindowRect )                  // object's bounding rectangle
{
    OBJWINDOWINFO *pObWindow;                // data for one object window
    HINSTANCE hInst;                         // program instance
    static idObWindow = 1;                   // window creation ID#

    hInst = GetWindowInstance( hwndParent );

    /* allocate an OBJWINDOWINFO block to store window-specific data */
    pObWindow = LocalAlloc( LPTR, sizeof(OBJWINDOWINFO) );

    if (pObWindow)
    {
        /* create the new window */
        pObWindow->hwndObject = CreateWindow( szObwinClass, NULL,
            WS_CHILD | WS_CLIPSIBLINGS | WS_VISIBLE | WS_BORDER,
            (int)lpObWindowRect->left, (int)lpObWindowRect->top,
            (int)lpObWindowRect->right - (int)lpObWindowRect->left,
            (int)lpObWindowRect->bottom - (int)lpObWindowRect->top,
            hwndParent, (HMENU)idObWindow, hInst, NULL );

        pObWindow->pNext = NULL;             // pointer to next node
        idObWindow++;                        // increment ID counter
    }

    return( pObWindow );
}

/*-------------------------------------------------------------------
        INSERT OBJECT WINDOW
        Append an object window to the end of the linked list.
   ------------------------------------------------------------------*/
```

```
void InsertObjWindow (
    PAPPOLESTREAM pStream,
    OBJWINDOWINFO *pObWindow )
{
    POBJWINDOWINFO pLast;

    if (pObWindow)
    {
        /* if list is empty, make this the first entry */
        if (!pStream->pObWindowList)
        {
            pStream->pObWindowList = pObWindow;
        }
        else
        {
            /* insert pObWindow at the end of existing ObjWindowList */
            pLast = pStream->pObWindowList;
            while (pLast)
            {
                if (pLast->pNext)                  // if not at end,
                {
                    pLast = pLast->pNext;          // advance one node
                }
                else                               // when pLast reaches end
                {
                    pLast->pNext = pObWindow;      // append new node
                    break;
                }
            }
        }
    }
    return;
}
/*------------------------------------------------------------------
        GET OBJECT WINDOW INFO
        Retrieve the information structure from a given HWND.
    ----------------------------------------------------------------*/

POBJWINDOWINFO GetObjWindowInfo ( HWND hWnd )
{
    PAPPOLESTREAM pStream;
    POBJWINDOWINFO pObWindow;
```

```
    pStream = GetOleStream();

    pObWindow = pStream->pObWindowList;

    while (pObWindow)
    {
        if (pObWindow->hwndObject == hWnd)
        {
            return( pObWindow );
        }
        pObWindow = pObWindow->pNext;
    }

    return( NULL );
}

/*-------------------------------------------------------------------
        SET CURRENT OBJECT WINDOW
        Make one window the active window.  Bring it to the front
        of all the object windows and give it the input focus.
        The active window is the selected window, and commands
        such as Copy and Delete operate on it.

        Returns a handle to the previously active object window, or
        NULL if passed a bad pointer.
        -------------------------------------------------------------*/

POBJWINDOWINFO SetCurrentObject (
    PAPPOLESTREAM pStream,
    OBJWINDOWINFO *pNewObWindow )
{
    OBJWINDOWINFO *pLastObWindow;

    /* if window is already active, do nothing */
    if (pNewObWindow == pStream->pCurObject)
    {
        return (pNewObWindow);
    }

    /* if the window handle is NULL, make no window active */
    if (pNewObWindow == NULL)
    {
        pStream->pCurObject = NULL;
        return( pStream->pCurObject );
    }
```

```
    /* change active window setting and bring new window to the top */
    pLastObWindow = pStream->pCurObject;
    pStream->pCurObject = pNewObWindow;
    BringWindowToTop( pNewObWindow->hwndObject );
    UpdateWindow( pNewObWindow->hwndObject );

    return( pLastObWindow );
}


/*------------------------------------------------------------------
        DELETE OBJECT WINDOW
        Destroy an object window and delete it from the linked
        list of object windows.

        Returns the next node on the list after the deleted one
        (or cycles back to the first node from the end of the list).
   ------------------------------------------------------------------*/
POBJWINDOWINFO DeleteObjWindow (
    PAPPOLESTREAM pStream,              // document I/O stream
    POBJWINDOWINFO pObWindow )          // info about window to delete
{
    POBJWINDOWINFO pListEntry;          // pointer to a list node
    POBJWINDOWINFO pNextObWindow;       // function's return value

    if (pObWindow == NULL)
    {
        return( NULL );
    }

    DestroyWindow( pObWindow->hwndObject );

    /* remove window from the master list */
    if (pObWindow == pStream->pObWindowList)         // root node?
    {
        /* make the second node be the root node */
        pStream->pObWindowList = pObWindow->pNext;
    }
    else
    {
        /* walk the list looking for the given window node */
        pListEntry = pStream->pObWindowList;
        while ((pListEntry != NULL) && (pListEntry->pNext != pObWindow))
        {
```

```
        pListEntry = pListEntry->pNext;
    }

    /* if we found the window, remove it from the list */
    if (pListEntry != NULL)                // did we reach the end?
    {                                      // no, we found the window
        pListEntry->pNext = pObWindow->pNext;
    }
}

/* set return value to the next node after the deleted one */
pNextObWindow = pObWindow->pNext;
if (pNextObWindow == NULL)
{
    /* if the deleted node was last, return a pointer to the first node */
    pNextObWindow = pStream->pObWindowList;
}

/* free the window info block */
LocalFree( (HANDLE)pObWindow );

return( pNextObWindow );
}
```

Processing Object Window Messages

The window procedure and message handlers for the child windows perform several important program tasks. Besides drawing the objects when the screen needs painting, they handle mouse messages when the user clicks an object to select it, double-clicks to activate it, or drags the mouse to move it around the client area. Also, the window procedure recognizes two user-defined messages:

- OBWIN_MSG_SETDATA assigns the window an OLE object to display.

- OBWIN_MSG_GETDATA asks the window which object it displays.

The first message causes the window to store its newly assigned object pointer as a window property, and in response to the second message the window retrieves its stored pointer. The **WM_DESTROY** handler removes the property before the window dies.

The logic for tracking the mouse is unchallenging and probably familiar, but two of the message handlers call OLE functions. Obwin_OnPaint calls **OleDraw**, causing

OleCli to examine the object's presentation data and display it. Because OleCli does not contact the server in response to **OleDraw**, you don't have to check for a delayed release afterward. The other procedure is DoDoubleClick, which calls **OleActivate**. The server always defines at least one verb for each object class it supports. If there are several verbs, the first one is considered primary. When the user activates an object, the client calls **OleActivate** to execute the object's primary verb. Usually the verb is Edit and the server appears, shows the object, and waits for the user to make changes. For some objects, such as wave sound packages, Edit is not a useful verb. Activating a sound package invokes Play instead, and the server plays the sound.

A more fully developed OLE client would be expected to add the full list of the current object's verbs to one of its menus. The client finds verb strings in the system registry in just the way it finds object class names.

```
/*---------------------------------------------------------------
        OBJECT WINDOW WNDPROC
        Process the messages for each object window.
    --------------------------------------------------------------*/

LRESULT WINAPI Obwin_WndProc (
    HWND hWnd,
    UINT uMessage,
    WPARAM wParam,
    LPARAM lParam )
{
    PAPPOLECLIENT pAppObject;

    switch (uMessage)
    {
        /* messages specific to this application */

        case OBWIN_MSG_SETDATA:                // attach object to window
            pAppObject = (PAPPOLECLIENT)wParam;
            SetProp( hWnd, szObwinClass, pAppObject );
            InvalidateRect( hWnd, NULL, TRUE );
            UpdateWindow( hWnd );
            break;

        case OBWIN_MSG_GETDATA:                // get object from window
            pAppObject = GetProp( hWnd, szObwinClass );
            return( (LRESULT)pAppObject );
```

```
        /* Windows messages */

        HANDLE_MSG( hWnd, WM_PAINT, Obwin_OnPaint );

        HANDLE_MSG( hWnd, WM_LBUTTONDOWN, Obwin_OnLeftButtonDown );

        HANDLE_MSG( hWnd, WM_LBUTTONDBLCLK, Obwin_OnLeftButtonDown );

        HANDLE_MSG( hWnd, WM_MOUSEMOVE, Obwin_OnMouseMove );

        HANDLE_MSG( hWnd, WM_LBUTTONUP, Obwin_OnLeftButtonUp );

        HANDLE_MSG( hWnd, WM_DESTROY, Obwin_OnDestroy );

        default:
            return( DefWindowProc (hWnd, uMessage, wParam, lParam) );
    }
    return( 0 );
}

/*--------------------------------------------------------------------
        OBWIN_ONPAINT
        Display an object in the client area of a child window.
    --------------------------------------------------------------------*/

void Obwin_OnPaint ( HWND hWnd )
{
    PAINTSTRUCT ps;
    RECT rClient;
    PAPPOLECLIENT pAppObject;

    BeginPaint( hWnd, &ps );

    pAppObject = GetProp( hWnd, szObwinClass );
    if (pAppObject)
    {
        GetClientRect( hWnd, &rClient );
        OleDraw(                          // paint an OLE object
            pAppObject->pObjectData,      // the object
            ps.hdc,                       // DC for display
            &rClient,                     // bounding rect
            NULL,                         // window rect (for metafiles)
```

```
            NULL );                             // DC for formatting
    }
    EndPaint( hWnd, &ps );
    return;
}

/*------------------------------------------------------------------
        OBWIN_ONLEFTBUTTONDOWN
        When the left button goes down, the user is making an object
        active.  Once active it can be cut, deleted, or moved.  A
        double-click activates the object.
    ------------------------------------------------------------------*/

void Obwin_OnLeftButtonDown (
    HWND hWnd,
    BOOL bDoubleClick,
    int x,
    int y,
    UINT uKeyFlags )
{
    PAPPOLECLIENT pAppObject;           // info associated with this window
    PAPPOLESTREAM pStream;              // document's OLE I/O stream
    POBJWINDOWINFO pObWindow;           // info about an object window
    HWND hwndParent;                    // main program window

    hwndParent = GetParent( hWnd );

    /* if this is a double-click, process it differently */
    if (bDoubleClick)
    {
        DoDoubleClick( hWnd );
    }

    // Get the child window's rectangle and convert it to
    // coordinates relative to the parent window's origin.

    GetWindowRect( hWnd, &rObject );
    ScreenToClient( hwndParent, (LPPOINT)&rObject );
    ScreenToClient( hwndParent, (LPPOINT)&rObject.right );

    /* get the current mouse coordinates and convert them, too */
    ptPrev.x = x;
    ptPrev.y = y;
    ClientToScreen( hWnd, (LPPOINT)&ptPrev );
    ScreenToClient( hwndParent, (LPPOINT)&ptPrev );
```

```
        SetCapture( hWnd );                         // begin dragging
        bMouseDown = TRUE;

        /* make this window the active window */
        pAppObject = GetProp( hWnd, szObwinClass );
        if (pAppObject)
        {
            pStream = GetOleStream( );
            if (pStream)
            {
                pObWindow = GetObjWindowInfo( hWnd );
                SetCurrentObject( pStream, pObWindow );
            }
        }
        return;
        UNREFERENCED_PARAMETER( uKeyFlags );
}

/*-----------------------------------------------------------------

        DO DOUBLECLICK
        If the user double-clicks an object, the client should
        call OleActivate to execute the object's primary verb.
        Typically the verb is Edit and the server will appear,
        allowing the user to edit the selected object.
        ------------------------------------------------------------*/

void DoDoubleClick ( HWND hWnd )
{
    RECT rClient;
    PAPPOLECLIENT pAppObject;                // obj window's display area
    PAPPOLESTREAM pStream;                    // OLE object wrapper
    char szAppName[MAX_RSRCLEN];             // OLE I/O stream
    HINSTANCE hInst;                          // string naming application
    OLESTATUS OleStatus;                      // program instance
                                              // return from Ole functions

    GetClientRect( hWnd, &rClient );
    hInst = GetWindowInstance( hWnd );
    pStream = GetOleStream( );

    /* get a pointer to the object info associated with this window */
    pAppObject = GetProp( hWnd, szObwinClass );
    if (pAppObject)
    {
```

```
    /* can the object be activated? */
    if (pAppObject->dwType == OT_STATIC)    // object is not linked
    {                                        // or embedded and
        return;                              // cannot be activated
    }
    OLEWait( pAppObject );                   // be sure object's not busy

    // Tell the OleCli library how the server should identify
    // this object to the user on its window title bar.

    LoadString( hInst, IDS_CAPTION, szAppName, sizeof(szAppName) );
    OleStatus = OleSetHostNames(
        pAppObject->pObjectData,             // the object
        szAppName,                           // application name
        pStream->szDocName );                // document name
    MarkIfBusy( &OleStatus, pAppObject );    // WAIT_FOR_RELEASE?
    OLEWait( pAppObject );                   // wait for green light

    /* activate the object by performing its primary verb */
    OleStatus = OleActivate(
        pAppObject->pObjectData,             // the object
        OLEVERB_PRIMARY,                     // which verb
        TRUE,                                // server window appears?
        TRUE,                                // server window gets focus?
        hWnd,                                // document window
        &rClient );                          // document bounds
    MarkIfBusy( &OleStatus, pAppObject );    // WAIT_FOR_RELEASE?
    OLEWait( pAppObject );
    }
    return;
}

/*-------------------------------------------------------------------
        OBWIN_ONMOUSEMOVE
        Mouse movement messages matter only when the button is down
        and the user is dragging an object window.  In that case,
        move the window to the new mouse position.
    -----------------------------------------------------------------*/

void Obwin_OnMouseMove (
    HWND hWnd,
    int x,
```

```
    int y,
    UINT uKeyFlags )
{
    HWND hwndParent = GetParent( hWnd );

    if (!bMouseDown)
    {
        return;
    }

    /* record the new mouse coordinates */
    ptMouse.x = x;
    ptMouse.y = y;

    /* adjust the coordinates to the parent's screen. */
    ClientToScreen( hWnd, (LPPOINT)&ptMouse );
    ScreenToClient( hwndParent, (LPPOINT)&ptMouse );

    /* move the object window to its new location */
    OffsetRect( &rObject,
        (int)(ptMouse.x - ptPrev.x),                // delta x
        (int)(ptMouse.y - ptPrev.y) );              // delta y
    MoveWindow( hWnd,
        (int)rObject.left, (int)rObject.top,        // upper left
        (int)(rObject.right - rObject.left),        // width
        (int)(rObject.bottom - rObject.top),        // height
        TRUE );                                     // repaint

    /* current point becomes previous point for next drag message */
    ptPrev.x = ptMouse.x;
    ptPrev.y = ptMouse.y;

    return;
    UNREFERENCED_PARAMETER( uKeyFlags );
}

/*-------------------------------------------------------------
        OBWIN_ONLEFTBUTTONUP
        When the left button goes up, the user stops dragging
        an object around the document window.
    -------------------------------------------------------*/
static void Obwin_OnLeftButtonUp (
    HWND hWnd,
    int x,
```

```
    int y,
    UINT uKeyFlags )
{
    if (!bMouseDown)
    {
        return;
    }
    ReleaseCapture();
    bMouseDown = FALSE;

    return;
    UNREFERENCED_PARAMETER( hWnd );
    UNREFERENCED_PARAMETER( x );
    UNREFERENCED_PARAMETER( y );
    UNREFERENCED_PARAMETER( uKeyFlags );
}


/*-----------------------------------------------------------------
        OBWIN_ONDESTROY
        The child window may be destroyed if the user chooses
        New, Delete, Cut, or Exit.  In any case, we have no
        further need for the window's associated OLE object.
        ----------------------------------------------------------*/


void Obwin_OnDestroy ( HWND hWnd )
{
    PAPPOLECLIENT pAppObject;

    pAppObject = RemoveProp( hWnd, szObwinClass );
    if (pAppObject)
    {
        /* release the object and delete the wrapper */
        DeleteAppObject( pAppObject );
    }
    return;
}
```

We began our approach to OLE with a description of clients and servers, explaining how clients import data from servers into compound documents. Two system libraries, OleCli and OleSvr, together coordinate the interactions that permit one program to incorporate foreign objects seamlessly in its own documents. One of the techniques that enables OLE is the duplication of data in Native and presentation formats. For example, a drawing program might want to include text from a word processor. Because the text object includes a metafile, the client library easily draws the text on any program's screen. Because the object also includes the original data, complete with any internal formatting codes, it can always be passed back to the word processor for revision.

Virtual tables also help OLE to perform basic functions, such as drawing and saving, with any object. The client and the server both provide several sets of pointers to standard functions, such as Get and Put, for the OLE libraries to call when objects require certain kinds of manipulation that only the donor or the recipient can perform. Each set of function pointers is held in a structure called a virtual table, and each application adds its own fields to the virtual table by enclosing it in a larger customized structure called a wrapper. A client program needs its stream and object wrappers constantly for most OLE interactions.

From the user's point of view, OLE operations work through the clipboard. Besides Cut, Copy, and Paste, which recognize extended OLE formats and create links and embed objects, an OLE client is expected to provide additional commands such as Paste Link and Insert Object. To gather information about servers for the Insert Object command, the client must read the system registry by opening and enumerating keys and retrieving the values they contain.

But even after coming this far we've penetrated only halfway into the mysteries of OLE. Chapter 15 continues the same topic, moving now from clients to servers.

Writing an OLE Server

- The server's virtual tables

- Code for server methods

- Writing to the registry

- Features of OLE 2.0

This chapter steps through the looking glass to view the same OLE interactions we described in Chapter 14 from the opposite point of view. A client program brings mysterious objects into a familiar document, while a server sends a familiar object into unknown documents. A client calls the OLE libraries and a server is called by them. A client supplies only three methods in its virtual tables and chooses from over 50 OLE functions to perform its tasks. A server calls only a few OLE functions and exports many methods.

The sample code from this chapter is drawn from a commercial 2D CAD application called Smartdraw for Windows, written by Stephen Crane. From his program we have excerpted the procedures that perform the basic operations of an OLE server. To support its objects, every server calls functions from the OleSvr library (olesvr32.dll). To write an OLE server you must include the ole.h header file in your source code and link with the olesvr32.lib import library. All the server API functions interact with the OleSvr library, not directly with any client. The server library talks to the client library, and the client library talks to clients. Refer back to Figure 14.1 for a diagram of these interactions.

CONCEPTS

A full-featured application may both import and export OLE objects, acting sometimes as server and sometimes as client. Microsoft's Excel spreadsheet is a good example. It pastes objects from any server into its spreadsheets, and it exports spreadsheet cells and graphs to any client. Some applications act only as clients or only as servers. Paintbrush, for example, gives pictures to clients but doesn't import objects from other servers into its files. Its own documents are never compound documents. A third category for OLE programs is the mini-server, a program that exists only to export OLE objects and never loads or saves any documents of its own. Mini-servers can't be started by double-clicking them; only a client can invoke them. The Draw and WordArt programs that accompany Word for Windows are mini-servers. The File menu of the Draw program, for example, lacks commands to open and save, as you can see in Figure 15.1.

FIGURE 15.1:

File menu of a mini-server, characteristically lacking Open and Save commands

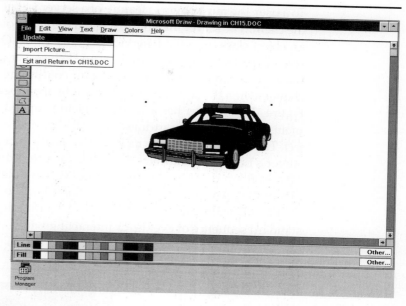

The action of a mini-server shows that servers generally do not initiate OLE actions. They run when a client needs them. For example, if a client calls `OleUpdate` because one of its objects is out of date, OleCli passes the request to OleSvr, which in turn calls a GetData routine in the server. The OleSvr library defines an API of server callback functions that every server must provide. For example, every server must have a GetData routine. OleSvr calls the server's functions, as you might expect, through a set of virtual tables. A server provides over 20 methods the OleSvr library can call to process requests from the client. Among other things, the callbacks create objects, pass object data, display objects, resize objects, render objects in different formats, and set the client's document name in the server window's caption bar.

The Server's User Interface

The user becomes aware of the server only when creating a new object or editing an old one. As long as the client only displays objects and updates links, the user never sees the server program. Sometimes the OLE libraries call the server without the user's knowledge. We'll explain how that happens when we discuss the server's programming interface.

To a user, the most obvious feature of a server is that it responds to actions taken in the client. The server materializes when the user double-clicks an object or chooses an object class from the Insert Object dialog box. Once the server appears on the screen, the features that mark it as an OLE server are its File and Edit menus, its window caption, and its dialog box for confirming Save commands, all of which change when the server is invoked to edit an embedded object. In the first part of Figure 15.2, the user has activated a picture embedded in a Microsoft Word document to edit it. The Smartdraw server has opened a document window for the object. The title bar shows the name of the *client's* document, not the server's, and the server's Edit menu indicates that when the user exits, the object will be returned to Microsoft Word. When the user chooses Exit and Return, the server asks for confirmation before sending the updated object back to the client. Its dialog box asks, "Update Document2 in Microsoft Word?" From the user's perspective, this is the standard sequence of events for interacting with any server.

FIGURE 15.2:

Modified title bar and File menu displayed by a server activated to edit an embedded object

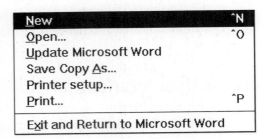

To summarize,

- Several items in the server's File and Edit menus change:

Original	Modified
Exit	Exit and return to <client>
Save	Update <client>
Save As	Save Copy As

- The title bar of the document window changes to

<application name>--<descriptive object class name> in <client document>

- where the descriptive name is the same string the server lists in the system registry to identify its objects for the user. In Paintbrush, for example, the modified title looks like this:

Paintbrush--Paintbrush Picture in CLIENT.DOC

- The message box that reminds the user when changes have not been saved also changes when the object is embedded in the client.

The Server's Programming Interface

The server often acts without the user's knowledge. When a client loads a compound document, for example, it usually checks with the OLE libraries to see if any of the document's linked objects have changed since the document was last opened. The libraries determine the answer by comparing file dates. If any of the links do need refreshing, then the OLE libraries must invoke the server to pass a revised version of the object. OleSvr launches the server program and calls one of its functions. The server reads its own data file, constructs a new version of the object, gives it to the OleSvr, and terminates. The server never shows its window on the screen, so the user doesn't know it ran.

The OleSvr library interacts with the server through two channels. The first is the command line. When the library launches the server, it passes information on the command line telling the server how to initialize itself, whether to show itself, and what operation to prepare for. By reading its command line, the server knows whether it has been invoked independently as a stand-alone application or as a participant in a transaction with an OLE client. OleSvr also controls servers by calling the functions supplied in the server's three virtual tables.

Object Handlers

To customize the services it provides for clients, a server application may choose to provide its own DLL of client functions. A library that replaces some of the functions from olecli32.dll is called an *object handler*. The server records its object handler in the system registry during installation. When the client creates an object, OleCli seeks a handler for the object class. If it finds one, it loads the DLL and calls the handler's exported functions instead of its own. The object handler can pass calls back to the OleCli library for default processing.

An object handler might, for example, replace the **OleDraw** function with a new version capable of rendering the server's native data directly in the client's window. Native data then effectively becomes a presentation format. Or a handler might play a sound when the user opens objects of its object class. Object handlers can usually respond more quickly than the usual chain of command from client through both libraries to server allows.

COMMANDS

To program a server, you must be able to write to the system registry, construct three virtual tables, and familiarize yourself with a small set of OleSvr API commands.

Writing to the System Registry

OLE servers have to enter themselves in the system registry. Besides the registry functions described in Chapter 14, a server needs commands to create new keys and to store key values. Smartdraw uses `RegCreateKey` and `RegCreateValue` because it has no need for anything more advanced, but we should mention that many of the registry functions have new extended versions that take into account the security features of Windows NT.

```
LONG RegCreateKeyEx(
    HKEY hKey,                          // an open key
    LPTSTR lpszSubKey,                  // name for new subkey
    DWORD dwReserved,                   // reserved; must be zero
    LPTSTR lpszClass,                   // class string
    DWORD dwOptions,                    // flag for special options
    REGSAM samDesired,                  // desired security access
    LPSECURITY_ATTRIBUTES lpsa,         // address of key security structure
    PHKEY phkResult,                    // buffer for opened handle
    LPDWORD lpdwDisposition );          // disposition value buffer
```

The key indicated in the first parameter should already be open. The second parameter gives a name for the new subkey to be created under hKey. The class name given in lpszClass becomes the class data associated with the key. (Every key must have a name and a class; storing a value as well is optional.) The option flags permit a distinction between volatile and nonvolatile registry entries. Volatile entries are lost whenever the system restarts. Volatile entries make sense for temporary settings and dynamic performance statistics. Under the **HKEY_PERFORMANCE_DATA** subkey, for example, the system records information about all the currently running threads and processes. These are volatile entries.

The samDesired parameter indicates the operations you want clearance to perform with the new key. It takes the form of a flag or combination of flags, such as **KEY_SET_VALUE**, **KEY_READ** | **KEY_WRITE**, or **KEY_ALL_ACCESS**. The lpsa parameter governs the access other processes may have to the new key. In phkResult the function returns a handle to the newly opened key, and the final parameter returns a flag telling whether the key was indeed new or existed previously.

For most OLE operations, the old registry functions suffice. It should be noted, however, that **RegSetValueEx** allows the insertion of key values in formats other than null-terminated strings (**REG_SZ**).

Virtual Table Structures

As you saw in Chapter 14, a client constructs one kind of virtual table for each of its documents and another for each of its objects. A server too has a virtual table structure for its documents and another for its objects, and also one more from which the OLE libraries control the server itself.

- **OLESERVERVTBL:** Functions that direct the server to open and edit new documents, to execute commands, to close connections, and to terminate

- **OLESERVERDOCVTBL:** Functions that direct the server to name, save, and close existing documents

- **OLEOBJECTVTBL:** Functions that direct the server to describe, display, and manipulate its objects

The following list shows which functions each virtual table must provide. The tables may provide other optional functions as well. When the server library wants the server to save a document, it calls the Save function. To close a document, it calls the Close function. To set a client document name in the server's window, it calls the SetHostNames function, and so on.

OLESERVERVTBL	OLESERVERDOCVTBL	OLEOBJECTVTBL
Create	Close	DoVerb
CreateFromTemplate	GetObject	EnumFormats
Edit	Execute	GetData
Execute	Release	QueryProtocol
Exit	Save	Release
Open	SetColorScheme	SetBounds
Release	SetHostNames	SetColorScheme
		SetData
		SetTargetDevice
		Show

As with the client, the system defines another structure to hold a pointer for each virtual table:

```
typedef struct _OLESERVER
{
    LPOLESERVERVTBL lpvtbl;
} OLESERVER;
```

```
typedef struct _OLESERVERDOC{
    LPOLESERVERDOCVTBL lpvtbl;
} OLESERVERDOC;

typedef struct _OLEOBJECT
{
    LPOLEOBJECTVTBL lpvtbl;
} OLEOBJECT;
```

The server uses these structures the same way the client uses its equivalents: as the first field in a wrapper structure of its own. Other fields in the wrapper may contain any data the server finds helpful in dealing with its documents and objects. Its object wrapper might, for example, include a handle to the object, a color for it, or a bounding rectangle. When the OleSvr library calls one of the server's object methods, it passes a pointer to one of the server's own object wrappers. The server identifies an object by the information the wrapper contains. A server should declare and initialize all the virtual tables and allocate an **OLESERVER** wrapper as it launches. The **OLESERVERDOC** and **OLEOBJECT** wrappers are needed when the server opens new documents or creates new objects.

Virtual Table Methods

Much of the energy spent on designing a server goes into writing the methods for its virtual tables. The individual methods may have any name, but they must follow particular prototypes, perform particular actions, and signal the outcome with particular return values. The prototypes appear in the virtual table definitions.

As an example, here's the definition of a virtual table for functions that process server documents. It comes from the ole.h header file. The suggested actions and possible return values for each method are documented in Microsoft's on-line help. Methods from all three virtual tables are implemented later in this chapter.

```
typedef struct _OLESERVERDOCVTBL
{
    OLESTATUS(CALLBACK* Save) (LPOLESERVERDOC);
    OLESTATUS(CALLBACK* Close) (LPOLESERVERDOC);
    OLESTATUS(CALLBACK* SetHostNames) \
        (LPOLESERVERDOC, OLE_LPCSTR, OLE_LPCSTR);
    OLESTATUS(CALLBACK* SetDocDimensions) \
        (LPOLESERVERDOC, OLE_CONST RECT FAR*);
    OLESTATUS(CALLBACK* GetObject) \
        (LPOLESERVERDOC, OLE_LPCSTR, LPOLEOBJECT FAR*, LPOLECLIENT);
```

```
OLESTATUS(CALLBACK* Release) (LPOLESERVERDOC);
OLESTATUS(CALLBACK* SetColorScheme) \
     LPOLESERVERDOC, OLE_CONST LOGPALETTE FAR*);
OLESTATUS(CALLBACK* Execute) (LPOLESERVERDOC, HGLOBAL);
} OLESERVERDOCVTBL;
typedef OLESERVERDOCVTBL FAR* LPOLESERVERDOCVTBL;
```

Putting Objects on the Clipboard

The primary channel for moving objects from the server to the client is the clipboard. From the server's side, however, OLE clipboard transactions look just like any other clipboard transaction. No special OLE functions are required. The only requirements are to offer the registered OLE data formats Native, OwnerLink, and ObjectLink.

When the user chooses Cut or Copy, the server calls the usual clipboard functions: **OpenClipboard**, **EmptyClipboard**, **SetClipboardData**, and **CloseClipboard**. A server should offer the object in as many formats as possible. Usually it offers first the formats it prefers, such as SYLK, TIFF, or RTF. After all, if the client understands the original data perfectly, importing it as an OLE object may not be necessary. Next the server offers the OLE formats—Native, OwnerLink, and ObjectLink— and along with them at least one presentation format. A presentation format is one the client library can draw by itself. Typically, the choices are **CF_ENHMETAFILE**, **CF_METAFILE**, **CF_BITMAP**, and **CF_DIB**. Every server should support a metafile format, and presentation metafiles should use the **MM_ANISOTROPIC** mapping mode to allow scaling.

Native data is whatever format the server uses internally. The other two OLE formats, OwnerLink and ObjectLink, are just as easy to manage because they consist of a short, three-part string. The three parts name the object class, the document, and the object itself. Both formats use the same string. The object class is the name that appears in the server's system registry entry; the document name is straightforward; and the object name is any string the server creates enabling it to identify an object within a document. Each section of the OwnerLink/ObjectLink string ends with a single null character, and an extra null terminates the entire string. This example names an object called widget, of class MyAppDrawing, from document Userwork.drw:

```
MyAppDrawing\Ouserwork.drw\Owidget\0\0
```

The client cannot embed an object unless the clipboard contains native data, OwnerLink data, and presentation data. The `OleCreateFromClip` function copies all three data sets into the file. The presentation data gets displayed, and if the user wants to edit the object, the native data gets sent back to the server. Linking an object requires only the ObjectLink and presentation data formats; the native data resides in the source document. Whether the clipboard allows an object to be linked, embedded, or both depends not only on which data formats the server has offered to the clipboard, but also on the order in which the formats were placed there. If the server sets OwnerLink on the clipboard before Native, for example, the object cannot be embedded. To avoid unexpected restrictions, enter formats with `SetClipboardData` in the following order:

1. Preferred formats (for clients that understand your data)

2. Native

3. OwnerLink

4. Presentation formats (at least a metafile)

5. ObjectLink

If you offer only one presentation format, it should be a metafile, preferably `CF_ENHMETAFILE`. If you offer several, the client will use the first acceptable one it finds. `CF_METAFILE` should precede `CF_DIB` and `CF_BITMAP` because metafiles scale better than bitmaps. (Remember too that as we mentioned in Chapter 9, the clipboard converts automatically between old and enhanced metafile formats if necessary.)

Not all servers need to support clipboard operations because clients can still reach any object class through the registry with the Insert Object command. A miniserver, which launches only in response to the Insert Object command, may have little use for clipboard commands. (Microsoft's Word Art server, for example, has no menu bar at all.)

OleSvr Commands

A client program has at its disposal over 50 commands that interact with the OleCli library. The OleSvr library relies more on the server's virtual tables and supports a much smaller API. We'll list the server commands here for reference and describe some in more detail when we reach the server code.

```
OleBlockServer
OleQueryServerVersion
OleRegisterServer
OleRegisterServerDoc
OleRenameServerDoc
OleRevokeServerDoc
OleRevokeObject
OleRevokeServer
OleSavedServerDoc
OleUnblockServer
```

The registration and revocation functions announce to OleSvr that some resource has become available or been withdrawn. The block and unblock commands come into play when a server initiates a sequence of actions that should not be interrupted, either for speed or to avoid reentrancy problems. Blocking the server makes the library hold subsequent calls to the server in a queue. Call `OleUnblockServer` to remove calls from the queue one by one.

CODE: THE SERVER PROGRAM

This section describes the actions of OLE servers using examples from Smartdraw. We have sometimes expanded the comments within the program but have always left the C code unchanged. The programming for an OLE server falls roughly into two main categories: those sections that initialize the server and those that respond to calls from the OLE libraries.

Initializing an OLE Server

On launching, the server checks the version number of the OLE libraries, verifies its entry in the system registry, initializes at least one virtual table for OleSvr, and reads its command line to determine what action to take.

Updating the System

Clients and servers alike should begin by checking the version number of the currently installed OLE system libraries. Generally an OLE application ships with a complete set of all three OLE libraries (olecli32.dll, olesvr32.dll, and shell32.dll), and if the application's libraries are more current than those already installed, the program should copy the new versions into the system directory or ask the user to do so. **OleQueryClientVersion** and **OleQueryServerVersion** return version numbers for the client and server libraries.

When a server starts up, it must also confirm that its entry in the registration database still exists, refreshing it if necessary. Since only one server may service requests for each object class, it is possible for another application to have overwritten the registration.

A server must record at least five pieces of information in the registry:

- The class name of its object

- A descriptive string naming the class more legibly for humans

- The StdFileEditing protocol

- The name of the server's executable file

- At least one verb to execute when an object is activated

The following list shows the location of each piece of data. On the left of each equal sign is the name of a subkey; on the right is the value stored in the subkey.

HKEY_CLASSES_ROOT\<class name> = <readable class name string>

HKEY_CLASSES_ROOT\<class name>\protocol\StdFileEditing\server = <executable file>

HKEY_CLASSES_ROOT\<class name>\protocol\StdFileEditing\verb\0 = <primary verb>

In addition, a server may choose to support some optional entries, such as a file extension for its data files, the StdExecute protocol for **OleExecute** commands, more verbs, and an object handler DLL.

HKEY_CLASSES_ROOT\.ext = <class name>

HKEY_CLASSES_ROOT\<class name>\protocol\StdFileExecute\server = <executable file>

HKEY_CLASSES_ROOT\<class name>\protocol\StdFileEditing\verb\1 = <secondary verb>

HKEY_CLASSES_ROOT\<class name>\protocol\StdFileEditing\verb\2 = <tertiary verb>

HKEY_CLASSES_ROOT\<class name>\protocol\StdFileEditing\handler32 = <handler DLL>

In Smartdraw, the ChkReg procedure updates the system registry. It records one object class, two file extensions, one verb, and a command line for invoking the program when the user clicks one of Smartdraw's data files from inside the File Manager.

```c
BOOL ChkReg (
    HANDLE hinst,                         // program instance
    LPSTR lpszApp)                        // object class ("Smartdraw")
{
    char szExec[_MAX_PATH + 3];           // program's executable file
    char keybuf[128];                     // buffer for building key value
    HKEY hApp;                            // handle to object class key
    HKEY hProto;                          // handle to StdFileEditing key

    // get full name of this program's executable file
    if (!GetModuleFileName (hinst, szExec, sizeof(szExec)))
        return (FALSE);

    // OLE registration (create class name key)
    if (RegCreateKey (HKEY_CLASSES_ROOT, lpszApp, &hApp)
            != ERROR_SUCCESS)
        return (FALSE);

    // create other OLE subkeys
    RegCreateKey (hApp, "protocol\\StdFileEditing", &hProto);
    RegSetValue (hProto, "server", REG_SZ, szExec, lstrlen (szExec));
    RegSetValue (hProto, "verb\\0", REG_SZ, "Edit", 4);
    RegCloseKey (hProto);

    // Shell registration (command line for invoking application)
    lstrcat (szExec, " %1");
```

```
RegSetValue (hApp, "shell\\open\\command", REG_SZ, szExec,
    lstrlen (szExec));

// supply descriptive string for class name
wsprintf (keybuf, "%s Drawing", lpszApp);
RegSetValue (hApp, "", REG_SZ, keybuf, lstrlen (keybuf));
RegCloseKey (hApp);

// specify the extensions the server recognizes
RegSetValue (HKEY_CLASSES_ROOT, ".dxf", REG_SZ, lpszApp,
    lstrlen (lpszApp));
RegSetValue (HKEY_CLASSES_ROOT, ".dx_", REG_SZ, lpszApp,
    lstrlen (lpszApp));

return (TRUE);
}
```

Initializing for OleSvr

Besides entering itself in the registry, the server must announce itself to the OleSvr library. There are four steps to the server's initialization:

1. Create the virtual function tables by assigning a function pointer to each required field in each table.

2. Register the three OLE clipboard formats—"Native", "OwnerLink", and "ObjectLink". (These are the same three formats the client registered in Chapter 14.)

3. Pass the OleSvr library a completed **OLESERVER** wrapper so the library can call functions from the server.

4. Read the command line that launched the server.

The Server's Data Structures

Smartdraw's private data structures OLESVR, OLESVRDOC, and OLESVROBJ are shown below. To understand them, it will help to know that Smartdraw is a multi-document interface application that opens a new child window for each new document. Also, each document window holds a single object. That makes the OLESVROBJ object wrapper very simple; it refers back to its containing document where all the fields describing an object are kept.

```
typedef struct olesvr_t {
    LPOLESERVERVTBL lpvtbl;              // server virtual table
    LHSERVER lh;                         // handle to the server
    HWND hframe;                         // server frame window
} OLESVR, FAR *LPOLESVR;

typedef struct olesvrdoc_t {
    LPOLESERVERDOCVTBL lpvtbl;           // document virtual table
    LHSERVERDOC lhd;                     // handle to a document
    LPOLESVR pSvr;                       // the server wrapper
    HWND hwnd;                           // document window (MDI)
    LPOLEOBJ pObj;                       // object in the document
    ATOM aCli, aObj;
    BOOL fRel;
    BOOL fClose;
} OLESVRDOC, FAR *LPOLESVRDOC;

typedef struct oleobj_t {
    LPOLEOBJECTVTBL lpvtbl;              // server's virtual table
    LPOLECLIENT lpcli;                   // client's virtual table
    LPOLESVRDOC pDoc;                    // object's document
} OLEOBJ, FAR *LPOLEOBJ;
```

Reading the Command Line

To determine why it was launched in the first place, the server examines the command line passed to WinMain as lpszCmdLine. If the command line is empty, then the user opened the application directly. The server should open an untitled document (see the next section), show its window, and wait for input. The user may also open the application directly by clicking an associated document in the File Manager. In that case the command line contains a document name, and the server should open the document immediately.

But sometimes OleSvr starts up applications in response to a request from a client. In that case, the command line begins with the −Embedding flag. This flag signals that the server was launched to operate on an object in some client application. If the command line contains no other information, the client needs help with an embedded object. If the flag is followed by a file name, the client needs help with a linked object from that file. Either way, the server should not show its window. It should register itself, open the file if one is named, and wait invisibly for instructions from the server library. If OleSvr calls the Show or DoVerb callback procedure, the server may then show itself.

The OLESvrInit Procedure

OLESvrInit performs all the initialization tasks. It sets up the three virtual tables, passes one to OleSvr to register with the library, registers the three clipboard formats, and scans the command line for the –Embedding flag and a file name.

```
BOOL OLESvrInit (
    HWND hframe,                    // program window
    LPSTR lpszApp,                  // application name ("Smartdraw")
    LPSTR FAR *lpcmd)               // program's startup command line
{
    char *szEmb = "Embedding";      // check for this on command line
    LPSTR p;                        // used for parsing the command line
    BOOL fEmb = FALSE;              // TRUE if "Embedding" is found
    HANDLE hinst = GetWindowWord (hframe, GWW_HINSTANCE);

    // 1. Set up all three virtual tables.

    // (MakeProcInstance is unnecessary for a Windows NT program,
    // but including it makes the source code work in both 16-
    // and 32-bit versions.)

    // the OLESERVERVTBL
    svrvtbl.Open = (LPVOID)MakeProcInstance((FARPROC)SvrOpen, hinst);
    svrvtbl.Create =
        (LPVOID)MakeProcInstance((FARPROC)SvrCreate, hinst);
    svrvtbl.CreateFromTemplate =
        (LPVOID)MakeProcInstance((FARPROC)SvrCreateFromTemplate, hinst);
    svrvtbl.Edit = (LPVOID)MakeProcInstance((FARPROC)SvrEdit, hinst);
    svrvtbl.Exit = (LPVOID)MakeProcInstance((FARPROC)SvrExit, hinst);
    svrvtbl.Release =
        (LPVOID)MakeProcInstance((FARPROC)SvrRelease, hinst);
    svrvtbl.Execute =
        (LPVOID)MakeProcInstance((FARPROC)SvrExecute, hinst);

    // the OLESERVERDOCVTBL
    svrdocvtbl.Save = (LPVOID)MakeProcInstance((FARPROC)DocSave, hinst);
    svrdocvtbl.Close =
        (LPVOID)MakeProcInstance((FARPROC)DocClose, hinst);
    svrdocvtbl.SetHostNames =
        (LPVOID)MakeProcInstance((FARPROC)DocSetHostNames, hinst);
    svrdocvtbl.SetDocDimensions =
        (LPVOID)MakeProcInstance((FARPROC)DocSetDocDimensions, hinst);
    svrdocvtbl.GetObject =
        (LPVOID)MakeProcInstance((FARPROC)DocGetObject, hinst);
```

```
svrdocvtbl.Release =
    (LPVOID)MakeProcInstance((FARPROC)DocRelease, hinst);
svrdocvtbl.SetColorScheme =
    (LPVOID)MakeProcInstance((FARPROC)DocSetColorScheme, hinst);
svrdocvtbl.Execute =
    (LPVOID)MakeProcInstance((FARPROC)DocExecute, hinst);

// the OLEOBJECTVTBL
objvtbl.QueryProtocol =
    (LPVOID)MakeProcInstance((FARPROC)ObjQueryProtocol, hinst);
objvtbl.Release =
    (LPVOID)MakeProcInstance((FARPROC)ObjRelease, hinst);
objvtbl.Show =
    (LPVOID)MakeProcInstance((FARPROC)ObjShow, hinst);
objvtbl.DoVerb =
    (LPVOID)MakeProcInstance((FARPROC)ObjDoVerb, hinst);
objvtbl.GetData =
    (LPVOID)MakeProcInstance((FARPROC)ObjGetData, hinst);
objvtbl.SetData =
    (LPVOID)MakeProcInstance((FARPROC)ObjSetData, hinst);
objvtbl.SetTargetDevice =
    (LPVOID)MakeProcInstance((FARPROC)ObjSetTargetDevice, hinst);
objvtbl.SetBounds =
    (LPVOID)MakeProcInstance((FARPROC)ObjSetBounds, hinst);
objvtbl.EnumFormats =
    (LPVOID)MakeProcInstance((FARPROC)ObjEnumFormats, hinst);
objvtbl.SetColorScheme =
    (LPVOID)MakeProcInstance((FARPROC)ObjSetColorScheme, hinst);

// 2.: register clipboard formats
cfNative    = RegisterClipboardFormat ("Native");
cfOwnerLink = RegisterClipboardFormat ("OwnerLink");
cfObjectLink= RegisterClipboardFormat ("ObjectLink");

// 3. Initialize OLESERVER wrapper and register server with
//     the OleSvr library as an MDI application.
Svr.lpvtbl = &svrvtbl;
Svr.hframe = hframe;
if (OLE_OK != OleRegisterServer (
                lpszApp,             // server name
                (LPOLESERVER)&svr,   // server wrapper
                &svr.lh,             // server handle (returned)
                hinst,               // program instance
                OLE_SERVER_SINGLE))  // single-instance program
     return (FALSE);
```

```
    // 4. Search for "Embedded" on the command line
    if (p = _fstrstr (*lpcmd, szEmb)) {
        char ch = p[-1];
        if (fEmb = (ch=='/' || ch=='-'))        // check for switch marker
            p += lstrlen (szEmb);               // move past "Embedding"

    for (; *p && isspace(*p); p++ );            // move past white space
    *lpcmd = p;

    // now lpcmd points to the word after -Embedding
    return (fEmb);                              // TRUE for -Embedding
}
```

Updating and Saving Linked or Embedded Objects

The pointer the libraries pass to identify an OLE object contains, as you already know, the server's **OLEOBJECT** wrapper structure. Less obvious is the fact that the client's object virtual table (**OLECLIENT**) is also contained in the same data structure. The DocGetObject procedure puts it there, as you'll see in a few pages. Smartdraw puts an **LPOLECLIENT** field in its object wrapper, and through it the server has access to the client's callback procedure—the notification procedure where the client receives signals about objects being painted, changed, or released. (The example in Chapter 14 titled this function OLEEvent.)

The server sometimes uses the client's callback function address to signal the client directly when an object changes. If the server opens a document to edit an embedded object, the client needs to be told when the user has made modifications. Ole-ClientCallBack sends a notification code directly to the client program.

```
static void OLEClientCallBack (
    LPOLEOBJ lpo,                       // object wrapper
    WORD msg )                          // notification code
{
    LPOLECLIENT lpc;                    // client's object wrapper

    // Verify valid pointers for the object wrapper, the
    // client's virtual table, and the callback function.
```

```
    if (lpo && (lpc=lpo->lpcli) && lpc->lpvtbl)
        // send a message to the client
        lpc->lpvtbl->CallBack (lpc, msg, (LPOLEOBJECT)lpo);
}
```

This function is called by a number of higher level functions, of which one is OLEChangedDoc. Smartdraw maintains a flag to mark a document "dirty" when it needs to be saved. Whenever the object becomes dirty, Smartdraw notifies the client of the modification by calling OLEChangedDoc.

```
void OLEChangedDoc (HWND hwnd)                   // MDI document window
{
    LPOLESVRDOC lpd = GetDocPtr (hwnd);        // retrieve document wrapper
    OLEClientCallBack (lpd->pObj, OLE_CHANGED);
}
```

When the user, while editing an object, selects the Update <client> command from the server's menu—or chooses Save in the case of a linked object—the server must notify the client that the changes have been committed. If the server contacted the client directly, the OLE libraries would not be aware of the object's new status, so this time the server must call an OLE function instead of sending **OLE_SAVED** directly to the client.

```
void OLESavedDoc (HWND hwnd)                     // MDI document window
{
    LPOLESVRDOC lpd = GetDocPtr (hwnd);        // retrieve document wrapper
    OleSavedServerDoc (lpd->lhd);              // lhd = document handle
}
```

Server Methods

The remainder of the server code excerpts show the operations invoked by the OleSvr library through the server's three virtual tables. Each procedure implements a different virtual table method. We'll present first the server methods, then the document methods, and then the object methods.

Create a Document for a Client's Embedded Object

When a user chooses the Insert Object menu command in an OLE client application, the OleSvr library launches the server with -Embedding on its command line.

The server starts but hides itself and doesn't create a document. OleSvr then invokes the Create method to make the server create a new document. Smartdraw's Create method is the procedure SvrCreate.

```
OLESTATUS CALLBACK SvrCreate (
    LPOLESERVER lpos,                         // server wrapper
    LHSERVERDOC lhd,                          // document handle
    OLE_LPCSTR lpclass,                       // object class
    OLE_LPCSTR lpdoc,                         // document name
    LPOLESERVERDOC FAR *lplpd)                // return document handle here
{
    LPOLESVR lps = (LPOLESVR)lpos;            // cast to app's own wrapper
    HWND hdocwnd;                             // new MDI child window
    LPOLESVRDOC lpDoc;                        // document wrapper

    // make the server visible
    ShowWindow (lps->hframe, SW_SHOWNORMAL);

    // create a new MDI window
    hdocwnd = SendMessage (lps->hframe, WM_COMMAND, IDM_NEW, TRUE);
    if (!hdocwnd)
        return (OLE_ERROR_NEW);              // signal failure to OleSvr

    lpDoc = AllocDoc (lps);                   // allocate new document wrapper
    lpDoc->lhd = lhd;                         // initialize wrapper fields
    lpDoc->hwnd = hdocwnd;
    SetDocPtr (hdocwnd, lpDoc);               // give the window its structure
    *lplpd = (LPOLESERVERDOC)lpDoc;           // return new wrapper
    return (OLE_OK);                          // signal success to OleSvr
}
```

This function reveals the server, creates a new untitled document window, allocates an **OLESVRDOC** structure, and associates it with the window using the application-defined SetDocPtr. Finally it casts the document pointer to its superclass and returns it to olesvr32.dll.

Other Server Operations

Most of the other server methods may be introduced more briefly and explained in their source code comments.

SvrOpen is called when a user activates a linked object. It receives the name of the file in which the object is stored. WUSR_OPENFILE is an application-specific window message that directs the frame window to open a disk file, and AllocDoc sets up a document wrapper in much the same way that the Client program's InitAppObject sets up an object wrapper.

```
OLESTATUS CALLBACK SvrOpen (
    LPOLESERVER lpos,                    // server wrapper
    LHSERVERDOC lhd,                     // document handle
    OLE_LPCSTR lpszDoc,                  // document name
    LPOLESERVERDOC FAR *lplpd)           // return document wrapper here
{
    LPOLESVR lps = (LPOLESVR)lpos;       // cast to app's wrapper
    HWND hdocwnd;                        // MDI document window
    LPOLESVRDOC lpDoc;                   // new document wrapper

    // Create new document window.
    // FALSE means don't use a progress meter.
    hdocwnd = SendMessage (lps->hframe, WUSR_OPENFILE,
                FALSE, (LPARAM)(LPVOID)lpszDoc);
    if (!hdocwnd)
        return (OLE_ERROR_NEW);
    lpDoc = AllocDoc (lps);              // allocate a document wrapper
    lpDoc->lhd = lhd;                    // initialize wrapper fields
    lpDoc->hwnd = hdocwnd;
    SetDocPtr (hdocwnd, lpDoc);          // give window its document info
    *lplpd = (LPOLESERVERDOC)lpDoc;      // return pointer

    // Make the new window visible top front
    SetWindowPos (lps->hframe, HWND_TOP, 0, 0, 0, 0,
        SWP_SHOWWINDOW | SWP_NOZORDER);
    BringWindowToTop (hdocwnd);
    return (OLE_OK);                     // return success
}
```

SvrCreateFromTemplate is called to create an embedded object from the contents of a server file.

```
OLESTATUS CALLBACK SvrCreateFromTemplate (
    LPOLESERVER lpos,                    // server wrapper
    LHSERVERDOC lhd,                     // document handle
    OLE_LPCSTR lpclass,                  // object class for new object
    OLE_LPCSTR lpszDoc,                  // document name
    OLE_LPCSTR lpszTpl,                  // template name
    LPOLESERVERDOC FAR *lplpd )          // pointer to new doc wrapper
```

```
{
    LPOLESVR lps = (LPOLESVR)lpos;        // cast to app's wrapper
    HWND hdocwnd;                         // MDI document window
    LPOLESVRDOC lpDoc;                    // new document wrapper

    // FALSE means don't use a progress meter
    hdocwnd = SendMessage (lps->hframe, WUSR_OPENFILE,
        FALSE, (LPARAM)(LPVOID)lpszTpl);
    if (!hdocwnd)
        return (OLE_ERROR_NEW);

    lpDoc = AllocDoc (lps);               // allocate new doc wrapper
    lpDoc->lhd = lhd;                     // initialize wrapper fields
    lpDoc->hwnd = hdocwnd;
    SetDocPtr (hdocwnd, lpDoc);           // give window its document info
    *lplpd = (LPOLESERVERDOC)lpDoc;       // return wrapper pointer
    return (OLE_OK);                      // return success
}
```

SvrEdit is called in preparation for editing an embedded object. The server does not display itself. It waits for a follow-up call to the SetData method in its object virtual table to send object data from the client back to the server.

```
OLESTATUS CALLBACK SvrEdit (
    LPOLESERVER lpos,                     // server wrapper
    LHSERVERDOC lhd,                      // document handle
    OLE_LPCSTR lpclass,                   // object class name
    OLE_LPCSTR lpdoc,                     // document name
    LPOLESERVERDOC FAR *lplpd)            // pointer to new doc wrapper
{
    LPOLESVR lps = (LPOLESVR)lpos;        // cast to app's wrapper
    HWND hdocwnd;                         // MDI document window
    LPOLESVRDOC lpDoc;                    // pointer to new doc wrapper

    // make new document window
    hdocwnd = SendMessage (lps->hframe, WM_COMMAND, IDM_NEW, TRUE);
    if (!hdocwnd)
        return (OLE_ERROR_NEW);

    lpDoc = AllocDoc (lps);               // allocate document wrapper
    lpDoc->lhd = lhd;                     // initialize wrapper fields
    lpDoc->hwnd = hdocwnd;
    SetDocPtr (hdocwnd, lpDoc);           // give window its doc info
```

```
    *lplpd = (LPOLESERVERDOC)lpDoc;        // return wrapper pointer
    return (OLE_OK);                       // return success
}
```

When an OLE transaction ends, if the server library wants the server application to quit it calls the Exit function from the application's **OLESERVERVTBL**. If the server is not required to close down, OleSvr calls the Release function instead. SvrExit tells the server to shut itself down unconditionally when, for example, a client quits without saving changes.

```
OLESTATUS CALLBACK SvrExit (LPOLESERVER lpos)
{
    LPOLESVR lps = (LPOLESVR)lpos;         // cast to app's wrapper
    ShowWindow (lps->hframe, SW_HIDE);     // prevent user actions
    OleRevokeServer (lps->lh);             // tell OleSvr we're gone
    DestroyWindow (lps->hframe);           // shut down program
    return (OLE_OK);
}
```

OleSvr calls the server's Release function when its interaction with the server ceases and the server may safely terminate. Calling SvrRelease signals the server that it is no longer needed and may shut down when the user closes it. If the server is hidden the user cannot close it, and the server should terminate at once.

```
OLESTATUS CALLBACK SvrRelease (LPOLESERVER lpos)
{
    LPOLESVR lps = (LPOLESVR)lpos;         // cast to app's wrapper

    // is window invisible and was a server handle created?
    if (!IsWindowVisible (lps->hframe) && lps->lh)
        // tell the window to close
        PostMessage (lps->hframe, WM_CLOSE, 0, 0);
    return (OLE_OK);
}
```

SvrExecute is called with a buffer containing a list of DDE commands for it to execute. Smartdraw doesn't support this feature.

```
OLESTATUS CALLBACK SvrExecute (
    LPOLESERVER lpos,                      // server wrapper
    HGLOBAL hcmds)                         // buffer full of commands
{
    return (OLE_ERROR_COMMAND);           // Smartdraw doesn't execute
}
```

Closing the Server

OLESvrTerm is called when the user shuts down the server. It notifies OleSvr by calling **OleRevokeServer** and, if required to do so, waits for further instructions. (We haven't bothered to list all the **FreeProcInstance** commands because they are necessary only for compatibility with Win16.)

```
void OLESvrTerm (void)
{
    // close registered documents
    OLESTATUS s = OleRevokeServer (Svr.lh);

    if (s==OLE_WAIT_FOR_RELEASE) {
        BOOL fRel = FALSE;                    // block release
        WaitFlag (&fRel);                     // wait for fRel to be TRUE
    }

    // Free the virtual table methods, one by one
    // (Necessary only for compiling under Win16)
    FreeProcInstance((FARPROC)objvtbl.QueryProtocol);
    // free the other object table methods...

    // free document virtual table methods
    FreeProcInstance((FARPROC)svrdocvtbl.Save);
    // free the other document table methods...

    // free server virtual table methods
    FreeProcInstance((FARPROC)svrvtbl.Open);
    // free the other server table methods...
}
```

Server Document Methods

When the server begins a new document, the server library needs to know about it. The server registers each new document, even untitled ones, by calling **OleRegisterServerDoc**. The server program keeps the OleSvr library constantly apprised of document events. When the server saves a document, it calls **OleSaveServerDoc**. When the user chooses Save As, the server calls **OleRenameServerDoc**. When a document closes, it calls **OleRevokeServerDoc**. The state of the server document matters to clients that import linked objects from it. **OleSaveServerDoc**, for example, sends an **OLE_SAVED** code to clients so they can update and redraw their linked objects.

Often a server updates data instead of saving it. When the client loads the server to edit an object, the object lives in the container document, not in a server document. The server adjusts its File menu by changing Save to Update. When the user chooses Update, the server calls **OleSaveServerDoc**. The client receives the **OLE_SAVED** code, requests the new data, and writes it to disk.

Creating a New Object

Once the containing document has been successfully created, OleSvr's next action is to create a new object in the server. It does this by calling svrdocvtbl.GetObject, which in Smartdraw points to the DocGetObject procedure.

```
OLESTATUS CALLBACK DocGetObject (
    LPOLESERVERDOC lpsd,                          // document wrapper
    OLE_LPCSTR lpszItem,                          // requested item
    LPOLEOBJECT FAR *lplpobj,                     // return pointer here
    LPOLECLIENT lpoc)                             // client's object wrapper
{
    LPOLESVRDOC lpd = (LPOLESVRDOC)lpsd;          // case to app's wrapper
    LPOLEOBJ lpo = farmalloc (sizeof(OLEOBJ));    // allocate wrapper
    if (!lpo)
        return (OLE_ERROR_MEMORY);

    lpo->lpvtbl = &objvtbl;                       // put VTBL in wrapper
    lpo->lpcli = lpoc;                            // include client's wrapper
    lpo->pDoc = lpd;                              // set document in wrapper
    *lplpobj = (LPOLEOBJECT)lpo;                  // return new wrapper
    lpd->pObj = lpo;                              // set object in doc wrapper
    return (OLE_OK);
}
```

Other Document-Level Operations

Smartdraw's exported OLE objects are user-drawn graphics, and Smartdraw desires to preserve their size and color in any context. It therefore ignores advisory calls that inform the server when the client attempts to resize a document or to suggest a color palette.

DocSetHostNames tells the server the names of the current object and client. It enables the server to change the document window's title bar.

```
OLESTATUS CALLBACK DocSetHostNames (
    LPOLESERVERDOC lpsd,                    // document wrapper
    OLE_LPCSTR lpszClient,                  // client app name
    OLE_LPCSTR lpszDoc)                     // client document name
{
    char buf[256];
    char fmt[32];                           // for building window title
    LPOLESVRDOC lpd = (LPOLESVRDOC)lpsd;    // format string (from .res)
                                            // cast to app's wrapper

    // construct a window title string and display it
    LoadString (GetWindowWord (lpd->hwnd, GWW_HINSTANCE),
        IDS_OLETITLE, fmt, sizeof(fmt));
    wsprintf (buf, fmt, lpszDoc, lpszClient);
    MakeDocTitle (lpd->hwnd, buf);          // set window caption

    // save names for future reference
    lpd->aCli = AddAtom (lpszClient);       // save name of client
    lpd->aObj = AddAtom (lpszDoc);          // save name of document

    return (OLE_OK);
}
```

DocSetDocDimensions informs the server that the client has changed the dimensions of the object. Smartdraw ignores this notification, choosing to preserve the original size of its objects.

```
OLESTATUS CALLBACK DocSetDocDimensions (
    LPOLESERVERDOC lpsd,                    // document wrapper
    OLE_CONST RECT FAR *lpr)                // client's new size for doc
{
    // Smartdraw ignores this notification and
    // uses its own size calculations for the document.
    return (OLE_OK);
}
```

DocExecute conveys a list of document-related DDE commands for the server to execute. Smartdraw does not service any DDE requests.

```
OLESTATUS CALLBACK DocExecute (
    LPOLESERVERDOC lpsd,                    // document wrapper
    HGLOBAL hglob)                          // buffer full of commands
{
    return (OLE_ERROR_COMMAND);            // Smartdraw doesn't execute
}
```

DocSetColorScheme recommends a logical color palette to the server for drawing a document. The server, if it wants to follow the recommendations, should make its own copy of the **LOGPALETTE** array and construct its own logical palette. The first color in the array is recommended for the foreground, the second for the background.

```
OLESTATUS CALLBACK DocSetColorScheme (
    LPOLESERVERDOC lpsd,                    // document wrapper
    OLE_CONST LOGPALETTE FAR *lplogp)       // recommended palette
{
    return (OLE_ERROR_PALETTE);             // Smartdraw doesn't use it
}
```

DocSave asks the server to save a linked object in its file.

```
OLESTATUS CALLBACK DocSave (LPOLESERVERDOC lpsd)
{
    LPOLESVRDOC lpd = (LPOLESVRDOC)lpsd;    // cast to app's wrapper

    // tell document window to save its object
    SendMessage (lpd->hwnd, WM_COMMAND, IDM_SAVE, 0);
    return (OLE_OK);
}
```

DocClose is called to close the specified document. By calling **OleRevokeServerDoc** from inside DocClose, we arrange for a follow-up call to DocRelease, where the rest of the cleaning up occurs.

```
OLESTATUS CALLBACK DocClose (LPOLESERVERDOC lpsd)
{
    LPOLESVRDOC lpd = (LPOLESVRDOC)lpsd;        // cast to app's wrapper
    lpd->fClose = TRUE;                         // mark document closed
    return (OleRevokeServerDoc (lpd->lhd));     // OleSvr calls DocRelease
}
```

DocRelease is called when a document is no longer needed. It releases atoms, frees the object wrapper, and closes the document window.

```
OLESTATUS CALLBACK DocRelease (LPOLESERVERDOC lpsd)
{
    LPOLESVRDOC lpd = (LPOLESVRDOC)lpsd;     // cast to app's doc wrapper

    if (lpd->aObj) {                         // were atoms created?
        DeleteAtom (lpd->aObj);              // release them
        DeleteAtom (lpd->aCli);
    }
```

```
    if (lpd->pObj)                                     // was an object created?
        farfree (lpd->pObj);

    lpd->pObj = 0;                                      // set pointer to NULL
    lpd->fRel = TRUE;                                   // mark object released

    // tell document window to close
    if (lpd->fClose) {                                 // tell window to close
        lpd->fClose = FALSE;                           // don't ask to save changes
        PostMessage (lpd->hwnd, WM_CLOSE, TRUE, 0);
    }
    return (OLE_OK);                                   // return success
}
```

Server Object Methods

The final set of methods deals with individual server objects. The first method, Obj-EnumFormats, is called to determine which data formats the server supports for an object. Each time it is called, ObjEnumFormat returns a different clipboard format, beginning with the most descriptive one, usually Native. When it has cycled through all its formats, it finally returns 0. The first time ObjEnumFormats is called, the ocf parameter is **NULL**. On each successive call, ocf carries the last value ObjEnum-Formats returned to the OLE libraries. The server sets up if statements like these to return, one by one, values for all the data formats the server chooses to support.

```
OLECLIPFORMAT CALLBACK ObjEnumFormats (
    LPOLEOBJECT lpoo,                                  // object wrapper
    OLECLIPFORMAT ocf)                                 // a clipboard format ID
{
    OLECLIPFORMAT cf;
    extern UINT cfNative;                              // three formats, all
    extern UINT cfOwnerLink;                           //    registered during
    extern UINT cfObjectLink;                          //    initialization.

    if (!ocf) cf=cfNative;
    else if (ocf==cfNative) cf=cfOwnerLink;
    else if (ocf==cfOwnerLink) cf=CF_METAFILEPICT;
    else if (ocf==CF_METAFILEPICT) cf=cfObjectLink;
    else if (ocf==cfObjectLink) cf=0;
    return (cf);
}
```

ObjShow directs the server to show or hide the specified object. Smartdraw has only one object per document.

```
OLESTATUS CALLBACK ObjShow (
    LPOLEOBJECT lpoo,                               // object wrapper
    BOOL bFocus)                                    // TRUE to take input focus
{
    LPOLEOBJ lpo = (LPOLEOBJ)lpoo;                  // cast to app's wrapper

    // make server window visible
    ShowWindow (lpo->pDoc->pSvr->hframe, SW_SHOWNORMAL);
    if (bFocus)                                     // take input focus?
        SetFocus (lpo->pDoc->hwnd);
    return (OLE_OK);
}
```

ObjSetTargetDevice receives a handle to an **OLETARGETDEVICE** structure with which to modify the device context when rendering the object. Even if the server ignores the information, as Smartdraw does, it still must free the handle containing the data. If OleSvr passes **NULL** for the structure, then the target device is the current display device.

```
OLESTATUS CALLBACK ObjSetTargetDevice (
    LPOLEOBJECT lpoo,                               // object wrapper
    HGLOBAL hdev)                                   // StdTargetDevice structure
{
    if (hdev) GlobalFree (hdev);                    // Smartdraw ignores it
    return (OLE_OK);
}
```

ObjGetData is called when a client requests the object's data in a specified format, perhaps because it is saving the object to a stream. (GetNative is an application-supplied routine also used when putting Native format data on the clipboard.)

```
OLESTATUS CALLBACK ObjGetData (
    LPOLEOBJECT lpoo,                               // object wrapper
    OLECLIPFORMAT ocf,                              // requested format
    HANDLE FAR *phdata)                             // return data handle here
{
    LPOLEOBJ lpo = (LPOLEOBJ)lpoo;                  // cast to app's wrapper
    HANDLE hData;                                   // handle to requested data
    HWND hwnd = lpo->pDoc->hwnd;                    // object's document window
    extern UINT cfNative;                           // OLE clipboard formats
    extern UINT cfOwnerLink;                        //     initialized when
    extern UINT cfObjectLink;                       //     server launched
```

```
    // The subroutines called here each allocate a memory
    // buffer, fill it with a representation of the object
    // in the requested format, and return a handle.

    if (ocf==cfNative)
        hData = GetNative (hwnd, TRUE);
    else if (ocf==CF_METAFILEPICT)
        hData = GetMetaPict (hwnd, TRUE);
    else if (ocf==cfOwnerLink)
        hData = OLEGetLink ("");
    else if (ocf==cfObjectLink)
        hData = OLEGetLink ("");
    else
        return (OLE_ERROR_MEMORY);          // return failure
    *phdata = hData;                        // handle to be received
    return (OLE_OK);                        // return success
}
```

ObjSetData is called when the client is supplying data from an object. This typically occurs when loading an object from a client's stream. (SetNative is another routine defined by the enclosing application.)

```
OLESTATUS CALLBACK ObjSetData (
    LPOLEOBJECT lpoo,                       // object wrapper
    OLECLIPFORMAT ocf,                      // format of given data
    HANDLE hdata)                           // data in ocf format
{
    LPOLEOBJ lpo = (LPOLEOBJ)lpoo;          // cast to app's wrapper
    extern UINT cfNative;                   // native data format

    if (ocf!=cfNative)
        return (OLE_ERROR_FORMAT);          // can only receive native

    // set the given data as the object for its associated window
    if (!SetNative (lpo->pDoc->hwnd, hdata))
        return (OLE_ERROR_MEMORY);          // return failure

    return (OLE_OK);                        // return success
}
```

ObjDoVerb requests the server to perform one of the verbs registered for an object class. Smartdraw supports only Edit.

```
OLESTATUS CALLBACK ObjDoVerb (
    LPOLEOBJECT lpoo,                      // object wrapper
    UINT vb,                               // number of requested verb
    BOOL fShow,                            // TRUE to show obj window
    BOOL fFocus)                           // TRUE to take input focus
{
    // Smartdraw's primary (and only) verb is Edit. All
    // Smartdraw needs to do for the Edit verb is display
    // the object in its window so the user can get at it.

    if (vb==0)                             // if the verb is Edit
        ObjShow (lpoo, fFocus);           // always show the window

    return (vb==0? OLE_OK: OLE_ERROR_DOVERB);
}
```

ObjRelease is called by the client when it no longer cares about the specified object.

```
OLESTATUS CALLBACK ObjRelease (LPOLEOBJECT lpoo)
{
    LPOLEOBJ lpo = (LPOLEOBJ)lpoo;         // cast to app's wrapper

    // If the client has released the object, then there's no point
    // in retaining our pointer to the now-defunct OLECLIENT structure.
    lpo->lpcli = 0;                        // lose client's VTBL

    return (OLE_OK);
}
```

ObjSetBounds informs the server if the bounding rectangle for an object has changed in a client document. Smartdraw ignores this notification.

```
OLESTATUS CALLBACK ObjSetBounds (
    LPOLEOBJECT lpoo,                      // object wrapper
    OLE_CONST LPRECT r)                    // new bounding rectangle
{
    return (OLE_OK);                       // Smartdraw ignores it
}
```

ObjSetColorScheme passes the client's color preference for an object. As in the case of document preferences, Smartdraw ignores it because its objects already have defined sizes and colors.

```
OLESTATUS CALLBACK ObjSetColorScheme (
    LPOLEOBJECT lpoo,                      // object wrapper
    OLE_CONST LOGPALETTE FAR *lplogp)      // suggested palette
```

```
{
    return (OLE_OK);                          // Smartdraw ignores it
}
```

A PREVIEW OF OLE 2.0

As we write this book, Microsoft has begun beta-testing OLE 2.0. The 32-bit version of OLE 2.0 is scheduled for release soon after Windows NT appears. We close the chapter with a brief overview of the new OLE, considering how it addresses the limitations of OLE 1.0 and what new features it provides.

The features of OLE 2.0 visible to the user include

- Editing objects directly in the client document window without switching to the server's window
- Moving and copying OLE objects by dragging and dropping them
- Tracking links even when files move
- Redrawing and printing objects more quickly
- Programming applications more easily, sometimes even with a single macro language for controlling a variety of programs
- Interacting fully with existing OLE 1.0 clients and servers

Internally, the basic conceptual model that underlies all these features is the ability to associate *interfaces* with *objects*. Microsoft defines an interface as a related group of public functions implemented by an object, a definition that clearly relates to the virtual tables of OLE 1.0. Users, both programmers and macro-writers, plug in to an object's interface to use the object. Every object is represented by a DLL that handles objects of its class, and the DLL exports functions anyone can use. The system supplies many prebuilt interfaces, and a single object may derive its own interface from a combination of preexisting ones. All interfaces derive from the fundamental IUnknown root interface, but an object might, for example, also incorporate the IStream interface for data streams or the IDragSource interface to be a drag-and-drop server.

OLE 2.0 provides a potential solution to "software bloat," the seemingly inexorable tendency of applications to grow with each new release as more and more functionality is added; it permits the division of an integrated application into pluggable components. Since it is merely a set of guidelines, it is likely that large applications will evolve into families of components that understand each other well. (Similar family relations appear in some Aldus products, which are built around a common core of DLLs.)

Limitations of OLE 1.0 Corrected by OLE 2.0

When a user activates an embedded object in a compound document under OLE 1.0, the work context changes as the theater of action moves to the server's window. OLE 2.0 avoids the disorienting shift with *in-place* activation: The document window remains unchanged, but the server takes over the menu, title bar, and even the tool bar of the same window where the compound document appears. The two views of a window in Figure 15.3 illustrate in-place activation. The menus have changed in the second view because the user has activated an OLE object.

The time required to switch between client and server while editing and updating can be quite long, particularly where large objects are involved. The delay occurs because OLE 1.0 reads objects in their entirety. OLE 2.0 permits objects greater control over how they are moved to and from their streams, allowing them to be loaded on demand. To optimize speed and memory usage, objects may even be loaded in pieces.

The asynchronous operation of some OLE 1.0 commands produces some repetitious and awkward message-polling in an OLE client. OLE 2.0 moves the message loop into the OLE system DLLs, freeing the program from some of its tedious chores.

When the user moves a file containing a linked object, the link must be repaired manually. OLE 2.0 reduces the problem by storing a relative path to the object in addition to the absolute path kept by OLE 1.0. Only if the linked object is moved relative to the document can the link be broken.

OLE 1.0 provides limited control over object size and page layout. Since objects must be rectangular, oddly shaped objects are hard to place. OLE 2.0 allows objects to be broken up into multiple rectangular pieces and printed across page breaks.

FIGURE 15.3:

Two views of the same window, showing how in-place activation makes the client's menu bar accessible to a server program

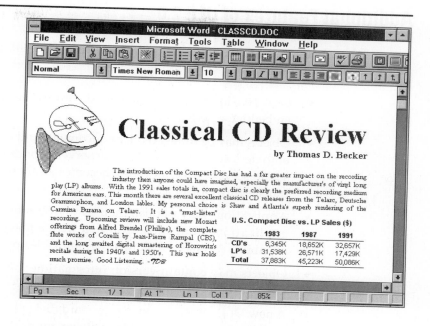

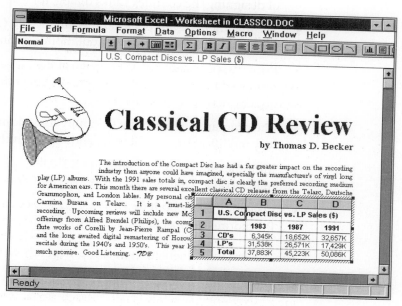

Additional Features of OLE 2.0

Besides the features we've already mentioned, OLE 2.0 offers these additional capabilities:

- OLE 2.0 allows objects to be nested within others. A link may be made to an embedded object.

- Objects may be dragged out of documents and dropped onto other objects, onto desktop icons, or onto other servers (for example, a printer server or a sound server). Drag-and-drop becomes an alternative to the clipboard for transferring OLE objects.

- Applications may publish their own OLE interfaces, facilitating inter-application commands. Coupled with a macro language, the interface capability facilitates making programmable applications.

- Objects may contain version information about the application that created them.

- A new DLL containing many standard dialog boxes relieves the programmer of designing the complex Links dialog, for example.

- The default behavior of OLE 2.0 is identical to OLE 1.0. OLE 1.0 applications run on an OLE 2.0 system without modification.

- Primary specification in C++ is one of the biggest changes. A C API is still promised for compatibility, but the system is clearly moving toward an object-oriented specification.

- The programmer has more flexibility in deciding whether to *commit* or *roll back* modifications, facilitating Undo commands.

- Multiple platforms will support OLE 2.0. Expect to see it on the Apple Macintosh as well as 16-bit Windows and Windows NT.

- Instead of being built on DDE, OLE 2.0 uses a new Lightweight Remote Procedure Call mechanism (LRPC).

The current implementation of LRPC depends on shared memory to operate and does not make true procedure calls. When OLE 2.0 libraries converse with OLE 1.0 libraries, both interlocutors still speak in DDE.

Programming OLE 2.0

OLE 2.0 introduces the biggest programming paradigm shift since Windows itself was introduced. It continues the trend toward a more object-oriented style of programming, using virtual tables and methods, defining interfaces to objects through which all communication takes place. The basic interface is called IUnknown and contains the members AddRef, QueryInterface, and Release. All objects that the system manipulates must derive their interfaces from this base class. Thus, in C the interface IMyInterface would be defined in pseudo-C as follows:

```
typedef struct imyinterface_t
{
    AddRef( . . . );
    Release( . . . );
    QueryInterface( . . . );
    MyMethod1( . . . );
    . . .
} IMyInterface;
```

When an object containing this interface is instantiated in a C program, the member function pointers must be initialized manually. In C++, the compiler performs the initialization.

The AddRef method causes the object to increment a reference count. Release decrements the count and frees the interface when the count reaches 0. Whatever the language, the onus is on the programmer to increment an interface's reference count when a pointer is copied and decrement it when the pointer passes out of scope.

QueryInterface allows the system to perform a form of negotiation with the object to discover which other standard interfaces it supports. (All interfaces have system-wide unique identifiers.) For example, a container application that allows objects to be dragged and dropped on it may provide an interface derived from IUnknown, which contains the IDragDrop interface.

Since Microsoft evidently hopes that OLE 2.0 will become the standard form of interaction with future Windows systems, a shift to C++ seems inevitable. Using C is simply too much trouble.

Looking beyond OLE 2.0

The primary problem with OLE is the false duality of links and embedded objects. This has its roots in the duality of Windows and DOS, where objects stored in the file system (DOS) may be modified without the knowledge of the object management system. The obvious solution is to merge the file system and object management systems to provide a seamless, persistent object storage system. Microsoft is already at work on a Windows Objects product, known for now as Cairo. It is a distributed-object operating system, and its object model is the same as that of OLE 2.0. OLE 2.0 and Cairo provide the same programming model for inter-application, system, and network services, and Cairo's services will absorb many of the OLE 2.0 interfaces.

This chapter completes our treatment of Object Linking and Embedding. The operations of an OLE server complement the operations of the client, described in Chapter 14. Client programs initiate OLE transactions, and the OLE libraries invoke servers to perform them. From the system's point of view, an OLE server looks like a set of custom procedures for performing standard tasks with a particular kind of data object. The system doesn't care what the data is. By calling the standard functions from the server's three virtual tables, the OLE libraries can cause objects of any class to be created, edited, saved, displayed, resized, and released. The virtual tables divide the server's methods into three groups: general server functions, server document functions, and object functions.

Besides supplying functions to fill virtual tables, an OLE server maintains entries in the system registry and puts objects on the clipboard. The registry records information about all the object classes available from all the currently installed servers. From reading the registry, the OLE libraries can locate the programs that support objects from the client's compound documents. It is the glue that connects objects to the programs that can edit them. The clipboard is the medium through which objects are transferred.

The appeal of OLE lies in the potential for integrating diverse data formats seamlessly in a single document. The more data formats the system itself supports, the more potentially powerful OLE becomes. Starting with Windows 3.1, Microsoft incorporated in the Windows system an API for dealing with diverse sound and video formats of multimedia applications. Chapter 16 demonstrates the multimedia API under Windows NT.

Programming for Multimedia

- **Controlling multimedia devices**

- **Waveform sounds**

- **Reading and writing multimedia RIFF files**

- **Playing, recording, and mixing sounds**

A guiding principle behind the design of the Windows system has always been integration. Concurrent programs can exchange data, send each other messages and commands, and cooperate in combining linked and embedded objects to create compound documents. The addition of a multimedia API to Windows 3.1 furthered the goal of integration by embracing new ranges of data. Besides text and graphics, audio and video data in many formats now has a place in the general PC market. For about the price of a large hard disk you can add a sound board and a CD-ROM drive to your computer and play audio CDs, watch movies, record sounds to the disk, and create animation sequences. Multimedia seems to promise most for the education and entertainment fields, but business too will appreciate the new flexibility and variety of choices in presenting information.

After explaining the general concepts of Windows multimedia, this chapter builds a program modeled on the Windows Sound Recorder. You will learn the high-level commands for operating any multimedia device and the file I/O commands for reading and writing many kinds of multimedia data. You will also see how to play sounds, record them, change their volume, and combine them. The ShowWave example program introduces basic techniques needed for many multimedia operations.

CONCEPTS

This section introduces the basic components and capabilities of multimedia programming for Windows. The section "Commands" later in this chapter covers in more detail the high-level device commands, RIFF files, and waveform sound.

What Is Multimedia?

Windows multimedia is a collection of capabilities for dealing with audio and visual peripherals. Its purpose is to allow the integration of many different data formats in a single system environment. Windows' multimedia features include three different components: audio and visual hardware devices, drivers for those devices, and a generalized API that translates programming commands into instructions for any multimedia driver.

Multimedia operations are data intensive; they make great demands on the CPU to process comparatively large quantities of data rapidly. The devices that store the data must meet certain function and protocol standards in order to work effectively. To encourage the proliferation of multimedia-capable systems, Microsoft consulted with a number of hardware and software companies to develop a Multimedia PC specification establishing minimum system capabilities for multimedia computing. Hardware and software products compatible with this standard carry the MPC trademark. For example, to carry the MPC mark a CD-ROM drive must transfer data at a minimum rate of 150K per second without utilizing more than 40 percent of the CPU's power. It must also have an average seek time of 1 second.

Windows NT recognizes the following types of multimedia devices:

Device Type	Description
animation	Animation device
cdaudio	Audio CD player
dat	Digital audio tape player
digitalvideo	Digital video (not GDI) in a window
other	Undefined MCI device
overlay	Overlay device (analog video in a window)
scanner	Image scanner
sequencer	MIDI sequencer
videodisc	Videodisk player
waveaudio	Device that plays digitized waveform sounds

The list of drivers suggests the range of hardware and data formats that Windows now expects to encounter—devices and data formerly inaccessible to most Intel-based PC users. Besides these drivers, multimedia also brought to Windows enhanced display drivers for high-resolution adapters and gray-scale VGA, the Sound Recorder and Media Player applications, and several applets in the Control Panel for installing devices and setting system sounds.

Beyond the hardware and drivers, however, the multimedia services include a layer of software defining (predictably) a device-independent interface for programs to use multimedia. A single set of commands will, for example, play sounds on any waveform device. Under Windows 3.1, the multimedia services reside in mmsystem.dll. Win32 moves them to winmm.dll. The layer of Win32 that interprets multimedia commands is called WinMM.

Four Command Sets

The system provides four different ways to manage multimedia services: two high-level command sets, one low-level command set, and a set of file I/O commands.

The low-level and the high-level commands control the same multimedia devices. The low-level commands are more powerful, and the high-level commands are more convenient. To record a sound, for example, the low-level functions make you repeatedly send the device an empty buffer and wait for it to come back full. But the low-level functions will also let you mix a new sound with an old sound as you record, scale the pitch and playback rates, change the device volume setting, record a MIDI song, and send custom messages defined by the driver. Also, since all the high-level commands are implemented internally through the low-level commands, you can get better performance by calling the low-level commands directly.

Low-level commands interact with drivers for particular devices. The more generalized high-level commands interact with drivers for logical devices. Windows NT comes with three: a MIDI sequencer, a CD player, and a waveform audio player. These generic drivers translate high-level commands into low-level function calls for particular drivers. The high-level API defined by the generic drivers is called the Multimedia Command Interface (MCI). MCI commands shield you from many small details of managing data streams, but at the expense of some flexibility. The high-level commands give the same kind of control that, for example, wsprintf gives for string output. Sometimes you really do need low-level commands like lstrcat and _fcvt, but the high-level commands are usually much easier to use.

Only specialized programs require the low-level multimedia functions. The high-level functions can play MIDI files, movies, videodisks, and CD-ROMs, and they can record as well as play waveform sounds. Like many multimedia programs, ShowWave has no need for the low-level commands, and we'll say little more about them.

The Multimedia Command Interface supports two parallel sets of high-level MCI functions: a command interface and a message interface. Command strings and command messages do the same thing, but strings are useful for authoring systems where the user writes command scripts to control a device. The function `mciSend-Command` sends drivers messages like `MCI_OPEN` and `MCI_PLAY`. The parallel function `mciSendString` sends strings like "open c:\sounds\harp.wav" and "play waveaudio to 500".

Besides the low-level commands, the MCI commands, and the MCI strings, a fourth command set facilitates reading and writing with multimedia data files. The Multimedia I/O (MMIO) commands understand the organization of files in the standard RIFF format and also perform buffering, a useful optimization for data-intensive multimedia programs.

The Multimedia Timer

Since timing is often critical in multimedia—particularly for playing MIDI music and for coordinating different devices during a presentation—WinMM also includes enhanced timer services. The multimedia timer does not send `WM_TIMER` messages; instead it is based on interrupts. The CPU regularly receives interrupt signals from the computer's timer chip, and the multimedia timer invokes a callback function from your program during those interrupts. Interrupt-driven timer signals are much more regular because no time is lost waiting for the application's message queue to empty. Furthermore, the multimedia timer is accurate down to about 10 (MIPS) or 16 (Intel) milliseconds, but the smallest effective interval for `SetTimer` is about 55 milliseconds, and even that resolution isn't guaranteed because of message queue delays. The timer resolution varies from system to system; you can determine the resolution by calling `timeGetDevCaps`.

The drawback of real-time interrupt processing is that it can significantly slow other applications and degrade system performance.

Multimedia Animation

WinMM includes animation capabilities. By opening an `mmmovie` device you can play animation files called *movies*. Multimedia animation does not provide new GDI functions to create moving images. It works very much like the audio device, translating a data file into output. The movie player reads from a RIFF file (one containing RMMP format chunks). Movie files can support casts, scores, inks, transitions, palette effects, audio, and other animation structures. You open the movie player device with the **MCI_OPEN** command message, play the movie with **MCI_PLAY**, and finish with **MCI_CLOSE**. Some other command messages are specific to movie files; **MCI_STEP**, for example, changes the current position forward or backward a set number of movie frames. **MCI_WINDOW** sets or adjusts the window where the movie appears. But in general the MCI commands for movies work the same way as the commands for sound, and when you have learned one set you can easily learn the other.

Creating movie files is more difficult than playing them. You need a high-level tool for designing animation. Microsoft's Video for Windows 3.1 is one choice; the MacroMind Director is another. Although the MacroMind Director runs on the Macintosh, its data files easily convert to Windows' multimedia format. (As of this writing, there is not yet a native Win32 animation tool.)

Sound Data Formats

Digitized sounds for the PC generally come in one of three common forms. One is the Compact Disc-Digital Audio format (also called "Red Book audio"). Commercial CDs use this data-intensive format to store high-quality digitized sound. Each second of sound consumes 176K of disk space. Another more compact storage format is defined by the Musical Instrument Digital Interface. MIDI is a standard protocol for communication between musical instruments and computers. MIDI files contain instructions for a synthesizer to play a piece of music. MIDI sound files take up less room and produce good quality sound, but recording them requires MIDI hardware. A third format, waveform files, produces adequate sound without a synthesizer and consumes less disk space than the CD Digital Audio format. *Waveform audio* is a technique for re-creating sound waves by sampling the original sound at discrete intervals and recording a digital representation of each sample. The rest of this chapter concerns itself with waveform files.

To store sound as waveform data, a digitizer measures the sound at frequent intervals. Each measurement forms a snapshot called a *sample*. With smaller intervals and more frequent samples, the sound quality improves. Sound travels in waves; by sampling frequently we can plot more points on the wave and reproduce it more accurately. WinMM supports three sampling rates: 11.025 kHz, 22.05 kHz, and 44.1 kHz. One kilohertz equals 1000 times per second; 44.1 kHz is 44,100 times per second. In a .WAV file digitized with a sampling rate of 11.025 kHz, each millisecond contains about 11 samples.

The human ear stops perceiving high-pitched sounds when they reach a frequency near 20 kHz. For a recording to capture a sound, it must sample at a rate at least twice the frequency of the sound, so a sampling rate of 44.1 kHz captures the full range of perceptible frequencies. Commercial audio compact disks sample at 44.1 kHz. The lower sampling rates, which are fractions of 44.1, reproduce sound less well but take up less room in storage.

COMMANDS

A program that uses the WinMM commands must include the mmsystem.h header file and link with the winmm.lib library. When porting from Windows 3.1, be sure to change your makefile to use winmm.lib instead of mmsystem.lib.

Three Easy Ways to Play Sounds

Waveform files conventionally have the .WAV extension. To produce waveform sounds, most programs will rely on one of three simple commands: **MessageBeep**, **sndPlaySound**, or **PlaySound**. All three work best with short .WAV files. **MessageBeep** plays only sounds configured in the registry for warnings and errors. **sndPlaySound** plays sounds directly from .WAV files or from memory buffers. **PlaySound**, new in Win32, resembles **sndPlaySound** but differs in two respects: It does not play sounds from memory, and it does play sounds stored as resources of type WAVE.

MessageBeep takes one parameter naming one of five system sounds configured in the Control Panel. By pairing every call to **MessageBox** with a **MessageBeep**, you can make your program play sounds the user selects to indicate different levels of warning. If **MessageBox** displays the **MB_ICONHAND** icon, **MessageBeep** should pass **MB_ICONHAND** as its parameter. The sound produced depends on the SystemHand entry in the system registry. (You should allow the user to disable your program's message beeps. If many errors occur, the repeated yellow-alert sirens and broken dishes crashing may grow irritating.)

Here are the possible parameter values and their corresponding registry entries. Through the Control Panel or the Registry Editor, the user may associate any .WAV file with these signals.

0xFFFFFFFF	**Standard Beep through PC speaker**
MB_ICONASTERISK	SystemAsterisk
MB_ICONEXCLAMATION	SystemExclamation
MB_ICONHAND	SystemHand
MB_ICONQUESTION	SystemQuestion
MB_OK	SystemDefault

Like all the sound functions, **MessageBeep** requires an appropriate device driver in order to play a waveform sound. The normal PC speaker is not an adequate device for multimedia.

With **sndPlaySound** you can play any system sounds named in the registry and configured from the Control Panel—there may be others besides the standard five—or you can play .WAV files directly.

```
BOOL sndPlaySound(
    LPCTSTR lpszSoundName,          // file or registry key
    UINT uFlags );                  // SND_ option flags
```

The first parameter names a registry entry such as SystemStart or SystemQuestion; alternatively, it may contain a full path name pointing to a .WAV file. **sndPlaySound** requires enough memory to load the full sound into memory. It works best with sound files no larger than about 100K.

The second parameter expects a flag controlling how the sound is played. Here are some possible values:

- **SND_MEMORY** identifies the first parameter as a pointer to an object in memory and not to a file name or system sound.

- **SND_SYNC** finishes playing sound before returning control to the program.

- **SND_ASYNC** returns control to the program immediately and plays sound in the background.

- **SND_ASYNC | SND_LOOP** return control to the program immediately and play the sound continuously in the background until the program calls **sndPlaySound** with **NULL** for the first parameter.

- **SND_NODEFAULT** instructs the function to make no noise at all if for any reason it cannot find or play the sound. Normally **sndPlaySound** feels obligated to produce a noise of some sort on every call and if all else fails will at least play the SystemDefault sound.

To play sounds compiled as resources, **PlaySound** is the best choice. **sndPlaySound** can also play sounds from the program's resources, but only if you load them into memory first and set the **SND_MEMORY** flag. Chapter 10 shows how to load resources using the commands **FindResource**, **LoadResource**, and **LockResource**. After playing the sound, release the resource with **FreeResource**. **PlaySound**, however, deals with resources more conveniently.

```
BOOL PlaySound(
    LPCTSTR lpszSoundName,              // file or resource name
    HANDLE hModule,                     // source for resource sounds
    DWORD dwFlags );                    // sound type and option flags
```

The function interprets the first parameter according to the option flags.

- **SND_ALIAS:** Plays a sound from the system registry. The first parameter is an alias from the registry, such as SystemAsterisk or SystemHand.

- **SND_FILENAME:** Plays a sound from a .WAV file, just as **sndPlaySound** does. The first parameter points to a file name.

- **SND_RESOURCE:** Plays a sound from a program's resources. The first parameter is a resource ID string, possibly returned from the **MAKEINTRESOURCE** macro.

These three flags are mutually exclusive. In addition to them, **PlaySound** recognizes some of the same flags defined for **sndPlaySound**, such as **SND_NODEFAULT** and **SND_ASYNC**. (It does not recognize **SND_MEMORY**.)

The second parameter, hModule, is ignored unless dwFlags includes **SND_RESOURCE**, in which case hModule identifies the program whose resources contain the WAVE data named in lpszSoundName. The handle may belong to an instance rather than a module and may be acquired, for example, from **GetModuleHandle**, **LoadLibrary**, or **GetWindowLong**.

Windows NT does not define a WAVE keyword to use in resource files the way you use **ICON** or **BITMAP**, but you can always define your own resource types.

<resname> WAVE <filename>   // add sound to program's resources

<resname> is a name you choose for your resource and <filename> points to a .WAV file. **PlaySound** always looks for resources identified as type "WAVE".

But **MessageBeep**, **sndPlaySound**, and **PlaySound** have limits. In order to control where in a sound the playback starts, to record sounds, to mix them and change their volume, and to save new sound files, we need more commands.

Media Control Interface (MCI)

The Media Control Interface is the easiest way to program for multimedia. MCI operations take the form of command messages sent to devices. Generally you begin an operation by opening a device; then you send commands, such as **MCI_PLAY** or **MCI_STOP**, to make the device play, stop, record, or rewind; and finally you close the device.

The most important and most versatile of the MCI functions is **mciSendCommand**. This function is to multimedia what **Escape** is to printing: a route for sending any of many possible signals to a device. **mciSendCommand** expects four parameters:

```
MCIERROR mciSendCommand(
    MCIDEVICEID mciDeviceID,        // identifier for a MM device
    UINT uMessage,                  // a command message number
    DWORD dwFlags,                  // flags modifying command action
    DWORD dwParamBlock );           // structure full of relevant info
```

The first parameter addresses a particular device. When you open a device, **mciSendCommand** gives you a device ID; in subsequent commands the device ID tells Windows where to deliver the message. The second parameter, **uMessage**, is a constant like **MCI_PLAY** or **MCI_STOP**. ShowWave sends the following messages:

- **MCI_OPEN** opens a device (to begin an interaction).

- **MCI_CLOSE** closes a device (to end interaction).

- **MCI_SET** changes device settings.

- **MCI_PLAY** begins playback.

- **MCI_STOP** interrupts current action.
- **MCI_RECORD** begins recording.
- **MCI_SAVE** saves a recorded sound in a file.

Other messages might, for example, make the device pause, seek to a location in the device element, or retrieve information about the device.

The third parameter, dwFlags, usually combines several bit flags that help Windows interpret the command. The set of possible flags varies for each message, but a few are common to all messages. For example, **mciSendCommand** normally works asynchronously. When it initiates a device operation, it doesn't wait for the device to finish. It returns immediately and the device continues to operate in the background. If you want to know when the operation ends, setting the **MCI_NOTIFY** flag causes WinMM to send you a termination message. You might, for example, want to close the audio device when a sound finishes playing. On the other hand, sometimes you don't want to proceed until you are certain the device operation succeeded. The **MCI_WAIT** flag forces the command to run synchronously. Program execution stops at **mciSendCommand** until the device finishes the requested task.

The final parameter for **mciSendCommand**, dwParamBlock, also varies from message to message. It is always a structured variable holding either information the device may need to execute the command or empty fields for information the device may return after executing the command. Here are the parameter block data structures needed for ShowWave:

Data Structure	Associated Message
MCI_OPEN_PARMS	MCI_OPEN
MCI_SET_PARMS	MCI_SET
MCI_PLAY_PARMS	MCI_PLAY
MCI_RECORD_PARMS	MCI_RECORD
MCI_SAVE_PARMS	MCI_SAVE

The fields of these structures might hold a file name, positions in the file at which to start or stop playing, a device ID, or the address of a callback function to receive the asynchronous completion message. We'll consider each structure in more detail as we encounter it in the ShowWave program.

One consideration shaping the design of the MCI was clearly extensibility. As other devices and other technologies find their way into Windows PCs, the set of MCI command messages and parameter block structures can easily expand to accommodate them. New drivers can define their own messages and structures.

Multimedia File I/O

Multimedia data files conform to the standard RIFF format. Multimedia programmers need to understand the structure of a RIFF file and to learn the MMIO functions for reading and writing them.

RIFF Files

The Resource Interchange File Format (RIFF) protocol is a tagged file structure, meaning that a file can be divided into a series of irregular sections marked off by *tags*, or short strings. The tags in RIFF files are four-character codes, such as "RIFF", "INFO", and "PAL ". (The fourth character in "PAL " is a space.) Each tag begins a *chunk*. The most important chunks begin with the tag "RIFF". RIFF chunks are allowed to contain other chunks, sometimes called *subchunks*. RIFF files always begin with a RIFF chunk, and all the remaining data is organized as subchunks of the first one.

Every chunk has three parts: a tag, a size, and some binary data. The tag tells what kind of data follows. The size, a **DWORD**, tells how much data the chunk contains. At the end of the data comes the tag for the next chunk (if any). A waveform file always has at least two subchunks, one for the format and one for the sound data, and may have more. Some chunks might carry copyright and version information; others might hold a list of *cues*, locations in the file that coordinate with events in some other chunk or file.

RIFF chunks differ from most others in that their data fields—the binary data section—always begin with another four-letter code indicating the file's contents. The "RIFF" tag identifies a RIFF file, and the form code tells us to expect subchunks appropriate for a waveform ("WAVE"), a MIDI sound ("RMID"), a DIB ("RDIB"), a movie file ("RMMP"), or a palette file ("PAL ").

Since RIFF files need so many of these four-character codes, there's a macro for creating them: **mmioFOURCC**. This command stores a "RIFF" tag in one field of a chunk information structure:

```
MMCKINFO mmckinfo.ckid = mmioFOURCC( 'R', 'I', 'F', 'F' );
```

The **MMCKINFO** structure holds information describing a single chunk. When reading data, the system fills out fields describing the current chunk for you. When writing data, you fill out the information for the system to store.

```
/* RIFF chunk information data structure */
typedef struct _MMCKINFO
{
    FOURCC  ckid;                 // chunk ID
    DWORD   cksize;               // chunk size
    FOURCC  fccType;              // form type or list type
    DWORD   dwDataOffset;         // offset of data portion of chunk
    DWORD   dwFlags;              // flags used by MMIO functions
} MMCKINFO;
```

FOURCC is a new data type based on the **DWORD** type. Each character in the code fills one of the 4 bytes in a **DWORD**. The third field, **fccType**, is the form tag we said follows every "RIFF" tag. The **fccType** field is irrelevant for non-RIFF chunks because they don't have forms. Figure 16.1 illustrates parent chunks (or superchunks) and subchunks in a RIFF file.

FIGURE 16.1:

Structure of a RIFF file

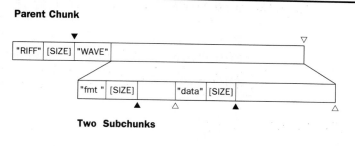

Parent Chunk

Two Subchunks

▲ Descend points
△ Ascend points

The Multimedia File I/O Functions

You've already encountered two sets of file I/O functions, one in the C runtime libraries and one in the Windows API. The WinMM API includes yet another set, having special features for chunky RIFF files. The multimedia file I/O functions understand chunks better than do other functions. In addition, they allow buffered file access. (The Windows NT system caches file I/O by default, but functions that do their own additional buffering can still improve performance.) The command that opens a file also controls the buffer settings.

```
HMMIO mmioOpen(
    LPTSTR lpszFilename,          // name of file to open
    LPMMIOINFO lpmmioinfo,        // place to put file info
    DWORD fdwOpen );              // option flags
```

The first parameter names the file, and the second stores information about its current state. Unless you want to change a default setting, such as the size of the I/O buffer (8K), lpmmioinfo should be **NULL**. The third parameter contains a variety of option flags. Here are some of them:

- **MMIO_READ** allows reading only.

- **MMIO_WRITE** allows writing only.

- **MMIO_READWRITE** allows reading and writing.

- **MMIO_CREATE** creates a new file.

- **MMIO_DELETE** deletes an existing file.

- **MMIO_EXCLUSIVE** prevents other programs from using the file.

- **MMIO_DENYWRITE** prevents other programs from changing the file.

- **MMIO_ALLOCBUF** enables buffered I/O.

In the C libraries, fopen begins buffered I/O and _open begins unbuffered I/O. The **MMIO_ALLOCBUF** flag makes the same distinction for the multimedia file I/O procedures. The system responds by allocating a default buffer of 8K. (To make the buffer larger or smaller, set a value in the **MMIOINFO** structure or call **mmioSetBuffer**.)

mmioOpen returns a handle of type **HMMIO**, meaning a handle to a multimedia file. Multimedia file handles are not compatible with other file handles; don't use them with the other C or Win32 file functions.

The functions **mmioRead**, **mmioWrite**, and **mmioClose** perform easily recognizable file operations. A few other I/O functions deal specifically with RIFF data chunks. To put a new chunk in a file, call **mmioCreateChunk**. This command writes a chunk header—the tag, the size, and, for RIFF and LIST chunks, a form code as well. It leaves the file pointer on the byte where you will begin writing the chunk's data with **mmioWrite**.

```
MMRESULT mmioCreateChunk(
    HMMIO hmmio,                    // handle of RIFF file
    LPMMCKINFO lpmmcki,            // description of new chunk
    UINT uOptions );               // creation options
```

To write a RIFF or LIST superchunk set an option flag, either **MMIO_CREATERIFF** or **MMIO_CREATELIST**.

Moving the file pointer from chunk to chunk calls for **mmioDescend** and **mmioAscend**. *Descending* into a chunk means advancing the file pointer past the tag and size fields to the beginning of the chunk's binary data. *Ascending* from a chunk means advancing the pointer to the end of its data.

```
MMRESULT mmioDescend(
    HMMIO hmmio,                    // handle of RIFF file
    LPMMCKINFO lpmmcki,            // place to put chunk info
    LPMMCKINFO lpmmckiParent,      // optional parent structure
    UINT uSearch );                // search option flags

MMRESULT mmioAscend(
    HMMIO hmmio,                    // handle of RIFF file
    LPMMCKINFO lpmmcki,            // place to put chunk info
    UINT uReserved );              // reserved; must be zero
```

After each descent, **mmioDescend** returns information about the chunk through the **MMCKINFO** parameter. You can also make **mmioDescend** search for a chunk of a certain type and descend into it. To initiate a search, the last parameter should contain **MMIO_FINDCHUNK**, **MMIO_FINDLIST**, or **MMIO_FINDRIFF**. The search begins at the current file position and stops at the end of the file. **mmioAscend**, besides advancing to the end of a chunk, helps build new chunks. Called after you write new data, it pads the chunk to an even byte boundary and writes the data size in the chunk's header.

About WAVE Chunks

Every waveform in a RIFF file is required to contain a chunk tagged "fmt ". (Lowercase tags indicate subchunks in a larger form.) The **PCMWAVEFORMAT** structure defines the contents of the format subchunk. ShowWave reads the format information to confirm that the sound is playable. It also remembers the sampling rate (nSamplesPerSecond) for calculating file positions and scroll bar ranges.

```
/* general waveform format (information common to all formats) */
typedef struct waveformat_tag {
    WORD wFormatTag;               // format type
    WORD nChannels;                // number of channels (1 = mono; 2 = stereo)
    DWORD nSamplesPerSec;          // sample rate
    DWORD nAvgBytesPerSec;         // for buffer estimation
    WORD nBlockAlign;              // block size of data
} WAVEFORMAT;

/* specific waveform format structure for PCM data */
typedef struct pcmwaveformat_tag
{
    WAVEFORMAT wf;
    WORD wBitsPerSample;
} PCMWAVEFORMAT;
```

PCM stands for "pulse control modulation." Currently PCM is the only format category defined for .WAV files, so the value in the **wFormatTag** field of a **WAVEFORMAT** structure should be **WAVE_FORMAT_PCM**. The **PCMWAVEFORMAT** structure adds to the general wave data a single field for bits per sample; this describes the space required to hold the data for a single sound sample. The common values on personal computers are 8 and 16 bits. A monaural wave sound sampled for 1 second at 11 kHz and 8 bits per sample contains 11,000 different samples of 8 bits each, for a total of about 11K. A stereo waveform samples in two channels simultaneously. If each channel records 8 bits at a time then a single full sample is 16 bits. A 1-second 11 kHz stereo waveform with a **wBitsPerSample** value of 8 would fill 22K.

CODE: THE SHOWWAVE PROGRAM

The ShowWave program imitates the Sound Recorder that comes with Windows NT. It reads and writes waveform files, plays and records wave sounds, mixes sounds from several files, and adjusts the volume of a sound. Without a sound card you can still run the program to open, close, mix, scroll through, and save sound files, but the program will be deaf and dumb, unable to play or record anything.

ShowWave is made up of several modules. Here they are in the order we'll present them:

File	Purpose
mci.c	Sends commands to audio device
mmio.c	Reads and writes waveform data
winmain.c	Contains `WinMain` and the About box procedure
showwave.c	Responds to dialog box controls
graphwin.c	Manages the custom control used for the program's graph

The first two modules contain general procedures for performing basic sound operations such as playback and record. Winmain.c registers and creates the program's window and runs the About box. The fourth module, showwave.c, calls the appropriate functions in response to input from the user. Graphwin.c manages the sound graph at the center of the program's window, visible in Figure 16.2. When

FIGURE 16.2:

ShowWave dialog box

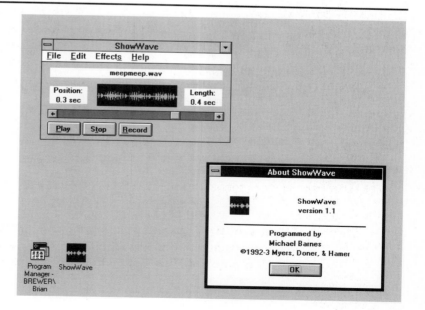

the user scrolls with the scroll bar, the graph display shows the sound wave in different parts of the file. To paint the graph display, we create a custom control and write a window procedure for it. (Another solution would be to subclass a standard control.)

Following are the program's header files and resource script. A few oddities may strike you in the main dialog box's resource template. We haven't used the **MENU** keyword before, but dialog boxes may have menus just as overlapping windows do. Also, the dialog template refers to two custom window classes: GraphClass and ShowWaveClass. Defining new classes for a dialog control and for the dialog itself makes it possible to assign nonstandard properties to both windows. The control in the center of the program window represents the current wave sound as a graph. When the user scrolls through the file, the graph changes to represent different parts of the sound. The custom class for the graph window lets us write the window's paint procedure for graphing the sound. The custom class for the main dialog window lets us assign the dialog an icon to display when minimized.

```
#
#    NMake file for the SHOWWAVE program
#


#
#    Set target and dependencies
#

all: showwave.exe
showwave.exe: winmain.obj showwave.obj graphwin.obj mmio.obj \
    mci.obj showwave.rbj
winmain.obj: winmain.c showwave.h rsrc.h
showwave.obj: showwave.c showwave.h rsrc.h
graphwin.obj: graphwin.c showwave.h
mmio.obj: mmio.c rsrc.h
mci.obj: mci.c rsrc.h
showwave.rbj: showwave.rc rsrc.h


#
#    Define macros for command-line options and library modules
#
```

```
!IFDEF NODEBUG
CFLAGS = -c -G3 -Os -W4 -D_X86_=1 -DWIN32
LFLAGS = -subsystem:windows
!ELSE
CFLAGS = -c -G3 -Od -W4 -Zi -D_X86_=1 -DWIN32
LFLAGS = -debug:full -debugtype:cv -subsystem:windows
!ENDIF

OBJS = winmain.obj showwave.obj graphwin.obj mmio.obj mci.obj showwave.rbj
LIBS = libc.lib ntdll.lib kernel32.lib user32.lib gdi32.lib winmm.lib \
       comdlg32.lib

#
#    Define compiling rules
#

.c.obj:
     cl386 $(CFLAGS) $*.c

.rc.rbj:
   rc -DWIN32 $*.rc
   cvtres -i386 $*.res -o $*.rbj

.obj.exe:
   link32 $(LFLAGS) -out:$*.exe $(OBJS) $(LIBS)

=======================================================================

/*----------------------------------------------------------------


         RSRC.H

         Resource identifier definitions for the SHOWWAVE program


   ----------------------------------------------------------------*/
/*----------------------------------------------------------------
         ICONS
   ----------------------------------------------------------------*/

#define IDI_WAVE                    1000
/*----------------------------------------------------------------
         DIALOG TEMPLATES
   ----------------------------------------------------------------*/
```

```
#define DLG_MAIN                    1000
#define DLG_ABOUT                   1010


/*------------------------------------------------------------------
            DIALOG ITEM IDs
  ----------------------------------------------------------------*/


/* For DLG_MAIN: */
#define IDD_FILETITLE               200
#define IDD_POSITION                210
#define IDD_SHOWWAVE                220
#define IDD_LENGTH                  230
#define IDD_SCROLLBAR               240
#define IDD_PLAY                    250
#define IDD_STOP                    260
#define IDD_RECORD                  270


/*------------------------------------------------------------------
            MENU TEMPLATE
  ----------------------------------------------------------------*/


#define IDM_MAIN                    1000

/*------------------------------------------------------------------
            MENU ITEMS
  ----------------------------------------------------------------*/


/* main menu item IDs */
#define IDM_NEW                     110
#define IDM_OPEN                    120
#define IDM_SAVE                    130
#define IDM_SAVEAS                  140
#define IDM_EXIT                    150

#define IDM_MIXWITHFILE             160

#define IDM_INCREASEVOLUME          170
#define IDM_DECREASEVOLUME          180

#define IDM_ABOUT                   190


/*------------------------------------------------------------------
            STRINGS
  ----------------------------------------------------------------*/
```

```
#define IDS_CAPTION              1000      /* window caption */

#define IDS_CANTOPENFILE         1100      /* MMIO error messages */
#define IDS_NOTWAVEFILE          1110
#define IDS_CORRUPTEDFILE        1120
#define IDS_CANTREADFORMAT       1130
#define IDS_UNSUPPORTEDFORMAT    1140
#define IDS_NOWAVEDATA           1150
#define IDS_OUTOFMEMORY          1160
#define IDS_CANTREADDATA         1170
#define IDS_CANTWRITEWAVE        1180
#define IDS_CANTWRITEFORMAT      1190
#define IDS_CANTWRITEDATA        1200

#define IDS_TIMEFMT              1210      /* program strings */
#define IDS_UNTITLED             1220
#define IDS_CONFIRMCLOSE         1230
#define IDS_OVERWRITE            1240
#define IDS_BADFREQUENCY         1250
#define IDS_BADRECORDFILE        1260

/*-----------------------------------------------------------------
      MAXIMUM LENGTH OF RESOURCE STRINGS
  -------------------------------------------------------------*/

#define MAX_RSRC_STRING_LEN 80

=================================================================

/*-----------------------------------------------------------------


      SHOWWAVE.H

      Declarations for the ShowWave sound program.

  -------------------------------------------------------------*/

/*-----------------------------------------------------------------
      PROGRAM CONSTANTS
  -------------------------------------------------------------*/

/* Values for PCM waveform data */
/* NOTE: dependent on the Bits Per Sample (in this demo: 8) */
#define MAXVALUE         255       // max value for one 8-bit sample
#define MIDVALUE         128
```

```
#define MINVALUE          0          // min value for one 8-bit sample

#define RGB_WHITE         RGB( 0xFF, 0xFF, 0xFF )
#define RGB_GREEN         RGB( 0x00, 0xFF, 0x00 )

/*------------------------------------------------------------------
         GLOBAL VARIABLES
     --------------------------------------------------------------*/

extern LPSTR lpWaveData;            // data from current .WAV file
extern DWORD dwWaveDataSize;        // size of .WAV file data
extern DWORD dwCurrentSample;       // position in current sound
extern DWORD dwSamplesPerSec;       // sampling rate for current sound

/*------------------------------------------------------------------
         MACROS
     --------------------------------------------------------------*/

/* message cracker for MCINOTIFY message */

/* void Cls_OnMCINotify(HWND hwnd, UINT uCode, UINT uDevID); */
#define HANDLE_MM_MCINOTIFY(hwnd, wParam, lParam, fn) \
        ((fn)((hwnd), (UINT)(wParam), LOWORD(lParam)), OL)

/*------------------------------------------------------------------
         FUNCTION PROTOTYPES
     --------------------------------------------------------------*/

/* SHOWWAVE.C */
LRESULT WINAPI ShowWave_WndProc( HWND hDlg, UINT uMsg, WPARAM wParam,
    LPARAM lParam );
BOOL QuerySave( HWND hDlg );

/* GRAPHWIN.C */
BOOL RegisterGraphClass( HINSTANCE hInstance );

/* MMIO.C */
BOOL ReadWaveData( HWND hWnd, LPSTR lpszFileName, LPSTR *lplpWaveData,
    DWORD *lpdwWaveDataSize, DWORD *lpdwSamplesPerSec );
BOOL WriteWaveData( HWND hWnd, LPSTR lpszFileName, LPSTR lpWaveData,
    DWORD dwWaveDataSize, DWORD dwSamplesPerSec );

/* MCI.C */
BOOL OpenDevice( HWND hWnd, LPSTR lpszFileName, MCIDEVICEID *lpuDeviceID );
VOID CloseDevice( HWND hWnd, MCIDEVICEID mciDevice );
```

```
BOOL SetTimeFormat( HWND hWnd, MCIDEVICEID mciDevice );
BOOL BeginPlay( HWND hWnd, MCIDEVICEID mciDevice, DWORD dwFrom );
VOID StopPlay( HWND hWnd, MCIDEVICEID mciDevice );
BOOL BeginRecord( HWND hWnd, MCIDEVICEID mciDevice, DWORD dwTo );
BOOL SaveRecord( HWND hWnd, MCIDEVICEID mciDevice, LPSTR lpszFileName );

/* WINMAIN.C */
BOOL WINAPI About_DlgProc( HWND hDlg, UINT uMsg, WPARAM wParam,
    LPARAM lParam );

=============================================================================

/*-------------------------------------------------------------------


       SHOWWAVE.RC


       The resource script for the SHOWWAVE program.

    -------------------------------------------------------------------*/

#include <windows.h>
#include "rsrc.h"

IDI_WAVE ICON wave.ico

IDM_MAIN MENU
BEGIN
    POPUP "&File"
    BEGIN
        MENUITEM "&New",                IDM_NEW
        MENUITEM "&Open...",            IDM_OPEN
        MENUITEM "&Save",               IDM_SAVE
        MENUITEM "Save &As...",         IDM_SAVEAS
        MENUITEM SEPARATOR
        MENUITEM "E&xit",               IDM_EXIT
    END
    POPUP "&Edit"
    BEGIN
        MENUITEM "&Mix with File...",   IDM_MIXWITHFILE
    END
    POPUP "Effect&s"
    BEGIN
        MENUITEM "&Increase Volume (by 25%)",IDM_INCREASEVOLUME
        MENUITEM "&Decrease Volume",    IDM_DECREASEVOLUME
    END
```

```
    POPUP "&Help"
    BEGIN
        MENUITEM "&About ShowWave...",   IDM_ABOUT
    END
END


STRINGTABLE LOADONCALL MOVEABLE DISCARDABLE
BEGIN
    /* window caption: */
    IDS_CAPTION               "ShowWave"

    /* MMIO Errors: */
    IDS_CANTOPENFILE          "Cannot open file."
    IDS_NOTWAVEFILE           "Not a WAVE file."
    IDS_CORRUPTEDFILE         "File is corrupted."
    IDS_CANTREADFORMAT        "Cannot read FMT chunk."
    IDS_UNSUPPORTEDFORMAT     "File must be an 8-bit mono PCM WAVE file."
    IDS_NOWAVEDATA            "File contains no WAVE data."
    IDS_OUTOFMEMORY           "Out of Memory."
    IDS_CANTREADDATA          "Cannot read DATA chunk."
    IDS_CANTWRITEWAVE         "Cannot write WAVE chunk."
    IDS_CANTWRITEFORMAT       "Cannot write FMT chunk."
    IDS_CANTWRITEDATA         "Cannot write DATA chunk."

    /* program message strings: */
    IDS_TIMEFMT               "%u.%u sec"
    IDS_UNTITLED              "(Untitled)"
    IDS_CONFIRMCLOSE          "Save changes to %s?"
    IDS_OVERWRITE             "Overwrite file?"
    IDS_BADFREQUENCY          "Cannot mix in a file with differing sample rate."
    IDS_BADRECORDFILE         "Cannot record over existing WAVE data."
END

DLG_ABOUT DIALOG 45, 45, 165, 115
STYLE DS_MODALFRAME | WS_POPUP | WS_CAPTION | WS_SYSMENU
CAPTION "About ShowWave"
FONT 8, "Helv"
BEGIN
    ICON            IDI_WAVE, -1, 20, 20, 20, 20
    CTEXT           "ShowWave", -1, 50, 20, 105, 10
    CTEXT           "version 1.1", -1, 50, 30, 105, 10
    CONTROL         "", -1, "Static", SS_BLACKRECT, 15, 50, 135, 1
    CTEXT           "Programmed by", -1, 10, 55, 145, 10
```

```
        CTEXT           "Michael Barnes", -1, 10, 65, 145, 10
        CTEXT           "©1992-3 Myers, Doner, && Hamer", -1, 10, 75, 145, 10
        DEFPUSHBUTTON   "OK", IDOK, 58, 90, 50, 14, WS_GROUP
END


DLG_MAIN DIALOG 1, 100, 180, 92
STYLE WS_MINIMIZEBOX | WS_POPUP | WS_CAPTION | WS_SYSMENU
CLASS "ShowWaveClass"
CAPTION "ShowWave"
FONT 8, "Helv"
BEGIN
        CTEXT           "(Untitled)", IDD_FILETITLE, 8, 6, 164, 10
        CTEXT           "Position:", -1, 8, 25, 36, 10
        CTEXT           "0.0 sec", IDD_POSITION, 8, 35, 36, 8
        CONTROL         "", IDD_SHOWWAVE, "GraphClass", 0x0000, 53, 22, 76, 23
        CTEXT           "Length:", -1, 136, 25, 36, 10,
        CTEXT           "0.0 sec", IDD_LENGTH, 136, 35, 36, 8,
        SCROLLBAR       IDD_SCROLLBAR, 6, 49, 168, 9, WS_TABSTOP
        PUSHBUTTON      "&Play", IDD_PLAY, 6, 62, 32, 14, WS_TABSTOP
        PUSHBUTTON      "S&top", IDD_STOP, 40, 62, 32, 14, WS_TABSTOP
        PUSHBUTTON      "&Record", IDD_RECORD, 74, 62, 32, 14, WS_TABSTOP
END
```

The MCI Module

In the MCI module we've isolated all the **mciSendCommand** function calls and built a separate routine for each command message. All the procedures are short, and most follow this basic pattern:

1. Initialize a parameter block.

2. Send a command.

3. Check for errors.

4. Return a value.

The module's eight procedures are described at the top of the mci.c file:

```
/*--------------------------------------------------------------


        MCI.C
        Routines for the SHOWWAVE program to manipulate audio using
        the Multimedia Command Interface (MCI).

        PUBLIC FUNCTIONS
                OpenDevice          open audio device
                CloseDevice         close audio device
                SetTimeFormat       choose millisecond time format
                BeginPlay           begin sound playback
                StopPlay            end sound playback
                BeginRecord         begin recording
                SaveRecord          save recording


        PRIVATE FUNCTION
                ReportMCIError      show error message for user

        program by Michael Barnes
        copyright 1992, 1993 by Brian Myers, Chris Doner, & Eric Hamer
        from Mastering Windows NT Programming
        ------------------------------------------------------------*/

#define STRICT
#include <windows.h>
#include <windowsx.h>
#include <mmsystem.h>          // multimedia definitions
#include "rsrc.h"              // program resource ID definitions

/*------------------------------------------------------------
        FUNCTION PROTOTYPE
        ------------------------------------------------------------*/

static void ReportMCIError( HWND hWnd, DWORD dwError );
```

Opening and Closing a Device

Opening a device is like opening a file; it announces your intention to exchange in-formation with some piece of hardware and tells the system to create whatever internal structures are needed to manage the interaction. The system gives you a device ID number that, like a file handle, identifies your partner in the exchange.

When the interaction ends you close the device, the system releases any related memory resources, and the device ID becomes invalid.

All multimedia devices respond to the **MCI_OPEN** and **MCI_CLOSE** messages. (The other three messages to which all drivers must respond are **MCI_GETDEVCAPS**, **MCI_STATUS**, and **MCI_INFO**, all of which request information about the device.)

Every **MCI_OPEN** command is accompanied by an **MCI_OPEN_PARMS** structure, defined in mmsystem.h:

```
/* parameter block for MCI_OPEN command message */
typedef struct tagMCI_OPEN_PARMS {
    DWORD dwCallback;              // window handle
    MCIDEVICEID wDeviceID;        // number identifying device
    LPCTSTR lpstrDeviceType;      // type of device to open
    LPCTSTR lpstrElementName;     // input element for device
    LPCTSTR lpstrAlias;           // optional
} MCI_OPEN_PARMS;
```

The **dwCallback** field appears in all the parameter structures. It works in tandem with the **MCI_NOTIFY** flag. Any **mciSendCommand** function call that asks for a notification message must include a window handle in the low-order word of the **dwCallback** field. This way, when the operation ends the system can send an **MM_MCINOTIFY** message to the window you named. You'll see how to answer the notification message when we reach the showwave.c module.

The **wDeviceID** field must be empty when you open a device; WinMM assigns an ID to the device you open and places the ID in the **wDeviceID** field. After opening any device you will want to save the ID number.

When Microsoft first released the Multimedia Extensions as a separate product enhancing Windows 3.0, the second and third fields were declared to be type **WORD**. In Windows 3.1 they changed to the polymorphic type **UINT**, and in Win32 the ID field changed again to the newly defined **MCIDEVICEID** type. For backward compatibility, however, both fields still incongruously retain the "w" prefix. In the transition from Windows 3.1 to Windows NT, the **MCI_OPEN_PARMS** structure has also lost an unused field, **wReserved0**.

The **lpcstrDeviceType** field names the sort of device you need for your data. The type name comes from the system registry, where you find entries like these:

```
AVIVideo : REG_SZ : mciavi32.dll
WaveAudio : REG_SZ : mciwave.dll
```

```
Sequencer : REG_SZ : mciseq.dll
CDAudio : REG_SZ : mcicda.dll
```

(To find these entries with the Registry Editor, go to HKEY_LOCAL_MACHINE and descend through SOFTWARE to Microsoft to Windows NT to CurrentVersion to MCI and MCI32.)

ShowWave requests a device of type WaveAudio in order to play .WAV files.

The lpstrElementName field designates a data source for a compound device. Windows distinguishes between simple devices and compound devices. A *simple device* doesn't need the name of a file in order to operate; a *compound device* does. For example, a program cannot choose what a CD player will play; the player plays only whatever compact disk the drive contains. A CD player is a simple device. A waveform sound driver, on the other hand, might play any of many different files currently available in the system; you must specify the file. The waveaudio device is always a compound device. A *device element* is whatever input or output medium your program connects with the device. The device element is usually a file, so the lpstrElementName field usually contains a file name.

The final field, lpstrAlias, allows you to provide a synonym for naming the device you open. Aliases matter only for the MCI string command interface.

You don't have to fill out all the fields in the parameter block. You might, for example, provide only the element name and let the system choose a matching device by looking at the file's extension—a waveaudio device for a .WAV file, a sequencer for a .MID file. Or if you just want information about the device, you might open it by supplying the type without any element. The flags parameter of the mciSend-Command function tells the system which fields to read. Here is an example:

```
/*-------------------------------------------------------------------
        OPEN DEVICE
        Open a waveaudio device
    ------------------------------------------------------------------*/

BOOL OpenDevice (
    HWND hWnd,
    LPSTR lpszFileName,
    MCIDEVICEID *lpmciDevice )
{
    DWORD dwRet;
    MCI_OPEN_PARMS mciOpenParms;
```

```
    /* open the compound device */
    mciOpenParms.lpstrDeviceType  = "waveaudio";
    mciOpenParms.lpstrElementName = lpszFileName;
    dwRet = mciSendCommand( 0,                              // device ID
                MCI_OPEN,                                   // command
                MCI_OPEN_TYPE | MCI_OPEN_ELEMENT,           // flags
                (DWORD)(LPVOID)&mciOpenParms );             // param block

    if (dwRet != 0)
    {
        ReportMCIError( hWnd, dwRet );
        return( FALSE );
    }

    /* set return values */
    *lpmciDevice = mciOpenParms.wDeviceID;
    return( TRUE );
}
```

The first parameter for **mciSendCommand** can only be 0 because the device is not open and has not yet been assigned an ID. The third parameter combines two flags. The first, **MCI_OPEN_TYPE**, tells the system to read the **lpstrDeviceType** field of the parameter block because we have put a string there. The second flag, **MCI_OPEN_ELEMENT**, says to read the **lpstrElementName** field as well. Because we have omitted the **MCI_OPEN_ALIAS** flag, the system will ignore any value in the **lpstrAlias** field.

Our OpenDevice procedure returns **TRUE** or **FALSE** to indicate its success; if it succeeds then it also returns the device ID in its third parameter. The device ID will be needed for subsequent operations—for example, closing the device:

```
/*-------------------------------------------------------------------
        CLOSE DEVICE
        Close a multimedia device
    -------------------------------------------------------------------*/

void CloseDevice (
    HWND hWnd,
    MCIDEVICEID mciDevice )
{
    DWORD dwRet;
```

```
dwRet = mciSendCommand( mciDevice,
                        MCI_CLOSE,
                        MCI_WAIT,
                        (DWORD)NULL );

if (dwRet != 0)
{
    ReportMCIError( hWnd, dwRet );
}
return;
}
```

CloseDevice expects a device ID as part of its input. No other input is needed; the **MCI_CLOSE** command doesn't even use a parameter block.

Setting the Time Format

When ShowWave asks the waveaudio device to play a sound, it always specifies a location in the file from which to begin. With the program's scroll bar the user can move to any part of the file before starting playback. ShowWave and the driver have to agree on units for measuring the file. The possible units for waveform files are bytes, samples, and milliseconds. Measuring files in bytes makes intuitive sense. A sample is, as we said, a discrete instant of digitized sound. To measure a file in samples means counting each individual snapshot of the sound wave. Samples are taken at a constant rate, so every millisecond of sound contains the same number of samples. A sound recorded with a sampling rate of 22.5 kHz contains about 22 samples in every millisecond. Because milliseconds mean more to most users than do samples or bytes, ShowWave chooses the **MM_FORMAT_MILLISECONDS** format. Choosing a format means sending the **MCI_SET** command message with the **MCI_SET_PARMS** parameter block:

```
/* parameter block for MCI_SET command message */
typedef struct tagMCI_SET_PARMS {
    DWORD dwCallback;              // window for MM_MCINOTIFY message
    DWORD dwTimeFormat;           // time format constant
    DWORD dwAudio;                // audio output channel
} MCI_SET_PARMS;
```

dwTimeFormat may be **MM_FORMAT_BYTES**, **MM_FORMAT_SAMPLES**, or **MM_FORMAT_MILLISECONDS**. ShowWave doesn't play stereo, so we ignore the **dwAudio** field.

```
/*----------------------------------------------------------------
            SET TIME FORMAT
            Set time format.  Use milliseconds (not bytes or samples).
       ----------------------------------------------------------------*/
BOOL SetTimeFormat (
    HWND hWnd,
    MCIDEVICEID mciDevice )
{

    DWORD dwRet;
    MCI_SET_PARMS mciSetParms;

    /* set time format to milliseconds */
    mciSetParms.dwTimeFormat = MCI_FORMAT_MILLISECONDS;
    dwRet = mciSendCommand( mciDevice,
                            MCI_SET,
                            MCI_SET_TIME_FORMAT,
                            (DWORD)(LPVOID)&mciSetParms );

    if (dwRet != 0)
    {
        ReportMCIError( hWnd, dwRet );
        return( FALSE );
    }

    return( TRUE );                                // success
}
```

The **MCI_SET_TIME_FORMAT** flag tells the system to read the value in the **dwTime-Format** field of **mciSetParms**.

Playing a Sound

For modularity, PlayBack makes no assumptions about the device settings. It resets the time format before each operation. The **MCI_PLAY** command initiates playback, and its parameter block is called **MCI_PLAY_PARMS**:

```
/* parameter block for MCI_PLAY command message */
typedef struct tagMCI_PLAY_PARMS {
    DWORD dwCallback;                  // window for MM_MCINOTIFY
    DWORD dwFrom;                      // starting point
    DWORD dwTo;                        // ending point
} MCI_PLAY_PARMS;
```

By default, the Play command starts at the current position in the file and plays to the end, but **dwFrom** and **dwTo**, if they are flagged, direct WinMM to start and stop at other points. You may express the starting and stopping points in bytes, samples, or milliseconds, but you should tell the driver in advance which units to expect. (By default, drivers work in milliseconds.)

```
/*-------------------------------------------------------------
        BEGIN PLAYBACK
    --------------------------------------------------------------*/

BOOL BeginPlay (
    HWND hWnd,
    MCIDEVICEID mciDevice,
    DWORD dwFrom )
{
    DWORD dwRet;
    MCI_PLAY_PARMS mciPlayParms;

    /* set time format to milliseconds */
    if (!SetTimeFormat( hWnd, mciDevice ))
    {
        return( FALSE );
    }

    // The callback window will be notified with an MM_MCINOTIFY message
    // when playback is complete.  At that time, the window procedure
    // closes the device.

    mciPlayParms.dwCallback = (DWORD)(LPVOID)hWnd;
    mciPlayParms.dwFrom = dwFrom;
    dwRet = mciSendCommand( mciDevice,
                            MCI_PLAY,
                            MCI_FROM | MCI_NOTIFY,
                            (DWORD)(LPVOID)&mciPlayParms );

    if (dwRet != 0)
    {
        ReportMCIError( hWnd, dwRet );
        return( FALSE );
    }

    return( TRUE );                              // success
}
```

The **MCI_FROM** flag signals the presence of a value in the **dwFrom** field. The **MCI_ NOTIFY** flag tells the system to send us a message when the sound stops playing. Sounds can be quite long, so we let WinMM take over and continue to play the sound in the background while ShowWave moves on to the next procedure. When WinMM reaches the end of the .WAV file it addresses an **MM_MCINOTIFY** message to the window named in the **dwCallback** field. Look for an **MM_MCINOTIFY** message handler when we reach **ShowWave_WndProc**. It is the completion routine for asynchronous multimedia operations.

The notify message won't arrive until after the wave device reaches the **dwTo** point or the end of the file. In its **wParam**, the message carries a result code indicating whether the operation finished normally, was interrupted or superseded by another command to the device, or failed from a device error. The low word of the **lParam** carries the device ID.

Stopping a Sound

The **MCI_STOP** command interrupts an operation already in progress. If the user begins playing a long sound and then decides not to listen after all, clicking the Stop button sends an **MCI_STOP** command to abort the playback. Like the **MCI_CLOSE** message, this uses no parameter block.

```
/*----------------------------------------------------------------
        STOP PLAY
        Terminate playback
   -------------------------------------------------------------*/
void StopPlay (
    HWND hWnd,
    MCIDEVICEID mciDevice )
{
    DWORD dwRet;

    dwRet = mciSendCommand( mciDevice,
                            MCI_STOP,
                            MCI_WAIT,
                            (DWORD)NULL );
```

```
    if (dwRet != 0)
    {
        ReportMCIError( hWnd, dwRet );
    }
    return;
}
```

If we were to send **MCI_STOP** with **MCI_NOTIFY** instead of **MCI_WAIT**, the window procedure would receive *two* notification messages. The first, **MCI_NOTIFY_ABORTED**, would tell us that playback ended before reaching the terminal point. The second, **MCI_NOTIFY_SUCCESSFUL**, would indicate successful completion of the Stop command.

Recording a Sound

Sound boards generally include a jack so you can plug a microphone directly into your computer and record straight to disk. The **MCI_RECORD** message directs the sound device to accept input from a microphone.

```
/* parameter block for MCI_RECORD command message */
typedef struct tagMCI_RECORD_PARMS {
    DWORD dwCallback;                  // window for MM_MCINOTIFY
    DWORD dwFrom;                      // starting point
    DWORD dwTo;                        // ending point
} MCI_RECORD_PARMS;
```

The **dwFrom** and **dwTo** fields name points in an existing file where the recorded information should be written. In a new file only the **dwTo** field matters; new files must always begin at 0. Without the **MCI_TO** flag and a **dwTo** value, recording continues until either the disk fills up or the driver receives a stop command. (To get a new file, give **MCI_OPEN** a null string ("") for the element name.)

```
/*-------------------------------------------------------------------
        BEGIN RECORD
   ----------------------------------------------------------------*/


BOOL BeginRecord (
    HWND hWnd,
    MCIDEVICEID mciDevice,
    DWORD dwTo )
{
    DWORD dwRet;
    MCI_RECORD_PARMS mciRecordParms;
```

```
/* set time format to milliseconds */
if (!SetTimeFormat( hWnd, mciDevice ))
{
    return( FALSE );
}


// Begin recording for the specified number of milliseconds.
// The callback window will be notified with an MM_MCINOTIFY message
// when recording is complete.  At that time, the window procedure
// saves the recording and closes the device.

mciRecordParms.dwCallback = (DWORD)(LPVOID) hWnd;
mciRecordParms.dwTo = dwTo;
dwRet = mciSendCommand( mciDevice,
                        MCI_RECORD,
                        MCI_TO | MCI_NOTIFY,
                        (DWORD)(LPVOID)&mciRecordParms );

if (dwRet != 0)
{
    ReportMCIError( hWnd, dwRet );
    return( FALSE );
}

return( TRUE );                                 // success
}
```

Saving a Recorded Sound

The **MCI_SAVE** command instructs a driver to save the current recording to disk. If you record and then close without sending **MCI_SAVE**, the data will be lost.

```
/* parameter block for MCI_SAVE command message */
typedef struct tagMCI_SAVE_PARMS {
    DWORD dwCallback;                   // window for MM_MCINOTIFY
    LPCTSTR lpfilename;                 // name of disk file
} MCI_SAVE_PARMS;
```

The string in **lpfilename** names the output file.

```
/*----------------------------------------------------------------
        SAVE RECORD
        Save recording
    ---------------------------------------------------------------*/
```

```
BOOL SaveRecord (
    HWND hWnd,
    MCIDEVICEID mciDevice,
    LPSTR lpszFileName )
{
    DWORD dwRet;
    MCI_SAVE_PARMS mciSaveParms;

    // Save the recording to the specified file.  Wait for
    // the operation to complete before continuing.

    mciSaveParms.lpfilename = lpszFileName;
    dwRet = mciSendCommand( mciDevice,
                            MCI_SAVE,
                            MCI_SAVE_FILE | MCI_WAIT,
                            (DWORD)(LPVOID)&mciSaveParms );

    if (dwRet != 0)
    {
        ReportMCIError( hWnd, dwRet );
        return( FALSE );
    }

    return( TRUE );                               // success
}
```

Handling Errors

The last function in the MCI module handles errors in any of the other functions. It puts up a message box telling the user what happened, as shown in Figure 16.3.

FIGURE 16.3:

Error message from ShowWave

The error procedure needs two strings. The first, the program title for the caption bar, it loads from the string table; the second, an error message, it gets directly from

MCI. The `mciGetErrorString` function retrieves a string describing a WinMM error. `mciSendCommand` returns detailed error codes that ShowWave dutifully stores in its dwResult variable. If the return value is not 0 an error has occurred and ShowWave calls `ReportMCIError`. Given the dwResult error code, `mciGetErrorString` returns an appropriate string. The mmsystem.h file defines about 90 different error codes. Some of them, like **MCIERR_INVALID_DEVICE_ID**, can happen any time; others, like **MCIERR_CANNOT_LOAD_DRIVER**, arise only during a specific command (in this case, Open); still others are peculiar to one device. **MCIERR_WAVES_OUTPUTSINUSE**, for example, indicates that all waveform devices are already busy.

```
/*-------------------------------------------------------------------
        REPORT MCI ERROR
        Report given MCI error to the user
   ----------------------------------------------------------------*/
static void ReportMCIError (
    HWND hWnd,
    DWORD dwError )
{

    HINSTANCE hInstance;
    char szErrStr[MAXERRORLENGTH];
    char szCaption[MAX_RSRC_STRING_LEN];

    hInstance = GetWindowInstance( hWnd );
    LoadString( hInstance, IDS_CAPTION, szCaption, sizeof(szCaption) );
    mciGetErrorString( dwError, szErrStr, sizeof(szErrStr) );
    MessageBox( hWnd, szErrStr, szCaption, MB_ICONEXCLAMATION | MB_OK );

    return;
}
```

The MMIO Module

If ShowWave only played and recorded it wouldn't need the MMIO module. Several of its functions, however, require the program to manipulate the data in sound files directly. Most obviously, to draw the sound wave it must read samples from the .WAV file. Also, since the user can modify sounds in memory by mixing them or changing the volume, sometimes ShowWave must save data into a new file. The MMIO module contains one function to read wave data, one to write wave data, and one to handle file errors.

Reading the .WAV File

The `ReadWaveData` procedure loads all the data from a .WAV file into memory. It performs the following steps:

1. Opens the file.

2. Finds the `WAVE` chunk.

3. Locates the `fmt` subchunk and confirms that the sound is in a suitable format.

4. Finds the `data` subchunk and loads it into memory.

5. Closes the file.

```
/*-------------------------------------------------------------

        MMIO.C
        Routines to read from and write to multimedia RIFF files
        with a "WAVE" format.

        PUBLIC FUNCTIONS
            ReadWaveData            read info from a .WAV file
            WriteWaveData           write info to a .WAV file

        PRIVATE FUNCTION
            ReportError             tell user what went wrong

        program by Michael Barnes
        copyright 1992, 1993 by Brian Myers, Chris Doner, & Eric Hamer
        from Mastering Windows NT Programming
        -----------------------------------------------------------*/


#define STRICT
#include <windows.h>
#include <windowsx.h>
#include <mmsystem.h>           // multimedia definitions
#include "rsrc.h"               // program resource ID definitions


/*-------------------------------------------------------------
        FUNCTION PROTOTYPE
        -----------------------------------------------------------*/


static void ReportError( HWND hWnd, int iErrorID );
```

```
/*-------------------------------------------------------------------
        READ WAVE DATA
        Read waveform data from a RIFF file into a memory buffer.

        RETURN
        TRUE if we successfully fill the buffer, otherwise FALSE.
        If the function returns TRUE, then the last three parameters
        return information about the new buffer.
        -------------------------------------------------------------*/
BOOL ReadWaveData (
    HWND  hWnd,
    LPSTR lpszFileName,
    LPSTR *lplpWaveData,            // points to buffer
    DWORD *lpdwWaveDataSize,        // size of buffer
    DWORD *lpdwSamplesPerSec )      // sampling rate
{
    HMMIO           hmmio;          // file handle
    MMCKINFO        mmckinfoWave;   // description of "WAVE" chunk
    MMCKINFO        mmckinfoFmt;    // description of "fmt " chunk
    MMCKINFO        mmckinfoData;   // description of "data" chunk
    PCMWAVEFORMAT   pcmWaveFormat;  // contents of "fmt " chunk
    LONG            lFmtSize;       // size of "fmt " chunk
    LONG            lDataSize;      // size of "data" chunk
    LPSTR           lpData;         // pointer to data buffer

    /* open the given file for reading using multimedia file I/O */
    hmmio = mmioOpen( lpszFileName, NULL, MMIO_ALLOCBUF | MMIO_READ );
    if (hmmio == NULL)
    {
        ReportError( hWnd, IDS_CANTOPENFILE );
        return( FALSE );
    }
```

The **mmioOpen** command takes three parameters: a file name, a structure for extra parameters, and some operation flags. The extra parameters matter only for changing the size of the file I/O buffer, for opening a memory file, or for naming a custom I/O procedure to read the file. Since ReadWaveData does none of these, the parameter is **NULL**.

MMIO_ALLOCBUF turns on I/O buffering. The other flag, **MMIO_READ**, opens the file for reading only. **mmioWrite** will return an error for files opened with **MMIO_READ**.

```
/* locate a chunk with a "WAVE" form type */
mmckinfoWave.fccType = mmioFOURCC('W','A','V','E');
if (mmioDescend( hmmio, &mmckinfoWave, NULL, MMIO_FINDRIFF ) != 0)
{
    ReportError( hWnd, IDS_NOTWAVEFILE );
    mmioClose( hmmio, 0 );
    return( FALSE );
}
/* find the format subchunk */
mmckinfoFmt.ckid = mmioFOURCC('f','m','t',' ');
if (mmioDescend( hmmio, &mmckinfoFmt, &mmckinfoWave,
                 MMIO_FINDCHUNK ) != 0)

{
    ReportError( hWnd, IDS_CORRUPTEDFILE );
    mmioClose( hmmio, 0 );
    return( FALSE );
}
```

After opening the file, we next locate and verify the data. The first **mmioDescend** command looks for a "RIFF" tag followed by a WAVE code. If that works, the second command looks for the waveform's format subchunk.

To find the first chunk we fill out only one field in the chunk info structure: **fccType**. The form type we seek is WAVE. The **ckid** field (chunk ID) ought to be RIFF, but the **MMIO_FINDRIFF** flag adequately describes that part of our target. The Descend command also recognizes three other flags: **MMIO_FINDCHUNK**, **MMIO_FIND-RIFF**, and **MMIO_FINDLIST**. In effect, the **FINDCHUNK** flag says to search for whatever is in the **ckid** field, and the other flags say to match the **fccType** field with a RIFF or LIST chunk.

mmioDescend takes four parameters: an **HMMIC** file handle, a description of the target chunk, a description of its parent chunk, and some operation flags. RIFF chunks don't have parents, so we leave the third field **NULL**, but the format chunk is always a subchunk of some parent. (Pardon the mixed metaphor; the terminology comes from the Microsoft manuals. Perhaps "superchunk" would be clearer than "parent.") Only RIFF and LIST chunks can have subchunks.

To find the format subchunk we put "fmt " in the target info structure and "WAVE" in the parent info structure. **mmioDescend** will stop looking for "fmt " if it reaches the end of the current WAVE chunk. In this case the file is unusable, perhaps corrupted, because you can't interpret a WAVE without its format specifications.

The second Descend command left the file pointer at the beginning of the data in the format subchunk. Next we load the format information into memory for verification:

```
/* read the format subchunk */
lFmtSize = (LONG)sizeof( pcmWaveFormat );
if (mmioRead( hmmio, (LPSTR)&pcmWaveFormat, lFmtSize ) != lFmtSize)
{
    ReportError( hWnd,IDS_CANTREADFORMAT );
    mmioClose( hmmio, 0 );
    return( FALSE );
}

/* ascend out of the format subchunk */
if (mmioAscend( hmmio, &mmckinfoFmt, 0 ) != 0)
{
    ReportError( hWnd, IDS_CANTREADFORMAT );
    mmioClose( hmmio, 0 );
    return( FALSE );
}

/* make sure the sound file is an 8-bit mono PCM WAVE file */
if ((pcmWaveFormat.wf.wFormatTag != WAVE_FORMAT_PCM)
    || (pcmWaveFormat.wf.nChannels != 1)
    || (pcmWaveFormat.wBitsPerSample != 8))
{
    ReportError( hWnd, IDS_UNSUPPORTEDFORMAT );
    mmioClose( hmmio, 0 );
    return( FALSE );
}
```

mmioRead expects a file handle, a pointer to a memory buffer, and a byte quantity. **lFmtSize** contains the number of bytes in a **PCMWAVEFORMAT** structure and **mmioRead** loads that many bytes from the disk.

The Ascend command advances the file position pointer past the last byte of the format chunk, ready for the next file operation. **mmioAscend** takes only three parameters because it never needs to think about the enclosing superchunk in order to find the end of a subchunk.

For clarity, we've limited ShowWave to one-channel sounds with 8 bits per pixel. To allow other ratings you could add a few variables and modify the scroll bar code. More on that in the section "Scrolling While Playing or Recording" later in this chapter.

We've verified the data format and now at last we can load it into memory. We'll find the data subchunk, determine its size, allocate a memory buffer for it, and read the data into the buffer.

```
/* find the data subchunk */
mmckinfoData.ckid = mmioFOURCC('d','a','t','a');
if (mmioDescend( hmmio, &mmckinfoData, &mmckinfoWave,
                 MMIO_FINDCHUNK ) != 0)
{
    ReportError( hWnd, IDS_CORRUPTEDFILE );
    mmioClose( hmmio, 0 );
    return( FALSE );
}

/* get the size of the data subchunk */
lDataSize = (LONG)mmckinfoData.cksize;
if (lDataSize == 0)
{
    ReportError( hWnd,IDS_NOWAVEDATA );
    mmioClose( hmmio, 0 );
    return( FALSE );
}

/* allocate and lock memory for the waveform data */
lpData = GlobalAllocPtr( GMEM_MOVEABLE, lDataSize );
if (!lpData)
{
    ReportError( hWnd, IDS_OUTOFMEMORY );
    mmioClose( hmmio, 0 );
    return( FALSE );
}

/* read the data subchunk */
if (mmioRead( hmmio, (LPSTR)lpData, lDataSize ) != lDataSize)
{
    ReportError( hWnd, IDS_CANTREADDATA );
    GlobalFreePtr( lpData );
    mmioClose( hmmio, 0 );
    return( FALSE );
}
```

Finding the `data` chunk is just like finding the `fmt` chunk. **mmioDescend** fills the **mmckinfoData** variable with information that includes the size of the data. `lData-Size` tells us how much space to allocate from memory and how many bytes to read from the file.

To finish `ReadWaveData`, we close the file and return through the procedure's parameters three values: a pointer to the new memory object, the number of data bytes in the object, and the sampling rate:

```
/* close the file */
mmioClose( hmmio, 0 );

/* set return variables */
*lplpWaveData = lpData;
*lpdwWaveDataSize = (DWORD)lDataSize;
*lpdwSamplesPerSec = pcmWaveFormat.wf.nSamplesPerSec;
return( TRUE );
}
```

Writing the .WAV File

`WriteWaveData` transfers a wave sound from a memory buffer to a disk file. When the user modifies an existing sound or records a new one, `WriteWaveData` saves the result. It performs these steps:

1. Opens the file

2. Creates the `RIFF` superchunk with a `WAVE` format type

3. Creates the `fmt` subchunk; fills in its size and data fields

4. Creates the `data` subchunk; fills in its size and data fields

5. Ascends to the end of the file, causing the total size to be written in for the superchunk

6. Closes the file

```
/*-----------------------------------------------------------
     WRITE WAVE DATA
     Transfer waveform data from a memory buffer to a disk file
   -----------------------------------------------------------*/
```

```
BOOL WriteWaveData (
     HWND hWnd,                          // main window
     LPSTR lpszFileName,                 // destination file
     LPSTR lpWaveData,                   // data source buffer
     DWORD dwWaveDataSize,               // size of data in buffer
     DWORD dwSamplesPerSec )             // sampling rate
{
     HMMIO           hmmio;              // file handle
     MMCKINFO        mmckinfoWave;       // description of "WAVE" chunk
     MMCKINFO        mmckinfoFmt;        // description of "fmt " chunk
     MMCKINFO        mmckinfoData;       // description of "data" chunk
     PCMWAVEFORMAT   pcmWaveFormat;      // contents of "fmt " chunk
     LONG            lFmtSize;           // size of "fmt " chunk
     LONG            lDataSize;          // size of "data" chunk

     /* open the given file for writing using multimedia file I/O */
     hmmio = mmioOpen( lpszFileName, NULL,
                     MMIO_ALLOCBUF | MMIO_WRITE | MMIO_CREATE );

     if (hmmio == NULL)
     {
         ReportError( hWnd, IDS_CANTOPENFILE );
         return( FALSE );
     }

     /* create a "RIFF" chunk with a "WAVE" form type */
     mmckinfoWave.fccType = mmioFOURCC( 'W','A','V','E' );
     if (mmioCreateChunk( hmmio, &mmckinfoWave, MMIO_CREATERIFF ) != 0)
     {
         ReportError( hWnd, IDS_CANTWRITEWAVE );
         mmioClose( hmmio, 0 );
         return( FALSE );
     }
```

This **mmioOpen** command tells the system we want to buffer our file operations, write without reading, and create the file if it doesn't already exist. **mmioCreate-Chunk** expects three parameters: a file handle, a structure describing the new chunk, and an optional flag for creating superchunks.

The **MMCKINFO** structure has a field called **dwDataOffset**. **mmioCreateChunk** returns a value there telling where in the file the new chunk's data area begins. It also leaves the file pointer on the first byte of the new data area.

mmioCreateChunk cannot insert new chunks into the middle of a file. If the file pointer is not at the end of the file, old data will be overwritten.

Having established the main RIFF chunk, we next create and initialize the format subchunk:

```
/* store size of the format subchunk */
lFmtSize = (LONG)sizeof( pcmWaveFormat );

// Create the format subchunk.
// Since we know the size of this chunk, specify it in the
// MMCKINFO structure so MMIO doesn't have to seek back and
// set the chunk size after ascending from the chunk.

mmckinfoFmt.ckid = mmioFOURCC( 'f', 'm', 't', ' ' );
mmckinfoFmt.cksize = lFmtSize;
if (mmioCreateChunk( hmmio, &mmckinfoFmt, 0 ) != 0)
{
    ReportError( hWnd, IDS_CANTWRITEFORMAT );
    mmioClose( hmmio, 0 );
    return( FALSE );
}


/* initialize PCMWAVEFORMAT structure */
pcmWaveFormat.wf.wFormatTag       = WAVE_FORMAT_PCM;
pcmWaveFormat.wf.nChannels        = 1;
pcmWaveFormat.wf.nSamplesPerSec   = dwSamplesPerSec;
pcmWaveFormat.wf.nAvgBytesPerSec  = dwSamplesPerSec;
pcmWaveFormat.wf.nBlockAlign      = 1;
pcmWaveFormat.wBitsPerSample      = 8;

/* write the format subchunk */
if (mmioWrite( hmmio, (LPSTR)&pcmWaveFormat, lFmtSize ) != lFmtSize)
{
    ReportError( hWnd, IDS_CANTWRITEFORMAT );
    mmioClose( hmmio, 0 );
    return( FALSE );
}


/* ascend out of the format subchunk */
if (mmioAscend( hmmio, &mmckinfoFmt, 0 ) != 0)
{
    ReportError( hWnd, IDS_CANTWRITEFORMAT );
```

```
    mmioClose( hmmio, 0 );
    return( FALSE );
}
```

Remember that every chunk contains a tag, a size, and some data. **mmioCreate-Chunk** leaves a space for the size, but if the **cksize** field is 0 then the space remains blank until the next **mmioAscend** seals off the new chunk. Normally, **mmioAscend** has to calculate the data size, move back to the size field and fill it in, and then move forward to the end of the data. By providing the size straight off we avoid the extra backward motion, saving the time of two disk accesses.

The value in the global variable **dwSamplesPerSecond** defaults to 22,050 (22.05 kHz), but it changes whenever ReadWaveData loads a new file. (Choosing New from the File menu resets the value.) Because ShowWave restricts itself to one-channel sounds with 8 bits per sample, every sample always contains 1 byte. This is why we can put the same value in the **nSamplesPerSecond** and **nAvgBytesPerSecond** fields of the **pcmWaveForm** variable.

The **nBlockAlign** field tells how many bytes one sample fills. The size of a sample must be rounded up to the nearest byte. A 12-bit-per-sample sound, for example, would align on 2-byte boundaries. Four bits would be wasted in each block, but when loaded into memory the extra padding speeds up data access. The CPU always fetches information from memory in whole bytes and words, not bits.

You may wonder why we call **mmioAscend** when the write operation has already moved the file position to the end of the format data. Again the answer has to do with alignment and access speed. A chunk's data area must always contain an even number of bytes so that it aligns on word (2-byte) boundaries. If the data contains an odd number of bytes, the final **mmioAscend** adds padding. Otherwise it has no effect. **mmioCreateChunk** should nearly always be followed eventually by **mmioAscend**.

The format chunk written, we next perform the same steps to create the data chunk:

```
/* store size of the "data" subchunk */
lDataSize = (LONG)dwWaveDataSize;

/* create the "data" subchunk that holds the waveform samples */
mmckinfoData.ckid   = mmioFOURCC( 'd', 'a', 't', 'a' );
mmckinfoFmt.cksize = lDataSize;
if (mmioCreateChunk( hmmio, &mmckinfoData, 0 ) != 0)
{
    ReportError( hWnd, IDS_CANTWRITEDATA );
```

```
      mmioClose( hmmio, O );
      return( FALSE );
   }

/* write the "data" subchunk */
if (mmioWrite( hmmio, lpWaveData, lDataSize ) != lDataSize)
{
    ReportError( hWnd, IDS_CANTWRITEDATA );
    mmioClose( hmmio, O );
    return( FALSE );
}

/* ascend out of the "data" subchunk */
if (mmioAscend( hmmio, &mmckinfoData, O ) != 0)
{
    ReportError( hWnd, IDS_CANTWRITEDATA );
    mmioClose( hmmio, O );
    return( FALSE );
}
```

That **mmioAscend** command moves to the end of the data subchunk, but remember we are still inside the RIFF superchunk. We've called **mmioCreateChunk** three times but **mmioAscend** only twice. One more to go:

```
/* ascend out of the "WAVE" chunk -- causes size to be written */
if (mmioAscend( hmmio, &mmckinfoWave, O ) != 0)
{
    ReportError( hWnd, IDS_CANTWRITEWAVE );
    mmioClose( hmmio, O );
    return( FALSE );
}

/* close the file */
mmioClose( hmmio, O );

return( TRUE );
}
```

Before creating each subchunk we put a size value in the **cksize** field, so WinMM knew the chunk size from the beginning. But for the first chunk, the parent chunk, we provided only a format type (WAVE). The final **mmioAscend** completes the creation of the first chunk. It computes the size and records it right after the "RIFF" tag at the beginning of the file.

Handling Errors

mciGetErrorString works only with the error returns from **mciSendCommand**; the file I/O procedures have no equivalent function for error messages. We put our own messages in showwave.rc and wrote **ReportError** to display them:

```
/*------------------------------------------------------------------
        REPORT ERROR
        Report given error to the user
        ----------------------------------------------------------*/

static void ReportError (
    HWND hWnd,
    int iErrorID )
{
    HINSTANCE hInstance;
    char szErrStr[MAX_RSRC_STRING_LEN];
    char szCaption[MAX_RSRC_STRING_LEN];

    hInstance = GetWindowInstance( hWnd );
    LoadString( hInstance, iErrorID, szErrStr, sizeof(szErrStr) );
    LoadString( hInstance, IDS_CAPTION, szCaption,
                sizeof(szCaption) );
    MessageBox( hWnd, szErrStr, szCaption,
                MB_ICONEXCLAMATION | MB_OK );
    return;
}
```

The WinMain Module

WinMain registers window classes for the main window and the sound graph control. The custom window classes let us paint the control window and assign an icon to the dialog window. This module also contains the About box procedure.

```
/*------------------------------------------------------------------

        WINMAIN.C

        Routines from the SHOWWAVE program to register and create
        the main program window.
```

```
        PUBLIC FUNCTIONS
              WinMain              create windows and poll for messages
              About_DlgProc    handle messages for the About box
        PRIVATE FUNCTION
              RegisterShowWaveClass    create class for main window

        program by Michael Barnes
        copyright 1992, 1993 by Brian Myers, Chris Doner, & Eric Hamer
        from Mastering Windows NT Programming
--------------------------------------------------------------------*/

#define STRICT
#include <windows.h>
#include <windowsx.h>
#include <mmsystem.h>        // multimedia definitions
#include "showwave.h"        // program variables and functions
#include "rsrc.h"            // program resource ID definitions

/*------------------------------------------------------------------
         FUNCTION PROTOTYPE
  --------------------------------------------------------------------*/

int WINAPI WinMain( HINSTANCE hinstThis, HINSTANCE hinstPrev,
    LPSTR lpszCmdLine, int iCmdShow );
BOOL RegisterShowWaveClass( HINSTANCE hInstance );

/*------------------------------------------------------------------
         GLOBAL VARIABLES
  --------------------------------------------------------------------*/

LPSTR lpWaveData       = NULL;    // huge pointer to sound data
DWORD dwWaveDataSize  = 0;        // size of lpWaveData buffer
DWORD dwCurrentSample = 0;        // position in the current sound
DWORD dwSamplesPerSec = 22050;    // default sampling rate

/*------------------------------------------------------------------
         STATIC VARIABLE
  --------------------------------------------------------------------*/

static char szShowWaveClass[] = "ShowWaveClass";

/*------------------------------------------------------------------
         WINMAIN
  --------------------------------------------------------------------*/
```

```
int WINAPI WinMain (
    HINSTANCE hinstThis,
    HINSTANCE hinstPrev,
    LPSTR lpszCmdLine,
    int iCmdShow )
{
    if (!RegisterGraphClass( hinstThis ))          // wave graph
    {
        return( 0 );
    }

    if (!RegisterShowWaveClass( hinstThis ))      // program window
    {
        return( 0 );
    }

    /* create and display the main program window */
    DialogBox( hinstThis,
        MAKEINTRESOURCE(DLG_MAIN),
        NULL,
        (DLGPROC)ShowWave_WndProc );

    return( 0 );
    UNREFERENCED_PARAMETER( hinstPrev );
    UNREFERENCED_PARAMETER( iCmdShow );
    UNREFERENCED_PARAMETER( lpszCmdLine );
}

/*-------------------------------------------------------------------
        ABOUT DIALOG PROCEDURE
        Handle messages for the About box.
    --------------------------------------------------------------*/

BOOL WINAPI About_DlgProc (
    HWND hDlg,
    UINT uMsg,
    WPARAM wParam,
    LPARAM lParam )
{
    switch (uMsg)
    {
        case WM_INITDIALOG:
            return( TRUE );
```

```
        case WM_COMMAND:
            EndDialog( hDlg, 0 );
            return( TRUE );;

        default:
            return( FALSE );
    }

    UNREFERENCED_PARAMETER( uMsg );
    UNREFERENCED_PARAMETER( wParam );
    UNREFERENCED_PARAMETER( lParam );
}

/*-------------------------------------------------------------------
        REGISTER SHOWWAVE CLASS
        Register a window class for the main dialog box window.
   ----------------------------------------------------------------*/
BOOL RegisterShowWaveClass ( HINSTANCE hInstance )
{
    WNDCLASS WndClass;

    WndClass.style          = 0;
    WndClass.lpfnWndProc    = ShowWave_WndProc;
    WndClass.cbClsExtra     = 0;
    WndClass.cbWndExtra     = DLGWINDOWEXTRA;
    WndClass.hInstance      = hInstance;
    WndClass.hIcon          = LoadIcon( hInstance, MAKEINTRESOURCE(IDI_WAVE) );
    WndClass.hCursor        = LoadCursor( NULL, IDC_ARROW );
    WndClass.hbrBackground  = (HBRUSH)(COLOR_BTNFACE + 1);
    WndClass.lpszMenuName   = MAKEINTRESOURCE( IDM_MAIN );
    WndClass.lpszClassName  = szShowWaveClass;

    return( RegisterClass(&WndClass) );
}
```

The ShowWave Module

The MCI and MMIO modules provide a modular set of tools that any program might use to manipulate .WAV files. The showwave.c module runs the program's main window, a modal dialog box, and in response to commands from the user it calls functions from the other modules to play and record sounds.

ShowWave_WndProc mixes characteristics of a window procedure and a dialog procedure. Like a window procedure, it calls **DefWindowProc** and returns an **LRESULT**; like a dialog procedure, it receives **WM_INITDIALOG** rather than **WM_CREATE**. Because the window is launched by the **DialogBox** command, it initializes like a dialog box. Because the window has its own custom window class, it must have its own window procedure and does not use the default **DefDlgProc** processing.

```
/*-----------------------------------------------------------------

    SHOWWAVE.C

    Routines for handling the SHOWWAVE window, the modeless dialog
    that serves as the main window for the ShowWave program.
    Primarily these routines maintain the program window and
    respond to commands from the user.

    PUBLIC FUNCTIONS
        ShowWave_WndProc            callback function for main window

    MESSAGE HANDLING FUNCTIONS
        ShowWave_OnInitDialog       initialize ShowWave modeless dialog box
        ShowWave_OnCtlColor         set dialog box's background color
        ShowWave_OnCommand          handle menu commands
        ShowWave_OnHScroll          handle waveform data scrolling
        ShowWave_OnTimer            handle timer request to update display
        ShowWave_OnMCINotify        handle MM_MCINOTIFY message
        ShowWave_OnQueryEndSession  handle request to end demo window session
        ShowWave_OnDestroy          handle window destruction

    OTHER PRIVATE FUNCTIONS
        PaintWaveData               paint the waveform data
        UpdateFileTitleText         update file title text
        UpdateTimeText              update Position and Length text
        ConfirmClose                confirm closing a dirty file with user
        GetFileName                 invoke the file name common dialog boxes
        FreeGlobalWaveData          free global waveform data
        CloseAudioDevice            close an opened waveform audio device
        CloseTimerDevice            kill an active timer
        NewWaveFile                 start work on a new .WAV file
        OpenWaveFile                open a new .WAV file
        SaveWaveFile                save waveform data to disk
        MixWithFile                 mix another .WAV file into current file
```

```
                    ChangeVolume              change the playback volume
                    PlayWaveFile              play waveform data
                    RecordWaveFile            record waveform data

             program by Michael Barnes
             copyright 1992, 1993 by Brian Myers, Chris Doner, & Eric Hamer
             from Mastering Windows NT Programming
             -----------------------------------------------------------------*/

#define STRICT
#include <windows.h>
#include <windowsx.h>
#include <commdlg.h>                // common dialog box (for file names)
#include <mmsystem.h>               // multimedia definitions
#include <stdlib.h>                 // _MAX_* constants
#include "showwave.h"               // program variables and functions
#include "rsrc.h"                   // program resource ID definitions

/*-----------------------------------------------------------------
          PROTOTYPES FOR PRIVATE FUNCTIONS
  -----------------------------------------------------------------*/

static BOOL ShowWave_OnInitDialog( HWND hDlg, HWND hWndFocus, LPARAM lParam );
static HBRUSH ShowWave_OnCtlColor( HWND hDlg, HDC hDC, HWND hCtl, int iType );
static void ShowWave_OnCommand( HWND hDlg, int iCmd, HWND hCtl, UINT uCode );
static void ShowWave_OnHScroll( HWND hDlg, HWND hCtl, UINT uCode, int iPos );
static void ShowWave_OnTimer( HWND hDlg, UINT uID );
static void ShowWave_OnMCINotify( HWND hDlg, UINT uCode, UINT uDevID );
static BOOL ShowWave_OnQueryEndSession( HWND hDlg );
static void ShowWave_OnDestroy( HWND hDlg );

static void PaintWaveData( HWND hDlg );
static void UpdateFileTitleText( HWND hDlg );
static void UpdateTimeText( HWND hDlg );
static BOOL GetFileName( HWND hDlg, BOOL bOpenName, LPSTR lpszFile,
    int iMaxFileNmLen, LPSTR lpszFileTitle, int iMaxFileTitleLen );
static void FreeGlobalWaveData( void );
static void CloseAudioDevice( HWND hDlg );
static void CloseTimerDevice( HWND hDlg );
static void NewWaveFile( HWND hDlg );
static void OpenWaveFile( HWND hDlg );
static void SaveWaveFile( HWND hDlg, BOOL bAskForName );
static void MixWithFile( HWND hDlg );
```

```
static void ChangeVolume( HWND hDlg, BOOL bIncrease );
static void PlayWaveFile( HWND hDlg );
static void RecordWaveFile( HWND hDlg );


/*-------------------------------------------------------------------
          STATIC VARIABLES
     -------------------------------------------------------------*/

static char szOFNDefExt[]      = "WAV";  // for file name dialog
static char *szOFNFilter[]     =
{
    "Sound Files (*.WAV)\0 *.WAV\0, All Files(*.*)\0    *.* \0\0"
};

static int iHScrollPos = 0;              // scroll bar thumb position

static char szFileName[_MAX_PATH];       // file handling
static char szFileTitle[_MAX_FNAME];
static BOOL bIsFileDirty = FALSE;

static UINT uTimerID  = 0;               // MCI symbols and variables
static MCIDEVICEID mciDevice = 0;
static char szTempFileName[_MAX_PATH];   // stores new unnamed sounds
#define TMRPLAY          1               // timer event IDs
#define TMRRECORD        2

static HBRUSH hbrBackgnd;                // for dialog box's background


/*-------------------------------------------------------------------
          SHOWWAVE DIALOG PROCEDURE
          Sort out messages for the program's main window, the ShowWave
          dialog box.
     -------------------------------------------------------------*/

LRESULT WINAPI ShowWave_WndProc (
    HWND hDlg,
    UINT uMsg,
    WPARAM wParam,
    LPARAM lParam )
{
    switch (uMsg)
    {
        HANDLE_MSG( hDlg, WM_INITDIALOG, ShowWave_OnInitDialog );

        HANDLE_MSG( hDlg, WM_CTLCOLORSTATIC, ShowWave_OnCtlColor );
```

```
        HANDLE_MSG( hDlg, WM_CTLCOLORBTN, ShowWave_OnCtlColor );

        HANDLE_MSG( hDlg, WM_COMMAND, ShowWave_OnCommand );

        HANDLE_MSG( hDlg, WM_HSCROLL, ShowWave_OnHScroll );

        HANDLE_MSG( hDlg, WM_TIMER, ShowWave_OnTimer );

        HANDLE_MSG( hDlg, MM_MCINOTIFY, ShowWave_OnMCINotify );

        HANDLE_MSG( hDlg, WM_QUERYENDSESSION, ShowWave_OnQueryEndSession );

        HANDLE_MSG( hDlg, WM_DESTROY, ShowWave_OnDestroy );

        default:
            return( DefWindowProc(hDlg, uMsg, wParam, lParam) );
    }
}


/*------------------------------------------------------------------
        SHOWWAVE_ONINITDIALOG
        Handle WM_INITDIALOG here. Initialize program settings.
  ----------------------------------------------------------------*/
static BOOL ShowWave_OnInitDialog (
    HWND hDlg,
    HWND hwndFocus,
    LPARAM lParam )
{
    char szTempPath[_MAX_PATH];

    /* create a brush for painting the dialog box's background */
    hbrBackgnd = CreateSolidBrush( GetSysColor(COLOR_BTNFACE) );

    /* get file name for temporary storage of waveform data */
    GetTempPath( sizeof(szTempPath), szTempPath );
    GetTempFileName( szTempPath, "SWT", O, szTempFileName );

    /* start out with an empty wave file */
    FORWARD_WM_COMMAND( hDlg, IDM_NEW, NULL, O, PostMessage );

    /* do nothing with the focus */
    return( TRUE );
```

```
        UNREFERENCED_PARAMETER( hwndFocus );
        UNREFERENCED_PARAMETER( lParam );
}

/*-------------------------------------------------------------

        SHOWWAVE_ONCTLCOLOR
        Process WM_CTLCOLOR messages here.  Give text controls
        a white background.  Shade other parts of dialog.

        RETURN
        A brush handle to use in painting the background.  The
        handle used is declared with the other static variables
        near the top of this file.
        -------------------------------------------------------*/

static HBRUSH ShowWave_OnCtlColor (
        HWND hDlg,                          // parent dialog window
        HDC hDC,                            // DC for control's client area
        HWND hCtl,                          // control window
        int iType )                         // type of control
{
        switch (iType)
        {
                case CTLCOLOR_STATIC:
                        /* colors for static text controls */
                        SetTextColor( hDC, GetSysColor(COLOR_BTNTEXT) );
                        SetBkColor( hDC, RGB_WHITE );
                        return( GetStockBrush(WHITE_BRUSH) );

                default:
                        /* any other controls */
                        SetTextColor( hDC, GetSysColor(COLOR_BTNTEXT) );
                        SetBkColor( hDC, GetSysColor(COLOR_BTNFACE) );
                        return( hbrBackgnd );
        }

        return;
        UNREFERENCED_PARAMETER( hDlg );
        UNREFERENCED_PARAMETER( hCtl );
}
```

ShowWave stores newly recorded sounds in the temporary file until they have names, so the dialog initialization handler generates a name for the file by calling **GetTempPath** and **GetTempFileName**. These commands generate a full path with a unique file name suitable for storing temporary data. If the environment defines a

TEMP variable, the path takes it into account. The second and third parameters of **GetTempFileName** are for alphabetic and numeric elements to be combined in the file name. SWT stands for "ShowWave Temporary." Since we haven't provided a number, Windows will append digits drawn from the current system time to create a unique name. The new name is returned in the final parameter.

Responding to Commands

Some of the **WM_COMMAND** messages come from the menu, some from buttons on the dialog box. A different procedure handles each command. StopPlay appeared earlier in the MCI module.

```
/*-------------------------------------------------------------------
        SHOWWAVE_ONCOMMAND
        Handle WM_COMMAND messages here.  Respond to actions from
        each dialog control and from the menu.
        ------------------------------------------------------------------*/
static void ShowWave_OnCommand (
    HWND hDlg,
    int iCmd,
    HWND hCtl,
    UINT uCode )
{
    switch (iCmd)
    {
        case IDM_NEW:                           // clear data buffer
            NewWaveFile( hDlg );
            break;

        case IDM_OPEN:                          // load a disk file
            OpenWaveFile( hDlg );
            break;

        case IDM_SAVE:                          // save to disk file
        case IDM_SAVEAS:
            SaveWaveFile( hDlg, (iCmd==IDM_SAVEAS) );
            break;

        case IDM_EXIT:                          // end program
            FORWARD_WM_CLOSE( hDlg, PostMessage );
            break;
```

```
    case IDM_MIXWITHFILE:                    // mix two sounds
        MixWithFile( hDlg );
        break;

    case IDM_INCREASEVOLUME:                 // make louder
    case IDM_DECREASEVOLUME:                 // make softer
        ChangeVolume( hDlg, iCmd==IDM_INCREASEVOLUME );
        break;

    case IDM_ABOUT:                          // show About box
        DialogBox( GetWindowInstance(hDlg),
            MAKEINTRESOURCE(DLG_ABOUT),
            hDlg, About_DlgProc );
        break;

    case IDD_PLAY:                           // play a sound
        PlayWaveFile( hDlg );
        break;

    case IDD_RECORD:                         // record a sound
        RecordWaveFile( hDlg );
        break;

    case IDD_STOP:                           // interrupt device
        if (mciDevice)
        {
            StopPlay( hDlg, mciDevice );
        }
        break;

    default:
        break;
    }

return;
UNREFERENCED_PARAMETER( hCtl );
UNREFERENCED_PARAMETER( uCode );
}
```

Scrolling the Wave Image

Windows translates scroll bar input into one of eight SB_ notification codes delivered through the first parameter of a **WM_HSCROLL** message. The nine signals reflect the actions described in Figure 16.4. Each program decides for itself what the signals mean. The SB_ signals are named for their most common application, paging through a document. **SB_TOP** and **SB_BOTTOM** indicate opposite ends of the data. **SB_LINEUP** and **SB_LINEDOWN** move through the data by the smallest permissible increment, usually 1. The page scrolling messages move at whatever intermediate increment the programmer decides is convenient.

FIGURE 16.4:

Scroll bar commands

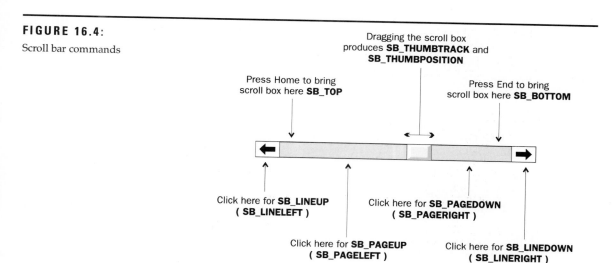

The range of ShowWave's scroll bar measures the current sound in hundredths of a second. Line commands scroll in tenths of a second; page commands scroll in full seconds. When the new position is reached, we store it in dwCurrentSample, move the scroll bar thumb, update the dialog text that says how many seconds we have progressed into the file, and call another procedure to repaint the wave graph. The value in dwCurrentSample measures the current position in samples. The assignment statement converts hundredths of a second to samples. It assumes each sample contains 8 bits.

```
/*--------------------------------------------------------------

    SHOWWAVE_ONHSCROLL
    Process WM_HSCROLL messages here.  Advance through the
    sound file according to the user's signals from the scroll
    bar.
    --------------------------------------------------------*/
```

```
static void ShowWave_OnHScroll (
    HWND hDlg,
    HWND hCtl,
    UINT uCode,
    int iPos )
{
    int iMinPos, iMaxPos;

    ScrollBar_GetRange( hCtl, &iMinPos, &iMaxPos );

    switch (uCode)
    {
        case SB_LINEUP:
            iHScrollPos -= 11;
            break;

        case SB_LINEDOWN:
            iHScrollPos += 11;
            break;

        case SB_PAGEUP:
            iHScrollPos -= 101;
            break;

        case SB_PAGEDOWN:
            iHScrollPos += 101;
            break;

        case SB_TOP:
            iHScrollPos = iMinPos;
            break;

        case SB_BOTTOM:
            iHScrollPos = iMaxPos;
            break;

        case SB_THUMBPOSITION:
        case SB_THUMBTRACK:
            iHScrollPos = iPos;
            break;

        default:
            return;
    }
```

```
        /* update scroll bar thumb */
        iHScrollPos = max( iMinPos, min(iHScrollPos, iMaxPos) );
        ScrollBar_SetPos( hCtl, iHScrollPos, TRUE );

        /* set current sample */
        dwCurrentSample = (iHScrollPos*dwSamplesPerSec) / 100;

        /* set position and length text */
        UpdateTimeText( hDlg );

        /* paint the waveform data */
        PaintWaveData( hDlg );
        return;
}
```

Scrolling While Playing or Recording

While ShowWave plays or records a sound, we'd like the scroll bar thumb to move forward and the sound wave to scroll with it. As you'll see in a minute, ShowWave always begins a timer at the same time it begins playing or recording. Show-Wave_OnTimer responds to the **WM_TIMER** messages.

```
/*-------------------------------------------------------------------

        SHOWWAVE_ONTIMER
        Handle WM_TIMER messages here.  Update display to show
        current position in sound file.
        ----------------------------------------------------------------*/

void ShowWave_OnTimer (
    HWND hDlg,
    UINT uID )
{
    int   iMaxPos;
    HWND  hwndScrollBar = GetDlgItem( hDlg, IDD_SCROLLBAR );

    if (uID == TMRPLAY)
    {
        /* set the new scroll bar position */
        FORWARD_WM_HSCROLL( hDlg, hwndScrollBar, SB_LINEDOWN, 0,
                            SendMessage );
    }
    else
    {
```

```
/* set the new waveform data */
dwWaveDataSize += dwSamplesPerSec/10;

/* set the new scroll bar range */
iMaxPos = (int)((dwWaveDataSize*100) / dwSamplesPerSec );
ScrollBar_SetRange( hwndScrollBar, 0, iMaxPos, FALSE );

/* set the new scroll bar position */
FORWARD_WM_HSCROLL( hDlg, hwndScrollBar, SB_BOTTOM, 0,
                    SendMessage );
    }
    return;
}
```

The timer messages arrive ten times each second. The uID value is set when the timer begins and will be either TMRPLAY or TMRRECORD. If the timer is marking progress during a Play operation, we send ourselves a scroll message to advance the thumb one tenth of a second further into the sound wave.

While ShowWave records, the size of the file through which we're scrolling changes. The scroll bar thumb is always at the right end of the bar because we're always at the end of the recorded data, but as more data comes in the file size increases and the scroll bar range must increase, too. First we update the global variable dwWaveDataSize, adding to it the number of bytes received every tenth of a second. (Remember that with 8 bits per sample, each sample adds 1 byte to the file size.) Then we convert the new file size into hundredths of a second and set that as the scroll bar's new maximum range. And again we send ourselves another scroll message to keep the thumb at the end of the bar.

Ending a Play or Record Operation

Playing and recording continue in the background until the user clicks Stop or the device reaches the end of its input element. When the action ends, WinMM sends the **MM_MCINOTIFY** message that we requested with the **MCI_NOTIFY** flag. The windowsx.h file does not include message-handler macros for any multimedia messages, so we wrote HANDLE_MM_MCINOTIFY and put it in showwave.h. When the notify message comes we have to close the device and kill the timer.

```
/*----------------------------------------------------------------
          SHOWWAVE_ONMCINOTIFY
          Handle MM_MCINOTIFY messages here.  Clean up after a playback
          or recording operation terminates.
     --------------------------------------------------------------*/
static void ShowWave_OnMCINotify (
     HWND hDlg,
     UINT uCode,
     MCIDEVICEID mciDevice )
{
     int   iMaxPos;
     HWND hwndScrollBar = GetDlgItem( hDlg, IDD_SCROLLBAR );

     if (uTimerID == TMRPLAY)
     {
         /* close devices */
         CloseAudioDevice( hDlg );
         CloseTimerDevice( hDlg );
         if (uCode == MCI_NOTIFY_SUCCESSFUL)
         {
             FORWARD_WM_HSCROLL( hDlg, hwndScrollBar, SB_BOTTOM, 0,
                                 SendMessage );
         }
     }
     else
     {
         /* save recording and close devices */
         SaveRecord( hDlg, mciDevice, szTempFileName );
         CloseAudioDevice( hDlg );
         CloseTimerDevice( hDlg );

         /* set file dirty flag */
         bIsFileDirty = TRUE;

         /* read new waveform data */
         ReadWaveData( hDlg, szTempFileName,
                       &lpWaveData,
                       &dwWaveDataSize,
                       &dwSamplesPerSec );

         /* set the new scroll bar range */
         iMaxPos = (int)((dwWaveDataSize*100) / dwSamplesPerSec);
         ScrollBar_SetRange( hwndScrollBar, 0, iMaxPos, FALSE );
```

```
    /* set the new scroll bar position */
    FORWARD_WM_HSCROLL( hDlg, hwndScrollBar, SB_BOTTOM, 0,
                            SendMessage );
}

return;
 UNREFERENCED_PARAMETER( mciDevice );
}
```

This time we determine which action has stopped by testing a global variable, uTimerID, that we set when the timer started. If the device was playing sound and the sound ended successfully, we finish the scroll action by advancing the thumb to the end of the bar.

When ShowWave records a sound the new data accumulates in a temporary file. When the recording ends, the program lifts the entire sound into a memory buffer so it can be the current sound. Since the user has not yet given the new sound a name and saved it, we mark the current file "dirty." And again we finish the scroll operation by updating the scroll range and moving the thumb to the end.

Ending the Program

The last few message-handling functions help the program close down without losing data or leaving objects behind.

```
/*--------------------------------------------------------------------
        SHOWWAVE_ONQUERYENDSESSION
        Handle WM_QUERYENDSESSION messages here.  Give the user a
        chance to save any open file before program ends.
        -------------------------------------------------------------*/

static BOOL ShowWave_OnQueryEndSession ( HWND hDlg )
{
    return( QuerySave(hDlg) );
}


/*--------------------------------------------------------------------
        SHOWWAVE_ONDESTROY
        Handle WM_DESTROY message here.  Close all devices.
        -------------------------------------------------------------*/

static void ShowWave_OnDestroy ( HWND hDlg )
{
```

```
    OFSTRUCT of;

    DeleteBrush( hbrBackgnd );
    FreeGlobalWaveData( );                                  // release buffer
    CloseAudioDevice( hDlg );                               // close devices
    CloseTimerDevice( hDlg );
    OpenFile( szTempFileName, &of, OF_DELETE );      // delete temp file

    PostQuitMessage( 0 );                                   // send WM_QUIT
    return;
}
```

To clean up, we delete the background brush created in ShowWave_OnInitDialog, release the buffer where the current sound is held, close the audio device if it's open, kill the timer if it's running, and delete the temporary file we opened on initializing. Here are the cleanup functions:

```
/*----------------------------------------------------------------
        QUERY SAVE
        Ask user to confirm loss of unsaved file before closing
    ----------------------------------------------------------------*/
BOOL QuerySave ( HWND hDlg )
{
    HINSTANCE hInstance;
    char szText[MAX_RSRC_STRING_LEN];
    char szCaption[MAX_RSRC_STRING_LEN];
    char szFormat[MAX_RSRC_STRING_LEN];
    int  iRet;

    /* is file dirty? */
    if (!bIsFileDirty)
    {
        return( TRUE );
    }

    /* see if user wants to save the modifications */
    hInstance = GetWindowInstance( hDlg );
    LoadString( hInstance, IDS_CAPTION,      szCaption, sizeof(szCaption) );
    LoadString( hInstance, IDS_CONFIRMCLOSE, szFormat,  sizeof(szFormat)  );
    wsprintf( szText, szFormat, (LPSTR)szFileTitle );

    iRet = MessageBox( hDlg, szText, szCaption,
                    MB_YESNOCANCEL | MB_ICONQUESTION );
```

```
    if (iRet == IDYES)
    {
        FORWARD_WM_COMMAND( hDlg, IDM_SAVE, NULL, 0, SendMessage );
    }
    return( iRet != IDCANCEL );
}
/*------------------------------------------------------------------
        FREE GLOBAL WAVE DATA
        Free storage associated with the global waveform data
  ----------------------------------------------------------------*/

static void FreeGlobalWaveData ( void )
{
    if (lpWaveData)
    {
        GlobalFreePtr( lpWaveData );
        lpWaveData = NULL;
    }
    return;
}

/*------------------------------------------------------------------
        CLOSE AUDIO DEVICE
        Close an opened waveform audio device
  ----------------------------------------------------------------*/

static void CloseAudioDevice ( HWND hDlg )
{
    if (mciDevice)
    {
        CloseDevice( hDlg, mciDevice );
        mciDevice = 0;
    }
    return;
}

/*------------------------------------------------------------------
        CLOSE TIMER DEVICE
        Kill an active timer; stop receiving WM_TIMER messages
  ----------------------------------------------------------------*/

static void CloseTimerDevice ( HWND hDlg )
```

```
{
    if (uTimerID)
    {
        KillTimer( hDlg, uTimerID );
        uTimerID = 0;
    }
    return;
}
```

QuerySave tests bIsFileDirty to see whether the current sound has been saved. If not, we put up a message box asking the user what to do. The user chooses Yes (to save), No (to end without saving), or Cancel (to avoid ending after all). The function returns **TRUE** unless the user cancels.

Displaying Information in Static Controls

The next procedures change static controls in the dialog box to make them show current information.

```
/*------------------------------------------------------------------

        PAINT WAVE DATA
        Repaint the dialog box's GraphClass display control
    ------------------------------------------------------------------*/

static void PaintWaveData ( HWND hDlg )
{
    HWND hwndShowWave = GetDlgItem( hDlg, IDD_SHOWWAVE );

    InvalidateRect( hwndShowWave, NULL, TRUE );
    UpdateWindow( hwndShowWave );
    return;
}


/*------------------------------------------------------------------

        UPDATE FILE TITLE TEXT
        Set a new file name in the dialog box's static file name control
    ------------------------------------------------------------------*/

static void UpdateFileTitleText ( HWND hDlg )
{
    Static_SetText( GetDlgItem(hDlg, IDD_FILETITLE), szFileTitle );
    return;
}
```

```
/*-----------------------------------------------------------------
        UPDATE TIME TEXT
        Update the static dialog controls that show the scroll
        thumb's current position and the playing time for the
        current .WAV file.
   -----------------------------------------------------------------*/

static void UpdateTimeText ( HWND hDlg )
{
    DWORD dwFrac;
    UINT  uSecs, uTenthSecs;
    char  szText[MAX_RSRC_STRING_LEN];
    char  szFormat[MAX_RSRC_STRING_LEN];

    /* get the format string */
    LoadString( GetWindowInstance(hDlg), IDS_TIMEFMT, szFormat,
                sizeof(szFormat) );

    /* update position text */
    dwFrac      = ((dwCurrentSample*100) / dwSamplesPerSec) / 10;
    uSecs       = (UINT)(dwFrac / 10);
    uTenthSecs = (UINT)(dwFrac % 10);
    wsprintf( szText, szFormat, uSecs, uTenthSecs );
    Static_SetText( GetDlgItem(hDlg, IDD_POSITION), szText );

    /* update length text */
    dwFrac      = ((dwWaveDataSize*100) / dwSamplesPerSec) / 10;
    uSecs       = (UINT)(dwFrac / 10);
    uTenthSecs = (UINT)(dwFrac % 10);
    wsprintf( szText, szFormat, uSecs, uTenthSecs );
    Static_SetText( GetDlgItem(hDlg, IDD_LENGTH), szText );

    return;
}
```

Resetting the Program

When the user chooses New from the File menu, the program must discard any current data and reset all its variables. NewWaveFile also updates the static dialog box controls and effectively disables the scroll bar by making its range very small.

```
/*-------------------------------------------------------------------
        NEW WAVE FILE
        Start work on a new .WAV file.  Reset variables and update
        display.  Called in response to the New command.
    -------------------------------------------------------------------*/

static void NewWaveFile ( HWND hDlg )
{
    HINSTANCE hInstance;
    HWND hwndScrollBar = GetDlgItem( hDlg, IDD_SCROLLBAR );

    /* close the old Wave file */
    if (!QuerySave( hDlg ))
    {
        return;
    }

    /* set file name and title */
    hInstance = GetWindowInstance( hDlg );
    LoadString( hInstance, IDS_UNTITLED, szFileTitle,
                sizeof(szFileTitle) );
    szFileName[0] = '\0';
    FreeGlobalWaveData( );                  // delete old waveform data
    bIsFileDirty = FALSE;                   // set file dirty flag
    UpdateFileTitleText( hDlg );            // set file name text

    /* set the new waveform data */
    dwCurrentSample = 0;
    lpWaveData      = NULL;
    dwWaveDataSize  = 0;
    dwSamplesPerSec = 22050;

    /* set the new scroll bar range */
    ScrollBar_SetRange( hwndScrollBar, 0, 1, FALSE );

    /* set the new scroll bar position */
    FORWARD_WM_HSCROLL( hDlg, hwndScrollBar, SB_TOP, 0, SendMessage );

    return;
}
```

Getting a File Name

GetFileName calls the common dialog box for opening or saving files. You saw similar code in Chapter 10.

```
/*------------------------------------------------------------------
        GET FILE NAME
        Invoke the File Open or File Save As common dialog box.
        If the bOpenName parameter is TRUE, the procedure runs
        the OpenFileName dialog box.

        RETURN
        TRUE if the dialog box closes without error.  If the dialog
        box returns TRUE, then lpszFile and lpszFileTitle point to
        the new file path and name, respectively.
------------------------------------------------------------------*/

static BOOL GetFileName (
    HWND hDlg,
    BOOL bOpenName,                     // open file or save as
    LPSTR lpszFile,                     // buffer for file path
    int iMaxFileNmLen,                  // max file path length
    LPSTR lpszFileTitle,                // buffer for file name
    int iMaxFileTitleLen )              // max file name length
{
    OPENFILENAME ofn;

    /* initialize structure for the common dialog box */
    lpszFile[0] = '\0';
    ofn.lStructSize         = sizeof( OPENFILENAME );
    ofn.hwndOwner           = hDlg;
    ofn.hInstance           = NULL;
    ofn.lpstrFilter         = szOFNFilter[0];
    ofn.lpstrCustomFilter   = NULL;
    ofn.nMaxCustFilter      = 0;
    ofn.nFilterIndex        = 1;
    ofn.lpstrFile           = lpszFile;
    ofn.nMaxFile            = iMaxFileNmLen;
    ofn.lpstrFileTitle      = lpszFileTitle;
    ofn.nMaxFileTitle       = iMaxFileTitleLen;
    ofn.lpstrInitialDir     = NULL;
    ofn.lpstrTitle          = NULL;
    ofn.nFileOffset         = 0;
    ofn.nFileExtension      = 0;
    ofn.lpstrDefExt         = szOFNDefExt;
```

```
ofn.lCustData        = 0;
ofn.lpfnHook         = NULL;
ofn.lpTemplateName   = NULL;

/* invoke the common dialog box */
if (bOpenName)                                       // open a file
{
    ofn.Flags = OFN_HIDEREADONLY | OFN_PATHMUSTEXIST |
                OFN_FILEMUSTEXIST;
    return( GetOpenFileName(&ofn) );
}
else                                                 // Save As...
{
    ofn.Flags = OFN_HIDEREADONLY | OFN_OVERWRITEPROMPT;
    return( GetSaveFileName(&ofn) );
}
}
```

Opening a Data File

The procedure that responds when the user chooses Open from the File menu asks the user to choose a file and then passes the name to ReadWaveData in the MMIO module. When the program loads new data, it resets the scroll bar range and pushes the thumb back to 0.

```
/*------------------------------------------------------------------
        OPEN WAVE FILE
        Open a new .WAV file
    ------------------------------------------------------------------*/
static void OpenWaveFile ( HWND hDlg )
{
    int   iMaxPos;
    HWND hwndScrollBar = GetDlgItem( hDlg, IDD_SCROLLBAR );

    /* close the old Wave file */
    if (!QuerySave( hDlg ))
    {
        return;
    }
```

```
/* get a Wave file to open */
if (!GetFileName( hDlg, TRUE,
                  szFileName,
                  sizeof(szFileName),
                  szFileTitle,
                  sizeof(szFileTitle) ))
{
    return;
}

FreeGlobalWaveData( );              // delete old waveform data
bIsFileDirty = FALSE;               // set file dirty flag
UpdateFileTitleText( hDlg );        // set file name text

/* read new waveform data */
dwCurrentSample = 0;
ReadWaveData( hDlg,
              szFileName,
              &lpWaveData,
              &dwWaveDataSize,
              &dwSamplesPerSec );

/* set the new scroll bar range */
iMaxPos = (int)((dwWaveDataSize*100) / dwSamplesPerSec );
ScrollBar_SetRange( hwndScrollBar, 0, iMaxPos, FALSE );

/* set the new scroll bar position */
FORWARD_WM_HSCROLL( hDlg, hwndScrollBar, SB_TOP, 0, SendMessage );

return;
}
```

Saving New Data

With the procedures we've already defined, writing a wave file to disk is easy. SaveWaveFile spends most of its time ensuring that we have a file name and that we don't write over important data.

```
/*-----------------------------------------------------------------
        SAVE WAVE FILE
        Save waveform data to disk.  If the second parameter is TRUE,
        or if the current data does not yet have a file name, this
        procedure will request a name.
    ----------------------------------------------------------------*/
```

```
static void SaveWaveFile (
    HWND hDlg,
    BOOL bAskForName )
{
    HINSTANCE hInstance;
    BOOL bSave;
    char szText[MAX_RSRC_STRING_LEN];
    char szCaption[MAX_RSRC_STRING_LEN];
    int  iRet;

    /* anything to save? */
    if (!lpWaveData)
    {
        return;
    }

    /* if renaming or no name, prompt user for name */
    if ((bAskForName) || (szFileName[0] == '\0'))
    {
        /* get the name of the wave file to save as */
        bSave = GetFileName( hDlg, FALSE,
                             szFileName,  sizeof(szFileName),
                             szFileTitle, sizeof(szFileTitle) );
    }
    else
    {
        /* no new name; confirm overwriting old file */
        hInstance = GetWindowInstance( hDlg );
        LoadString( hInstance, IDS_OVERWRITE, szText,
                    sizeof(szText) );
        LoadString( hInstance, IDS_CAPTION, szCaption,
                    sizeof(szCaption) );
        iRet = MessageBox( hDlg, szText, szCaption,
                    MB_YESNO | MB_ICONQUESTION );
        bSave = (iRet == IDYES);
    }

    /* save to the wave file */
    if (bSave)
    {
        /* set file dirty flag */
        bIsFileDirty = FALSE;
```

```
    /* set file name text */
    UpdateFileTitleText( hDlg );

    /* write out the waveform data */
    WriteWaveData( hDlg, szFileName,
                   lpWaveData,
                   dwWaveDataSize,
                   dwSamplesPerSec );
    }
    return;
}
```

Mixing Two Sounds Together

ShowWave's Edit menu gives the user a Mix command. To mix one sound with another you average them; that is, you add together each pair of samples and divide by two. When you play the combined sounds you should hear both components simultaneously.

```
/*-------------------------------------------------------------------
        MIX WITH FILE
        Mix a .WAV file into the current waveform data, combining
        the data from both into a single recording.  Mixing begins
        at the current point in the current file.  Mixing stops if
        we reach the end of the current file; it will not extend
        the current file.
        -----------------------------------------------------------*/

static void MixWithFile ( HWND hDlg )
{
    HINSTANCE hInstance;
    char  szMixFile[_MAX_FNAME];          // name of second .WAV file
    LPSTR lpMix;                          // data from second file
    DWORD dwMixSize;                      // size of new data
    DWORD dwMixSPS;                       // samples per second
    char  szErrStr[MAX_RSRC_STRING_LEN];
    char  szCaption[MAX_RSRC_STRING_LEN];
    LPSTR lpDest, lpSrc;                  // pointers for data transfer
    DWORD dw;                             // loop variable
    int   iMaxPos;                        // scroll bar range
    HWND  hwndScrollBar = GetDlgItem( hDlg, IDD_SCROLLBAR );
```

```
/* get a .WAV file to mix with */
if (!GetFileName( hDlg, TRUE,
                  szMixFile,
                  sizeof(szMixFile),
                  NULL, 0 ))
{
    return;                                 // no file name
}

/* read waveform data */
if (!ReadWaveData( hDlg,
                   szMixFile,
                   &lpMix,
                   &dwMixSize,
                   &dwMixSPS ))
{
    return;                                 // error reading data
}

/* mix data */
if (!lpWaveData)
{
    /* set file dirty flag */
    bIsFileDirty = TRUE;

    /* set the new waveform data */
    dwCurrentSample = 0;
    lpWaveData      = lpMix;
    dwWaveDataSize  = dwMixSize;
    dwSamplesPerSec = dwMixSPS;

    /* set the new scroll bar range */
    iMaxPos = (int)((dwWaveDataSize*100) / dwSamplesPerSec );
    ScrollBar_SetRange( hwndScrollBar, 0, iMaxPos, FALSE );

    /* set the new scroll bar position */
    FORWARD_WM_HSCROLL( hDlg, hwndScrollBar, SB_TOP, 0, SendMessage );
}
else
{
    /* for demo, use only matching frequencies */
    if (dwSamplesPerSec != dwMixSPS)
    {
        hInstance = GetWindowInstance( hDlg );
```

```
      LoadString( hInstance, IDS_BADFREQUENCY, szErrStr,
                  sizeof(szErrStr) );
      LoadString( hInstance, IDS_CAPTION, szCaption,
                  sizeof(szCaption) );
      MessageBox( hDlg, szErrStr, szCaption,
                  MB_ICONEXCLAMATION | MB_OK );
      GlobalFreePtr( lpMix );
      return;
   }

   /* mix new file into waveform at current position (lpDest) */
   lpSrc  = lpMix;
   lpDest = lpWaveData + dwCurrentSample;
   for (dw = 0; dw < (dwWaveDataSize-dwCurrentSample); dw++)
   {
      /* merge one source and destination sample */
      *lpDest = (BYTE)(((int)(BYTE)*lpDest + (BYTE)*lpSrc) / 2);
      lpSrc++;                 // increment transfer pointers
      lpDest++;
      if (lpSrc >= (lpMix+dwMixSize))
      {
          break;              // reached end of original data
      }
   }

   /* clean up */
   GlobalFreePtr( lpMix );    // free memory
   bIsFileDirty = TRUE;       // set file dirty flag
   PaintWaveData( hDlg );     // paint the new waveform data
   }
   return;
}
```

MixWithFile begins by asking for the name of a .WAV file to open and reading the data into a second memory buffer, lpMix. If there is no current sound—if the user has not already opened another file— the new "mix" sound simply becomes the current sound. We mark the new file unsaved, set the global variables, and give the scroll bar new range values based on the length of the new sound.

But normally the user will already have loaded a sound and we'll need to combine two sets of data. For demonstration purposes ShowWave mixes only sounds that have the same sampling rate. To mix sounds with different rates you would skip over some samples in the faster sound. For example, if one had a sampling rate of

11 and the other of 22, you would average every other sample from the second sound with one sample from the first.

The for loop that averages bytes together starts with the current position in the current sound. The user may already have played or scrolled partway through the file. The loop continues averaging bytes until it reaches the end of either sound and then stops. The new sound is cut off if it extends past the end of the old one. You could allow mixing to expand the current sound by calling **GlobalReallocPtr** to expand the **lpWaveData** buffer.

The line that averages two samples performs some type-casting to ensure that the compiler uses integers (which have 2 bytes) when it multiplies and divides. Even though the answer always fits in a byte, the intermediate product of two samples often overflows that limit.

Changing the Volume

The Effects menu lets the user make the current sound louder or softer. Like mixing, this effect involves modifying the samples mathematically. To understand the calculation, consider the diagram of a sound wave in Figure 16.5. The wave undulates above and below a middle point, called the *baseline*. When the wave swings very high and low, far away from the baseline, the sound it makes is loud. Quiet sounds have low peaks and shallow troughs. You can make a quiet sound loud by raising the peaks and lowering the troughs.

FIGURE 16.5:

Diagram of a sound wave

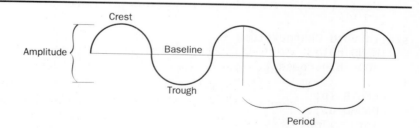

When a digitizer samples a sound wave, it notes where the wave falls in relation to the baseline at any given moment. When recording with 8 bits per sample, the range of the largest wave is divided into 256 different regions. Each sample names one of the regions. Sixteen-bit samples perceive 65,536 regions in the same amplitude and so record much finer distinctions. ShowWave works with 8-bit samples, so a value of 128 represents the baseline. To change the volume of a sound sample, first you determine its distance from the baseline:

WaveHeight = sample − baseline

Samples with values less than 128 produce negative heights, indicating a trough in the wave. To increase the volume by 25 percent you multiply each height by 1.25:

LouderHeight = (WaveHeight * 125) / 100;

Finally, you have to be sure the new value doesn't fall outside the possible range of 8-bit values. Amplitudes greater than 255 or less than 0 are not permitted.

LouderSample = LouderHeight + baseline

LouderSample = max(0, min(LouderSample, 255))

For 16-bit samples, make LouderSample type **LONG** and change the second calculation to this:

LouderSample = max(−32768, min(LouderSample, 32767))

ShowWave can either increase or decrease the volume by 25 percent. To decrease the volume, multiply each height by 0.75.

```
/*-------------------------------------------------------------------
        CHANGE VOLUME
        Increase/decrease the volume of the waveform data playback
    ----------------------------------------------------------------*/

static void ChangeVolume (
    HWND hDlg,
    BOOL bIncrease )
{
    LPSTR lp;
    DWORD dw;
    int   iTmp, iFactor;

    /* anything to change? */
    if (!lpWaveData)
    {
        return;
    }
```

```
/* change the volume of the waveform data */
lp       = lpWaveData;
iFactor = (bIncrease ? 125 : 75);
for (dw = 0; dw < dwWaveDataSize; dw++)
{
    iTmp = (((int)(BYTE)(*lp) - MIDVALUE) * iFactor) / 100;
    *lp = (BYTE)max( MINVALUE, min(iTmp+MIDVALUE, MAXVALUE) );
    lp++;
}

/* set file dirty flag */
bIsFileDirty = TRUE;

/* paint the new waveform data */
PaintWaveData( hDlg );

return;
}
```

Playing a Sound

BeginPlay from the MCI module plays a sound, but PlayWaveFile performs some additional housekeeping chores before calling that core function.

```
/*-------------------------------------------------------------------
        PLAY WAVE FILE
        Play waveform data
    -----------------------------------------------------------------*/

static void PlayWaveFile ( HWND hDlg )
{
    LPSTR lpsz;
    DWORD dwFrom;
    int   iMinPos, iMaxPos;
    HWND  hwndScrollBar = GetDlgItem( hDlg, IDD_SCROLLBAR );

    /* anything to play? */
    if (!lpWaveData)
    {
        return;
    }
```

```
/* get waveform file to play */
if (!bIsFileDirty)
{
    lpsz = szFileName;
}
else
{
    /* temporarily store waveform data to disk for playing */
    WriteWaveData( hDlg, szTempFileName, lpWaveData,
                   dwWaveDataSize, dwSamplesPerSec );
    lpsz = szTempFileName;
}

/* if current position is end of sound, reset to beginning */
ScrollBar_GetRange( hwndScrollBar, &iMinPos, &iMaxPos );
if (iHScrollPos == iMaxPos)
{
    FORWARD_WM_HSCROLL( hDlg, hwndScrollBar, SB_TOP, 0, SendMessage );
}

/* convert current sample position to milliseconds */
dwFrom = (dwCurrentSample*1000) / dwSamplesPerSec;
/* play waveform file */
if (OpenDevice( hDlg, lpsz, &mciDevice ))
{
    if (!BeginPlay( hDlg, mciDevice, dwFrom))
    {
        CloseAudioDevice( hDlg );
        return;
    }

    /* set timer to update display */
    uTimerID = TMRPLAY;
    SetTimer( hDlg, uTimerID, 100, NULL );
}
return;
}
```

Since BeginPlay must play from a disk file, first we have to decide which file to pass it. If the sound in memory has not changed since the user loaded it, ShowWave reads from the sound's original file. But if the user has changed the sound by mixing it or adjusting its volume, ShowWave deposits the sound in the temporary file we created on initialization.

If the user has scrolled partway through the current sound, we should start playing at the current position. The static variable iHScrollPos remembers where the scroll bar thumb is. If the user has scrolled to the end of the file then PlayWaveFile sends a message to reset the thumb at the beginning. ShowWave_OnHScroll answers the message, updating both iHScrollPos and dwCurrentSample to reflect the new file position.

Having guaranteed that the starting point is not the end of the file, PlayWaveFile opens the audio device and calls BeginPlay. The sound starts and BeginPlay returns immediately. The **SetTimer** command causes Windows to send us **WM_TIMER** messages every tenth of a second while the sound continues to play. You already saw how ShowWave_OnTimer responds to each message by advancing the scroll bar thumb and scrolling the wave graph.

Recording a Sound

The code for recording closely resembles the code for playing sound. The opening chores differ, however. Although the high-level audio commands allow you to insert newly recorded sound into an existing wave sound, not all devices support the **MCI_RECORD_INSERT** flag with the **MCI_RECORD** command. For simplicity, Show-Wave insists on recording to an empty file, and the opening if statement enforces the restriction.

We have also somewhat arbitrarily limited the recording to 20 seconds. You can interrupt the recording any time before that by clicking the Stop button. If you prefer to leave the recording time open ended, modify BeginPlay by removing the **MCI_TO** flag. (Or you might conditionally remove the flag only if the dwTo parameter is 0.)

```
/*--------------------------------------------------------------------
        RECORD WAVE FILE
        Record waveform data
    ------------------------------------------------------------------*/

static void RecordWaveFile ( HWND hDlg )
{
    HINSTANCE hInstance;
    char szErrStr[MAX_RSRC_STRING_LEN];
    char szCaption[MAX_RSRC_STRING_LEN];
```

```
/* for demo purposes, record only onto new wave files */
if (lpWaveData)
{
    hInstance = GetWindowInstance( hDlg );
    LoadString( hInstance, IDS_BADRECORDFILE, szErrStr,
                sizeof(szErrStr) );
    LoadString( hInstance, IDS_CAPTION, szCaption,
                sizeof(szCaption) );
    MessageBox( hDlg, szErrStr, szCaption,
                MB_ICONEXCLAMATION | MB_OK );
    return;
}
/* record waveform data into a new file */
if (OpenDevice( hDlg, "", &mciDevice))
{
    /* set recording to stop after 20 seconds */
    if (!BeginRecord( hDlg, mciDevice, 20000))
    {
        CloseAudioDevice( hDlg );
        return;
    }

    /* set timer to update display */
    uTimerID = TMRRECORD;
    SetTimer( hDlg, uTimerID, 100, NULL );
}
return;
}
```

The GraphWin Module

The Fonts Dialog program paints sample text in a static control. To modify the control's behavior (to intercept its **WM_PAINT** messages), we subclassed the control. ShowWave demonstrates another way to accomplish the same thing. The static control that graphs the sound wave has its own custom window class. Here's the resource script text that defined the Fonts Dialog preview control:

```
CONTROL    "", IDD_SAMPLE, "Static", SS_BLACKFRAME, 8, 79, 288, 64
```

The third item in a **CONTROL** statement—here, **Static**—names the control's window class. **Static** is a window class built into the system, as are, for example, **Button**, **ComboBox**, and **ScrollBar**. Each class has its own window procedure. Nothing prevents you from naming a class of your own invention when you define a control:

```
CONTROL    "", IDD_SHOWWAVE, "GraphClass", 0x0000, 53, 22, 76, 23
```

GraphClass names a window class that ShowWave registers when it initializes. The graphwin.c module contains the three procedures that support our Graph-Class window. RegisterGraphClass tells the system about the new class when the program begins, Graph_WndProc receives messages for the control, and Graph_OnPaint draws the sound wave.

```
/*-------------------------------------------------------------------

           GRAPHWIN.C

      Routines to handle the Graph window from the SHOWWAVE
      program.  The Graph window is the control in the center
      of the program's modeless dialog box where a graph of
      the current sound wave appears.

      PUBLIC FUNCTIONS
           Graph_WndProc         window procedure for graph control
           RegisterGraphClass    register graph control window class

      PRIVATE FUNCTION
           Graph_OnPaint         paint wave line in graph control

      program by Michael Barnes
      copyright 1992, 1993 by Brian Myers, Chris Doner, & Eric Hamer
      from Mastering Windows NT Programming
      -------------------------------------------------------------*/

#define STRICT
#include <windows.h>
#include <windowsx.h>
#include <mmsystem.h>          // multimedia definitions
#include "showwave.h"          // program variables and functions

/*-------------------------------------------------------------------
           FUNCTION PROTOTYPES
      -------------------------------------------------------------*/

LRESULT WINAPI Graph_WndProc( HWND hWnd, UINT uMsg, WPARAM wParam,
    LPARAM lParam );
static void Graph_OnPaint( HWND hWnd );
```

```
/*--------------------------------------------------------------------
        STATIC VARIABLES
   ----------------------------------------------------------------*/

static char szGraphClass[] = "GraphClass";

/*--------------------------------------------------------------------
        MACROS
   ----------------------------------------------------------------*/

#define RECTWIDTH( r )  ((r.right) - (r.left) + 1)
#define RECTHEIGHT( r ) ((r.bottom) - (r.top) + 1)

/*--------------------------------------------------------------------
        REGISTER GRAPH CLASS
        Register the window class for the dialog box's wave graph
        control window.  The main dialog box's resource template
        names this window class for one of its controls.  This
        procedure must be called before CreateDialog.
   ----------------------------------------------------------------*/

BOOL RegisterGraphClass ( HINSTANCE hInstance )
{
    WNDCLASS wc;

    wc.style         = 0;
    wc.lpfnWndProc   = Graph_WndProc;
    wc.cbClsExtra    = 0;
    wc.cbWndExtra    = 0;
    wc.hInstance     = hInstance;
    wc.hIcon         = NULL;
    wc.hCursor       = LoadCursor( NULL, IDC_ARROW );
    wc.hbrBackground = GetStockBrush( BLACK_BRUSH );
    wc.lpszMenuName  = NULL;
    wc.lpszClassName = szGraphClass;

    return( RegisterClass(&wc) );
}
```

```
/*--------------------------------------------------------------------
        GRAPH WNDPROC
        Receive messages for the main dialog box's sound graph window.
    --------------------------------------------------------------------*/
LRESULT WINAPI Graph_WndProc (
    HWND hWnd,
    UINT uMsg,
    WPARAM wParam,
    LPARAM lParam )
{
    switch (uMsg)
    {
        /* paint the green sound graph line */
        HANDLE_MSG( hWnd, WM_PAINT, Graph_OnPaint );
        default:
            return( DefWindowProc(hWnd, uMsg, wParam, lParam) );
    }
}
```

The window procedure intercepts only one message, **WM_PAINT**, and in every other case the window accepts the standard message responses from the default window procedure. (Dialog box controls are not themselves dialog boxes, so they call **DefWindowProc** and not **DefDlgProc**.)

Our **GraphClass** window isn't really a full-blown control. Real controls must be careful with global or static variables because, unlike child windows, they do not have separate data segments for each window instance. Changing one static variable for one control would change that variable for all controls of the same class. Also, a control should answer the **WM_GETDLGCODE** message to tell the parent dialog box what keyboard input it wants. (GraphClass doesn't want any and would respond with **DLGC_STATIC**.) A tightly designed custom control can be compiled into a dynamic-link library (see Chapter 11) and made available to all applications, including the Dialog Editor. To do that you would have to write and export a small set of standard control functions.

Drawing the Sound Wave

Rather than connecting points on the wave curve, ShowWave represents each sample as a vertical line. The wave height indicated in the sample determines the height of the vertical line. Each line extends an equal distance above and below the baseline, coloring in the space over and under each wave. Solid shapes show up better in the small graph window than a single wave line could. In Figure 16.6 you can see how the vertical lines fill the wave.

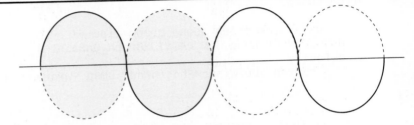

FIGURE 16.6:

How ShowWave draws the sound wave

```
/*----------------------------------------------------------------
            GRAPH_ONPAINT
            Handle WM_PAINT messages for the Graph window.  Draw
            the green wave graph.
      --------------------------------------------------------------*/

static void Graph_OnPaint ( HWND hWnd )
{
    PAINTSTRUCT ps;
    HDC    hDC;
    HPEN   hPen, hpenOld;        // green pen for drawing columns
    RECT   rClient;              // size of graph control window
    int    iBase;               // vertical position of baseline
    LPSTR  lp;                   // points to one sample in wave data
    DWORD  dwMaxStart;           // maximum value for starting point
    int    iYScale;             // vertical scaling factor
    int    iCol;                // horizontal position of a column
    int    iColHeight;          // height of a column

    /* begin paint processing */
    hDC = BeginPaint( hWnd, &ps );
```

```
/* create a pen for drawing graph */
if (GetDeviceCaps(hDC, NUMCOLORS) > 2)
{
    hPen = CreatePen( PS_SOLID, 1, RGB_GREEN );      // color display
}
else
{
    hPen = CreatePen( PS_SOLID, 1, RGB_WHITE );      // mono display
}

if (hPen)
{
    /* select the pen */
    hpenOld = SelectPen( hDC, hPen );

    /* draw the waveform baseline */
    GetClientRect( hWnd, &rClient );
    iBase = RECTHEIGHT(rClient) / 2;
    MoveToEx( hDC, 0, iBase, NULL );
    LineTo( hDC, (int)rClient.right, iBase );

    /* graph waveform data */
    if (lpWaveData)
    {
        /* set the current sample position in the waveform data */
        dwMaxStart = dwWaveDataSize - RECTWIDTH(rClient) - 1;
        lp = lpWaveData + min( dwCurrentSample, dwMaxStart );

        /* determine the height scaling factor */
        iYScale = ((MAXVALUE-MINVALUE) + 1) /   // amplitude
                  (RECTHEIGHT(rClient) - 4);    // control height

                  // Subtracting 4 from the height ensures a small
                  // margin above and below the biggest waves

        /* paint samples from the waveform data */
        for (iCol = (int)rClient.left;
            iCol <= (int)rClient.right;
            iCol++)
```

```
    {
        iColHeight = ((int)(BYTE)(*lp++) - MIDVALUE) / iYScale;
        if (iColHeight != 0)
        {
            /* figure absolute value of column height */
            if (iColHeight < 0)
            {
                iColHeight = -iColHeight;
            }

            /* draw line from below base to above base */
            MoveToEx( hDC, iCol, iBase-iColHeight, NULL );
            LineTo( hDC, iCol, iBase + (iColHeight+1) );
        }
    }
}
/* restore the DC and delete the pen */
SelectPen( hDC, hpenOld );
DeletePen( hPen );
}

/* end paint processing */
EndPaint( hWnd, &ps );
return;
}
```

Graph_OnPaint represents the baseline with a horizontal line bisecting the graph window. The first vertical line on the left side of the control window will represent the current sample. If the user has scrolled to a point near the end of the file and only a few samples remain, the wave graph might not extend all the way across the window. To avoid leaving part of the graph empty, the program imposes a maximum value for the starting point. If the graph control is, for example, 50 pixels wide, the graph must not begin less than 50 samples from the end.

The heights must of course be scaled to fit inside the window. A line extending the full height of the window must represent the maximum possible amplitude. With 8-bit samples, the maximum is 256. ShowWave calculates the line height with the following formulas:

Scale factor = maximum amplitude / window height

column height = sample height / scale factor

To preserve a small margin of 2 pixels below and above the tallest waves, Show-Wave subtracts 4 from the window height when figuring the scale factor.

The loop that draws each column begins by figuring the sample height and scaling it down to fit in the window. It draws each column by moving to a point below the baseline and drawing upward to a point an equal distance above the baseline. Because the columns extend on both sides of the baseline, the height of each column is twice the height of the sample.

We could call the C library function abs to get the absolute value of iColHeight, but then the compiler would add library code to the .EXE file. The if statement takes up less memory.

Other Ideas for ShowWave

Although the 8-bit sample size is common, you might want to allow ShowWave to work with 16-bit samples as well. We've described several places where ShowWave makes calculations that assume 8-bit samples—particularly in changing the volume, drawing the sound wave, and moving the scroll bar thumb. Any place that assumes a sample is a **BYTE** or refers to the manifest constants MINVALUE, MIDVALUE, and MAXVALUE would need to be changed. 16-bit samples range in value from −32,768 to 32,767, with a midpoint of 0.

You also know enough to add stereo sound. MixWithFile and ChangeVolume would have to do everything twice, once for the left channel and once for the right. To draw the sound wave you could average both channels together or let the user choose which channel to see. In a stereo data chunk the channels are interleaved:

Sample one: channel 0 sample, channel 1 sample

Sample two: channel 0 sample, channel 1 sample

and so on.

MixWithFile might be modified to permit expanding the original sound. To do this, you would have to reallocate the buffer periodically.

The MCI_OPEN command reloads the waveaudio driver each time you open the device. From working with printers you know that loading the driver causes a noticeable lag. ShowWave could load the driver once on opening and close it once at the end. In between it would open and close individual device elements. The very first Open command would specify a device type but no device element; subsequent commands would open and close with an element name. The final close would again omit the element.

Several programs may open one device simultaneously, so holding it open won't cause trouble. (Whether different programs can share the same device *element* depends on the flags they use with MCI_OPEN.)

With EnableWindow and EnableMenuItem you could disable buttons and menu commands not currently available. For example, all the buttons should be disabled until the user loads a sound. Stop should be disabled unless a playback or record message is in progress.

Finally, you could add MessageBeep commands to the program's error messages. Those who favor restraint in interface design will limit audio signals to the more critical errors or allow the user to choose whether and when to hear error sounds.

This chapter began with a general discussion of the hardware for multimedia applications and the WinMM translation layer that permits Windows programs to manipulate multimedia files in a device-independent manner. Windows works with files that contain data for wave sounds, MIDI music, animation, and analog video, among others.

WinMM was designed to be extensible. When other data types appear, new chunk formats can expand the RIFF standards. The MCI commands could send new messages, and their parameter structures could easily acquire new fields to accommodate more input. The high-level MCI commands establish a general protocol for opening and operating many very different devices.

For a sample program we chose to work with waveform audio because its hardware requirements are less demanding; many machines now have inexpensive sound cards. The ShowWave program demonstrates a full range of MCI command messages for opening and closing a device, playing and recording sounds, and interrupting operations. The MMIO module shows off the group of WinMM functions that facilitate reading and writing chunks of a RIFF file.

Having read this far, you have passed well beyond the beginning stages of Windows programming and have come to understand such advanced topics as threads, processes, synchronization, pipes, virtual memory, exception handling, enhanced metafiles, DDEML, and multimedia. Thorough as we have been, more remains. Windows NT is too large a system for one book to explain everything. The final chapter prepares you to proceed into new fields on your own, providing the background for exploring even more mysteries.

Surveying Advanced Features

 System security

Network APIs

Unicode text

Console API for character-based programs

The final chapter of this book prepares you for further adventures in Windows NT. To reward you for having mastered everything from `AngleArc` to `ZeroMemory`, we now pass on the keys to four new enhancements for your programs. The following sections describe system security, the network APIs, Unicode text, and the console API. We'll explain what each feature is, what it does, how it works, and why you might consider using it.

The security system protects resources by comparing an object's protection status to a user's clearance level whenever a process tries to use a secure resource. The network commands communicate with processes on remote machines. Unicode replaces ASCII as a standard for the internal representation of character symbols; it has the advantage of recognizing many different international alphabets. Finally, the console API is for writing programs with a character-based interface. All of these features address special needs rather than general tasks most programs might use. Each section presents an overview of its topic. The goal is to introduce the main features so you can make intelligent choices about which facilities will meet your needs.

SYSTEM SECURITY

We've skirted around issues of security several times in this book. When Chapter 4 explained how to create threads, it simply passed **NULL** for the **LPSECURITY_AT-TRIBUTES** parameter, and most of the other sample programs that create objects continued to ignore the security parameter. Chapter 12 observed that the NTFS file system supports more security attributes than either FAT or HPFS, but it did not explain the features in any detail. Now is the time to fill in those gaps.

A security system concerns itself with users and objects. Whenever a user wants an object, the security system intervenes to determine whether the user should be allowed access. If the user's privilege level matches the object's protection level, then access is allowed. In order for a security system to make such decisions, users and objects both must carry security information with them. The user's list of access rights must be compared to the object's list of protections. In Windows NT, the user has an *access token* and the object has a *security descriptor*. The security system regulates every access by comparing the user's token to the object's descriptor.

At its most basic level, then, the operation of a security system is straightforward and simple. In practice, however, a good security system must be complex in order to be flexible. The access token and security descriptor objects contain many different pieces so that, for example, an object can permit or deny different rights to each individual user. Users can belong to one or more groups and derive different rights from each one. Users from the accounting department might be one group; guests logging in remotely might be another. An administrator can override group settings to make exceptional privilege adjustments for an individual user. A troublesome member of your Power Users group, for example, could be prevented from debugging any processes. Windows NT also produces audit reports showing who has used which resources. An object's security descriptor can be set to generate audit signals when particular kinds of access occur or when illegal access is attempted. The complexity of the security system and its APIs results from the need to allow all these ways of regulating access.

As you have already seen, however, security considerations have little effect on how a programmer uses most of the Win32 APIs, and unless your project has particular security needs you can ignore the security system entirely. NTFS files, for example, can be protected automatically without any effort from the program that creates them. The system administrator (meaning anyone belonging to the security group called "Administrators") can create a private, protected directory for each user. Files inherit their security descriptors from the directories where they are created, so any file created in the user's private directory would be protected from other users. Some applications, however, do need to be aware of security. You would need to think of security when programming a server that manages protected data for a variety of clients. You also need security to change system-wide resources such as the system time or to modify an object's security settings.

The sections that follow first explain the structure of a security descriptor and an access token. Understanding the pieces that compose these two objects is essential for understanding how to program with the security API. Most of the security commands manipulate parts of a descriptor or a token. After we explain what descriptors and tokens are, we'll consider how the two are compared to evaluate access requests, how and why one process can impersonate another, and what a server does to make itself secure. Finally, we'll modify the Threads program from Chapter 4 to show how to restrict access to an object.

Identifying the User

The access token, which identifies a user, contains three pieces, as shown in Figure 17.1. First, a serial number identifies the individual user. The serial number, which is unique within an entire system of linked stations, is called a *security identifer* (*SID*). Next follows a variable-length list of other SIDs identifying groups to which the user belongs. When creating a new account, the system administrator grants the new user membership in one or more groups. Groups are defined by the set of access rights they carry, and their use eliminates the need to mark individual rights one by one for each new user. The administrator creates accounts and regulates group membership through the User Manager utility, shown in Figure 17.2.

FIGURE 17.1:

The parts of a user's access token. The SID is a security identifier uniquely naming a user or group; a LUID is a locally unique identifier designating a privilege that may be granted or denied.

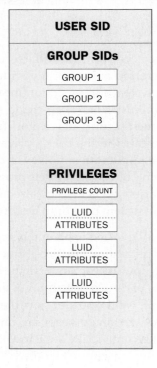

ACCESS TOKEN
Identifies the user

The User Manager, an administrative utility for regulating user accounts

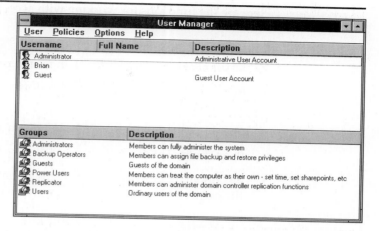

The third section of a user's access token is a variable-length list of privileges. By attaching privileges that grant or deny authority for specific actions, the administrator can customize a user's account. For example, one user in a company might be given responsibility for running a tape drive to back up the entire system regularly. Backing up requires a particular access right to read all the files on the drive. Rather than creating a group of backup operators for just one user, the administrator may choose to attach the backup privilege to the user's access token.

Access Token Commands

An access token is a system object, just like processes, threads, pipes, events, and many other objects we've introduced in earlier chapters. **OpenProcessToken** returns a handle to the access token for a given process, and **GetTokenInformation** retrieves the pieces that compose an access token. In order to read information from the token you retrieve, you must ask **OpenProcessToken** for the **QUERY_TOKEN** access right, and the function will fail if you do not have that privilege. The winnt.h header file defines a set of structures to hold different kinds of information from an access token, so the information buffer filled by **OpenProcessToken** is usually cast to a type such as **TOKEN_USER**, **TOKEN_GROUPS**, or **TOKEN_PRIVILEGES**.

If **OpenProcessToken** has granted you **TOKEN_WRITE** privileges, then you will be able to modify parts of the token by calling **SetTokenInformation**. Modifying a token is a powerful action because with it you can change a user's group memberships and add or subtract privileges.

Here are the functions for working with access tokens:

- **AdjustTokenGroups**: Modifies a token's group affiliations
- **AdjustTokenPrivileges**: Changes the privileges in an access token
- **GetTokenInformation**: Extracts information selectively from an access token object
- **OpenProcessToken**: Returns a handle to a process's access token
- **OpenThreadToken**: Returns a handle to a thread's access token
- **SetTokenInformation**: Modifies a token's primary group, default DACL, or the owner SID assigned to objects created for the token.

The Security Identifier (SID)

The serial number that identifies a single user or group of users has several parts: a revision level, an identifier authority, a domain, and a user. The common shorthand for listing an SID value looks like this:

```
S-1-4138-54-41
```

The initial "S" conventionally signals the beginning of a written SID value. The number 1 is the revision level, and 4138 is the identifier authority, indicating who created the SID. An "authority" is responsible for assigning ID numbers to all its users, and within one authority's domain all users have a unique number. Other values, called subauthorities, may follow the authority. The chain of subauthorities represents a hierarchy of domains. One subauthority may represent a company, the next a division within the company, the next a department within the division, and the last a particular user or group of users within the department. Because each subauthority designates a group within the next higher subauthority, subauthorities are also called relative identifiers (RIDs). They are defined by relation to another larger group. In the example, 54 and 41 are subauthorities. Combining authorities and subauthorities produces SIDs unique within a linked set of domains.

You receive an SID when you log on. A logon process within the system validates your password by comparing it to the one stored in the Security Account Manager (SAM) database, located in the system registry. The logon process assigns you an SID and fills out the rest of your access token by reading your groups and privileges from the database. The first process you start—usually the Program Manager—receives the new access token from the logon process, and every program you launch from the Program Manager inherits the same token. Your access token identifies you as the owner of each new process you start. Each process receives a separate copy of the access token so that a temporary modification of your privileges in one process doesn't automatically grant the same new privilege to all your other processes.

Once you have an SID, you are a *subject*. Several subjects may be active on one machine if some have reached it from a remote source. Also, the parts of the system that run in user mode (for example, the Win32 subsystem) are considered subjects and operate under their own set of security restraints.

The SID Commands

To allow for future modifications to the structure of an SID, the Win32 API includes a number of functions for parsing, reading, and comparing the information in an SID. Use the Win32 commands rather than reading the information directly.

- **EqualPrefixSid:** Compares two SIDs and returns **TRUE** if they match except for their final subauthority values

- **EqualSid:** Compares two SIDs and returns **TRUE** if they match exactly

- **GetLengthSid:** Returns the length of a given SID in bytes

- **GetSidIdentifierAuthority:** Returns a pointer to the identifier authority component of an SID

- **GetSidLengthRequired:** Returns the size in bytes of an SID with a given number of authorities; call this before allocating a buffer

- **GetSidSubAuthority:** Returns a pointer to a given subauthority, identified by its sequential position, in an SID

- **GetSidSubAuthorityCount:** Returns the number of subauthorities present in a given SID

- **IsValidSid:** Tests whether the given SID possesses a recognizable version number and no more than the maximum number of subauthorities

Two more functions read information from the SAM database.

- **LookupAccountName:** Given an account name, retrieves the corresponding SID
- **LookupAccountSid:** Given an SID, retrieves the corresponding account name

To retrieve your own SID, pass the handle from **GetCurrentProcess** to **OpenProcessToken**. Alternatively, you can call **GetUserName** to retrieve the account name for the current thread and then call **LookupAccountName** to find the corresponding SID.

Another set of commands helps to construct new SIDs from scratch.

- **AllocateAndInitializeSid:** Allocates and initializes a new SID
- **CopySid:** Copies an SID to a buffer
- **FreeSid:** Releases an SID previously allocated by **AllocateAndInitializeSid**
- **InitializeSid:** Initializes an SID structure but not its subauthorities

AllocateAndInitializeSid allocates a buffer for an SID and fills the buffer with information from its parameters. Here is the function's prototype:

```
BOOL AllocateAndInitializeSid(
    PSID_IDENTIFIER_AUTHORITY psia,    // address of identifier authority
    BYTE bSubAuthorities,              // number of subauthorities to append
    DWORD dwSubAuthority0,             // subauthority 0
    DWORD dwSubAuthority1,             // subauthority 1
    DWORD dwSubAuthority2,             // subauthority 2
    DWORD dwSubAuthority3,             // subauthority 3
    DWORD dwSubAuthority4,             // subauthority 4
    DWORD dwSubAuthority5,             // subauthority 5
    DWORD dwSubAuthority6,             // subauthority 6
    DWORD dwSubAuthority7,             // subauthority 7
    PSID *lppsid );                    // address of pointer to SID
```

If you pass predefined constants to **AllocateAndInitializeSid**, it is possible to construct SIDs that represent standard users and groups such as the group of local users, users connected remotely by telephone, the creator of an object, the guest user account, or the system subject. Typically these predefined values are used to construct ACE entries granting and restricting access rights. The sample code in the section "An Example: Creating a New Security Descriptor" shows how to construct an SID.

Privileges

A privilege is a structure attached to an access token. It grants or denies the right to perform a particular action or a set of related actions. A privilege has two states: enabled or disabled, granted or denied. A privilege overrides any other settings attached to a user's account or a user's groups. The system administrator assigns privileges to groups or to individual users through the User Manager (shown in Figure 17.2). A process can do the same thing through the security API if its owner's access token grants the privilege called SeSecurityPrivilege.

The winnt.h header defines identifiers for the following privileges:

- **SE_ASSIGNPRIMARYTOKEN_NAME:** Assigns a token to a process

- **SE_AUDIT_NAME:** Generates audit log entries

- **SE_BACKUP_NAME:** Reads all files in order to back up the system

- **SE_CHANGENOTIFY_NAME:** Receives notification when files or directories change

- **SE_CREATE_PAGEFILE_NAME:** Creates the system's memory-paging file

- **SE_CREATE_PERMANENT_NAME:** Creates permanent objects (useful for device drivers)

- **SE_CREATE_TOKEN_NAME:** Creates a primary token

- **SE_DEBUG_NAME:** Debugs a process

- **SE_INC_BASE_PRIORITY_NAME:** Raises a process's base scheduling priority

- **SE_INCREASE_QUOTA_NAME:** Increases a process's resource quota

- **SE_LOAD_DRIVER_NAME:** Loads and unloads removable drivers

- **SE_LOCK_MEMORY_NAME:** Locks physical memory pages

- **SE_PROF_SINGLE_PROCESS_NAME:** Profiles information for a single process

- **SE_REMOTE_SHUTDOWN_NAME:** Shuts down the system through a network

- **SE_RESTORE_NAME:** Restores files from a backup

- **SE_SECURITY_NAME:** Performs security-related functions, such as viewing system audits

- **SE_SHUTDOWN_NAME:** Shuts down a local system

- **SE_SYSTEM_ENVIRONMENT_NAME:** Modifies configuration information stored in nonvolatile RAM

- **SE_SYSTEM_PROFILE_NAME:** Gathers profiling information for the entire system

- **SE_SYSTEMTIME_NAME:** Modifies the system's time setting

- **SE_TAKE_OWNERSHIP_NAME:** Takes ownership of an object without having discretionary access

- **SE_TCB_NAME:** Acts as a part of the system (some subsystems belong to the "trusted computer base")

- **SE_UNSOLICITED_INPUT_NAME:** Reads unsolicited input from a terminal

Each privilege can be represented in three different ways: as a string recognized on any system, as a 64-bit numeric ID for the local machine, and as a descriptive string for users. The SE_ symbols in the preceding list are defined in winnt.h as strings.

```
#define SE_SYSTEMTIME_NAME          TEXT("SeSystemtimePrivilege")
```

"SeSystemtimePrivilege" is the string recognizable on different systems. Some of the functions for dealing with privileges translate from one representation to another.

- **LookupPrivilegeValue:** Given a privilege string (such as **SE_SYS-TEMTIME_NAME**), returns a local ID

- **LookupPrivilegeDisplayName:** Given a privilege string, returns a descriptive string such as "Change the system time."

- **LookupPrivilegeName:** Given a privilege's local ID, returns the privilege string

- **PrivilegeCheck:** Tells whether a given access token possesses particular privileges

The 64-bit local ID that identifies a privilege is called a "locally unique identifer," or **LUID**. The privileges attached to an access token are composed of one **LUID** and one attribute each. The attribute tells whether the privilege is being granted or denied.

```
typedef LARGE_INTEGER LUID, *PLUID;

typedef struct _LUID_AND_ATTRIBUTES {
    LUID Luid;                              // a particular privilege
    DWORD Attributes;                       // 32 1-bit flags
} LUID_AND_ATTRIBUTES, * PLUID_AND_ATTRIBUTES;
```

The flags in the **Attributes** field mean different things for different privileges, but all the flags grant or deny rights.

The following code changes an access token by adding a privilege to permit changing the system time:

```
HANDLE hToken;                              // process's access token
LUID luidSetTime;                           // ID for SeSystemtimePrivilege
TOKEN_PRIVILEGES tkp;                       // wrapper for array of privileges

/* get a handle to the process's access token */
OpenProcessToken( GetCurrentProcess(),      // process handle
    TOKEN_ADJUST_PRIVILEGES | TOKEN_QUERY,  // requested access rights
    &hToken );                              // place for token handle

/* get the local identifier for the time-setting privilege */
LookupPrivilegeValue( NULL,                 // system to query (local)
    SE_SYSTEMTIME_NAME,                     // privilege name string
    &luidSetTime );                         // place for privilege ID

/* initialize a structure representing the set of desired privileges (1) */
tkp.PrivilegeCount = 1;
tkp.Privileges[0].Luid = luidSetTime;
tkp.Privileges[0].Attributes = SE_PRIVILEGE_ENABLED;

/* modify the access token */
AdjustTokenPrivileges( hToken,
    FALSE,                                  // token to modify
    &tkp,                                   // TRUE to disable all privileges
    sizeof(TOKEN_PRIVILEGES),               // array of new privilege settings
    NULL,                                   // size of the array
    NULL );                                 // place for old privileges
                                            // size of old privileges
```

The **TOKEN_PRIVILEGES** structure is a wrapper for an array of **LUID_AND_ATTRIBUTE** pairs preceded by a **DWORD** header telling how many elements the array contains. Use the wrapper to process a set of privileges in a single function call.

For simplicity we have omitted error checking. **AdjustTokenPrivileges** always returns **TRUE**, so to test its result you must call **GetLastError**. **ERROR_SUCCESS** indicates that all requested privileges were granted. If all the functions succeed, then after running this code the process will be able to issue commands that change the system time. **AdjustTokenPrivileges** will not succeed if the user running the program does not have the right to change the system time (**SE_SYSTEMTIME_NAME**).

Protecting the Object

Having considered the pieces that compose a user's access token, we now move on to the pieces of an object's security descriptor. A security descriptor, diagrammed in Figure 17.3, begins with a set of flags indicating the structure's revision level, its format, whether the SACL and DACL pieces are present, and whether they were assigned by default. Next comes an SID naming the object's owner. The third element, a group SID, is included for the use of POSIX and Macintosh clients. When programming for the Win32 subsystem, you can ignore the group. The System Access Control List (SACL) tells when to make entries for this object in the audit log. The system can record for the administrator when any user, or a particular user, or any member of a certain group uses or tries to use the object in particular ways. The SACL sets the audit conditions. The final component of a security descriptor is its Discretionary Access Control List (DACL). It contains a list of variable length, and each item in the list grants or denies particular access rights to a user or a group.

FIGURE 17.3:

The pieces of an object's security descriptor

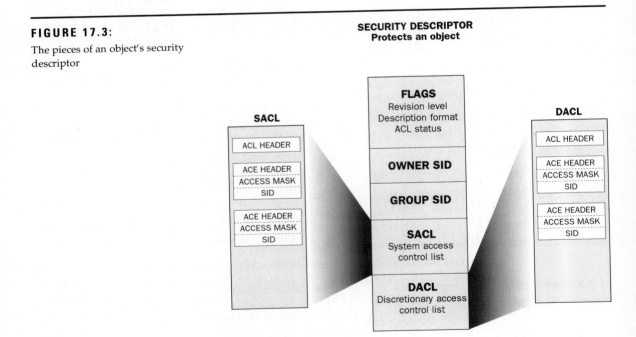

1120

We'll save the security descriptor flags for later, and you already know what an SID looks like. The SID naming the owner of an object can always be changed to any group SID in the owner's access token. A group SID allows all group members to act as the object's owner. The owner of an object can modify or replace the object's DACL, granting discretionary access to whomever the owner chooses. As a result, the owner usually cannot be prevented from exercising any access rights on the object. The DACL is the piece that sets permissions for an object, and the rest of this section describes how it works.

Access Control Lists (ACLs)

The SACL and the DACL are structurally alike. (Incidentally, the acronyms are pronounced "sackle" and "dackle.") Both ACLs contain a list of items associating SIDs with access rights. Each SID names a user or group. In a DACL, each list item grants or denies access rights for the SID. In a SACL, the indicated rights are neither granted nor denied; they are simply flagged for audit control. Whenever any user attempts to exercise a right flagged in the SACL, the system produces a message. Reading and modifying the SACL and DACL require privileges that can be granted or denied to a user.

The diagram in Figure 17.3 sets out the structure of an access control list. The list begins with a header of type **ACL**:

```
typedef struct _ACL {
    BYTE AclRevision;            // ACL_REVISION
    BYTE Sbz1;                   // unused (should be 0)
    WORD AclSize;                // size of list in bytes
    WORD AceCount;               // number of ACEs in list
    WORD Sbz2;                   // unused (should be 0)
} ACL;
```

The two extra fields are padding to keep the entire structure aligned on 32-bit boundaries. After the **ACL** come the list items associating SIDs with access rights.

Access Control Entry (ACE)

Each item in an access control list is called an access control entry (ACE); an ACL is a list of ACEs. In the current implementation there are three different kinds of

ACEs, but they are all defined alike. Here is one of them.

```
typedef struct _ACCESS_ALLOWED_ACE {
    ACE_HEADER Header;          // info about this ACE
    ACCESS_MASK Mask;           // access mask of bit flags
    DWORD SidStart;             // the SID starts here
} ACCESS_ALLOWED_ACE;
```

The other two ACE types are **ACCESS_DENIED_ACE** and **SYSTEM_AUDIT_ACE**. The access mask field in all these ACEs is a 32-bit quantity composed of bit flags that are set to indicate particular access rights. In an access-allowed ACE, setting a bit flag grants a right. In an access-denied ACE, setting a flag denies a right. In a system audit ACE, setting a flag makes an action generate audit log entries. The meaning of specific flags varies from object to object. The allowed and denied ACE types occur only in a discretionary ACL. All the ACEs in a system ACL are system audit ACEs.

SIDs vary in length. The **SidStart** field is defined as a **DWORD**, but its value is likely to be longer. In order to parse an ACE, therefore, you have to know its length. That information is in the ACE header.

```
typedef struct _ACE_HEADER {
    BYTE AceType;               // the type (or purpose) of the ACE
    BYTE AceFlags;              // audit and inheritance flags
    WORD AceSize;               // size of ACE in bytes
} ACE_HEADER;
```

The **AceType** field identifies the ACE as one of three types:

- **ACCESS_ALLOWED_ACE_TYPE:** Grants rights in a DACL

- **ACCESS_DENIED_ACE_TYPE:** Denies rights in a DACL

- **SYSTEM_AUDIT_ACE_TYPE:** Flags rights for auditing in a SACL

The header files define a fourth type of ACE, **SYSTEM_ALARM_ACE_TYPE**. When implemented it will enable a SACL to generate alarms as well as entries in the audit log. The first release of Windows NT does not, however, support alarms.

The flags combined in the **AceFlags** field determine whether other objects inherit this object's SACL and DACL settings. Objects sometimes inherit security protection when they are placed in a container object. For example, a directory is an object that contains other objects. When a file is created inside a containing directory, it may inherit protection. Whether it does depends on the inheritance flags in the directory's access control lists.

- **CONTAINER_INHERIT_ACE:** Subdirectories inherit from their parent directory protections marked with this flag.

- **INHERIT_ONLY_ACE:** The ACE is present only to be inherited. It does not apply to the container object, but anything in the container inherits it.

- **NO_PROPAGATE_INHERIT_ACE:** Prevents the **OBJECT_INHERIT_ACE** and **CONTAINER_INHERIT_ACE** flags from being inherited. Prevents an ACE inherited at one level from being passed on to objects at lower levels.

- **OBJECT_INHERIT_ACE:** Non-container objects inherit the ACE, but subcontainers do not. New files inherit it, but new subdirectories do not.

Besides the four inheritance flags, the **AceFlags** field of an ACE header may contain one of two audit flags. Only the ACEs in a SACL use these flags.

- **FAILED_ACCESS_ACE_FLAG:** Generates an audit log entry when an attempt to exercise the indicated access right fails

- **SUCCESSFUL_ACCESS_ACE_FLAG:** Generates an audit log entry when an attempt to exercise the indicated access right succeeds

Although all the currently defined ACE structures contain exactly the same three fields, in subsequent releases they may not. All ACEs, however, will always begin with an **ACE_HEADER**, and the **AceType** field indicates which structure to use in parsing what follows. Also, although ACEs come in different lengths because they contain a variable-length SID, successive ACEs in a list must begin on **DWORD**-aligned boundaries.

The Access Mask Field

To review, a security descriptor contains two access control lists (ACLs). Each ACL contains a list of access control entries (ACEs). Each ACE has three pieces: a header, an access mask, and an SID. Usually the ACLs are assigned to an object by default, but sometimes a program constructs ACLs from scratch. Doing so requires some knowledge of the flags in the access mask. The winnt.h header gives the following illustration and definition to describe an access mask:

```
//      3 3 2 2 2 2 2 2 2 2 2 2 1 1 1 1 1 1 1 1 1 1
//      1 0 9 8 7 6 5 4 3 2 1 0 9 8 7 6 5 4 3 2 1 0 9 8 7 6 5 4 3 2 1 0
//      +---------------+---------------+-------------------------------+
//      |G|G|G|G|Res'd|A| StandardRights|          SpecificRights       |
//      |R|W|E|A|     |S|               |                               |
//      +-+-----------+-+---------------+-------------------------------+
//
//      typedef struct _ACCESS_MASK {
//          WORD  SpecificRights;
//          BYTE  StandardRights;
//          BYTE  AccessSystemAcl : 1;
//          BYTE  Reserved : 3;
//          BYTE  GenericAll : 1;
//          BYTE  GenericExecute : 1;
//          BYTE  GenericWrite : 1;
//          BYTE  GenericRead : 1;
//      } ACCESS_MASK;
//      typedef ACCESS_MASK *PACCESS_MASK;
```

The access mask is 32 bits long. The low-order word, whose meaning changes from object to object, designates specific rights. The high-order word is divided into bits for standard rights and generic rights. These bit fields retain the same meaning for all objects. We'll explain them in a minute.

The **Mask** field of an ACE structure is defined as type **ACCESS_MASK**, but an **AC-CESS_MASK** is not actually defined as a structure.

```
typedef DWORD ACCESS_MASK;
```

Defining it as a **DWORD** allows the programmer to build masks by combining flags with an OR operator rather than toggling fields named within a structure.

Standard Access Rights

The easiest flags to explain and to use are the standard rights. They are standard for all objects and always have the same meaning.

```
#define DELETE          (0x00010000L)   // delete an object
#define READ_CONTROL    (0x00020000L)   // query owner, DACL, and descriptor
#define WRITE_DAC       (0x00040000L)   // modify or remove the DACL
#define WRITE_OWNER     (0x00080000L)   // change the object's owner
#define SYNCHRONIZE     (0x00100000L)   // pass object to a Wait command
```

A few more symbols give alternate ways to refer to some of the standard rights or to a particular combination of them.

```
// Combines DELETE, READ_CONTROL, WRITE_DAC, WRITE_OWNER,
// and SYNCHRONIZE access.

#define STANDARD_RIGHTS_REQUIRED    (0x000F0000L)

// Standard read, write, and execute are currently
// synonyms for READ_CONTROL.

#define STANDARD_RIGHTS_READ        (READ_CONTROL)
#define STANDARD_RIGHTS_WRITE       (READ_CONTROL)
#define STANDARD_RIGHTS_EXECUTE     (READ_CONTROL)

// Combines all the standard rights flags in one symbol.

#define STANDARD_RIGHTS_ALL         (0x001F0000L)
```

Specific Rights

The standard rights are convenient because they are the same for all objects, but clearly most objects need more kinds of protection than the standard rights provide. Standard rights, for example, don't allow for changing the data in a file, creating a process, terminating a thread, or modifying an event state. Actions that apply only to a certain kind of object must be defined individually as specific rights using flags in the lower 16 bits of the access mask. Here, for example, are the specific rights flags for a file object, as defined in winnt.h:

```
#define FILE_READ_DATA            ( 0x0001 )    // file & pipe
#define FILE_LIST_DIRECTORY       ( 0x0001 )    // directory

#define FILE_WRITE_DATA           ( 0x0002 )    // file & pipe
#define FILE_ADD_FILE             ( 0x0002 )    // directory

#define FILE_APPEND_DATA          ( 0x0004 )    // file
#define FILE_ADD_SUBDIRECTORY     ( 0x0004 )    // directory
#define FILE_CREATE_PIPE_INSTANCE ( 0x0004 )    // named pipe

#define FILE_READ_EA              ( 0x0008 )    // file & directory

#define FILE_WRITE_EA             ( 0x0010 )    // file & directory
```

```
#define FILE_EXECUTE              ( 0x0020 )    // file
#define FILE_TRAVERSE             ( 0x0020 )    // directory

#define FILE_DELETE_CHILD         ( 0x0040 )    // directory

#define FILE_READ_ATTRIBUTES      ( 0x0080 )    // all

#define FILE_WRITE_ATTRIBUTES     ( 0x0100 )    // all
```

The header files define a different set of specific access rights for each object. (Other objects include, for example, registry keys, semaphores, processes, and access tokens.) Bit 0 in a file's access mask means **FILE_READ_DATA**, but for an event the same bit means **EVENT_QUERY_STATE**, and for an access token it means **TOKEN_ASSIGN_PRIMARY**. You can always request all the specific rights for any object with this symbol.

```
#define SPECIFIC_RIGHTS_ALL       (0x0000FFFFL)
```

Two more symbols are usually listed with the standard rights although their cases are exceptional. The **ACCESS_SYSTEM_SECURITY** flag must be requested in order to read or write any system ACL. The **ACCESS_SYSTEM_SECURITY** bit does not belong to the standard rights byte, and it cannot be used in an ACL. The **MAXIMUM_ALLOWED** flag tells the system to compare the access token to the security descriptor and grant all the rights this user is permitted. The advantages of requesting the maximum allowed rights are that the request cannot fail and you don't have to discover by trial and error what rights you may receive. The disadvantages are that you cannot count on **MAXIMUM_ALLOWED** to give you a particular right you may need, and waiting for the system to figure the maximum takes longer. It is usually better to anticipate the smallest set of rights you require and to request them specifically. Like **ACCESS_SYSTEM_SECURITY**, **MAXIMUM_ALLOWED** may not appear in an ACL. In other words, both are used to formulate requests, never to set protections on an object.

After requesting the **MAXIMUM_ALLOWED** rights, you can call these functions to determine whether particular rights were granted:

```
AreAllAccessesGranted

AreAnyAccessesGranted
```

Generic Access Rights

Because it's difficult to keep track of all the specific rights for each different kind of object, Microsoft dedicated the upper 4 bits of an access mask to signal generic rights. They are **GENERIC_READ**, **GENERIC_WRITE**, **GENERIC_EXECUTE**, and **GENERIC_ALL**. The system translates any request for generic rights into a request for a set of specific rights. Generic rights map to different sets of specific rights for different objects. Each type of object defines its own generic mapping scheme. As a result, you can always ask for **GENERIC_READ** in order to query the object for information. For example, a request for **GENERIC_READ** rights to a file produces a handle with the following permissions:

- **STANDARD_RIGHTS_READ:** Queries owner, DACL, and security descriptor
- **FILE_READ_DATA:** Reads data from the file
- **FILE_READ_ATTRIBUTES:** Queries the file's storage attributes
- **FILE_READ_EA:** Queries the file's extended attributes
- **SYNCHRONIZE:** Passes the file handle to a Wait command

GENERIC_READ maps to a different set of permission flags for each object, but it always grants the privileges needed to perform whatever queries the object supports. To consider another example, a *window station* is an internal structure representing a combination of keyboard, mouse, and screen. A window station contains desktops, and desktops contain windows and menus. Window stations and desktops contain other objects, just as directories do. Desktops inherit security attributes from the window station, and windows inherit them from the desktop. **GENERIC_READ** for a window station maps to these rights:

- **STANDARD_RIGHTS_READ:** Queries owner, DACL, and security descriptor

- **WINSTA_ENUMDESKTOPS:** Enumerates desktop objects contained in the station

- **WINSTA_ENUMERATE:** Enumerates the window station

- **WINSTA_READATTRIBUTES:** Reads color settings and other station attributes

- **WINSTA_READSCREEN:** Accesses the contents of the screen

Many of the generic right mappings are described in the on-line help file. (Search for the Securities Overview topic, and then browse through the topics with names like File and Directory Objects or Kernel Objects.)

In other chapters, we have sometimes passed **GENERIC_READ** and **GENERIC_WRITE** to functions that return object handles. We used them, for example, when requesting either read or write access to files. **CreateNamedPipe** doesn't recognize the generic flags directly, but the pipe's open mode implies a set of access rights.

- **PIPE_ACCESS_DUPLEX: GENERIC_READ, GENERIC_WRITE**, and **SYNCHRONIZE**
- **PIPE_ACCESS_INBOUND: GENERIC_READ** and **SYNCHRONIZE**
- **PIPE_ACCESS_OUTBOUND: GENERIC_WRITE** and **SYNCHRONIZE**

Getting an Object's Security Descriptor

One set of security functions retrieves or assigns security descriptors. Which function you call depends on the type of object you want to manipulate. Use of these functions requires the **SE_SECURITY_NAME** privilege.

`GetFileSecurity`	For files, directories,
`SetFileSecurity`	pipes, and mailslots
`GetKernelObjectSecurity`	For processes, threads, access tokens,
`SetKernelObjectSecurity`	synchronization objects
`GetUserObjectSecurity`	For window stations, desktops,
`SetUserObjectSecurity`	windows, and menus
`RegGetKeySecurity`	For system registry keys
`RegSetKeySecurity`	
`QueryServiceObject= Security`	For executable service objects
`SetServiceObjectSecurity`	

This list also indicates most of the objects that can be secured. Most securable objects can have names: pipes, files, file-mapping objects, and synchronization objects, for example, can all be named. The name enables different processes to share the object. Objects that can't be shared often don't need security. Critical sections, for example, don't need to be secured because they are always local to a process. Since they cannot be shared, protection is irrelevant. Events, mutexes, and semaphores are securable. All nameable objects are securable, but only a few unnameable objects are. Processes and threads fall into this exceptional category.

Occasionally objects that you expect to be securable may not be. Files and directories are securable only under NTFS. The security commands have no effect on FAT and HPFS files. Also, if you create a nameable object but do not give it a name, the system ignores its security descriptor. For example, a file-mapping object without a name cannot be secured. Of course, without a name it cannot be shared either, so security is usually irrelevant.

Note that access tokens count as kernel objects. Though we didn't show it in Figure 17.1, an access token, like any securable object, has a security descriptor of its own to protect it.

Parsing a Security Descriptor

Security descriptors come in two formats, absolute and self-relative. An *absolute* descriptor is self contained; all its pieces follow each other consecutively in memory. A *self-relative* descriptor does not contain its SACL and DACL; instead it holds pointers to them. The self-relative format is convenient when creating a series of objects with identical access control lists; all may contain pointers to the same ACLs. In order to store a security descriptor, however, or to transmit it to another process, it must be converted to absolute format. All the descriptors retrieved by Win32 functions are self relative. Win32 functions that ask for an SID accept either format. Two commands convert from one format to the other:

```
MakeAbsoluteSD

MakeSelfRelativeSD
```

Although some of its internal structures are documented, a security descriptor (like an access token) is meant to be an opaque object. Programs should not try to parse and manipulate directly the ACLs and SIDs that compose a security descriptor. Rely instead on the security API to extract and modify individual pieces. This indirection protects a program from breaking on future versions if the internal structures change. These functions retrieve information from a descriptor:

- **GetSecurityDescriptorControl:** Revision level and control flags

- **GetSecurityDescriptorDacl:** Discretionary ACL

- **GetSecurityDescriptorGroup:** Primary group

- **GetSecurityDescriptorLength:** Length in bytes of a security descriptor

- **GetSecurityDescriptorOwner:** Owner of a security descriptor

- **GetSecurityDescriptorSacl:** System ACL

A descriptor's control flags tell whether the DACL and SACL are present, whether the owner, the group, or either ACL was assigned a default value, and whether the descriptor is in absolute or self-relative format.

To build a security descriptor from scratch, begin by calling **InitializeSecurity-Descriptor** to set up a **SECURITY_DESCRIPTOR** structure. The result is a blank descriptor in absolute format, empty except for a revision level. Call some of these functions to fill the security descriptor with more information.

- **SetSecurityDescriptorDacl:** Replaces the list of protections

- **SetSecurityDescriptorGroup:** Replaces the group attribute

- **SetSecurityDescriptorOwner:** Assigns the object a new owner

- **SetSecurityDescriptorSacl:** Replaces the list of audit conditions

After constructing or modifying a security descriptor, call **IsValidSecurityDescriptor** to confirm that the result is usable.

Access Control List Commands

The functions just listed can add access control lists to a descriptor, but you still need to know how to construct an access control list. ACLs are manipulated by another set of security commands:

- **GetAclInformation:** Retrieves revision or size information from the header of an access control list

- **GetSecurityDescriptorDacl:** Copies the DACL from a security descriptor

- **GetSecurityDescriptorSacl:** Copies the SACL from a security descriptor

- **InitializeAcl:** Puts starting values in an empty buffer to initialize a blank ACL structure

- **IsValidAcl:** Verifies the revision level and structure of an ACL

- **SetAclInformation:** Alters the revision level stored in an ACL header
- **SetSecurityDescriptorDacl:** Replaces a security descriptor's old DACL with a new one
- **SetSecurityDescriptorSacl:** Replaces a security descriptor's old SACL with a new one

Access Control Entry Commands

Seven more commands deal with the access control entries in an ACL:

- **AddAccessAllowedAce:** Appends an **ACCESS_ALLOWED_ACE** structure to an ACL
- **AddAccessDeniedAce:** Appends an **ACCESS_DENIED_ACE** structure to an ACL
- **AddAuditAccessAce:** Appends a **SYSTEM_AUDIT_ACE** structure to an ACL
- **AddAce:** Inserts a list of new ACEs at any position within an existing ACL
- **DeleteAce:** Removes one ACE from any position within an existing ACL
- **GetAce:** Retrieves a pointer to the ACE at a given position within an existing ACL
- **FindFirstFreeAce:** Retrieves a pointer to the first free byte in an existing ACL

The first three functions construct a new ACE from information given in the parameters and add the ACE to the end of an existing ACL. If the ACL's buffer is too small, the Add functions fail. The last four functions are frequently used along with **GetAclInformation**, which retrieves, among other things, the number of ACEs in an ACL and the number of used and unused bytes in the ACL buffer. **AddAce** and **DeleteAce** allow you some control over how the ACEs in a list are ordered. The order matters when evaluating an access request, as we'll explain shortly.

To change an object's protection you modify its DACL. If you have the right privileges, you can alter the existing ACEs, delete old ones, or add new ones. In order to add ACEs to an ACL that is already full, you have to create a new, larger ACL, copy the old ACEs, and then append the new ones. The algorithm involves these steps:

1. Get the object's security descriptor (with a function such as **GetFileSecurity** or **GetKernelObjectSecurity**).

2. Call **GetSecurityDescriptorDacl** to get the original DACL.

3. Call **GetAclInformation** to determine the number of ACEs in the original DACL.

4. Call **InitializeAcl** to create a new, larger DACL.

5. Copy the old ACEs to the new DACL by calling **AddAce** in a `for` loop.

6. Call **AddAce** (or other Add functions) to append new ACEs.

7. Call **SetSecurityDescriptorDacl** to replace the original DACL with the new DACL.

8. Reattach the modified security descriptor to the object (with a function such as **SetFileSecurity** or **SetKernelObjectSecurity**).

You can control the order of ACEs by adding some to the new, empty ACL before copying the old ones. For example, you may want to make any calls to **AddAccess-DeniedAce** between steps 4 and 5.

By calling **InitializeAcl** and then setting the empty, initialized ACL in place with **SetSecurityDescriptorDacl**, you can deny all access to the object. The rule is that a DACL denies all rights unless they are explicitly granted. An empty DACL grants no rights, so no access is possible. An empty DACL, however, is not the same thing as a nonexistent DACL. If you call **SetSecurityDescriptorDacl** with a **NULL** pointer in place of a new ACL, then the security descriptor has no DACL at all. In this case, all access is granted to everyone. The system interprets the absence of a DACL as an absence of protection.

Only an object's owner can change an object's discretionary ACL. A system administrator can change it only by first assuming ownership of the object.

Securing New Handles

When a new object is created, it may acquire its security descriptor from a variety of possible sources. First, the **SECURITY_ATTRIBUTES** parameter passed to the creation function may contain a descriptor. In a few pages we'll show you a sample program that creates a descriptor and attaches it in this way. More often, however, the structure's descriptor field is left **NULL**, and the system constructs a descriptor from various default values. Some of the defaults are taken from the creator's access token. Besides the token components shown in Figure 17.1, an access token contains an owner SID and a default DACL. When the system becomes responsible for assigning ownership to a new object, it looks first to the owner SID held in the creator's access token. The owner SID must be that of the user or one of the user's groups. If that SID is for any reason unsuitable, the system takes the user SID from the access token. The default primary group also comes from the creator's access token.

When the creator does not provide a DACL, the system begins with the parent object's DACL and searches for inheritable ACEs. If it finds none or if there is no parent object, it then turns to the security descriptor that protects the creator's access token. If the security descriptor does not contain a default DACL, then the system looks for one in the creator's access token. If no default DACL appears anywhere, the object is created without a DACL and has no protection. All access is granted to all users. The default SACL is sought in a similar series of places.

When a child process inherits a handle from its parent, the new handle has exactly the same security attributes as the original. **DuplicateHandle**, however, can produce copies that differ from their originals. One of the function's parameters is an access mask, so the new handle may allow different actions. When **DuplicateHandle** copies a handle from one process to make a handle for an unrelated process, it must take into account the privileges of the receiving process. It is possible for **Duplicate-Handle** to produce a handle that allows more access rights than either the source process or the calling process could receive. No security breach occurs, however, because only the destination process can use the new handle.

Evaluating Access Requests

In each access, it isn't enough to know who the subject is (access token) and how the object is protected (security descriptor). You also have to know what the subject wants to do. Every access request needs a third component, describing the desired actions. This takes the form of a bitmask with flags set to request permission for particular actions. The programmer often creates a bitmask when calling particular functions such as **OpenFileMapping** by joining flags such as **GENERIC_READ** and **GENERIC_WRITE**. The system compares the access request bitmask to the access masks in the object's security descriptor to determine whether the given subject may receive the requested access. The handle returned works only with the requested access. All handles are not alike. If one object has been opened twice, each handle may permit different kinds of access.

You must decide which access rights to request. Requesting more rights than you need increases the chances of being refused, but requesting fewer rights than you need will prevent some of your code from working. It's easy to request all possible rights by specifying symbols such as **EVENT_ALL_ACCESS** or **GENERIC_ALL**, but such requests slow down the program while the system determines the specific mask mapping and then compares all possible rights to all the entries in the SACL and the DACL. Symbols that represent large sets of rights are better used in an ACE than in an access request. Besides, using a limited set of access rights sometimes aids in debugging by preventing you from performing accidentally actions you did not intend. Knowing what to request sometimes requires careful planning, but requesting only the rights you need is good programming style.

Order of Evaluation

The order of ACEs in a DACL is significant. Conflicts can arise when a user belongs to several groups with different privileges and when several ACEs in one DACL grant and deny rights to the same user. What happens if the ACEs contradict each other?

First, rights acquired from membership in groups are cumulative. If any one of your groups allows you access to a file, then you may access the file, even if you also belong to groups to whom the file is restricted.

The second situation—conflicting ACEs—is more complex. It helps to understand how the system evaluates an access request. The system walks through the list of ACEs in a DACL one by one, in order from first to last. As it reads each ACE, it checks whether the SID matches any SID in the user's access token. (It might match the user's own ID, or it might match one of the user's groups.) When the system encounters a matching SID in an **ACCESS_ALLOWED_ACE**, it compares the allowed rights to the requested rights and clears the matching bits from the request mask. If all the desired bits are cleared, the search ends and access is granted. When the system encounters a matching SID in an **ACCESS_DENIED_ACE**, it compares the denied rights to the requested rights. If any match, then the search ends immediately and access is denied. An explicit denial of any one requested right causes the entire request to fail.

Denial ACEs, therefore, must come early in the list in order to have their intended effect. Consider a DACL with two ACEs. One grants the user all access rights and another denies the same user deletion rights. Suppose the user requests **GE-NERIC_ALL** rights. The success of the request depends on the order of the ACEs. If the entry granting all access comes first, then all the bits of the requested access mask are cleared on the first comparison and the search ends in success. If the entry denying access comes first, then the first comparison meets an explicit denial of one requested right, and the search ends in failure.

The search ends, then, as soon as all the requested access rights have been granted or as soon as any one of them is denied. If the seach reaches the end of the DACL without clearing all the requested access bits, the request fails.

Conventionally, all the restrictive ACEs precede all the permissive ACEs in a DACL. A list obeying this convention is said to follow *canonical order.* The File Manager under Windows NT has an ACL editor where users with sufficient clearance can modify the protection set on a file. The System Registry has a similar editor for modifying the protection set on registry keys. Both editors always enforce the canonical form. The programming commands for adding and deleting ACEs do not enforce canonical form.

Impersonation

A potential security loophole appears when different processes cooperate in performing some action. In particular, client and server processes are likely to have different access tokens, especially if they are running on different machines. A client that cannot access certain resources might be able to reach them anyway by calling a server with higher clearance. Clients typically talk to servers through network commands, through pipes, or through DDE. In every case, the server must assume responsibility for security. It is up to the server to block the loophole by refusing to give the client anything it should not have.

A server may adopt one of several strategies. It might, for example, maintain its own private database of users and passwords so that users would log on to the server as a separate step. However, the server must then check every access request itself rather than rely on the system's security to prevent unauthorized actions. Or a server might ask for the client's user logon name and system password, but there are no commands to check their validity through the System Access Manager (SAM).

Sometimes you can confirm a name and password by passing them to **WNetAdd-Connection2** and attempting to connect to a dummy network share. If the call succeeds, the name and password are valid. But for the server to receive any password directly it must be sent across the network, a practice best avoided where possible.

The Win32 API allows a less cumbersome alternative called *impersonation*. The server thread may temporarily assume the client's security context, attempt to perform certain actions, and then resume its original security context. The server may even *gain* rights by impersonating a client with high clearance. Impersonation is available to servers communicating with their clients through DDE, named pipes, or the remote procedure call (RPC) facility. Here are the relevant commands:

```
DdeImpersonateClient

ImpersonateDDEClientWindow

ImpersonateNamedPipeClient

RpcImpersonateClient

RpcRevertToSelf

RevertToSelf
```

The first four functions alter the security context of the thread that calls them. The last two restore the original settings. A thread can control the degree to which other threads may impersonate it by setting an impersonation level with **Impersonate-Self** or **DuplicateToken**.

Sometimes it is not possible to impersonate a client. The impersonation commands do not work across a TCP/IP connection, for example. In these cases the server must resort to other strategies. The Win32 API does not yet offer a convenient solution for situations where impersonation does not work.

A Protected Server

Another security problem servers face is protecting their own data. Impersonation works well to protect objects such as files to which the system has already attached a security descriptor, but it does not help the server protect its own private objects. Suppose, for example, a database server wants to protect its database records. The following commands allow a server to create, modify, query, and release security descriptors for its own objects:

- **CreatePrivateObjectSecurity:** Creates a security descriptor for an object defined by the server

- **DestroyPrivateObjectSecurity:** Releases a private object's security descriptor

- **GetPrivateObjectSecurity:** Retrieves information selectively from a given security descriptor

- **SetPrivateObjectSecurity:** Alters the information in a security descriptor

These commands do not attach the new security descriptor to a private object. It is up to the server to remember which descriptors go with which objects. In the database example, the server would probably store a descriptor as a field in each record. (Security descriptors have variable lengths, so storing them in a database file takes some extra work.) The server might use the descriptors to grant specific rights for reading customer data, reading employee data, reading the salary field in an employee record, altering a customer's billing information, or whatever other actions need securing.

To use the private object descriptors, the server must also perform the security checks explicitly. The server defines a **GENERIC_MAPPING** for each type of object and calls **MapGenericMask** to begin each access request. **AccessCheck** takes the object's descriptor, the client's access token, and several other pieces of information, evaluates the request, and tells the server the result.

The C2 Security Rating

Microsoft hopes to enhance the appeal of Windows NT for government-related work by having the system evaluated for use at installations with a C2 security rating. The National Security Agency (NSA) defines different sets of security policies for different ratings and evaluates operating systems for their compliance. A product that passes the evaluation is added to the Evaluated Products List. Sites that use evaluated products can in turn have their installation certified to comply with a particular security level. (Only installations become certified, not systems.) Some parts of the Windows NT security system were designed to implement C2 policies.

Speaking very generally, the essence of the C2 security policy is Discretionary Access Control (DAC). In plain English, DAC calls for the owner of an object to have complete discretionary control over who may access the object and how. Also, the system can track every attempted access and produce an audit report for the system administrator. The next higher security rating, B level, calls for Mandatory Access Control (MAC), where objects have a security level over which the owner has no control. A file rated "top secret," for example, can never be made available to users cleared only for "secret" information. Other security features of Windows NT that answer C2-level requirements include

- Identifying each user with a unique number for auditing purposes

- Zeroing memory after it is freed by a process

- Allowing only administrators to set and see audit data

As of this writing, the C2 evaluation is still in progress.

An Example: Creating a Security Descriptor

To show how a program manipulates security structures, we've modified the Threads program from Chapter 4 to protect its mutex. In the revised version, only an administrator can select the Use Mutex command to make the threads take turns one at a time drawing their shapes.

Several possible approaches could accomplish this goal. One would be to extract the SID from the process's access token and call **LookupAccountSid** to retrieve the account name, which is the name the user gives to log on. That would work if the program knew in advance the names of the accounts it wanted to recognize. Or you could look up the names associated with the access token's group SIDs in order to recognize particular groups.

We have chosen instead to create a security descriptor from scratch and assign it to the new mutex. The descriptor names the Administrators group as the object's owner, and the descriptor's DACL contains only one ACE, granting rights to Administrators only. When a non-administrator runs the program, **CreateMutex** fails. **CreateMutex** always requests **MUTEX_ALL_ACCESS** rights to the new object, but the security descriptor we attach to the new object allows access only to administrators. What actually happens is that **CreateMutex** does create the mutex, but the security protection prevents the command from inserting the object in the process's handle table, so the mutex is immediately destroyed and the command returns **FALSE**. After **CreateMutex** fails, **GetLastError** and **FormatMessage** produce the message shown in Figure 17.4. The program still runs, but the Use Mutex command has no effect.

FIGURE 17.4:

Error message the system produces when a user tries to open an object for which it has inadequate privileges

The protected mutex approach has for us the pedagogical advantage of demonstrating how to create a security descriptor. First we create the pieces: an SID for the Administrators group, a DACL, and an access-allowed ACE. Then we initialize the new descriptor and attach the owner and the DACL to it. **IsValidSecurity-Descriptor** tests the success of our construction. Finally we create the mutex, protecting it with the new descriptor.

```
/*-----------------------------------------------------------------

   MAKE SECURE MUTEX

   Creates a mutex object.  Constructs for the new mutex a DACL
   that allows access only to administrators.  The creation
   function fails when this procedure is run under a non-
   administrative account.

   Builds a blank DACL and an SID representing the group of
   Administrators.  Adds to the DACL a single ACE granting full
   access to members of the Administrators group. Passes the
   resulting security descriptor to CreateMutex. The nascent
   mutex, protected by the new descriptor, will not allow access
   to anyone other than an administrator.

   RETURN: a handle to the new mutex, or NULL for failure.
-----------------------------------------------------------------*/
```

```
HANDLE MakeSecureMutex ( void )
{
    SID_IDENTIFIER_AUTHORITY siaAuthority = SECURITY_NT_AUTHORITY;
    PSID psidAdmin;                        // pointer to admin SID
    SECURITY_DESCRIPTOR SecurityDesc;      // new security descriptor
    SECURITY_ATTRIBUTES SecurityAttr;      // info for CreateMutex
    DWORD dwDaclSize;                      // size of new DACL
    BOOL bTest;                            // for testing results

    // 1. Create the pieces that become part of the security
    // descriptor.  These include an SID, an ACE, and a DACL.

    /* build a new SID identifying the group of Administrators */
    bTest = AllocateAndInitializeSid(
        &siaAuthority,                     // identifier authority (NT)
        2,                                 // two valid subauthorities
        SECURITY_BUILTIN_DOMAIN_RID,       // the system domain
        DOMAIN_ALIAS_RID_ADMINS,           // group of administrators
        0, 0, 0, 0, 0, 0,                  // unused SIDs
        &psidAdmin );                      // new SID buffer
    if (!bTest)
    {
        ShowErrorMsg( __LINE__ );
        return( NULL );                    // could not make SID
    }

    /* calculate the size of the DACL */
    dwDaclSize = sizeof(ACL)               // ACL header structure
        + sizeof(ACCESS_ALLOWED_ACE)       // one access control entry
        - sizeof(DWORD)                    // size of ACE's SidStart field
        + GetLengthSid(psidAdmin);         // full length of the ACE's SID

    /* allocate memory for the DACL */
    pDacl = GlobalAllocPtr( GHND, dwDaclSize );
    if (!pDacl)
    {
        ShowErrorMsg( __LINE__ );
        return( NULL );                    // memory allocation failed
    }

    /* initialize the new DACL */
    bTest = InitializeAcl( pDacl,          // empty ACL buffer
        dwDaclSize,                        // size of buffer
        ACL_REVISION2 );                   // current ACL revision level
```

```
if (!bTest)
{
    ShowErrorMsg( __LINE__ );
    return( NULL );                   // ACL initialization failed
}


// Allocate and insert in the DACL a new ACE granting
// all possible access to the group of Administrators.

bTest = AddAccessAllowedAce(
    pDacl,                            // existing DACL
    ACL_REVISION2,                    // ACL revision level
    GENERIC_ALL,                      // desired rights
    psidAdmin );                      // group to receive the rights
if (!bTest)
{
    GlobalFreePtr( pDacl );
    ShowErrorMsg( __LINE__ );
    return( NULL );                   // failed to add new ACE to DACL
}


// 2. Initialize the security descriptor, attach the new DACL, and make
// Administrators own the mutex.  Test the new descriptor's validity.

/* put starting values in a new security descriptor */
bTest = InitializeSecurityDescriptor(
    &SecurityDesc,                    // blank security descriptor
    SECURITY_DESCRIPTOR_REVISION);    // current revision level
if (!bTest)
{
    ShowErrorMsg( __LINE__ );
    return( NULL );                   // could not initialize descriptor
}


/* attach the new DACL to the new security descriptor */
bTest = SetSecurityDescriptorDacl(
    &SecurityDesc,                    // incomplete security descriptor
    TRUE,                             // make DACL present flag TRUE
    pDacl,                            // the new DACL
    FALSE );                          // the DACL is not a default DACL
if (!bTest)
{
```

```
        GlobalFreePtr( pDacl );
        ShowErrorMsg( __LINE__ );
        return( NULL );                    // couldn't attach DACL
}

/* set the Administrators group SID as object owner */
bTest = SetSecurityDescriptorOwner(
        &SecurityDesc,                     // incomplete security descriptor
        psidAdmin,                         // address of pointer to new owner
        FALSE );                           // the owner is not a default owner
if (!bTest)
{
        GlobalFreePtr( pDacl );
        ShowErrorMsg( __LINE__ );
        return( NULL );                    // unable to attach owner SID
}

/* did we construct the security descriptor correctly? */
if (!IsValidSecurityDescriptor( &SecurityDesc ))
{
        GlobalFreePtr( pDacl );
        ShowErrorMsg( __LINE__ );
        return( NULL );                    // descriptor is unusable
}

// 3. Create the mutex using the newly created security descriptor.
// Creation will fail when attempted by a non-administrator.

/* put the new security descriptor in a SECURITY_ATTIBUTES structure */
SecurityAttr.nLength = sizeof(SECURITY_ATTRIBUTES);
SecurityAttr.lpSecurityDescriptor = &SecurityDesc;
SecurityAttr.bInheritHandle = FALSE;

// Create the mutex.  The object must be assigned a name,
// even though we don't intend to share it, in order to
// be securable.

hDrawMutex = CreateMutex(
        &SecurityAttr,                     // the security attributes
        FALSE,                             // this thread doesn't want mutex
        "threads_mutex" );                 // name for mutex object
```

```
if (!hDrawMutex)
{
    GlobalFreePtr( pDacl );        // couldn't create mutex
    ShowErrorMsg( __LINE__ );
}

return( hDrawMutex );
}
```

We've also made minor changes in other parts of the program to accommodate the secure mutex. If the **WM_CREATE** handler fails to produce a mutex, initialization now proceeds anyway. Also, pDacl must be a global variable because it points to a buffer allocated dynamically that becomes part of the security descriptor. The **WM_DE-STROY** handler releases the buffer. Alternatively, we could call **MakeAbsoluteSD** to convert the descriptor from self-relative to absolute format. Then the information in pDacl would no longer be needed and the buffer could be released within the procedure.

The mutex must be named even though no program tries to share it. The system ignores any security information stored in a nameless but nameable object.

A common programming error in code like this is to omit the **SECURITY_ATTRIBUTES** structure and pass the creation function a **PSECURITY_DESCRIPTOR** instead. Because winnt.h defines the security descriptor pointer as type **LPVOID**, the compiler does not object. The error does, however, produce unpredictable behavior at run time.

PROGRAMMING FOR NETWORKS

Chapter 1 explained that Windows NT boasts built-in network capabilities. Any NT workstation can connect to any other as a network peer, and all may share their files and printers with each other. The I/O manager can parse device names that refer to remote machines and translate device-independent network commands through network transports into specific protocols. Windows NT can communicate through a variety of transport protocols and network adapters. The first release comes with NBF, TCP/IP, and DLC transports. NBF is derived from IBM's NetBEUI protocol. TCP/IP is popular in wide-area networks (WANs) such as the Internet. Many mainframes use DLC. All of these transports operate at the system level, below the programming interface. Not surprisingly, Windows NT also supports several industry-standard network programming interfaces including NetBIOS, sockets, and the Windows Network (WNet) interface. A version of the LAN Manager API is supported too, at least for now. Finally, the system's networking capabilities extend to distributed processing. Through the remote procedure call (RPC) facility, Windows NT helps programmers split a single program to run divided on different machines in order to make the best possible use of CPU power in a network.

Network programming is a vast and complex topic, and all we can aim for here is a description and comparison of the various options a programmer faces in deciding among the system's various networking options.

The Network Commands

The following list summarizes the network command sets available to Windows NT programmers:

- **File I/O API: `CreateFile`, `ReadFile`**, and **`WriteFile`** can reach remote machines. Named pipes and mailslots, which are also implemented through the File Manager, enable remote processes to communicate. The file and pipe commands by themselves will satisfy the network needs of many programs.

- **WNet API:** First introduced in Windows 3.0, the Windows Network API now consists of 12 functions for enumerating network resources and making and breaking network connections.

- **Windows Sockets:** The popular socket paradigm is a specification for a network-independent programming interface. Network suppliers can write protocols that conform to the socket conventions, and programs that use the conventions will work with any compliant network.

- **Remote Procedure Call (RPC) facility:** This facility allows programmers to write split applications that span several machines. A simple procedure call on one machine can invoke a routine that runs on another machine. The RPC facility helps create programs that perform distributed processing.

- **NetDDE:** NetDDE is a redirector that forwards DDE messages to remote machines. It is not present in our beta version, but Microsoft promises it for the system's first public release. It will be based on the NetDDE facility from Windows for Workgroups. The Win32 version will make use of the Windows NT security system.

- **Netbios:** For the convenience of developers porting network applications written for the IBM NetBIOS system, Win32 offers the **Netbios** command. Mailslots and named pipes can usually accomplish the same things.

- **Windows Networking APIs:** These commands provide some of the functionality available in LANManager 2.x. They work only on LANMan networks, only in Unicode, are not part of the public Win32 API, and may not be supported in future releases.

The remaining sections consider in more detail sockets, the Windows networking APIs, and RPC.

Windows Sockets

The sockets programming paradigm originated in Berkeley UNIX as a local inter-process communication mechanism and evolved into a network mechanism. Its commands abstract a conceptual model from the networking software. Sockets are a programming convention for network suppliers and API designers. The convention was developed by cooperating vendors in the TCP/IP networking community. So far all its implementations work only in the family of TCP/IP networks, but eventually it will support others as well. The socket standard is still developing, and discussions of it occur on the Internet. To subscribe to a mailing list for socket discussions, send E-mail to this address:

    winsock-request@microdyne.com

USENET participants can find the same discussions cross-posted in alt.winsock.newsgroup.

The inclusion of sockets in NT should help UNIX developers port programs to Windows. Microsoft's implementation of the convention, called Windows Sockets, is consistent with release 4.3 from Berkeley Software Distribution. The Windows Sockets API is intended for both 16-bit and 32-bit Windows, presenting a uniform interface for all versions. In Windows NT the command parameters are widened to 32 bits. In all versions Microsoft adds some extra commands that modify the socket paradigm to work more efficiently in message-driven programs. Use of the extended commands is recommended but optional.

What Is a Socket?

A *socket* is a communication end point, like one end of a pipe. A program creates a socket to send and receive messages. There are two kinds of sockets. A *stream socket* works with bidirectional, sequenced, reliable, non-duplicated streams of data. In a less reliable stream—one where packets may arrive in duplicate, sporadically, and out of sequence—use *datagram sockets* instead. Streams connect two points; datagram sockets are open channels that do not link specific partners. Stream connections are useful for applications that exchange large amounts of data or data that must be processed in a particular order. Sending the contents of a file from one program to another, for example, requires a stream socket because all the data must be received in the order sent, and losing any part of the transmission may invalidate the result. Datagram sockets often make good network daemons. A talk daemon, for example, would receive single messages from a variety of senders requesting connections to other users. In response to each request, the daemon might create a new stream socket to connect the two participants. The primary datagram socket continues to listen for sporadic signals that arrive in no particular order from other users.

Clearly, sockets resemble pipes and mailslots, but there are important differences. Pipes and mailslots can use the system's security mechanisms; sockets cannot. Not only do pipes and mailslots have security descriptors to protect them from unauthorized users, pipes also support impersonation to help servers maintain security when they act on behalf of their clients. Sockets make no such provisions. Sockets, however, can connect to UNIX platforms where named pipes and mailslots are usually not supported. OS/2, DOS, and LAN Manager for UNIX stations can communicate through sockets. Furthermore, the Windows extensions to the socket API make the process message driven so that a window can receive messages when, for example, a socket is ready to read or write.

Socket Programming

The code for socket functions comes from a DLL. Different vendors may supply different versions of the DLL to support sockets for various network implementations. For 16-bit Windows, the library is winsock.dll. For Windows NT, it is wsock32.dll. Windows NT socket programs must include the winsock.h header and link to wsock32.lib. They must call **WSAStartup** to initialize the socket library and **WSACleanup** before releasing the library. (These two functions belong to the Windows socket extensions and are not part of the standard socket convention. Note that you do not need to initialize the **WSAData** structure before calling **WSAStartup**.)

A socket server generally creates a datagram socket that waits to hear from clients. Whenever a new client contacts the listening socket, the server accepts the connection by spinning off a new socket dedicated to the client. The life cycle of a client's socket typically progresses through the following stages:

1. The socket is created (**socket**).

2. The socket is bound to an address (**bind**).

3. The socket is connected to a server (**connect**).

4. The socket receives and transmits data (**recv** and **send**).

5. The socket is closed (**closesocket**).

The binding stage associates a socket with a three-part name. The name contains a host address, a protocol number, and a port number. Clients may access servers by name or by address.

Here are a few functions and a structure to show what the API looks like:

```
/* create a new socket */
SOCKET PASCAL FAR socket(
    int af,                         // address format
    int type,                       // stream or datagram
    int protocol );                 // 0 to accept any underlying protocol

/* give the new socket a name (which implies an I/O port, too) */
int PASCAL FAR bind(
    SOCKET s,                       // socket identifier
    const struct sockaddr FAR * name,   // tripartite socket name
    int namelen );                  // length of name

/* structure describing an address for binding */
struct sockaddr{
    u_short sa_family;              // identifies format of name that follows
    char sa_data[14];               // tells network where to deliver data
};

/* receive data through a socket */
int PASCAL FAR recv(
    int s,                          // socket identifier
```

```
char FAR * buf,          // place to put incoming data
int len,                 // size of input buffer
int flags );             // function semantics flags
```

Because the Internet and Intel differ in how they order the bytes within a word, data must sometimes be converted as it is passed into or out of a socket function. The network and the host may or may not follow different formats. For good style and portability, every socket program should call the socket conversion functions. The four functions take a short or a long integer and switch the byte order from network to host format or from host to network.

htons:	Host to network short
ntohs:	Network to host short
htonl:	Host to network long
ntohl:	Network to host long

When the host and network use the same order, these functions have no effect. It is not necessary to convert data that you receive through a socket, only information you pass to or receive from the network directly, such as IP addresses and port numbers.

The sockets library also maintains a database of information about hosts, protocols, and services. Some database socket functions convert between string and binary representations of a system or service. The database functions make a master database of network stations visible from a group of machines.

Socket programming allows multithreading, but as with files, the programmer must synchronize access to a socket with a mutex or other synchronizing mechanism. Sockets also come in blocking and non-blocking versions. A socket that causes some commands to block makes problems for the nonpreemptive 16-bit Windows system, so for cross-platform compatibility you should use non-blocking sockets. Programs destined only for NT systems may block without affecting overall system performance.

Microsoft adds 16 unconventional functions of its own to the standard socket API. The new functions all begin with "WSA," for Windows Sockets Interface. All of them help sockets run in a manner more suited to the message-based Windows programming model. Any socket program that will not be ported to a non-Windows platform should use the WSA extensions. The primary attraction of the extensions is **WSAAsynchSelect**, which associates a socket with a window and requests to receive window messages when particular events occur, such as readiness for reading or writing, the arrival of an incoming connection, and the closing of the socket. Other WSA functions match the standard database functions but work asynchronously so that a thread need not block waiting for a response while the system resolves a reference through the network. Win16 applications particularly benefit from asynchronicity, but another WSA function is aimed specifically at Win32. **WSAGetLastError** retrieves information about the last Windows Sockets error. The sockets library maintains error information independently for each thread, so a multithreading application won't overwrite one thread's errors with another's. Without this extension the socket functions would have to report errors through errno, which is not specific to particular threads.

The Windows Networking API

The Windows Networking API exists in Windows NT largely to attract developers who might port applications from LAN Manager systems. Unlike Windows Sockets, the LANMan API seems to have a limited future in NT. Sockets are a growing standard with many enthusiasts, and the potential to expand and regularize network programming over many different network protocols is a goal in keeping with the device independence Windows NT manifests at many levels. The Windows Networking API has no such expansive mission.

Even though the Windows NT LANMan library does not port all the original LANMan functions, it is still the richest of the networking APIs available through Windows NT. The DLL that supports the LANMan API for Windows NT is not considered part of the Win32 API. The documentation that accompanies the LANMan library warns that the library represents an interim solution for porting LAN Manager applications and may not be supported in the future. Furthermore, the LANMan commands have not been tested as thoroughly as have the public Win32 APIs. Potential users should also be warned that the functions in netapi32.lib work only with Unicode text and only on LAN Manager networks.

(We are unable to determine for certain what parts of the LANMan API will ship with the first release of Windows NT. You may have the netapi32 library without the accompanying documentation, ntlmapi.doc. You can download the full package, lmapi.zip, from the MSWIN32 forum of CompuServe.)

It is unfortunate, given all the caveats, that the Windows Network API includes useful commands not otherwise available to Windows NT programmers. For example, the only way for a server to determine a client's home directory is through **NetUserGetInfo**. Only **NetUserEnum** can list all the users in a domain.

The following list summarizes families of related functions within the LAN Manager API. Many of them duplicate functions already available in parts of the Win32 API, in which case the documentation urges developers to use the Win32 commands.

- **Access APIs:** Query and modify an object's security information. Use the Win32 security API to perform the same functions. These LANMan commands work only when used to access a remote system that is not running Windows NT.

- **Alert APIs:** Raise signals when particular process or hardware events occur.

- **Auditing APIs:** Administrate the audit log. Used only for remote systems not running NT.

- **Buffer Manipulation APIs:** Allocate, reallocate, and release the data buffers that hold data returned from some network calls.

- **Configuration APIs:** Get information about the current network configuration. You should use the registry commands instead to query any Windows NT machine.

- **Connection API:** List a server's connections to shared resources.

- **Domain APIs:** Get information about a domain.

- **Error-Logging APIs:** Report errors and audits. Use these commands only for remote non-NT machines. For NT machines, use instead event log commands such as **ReadEventlog** and **ReportEvent**.

- **File APIs:** Monitor and close a server's file, device, and pipe resources.

- **Global Group APIs:** Manage user security groups whose members are drawn from several domains.

- **Local Group APIs:** Manage user security groups whose members are drawn from a single workstation or Advanced Server domain.

- **Message APIs:** Send and receive messages for users or applications. Register aliases for entities that want to receive messages.

- **Remote Utility API:** Get time-of-day information from a remote server.

- **Replicator APIs:** Control the NT Replicator service, which maintains duplicate directories on connected machines.

- **Server APIs:** Administrate system servers. Enumerate, query, and control system resources and settings. `WNetEnumResource` can perform some of these tasks.

- **Service APIs:** Enumerate, query, and control system services. You should use the Win32 Service API instead.

- **Session APIs:** Add, delete, enumerate, and query connections between workstations and servers.

- **Share APIs:** Control shared resources such as printers, pipes, and directories.

- **Statistics APIs:** Gather accumulated operating statistics for workstations or servers. Statistics include, for example, bytes transmitted, number of read operations, number of failed completion routines, and number of LANMan connections.

- **Transport APIs:** Bind and unbind network transports managed by the server or the redirector.

- **Use APIs:** Establish and query connections between workstations and servers. Use `WNetAddConnection2` and `WNetCancelConnection2` instead.

- **User APIs:** Administrate user accounts in the Security Account Manager (SAM).

- **User Modal APIs:** Manage system-wide security system parameters.

- **Workstation APIs:** Control the operation, user access, and resource sharing of local and remote workstations.

The Remote Procedure Call (RPC) Facility

Simply put, using a remote procedure call is like calling a library function when the library happens to reside on a remote machine. To continue the analogy, the RPC facility resembles a linker that resolves references to functions in remote modules. It silently adds the glue that makes the pieces stick together.

In designing the RPC facility, Microsoft followed guidelines set for Data Communications Exchange by the Open Software Foundation. The guidelines for remote procedure calls form one part of the OSF specification for a complete distributed computing environment. Programs that use Microsoft's tools for RPCs can communicate with other implementations of the OSF/DCE specification.

With remote procedure calls, a program can split itself into halves that run as distinct processes on different machines. One half acts as a server to the other half, the client. Though such a scheme has many uses, the main attraction is distributed processing. Any parts of a program that make intensive use of the CPU might benefit from relocating to a more powerful workstation. The client handles the lighter jobs, such as managing the user interface, and delegates the heavier chores to a machine better equipped to perform them. *Distributed processing* is a way of using the best tool for each job. It makes CPU power a shareable resource, just like printers and disk drives.

You've already seen several other ways a client can enlist a server's resources. A remote procedure call facility could be built from sockets, pipes, or DDE, to name a just a few suitable interprocess communication (IPC) methods. Two features distinguish Microsoft's remote procedure calls from other IPC models. First, the source code for a remote procedure call looks just like any other procedure call. You define the procedure, its parameters, and its return value, and the RPC invisibly transmits the information over the network. RPC does require some extra work from programmers, but in this respect it offers the easiest, most flexible, and most familiar paradigm for communicating between client and server. The other distinguishing feature is that Microsoft's RPC facility is not tied to any one underlying IPC mechanism. It can run using NetBIOS, sockets, or named pipes. If the client and server happen to occupy the same workstation, then the RPC can even work through the system's local procedure call (LPC) facility. This too makes remote procedure calls an unusually flexible and portable IPC facility. In fact, the Windows Networking API that imitates the LAN Manager is built on RPCs.

How RPC Works

The RPC facility works by attaching stubs to the client for every procedure called remotely. The stubs replace the remote procedures. The client makes normal procedure calls as though all the routines were local, but some of the calls invoke RPC stubs instead of program procedures. A stub translates a call into network signals. The signals reach a corresponding stub in the remote server. The server's stub receives the procedure parameters and calls the actual server procedure. The server blindly passes the return value back to the server stub, which transmits the result back to the client stub. Although the client and the server both think they are calling or responding to local procedure calls, in fact each interacts only with the RPC stubs.

The sequence of exchanges just described actually involves one other component as well. The Windows NT system directory contains RPC dynamic-link libraries. The RPC client stubs pass the parameters to an RPC client library, which in turn forwards them through the network transports to a remote RPC server library. The server library calls the server stubs. Figure 17.5 illustrates the complete sequence. Remote procedure calls can use different transport mechanisms by calling different versions of the RPC client and server libraries. For example, rpcltc1.dll and rpclts1.dll connect the client and server, respectively, though a named pipe, while rpcltc3.dll and rpclts3.dll use TCP/IP. The libraries for different transports are remembered in the system registry. There are also versions of the RPC libraries for different operating systems. 16-bit Windows and MS-DOS can both run RPC clients.

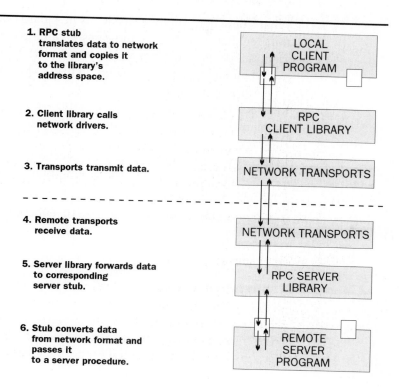

FIGURE 17.5:

How the RPC run-time libraries intervene to pass procedure parameters from the client to the server and a return value from the server to the client

1. **RPC stub translates data to network format and copies it to the library's address space.**

2. **Client library calls network drivers.**

3. **Transports transmit data.**

4. **Remote transports receive data.**

5. **Server library forwards data to corresponding server stub.**

6. **Stub converts data from network format and passes it to a server procedure.**

LOCAL CLIENT PROGRAM

RPC CLIENT LIBRARY

NETWORK TRANSPORTS

NETWORK TRANSPORTS

RPC SERVER LIBRARY

REMOTE SERVER PROGRAM

The Interface Definition

The client and server stubs, in order to cooperate, require a very precise template describing who passes what to whom. The programmer supplies this information in an interface definition file. The items in an interface definition file describe the function prototypes for the remote procedures, but with more detail than normal prototypes provide. Consider, for example, a database server. Suppose it contains a function called FindRecord that receives a last name and searches for a matching record. FindRecord returns the matching record's number. This might be the prototype:

```
int FindRecord( unsigned char * pszLookup );
```

Here's how the same function would be described in the interface definition file shared by client and server:

```
#define MAX_STRLEN 512

int FindRecord( [out, string, size_is(MAX_STRLEN)]
    unsigned char * pszLookup );
```

What's new here are the three items in square brackets. They describe the one parameter that follows. out indicates a value passed from client to server. string identifies the parameter as an array of characters. The entire array needs to be transmitted, not just the pointer stored in pszLookup. size_is sets an upper boundary on the size of the string. This description of a function prototype is expressed in the Interface Design Language (IDL). Microsoft's particular implementation of this standard is called the Microsoft Interface Design Language. The interface file the programmer builds receives the extension .IDL, and the special compiler that builds stub code from the IDL file is called the MIDL compiler. To communicate across a network with RPC, the programmer learns the IPC language, not network commands. Here is a complete IDL file:

```
[ uuid( C2557720-CA46-1067-B31C-00DD010662DA ),
  version( 1.0 ),
  pointer_default( reference )
] interface database
{
    #define MAX_STRLEN 512
```

```
int FindRecord( [in, out, string, size_is(MAX_STRLEN)]
    unsigned char * pszLookup );

void ShutDown( void );
}
```

The complete file contains several important pieces of information besides the extended prototypes. A universal unique identifier (uuid) distinguishes each RPC interface from any others that may be active. It always has the five-part form you see here and is generated mechanically to ensure uniqueness. A small utility called uuidgen.exe takes care of that. The client and server use the uuid to identify each other. The version is optional; it is useful when different versions of the same interface need to be distinguished. The `pointer_default` attribute tells the compiler how to treat pointer parameters. The keyword `reference` here indicates that by default pointers should be considered constants. They may not be **NULL**, their value may not change during a procedure call, and no other name in the procedure may refer to the same storage—no aliases are allowed. All these attributes influence the way the RPC facility must handle the values it transmits.

After the square brackets comes the name of the interface. The square brackets enclose the interface header, and the curly brackets enclose the interface body. The body contains extended function prototypes. This time we've modified `FindRecord` by marking its parameter with both `in` and `out`. That would be appropriate if the function used the `pszLookup` pointer to return a value to the caller. If the caller passed in a last name, `FindRecord` might use the string buffer to pass back the full name from the matching record. We've also added the `ShutDown` prototype because most RPC interfaces provide a way for the client to tell the server when to end the conversation.

The Attribute Configuration File (.ACF)

Besides the interface definition, the MIDL compiler needs to see a configuration file, conventionally named with an .ACF extension. The configuration file contains RPC data and attributes that do not affect how data is transmitted. In the simplest case, the ACF file contains only information about the handle used to bind the client and server.

```
[implicit_handle(handle_t ImpHandle)]
interface database
{

}
```

This example declares a handle and asks for it to be considered implicit so that the client need never refer to it directly.

In RPC terms, *binding* is the process of establishing a connection between the client and server. (Contrast the use of the same term in the socket API, where "binding" merely associates a socket with a name, and `connect` is a separate command.) Binding a client to a server results in a handle. The handle represents the connection and, like a socket or a DDE conversation handle, must frequently be passed in function calls. By declaring the handle implicit, we direct the MIDL compiler to supply this handle automatically wherever the client stubs require it. The client's source file need never refer to the handle explicitly. Some clients, however, might prefer an explicit handle in order to choose a server dynamically at run time.

From the IDL and ACF files, the MIDL compiler generates source code for the client and server stubs. The C compiler processes these along with all the other source files, and the linker joins the resulting object files into a single executable file.

The Main Program

There are a few chores an RPC program must handle in its own source code. It calls RPC functions to initialize its binding handle, and it adds a few user-supplied procedures for the RPC libraries to call. Often `midl_user_allocate` and `midl_user_free` are enough. Like the Get and Put stream functions in OLE clients, these functions are called by the libraries to perform common basic actions over which the program itself sometimes needs to exercise control. The allocate and free functions are called whenever the library needs to allocate or release memory, which it frequently does in order to create data buffers for network transmissions. Most programs can implement both procedures with simple calls to `malloc` and `free` or `GlobalAlloc` and `GlobalFree`.

Considering how successfully the RPC facility has so far managed to avoid requiring special RPC code in the source file, you may be surprised to learn that there are nearly a hundred RPC routines that clients and servers can call directly. In the simplest case, which is all we're considering here, the program can avoid them by letting the MIDL compiler and the RPC libraries handle most of the details. But RPC programs can also choose to take a much more active part in managing their network activities. The program's freedom to intervene makes RPC a very flexible networking mechanism.

UNICODE

Unicode is a convention, like ASCII, for representing characters with numbers. Unlike ASCII and ANSI, Unicode represents each character with 2 bytes rather than 1, allowing for the possibility of up to 65,536 different symbols. That's enough to include all the characters in all the alphabets commonly used on computers anywhere, along with technical symbols and special characters, and still have room to spare. In theory, a single font could contain all the characters for all the alphabets Unicode recognizes. The list includes Latin, Greek, Han, Hiragana, and Katakana, among others. In practice, one font is unlikely to contain all the possible characters, and you will still choose different fonts in order to see different alphabets.

Our beta version of Windows NT comes with a single Unicode font containing over 1000 characters from different alphabets. It is called uclucida.ttf, and the setup program does not install it. You may have to do that yourself through the Control Panel. Unless you install a Unicode font, you won't be able to see any Unicode characters. Part of the Unicode Lucida font appears in Figure 17.6.

FIGURE 17.6:

Microsoft's sample program NT Fonts displaying part of a Unicode font

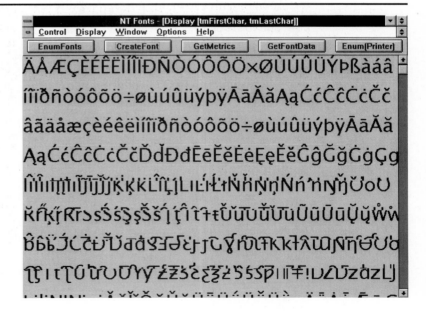

The advantage of Unicode is that it represents all characters with a single standard convention. A number that means ÿ on one machine won't slip over to ² on another machine; changing a code page no longer changes what the character codes represent. A single binary file may contain all the strings it ever needs for any of the countries where it runs. Programs that use Unicode can name any character without worrying about whether it will be interpreted as an OEM or an ANSI character. Programs can process characters from Asian alphabets without laboriously parsing each string to find the double-byte characters (DBCS).

Unicode promises the most advantages for programs that process multilingual text or that sell in foreign markets. At least for now, most projects probably have no real need for Unicode. Still, adapting a program to be compatible with Unicode is very easy, and procedures that anticipate the possibility of Unicode characters transfer more easily to other programs.

Unicode characters, being a different size, have different variable types. **WCHAR**, for wide character, is the type for a single character, and **LPWSTR** is a pointer to a Unicode string. Making a program use Unicode means changing the variable types. The header files make the change easy. A well-written program can change from using ANSI to Unicode by the addition of one line:

```
#define UNICODE
```

A program may decide to use only Unicode strings, only ANSI strings, or to mix both at once. The system itself always uses Unicode internally. Resources, for example, are always stored as Unicode. If you run a hex viewer to inspect the string table in an .EXE file, you'll see that the character codes alternate with zeros. In Unicode, the Latin alphabet characters keep their familiar ASCII values, but they are of course expanded to 2-byte quantities. "A" is 0x41 in ASCII and 0x0041 in Unicode.

The move to wide characters affects any part of a program that works with text, including, to name a few, window messages, resource strings, function calls, command-line arguments, and file names. For the most part the system handles the new situations very well with very little effort from the programmer, but there are a few 1-byte habits a programmer needs to avoid. We'll point them out as we proceed.

Generic Text

Given that ANSI characters and wide characters count as different data types, text-processing functions have to come in pairs, one for each kind of string. A quick glance through the header files turns up many such pairs:

```
UINT WINAPI GetDlgItemTextA(
    HWND hDlg,
    int nIDDlgItem,
    LPSTR lpString,
    int nMaxCount);

UINT WINAPI GetDlgItemTextW(
    HWND hDlg,
    int nIDDlgItem,
    LPWSTR lpString,
    int nMaxCount);
```

These two prototypes for the function that retrieves text from a dialog control differ in their names and in the type declared for the string parameter. **GetDlgItemTextA** retrieves an ANSI string, and its third parameter is type **LPSTR**. **GetDlgItemTextW** retrieves a wide-character string, and its third parameter is type **LPWSTR**. But what about the more familiar function, **GetDlgItemText**—what does it do?

```
#ifdef UNICODE
#define GetDlgItemText  GetDlgItemTextW
#else
#define GetDlgItemText  GetDlgItemTextA
#endif
```

The function **GetDlgItemText** doesn't really exist. It's only a macro. When the symbol UNICODE is defined, **GetDlgItemText** maps to **GetDlgItemTextW** and retrieves a string composed of wide characters. Otherwise it maps to **GetDlgItemTextA** and retrieves a string of 8-bit characters. Many Win32 functions come in similar W/A pairs with a generic macro for calling either one. When the documentation says a function is "Unicode-enabled," it usually means that two parallel versions of the function exist. You can identify Unicode-enabled functions by the globe icon that marks their entries in the on-line help file, as in Figure 17.7.

FIGURE 17.7:

Help file entry with a globe icon indicating the ability to work with Unicode strings

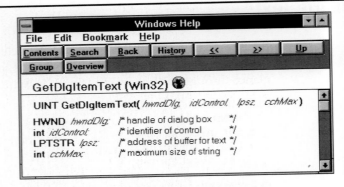

To indicate the pervasiveness of these dual APIs, here is a list of a few other functions that map through a macro to different versions for different text formats:

```
AddAtom

CharUpper

CreateWindow

DefDlgProc

ExtTextOut

LoadAccelerators

lstrlen

OpenMutex

OutputDebugString

RegEnumKey

RegisterClipboardFormat

RemoveDirectory
```

The list probably makes you think of several questions at once. We'll start with **CharUpper**. When UNICODE is not defined, it converts ANSI characters from lower- to uppercase. With UNICODE defined, it converts wide characters to uppercase. And yes, it works with any character in a Unicode font. Besides associating numbers with characters, the full Unicode standard defines some of the semantic rules for manipulating fonts in different alphabets. The rules include mapping lower- to uppercase, recognizing numeric digits, and sorting in alphabetical order. **IsAlphaNumeric** and **lstrcmp** work correctly with a full Unicode symbol set. The rules for sorting and comparing differ from language to language. These cosmopolitan commands choose their rules to match the user's language setting as recorded in the Control Panel.

lstrlen is also enabled for Unicode. It always counts the number of *characters* in a string, not the number of bytes. Text format becomes an issue for file names, too. NTFS does permit names to be stored on the disk in Unicode, but FAT and HPFS do not. Functions such as **RemoveDirectory** that read file names can always deal correctly with any format they find on the disk, but they are typed to expect only one format in their parameters. **RemoveDirectoryA** expects to receive ANSI strings, and **RemoveDirectoryW** expects to receive Unicode strings.

It isn't enough to have generic-text macros just for the functions. You have to worry about variables, too. If you want to compile both an ANSI and a Unicode version of your program and you want to pass szClassName to the generic macro **Create-Window**, then you have to allow for two different declarations of szClassName.

```
#ifdef UNICODE
LPWSTR szClassName[256];              // that's 256 characters, not 256 bytes
#else
LPSTR szClassName[256];              // 256 characters and 256 bytes
#endif
```

That causes szClassName to be a wide string for **CreateWindowW** and an ANSI string for **CreateWindowA**. The header files, however, provide a more elegant solution in the form of a generic text type: **TCHAR**.

```
//
// Neutral ANSI/UNICODE types and macros
//
#ifdef  UNICODE
typedef WCHAR TCHAR, *PTCHAR;
typedef LPWSTR PTSTR, LPTSTR;
#else   /* UNICODE */
typedef char TCHAR, *PTCHAR;
typedef LPSTR PTSTR, LPTSTR;
#endif /* UNICODE */
```

A variable of type **TCHAR** changes according to the state of the UNICODE symbol. **TCHAR** is polymorphic, sometimes 8 bits wide and sometimes 16. Now we can declare szClassName more simply.

TCHAR szClassName;

To put it another way, the polymorphic types in the left column always change to one of the corresponding types in the other columns, depending on whether UNICODE is defined.

Generic Text	ANSI Text	Wide Text
TCHAR	CHAR	WCHAR
LPTSTR	LPSTR	LPWSTR
LPTCH	LPCH	LPWCH

The C runtime libraries come with a tchar.h header that does for C functions approximately what the Windows headers do for Windows code. If _UNICODE is defined, **TCHAR** becomes wchar_t, and otherwise simply char.

Choose the generic text types for your programs wherever possible. Code that relies on neutral types can be reused more freely because it makes no assumptions about the text it receives. In any case, be aware of the problems that may arise from using non-generic variable types, such as **LPSTR**, with generic functions, such as **ExtTextOut**. Bugs will appear if you later define UNICODE because **ExtTextOutW** will expect wide characters.

Converting Strings

Some programs cannot limit themselves to generic types because they need to manipulate the text format directly. A server that receives ANSI strings from its clients might, for example, convert them to Unicode before saving them. Such a program might sometimes call explicitly typed functions, such as **ExtTextOutA**, depending on the particular string it needs to handle.

The Win32 API includes a number of conversion routines, but there is no reliable way to convert an unknown string that might be either Unicode or ANSI. It is difficult to determine the text format given a random set of bytes, particularly a short set. When the format is known, however, you can easily convert from one to the other.

```
MultiByteToWideChar

WideCharToMultiByte
```

Other functions convert between the OEM character set built into a computer and an ANSI or Unicode character set.

```
CharToOem

CharToOemBuff

OemToChar

OemToCharBuff
```

When UNICODE is defined, these functions convert between wide characters and OEM characters. Without UNICODE, they convert between OEM and ANSI.

Implementation Details

The following sections present some smaller facts that will help you write wide-character programs.

Unicode String Constants

Just as you can mark hexadecimal values in source code with the prefix "0x" and character constants with a backslash, so you can mark wide-character strings by preceding them with "L".

```
LPWSTR lpszUnicode[] = L"This string uses wide characters.";
```

For neutral declarations, use the **TEXT** macro to add the L prefix only when UNICODE is defined.

```
LPTSTR lpszGeneric[] = TEXT( "This string may be using wide characters." );
```

String Buffer Size and Length

When a function asks for the length of a text buffer as one parameter, measure the buffer in characters, not bytes.

```
LPTSTR szResString[40];
int iLoaded;

iLoaded = LoadString( hInst,                          // program instance
    IDS_RESSTRING,                                    // resource identifer
    szResString,                                      // buffer for string
    sizeof(szResString) / sizeof(TCHAR) );   // size of buffer in characters
```

sizeof returns a byte count that must be divided by sizeof(TCHAR) in order to produce a count of characters when UNICODE is defined. The function's return value also counts characters, not bytes. **LoadStringW** returns half the number of bytes loaded because it is counting characters. Contrast **GlobalAlloc**, for example, which always requires a byte count, not a character count, because it is allocating a block of untyped memory. **ReadFile** and **WriteFile** too work with data buffers, not strings, and so count bytes rather than characters.

When UNICODE is defined, this calculation determines a size in bytes, not a length in characters:

```
LPTSTR lpszEnd, lpszStart;
int iCount;

iCount = lpszEnd - lpszStart;
```

Here is the correct way to determine the length:

```
iCount = (lpszEnd - lpszStart) / sizeof(TCHAR);
```

In contrast, the next operation works regardless of the UNICODE setting because it increments the pointer in character units, not in byte units:

```
LPTSTR lpszText;
TCHAR tchNext;

tchNext = *lpszText++;
```

OemToCharBuff and File Names

When UNICODE is not defined and a program is reading from a FAT disk, Windows NT faces the same problem that Windows 3.1 does: It needs to convert the file names from OEM to ANSI characters by calling **OemToCharBuff**. When UNICODE is defined, however, no conversion is necessary because the wide-character versions of the file I/O functions automatically convert the strings to wide format. A program that works with generic text types should define a macro something like this:

```
#ifdef UNICODE
#define OEMTOCHARBUFF( (lpszOem), (lpszAnsi), (dwSize) )
#else
#define OEMTOCHARBUFF( (lpszOem), (lpszAnsi), (dwSize) ) \
        OemToCharBuff( (lpszOem), (lpszAnsi), (dwSize) )
#endif
```

When the program uses Unicode, the conversion command disappears.

The Byte-Order Mark

Problems arise when an Intel-based computer and a Macintosh attempt to exchange Unicode plain text files because the two systems place the high- and low-order bytes of a word in reverse order. Therefore Unicode text files conventionally begin with a byte-order mark, 0xFEFF. When you save a Unicode file, always begin with that mark. When you read a Unicode file, always confirm that the first word is 0xFEFF. If you discover a file that begins 0xFFFE, then you have a byte-reversed Unicode file. You can either warn the user of the error or reverse all the bytes yourself.

The byte-order mark does not cause the file to be stored in a particular format. It simply helps the receiver identify the format. The byte marker also makes a good way to test whether or not a file contains Unicode text. It is not infallible, however, because of course other files could conceivably happen to begin with those 2 bytes. To determine whether a file contains Unicode text, you might also check for a higher variation in low-order bytes than in high-order bytes. When ASCII or ANSI text is converted to Unicode, for example, every other byte is 0. Sometimes you can determine the format of line-oriented text files by discovering the repeated linefeed and carriage-return characters. If you always find 0x000A and 0x000D rather than 0x0A and 0x0D, then you probably have Unicode. Finally, if the file size is odd then you probably do not have Unicode.

Incidentally, the first 128 characters of the Unicode standard are the same as the first 128 characters of the ASCII standard. Even the control codes are the same. 0x000D can be treated as a carriage return, 0x0007 as a bell.

Window Messages

When a `WM_CHAR` message delivers keyboard input to a window, does it deliver ANSI or Unicode characters? When you send strings to a list box, which format does the system expect? To resolve questions like these, the Win32 subsystem assigns windows a text type. Wide-character windows transact all their business in Unicode, while ANSI windows use only ANSI strings. When one window sends a message to a window of a different type, the system converts the message automatically. So every `WM_CHAR` message always delivers its character using the window's chosen format. And when the system delivers a string to a list box, it always presents the string in whatever format the list box window prefers.

A program chooses a type for its window when it registers the window class. All the windows of one class use the same text type. `RegisterClassA` creates classes that receive ANSI strings, and `RegisterClassW` creates classes that receive wide-character strings. A program may call either one explicitly or make an implicit choice with the `RegisterClass` macro and the UNICODE symbol. `IsWindowUnicode` tells whether a particular window is registered as a Unicode recipient. Note that a window procedure may send messages or call functions of either type, regardless of its own class. The window class governs only what the window procedure receives, not what it does.

A window's registered class affects all the messages in this list:

CB_ADDSTRING	WM_ASKCBFORMATNAME
CB_DIR	WM_CHAR
CB_FINDSTRING	WM_CHARTOITEM
CB_GETLBTEXT	WM_CREATE
CB_INSERTSTRING	WM_DEADCHAR
CB_SELECTSTRING	WM_DEVMODECHANGE
	WM_GETTEXT
EM_GETLINE	WM_MDICREATE
EM_REPLACESEL	WM_MENUCHAR

EM_SETPASSWORDCHAR   WM_NCCREATE

WM_SETTEXT

LB_ADDFILE   WM_SYSCHAR

LB_ADDSTRING   WM_SYSDEADCHAR

LB_DIR   WM_WININICHANGE

LB_FINDSTRING

LB_GETTEXT

LB_INSERTSTRING

LB_SELECTSTRING

The system's translation from Unicode to ANSI works even for subclassed windows. **SetWindowLongA** inserts a window procedure that wants ANSI messages, and **SetWindowLongW** inserts a window procedure that wants Unicode messages. **CallWindowProc** performs any necessary conversion when it forwards a message to the supplanted window procedure.

Command-Line Arguments

The third parameter of WinMain points to a string that cannot be typed neutrally.

```
int WINAPI WinMain(
    HANDLE hInstance,
    HANDLE hPrevInstance,
    LPSTR lpszCmdLine,                 // an ANSI string
    int iCmdShow );
```

Until a program registers a window class, the system cannot know whether the program wants ANSI or Unicode arguments. It always delivers ANSI arguments. To receive the arguments as Unicode, use **GetCommandLineW** (or **GetCommandLine** with UNICODE defined).

Guidelines for Generic-Text Applications

The following guidelines summarize the major points to remember when converting a program to be compatible with Unicode.

- Declare all character and string variables using generic types such as **TCHAR**, **LPTSTR**, and **LPTCH**. Eliminate **CHAR** and **LPSTR**.

- Do not declare non-text data buffers using type **LPTSTR**. Use **LPBYTE** or **LPVOID**.

- Always divide the size of a text buffer by sizeof(TCHAR) to compute this length.

- Mark all literal strings with the **TEXT** macro. Cast all character constants to type **TCHAR**. Be especially careful with '\0' because a null-terminated Unicode string must end with 0x0000, not 0x00. Where possible, move strings into the resources.

- Change code that assumes 255 is the largest possible value for a character.

An Example: ShowErrorMsg

As an example of generic text coding, we offer yet another version of the **Show-ErrorMsg** procedure.

```
#define UNICODE
#include <windows.h>

/*----------------------------------------------------------------
        SHOW ERROR MESSAGE
        Receives line number where error occurred and displays it
        as part of a system error message describing the most
        recent error.
        ----------------------------------------------------------*/

void ShowErrorMsg ( int iLine )
{
    LPTSTR pBuffer;                              // temporary message buffer
    LPTSTR pMessage;
```

```
/* retrieve a message from the system message table */
FormatMessage(
    FORMAT_MESSAGE_ALLOCATE_BUFFER | FORMAT_MESSAGE_FROM_SYSTEM,
    NULL,                               // ignored
    GetLastError(),                     // message ID
    MAKELANGID(LANG_ENGLISH, SUBLANG_ENGLISH_US),   // message language
    (LPTSTR)&pBuffer,                   // address of buffer pointer
    0,                                  // minimum buffer size
    NULL );                             // no other arguments

/* allocate a larger buffer and append the line number to the end */
pMessage = LocalAlloc( LHND,
    (lstrlen(pBuffer) * sizeof(TCHAR))
    + (15 * sizeof(TCHAR)) );
wsprintf( pMessage, TEXT("%s (line %u)"), (LPTSTR)pBuffer, iLine );

/* display the message in a message box */
MessageBox( NULL, pMessage, TEXT("Console Message"),
            MB_ICONEXCLAMATION | MB_OK );

/* release the buffers allocated by FormatMessage and by us */
LocalFree( pBuffer );
LocalFree( pMessage );

return;
}
```

A number of small changes were necessary to support Unicode. First, the two string buffer parameters were changed from type **LPSTR** to type **LPTSTR**. With UNICODE defined, **FormatMessage** becomes **FormatMessageW** and copies wide characters into the message buffer, but the source code for this command hasn't changed. When figuring the necessary buffer size for the full message, we've had to be sure **LocalAlloc** bases its calculations on the byte size rather than the character length of pBuffer. **lstrlen** returns a character length, and 15 is the number of extra spaces we add to make room for the line number. Both quantities measure characters, so multiplying by sizeof(TCHAR) converts them to bytes. The **TEXT** macro prefixes an "L" to the format string in **wsprintf** to mark a Unicode constant. It appears again in **MessageBox** to make sure the window caption also uses wide characters.

We revised **ShowErrorMsg** in order to use it in a short sample program that shows off the console window functions, to which we now turn.

THE CONSOLE API

A *console* is a window where Win32 runs character-mode applications. A program running in a console window typically does not have a graphics user interface, is not message driven, and begins with `main` rather than `WinMain`. The console environment supports standard I/O streams and line-oriented C runtime commands such as `printf` and `gets`. The MS-DOS subsystem creates console windows to run its processes, and we've used console windows in this book for short demonstration programs like those on structured exception handling in Chapter 6. Presumably Microsoft added consoles in order to attract developers who might then be more likely to port their character-based applications, perhaps originally written for POSIX or DOS, to Windows NT.

But consoles are good for more than compatibility and easy ports. Until now our simple console examples have ignored the set of console commands included in the Win32 API. You can write console programs without using console commands, but the commands make console windows significantly more flexible. With or without the console commands, the console facility makes it possible for short programs to avoid the high code overhead of a message queue and a graphics interface. The Windows programming model does not lend itself to quick-and-dirty utilities. Also, console windows can be handy for debugging. A GUI application might easily open an auxiliary console for the sake of printing trace messages.

A console consists of an input buffer, an output buffer, and a window. The input buffer is a queue and features the ability to handle mouse events as well as keystrokes. The output buffer is a two-dimensional array of characters. The console window shows a view of the output buffer. Output commands write to the output buffer, and the output becomes visible in the window. If the buffer is larger than the window, the programmer can remap the window to show different views of the buffer. The console API supports scrolling, moving blocks of text, changing character color attributes, running full-screen or windowed, and using raw or cooked I/O modes. It does not support ANSI escape sequences, but they may be added in a later release.

To build a console application, write a program that uses `main` instead of `WinMain`. Avoid calling GUI output functions such as **Rectangle** and **BitBlt**. On the compiler command line, use this switch:

```
-subsystem:console
```

There are no other requirements. Except for the output commands, a console application may call any Win32 commands that a GUI program calls. Console applications may load resources, create popup GUI windows, run multiple threads, participate in DDEML conversations, talk through pipes, or read the system registry.

(To load resources, a console program needs an instance handle. It can call **GetModuleHandle** with a **NULL** parameter and use that handle instead.)

The Console Commands

The console API makes provisions for creating and releasing a console; changing the size of the output buffer; reading from and writing to the three standard devices stdin, stdout, and stderr; performing high- and low-level I/O; and adjusting the I/O modes.

Creating a Console

The console programs we wrote in Chapter 6 do not create new consoles. They run from the command line in the command window, and any output they produce goes to the window where they were launched. By default a new console application inherits the parent's console and the two processes share one window. A process that wants a window of its own calls **FreeConsole** to release itself from the inherited console and **AllocConsole** to create a new one.

```
BOOL AllocConsole( void );
BOOL FreeConsole( void );
```

When the user launches a console application through the Program Manager, the parent process (Program Manager) has no console for the child to inherit. The new process still receives a console, however, because console applications are usually initialized with a console if the parent lacks one. (To avoid creating a console, use the **DETACHED_PROCESS** flag with **Create Process**.)

To use the console API, a program needs handles to the input and output buffers. Call **GetStdHandle** to acquire them. **STD_INPUT_HANDLE** retrieves the input queue; **STD_OUTPUT_HANDLE** and **STD_ERROR_HANDLE** both reach the output buffer. Recall from Chapter 5, however, that the parent may have chosen to redirect any of these handles to other devices. A console program may redirect its own handles with

SetStdHandle. To retrieve input and output buffer handles that ignore redirection, call **CreateFile** and ask for the CONIN$ or CONOUT$ device.

Pass the I/O handles to the console APIs in order to manipulate the window and the buffers. The handles also work with standard C library routines such as puts and scanf.

- **GetConsoleScreenBufferInfo:** Fills a structure with information about the size of the window and of the output buffer, about the cursor position, and about the current color attributes

- **GetLargestConsoleWindowSize:** Retrieves the maximum allowable window size

- **SetConsoleTitle:** Provides a string for the console window's title bar

- **GetConsoleTitle:** Retrieves the string showing in the console window's title bar

The structure **GetConsoleScreenBufferInfo** fills looks like this:

```
typedef struct _CONSOLE_SCREEN_BUFFER_INFO { /* csbi */
    COORD dwSize;                    // current size
    COORD dwCursorPosition;          // where cursor is now
    WORD wAttributes;                // color flags
    SMALL_RECT srWindow;             // window position
    COORD dwMaximumWindowSize;       // maximum window size
} CONSOLE_SCREEN_BUFFER_INFO ;
```

The structures **COORD** and **SMALL_RECT** resemble **POINT** and **RECT**, but all the fields are **SHORT** instead of **LONG**. The console commands always measure the window and buffer sizes in characters. The buffer might be 80 characters wide and 40 across, while the window might only be 20 x 20. If the cursor is at the upper-left corner, then **dwCursorPosition** names the point (0, 0). The maximum window size varies with the font and the display size. In calculating the maximum window size, **GetConsoleScreenBufferInfo** also takes into account the size of the output buffer. The window may not be made larger than the buffer. Console windows abhor a vacuum and will not expand beyond the buffer they expose. To find out how large the window could be if it had a bigger buffer, call **GetLargestWindowConsoleSize**.

Managing the Buffer and the Window

The output buffer is a two-dimensional array of structures that hold a character and an attribute each. The character field tells what text to show at a given location on the screen, and the attribute field tells what colors to use for the character's foreground and background. You can expand and shrink the buffer. Shrinking the buffer loses data. When a small window is attached to a large buffer, you can slide the buffer to show different areas through the window. You can also create extra buffers and switch between them. The window shows a view of the active buffer. Only one buffer may be active at a time, but you can read to and write from buffers even when they are not visible. The position, appearance, and visibility of the cursor are maintained independently for each output buffer.

- `CreateConsoleScreenBuffer`: Creates a new output buffer
- `SetConsoleScreenBufferSize`: Changes the size of an output buffer
- `SetConsoleActiveScreenBuffer`: Selects an output buffer for the window to use
- `CloseHandle`: Releases an output buffer
- `GetConsoleCursorInfo`: Finds out where the cursor is
- `SetConsoleCursorInfo`: Moves the cursor to a new position
- `SetConsoleWindowInfo`: Sets the size and position of the console window; determines what part of the output buffer is visible
- `ScrollConsoleScreenBuffer`: Transfers the contents of a square block in the output buffer from one place to another

I/O Modes

When first created, a console's input buffer operates with line-oriented input, echoes keys to the screen, and processes keystrokes. Processing input means correctly handling keys such as the backspace and carriage return. All three of these features are modes you can turn on and off. With all three modes on, the console input stream delivers *cooked input*. Turning them off produces *raw input*, where none of the keystrokes has been interpreted. The backspace and carriage return come through the queue just like any other characters, and the receiving program must decide what to do with them.

The default output modes call for processed output and line wrapping. Processed output interprets keystrokes just the way processed input does. Tabs expand, bells sound, and backspaces space back. Line wrapping causes the cursor to move down automatically when it reaches the end of a line. Otherwise it would stick at the right edge of the window and characters that overflowed the line would be written on top of each other. To query or alter any of these modes, call **GetConsoleMode** or **SetConsoleMode**.

Here, for example, are the commands to prevent input from echoing to the screen:

```
DWORD dwConMode;                              // console's input mode

hStdIn = GetStdHandle( STD_INPUT_HANDLE );    // get handle to input buffer
GetConsoleMode( hStdIn, &dwConMode );         // retrieve current modes
SetConsoleMode( hStdIn,
    (dwConMode & ~ENABLE_ECHO_INPUT) );       // suppress echo bit
```

Input Commands

The high-level input commands are **ReadFile** and **ReadConsole**. **ReadFile** (like **WriteFile**) cannot handle Unicode text, while **ReadConsole** can. The file I/O functions always process data as a stream of bytes, but the console functions always process text and can convert between ANSI and Unicode. Defining UNICODE in a console application causes **ReadConsole** (or really **ReadConsoleW**) to return wide characters from the input queue. **ReadFile**, however, can read from pipes and communication devices, which **ReadConsole** cannot do. If a console's I/O handles have been redirected to other devices, then **ReadFile** may be necessary.

ReadFile and **ReadConsole** both ignore non-keyboard events in the input queue. By using low-level input commands you can receive and respond to mouse events and window-sizing events as well. In cooked mode, both Read commands return when the user presses Enter. In raw mode, they return as soon as one or more characters appear in the input queue. It is possible to wait on a console input handle. In other words, you can pass hStdIn to a command like **WaitForSingleObject** in order to block while waiting for input.

To respond to mouse actions or window-size changes, you need low-level input commands that recognize these events when they appear in the input queue.

- **ReadConsoleInput:** Takes one or more input records from the queue

- **PeekConsoleInput:** Copies one or more input records from the queue without removing them

- **GetNumberOfConsoleInputEvents:** Determines how many input records are waiting on the queue

- **WriteConsoleInput:** Appends input records to the queue

- **FlushConsoleInputBuffer:** Discards all input records pending in the queue

Input records contain two fields: a type and an event record. The type field tells what kind of event the record field describes.

```
typedef struct _INPUT_RECORD { /* ir */
    WORD EventType;
    union {
        KEY_EVENT_RECORD KeyEvent;
        MOUSE_EVENT_RECORD MouseEvent;
        WINDOW_BUFFER_SIZE_RECORD WindowBufferSizeEvent;
        MENU_EVENT_RECORD MenuEvent;
        FOCUS_EVENT_RECORD FocusEvent;
    } Event;
} INPUT_RECORD;
```

Key events record keystrokes. Mouse events report movement and button presses. The mouse and key events carry extended information about the state of toggle keys and control keys. Buffer-size events occur when something the user does causes the buffer size to change. Menu and focus events are used internally and should be ignored; they come into play when the console window's system menu is activated or the window gains or loses input focus. The sample program in the section "Example: Mouse Input" later in this chapter reads mouse messages.

Output Commands

The high-level output commands are **WriteFile** and **WriteConsole**. Use **WriteFile** when the output stream may have been redirected to a pipe or a port. Use **WriteConsole** (with UNICODE) to work with wide characters. Of course, C runtime routines such as `printf` and `puts` work with consoles, too. The console API also includes a command for setting text colors. **SetConsoleTextAttribute** sets text and background colors for subsequent output commands. (It does not modify the color of text that was already written.)

- **WriteConsoleOutput:** Copies text and color attributes from a memory buffer to a rectangular block in the output buffer

- **WriteConsoleOutputCharacter:** Copies characters from a memory buffer to consecutive cells in the output buffer

- **WriteConsoleOutputAttribute:** Copies color attributes from a memory buffer to consecutive cells in the output buffer

- **FillConsoleOutputCharacter:** Copies one character to consecutive cells in the output buffer

- **FillConsoleOutputAttribute:** Copies one set of color attributes to consecutive cells in the output buffer

The buffer stores color attributes with each character code. The buffer is a two-dimensional array of structures like this:

```
typedef struct _CHAR_INFO { /* chi */
    union {                  /* Unicode or ANSI character  */
        WCHAR UnicodeChar;
        CHAR AsciiChar;
    } Char;
    WORD Attributes;         /* text and background colors */
} CHAR_INFO, *PCHAR_INFO;
```

The attributes field combines color flags drawn from this list:

> FOREGROUND_BLUE
>
> FOREGROUND_GREEN
>
> FOREGROUND_RED
>
> FOREGROUND_INTENSITY
>
> BACKGROUND_BLUE
>
> BACKGROUND_GREEN
>
> BACKGROUND_RED
>
> BACKGROUND_INTENSITY

To indicate a black background, don't use any background flags. To indicate a white background, combine all four flags with OR. To make the text appear in bright cyan letters, combine the foreground flags for blue, green, and intensity.

Because the output buffer is just an array, it is possible to read data back from it.

- **ReadConsoleOutput:** Copies characters with their attributes from the screen buffer to a memory buffer
- **ReadConsoleOutputCharacter:** Copies characters from the screen buffer to a memory buffer
- **ReadConsoleOutputAttribute:** Copies color attributes from the screen buffer to a memory buffer

To copy rectangular blocks of text with attibutes from place to place or buffer to buffer, call **ReadConsoleOutput** and **WriteConsoleOutput** together.

The Console and OEM Characters

For compatibility with DOS, the console commands default to the OEM code page rather than the ANSI code page. This means, for example, that when a DOS program uses the IBM extended line-drawing characters to construct its screen, it still gets line-drawing characters from the console. Problems can arise, however, when console commands try to display strings acquired through other Win32 APIs because the others use ANSI characters. For example, if a string retrieved with **GetFullPathName** happens to use certain ANSI characters, the string will not display correctly when **WriteConsole** tries to display it with OEM characters.

One solution is to use Unicode. Only the 8-bit console functions use OEM characters. With UNICODE defined, **GetFullPathNameW** and **WriteConsoleW** speak the same dialect. Another solution is to call **SetFileApisToOEM**, forcing the 8-bit file I/O commands such as **GetFullPathNameA** to use OEM characters.

Assigning a Program Icon

Console programs can have a program icon just as GUI applications do. The program's icon appears automatically in the Program Manager group. It also appears if you launch the program through the Program Manager and minimize the console window. Follow the usual procedures to put an icon in the program's resource file.

1. Draw an icon.

2. Write a resource file that refers to the icon.

   ```
   MyIcon ICON myicon.ico
   ```

3. Compile the resource file in the normal way using rc.

4. Call CvtRes to convert the .RES file into an .RBJ file.

5. Add the .RBJ file name to the Link32 command line.

That's all you do. Because console applications don't register a window class you can't attach the icon to the window in the same way, but the Program Manager will notice the icon anyway and load it.

Bringing Up a Dialog Window

A console application is allowed to create dialog boxes, but the dialog box is likely to appear behind the console rather than in front of it. If the console window is large the dialog box may be completely hidden, and the user may not even be aware of it. Console windows don't expect to find themselves related to other windows on the desktop, and they aren't prepared to yield focus the way a GUI window does instinctively. The solution is for the dialog box to promote itself during initialization.

```
case WM_INITDIALOG:
    SetForegroundWindow( hDlg );
```

This doesn't solve the problem for message boxes because you can't initialize them yourself. Console programs should probably avoid message boxes and create small dialog boxes from scratch instead.

Example: Mouse Input

This sample program, called Console, demonstrates a number of the console commands, including mouse input. It also defines UNICODE and observes the coding rules for generic text types. It calls the ShowErrorMsg procedure listed earlier in the Unicode section.

When the program begins, it asks the user to enter a string. Then it clears the screen and enters a loop waiting for the user to click with the mouse. Console prints the user's string wherever the user clicks with the mouse. A double-click ends the program. Figure 17.8 shows the Console program in action.

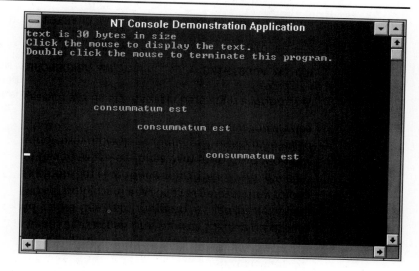

As it initializes, Console enlarges the window to its maximum size and expands the output buffer to match. Although console programs can change the size of a window, the console API does not allow for them to change their position on the screen. If the expanded window extends off the screen, the user has to position it manually.

During initialization, the program also calls **SetConsoleMode** to enable mouse input. This call is not necessary because mouse input is enabled by default. We included the call anyway to show how to change the mode.

After the user enters a string, Console prints the size of the string. It does this as a way of showing that Unicode is enabled. If you type a five-character string, Console will inform you that the string occupies 10 bytes.

```
/*-------------------------------------------------------------------

            CONSOLE

    Sets up a console window, asks the user to enter a string,
    and displays the string in the window wherever the user
    clicks the mouse.  Demonstrates the console API and Unicode
    string types.

        Functions

            main                    initialization and main input loop
            MaximizeConsoleWindow   set window to maximum size
            ClearScreen             erase everything from console window
            ShowErrorMsg            display message if an error occurs

        from Mastering Windows NT Programming
        copyright 1993 by Brian Myers & Eric Hamer

    ----------------------------------------------------------------*/


#define UNICODE

#include <windows.h>
#include <stdio.h>

/*-------------------------------------------------------------------
            FUNCTION PROTOTYPES
    ----------------------------------------------------------------*/


BOOL MaximizeConsoleWindow( HANDLE hConsole );
BOOL ClearScreen( HANDLE hStdOut );
void ShowErrorMsg( int iLine );

/*-------------------------------------------------------------------
            MAIN
            Initializes the console, asks the user for a string, and
            enters the program's main loop.  Whenever the user clicks
            the mouse, the program shows the string.
    ----------------------------------------------------------------*/


int main ( void )
{
    LPTSTR szCaption = TEXT( "NT Console Demonstration Application" );
    HANDLE hStdIn;                              // input buffer handle
```

```
HANDLE hStdOut;                    // output buffer handle
INPUT_RECORD UserInput;            // entry from input queue
COORD Coord;                       // a cell position in window
TCHAR szText[256];                 // string entered by user
DWORD dwConMode;                   // console's input mode
BOOL bDone;                        // TRUE to end program

DWORD dwCharsRead;                 // function return values
DWORD dwCharsWritten;
DWORD dwRecsRead;
BOOL bTest;

// This program wants to run in its own window.  Release
// the inherited console and allocate a new one.

bTest = FreeConsole( );
if (!bTest)
{
    ShowErrorMsg( __LINE__ );
    return( 1 );
}

bTest = AllocConsole( );
if (!bTest)
{
    ShowErrorMsg( __LINE__ );
    return( 1 );
}

/* set the new console's title */
bTest = SetConsoleTitle( szCaption );
if (!bTest)
{
    ShowErrorMsg( __LINE__ );
    return( 1 );
}

/* retrieve the standard input and output handles */
hStdOut = GetStdHandle( STD_OUTPUT_HANDLE );
hStdIn = GetStdHandle( STD_INPUT_HANDLE );

/* retrieve I/O modes so we can modify them */
bTest = GetConsoleMode( hStdIn, &dwConMode );
```

```
if (!bTest)
{
    ShowErrorMsg( __LINE__ );
    return( 1 );
}

/* ask to receive mouse input */
bTest = SetConsoleMode( hStdIn,
    (dwConMode | ENABLE_MOUSE_INPUT) );
if (!bTest)
{
    ShowErrorMsg( __LINE__ );
    return( 1 );
}

/* resize the console and clear it */
bTest = MaximizeConsoleWindow( hStdOut );
if (!bTest)
{
    ShowErrorMsg( __LINE__ );
    return( 1 );
}

/* tell the user to enter a string */
printf( "Enter a character string:  " );

/* read the string and terminate it */
ReadConsole( hStdIn,
    szText,
    sizeof(szText),
    &dwCharsRead,
    NULL );
szText[dwCharsRead - 1] = (TCHAR)'\0';

ClearScreen( hStdOut );              // draw black all over the window

/* the size reported here shows whether the program is using Unicode */
printf( "Your string is %d bytes in size.\n",
    (lstrlen(szText) - 1) * sizeof(TCHAR) );

/* tell the user to click with the mouse */
printf( "Click the mouse to display the text.\n" );
printf( "Double click the mouse to terminate this program.\n" );
```

```
// This is the main program loop.
// Reads events, waiting for mouse clicks.  One click
// means draw the user's string; two clicks means quit.

bDone = FALSE;
while (!bDone)
{
    /* read the user event */
    bTest = ReadConsoleInput(
        hStdIn,                     // input buffer
        &UserInput,                 // buffer for one record
        1,                          // number of records to read
        &dwRecsRead );              // number of records read
    if (!bTest)
    {
        bDone = TRUE;
    }

    if (UserInput.EventType == MOUSE_EVENT)
    {
        // If a button has been clicked, retrieve the
        // coordinates and display the text.

        if (UserInput.Event.MouseEvent.dwEventFlags == 0 &&
            UserInput.Event.MouseEvent.dwButtonState)
        {
            Coord.X = UserInput.Event.MouseEvent.dwMousePosition.X;
            Coord.Y = UserInput.Event.MouseEvent.dwMousePosition.Y;

            bTest = SetConsoleCursorPosition( hStdOut, Coord );
            if (bTest)
            {
                WriteConsole( hStdOut,  // buffer handle
                    szText,             // text to write
                    lstrlen(szText),    // number of chars in text
                    &dwCharsWritten,    // number of chars written
                    NULL );             // reserved, unused
            }
        }
    }
```

```
            /* check for a double click */
            if (UserInput.Event.MouseEvent.dwEventFlags == DOUBLE_CLICK)
            {
                bDone = TRUE;
            }
        }
    }

    return( 0 );
}


/*-------------------------------------------------------------------
        MAXIMIZE CONSOLE WINDOW
        resize and clear the console window
    -------------------------------------------------------------*/

BOOL MaximizeConsoleWindow ( HANDLE hConsole )
{
    CONSOLE_SCREEN_BUFFER_INFO ConBufInfo;  // info about the buffer
    SMALL_RECT WindowRect;                  // console window position
    COORD ConsoleSize;                      // console buffer size
    COORD WindowMax;                        // console window size
    SHORT nMaxWidth, nMaxHeight;            // max window dimensions
    WORD wSize;                             // size in cells of console buffer
    BOOL bTest;                             // function return value

    /* get the size of the current console */
    bTest = GetConsoleScreenBufferInfo( hConsole, &ConBufInfo );
    if (!bTest)
    {
        return( FALSE );
    }

    /* determine the maximum allowable window size */
    WindowMax = GetLargestConsoleWindowSize( hConsole );
    nMaxWidth  = WindowMax.X;
    nMaxHeight = WindowMax.Y;

    /* calculate the number of character cells in the current output buffer */
    wSize = (WORD)(ConBufInfo.dwSize.X * ConBufInfo.dwSize.Y);

    /* initialize WindowRect and ConsoleSize to maximum values */
    WindowRect.Left   = 0;
    WindowRect.Top    = 0;
    WindowRect.Right  = (SHORT)(nMaxWidth - 1);
```

```
        WindowRect.Bottom = (SHORT)(nMaxHeight - 1);
        ConsoleSize.X     = nMaxWidth;
        ConsoleSize.Y     = nMaxHeight;

        /* if current buffer is not set to the window's maximum size */
        if (wSize < (nMaxWidth * nMaxHeight))
        {
            /* set the size of the console buffer */
            bTest = SetConsoleScreenBufferSize( hConsole, ConsoleSize );
            if (bTest)
            {
                /* now expand the window to its maximum size */
                bTest = SetConsoleWindowInfo(
                    hConsole,                 // console output
                    TRUE,                     // using absolute coordinates
                    &WindowRect );            // new position
                if (!bTest)
                {
                    ShowErrorMsg( __LINE__ );
                }
            }
            else
            {
                ShowErrorMsg( __LINE__ );
            }
        }
        if (!bTest)                           // if anything failed
        {
            return( FALSE );                  // then quit
        }

    return( TRUE );
}


/*-------------------------------------------------------------------
        CLEAR SCREEN
        Writes black blank characters all over the window.  (Erases
        only what is visible in the window, not other parts of the
        buffer.)
    --------------------------------------------------------------*/

BOOL ClearScreen( HANDLE hStdOut )
{
    CONSOLE_SCREEN_BUFFER_INFO ConBufInfo;  // info about the buffer
    COORD Cursor;                           // point where cursor is
```

```
WORD wSize;                             // size of buffer in chars
BOOL bTest;                             // function return values
DWORD dwCharsWritten;

/* get the size of the current console */
bTest = GetConsoleScreenBufferInfo( hStdOut, &ConBufInfo );
if (!bTest)
{
    return( FALSE );
}
/* determine number of character cells in visible window */
wSize = (WORD)(ConBufInfo.dwSize.X * ConBufInfo.dwSize.Y);

/* now fill the screen with blanks, starting at (0, 0) */
Cursor.X = 0;
Cursor.Y = 0;

bTest = FillConsoleOutputCharacter(
    hStdOut,                           // console output
    TEXT(' '),                         // character to write
    wSize,                             // number of cells to fill
    Cursor,                            // cursor COORD position
    &dwCharsWritten );                 // number of cells filled
if (!bTest)
{
    ShowErrorMsg( __LINE__ );
    return( FALSE );
}

bTest = FillConsoleOutputAttribute(
    hStdOut,                           // console output
    0L,                                // write black attributes
    wSize,                             // number of cells to fill
    Cursor,                            // cursor COORD position
    &dwCharsWritten );                 // number of cells filled
if (!bTest)
{
    ShowErrorMsg( __LINE__ );
    return( FALSE );
}
```

```
/* put the cursor at (0, 0) */
SetConsoleCursorPosition( hStdOut, Cursor );

    return( TRUE );
}
```

When Console pulls an input record from the queue, it tests for the type **MOUSE_EVENT**. A mouse event record has the following form:

```
typedef struct _MOUSE_EVENT_RECORD { /* mer */
    COORD dwMousePosition;
    DWORD dwButtonState;
    DWORD dwControlKeyState;
    DWORD dwEventFlags;
} MOUSE_EVENT_RECORD;
```

The bits in the **dwButtonState** field tell which buttons, if any, were pressed. **dwControlKeyState** records the state of the Shift, Alt, Ctrl, Num Lock, Caps Lock, and Scroll Lock keys. **dwEventFlags** is 0 for a mouse button action, **MOUSE_MOVED** if the position has changed, and **DOUBLE_CLICK** for a double click.

In this chapter we've surveyed four topics that may help you with specialized tasks. We began with security. Security information is built into Windows NT at a low level because the object manager, which creates all system objects, can attach security descriptors to any of them. The security descriptor tells who may use the object and how. In order to evaluate any attempt to use an object, the system compares the object's security descriptor to the user's access token and an access mask requesting permission for particular actions. The access token contains privileges assigned by the system administrator and usually derived through membership in certain system user groups, such as Power Users and Backup Operators. A sample program showed how to protect an object by creating its security descriptor from scratch.

From security we moved to networks, a large topic that we could only survey generally. Networks are related to security because networks let many users share resources on remote machines. Network capabilities are built into Windows NT, and any NT workstation can link up to any other as a peer. In its usual voracious desire to incorporate as many industry standards as possible, Microsoft has provided a bewildering variety of ways for programmers to write for a network. There are pipes, a WNet interface for managing connections, a **Netbios** function, Network DDE, a sockets API, a LAN Manager API, and a remote procedure call facility for distributed processing.

The third topic was Unicode, a standard for storing text characters as numeric data. Because Unicode uses 2 bytes to represent each character, it can accommodate in a single font all the characters and symbols from a large number of alphabets. Giving each character an absolute representation eliminates problems that arise from transferring data between machines that use limited code sets and different code pages. Internally, Windows NT uses Unicode exclusively to represent text. Programming for Unicode is less a matter of calling special Unicode commands and more a matter of remembering to use generic text variable types. A well-designed source file can produce either ANSI or Unicode binaries simply by redefining the UNICODE symbol.

Finally, we surveyed the commands available for managing the console windows, which support character-based applications. A console consists of an input buffer, an output buffer, and a window. The console API allows you to create a console, read from its input buffer and write to its output buffer, create multiple buffers and switch between them, remap the window to expose different views of the same buffer, and handle I/O through standard device streams that accommodate processed or unprocessed data operations, redirection, and standard C library text commands. Besides helping people port character-based programs to Windows NT, the console facility makes small utility programs more practical because they can be created without the overhead of a graphics user interface.

INDEX

Note to the Reader: **Boldfaced** page numbers indicate definitions of terms and the principal discussions of topics. *Italic* page numbers indicate illustrations.

As in the text, no formal distinction is made in the index between commands and functions.

Numbers and Symbols

16-bit Windows. *See* Windows for DOS
32-bit Windows. *See* Win32 entries;
    Windows NT
* (asterisk)
    commenting with /*, 307
    in mailslot names, 209–210
\ (backslash)
    for ASCII code sequences, 248
    named pipes and, 189–190
    object names and, 15, *16*
. (period), named pipes and, 190
; (semicolon), commenting with, 307
/ (slash), commenting with /*, 307

A

AbnormalTermination, 289
AbortPath, 412
Access APIs, 1150
access control entries (ACEs), 759, **1121–
    1123**, 1134–1135
    access control entry commands, 1131–
    1132
access control lists (ACLs), **18**, **1120–
    1128**, *1120*, 1134–1135
    access control list commands, 1130–
    1131
    Discretionary Access Control Lists
      (DACLs), 1120–1121

System Access Control Lists (SACLs),
    1120–1121
access mask field, 1123–1124
access mode parameter, named pipe, 190
access requests, evaluating, **1133–1135**
access rights
    generic, 1126–1128
    locking and unlocking files, 745–747
    object handles and, 18
    specific, 1125–1126
    standard, 1124–1125
access token commands, 1113–1114
access tokens, **14**, **1110–1113**, *1112*, 1129
    object manager and, 18
access violation exceptions, 277
AccessCheck, 1137
ACEs. *See* access control entries
.ACF (attribute configuration files),
    1155–1156
ACLs. *See* access control lists
AddAccessAllowedAce, 1131
AddAccessDeniedAce, 1131
AddAce, 1131
AddAtom, 1160
    AddAuditAccessAce, 1131
AddItem procedure, List program,
    365–369
AddRef method, 1015
address space, **329–331**, *330*, *331*

C

H

Q

R

AN $800 SEMINAR DISGUISED AS A BOOK

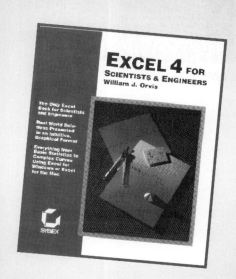

A MONARCH'S MANUAL.

235pp. ISBN: 1293-5.

Whether you are new to the game or an old pro, *Civilization Strategies & Secrets* tells you everything you need to know about Civilization—the dynamic game of world domination.

This compact guide shows you how to choose long and short-term goals, create cities, open trade relationships, build infrastructure and more. In short, you learn to govern.

What's more, you get something every monarch wishes they had— tried and true winning strategies for successfully running a government. Experienced Civilization players give you tips and tricks they've used to create civilizations that work. So unlike real rulers with daunting problems, you can guarantee that your civilization will always be the best it can be.

SYBEX. Help Yourself.

2021 Challenger Drive
Alameda, CA 94501
800- 227-2346

SYBEX

SYBEX

FREE BROCHURE!

Complete this form today, and we'll send you a full-color brochure of Sybex bestsellers.

Please supply the name of the Sybex book purchased.

_____

How would you rate it?

_____ Excellent _____ Very Good _____ Average _____ Poor

Why did you select this particular book?

_____ Recommended to me by a friend

_____ Recommended to me by store personnel

_____ Saw an advertisement in _____

_____ Author's reputation

_____ Saw in Sybex catalog

_____ Required textbook

_____ Sybex reputation

_____ Read book review in _____

_____ In-store display

_____ Other _____

Where did you buy it?

_____ Bookstore

_____ Computer Store or Software Store

_____ Catalog (name: _____

_____ Direct from Sybex   )

_____ Other: _____

Did you buy this book with your personal funds?

_____ Yes _____ No

About how many computer books do you buy each year?

_____ 1-3 _____ 3-5 _____ 5-7 _____ 7-9 _____ 10+

About how many Sybex books do you own?

_____ 1-3 _____ 3-5 _____ 5-7 _____ 7-9 _____ 10+

Please indicate your level of experience with the software covered in this book:

_____ Beginner _____ Intermediate _____ Advanced

Which types of software packages do you use regularly?

_____ Accounting	_____ Databases	_____ Networks
_____ Amiga	_____ Desktop Publishing	_____ Operating Systems
_____ Apple/Mac	_____ File Utilities	_____ Spreadsheets
_____ CAD	_____ Money Management	_____ Word Processing
_____ Communications	_____ Languages	_____ Other _____

(please specify)

Which of the following best describes your job title?

_____ Administrative/Secretarial   _____ President/CEO

_____ Director   _____ Manager/Supervisor

_____ Engineer/Technician   _____ Other _____
                                                      (please specify)

Comments on the weaknesses/strengths of this book: _____

_____

_____

_____

_____

Name _____

Street _____

City/State/Zip _____

Phone _____

PLEASE FOLD, SEAL, AND MAIL TO SYBEX

SYBEX, INC.
Department M
2021 CHALLENGER DR.
ALAMEDA, CALIFORNIA USA
94501

SYBEX

SEAL

ABOUT THE DISK

What's on the Disk?

The companion disk contains all of the source code used in *Mastering Windows NT Programming*. For complete installation instructions and more information about the disk, see the Introduction to this book.

How Can I Get a 3½" Disk?

Send $5.00, plus proof of purchase, and your written request to:

SYBEX Inc.
Customer Service Department
2021 Challenger Drive
Alameda, CA 94501
(800) 227-2346

Please include your name, complete mailing address, and the following reference number: 1264-1. Without the reference number, your request cannot be processed. Please allow six weeks for delivery.